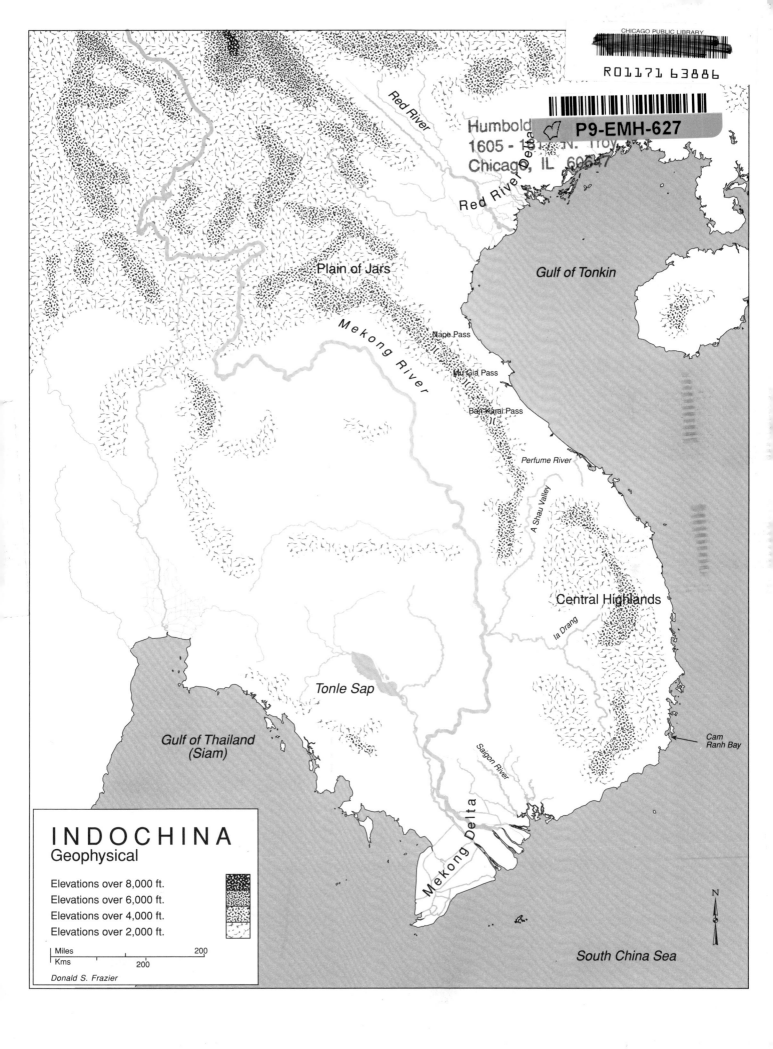

Red River

Red River Delta

Gulf of Tonkin

Plain of Jars

Mekong River

Nape Pass

Mu Gia Pass

Ban Karai Pass

Perfume River

A Shau Valley

Central Highlands

Ia Drang

Tonle Sap

Gulf of Thailand
(Siam)

Saigon River

Cam
Ranh Bay

Mekong Delta

South China Sea

INDOCHINA
Geophysical

Elevations over 8,000 ft.
Elevations over 6,000 ft.
Elevations over 4,000 ft.
Elevations over 2,000 ft.

Miles   200
Kms   200

Donald S. Frazier

N

ENCYCLOPEDIA
OF THE
VIETNAM WAR

Editorial Board

ENCYCLOPEDIA OF THE VIETNAM WAR

EDITOR

STANLEY I. KUTLER

University of Wisconsin–Madison

CHARLES SCRIBNER'S SONS
Macmillan Library Reference USA
Simon & Schuster Macmillan
NEW YORK
Simon & Schuster and Prentice Hall International
LONDON MEXICO CITY NEW DELHI SINGAPORE SYDNEY TORONTO

Charles Scribner's Sons
An Imprint of Simon & Schuster Macmillan
1633 Broadway
New York, New York 10019

1 3 5 7 9 11 13 15 17 19 20 18 16 14 12 10 8 6 4 2

LIBRARY OF CONGRESS CATALOGING-IN-PUBLICATION DATA

Encyclopedia of the Vietnam War / editor, Stanley I. Kutler.
    p. cm.
   Includes bibliographical references and index.
   ISBN 0-13-276932-8 (alk. paper)
   1. Vietnamese Conflict, 1961–1975—Encyclopedias. I. Kutler,
Stanley I.
DS557.7.E53 1996
959.704'3'03—dc20   95–20940
                                                      CIP
The paper in this publication meets the requirements of ANSI/NISO Z39.48-1992 (Permanence of Paper).

Editorial and Production Staff

Managing Editors
Paul Bernabeo   Stephen Wagley

Project Editor
Steven J. Tirone

Assistant Project Editors
John B. Roseman   Sarah Gardner Cunningham

Manuscript Editor
John W. Hopper

Proofreaders
Susan L. Andrews   Rachel Benzaquen   Sabrina Bowers
Mary Flower   Christine A. Gibbs   John N. Jones

Compositor
Compset, Inc.

Cartographer
Donald S. Frazier

Indexer
Olive Holmes, EDINDEX

Case Designer
Irena Lubenskaya

Production Director
Richard Hollick

Publisher
Karen Day

President, Macmillan Library Reference
Gordon Macomber

Contents

Maps

Introduction

Twenty years after the fall of Saigon, the guns of the Vietnam War are silent. But its history remains profoundly fascinating and controversial to the generation that fought and lived through it. Later generations have been equally attracted to the events in Vietnam and their ramifications throughout the world. In Vietnam, of course, the war remains a vivid, searing memory, and its devastating effects are readily apparent throughout the land. In the United States, the war has cast a long shadow since 1975, touching the nation's politics, culture, military structure and strategy, and foreign policy. President George Bush, in 1989, lamented that the war still divided Americans. But he insisted that "the statute of limitations" has been reached and that a great nation could not "long afford to be sundered by a memory." After committing American troops in the Gulf War, Bush proclaimed that the "Vietnam Syndrome," which he contended had long paralyzed the nation's will, had been overcome. But a year later, Bush unhesitatingly exploited the memories of the Vietnam conflict when he questioned Bill Clinton's patriotism for opposing the war.

The Vietnam War is usually divided into two parts: the first, the French attempt to maintain their colonial hold on Indochina from 1945 to 1954; the second, the subsequent conflict between the politically divided sections, commonly referred to as North and South Vietnam. During this latter period, the United States intervened against the communist North, first with economic and military material aid to the noncommunist South, and later, with more than half a million troops and massive firepower. The struggle became America's longest war, longer than its participation in the two world wars and the Korean War combined. For Vietnamese the conflict dated back to the nineteenth century, when forcible and passive resistance to the imposition of French rule began.

Years after the war ended, an American military officer testified in a court case that "Vietnam is one

long blur, sir." For most Vietnamese, however, the war always clearly focused on national independence; for some, it was an ideological contest either for or against communism. But during the years of American involvement, Americans—in Vietnam and at home—were deeply divided, even confused, over the nature, purpose, and morality of that war. More than two decades since its end, many incidents and events remain shrouded in controversy and ambiguity.

Still, we struggle to make sense of what happened in Vietnam and the United States during that long conflict. This encyclopedia is designed as a basic reference for defining the actors, battles, weapons, and issues of the period. We have attempted to define the "who" and the "what." But all historical study must engage the "why"—the meaning and significance of events. Often the answers are complex and varied. We have included as many of those viewpoints as possible. We also have been mindful of Vietnamese perspectives, including the impact of the war on their society and how they perceived events. As relations between the United States and Vietnam develop more openly and cordially in the future, we should gain added knowledge and insight of events from the Vietnamese point of view.

This volume contains two types of entries. Long interpretive essays, written by leading experts, provide in-depth coverage of major topics related to the war. These include articles on the land and the peoples of Vietnam, the French colonial era, the background to American military intervention, the military history of the war, its impact on both the Vietnamese and American peoples, the peacemaking efforts, the role of the American media, the cultural impact of the war in the United States, and a treatment of the war's ongoing effects in the United States. The second type of entry comprises topical articles from fifty to five thousand words long dealing with the people and events of the war and its surrounding history.

The Vietnam War was a complex and multifaceted episode. For Vietnam and the United States the war was a major event in their histories. Much of the rest of the world, too, felt its effects in varying ways. The Vietnam War demands our attention if we are to gain a larger historical understanding of the last half of the twentieth century. Such understanding will change over time; history inevitably produces waves of revisionism. However future historians and generations choose to view the event, they must ground their interpretations in its factual content. This encyclopedia will, it is hoped, help in that endeavor.

Stanley I. Kutler
Madison, Wisconsin
July 1995

Directory of Contributors

DALE ANDRADÉ
U.S. Army Center of Military History

Easter Offensive
Pacification

DANIEL T. BAILEY
Madison, Wisconsin

Military Assistance Advisory Group–Vietnam
(MAAG–V)
Military Assistance Command, Vietnam (MACV)
Order of Battle
U.S. Military

ELLEN BAKER
Madison, Wisconsin

Acheson, Dean
Australia
Canada
China, Republic of (Taiwan)
Cooper, Chester
France
Free-fire Zones
Great Britain
Haig, Alexander M.
India
Indonesia
International Commission for Supervision and
Control
International Reaction
Kennedy, Edward M.
Kennedy, Robert F.
Korea, Republic of
Malaysia
Military Revolutionary Council
Montagnards
New Zealand
Ngo Dinh Can
Nuclear Weapons
Pearson, Lester

Poland
Prostitution
Thompson, Robert G. K.
Tran Van Huong
Tran Van Tra
Wilson, Harold

WILLIAM C. BERMAN
University of Toronto

Congress, U.S.
Fulbright, J. William

THOMAS R. CANTWELL
Burwood, N.S.W., Australia

Army of the Republic of Vietnam (ARVN)
Le Nguyen Khang
Medical Support
National Liberation Front (Viet Cong)
People's Army of Vietnam (PAVN)
Republic of Vietnam Armed Forces (RVNAF)
Ngo Quang Truong
Pathet Lao
Provincial Reconnaissance Units (PRU)
Regional Forces/Popular Forces
Special Forces, ARVN

TIMOTHY N. CASTLE
Office of the Secretary of Defense

Laos
Phoumi Nosavan
Souphanouvong
Souvanna Phouma

GRAHAM A. COSMAS
U.S. Army Center of Military History

Army, U.S.
Atrocities
My Lai

ROBERT DALLEK
University of California, Los Angeles

Johnson, Lyndon B.

DAVID A. DAWSON
United States Marine Corps

Project 100,000

JEAN DELMAS
Paris

Colonialism

VINCENT H. DEMMA
U.S. Army Center of Military History

Strategy and Tactics

WILLIAM J. DUIKER
Penn State University

Ho Chi Minh
Lao Dong
Le Duan
National Liberation Front (NLF)
People's Liberation Armed Forces (PLAF)
Provisional Revolutionary Government (PRG)
Vietnam
Vietnam, Republic of (RVN)

KELLY EVANS-PFEIFER
Madison, Wisconsin

Adams, Sam
Amnesty
Arnett, Peter
Body Count
Brezhnev, Leonid
Bui Diem
Bundy, McGeorge
Bundy, William
Bush, George
Carter, Jimmy
Casualties
Clifford, Clark
Con Son
Cronkite, Walter
Democratic Party, U.S.
Dobrynin, Anatoly
Domino Theory
Fall, Bernard
Federal Bureau of Investigation

Fishel, Wesley
Fonda, Jane
Fortas, Abe
Friendly Fire
Galbraith, John Kenneth
Gelb, Leslie
Goldman, Eric F.
Great Society
Guam Conference
Halberstam, David
Hardhats
Hawks and Doves
Hersh, Seymour
Hoopes, Townsend
Humphrey, Hubert H.
Huston Plan
International War Crimes Tribunal
Kennan, George
Khrushchev, Nikita
King, Martin Luther, Jr.
Korean War
Kosygin, Alexei N.
LeMay, Curtis
Lippmann, Walter
McCloy, John J.
McNaughton, John T.
McPherson, Harry
Meany, George
Michigan State University Vietnam Advisory
    Group (MSUVAG)
Mitchell, John
Munich Analogy
National Security Action Memorandum (NSAM)
    263
National Security Action Memorandum (NSAM)
    288
New Left
Nguyen Co Thach
Pentagon Papers
Plumbers
Post-traumatic Stress Syndrome (PTSS)
POW/MIA Controversy
Public Opinion, American
Read, Benjamin
Reagan, Ronald W.
Reeducation Camps
Republican Party
Richardson, Elliot
Rogers, William P.
Schlesinger, James
Sheehan, Neil

GLEN GENDZEL (cont.)
Jones, David C.
Komer, Robert W.
Laird, Melvin R.
LAM SON 719
Lansdale, Edward G.
Le Duc Tho
Lemnitzer, Lyman
Le Van Kim
McCain, John S., Jr.
McCain, John S., III
McConnell, John P.
Martin, Graham A.
Momyer, William W.
Moorer, Thomas H.
National Bank of Vietnam
New Mobe
Nguyen Chanh Thi
Nguyen Khanh
Nitze, Paul
Nolting, Frederick E.
Normalization
O'Daniel, John W.
Paris Accords
Pham Hung
Pham Van Dong
Phan Huy Quat
Radford, Arthur W.
RAND Corporation
Ridgway, Matthew B.
Rostow, Eugene V.
Rostow, Walt Whitman
Saigon
SAM Missiles
Schlesinger, Arthur M., Jr.
Seabees
SEALs
Search and Destroy
Search and Rescue
Selective Service
Sharp, U. S. Grant
Son Tay Raid
Special Forces, U.S. Army
Stilwell, Richard G.
Stockdale, James B.
Taylor, Maxwell D.
Taylor–McNamara Report
Taylor–Rostow Report
Trang Sup
Tran Thien Khiem
Tri Quang

Truong Chinh
Tunnels
Twining, Nathan F.
Vann, John Paul
Van Tien Dung
Viet Minh
Viet Nam Quoc Dan Dang (VNQDD)
Vogt, John W., Jr.
Weyand, Frederick C.
Wheeler, Earle G.
Williams, Samuel T.
Xuan Thuy
Zumwalt, Elmo R., Jr.

AMY GOLDEN
Madison, Wisconsin

Cambodia

ELLEN D. GOLDLUST
Madison, Wisconsin

Agricultural Reform Tribunals
An Loc
Ap Bac
Ap Bia
A Shau Valley
Ban Me Thuot
Bay Vien
Berger, Samuel D.
Binh Gia
Booby Traps
Bui Phat
Bui Tin
Cao Bang
Case, Clifford
Chapman, Leonard
Claymore Mines
Cluster Bombs
Con Thien
Cooper, John Sherman
Cushman, Robert
Dak To
Daniel Boone Operations
Democratic National Convention, 1968
Dong Xoai
Ely, Paul
FANK (Forces Armées Nationales Khmères)
Four-Party Joint Military Commission
Freedom Birds
Free World
Gravel, Mike

Greene, Wallace
Hanoi Hannah
Hanoi Hilton
Ho Chi Minh Trail
Johns Hopkins Speech
Loc Ninh
Long Binh
Manila Conference
Mayaguez Incident
Mekong River and Delta
Midway Island Conference
Nguyen Chi Thanh
Nguyen Ngoc Loan
Pathfinders
Perot, H. Ross
Porter, William
Pueblo Incident
Quang Tri
Rheault, Robert
Short-timer
Smart Bombs
Song Be
Tan Son Nhut
Teach-ins
Vietnamization
Westmoreland-CBS Libel Suit
Xuan Loc

JEFFREY GREENHUT
Howard Community College

Medical Support
U.S. Military

JOHN F. GUILMARTIN JR.
The Ohio State University

Air Force U.S.
ARC LIGHT
B-52
Casualties
COMMANDO HUNT
FLAMING DART
F-111
Helicopters
LINEBACKER and LINEBACKER II
MENU
Monsoon
NIAGARA
PIERCE ARROW
RANCH HAND
ROLLING THUNDER

K. E. HAMBURGER
United States Army (ret.)

Abrams, Creighton
Westmoreland, William

WILLIAM M. HAMMOND
U.S. Army Center of Military History

Media and the War

HAN TIE
Madison, Wisconsin

China, People's Republic of (PRC)
Mao Zedong
Zhou Enlai

GEORGE C. HERRING
University of Kentucky

Diplomacy

ARNOLD R. ISAACS
Towson State University

American Perspectives

VICTOR JEW
Michigan State University

Air America
Argenlieu, Georges Thierry D'
August Revolution
Ball, George
Bidault, Georges
Bowles, Chester
Caravelle Group
Castries, Christian de
Conscientious Objectors
Élysée Agreement
Enthoven, Alain
European Defense Community
Faure, Edgar
Fontainebleau Conference
Gaulle, Charles de
Justice, Department of
Katzenbach, Nicholas
Laniel, Joseph
Lattre de Tassigny, Jean de
Leclerc, Jacques Philippe
Mendès-France, Pierre
National Assembly Law 10/59
Navarre, Henri
Navarre Plan
Roosevelt, Franklin D.

ALLAN R. MILLETT
The Ohio State University

Combined Action Program
Marines, U.S.

THOMAS MYERS
Saint Norbert College

Art and Literature

NGÔ VIÑH LONG
University of Maine

Ngo Dinh Diem
Ngo Dinh Nhu
Ngo Dinh Nhu (Madame Nhu)
Nguyen Cao Ky
Nguyen Van Thieu
Veterans
    Vietnamese Veterans
Vietnamese Perspectives

JAMES S. OLSON
Sam Houston State University

Antiwar Movement

LEO P. RIBUFFO
George Washington University

Eisenhower, Dwight D.
Ford, Gerald R., Jr.
Goldwater, Barry
McCarthy, Eugene J.
McGovern, George

RANDY W. ROBERTS
Purdue University

Antiwar Movement

ANDREW J. ROTTER
Colgate University

Prelude to U.S. Combat Intervention

WILLIAM PAUL SCHUCK
San Francisco, California

Agnew, Spiro T.
American Friends of Vietnam
Chicago Seven
Clergy and Laity Concerned about Vietnam
Coffin, William Sloane
COWIN Report
Dean, John Gunther
Forrestal, Michael
Habib, Philip

Heath, Donald
Honolulu Conferences
Jackson State College
Kent State University
Mayday Tribe
Mendelhall, Joseph
Murphy, Robert D.
Napalm
National Committee for Peace and Freedom in
    Vietnam
National Council of Reconciliation and Concord
Nguyen Huu Tho
Richardson, John H.
Romney, George
San Antonio Formula
Silent Majority Speech
Spock, Benjamin
Vietnamese Information Group
Vietnam Moratorium Committee
Vietnam Veterans against the War

ROBERT D. SCHULZINGER
University of Colorado at Boulder

Kissinger, Henry
Nixon, Richard M.
State, Department of

JACK SHULIMSON
Marine Corps Historical Center

Amphibious Landing Operations
Khe Sanh
Krulak, Victor H.
Shoup, David M.
Walt, Lewis W.

PAUL M. TAILLON
Madison, Wisconsin

Agency for International Development (AID)
Central Office for South Vietnam (COSVN)
Commercial-Import Program
Da Nang
DeSoto Missions
Détente
Donovan, William J.
Dulles, Allen
Dulles, John Foster
Eden, Anthony
Elections, South Vietnamese, 1955
Geneva Conference, 1954
Geneva Conference, 1962
Gulf of Tonkin Resolution

Chronology

Date	Southeast Asia	United States	The War
Early History			
Early seventh century BC	Dong Son era begins; the kingdom of Van Lang forms in the Red River Delta, eventually expanding into surrounding mountainous areas to form Au Lac.		
Late third century BC	Chinese general Chao T'o (Trieu Da) conquers Au Lac and establishes the independent kingdom of Nam Viet ("Southern Viet") under his rule.		
111 BC	Chinese Han dynasty conquers Nam Viet.		
AD 39	Trung sisters lead unsuccessful revolt against Chinese rule.		
938 January	Battle of Bach Dang River; Vietnamese under Ngo Quyen defeat Chinese.		
939	Ngo Quyen becomes king of new independent Nam Viet.		
966	Bo Linh declares himself emperor, naming his empire Dai Co Viet.		
1009	Ly Thai To becomes emperor, establishing Ly dynasty.		
1225	Tran dynasty replaces Ly dynasty.		
1288 April	Second battle of Bach Dang River; Vietnamese under Tran Hung Dao defeat invading Mongols.		
1407	Chinese Ming dynasty reoccupies Vietnamese state, known as Dai Viet.		

Date	Southeast Asia	United States	The War
1426	Le Loi defeats Chinese, reestablishing independent Dai Viet and establishing Le dynasty.		
1492 October		Columbus lands at San Salvador.	
Late sixteenth century	Vietnam fragments politically and is divided by the Trinh and the Nguyen.		
1627	French missionary Alexandre de Rhodes codifies *quoc ngu,* an adaption of the Roman alphabet to the Vietnamese language.		
1771	Tay Son Rebellion begins under Nguyen Hue, deposing the Nguyen and later the Trinh.		
1776 July		Declaration of Independence signed.	
1778 December	Nguyen Hue declares himself emperor.		
1779 January	Nguyen Hue attacks and defeats Chinese forces at Thang Long (Hanoi) during Tet.		
1787 September		Constitution of the United States signed.	
1802 June	Nguyen Anh, after defeating Tay Son forces with the aid of French missionary Pigneau de Béhaine, becomes emperor Gia Long, establishing his capital at Hue.		

The Colonial Era

Date	Southeast Asia	United States	The War
1858	French fleet under Adm. Rigault de Genouilly bombards Tourane (Da Nang) and captures Saigon.		
1862 June	Vietnam cedes the three eastern provinces of Cochinchina to France under the Treaty of Saigon.		

Date	Southeast Asia	United States	The War
1863 August	France imposes protectorate on Cambodia.		
1867	France occupies the three western provinces of Cochinchina.		
1883 August	France extends protectorate to Annam and Tonkin under the Treaty of Hue, effectively establishing control of Vietnam.		
1887	France creates the Union Indo-Chinoise, which administratively unifies Tonkin, Annam, Cochinchina, and Cambodia.		
1893	France imposes protectorate on Laos.		
1930 February	Ho Chi Minh creates the Indochinese Communist Party.		
1940 March	Japan occupies French Indochina but retains French colonial administration.		
1941 May	Viet Minh established.		
1945 March	Japanese eliminate French rule; Bao Dai proclaims independent Vietnam under Japanese protectorate.		
April		Franklin D. Roosevelt dies; Harry S. Truman becomes president.	
August	Japan surrenders; August Revolution; Bao Dai abdicates.		
September	Ho Chi Minh proclaims the creation of the Democratic Republic of Vietnam (DRV).		
November	Ho Chi Minh dissolves the Indochinese Communist Party.		
1946 March	French declare Vietnam an independent state within the French Union.		
May	Fontainebleau conference begins, lasting until September.		

Date	Southeast Asia	United States	The War
June	Argenlieu proclaims State of Cochinchina.		

The Indochina War

Date	Southeast Asia	United States	The War
1946 November			French naval forces bombard Haiphong, initiating the Indochina War.
1949 March	Élysée Agreement is signed, creating the nominally independent State of Vietnam under former emperor Bao Dai.		
1950 January	The DRV is recognized by the People's Republic of China, the Soviet Union, and Yugoslavia.		
February	The French-organized State of Vietnam is recognized by the United States and Britain.		
July		U.S. begins providing military and economic aid to French effort in Indochina.	
September		U.S. Military Advisory Group–Indochina established.	Battle of Cao Bang.
October			Battle of Lang Son.
1951 February	The Lao Dong Party is created.		
November			Battle of Hoa Binh begins, lasting until February 1952.
1952 November		Dwight D. Eisenhower elected president.	Battle of Na San.
1954 March			Battle of Dien Bien Phu begins, lasting until May 1954.
April		Eisenhower rejects French request for U.S. military intervention at Dien Bien Phu.	
May	Robert Capa killed.		
June	Ngo Dinh Diem is chosen as the State of Vietnam's prime minister by Bao Dai.		

Date	Southeast Asia	United States	The War
July	Geneva agreements signed, partitioning Vietnam at the 17th Parallel pending a national referendum; International Supervision and Control Commission established.		
September	Southeast Asia Treaty Organization (SEATO) established.		
October		J. Lawton Collins sent as special envoy to Diem government, bringing assurances of direct U.S. aid.	Final withdrawal of French troops from Hanoi.
1955 April	Binh Xuyen and Cao Dai defeated by Diem's forces.		
July	Diem refuses to proceed with national elections, rejecting the Geneva accords.		
September	Cambodia becomes independent; Norodom Sihanouk abdicates as king to become prime minister.		
October	Diem deposes Bao Dai by referendum; declares the establishment of the Republic of Vietnam.		

Prelude to U.S. Combat Intervention

Date	Southeast Asia	United States	The War
1955 November		U.S. Military Advisory Group–Vietnam formed from U.S. Military Advisory Group–Indochina.	
1957 June			Last French military advisers leave Republic of Vietnam.
October			Communist insurgency commences in Republic of Vietnam.
1959 May			*Group 559* established.
July		First U.S. casualties of the Vietnam War, Maj. Dale Buis and Sgt. Chester Ovnand, killed at Bien Hoa.	

Date	Southeast Asia	United States	The War
August	National Assembly Law 10/59 enacted.		
September			*Group 959* established.
October			*Group 759* established.
1960 April	Caravelle Group petitions Diem.		
August	Laotian government overthrown by Kong Le.		
November	Unsuccessful coup attempt against Diem.	John F. Kennedy elected president.	
December			National Liberation Front established.
1961 April		Frederick Nolting replaces Elbridge Durbrow as ambassador to South Vietnam.	
May	Geneva Conference convened in response to Laotian crisis, lasting until July 1962.	Vice President Lyndon B. Johnson visits Vietnam.	
1962 February		U.S. Military Assistance Command, Vietnam formed from U.S. Military Advisory Group–Vietnam, with Paul D. Harkins as commander.	Strategic Hamlet program initiated.
1963 January			Battle of Ap Bac.
April	Buddhist demonstrations begin and continue into August.		
June	First of seven Buddhist monks commits self-immolation to protest Diem's policies.		
November	Diem and Nhu assassinated; Duong Van Minh, as head of Military Revolutionary Council, assumes control of South Vietnam.	Kennedy assassinated; Lyndon B. Johnson becomes president.	
1964 January	Nguyen Khanh seizes power from Minh.		
June		William C. Westmoreland replaces Harkins; Maxwell Taylor replaces Lodge.	
August		Congress adopts Gulf of Tonkin Resolution.	Gulf of Tonkin incidents.
December			Viet Cong bomb U.S. officers quarters at Brinks Hotel, Saigon; battle of Binh Gia.

Date	Southeast Asia	United States	The War
1965 February	Khanh flees South Vietnam and Phan Huy Quat becomes prime minister.		Viet Cong attack U.S. base at Pleiku; U.S. retaliates with FLAMING DART air attacks; Viet Cong attack U.S. billet at Qui Nhon.

The Vietnam War

Date	Southeast Asia	United States	The War
1965 March		University of Michigan faculty organize first teach-in.	ROLLING THUNDER begins; U.S. Marines, the first U.S. combat troops committed to Vietnam, land at Da Nang; Viet Cong bomb U.S. embassy at Saigon.
April		Johnson delivers Johns Hopkins speech.	
May		Johnson announces six-day pause in the U.S. bombing of North Vietnam.	
June	Nguyen Cao Ky becomes South Vietnamese prime minister.		First ARC LIGHT strike launched, the first use of B-52s in combat.
July		Lodge reappointed as amabssador to South Vietnam, replacing Taylor; Johnson approves Westmoreland's request for an additional forty-four maneuver battalions.	
August		Henry Cabot Lodge replaces Nolting.	Operation STARLITE. Operation SILVER BAYONET begins, lasting until November.
November		Antiwar demonstrations become widespread.	Battles of the Ia Drang.
December		Johnson announces a thirty-seven day bombing pause.	
1966 January			Operation MASHER/WHITE WING begins, lasting until March.
February		Honolulu conference.	
March	Buddhist antigovernment protests begin in Hue and Da Nang, lasting until June.		

Date	Southeast Asia	United States	The War
April			First use of B-52s against targets in North Vietnam, in strikes on the Mu Gia pass.
October		Manila conference.	
1967 January			Operation CEDAR FALLS.
February	Bernard Fall killed.		Operation JUNCTION CITY begins, lasting until May.
March		Guam conference.	Battle of Con Thien begins, lasting until October.
May		Ellsworth Bunker replaces Lodge; Robert W. Komer becomes Westmoreland's deputy as head of CORDS. Johnson meets with Soviet Prime Minister Alexei N. Kosygin at Glassboro, New Jersey.	
August		Trial of the Chicago Seven begins, lasting until February.	
September	Nguyen Van Thieu elected president of South Vietnam, Ky vice president.	San Antonio speech.	
Autumn			"Border battles" of Song Be, Loc Ninh, and Dak To.
1968 January	Sihanouk meets with U.S. emissary Chester Bowles.		Siege of Khe Sanh begins, lasting until early April; Tet Offensive begins, lasting until late February; North Korea seizes USS *Pueblo*.
February		Westmoreland requests 206,000 additional U.S. troops; Clark Clifford replaces Robert McNamara.	U.S. and ARVN troops recapture Hue from PAVN forces.
March		Creighton Abrams replaces Westmoreland; "wise men" meet; Johnson announces a partial bombing halt and that he will not seek reelection as president.	My Lai massacre.
April		Martin Luther King Jr. assassinated.	

Date	Southeast Asia	United States	The War
May	U.S. and DRV begin negotiations in Pais.		"Mini Tet" offensive.
June		Robert F. Kennedy assassinated.	Khe Sanh abandoned.
August		Democratic national convention at Chicago.	Second "mini Tet" offensive.
October		Johnson announces a total cessation of bombing of North Vietnam.	
November		Richard W. Nixon elected president.	
1969 January	Republic of Vietnam and Provisional Revolutionary Government join Paris peace talks.		
February			Communist forces implement "high point" strategy, rocketing and mortaring South Vietnamese cities. Secret bombing of Cambodia begins, lasting until August 1973.
June		Midway Island conference; Nixon announces Vietnamization.	
September	Death of Ho Chi Minh.		
1970 October		First Moratorium antiwar protest.	
November		"Silent majority" speech; My Lai massacre revealed.	
March			ARVN forces begin cross-border operations into Cambodia.
April	Lon Nol seizes power in Cambodia, deposing Sihanouk.	Mass demonstration supporting Nixon's Vietnam policies, Washington, D.C.	Incursion into Cambodia begins, lasting until June.
May		Widespread antiwar protests; Kent State; Jackson State.	
November		Trial of Lt. William L. Calley Jr. begins, lasting until March 1971.	
December		Congress repeals Gulf of Tonkin Resolution.	
1971 January			ARVN Operation LAM SON 719 begins, lasting until April, supported by U.S. Operation DEWEY CANYON II.

Date	Southeast Asia	United States	The War
April		Massive antiwar protests occur in Washington, D.C., and San Francisco, including Dewey Canyon III protest by Vietnam veterans.	
June		*New York Times* begins publication of the Pentagon Papers.	
October	Thieu reelected president of South Vietnam.		
December			U.S. aircraft begin attacks on PAVN forces in North Vietnam massing in preparation for the Easter Offensive.
1972 February		Nixon visits the People's Republic of China.	
March			Easter Offensive begins.
April			Siege of An Loc begins, lasting until June.
May			Quang Tri City is captured by PAVN forces; Operation LINEBACKER begins, lasting until October.
June		Watergate break-in; Frederick C. Weyand replaces Abrams.	
August			The last U.S. ground combat troops withdraw from Vietnam.
September			ARVN forces recapture Quang Tri City.
November		Nixon reelected president.	
December			Operation LINEBACKER II.
1973 January		Draft ends.	Paris peace accords signed.
February			Communists release 588 U.S. POWs in Operation Homecoming.
March			The last U.S. troops leave Vietnam.
April			The last U.S. POWs are released.
June		Graham Martin replaces Bunker; Congress bans bombing of Cambodia as of August.	

Date	Southeast Asia	United States	The War
October		Vice President Spiro T. Agnew resigns and is replaced by Gerald R. Ford Jr.	
November		Congress overrides Nixon's veto of the War Powers Act.	
1974 January	Fall of South Vietnam's Phuoc Long province.		
August		Nixon resigns; Ford becomes president.	
September		Ford pardons Nixon.	
1975 March			Fall of Ban Me Thuot; Thieu orders abandonment of northern South Vietnam; fall of Hue and Da Nang; Ho Chi Minh Campaign begins.
April	Khmer Rouge assume power in Cambodia; reunification of Vietnam under communist rule.		Fall of Phnom Penh; fall of Saigon.
May			*Mayaguez* incident.
August	Pathet Lao assume control of Laos.		

Aftermath

Date	Southeast Asia	United States	The War
1976 November		Jimmy Carter elected president.	
1977 January		Carter pardons most Vietnam War draft evaders.	
1978 November	Vietnam and the Soviet Union sign mutual defense pact.		
December	Exodus of "boat people" from Vietnam begins.	U.S. establishes full diplomatic relations with People's Republic of China.	Vietnam invades Cambodia.
1979 February			Chinese invasion of Vietnam begins, lasting until March.
1980 November		Ronald Reagen elected president.	
1982 November		Vietnam Veterans Memorial dedicated.	
1984 May		A $180 million out-of-court settlement between seven manufacturers of Agent	

Date	Southeast Asia	United States	The War
1984 May		Orange and Vietnam veterans is announced; an unknown U.S. casualty of the Vietnam War is interred at Arlington National Cemetery.	
November		A statue of three servicemen, added to the Vietnam Veterans Memorial after protests by veterans, is dedicated.	
1986 December	Vietnam initiates economic reforms.		
1988 November		George Bush elected president.	
1989 September			Vietnam withdraws the bulk of its troops from Cambodia.
1990 August	Under United Nations auspices, Cambodian factions agree to form a coalition government and to hold national elections.		
1992 November		Bill Clinton elected president.	
1994 February		Clinton lifts embargo on trade with Vietnam.	
1995 July		Clinton announces recognition of Vietnam.	

Common Abbreviations and Acronyms Used in This Work

AAA	antiaircraft artillery
AB	Air Base
ABC	American Broadcasting Company
Adm.	admiral
AFB	Air Force Base
AID	Agency for International Development
ARVN	Army of the Republic of Vietnam
BBC	British Broadcasting Corporation
Brig.	brigadier
Capt.	captain
CBS	Columbia Broadcasting System
CIA	Central Intelligence Agency
CIDG	Civilian Irregular Defense Group
CINCPAC	Commander-in-Chief, Pacific
cm	centimeter(s)
Col.	colonel
Comdr.	commander (naval rank)
COMUSMACV	Commander, U.S. Military Assistance Command, Vietnam
CORDS	Civil Operations and Revolutionary Development Support
COSVN	Central Office for South Vietnam
CTZ	Corps Tactical Zone
D	Democrat
diss.	dissertation
DMZ	Demilitarized Zone
DRV	Democratic Republic of Vietnam
ed.	editor (pl., eds.); edition
e.g.	*exempli gratia,* for example
et al.	*et alii,* and others
fl.	*floruit,* active during
Gen.	general
HE	high explosive
HEAT	high explosive antitank
HQ	headquarters
i.e.	*id est,* that is
JCS	Joint Chiefs of Staff
JGS	Joint General Staff
kg	kilogram(s)

km	kilometer(s)
Lt.	lieutenant
MAAG–V	Military Assistance Advisory Group–Vietnam
MACV	Military Assistance Command, Vietnam
Maj.	major
mm	millimeter(s)
MR	Military Region
NBC	National Broadcasting Company
NCO	noncommissioned officer
n.d.	no date (of publication)
NLF	National Liberation Front
no.	number (pl., nos.)
n.p.	no place (of publication)
NVA	North Vietnamese Army
p.	page (pl., pp.)
PAVN	People's Army of Vietnam
pl.	plural
PLAF	People's Liberation Armed Forces
PRC	People's Republic of China
PRG	Provisional Revolutionary Government
pt.	part (pl., pts.)
Pvt.	private
R	Republican
Rein.	Reinforced
Rep.	Representative
ret.	retired
rev.	revised
RF/PF	Regional Forces/Popular Forces
RVN	Republic of Vietnam
RVNAF	Republic of Vietnam Armed Forces
SAM	surface-to-air missile
SEATO	Southeast Asia Treaty Organization
sec.	section (pl., secs.)
Sen.	Senator
Sgt.	sergeant
U.K.	United Kingdom
U.S.	United States
USAF	United States Air Force
USARV	United States Army, Vietnam
USMC	United States Marine Corps
USN	United States Navy
USS	United States ship
USSR	Union of Soviet Socialist Republics
VC	Viet Cong
VNAF	Republic of Vietnam Air Force
VNN	Republic of Vietnam Navy
vol.	volume (pl., vols.)

ENCYCLOPEDIA
OF THE
VIETNAM WAR

A

Abrams, Creighton (1914–1974), general, U.S. Army; commander, U.S. Military Assistance Command, Vietnam (COMUSMACV), 1968–1972; U.S. army chief of staff, 1972–1974. Creighton W. Abrams Jr. was commissioned into the cavalry as a member of the West Point class of 1936. Abrams, one of the most noted tank commanders of World War II, led Gen. George Patton's armored relief column to Bastogne during the Battle of the Bulge.

Assigned to the Pentagon during the early 1960s, Abrams commanded federal troops during civil rights protests in the South, and his skill in handling these situations was a factor in President Johnson's subsequent confidence in his abilities. Abrams was vice chief of staff for the U.S. Army during the U.S. buildup in Vietnam, and President Johnson chose him to be deputy COMUSMACV early in 1967. As deputy commander, Abrams had differences with Westmoreland over command policies, relations with the other services, and most importantly, tactics and strategy. But Westmoreland typically bypassed or ignored staff officers, and Abrams was no exception.

As General Westmoreland's deputy, Abrams's primary responsibilities lay in modernizing the Army of the Republic of Vietnam (ARVN) and, in cooperation with Robert W. Komer, managing pacification programs in South Vietnam. By the end of 1967, Abrams was expressing increased confidence in the fighting abilities of the ARVN, in some measure justified by its subsequent performance in the Tet Offensive one month later.

When the communist forces unleashed the Tet Offensive in February 1968, Westmoreland sent Abrams to the northern provinces (I Corps) to coordinate operations between the recently repositioned U.S. Army airmobile divisions, the U.S. Marines, and the South Vietnamese forces.

With the decision to push for negotiations in the aftermath of the Tet Offensive, President Johnson assigned Westmoreland U.S. Army chief of staff and Abrams as his successor as COMUSMACV. Abrams's crucial tasks were to oversee the Vietnamization of the war and, by 1969, to proceed with the withdrawal of U.S. forces at an accelerating pace. The destruction of most large Viet Cong units in South Vietnam during the Tet Offensive meant that U.S. tactics could shift from the earlier search-and-destroy operations, which often involved brigade-size or larger units, to much smaller-scale operations largely limited to local patrolling and pacification missions. Exceptions to the usually

1

small operations during Abrams's tenure were the invasions of Cambodia and Laos, both of which were intended to push North Vietnamese forces away from South Vietnamese borders to buy time for negotiations. Abrams's service spanned the period when the war became more unpopular with the American people. Despite Abrams's and Westmoreland's best efforts, dissent and drug use increasingly reduced the effectiveness of U.S. forces in Vietnam.

With the signing of the Paris peace accords in 1972, President Nixon nominated Abrams to succeed Westmoreland as U.S. Army chief of staff. According to former defense secretary Melvin Laird, Nixon favored Alexander Haig for chief of staff, but Laird insisted on naming Abrams. Laird maintained that the respect of Abrams's fellow officers made him the obvious choice despite civilian political opposition. Laird recognized that Abrams had a difficult task, but "he had an understanding of our country . . . that few military men have."

The last two years of Abrams's life were devoted to the formidable task of rebuilding a U.S. Army that was in disarray. In addition to the trauma of fighting an unpopular war, the army and the armed forces as a whole underwent a precipitate reduction in size and experienced a sense of alienation from American society. Also during Abrams's tenure, the draft was ended; the military services became entirely volunteer forces, with attendant short-term disruption. Abrams died of lung cancer in 1974 while chief of staff.

General Creighton Abrams enjoyed enormous respect within the U.S. Army, although he is little-known or appreciated by the American people. He commanded at every level, from the platoon to the entire U.S. Army. His persona was that of a traditional profane, hard-drinking, cigar-smoking tanker. One reporter described his appearance as resembling "an unmade bed smoking a cigar"—a description Abrams is said to have enjoyed. His contemporaries, however, paint a far subtler portrait. Many thought him one of the best thinkers in the military, certainly at the pinnacle of analytical ability. He read widely and seriously, and enjoyed classical music. Soldiers and politicians alike respected his unquestioned integrity. His relations with Vietnamese forces were good, and he was unusually sensitive to the impact of the war on Vietnamese society and life.

Having seen how the media often savaged Westmoreland despite his efforts to curry favor, Abrams refused to give press conferences. Instead, he granted individual reporters long and detailed interviews, impressing them with his intelligence and grasp of nuance. As a result, Abrams enjoyed positive press throughout the war.

General Abrams is one of the great yet little-known military figures in U.S. history. His life of service, culminating in his assignment as COMUS-MACV during the most difficult period of the Vietnam War and as U.S. Army chief of staff in the war's aftermath, merits greater recognition of his contributions.

BIBLIOGRAPHY

"Changing of the Guard." *Time,* 19 April 1968, 25.

DAVIDSON, PHILLIP B. *Vietnam at War: The History: 1946–1975.* 1991.

HOLLIS, HARRIS W. "The Heart and Mind of Creighton Abrams." *Military Review* (April 1985): 58.

LANGGUTH, A. J. "General Abrams Listens to a Different Drummer." *New York Times Magazine,* 5 May 1968, 28.

SORLEY, LEWIS. *Thunderbolt: General Creighton Abrams and the Army of His Times.* 1992.

K. E. HAMBURGER

Acheson, Dean (1893–1971), U.S. secretary of state, 1949–1953; one of the "wise men" during Lyndon B. Johnson's presidency. Dean Acheson began his tenure as secretary of state somewhat supportive of Southeast Asian nationalism. Although he encouraged President Truman to provide assistance to France in its war against the Viet Minh in Indochina, he viewed France and the Netherlands, which was determined to retain its East Indies colonial empire, as the primary obstacles to peaceful development in Southeast Asia. Acheson's views soon changed, however, and by 1950 he interpreted Vietnamese nationalism as merely a front for Soviet or Chinese communism. He declared that the United States had only two choices in Vietnam: to support Ho Chi Minh (leader of the Viet Minh and a communist, and therefore unacceptable to the United States) or to support former emperor Bao Dai.

During the 1960s Acheson served as one of the "wise men," unofficial advisers to President Johnson. In a meeting of fellow wise men on 26 March 1968, Acheson sharply repudiated his previous endorsement of the Johnson administration's escalation policy, declaring that the United States could not prevent a North Vietnamese victory and, consequently, should seek to end the war.

BIBLIOGRAPHY

KARNOW, STANLEY. *Vietnam: A History.* 1991.

WILLIAMS, WILLIAM APPLEMAN, et al., eds. *America in Vietnam: A Documentary History.* 1985.

ELLEN BAKER

Adams, Sam (died 1988), Central Intelligence Agency (CIA) analyst, 1963–1973. Adams reviewed agent field reports about the strength of Viet Cong and People's Army of Vietnam (PAVN) forces and came to the controversial conclusion that the U.S. military intentionally underestimated the number of enemy troops to bolster claims of progress and to justify further escalation. Adams's charges became the basis for a controversial "60 Minutes" television piece that resulted in Gen. William Westmoreland's multimillion-dollar libel suit against the CBS network.

BIBLIOGRAPHY

ADAMS, SAM. *War of Numbers: An Intelligence Memoir.* 1994.

KARNOW, STANLEY. *Vietnam: A History.* 1991.

KOWET, DON. *A Matter of Honor.* 1984.

KELLY EVANS-PFEIFER

African Americans. The Vietnam War provoked growing opposition from African Americans, both civilians and members of the armed forces. Although African Americans largely supported U.S. intervention until the late 1960s, polls indicate that they turned overwhelmingly against the war—more rapidly and in greater proportion than white Americans. In the military, African American soldiers grew increasingly critical of racial inequities. Their growing concerns, empowered by the civil rights movement and burgeoning black militancy, contributed to increased racial antagonism in the armed forces.

Black military personnel supported U.S. policy toward Vietnam in the initial years of the war. Since the desegregation of the armed forces during the Korean War, African Americans had viewed the military as a haven for economic advancement, and attempts by the military to address racial bias, such as discrimination in off-base housing, had drawn praise from many prominent African American career military personnel. African Americans' enthusiasm reflected and reinforced the generally high morale of the armed forces early in the war.

By 1968, however, there was a new critical attitude among African American soldiers. Influenced by the influx of African American draftees and the expanding civil rights movement, black soldiers questioned the continuing patterns of racial inequality in the military. For instance, in 1969 African Americans accounted for 13.3 percent of all the personnel in the U.S. Army and Marine Corps combined, but they made up only 3 percent of the officer corps of the army and less than 1 percent of the marine officer corps. Many African Americans, who often lacked technical training, performed the lowest level menial duties in rear areas. The military justice system, as congressional and U.S. military studies confirm, dealt more harshly with African American soldiers than with white soldiers.

Most ominously, soldiers expressed resentment at the preponderance of blacks in hazardous combat duty. In the late 1960s, African Americans accounted for roughly 11 percent of the total U.S. population. According to *New York Times* reporter Thomas A. Johnson, African Americans made up approximately 20 percent of combat platoons and 25 percent of high-risk paratrooper units in Vietnam. Although the precise makeup of U.S. casualties remains disputed, evidence indicates that there was a disproportionately high number of casualties among African Americans, particularly for the initial years of the Vietnam War. Pentagon statistics report that blacks suffered nearly 25 percent of U.S. fatalities in late 1965 and early 1966. The Defense Department, alarmed at the high rates, initiated policies to reduce that number, and Pentagon estimates subsequently put African American fatalities at 13.5 percent in 1967 and 14 percent in 1970.

U.S. draft policies contributed to the disproportionate number of African American soldiers in dangerous or less desirable duties. "Project 100,000," begun by the Johnson administration in 1966, lowered mental and physical requirements for inductees. Justified as a social welfare scheme, the project promised remedial and technical education for the "New Standards Men." In practice, the approximately 360,000 draftees (40 percent African American) received limited training, and the result of the program was that many of the poorest Americans were sent to combat duty in Vietnam. Critics charge that the program was intended primarily to avoid calling up additional reserves or repealing the college draft deferral for manpower needs.

In the late 1960s, racial violence engulfed the military services. In 1967, a race riot erupted at the

CHAPPIE JAMES. U.S. Air Force Col. Daniel "Chappie" James Jr. converses with Col. Robin Olds (left), Thailand, 1967. *National Archives*

U.S. Army stockade at Long Binh, Vietnam. In 1969, the marine base at Camp Lejeune, North Carolina, experienced virtual warfare between black and white marines who had just returned from Vietnam. Racial incidents also occurred on the U.S. aircraft carrier *Kitty Hawk* en route to Vietnam in 1972 and on U.S. bases in Germany in the early 1970s. African American challenges to racial insults or perceived discrimination in duty assignments and promotions often served as the impetus for violence. Some scholars, such as Richard Dello Buono, stress the role of a racist white officer corps as an instigator for violent incidents. Others argue that conflict occurred most often between white and African American infantrymen who were nearing the end of their service tours in Vietnam. Ironically, there is evidence that racial incidents occurred more frequently on rear base areas because combat duty may have promoted cooperation within units.

The Vietnam War divided African American elites in the United States. Many prominent civil rights leaders initially refrained from challenging Lyndon Johnson's policies because they viewed the president as a champion of civil rights legislation and the War on Poverty. In January 1966, however,

Martin Luther King Jr. spoke out as a peace advocate. More militant African Americans, such as members of the Student Nonviolent Coordinating Committee (SNCC), railed against the "white man's war," and challenged U.S. policy as racist oppression of nonwhite peoples. Many antiwar African Americans assailed the disproportionately high rates of African American fatalities in Vietnam. Poll data indicate that a majority of black Americans had turned against the war by 1969. By 1971, a Gallup poll found that 83 percent of black Americans believed the war was a mistake, significantly higher than the 67 percent of white Americans.

Racial friction in the U.S. armed forces subsided in the mid 1970s. The onset of the volunteer army, and meliorative racial programs instituted by the U.S. military contributed to the decline. Since the Vietnam War, the armed forces have attracted increasing numbers of African American men and women. As Bernard Nalty suggests, many African American high school graduates value the economic opportunities available in the military. In 1991, African American soldiers accounted for nearly 25 percent of the U.S. military personnel in the Persian Gulf War, just above their proportion in the armed forces worldwide.

BIBLIOGRAPHY

DELLO BUONO, RICHARD A. "The Vietnam War and African Americans." *The African American Encyclopedia.* Edited by Michael Williams. 1993.

JOHNSON, THOMAS A. "The U.S. Negro in Vietnam." *New York Times,* 29 April 1968.

KING, WILLIAM M., ed. "A White Man's War: Race Issues and Vietnam." *Vietnam Generation* (Spring 1989).

NALTY, BERNARD C. *Strength for the Fight: A History of Black Americans in the Military.* 1986.

TERRY, WALLACE. *Bloods: An Oral History of the Vietnam War by Black Veterans.* 1984.

YARMOLINSKY, ADAM. *The Military Establishment: Its Impact on American Society.* 1971.

ADAM LAND

Agency for International Development (AID).

A part of the State Department, the Agency for International Development originated out of the Foreign Assistance Act of 1961. Taking over the functions of its predecessors—the International Cooperation Administration and the Development Loan Fund—AID became the principal U.S. agency responsible for the design and implementation of nonmilitary U.S. development and assistance programs. Providing loans and grants—over $2 billion per year by 1965—AID programs emphasized long-range plans to build the economies of less developed countries and attempted to direct U.S. development aid to the areas of health, agriculture, population planning, education, and energy. Complementing the money AID invested, the agency sent specialists abroad to support the implementation of projects and the training of foreign nationals.

Between 1962 and 1975, South Vietnam received by far the largest portion of AID economic assistance. In 1967 alone the agency's budget allocated more than $550 million for Vietnam, the majority through the Commercial-Import Program (CIP). Between the early 1960s and 1972, AID attempted to establish self-help projects, schools, health clinics, and farming cooperatives. The agency provided funds for the construction and renovation of 20 hospitals and the building of more than 170 district, 370 village, and 400 hamlet maternity dispensaries. More than 774 American physicians, contracted by AID, served sixty-day tours of duty in these hospitals. Seeking to bring a measure of collectivity to the villages, AID workers in 1966 instituted village elections in "secure" areas. In the late 1960s, AID commissioned plans for the postwar development of South Vietnam, believing that the United States would win the war and "modernize" the country.

Although Congress had separated military and economic assistance in its 1961 legislation, policymakers considered foreign assistance to Southeast Asia part of containment policy. Particularly in South Vietnam, they saw long-term economic development as insurance against revolution, and a significant part of AID assistance went to police forces and counterinsurgency programs. In 1955, the International Cooperation Administration, under the cover of a Michigan State University advisory group, had financed a team of Central Intelligence Agency (CIA) specialists to teach South Vietnamese police forces and intelligence services techniques that could be used against the Viet Cong guerrillas. In the mid 1960s, AID's Office of Public Safety coordinated an effort to enlarge and upgrade the South Vietnamese police force, emphasizing "law enforcement" with more local roots for the rural population. AID representatives, however, were most successful when working with villagers individually or with the Hoa Hao and the Catholics, the only two independent organizations in rural areas that were able to resist Viet Cong guerrilla infiltration.

AID literature extolled South Vietnam as a success story in the 1950s and early 1960s. But by the late 1960s, as the war became more unpopular in the United States and after revelations of CIA involvement in AID programs, AID's public image suffered. The AID's overall efforts to help stabilize and maintain the government of South Vietnam by providing economic and development assistance proved ill-conceived. The disruption caused by the war, the corruption of government officials, and the heavy-handedness of the South Vietnamese government undermined the agency's programs. By the end of the decade, AID programs had little lasting effect, and only the U.S. military presence prevented the government's collapse.

BIBLIOGRAPHY

GIBSON, JAMES WILLIAM. *The Perfect War: Technowar in Vietnam.* 1986.

KOLKO, GABRIEL. *Anatomy of a War: Vietnam, the United States, and the Modern Historical Experience.* 1985.

WOOD, ROBERT E. *From Marshall Plan to Debt Crisis: Foreign Aid and Development Choices in the World Economy.* 1986.

PAUL M. TAILLON

Agent Orange. *See* Chemical Warfare.

Agnew, Spiro T. (1918–), governor of Maryland, 1967–1969; U.S. vice president, 1969–1973. As Richard M. Nixon's vice president, Agnew harshly criticized antiwar protesters and the news media, particularly in a speech on 13 November 1969 in Des Moines. He attacked the media for its liberal eastern bias. Agnew's efforts contributed to Nixon's "silent majority" strategy to marshal support in the wake of antiwar protests. Agnew resigned in October 1973, after strong allegations of criminal conduct while governor and vice president were raised against him. He was succeeded by Gerald R. Ford Jr.

BIBLIOGRAPHY

COYNE, JOHN R., JR. *The Impudent Snobs: Agnew vs. the Intellectual Establishment.* 1972.
SMALL, MELVIN. *Johnson, Nixon, and the Doves.* 1988.

WILLIAM PAUL SCHUCK

Agricultural Reform Tribunals. The Democratic Republic of Vietnam (DRV) operated agricultural reform tribunals between 1954 and August 1956 as part of its campaign to destroy landlords in rural North Vietnam, in keeping with Marxist ideology. Few peasants owned more than a few acres, however. Nevertheless, because the tribunals had quotas of landlords to fill, thousands of alleged landlords were killed and thousands more were banished to labor camps, many of them victims of unsubstantiated accusations made by those wishing to settle old scores. Consequently, the country's economy, already weak, was further debilitated. The tribunals sparked a peasant revolt in November 1956 in Ho Chi Minh's native province, Nhge An, and he sent in a division of North Vietnamese Army troops to quell it.

BIBLIOGRAPHY

FENN, CHARLES. *Ho Chi Minh: A Biographical Introduction.* 1973.
KARNOW, STANLEY. *Vietnam: A History.* 1991.
LACOUTURE, JEAN. *Ho Chi Minh: A Political Biography.* 1968.

ELLEN D. GOLDLUST

Aiken, George (1892–1984), U.S. senator (R-Vt.), 1941–1975; member, Senate Foreign Relations

SPIRO T. AGNEW. At right, with Richard M. Nixon. *Library of Congress*

Committee, 1954–1975. Aiken initially supported U.S. military intervention in Vietnam. By 1966, however, he opposed the war as a mistaken policy and urged President Johnson to declare the United States the winner, withdraw the troops, and end the war.

BIBLIOGRAPHY

DIETZ, TERRY. *Republicans and Vietnam, 1961–1968.* 1986.

JENNIFER FROST

Air America. A creation of the Central Intelligence Agency's Directorate for Plans, Air America became one of the largest commercial proprietary corporations of the Central Intelligence Agency (CIA). Air America was a conglomerate airline wholly owned by the CIA. It supported covert and paramilitary activities, flying missions in Laos, Vietnam, and Cambodia, where it ferried people and supplies when the use of U.S. military aircraft was undesirable. Personnel carried by Air America included visiting VIPs (e.g., former vice president Richard Nixon in 1965), prisoners, U.S. casualties, and CIA operatives from the Special Operations Group and the Phoenix program. Air America also transported opium grown by U.S.-backed Hmong tribesmen in northeastern Laos, U.S. proxies fighting the so-called secret war against the Pathet Lao. The sale of opium was key to the Hmong's financial survival, and Air America proved vital to maintaining this drug-based lifeline. Air America eventually proved to be too visible, and revelations about its illegal activities led to cutbacks in large proprietary activity by the CIA.

BIBLIOGRAPHY

McCoy, Alfred. *The Politics of Heroin in Southeast Asia.* 1972.

Robbins, Christopher. *Air America.* 1979.

VICTOR JEW

Air Force, U.S. The U.S. Air Force, established in 1947, was the preeminent air force in the Vietnam War. The U.S. Army controlled more aircraft (mainly helicopters) and the U.S. Navy and Marine Corps performed many of the same missions, but the U.S. Air Force dropped more destructive energy than the others combined and left its mark on the conflict through a strongly held belief in the strategic decisiveness of centrally controlled air power. The air force entered Vietnam with strike assets divided between the Strategic Air Command (SAC) and the Tactical Air Command (TAC) and overseas tactical air forces, notably the Pacific Air Forces (PACAF). The air force also possessed a globe-circling transport fleet, the Military Air Transport Service (MATS, later Military Airlift Command [MAC]). Many transport aircraft were also assigned to TAC and the overseas air forces. The active duty force was backed by Air National Guard and Air Force Reserve units.

The Air Force in Southeast Asia. The air force combat commitment to Vietnam began in late 1961 when President Kennedy sent air commando units equipped with propeller-driven, piston-engine A-26 bombers, T-28 ground attack-trainer aircraft, and C-123 transports modified to spray defoliants, notably Agent Orange, and insecticides. In 1964–1965, there was a massive air force buildup in Southeast Asia under President Johnson. Command relationships were complex and were marked by attempts, strongly resisted by the navy and partic-

ularly by the marines, to bring all fixed-wing air power under air force control. Air force operations were controlled by the Seventh Air Force (2d Air Division before April 1966) in Saigon except for B-52 ARC LIGHT strikes, which began on 18 June 1965 and were controlled directly by SAC.

The air force's war was divided into five distinct campaigns. The first, in South Vietnam, was waged in support of ground forces, primarily by aircraft based there. These included tactical fighters, notably F-100s, F-4s, and propeller-driven piston-engine A-1s, and a large tactical airlift fleet, notably C-123s and C-7s obtained from the army.

The second air force campaign was the ROLLING THUNDER offensive against North Vietnam, which began on 2 March 1965 and was driven by Secretary of Defense Robert McNamara's theory of graduated escalation that featured tight control of targets, and even tactics, by President Johnson. Thailand-based F-105 and F-4 fighter bombers were air force mainstays of the war over North Vietnam. Fought in conjunction with carrier-based navy air power, the campaign was waged in the face of unprecedentedly dense concentrations of antiaircraft artillery, Soviet-built SA-2 surface-to-air missiles (SAMs), and limited, but effective, use of MiG-17 and MiG-21 interceptor aircraft. The air force response to these defenses included standoff jamming aircraft, which used electronic counter-measures (ECM) to jam defensive radar while out of antiaircraft range, and specialized "Wild Weasel" anti-SAM strike fighters. ROLLING THUNDER was severely curtailed by President Johnson on 31 March 1968 and cancelled on 31 October as part of a U.S. peace initiative. President Nixon's LINEBACKER and LINEBACKER II campaigns, March–October and 18–29 December 1972, respectively, were extensions of ROLLING THUNDER.

The third air force campaign, conducted under the code names STEEL TIGER, TIGER HOUND, and COMMANDO HUNT, was an interdiction campaign against the Ho Chi Minh Trail, the network of communist supply lines in southern Laos and northeastern Cambodia. This campaign was waged primarily by Thailand-based air force units, the later stages featured the extensive use of small, air-dropped seismic and acoustic sensors to detect the movement of troops and vehicles along the trail, forming the so-called McNamara Line. [*See* Barrier Concept.]

The fourth campaign (December 1963–February 1973) was in northern Laos in support of the Royal Laotian Army, guerrillas trained and supplied

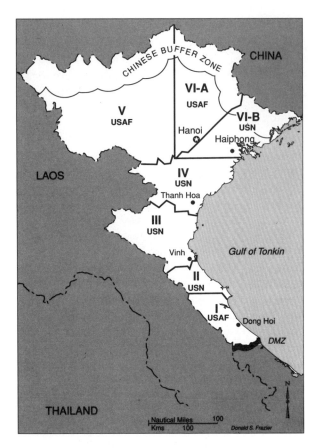

**U.S. AIR FORCE–U.S. NAVY ROUTE
PACKAGES.** Imposed in December 1965 by Adm. U. S.
Grant Sharp, CINCPAC, the so-called route packages
divided responsibility for bombing operations over North
Vietnam between the U.S. Navy and the U.S. Air Force. As
the map indicates, coastal targets were primarily reserved
for carrier-based Navy aircraft; inland targets were usually
allowed to longer-range Air Force aircraft mostly operating
from bases in Thailand and South Vietnam. Operations were
strictly forbidden within a buffer zone along the Chinese
border. (Map adapted from Barrett Tillman and John B.
Nichols, *On Yankee Station.* Naval Institute Press, 1987.)

by the Central Intelligence Agency (CIA), and Thai
ground forces. Much smaller than the other campaigns and never openly acknowledged, it was controlled by the various U.S. ambassadors to Laos. The
fifth campaign was in support of the Lon Nol government of Cambodia and lasted from March 1969
until August 1973.

**Air Force Efforts Extended Beyond Bomb-
ing.** The airlift capacity of the air force played a
major role in the Vietnam War. After the initial
buildup, most military personnel arrived in Vietnam
and returned home aboard MAC transports and
civilian jetliners operating under MAC contract.
Turboprop C-130 transports were used throughout

Southeast Asia and the Pacific. Air force airborne
forward air controllers (FACs), who directed air
strikes from propeller-driven light aircraft, were a
major feature of the war in South Vietnam, along
the Ho Chi Minh Trail, and in northern Laos. Technical and tactical air force contributions to the U.S.
war effort included the extensive use of air refueling; the development of fixed-wing, side-firing
gunships (notably the AC-47 and AC-130); and the
creation of a specialized combat rescue organization
based on long-range, air-refuelable HH-3E and
HH-53C helicopters.

Losses and Achievements. The air force lost
2,257 aircraft, 1,737 of them combat losses including 33 helicopters, and 2,584 personnel killed in action (KIA). The casualty profile differed sharply
from that of the army and Marine corps but resembled that of the navy in that most KIAs were officer
aviators. Casualties, defined as those killed in action
or wounded seriously enough to require hospital-
ization, comprised only 1.2 percent of air force personnel who served in Southeast Asia, as opposed to
22.5 percent for the marines and 9.5 percent for the
army. However, 65 percent of those killed in action
were officers. The median rank of air force KIAs was
captain (653 lost); more majors were killed in action
(399) than first lieutenants (236) and nearly as many
colonels (184) as lieutenant colonels (187).

The air force was the largest player in the air
power arena, and air power played a major role in
sustaining South Vietnam militarily, inflicted heavy
losses on North Vietnamese and Viet Cong forces,
and reduced the toll on U.S. and allied ground
forces. The air force left Vietnam with an unshaken
faith in air power's strategic decisiveness, but air
power did not win the war, and detractors argue
that it could not have done so. Advocates respond
that air power was not given a chance, citing the
dramatic operational success of the LINEBACKER
campaigns in achieving Nixon's objectives and arguing that Johnson and McNamara's micro-man-
agement of ROLLING THUNDER doomed it to failure.
It is important to note, however, that Nixon's policy
objectives in 1972–1973 were far more modest than
Johnson's in 1965–1968. Tactically, the air force re-
learned the value of realistic combat-oriented training, a lesson administered by losses to MiGs in
air-to-air combat. Following the navy's lead, it responded by creating aggressor squadrons trained to
simulate Soviet-bloc air-to-air tactics and by initiating the Red Flag series of exercises in late 1974.

[*See also* ARC LIGHT; LINEBACKER and LINE-
BACKER II; Medical Support, *article on* U.S. Military;

MENU; RANCH HAND; ROLLING THUNDER; Search and Rescue; Women, U.S. Military, *article on* Women in the Air Force (WAF).]

BIBLIOGRAPHY

MORROCCO, JOHN. *Rain of Fire: Air War 1969–1973.* Vol. 14 of *Vietnam Experience Series.* 1985.

MORROCCO, JOHN. *Thunder from Above: Air War, 1941–1968.* Vol. 9 of *Vietnam Experience Series.* 1984.

SCHLIGHT, JOHN. *The War in South Vietnam: The Years of the Offensive, 1965–1968.* 1988.

TILFORD, EARL H., JR. *Setup: What the Air Force Did in Vietnam and Why.* 1991.

JOHN F. GUILMARTIN JR.

Ali, Muhammad (1942–), born Cassius Clay; American heavyweight boxing champion (1964–1967). Drafted in 1966, Ali, a Black Muslim, unsuccessfully applied for conscientious objector status on religious grounds. When he refused to report for duty, he was stripped of his boxing title and in June 1967, was convicted of violating the Selective Service Act, fined $10,000, and sentenced to five years in prison. The Supreme Court, in *Clay v. United States* (403 U.S. 698 [1971]), reversed the conviction.

BIBLIOGRAPHY

HAUSER, THOMAS. *Muhammad Ali: His Life and Times.* 1991.

JENNIFER FROST

Amerasians. After the end of the Vietnam War, Amerasian children—whose fathers were U.S. servicemen and whose mothers were Vietnamese women—were a significant and visible group in Vietnam, and most sought to emigrate to the United States. Amerasians also exist in other countries where Americans served, in Korea, Laos, and Thailand. The most commonly accepted estimate of the number of Amerasians in Southeast Asia is 30,000, but estimates range from 10,000 to 200,000. Of these, most (65–75 percent) were fathered by Euro-American soldiers, the rest by African Americans. Amerasian children, particularly those of African American parentage, were illtreated and discriminated against in Vietnam.

U.S. immigration policy toward Amerasians evolved during the 1980s. In 1982, Congress passed legislation accepting Amerasians as U.S. citizens. However, because the United States and Vietnam had not yet established diplomatic relations, Amerasians in Vietnam were excluded from the bill. Af-

ter much criticism, the U.S. government qualified for entrance to the United States any person born in Vietnam between 1 January 1962 and 1 January 1976 and who was fathered by a citizen of the United States. Amerasians are not required to prove their paternity; they simply must have observable physical characteristics of an African American or Euro-American. Even after this change in policy, Amerasian emigration from Vietnam proceeded slowly until the Amerasian Homecoming Act of 1987 set a timetable for bringing all Amerasians and their family members to the United States. By 1990, about 22,000 Amerasian refugees had settled in the United States. Many of these Amerasians, however, were confused about their own ethnic identity and were not always accepted in the Vietnamese American community. Thus, resettlement in the United States has proved a difficult process for many.

BIBLIOGRAPHY

RUTLEDGE, PAUL JAMES. *The Vietnamese Experience in America.* 1992.

JENNIFER FROST

American Antiwar Movement. *See* Antiwar Movement.

American Friends of Vietnam. Supporters of South Vietnam's the embattled formed the American Friends of Vietnam in 1955 to promote American support for the embattled president of South Vietnam. Professor Wesley Fishel of Michigan State University led the organization, which consisted largely of American mainstream liberals. Charter members included Sen. John F. Kennedy, the historian Arthur M. Schlesinger Jr., and Norman Thomas, the perennial socialist presidential candidate. The group acted as an unofficial lobby for Diem's government until support for Diem waned in the early 1960s.

The organization became active again in 1965 after a wave of teach-ins on college campuses questioned President Lyndon Johnson's Vietnam policies. National Security Council aide Chester Cooper recommended using pro-administration Vietnam experts not officially tied to the White House to defend Johnson's policies. The administration turned to the Friends of Vietnam to organize this effort. In 1965 and 1966, the Friends organized a speaker's bureau of pro-administration Vietnam experts and arranged more than one hundred speeches, many on college campuses. In the fall of 1965, the organization also produced a newsletter, *Vietnam Perspectives,* to counter the antiwar *Viet Report.*

An April 1966 *Ramparts* article exposing Fishel's and Michigan State's deep ties to the South Vietnamese government undermined the organization. By late 1966, the group was weak but it had temporarily assisted in limiting the erosion of support for Johnson's policies.

BIBLIOGRAPHY

SCHEER, ROBERT, and HINCKLE, WARREN. "The Viet-Nam Lobby." *Ramparts* (July 1965).
SMALL, MELVIN. *Johnson, Nixon, and the Doves.* 1988.

WILLIAM PAUL SCHUCK

American Perspectives

"We've All Been There"—The War and American Memory

The Veteran's Changing Image
A Divided Generation
Vietnam's Contradictory Lessons
A Darkened Vision of America
Learning about the War
Refugees from a Long War
New Americans

"Dear Michael: Your name is here but you are not. I made a rubbing of it, thinking that if I rubbed hard enough I would rub your name off the wall and you would come back to me. I miss you so."

No one leaves notes or offerings at Washington's many other monuments. But the Vietnam Veterans Memorial is unlike any other monument. From the moment of its dedication, the wall with its 58,196 names inscribed on slabs of polished black granite has seemed to give physical form to a whole nation's feelings of pain and loss. The names unify, while other words about the war continue to divide. "It doesn't say whether the war was right or wrong," a man whose son was wounded in Vietnam, but survived, said about the wall. ". . . It just says, 'Here is the price we paid.' "

The memorial's emotional power is easier to describe than to explain. In part it comes from the names, which make the war's loss personal and concrete and immediate instead of distant and abstract. In part it comes from the reflecting surface, where those looking at the wall can also see the sky and trees and their own faces mirrored in the black stone behind the names of the dead.

There is a kind of mystery in those reflected images. It is as if the stone surface really became what its creator, Maya Ying Lin, imagined: a meeting-place "between the sunny world and the quiet dark world beyond, that we can't enter." That sense of closeness between the dead and living may explain why visitors so often do not just look but touch, as if they can send their messages of sorrow and love through their fingertips. At the memorial, communication with the dark world seems possible. Thus, along with tears and touching, the wall of names became a place for tokens of remembrance: not only letters but photographs, old dogtags and decorations, flags, religious medals, birthday and Christmas cards, faded scraps of uniforms and military equipment, souvenirs of war and high school and childhood.

These offerings expressed love and grief for the dead and often something more: a laying down of burdens, a release from the past. People came there to make peace with their memories—like a former marine sergeant named Frederick Garten, who left a ring and a note: "This wedding ring belonged to a young Viet Cong fighter. He was killed by a Marine unit in the Phu Loc province of South Vietnam in May of 1968. I wish I knew more about this young man. I have carried this ring for 18 years and it's time for me to lay it down. This boy is not my enemy any longer."

Lin's design (selected when she was only twenty-one years old and studying architecture at Yale University) was at first bitterly denounced by those favoring a more conventionally patriotic monument. But criticism was quickly overwhelmed by the public's reaction. Rarely in the long history of art, if ever, has an object crafted from stone affected a society's emotions so widely and deeply as the Vietnam memorial.

Most intense and dramatic, perhaps, was its impact on the veterans themselves, for whom the wall represented a place for healing and the end of the long silence in which most had shrouded their experiences for many years.

The Veteran's Changing Image. "You don't go to war, come home, and not talk about it," Bobby Muller once said. Muller, a disabled veteran and founder of the Vietnam Veterans of America, thus pinpointed the special pain of that war's soldiers—that when they came home, the country that sent them to war did not want to hear what happened to them there.

The popular folklore of returning soldiers being cursed or spit on was almost certainly exaggerated, but the experience of being silenced (which felt a good deal like being shunned) was common to nearly every veteran. Not infrequently, veterans reentered civilian life and told no one, not even wives or girlfriends, that they had served in Vietnam. And because their experiences remained untold they were also in a sense incomplete; the war remained within them "like a buried piece of shrapnel working its way to the surface," as one of them wrote.

After an unpopular, unsuccessful, and morally confusing war, most Americans, it seemed, just wanted to forget it as quickly as possible. The veterans were an uncomfortable reminder of a subject no one wanted to speak about, or remember. Though the failure of American policy was surely not the fault of the young men who were sent to do the fighting, they were often made to feel as if they alone carried the stigma of failure and the moral burden of violence.

"In past wars," Jack Smith, a psychologist and Marine Corps veteran, explained to the author Myra MacPherson, "through cleansing acts, society *shared* the blame and responsibility" with its soldiers; "victory banners, medals, and parades were ways of recognizing the tasks they did in the country's name." But after the Vietnam War, "the responsibility and blame was left on the heads of the guys who fought it. They were left to sort out who was responsible for what."

Because there was no victory and because America reached no consensus, no comforting myth to tell its soldiers why they had fought, it was also left to each veteran to find, alone, the meaning of his or her experience. Many could not. "I want it to have been worth *something,*" the poet W. D. Ehrhart, who was badly wounded in the war, burst out to a friend after coming home, "and I can't make myself believe that it was."

The memorial and the public response to it released many veterans from their silence and represented an expression of respect, however belated, for their sacrifice. It was not coincidental that Vietnam, almost unmentioned for nearly a decade after U.S. troops came home, became highly visible in American popular culture almost as soon as the wall was dedicated. The 1980s saw a proliferation of movies, books, and television shows depicting the war, or with Vietnam veterans shown in a favorable light—even a heroic one.

But the veteran's new image was not, as some shrewd critics noticed, exactly in the tradition of earlier war heroes. "The stereotype has been shattered," observed Joseph Ferrandino of Columbia University, but instead of being transformed into a conventional patriotic hero, literature's "new" Vietnam veteran represented something quite different.

> He is not a hero because he sacrificed himself for something "larger." He is a hero because he survived. He survived for no reasons other than he wanted to live, to raise a family, see the future. . . . The Viet Vet, as cultural hero, depends on no one but himself for survival. After having been fooled by his government and rejected by his peers, he holds everyone in equal distrust.

The veteran, in other words, was not an icon of faith or selflessness, but of skepticism, alienation, and individual survival as the supreme value; still a symbol of courage, perhaps, but one fitting a more cynical and selfish time. In a way this mirrored the soldiers' experience of the war itself, in which—particularly after the United States began withdrawing—there seemed no reason for fighting *other* than for their own survival. "I didn't care who won," recalled William Frassanito, who was sent to Vietnam in 1970. "I just wanted to make sure I got home. . . . I was taking one guy over, and bringing one guy back."

Public recognition and a changing image began to erase the stigma many veterans felt they carried. They welcomed the respect the country was finally ready to give. But for many vets, it was still not easy to interpret and absorb their own experience. In the spring of 1985, shortly after New York City's long overdue parade for Vietnam veterans, playwright David Berry described to a friend how torn he had felt—reluctant to march because he felt the parade was being used to glorify and justify the war, but equally reluctant not to march because that would be turning his back on his fellow veterans.

The dilemma kept him sleepless for the entire night before the parade, Berry said; and as he lay awake he kept asking himself another question, too: fifteen years after coming home, he thought, why did he still feel trapped in the war? "When am I going to stop brooding about Vietnam and get on with the rest of my life?"

A Divided Generation. Not just the veterans, but an entire generation, seemed unable to turn the page on the war. Many men who had avoided service also found difficulty in coming to terms with their Vietnam history—particularly those who felt, as many did, that they had benefited from a system that favored upper-middle-class, college-educated men over those from less privileged backgrounds.

In an article titled "What Did You Do in the Class War, Daddy?" writer James Fallows recalled how, after graduating from Harvard University in 1969, he escaped the draft by starving himself below the 120-pound weight requirement. One didn't have to be a Harvard graduate to use that technique. But boys from farms or from working-class or black or Hispanic neighborhoods weren't as practiced or as diligent in searching out the many ways to exploit the draft law's loopholes; nor did they as easily find the sympathetic doctors and psychiatrists who helped large numbers of college graduates obtain draft exemptions on medical grounds.

On the day of his own draft physical, Fallows recalled, as he and his Cambridge friends pursued their carefully planned strategies to escape the army, another busload of young men arrived from working-class Chelsea: "It had clearly never occurred to them that there might be a way around the draft. They walked through the examination lines like so many cattle off to slaughter. I tried to avoid noticing, but the results were inescapable. While perhaps four out of five of my friends

THE FALL OF SAIGON. That this photograph was taken by a North Vietnamese photographer underscores the urgency of the last-minute evacuation of U.S. personnel and select Vietnamese from Saigon, Operation FREQUENT WIND, 29–30 April 1975. *Reuters*

from Harvard were being deferred, just the opposite was happening to the Chelsea boys."

Fallows's recollections pinpointed a key fact about the Vietnam era. Instead of being a unifying experience, as military service had been in World War II (when college graduates were overrepresented, instead of underrepresented, in the riskiest combat assignments), the makeup of the Vietnam-era army contributed to a widening of class divisions in American society—a widening that was already under way as the result of other trends: the bifurcation of cities and suburbs, the loss of upward mobility as highly paid manufacturing jobs grew scarcer, and an educational system that increasingly seemed to serve the "haves" much better than the "have-nots."

The all-volunteer army, a direct legacy of Vietnam, clearly perpetuated that social gap. Without the draft, few men or women from upper-middle-class backgrounds chose to accept the regimentation and relatively modest compensation of a military career. Ironically, once the war in Vietnam was over, the armed forces also increasingly shut their doors to those from the poorest backgrounds, for whom military service had once offered a route to education, economic security and higher social status. New technology demanded better-educated soldiers; lower force levels enabled the services to recruit much more selectively. School dropouts or youngsters with minor criminal records could rarely qualify for enlistment. By the 1990s, neither the elite nor the very poor were to be found in uniform in significant numbers; the absence of that shared experience also meant, almost surely, less sense of common citizenship or a shared destiny as Americans.

As members of the Vietnam generation began to climb the rungs of America's political ladder, there were insistent echoes of the divide between those who had served in Vietnam and those who had not. When it was discovered during the 1988 election campaign that George Bush's running mate, Dan Quayle, had done his wartime military service in the Indiana National Guard instead of the regular armed forces, many critics instantly concluded that Quayle had been able to dodge Vietnam only because he came from a wealthy and influential family. Quayle insisted he had not been trying to avoid going to Vietnam. But as most men of his generation could remember, joining the National Guard was a virtual guarantee against being sent to the war zone; it was also an option very rarely available to young men facing the wartime draft.

Four years later during the 1992 presidential primaries, a similar furor erupted over the draft record of Gov. Bill Clinton of Arkansas. Clinton, after getting his draft notice, had delayed being inducted by promising to join the University of Arkansas ROTC (Reserve Officer Training Corps) program but had then re-neged, withdrawing his commitment just before he escaped the draft altogether by receiving a high number in the draft lottery that began in late 1969. Clinton (one of whose opponents in the 1992 primaries was Sen. Bob Kerrey of Ne-braska, a Medal of Honor winner in Vietnam) opposed the war, unlike Quayle, and acknowledged he had hoped to avoid it; thus he was spared the charge of hypocrisy frequently leveled at Quayle.

The two controversies drew heavy press coverage and the customary din of partisan commentary, pro and con. The issue certainly left a residue in voters' minds, particularly about Clinton, but neither his nor Quayle's draft history seemed to have a strong impact on voters' decisions. (Nor, for that matter, did Kerrey's heroic war record, or George Bush's.) The subject continued to dog Clinton from time to time during the 1992 campaign and after his election— most visibly on the first Memorial Day of his presidency, when veterans booed and demonstratively turned their backs on him during a ceremony at the Viet-nam memorial. The fact that Clinton had never served in the armed forces was an underlying factor in his often strained relations with the military leadership. In general, though, while his Vietnam record was clearly not a political asset, the country did not appear to hold it too strongly against him, either. Veterans' groups, including Vietnam Veterans of America, opposed Clinton's decision in early 1994 to lift the long-standing U.S. trade embargo against Vietnam, but even that did not provoke sustained controversy.

The relatively moderate response to Clinton's draft history suggested that Americans were not so quick, after all, to judge decisions made years earlier by young men in a troubled time. Unforgiving voices were still raised on both sides, but for most Americans the issues of a confusing and troubling war were still am-biguous, still defying easy or simple judgments, as the Vietnam generation moved on through middle age.

Vietnam's Contradictory Lessons. Like a weird relative popping out of the attic, Vietnam kept unexpectedly reappearing in American political debate, sometimes as text, sometimes as subtext. Like the veterans, "the rest of the coun-try can't seem to forget, either," wrote the novelist and journalist Jack Fuller, "but it doesn't know what exactly to remember."

It sees Vietnam everywhere, a ghost in every conflict. Vietnam in Angola. Vietnam in Nicaragua. Vietnam in El Salvador, in Guatemala, in Beirut. The ghost whispers contradictory messages. To some it says, "Stay out." To others it says, "Fight this one to win." . . . From time to

HOMECOMING. USAF Capt. Michael S. Kerr holds his wife, Jerri, as their children, Rick and Michele, look on, 7 March 1973, Travis AFB, California. Capt. Kerr was shot down over North Vietnam 16 January 1967. *United Press International*

time, politicians have proclaimed that we have finally put the war behind us. But we have always proven them wrong.

Through the 1980s, Americans generally saw Vietnam's lessons in the light of their own ideologies. Those favoring a muscular, activist foreign policy, usually agreeing that Vietnam was lost by Washington's timidity rather than by flawed policy, railed against a "Vietnam syndrome" that they felt crippled American leaders by constraining the use (or threat) of military force. On the other side of the debate were those who regarded the war as a tragic error born of arrogance, a misplaced confidence in military force, and a distorted strategic vision that failed, as the historian Barbara Tuchman observed, to see "that problems and conflicts exist among other peoples that are not soluble by the application of American force or American techniques or even American goodwill."

The ghost also whispered to the military itself, which came out of Vietnam so scarred that even twenty years later the wound still seemed fresh. The Vietnam

THE WALL. Relatives of soldiers killed in the Vietnam conflict mourn at the newly dedicated Vietnam Veterans Memorial, Washington, D.C., 11 November 1982. *United Press International*

War had been a painfully harsh test of nearly every aspect of U.S. military doctrine. (As early as 1969, one defense consultant's study ruefully observed that "the enemy, on purpose or not, has managed in the course of the Vietnam war to pulverize almost all of our military and strategic concepts.") Post-Vietnam U.S. military leaders were extraordinarily reluctant to get into any war that might prove long or inconclusive or ambiguous in result. Determined never to fight again without full public support, the military demanded authority to use enough force to assure a short, if brutal, conflict with an absolute minimum of American losses. As demonstrated in the 1983 Grenada invasion, in Panama, and in the Persian Gulf War, senior commanders also favored the tightest possible controls on news coverage of future wars, to assure that as far as possible, reporting would show the military and U.S. policies in a favorable light.

The Cold War ended and new conflicts brought new place names into the policy debates of the 1990s: Kuwait, Somalia, Haiti, Bosnia. But Vietnam still hovered over every crisis. During the buildup for the 1991 war against Iraq, President Bush at times sounded almost frantic in his assurances that this would not be another frustrating quagmire. In one press conference in December 1990 he declared three times in the space of six sentences that the Persian Gulf would not be "another Vietnam."

Explicitly and implicitly, once the fighting began, the Gulf War became in part a ritual exorcism of Vietnam. The flags and yellow ribbons fluttering outside millions of American homes and shops, symbolizing patriotism and support for troops in the Gulf, also expressed a kind of apology for not having given the same sympathetic support to American soldiers in Vietnam. News coverage was more celebratory than skeptical, and the U.S. theater commander, Gen. Norman Schwarzkopf, became an instant national hero. "The specter of Vietnam has been buried forever in the desert sands of the Arabian Peninsula," President Bush declared in a broadcast to U.S. forces after Iraq's surrender.

But the specter would not stay buried. It reappeared with every proposal to use military force—to end starvation and violent anarchy in Somalia; to restore an elected president in Haiti; to stop civil war and "ethnic cleansing," with its echoes of Nazi atrocities, in the former Yugoslav republic of Bosnia. In every case, U.S. policymakers were constrained by an overriding political need to avoid any step that even hinted at a repetition of Vietnam. Public misgivings were so strong that even relatively low U.S. casualties came to seem a prohibitive risk. In October 1993, when eighteen Americans died in a single botched battle in Somalia, the resulting uproar forced the Clinton administration to announce that all U.S. forces would be pulled out in less than six months.

Vietnam loomed most palpably over Bosnia, where Serb atrocities outraged the world but brought no military response. For years, the U.S. government was paralyzed by arguments eerily full of Vietnam echoes, but with weird distortions, as if heard on an old, warped record. Among liberals who had scoffed at the old "domino theory" (stop Communism in Vietnam or it will roll over the rest of Southeast Asia), many now espoused a new version of the same dubious logic (stop ethnic violence in Bosnia or it will spread to the rest of Eastern Europe). Conservatives who had called it faint-hearted not to stay the course in Vietnam now warned against a Bosnian "quagmire."

Almost everyone, though, accepted the assumption that Americans would not support—for any reason—a large-scale military intervention in Bosnia or any policy at all that might lead to U.S. casualties there. And it was clear throughout the debate that memories of Vietnam, far more than the realities of Bosnia, set the political limits on American decisions. As *Newsweek*'s Meg Greenfield wrote tartly in early 1994, "the Vietnamese may be in terrible shape, but they have certainly got their revenge. Merely mention the possible use of our military now any place on Earth and you will hear the pessimistic refrain: it will mean 500,000 ground troops, the military will fail, the wily enemy will prevail, the terrain is inhospitable, we will be hated, etc."

The Gulf War, instead of permanently vanquishing Vietnam's legacy as it was supposed to, faded quickly from the American memory. The sense of righteous success in the Gulf hardly outlasted the shooting; the vision of a new international order dominated by American power was equally fleeting. As the world moved on into the multiple confusions of the post–Cold War era, U.S. policy, in many important respects, was still imprisoned in the past.

A Darkened Vision of America.   In any case, Vietnam's shadow reached far beyond questions of foreign policy or military strategy. Vietnam had to do with America's fundamental vision of itself. It was not the only reason for the darkening of that vision, but it was perhaps the most powerful symbol of lost ideals and faith. The post-Vietnam consciousness circled back on itself to mold the popular image of the war and recent American history (a process epitomized in the 1992 movie *JFK,* in which director Oliver Stone, who had served in Vietnam and also made the most realistic of all Hollywood's movies about the war, asserted that senior members of America's military, intelligence, and foreign-policy leadership successfully carried out a gigantic conspiracy to murder President Kennedy precisely to keep him from ending the war in Vietnam. Millions of Americans, evidently, found nothing preposterous in that premise or in Stone's cynical vision of American leaders and institutions, just as millions were ready to believe that senior civilian and military officials had engaged in a twenty-year cover-up of evidence that U.S. prisoners were still captive in Vietnam.)

The country's division over Vietnam lay close to the heart of a cultural divide that still marked American political life a generation later. In 1980, 1984, and 1988, voters chose conservative presidents at least partly because of "values" issues arising directly from the turmoil of the war years. Fairly or not, many Americans still associated liberalism, and to some extent the entire Democratic Party, with lack of patriotism, permissiveness about sex and drugs and crime, contempt for traditional tastes and beliefs, and disrespect for authority. If the Vietnam era saddled liberals with a lingering image of cultural radicalism, though, it also burdened conservatives, miring them in nostalgic myths that took no account of the great changes in American life and had "little basis," as the Republican commentator Kevin Phillips once acknowledged, "in the political and economic facts of the world we live in today."

Ronald Reagan's 1980 declaration that Vietnam was "in truth, a noble cause," was not just a reinterpretation of the past, but an effort to recapture it. Implicit in Reagan's phrase was a yearning for a country that once again trusted its leaders and symbols, exulted in its power, and had no doubts that America was right and its enemies were wrong. Vanquishing Vietnam's legacy of doubt and moral confusion was more complicated than Reagan or his associates seemed to believe, however. It wasn't coincidental that Vietnam was inescapably entwined with the roots of his administration's greatest scandal: the Iran-contra affair.

Vietnam was the common link in the backgrounds of Oliver North, his boss Robert McFarlane, and others involved in secret arms sales to Iran and the murky "Enterprise" network that illegally armed Nicaraguan rebels. The strands connecting Vietnam and Iran-contra were clearest, perhaps, in the case of North, the most celebrated and flamboyant character in the drama. Risking his life in Viet-

VICTIMS AS WELL. A Vietnamese girl, having torn off all her clothing after being spattered by napalm, flees down Route 1 near Trang Bang, South Vietnam, 8 June 1972. Such images made a powerful impact on American audiences. *National Archives*

nam and then seeing his country abandon the fight left North "quite cynical about government," his mentor and fellow marine McFarlane told congressional investigators. Honor, to North and others seared by Vietnam, was not in observing the letter of laws made by timid politicians; it was in making sure the United States did not betray others as, North believed, it had betrayed its Vietnamese allies. Speaking about the Nicaraguan guerrillas, but surely remembering the Vietnamese as well, North lectured his congressional inquisitors: "Armies need food and consistent help. They need a flow of money, of arms, clothing and medical supplies. The Congress of the United States allowed the executive to encourage them to do battle, and then abandoned them. . . . It does not make sense to me."

North's intentions may have been honorable. But the Vietnam echoes that sounded so insistently throughout his testimony and the entire scandal recalled another harsh truth that had been taught by Vietnam: good intentions, even when accompanied by energy and courage, are not enough to make mistaken policies wise or failed ones successful.

VIETNAMESE REFUGEES. U.S. Navy crewmen aboard the USS *Blue Ridge* carry two Vietnamese children brought aboard by a VNAF helicopter, 29 April 1975. Photograph by An Homely. *National Archives*

Learning about the War. If even participants' memories were muddy ("Vietnam is one long blur, sir," a retired colonel testified in the 1984 Westmoreland-CBS libel trial), Vietnam was an even more confusing subject to Americans coming of age after the war was over.

To many the war seemed like a messy and embarrassing family scandal that no one wanted to tell them the truth about, but which they needed to understand because it was part of their past, too. "Vietnam seems to be another word for mistakes or dishonesty or whatever," Kevin T. Farrell, a twenty-two-year-old college student from Maryland, wrote in 1989. ". . . I really just want to know what happened and why." Nearly twenty-five years after the war and the domestic turmoil associated with it, however, what happened and why were still matters of sharp disagreement.

There was no consensus on broad moral judgments or even on such factual questions as (to mention a few of many possible examples): What was the impact and effectiveness of U.S. air power as it was employed in Vietnam? How did American opinion on the war evolve, how was it influenced by the antiwar movement and by press and television coverage, and how did public attitudes affect policymakers' decisions? Were U.S. forces "winning" or "losing" during the period of escalation (1965–1967), and what was a valid means of measuring military success, anyway?

In colleges and universities, Vietnam became a popular subject. But the many unresolved questions of fact and interpretation continued to confound teachers and students alike. It was comparable, the historian Ronald H. Spector observed, to teaching the American Civil War without knowing "whether the Battle of Gettysburg was a result of Lee's invasion of the North or Meade's invasion of the South, whether the Union blockade really made any difference, and whether railroads and rifled weapons were of any importance." Many instructors took the easier route of teaching what amounted to courses in 1960s nostalgia, inviting veterans and war protestors to share their memories with students. (Some "taught" the war by having students dress up in camouflage and camp out in the woods for a couple of days.)

Such courses may have taught something about the American experience of frustration, disillusion, and moral confusion, but they were not very useful in explaining the difficult and complicated story of the war that actually happened *there,* among 50 million Vietnamese, Lao, and Cambodians. The war curious young Americans learned about often seemed to be one that took place chiefly in America's imagination, connected only tenuously with the real historical event. Quite literally, the word "Vietnam" ceased to mean a real country on the far side of the Pacific Ocean with its own history and traditions and circumstances and became instead, just as Kevin Farrell wrote, "another word for mistakes or dishonesty or whatever."

For a new generation of Americans, the chief obstacle to understanding Vietnam may not have been, after all, the "incomplete and profoundly confused" knowledge (as Spector called it) of the facts, but an unbridgeable gap separating its experience and consciousness from that of America before Vietnam. No one growing up in the cramped, contentious, cynical society of the 1980s and 1990s could fully imagine the sunny and unconscious self-assurance (or arrogance) of a time when America's resources seemed limitless and its power seemed certain to prevail. President Kennedy's famous inaugural pledge that Americans would "pay any price, bear any burden, meet any hardship, support any friend, oppose any foe, to assure the survival and success of liberty" could never sound, after Vietnam, exactly the way it did when the words were spoken.

Nor was there any path back to that earlier consciousness. "We're not going to have another Vietnam now because we've already had Vietnam," Don Oberdorfer, one of America's wisest and most respected journalists, once remarked, meaning that America would never again be unaware of the risks and uncertainties of stepping into another country's violence. By the same premise, it was also true that the United States could never again be the same country it was before Vietnam, no matter how often presidents or other leaders evoked nostalgic visions of a more trusting and unified past. "Vietnam Vietnam Vietnam, we've all been there," Michael Herr wrote in the closing lines of his book *Dispatches.* Nearly a quarter-century after the war that was true, in a sense, even for Americans who were children during the war, or not yet born.

Refugees from a Long War.   "They were always at the edges, when we saw them at all," one writer remembered,

at the edges of the battlefield, at the edges of the television screens and magazine photographs, at the edges of our awareness. Small brown men and women with skinny legs and arms, wearing shorts and singlets or loose black pajamas, faces deeply shadowed under cone-shaped straw hats. Trudging away from battles; squatting in fields under soldiers' rifles and whirling helicopter blades, waiting to be "relocated" to somewhere the authorities had decided they must go; standing silent on Vietnamese roadsides as the machines of war clanked past. . . . Their security and freedom were supposed to be what the war was about, but in fact American soldiers and officials and civilians at home only rarely gave any thought to the actual experience of the people among whom we fought and eventually failed.

After the war, too, the experience of the Vietnamese (not to mention the Lao and Cambodians) remained remarkably shadowy in America's memories, despite the arrival of approximately 1 million Indochinese in the United States between 1975 and 1991. From time to time, images of frightened refugees on rickety, overcrowded boats reminded Americans of the country we had left behind. The images faded quickly, but the tragedy didn't. Through the 1980s and into the 1990s, refugee camps across Asia housed well over half a million Vietnamese, Lao, and Cambodians. Camp conditions generally reflected a policy called "humane deterrence," a term that belongs in the same class with such euphemisms as "reeducation" and "final solution." It meant keeping camp life as harsh as world opinion would allow, in order not to encourage more refugees to follow. But for more than a decade refugees kept coming, risking death at sea or the likelihood of many years behind barbed wire. Several hundred thousand displaced Cambodians finally returned home in the early 1990s, but in early 1995, more than 40,000 Vietnamese, between 17,000 and 25,000 Lao, and a small number of Cambodians were still in camps or other temporary refuges, generally in dismal circumstances and with little hope of finding new homes elsewhere.

The refugee exodus reflected the grim conditions of life under those who had "won" the war. In Cambodia, after mass slaughters during the Khmer Rouge era (1975–1978) and many more years of continuing violence and devastation, warring factions signed a peace agreement in October 1991, and an election for a new government was successfully carried out, under United Nations supervision, in May 1993. But peace was still fragile and the tasks of rebuilding the country and resettling refugees remained formidable. In Vietnam, following what its new rulers chose to call the "liberation" of the country, the old revolutionaries proved disastrously inept at peacetime government. Outmoded Marxist-Leninist doctrines, combined with blundering management and widespread corruption, led to deepening economic misery and all but destroyed the wartime mystique of national unity and sacrifice. If it was possible to imagine American commanders years after the war lying awake and asking themselves in the dark, *"How did we lose?,"* it was equally possible to imagine the Vietnamese communists whispering in their own anguished nights, *"What did we fight for?"*

In 1986, with the economy in a virtual state of collapse, a new party leadership under General Secretary Nguyen Van Linh launched a program known as *doi moi,* or "renovation," embracing economic reforms roughly parallel to those in Mikhail Gorbachev's Soviet Union and Deng Xiaoping's China. The lifting of the U.S. trade embargo in 1994 raised hopes of even swifter economic growth. By the mid 1990s, *doi moi* had begun to create a new prosperity and with it, inevitably, a gradual loosening of the party's totalitarian grip. Vietnam was not yet a democracy, but its entrepreneurs, its artists and its people as a whole—a majority of them now too young to remember the war at all—were becoming used to personal and political freedoms greater than Vietnamese had known for many years.

New Americans. Far from Vietnam and its hardships and its tattered revolutionary myths, a million Indochinese immigrants in the United States were writing a new chapter in a very old American story.

"I have freedom for myself, to work, to live, freedom to do everything," said one Vietnamese who began in America as a farm laborer, eventually achieved modest success as a businessman, and felt that "everything is very smooth for us in America." But like millions of immigrants before him, he also found in American freedom a kind of loneliness:

> We have all the material comforts, very good. But the joy and sentiment are not like we had in Vietnam. There, when we went out from the home, we laughed, we jumped. And we had many relatives and friends to come to see us at home. Here in America, I only know what goes on in my home; my neighbor knows only what goes on in his home. . . . I still remember the small road, the trees in the village where I grew up. Vietnam is forever in my mind.

As with other immigrants, too, a painful gap separated parents from their American-born children, who would never remember Vietnam or fully accept Vietnamese traditions. In a poem written in the style of a *truyen,* a traditional verse narrative, one Vietnamese woman wrote about celebrating the Tet festival, with its special meals, after coming to the United States:

> How silly I felt each noontime
> alone in my house
> surrounded by little saucers of food,
> no one to share them with
> no neighbors around me celebrating.
>
> I'd asked my children to take time off
> the way I had.
> They said, "What for?
> So we can sit around the table
> and stare at each other?"
>
> I said I did this not for them
> but for our ancestors.
> Inside I was sad
> feeling myself on a desert
> knowing my customs will die with me.

[From *Shallow Graves,* copyright © 1986 by Wendy Wilder Larsen and Tran Thi Nga (New York: Random House, 1986). Reprinted with permission.]

As relations between the United States and Vietnam slowly unfroze in the 1980s, Vietnamese-Americans and veterans began traveling back to Vietnam in steadily increasing numbers, to satisfy curiosity or to revisit the past or to make peace with troubled memories. One of those making the journey was William Broyles Jr., who had served in Vietnam as a Marine Corps lieutenant and returned in 1984. At a Viet Cong cemetery near his old combat base, which the U.S. Marines called Hill 10, Broyles came upon a gravestone inscribed with a Vietnamese name and the dates 1944–1969. Those might have been the dates over his own grave, Broyles wrote in his book *Brothers in Arms.* But he had survived, while his former enemy lay there in the now-peaceful field "where boys sang songs to water buffalo as he no doubt had done, and his ancestors before him. And I stood, a tourist from the land of his old enemy, and looked upon his grave and thought how it might have been my own. I had felt this way," he added, "when I first visited the Vietnam Veterans Memorial and saw my own face reflected from the names of my comrades who had died."

A few months before, on the fortieth anniversary of D-Day, ceremonies in Normandy had commemorated the Allied landing there in World War II. On Hill 10, Broyles stood amid the ghosts of his memories and thought about the flags rippling in Normandy and the rows of white crosses over the soldiers buried there, and the infinitely sad difference between their war and his. "There are times when such costs must be paid," he thought. "We had to fight the Nazis. We did not have to fight here."

[*See also* Amerasians; Amnesty; Embargo; Normalization; Post-traumatic Stress Syndrome (PTSS); POW/MIA Controversy; Veterans, *article on* American Veterans; Vietnamese Perspectives; Vietnam Syndrome; Vietnam Veterans Memorial.]

BIBLIOGRAPHY

BROYLES, WILLIAM, JR. *Brothers in Arms: A Journey from War to Peace.* 1986.
EHRHART, W. D. *Passing Time.* 1989.
FALLOWS, JAMES. "What Did You Do in the Class War, Daddy?" *Washington Monthly,* October 1975, 5–19.
FREEMAN, JAMES A. *Hearts of Sorrow: Vietnamese-American Lives.* 1989.
LARSEN, WENDY WILDER, and TRAN THI NGA. *Shallow Graves: Two Women and Vietnam.* 1986.
MACPHERSON, MYRA. *Long Time Passing: Vietnam and the Haunted Generation.* 1984.
PALMER, LAURA. *Shrapnel in the Heart: Letters and Remembrances from the Vietnam Veterans Memorial.* 1987.
SPECTOR, RONALD H. "What Did You Do in the War, Professor?—Reflections on Teaching about Vietnam." *American Heritage,* December 1986, 98–102.
TIMBERG, ROBERT. "The Private War of Ollie and Jim." *Esquire,* March 1988, 145–155.
TUCHMAN, BARBARA W. *The March of Folly: From Troy to Vietnam.* 1984.

ARNOLD R. ISAACS

Amnesty. Amnesty is defined as a general pardon for political crimes against a government. Historically, amnesty decrees or pardons have been issued following wars to address the legal status of those who opposed the wars. The issue of amnesty in the context of the Vietnam War, like the war itself, proved emotional and difficult to resolve. It involved such complexities as the political and moral nuances of the terms *pardon* and *amnesty,* and disagreements over which groups—draft resisters, deserters, veterans with anything less than honorable discharges—should be granted relief.

Following the end of the draft in the United States in 1972 and the withdrawal of all U.S. troops from Vietnam the following year, approximately 281,300 civilians, including draft fugitives, nonregistrants, convicted draft offenders, and expatriates, along with an estimated 566,000 military personnel required some form of amnesty. Civilians needed amnesty to have legal charges dismissed or to return from exile. Some specifically sought amnesty for moral reasons: they considered *amnesty* an acknowledgment by the government that those who had opposed the war were in fact morally correct, while a *pardon* would be an admission that they had been wrong but were being forgiven by the government.

Veterans with less-than-honorable discharges needed amnesty to erase the negative stigma. Deserters required amnesty to free them from the threat of legal action by the U.S. military and, most likely, incarceration in a military prison for having been absent without leave (AWOL).

The U.S. government took no official action on the issue for several years. Conservatives and veterans' groups hotly opposed amnesty, especially for draft resisters. President Gerald Ford initiated amnesty action with a clemency program of "earned reentry" based on case-by-case reviews and the option of alternative service, which applied to both civilians and military personnel. Few people participated in the Ford program, leaving hundreds of thousands without resolution of their situation.

The 1976 Democratic Party platform advocated amnesty for all who were "in legal or financial jeopardy because of their peaceful opposition to the Vietnam War." Jimmy Carter's first action as president in 1977 was to issue an unconditional "blanket pardon." Former military personnel were offered a "Special Discharge Review Program" with case-by-case reviews and the possibility of discharge upgrades.

BIBLIOGRAPHY

BASKIR, LAWRENCE M., and WILLIAM A. STRAUSS. *Chance and Circumstance.* 1978.

MACPHERSON, MYRA. *Long Time Passing.* 1984.

KELLY EVANS-PFEIFER

Amphibious Landing Operations.

The term amphibious operations has a very specific military definition: an assault from the open sea by a landing force across the shore. During the Vietnam War, U.S. amphibious capability remained nearly the exclusive domain of the amphibious task groups of the Seventh Fleet, consisting usually of a Marine Corps battalion landing team (a self-sustaining U.S. Marine infantry battalion reinforced with small support detachments) and a helicopter squadron embarked upon the ships of a U.S. Navy amphibious ready group. The Marine Corps battalion and helicopter squadron were referred to as the Special Landing Force (SLF) of the Seventh Fleet.

The most successful amphibious operation in the war was the first, Operation STARLITE (so named because of a typographical error by a clerk who misread the original name Satellite for Starlight and misspelled the latter word). In August 1965, three Marine Corps battalions, including the SLF battalion, surprised the *1st Viet Cong Regiment* on the small Van Tuong Peninsula just southeast of Chu Lai. From 18 to 24 August, the U.S. Marines killed more than six hundred Viet Cong soldiers, but sustained heavy casualties themselves, including fifty-one dead and more than two hundred wounded.

After STARLITE, the Seventh Fleet Marine SLF, in coordination with the U.S. Military Assistance Command, Vietnam (USMACV), undertook numerous amphibious raids. During these raids, from 1965 through 1969, the Marine Corps amphibious forces conducted more than seventy landings. The Marine SLF units (eventually consisting of two marine SLFs, Alpha and Bravo, each embarked in the ships of an amphibious ready group) landed at sites along the entire coast of South Vietnam. None of the raids was as successful as STARLITE, and most resulted in largely unopposed landings. Still, the Marine SLF units helped keep North Vietnamese and Viet Cong coastal forces off balance and served as a means to reinforce allied units already engaged. Until late 1967, the SLF units also permitted MACV some leverage because they did not count against "in-country" troop strength figures. For the Marine

Corps command in Vietnam, III Marine Amphibious Force (III MAF), the amphibious forces provided a means of refitting and replenishing units stationed ashore in I Corps through a system of battalion and helicopter rotations to and out of SLF units.

The existence of the amphibious forces caused problems. There were interservice debates about command and control of the amphibious forces once they came ashore. The creation of amphibious operational areas that included restrictive air lanes added to the problems. By 1967, these disputes became so persistent that MACV limited the Seventh Fleet SLF amphibious operations to I Corps, the five northern provinces of South Vietnam, controlled by III MAF. For much of 1968, during the Tet Offensive, the battle for Khe Sanh, and the heavy fighting along the demilitarized zone (DMZ), marine SLF battalions spent extended periods ashore, acting as merely additional III MAF infantry battalions. In the latter half of 1968, the marines reconstituted the SLF battalions as the Seventh Fleet amphibious reserve, but SLF battalion operations in Vietnam ceased in 1969.

While Marine Corps SLFs enjoyed only limited success, their mere existence provided the U.S. command with several advantages. The SLFs made up a reserve that could arrive quickly from over the horizon to reinforce or support U.S. or South Vietnamese forces in ongoing engagements. They were also the linchpin of MACV contingency planning for any amphibious envelopment of North Vietnamese forces south of Vinh in North Vietnam. While the SLFs undertook no landings in North Vietnam, Seventh Fleet amphibious ships with U.S. Marines conducted feints toward the north in 1971 during the South Vietnamese incursion into Laos and again in 1972 during the North Vietnamese Easter Offensive. In 1975, as part of Operation FREQUENT WIND, the Seventh Fleet amphibious forces (then designated Marine Amphibious Units [MAUs] rather than SLFs) evacuated the last U.S. personnel and several South Vietnamese officials and their families from Saigon before the North Vietnamese entered the city.

The other comparable waterborne campaigns of the Vietnam War included Operations MARKET TIME and MARKET GARDEN, conducted by U.S. Navy coastal and river surveillance forces including U.S. Coast Guard cutters and intended to prevent infiltration from the sea and along inland water passages. In mid 1966, a joint Army-Navy Mobile Riverine

AMPHIBIOUS LANDING. The first U.S. combat soldiers deployed to Vietnam, troops of the 9th Marine Expeditionary Brigade, come ashore at Da Nang, 8 March 1965. *National Archives*

Force was authorized, which deployed in early 1967 and eventually consisted of two brigades of the U.S. Army 9th Infantry Division which operated with the U.S. Navy river assault squadrons of Task Force 117 in the upper Mekong Delta. MACV abolished this force in August 1969. While occasionally mistakenly referred to as amphibious operations neither the joining Mobile Riverine Force nor the separate MARKET TIME and MARKET GARDEN operations can be considered such, either in organization or concept.

BIBLIOGRAPHY

U.S. MARINES, HISTORY AND MUSEUM DIVISION. *U.S. Marines in Vietnam, 1954–64: The Advisory and Combat Assistance Era.* 1977.

U.S. MARINES, HISTORY AND MUSEUM DIVISION. *U.S. Marines in Vietnam, 1954–73: An Anthology and Annotated Bibliography.* 2d ed. 1985.

U.S. MARINES, HISTORY AND MUSEUM DIVISION. *U.S. Marines in Vietnam, 1965: The Landing and the Buildup.* 1978.

U.S. MARINES, HISTORY AND MUSEUM DIVISION. *U.S. Marines in Vietnam, 1967: Fighting the North Vietnamese.* 1984.

U.S. MARINES, HISTORY AND MUSEUM DIVISION. *U.S. Marines in Vietnam, 1969: High Mobility and Standdown.* 1988.

U.S. MARINES, HISTORY AND MUSEUM DIVISION. *U.S. Marines in Vietnam, 1971–73: The War that Would Not End.* 1992.

U.S. MARINES, HISTORY AND MUSEUM DIVISION. *U.S. Marines in Vietnam, 1973–75: The Bitter End.* 1990.

JACK SHULIMSON

Angkor Wat. A massive Hindu temple complex in Cambodia, Angkor Wat was the scene of guerrilla fighting during the Vietnamese invasion of Khmer Rouge–controlled Democratic Kampuchea. Built between the ninth and twelfth centuries AD, the huge complex, center of an agricultural empire, was abandoned when the nation became Buddhist. French explorers rediscovered it in 1858. Providing inspiration as well as attracting tourism, the temple complex is currently undergoing restoration.

BIBLIOGRAPHY

BECKER, ELIZABETH. *When the War Was Over.* 1987.

KIERNAN, BEN, and CHANTHOU BOUA, eds. *Peasants and Politics in Kampuchea, 1942–1981.* 1982.

PARKES, CARL. *Southeast Asia Handbook.* 1990.

SANDRA C. TAYLOR

An Loc, capital of Binh Long province, located approximately 110 kilometers (70 miles) north of Saigon on the road from Saigon to Loc Ninh; site of a major Easter Offensive battle, April–May 1972. Viet Cong (VC) and North Vietnamese Army (NVA) troops besieged South Vietnamese forces in An Loc after taking Loc Ninh. South Vietnamese president Nguyen Van Thieu rushed a division of the Army of the Republic of Vietnam (ARVN) to defend An Loc, but the division never reached the city because the *VC 7th Division* had blocked the road. On 11 May the VC and NVA forces launched a climactic attack, but they were decimated by U.S. Air Force B-52 air strikes, and withdrew in July. Without the U.S. air support, the ARVN forces would not have held the city.

BIBLIOGRAPHY

CLARKE, JEFFREY J. *United States Army in Vietnam—Advice and Support: The Final Years, 1965–1973.* 1988.
DAVIDSON, PHILLIP B. *Vietnam at War—The History: 1946–1975.* 1988.
PALMER, DAVE RICHARD. *Summons of the Trumpet: U.S.-Vietnam in Perspective.* 1978.

ELLEN D. GOLDLUST

Antiaircraft Defenses. In 1964, when U.S. pilots first flew over North Vietnam, they encountered no jet fighters, no surface-to-air missiles (SAMs), and only a smattering of obsolete antiaircraft artillery (AAA). Soon they faced the most formidable air defense system in the history of warfare. In 1965, North Vietnam began deploying the latest Soviet-made Fan Song radar, SA-2 Guideline SAMs, and MiG-17 fighter aircraft; supersonic MiG-21 fighters appeared one year later. But the greatest threat came from AAA: Hanoi was said to resemble "an armed porcupine," bristling with thousands of AAA batteries atop tall buildings. Restricted targets, such as dikes or hospitals, were also favored sites for AAA emplacements. North Vietnam deployed practically every antiaircraft weapon in the Soviet and Chinese arsenals, ranging from 12.7mm machine guns to 130mm heavy artillery. AAA batteries with interlocking fields of fire surrounded the few approved bombing routes and target areas. One veteran pilot called the sky above North Vietnam "an awesome curtain of exploding steel," where some 8,000 airmen lost their lives.

Flying high to avoid AAA fire exposed U.S. pilots to guided-missile attack. The SA-2 was effective to 26,000 meters (85,000 feet), could reach Mach 2.5, and packed a 130-kilogram (285-pound) warhead.

ANGKOR WAT. *National Archives*

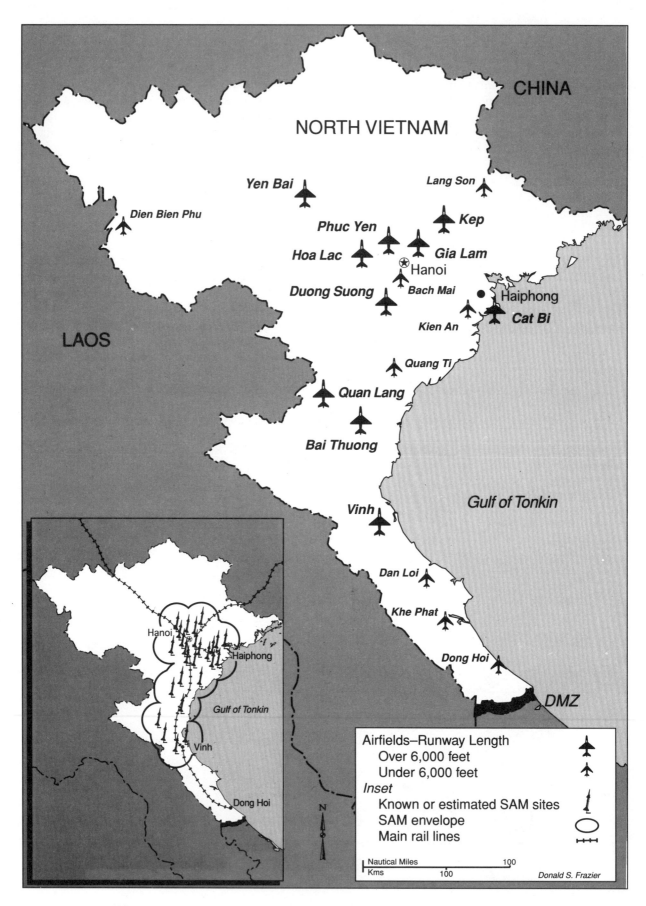

NORTH VIETNAM'S AIR DEFENSES.   SAM sites as of early 1969; key airfields as of 1972.
(Map adapted from Barrett Tillman and John B. Nichols, *On Yankee Station*. Naval Institute Press, 1987.)

The notorious "SAM Triangle" around Hanoi, Haiphong, and Vinh contained 60 multiple-launcher SAM sites by 1966, and more than 150 sites one year later. The number of SAM launches increased from 200 in 1965 to 3,500 in 1967, and to more than 4,200 during Operation LINEBACKER II, in which the United States lost fifteen B-52s and eleven other aircraft in just twelve days in December 1972. The use of evasive maneuvers, SAM suppression strikes by "Wild Weasel" aircraft equipped with radar-homing missiles, and electronic countermeasures (ECMs) gradually reduced U.S. losses per 1,000 sorties from 2.38 in 1967 to 1.80 in 1972. But, as a veteran pilot recalled, "Ninety-nine percent of the time as I dropped my bombs, somebody was shooting at me."

Even during halts in the bombing of the North, pilots on missions over South Vietnam or the Ho Chi Minh Trail ran a deadly gauntlet of enemy fire from small arms, machine guns, and mobile M38/39 37mm or ZSU 57mm AAA batteries. Slow moving, low flying helicopters proved especially vulnerable to ground fire as the war progressed, casting doubt on the U.S. Army's new airmobility doctrine. Nearly eight hundred helicopters were lost or damaged during Operation LAM SON 719, the invasion of Laos in 1971, preventing the resupplying of trapped units of the Army of the Republic of Vietnam (ARVN). During the Easter Offensive in 1972, North Vietnamese Army (NVA) troops equipped with shoulder-fired SA-7 Strella portable SAMs inflicted significant losses on combat support aircraft. U.S. air superiority was never threatened in the Vietnam War, but North Vietnam attained "air deniability" that limited the use of that superiority.

[*See also* SAM Missiles.]

BIBLIOGRAPHY

BEARDEN, THOMAS E. "What Really Happened in the Air Defense Battle of North Vietnam?" *Air Defense Magazine* (April–June 1976).

ANTIAIRCRAFT ARTILLERY. North Vietnamese antiaircraft cannon at Thanh Hoa. *Ngô Viñh Long*

BROUGHTON, JACK. *Going Downtown: The War against Hanoi and Washington.* 1988.
BROUGHTON, JACK. *Thud Ridge.* 1985.
BURBAGE, PAUL, et al. *The Battle for the Skies over North Vietnam.* 1976.
DAVIS, LARRY. *Wild Weasel: The SAM Suppression Story.* 1986.
TILFORD, EARL H., JR. *SETUP: What the Air Force Did in Vietnam and Why.* 1991.
WERRELL, KENNETH P. *Archie, Flak, AAA, and SAM.* 1988.

GLEN GENDZEL

Antiwar Movement

The ghost of Vietnam was lurking in the shadows of the Gulf War parades. The war with Iraq ended in the spring of 1991, and the GIs gradually began returning home from the Middle East. The demobilization was a gradual and steady process. They were treated as conquering heroes; no ancient Roman legion marching down the Appian Way from adventures abroad ever received a more enthusiastic welcome. Small towns and large cities across the country rolled out the red carpet and staged military parades complete with tanks, armor, high school marching bands, overhead jet fighters flying in formation, artillery pieces, Boy Scout and Girl Scout troops, and soldiers—lots of soldiers. The demand for soldiers to march in parades was so high that large military bases in the United States actually had some of their day-to-day operations disrupted by the need to supply units for the weekly parades.

The most striking image in those parades was not the military hardware or spit-and-polished young men and women marching in unison. The victory celebrations also attracted tens of thousands of middle-aged warriors—some balding and overweight, wearing flak jackets and faded military green, walking down the streets of America, or rolling down them in wheelchairs, with smiles on their faces. They had pinned their old medals on again. Vietnam vets were finally getting their due, their parades, delayed by fifteen or twenty or twenty-five years of guilt, angst, and anger over what had taken place in Indochina and in the United States. For millions of Americans, the Gulf War provided the opportunity for an act of mass, collective repentance. After a decade of films and books like *Coming Home, Platoon, Born on the Fourth of July,* and *Full Metal Jacket,* the whole country seemed anxious to atone for the wretched way they had treated those same Vietnam veterans a generation ago.

The Vietnam War, because of its peculiar nature—so bloody yet undeclared, so efficient yet so unpopular—had an extraordinary impact on American culture, shaping the way Americans view themselves and their history. Few experiences in American history have been more painful or confusing. W. D. Earhart, in his novel *Vietnam-Perkasie* (1983), captures that pain in describing the battle for the city of Hue in 1968:

> I fought back passionately, in blind rage and pain, without remorse, conscience or deliberation. I fought back . . . at the Pentagon Generals and the Congress of the United States, and the *New York Times;* at the draft-card burners, and the Daughters of the American Revolution . . . at the teachers who taught me that America always had God on our side and always wore white hats and always won; at the Memorial Day parades and the daily Pledge of Allegiance . . . at the movies of John Wayne and Audie Murphy, and the solemn statements of Dean Rusk and Robert McNamara (p. 214).

In 1975, when the helicopters took off from the U.S. embassy in Saigon, the vast majority of Americans, for a complex variety of reasons, were disgusted with the war and the politicians who had pursued it. Thirteen years earlier, with the Vietnam quagmire becoming increasingly messy, President John F. Kennedy incredulously recalled, "You know, Eisenhower never mentioned it, never uttered the word, Vietnam."

Under Eisenhower and Kennedy. During the Eisenhower years, a few voices expressed concern about what was happening in Southeast Asia. One of them was Graham Greene, whose 1955 novel, *The Quiet American,* took exception to U.S. policy there. The central character was Alden Pyle, an American who believed in coldly passionate abstractions—democracy, freedom, monolithic communism, falling dominoes, and the love of God. Greene's objective was to expose the fallacies of U.S. military policy in Vietnam. Stationed in Saigon as a war correspondent in the early 1950s, Greene watched the French leave and the Americans arrive. The Americans had young, fresh faces and crew cuts; they were Alden Pyles intent on doing good "not to any individual person but to a country, a continent, a world." That was the problem: Americans defined *good* and *evil* in universal abstractions. Few Americans were ready for Greene's prophetic message, delivered through the character Thomas Fowler, who tells Pyle: "In five hundred years there may be no New York or London, but they'll be growing paddy in these fields. . . . Do you think the peasant sits and thinks of God and Democracy when he gets inside his mud hut at night? . . . Isms and ocracies. Give me facts." In the end, Alden Pyle is murdered. Michael Herr, in his book *Dispatches* (1977), said: "Maybe it was already over for us in Indochina when Alden Pyle's body washed up under the bridge at Dakao, his lungs full of mud."

The Old Left. Throughout the 1950s and early 1960s, the Old Left—members of traditionally socialist political groups and pacifists—was beginning to marshal its forces against the growing U.S. involvement in Southeast Asia. In 1954, as the Eisenhower administration considered military intervention to rescue the French garrison at Dien Bien Phu, the Friends Committee on National Legislation, a Quaker pacifist group, cautioned against U.S. involvement in a war in Vietnam, characterizing the conflict there as an internal revolution against a despotic regime. Instead, they called on U.S. policymakers to implement a general settlement in Asia that "would shift the emphasis of the conflict from a military basis to a political and economic basis." Another Quaker group, the American Friends Service Committee, called on the United States to avoid military intervention in Vietnam in favor of a political settlement.

A. J. Muste, one of America's veteran pacifists, headed the Fellowhip of Reconciliation (FOR) during the 1950s and early 1960s. First established in 1914 during World War I, the FOR had long been the most influential pacifist group in Great Britain and the United States. In October 1964, Muste and the FOR issued the first public statement endorsing draft resistance to protest the increasing number of U.S. military advisers being sent to Vietnam: the Declaration of Conscience Against the War in Vietnam. The War Resisters League (WRL) was even more active. Founded in 1923 as a secular pacifist organization, the WRL had opposed U.S. involvement in World War II and the Korean War. By 1963, under the leadership of David Dellinger, the WRL focused its protests on the expanding U.S. military advisory effort in Vietnam. On 16 May 1964, the WRL sponsored a demonstration in New York City at which twelve men burned their draft cards. In December 1964, the WRL organized the first nationwide demonstration against the Vietnam War.

Opposition within the Government.   Except for the pacifists, however, the antiwar movement was a tiny, fringe force in U.S. politics. It also lacked any official voice in the Eisenhower and Kennedy administrations. There were some exceptions, a few Cold Warriors who had serious concerns about the war on pragmatic grounds. In November 1961 Undersecretary of State George Ball voiced his opposition to a proposal by Gen. Maxwell Taylor and national security adviser Walt W. Rostow for placement of an 8,000-man logistical task force in South Vietnam to serve as soldiers and/or economic and political workers. Ball told Kennedy that the geography of Indochina "was totally unsuitable for the commitment of American forces," and that any serious U.S. military effort there "would have the most tragic consequences." Ball then uttered the prophetic warning that has endeared him to a generation of scholars who opposed the Vietnam War: "If we go down that road we might have, within five years, 300,000 men in the rice paddies of the jungles of Viet-Nam and never be able to find them. . . . You [Kennedy] better be damned careful." Kennedy looked askance at Ball and said, "George, you're crazier than hell."

Kennedy received a similar message from several other advisers. John Kenneth Galbraith, a Harvard economist, told the president in April 1962 that Vietnam "could expand step by step into a major, long-drawn-out indecisive military involvement." A few days later W. Averell Harriman, former ambassador to the Soviet Union, warned the president that President Ngo Dinh Diem of South Vietnam "is a losing horse in the long run." George Kennan, another former ambassador to the Soviet Union and author of the famous "containment" doctrine, urged Kennedy to be careful, to realize that nationalism, not communism, was the real force at work in Southeast Asia.

There were also a few early critics in Congress. In a speech on 10 March 1964, Sen. Ernest Gruening of Alaska deplored the waste of American lives and resources "in seeking vainly in this remote jungle to shore up self-serving corrupt dynasties or their self-imposed successors, and a people [South Vietnam] that has demonstrated that it has no will to save itself. . . . All Vietnam is not worth the life of a single American boy. . . . The loss of any American lives in Vietnam will someday be denounced as a crime." Five months later, when President Lyndon B. Johnson used the Gulf of Tonkin incident as a cause célèbre and asked Congress for unlimited authority to wage war against North Vietnam, the vote in the Senate was 98 to 2 in favor; only Sen. Wayne L. Morse of Oregon and Gruening dissented.

The Press Corps.   There were also some vocal critics among the American press corps in Saigon. From the very beginning of the conflict in the early 1960s, officials of the Kennedy, Johnson, and Nixon administrations criticized the press for impeding the war effort. They wanted reporters to deliver positive news to the public, or at least news that reflected official opinion. Most journalists did just that, uncritically passing on the official version of events. But there were some renegades who kept reporting a steady decline in Vietnamese support for Diem and steady increases in the strength of the Viet Cong. David Halberstam of the *New York Times,* Neil Sheehan of United Press International (UPI), Nick Turner of Reuters, Peter Arnett of the Associated Press, Bernard Kalb and Peter Kalisher of CBS, James Robinson of NBC, Charles Mohr of *Time,* François Sully of *Newsweek,* Pepper Martin of *U.S. News & World Report,* and Stanley Karnow of *Time* consistently argued that the regime of Ngo Dinh Diem was isolated and paranoid, that a stable democracy would never develop as long as the Ngo family held power. In short, the United States and South Vietnam were losing.

ANTIWAR RALLY. Protestors against the Vietnam War demonstrate in New York City's Bryant Park, 15 April 1970. The coffin at center represents Vietnam dead. *National Archives*

American Military Intervention. But the opposition of Old Left pacifist groups, some Cold Warriors, a few reporters, and a few members of Congress was not enough, and early in 1965 the Johnson administration made the decision to escalate the war by sending regular U.S. ground troops to South Vietnam. When Dwight Eisenhower left the White House in 1961, there were only about 700

U.S. troops in South Vietnam. That number had increased to nearly 17,000 by the time Kennedy was assassinated in 1963. At the end of 1965, more than 180,000 U.S. soldiers were already there, and preparations were under way to send another 160,000 troops. Draft calls were escalating just as quickly as were American casualties.

At first, the general public rallied behind President Lyndon B. Johnson and the troops in Vietnam, expecting the vaunted U.S. military machine to crush the Viet Cong guerrillas with overwhelming firepower, technological superiority, and individual courage. Robin Moore's 1965 novel, *The Green Berets,* rocketed to the top of the best-seller lists, its simplistic plot depicting elite U.S. forces rescuing South Vietnam from its own incompetence and the immoral aggression of the Viet Cong. Barry Sadler's "Ballad of the Green Berets" made its way to the top of the popular music charts later in the year. The United States was at war and most Americans supported the commitment.

The administration's decision to Americanize and militarize the conflict in Vietnam jump-started the antiwar movement in the United States, broadening its narrow base to include new elements in American society. Student groups, New Leftists, and civil rights activists took a critical look at the war. More than thirty new antiwar organizations were formed in 1965, and they were represented by the National Coordinating Committee to End the War in Vietnam, an umbrella organization established in August in Madison, Wisconsin.

Religious Opposition. Theological and social liberals in the mainstream Protestant denominations were not comfortable with Johnson's decisions to escalate. They reacted immediately to the escalation, forming Clergy and Laity Concerned About Vietnam (CALCAV) to mobilize the religious community to take an ecumenical stand against the war. It attracted some conservatives and radicals and functioned as one of the first important channels for Jewish and Catholic peace activism. Originating in New York in 1965, CALCAV served as a protest vehicle for clergy and laity from churches that were silent on the war issue. Established to help defend the right to dissent, CALCAV, which was clearly in the mainstream of American life, argued that nothing was accomplished by escalating the war and advocated a negotiated settlement. Adopting a moderate tone and asserting its patriotic motivation in opposing the Vietnam War, CALCAV combined moral and pragmatic arguments in voicing its condemnation of the war. Always careful to avoid extreme arguments and tactics, CALCAV expressed its opposition in ways that kept it on good terms with its primarily white, middle-class, religiously motivated constituency, which proved to be the source of a great deal of its success.

Students and the Counterculture. American universities proved to be fertile ground for the antiwar movement. The intellectual left, which had been inactive in the Eisenhower era, was generally unable to function as an early critic of war policy because of its connection with the liberal bipartisanship of diplomacy in the period after World War II. In the early 1960s, few of them spoke out against the war, even though the seeds of all the principal arguments that were used later in the Johnson administration existed while Kennedy was president. A symbiotic relationship existed between the Kennedy administration and the intelligentsia, and Johnson began his presidency with noticeable attempts to court the intellectual community. That changed, however, when Johnson ordered 3,000 Marines into Da Nang on 10 March 1965. They were the first contingent of regular combat troops sent to Vietnam. At the University of Michigan in Ann Arbor, several faculty members organized a "teach-in"—patterned after the

1960s civil rights "sit-ins"—for 24 March 1965. More than 3,500 students attended the teach-in, during which faculty members discussed the nature of the war. Similar teach-ins occurred at campuses across the country in the spring of 1965, culminating with the "National Teach-In" at 122 colleges and universities on 15 May 1965.

The protests soon spread beyond the campuses, confirming the youth counterculture's sense of alienation and betrayal. Folksingers such as Phil Ochs, Bob Dylan, and Joan Baez sang at protest rallies around the country, calling for an immediate end to the war. Phil Ochs organized a number of "War Is Over" rallies across the country. At a White House garden party for artists and intellectuals in June 1965, writer John Hersey, poets Stanley J. Kunitz and Robert Lowell, editor Robert B. Silvers, cultural critic Dwight MacDonald, and others embarrassed President Lyndon B. Johnson with their public opposition to the war. Their behavior irritated the president, and after the party he said to an aide, "At least nobody pissed in the punch bowl."

Until the escalation of the war, the public antiwar movement had largely been confined to the Old Left, but by the summer of 1965, New Left groups also became active in opposition to the Vietnam conflict. The most prominent of those organizations was the Students for a Democratic Society (SDS), founded in January 1960 by a group of students who had been politically associated with the Socialist Party. Tom Hayden emerged as its first leader, and SDS was active in the civil rights movement. By 1964, especially after the Gulf of Tonkin incident, SDS began to organize campus demonstrations and teach-ins against the war and circulated "We Won't Go" petitions among draft-age men. On 17 April 1965, SDS sponsored a demonstration in Washington, D.C., that brought more than 20,000 protesters to the city. SDS membership increased from 2,000 to nearly 30,000 members during the next year. Other New Left groups—the Catholic Peace Fellowship, the Emergency Citizens' Group Concerned About Vietnam, the "Another Mother for Peace" organization, and the National Emergency Committee of Clergy Concerned About Vietnam—also became active in opposing the war.

The Civil Rights Movement. In mid 1965, just as the escalation of the war accelerated, some civil rights leaders became concerned about the effect of the war on President Lyndon B. Johnson's Great Society programs and on the civil rights movement. In the summer of 1965 Rev. James Bevel, a close associate of Martin Luther King Jr. in the Southern Christian Leadership Conference, called for an alliance between the civil rights movement and the antiwar movement. Although Martin Luther King Jr. openly denounced the Vietnam War in July 1965 because it was diverting attention and national resources away from domestic programs designed to assist poor people and minorities, he stopped short of linking the two movements together.

As American casualties mounted in 1966, the antiwar movement gained strength and the civil rights movement became more intimately involved with it. At the end of 1965, 636 Americans had been killed in action (KIA) during the entire war; one year later that number had increased to 6,644. Antiwar leaders denounced the conflict in more shrill terms, and civil rights leaders, especially Martin Luther King Jr., noticed a troubling trend in the grisly statistics. In 1965–1966, African Americans constituted more than 20 percent of the casualty deaths in Vietnam, a number higher than their percentage in the American population. African American men were more likely to be drafted than whites, more likely to be assigned to infantry platoons, and more likely to enter combat. Civil

THE OLD LEFT. American veterans of the Spanish Civil War protest the Vietnam War at the Lincoln Memorial, Washington, D.C., 21 October 1967. Photograph by Frank Wolfe. *Lyndon Baines Johnson Library*

rights leaders condemned as racist the army and marine policies that produced such statistics, and in the mind of Martin Luther King Jr. the antiwar movement and the civil rights movement began to fuse. Early in 1967, he formally linked the two movements, arguing that the Vietnam War was destroying the civil rights and antipoverty movements in the United States and creating an African American bloodbath on the other side of the world.

Even before King's conversion to the antiwar cause, heavyweight boxing champion Muhammad Ali voiced his opposition to the war. Early in 1966, Ali learned that his Selective Service classification was 1-A, which made him immediately eligible for military service. The press bombarded him with questions: How did he feel about the war in Vietnam? Did he think the war was just? What did he think about the Gulf of Tonkin Resolution? Ali replied, "I ain't got no quarrel with them Vietcong." He subsequently refused induction. The reporters had their headline, and the United States had a new symbol for resistance to the Vietnam War.

An Antiwar Movement. Late in 1966, with the number of U.S. troops in South Vietnam approaching 385,000, the antiwar movement began making new converts in the liberal political establishment. A number of former Kennedy administration officials and advisers spoke out against the war, urging President Johnson to end the bombing of North Vietnam and seek a negotiated settlement. Arthur M. Schlesinger Jr., a professor of history at Harvard and former Kennedy adviser, wrote *The Bitter Heritage* in 1966, which criticized U.S. policymakers for confusing communism with nationalism, backing the dictatorial regime of Ngo Dinh Diem, and conducting a futile war. John Kenneth Galbraith wrote *A Moder-*

ate's View of Vietnam in 1966, calling on the United States to adopt an enclave strategy and seek a negotiated settlement. Former general David Shoup, commandant of the Marine Corps during the Kennedy administration, testified in May 1966 that "I don't think the whole of Southeast Asia, as related to the present and future safety and freedom of this country, is worth the life or limb of a single American." James Gavin, a retired general and Kennedy's ambassador to France from 1961 to 1963, made a similar argument before the Senate Foreign Relations Committee in 1966. George Kennan testified before the same committee in May 1966, stating that Vietnam had no military, political, or economic significance to the United States.

The rising antiwar sentiment among political liberals in the United States was reflected in Congress as well. Senators Wayne Morse and Ernest Greuning were no longer alone. Sen. George Aiken, a Republican from Vermont, broke ranks with Lyndon Johnson in 1966 and publicly told the president "to declare the United States the winner and begin de-escalation." Sen. Clifford Case, a Republican from New Jersey, began calling for withdrawal as well. Republican Mark Hatfield won a Senate seat from Oregon in 1966 because of his antiwar platform. In New York, Republican senator Jacob Javits spoke out against the war. Other Republicans including Gov. Nelson Rockefeller of New York, Gov. William Scranton of Pennsylvania, Mayor John Lindsay of New York City, and Sen. Hugh Scott of Pennsylvania began expressing serious misgivings about the Vietnam War.

President Lyndon B. Johnson could explain away Republican opposition as partisanship; it was the defection of liberal Democrats that really frustrated him and weakened his presidency. During 1966 Johnson began to lose the support of some of the most powerful Democrats in the U.S. Senate. Sen. Mike Mansfield, the majority leader from Montana, had urged the president since 1964 to avoid an escalation of the conflict, and in 1966 Mansfield went public with his criticism. Sen. Frank Church of Idaho called on Johnson to end the bombing of North Vietnam in 1966 and negotiate a settlement. Sen. J. William Fulbright of Arkansas, a longtime friend of Lyndon B. Johnson and a supporter of the administration, accused the president in 1966 of confusing nationalism with communism and demanded a withdrawal from Indochina. Fulbright also staged a series of critical hearings by the Senate Foreign Relations Committee in 1966 and 1967. Sen. Vance Hartke of Indiana wrote a public letter to the president in January 1966 calling for an end to the war. Senators George McGovern of South Dakota, Robert Kennedy of New York, Edward Kennedy of Massachusetts, and Eugene McCarthy of Minnesota also began to make public their doubts about the war late in 1966 and early in 1967.

Throughout 1966 and early 1967, the antiwar movement, enjoying increasing legitimacy within the political establishment, gained momentum, becoming more visible and more vocal in its protests. In January 1967 Rev. James Bevell of the Southern Christian Leadership Conference was named director of the Spring Mobilization to End the War in Vietnam, a coalition group composed of academics, students, and Old and New Left organizations. The group sponsored mass demonstrations for the spring; on 15 April 1967, more than 130,000 demonstrators marched in New York City and another 70,000 protested in San Francisco. It was the largest antiwar demonstration to date and the event was widely reported in the media.

Six months later the Spring Mobilization's demonstration was dwarfed by the March on the Pentagon demonstration at the end of October. More than 100,000 people descended on Washington, D.C., to protest the war, and more than 50,000 of them actually marched on the Pentagon, where U.S. Army troops had to be called out to keep them from entering the building. It was a media circus. Folksinging troubadors performed antiwar ballads, smiling hippies placed flower stems down the barrels of army M-16 rifles, earnest professors lectured on the terrible price of war, peace activists preached their jeremiads, and photographers and film crews recorded the event for the world and for history. Around the world—in London, Paris, Moscow, Beijing, Hanoi, and Peoria— people knew that the war was unpopular and becoming more and more unpopular every day.

Despite the antiwar movement's growing influence and visibility, it was an uneasy coalition of disparate groups whose ideological differences created constant internal tension and bickering. Such black power advocates as H. Rap Brown, Stokely Carmichael, Bobby Seale, and Eldridge Cleaver began criticizing the nonviolent civil disobedience tactics of Martin Luther King Jr., and their rhetoric of protest and violence fractured the civil rights movement directly and the antiwar movement indirectly. They condemned the Vietnam War as a conscious effort by white politicians to carry out genocide against African Americans, and they accused such mainstream black leaders as Ralph Abernathy, Roy Wilkins, and Martin Luther King Jr. of being collaborators in the destruction. New Left groups such as Students for a Democratic Society became increasingly militant and frequently violent in their antiwar demonstrations. SDS students seized campus buildings, sought to drive Central Intelligence Agency (CIA), Reserve Officers Training Corps (ROTC), and Dow Chemical recruiters off campus, picketed or attacked military induction centers, and committed arson. During what was called "Stop the Draft Week" in October 1967, Carl Davidson of SDS said, "We must tear them [induction centers] down, burn them down if necessary." The violence and militancy of the black power advocates and the New Left radicals alienated the Old Left pacifists and mainstream liberals who opposed the war.

The Democratic Party. Partly because of their alienation from the violent elements within the antiwar movement, during the last half of 1967 the mainstream liberals channeled their antiwar energies into the politics of the Democratic Party. On 30 November 1967, Sen. Eugene McCarthy of Minnesota was announced as a candidate for the 1968 Democratic presidential nomination against President Lyndon B. Johnson, claiming that "Vietnam is draining the material and moral resources of the country from our really pressing problems." Two months later, the Viet Cong launched the Tet Offensive. Although the Viet Cong suffered a massive tactical defeat, their ability to stage such a broad-based attack, after so much U.S. military action against them and so much positive rhetoric from the Johnson administration, stunned the American public, transforming the Tet campaign from a tactical victory into a strategic defeat for the United States. Walter Cronkite, the anchorman of CBS News, was personally stunned by Tet, and after a visit to South Vietnam during the last two weeks of February 1968, he reported it likely that "the bloody experience of Vietnam is to end in stalemate." His comments especially upset Lyndon Johnson, who admitted, "If I have lost Walter Cronkite, I have lost Mr. Average American Citizen." Eugene McCarthy made a surprisingly good showing against Johnson in the 12 March New Hampshire primary election, and when Sen. Robert Kennedy of New York announced his own candidacy for the Democratic nomination a few days later, Johnson decided not to seek reelection. The Vietnam War, and the movement against it, had destroyed his presidency.

MORATORIUM DAY PEACE PARADE. Washington, D.C., 15 November 1969. *National Archives*

Vice President Hubert Humphrey then announced his candidacy for the presidency, and the Democratic Party became the focal point of the antiwar movement. New Left groups escalated the militancy and rhetoric of their protests throughout 1968. From March through May 1968, the SDS chapter at Columbia University, led by student Mark Rudd, staged several seizures of campus buildings, leading to violent confrontations with the New York City police and a shutdown of the entire campus. Under SDS pressure, Columbia agreed to cut its ties to the Institute of Defense Analysis, extend amnesty to the demonstrators, and abandon its plans to build a gymnasium at Morningside Park, which had alienated minority residents who would lose their apartments in the demolition.

The 1968 Convention. Later in the summer, at the Democratic National Convention in Chicago, the antiwar movement was on display for the entire world. Inside the convention hall, Democratic politicians jockeyed for position. Robert Kennedy had been assassinated after winning the California primary in June, and Senators Eugene McCarthy, George McGovern, and Edward Kennedy took up the antiwar banner. Hubert Humphrey, who eventually won the nomination, had to walk a political tightrope, hoping to maintain his contacts with the left wing of the party without alienating President Lyndon B. Johnson, who was still trying to orchestrate the party's platform.

Outside the convention hall, however, antiwar activists had gathered, and most of the major New Left groups were represented in the streets and parks of downtown Chicago. Bobby Seale was there representing the Black Panthers. Tom Hayden headed the contingent from SDS. YIPPIE (Youth International Party) leaders Jerry Rubin and Abbie Hoffman were also in Chicago, as were David Dellinger and other old-line pacifists and their representatives in such groups as Clergy and Laity Concerned About Vietnam and the War Resisters' League. When Mayor Richard Daley ordered the Chicago police to quell the demonstrations, downtown Chicago became the scene of what was later called a "police riot," when officers violently waded into the demonstrators with dogs, horses, and billy clubs. To millions of Americans, the televised images of the demonstrations and the police attacks were proof that the Democratic Party was incapable of leading the country out of the social and political morass.

The Trial of the Chicago Seven. The subsequent trial of the so-called Chicago Seven—on charges of conspiracy and crossing state lines with the intent to commit riot—in August 1969 was political theater. Judge Julius Hoffman presided at the trial, and he frequently denied defense motions and mispronounced the names of defendants and their attorneys. Insults and epithets went back and forth between the judge and the defendants. The defendants sought to make the Vietnam War, racism, and domestic repression the main issues of the trial; they even draped the Viet Cong flag across their defense tables. When Bobby Seale refused to comply with Hoffmann's demands to be quiet, the judge had him gagged and bound to a chair. Seale then resorted to banging his leg chains on the floor. Hoffman found the defendants and their attorneys guilty of 125 counts of contempt. Seale's case was soon declared a mistrial and he was sentenced to four years in prison on charges of contempt. The trial for the others went on for four months before the defendants were found not guilty of conspiracy. All of them, however, were convicted of intent to riot and sentenced to five years in prison. Three years later, a federal appeals court acquitted them on all charges, criticizing Judge Hoffman for gross judicial misbehavior during the trial.

Voices on the Right. By that time the antiwar coalition was rapidly acquiring a new political element on the right. President Lyndon B. Johnson had tried to walk the middle ground between critics on the left who wanted the United States out of the war and critics on the right who were demanding a more aggressive military policy. In the end, he satisfied neither. Frustration with the Vietnam War was not confined to those of the left wing who believed that the war was immoral and that the United States simply had no business there. There were millions more—represented by former Military Assistance Command, Vietnam

(MACV), Gen. William Westmoreland, Adm. Ulysses S. Grant Sharp, and Senators Barry Goldwater of Arizona, Richard Russell of Georgia, Strom Thurmond of South Carolina, and Russell Long of Louisiana—who began to insist that if the United States was not going to "win the war," the only sensible option was disengagement.

The Nixon Years. Richard Nixon, who secured the Republican presidential nomination, took advantage of those sentiments by hinting that he would bring an end to the war, and in the election of 1968 Nixon narrowly defeated Hubert Humphrey for the presidency. After entering the White House in January 1969, Nixon waited several months before initiating any policy changes, and the delay galvanized the antiwar movement. On 26 March, Women's Strike for Peace pickets carried out the first large-scale antiwar demonstration since the inauguration. Nixon soon announced Vietnamization—turning the war gradually over to the South Vietnamese. In June 1969 the president informed the American public that he was planning to withdraw 25,000 of 543,000 soldiers from Vietnam.

Moratorium Day. For most people in the antiwar movement, however, Nixon was moving too slowly to end the war. Between his inauguration in January 1969 and the departure from Vietnam of the 9th Infantry Division in August 1969, more than 7,000 U.S. soldiers died in Vietnam. Two antiwar groups—the Vietnam Moratorium Committee and the reconstituted New Mobilization Committee to End the War in Vietnam—decided to sponsor an ongoing series of nationwide protests, in large cities and small towns, on a monthly basis beginning in October 1969. Sam Brown, who had organized student volunteers for Sen. Eugene McCarthy's 1968 presidential bid, founded what became known as the Moratorium Day Demonstrations—taking a day off from work or school to protest the war. Millions participated in the demonstrations on 15 October 1969. Thousands of soldiers in South Vietnam wore black armbands to support the demonstrations. In the United States, millions of drivers left their headlights on all day as a symbol of opposition. More than 100,000 people gathered in the Boston Common, and Mayor John Lindsay of New York City declared 15 October a day of mourning and ordered all flags flown at half-staff. The United Automobile Workers and the Chemical Workers of America unions endorsed the Moratorium Day demonstrations and sent their delegations to picket. Coretta Scott King, the widow of Martin Luther King Jr., led a candlelight vigil in Washington, D.C.

The Moratorium Day rallies in mid-October brought a powerful response from the president. Most Americans experienced real political agony in the late 1960s, wanting to rally around the flag and support the administration's policies and the GIs, but hoping at the same time to extricate the United States from Vietnam honorably. They did not want the United States simply to turn its back on Vietnam and leave, if for no other reason than the need to redeem the blood of nearly 40,000 Americans who had died there. Sensing that fundamental political reality, President Richard Nixon delivered his famous Silent Majority speech on 3 November 1969. The president made a patriotic appeal to "the great silent majority" of Americans to support his search for a "just and lasting peace" as an alternative to immediate withdrawal which, he stated, would lead to "a collapse of confidence in American leadership, not only in Asia but throughout the world." Nixon outlined the history of U.S. involvement in Vietnam since his inauguration, stated that the previous administrations had "Americanized the war," and claimed that his administration would henceforth "Vietnamize the search for

KENT STATE   On 4 May 1970, National Guard troops shot and killed four students at Kent University, Ohio, during a protest against the U.S. and ARVN incursion into Cambodia. The killings increased antiwar sentiment. Photograph by John Filo. *AP/World Wide Photographs*

peace." To this end, he described a plan of withdrawal of U.S. forces from Vietnam to correspond with the buildup and strengthening of South Vietnam's forces. He then attacked the antiwar movement as a "vocal minority" and stated that "North Vietnam cannot defeat or humiliate the United States. Only Americans can do that."

High-water Mark of Protest.   At first, Nixon's appeal to the silent majority had little effect. Twelve days after the speech, Sam Brown orchestrated another Moratorium Day series of demonstrations. Even more people participated than in October. The day after the November 1969 Moratorium Day demonstrations, news of the My Lai massacre was printed and broadcast around the world, and antiwar groups used it as evidence that the U.S. war machine was out of control in South Vietnam. In May 1969 the *New York Times* had exposed the secret bombing of Cambodia, and the Nixon administration was criticized for widening the "credibility gap." When President Nixon ordered the invasion (Nixon called it an incursion) of Cambodia at the end of April 1970, he was subjected to intense criticism and protests from students, faculty, business groups, and the press, which resulted in the Kent State University killings and protest demonstrations at more than 70 percent of American colleges and universities. In the wake of the Cambodian invasion and the killings at Kent State, Congress prohibited the introduction of U.S. ground troops into Laos or Thailand.

But the protests against My Lai and the Cambodian invasion marked the high-water mark of the antiwar movement. It began to lose support, partly because of continuing ideological squabbles within the movement. The most radical elements of the movement self-destructed in an escalation of their own rhetoric and tactics. In May 1968, for example, Philip and Daniel Berrigan, the Catholic antiwar activists, broke into Selective Service offices in Catonsville, Maryland, and destroyed draft records with homemade napalm to protest the war. The Berrigans and their associates became known as the "Catonsville Nine." In 1969, the SDS formally allied with "Third World Revolutionaries," and at its March 1969 "War Council," SDS resolved to promote "armed struggle as the only road to revolution in the heartland of a worldwide monster [the United States]." Most Americans would not support such radical movement.

But the steady implementation of the Vietnamization policy was the real reason behind the decline of the antiwar movement. Nixon's appeal to patriotism in the Silent Majority speech and his promise to bring the troops home marked the beginning of the end of the massive antiwar demonstrations of the Vietnam era. Nixon withdrew the 3d Marine Division from South Vietnam two weeks after the speech, and by 31 December 1969, U.S. troop levels were down to 475,000; they fell to 334,600 at the end of 1970.

The antiwar movement was not moribund, however. Among the most influential antiwar groups toward the end of the conflict was the Vietnam Veterans Against the War (VVAW). Formed in 1967 by six Vietnam veterans who opposed the war, the VVAW eventually became one of the most influential antiwar groups. Its membership swelled to include thousands of veterans, and even Americans who hated the antiwar movement were willing to listen to men and women who had served in Vietnam. In February 1971, the VVAW sponsored the so-called Winter Soldier Investigation in Detroit, Michigan. The hearings were prompted in part by VVAW outrage over administration claims that the My Lai massacre was an aberration. Dozens of soldiers testified that atrocities were hardly an aberration, that on the contrary, they were commonplace. Two months later, the VVAW sponsored what it called Dewey Canyon III (DEWEY CANYON and (DEWEY CANYON II were military operations in Laos). More than 1,000 veterans, led by men in wheelchairs and mothers of men killed in combat, held a memorial service at the Tomb of the Unknown Soldier. They were then refused permission to lay wreaths on the graves of fallen comrades at Arlington Cemetery. They camped out on the mall in defiance of a court order, and on 23 April 1971, more than 1,000 veterans threw medals they had won in Vietnam over police barricades on the Capitol steps.

The Pentagon Papers. Two months later, the *New York Times* began publishing a series of articles based upon the Pentagon Papers, a secret Defense Department account of U.S. involvement in Indochina. Secretary of Defense Robert McNamara had ordered the study in 1967 and it was completed in 1968. Daniel Ellsberg, one of the contributors to the study, had secretly photocopied thousands of pages and given them to J. William Fulbright, chairman of the Senate Foreign Relations Committee. In June 1971, Ellsberg also gave them to the *New York Times*. The Pentagon Papers immediately become a cause célèbre primarily because they revealed duplicity in the Johnson administration—government officials telling the public one thing and actively pursuing different military and political policies, in particular being involved in Indochina sooner and to a greater extent than the public was aware. Public cynicism about the war deepened.

All America's previous wars had generated some opposition, but the dissent had usually been tangential and peripheral. It was different for the Vietnam War. Opposition began among pacifists in the political fringe of the Old Left but then spread to students, academics, artists, intellectuals, clergy, civil rights activists, writers, politicians, journalists, and entertainers. Some demanded an end to the war because they felt it was immoral, others because it was poorly conceived and unwinnable, and still others because the United States refused to employ the full range of its military power to achieve a military victory. By the early 1970s opposition to the Vietnam War was endemic to American political culture, affecting almost every segment of American society. Modern mass communications magnified and popularized opposition and gave it a powerful immediacy. President Richard Nixon's desperate attempt to secure a peace treaty before the presidential election of 1972 is a symbolic testament to the desire of most Americans to withdraw from Vietnam.

Withdrawal and Aftermath. But that did not imply widespread support for an immediate U.S. withdrawal. Most Americans wanted to give President Nixon a chance to secure "peace with honor," and many believed he could. On 1 January 1971, there were 334,600 U.S. troops in South Vietnam; one year later, there were only 156,800. In 1969, 9,400 U.S. troops died in Vietnam; in 1971, the number fell to 1,400. Relatively few of the U.S. soldiers in Vietnam at the beginning of 1972 were combat troops; most were playing a support role to South Vietnamese personnel. American casualties continued to decline. In 1972, only 300 U.S. soldiers were killed in action.

A substantial majority of Americans believed the president was making real progress in extricating the country from a terrible situation. When North Vietnam unleashed the Easter Offensive in March 1972 in an attempt to overrun South Vietnam, Nixon suspended the Paris peace talks, which had been going on ineffectively since March 1969. He then launched Operation LINEBACKER, a ferocious, long-term strategic bombing campaign over North Vietnam designed to force North Vietnam into serious negotiations. In May 1972, Nixon decided to do what conservative critics had long demanded: mine the North Vietnamese ports of Haiphong, Cam Pha, Hon Gai, and Thanh Hoa. The Easter Offensive continued through the summer of 1972, but North Vietnam lost more than 100,000 troops in the campaign. In October, the politburo in Hanoi expressed the desire to negotiate. Nixon ended the bombing on 22 October 1972, and the United States and North Vietnam reached a tentative agreement to end the war and to return prisoners of war (POWs).

In the presidential election of 1972, the American people confirmed their support for President Nixon and his success in ending the war. The Democrats nominated Sen. George McGovern of South Dakota on an antiwar platform. McGovern campaigned on the theme of an immediate, unilateral U.S. withdrawal from Vietnam. Nixon countered by arguing that a wholesale U.S. flight from Indochina would send the wrong message to allies and enemies alike, compromising U.S. commitments around the world. The American public agreed, and in the November election, Nixon received 61 percent of the popular vote and 521 of 538 votes in the Electoral College to win reelection. Between February and April 1973, the end of the war was symbolized by the return of 591 U.S.

THE RESPONSE OF THE RIGHT. Demonstrators march up Pennsylvania Avenue in support of "Victory in Vietnam," Washington, D.C., 1970. The opinion of many conservatives toward the war was "win or get out." *National Archives*

POWs. By that time, the number of U.S. troops in South Vietnam had decreased to 20,000.

U.S. military forces were out of South Vietnam, but many Americans doubted the viability of the South Vietnamese government and the willingness of the North Vietnamese to abide by the 1973 Paris peace accords. They feared that any resumption of hostilities would bring new requests by South Vietnam for U.S. military assistance, and from 1973 to 1975 an intense debate raged in Congress over the future of the U.S. commitment in Indochina. By the summer of 1973, abundant evidence from the Pentagon Papers and the *New York Times* exposé of the secret bombing campaigns in Cambodia and Laos proved that the Nixon administration had deliberately falsified statistics, data, and reports to Congress to hide the extent of questionable U.S. military activity in Vietnam, Cambodia, and Laos. In July, Congress responded by formulating the War Powers Resolution, which required the president to report to Congress within forty-eight hours if he committed U.S. troops to a foreign conflict or if he "substantially" increased the number of combat troops in a foreign country, Unless Congress approved the president's action within sixty days, the commitment would have to be terminated.

President Nixon viewed the resolution as an intolerable restriction on the powers of the presidency. He spoke out vigorously against the resolution and tried to marshal opposition to it in Congress. But by the fall of 1973, the Watergate scandal was taking its toll on his presidency. The Senate Select Committee on Presidential Campaign Activities (Watergate Committee) investigation of the Watergate cover-up, which began in the summer, kept generating new information that, on a weekly basis, eroded the administration's claims of innocence. The so-called Saturday night massacre in October, in which Nixon fired Watergate special prosecutor Archibald Cox, led to the resignations of Attorney General Elliot Richardson and Assistant Attorney General William Ruckleshaus. The Nixon administration was politically impotent. Congress passed the War Powers Resolution and Nixon vetoed it, but on 7 November 1973, Congress overrode the veto and the resolution went into effect.

Beginning in mid 1974, as North Vietnamese violations of the Paris peace accords became more abundant and the conflict in Vietnam threatened to escalate again, Congress began limiting aid to South Vietnam. North Vietnam launched attacks late in 1974 and a major offensive in March 1975. South Vietnamese military forces collapsed. President Gerald Ford requested $300 million in emergency aid for South Vietnam in late January 1975 and another $722 million on 10 April, alienating many members of Congress with his prowar rhetoric. Congress appropriated only $300 million, and use of that money was limited to evacuating Americans from the war zone and "humanitarian" assistance. Opponents of the war thus had the last word. North Vietnamese forces entered Saigon on 1 May 1975, ending the Vietnam War.

[*See also* African Americans; Chicago Seven; Congress, U.S.; Conscientious Objectors; Democratic National Convention, 1968; Hawks and Doves; Jackson State College; Kent State University; New Left; New Mobe; Public Opinion, American; Silent Majority Speech; Students for a Democratic Society (SDS); United States of America; University of Wisconsin Bombing; Vietnam Moratorium Committee; Vietnam Veterans against the War; Weathermen; Winter Soldier Investigation.

BIBLIOGRAPHY

BASKIR, LAWRENCE M., and WILLIAM A. STRAUSS. *Change and Circumstance: The Draft, the War, and the Vietnam Generation.* 1978.

BERMAN, WILLIAM C. *William Fulbright and the Vietnam War: The Dissent of a Political Realist.* 1988.

DeBENEDETTI, CHARLES, and CHARLES CHATFIELD. *An American Ordeal: The Antiwar Movement of the Vietnam Era.* 1990.

FAIRCLOUGH, ADAM. "Martin Luther King, Jr., and the War in Vietnam." *Phylon* 45 (1984): 19–39.

FISHER, RANDALL M. *Rhetoric and American Democracy: Black Protest through Vietnam Dissent.* 1985.

HALL, MITCHELL K. *Because of Their Faith: CALCAV and Religious Opposition to the Vietnam War.* 1990.

LEVY, DAVID W. *The Debate over Vietnam.* 1991.

MECONIS, CHARLES. *With Clumsy Grace: The American Catholic Left, 1961–1977.* 1979.

MILLER, JAMES. *"Democracy Is in the Streets": From Port Huron to the Siege of Chicago.* 1987.

POWERS, THOMAS. *Vietnam: The War at Home, Vietnam and the American People, 1964–1968.* 1984.

ROTHMAN, STANLEY, and S. ROBERT LICHTER. *Roots of Radicalism: Jews, Christians, and the New Left.* 1982.

SMALL, MELVIN. *Johnson, Nixon, and the Doves.* 1988.

SURREY, DAVID S. *Choice of Conscience: Vietnam Era Military and Draft Resisters in Canada.* 1982.

TURNER, KATHLEEN J. *Lyndon Johnson's Dual War: Vietnam and the Press.* 1985.

UNGER, IRWIN. *The Movement: A History of the American New Left, 1959–1972.* 1974.

VOGELGESANG, SANDY. *The Long Dark Night of the Soul: The American Intellectual Left and the Vietnam War.* 1974.

WITTNER, LAWRENCE S. *Rebels against War: The American Peace Movement, 1933–1983.* 1984.

ZAROULIS, NANCY, and GERALD SULLIVAN. *Who Spoke Up? American Protest against the War in Vietnam, 1963–1975.* 1985.

RANDY ROBERTS AND JAMES S. OLSON

Ap Bac, South Vietnamese village in Mekong Delta, 65 kilometers (40 miles) southwest of Saigon. In early January 1963 Army of the Republic of Vietnam (ARVN) forces attacked Viet Cong guerrilla positions in the area. The guerrillas inflicted heavy casualties on the South Vietnamese, largely because of the poor performance of the ARVN officers. Although the Viet Cong forces eventually abandoned their positions, their success against the ARVN forces provided them with an important psychological boost.

BIBLIOGRAPHY

KARNOW, STANLEY. *Vietnam: A History.* 1991.

PALMER, DAVE RICHARD. *Summons of the Trumpet: U.S.-Vietnam in Perspective.* 1978.

ELLEN D. GOLDLUST

Ap Bia. Ap Bia mountain, located in the A Shau Valley less than two kilometers (one mile) from the Laotian border with South Vietnam, was the site of one of the bloodiest single battles of the Vietnam War. From 10 to 20 May 1969, as part of Operation APACHE SNOW, Army of the Republic of Vietnam (ARVN) units and elements of the U.S. Army's 101st Airborne Division fought to take the mountain from an entrenched Viet Cong force. Both sides sustained high numbers of casualties; the carnage led U.S. troops to nickname the battle "Hamburger Hill." Though they ultimately succeeded in occupying the hill, the ARVN and U.S. forces withdrew only one week later. The apparently pointless battle, which received extensive publicity in the American press, resulted in a public outcry in the United States and greatly increased antiwar sentiment.

BIBLIOGRAPHY

DAVIDSON, PHILLIP B. *Vietnam at War—The History: 1946–1975.* 1988.
KARNOW, STANLEY. *Vietnam: A History.* 1991.
LIPSMAN, SAMUEL. *Fighting for Time.* 1983.
STANTON, SHELBY L. *The Rise and Fall of an American Army: U.S. Ground Forces in Vietnam, 1965–1973.* 1985.

ELLEN D. GOLDLUST

ARC LIGHT. ARC LIGHT was the code name for high-altitude B-52 bombing raids in support of U.S. and Army of the Republic of Vietnam (ARVN) operations in South Vietnam and Laos. Dropped from B-52s flying above 30,000 feet, the bombs, unseen and unheard until they began exploding, wrought enormous destruction in the impact areas. The first ARC LIGHT strike targeting communist forces' rear areas occurred on 18 June 1965, marking the debut of U.S. Air Force Strategic Air Command (SAC) firepower in Vietnam; the last was on 18 August 1973. Prior to ARC LIGHT, B-52s were used exclusively as part of the U.S. strategic nuclear force and as a pillar of the SIOP (Single Integrated Operational Plan), the U.S. war plan for a nuclear exchange with the Soviet Union.

ARC LIGHT strikes were first mounted from Andersen Air Force Base in Guam, which was more than 3,200 kilometers (2,000 miles) from Vietnam. These great distances required that the B-52s refuel in flight, usually on the return trip, from KC-135 jet tankers. Beginning in July 1967, B-52s also operated from the U Tapao Royal Thai Naval Base near Bangkok, which was only some 800 kilometers (500 miles) from the target areas, and therefore did not require in-flight refueling. Because of SAC concerns that classified B-52 electronic warfare systems designed to defeat Soviet radar and surface-to-air missile (SAM) defenses might be compromised over North Vietnam, and for diplomatic reasons, ARC LIGHT strikes were largely confined to South Vietnam, which absorbed more than 80 percent of the total. Targets immediately across the Laotian border were hit from December 1966 on, and there were occasional strikes against transportation and infiltration targets in southernmost North Vietnam.

The B-52s bombed by radar, at first using radar reflectors brought into the target area by helicopter and later under guidance from ground-based Skyspot radars. Most ARC LIGHT strikes were against North Vietnamese Army (NVA) or Viet Cong base areas. Their effectiveness, however, was a matter of debate:

Since the targets were in heavily jungled terrain deep in hostile territory, post-strike aerial photography generally yielded inconclusive intelligence, and ground teams were rarely sent in. Many such raids struck empty jungle, but intelligence suggested, and postwar accounts confirmed, that they were highly destructive, greatly feared, and had a serious impact on the morale of North Vietnamese and Viet Cong forces.

The effectiveness of B-52s in direct support of ground troops is beyond doubt. First used in tactical support of ground troops in the Ia Drang battles of mid-November 1965, such ARC LIGHT strikes were employed within 900 meters (3,000 feet) of friendly troops and devastated the NVA forces attacking Khe Sanh in 1968 and Pleiku and An Loc in 1972. Ironically, until Nixon's bombing escalation in the wake of the 1972 Easter Offensive, B-52 strategic bombers provided tactical support for ground forces in the South, while strategic targets in the North were attacked by tactical fighters and attack aircraft.

BIBLIOGRAPHY

SCHLIGHT, JOHN. *The Years of the Offensive, 1965–1968.* 1988.

JOHN F. GUILMARTIN, JR.

Argenlieu, Georges Thierry D' (1884–1964), French high commissioner for Indochina, August 1946–April 1947. Appointed by De Gaulle, d'Argenlieu zealously reestablished French authority in Indochina. He preempted the Fontainebleau Conference by unilaterally and without authority declaring the Republic of Cochinchina in southern Vietnam. The bombardment of Haiphong in November 1946, which he ordered, led to open warfare with the Viet Minh in December.

BIBLIOGRAPHY

HAMMER, ELLEN J. *The Struggle for Indochina.* 1954.
KARNOW, STANLEY. *Vietnam: A History.* 1991.

VICTOR JEW

Army, U.S. When the U.S. Army entered the Vietnam conflict, it was at a high point in internal efficiency and public prestige. The service had benefited greatly from the flexible response strategy instituted by President John F. Kennedy and Secretary of Defense Robert McNamara, which emphasized the buildup of U.S. conventional forces to deter and if necessary defeat communist expansionism without early resort to nuclear weapons. Under Kennedy, the active army grew from eleven to sixteen divisions and to a strength of nearly 1 million men, backed by a National Guard and Reserve of much enhanced readiness. All U.S. Army divisions were restructured on the flexible ROAD (Reorganization Objective Army Division) pattern of three task-organized brigades, a formation adaptable to many types and levels of combat. Adding to its mobility and firepower, the army developed new helicopter-borne airmobile assault units and tactics. Preparing to counter communist-supported "wars of national liberation," the service expanded its green-beret-wearing Special Forces to provide counterinsurgency training and assistance to U.S. allies in the developing world. Throughout these changes, the army remained essentially a force of draftee citizen-soldiers, commanded by officers who were graduates of the college Reserve Officers' Training Corps (ROTC) program.

The U.S. Army Enters the War. The army entered the Vietnam War gradually. President Kennedy initially sent in Special Forces and military advisers as well as helicopter companies and other support units, to enhance the mobility and combat effectiveness of the Army of the Republic of Vietnam (ARVN). As the insurgency expanded and a series of South Vietnamese governments foundered

INFANTRYMEN. Soldiers of the U.S. 1st Infantry Division (the "Big Red One") attend memorial services for dead comrades, 1965. *National Archives*

politically and militarily, the United States incrementally increased the number of army advisers and support troops to nearly 16,000 and committed them fully to armed combat against the insurgents. In 1965, President Lyndon Johnson, to save South Vietnam from total defeat by Viet Cong guerrillas and North Vietnamese Army (NVA) forces, who seemed to be moving into large-unit conventional warfare, sent U.S. combat divisions to South Vietnam to accompany the Operation ROLLING THUNDER bombing offensive against the North. By late 1968, the U.S. Army force in Vietnam, then at its peak strength, included seven divisions, six regiments and separate brigades, and large combat and service support elements as well as a substantial advisory contingent—a total of more than 365,000 men. By the war's end, U.S. Army casualties in Vietnam totaled more than 47,000 dead, 200,000 wounded, and nearly 2,000 captured or missing in action (MIA), a toll larger than that of the Korean conflict.

Success and Failure. The army's performance in Vietnam was mixed. Logistically, the service, much aided by the McNamara reforms in defense management, rapidly installed a modern support structure in an underdeveloped country while simultaneously carrying on active combat operations. The army's soldiers in Vietnam probably were the best supplied and equipped and received the most rapid and effective medical care of any fighting men in any U.S. war. Tactically, U.S. units engaged elite enemy forces on their own ground and defeated them. The army's ROAD division and airmobile units and tactics met the test of combat. Indeed, the helicopter revolutionized every aspect of operations from fire support to medical evacuation, establishing itself beyond doubt as a significant new weapon of war. Army troops also performed effectively in antiguerrilla and pacification missions, although their dependence on heavy firepower at times was counterproductive in such operations.

Yet logistical and tactical successes did not result in victory. The army broadly had two primary missions in Vietnam: the destruction of the organized North Vietnamese and Viet Cong military units; and the development of an ARVN that was capable of bringing security and government control to the countryside, ultimately replacing U.S. forces in the overall defense of South Vietnam. While U.S. troops defeated large NVA units when they engaged them, the NVA and Viet Cong forces, with superior intelligence and knowledge of the terrain, regularly

WILLIAM C. WESTMORELAND. Circa 1967. *National Archives*

evaded combat at will and when hard pressed withdrew to base areas in Cambodia, Laos, and North Vietnam where the Americans, because of Johnson's decision to limit the war, were not allowed to pursue them. The U.S. Army advisory and assistance effort never overcame the ARVN's fundamental deficiencies in leadership, training, and motivation and suffered as well from confusion of purpose. Vacillating between trying to prepare the ARVN for counterinsurgency and for a conventional Korea-style war, U.S. Army advisers produced a force not truly effective in either mission.

The War's Internal Toll on the Army. As the war dragged on, its cost to the U.S. Army reached nearly catastrophic proportions. Because President Johnson decided, for domestic political reasons, not to mobilize the National Guard and Reserves for the conflict, the army had to sustain its combat forces by stripping key personnel from units in the United States and Europe and by filling its ranks in Vietnam largely with short-term draftees and inexperienced company-grade officers and noncommissioned officers. The quality of army leadership and training inevitably declined, a decline that many in and outside the army believe was accelerated by the policy of continually cycling soldiers through

Vietnam on one-year tours. Especially after the Tet Offensive of 1968, the U.S. Army in Vietnam and worldwide was beset by a succession of internal scandals, culminating in revelation of the major atrocity at My Lai. The army leadership struggled in vain to stem political and racial dissension, drug abuse, and a general decline in discipline. As the Vietnam War became unpopular with Americans at home, so did the army, the service most identified with the conflict. The army's loss of internal cohesion and public support had become so great by the early 1970s that many of its commanders expressed relief at the final U.S. military withdrawal from a war that seemed to threaten the complete destruction of their service.

Rebuilding after the War. The army devoted itself in the decades following Vietnam to the task of rebuilding cohesion, discipline, and professionalism in what was now an all-volunteer force and to making up for time lost in the war in developing and assimilating new weapons and equipment. That rebuilding process produced impressive results, as the army's performance in the Gulf War of 1991 attested. Nevertheless, the wounds of Vietnam persisted, both within the army and in the army's relationship to the larger society which it serves and from which it ultimately draws its strength.

[*See also* Casualties; Discipline, *article on* U.S. Military; Drugs and Drug Use; Helicopters; Medical Support, *article on* U.S. Military; Military Assistance Advisory Group-Vietnam (MAAG-V); Military Assistance Command; Vietnam (MACV); Pacification; Project 100,000; Special Forces, U.S.; Women, U.S. Military, *article on* Women's Army Corps (WAC).]

BIBLIOGRAPHY

CLARKE, JEFFREY. *Advice and Support: The Final Years.* 1988.
HAUSER, WILLIAM L. *America's Army in Crisis.* 1973.
KINNARD, DOUGLAS. *The War Managers.* 1985.
SPECTOR, RONALD H. "The Vietnam War and the Army's Self-Image." In *Second Indochina War Symposium: Papers and Commentary,* edited by John Schlight. 1986.
WEIGLEY, RUSSELL F. *History of the United States Army.* 1984.

GRAHAM A. COSMAS

Army of the Republic of Vietnam (ARVN).

Created by the United States in 1955, the ARVN represented the land forces component within the larger entity called the Republic of Vietnam Armed Forces (RVNAF), which included a navy and air force. The ARVN's mission was to neutralize the military and political threats generated by the People's Army of Vietnam (PAVN) and its southern ally, the National Liberation Front (NLF). Most attention has focused on the ARVN's demise in 1975, leaving the misleading impression that this army was short-lived. In retrospect the ARVN represented the largest, and last, Vietnamese army sponsored by foreigners to preserve the nation's independence.

French Colonial Armies. The first Vietnamese military force created by a Western nation to fight Vietnamese opponents dates from 1879. In that year, the French organized the Regiment de Tirailleurs Annamites (the Annamite Rifles) in Saigon; four years later, a companion unit, the Régiment de Tirailleurs Tonkinois (the Tonkin Rifles) was formed in Hanoi. Together they assisted colonial army units in enforcing French policies in Vietnam, which earned them public scorn.

As France's control of Vietnam tightened, Vietnamese society divided into two basic groups. The first represented those who, by choice or subjection, complied with colonial rule. The second group was composed of Vietnamese Resistance leaders and their followers who were intent on reestablishing an independent Vietnam, basing their claims on the Vietnamese people's long-established resentment of foreign interference or invasion. Thus, they found psychological strength and support in Vietnam's traditions and history. Conversely, Vietnamese aligned with the French could not credibly argue that they represented the aspirations and will of the people—which resulted in a negative image that they and their successors never successfully overcame. The ARVN inherited this ideological dilemma.

France believed its presence in Vietnam was "just," based on Western perceptions of empire, and it took steps to attain a variety of goals at local expense. For example, during World War I, some 48,000 Vietnamese laborers were conscripted and sent to the western front in Europe: 10,000 died and another 15,000 were wounded, a casualty rate in excess of 50 percent. The Vietnamese were praised for their sacrifices in government reports, but there were few welfare or repatriation benefits for them. Veterans received little, if any, psychological support or material rewards for their services to France, resulting in a negative legacy from the Vietnamese perspective. This exploitation continued in future years because the viability of French rule in Vietnam depended on local manpower. In 1940 there were 60,000 Vietnamese troops, mostly conscripts, serving in the French colonial army in Vietnam; North African (40,000) and European (20,000) troops provided the remainder. France expected a degree of loyalty from the Vietnamese troops that did not materialize, however, because of the conclusion of World War II, continued Vietnamese antagonism toward colonial rule, and Vietnamese resentment over French collaboration with the Japanese occupation of Vietnam. By October 1946, 39,610 Vietnamese troops had deserted, more than 50 percent of the Vietnamese contribution to the colonial army's strength in Vietnam at that time.

Two years later, the French Indochina War against the Viet Minh had intensified and the colonial army had yet to find a military solution. Furthermore, defense priorities in Europe required a decrease in the number of French personnel serving in Vietnam, and growing antiwar sentiment among the French public had increased to the point at which government officials felt insecure about France's position in the war. Funding was unreliable; without U.S. assistance the entire French war effort would have ground to a halt. The Vietnamese National Army (VNA), the ARVN's predecessor, was created in this unsettled atmosphere. If other realistic options had existed, however, it is unlikely that the VNA would have emerged at all because, overall, the French high command had viewed its local troops indifferently or negatively since at least 1914. Subservience, not equality, characterized Franco-Vietnamese relations. Now the French demanded even greater sacrifices from the Vietnamese than ever before. However, the degree of cooperation the French anticipated once again did not materialize: in 1953 only 10,000 Vietnamese responded to their draft notices, only 20 percent of the desired quotas. Furthermore, desertion was widespread, as more than 4,000 Vietnamese troops left the army illegally after the French surrendered at Dien Bien Phu in May 1954.

The American Model. Within twelve months, the United States transformed the fragmented VNA, whose loyalty to foreigners was questionable, into the new Army of the Republic of Vietnam. The ARVN was organized along the lines of Western forces, emphasizing conventional methods of warfare that included artillery, armor, and large-scale infantry formations. This format complemented the U.S. government's global outlook in the 1950s: specifically, the People's Republic of China (PRC) had been identified as a potential threat that required the creation of armies in select Asian nations, armies that could be integrated with U.S. forces to thwart the PRC's expansionism. By 1960, this prognosis had proved faulty, but by then it was too late to alter the U.S. approach to training the ARVN. In addition, U.S. advisers were products of their own system and could only teach what they knew. Thus, little, if any, emphasis was placed on the political aspects of a war of national liberation such as that espoused by North Vietnam.

The United States classified the conflict in Vietnam a "low-intensity conflict," and mistakenly believed that it could be rapidly solved by the South Vietnamese army. It became clear during the war that the ARVN's conventional format reduced its ability to deal with small groups of highly mobile guerrilla soldiers operating primarily at night. The ARVN's methods became predictable; its divisions were basically tied to specific areas of responsibility, from which they rarely moved. Armored units, with their noise and bulk, could not move secretly, and artillery batteries were useless at night. Ironically, these limitations had also been a primary cause of Franco-Vietnamese failures during the Indochina War, yet their significance was downplayed by a confident, results-oriented Military Assistance Advisory Group–Vietnam (MAAG-V), which was responsible for training the ARVN.

The ARVN's first encounter against an armed adversary took place soon after Ngo Dinh Diem became South Vietnam's first president. Previously, some French intelligence officials, in conjunction with the Binh Xuyen, a Vietnamese criminal organization, had established a gambling, prostitution, and opium empire, which Diem vowed to extinguish. Superior numbers and firepower enabled the ARVN to defeat the Binh Xuyen in 1955, but this did not present a real test for the army. To further consolidate Diem's military power, the Hoa Hao and Cao Dai religious sect armies, incorporated into the French colonial army in the late 1940s, were bribed by U.S. Army colonel Edward Lansdale into pledging their allegiance to Diem. The ARVN's first major engagement against the Viet Cong occurred at Ap Bac in 1963 and revealed serious deficiencies in command and control, tactics, and the judicious use of resources. A fundamental cause of the ARVN's failure was its operational format, yet MAAG-V again discounted the possibility that the U.S. approach to training the ARVN might be inappropriate for local conditions. Instead, the ARVN was uncharitably labeled incompetent.

ARVN AIRMOBILE OPERATIONS. U.S. helicopters land on the fringe of a pineapple plantation in the Mekong Delta to pick up South Vietnamese rangers joining U.S. troops in a sweep southwest of Saigon. *National Archives*

The massacre of a Vietnamese marine unit at Binh Gia, east of Saigon, in 1964 gave support to the views of those Pentagon analysts who believed that the ARVN was incapable of settling the ever growing insurgency. Within a year, U.S. forces were committed to the conflict, which had both positive and negative influences on the ARVN. On the positive side, the ARVN, now supported directly by U.S. military forces, seemed incapable of losing. A series of decisions at the Honolulu and Manila conferences in 1966, however, reassigned 50 percent of the ARVN's total strength to pacification duties, thus preventing novice troops from acquiring valuable combat experience, which they would later need. At this point, one of the original U.S. objectives in South Vietnam—to make the ARVN self-sufficient—was lost in the shuffle as U.S. units attempted to succeed where ARVN units had previously failed. The U.S. presence overwhelmed the ARVN, but by 1969 it was clear that U.S. forces had not found a satisfactory military solution. The conflict had escalated to a point at which it became a vendetta, with the U.S. government's credibility at stake.

Vietnamese Contexts. It is important to remember that the two largest armies in the conflict—the ARVN and the People's Army of Vietnam (PAVN)—were both Vietnamese. They shared a common history, language, values, and spiritual beliefs. All Vietnamese troops, from both the North and South, lived, fought, and died in similar surroundings. Both armies received enormous amounts of financial and military assistance from foreign nations, but ultimately the Vietnamese settled the conflict between themselves. Observed as a whole, the ARVN did not have the strength of purpose that was ingrained within the ranks of the PAVN. Although ARVN units performed credibly on many occasions, the army was also rife with apathy, corruption, indifference, unreliability, and desertion. In retrospect, the fanaticism, diligence, and dedication of a minority of personnel within the ARVN, could not offset the accumulated shortfalls of the majority, which eventually wore the army down. The ARVN's demise was caused by internal and external factors, but ultimately it was the very nature of the ARVN that caused it to fail.

To succeed, the ARVN needed to find an acceptable image that went beyond the concept of anticommunism in order to satisfy the Vietnamese people's definition of a truly Vietnamese fighting force. This task was difficult as it ultimately required the people to ignore past activities and precedents and accept the United States as the ARVN's patron. A wide variety of political emotions, including communist and anticommunist sentiments, was present in South Vietnam. The division of the country at the 17th parallel into North and South Vietnam in 1954 caused significant demographic changes. It provided Vietnamese Francophiles and northern Catholics with a convenient sanctuary in the south. However, tens of thousands of Cochinchinese had their ancestral roots in the south and did not migrate north unless they were intensely political. The support of this "silent majority" was crucial to the South Vietnamese government because the conflict, except for the air war, was contested in the South, not the North. The ARVN and the PAVN both required the silent majority's support, albeit for opposite political ideologies. Ultimately the ARVN and the South Vietnamese government failed to gain this support, leading to a PAVN victory.

Dedication to a legitimate government is a Confucian ethic with strong Vietnamese roots. Historically, any Vietnamese military or civilian leader was expected to display morality, ability, and stability. Local traditions do not separate a person's qualifications from his or her private life. Simply expressed, leadership was not a cold, detached concept, but an expression of self-worth. The government of North Vietnam and the conduct of its leaders complemented this all-important ideal. Conversely, successive governments in South Vietnam were perpetually involved with political intrigue, excessive corruption, and instability, which diminished popular support and eroded the ARVN's morale. As the government's enforcement branch, the ARVN could neither escape political criticism nor justify the conduct of its leaders. The United States was partly to blame for this problem as it allowed a military clique to remove President Diem by force in 1963. Henceforth, the U.S. government was required to deal with a variety of military leaders who were unqualified for political duties. As the war escalated, political jousting and infighting surged as favorite sons fell into disgrace and aspirants jockeyed for national recognition. The ARVN's morale suffered as a result.

South Vietnamese troops had little material, financial, or welfare benefits to guarantee their loyalty. In April 1968, an ARVN private earned US$467 per

MASS ARRESTS. South Vietnamese troops holding a group of suspected Viet Cong, Kien Tuong province, 1967. *National Archives*

annum; generals were also poorly paid (US$2,500 per year), which prompted many senior officers to use their rank to conduct illegal activities. Overall, the average pay of all ranks in the RVNAF in 1968 was US$108 monthly, while the cost of living was between US$117 and US$120. Thus, Vietnamese soldiers, sailors, and airmen could not exist on their wages. Poverty was also a fact of life among the PAVN and Viet Cong forces. The average cadre (in 1968–1969) was paid 60 piasters (US$.75) monthly and political cadres earned 75 piasters (US$.93). Again, both Vietnamese armies had few incentives to motivate them. Ultimately the conflict was decided in favor of those who overcame mental anxieties and sacrificed personal desires to complement the war effort.

Desertion. Desertion was a fundamental cause of the ARVN's demise and South Vietnam's downfall. Men of the ARVN left their ranks and disappeared for extended periods of time. Some returned and rejoined the army under different names, while others never returned. Soldiers usually deserted for socioeconomic reasons; defection to the PAVN or the Viet Cong was rarely a motive. The South Vietnamese government was beset by numerous problems, including developing its armed forces, maintaining an unbalanced economy, and fighting a war against a determined adversary. Accordingly, austerity measures became the rule, not the exception. This modus operandi reached a crisis in 1968, when all leaves were canceled and military personnel were informed that they must serve until the war ended. In addition, the government enacted its most ambitious conscription system, which included all males aged 16–50 in full- or part-time duties. However, this legislation did not deter desertions.

The results of these measures were staggering. Between 1965 and 1972 approximately 840,000 troops deserted, 120,000 per year. Desertions exceeded casualties by 6 to 1. The average deserter was aged 17–21, held the rank of private, and had served less than six months. The ARVN had the highest desertion rate (60 percent) of all ground units; the Regional Forces (23 percent) and Popular Forces (17 percent) accounted for the remainder. The ARVN's infantry divisions, those closest to the conflict, had the greatest number of deserters. The 25th and 5th divisions, located in III Corps Tactical Zone (CTZ) near Saigon, had the worst desertion rates: between 1965 and 1972, the 25th Division lost more than 8,400 troops, 1,200 men annually; the 5th Division ranked second. Within the ARVN's elite forces, the rangers had the greatest overall desertion rate (55 percent), followed by the airborne unit (30 percent) and the marines (15 percent). Of the entire RVNAF, 80 percent of all desertions occurred in the ARVN's combat units, 12 percent in the navy, and 8 percent in the air force.

ARVN deserters significantly reduced unit strengths, compromised potential operations, and eroded the army's identity and integrity. Despite these problems, on numerous occasions over twenty years, the men of the ARVN held their ranks and engaged PAVN and Viet Cong forces with a determination that rivaled that of any highly motivated fighting force. What converted apathy into aggressiveness was leadership, a quality rarely found within the ARVN's senior ranks. The ARVN was motivated and held together by lieutenants and captains who had graduated from the nation's military schools and academies. These junior officers, who had been subjected to intense anticommunist propaganda while in training, performed with diligence, although frequently their responsibilities were frustrated by large groups of unmotivated troops. The successes of the ARVN are a tribute to its junior officers, without whose sacrifices and talents the army would have collapsed earlier than 1975.

The average ARVN soldier believed in South Vietnam and the cause of anticommunism but was still prepared to place himself above the war effort—a problem that was never solved. Soldiers' attitudes

LOOTING. ARVN soldiers with a stolen chicken. *U.S. Army*

were influenced as much by family or personal desires and prejudices as by army training. They lived in a perpetual state of anxiety—the war continued with no end in sight, and there was no relief except through desertion. The PAVN, by its continued presence in the field despite staggering losses, maintained a strong psychological advantage, which unnerved ARVN troops. The shortcomings of U.S. military units also undermined ARVN troops' morale. Accordingly, the ARVN adopted an overly cautious approach in which potential risks were carefully scrutinized before commitment. There were numerous occasions when ARVN units and their PAVN and Viet Cong counterparts avoided direct confrontation when mutual odds and outcomes were unknown, objectives questionable, or when support was unreliable or nonexistent. Under these circumstances, both armies at times conducted reputation-saving silent retreats.

Fighting the War. North Vietnam's enemies were the United States and its allies, not the people of Vietnam, which included the members of the

ARVN, a point that was continually stressed in North Vietnamese propaganda. Both Vietnamese opponents would have preferred to settle their differences between themselves, but the influence of foreign patrons, which demanded a military solution, plunged the Vietnamese into a head-on confrontation. A reality of the conflict was the degree to which ARVN and U.S. operations were frequently compromised by faulty intelligence, misjudgments, and a poor performance by South Vietnamese troops. When the ARVN's behavior is assessed strictly on the basis of U.S. military criteria, it was often guilty of avoiding combat. Viewed another way, however, the ARVN's behavior was an extension of how its troops viewed themselves, the future, the nation of Vietnam irrespective of political ideologies, and a genuine hope that a peaceful settlement could be found.

By 1969, the ARVN contained nearly 1 million troops representing ten divisions, marine, ranger, and airborne units, artillery and armored commands, plus a territorial forces network. By that year the ARVN, as well as U.S. forces, had failed permanently to eliminate the operations of the PAVN and the Viet Cong yet had paid a high cost in lives and casualties because of faulty strategies and a basic reliance on a war of attrition, that is, sustained massive firepower supplemented by a prodigious waste of human resources. North Vietnam considered the entire country a single battlefield where all resources—human, material, and geographic—were essential components in a conflict that emphasized political, not military, issues. Conversely, the South Vietnamese and U.S. approach was geographically fragmented, psychologically disjointed, and functionally unsound, which left them, on most occasions, in disadvantageous defensive positions.

Tet Offensive and its Aftermath. North Vietnam's 1968 Tet Offensive was an ambitious plan that attempted to humble the ARVN by a complete reversal of tactics. For the first time during the Vietnam War the PAVN resorted to conventional tactics that did not rely extensively on snipers, mines, and booby traps. This provided the ARVN with an opportunity to show initiative in the type of battle for which it had been trained. However, its successes and those of U.S. forces were obscured by media coverage that focused on U.S. and South Vietnamese vulnerability in South Vietnam and strengthened the position of critics who argued that the United States should disengage immediately. When South Vietnamese officials came to understand fully that as a consequence of Vietnamization (1969–1972) direct U.S. military intervention would gradually cease, the ARVN's post–Tet Offensive elation was replaced by wary pessimism. Upgrading the RVNAF materially and financially so that it could assume complete control of the war—the essence of Vietnamization—would only succeed if the South Vietnamese were capable of fulfilling such a task.

The arrival of U.S. forces in 1965 brought with it an unprecedented demand for war matériel and supplementary resources, the majority of which was assigned to U.S. units instead of ARVN units. At the same time, the United States had not sufficiently developed an independent logistical command within the RVNAF by 1969. At best, the ARVN's ability to sustain itself was rudimentary. Nevertheless, the implications of Vietnamization forced the RVNAF to assume duties well beyond its ability, especially in the critical area of logistics. For example, in 1972 the RVNAF required 381,000 specific items on a continual basis. These included ammunition, uniforms, spare parts, and other items essential to the war effort. The Vietnamese Air Force (VNAF), with a variety of aircraft at its disposal, needed 192,000 lines of supply, the ARVN 127,000, and the Vietnamese Navy (VNN) 62,000.

Not unexpectedly, the South Vietnamese found these new demands daunting, if not impossible to fulfill. As a result, on-the-job training occurred concurrently with regular duties; staff with no logistical background often were in charge of vital areas beyond their comprehension. Predictably, results were poor; services malfunctioned, or ceased to exist, which directly influenced the war effort. Critical problems also existed in intelligence gathering and analysis, a luxury the ARVN had previously enjoyed thanks to U.S. resources. On the positive side, U.S. advisory assistance and tactical air support was still present, although it was known that these assets also would be withdrawn. Overall, the ARVN in 1969 was incapable of managing its war effort independently because of ongoing, seemingly uncorrectable, internal problems and continued reliance on the United States. The army's vulnerable status was again confirmed in Cambodia and Laos and during the 1972 Easter Offensive.

Cambodian Offensive. The Cambodian offensive, or Operation TOAN THANG (TOTAL VIC-

TORY), was launched on 30 April 1970 to prove that the U.S. policy of Vietnamization was effective. The overall plan was for U.S. and ARVN forces to strike west into Cambodia and interdict the southern extremities of the Ho Chi Minh Trail, near Mimot and Snoul, and destroy the Central Office for South Vietnam (COSVN), the NLF's political and administrative headquarters known to operate on both sides of the border. Attempts at secrecy were unsuccessful; the ARVN conducted two daylight probes into Cambodia, one on 4 May and one on 20 May, which alerted even the most casual observers that a larger campaign would follow. The ARVN's manpower commitment was impressive; more than 50,000 troops served in Cambodia before all the associated operations were canceled in January 1971. The results of the campaign were mixed and subject to interpretation. The ARVN claimed to have killed some 11,000 PAVN and Viet Cong troops and to have captured another 2,300. But these figures could have been exaggerated because of the ARVN's faulty reporting systems, which often relayed fabricated information. Furthermore, 25,000 weapons and 2,500 tons of ammunition were reportedly seized, which represented the ARVN's greatest seizure of matériel on Cambodian soil.

On the negative side, the campaign's primary objectives—destruction of the southern extremities of the Ho Chi Minh Trail and COSVN—were not achieved. Isolated small-unit actions—not a general engagement—characterized the military aspect of the operations. On most occasions, PAVN and Viet Cong forces withdrew and fled deeper into Cambodia, which aggravated an already difficult situation. In retrospect, the campaign again revealed the ARVN's organizational weaknesses: command and control was weak and ineffective, and units maneuvered independently and frequently fired on each other. A major assumption was that the ARVN could hold areas cleared by U.S. troops, but this did not occur. Instead a prodigious waste of war matériel, highlighted by the unbridled use of firepower, including B-52 bombings, resulted in the destruction of vast amounts of Cambodian territory that had little or no strategic value. Looting was widespread: some ARVN officers hijacked expensive motor vehicles and sacred relics, usually stone sculptures, which were photographed being carried to Saigon in slings beneath ARVN helicopters. Thus, the Cambodian incursion was not a "showpiece of Viet-

namization," as President Nixon claimed. Instead, it was a reminder that the ARVN still relied heavily on U.S. advisers, logistical networks, and tactical air support, shortfalls that were not the fault of the average soldier.

In Cambodia the ARVN had encountered PAVN and Viet Cong forces that preferred to withdraw rather than participate in a protracted campaign with questionable outcomes. However, this was not the case in Laos. In late January 1971, the Military Assistance Command, Vietnam (MACV), decided to erase the memory of the ARVN and U.S. setbacks in Cambodia by launching a new offensive in Laos, Operation LAM SON 719. The target was Tchepone, located just inside the Laotian border at the western terminus of Route 9. This road, which extended from Dong Ha, on the coast of South Vietnam, into Laos, intersected the Ho Chi Minh Trail, the campaign's military objective. No major operation in the ARVN's history had been planned so hastily; Gen. Creighton Abrams, commander of MACV, gave Gen. Hoang Xuan Lam only three weeks to prepare. Lam and his subordinates expressed severe reservations about the mission but were less skeptical when informed by U.S. intelligence that the PAVN forces near Tchepone were weak and had no immediate plans for a new offensive. This assessment was incorrect—the PAVN–Pathet Lao forces in the Tchepone area numbered some 42,000 troops, and they had been preparing for a border offensive since October 1970.

Operation LAM SON. Despite the ARVN's misgivings, MACV launched Operation LAM SON 719 in early February. Approximately 17,000 South Vietnamese troops participated, representing the 1st Division, plus marine, airborne, and ranger battalions. Ultimately they encountered no fewer than 30,000 PAVN–Pathet Lao forces supported by 10,000–20,000 reserves, while the ARVN had none. To succeed, the ARVN had to advance into Laos while simultaneously creating fire support bases along the way. U.S. tactical air support and helicopter resources were available, but U.S. advisory staff did not participate in order to adhere to Vietnamization schedules. Most important, no alternative strategies were developed that could be implemented if the ARVN walked into a trap, which is exactly what occurred.

On 8 February, the ARVN's convoys (some 300 trucks and 50 armored vehicles) crossed the Laotian frontier. Three days later PAVN artillery fire erupted

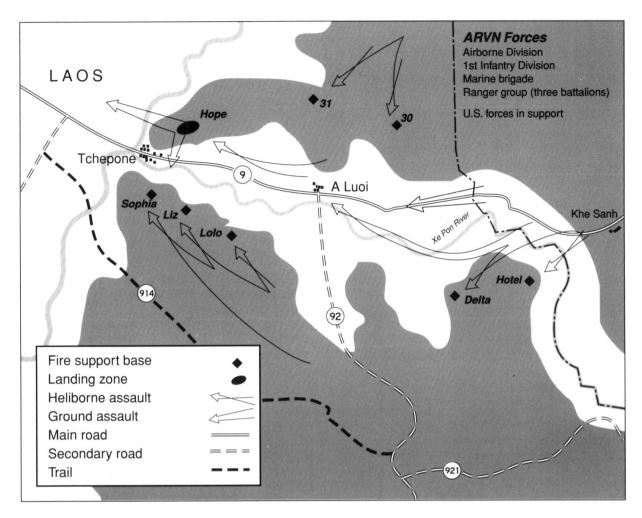

OPERATION LAM SON 719. 8 February–9 April 1971.

along the ridges of the Co Roc escarpment, which flanked Route 9 into Tchepone. For the next five weeks the ARVN fought desperately to retreat from Laos, a retreat highlighted by U.S. aircraft destroying discarded ARVN equipment, the loss of essential intelligence data, plus the abandonment of eighteen fire support bases established during the campaign. U.S. helicopter crews flew 90,000 sorties supporting, or rescuing, ARVN troops, many of whom were photographed hanging onto skids en route to safety. Casualties were high: the ARVN lost 8,000 men, 45 percent of its entire command; PAVN casualties numbered 5,000. Overall, the operation was a disaster; the ARVN did not achieve its objectives and showed that it still relied on U.S. support.

The Easter Offensive. By 1972, the ARVN's control of I CTZ was questionable. The 1st Divi-

sion, the army's best, was being rebuilt after its battering in Laos the previous year. Furthermore, the withdrawal of U.S. forces from the region required the creation of a new division, designated the 3d. On 30 March, North Vietnam launched its Eastern Offensive, or the Nguyen Hue campaign, which pushed ARVN forces from the demilitarized zone (DMZ) back to Quang Tri. For most of April, the ARVN conceded territory and withdrew in disorder, highlighted by the collapse of the 3d Division on two separate occasions. The 3d Division was eventually reconstituted, but at a cost of $37.6 million only fifteen months after its creation. Command and control, as in Laos, was noticeably absent within the ARVN. Gen. Hoang Xuan Lam, the I CTZ commander, frequently clashed with Gen. Vu Van Giai, the 3d Division's senior officer, which left the army confused and directionless. Five hours before the offensive began, General Giai ignored intelligence warnings and military prudence by rotating two of the 3d Division's regiments from secured positions, which left them exposed and in motion when the attack commenced. Content with the situation, Giai flew to Saigon for the weekend.

On 3 May, Lam and Giai were relieved of command. Gen. Ngo Quang Truong, the IV CTZ commander, replaced Lam and launched Operation LOI PHONG (THUNDER HURRICANE) within days of his appointment. By mid-September the ARVN had reestablished its position in northern South Vietnam under General Truong's leadership. At the same time, however, his victories were partially due to enormous U.S. air support, particularly tactical air strikes, which isolated PAVN units and destroyed their sanctuaries. Overextended, undersupplied, and without reinforcements, the PAVN was eventually forced to withdraw. The results of the Easter Offensive proved that the ARVN, when led well, responded with determination, but at the same time, the ARVN's reliance on U.S. support cannot be underestimated. This U.S. assistance was gradually reduced and then withdrawn completely, which helped determine the ARVN's fate.

The End of the War. In July 1973, Congress passed Public Law 93-50, which ended funding for any U.S. military activities in Cambodia, Laos, North Vietnam, and South Vietnam. The greatest consequence of the law, which took effect on 15 August, was that the ARVN no longer had U.S. air support. Financially, South Vietnam needed $1.45 billion for the calendar year 1975, but Congress provided only $700 million. In December 1974 and January 1975, PAVN forces attacked Phuoc Long province, northeast of Saigon, to determine how the United States would react to PAVN military actions. Outnumbered and outgunned, the ARVN fought with determination, but at great cost; the 18th Division and the 7th Ranger Group lost 4,500 troops killed or wounded by the PAVN's sustained artillery barrages. The congressional legislation had prohibited intervention by U.S. air power, and the ARVN was on its own for the remainder of the war.

In the field, the ARVN's ability to control all of South Vietnam was questionable. Desertion—the army's greatest problem—soared to unprecedented levels. Between April and December 1974, nearly 176,000 men deserted. President Thieu's decision in March 1975 to split South Vietnam in half by abandoning the Central Highlands was a desperate reaction to a hopeless situation. To succeed, the plan required senior officers to organize and execute a timely withdrawal from Pleiku and Kontum before initiating a counteroffensive to retake Ban Me Thuot, which had already fallen. But no ARVN general or consortium of generals had sufficient experience to conduct such an operation.

Gen. Pham Van Phu, a Thieu loyalist, was placed in charge of the evacuation. On 14 March, Phu convened a meeting with Gen. Pham Van Tat, the ARVN ranger commander of II Corps, and Generals Tran Van Cam and Pham Ngoc Sang. Phu reconfirmed Thieu's orders and ordered that Pleiku be evacuated in forty-eight hours, by March 16. Phu added that he would fly to Nha Trang on 15 March in order to establish a new operations center, an unanticipated revelation. Prior to departing, Phu ordered Generals Tat and Cam to jointly supervise all operations, which immediately resulted in command-and-control problems because neither officer was sure what to do. To make matters worse, Col. Le Khac Ly, Phu's chief of staff, was also told to assist with the evacuation. Phu then flew to Nha Trang and never returned to the Central Highlands. He killed himself in Saigon on 30 April.

The evacuation convoys ran a guantlet down Route 7-B toward the coast. Some 60,000 troops departed Pleiku, yet only 20,000 arrived at Tuy Hoa, a loss of 66 percent. The retreat from the Central Highlands was a disaster, as equipment worth $254 million was lost, stolen, or destroyed, including 20,000 tons of ammunition. On 19 March, President Thieu ordered General Truong to Saigon and told him to hold Da Nang, Hue, and Chu Lai; and to abandon the remainder of I Corps. The following day Truong, then back in Da Nang, was told to hold only Da Nang, nothing more. That same night, Thieu announced on television that I Corps and II Corps were being abandoned, which led to panic in the nation. During the next ten days, seventeen provinces were lost as the ARVN's control weakened. On 25 March, Truong abandoned Hue, believing that the promised rescue ships would arrive. Some vessels, although not enough, did arrive; but those that were to be sunk to provide a nautical bridge over the Cau Tu Hien estuary did not materialize. Consequently, troops were forced to ford the inlet independently, a situation that also occurred at Tuan An inlet north of Hue. High tides, strong currents, and bad weather took its toll: hundreds drowned and thousands more were stranded. Most of the soldiers of the 1st and 2d divisions, whose senior officers, except for Truong, had fled, remained in disorder awaiting more ships, which never arrived. Truong eventually departed with 2,000 troops from the 2d Division, only a fraction of the division's total strength.

When Da Nang was threatened on 28 March, panic engulfed the city, now swollen with 120,000 refugees and more than 20,000 troops. Only 6,000 marines (45 percent) boarded relief ships, but very few troops of the 3d Division escaped; some 5,000 men (40 percent) of the 3d Division reached the departure point, but only 1,000 boarded the ships. The PAVN captured Da Nang on 30 March after a twenty-four-hour episode highlighted by an absence of gunfire as the ARVN fled. The ARVN lost two marine brigades and one division (the 3d); a variety of RF/PF units ceased to exist. In addition, the 1st and 2d divisions were no longer combat effective because of the losses they had sustained during their retreats from Hue and Quang Ngai.

An absence of command and control, highlighted by vague orders that frequently were disobeyed or countermanded, characterized the ARVN's battle actions for most of April, while the PAVN spearheaded its way south at a much more rapid pace than it had anticipated. The flight of the ARVN's senior commanders from their units broke the army's back. When led well, the ARVN could still respond with determination, such as during the 18th Division's last stand at Xuan Loc, outside Saigon. But it was too late; on 30 April 1975 the ARVN surrendered, its men deflated by remorse, fear, humiliation, and hate.

[See also Civilian Irregular Defense Groups (CIDG); Discipline, article on Republic of Vietnam Armed Forces; Joint General Staff; Medical Support, article on Republic of Vietnam Armed Forces; Order of Battle, article on Republic of Vietnam Armed Forces; Provincial Reconnaissance Units (PRU); Regional Forces/Popular Forces; Vietnamization.]

BIBLIOGRAPHY

CANTWELL, THOMAS R. "The Army of South Vietnam: A Military and Political History, 1955–75." Ph.D. diss., University of New South Wales, Sydney, Australia, 1989.

CLARKE, JEFFREY J. *Advice and Support: The Final Years, 1965–1973.* 1988.

KREPINEVICH, ANDREW F., JR. *The Army and Vietnam.* 1986.

THOMAS R. CANTWELL

Arnett, Peter (1934–), Associated Press correspondent in Vietnam 1962–1975. The longest-serving reporter in South Vietnam, Arnett often clashed with officials over his critical reporting of problems within the South Vietnamese government and the U.S. military. Labeled a "traitor" by some, Arnett was regarded by many of his peers as the best Vietnam War correspondent.

BIBLIOGRAPHY

HAMMOND, WILLIAM M. *Public Affairs: The Military and the Media 1962–1968.* 1989.

KARNOW, STANLEY. *Vietnam: A History.* 1991.

KELLY EVANS-PFEIFER

Art and Literature

American Cultural Images of the Vietnam War

Aesthetic Fields of Fire
The Camera's Eye
  Photography
  Documentary Films
  Television Documentaries
  Television
  Hollywood Film, 1948–1975
  Hollywood Film, 1976–1985
  Hollywood Film since 1986
Literary Landing Zones

Poetry
Drama
Oral History
Memoirs
Novels

In 1990, Tim O'Brien, one of America's most celebrated writers on the Vietnam War, published a remarkable work of fiction called *The Things They Carried*. A free play of remembrance and invention, O'Brien's work is also a treatise on how the Vietnam War may be represented in art. In the chapter entitled "How to Tell a True War Story" the author identifies both the aesthetic and political realities of representations of the war in art and literature. He asserts that strict adherence to fact is a dead end, for what the artist really seeks is truth. As O'Brien reveals, "A thing may happen and be a total lie; another thing may not happen and be truer than the truth."

All artists begin with facts, suggests O'Brien, but they are only the necessary points of departure for creative imagination, for historical judgment, for cultural connection. The Vietnam War deformed and reconstituted many deeply ingrained patterns of national myth; from its beginning (both historians and artists have difficulty establishing a date), the war was always something beyond a chronological, objectively recordable event. For all, but perhaps especially for the artist, the war is a persistent challenge to fashion appropriate forms of symbolic history to represent the human truth of the event. Until those forms are created—artifacts faithful not merely to facts but also to the artist's necessary vision—there can be no lasting peace or understanding for the United States and Vietnam, no true cultural coming to terms.

As American artists of the Vietnam War have shaped the malleable history of the war into symbolic gestures, however, they have entered artistic combat zones and have undertaken imaginative tours of duty with heavy responsibilities. In the postwar United States, battles have continued to rage in the realms of high art and popular culture for possession of national memory. Reflecting the larger national debates on the war, American aesthetic response to the Vietnam War offers striking oppositions: "hawk" versus "dove," art versus ideology, fact versus imagination, "national tragedy" versus "noble cause."

Aesthetic Fields of Fire. There is no more powerful symbol of the aesthetic-ideological debate than the Vietnam Veterans Memorial in Washington, D.C. Collective cultural artifact, personal artistic statement, and heated historical exchange, Maya Lin's black reflecting wall and Frederick Hart's statue of three soldiers stand in uneasy tension: the postmodern to the traditional, the ambiguous to the obvious, the challenging to the embracing. Representing the entire arrangement of aesthetic responses that surround it like the blocks of Stonehenge, the Vietnam Veterans Memorial reflects the war in the most appropriate way. Tragedy and honor, dark metaphor and bright message, the wall and the statue as antagonistic American symbols capture the depth and intensity of the larger, ongoing national debate. As each new artistic creation—painting, statue, photograph, film, song, poem, play, story, or novel—figuratively takes its place in the expanding archive that rings the symbolic epicenter in Washington, it joins a national dialogue sometimes harmonious, often cacophonous, always demanding.

One need only examine the fine art and pop art created between 1965 and 1973, the period of U.S. involvement in combat, to find the origins of the debate. During those years, established artists such as Robert Rauschenberg, Nancy

Spero, James Rosenquist, Richard Hamilton, and many others created art in powerful political opposition to the war. Ed Keinholz's *11th Hour Final* (1968), for example, featured a television embedded in concrete across whose screen is emblazoned the nightly body count. Individual artists and art collectives offered striking antiwar images at the same time that the armed services were commissioning military and civilian combat artists to journey to Vietnam to draw or paint their personal visions. In 1966, the Department of the Army began sending not only active-duty soldiers but also professional artists (all from the Salmagundi Club in New York) to Vietnam. Those artists eventually produced about two thousand pieces of art: some predictably traditional and politically safe; some more personal and ambiguous. Augustine Acuna's *Body Count* (1966), for example, is an ink drawing of an armed U.S. soldier reaching down to a young, dead Vietnamese, the image condemning rather than validating the strategy of attrition. Gerald W. Dokken's *Monk* (1970) is an ink and watercolor drawing of a Buddhist monk walking with eyes cast down within the horrors of war. Much American art was less ambiguous, however. There were between twenty thousand and forty thousand pieces of dissident poster art created between 1965 and 1973, many of them graphic attempts to depict the historical obscenity the artists perceived the war to be. Toni Ungerer's poster, *Kiss for Peace,* for example, showed a U.S. infantryman forcing a bound, naked Vietnamese prisoner to lick the buttocks of Lady Liberty. American fine, pop, and official visual art on the Vietnam War has been a true battlefield of symbolic responses.

American popular music produced during and after the war has offered similar lessons in artistic consensus and disagreement. In the late 1960s, Sgt. Barry Sadler's "The Ballad of the Green Berets" coexisted with folk artist Phil Ochs's "Draft Dodger Rag" and the rock group the Doors' "The Unknown Soldier." Sadler's homage to the U.S. Special Forces, however, was soon overwhelmed by voices of opposition. Ochs and fellow folk artists Tom Paxton, Joan Baez, Arlo Guthrie, Judy Collins, Joni Mitchell, and Bob Dylan comprised a formidable platoon of acoustic response. The folk artists were joined, and perhaps overwhelmed, by the volume and intensity of rock artists: the Doors' antiwar sentiments were amplified in the Animals' "Sky Pilot," the Byrds' "Draft Morning," Creedence Clearwater Revival's "Fortunate Son," Jimi Hendrix's "Machine Gun," and Country Joe and the Fish's "I-Feel-Like-I'm-Fixin-to-Die-Rag," the unofficial anthem of the counterculture that found in August 1969 its collective ecstasy at the Woodstock music and arts festival in New York and its hidden darknesses later that year with the Rolling Stones and the Hell's Angels in Altamont, California.

The postwar period has offered debates in art that have been even more energetic, divisive, and surreal than those of the war years. Artists insisting that the war's tragic lessons never be forgotten have stood in opposition to those busily reinscribing traditional notions of honor, patriotism, and national will—and to those who would use the war to secure profits, ratings points, or appearances on best-seller lists. For better or worse, the Vietnam War has become a cultural industry with branches in academia, entertainment, fine art, and pop art, and the consumers of the cultural products often comprise very different audiences with varying political beliefs.

In the postwar years, the image of the Vietnam veteran has often been the central issue in the ongoing struggle for possession of collective memory. How the veteran has been represented, remembered, valorized, or excoriated in high and low art has been a powerful register of how serious, extensive, and inconsistent the debate has been. In mass-produced art and culture, the symbols have been strong and disturbing. Such magazines as *Soldier of Fortune, New Breed,* and *Vietnam Combat* have attempted to salve and reenergize wounded American male pride and aggressiveness. Action-adventure novels featuring reconstituted Vietnam vets have flowed from paperback houses and filled stacks in grocery and discount stores. Comic books have offered updated versions of Sergeant Rock and GI Joe to the adolescent mind. Historical romances about Vietnam such as Danielle Steele's *Message from Nam* have been on the *New York Times* best-seller list. Rambo toys, featuring the mythic avenger created by Hollywood's Sylvester Stallone, have been offered to children with the manufacturer's product claim, "If the Army can't, Rambo can!"

Although the Vietnam War is being mythically refought and won within certain nooks and crannies of American popular culture, there has been a consistent artistic counterforce to that trend. Seeking to complicate rather than to simplify, many serious artists have succeeded in keeping the painful and challenging lessons of the war in the public eye. The Vietnam War, the "living-room war" as some have called it, was captured in millions of words and images and transmitted to millions on televisions as it occurred. It is not surprising that the most powerful and enduring symbolic representations of the war have come through the celluloid image and the printed word. The quantity of artistic response has been monumental, and the quality of the art reveals that in aesthetic power and vision the war was anything but a limited engagement. In the camera's eye, on the printed page, the facts and fictions of the Vietnam War have blended freely into resonant symbolic history—art of significant cultural vision and depth.

The Camera's Eye. The cultural significance of the Vietnam War has been determined greatly by the quantity and quality of its recorded visual images. In photography, documentary film, television, and Hollywood film, the pictorial history has been powerful and controversial.

Photography. Perhaps the most famous photograph of the Vietnam War appeared on 1 February 1968 during the Tet Offensive. The picture is a close view of Nguyen Ngoc Loan, chief of the South Vietnamese national police, holding a pistol to the head of a cringing prisoner moments before pulling the trigger outside the Au Quang Pagoda in Saigon. Taken by Associated Press photographer Eddie Adams, the picture captured the particular brutalities and inconsistencies of the war. Like many of the other striking images of the war—of Buddhist monks ablaze in protest, of combat assaults into hot landing zones, of weary U.S. Marines at Hue and Khe Sanh, of South Vietnamese troops stampeding toward Saigon in 1975—Adams' photo seems a hybrid form of cultural response: one part that of composed, self-conscious art; another part, the serendipitous capturing of raw fact. Some of the greatest photography of the war is not battle action; rather, it is images of minds and bodies in repose or contemplation, in frozen moments of hope or fear. The best pictures are the visual chronicle of a country and people at war and, sometimes, at peace, and in the most memorable photos, the beauty and hidden terrors of Vietnam are seldom far apart.

The mixed-media nature of the Vietnam War manifested itself in some of the finest collections of photography. Tim Page, a figure Michael Herr made famous in his piece of New Journalism (a brand of reporting that is personal, dramatic, and often participatory, incorporating the techniques and devices of the novel or short story) called *Dispatches,* also wrote the text that accompanies his photos in *Tim Page's Nam* (1983) and *Ten Years After: Vietnam Today* (1987). Other photographers collaborated with notable Vietnam writers: the photography of Julene Fischer and the Picture Staff of Boston Publishing Company joined narrative by National Book Award–winning novelist Robert Stone (*Dog Soldiers*) in *Images of War* (1986); the photographic art of Dick Durrance was accompanied by an introductory essay by memoirist Ron Kovic *(Born on the Fourth of July)* in *Where War Lives* (1988); and Geoffrey Clifford's pictures met the voice of poet John Balaban *(After Our War)* in *Vietnam: The Land We Never Knew* (1989). Culturally interpretive, intensely personal, the work of the best still-camera artists has kept the war firmly lodged in collective memory and has provided a visual history for future generations.

Documentary Films. The same may be said for documentary filmmakers. Defining the documentary film as both personal aesthetic and political statement, directors often used the techniques of the art or Hollywood film to stake their claims to historical legitimacy. Documentary films made relatively early in the war often offered a cinema vérité style and a tentative, ambiguous appraisal of the war and its principal American actor, the infantry soldier. Such films as Pierre Schoendorffer's *The Anderson Platoon* (1967), which follows the exploits of a U.S. Army unit in the Central Highlands, and Eugene Jones's *A Face of War* (1968), which documents the actions of a U.S. Marine company, appeared to tell their stories with high objectivity, allowing the camera and microphone to capture image and word without bias. Captured by both films, however, were many of the features of the Vietnam War—difficulties of terrain, language, and climate; fruitless patrols and village searches; the youth and frustration of U.S. soldiers—that would become prominent features in the expensive Hollywood treatments of the late 1970s and after.

The documentaries that appeared in 1969 showed how divisive the war had become and how adversarial were many independent filmmakers to the official story. The Department of Defense produced *The Battle of Khe Sanh* and the U.S. Navy made *Men with Green Faces,* films that attempted to validate the efforts of the U.S. military in Vietnam. In 1969, however, the radical film collective Newsreel also produced *The People's War,* a tribute to North Vietnamese and Viet Cong forces in Vietnam, and independent filmmaker Emile de Antonio offered *In the Year of the Pig,* a very personal statement on the folly of U.S. involvement in Vietnam that used historical footage and interviews with well-known voices in carefully composed juxtapositions. Pauline Kael contended that the obvious hero in de Antonio's Oscar-nominated film is Ho Chi Minh; in reality, it is the critical voices of Roger Hilsman, Paul Mus, Harrison Salisbury, and David Halberstam who make the case against U.S. intervention in counterpoint to the prowar testimony of John Foster Dulles, Curtis LeMay, George Patton Jr., and others.

Emile de Antonio's technique of cinematic collage was used to even more controversial effect in 1974 when Peter Davis made *Hearts and Minds,* a film that won a Best Documentary Oscar and prompted a "hawk" versus "dove" firefight at the Academy Awards ceremony. The pro- and antiwar wings of the Academy exchanged verbal jibes on camera while millions of Americans watched at home, reminded again in an unexpected context of how polarized America remained, of how impossible it was to separate art from politics within the symbolic history of the war. Like de Antonio's film, *Hearts and Minds* is a collage of interview and archival footage with a specific political and artistic agenda. Within carefully crafted, ironic juxtapositions of word and image, the film condemned U.S. involvement as it elicited emotional response.

Televison Documentaries. Television documentary in the 1980s showed no slackening of the battle for cultural possession of the war. In 1983, WGBH, Boston public television, produced the thirteen-part *Vietnam: A Television His-*

tory, a series that seemed to many a worthy attempt to offer a balanced view of the war from multiple perspectives: North Vietnamese, Viet Cong, South Vietnamese, and American. In 1985 the conservative media watchdog organization Accuracy in Media responded with two programs on the perceived "liberal bias" of the WGBH series: *Television's Vietnam: The Real Story* and *Television's Vietnam: The Impact of Media.* Once again, the liberal-conservative battle was joined as artful documentary revealed itself to be anything but objective and value-free. Cable television also joined the debate. In 1987 Home Box Office (HBO) produced *Dear America: Letters Home from Vietnam,* a collage of music, documentary footage, and the real correspondence of military personnel read by such Hollywood voices as Robert De Niro, Kathleen Turner, Martin Sheen, and Michael J. Fox. The HBO film made the argument in song, word, and image that the personal sacrifices and sufferings of U.S. soldiers rather than the larger historical and political realities of the war and the Vietnamese people were the most important narratives. With its Hollywood resonance and slick production, *Dear America* revealed what lay behind the apparent objectivity and historical immediacy of documentaries that preceded it. Shattering the illusion of political neutrality, loyal to their personal visions, the most powerful documentary filmmakers offered passionate art and, often, even more passionate politics.

Television. The symbolic history of the war within American television has been an inconsistent legacy. In the 1970s, it seemed that every police or action-adventure show featured a deranged veteran or walking time bomb intent on bringing the war back home. From the Honolulu of "Hawaii Five-O" through "The Streets of San Francisco" to the New York avenues of "Kojak," every TV urban center seemed rife with symbolic scapegoats of Vietnam. In the 1980s, as American attitudes metamorphosed, television drama reinscribed the veterans' heroism and sacrifice. Such series as "The A-Team," "Simon and Simon," "Miami Vice," and "Magnum PI" featured the Vietnam veteran as reconstituted hero, the urban maverick or team player (if the other team members were vets) who distrusted authority and lived by his own ethical code, one that often took him to the border of legality or beyond. Only three prime-time series, however, made life in the war zone their subject. Like the Hollywood film on which it was based, the series "M★A★S★H" (1972–1983) offered a group of army surgeons and nurses in the Korean War whose attitudes and actions always conjured images of Vietnam. Like "Tour of Duty" (1987–1990) and "China Beach" (1988–1991), "M★A★S★H" focused on the human story with little attempt to deal with the history or politics of the war. "Tour of Duty," which featured the exploits of an infantry platoon, and "China Beach," which portrayed nurses in Vietnam, like the documentary *Dear America,* remythologized individual American heroism in a morally ambiguous, politically charged war zone that defied larger historical analysis. Although dramatizing the human story at the expense of history and politics was standard operating procedure for the series, a few television films were more polemical, perhaps because of their literary sources. *Friendly Fire* (1979), from C. D. B. Bryan's book, and *A Rumor of War* (1980), from Philip Caputo's memoir, were attempts by major networks to tell human stories that did seek to foster a serious cultural-historical response from the audience.

Hollywood Film, 1948–1975. The mixtures of art, politics, and history found in Hollywood treatments of the war have been variable and controversial. Realistic, romantic, surreal, and even fantastic, the symbolic history of the war in commercial cinema has offered a variety of artistic styles and cultural agendas but also some clear patterns of response in discernible stages. Alan Ladd and Veronica

Lake began Hollywood's romance with Vietnam in *Saigon* (1948), and a cluster of conservative visions concerned with tumbling dominoes appeared in the 1950s: Samuel Fuller's *China Gate* (1957), whose title reveals its ignorance of historical Vietnamese-Chinese antagonism, Joseph L. Mankiewicz's *The Quiet American* (1958), which transforms Graham Greene's dangerously innocent Alden Pyle into a real American hero done in by European duplicity and communist venality, and James Clavell's *Five Gates to Hell* (1959).

The period 1961–1975 offered several types of symbolic Vietnams in American film. During the advisory period, George Englund's *The Ugly American* (1963), from the 1958 novel by William Lederer and Eugene Burdick, offered a Cold War parable of what U.S. political and diplomatic blindness could produce in Southeast Asia. It was not until deep into the full combat period, however, 1968 and after, that Hollywood arrived in force. John Wayne's anomalous *The Green Berets* (1968), produced and directed by Wayne, was a film that could have been written by John Foster Dulles and directed by John Ford, a mythic pastiche combining tumbling dominoes and the symbols and plot devices of Wayne's World War II films and westerns. *The Green Berets* was anomalous in another way as well: it depicted life in the combat zone, whereas the other films of the period largely symbolized Vietnam within stateside settings. One group depicted political unrest at home, campus antiwar movements, the alienation and confusion of youth toward the war. Such films as *Medium Cool* (1969), *Alice's Restaurant* (1969), *Getting Straight* (1970), *The Strawberry Statement* (1970), and *The Trial of the Catonsville Nine* (1972) spoke strongly to their increasingly radicalized, disaffected audiences. Another group of films depicted the cultural effects of Vietnam in a strangely different form. The returned veteran was portrayed as a rebel or scapegoat in a number of Hollywood products. America's deep ambivalence toward its returned warriors played itself out in such low-budget motorcycle gang movies as *The Losers* (1971), *Chrome and Hot Leather* (1971), and *Welcome Home, Soldier Boys* (1972).

Hollywood Film, 1976–1985. The period 1976–1985 is notable for two major groups of films. In the late 1970s, major studios, writers, and directors began a serious, complex reappraisal of the Vietnam War. Symbolic representations of the returned veteran continued, but in richer, more considered works such as Martin Scorsese's *Taxi Driver* (1976), Hal Ashby's *Coming Home* (1978), and Karel Reisz's *Who'll Stop the Rain?* (1978). Hollywood also journeyed into the combat zone in a serious way: Ted Post's *Go Tell the Spartans* (1978) was a complex depiction of the advisory period, and Sidney J. Furie's *The Boys in Company C* (1978) was an early attempt to dramatize the training and combat experience of an infantry unit in Vietnam. The two films with the greatest impact on critics and audiences in the late 1970s were Michael Cimino's *The Deer Hunter* (1978) and Francis Ford Coppola's *Apocalypse Now* (1979). Cimino's film, the symbolic Vietnam journey and return of three young men from a Pennsylvania steel town, won the Best Picture Oscar, and Coppola's surreal reworking of Joseph Conrad's *Heart of Darkness* in Vietnam and Cambodia was nominated the following year for the same award. Both films produced controversy. *The Deer Hunter* was faulted for its one-sided depiction of the North Vietnamese and Viet Cong as cruel or sadistic, and many critics took Coppola to task for his symbolic, surrealistic version of the war in which soldiers surf during combat assaults and a demented officer says wistfully, "I love the smell of napalm in the morning." Both films, however, dramatized the shattering personal lessons and the deadly mythic overload of the Vietnam War. Together, Cimino and Coppola argued passionately for the integrity of the individual artist's vision in symbolic and cultural significance.

Hollywood versions of the Vietnam War in the early 1980s offered divergent substance and style—and one significant new trend with important cultural ramifications. Films with special focus included John Sayle's *Return of the Secaucus Seven* (1980), a reappraisal of the counterculture; Haile Gerima's *Ashes and Embers* (1982), one of the few serious treatments of African American veterans; Roland Joffe's *The Killing Fields* (1984), a sweeping epic of the tragedy of Cambodia; and Louis Malle's *Alamo Bay* (1985), a depiction of American and Vietnamese fisherman on the Gulf Coast of the United States.

A significant new type of film, however, featured veterans returning to Vietnam to rescue imprisoned comrades. Symbolically refighting and winning the war in mythic terms, these films often simplistically reinscribed damaged notions of American honor, courage, and patriotism at the expense of the war's larger history and the Vietnamese people. The Vietnam avenger first appeared as John Rambo (Sylvester Stallone) in *First Blood* (1982) but soon went through many permutations. Stallone returned in *Rambo: First Blood Part II* (1985) and *Rambo III* (1988), actor and martial arts champion Chuck Norris made three *Missing in Action* films between 1984 and 1988, and the team rescue concept was featured in *Uncommon Valor* (1983). Overall, the films that dealt with Americans listed as missing in action (MIA) were unique reminders of the tendency of pop culture to reduce complex cultural events to simple narratives. Stallone's Rambo, largely ignoring the damage done to Vietnam, spoke for all of the other heroes of the genre when he said, "We just want our country to love us as much as we love it."

Hollywood Film since 1986. From 1986 onward new artistic and political agendas have appeared in commercial films. The platoon or rifle squad as symbolic cultural microcosm has been the focus of major films set in the combat zone: Oliver Stone's *Platoon* (1986), Stanley Kubrick's *Full Metal Jacket* (1987), and John Irvin's *Hamburger Hill* (1987). Stone's film, a dark romance covered with a thick veneer of cinematic realism, and Kubrick's, a minimalist piece of black humor and visual poetry, like Cimino's and Coppola's films of the 1970s, have had the greatest cultural impact. While Stone worked to establish the battlefield bildungsroman as a workable form, Kubrick undermined it in word and image at every turn. *Platoon* portrayed opposing good and bad sergeants as a symbolic Christ and Captain Ahab and a young quester (Charlie Sheen) who speaks in classical tones; *Full Metal Jacket* offered a hero named Joker (Matthew Modine) who asks questions resonant with popular myth—"Is that you, John Wayne? Is this me?"—and concludes with young U.S. Marines singing the Mickey Mouse Club theme song after fighting the Battle of Hue. Vietnam as reconstituted frontier, as postmodern trash heap—such were the striking oppositions in the films of the late 1980s.

Recent films suggest an increasingly diversified future for the Vietnam War in documentary and commercial cinema. *Aliens* (1986), directed by Vietnam veteran James Cameron, offered striking images of the war mixed with its science-fiction elements, and *Good Morning, Vietnam* (1987) gave the war a tragicomic treatment. The return to society—"the World" as the vets called it—continues to be a prime narrative in such films as *Gardens of Stone* (1987), *In Country* (1988), *Jacknife* (1989), and *Born on the Fourth of July* (1989). The director of the latter, Oliver Stone, has also offered *JFK* (1991), a film that argues John Kennedy was killed by a conspiracy of those who opposed his Vietnam policies, and *Heaven and Earth* (1993), a film treatment of the memoirs of Le Ly Hayslip that has shown Americans the war from a Vietnamese perspective. There have been interesting overlappings of the style and substance of commercial and documentary filmmaking: *84 Charlie Mopic* (1989), a fictional film, has the look and feel of *The Anderson Platoon* or *A Face of War; Hearts of Darkness* (1991), a documentary, is a metacommentary on the making of *Apocalypse Now* in which the border between fact and fiction is difficult to trace. Overall, Vietnam War filmmakers have created a complex archive of symbolic history resonant and demanding on every cultural level. The camera's eye was in Vietnam from the beginning and has remained there, but no more so than the pen of the poet, dramatist, oral historian, memoirist, or novelist.

Literary Landing Zones. The American response in poetry to the Vietnam War is a full and diversified bookshelf supporting a wide range of style and substance within two main groupings. Such established noncombatant poets as Daniel Berrigan, Robert Bly, Denise Levertov, Allen Ginsberg, and William Stafford comprised the more political voices whose body of work was sporadic but intensely felt and expressed. It was the civilian poets who featured in their verse the antiwar movement and other domestic upheavals and who offered the large political critiques.

Poetry. Although several notable American civilian poets made strong cultural statements, the larger and more important corpus of poetry has come from veterans, with such soldier-poets as Michael Casey, Jan Barry, W. D. Ehrhart, D. C. Berry, John Balaban, D. F. Brown, Walter McDonald, Yusef Komuyakaa, and Bruce Weigl establishing themselves as powerful voices in American poetry. Two important early collections of poems were *Winning Hearts and Minds: War Poems by Vietnam Veterans* (1972), edited by Larry Rottman, Jan Barry, and Basil T. Paquet, and *Demilitarized Zones: Veterans After Vietnam* (1976), edited by W. D. Ehrhart.

Artistically or politically, the poet-veterans belong to no single school, but there are traceable patterns and repeated arguments within their poems: careful re-creation in often minute detail of the experience of war—the sights, smells, sounds, frequent pain, and occasional beauty of life in the combat zone; concerted efforts to re-create faithfully in image and symbol the emotional and spiritual truths of the war; the prime task of tracing the ongoing exchange between original experience and postwar memory. Two fine achievements were Michael Casey's *Obscenities* (1972) and D. C. Berry's *saigon cemetery* (1972), early examples of how the poet-veterans would strive to build worthy unions of experience and remembrance. Other veterans have published substantial bodies of work, unfolding statements and restatements in short and long poems of the chimerical nature of personal and cultural memory. Important works include John Balaban's *After Our War* (1974) and *Coming Down Again* (1985); W. D. Ehrhart's *To Those Who Have Gone Home Tired* (1984); Yusef Komunyakaa's *Copacetic* (1984) and *Dien Cai Dau* (1988); Walter McDonald's *Caliban in Blue* (1976) and *After the Noise of Saigon* (1988); and Bruce Weigl's *A Romance* (1979), *The Monkey Wars* (1985), and *Song of Napalm* (1988). In addition to his own poetic accomplishments, Ehrhart also edited two key collections that have kept major and minor American poetic voices available to audiences: *Carrying the Darkness: The Poetry of the Vietnam War* (1985) and *Unaccustomed Mercy: Soldier-Poets of the Vietnam War* (1989).

Although the poet-veterans are distinctive individual voices, there have been many consistent concerns within their poetic testimony. Many have spoken of America's cultural blindness in Vietnam and its tragic consequences. In Jan Barry's "In the Footsteps of Genghis Khan," for instance, the poet finds terrible historical repetition in the U.S. involvement, asserting that Americans are merely the newest invaders. The best poets have also used the imagistic and symbolic power of the lyric to capture the effects of Vietnam on both the mind and senses. Bruce Weigl's "Mines" is a typical response, a poem in which hidden booby traps and the horrors of personal locomotion speak volumes for other, larger dangers to body and soul. Ultimately, the most striking poems have combined both poetic operations, combining specific personal experience in the combat zone with the problem of ongoing cultural memory and connection. Using the lyric as both polemical field weapon and emotional flak jacket, the finest soldier-poets have refused to allow the nation to ignore or forget their historical experience and its symbolic significance.

Drama. The history of the important American drama of the Vietnam War extends from Barbara Garson's *MacBird* (1967) to *Miss Saigon* in the 1990s. Again, there is no consensus among playwrights on appropriate style or subject of Vietnam War drama. One pattern has been established, however; unlike the poems, novels, and films, few of the major plays have been set in the war zone itself. Most have re-created the emotional truths of the war through symbol, surreal image, memory devices, historical extension and projection, mythic, satirical, or poetic disjunctures.

Such plays as Ron Cowen's *Summertree* (1968) and Stephen Metcalfe's *Strange Snow* (1983) have come in the form of traditional realism, but many playwrights deliberately broke the dramatic illusion for artistic and political effect. Emily Mann's *Still Life* (1979) was rife with Brechtian alienation effects that deny an audience traditional cultural response to war. Amlin Gray's *How I Got That Story* (1979) contained only two actors: one playing a naive reporter from the Midwest; the other, Historical Event, playing twenty-one roles in one that included American and Vietnamese soldiers, a nun, another reporter, and Vietnamese peasants and prostitutes. David Rabe's *Sticks and Bones* (1972) offered the war as the television situation comedy universe of Ozzie and Harriet in which son David, as a damaged Vietnam veteran, must contend with the deadly mythic underpinnings of American fantasy and pop culture. Arthur Kopit's *Indians* (1969), featuring Buffalo Bill and territorial imperatives, linked the war symbolically and historically to the deeper, persistent tendencies toward cultural imperialism and genocidal blindness.

Other important plays produced during the war and after included Terrence McNally's *Botticelli* (1968), John Guare's *Muzeeka* (1971), Tom Cole's *Medal of Honor Rag* (1977), and Michael Weller's *Moonchildren* (1980). The Vietnam War playwright, however, who established himself most as a major voice in American drama is David Rabe. His trilogy of Vietnam plays—*The Basic Training of Pavlo Hummel* (1971), *Sticks and Bones,* and *Streamers* (1976)—garnered critical acclaim and a number of prestigious drama awards. Rabe's plays, full of sudden disjuncture, mythic overload, and psychic violence, brought Vietnam home to audiences as they helped to redefine the form and substance of American theater.

Oral History. Another principal American form of bearing witness to the personal truths of the Vietnam War has been oral history. Assembling choruses of sometimes complementary, often contradictory, individual voices, oral historians have adapted to print the techniques of the documentary filmmaker, editing, blending, and shaping discrete testimony into collective personal history. Editor Mark Baker used anonymous voices and personal, often polemical, connecting commentary in *Nam* (1981), whereas Al Santoli employed fewer but identified speakers in *Everything We Had* (1981) and *To Bear Any Burden* (1986). Two other oral histories of special value and focus are *In the Combat Zone: An Oral History of American Women in Vietnam* (1984), edited by Kathryn Marshall, and *Bloods: An Oral History of the Vietnam War by Black Veterans* (1984), compiled by Wallace Terry.

Memoirs. The personal memoir and the novel, traditionally the most expansive personal and cultural explorations of Americans at arms, were once again put to memorable use in Vietnam. In 1963, Richard Tregaskis published *Vietnam Diary,* a rather traditional memoir largely supportive of the U.S. involvement in Vietnam. It was a work more akin in tone and style to depictions of World War II experience than the new cultural data of Vietnam. Other writers who followed put the memoir to new artistic and polemical uses as they offered their personal narratives as symbolic history. Important works written during the war years include Ronald J. Glasser's *365 Days* (1971), Joe Haldeman's *War Year* (1972), and Tim O'Brien's *If I Die in a Combat Zone* (1973), early examples of how personal experiential truth could be forged into demanding cultural statement. Like the best American poems on the war, the most powerful memoirs have combined faithfulness to facts with larger moral and historical probings. In *If I Die in a Combat Zone,* for example, O'Brien used the specific transgressions of himself and his comrades to draw larger cultural conclusions. Recounting how his company struck back at the enemy by burning villages, finding the deadly center of his country's most unpopular war, he concluded darkly, "It was good, just as pure hate is good."

Not all memoirists shared O'Brien's tragic vision. General William Westmoreland attempted to justify the U.S. involvement in *A Soldier Reports* (1976), but his personal version of the war met harsh response in Ron Kovic's *Born on the Fourth of July* (1976), Gloria Emerson's *Winners and Losers* (1976), Philip Caputo's *A Rumor of War* (1977), and Michael Herr's *Dispatches* (1977). Kovic's and Caputo's works were the battlefield autobiography as journey through American myth and its personal and historical consequences; bildungsroman as literary memoir, both writers created themselves as symbolic figures who move from innocence to experience, from transgression to expiation. Kovic's memoir was a fiercely polemical condemnation of the price paid by the foot soldier for American cultural blindness in Vietnam, whereas Caputo's was a more classical, poetic, and meditative narrative of one man's initiation, a vainglorious quest that resulted in Caputo saying of himself and his fellow warriors, "We left Vietnam peculiar creatures, with young shoulders that bore rather old heads."

Emerson's and Herr's books were important examples of personal journalism as memoir. Both historical witnesses immersed themselves in the voices, rhythms, and strange cultural recesses of the war and produced documents of both distinctive personal voice and larger cultural judgment. Emerson's work was a true collage of Vietnam voices interacting with her own controlling, interpretive persona. Herr's was the hip articulation of the spaced-out, rock 'n' roll-drenched journalist, the romantic seeker who tells what traditional reporting cannot. In *Dispatches,* Herr played the role of the New Journalist in Vietnam, and, powered by both the exhilaration and loathing he felt in the combat zone, he summarized the experience with a dark irony shared by many: "Vietnam was what we had instead of happy childhoods."

American memoirs of the Vietnam War have rendered important historical testimony from other perspectives as well. Lynda Van Devanter's *Home Before Morning* (1983) was an autobiographical account of the role of the nurse in Vietnam, whereas Charles Mason's *Chickenhawk* (1984) offered the airborne perspective of a helicopter pilot. Of special significance were *When Heaven and Earth Changed Places* (1989) and *Child of War, Woman of Peace* (1993), the memoirs of Le Ly Hayslip, a writer whose transformation from Vietnamese villager to U.S. citizen was a symbolic journey from war to peace from two cultural perspectives. Other important memoirs by soldiers and correspondents include Frederick Downs's *The Killing Zone* (1978), William Broyles's *Brothers in Arms* (1986), W. D.

Ehrhart's *Going Back: An Ex-Marine Returns to Vietnam* (1987), Neil Sheehan's *A Bright Shining Lie: John Paul Vann and America in Vietnam* (1988), and Michael Norman's *These Good Men* (1990).

Novels. The Vietnam War novel has been an artistic combat zone of serious political and historical firefights both during the war and after, but two novels from the 1950s—one British, Graham Greene's *The Quiet American* (1955); one American, William Lederer's and Eugene Burdick's *The Ugly American* (1958)—were strong warnings in prose fiction of what American cultural innocence and ignorance would lead to in Southeast Asia. Greene's story of a zealous but dangerously inexperienced American operative in Vietnam was read in many quarters as a spiteful example of anti-Americanism; Lederer's and Burdick's Cold War fable of American arrogance unleashed in Indochina was perceived in the State Department as simplistic or alarmist. Both novels as symbolic realism pointed to the real possibility of a historical quagmire and a cultural tragedy for America in Vietnam.

Despite the accurate prophecy in art of the 1950s novels, American novelists from 1965 onward were faced with serious questions about appropriate fictional forms for the living narrative raging before their eyes. Debates regarding style and content surrounded author, critic, and audience in three key stages. The full combat period for America in Vietnam, 1965–1973, saw the production of both traditional and experimental novels. Few prominent American novelists produced works with Vietnam themes during the war years: Norman Mailer's *Why Are We in Vietnam?* (1967), a surreal Vietnam parable featuring a symbolic bear hunt in Alaska, and Kurt Vonnegut's *Slaughterhouse-Five* (1969), a fiction on the bombing of Dresden with a Vietnam subtext, proved the exceptions. Instead, the war years saw the appearance of works by lesser-known novelists, journalists, and combat veterans.

Robin Moore's *The Green Berets* appeared in 1965, but as homage to the Special Forces and U.S. involvement, like John Wayne's film treatment, it proved an anomalous artistic and political statement. Most of the lasting literature assumed an adversarial position toward the war. Two realistic parables asserting that Vietnam was already a quagmire for America appeared in 1967: Daniel Ford's *Incident at Muc Wa* and David Halberstam's *One Very Hot Day.* Other writers chose a variety of styles for their criticisms: William Eastlake's *The Bamboo Bed* (1968) and Asa Baber's *The Land of a Million Elephants* (1970) were elaborate symbolic fantasies and James Park Sloan's *War Games* (1971) employed metafictional black humor as its historical register, consciously and consistently placing its status as story, as imaginative artifice, in the foreground. Some novelists chose more traditional styles, with Josiah Bunting's *The Lionheads* (1972), William Pelfrey's *The Big V* (1973), William Turner Huggett's *Body Count* (1973), and Robert Roth's *Sand in the Wind* (1973) attempts to adapt literary realism to the cultural facts of Vietnam. The American novels written during the war, however, while garnering respectable sales and critical response, did not achieve the prominence of the second stage of the Vietnam novel's evolution. The works of the war years varied widely in quality as well, with well-wrought novels often joined by fictions of passionate but ephemeral literary voices.

The period 1974–1980 marked the appearance of early works by major novelists who would continue to render significant Vietnam War fiction in the next decade and beyond. A few important novels such as John Clark Pratt's *The Laotian Fragments* (1974) and Charles Durden's *No Bugles, No Drums* (1976) were the first and last major Vietnam fictions by their authors. Many works of the period, however, were only initial renderings by a notable group of American writers. The rich second flowering of novels included Ward Just's *Stringer* (1974), Robert Stone's *Dog Soldiers* (1974), Tim O'Brien's *Northern Lights* (1975) and *Going After Cacciato* (1978), Larry Heinemann's *Close Quarters* (1977), Winston Groom's *Better Times Than These* (1978), James Webb's *Fields of Fire* (1978), and Gustav Hasford's *The Short-Timers* (1979). The styles and political agendas of these major voices were widely divergent: Webb's traditional, realistic reinscription of honor and duty spoke in counterpoint to Hasford's darkly humorous subversion of those same myths; Groom's attempt to reinstate the large novel of sociological realism stood in stark opposition to the American magical realism of O'Brien's *Going After Cacciato*. The second-stage novelists, however, found wider readership and significant critical acclaim, with O'Brien and Stone winning National Book Awards in the 1970s.

From 1981 to the mid 1990s, there have been major new works by established voices, distinctive combat-zone and postwar fictions by new writers, and major novels by important women novelists. Stone, Webb, Groom, Just, O'Brien, Heinemann, and Hasford all rendered worthy new novels in the 1980s and 1990s, with Heinemann's *Paco's Story* (1986) winning the National Book Award, but they were joined by other important contributors, some with multiple achievements. Robert Olen Butler offered *The Alleys of Eden* (1981) and several other novels, Nicholas Proffitt published *Gardens of Stone* (1983) and *The Embassy House* (1986), John DelVecchio published *The 13th Valley* (1982) and *For the Sake of All Living Things* (1990), and Tim Mahoney garnered notice with *Holloran's World War* (1985) and *We're Not Here* (1988). Other significant novels of the period include Jack Fuller's *Fragments* (1984), Donald Tate's *Bravo Burning* (1986), Joseph Ferradino's *Firefight* (1987), and Philip Caputo's *Indian Country* (1987).

Important works set in the combat zone continue to appear, but the newer writing has shown a marked shift to narratives set in postwar America that connect the war to larger, deeper patterns in national culture. Significant novels by women have been a major part of the new historical project: Joan Didion's *Democracy* (1984) connected Vietnam to a deeper legacy of American imperatives; Jayne Anne Phillips's *Machine Dreams* (1984) was a generational saga that enfolded the Vietnam War within larger national stories; Bobbie Ann Mason's *In Country* (1985) connected American past to present in the symbolic quest of a young Kentucky girl to learn about her father, who was killed in action, and the war.

Symbolic of all postwar America that did not experience Vietnam firsthand but that seeks its lessons, Mason's protagonist, Samantha "Sam" Hughes, "humps the boonies" in her imagination, making a necessary spiritual journey as she reminds readers that the Vietnam War continues to live within many American hearts and minds. At novel's end, with her dead father's mother and her debilitated Vietnam veteran uncle, she ends her symbolic quest at Maya Lin's wall, gaining not historical knowledge but rather necessary empathy, the beginning of personal understanding. Like Mason's young seeker, all of the American artists of the Vietnam War—painters, poets, dramatists, filmmakers, fiction writers—have lived paradoxically with both certain failure and notable success. By creating the symbolic history of the war—while the guns were blazing and long after they have fallen silent—they have reminded the world of how demanding and complex the Vietnam War was and continues to be, of how true Tim O'Brien's description of a true war story remains. By telling necessary "lies" in art—by moving toward the truth without ever fully capturing it—they have brought us constantly closer to true cultural illumination, to private and collective peace.

BIBLIOGRAPHY

ANDREGG, MICHAEL, ed. *Inventing Vietnam: The War in Film and Television.* 1991.

BEIDLER, PHILIP D. *American Literature and the Experience of Vietnam.* 1982.

BEIDLER, PHILIP D. *Re-Writing America: Vietnam Authors in Their Generation.* 1991.

DITTMAR, LINDA, and GENE MICHAUD, eds. *From Hanoi to Hollywood: The Vietnam War in American Film.* 1990.

GILMAN, OWEN W., JR., and LORRIE SMITH, eds. *America Rediscovered: Critical Essays on Literature and Film of the Vietnam War.* 1990.

JASON, PHILIP K., ed. *Fourteen Landing Zones: Approaches to Vietnam War Literature.* 1991.

JEFFORDS, SUSAN. *The Remasculinization of America: Gender and the Vietnam War.* 1989.

MYERS, THOMAS. *Walking Point: American Narratives of Vietnam.* 1988.

ROWE, JOHN CARLOS, and RICK BERG, eds. *The Vietnam War and American Culture.* 1991.

SEARLE, WILLIAM J., ed. *Search and Clear: Critical Responses to Selected Literature and Films of the Vietnam War.* 1988.

THOMAS MYERS

A Shau Valley, located in Thua Thien province, near Laos; main entry point of the Ho Chi Minh Trail into South Vietnam. The A Shau Valley was a vital conduit into U.S. I Corps tactical zone, the northern military region of South Vietnam. North Vietnamese forces vigorously defended the valley against repeated U.S. and South Vietnamese attacks, none of which succeeded for more than a brief period. One of the most famous battles of the war, Ap Bia (known by the nickname Hamburger Hill), took place in the valley from 10 to 20 May, 1969.

BIBLIOGRAPHY

LIPSMAN, SAMUEL. *Fighting for Time.* 1983.

PEARSON, WILLARD. *The War in the Northern Provinces, 1966–1968.* 1975.

STANTON, SHELBY L. *The Rise and Fall of an American Army: U.S. Ground Forces in Vietnam, 1965–1973.* 1985.

ELLEN D. GOLDLUST

Atrocities. Often considered synonymous with war crimes, atrocities are defined by various international treaties and conventions. In the U.S. armed forces, these conventions are incorporated into the Uniform Code of Military Justice, and breaches of them by U.S. soldiers are supposed to be prosecuted through the military judicial system. These rules of warfare are quite extensive and complex. In general, they are intended to restrict the use of inhumane weapons and tactics and to protect prisoners of war (POWs) and noncombatants against murder, torture, and other abuse.

The Vietnam War witnessed many breaches of these restraints by both sides, arising from the violence of combat, the political and ideological hatreds of civil strife complicated by foreign intervention, and the unconventional nature of the struggle. The established international laws of armed conflict were difficult if not impossible to apply, and each side had its own definitions of what constituted legitimate acts of war.

Many abuses resulted from the chaos of the battlefield, the decentralized character of operations, and the widely varying discipline and training of the participating forces. Most instances of killing of captured or wounded soldiers and mutilation of the dead fall into this category, as do individual acts of murder, rape, and robbery by soldiers of both sides—crimes common among fighting men from time immemorial. Common, too, was the exaction of food and other supplies from peasants by soldiers of both Vietnamese factions, although the Viet Cong guerrillas regularized theirs as a form of taxation.

The fate of prisoners was often dire because of these same factors but also because of political considerations. North Vietnam, which declared captured U.S. airmen to be war criminals, subjected them to torture and abuse and compelled them to participate in anti–United States propaganda broadcasts. On the allied side, U.S. forces in the main treated prisoners in conformity with the Geneva and Hague conventions; but the South Vietnamese and South Koreans, who were not under U.S. command, frequently did not. South Vietnamese troops, despite continual U.S. efforts to improve their conduct, often brutalized prisoners, especially during interrogations. South Vietnamese prison camps often fell short of international standards, as the well-publicized case of the Con Son "tiger cages" attested.

U.S. forces used some weapons and tactics that came very close to or crossed the line of the permissible, notably the widespread employment of riot gases and herbicides, although a legal and moral defense can be made for the use of both. On the other hand, U.S. bombing of North Vietnam, while far from pinpoint in precision, avoided the sort of indiscriminate area attacks common in World War II.

Many other actions that could be considered atrocities under the established international conventions grew out of the special characteristics of a people's revolutionary struggle in which both sides found it expedient to abolish the distinction between soldier and civilian, combatant and noncombatant, which is at the heart of the rules of warfare. Viet Cong guerrillas used terror, including systematic murder and kidnapping of civilians, as an indispensable—and in their eyes legitimate—weapon for breaking down government control over the population and establishing their own. The execution of some 2,800 persons in Hue during the 1968 Tet Offensive by North Vietnamese forces was an unusually large-scale instance of such elimination of "tyrants" and "traitors," that is, supporters of the South Vietnamese government. Lesser acts of terror took a steady toll of civilians as well as military personnel. The United States and its allies countered Viet Cong terror with their own campaigns to find and "neutralize"—which in some instances meant assassinate—the Viet Cong's clandestine political and administrative leaders.

Civilians participated in hostilities and concomitantly became victims of them. Peasants under Viet Cong control planted mines and booby traps that killed and maimed U.S. soldiers, provoking fear, hatred, and a desire to retaliate among the GIs. Those feelings, combined with poor unit leadership and training, contributed to the largest single U.S. atrocity of the war, the slaughter of several hundred civilians by soldiers of the Americal Division at My Lai in March 1968. Fighting an enemy that regularly used villages as fortified positions, allied troops bombed and shelled such places out of necessity. While U.S. and South Vietnamese pacification programs emphasized bringing security to the peasants where they were—often in Viet Cong–controlled areas—the U.S. and South Vietnamese forces at times forcibly relocated entire village populations in order to deprive the Viet Cong guerrillas of their source of support and to create free-fire zones in which U.S. forces could use their firepower.

In the United States, the widely publicized brutalities of the conflict contributed to popular disillusionment with the Vietnam War, although they likely had less effect on public opinion than did the growing numbers of American casualties and the apparent lack of military progress. The U.S. armed forces, embarrassed by the My Lai revelations, intensified their training in the law of war, strengthened their procedures for reporting war crimes, and reemphasized in their counterinsurgency doctrine restraint in the use of firepower and humane treatment of civilians. These reforms influenced the behavior of U.S. forces during operations in Grenada, Panama, Kuwait, and Somalia but have yet to be tested in a counterinsurgency situation as severe as that in Vietnam. Subsequent conflicts around the world have demonstrated that the problem of applying rules designed for limited international war to civil and revolutionary struggles is far from solved.

[*See also* My Lai; Tiger Cages.]

BIBLIOGRAPHY

LEWY, GUENTER. *America in Vietnam*. 1978.
TAYLOR, TELFORD. *Nuremberg and Vietnam: An American Tragedy*. 1971.
WELLS, DONALD A. *The Laws of Land Warfare: A Guide to the U.S. Army Manuals*. 1992.

GRAHAM A. COSMAS

Attrition Strategy. Despite occasional forays into counterinsurgency doctrine, attrition strategy guided the U.S. war effort in Vietnam from start to finish. It was a strategy by default: U.S. commanders, denied permission to invade North Vietnam, tried to break the will of communist forces by killing their soldiers and destroying their equipment until they gave up. The assumption was that losses would grow unacceptable and that North Vietnam would withdraw support for insurgency in South Vietnam. Americans compiled meticulous body counts to chart the attrition of the communists' will. "If we just keep up the pressure," insisted Gen. Earle Wheeler, chairman of the Joint Chiefs of Staff, "those little guys will crack." The United States killed nearly 1 million communist soldiers while suffering fewer than 50,000 battle deaths—but in the end the Americans, not their opponents, lost the will to fight.

Attrition strategy failed in Vietnam for two reasons. First, despite enormous U.S. firepower, Viet Cong and North Vietnamese forces could control the pace and intensity of battle and hence manage their own attrition. They initiated most military engagements and pulled back when battles turned against them. They sought sanctuary across borders that Americans could not cross and received supplies from foreign sources that Americans could not interdict. U.S. and South Vietnamese troops wore themselves out in vain pursuit of an elusive foe, hoping for a decisive set piece battle while neglecting the vital tasks of nation-building and population security. "We fought a military war," wrote Henry Kissinger in 1969, while "our opponents fought a political one." North Vietnam measured success not with body counts but with increasing control of the land and people of South Vietnam.

Second, North Vietnam could absorb staggering losses and still continue the war indefinitely. Gen. William Westmoreland, commander U.S. Military Assistance Command, Vietnam (COMUSMACV), complained that he would have been "sacked overnight" for taking such enormous casualties. North Vietnam lost about 3 percent of its population to battle deaths, a level nearly unprecedented in the history of warfare, but pressed on with the two-thousand-year struggle for national independence. By contrast, U.S. support for the war flagged with each new communist offensive that implied that no end was in sight. To inflict truly unacceptable losses would have required greater commitments than the United States was prepared to make in Vietnam. The North Vietnamese had their own version of attrition. "You can kill ten of my men for every one I kill of yours," Ho Chi Minh had taunted the French decades earlier, "but even at those odds, you will lose and I will win." In the end, attrition took a greater toll on American public opinion than on North Vietnam's impervious will.

BIBLIOGRAPHY

FRIZZELL, DONALDSON D. "The Strategy of Attrition." In *The Lessons of Vietnam.* Edited by D. D. Frizzell and W. S. Thompson.

KREPINEVICH, ANDREW F., JR. *The Army and Vietnam.* 1986.

MUELLER, JOHN E. "The Search for the 'Breaking Point' in Vietnam." *International Studies Quarterly* 4 (1980): 497–519.

WESTMORELAND, WILLIAM C. "A War of Attrition." In *The Lessons of Vietnam.* Edited by D. D. Frizzell and W. S. Thompson. 1977.

GLEN GENDZEL

August Revolution. On 16 August 1945 Ho Chi Minh formed the National Liberation Committee and called for a general insurrection. On 19 August the Viet Minh, led by Ho, seized power in Hanoi, initiating a revolution against the defeated Japanese and the resurgent French. On 2 September Ho Chi Minh proclaimed Vietnamese independence and the establishment of the Democratic Republic of Vietnam (DRV).

BIBLIOGRAPHY

The Pentagon Papers: The Defense Department History of United States Decisionmaking on Vietnam. Senator Gravel Edition. Vol. 1. 1971.

DEVILLERS, PHILLIPE, and JEAN LACOUTURE. *End of a War, Indochina, 1954.* 1969.

VICTOR JEW

Australia. Australia's military involvement in Vietnam began in 1962, when it sent the thirty-man Australian Army Training Team Vietnam, composed of jungle warfare specialists, to train South Vietnamese army forces. In April 1965 Australia deployed its first combat troops, the 1st Battalion of the Royal Australian Regiment, which was attached to the U.S. 173d Airborne Brigade at Bien Hoa. By September 1965, Australia had supplemented the initial battalion of 778 men with units of artillery, air reconnaissance, and engineers, totaling 1,477 personnel. Throughout its participation, Australia relied heavily on U.S. logistical support; and as a result only a small percentage of its troops engaged in support services.

In contrast to the United States, Australia rotated entire regiments, rather than individuals, into and out of Vietnam; but like the United States, it conscripted soldiers to fill its ranks. Australia coordinated its military forces with those of New Zealand. With its military contribution expanding, in 1966 Australia established a base camp in III Corps in Phuoc Tuy province. It added air force and naval units in 1967; the number of troops reached its peak of 7,672 in 1969. By 1971, all personnel had re-

AUSTRALIAN TROOPS. A contingent of the Royal Australian Air Force (RAAF) arrives at Tan Son Nhut airport, 10 August 1964. *National Archives*

turned to Australia except for the Australian Army Assistance Group (AAAG), which was created in March 1972 to train South Vietnamese and Khmer Republic forces and remained until January 1973. A total of 386 Australians were killed in action and 2,193 wounded in action. In addition to military aid, Australia provided civil services to South Vietnam valued at more than $10.5 million in the period 1966–1968, and another $230,000 in 1969–1970.

The Australian public initially supported the nation's commitment of troops, believing that keeping South Vietnam free of communist domination was vital to its own interest. But support for the war had declined by the late 1960s. The opposition Labour Party supported the United States's first bombing of North Vietnam in February 1965, but as its left-wing faction gained more power by 1969, the party demanded a reduction in the number of troops. When the Labour Party came to power in 1972 it recognized the Democratic Republic of Vietnam (DRV) and withdrew the remaining Australian troops by 1973.

BIBLIOGRAPHY

FROST, FRANK. *Australia's War in Vietnam.* 1987.

KING, PETER, ed. *Australia's Vietnam: Australia in the Second Indochina War.* 1983.

LARSEN, STANLEY ROBERT, and JAMES LAWTON COLLINS JR. *Allied Participation in Vietnam.* 1975.

ELLEN BAKER

AWOL. *See* Discipline: U.S. Military.

B

Ball, George (1909–), U.S. undersecretary of State, 1961–1966. George W. Ball skillfully dissented from the optimistic war policies of the Kennedy and Johnson administrations. He objected to the Taylor-Rostow report in November 1961, predicting "the most tragic consequences" if the United States committed itself to a military role in Vietnam. Ball saw the recommended 8,000-man logistical task force as a down payment for disaster, predicting that within five years 300,000 U.S. soldiers would be mired in a hopeless war. Ball's advice, however, was dismissed by Kennedy. In the Johnson administration, Ball continued to argue against U.S. military escalation in Vietnam. From 31 May 1964 to 21 April 1966 he submitted eighteen memoranda and talking papers in which he skillfully refuted the arguments for expanding the war. When Johnson's advisers endorsed an air offensive against North Vietnam in the fall of 1964, Ball dissented, rebutting each argument for and prediction of bombing's effectiveness. He argued that an air war would not necessarily demoralize the North nor strengthen the South; that North Vietnam might raise the stakes by sending a flood of North Vietnamese Army regulars into South Vietnam, thus forcing the United States to match their troop commitment. Ball argued that the conse-quences of military escalation could not be easily calibrated or controlled, that "once on the tiger's back, we cannot be sure of picking the place to dismount." Ball was a lonely dissenter, whose views encountered stiff resistance from Dean Rusk, Robert McNamara, and McGeorge Bundy. He resigned in September 1966.

BIBLIOGRAPHY

DI LEO, DAVID. *George Ball, Vietnam and the Rethinking of Containment.* 1991.
HERRING, GEORGE C. *America's Longest War: The United States and Vietnam, 1950–1975.* 1986.

VICTOR JEW

Ban Me Thuot, South Vietnamese town, located in Darlac province, in the Central Highlands. In a major battle of the Spring Offensive, fought 10–11 March 1975, Ban Me Thuot was captured by three North Vietnamese Army (NVA) divisions, prompting President Nguyen Van Thieu to withdraw all South Vietnamese forces from the Central Highlands. This withdrawal of Army of the Republic of Vietnam (ARVN) forces and the flow of refugees collapsed into what journalists dubbed the "Convoy

GEORGE BALL. Testifying before a Senate Armed Services Subcommittee, 27 February 1962. *National Archives*

of Tears," in which thousands died from starvation and NVA or ARVN shellfire.

BIBLIOGRAPHY

CLARKE, JEFFREY J. *United States Army in Vietnam—Advice and Support: The Final Years, 1965–1973.* 1988.
DAVIDSON, PHILLIP B. *Vietnam at War—The History: 1946–1975.* 1988.

ELLEN D. GOLDLUST

Bao Dai (1913–), emperor of Annam (1925; reigned 1932–1945); emperor of Vietnam (1949–1955). Bao Dai was crowned in 1925 and retained regal palaces at Hue and Da Lat. He collaborated with Japanese occupiers during World War II but abdicated in 1945 when Ho Chi Minh proclaimed the Democratic Republic of Vietnam. Bao Dai then took a common name and went to Hanoi, where he was appointed a "supreme adviser" to the new government. Subsequently he retired to the French Riviera. In 1949 the French, desiring a Vietnamese figurehead for their newly proclaimed Republic of Vietnam restored him as emperor, and in 1950 the United States recognized the regime (often referred to as the "Bao Dai solution"). He was uninterested in ruling the country and had no real power. Much of the U.S. monetary aid funneled to the South Vietnamese to defeat the Viet Minh was deposited by Bao Dai outside the country for use upon his eventual departure. He installed Ngo Dinh Diem as prime minister in 1954, swearing him to defend Vietnam against the communists, and if necessary, against the French. Five months later, in 1955, Diem deposed Bao Dai in a referendum.

BIBLIOGRAPHY

FITZGERALD, FRANCES. *Fire in the Lake: The Vietnamese and the Americans in Vietnam.* 1982.
KARNOW, STANLEY. *Vietnam: A History.* 1991.

SANDRA C. TAYLOR

Barrier Concept. Throughout the Vietnam War, no amount of U.S. bombing could stop the flow of men and supplies along the Ho Chi Minh Trail from North Vietnam into South Vietnam. Building a 100-kilometer (60-mile) anti-infiltration barrier across the demilitarized zone (DMZ) and Laos to interdict the trail was a solution first proposed by Prof. Roger Fisher of Harvard Law School in 1966. After scientists at the Institute for Defense Analysis added technological details, Lt. Gen. Alfred D. Starbird took charge of the plan. As an alternative to escalation, the barrier appealed to policymakers despite its estimated $1 billion price tag. In a memo to President Johnson in October 1966, Secretary of Defense Robert McNamara called for "an interdiction zone covered by air-laid mine and bombing attacks pin-pointed by air-laid acoustical sensors." Construction of the so-called McNamara Line began with Operation DYE MARKER in April 1967, when U.S. Marines cleared 11.6 kilometers (8 miles) of land along the DMZ and sowed it with barbed wire, mines, and sensors. Problems soon developed: the government of Laos rejected a cross-border barrier; PAVN shelling slowed construction; and U.S. military commanders never embraced a static "jungle Maginot line," complaining it would tie down thousands of men who could better be used for search-and-destroy missions. By 1968, the diversion of U.S. manpower for defense of Khe Sanh halted construction of the barrier. A marine commander thought the barrier concept typified "the Defense Department's Alice in Wonderland approach" to the Vietnam War. Later, however, air-delivered seismic intrusion detectors (ADSIDs) developed for the McNamara Line helped pinpoint air strikes against convoys along the Ho Chi Minh Trail.

BIBLIOGRAPHY

CORSON, WILLIAM R. *The Betrayal.* 1968.

DICKSON, PAUL. *The Electronic Battlefield.* 1976.

HAMILTON, ANDREW. "Vietnam—Fencing in the North." *New Republic,* 8 July 1967.

"McNamara's Gimmick." *Nation,* 25 September 1967.

NORMAN, LLOYD. "McNamara's Fence: Our Eyes and Ears along the Demilitarized Zone." *Army* 18 (August 1968).

PEARSON, WILLARD. *The War in the Northern Provinces.* 1978.

GLEN GENDZEL

Bay Vien, born Le Van Vien; leader of the Binh Xuyen, Saigon's preeminent criminal organization. Through payoffs to emperor Bao Dai and with French approval, Bay Vien became a general in the South Vietnamese army and head of the national police. After the Diem government defeated the Binh Xuyen in 1955, Bay Vien fled to Paris.

BIBLIOGRAPHY

KARNOW, STANLEY. *Vietnam: A History.* 1991.

OLSON, JAMES, and RANDY ROBERTS. *Where the Domino Fell: America and Vietnam, 1945 to 1990.* 1991.

ELLEN D. GOLDLUST

Ben Suc, South Vietnamese village controlled by Viet Cong guerrillas, located at the heart of the Iron Triangle tunnel complex. As part of Operation CEDAR FALLS in January 1967, over 30,000 U.S. and South Vietnamese troops razed the village of Ben Suc, fifty kilometers (thirty miles) from Saigon in Binh Duong province. All six thousand residents were forcibly relocated so the Viet Cong–controlled village could become a free-fire zone. The operation was ultimately unsuccessful, however, for the tunnels beneath the village were rebuilt, the deepest still intact after CEDAR FALLS and JUNCTION CITY. One year later, Ben Suc served as a base for Viet Cong guerrillas during the Tet Offensive.

BIBLIOGRAPHY

ROGERS, BERNARD WILLIAM. *Cedar Falls–Junction City: A Turning Point.* 1974.

SCHELL, JONATHAN. *The Village of Ben Suc.* 1967.

GLEN GENDZEL

Ben Tre, South Vietnamese city, capital of Kien Hoa province in the Mekong Delta region. Ben Tre fell to Viet Cong guerrillas during the Tet Offensive. Half of the city, with a population of 35,000, was destroyed by U.S. bombs and shells as U.S. forces retook it in February 1968, killing or wounding about two thousand civilians in the process. Ben Tre is famous because a U.S. Army major explained: "It became necessary to destroy the town in order to save it."

BIBLIOGRAPHY

BRAESTRUP, PETER. *Big Story: How the American Press and Television Reported and Interpreted the Crisis of Tet 1968 in Vietnam and Washington.* 1977.

OBERDORFER, DON. *Tet! The Turning Point of the Vietnam War.* 1983.

GLEN GENDZEL

Berger, Samuel D. (1911–), U.S. deputy ambassador to South Vietnam, 1968–1972. Berger acted as liaison between the United States and the South Vietnamese government and military. He believed that South Vietnamese president Nguyen Van Thieu could serve as the head of a viable civilian, anticommunist government and urged the United States to support Thieu. Berger also supported the invasions of Cambodia and Laos.

BIBLIOGRAPHY

DOUGAN, CLARK, and STEVEN WEISS. *The Vietnam Experience, 1968.* 1983.

U.S. DEPARTMENT OF STATE. *Biographic Register.* 1974.

ELLEN D. GOLDLUST

Berrigan Brothers. Daniel Berrigan (1921–), and Philip Berrigan (1923–), American Roman Catholic priests; active spokesmen for Clergy Concerned about Vietnam (later Clergy and Laity Concerned About Vietnam [CALCAV]), an interdenominational peace group. Daniel gained national prominence in 1965 when church superiors, strongly anticommunist and supporters of the Vietnam War, ordered him to travel on a mission in Latin America to halt his antiwar activities in the United States. This action provoked protests from Berrigan's supporters led by his brother Philip, and church superiors allowed Daniel to return to the United States in early 1966.

B-52 STRATOFORTRESS. In October 1965, a Strategic Air Command B-52 strikes a target near the South Vietnamese coast with a cascade of 750-pound bombs. *National Archives*

By 1967, believing that vocal criticism of the war was ineffective, the Berrigan brothers and CALCAV urged peace advocates to engage in civil disobedience. In 1968, they and other members of the "Catonsville 9" used homemade napalm to burn hundreds of records from a Maryland draft board. Tried and convicted, Daniel and Philip Berrigan respectively served terms of sixteen and thirty-two months in federal prison in the early 1970s. Both brothers, critical of the proliferation of nuclear weaponry, continued their peace activism and civil disobedience during the 1970s and 1980s.

BIBLIOGRAPHY

HALL, MITCHELL K. *Because of Their Faith: CALCAV and Religious Opposition to the Vietnam War.* 1990.

MECONIS, CHARLES A. *With Clumsy Grace: The American Catholic Left, 1961–1975.* 1979.

JENNIFER FROST

B-52. B-52s, U.S. Air Force strategic bombers, dropped huge quantities of bombs from high altitude in support of U.S. and Army of the Republic of Vietnam (ARVN) ground operations in South Vietnam, along the Ho Chi Minh Trail, on Cambodia in Operation MENU raids, and in the LINEBACKER II "Christmas bombing" of North Vietnam. Designed for the U.S. Strategic Air Command (SAC) as a nuclear bomber by the Boeing Aircraft Company, the eight-engine B-52 was the first true intercontinental jet bomber and one of the most successful military aircraft ever built. The B-52's precursor was the

B-47, a Boeing medium bomber of radical design, which entered service in the early 1950s. The B-47's thin, swept-back wings and jet engines suspended from underwing pylons inspired not only the B-52, but also the Boeing 707, the first truly successful commercial jet, and its basic military version, the C-135, the KC-135 tanker version of which played a major role in Vietnam. The B-52 design began as a turboprop in 1945–1946 and solidified in 1948 when the Pratt and Whitney J-57 engine, far more efficient than earlier turbojets, promised to combine jet speed with long range. Far-sighted Air Force procurement officials stipulated that the bomber

have a conventional as well as a nuclear ordnance capability. The B-52's immense 185-foot wingspan and capacious fuselage, provided to enable it to fly above the range of Soviet antiaircraft artillery and to increase its range, also enabled the B-52 to drop enormous loads of 500-, 750-, and 1,000-pound high-explosive, general-purpose bombs from altitudes well above 30,000 feet, out of sight and hearing from the ground. On occasion, time-delay fuses were used for area denial and harassment, and armor-piercing 1,000-pound bombs were used to penetrate underground facilities. Bombs, typically dropped by three-aircraft cells in closely spaced

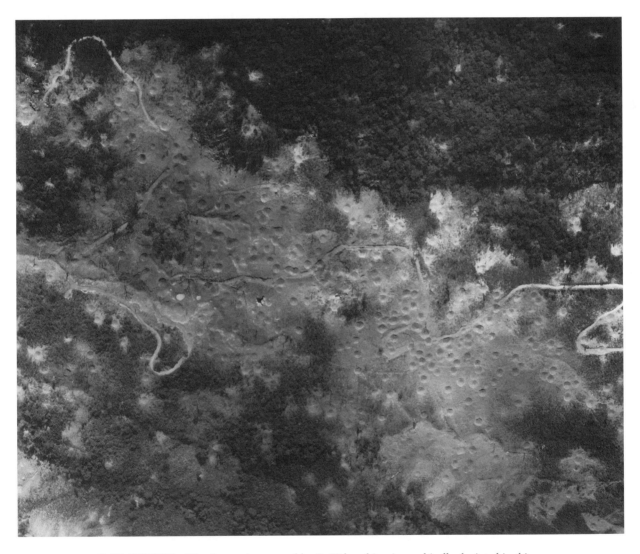

B-52 STRIKE. The devastation caused by B-52 bombing is graphically depicted in this reconnaissance photo of North Vietnam's Route 15, heavily cratered after a 27 April 1966 B-52 strike. The road fed into Laos and the Ho Chi Minh Trail through the Mu Gia pass, a frequent target of the B-52. *Archive Photos*

strings, fell in long strips, leaving enormous swaths of destruction from blast and cratering.

The air force purchased 742 B-52s in models A through H between 1953 and 1962. The first ARC LIGHT strikes were carried out by B-52Fs modified to carry twenty-four 750-pound bombs externally on underwing racks. The B-52Fs were replaced beginning in December 1965 by B-52Ds with "Big Belly" bomb bays, modified to carry eighty-four 500-pound bombs or forty-two 750-pound bombs, a total bomb load of some 60,000 pounds, as opposed to 38,000 pounds for the model F. Many older B-52s were retired from service in the 1960s, and about half the B-52s used in the LINEBACKER campaigns were G models, optimized for the nuclear role with "wet" (i.e., fuel-filled) wings and less than half the conventional bomb load of the model Ds. Until LINEBACKER, B-52s were used only in low-threat areas and the crews fought a remote, almost antiseptic, war—which earned them the sobriquets "monkey killers" and "splinter makers" among tactical aircrews, the implication being that the B-52s, attacking well above the range of enemy guns, destroyed only jungle vegetation and animals. Despite initially heavy losses, B-52s proved highly effective in the 1972 "Christmas bombings," destroying railroad yards and industrial targets in North Vietnam with minimal collateral damage outside the target areas. The B-52 was a mainstay of the nuclear deterrent through the end of the Cold War, served effectively in the Persian Gulf War of 1991, and remains in service.

BIBLIOGRAPHY

KNAACK, MARCELLE S. *Post–World War II Bombers, 1945–1973, U.S. Air Force Encyclopedia of Aircraft and Missile Systems.* Vol. 2, 1988.

JOHN F. GUILMARTIN JR.

Bidault, Georges (1899–1983), premier of the French Fourth Republic, July–December 1946, October 1949–June 1950; minister of foreign affairs, 1953–1954; leader of the Mouvement Républicain Populaire (MRP), the Christian-Democratic party that he helped to found after World War II. Elected premier at the time of the Fontainebleau Conference in 1946, Bidault represented a rightward shift in the government. As foreign minister he was a stalwart proponent for the maintenance of the postwar French empire. He allowed High Commissioner Georges d'Argenlieu to pursue aggressive and provocative policies in Vietnam including the bombardment of Haiphong in November 1946. Eight years later, when defeat at Dien Bien Phu appeared imminent, Bidault implored the Eisenhower administration to intervene militarily, offering to disguise U.S. warplanes with French markings. Bidault later claimed that Secretary of State John Foster Dulles offered the use of two tactical nuclear bombs to save the deteriorating French situation, an assertion angrily denied by Dulles. When the garrison at Dien Bien Phu fell, Bidault reversed himself and appeared sincere in seeking a French withdrawal. However, with the demise of the Laniel government in June 1954, Bidault's ministerial duties relating to Indochina came to an end.

BIBLIOGRAPHY

HAMMER, ELLEN J. *The Struggle for Indochina.* 1954.
WALL, IRWIN. "Georges Bidault." In *Historical Dictionary of the French Fourth and Fifth Republics, 1946–1991,* edited by Wayne Northcutt. 1992.

VICTOR JEW

Bien Hoa, South Vietnamese city, capital of Bien Hoa province. Viet Cong guerrillas attacked the South Vietnamese air base at Bien Hoa on 1 November 1964. A predawn mortar bombardment destroyed six and damaged fourteen of the twenty B-57 bombers stationed there, killing five Americans and two South Vietnamese. Some 32 kilometers (20 miles) from Saigon, Bien Hoa became a major U.S. air base and the headquarters of III Corps. By 1969, 220 U.S. Air Force and 75 South Vietnamese air force planes were based at Bien Hoa. The base was overrun in the North Vietnamese Spring Offensive of April 1975.

BIBLIOGRAPHY

"Bien Hoa." *Air Force Times,* 10 April 1968.
FLYNN, JOHN. "U.S. Bombers Are Blasted in Vietnam: Bien Hoa Airbase." *LIFE,* 13 November 1964.
FOX, ROGER P. *Air Base Defense in the Republic of Vietnam, 1961–1973.* 1979.

GLEN GENDZEL

Big Minh. *See* Duong Van Minh.

Binh Gia, town in Quang Ngai province on Vietnam's coastal plain. On 29 May 1965 Viet Cong

GEORGES BIDAULT. At left, with John Foster Dulles. *Archive Photos*

forces attacked Binh Gia, destroying two South Vietnamese battalions, which dropped their weapons and fled. The performance of the South Vietnamese troops led Gen. William Westmoreland to send a message on 7 June to Adm. Ulysses S. Grant Sharp, Commander-in-Chief, Pacific (CINCPAC), in which Westmoreland concluded that the South Vietnamese could not defeat the Viet Cong without massive U.S. assistance.

BIBLIOGRAPHY

DAVIDSON, PHILLIP B. *Vietnam at War—The History: 1946–1975.* 1988.

MAITLAND, TERRENCE, and PETER MCINERNEY. *A Contagion of War.* 1983.

The Marines in Vietnam, 1954–1973: An Anthology and Annotated Bibliography. 1983.

ELLEN D. GOLDLUST

Binh, Nguyen Thi. *See* Nguyen Thi Binh.

Binh Xuyen. Named for a village south of the Saigon-Cholon area, Saigon's preeminent criminal organization from the 1940s to 1955 originated from a fusion of bandit gangs, some of whose members were released from the penal colony of Poulo Condore (Con Son) by the Japanese during World War II. Under the leadership of Bay Vien, the Binh Xuyen became a well-disciplined paramilitary organization serving whichever client paid the best— the Japanese, the French, or the Viet Minh. In September 1945 the gang, which was involved in protection rackets, drugs, gambling, prostitution, and other vices for which Saigon was known, became politically active. Joining a Viet Minh–sponsored general strike, it infiltrated a Saigon suburb, killed 150 French and Eurasians, and mutilated many hostages. But Vien became unreliable to the Viet Minh, who put a price on his head. The Binh Xuyen joined alternately with the Hoa Hao and the Cao Dai sect armies challenging the French for power. By 1951 Vien was backing Emperor Bao Dai and providing him with money for gambling. The gang soon rivaled the Viet Cong guerrillas as threats to Premier Ngo Dinh Diem's government. In spring 1955 some 40,000 Binh Xuyen troops, along with the sect armies, attacked Diem's army but were defeated and retreated to Cholon. Although U.S. adviser Edward Lansdale and others encouraged Diem to compromise, he insisted on eliminating the gang. Ngo Dinh Nhu's success in breaking up the gang convinced the Americans of Diem's viability against the communists, who acquired members from the defeated organization. Bay Vien retired with a fortune to France.

BIBLIOGRAPHY

HERRING, GEORGE C. *America's Longest War: The United States and Vietnam, 1950–1975.* 1986.
KARNOW, STANLEY. *Vietnam: A History.* 1991.

SANDRA C. TAYLOR

Blacks. *See* African Americans.

Boat People. *See* Refugees.

Body Count. Unlike previous wars, the Vietnam conflict was a war of attrition rather than a war for territory along a specific front. Guerrilla fighting in the dense jungles involved ambushes, quick firefights, and retreats to bases. Troops did not hold ground, the traditional measure of military success. Both the U.S. military and the American public, however, needed a measurement of success for the war, and since territorial measures were not applicable, the body count became the yardstick. The body count was just that: casualty statistics to indicate the damage U.S. and Army of the Republic of Vietnam (ARVN) forces were inflicting upon the Viet Cong guerrillas (VC) and North Vietnamese Army (NVA) regulars. The body counts were regularly announced to the media to indicate how the conflict was progressing.

From the outset the body count concept was troubling. U.S. and ARVN troops continually dealt with Viet Cong guerrillas, NVA regulars, and hostile peasants, and the U.S. military's unwritten rule for determining body counts became: "If it's dead, it's VC." Some argue that the use of body count as a measure desensitized U.S. troops and officers as well as contributed to understandable tensions between Vietnamese civilians and the U.S. military. As the war continued, pressure from U.S. officials in Washington, who wanted to show the American public that the war was going well, led to routine inflation of body counts throughout the chain of command. By the time field reports had filtered through the ranks to leaders in Vietnam and the United States, body count figures often had been increased by as much as 30 percent. The exact figure is indeterminable, but most agree that the counts were routinely and significantly exaggerated.

Revelations of inaccurate body counts contributed to public mistrust of the U.S. government's handling of the war, while the brutality of using such a measure caused many to question the war's morality. Ironically, the body count, intended to assure the American public and political leaders of the war's progress, eventually undermined support for continued U.S. involvement.

BIBLIOGRAPHY

HERRING, GEORGE C. *America's Longest War: The United States and Vietnam, 1950–1975.* 1986.
ISAACS, ARNOLD R. *Without Honor.* 1983.

KELLY EVANS-PFEIFER

Booby Traps. Booby traps are concealed explosives or other deadly devices that are activated when someone unwittingly steps on, lifts, or moves something seemingly harmless. Viet Cong guerrillas extensively used booby traps such as hidden pits with stakes in them (known as punji pits) or hand grenades or other explosives attached to trip wires. These weapons accounted for more than 10 percent of all Americans killed or wounded during the Vietnam War.

BIBLIOGRAPHY

DOLEMAN, EDGAR C., JR. *The Vietnam Experience: Tools of War.* 1984.
GOLDMAN, PETER, and TONY FULLER. *Charlie Company: What Vietnam Did to Us.* 1983.
QUICK, JOHN. *Dictionary of Weapons and Military Terms.* 1973.

ELLEN D. GOLDLUST

JUNGLE BOOBY TRAP FACTORY. Unexploded U.S. bombs and shells provide the raw material for crude but effective Viet Cong mines and booby traps. *Center of Military History*

Bowles, Chester (1901–1986), U.S. undersecretary of state, 1961; ambassador to India, 1963–1969. In 1961, Bowles opposed the Taylor-Rostow recommendations for increased military support for the Diem regime, urging instead that Vietnam, like Laos, be made neutral. It was not a propitious time to disagree with the Kennedy administration, however, because the White House had suffered three embarrassments that year: the Bay of Pigs fiasco, Khrushchev's ill-mannered treatment of Kennedy in Vienna, and the sealing off of Berlin and the construction of the Berlin Wall. Bowles was dismissed and reassigned as "roving ambassador." The silencing of Bowles chilled any opposition that may have arisen in the 1961–1963 Kennedy White House. During the Johnson administration, Bowles headed a 1968 mission to Cambodia that helped lead to the Cambodian invasion.

BIBLIOGRAPHY

Di Leo, David. *George Ball, Vietnam and the Rethinking of Containment.* 1991.

Schaffer, Howard B. *Chester Bowles: New Dealer in the Cold War.* 1993.

VICTOR JEW

Bradley, Omar N. (1893–1981), general, U.S. Army; chairman, Joint Chiefs of Staff (JCS), 1947–1953. During the Indochina War, General Bradley helped draft JCS contingency plans to assist the French by bombing and blockading China in 1952. After retirement, Bradley visited Vietnam in 1967 and declared "this is a war at the right place, at the right time and with the right enemy—the Communists." In 1968, he was one of the few "wise men" of President Johnson's Special Advisory Group (SAG) to advise against withdrawal from Vietnam.

BIBLIOGRAPHY

Bradley, Omar N. "My Visit to Vietnam." *Look,* 14 November 1967.

Bradley, Omar N., and Clay Blair. *A General's Life.* 1983.

Joint Chiefs of Staff. Memorandum to the Secretary of Defense, 18 April 1952. U.S. Department of State. Part 1 of *Indochina.* Vol. 12 of *Foreign Relations of the United States, 1952–1954.* 1982.

Kirkpatrick, Charles E. *Omar Nelson Bradley: The Centennial.* 1992.

GLEN GENDZEL

Brezhnev, Leonid (1906–1982), first secretary general of the Soviet Communist Party, 1964–1982. Brezhnev replaced Nikita Khrushchev in 1964 and immediately changed the Soviet Union's Vietnam policy. Under Khrushchev, the Soviet Union was not very active in promoting communism in Southeast Asia; China was North Vietnam's chief source of aid. Brezhnev, however, did not want the USSR to cede Asia to Chinese influence, and consequently, he involved the Soviet Union more deeply in the Vietnam conflict. The Soviet Union significantly increased military aid to the Democratic Republic of Vietnam, particularly high-technology equipment such as surface-to-air missiles (SAMs) and sophisticated radar systems, which the Chinese could not provide.

By the early 1970s, however, Brezhnev began to view détente with the United States as more vital to Soviet interests than was a communist victory in Vietnam. Aid to Vietnam was costly and the USSR desired an end to the conflict. Nixon and Kissinger tried to make a U.S.-USSR nuclear arms reduction agreement contingent on the Soviet Union pressuring North Vietnam to negotiate. Although Brezhnev rejected such linkage, he did not cancel his May 1972 Moscow summit with Nixon despite the initiation of the U.S. LINEBACKER bombing campaign against North Vietnam.

BIBLIOGRAPHY

HERRING, GEORGE C. *America's Longest War: The United States and Vietnam, 1950–1975.* 1986.
KARNOW, STANLEY. *Vietnam: A History.* 1991.

KELLY EVANS-PFEIFER

Britain. *See* Great Britain.

Brown, George S. (1918–1978), general, U.S. Air Force; commander, Seventh Air Force, 1968–1970; Air Force chief of staff, 1973–1974; chairman, Joint Chiefs of Staff, 1974–1978. From August 1968 to September 1970 George S. Brown, a highly decorated World War II veteran, commanded the Seventh Air Force in Vietnam, which bombed Cambodia. During the confirmation hearings in 1973 for his appointment as chairman of the Joint Chiefs of Staff (JCS), Brown defended his concealment of the secret bombing of Cambodia under sharp questioning from Congress. As JCS chairman he criticized Congress for withholding

aid when South Vietnam collapsed, and he drew fire for public attacks on "the Jewish influence in this country" and U.S. military aid to Israel.

BIBLIOGRAPHY

"The Airman in Charge of Southeast Asia." *Airman* 13 (January 1969).
BERGER, CARL, ed. *The United States Air Force in Southeast Asia, 1961–1973.* 1977.
KORB, LAWRENCE J. *The Joint Chiefs of Staff: The First Twenty-five Years.* 1976.
PURYEAR, EDGAR F., JR. *George S. Brown, General, U.S. Air Force: Destined for Stars.* 1983.

GLEN GENDZEL

Buddhists. Buddhists became a significant political constituency in South Vietnam during the 1950s and 1960s. Buddhism was the dominant popular religion in Vietnam, and in contrast to Confucianism's concern for social order and hierarchy, Buddhism emphasized a faith that transcended politics and society and that promoted equality and community among individuals. According to an old saying, "the Vietnamese are Confucians in peacetime, Buddhists in times of trouble." Popular forms of Buddhism, such as the Hoa Hao, gained in prominence during Vietnam's anticolonial struggle against the French.

Although strongly anticommunist, Buddhists had little political influence in the regime of President Ngo Dinh Diem. The Catholic Diem largely appointed Catholics to fill important government positions and, in addition to suppressing political opposition, issued edicts that limited the religious freedom of Buddhists. On 8 May 1963, the government prohibited Buddhists from carrying flags on the birthday of the Buddha. Crowds gathered in Hue to protest, and government troops fired to disperse the dissidents, killing nine people. Diem's government blamed Viet Cong guerrillas for the deaths and never admitted responsibility. The Buddhist leadership quickly organized protests against the Diem regime. On 11 June, in Saigon, Quang Duc, a Buddhist bonze (or monk), set himself on fire to protest the regime's policies. Vast demonstrations in the cities broke out, followed by the self-immolation of six more bonzes by autumn. On 21 August, Diem's brother, Ngo Dinh Nhu, responded to the protests with a raid on the Buddhist Xa Loi pagoda in Saigon, in which more than thirty bonzes were killed. Similar raids were carried out

BUDDHIST MONKS. In Phnom Penh, Cambodia, 1960. *National Archives*

in Hue and other cities, and these blatant, repressive actions against Buddhists encouraged the successful military coup against the Diem government in November 1963.

Over the next three years, Buddhists continued to organize, to protest the military governments and U.S. presence in Vietnam, and to demand elections and the return of a civilian government. Buddhist leaders organized the United Buddhist Church of Vietnam in January 1964, which was widely supported. Sharp divisions existed among Buddhists, however; Thich Tri Quang, the militant leader of Buddhists in Hue and Da Nang, and Thich Tam Chau, a political moderate in Saigon, disagreed on goals and tactics for the Buddhist movement. Buddhist opposition nevertheless challenged and undermined the military government of General Nguyen Khanh and the nominally civil-

ian government of Tran Van Huong during 1964 and 1965. Protests against the military junta of Generals Nguyen Cao Ky and Nguyen Van Thieu failed, however. In March 1966, the United Buddhist Church demanded that the junta hold elections for a civilian government, and urban popular protests and divisions within the military followed. In response, General Thieu convened a National Political Congress and promised to hold elections, while General Ky, who refused to relinquish power, planned a military action. In May, with the tacit approval of the United States, Ky ordered troops to Da Nang, where hundreds of civilians were killed and wounded, and laid siege to Hue to crush all opposition.

After this sound defeat, Tri Quang, the Buddhist leader of Hue, was placed under house arrest, and Buddhists largely abandoned political activity.

BUDDHIST PROTEST. Quang Duc, a Buddhist monk for fifty-one years, immolates himself to protest Ngo Dinh Diem's policies, Saigon, 11 June 1963. Photograph by Malcolm Browne. *AP/Wide World Photos*

Caught between the corruption of the U.S.-sponsored military government and the communists, Buddhists were beset by political paralysis and hopelessness, a mood shared by many urban residents. On 11 June 1970, marking the anniversary of the self-immolation of Quang Duc and in response to the invasion of Cambodia, a Saigon bonze set himself on fire. This action, unlike earlier self-immolations, failed to spark additional protests. Reflecting a sense of futility, the Buddhist leadership chose not to capitalize upon the situation, stating merely that the self-immolation was an indication of the desire for peace. During the last years of the war, the Buddhists were an insignificant political force.

BIBLIOGRAPHY

FitzGerald, Frances. *Fire in the Lake: The Vietnamese and the Americans in Vietnam.* 1982.
HAMMER, ELLEN. *Vietnam: Yesterday and Today.* 1966.

JENNIFER FROST

Bui Diem (1923–), Republic of Vietnam's ambassador to the United States, 1966–1972. Bui Diem served as the liaison between the U.S. government and South Vietnam on a number of issues, including conditions for peace negotiations. In 1968, Bui Diem was the liaison between President Nguyen Van Thieu and Anna Chennault, who worked behind the scenes to drum up support for Nixon's presidential candidacy in the belief that Nixon would take a harder line against the Democratic Republic of Vietnam than would Hubert Humphrey, the Democratic U.S. presidential candidate.

BIBLIOGRAPHY

KARNOW, STANLEY. *Vietnam: A History.* 1991.
NGUYEN TIEN HUNG and JERROLD SCHECTER. *The Palace File.* 1986.

KELLY EVANS-PFEIFER

Bui Phat, refugee slum on the edge of Saigon. Bui Phat was an example of the slums in numerous South Vietnamese cities, slums created by peasants who migrated from the north to the south in the wake of the 1954 Geneva Accords. These shanty towns expanded as South Vietnamese also became refugees, a result of U.S. bombardment of the south, establishment of free-fire zones, and the use of search-and-destroy tactics.

The people in these slums, who represented 40–50 percent of the population of South Vietnam, became economically dependent on the U.S. presence in Vietnam and thus resisted efforts by both Viet Cong guerrillas and Buddhists to organize protests against the U.S. presence.

BIBLIOGRAPHY

FITZGERALD, FRANCES. *Fire in the Lake: The Vietnamese and the Americans in Vietnam.* 1982.

ELLEN D. GOLDLUST

Bui Tin (1924–), officer, People's Army of Vietnam (PAVN); journalist; government official. Bui Tin joined the Viet Minh in 1945 and fought at Dien Bien Phu. In 1963, he infiltrated South Vietnam to gather intelligence for the North Vietnamese war effort, and he later became a colonel in the PAVN. Bui wrote for the Communist Party newspaper, *Nhan Dan,* and the army newspaper, *Quan Doi Nhan Dan.* He accepted the South Vietnamese government's surrender as the ranking PAVN officer in Saigon in 1975. In 1990, while in Paris on official business, Bui Tin released a "citizen's petition" that was extremely critical of the regime of the Socialist Republic of Vietnam, which resulted in his expulsion from the Communist party.

BIBLIOGRAPHY

BOWMAN, JOHN S., ed. *The Vietnam War: An Almanac.* 1985.
"Ex-Follower of Ho Chi Minh Scolds Vietnam in Broadcasts." *New York Times,* 29 December 1990.
KARNOW, STANLEY. *Vietnam: A History.* 1991.

ELLEN D. GOLDLUST

Bundy, McGeorge (1919–), national security adviser, 1961–1966. Bundy was a key player in the formulation of U.S. Vietnam policy, from the early advisory role through escalation. Under Kennedy,

Bundy dealt with the Diem regime and sought to ensure a democratic South Vietnam without having the United States assume sole responsibility for the fight against the insurgent communists. After Kennedy's assassination, Bundy became more prowar. By late 1964, he favored a sustained bombing campaign against North Vietnam and an expanded U.S. combat role. After the initial troop commitment, Bundy supported subsequent buildups, arguing that unilateral deescalation would devastate U.S. credibility. He also believed that a strong military presence would strengthen the hand of the United States and South Vietnam in any peace negotiations and thus took a hard line on preconditions for talks. By 1966, however, Bundy began to question the unending escalation and his concerns led to his resignation. Later, as one of the "wise men," he continued to advise Johnson on an informal basis. He supported deescalation and eventual withdrawal in the watershed 1968 "wise men" meeting and undoubtedly affected Johnson's policies profoundly.

BIBLIOGRAPHY

KAHIN, GEORGE MCT. *Intervention: How America Became Involved in Vietnam.* 1986.
KARNOW, STANLEY. *Vietnam: A History.* 1991.

KELLY EVANS-PFEIFER

Bundy, William P. (1917–), Central Intelligence Agency (CIA), 1951–1961; assistant secretary of defense for international security affairs, 1961–1963; assistant secretary of state for Far Eastern affairs, 1964–1968. Along with his younger brother McGeorge, William Bundy had a significant hand in the drafting of U.S. policy in Vietnam. He advocated a U.S. military presence in Vietnam but did not initially favor a ground combat role. Bundy instead pushed for air strikes against military and industrial targets in the North and the mining of Haiphong harbor.

By 1964 Bundy believed that the administration needed congressional approval for further action in Vietnam. And so, he and aides drafted the Gulf of Tonkin Resolution, perhaps the most significant document of the war, as it provided Johnson with the ability to escalate the conflict as he saw fit. In 1964–1965, Bundy headed a working group to formulate U.S. policy recommendations. He opposed a large U.S. troop buildup, fearing that the fight would become essentially the responsibility of the United States, although he supported a limited

ELLSWORTH BUNKER. At right, with William C. Westmoreland (left) and Earle G. Wheeler. *U.S. Air Force*

enviable and least assailable reputation in American government" when President Johnson appointed him ambassador to South Vietnam in 1967. Bunker told reporters that "military power—important as it is—cannot alone provide any lasting answer to the real problems in Vietnam." He ignored repression in South Vietnam and shored up the Saigon government with praise while revamping pacification and counterinsurgency efforts in the countryside. Opposition politicians accused Bunker of meddling in South Vietnam's elections when he openly endorsed President Thieu in 1967 and 1971.

Bunker loyally supported President Nixon's policy of Vietnamization, stating that "the yardstick of our success is not what we do, but what the Vietnamese do for themselves." He accompanied Henry Kissinger during the stormy sessions that persuaded President Thieu to accept the Paris peace accords in 1973. Bunker resigned after the cease-fire. "I'm an old-fashioned patriot," he once said. "I have always assumed that my country was fundamentally right in its dealings with others."

combat troop commitment of 100,000 men. Nevertheless, he preferred sustained bombing campaigns against North Vietnam. By 1967, Bundy walked the line between the prowar and antiwar factions within the administration. The rapid U.S. escalation concerned him, although he consistently supported the notion of a divided Vietnam with an anticommunist south.

BIBLIOGRAPHY

KAHIN, GEORGE McT. *Intervention: How America Became Involved in Vietnam.* 1986.
KARNOW, STANLEY. *Vietnam: A History.* 1991.

KELLY EVANS-PFEIFER

Bunker, Ellsworth (1894–1984), U.S. ambassador to South Vietnam, 1967–1973. Heir to a fortune in the sugar business, Ellsworth Bunker served as ambassador to Argentina, India, Italy, and Nepal in the 1950s. He mediated several international conflicts as a State Department troubleshooter in the 1960s, earning praise for his efforts in the Dominican crisis of 1965–1966. According to journalist David Halberstam, Bunker had "the most

GEORGE BUSH. *Library of Congress*

BIBLIOGRAPHY

HALBERSTAM, DAVID. *The Best and the Brightest.* 1992.
PIKE, DOUGLAS, ed. *The Bunker Papers: Reports to the President from Vietnam, 1967–73.* 1990.
SZULC, TAD. *The Illusion of Peace: Foreign Policy in the Nixon Years.* 1978.

GLEN GENDZEL

Bush, George (1924–), U.S. representative (R-Tex.), 1966–1970; U.S. ambassador to the United Nations, 1971–1973; U.S. envoy to China, 1974; director of the Central Intelligence Agency (CIA), 1975–1976; vice president, 1981–1989; president, 1989–1993. George Walker Bush endorsed U.S. involvement in Vietnam as a member of Congress and supported the escalation policies of Presidents Johnson and Nixon. Bush did not denounce anti-war protestors, and had a reputation of balancing his support for the war with understanding for its opponents. As president, Bush claimed that the Persian Gulf War victory laid to rest the Vietnam Syndrome, the fear of military entanglement inspired in U.S. policymakers and the public by the experience of the Vietnam War.

BIBLIOGRAPHY

DUFFY, MICHAEL, and DAN GOODGAME. *Marching in Place: The Status Quo Presidency of George Bush.* 1992.
ROTHENBERG, RANDALL. "In Search of George Bush." *New York Times Magazine,* 6 March 1988.
WOODWARD, BOB. *The Commanders.* 1991.

KELLY EVANS-PFEIFER

C

Calley, William L., Jr. (1943–), second lieutenant, U.S. Army, 23d Infantry Division (Americal), 1967–1969. Calley was the only U.S. soldier convicted of a crime in the My Lai massacre. On 16 March 1968, U.S. troops killed 347 South Vietnamese—mostly women, children, and elderly—on a search-and-destroy operation in the hamlet of My Lai, part of the northern coastal village of Song My. Calley directed the activities of his platoon in the atrocity and was subsequently charged with killing 109 Vietnamese. In March 1971 a court-martial convicted Calley of the premeditated murder of at least 22 people and sentenced him to life in prison. President Nixon, however, intervened to review the case. The secretary of the army eventually reduced the sentence to ten years, and Calley gained parole in November 1974. During his incarceration, Calley received considerable domestic support from veterans' groups and conservative political organizations, who charged that he was made a scapegoat for a flawed Vietnam policy.

BIBLIOGRAPHY

CALLEY, WILLIAM L. *Lieutenant Calley: His Own Story.* 1971.
LEWY, GUENTER. *America in Vietnam.* 1978.

ADAM LAND

Cambodia. Once the center of a powerful empire, Cambodia became the battleground for more powerful nations during the Vietnam War. The kingdom of Angkor dominated the Southeast Asian mainland from the ninth through the fourteenth centuries, but thereafter Cambodian influence declined, and the country never regained its former glory. Beginning in the late eighteenth century, the Khmer people struggled to limit the expansion of the Chakri and Nguyen dynasties of neighboring Thailand and Vietnam. Ultimately, to avoid domination by either, King Norodom signed a treaty in 1863 that allowed France to make Cambodia a protectorate. That relationship lasted until Japanese forces occupied Indochina in 1940. The French continued to administer Cambodia, however, and in 1941 France deemed Prince Norodom Sihanouk (grandson of King Norodom) a pliable ally and made him king, in place of his cousin Prince Sirik Matak, who was more directly in the line of succession.

An Independent Cambodia. Sihanouk proved an astute political operator, however, hardly the figurehead the French had sought. After the Japanese defeat, Ho Chi Minh's nine-year fight for independence in Vietnam inspired Cambodians on both the left and right to oppose continued French rule. Sihanouk launched an international campaign for Cambodian independence in 1952, using French military reverses in Vietnam and Laos as leverage. After the French defeat at Dien Bien Phu in 1954, France granted Cambodia complete independence at the Geneva Conference. Sihanouk declared himself the "father of Cambodian independence," but as king he was not permitted to participate in the country's first democratic elections. Opting for political power instead of the ceremonial throne, Sihanouk abdicated in 1955, and easily won election to the presidency. Peasants provided his main support, as they revered him as a god-king. But his power ultimately rested on his ability to maintain Cambodia's neutrality by subsuming rival domestic forces and balancing competing international interests.

Domestically, Sihanouk set out to include or neutralize his former political adversaries. The Geneva accords assisted him by leaving the Cambodian communists without a territorial base. Acting on the advice of Viet Minh leaders, some party members fled to Hanoi, others went underground in Cambodia, while a few allowed themselves to be incorporated into the government. At the same time, Sihanouk co-opted leaders of the political right except for Son Ngoc Thanh, a popular nationalist who, with permission from South Vietnam and Thailand, established Khmer Serei camps in both countries. The United States also aided Thanh in efforts to foster good relations with South Vietnam and Thailand.

Shifting Alliances. Sihanouk's international strategy was to play the People's Republic of China (PRC), the United States, and Vietnam against one another to preserve peace in Cambodia as the conflict in South Vietnam escalated. In 1958 Ngo Dinh Diem's troops crossed the Cambodian border in pursuit of communist Viet Minh guerrillas. When the United States supported that action despite Sihanouk's protests, he turned to the PRC for assistance. Over the next five years, Sihanouk became convinced that North Vietnam would win its war against the South. Anticipating a communist Indochina, he broke relations with South Vietnam, and after Diem's assassination in November 1963, he renounced U.S. aid, which had been crucial to building the Cambodian army. Sihanouk's move planted seeds of discontent among military leaders, such as Defense Minister Lon Nol.

In 1965, Sihanouk deepened his international commitment to the left by severing diplomatic relations with the United States and allowing North Vietnam to build semipermanent base camps in eastern Cambodia, which facilitated the deployment of equipment and soldiers southward along the Ho Chi Minh Trail. In 1966, Sihanouk permitted the PRC to funnel supplies through the port of Sihanoukville to the base camps and ultimately to National Liberation Front (NLF) troops inside Vietnam. Chinese prime minister Zhou Enlai offered Sihanouk a share of the profits from the arms shipments, and a black market bonanza opened up. Sihanouk tolerated profiteering by military and government officials, and Lon Nol benefited enormously as a result.

Also in 1965, the United States committed ground troops to South Vietnam, and the intensified fighting forced more NLF guerrillas to seek refuge across the Cambodian border. Sihanouk felt his control slipping, and in an effort to stabilize his position, he engineered the election of a conservative Cambodian government in 1966. Yet he could not avert a serious peasant rebellion in the northwestern province of Battambang, which was brutally crushed by Lon Nol. When Sihanouk attempted to prosecute leftist members of his government for complicity in the uprising, they escaped from Phnom Penh and joined their comrades in the forest. The Battambang revolt convinced Cambodian communists (dubbed the Khmer Rouge by Sihanouk) that there was sufficient rural discontent to support an armed revolution against the existing government.

Communist Insurgency and U.S. Bombing. Cambodia's poorly equipped military could not fight communist insurgents and control the ever-increasing number of NLF troops in the east. Sihanouk needed outside support. The chaos of the Cultural Revolution after 1966 rendered the PRC both unreliable and menacing, so Sihanouk turned again to the United States, whose military position in Vietnam had strengthened substantially. Welcoming the possibility of closer ties to Cambodia, the United States sent Chester Bowles, then ambassador to India, to Phnom Penh. What transpired at their meeting is disputed, but it appears that Sihanouk sought recognition of Cambodia's borders and assurance that the United States would not bomb his country. Bowles seems to have agreed, but he explained that the United States might have to send forces across the border in "hot pursuit" of NLF forces. Sihanouk replied that he was "not opposed to hot pursuit in uninhabited areas" to free his country from Viet Cong incursions, as long as no

Cambodians were harmed. President Richard Nixon and his national security adviser Henry Kissinger later used Sihanouk's conditional acceptance of "hot pursuit" as implied consent for a full-scale bombing program.

In early 1969, Nixon approved the covert MENU bombings of NLF sanctuaries in Cambodia. [For discussion of the military aspects of the bombing of Cambodia, see MENU.] Meanwhile, infiltration of the People's Army of Vietnam (PAVN) from North Vietnam into Cambodia had increased, and large numbers of PAVN forces fled deeper into Cambodia to avoid U.S. aerial attacks. Before the bombings the Khmer Rouge had an armed force of only about 4,000 guerrillas. But the 29,000 tons of bombs dropped during the MENU campaign disrupted the lives of rural Cambodians, who were increasingly unhappy with their government's inability to protect them. The Khmer Rouge benefited most as general discontent turned to anger—by April 1975 the guerrilla force would grow to an estimated 80,000 armed soldiers. Frustrated by MENU's failure to eradicate the North Vietnamese and NLF bases in Cambodia, Gen. Creighton Abrams revived the military's call for a ground invasion of Cambodia. Knowing that Sihanouk would not approve such a plan, the U.S. government approached Lon Nol, a career officer and now Sihanouk's prime minister.

The Ouster of Sihanouk. While Sihanouk was in Paris for health reasons in March 1970, his rivals conspired to oust him. Together, Lon Nol and Sirik Matak, who had ties to the Central Intelligence Agency (CIA), undermined Sihanouk's policy of neutrality. They encouraged crowds to sack the North Vietnamese and NLF embassies, ordered PAVN soldiers out of Cambodia, and closed the port at Sihanoukville. On 18 March the new leaders announced the end of Sihanouk's rule and proclaimed a new government, which the United States immediately recognized. While direct CIA assistance has not been established, former agents note that the CIA generated misinformation to aid the plotters and sent agency-backed Khmer Serei troops into Cambodia. After the coup, Lon Nol launched pogroms against ethnic Vietnamese in an attempt to unite the Cambodians, but the people remained divided. Phnom Penh residents supported the new government, while many rural Cambodians retained their loyalty to Sihanouk who, in a remarkable turn of events, became the titular head of the Khmer Rouge.

Sihanouk arrived in Beijing the day after the coup, and at the insistence of Zhou Enlai agreed to lead the Khmer Rouge. Although he actually had no authority over the Khmer Rouge, which was led by Pol Pot and a shadowy central committee, Sihanouk's name provided needed credibility among the peasants. North Vietnam also increased its aid to the insurgents. Formerly only a marginal group, the Khmer Rouge emerged as a viable political alternative when President Nixon approved the invasion of Cambodia by ground forces.

The U.S. Incursion into Cambodia. Confident of Lon Nol's support, Nixon sent U.S. and Army of the Republic of Vietnam (ARVN) troops and B-52 bombers into eastern Cambodia in April 1970. The plan permitted the invasion forces to move only 30 kilometers (19 miles) into the country, so PAVN forces took refuge beyond that line, embroiling previously unaffected Cambodian villages in the war. Within the 30-kilometer battle area, ARVN forces ransacked villages and murdered innocent civilians to exact revenge for the post-coup pogroms against ethnic Vietnamese. The invasion ignited domestic protests in the United States, and when the troops withdrew at the end of May they had failed to achieve any of their major objectives, particularly the capture of the Vietnamese communist command post for operations in South Vietnam (Central Office for South Vietnam, COSVN). Far from driving PAVN troops from Cambodia, the invasion pushed them deeper into the country, thus increasing dissatisfaction with Lon Nol's government and building peasant support for the Khmer Rouge.

After the invasion, the United States provided military support for Lon Nol's failing government from 1970 to 1973, channeling most of the U.S. air power in Indochina into Cambodia to prevent the increasingly strong Khmer Rouge from taking Phnom Penh. U.S. bombs destroyed about 20 percent of the property in the region and forced 2 million Cambodians to become refugees. Most moved into Phnom Penh, the population of which soared from 600,000 in 1970 to 1.2 million in 1975. When Congress forced Nixon to halt the bombing in August 1973, 539,000 tons of bombs had been dropped on Cambodia. The air assault temporarily curtailed the Khmer Rouge's ground advance, but it expanded their influence over those who were displaced by or lost relatives to the bombing.

Under Khmer Rouge Rule. A Khmer Rouge takeover seemed imminent by the end of 1974.

Cambodian national forces blocked the Khmer Rouge's assault on Phnom Penh until late 1974, when a war-weary U.S. Congress dramatically slashed aid shipments. The Khmer Rouge guerrillas steadily advanced as resistance crumbled. On 17 April 1975 Khmer Rouge troops marched into Phnom Penh and ushered in a tragic new era in Cambodian history. The Khmer Rouge set the year at Zero and renamed the country Democratic Kampuchea. Within hours of their victory, they forcibly evacuated all urban centers. Residents had to leave all their belongings and march into the countryside where cadres assigned them to work camps. Cambodians labored from dawn to dusk in exchange for paltry portions of rice gruel. Khmer Rouge cadres systematically killed all educated people. They tortured and slaughtered thousands of government officials, military officers, teachers, doctors, engineers, and anyone else thought unsuitable for reeducation.

The intensely nationalistic and xenophobic Khmer Rouge renounced their ties to North Vietnam and accepted support only from the PRC. They broke diplomatic and trade ties with virtually all countries and launched a program to achieve self-sufficiency through rice production as the great kingdoms of Angkor had done. Sihanouk was appalled, but he was powerless to act. He resigned as head of state in 1976 and was confined to house arrest in Phnom Penh. Poor planning and internal corruption combined with a year of drought to create a severe food shortage. Malnutrition, a malaria epidemic, and a Khmer Rouge refusal to use modern medicine resulted in the deaths of hundreds of thousands of Cambodians. By the end of 1978, about 1 million people (one-seventh of the population) had been killed or had died of starvation or disease.

Vietnamese Invasion. Disputes between the reunited Vietnam and Democratic Kampuchea persisted and ultimately led to the Vietnamese invasion and occupation of Kampuchea. Prodded by the PRC, the Khmer Rouge engaged in border provocations with the Socialist Republic of Vietnam (SRV) after 1977. Those attacks and the Pol Pot government's resistance to the SRV's hegemonic designs on Indochina spurred an invasion by SRV forces. In January 1979, the SRV seized Phnom Penh and placed into power the Cambodian communists, who had fled to Hanoi in 1954. The Khmer Rouge leadership returned to the forest, where it joined two other groups (one led by Sihanouk) in armed opposition to the government. The Vietnamese puppet regime lasted until the United Nations–supervised elections in 1993, which resulted in a coalition government representing three of the country's four major factions. The Khmer Rouge refused to participate in the elections and continued to contest their legitimacy. Sihanouk resumed the throne as king in September 1993. Outlawed by the government in 1994, the Khmer Rouge, armed with Chinese weapons and backed by powerful Thai elements, continued to control portions of the countryside and to contribute to overall instability in Cambodia.

BIBLIOGRAPHY

CHANDLER, DAVID P. *The Tragedy of Cambodian History: Politics, War, and Revolution since 1945.* 1991.
KARNOW, STANLEY. *Vietnam: A History.* 1991.
KIERNAN, BEN. *How Pol Pot Came to Power: A History of Communism in Kampuchea, 1930–1975.* 1985.
SHAWCROSS, WILLIAM. *Sideshow: Kissinger, Nixon, and the Destruction of Cambodia.* 1979.
VICKERY, MICHAEL. *Cambodia, 1975–1982.* 1984.

AMY GOLDEN

Cambodian Incursion. On 1 May 1970, the U.S. Army commenced a series of operations against North Vietnamese and National Liberation Front (NLF) bases inside Cambodia. The Nixon administration sought to bolster the new pro-U.S. government in Cambodia, which had overthrown neutralist Prince Norodom Sihanouk in March. The coup had destabilized the country and brought about military hostilities with the North Vietnamese after the regime challenged communist bases in Cambodia. Previously, the United States had carefully avoided widening the ground war beyond South Vietnam. President Nixon, however, defiantly committed U.S. troops to support the new regime rather than rely on the Army of the Republic of Vietnam (ARVN) and U.S. air power. The U.S. military command favored U.S. military participation to ensure destruction of enemy sanctuaries, a tactical strike advocated by top generals since 1967. Moreover, President Nixon was determined to signal a hard-line stance in peace negotiations with North Vietnam and to show his resolve to political adversaries at home and abroad.

In the main Cambodian operation, nearly 12,000 U.S. Army and 8,000 ARVN troops attacked a 160-kilometer (100-mile) long border region northwest of Saigon. Elements of the 1st U.S. Cavalry Division targeted the suspected communist command center, the Central Office for South Vietnam (COSVN), in the "Fish Hook" region, while ARVN forces entered the "Parrot's Beak" to the south. U.S. command expected a decisive battle, but the enemy retreated quickly to the west, offering limited resistance. Allied forces sped through the lowlands of the border area, capturing huge stocks of abandoned supplies. U.S. forces ventured only 30 kilometers (19 miles) into the country and departed Cambodian territory on 30 June 1970. During the two-month operation, North Vietnamese and Viet Cong forces lost an estimated 11,000 men while U.S. and ARVN forces suffered 976 fatalities (338 American) and 4,500 wounded. The ARVN, which had begun limited operations in Cambodia in late March, operated sporadically in the region until the 1973 Paris peace accords.

The Cambodian incursion had uncertain military results. Although U.S. and ARVN forces captured ample enemy matériel (including 23,000 individual weapons and 14 million pounds of rice) and disrupted supply lines, North Vietnamese and Viet Cong forces quickly restocked supplies with Soviet and Chinese aid and moved bases further into the interior of Cambodia. In justifying the incursion, the Nixon administration also trumpeted the destruction of communist headquarters in the South. But in truth, COSVN, the supposed North Vietnamese equivalent to the Pentagon, turned out to be a few abandoned huts. Commentators remain divided on the success of the larger goals for the incursion. Henry Kissinger claimed that the invasion successfully relieved pressure on the Cambodian government. He and others also maintained that the incursion seriously disrupted North Vietnamese and Viet Cong military operations, gaining for the United States an extra year to implement Vietnamization policies in South Vietnam. Critics, such as William Shawcross, argued that the United States lacked the resources to disrupt the Cambodian sanctuaries effectively, and they criticized U.S. policy for committing U.S. resources in support of a second unstable regime in the region. The Cambodian government, as well as its South Vietnamese counterpart, fell to communist forces in April 1975.

Nixon's decision to send U.S. ground forces into Cambodia, however, whatever its military value, provoked fierce reactions among the U.S. public, which reflected the weariness and disapproval of many Americans with the war in Vietnam. Antiwar fervor had subsided since the previous autumn, when in November 1969, President Nixon had effectively appealed to a "great silent majority" of Americans to support his policy of Vietnamization. Over the winter, Nixon announced continuing troop withdrawals and told the nation, "we finally have in sight just the peace we are seeking." However, Nixon's belligerent 30 April speech announcing the Cambodian invasion signaled to many Americans an ominous escalation of the war, and protests erupted around the country. More than 100,000 antiwar protestors demonstrated in Washington on 9 May, joined for the first time by many politically moderate citizens. Within the administration, several prominent National Security Council officials resigned. The U.S. Senate, alarmed at Nixon's widening of the war without congressional consultation, overturned the Gulf of Tonkin Resolution by a vote of 85 to 10 in July.

Student antiwar demonstrations escalated to unprecedented proportions, providing startling scenes of social unrest. In May 1970, U.S. campuses experienced the most intensive period of protests in history, with demonstrations at 1,350 colleges and universities. On 4 May, after protesters burned down a Reserve Officers' Training Corps (ROTC) building at Kent State University in Ohio, National Guard troops fired on a crowd of demonstrators, killing four students and wounding nine. Ten days later, Mississippi police fired on unarmed black student protestors at Jackson State University, killing two and wounding twelve. Some commentators argue that the administration's bitter diatribes against protesters contributed to the shootings. In general, many public figures, both pro- and antiwar, raised fears of a collapse of social cohesion. Public outcry subsided in the summer after Nixon withdrew troops from Cambodia and announced continuing U.S. troop withdrawals from Vietnam. Although the details of the U.S. invasion plan remain disputed, Nixon apparently hastily limited the scope and duration of U.S. military operations in Cambodia after the alarmed response by the U.S. public.

BIBLIOGRAPHY

DAVIDSON, PHILLIP B. *Vietnam at War: The History, 1946–1975.* 1988.

KISSINGER, HENRY. *Years of Upheaval.* 1982.

SHAWCROSS, WILLIAM. *Sideshow: Kissinger, Nixon, and the Destruction of Cambodia.* 1979.

WELLS, TOM. *The War Within: America's Battle over Vietnam.* 1994.

ADAM LAND

Cam Ranh Bay. When the U.S. military buildup began, Saigon was South Vietnam's only modern port, and at times more than one hundred merchant ships lay offshore awaiting dock space. A natural harbor at Cam Ranh Bay in Khanh Hoa province was chosen as the site for a new deepwater port. Some 25,000 navy Seabees, army engineers, and civilians from the Raymond-Morrison-Knudson Corporation began work on the port in May 1965, and it opened by the end of the year. The port had prefabricated concrete piers, a 10,000-foot jet runway, warehouses, fuel storage tanks, cargo cranes, hospitals, and barracks. Cam Ranh Bay, the largest of six seaports the United States built in South Vietnam, fell to the North Vietnamese Army in 1975 and became a Soviet naval base in 1978.

BIBLIOGRAPHY

DUNN, CARROLL H. *Base Development in South Vietnam, 1965–1970.* 1972.

GREELEY, BRENDAN M., JR. "Soviets Extend Air, Sea Power with Buildup at Cam Ranh Bay." *Aviation Week,* 2 March 1987.

NAVAL FACILITIES ENGINEERING COMMAND. *Southeast Asia: Building the Bases.* 1975.

GLEN GENDZEL

Canada. Canada maintained official neutrality throughout the Vietnam War, neither openly criticizing U.S. policy nor providing war matériel. Beginning in 1964, Canada sent $9.3 million in development assistance to South Vietnam, most of it consisting of medical supplies and training. Canadian diplomats, including Prime Minister Lester Pearson, occasionally served as envoys between Washington, D.C., and Hanoi.

Canada was an original member of the International Control Commission (ICC) established in 1954 as part of the Geneva accords. In 1973, the Paris accords reconstituted the ICC as the International Commission for Control and Supervision (ICCS). Canada continued as a member, but withdrew in July 1973 because it believed that North Vietnam was undermining the ICCS and because it believed that Poland and Hungary—also members of the commission—were hindering accurate reporting of the military situation in South Vietnam.

The Canadian government estimated that 30,000 Americans fled to Canada to evade the draft during the war. At the same time, a Canadian parliamentary committee in 1967 estimated that 7,000 Canadians were serving with U.S. forces in Vietnam. In the early 1990s, however, Canadian veterans agi-

CAM RANH BAY, 1965. *National Archives*

tated for a memorial to honor their services, claiming that 30,000–40,000 Canadians had participated in the Vietnam conflict. The Canadian government rejected their request and refused to provide funds or land, insisting that it had not been a Canadian war.

BIBLIOGRAPHY

LARSEN, STANLEY ROBERT, and JAMES LAWTON COLLINS JR. *Allied Participation in Vietnam.* 1975.

SUMMERS, HARRY G., JR. *Vietnam War Almanac.* 1985.

ELLEN BAKER

Can Lao. Created in 1954, Can Lao Nhan Vi Cach Mang Dang (Revolutionary Personalist Labor party) was South Vietnamese president Ngo Dinh Diem's secret network of political supporters, organized and controlled by Diem's brother Ngo Dinh Nhu. Comprised mostly of highly placed Catholic refugees from the north, the Can Lao during the height of its powers had more than twenty thousand followers, who spied and killed on behalf of Diem and Nhu and were rewarded with payoffs and political favors. The organization disintegrated after the brothers were assassinated in November 1963.

BIBLIOGRAPHY

DUCANSON, DENNIS J. *Government and Revolution in Vietnam.* 1968.

DURBROW, ELBRIDGE. "Despatch from the Ambassador in Vietnam to the Department of State, 2 March 1959." U.S. Department of State. *Vietnam.* Vol. 1 of *Foreign Relations of the United States, 1958–1960.* 1986.

SCIGLIANO, ROBERT G. "Political Parties in South Vietnam under the Republic." *Pacific Affairs* 33 (December 1960).

SHAPLEN, ROBERT. *The Lost Revolution: The U.S. in Vietnam, 1946–1966.* Rev. ed. 1966.

GLEN GENDZEL

Cao Bang, province on the North Vietnamese–Chinese border. During a North Vietnamese offensive against French border positions in October 1950, French forces garrisoned in Cao Bang attempted to evacuate the area. Viet Minh knowledge of the French plans, combined with poor French strategy, which included an evacuation route through untracked jungle, resulted in the massacre of fleeing French troops by Gen. Vo Nguyen Giap's forces. The collapse of Cao Bang led the French to abandon Lang Son and several other important posts in the region, leaving valuable military equipment behind. These events greatly weakened the French position in the area.

BIBLIOGRAPHY

DAVIDSON, PHILLIP B. *Vietnam at War—The History: 1946–1975.* 1988.

KARNOW, STANLEY. *Vietnam: A History.* 1991.

SPECTOR, RONALD H. *United States Army in Vietnam—Advice and Support: The Early Years, 1941–1960.* 1983.

ELLEN D. GOLDLUST

Cao Dai. A South Vietnamese religious sect, the Cao Dai originated in the Tay Ninh area in the 1920s and was inaugurated as a formal religion in 1926. Beginning with 28 leaders and 247 followers, it grew rapidly, preaching that the principal founders of all great religions are incarnations of the one supreme God (Cao Dai). Because it draws on all faiths except Islam, it is considered the supreme religion by its followers. From Catholicism it adopted a hierarchical organization, the cathedral and the idea of universal love. It added female cardinals along with nuns and venerates as saints such leaders as Sun Yat-sen, Vietnamese prophet Trang Trinh, Joan of Arc, Victor Hugo, Buddha, Jesus, and Confucius. Its principal shrine, located at Tay Ninh City, consists of a large cathedral and administrative headquarters. The Cao Daists favored the Progressive Forces Alliance, a party opposed to President Ngo Dinh Diem's authoritarian rule, and its adherents formed a private army, resisting attempts by Diem's U.S. adviser Edward Lansdale to bribe them into compliance. Instead, they joined the Hoa Hao and the Binh Xuyen gang to oppose Diem militarily in 1955, but Diem's forces crushed them. After its defeat, the sect, though split into a dozen or more factions, continued to exist as a religion, numbering about 3 million adherents, declining to about 2 million by the mid 1970s. The government of the Socialist Republic of Vietnam formally recognized the sect as a religion in 1986, and it continues to exist in Tay Ninh.

BIBLIOGRAPHY

ELIADE, MIRCEA, ed. *The Encyclopedia of Religion.* 1987.

FITZGERALD, FRANCES. *Fire in the Lake: The Vietnamese and the Americans in Vietnam.* 1982.

KARNOW, STANLEY. *Vietnam: A History.* 1991.

SANDRA C. TAYLOR

Cao Van Vien (1921–), general, Army of the Republic of Vietnam (ARVN); chief, Joint General Staff, 1965–1975. Gen. Cao Van Vien retained the top military post in South Vietnam through numerous government upheavals. He belonged to the so-called Young Turks faction of ARVN officers who took power in 1964, and he was a close ally of President Thieu. Gen. William Westmoreland met weekly with Vien, who resisted U.S. pressure to reform the ARVN or to replace corrupt officers. Robert Komer, the top U.S. pacification adviser, nonetheless considered Vien "energetic, hardworking, very low-profile and self-effacing." He always made a good impression on Americans. Vien was the first to propose the disastrous withdrawal from the Central Highlands that led to communist victory in April 1975. After gaining asylum in the United States, Vien worked at the U.S. Army Center for Military History and became a U.S. citizen in 1982. "We did the very best we could," he said of the war.

BIBLIOGRAPHY

CAO VAN VIEN and DONG VAN KHUYEN. *Reflections on the Vietnam War.* 1980.
CAO VAN VIEN. *The Final Collapse.* 1983.

GLEN GENDZEL

Caravelle Group. A group of eighteen former South Vietnamese government leaders and politicians met at the Caravelle Hotel in Saigon in late April 1960 to demand reforms within Ngo Dinh Diem's government. These reforms included more democracy, civil rights guarantees, and recognition for political opponents, as well as economic reforms and an end to the corruption that pervaded Diem's government. Most members of the group were arrested following the unsuccessful November 1960 coup attempt.

BIBLIOGRAPHY

The Pentagon Papers: The Defense Department History of United States Decisionmaking on Vietnam. Senator Gravel Edition. Vol. 1. 1971.

VICTOR JEW

Carter, Jimmy (1924–), governor of Georgia, 1970–1976; U.S. president, 1977–1981. As governor, James Earl Carter backed President Nixon's Vietnam policy and urged his fellow governors not to oppose the war and undermine public support. He criti-

JIMMY CARTER. *Archive Photos*

cized the press for its handling of the My Lai massacre story. As a Democratic presidential candidate in 1976, however, Carter denounced the Vietnam War as "immoral" and "racist." Upon assuming the presidency in 1977 he issued a blanket pardon for draft resisters, an action he believed necessary to begin a national reconciliation process. He considered a pardon as "forgiveness" as opposed to amnesty, which would have implied government recognition of draft resistance as morally correct. Carter explored the possibility of normalization of relations with the Socialist Republic of Vietnam, but Vietnamese demands for war reparations, unacceptable to the United States, foreclosed such a policy change.

BIBLIOGRAPHY

CARTER, JIMMY. *Keeping Faith: Memoirs of a President.* 1982.
OLSON, JAMES, and RANDY ROBERTS. *Where the Domino Fell.* 1991.

KELLY EVANS-PFEIFER

Case, Clifford P. (1904–1982), U.S. senator (R-N.J.), 1954–1978; ranking Republican on the Senate Foreign Relations Committee. Case criticized the war from 1967 onward, arguing that the conflict represented an unwarranted extension of executive power, that the South Vietnamese government could not become viable as the U.S. military increasingly took over its responsibilities, and that the war could not be won without "the destruction of South Vietnam and much of American might itself."

BIBLIOGRAPHY

DOUTH, GEORGE. *Leaders in Profile: The U.S. Senate.* 1975. Obituary. *New York Times,* 7 March 1982, 9 March 1982.

ELLEN D. GOLDLUST

Castries, Christian de (1902–1991), French army officer; commander of French garrison at Dien Bien Phu, 1953–1954. A protégé of Gen. Henri Navarre, Colonel Castries was selected to take charge of French forces at Dien Bien Phu because the terrain appeared suitable for tank maneuvers, and Navarre believed French armor would win his desired set-piece battle. Colonel Castries had an impressive record as a tank commander during World War II, yet this experience proved worthless as Dien Bien Phu became a muddy siege with the French dug in to World War I–like trenches. While he was the wrong tactical choice, Castries proved to be the right inspirational leader needed by a besieged and beleaguered army. He commanded the affection and loyalty of the Algerian and Moroccan conscripts in the French forces who believed Castries would never abandon them. Christian de Castries, who received a battlefield promotion from colonel to brigadier general at Dien Bien Phu, stayed with his men and was taken prisoner when the garrison fell in May 1954.

BIBLIOGRAPHY

KARNOW, STANLEY. *Vietnam: A History.* 1991.
New York Times Biographical Service. July 1991.
ROY, JULES. *The Battle of Dienbienphu.* 1963.

VICTOR JEW

Casualties. Casualties in war are traditionally defined as military personnel killed, wounded, or missing in action (MIA). The exact figures will never be known, but by that definition Vietnam War casualties 1945–1975 totaled at least 1.75 million deaths for all participants and more than twice that many wounded. Civilian casualties were even higher. Estimates of Vietnamese civilian deaths dur-

ing the U.S. phase of the war include some 300,000 South Vietnamese killed by both sides and 65,000 North Vietnamese killed by U.S. bombs. Tens of thousands of North Vietnamese peasants executed in the land redistribution campaign of 1954–1956 must be added to the total, as must at least 2 million Cambodians killed by the Khmer Rouge regime during 1975–1978 and many tens of thousands of boat people who died at sea fleeing Vietnam in the wake of the North Vietnamese victory. Laotian civilian losses to U.S. bombs and antiguerrilla operations accounted for tens of thousands as well. All these figures are controversial.

The causes and effects of military casualties in Vietnam differed for the various sides and from those of previous conflicts. Some 51 percent of U.S. Army combat deaths were caused by small arms fire, more than from any other cause; 35 percent were caused by fragments from artillery and mortar shells, rockets, and grenades. In contrast, during World War II and the Korean War only about one-third of combat deaths were caused by small arms fire, while shell fragments accounted for more than one-half. The same considerations apply to the Marine Corps, which also suffered a higher proportion of combat deaths from small arms fire, 41 percent, than it had in World War II or the Korean War. The shift is attributable partly to the increased effectiveness of rapid-fire infantry weapons, notably the AK-47, and partly to vastly improved medical care for combat casualties. Reflecting the guerrilla aspect of the war, the proportion of U.S. Army deaths caused by mines and booby traps was three times that of World War II and the Korean War, but still amounted to only 11 percent. The dreaded punji pits (camouflaged pits containing sharpened, excrement-smeared stakes) had no statistical effect on U.S. Army deaths and caused only 2 percent of wounds. About 18 percent of U.S. fatalities were from causes other than enemy action including disease, auto accidents, airplane crashes, friendly fire, homicide, suicide, and drug overdose.

U.S. casualties included 304,000 wounded, but helicopter battlefield casualty evacuation and prompt medical care saved the lives of tens of thousands who would have died in any previous conflict. Some 74,000 of them survived as quadriplegics or multiple amputees. Not all wounds were physical, and post-traumatic stress disorder (PTSD), called shell shock in World War II, received unprecedented attention during and after the conflict. While there is no evidence that PTSD was different in nature or

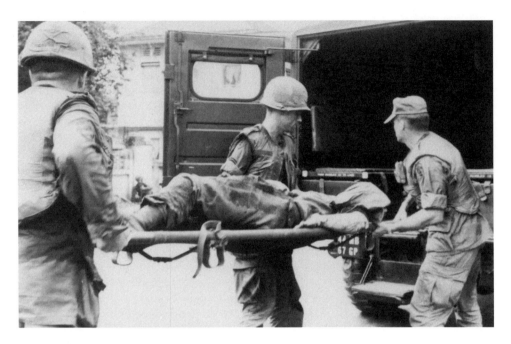

A LOST COMRADE. The body of a U.S. soldier is shipped out after being removed from the wreckage of a U.S. bachelor officers' quarters in Saigon attacked by Viet Cong during the Tet Offensive, 1968. *National Archives*

more common than in previous conflicts, the indifferent or hostile reception that many veterans received on their return to the United States may have exacerbated its effects.

Casualty figures for the Viet Minh during 1945–1954 and for North Vietnamese and Viet Cong forces, 1960–1975, are unreliable. Official records are not open to inspection; estimates of guerrilla casualties are notoriously unreliable because the distinction between combatant, civilian porter, and innocent bystander was rarely clear; and the numbers were manipulated by both sides. In early 1969, Gen. Vo Nguyen Giap told a Western journalist that the People's Army of Vietnam (PAVN) had lost 500,000 soldiers since 1964. A conservative estimate would add to that number at least 300,000 Viet Minh killed during the 1945–1954 period, and the PAVN sustained heavy casualties subsequently, particularly in the 1972 Easter Offensive. Pathet Lao and Khmer Rouge casualties numbered in the tens of thousands, but no reliable estimates are available. A high proportion of communist casualties were caused by fragments, blast, and flame produced by aerial munitions and artillery shells; medical care was limited and many communist soldiers died from wounds and diseases

that U.S. and allied forces, supported by an elaborate medical infrastructure, would have survived.

During 1945–1954, France and its Indochinese client states lost 94,581 military personnel killed and 78,127 wounded. The United States lost 58,159 killed, including 8 women, and 304,000 wounded during 1959–1975. The Republic of Vietnam Armed Forces (RVNAF) suffered some 224,000 killed and more than 1 million wounded, excluding losses in the final, victorious North Vietnamese offensive for which figures are unavailable. The Royal Laotian Army and its Central Intelligence Agency–supported guerrilla auxiliaries lost many thousands in the undeclared war in Laos, as did regular and irregular Thai forces fighting there. Though there are no reliable estimates, casualties in the 1970–1975 Cambodian civil war were heavy on both sides.

U.S. casualties became a focal point for opposition to the war in America as the number of casualties, the rate at which they were sustained, and the groups that incurred them changed dramatically with changes in policy. Between 1959 and the overt commitment of ground combat troops to South Vietnam in March 1965, fewer than 500 U.S. servicemen were killed in action in Southeast Asia, almost all of whom were professionals who had volunteered to serve there. As the scale and intensity of combat increased, casualties mounted dramatically and changed in incidence. During 1968–1969, 300 or more servicemen were killed in a single week on occasion, and in April 1969 the total reached 33,641, surpassing the total number killed in the Korean War. At the same time, the burden shifted from mature, professional noncommissioned officers (NCOs) and officers to low-ranking enlisted men in their teens and early twenties. The demographic profile of those most likely to be killed or wounded in Vietnam became a hotly debated issue in U.S. politics, with antiwar activists claiming that those most at risk were poor, poorly educated young draftees and that ethnic minorities, particularly African Americans, were overrepresented. There were elements of truth in this portrayal. The statistics on the youth of the U.S. Army and Marine Corps enlisted men who took the brunt of the casualties are shocking: 40 percent of enlisted marines and 16 percent of enlisted army personnel killed in Vietnam were teenagers and 70 percent of all American enlisted casualties were twenty-one years of age or younger. Of army and marine enlisted deaths, 50.2 percent were privates and lance corporals, amounting to 41.0 percent of all U.S. service personnel killed. The same age bias applied to army and marine officers: 50 percent of army and marine officer fatalities were first lieutenants or below and twenty-four or younger. African Americans comprised only about 11.0 percent of the young male population in the United States, but sustained 14.1 percent of enlisted casualties, and Hispanics were overrepresented as well. Draftees comprised only a bare majority of army enlisted deaths, 50.5 percent, and no less than 91.9 percent of enlisted marines killed in action were volunteers. In the aggregate, volunteers comprised 63.6 percent of enlisted deaths, and the figure rises to 70 percent when officers, 13.5 percent of the total, are included. Nearly two-thirds of enlisted personnel who served during the Vietnam War had high school diplomas, a higher proportion than that for World War II or the Korean War, and the vast majority of commissioned officer casualties had college degrees. Catholics, 25 percent of the U.S. population, suffered disproportionately, accounting for 28.9 percent of fatalities.

The U.S. Air Force and Navy casualty profiles were very different from those of the U.S. Army and Marine Corps. The air force lost more officers than enlisted men and the median officer rank of the casualty was captain; more majors were killed than first lieutenants, as were nearly as many lieutenant colonels and colonels. The navy lost more enlisted men than officers, many of them young medical corpsmen serving with the marines, but the navy officer casualty profile was similar to that of the air force, with aviators predominating and more lieutenant commanders and commanders killed in action than lieutenants.

BIBLIOGRAPHY

ABBOTT, WILLIAM F. "The Names on the Wall, a Closer Look: A Sociological Analysis and Commentary on Our 58,152 Vietnam Casualties." Based on the Department of Defense Southeast Asia Combat Area Casualties File (CACF) in the National Archives. 1992.

DAVIDSON, PHILLIP B. *Vietnam at War: The History, 1946–1975.* 1988.

FALL, BERNARD. *Hell in a Very Small Place: The Siege of Dien Bien Phu.* 1967.

FALL, BERNARD. *Street without Joy.* 1964.

KAHIN, GEORGE MCT. *Intervention: How America Became Involved in Vietnam.* 1986.

SUMMERS, HARRY G., JR. *Vietnam War Almanac.* 1985.

JOHN F. GUILMARTIN JR. AND
KELLY EVANS-PFEIFER

Catholics. Roman Catholics were the most organized religious group in South Vietnam during the years of the Vietnam War. During President Ngo Dinh Diem's rule, from 1954 until 1963, Roman Catholicism dominated politics and government. Diem's brother, Ngo Dinh Thuc, the archbishop of Hue, was an important leader of the South Vietnamese Catholic clergy. Diem knew that Catholics were a key constituency for his government, and he cultivated their support with political patronage and business favors. Catholics, although a minority of the population, held the prominent political and military appointments in the Diem regime. They also tended to be better educated and wealthier than most of the country. Catholics' privileged position in South Vietnam increasingly alienated the majority Buddhist population.

Beneficiaries of Diem's favor included many anticommunist, pro-Western Catholics who had left North Vietnam after the Geneva Accords of 1954 to live in South Vietnam. Fearing religious persecution by the communist government of North Vietnam, almost 700,000 Catholics relocated, and many commentators insisted that these refugees had "voted with their feet," choosing "democracy" over communism. Most Catholic northerners were peasants, and entire villages migrated south, often led by the local priest. This population influx increased the number of Catholics in South Vietnam from 461,000 to 1,137,000, or one in every 9.6 inhabitants, and laid a strong foundation for the Diem regime and for the war against the Viet Cong guerrillas.

Diem also established ties with such Catholics in the United States as Senators Mike Mansfield and John F. Kennedy and Cardinal Francis Joseph Spellman. These and other U.S. Catholics helped form the "Vietnam Lobby," which advocated support for Diem's government and, later, U.S. military intervention in Vietnam.

After the military coup against Diem and his assassination in 1963, Catholic influence in South Vietnam waned, although Catholics retained important positions in military, government, and civilian life. They remained a critical political force throughout the 1960s, often countering Buddhist activism and ensuring Catholic representation in the government of South Vietnam. With the fall of Saigon in 1975, many Catholics close to the government fled Vietnam.

BIBLIOGRAPHY

FitzGerald, Frances. *Fire in the Lake: The Vietnamese and the Americans in Vietnam.* 1982.
Hammer, Ellen. *Vietnam: Yesterday and Today.* 1966.
Wiesner, Louis A. *Victims and Survivors: Displaced Persons and Other War Victims in Viet-Nam, 1954–1975.* 1988.

Jennifer Frost

Catonsville Nine. *See* Berrigan Brothers.

Central Highlands, Isolated plateau at southern end of Truong Son Mountains in west-central South Vietnam, called Cao Nguyen Trung Phan, or Central Highlands. This region stretches from Darlac province in the north to Kontum province in the south and covers about 52,000 square kilometers (20,000 square miles) of tropical and bamboo forest interspersed with tea, tobacco, and coffee plantations. The principal towns are Dak To, Kontum, Pleiku, and Ban Me Thuot. Few Vietnamese settled the region despite centuries of colonization efforts, and the predominant ethnic groups are the Rhade and the Jarai. These seminomadic native inhabitants of the Central Highlands were called *montagnards*

(highlanders) by the French and *moi* (savages) or *ngoui thuong* (hillbillies) by the Vietnamese. An estimated 200,000 out of 800,000 highland tribesmen died during the Vietnam War, and most of the survivors became refugees.

Strategically vital to the defense of South Vietnam and the exit point for several spurs off the Ho Chi Minh Trail, the Central Highlands were the scene of fierce fighting during the war. Beginning in 1962, the U.S. Army Special Forces organized highlanders into Civilian Irregular Defense Groups (CIDGs) to screen South Vietnam against border infiltration along the Ho Chi Minh Trail. Viet Cong guerrilla attacks on Pleiku triggered the first large-scale U.S. bombing of North Vietnam in February 1965. In October 1965, the U.S. Army 1st Cavalry Division stopped a major North Vietnamese Army (NVA) offensive across the Central Highlands. Desperate battles around Kontum and heavy U.S. bombing blunted the NVA's Easter Offensive in 1972. North Vietnam's final offensive began with an armored thrust against Ban Me Thuot in March 1975, and South Vietnamese army defenses crumbled rapidly after withdrawing from the Central Highlands. Although promised autonomy by the communists, the montagnards since the war have been forced into villages, their leaders sent to reeducation camps, and their lands given to resettled Vietnamese.

BIBLIOGRAPHY

Hickey, Gerald C. *Free in the Forest: Ethnohistory of the Vietnamese Central Highlands, 1954–1976.* 1982.
Kelly, Francis J. *U.S. Army Special Forces, 1961–1971.* 1973.
Smith, Harvey H., et al. *Area Handbook for South Vietnam.* 1967.
Stanton, Shelby L. *The Green Berets at War.* 1985.
Turley, G. H. *The Easter Offensive, Vietnam, 1972.* 1985.

Glen Gendzel

Central Intelligence Agency. The primary function of the U.S. Central Intelligence Agency (CIA) is to give the president accurate, apolitical intelligence about the rest of the world. In Vietnam the CIA was heavily involved in intelligence-gathering and clandestine activities. During the war the agency sought to provide the president with information about the size, nature, and goals of the North Vietnamese government and the National Liberation Front (NLF) and to determine their intentions. The U.S. intelligence effort in Indochina was the largest in any one area since World War II; however, by the end of the Vietnam War, covert operations far surpassed the agency's intelligence-gathering efforts.

Early Involvement. U.S. intelligence operations in Indochina began in 1943 when the CIA's World War II predecessor, the Office of Strategic Services (OSS), worked to rescue downed U.S. aviators in the Japanese-occupied French colonies. The OSS also cooperated with the communist-led Viet Minh to harass and overthrow the Japanese. By 1945, OSS officer Archimedes Patti was so impressed with the leadership abilities of Ho Chi Minh that he encouraged the Vietnamese nationalist to seek U.S. assistance in ousting the French. Although French rule had been harsh, to President Harry S. Truman and his advisers Ho was indisputably a communist and therefore on the wrong side of the emerging Cold War, and so Ho's overtures went unanswered.

Although the OSS contributed leadership, certain precedents, and a penchant for action to the CIA, it was a wartime clandestine organization that ended in 1945. The CIA, established in 1947 by a provision of the National Security Act, was a direct descendent of the OSS and the Central Intelligence Group, an interim agency. The new agency encountered significant opposition based on fears that the CIA would become a domestic Gestapo and on suspicions generated by OSS director William "Wild Bill" Donovan's cloak-and-dagger image. The CIA also faced hostility from Federal Bureau of Investigation (FBI) director J. Edgar Hoover over a possible conflict of missions between the two agencies.

Critics and Champions. The agency's role in the Vietnam War was controversial both during the war and after the U.S. withdrawal. To its critics, which included disaffected employees, notably Victor Marchetti, John Marks, Frank McGehee, and Frank Snepp, it was a super-spy agency that specialized in assassinations, operated outside the mandate of its charter, and often charted its own course. Obsessed with the containment of communism, it conducted a secret war in Laos, using planes from Air America (its own airline) piloted by mercenaries who knowingly smuggled opium into South Vietnam. Because its budget was secret and its personnel, both regular employees and contract agents, were often unknown (at least in the United States), it could conduct covert operations without public scrutiny.

The agency's wartime activities were championed by some, perhaps none more vocal than William Colby, who spent sixteen years involved with the war and served as director of central intelligence (DCI) from 1973 to 1976. He believed that the United States failed in its efforts in Vietnam because of mistakes made by U.S. presidents and the Pentagon, and that the war was won, militarily, in 1972, only to be lost or abandoned in 1975. Opinions about the performance of the CIA break roughly along the lines of radicals disillusioned about the conduct of the war and moderates or conservatives, such as Colby, who believed that the war was "just" and that the end—victory—justified the means.

Political and military aspects of the war clearly raised differences of opinion between the CIA chiefs of station in Saigon and leaders of the Military Assistance Command, Vietnam (MACV). Gen. William Westmoreland preferred to fight the war by conventional means rather than with the self-defense techniques preferred by the CIA. Some activities, such as the Phoenix program, outraged antiwar activists in the United States, who considered it a CIA assassination plot. Presidents Lyndon Johnson and Richard Nixon personally distrusted the agency and both often ignored the information it provided and the results of its activities. Since the DCIs were frequently the bearers of bad news, they were isolated from the decision-making process. Johnson did not involve the DCIs in his "Tuesday luncheons" at which policy was determined, and Nixon continued that pattern. As a result, directors began to shape their intelligence to reflect the wishes of the president rather than the realities of the unsuccessful war.

An outline of the CIA's activities illustrates its successes and failures. During Dwight D. Eisenhower's presidency, it provided accurate intelligence, especially following France's defeat at Dien Bien Phu. After Ngo Dinh Diem became prime minister of the South, most agency analysts believed that he had little chance of victory in an election against Ho Chi Minh if elections to reunite the country were held in 1956, as specified at the Geneva Conference in 1954. The Saigon Military Mission, a CIA offshoot headed by Col. Edward J. Lansdale and Lucien Conein, aided Diem in establishing control. They covertly conducted heavy propaganda campaigns in the North and sabotage operations in Hanoi in a successful effort to encourage Catholics to flee to the South, thereby supposedly demonstrating communism's unpopularity and giving the Catholic Diem a large base of popular support. A group of Michigan State University professors, which included CIA intelligence officers, advised Diem on domestic and internal security affairs. The Vietnam CIA station was also involved in removing French influence and helping to create a new, anticommunist government under Diem. By the end of his administration Eisenhower was more concerned about the communist subversion in Laos than he was about that in Vietnam, where nation-building seemed to be successful.

President John F. Kennedy also distrusted the CIA, partly because it had failed to overthrow Fidel Castro in Cuba. He fired DCI Allen Dulles and appointed a new director in 1962. At first ignoring Vietnam in favor of Laos, by mid 1963 Kennedy was advised that the South Vietnamese government was on the verge of failure because of internal dissension. Furthermore, the president was told that Diem and his brother Ngo Dinh Nhu were ineffectually conducting the war and perhaps even considering negotiating with North Vietnam. Ambassador Henry Cabot Lodge recommended that the United States support a coup to remove the Ngo brothers; the CIA's Saigon station chief, John Richardson, and William Colby, however, supported Diem, citing his anticommunist achievements. The agency was not directly involved in the coup, but Conein was the liaison between U.S. embassy personnel, U.S. officials in Washington, and the Vietnamese plotters, who would not have proceeded without tacit U.S. approval and assurances of continued U.S. support of the South. Colby later considered the Ngo brothers' ouster and subsequent deaths one of the biggest errors the United States made in the war.

Conduct of the War. Although the CIA was not a policy-making body, its personnel held strong views about the conduct of the Vietnam War, views increasingly at variance with those of the president and top military leaders. President Lyndon Johnson disliked the agency, and he distrusted CIA intelligence as well as its views on how to win the "hearts and minds" of the Vietnamese people. The Civilian Irregular Defense Group (CIDG), created in 1961, was a case in point. The Coordinated Studies Group (which included CIA, Agency for International Development [AID], and U.S. Special Forces personnel) armed and assisted montagnard tribes, such as the Sre and Rhade, in the Central Highlands. These minority peoples hated the Vietnamese generally and

communists in particular, and they were eager defenders of their own lands. The CIA directed the CIDG until 1964, when MACV assumed control. The CIDG program and similar efforts collapsed with the Americanization of the war, as conventional military operations replaced programs like that of the CIDG, which aided local people in defending themselves. People's Action Teams, composed of small groups of peasants, and Revolutionary Development Teams likewise were CIA-inspired. The decision to emphasize conventional military actions run by Americans eventually undermined and doomed such self-defense efforts.

Pacification, nominally the task of the Army of the Republic of Vietnam (ARVN), continued to involve the CIA. To counter assassinations and intimidation by Viet Cong guerrillas, the CIA organized South Vietnamese teams to use similar methods and to "fight terror with terror." The various operations used groups with innocuous-sounding names such as Provincial Reconnaissance Units. Although members of such units were encouraged to use discipline and arrests rather than arbitrary killings, the perceived need to root out the Viet Cong Infrastructure (VCI) led to the creation of the infamous Phoenix program (Phuong Hoang). Organized in 1967 by the Office of Civil Operations and Revolutionary Development Support (CORDS), which coordinated all pacification attempts, the Phoenix program intimately involved CIA personnel. CORDS was a joint MACV-CIA organization working with Vietnamese Central Intelligence. (Like many other South Vietnamese government operations, it was patterned after a U.S. institution.) Through Phoenix the CIA obtained intelligence from CORDS interrogation centers, while the manpower ostensibly came from the South Vietnamese police and military. The program, although not directly run by the CIA, was linked to it by the American public, and Colby, who worked with CORDS and then served as deputy to the commander of MACV, was labeled a murderer by the public when he was nominated as DCI in 1973.

In its activities the CIA failed to penetrate the National Liberation Front (NLF) or the government of the Democratic Republic of Vietnam (DRV). It did, however, infiltrate the South Vietnamese government—as did the NLF. At the height of the war, more than one thousand personnel were employed by the agency in Saigon, with two to three times that many contract agents. Many Vietnamese CIA operatives were double agents, also serving the communists. Snepp estimated that 36 percent of the CIA's employees were involved in clandestine operations in 1974.

Problems of Credibility. CIA personnel became divided into two camps: prowar "hawks" and antiwar or antiescalation "doves," as were U.S. politicians and the American public. Initially opposed to aerial bombing of North Vietnam as a means of destroying the DRV's warmaking capacity, the agency reversed itself and issued a study in March 1966 that supported such bombing. This report advocated levels of bombing that would surpass Johnson's policy of restricting targets to military ones. But the negative reports of George A. Carver Jr., the CIA's special assistant for Vietnam, disillusioned Secretary of Defense Robert McNamara, who turned increasingly against escalation of the war. Johnson, who rejected CIA advice he did not wish to hear, decided not to escalate the air war. Similarly, intelligence officer Samuel Adams refused to accept the military's assessment of the communist military's order of battle, which he believed was far too optimistic. Adams took his complaint directly to Richard Helms. Helms did not argue the issue of communist military strength with President Johnson, but the 1968 Tet Offensive demonstrated the fallibility of the intelligence gathered on the situation in Vietnam. The agency's failure to accurately predict the timing and scale of an event it knew was eventually coming represented an intelligence disaster of the magnitude of Pearl Harbor. Helms's deference and fear of bringing bad tidings to Johnson damaged both the president's and the agency's credibility. The U.S. public was given its first glimpse of the conflicts between the agency and the military only in 1984, when Gen. William Westmoreland sued CBS News over a documentary based on Adams' allegations that Westmoreland had deliberately lowered estimates of North Vietnamese and Viet Cong troop strength before the Tet Offensive to strengthen the U.S. military's claims of progress in the war.

The agency's performance rating may have reached bottom in 1968, but its credibility was not rebuilt under Richard Nixon. Like Lyndon Johnson, Nixon disliked the agency, although he reluctantly retained Helms as DCI. Believing that the CIA was rife with effete, soft "ivy league liberals" and that it had been in part responsible for his loss of the 1960 election to Kennedy, Nixon, like Johnson, excluded Helms from policy discussions. Material in the leaked *Pentagon Papers,* however, portrayed the CIA

as more often right than wrong because its analysts had attempted to warn the administration from the outset that an air war would not destroy North Vietnam's will to resist. Nixon, who intended to pursue the bombing strategy, was annoyed, and when the CIA opposed his decision to escalate the war in Laos by increased aerial bombardment, he overruled it. In 1969 Nixon refused to allow Green Berets working for the CIA to testify in the murder case of a Vietnamese double agent; again the agency's reputation suffered.

The CIA was also involved in the war in Cambodia. Covert operations had been carried out in that country since the late 1950s. Following its mandate of strong opposition to communism and neutralism, the agency penetrated a right-wing group, the Khmer Serei, and encouraged the overthrow of Prince Norodom Sihanouk. The prince expelled the CIA from the country but later allowed it to return. Sihanouk was convinced the CIA had plotted his overthrow and wrote a memoir, *At War with the CIA,* when he was deposed in 1969. Although the agency was apparently innocent in this matter, its intelligence on Cambodia suffered from the same unreality as in Vietnam. Helms suppressed an intelligence report that indicated that the U.S. invasion of Cambodia would not prevent the North Vietnamese from continuing the war. When Helms, who wished to avoid antagonizing national security adviser Henry Kissinger, learned of the proposed invasion he did not even inform the CIA's special assistant for Vietnam, George Carver. Nixon's Cambodian incursion failed in its objectives, widened the war, and touched off demonstrations on college campuses throughout the United States.

The CIA was involved in the worst intelligence failures of the Vietnam War: the misjudgment regarding the size and locations of the Tet Offensive of 1968 and the failure to recognize that North Vietnam, the People's Republic of China, and the Soviet Union were using the Cambodian port of Sihanoukville as a major supply port for the Viet Cong and Khmer Rouge. The CIA, although not asked to write a national intelligence estimate (NIE) on the strength of People's Army of Vietnam (PAVN) forces in southern Laos, was nonetheless blamed by Nixon for the failure of Operation LAM SON 719, which targeted the Ho Chi Minh Trail in Laos. The American public was outraged most by the revelation of Operation Chaos, begun in 1967 by Helms on Johnson's orders to uncover possible foreign involvement in the domestic antiwar movement. Chaos included penetration of antiwar groups and provocation of acts of violence against antiwar groups in the United States, a violation of the CIA charter. Chaos was terminated in 1972 and made public in 1973. By the early 1970s the low morale within the agency over Operations Phoenix and Chaos, censorship of a book critical of the CIA by former CIA employees Victor Marchetti and John Marks, and the involvement of former CIA employees in the Watergate break-in precipitated a crisis. Nixon dismissed Helms when the DCI was reluctant to involve the agency in the Watergate coverup. James R. Schlesinger Jr., his successor, began a process of reform but was quickly moved to head the Defense Department and was succeeded as DCI by William Colby. Revelations about the agency's "family jewels" (propriatory corporations, such as Air America), its illegal domestic operations, plus the dismissal of some 1,500 employees (the bulk of whom were in operations) led to further internal reforms and changes.

The CIA's final days in Saigon were filled with ignominy. As Saigon was collapsing, station chief Tom Polgar and Ambassador Graham Martin failed to report to President Gerald Ford that the Thieu government would be unable to resist the North Vietnamese military campaign. According to former CIA employee Frank Snepp, this needlessly jeopardized thousands of Vietnamese who had worked for the agency, which did not even have time to destroy its files before fleeing Saigon. Events during the Vietnam War and the resulting internal feuds within the CIA left it significantly weakened and demoralized throughout the 1970s.

BIBLIOGRAPHY

BLUM, WILLIAM. *The CIA: A Forgotten History*. 1986.

COLBY, WILLIAM. *Honorable Men: My Life in the CIA*. 1978.

COLBY, WILLIAM, with JAMES MCCARGER. *Lost Victory*. 1989.

DESILVA, PEER. *Sub Rosa: The CIA and the Uses of Intelligence*. 1978.

JEFFREYS-JONES, RHODRI. *The CIA and the American Democracy*. 1989.

JOHNSON, LOCH K. *A Season of Inquiry: The Senate Intelligence Investigation*. 1985.

LEARY, WILLIAM M., ed. *The Central Intelligence Agency: History and Documents*. 1984.

MARCHETTI, VICTOR, and JOHN D. MARKS. *The CIA and the Cult of Intelligence*. 1980.

POWERS, THOMAS. *The Man Who Kept the Secrets: Richard Helms and the CIA*. 1979.

RANELAGH, JOHN. *The Agency: The Rise and Decline of the CIA*. 1987.

TROY, THOMAS F. *Donovan and the CIA*. 1981.

SANDRA C. TAYLOR

Central Office for South Vietnam (COSVN).

COSVN originated in 1961 when the southern and central branches of the Lao Dong Party (Vietnam Workers' Party) merged. The group was designated the Central Committee Directorate for the South, but Americans mistranslated the name as Central Office for South Vietnam. An advance element of the Communist Party's Central Committee, COSVN's purpose was to direct the People's Liberation Armed Force (the military arm of the National Liberation Front [NLF], or Viet Cong guerrillas) in the South. COSVN was first headed by Nguyen Van Linh, who had spent most of his career in the South; then Nguyen Chi Thanh, a northerner, assumed command in 1964, reflecting the NLF's expectation of military conflict with the United States.

In reality COSVN was no more than a mobile leadership group, but U.S. military leaders believed it to be a fixed headquarters with a bureaucratic structure that could be located and destroyed, presumably crippling the communist war effort in the South. Operating on this assumption, U.S. strategists, who believed COSVN to be located in Laos and later in Cambodia, launched several operations to destroy it, beginning with Operation JUNCTION CITY in 1967. Two years later, Gen. Creighton Abrams requested a short "surgical" B-52 strike against the Cambodian area known as the Fishook, where he believed COSVN was located—bombing that escalated into the sustained bombing campaign Operation MENU. In 1970, President Nixon authorized an incursion into Cambodia by 48,000 U.S. and 32,000 South Vietnamese troops, with the avowed purpose of destroying COSVN. Occupying a prominent place as a frequent subject of U.S. strategy and thinking, COSVN served to justify U.S. military operations in Cambodia, but the U.S. military never succeeded in locating or destroying it.

BIBLIOGRAPHY

ISAACS, ARNOLD R. *Without Honor: Defeat in Vietnam and Cambodia*. 1983.

TURLEY, WILLIAM S. *The Second Indochina War: A Short Political and Military History, 1954–1975*. 1986.

PAUL M. TAILLON

Chapman, Leonard (1913–), U.S. Marine Corps commandant, 1968–1971. Chapman, the first artillery officer to head the marines, served as commandant while U.S. forces were withdrawn from Southeast Asia under Richard Nixon's policy of Vietnamization. In 1968, largely in response to racial incidents on U.S. Marine bases in the United States, Chapman initiated programs to improve race relations in the corps. These policies included investigating discrimination against blacks in promotion and discipline matters and permitting the display of black cultural symbols. As commandant, Chapman maintained the corps' strict standards on drugs and discipline matters, even as other military services relaxed disciplinary regulations. Chapman also took advantage of the down-sizing of the corps to put through 15,000 administrative discharges for marines considered marginally competent. After Chapman's retirement as commandant on 31 December 1971, Nixon appointed him commissioner of immigration and naturalization, a post he held until May 1977.

BIBLIOGRAPHY

MOSKIN, J. ROBERT. *The U.S. Marine Corps Story.* 1982.
New York Times, 4 September 1969; 1 December 1971.
Washington Post, 22 May 1971; 1 December 1971.

ELLEN D. GOLDLUST AND ADAM LAND

Chemical Warfare. The use of riot control agents (RCAs) and herbicides by the United States in Southeast Asia during the Vietnam War was possibly the largest use of chemicals in combat, even though technically and legally the United States did not wage chemical warfare (CW). Consistent with its declared policy since World War II, the United States did not use lethal agents; however, semantic disputes characterized the propaganda war that was waged by all participants in the conflict. In November 1961—one month before the first herbicide operations and while the United States prepared an information program for peasants in target areas—Radio Hanoi charged that South Vietnam was using poison gas against crops. Documents captured from Viet Cong guerrillas showed that North Vietnam was aware of covert herbicide tests that had been carried out by the United States and planned to exploit these tests in a propaganda campaign; similarly, they had capitalized on U.S. warnings to peasants in herbicide target areas, publicizing them in propaganda efforts. As a result of this North Vietnamese

propaganda, various nations and private groups, including the philosopher and pacifist Bertrand Russell's so-called International War Crimes Tribunal, accused the United States of chemical or biological warfare. The U.S. government denied the charges, stating that the chemicals used were neither lethal agents nor agents proscribed under the Geneva Protocol of 1925 (which the United States did not sign until 1975); nor did they meet any clearly accepted definition of chemical weapons in international law. RCAs, originally developed for use by domestic police, temporarily incapacitate victims by suddenly causing crying, vomiting, coughing, sneezing, and combinations of these symptoms. More than fifty countries acknowledged that their police forces routinely used these agents. The United States, moreover, argued that these agents prevented casualties among noncombatants and even among North Vietnamese and Viet Cong forces, who sometimes surrendered when under attack with RCAs in circumstances in which lethal firepower would otherwise be needed. Critics responded that U.S. operations were actually chemical warfare because they produced deaths both directly and indirectly. Victims suffocated from lethal concentrations that built up in caves or tunnels, and at times RCAs were used to drive opposing forces into the open for attack with conventional weapons.

Herbicides. Herbicides were the first chemical agents used in the Vietnam War. In 1961, the Kennedy administration considered herbicidal operations in Vietnam as a measure of its commitment to the Diem government. These operations were conceived as part of Project Agile, commissioned to develop counterinsurgency techniques. The administration delayed the program until November for fear of adverse public reaction and doubts about the Diem government's concern for the welfare of the montagnards, who would be most affected. Even then herbicides were used only when and where they were clearly linked to ground operations, although tests were carried out to create "fire breaks" or open areas along South Vietnam's borders in August under the Advanced Research Projects Agency (ARPA). Operational flights to deliver defoliants began in January 1962, under the code name Operation RANCH HAND, and continued sporadically until January 1971. Separate crop-destruction missions, flown by the Vietnamese air force, began in October 1962. During the peak year of 1967, RANCH HAND involved 6,847 sorties, used 4.8 million gallons of herbicide, defoliated 1.2 million

DEFOLIATION. A U.S. Air Force C-123 sprays herbicides along a South Vietnamese highway, c. 1966. The spray from another airplane can be seen at right. *Archive Photos*

acres, and destroyed 60,000 hectares (148,000 acres) of crops.

Operation RANCH HAND suffered from a host of problems as U.S. government agencies wrangled over policy. Production and funding shortfalls led to using cheaper agents, including Agent Orange (so named for the color of a band that marked the drums, not for the color of the agent). The government also preempted civilian purchases of herbicides, the first preemption of a commercial product since that on nylon during World War II. Qualified pilots, adequate equipment and support, and protective escort flights were scarce. Ground commanders, who feared endangering their troops, sometimes banned RANCH HAND operations from their areas. RANCH HAND units also were often di-

verted to airlift, training, insecticide-spraying, flare- and leaflet-dropping, and even baiting North Vietnamese and Viet Cong gunners. The 1,200 RANCH HAND volunteers were the most shot-at and decorated U.S. Air Force unit in Vietnam; most of the decorations were Purple Hearts for wounds inflicted by small-arms ground fire. About 2 percent of all herbicides were applied around U.S. base perimeters by truck-mounted "buffalo turbines," improvised helicopter rigs, and backpack sprayers. The U.S. Navy also sprayed herbicides along riverbanks.

Tear Agents. During 1963–1964 the U.S. Army procured about 180 tons of CS powder, an RCA that is a powerful tear agent, for use in Southeast Asia. As with herbicides, it was used sparingly and cautiously at first, but soon became routine and widespread. CS was first used after a battle in early 1964 that had resulted in casualties among women and children, who had been used as shields by Viet Cong guerrillas. In December 1964, CS grenades were air-dropped in an attempt to rescue prisoners. In February 1965, the Military Assistance Command, Vietnam (MACV) authorized defensive-only use of RCAs. U.S. Marines used it in September after they discovered Viet Cong forces with women and children present in bunkers, tunnels, and "spider holes." The marines successfully captured about four hundred people without causing any serious injuries. In October Gen. William Westmoreland delegated authority for CS use to field commanders; and the next month MACV removed all previous restraints. By February 1966 the Department of Defense authorized use of RCAs to force the enemy out of shelters just before bombing raids. Tactics to clear tunnels included using powerful blowers to force CS into tunnels, which rendered them unusable for up to six months. CH-47 helicopters with improvised racks dropped 80-pound drums of CS with explosive burster charges on infiltration routes, rest areas, and base camps. Exploding bags of CS in enemy rice caches made food unusable. RCAs were used to defend perimeters, counter ambushes, prepare landing zones, and restrict terrain. The value of RCAs for close-in fighting was proved during the 1968 Tet Offensive.

Smoke. Chemical smokes were used for signaling and for concealment, as well as more innovative ways. Unlike in World War II, there were no large-area smoke operations; only one smoke generator company went to Vietnam. Small-scale uses for concealment, surprise, and tactical deception were common. The XM-52 smoke generator, "Smokey the Bear," was improvised to inject fog oil into helicopter exhaust, which created a dense white cloud that blocked visibility from the ground for up to eleven minutes. This technique was used to mask landing zones for assaults and medical evacuations. Artillery shell- and rocket warhead-delivered smoke produced great quantities suddenly and added the

SMOKE SCREEN. A U.S. Army UH-1 "Huey" lays down a smoke screen along a tree line on the edge of a landing zone, 11 May 1968. *Archive Photos*

burning effects of white phosphorous. Soldiers forced smoke into tunnels to locate hidden exits and to map tunnel complexes.

Flame Weapons. Conventional flame and flame field expedients (FFEs) produced casualties and had psychological effects. Vehicle-mounted flamethrowers were useful for attacking bunkers and tunnels but were a failure for clearing landing zones due to the dense jungle. Man-portable flamethrowers were used by both sides, though infrequently. In November 1967 a portable flamethrower was used by the North Vietnamese in an attack on a perimeter; two years later North Vietnamese soldiers were found with Soviet-made flamethrowers. In 1969 the U.S. Army developed the XM191 Flash flame projector, whose four rockets gave the soldier the ability to attack with flame but from a distance. A common FFE was the 55-gallon drum of napalm, or jellied gasoline, set to detonate by standard triggering devices. Exclusively deployed by U.S. Army Chemical Corps soldiers, FFEs in perimeter defenses for fire bases and remote outposts produced casualties, provided early warning of attack, lit the battlefield, and channeled attackers' movements into range of small-arms and machine-gun fire. Techniques were also devised to drop 55-gallon drums from helicopters onto suspected North Vietnamese Army (NVA) and Viet Cong locations, weapons caches, and potential landing zones. During April–May 1970, the 101st Airborne Division dropped 2,000 such drums. As in World War II and the Korean War, the marines used napalm for close ground support and in attempts to ignite grass and jungle vegetation. In November 1967 General Westmoreland ordered herbicide spraying to kill vegetation in the Iron Triangle to prepare it for wholesale burning. After the area was doused with gasoline, incendiary bombs and napalm ignited it. The effort failed, however, because the smoke from the fire caused a cloudburst that extinguished the flames. After the Tet Offensive of 1968, there were even attempts by the U.S. military to sow seeds of "American grass"—a coarse, dry type—from the air to enhance burning.

The Controversy over Chemical Agents. The issue of U.S. chemical activities in Vietnam became more persistent than the agents themselves, despite U.S. government efforts to prevent even an appearance that could be construed as chemical warfare. Fears existed that even the use of RCAs might encourage other countries to seek and use chemical weapons, and a study in 1969 concluded that that had likely happened. Efforts to deal with adverse reactions both domestically and abroad led U.S. administrations, beginning with that of President Nixon, to try to offset criticisms with efforts toward disarmament. In December 1969 the U.N. General Assembly resolved that any use of chemical warfare—including herbicides—violated international law. The United States rejected the resolution as outside the scope of the General Assembly; but in August 1971 the United States and the Soviet Union jointly submitted a draft ban on biological weapons. This draft led to bilateral chemical disarmament in the late 1980s. In 1975, President Ford prohibited the military use of RCAs outside the United States except under very special conditions or with presidential approval. In 1975 the U.S. Senate finally ratified the 1925 Geneva Protocol.

The use of chemicals—especially herbicides—in Vietnam inadvertently fueled the environmental movement. In 1962 Rachel Carson's *Silent Spring* sensitized the public to the dangers pesticides posed to the environment. That sensitivity was heightened by the numerous scientific, political, economic, and moral issues associated with wartime defoliation and crop destruction. Scientific criticism, Defense Department–sponsored studies, and even senior military reviews raised such questions. By 1969 possible links between herbicide exposure and veterans' health problems led to the banning of the main ingredient in the herbicides in use, suspension of the herbicide operations, renewed efforts to ratify the 1925 Geneva Protocol, and an independent review of herbicide use by the American Academy for the Advancement of Science. The last U.S. military herbicides were destroyed in 1977, the same year that the publicity of veterans' illnesses led to formation of several lobbying groups. The controversy over exposures, associated diseases and genetic effects, and liabilities led to an out-of-court settlement in 1984 between the manufacturers of the herbicides and the veterans' groups. The $180-million settlement provided an average of about $1,000 per veteran. In 1985 the U.S. government committed an additional $1 billion to related research.

BIBLIOGRAPHY

ADAMS, VALERIE. *Chemical Warfare, Chemical Disarmament.* 1990.

CECIL, PAUL F. *Herbicidal Warfare: The RANCH HAND Project in Vietnam.* 1986.

GOUGH, MICHAEL. *Dioxin, Agent Orange: The Facts.* 1986.

MANGOLD, TOM, and JOHN PENNYCATE. *The Tunnels of Cu Chi: The Untold Story of Vietnam.* 1985.

NEILANDS, J. B., G. H. ORIANS, E. W. PFEIFFER, ALJE VENNEMA, and ARTHUR H. WESTING. *Harvest of Death: Chemical Warfare in Vietnam and Cambodia.* 1972.

READ, RICHARD D. *Low-Intensity Conflict: A Chemical Corps Role?* 1989.

STOCKHOLM INTERNATIONAL PEACE RESEARCH INSTITUTE (SIPRI). *Ecological Consequences of the Second Indochina War.* 1976.

THOMAS, ANN VAN WYNEN, and A. J. THOMAS JR. *Legal Limits on the Use of Chemical and Biological Weapons: International Law, 1899–1970.* 1970.

JAMES W. WILLIAMS

Chennault, Anna (1925–), Chinese-born wife of "Flying Tigers" General Claire Chennault; friend and Washington, D.C., contact of South Vietnamese president Nguyen Van Thieu. Working with U.S. presidential candidate Richard M. Nixon's representatives, Chennault boosted Nixon's electoral chances in the 1968 U.S. presidential campaign when she successfully urged Thieu to delay committing to and attending the Paris peace talks.

ANNA CHENNAULT. With Richard M. Nixon and Henry Kissinger, 1971. *Richard Nixon Library*

BIBLIOGRAPHY

CHENNAULT, ANNA. *The Education of Anna.* 1980.

NGUYEN TIEN HUNG, and JERROLD L. SCHECTER. *The Palace File.* 1986.

JENNIFER FROST

Chicago Seven. The August 1968 Democratic National Convention held in Chicago attracted many antiwar protestors and violence erupted. Months later, on 29 March 1969, eight men were indicted in Federal court for conspiring and traveling over state lines to incite rioting at the convention. These eight men, the "Chicago Eight," were David Dellinger, a veteran pacifist and chairman of the New Mobe; founders of Students for a Democratic Society (SDS), Tom Hayden and Rennie Davis; Yippie organizers Abbie Hoffman and Jerry Rubin; academics Lee Weiner and John Froines; and Black Panther leader Bobby Seale.

The trial, which began in September 1969, attracted national attention. All defendants except Seale made public appearances during the trial, which was the target of several protests. The trial was a raucous spectacle marked by indecorous outbursts as the defendants and defense attorneys William Kuntsler and Leonard Weinglass sparred with the antagonistic Federal Judge Julius Hoffman. Hoffman found the defendants and attorneys in contempt 175 times.

Seale, in particular, was demonstrative because his ill lawyer was unavailable and Hoffman would not let him represent himself. After several courtroom outbursts, Hoffman had Seale bound and gagged. In November, Seale's case was severed from the others, leaving the "Chicago Seven."

In February 1970, Weiner and Froines were acquitted; the other defendants were convicted only of traveling over state boundaries to riot. The convictions, and most of the contempt charges, were overturned on appeal because of the inappropriate behavior of Judge Hoffman and prosecutors.

While the trial drew attention to Federal attempts to quell protests, the defendants' confrontational antics exacerbated tensions within the antiwar movement between peaceful moderates and the more radical elements.

BIBLIOGRAPHY

EPSTEIN, JASON. *The Great Conspiracy Trial: An Essay on Law, Liberty, and the Constitution.* 1970.

UNREST DURING THE TRIAL. Demonstrators attack a Chicago police captain during the trial of the Chicago Eight, 24 September 1969. *National Archives*

ZAROULIS, NANCY, and SULLIVAN, GERALD. *Who Spoke Up? American Protest against the War in Vietnam, 1963–1975.* 1984.

WILLIAM PAUL SCHUCK

China, People's Republic of (PRC).
From its longstanding tributary relationship with Imperial China, Vietnam was familiar with the Chinese threat to its independence and national identity. Beginning in the late nineteenth century, however, both countries suffered from incursions of Western imperialism, a development that established the basis for the collaboration between Vietnamese and Chinese peoples in their struggle against a mutual enemy as well as for the cooperation between the Communist parties of the two countries. As Vietnam's northern neighbor and one of the two largest socialist countries after World War II, the People's Republic of China (PRC) provided significant support to the Vietnamese communists following 1949.

The Potsdam Conference in 1945 authorized Nationalist Chinese troops to disarm the Japanese in Vietnam, but the Nationalist Chinese withdrew the next year, following an agreement with France. The PRC, in 1950, became the first country to recognize the Democratic Republic of Vietnam (DRV) under the leadership of Ho Chi Minh. After Ho Chi Minh's secret visit to Beijing in January 1950, the PRC dispatched a military advisory mission under Gen. Wei Guoqing, a training team led by Vice Minister of Defense Chen Geng, and a political advisory group of administrative experts headed by Lo Guibo. They helped the Vietnamese forces, now armed with weapons from China, to drive the French out of the border region and to win the battle at Dien Bien Phu.

In 1954, Premier Zhou Enlai of China led a concerted effort by the PRC, the Soviet Union, and the DRV at the Geneva Conference to arrange the French withdrawal from Indochina. After that, however, the PRC and the Soviet Union differed in their views on unifying Vietnam. The Soviet Union advocated peaceful coexistence between North and South Vietnam, while PRC leaders believed that unification of Vietnam could be realized only through protracted military struggle rather than through general elections. Despite reservations about the timing of armed struggle against the South Vietnamese government of Ngo Dinh Diem, the PRC became the first country to recognize the National Liberation Front (NLF) in South Vietnam. In 1961, Chairman

Mao Zedong told DRV Premier Pham Van Dong that the PRC was determined to support the NLF. At the request of Ho Chi Minh, the PRC provided 90,000 guns in 1962 and supplied most of the weapons for the armed forces of the South Vietnamese communists. The PRC also helped build a transport line to South Vietnam through Cambodia and a secret port on Hainan Island to ship supplies. China annually provided approximately $10 million of foreign currency for the guerrilla war in South Vietnam.

The PRC reacted strongly to the U.S. government's escalation of its role in the Vietnam War in February 1965. Mao Zedong and Zhou Enlai led a protest rally of more than 1 million people in Beijing, and the PRC government warned that "aggression against the DRV is aggression against China." At the request of Le Duan, head of the Vietnamese delegation to the PRC in April 1965, the PRC and the DRV signed an agreement to send Chinese air defense, engineering, railroad, and support troops to assist North Vietnam. The PRC government claimed that a total of 320,000 of its troops

served in Vietnam between January 1965 and July 1970, and that more than 1,000 died on Vietnamese soil. Moreover, the military aid from China accounted for probably 70 percent of the physical quantity of total military aid to North Vietnam, even though Chinese aid represented only 25 percent of the aid's total monetary value. The total value of PRC aid between 1949 and 1979 was estimated at $20 billion.

When Soviet leader Leonid Brezhnev appealed for "united action" by the socialist countries to assist the DRV in 1965, the PRC rejected the Soviet request for an air corridor over Chinese territory and the use of Chinese airfields to send military assistance to Vietnam; it did, however, give the USSR transit rights to ship arms by railroad. The PRC's resistance to the Soviet requests reflected partly the Sino-Soviet split and partly the Chinese view that the Soviet proposals violated Chinese sovereignty. This resistance increased the DRV's discontent with China. Moreover, as a result of the increase of Soviet involvement in Vietnam, and the impact of the Cultural Revolution in China, the

CHINESE DELEGATES AT GENEVA. PRC prime minister Zhou Enlai meets with his negotiating team. From left: Wang Chia Shiang, a vice minister of foreign affairs; unidentified; Zhou Enlai; Hsu Chin, chief interpreter; Wang Ping Nan, the delegation's chief of protocol and secretary general; Chang Wen Tien, a vice minister of foreign affairs; unidentified; and Li Ke Nung, a vice minister of foreign affairs. *National Archives*

PRC government did not support the early negotiations between the U.S. and the DRV in Paris, especially when the DRV announced the negotiations without advance notice to the PRC in 1968. But Mao Zedong told Pham Van Dong that he agreed with Vietnamese policy—to fight as well as to negotiate.

When the United States and the PRC began efforts to improve relations in 1971, the PRC for the first time since 1965 officially endorsed a DRV peace plan to end the Vietnam War. The action, however, aroused suspicion in the DRV, even though Zhou Enlai and Vice Premier Li Xiannian visited North Vietnam to offer explanations. Zhou even announced that the Indochina conflict was one of four major obstacles in the way of normalizing relations between the United States and the PRC. In fact, Chinese aid to North Vietnam continued in large quantities. After the 1973 Paris peace accords, Mao told Le Duan that despite the withdrawal of U.S. troops, South Vietnam's large military forces had to be dealt with "by war." Consequently, the PRC continued to provide substantial support to the DRV.

Although the PRC contributed greatly to the North Vietnamese victory, the Sino-Soviet-U.S. strategic triangle, as well as regional rivalries, complicated Sino-Vietnamese relations during this period. After the end of the Vietnam War, those relations deteriorated rapidly because of Vietnam's invasion of Cambodia and territorial disputes between Vietnam and the PRC. In 1979, Deng Xiaoping and other post-Mao Chinese leaders decided to "teach Vietnam a lesson" with a short, punitive border war. The conflict was inconclusive, and tensions between the two nations continued. In 1989, both nations took steps to begin a dialogue at the vice–foreign ministerial level. After a summit of the two countries' new leaders in Beijing in 1991, relations between China and Vietnam were normalized.

BIBLIOGRAPHY

CHEN, MIN. *The Strategic Triangle and Regional Conflicts: Lessons from the Indochina Wars.* 1992.

DUIKER, WILLIAM J. *China and Vietnam: The Roots of Conflict.* 1986.

TAYLOR, JAY. *China and Southeast Asia: Peking's Relations with Revolutionary Movements.* 1976.

HAN TIE

China, Republic of (Taiwan).

In 1956 Ngo Dinh Diem, in an effort to consolidate his control over South Vietnam, dissolved the *bangs*—a centuries-old form of self-government by Chinese nationals living in South Vietnam—and forbade foreign nationals from engaging in eleven key areas of the economy. Because many Chinese Nationalists were involved in those sectors of the economy, Taiwan retaliated by placing an embargo on rice exports and refused to lend money to the South Vietnamese.

Nevertheless, in the 1960s Taiwan sought a role in the Vietnam War in order to increase its legitimacy and enhance its status with the United States. The United States, fearing retaliation by the People's Republic of China (PRC) in the Straits of Formosa, kept Taiwan's involvement to a minimum. In October 1964 the Republic of China Military Assistance Advisory Group, Vietnam (RCMAAGV), went to South Vietnam to assist with political warfare, medical work, and the refugee situation; by 1965 the group included agricultural experts and engineers. Taiwan provided $3 million in economic and technical aid to South Vietnam between 1964 and 1970 and donated 5,000 tons of rice immediately following the 1968 Tet Offensive.

In June 1966 Gen. William Westmoreland decided that Chinese Nationalist troop participation would be militarily advantageous, but officials at the U.S. embassy in Saigon considered it politically unwise. The U.S. Military Assistance Command, Vietnam (MACV), and the RCMAAGV signed a military working agreement in December 1968 whereby the Free World Military Assistance Policy Council supervised the Chinese Nationalists, but under the direct command of a military commander designated by the Republic of China.

BIBLIOGRAPHY

LARSEN, STANLEY ROBERT, and JAMES LAWTON COLLINS JR. *Allied Participation in Vietnam.* 1975.

ELLEN BAKER

Christmas Bombings. See LINEBACKER and LINEBACKER II.

Church, Frank

(1924–1984), U.S. senator (D.-Idaho), 1957–1981; chairman, Senate Intelligence Committee, 1975–1976. An outspoken liberal, Sen. Frank Church was the fourth senator to turn against the Vietnam War in 1965. He cosponsored the Cooper-Church amendment in 1970 and the Case-Church amendment in 1973, both intended to cut off funding for the war. Church's investigation of U.S. intelligence agencies in the mid 1970s revealed rampant abuses in the wake of the Vietnam War. After a strong run for the presidency in 1976, Church lost his bid for reelection to the Senate in 1980.

BIBLIOGRAPHY

CHURCH, F. FORRESTER. *Father and Son: A Personal Biography of Senator Frank Church of Idaho by His Son.* 1985.

"The Making of a Muckraker." *The Economist* 258 (14 February 1976).

NAUGHTON, JAMES M. "Head of C.I.A. Inquiry: Frank Forrester Church." *New York Times,* 30 January 1975.

GLEN GENDZEL

CINCPAC. *See* Commander-in-Chief, Pacific (CINCPAC).

Civilian Irregular Defense Groups (CIDGs). To protect South Vietnam's western border in the remote Central Highlands, Col. Gilbert B. Layton of the Central Intelligence Agency (CIA) began training local self-defense units of montagnard tribesmen in 1961. U.S. Army Special Forces took over the program in 1963, reorganizing the village defense units into Civilian Irregular Defense Groups (CIDGs) under Operation SWITCHBACK. CIDGs conducted border surveillance from isolated mountain camps and defended against Viet Cong guerrilla infiltration or North Vietnamese Army (NVA) attack. The tribesmen, traditional objects of Vietnamese ethnic hatred, valued the CIDG program as protection from South Vietnam as well as from North Vietnam. They received salaries, medical care, and development aid. Soon the CIDGs showed more loyalty to their Green Beret patrons than to President Diem, who sent his own Luc Luong Dac Biet (LLDB) special forces officers to take nominal command in 1963.

MONTAGNARD STRIKE FORCE IN THE CENTRAL HIGHLANDS. *National Archives*

About forty thousand tribesmen eventually joined the CIDGs, and Green Berets led them on increasingly far-ranging missions. CIDGs were reorganized into mobile-strike or "Mike Force" battalions in 1965 so that the camps could lend mutual support when attacked.

The CIDG program was controversial. Although the CIDGs successfully defended their villages, they did not prevent infiltration into South Vietnam. U.S. commanders complained that the CIDGs drained highly trained U.S. manpower for static defense rather than for aggressive search-and-destroy missions, which were preferred by the Military Assistance Command, Vietnam (MACV). Gen. Bruce Palmer, army commander in Vietnam, considered the CIDGs a "dubious asset." South Vietnam's rulers in Saigon blamed the CIDGs for encouraging montagnard separatism and the FULRO (Front Unifié pour la Lutte des Races Opprimées) uprisings against the government in 1964–1965. As the Green Berets withdrew under Vietnamization in 1970–1971, the Saigon regime incorporated the CIDGs into the Army of the Republic of Vietnam (ARVN), and renewed ethnic strife led some former CIDGs to defect to the communists during the Spring Offensive in 1975.

BIBLIOGRAPHY

KELLY, FRANCIS J. *U.S. Army Special Forces, 1961–1971.* 1973.
SHACKLETON, RONALD A. *Village Defense: Initial Special Forces Operations in Vietnam.* 1975.
SIMPSON, CHARLES M. *Inside the Green Berets: The First Thirty Years.* 1983.
STANTON, SHELBY L. *The Green Berets at War.* 1986.
STIRES, FREDERICK H. *The U.S. Special Forces C.I.D.G. Mission in Vietnam.* 1964.

GLEN GENDZEL

Clark, Ramsey (1927–), deputy assistant attorney general, U.S. Department of Justice, 1965–1967; attorney general, 1967–1969. Son of Supreme Court justice Tom Clark, Ramsey Clark served as U.S. attorney general under President Lyndon Johnson. By 1967, Clark had privately become a peace advocate, drawing the ire of Johnson administration officials. Clark resisted policies to repress the antiwar movement, despite pressure from the administration and congressional sources. As acting attorney general in 1966, he opposed a proposal by the Selective Service system to induct draft resisters quickly into military service in Vietnam. He later allowed large, potentially violent demonstrations—including the 1967 March on the Pentagon—rather than repress such protests under his authority to prevent civil disorders. Clark also had limited enthusiasm for domestic intelligence against the antiwar movement, such as wiretapping of the telephones of peace activists. Federal Bureau of Investigation (FBI) chief J. Edgar Hoover, nominally under Clark's authority, independently pursued many of those programs at Johnson's behest.

In 1968, under pressure from the administration to move against draft resisters, Clark indicted several prominent antiwar figures, including Dr. Benjamin Spock and the Reverend William Sloan Coffin, for conspiracy to promote violation of draft laws. Clark deliberately targeted the perceived ringleaders of the resistance effort. The subsequent trial, despite a guilty verdict, worked in part to promote the peace movement by giving a broad public forum for the most articulate activists. After successful appeals by the defendants, the Justice Department dropped the charges against them.

After leaving office in 1969, Clark publicly joined the antiwar movement. In 1971, he represented Vietnam Veterans against the War (VVAW) in legal efforts to obtain permission for demonstrations in Washington, D.C. Clark toured North Vietnam in 1972 in a highly publicized survey of war damage, noting that North Vietnam had been "bombed back to the 17th century." In the early 1990s, Clark actively opposed U.S. policy in the Persian Gulf, forming the group Coalition to Stop US Intervention. In 1991 he visited Iraq and reported that U.S. air raids caused extensive civilian casualties.

BIBLIOGRAPHY

WELLS, TOM. *The War Within: America's Battle over Vietnam.* 1994.

ADAM LAND

Claymore Mines. The claymore mine is an antipersonnel mine designed to emit a fan-shaped spray of fragments about three feet above the ground when detonated. These mines were carried by infantry and were commonly used by U.S. forces during the Vietnam War to defend static positions. Viet Cong forces who captured claymores used them for booby traps.

BIBLIOGRAPHY

QUICK, JOHN. *Dictionary of Weapons and Military Terms.* 1973.
SHAFRITZ, JAY M., TODD J. A. SHAFRITZ, and DAVID B. ROBERTSON. *The Facts on File Dictionary of Military Science* 1989.

ELLEN D. GOLDLUST

Clear and Hold.

The clear-and-hold strategy emphasized population security in South Vietnam over battle attrition of North Vietnamese and Viet Cong forces. Not all strategists expected General Westmoreland's search-and-destroy tactics to win the Vietnam War. British counterinsurgency expert Sir Robert Thompson first recommended clear-and-hold tactics in 1961. Static defense of villages cleared of North Vietnamese or Viet Cong troops, he suggested, would deprive the Viet Cong guerrillas of their power base by emphasizing population security over battle attrition. Rather than chase insurgents in the jungle, U.S. forces should defend populated areas, where government officials and aid workers could operate safely. A secure population might prove more loyal to the South Vietnamese government. But U.S. commanders relegated such pacification chores to South Vietnamese forces, concentrating instead on pursuing the elusive enemy. Search and destroy remained the object of three out of four U.S. ground combat missions until 1968. U.S. Marines, however, practiced clear-and-hold tactics in I Corps with Combined Action Platoons (CAP) from 1966 to 1971.

BIBLIOGRAPHY

KREPINEVICH, ANDREW F., JR. *The Army and Vietnam.* 1986.
SCOVILLE, THOMAS W. *Reorganizing for Pacification Support.* 1982.
SHEEHAN, NEIL, ed. *The Pentagon Papers.* 1971.
WESTMORELAND, WILLIAM C. *A Soldier Reports.* 1976.

GLEN GENDZEL

Cleland, Joseph Maxwell

(1942–), captain, U.S. Army, 1967–1968; head of the Veterans Administration (VA), 1977–1981. A highly decorated triple amputee who was wounded in action near Khe Sanh, Max Cleland became the first Vietnam veteran to head the VA. He vowed to root out "bureaucratic rigor mortis" and stop the agency from treating Vietnam veterans as "social misfits." Cleland expanded counseling services, opened drug and al-

cohol treatment centers, and helped organize Vietnam Veterans Week in 1979. He was less successful, however, at expanding GI Bill benefits for veterans, and he continued the VA's official policy of denying most Agent Orange disability claims.

BIBLIOGRAPHY

BONIOR, DAVID E., STEVEN M. CHAMPLIN, and TIMOTHY S. KOLLY. *The Vietnam Veteran: A History of Neglect.* 1984.
CLELAND, MAX. "Raw Deal for Vietnam Vets?" *U.S. News and World Report,* 29 May 1978.
CLELAND, MAX. *Strong at the Broken Places: A Personal Story.* 1980.

GLEN GENDZEL

Clergy and Laity Concerned About Vietnam (CALCAV).

In October 1965, antiwar American clergymen organized an ad hoc committee that evolved into Clergy and Laity Concerned About Vietnam (CALCAV). Composed largely of liberal Protestants with some Jewish and Roman Catholic members, CALCAV was a moderate, mainstream, national organization. Using peaceful methods, CALCAV advanced a moral critique of the war. Some of its members, however, later turned to more extreme measures of arson and vandalism.

BIBLIOGRAPHY

HALL, MITCHELL K. *Because of Their Faith: CALCAV and Religious Opposition to the Vietnam War.* 1990.

WILLIAM PAUL SCHUCK

Clifford, Clark

(1906–), adviser to President Johnson; secretary of defense, 1968–1969. Clifford was deeply involved with Vietnam policy, from the initial combat troop commitment through escalation and the beginning of disengagement. Clifford's changing views on the war—at times favoring escalation, at other times, favoring withdrawal—in many ways mirrored those of the American public.

Clifford first participated in Vietnam policy deliberations in 1965 when President Johnson debated sending combat troops, a significant expansion of the U.S. involvement in Vietnam. Clifford joined Undersecretary of State George Ball as one of the few Johnson advisers to argue against such escalation. He felt the war might be unwinnable and questioned whether Vietnam's strategic importance warranted U.S. military commitment.

CLARK CLIFFORD. At right, with Walt Whitman Rostow. *Lyndon Baines Johnson Library*

After the combat troop deployment and escalation began, Clifford supported the effort and believed that the United States must take all steps necessary to ensure quick victory. Throughout 1966 and 1967, Clifford, bolstered by optimistic briefings by U.S. military officials, advised against bombing halts, which he thought would be viewed by North Vietnamese officials as a sign of weakness and therefore would not lead to negotiations. As one of the "wise men," Clifford supported further escalation and urged Johnson to stay the course.

When a disillusioned Robert MacNamara stepped down as secretary of defense in 1968, Johnson appointed Clifford his successor, believing Clifford would loyally back his Vietnam policies. Clifford, however, began to have doubts. When the military requested 206,000 additional troops after the Tet Offensive, Paul Warnke, Townsend Hoopes, and others at the Pentagon presented Clifford with their bleak assessment of U.S. involvement in Vietnam and the chances for a southern victory—concerns that the military could not adequately alleviate in Clifford's mind. Clifford became convinced that the United States must withdraw its forces from Vietnam, and he tried to persuade Johnson of the wisdom of such a course.

Knowing that many of the "wise men" had changed their views in the wake of the Tet Offensive, Clifford scheduled a historic meeting between the group and Johnson. Nearly all the "wise men"

shared Clifford's conviction that disengagement was the best policy option. Johnson felt betrayed by Clifford but was deeply affected nonetheless by Clifford and his other long-time advisers' belief in the war's futility. Shortly after the meeting Johnson denied the military's request for more troops and stunned the nation with his decision not to seek a second term. Clifford spent the last months of Johnson's presidency laying the groundwork for U.S. withdrawal and Vietnamization of the war, and he urged Nixon to ensure that all U.S. troops were out of Vietnam by 1970.

BIBLIOGRAPHY

CLIFFORD, CLARK. *Counsel to the President: A Memoir.* 1991.
HERRING, GEORGE C. *America's Longest War: The United States and Vietnam, 1950–1975.* 1986.
KARNOW, STANLEY. *Vietnam: A History.* 1991.

KELLY EVANS-PFEIFER

Clinton, Bill (1946–), governor of Arkansas, 1979–1981, 1983–1992, president of the United States, 1993–. The turmoil of the Vietnam War era reemerged as an issue during Bill (William Jefferson) Clinton's presidential campaign and early administration. In the late 1960s, Clinton played a minor role organizing antiwar demonstrations as a Rhodes scholar in England and, after losing his college draft deferment, avoided military induction in unusual circumstances. Clinton received a draft induction notice while at Oxford in 1968, though after the reporting date had passed. He subsequently obtained a temporary deferment from Arkansas draft officials. In the fall of 1969 after briefly committing to join the Reserve Officers' Training Corps, he put himself up for the draft. By this time the government had cut back military induction. Clinton received a high lottery number, assuring he would not be called into service.

Clinton's Vietnam record became a liability to the candidate when, before the New Hampshire primary, the national media obtained a 1969 Clinton letter to Arkansas draft officials in which he expressed opposition to the war and thanked them for "saving" him from the draft the previous year. Clinton's public statements before his presidential bid had downplayed his antiwar activities. The media seized upon the apparent inconsistencies in Clinton's account as well as on evidence of his uncertain draft status, escalating the issue into a widely debated, national controversy. Clinton's opponents attempted to use his record to impugn the candidate's honesty and character, though as polling research confirmed, the issue did not prove a decisive factor for most voters in either the Democratic primaries or general election.

Clinton's Vietnam record continued to affect his presidency. He suffered from strained relations with the armed forces, exacerbated in part by some military officials' resentment of the president's activities in the 1960s. As part of an effort to expand foreign markets for American businesses, Clinton ended the nineteen-year trade embargo on Vietnam by executive order on 3 February 1994. Recognizing his political vulnerability, the president gathered bipartisan support in Congress for the policy and emphasized Vietnam's cooperation on the issue of U.S. soldiers still listed as missing-in-action (MIA). The enduring controversy erupted perhaps most dramatically on Memorial Day 1993 when, at the Vietnam Veterans Memorial, some protesters and veterans jeered the president as he honored U.S. soldiers who died in the war. Clinton's Memorial Day speech was the first official visit by a U.S. president to the Vietnam Veterans Memorial, which was completed in 1982.

BIBLIOGRAPHY

ALLEN, CHARLES F., and JONATHON PORTIS. *The Comeback Kid: The Life and Career of Bill Clinton.* 1992.

APPLEBOME, PETER. "Clinton Draft Issue Doesn't Sway Most in Georgia." *New York Times,* 4 March 1992.

KELLY, MICHAEL, and DAVID JOHNSTON. "Campaign Focus on Vietnam Reviving Debates on the 1960s." *New York Times,* 9 October 1992.

ADAM LAND

BILL CLINTON. *The White House*

Cluster Bomb, an assembly of smaller bombs dropped from the air. After the cluster bomb is released, the cluster bomb subunits—usually fragmentation or incendiary bombs—separate and fall individually, broadening the area of impact. A U.S. innovation during the Vietnam War, these weapons were used mainly against personnel, but antitank and fuel-air (which create exploding concussive gaseous clouds) varieties were also deployed.

BIBLIOGRAPHY

DOLEMAN, EDGAR C., JR. *The Vietnam Experience: Tools of War.* 1984.

QUICK, JOHN. *Dictionary of Weapons and Military Terms.* 1973.

SHAFRITZ, JAY M., TODD J. A. SHAFRITZ, and DAVID B. ROBERTSON. *The Facts on File Dictionary of Military Science.* 1989.

ELLEN D. GOLDLUST

Coast Guard, U.S. South Vietnam had over 1,950 kilometers (1,200 miles) of coastline with at least 60,000 junks and sampans plying the waters of the South China Sea. During the Vietnam War, the U.S. Navy's first task was to prevent north to south infiltration of men and supplies by sea. Coastal surveillance and interdiction has always been a primary mission of the U.S. Coast Guard, and President Johnson ordered the first Coast Guard patrol boats to Vietnam in May 1965. They joined U.S. and South Vietnamese units of the Coastal Surveillance Force in Operation MARKET TIME, which closed down the sea infiltration route from North Vietnam and forced the North Vietnamese to shift their supply operations to the Ho Chi Minh Trail and to Cambodian ports. Coast Guard Squadron One began in Vietnam with fifty officers, two hundred enlisted men, and seventeen 83-foot patrol boats in 1965, adding nine more boats in 1966. As requirements for U.S. naval gunfire support increased, Coast Guard Squadron Three was formed in May 1967, consisting of five cutters armed with 5-inch guns. U.S. Coast Guard units patrolled the entire South Vietnamese coast from bases in Da Nang, Qui Nhon, Nha Trang, Vung Tau, and An Thoi. They confiscated hundreds of tons of supplies, performed six thousand fire support mis-

sions, and also provided such vital services as port security, explosives handling, sea rescue, navigation, and training. Coast Guardsmen in Vietnam suffered seven killed, fifty-three wounded, and one missing in action. As part of Vietnamization in 1971, the Coast Guard turned over all patrol boats and four cutters to South Vietnam.

BIBLIOGRAPHY

KAPLAN, H. R. "Coast Guard Played Vital Role in Viet War." *Navy* (November 1970): 31–34.
TULICH, EUGENE N. *The United States Coast Guard in South East Asia during the Vietnam Conflict.* 1975.

GLEN GENDZEL

Coffin, William Sloane (1924–), chaplain, Yale University, 1958–1975. A leading opponent of the Vietnam War, Coffin was an important founding member of the group that became Clergy and Laity Concerned About Vietnam (CALCAV). He was convicted with Dr. Benjamin Spock in 1968 for conspiring to encourage resistance to Selective Service laws, though the verdict was reversed on appeal and charges against both men were later dropped.

INTERDICTION AT SEA. Near the mouth of the Co Chien river, a Coast Guard cutter stands by as a communist trawler burns. The ship was intercepted while attempting to smuggle 250 tons of supplies to Viet Cong forces. *U.S. Navy*

BIBLIOGRAPHY

COFFIN, WILLIAM SLOANE, JR. *Once to Every Man: A Memoir.* 1977.
HALL, MITCHELL K. *Because of Their Faith: CALCAV and Religious Opposition to the Vietnam War.* 1990.

WILLIAM PAUL SCHUCK

COINTELPRO. *See* Federal Bureau of Investigation; Justice, Department of.

Colby, William (1920–), station chief, Central Intelligence Agency (CIA), Saigon, 1959–1962; deputy director, Civil Operations and Revolutionary Development Support (CORDS), 1968; director, the Phoenix program, 1969; director, CIA, 1973–1976. Colby entered intelligence work during World War II, serving in Europe with the Office of Strategic Services (OSS). After the war he served in Italy and Sweden, advancing in the newly created CIA through the Directorate for Plans. He arrived in Vietnam in 1959, serving as station chief in Saigon from 1959 to 1962. Chief of the CIA's Far East Division following the Saigon assignment, he remained involved with the Vietnam War until its end in 1975.

Colby strongly supported President Ngo Dinh Diem, although he urged Diem to curb his authoritarian ways. Colby worked with Diem's brother Nhu to conceive the Strategic Hamlet program, which he thought could maintain and protect a noncommunist population. He considered Diem's ouster and murder a grave mistake, and he thought that U.S. encouragement of the coup was the first of a series of errors made by the U.S. presidents and the Pentagon that led to the U.S. defeat.

In firm opposition to officials of the Military Assistance Command, Vietnam (MACV), Colby opposed the use of massive military force, which he felt alienated the Vietnamese people. He believed that pacification and the use of Vietnamese civilian defense forces, aided and supported by the CIA and Green Berets, would have been a more successful approach. In theory the Phoenix program, which Colby took over from Robert Komer, epitomized the type of approach he espoused. Phoenix was operated through the Agency for International Development (AID), and the manpower for it was supplied by the South Vietnamese. The program involved detaining and questioning individuals who were identified as Viet Cong by at least three different sources. Suspects were to be questioned only, but

Colby later conceded that 20,587 deaths had been recorded in connection with the program. (Other estimates were twice as high.) Although he staunchly denied charges that he allowed Phoenix to become an assassination program for personal vendettas, he and the Phoenix program became a focal point for the antiwar movement's opposition to the conflict.

Colby claimed that the Army of the Republic of Vietnam (ARVN), supported by U.S. air power, essentially defeated the Easter Offensive of 1972, but lack of U.S. congressional support and the withdrawal of U.S. troops lost the war. Colby maintained that the CIA approach would have won the conflict but that overmilitarization and Americanization lost it. His tenure as director of the CIA from 1973 to 1976 was controversial because he revealed to a Senate investigating committee the extensive illegal activities of the "family jewels" (the CIA's propriatary corporations, such as Air America) and the CIA's other illegal escapades during the war. After President Ford pressured him for his resignation, Colby returned to the practice of law.

BIBLIOGRAPHY

COLBY, WILLIAM. *Lost Victory.* 1989.
POWERS, THOMAS. *The Man Who Kept the Secrets: Richard Helms and the CIA.* 1979.

SANDRA C. TAYLOR

College Unrest. *See* Antiwar Movement; Jackson State College; Kent State University; New Mobe; Students for a Democratic Society (SDS); Teach-ins; University of Wisconsin Bombing.

Collins, James Lawton, Jr. (1917–), general, U.S. Army; special assistant to the Commander, Military Assistance Command, Vietnam (COMUSMACV), 1965–1966; senior adviser to South Vietnam's Regional Forces and Popular Forces (RF/PF), 1964–1965. Gen. William Westmoreland, COMUSMACV, made Collins his personal representative responsible for coordinating allied operations with South Vietnam's Joint General Staff and other allies in May 1965. Collins harshly criticized the ARVN officer corps, later suggesting that the United States should have insisted on removal of corrupt and incompetent officers. He believed that "getting the job done" was more important than making friends when advising and training an army. He also believed that when U.S. forces were withdrawn, the ARVN would be "strong enough to take their

J. LAWTON COLLINS. At center, Collins, the personal representative of the President of the United States, presents a check for $28,571,428.58 to President Ngo Dinh Diem of South Vietnam for refugee relief. Left to right: President Diem; Pham Van Huyen, commissioner general of refugees; Collins; unidentified; Randolph A. Kidder, U.S. chargé d'affaires; unidentified. *National Archives*

place." Collins wrote two books drawing on his experiences, and became the U.S. Army's chief of military history after the war.

BIBLIOGRAPHY

COLLINS, JAMES L., JR. *Development and Training of the South Vietnamese Army, 1950–1972.* 1975.
LARSEN, STANLEY ROBERT, and JAMES L. COLLINS JR. *Allied Participation in Vietnam.* 1975.

GLEN GENDZEL

Collins, Joseph Lawton (1896–1987), general, U.S. Army; special representative to South Vietnam, 1954–1955. Known as Lightning Joe in World War II, Gen. J. Lawton Collins was U.S. Army chief of staff during the Korean War. President Eisen-

hower sent him to South Vietnam to assess the situation and to recommend assistance for President Diem's army in November 1954. Collins recommended reducing U.S. support because of Diem's refusal to institute democratic reforms, warning that "Diem does not have the capacity to unify the divided factions in Vietnam." Collins specified that Diem could not "prevent the country from falling under Communist control." But this advice went unheeded in Washington, and General Collins was recalled in May 1955.

BIBLIOGRAPHY

ARNOLD, JAMES R. *The First Domino: Eisenhower, the Military, and America's Intervention in Vietnam.* 1991.
COLLINS, J. LAWTON. *Lightning Joe: An Autobiography.* 1979.

GLEN GENDZEL

Colonialism

Colonization marked Franco-Vietnamese relations for a century. The forced cohabitation was first accepted, then tolerated, and finally rejected. It was a story of missed opportunities between the people of the ancient Annam empire—freed from the heavy yoke of China, proud of its culture, attached to its traditions, yet open to modernism—and France, imperialist, yet firmly convinced that it was the bearer of the blessings of Western civilization. The separation was tragic, for France failed to grant the Vietnamese political emancipation in due time, although of all the French possessions, Indochina, with its culture and its level of economic development, was the most deserving of independence.

Indochina, Pearl of the French Empire, 1858–1939. At the 1931 Colonial Fair in Paris, the Indochina pavilion, a replica of the temple of Angkor, symbolized the splendor of the French colony in the Far East. It was viewed as the "Pearl of the Empire" for its cultural richness, its hard-working people, and its economic development over the seventy years of French rule.

The first French infrastructures in Indochina were established in the mid-nineteenth century as a result of initiatives by the French navy.

Missionaries had settled in Indochina, but the evangelization of the local population had never involved political domination by France. In fact, at the end of the eighteenth century, French bishop Pigneau de Béhaine advised Nguyen Anh, who soon took the name Gia Long, in his attempt to restore imperial power. The territory under Anh's rule extended east of the Annam cordillera from the Chinese frontier to the Camau peninsula and was populated by Annamites, who progressively migrated from the Red River Delta to the Mekong Delta. Thus, Gia Long, the emperor of Annam, ruled Vietnamese territory from Hanoi to Saigon, although the emperor of China, to whom he paid tribute, acknowledged him as prince of Vietnam. As a gesture of thanks, Gia Long protected missionaries. After 1830, however, Long's successors persecuted Christians, who numbered about 600,000 in 1850. Under the pretense of obtaining redress for the deaths of French and Spanish missionaries, French navy ships anchored at Tourane (Da Nang) in 1858, and French forces captured the forts of Saigon and occupied the neighboring territories, over which France imposed direct rule. Napoleon III, already involved in the Mexican military expedition after 1861, initially hesitated to engage in an additional overseas venture; but after noting the results obtained at so little cost by the navy he decided to pursue it. Cambodia willingly accepted status as a French protectorate to escape certain destruction by Siam and Annam. Cochinchina, torn away from the Annam empire, was conquered by 1870, and a French exploratory mission along the upper reaches of the Mekong River opened new possibilities for colonizing the Red River area.

The French Third Republic pursued the same policy as had Napoleon III. In 1885, after bloody fighting, China was forced to relinquish its sovereignty over Annam, and by 1887, with the exception of Siam, the French ruled the entire Indochinese peninsula. The French Indochinese Union comprised five entities, each with a different legal standing: they included a colony, Cochinchina, legally part of the French national territory whose inhabitants supposedly were French citizens (although most were not); three protectorates, Annam, Cambodia, and

SAIGON IN 1948. *National Archives*

the Laotian kingdom of Luang Prabang; and Tonkin, a protectorate carved out of Annam. Vietnam with its three *ky* (Cochinchina, Annam, and Tonkin) under the rule of the Annam emperor was gone. The French even outlawed the use of the word *Vietnam,* which became a symbol of nationalist claims throughout the colonial period up to the days of Ho Chi Minh and Ngo Dinh Diem.

A French governor-general headed the Indochinese Union and received his orders from the Colonial Office. There was only a semblance of political autonomy. This situation was challenged by the Annam emperors, particularly Duy Tan, deposed and exiled in 1915, and by a first generation of nationalists, who were inspired by Japan's victory over Russia in 1905 and who saw in Japan a model and a refuge. The nationalist movement, however, was successfully suppressed by such talented French commanders as Gen. Joseph Gallieni and Lyautey, who methodically pacified and organized the upper Tonkin and the frontier areas, allowing the governors-general to devote their efforts to economic development. Indochina worked on a principle of financial autonomy; that is, it was not supposed to receive support from the French treasury, but rather had to rely on its own resources for revenue. Thus, direct and indirect taxation (e.g., taxes on alcohol and salt, customs duties) placed a heavy burden on the local population, especially as governors-general developed infrastructure and built hospitals and schools. Although the French administration in charge of collecting taxes and duties soon became unpopular, improvements in infrastructure were notable: creation of road and railway networks; construction of irrigation systems that multiplied sevenfold the area of cultivable rice paddies in the Mekong delta; development of plantations of rubber trees; and of mining operations, especially of coal in Hongay; the combating of malaria; creation of a Pasteur Institute in Hanoi; development of a school system in French and Quoc Ngu (romanization of Vietnamese characters) and creation of a university and of the French School of the Far East for the preservation of cultural heritage (in Angkor).

By 1914, the territories seemed so well pacified that France left only 2,500 European military personnel in Indochina and sent thousands of Annamite infantrymen and workers to France for the war effort. That climate changed after 1918, however. A new generation of Vietnamese, who were schooled in the French system, entered maturity at the same time that powerful doctrines were emerging: Wilsonian principles; the Bolshevik Revolution and birth of the Third International; and the example of Sun Yat-sen in China, who attempted to apply his three principles—nationalism, democracy, and socialism. A powerful wave of nationalism rose against acculturation, the political monopoly of the French minority, and the French dominance over the Bank of Indochina and major industrial concerns.

In 1925 a leftist governor-general, A. Varenne, established the right of qualified Indochinese to become public servants, protected peasants against usury by creating a farmers' bank, and developed a set of labor laws. These measures were not sufficient, however, to satisfy even moderate nationalists, who hoped to see a progressive evolution toward a commonwealth, a road that the new emperor, Boa Dai, apparently favored upon his return to Indochina in 1932 after ten years of schooling in France. Bent on resuming control over interior affairs, he summoned to power a generation of new men, including the young Catholic mandarin, Ngo Dinh Diem. But Diem, skeptical of France's willingness to allow reforms, resigned after four months.

Stronger opposition to French rule erupted on two fronts. Young Tonkinese bourgeois founded the Viet Nam Quoc Dan Dang (VNQDD) in 1927, a party fashioned after the Chinese Kuomintang. The VNQDD's main theme was nationalism and its primary objective was the expulsion of the French. After numerous terrorist acts, the insurrection erupted on 9 February 1930, when Annamite infantrymen massacred their French officers in Yen Bay. The revolt was short-lived; VNQDD leaders were arrested, executed, or fled to China, and the party ceased to be a threat.

Another insurrection, led by Nguyen Ai Quoq, (who would take the name Ho Chi Minh in 1942) broke out on 1 May 1930 in northern Annam, in Quoq's native province. Quoq, a Comintern agent, had been a revolutionary militant in France in 1920 and was the founder in 1925 of Thanh Nien, which would become the Vietnamese Communist Party. Quoq established local soviets in the Nghe An area, but the army intervened. Repression was savage, the party was entirely dislocated, and Nguyen Ai Quoq was arrested in Shanghai by the British. Organized in 1930, the Vietnamese Communist Party became the Indochinese Communist Party (PCI), which included factions in Cambodia and Laos and followed orders from the Comintern. The Comintern's top priority was the revolutionary struggle against bourgeoisie (including Vietnamese bourgeoisie), and accordingly the PCI put nationalist goals at the bottom of its agenda. The victory of the Popular Front in the elections of 1936 in France enabled the PCI to become legal in Cochinchina, but the party was divided by numerous factions and remained under the close watch of the French police. After the Nazi-Soviet Pact of August 1939 the French government banned the PCI and the French Communist Party.

At that time two politico-religious sects formed in Cochinchina: the Cao Dai, whose "pope," Pham Conq Tac, ruled in Tay Ninh, and the Hoa Hao of Huynh Phu So, the "mad bonze." Their rapid development was a matter of concern when it became clear that they were linked to Prince Cuong De and his Japanese patrons.

Following the suppression of the insurrections of the VNQDD and Nguyen Ai Quoq in 1930–1931, nationalist and revolutionary activity was much reduced. The French government—even the socialist ministers of Léon Blum—did not introduce sweeping political changes in the Union for fear of encouraging secession. The government, however, continued its policy of economic development (the Trans-Indochina railroad was completed in 1937) and its large-scale sanitary efforts, which resulted in a demographic boom. By 1939 Indochina had 22 million inhabitants, of which 17 million were Vietnamese. Ten percent of the population was Catholic.

French Indochina during World War II. Before 1939 the French high command had realized that if Japan entered the war on the side of Germany and Italy, Indochina, so distant from France (12,000 kilometers/7,400 miles), could not possibly be protected. The total collapse of France in June 1940 confirmed this projection. As early as 20 June Japan gave an ultimatum to the French, demanding the right to cross Tonkin and to use airstrips for its war against China. Well aware of his isolation and receiving no signs of support from Great Britain or the United States, the governor-general of Indochina, Admiral Decoux, supported by the government of Marshal Pétain, signed a convention that granted Japanese troops the right to encamp and transit to the north of the Red River. In return, Japan recognized French sovereignty over Indochina. Completely cut off from France by 1941 except for cablegram communications, Admiral Decoux exerted unquestioned power and resolutely carried out the "national revolution" policy of the Vichy government. He developed production inside the country and commercial exchanges with the Far East, and to oppose the Japanese, he encouraged centuries-old Vietnamese traditions.

In the last quarter of 1940, Decoux confronted interior and exterior threats simultaneously, and those who opposed French colonial rule saw it as an opportunity to oust the French. As early as November 1940, Indochina's neighbor to the west, Siam, invaded and claimed Cambodian and Laotian territories. Although Decoux had only 60,000 men (including 15,000 Frenchmen and legionnaires) and a small and obsolete air force and navy to protect the entire Union, French ships surprised the moored Siamese fleet and destroyed it. Japan imposed mediation and forced France to sign a peace treaty in May 1941 that granted Siam the territories it claimed on the right bank of the Mekong River in Laos and the provinces of Battambang and of Siem Reap in Cambodia.

Between September and December 1940, the army intervened twice: first, in the Lang Son area to destroy armed gangs, some claiming to be affiliated with Prince Cuong De, still in exile in Japan; and second in Cochinchina, where the PCI launched an insurrection on 22 November 1940. The PCI insurrection was quelled so effectively that the PCI vanished from the political scene in southern Indochina, a cause of concern for Nguyen Ai Quoq, who was still in China. In the spring of 1941, Quoq went to Indochina to attend the plenary sessions of the

FRENCH INDOCHINA, 1887–1954.

PCI, which were held in the Cao Bang area. He insisted that the nationalist struggle against the colonizing powers take precedence over revolutionary struggle and agrarian reforms, and in response the plenum created a patriotic front, the Revolutionary League for the Independence of Vietnam (Vietnam Doc-lap Dong Minh, or Viet Minh), an exclusively Vietnamese organization that did not include Cambodians and Laotians. The immense task of sensitizing the people remained at hand. Only a hideout in the northern mountains and the embryo of a clandestine organization in the Red River Delta existed.

The French police were less worried about the PCI insurrection than about the activity of the Vietnamese nationalists, who were strengthened by the Japanese presence in Indochina; and the Japanese presence was subject to no restraint because the Vichy government had acknowledged in the Darlan-Kano agreements of July 1941 the principle of a common Franco-Japanese defense of Indochina, which meant that there was no restriction on the number of Japanese troops that could be stationed in Indochina. Some Japanese groups, such as the Kempetai (the Japanese secret police) in fact supported or financed anti-French activities. The Cao Dai, whose "pope" was deported to Madagascar by the French in 1941, supported Prince Cuong De and placed themselves under the protection of the Kempetai, as did some nationalist leaders such as Ngo Dinh Diem when the French police initiated massive arrests in 1943. After these upheavals,

BLOCKHOUSE. Part of the network of blockhouses and fortresses constructed by the French to guard against the Viet Minh. *National Archives*

quiet was restored, and Admiral Decoux found himself more isolated than ever. Gen. Charles de Gaulle, president of the French Committee of National Liberation, headquartered in Algiers since June 1943, was determined to involve the entire French colonial empire in the war against Germany and Japan. He therefore refused to acknowledge the authority of Admiral Decoux, who had never joined the Free France forces, and de Gaulle named a general to organize anti-Japanese resistance in Indochina. The subsequent quarrel between Decoux and de Gaulle's designee ended on 9 March 1945, when the Japanese assumed complete control over Indochina. All French officials were arrested, and French troops were either captured or killed; only 3,000 managed to escape to China, and a few formed underground groups in Laos. On 11 March the emperor of Annam, Bao Dai, proclaimed the independence of his empire, followed by a similar proclamation on 13 March by the young king of Cambodia, Norodom Sihanouk, and by the king of Laos on 8 April. Cochinchina was under direct Japanese administration; French sovereignty in Indochina was over.

While Bao Dai formed a government, the Viet Minh took advantage of the absence of any real authority and of Japanese neutrality to expand its activities and membership in Tonkin and Annam. It received discreet—but effective—assistance from the U.S. Office of Special Services (OSS), which wanted Viet Minh troops to fight against the Japanese. Relations with the south became very difficult after the U.S. Air Force destroyed the few north-south communication lines. Meanwhile, the leader of the PCI, Tran Van Giau, escaped from a French jail and rebuilt the southern Communist Party, which was not as militant as the Viet Minh and had a very limited presence.

August 1945 was a turning point. As the Japanese withdrew from Indochina, the Viet Minh rushed to seize power before the arrival of the Allied occupation troops, which were to take possession of two occupation zones that had been agreed upon at the Potsdam Conference: a Chinese zone north of the sixteenth parallel and a British zone south of it. Relying on cunning, convincing arguments, sympathizers, or negotiations, the Viet Minh seized power in Hanoi on 19 August and in Hue on 23 August, using very little force. On 25 August, Bao Dai abdicated and became citizen Vinh Thuy. Matters were more complex in Saigon. The Cao Dai and Hoa Hao religious sects, closely tied to the Japanese, had a majority position in the national front that was formed on 14 August, but Tran Van Giau's communists and the Viet Minh were so skillful that on 25 August the Nam Bo (formerly Cochinchina) Executive Committee was formed under the presidency of Tran Van Giau. In Hanoi, on 28 August, a provisional government headed by Ho Chi Minh was established. Despite its claims of a diversity of representation, officials from the north were overwhelmingly dominant, and its communist orientation was evidenced by the nomination of Vo Nguyen Giap to the ministry of the interior and of Pham Van Dong to the ministry of finance. On 2 September the government proclaimed the independence of the Democratic Republic of Vietnam (DRV). On the same day, Japan signed its surrender on the USS *Missouri,* a ceremony attended by Gen. Jacques Philippe Leclerc, newly appointed chief military commander of French troops in the Far East.

France's Return to Indochina, 1945–1946. The timing of the establishment of the DRV and the Japanese surrender emphasized the clash to come between two antagonistic aspirations: the Vietnamese assertion of a fragile independence in an uncertain and changing world, and the French determination to regain sovereignty over its colonial empire regardless of the misgivings of its U.S., Chinese, or British allies.

In its declaration of 24 March 1945, the Provisional Government of the French Republic had defined the future status of Indochina. Independence was out of the question; only the relative autonomy of the five countries that formed the former Union—Annam, Cambodia, Cochinchina, Laos, and Tonkin—was discussed. The countries would form an Indochinese Federation whose government would be headed by a French governor-general. An assembly whose voting mechanism was not explained "but in which French interests would be represented" would vote on taxes and the federal budget. The Indochinese Federation would be part of a "French Union" whose interests outside of the Union would be represented by France. Although such a plan was an improvement over Vietnam's prewar status, it was far less than nationalist desires: the rebuilding of Vietnam with its three *ky* and independence.

General de Gaulle, aware of President Franklin D. Roosevelt's misgivings about helping European powers recover their Asian colonies, hoped to assuage those feelings by including French troops in the fight against Japan. In that effort, a French force was being assembled when the Pacific war ended abruptly after atomic bombs were dropped on Hiroshima and Nagasaki. This freed the expeditionary force to be used by the French to regain control of Indochina.

On 15 August 1945, de Gaulle appointed Adm. Georges Thierry d'Argenlieu high commissioner for Indochina and General Leclerc chief military commander. Their mission was to restore French sovereignty over the Indochinese

Union. On 22 August, Leclerc landed in Kandy, Ceylon, Lord Mountbatten's headquarters, where he learned for the first time that the Potsdam decisions had partitioned Indochina into two Allied occupation zones. Uninformed about the complex situation in Indochina, he was told of the events in Hanoi and Saigon by DGER (the French counterpart of the OSS) agents. One of them, Jean Sainteny, was allowed, although reluctantly, to fly to Hanoi by OSS Major Archimedes Patti; the other agent was parachuted into Cochinchina. In Laos, where French underground troops were solidly implanted, the "loyalty of the local people who hate Annamites" could be relied upon. But in Tonkin, where "the Chinese and Japanese rouse a violently hostile minority," and in Cochinchina, the mood was hostile toward the French and local forces were clearly dominant. It was therefore impossible to reconquer these areas with limited means, especially because France's allies would not help them reinvade Indochina, particularly north of the sixteenth parallel. The Americans disapproved, the British hesitated for fear of antagonizing the United States and other allies, and the Chinese generals, who enjoyed great autonomy, disregarded the official policy of Chungking.

On 28 August 1945, the Chinese entered Tonkin to disarm Japanese troops located north of the sixteenth parallel. On 12 September the British occupation troops arrived in Saigon with an Indian division and a symbolic French detachment. It was followed on 5 October by General Leclerc and, between 15 October 1945 and February 1946, by the 50,000-strong French force that had been intended for use against the Japanese. This force arrived gradually because there were few ships available in France and because of U.S. priorities on the allocation of boats in the Allied maritime pool.

Flying from Saigon to Phnom Penh, General Leclerc convinced Norodom Sihanouk to acknowledge French sovereignty over Cambodia, hoping to restore power quickly in the colony of Cochinchina. But the return to Tonkin was fraught with dangers, and recovering Cochinchina was more difficult than anticipated. Revolutionary and nationalist agitation forced the British to step in to maintain law and order. The former French garrison, which had been jailed by the Japanese, were rearmed and assumed control of Saigon's public buildings on 23 September 1945. But a hundred or so French civilians were immediately killed. The Nam Bo Executive Committee fled Saigon and advocated a guerrilla war, the beginning of war in the south. The area was pacified up to Vinh Long when Admiral d'Argenlieu arrived in Saigon at the end of October. Despite raids by tanks and river-ships, there were not enough French troops to ensure a permanent French presence. The French had reason for concern. If the pacification of the south was slow and man-intensive, how much more so would the reconquest of Tonkin be—especially because it required landing troops in Haiphong harbor, which was occupied by the Chinese, and then raiding Hanoi, where Ho Chi Minh's government was assembling a Vietnamese army? While preparing the military operation, French officials attempted to negotiate the return of Tonkin to French control.

In Hanoi, Jean Sainteny contacted Ho Chi Minh as early as 15 October 1945. Fragile ties were formed, leading to discreet and difficult negotiations. Ho Chi Minh discussed the independence of Vietnam—of the three *ky*. Sainteny offered autonomy within the Union. He was noncommittal about the reunification of Vietnam and Cochinchina because Cochinchina was a colony and therefore part of the French national territory, about which only the French parliament could legislate. Two factors convinced Ho Chi Minh to reach an agreement: the weight of Chinese occupation that encouraged the activities of anti–Viet Minh Viet-

VIET BAC. President Ho Chi Minh at a secret fortification in the far north Viet Bac area during the Indochina War, c. 1946–1954. *Ngo Vinh Long*

namese nationalists, and the international isolation of his government, which no nation, not even the Soviet Union, had acknowledged.

Simultaneously, French representatives in Chungking successfully negotiated the withdrawal from northern Indochina of Chinese troops on 28 February 1946. In exchange, France surrendered all the privileges it had accrued in China after the "unequal treaties." A Franco-Vietnamese agreement was signed at the last minute in Hanoi on 6 March, the day the French navy anchored in Haiphong with a division of troops. The Chinese, despite the Chungking agreements, opened fire on the French, who counterattacked. That was the only serious incident that occurred as the French returned to Tonkin. A few days later, Leclerc arrived in Hanoi and was received by Ho Chi Minh.

What was the price for the peaceful return to Tonkin? The French government acknowledged the Democratic Republic of Vietnam as a "free state" with its own government, parliament, army, and treasury within the framework of the Indochinese Federation and of the French Union. The possible reunification of Cochinchina with Vietnam was to be decided by referendum. Meanwhile, the Vietnamese government welcomed the French army's taking over from the Chinese. An additional agreement, signed on 7 March, limited the French to 15,000 soldiers, stipulated that they were not to stay more than five years, and that they

OPERATION CAMARGUE. A French amphibious assault on the coastal strip of central Vietnam, 28 July 1953. The landings centered on the village of Tan An, between Quang Tri and Hue, and were intended to clear Highway 1 (the "Street without Joy" made famous by Bernard Fall's book of the same name) of Viet Minh. *National Archives*

were to be progressively replaced by Vietnamese troops. By accepting the last restriction, the French negotiators had granted more than they had been authorized to by the French government, and they were reproached by Admiral d'Argenlieu for having done so.

Ho Chi Minh, however, had failed to unify the three *ky* and was savagely criticized by other nationalist parties and by the left wing of the Viet Minh. Still, the French government acknowledged his leadership, and negotiations were scheduled to define the meaning of "free state" and its sphere of authority.

French War in Indochina, 1946–1954. During the following months, the ambiguities of the agreement became apparent. Ho Chi Minh was welcomed as a head of state in France, but the negotiations of the status of Vietnam and of the Federation stalled on the issues of the term *Doc-lap* and on Cochinchina. As a result, the only agreement signed was to extend the cease-fire.

There were a number of factors that led to the failure of the negotiations. One factor was that since de Gaulle's resignation in January 1946, France had not formulated a clear governmental policy on Indochina. Another was an action taken in Saigon by Admiral d'Argenlieu, who was unwilling to leave the future of Cochinchina in the hands of the Marxist Viet Minh. Thus, prior to the referendum that was to decide of the fate of Cochinchina, d'Argenlieu formed an independent Republic of Cochinchina whose president was a moderate nationalist educated in the French system. Vietnamese leaders in Hanoi viewed this as a provocation because Ho Chi Minh was still negotiating in Paris. General Leclerc, leaving his command in July 1946, held more balanced views. In Ho Chi Minh he saw a fervent nationalist, as well as a Marxist, with the potential to be the representative of an undeniable Vietnamese nationalism.

Actions by the Vietnamese also affected the negotiations. In Hanoi, with Ho Chi Minh absent, hardliners in the government, such as Giap, gained influence. They encouraged confrontation, thus increasing the number of incidents between French and Viet Minh troops. In the south the Nam Bo Executive Committee, headed by Nguyen Binh, rejected the cease-fire agreement and intensified its guerrilla activity.

In Haiphong, on 20 November 1946, the Viet Minh attacked French civilians, built barricades, and were subsequently fired upon by French artillery. These events foreshadowed the assaults on French garrisons in Hanoi, Tonkin, and Hue by Vietnamese militia and troops on 19 December. After the French command regained control, the government of Ho Chi Minh went into hiding in the impenetrable Viet Bac area to lead the fight against the French.

The next six years can be divided into two major phases: a colonial war (1947–1949) during which France attempted to quell the insurrection in an unfavorable international context, and a conflict (1949–1952) that became of international interest after Mao Zedong seized power in China in 1949. The Indochina War, like the Korean War, became part of the Cold War, with free world nations supporting one side and communist nations the other. In this case, the French received U.S. assistance, and the Viet Minh received support from the People's Republic of China (PRC) and the USSR.

Another important feature of the situation in Vietnam was the continuity of the Viet Minh leaders and their strategy, which contrasted sharply with the lack of French policy and the high turnover of French civil and military authorities in Indochina. Over a period of eight years, there were six different French high commissioners and chief commanders, which led to continual shifts in priorities and tactics.

The Viet Minh applied the Communist Party's principles of revolutionary war: the party's role was to define major objectives (national independence, popular democracy, and socialism) and mobilize the nation through ongoing education and organization of the masses, and to gradually form, from hidden sanctuaries if necessary, armed forces that could be deployed across the entire territory. The armed forces can be thought of as a three-layer pyramid: at the base was the people's militia (Tu Ve), in the middle were regional troops, and at the top were regular units (regiments and divisions). It was a slow process that required the collaboration—by free choice, by force, or by terror—of the entire population. It was a long-range strategy whose success depended on exhausting the forces of the enemy, a "giant entangled in the mesh of a giant net," and on the demobilizing lassitude of its public opinion.

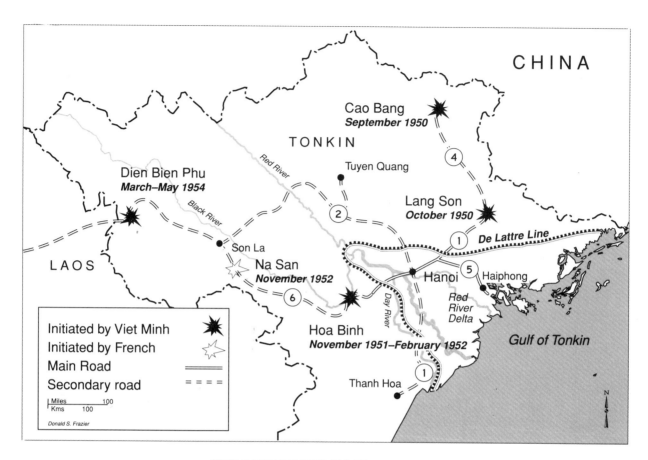

KEY BATTLES FOR TONKIN, 1950–1954.

The first few months of this type of struggle are crucial. The Viet Minh nearly collapsed in the fall of 1947 when its government narrowly escaped capture during the French offensive to wipe out the insurrection in the north. In the south, French pacification efforts succeeded despite rising urban terrorism.

French military successes, however, did not produce a lasting solution; the French found it necessary to commit an ever-increasing number of troops to maintain the war effort while the search for a political solution continued. In the Cold War climate of the late 1940s and early 1950s, and with the French Communist Party, which had been excluded from the government, ceaselessly campaigning against the "dirty war," negotiating with Ho Chi Minh, a communist and an agent of the Fourth International, was out of the question. It was difficult to find an acceptable and valid representative to negotiate a new status for Indochina within the French Union. The French government eventually chose former emperor Bao Dai. At first reticent, he accepted the position when the reunion of the three *ky,* that is, the rebirth of Gia Long's Vietnam with limited independence, was granted on 8 May 1949. Cambodia and Laos, where the situation was far quieter, also become part of the French Union.

Military Forces in 1953

French Troops	
French Expeditionary Corps in the Far East	
Standing Army	
French	55,000
Foreign Legion	19,000
North Africans	30,000
Africans	18,000
Indochinese	53,000
Total	**175,000**
Indochinese Reservists	55,000
Associated Armies	
National Vietnamese Army	200,000
National Cambodian Army	13,000
National Laotian Army	13,000
Total	**226,000**
Total French forces	**456,000**
Viet Minh Troops (estimated)	
Militia (Tu Ve)	150,000
Regional troops	75,000
Standing army	175,000
Total	**350,000**

France, after giving up its attempt to keep Cochinchina a separate entity and after granting Bao Dai what it had denied Ho Chi Minh three years before, hoped the war would become a civil war between two sides of a nation divided by opposite ideologies. But that would require the new Vietnamese state to assume military responsibilities. The size of the French expeditionary corps had doubled by 1946, adding from Foreign Legion and North African infantry regiments. After 1947, West African regiments were also deployed. Few units composed of French enlisted men were sent; most French military personnel were officers, who commanded the various units. Sending French conscripts to Indochina was out of the question because France had other priorities, including an insurrection in Madagascar and the formation of military units for the newly formed North Atlantic Treaty Organization (NATO). As early as 1946 Indochinese enlistees and "partisans" began joining the French forces of the expeditionary corps.

The interplay of political and economic interests led to a decision by the French High command to emphasize pacification of the south and thus concentrate forces there. At the same time, communist China offered the Viet Minh forces a rear base on the northern frontier of Tonkin where its troops could be trained and equipped. As the Viet Minh troops improved, the French found it increasingly difficult to send supplies to the French garrisons stationed between Cao Bang and Lang Son along Colonial Route 4. As French troops withdrew from Cao Bang, they were ambushed and 3,000 men were killed or captured. French troops subsequently withdrew from the whole area along Colonial Route 4, including Lang Son, leaving the Viet Minh in control of the area along the Chinese frontier. The failure of skilled French units fighting not against guerrillas but against Viet Minh regiments in a conventional warfare situation high-

THE END OF FRENCH RULE. The first Viet Minh troops to enter the French lines are escorted by French liaison officers, August 1954. *National Archives*

lighted the metamorphosis of the Viet Minh's capabilities. General Giap, chief commander of the Viet Minh army, recognized the weakness of the French position and the possibility of moving from guerrilla to conventional warfare, and deployed his first divisions against Hanoi.

The shock of the Cao Bang episode forced the French government to look for a "savior." Gen. Jean de Lattre de Tassigny accepted the command with the provision that he could wield full civilian and military powers. His arrival in Saigon on 19 December 1950 galvanized the depressed expeditionary corps: "I will be your leader," he promised. Three weeks later, between 14 and 17 January, his forces defeated the Viet Minh army in Vinh Yen. Giap had been overconfident and had made a mistake by shifting too quickly to conventional warfare. Lattre withdrew most French troops from the south, mustered his units in the Vinh Yen area, and authorized the use of napalm by the air force. After French forces again defeated Giap, this time at Dong Trieu, Lattre focused on Tonkin. He formed mobile units that were intended to push the Viet Minh out of the Red River Delta area, and he had a defensive line of fortresses and blockhouses built around the delta to pre-

WELCOMING THE NEW ORDER. Vietnamese Catholic boy scouts demonstrating in support of the victorious Viet Minh army, 1955. They hold a banner that reads: "Long live President Ho Chi Minh." *National Archives*

vent Viet Minh forces from infiltrating the area—a structure of questionable value considering the secret organization network that was already in place.

Lattre also led a major political effort to Vietnamize the war by inspiring feelings of national pride in the local youths: "Be a man. . . . [I]f you are a communist, join the Vietminh . . . if you are a patriot, fight for your fatherland, for this war is yours. France will only fight the war for you, if you fight along." The head of Bao Dai's government, Nguyen Van Tam, an anticommunist veteran, and his son, Col. Nguyen Van Hinh, the future chief of staff of the Vietnamese army, vigorously followed suit.

After a trip to the United States, where he glorified the common struggle against communism and requested more U.S. aid, Lattre died on 11 January 1952, suffering from cancer and from the memory of his son, killed in action in the delta area. The Lattre period was a positive interlude for the French in an otherwise steady process of degradation. Politically, the French Union was unraveling.

In Cambodia, Norodom Sihanouk, who had seized power, asked for complete independence and obtained it in 1953. In April 1954, Vietnam, under Bao Dai, was granted independence and full sovereignty.

After General de Lattre's death, the war intensified in the north. Giap stopped fighting in the delta, hoping to draw the French mobile units away from their bases in Tonkin and join battle in the upper Mekong area in the Central Highlands and Laos. French general Raoul Salan's strategy was to use air-land bases, well-defended bases along the Viet Minh's routes to Laos that could be easily resupplied by air, that had enormous firepower, and that could draw the Viet Minh divisions in to break them. Several bases were built, but this airplane-intensive strategy was too costly. Salan's successor, Gen. Henri Navarre, withdrew French forces from the base at Nasan, which had been built by Salan, and decided to build another in Dien Bien Phu to save Laos while launching a major operation to drive Viet Minh forces out of Annam. Navarre was to provide the government with a solid war plan before the start of the Geneva Conference, scheduled for 26 April 1954. But the fall of Dien Bien Phu on 7 May 1954 after a bloody siege (3,000 dead and 10,000 prisoners, half of them wounded) had international repercussions and changed the terms of the negotiations. The new French prime minister, Pierre Mendès-France, who favored ending the war, signed the Geneva Agreements on 20 July 1954. Vietnam was temporarily divided at the 17th Parallel into two states, pending the results of general elections to be held by July 1956 under the control of an international commission. Within ten months the forces of the French Union were to be south of the 17th Parallel and the Viet Minh forces to the north. Both were to withdraw from the kingdoms of Cambodia and Laos within two to three months.

The agreements contained a final declaration indicating approval by the United States, but U.S. officials did not sign the documents. Ngo Dinh Diem, the new leader of the Vietnamese government in Saigon, rejected the agreements.

On 5 May 1955, the last French troops in North Vietnam boarded ships in Haiphong. They withdrew for good in April 1956 from what used to be French Indochina. South Vietnam was now an independent state with its own national army, which was being trained by the U.S. Army. The French War was over.

[*See also* France; Navarre Plan; Ten-Pin Theory.]

BIBLIOGRAPHY

BODINIER, GILBERT. *Textes et documents sur l'Indochine.* Vol. 1, 1945–1946. Vol. 2, 1947. 1987, 1989.

DEVILLERS, PHILIPPE. *Histoire du Vietnam de 1946 à 1952.* 1952.

FALL, BERNARD. *Hell in a Very Small Place: The Siege of Dien Bien Phu.* 1967.

FALL, BERNARD. *The Vietminh Regime.* 1956.

FRANCHINI, PHILIPPE. *Les Guerres d'Indochine (Des origines de la présence française à la chute de Saïgon).* 1988.

GRAS, YVES. *Histoire de la guerre d'Indochine.* 1979.

HUYNH KIM KHANH. *Vietnamese Communism, 1925–1945.* 1982.

MUS, PAUL. *Vietnam, sociologie d'une guerre.* 1952.

JEAN DELMAS
TRANSLATED FROM THE FRENCH BY MARIE-JOSÉE SCHORP

Combined Action Program. Developed as part of the III Marine Amphibious Force's (III MAF) strategy of counterguerrilla operations and control of the rural population, the Combined Action Program (CAP) paired picked squads of U.S. marines with platoons of Popular Forces (PF), the government-sponsored Vietnamese village militia. Placed into operation in August 1965, the CAP eventually produced over one hundred Combined Action platoons in the densely populated coastal lowlands of South Vietnam's five northern provinces. At maximum strength in 1968–1969 the Combined Action Program controlled only about 2,500 marines. The CAP platoons were organized into companies, which, in turn, were responsible to four civil affairs groups.

The effectiveness of the CAP remains debatable, but the available statistics and personal testimony suggests that the CAP made the Vietnamese Popular Forces platoons more potent than their non-CAP counterparts. The program was too small, however, to produce dramatic results. In the I Corps area, the area in which the CAP operated, only one-tenth of all Popular Forces platoons (114 of 1,115) included U.S. marines. The CAP PF platoons, however, were responsible for 29 percent of all PF-inflicted deaths in the communist forces.

A rough analysis suggests that the CAP platoons were a sound investment compared with other RVN forces. During the period 1966–1970 Free World forces killed an average of 117,000 communist soldiers a year. Of these deaths, perhaps 20 percent were inflicted by some part of the South Vietnamese armed forces (an estimated 23,000 a year); of this casualty set, one-third of communist deaths (7,000 a year) came at the hands of the Regional Forces and Popular Forces (RF/PF). The number of RF/PF platoons throughout all of Vietnam varied between 5,000 and 8,000 during the same period, so the number of communist deaths was approximately one per RF/PF platoon per year. Yet the CAP platoons in the period 1966–1970 inflicted around 1,000 deaths a year or about ten per platoon per year. Overall the investment in RF/PF platoons looks sound; these forces accounted for one-third of the PAVN/VC killed each year by the South Vietnamese on one-fifth of the money spent on the RVN armed forces. By this measure the CAP platoons were the most effective portion of the Popular Forces.

The communist forces paid the CAP platoons the dubious honor of targeting them in most of their small unit attacks upon Vietnamese units in I Corps, especially in 1967 and 1968. More than half of the total deaths suffered by the entire RVN armed forces in 1967–1972 were inflicted on the Popular Forces (from 6,600 to 12,000 a year for this period). PF deaths in combat countrywide averaged 22 per 1,000 a year, which meant that CAP militiamen (3,000 to 4,000) died at an average rate of around 80 per year. In fact, such averaging misses the realities of combat: the surge of contacts during the Tet Offensive and the aggressive warfare throughout the first half of 1969. CAP Vietnamese died at rates three or four times higher than their non-CAP counterparts; the exchange ratio thus narrows to three or four CAP deaths against ten communist dead per platoon. When one considers the lack of access of CAP platoons to artillery and air support, their fighting effectiveness appears impressive. Their small size and vulnerability, however, meant that CAP units required marine combat units nearby to ensure quick reinforcement and fire support or they could be overrun and wiped out with relative ease.

For the U.S. marines who served in CAP platoons, Vietnam service could be as lethal as for their PF counterparts and even more dangerous than service in regular U.S. infantry battalions. During the six years in which U.S. marines served in CAP platoons, they suffered around 1,000 dead and wounded, a casualty rate of 75 percent for all CAP marines, with 16–18 percent of the casualties fatal. The risks of CAP service were well known, yet 60 percent of CAP marines extended their tours by several months to remain with their Vietnamese counterparts, who fought harder and deserted less than their non-CAP militia comrades.

After reaching an organizational high of 114 platoons in 1970, the Combined Action Program declined as III MAF withdrew. The modest CAP efforts at medical help for the villagers, small-scale construction, and other civic action activities were then passed to other agencies, largely Vietnamese. The last civil affairs group and Combined Action company disbanded in May 1971. Champions of the CAP insist that it played an important, although unappreciated, role in strengthening the Popular Forces, but critics point out that the CAP platoons' vulnerability to attack and some marine misbehavior in the villages made the program a questionable investment of lives and resources.

BIBLIOGRAPHY

ALLNUT, BRUCE C. *Marine Combined Action Capabilities: The Vietnam Experience.* 1969.

ANDERSON, CHARLES R. *Vietnam: The Other War.* 1982.

CORSON, WILLIAM R. *The Betrayal.* 1968.

PETERSON, MICHAEL E. *The Combined Action Platoons: The U.S. Corps' Other War in Vietnam.* 1989.

WEST, FRANCIS. *The Village.* 1985.

THAYER, THOMAS C. *War Without Fronts: The American Experience in Vietnam.* 1985.

ALLAN R. MILLETT

Commander-in-Chief, Pacific (CINCPAC).

During the Vietnam War, the office of Commander-in-Chief, Pacific, was held by four U.S. Navy admirals: Adm. Harry D. Felt, Adm. U. S. Grant Sharp, Adm. John S. McCain Jr., and Adm. Noel Gayler. They directed all U.S. ground, air, and sea forces in the Pacific Command (PACOM), one of several unified commands created after the Korean War to simplify administration of U.S. armed forces worldwide. Based on Gen. Douglas MacArthur's legendary Far Eastern Command, PACOM covered 220 million square kilometers (85 million square miles) from Alaska to the Indian Ocean—about one-sixth of the earth's surface—including the entire Southeast Asian area of operations. During the Vietnam War, the commander of the U.S. Military Assistance Command, Vietnam (COMUSMACV), in Saigon reported to CINCPAC in Honolulu, who in turn reported to the Joint Chiefs of Staff in Washington. Many military analysts considered this long chain of command a cumbersome obstacle to flexibility in the war. Furthermore, U.S. Air Force, Navy, and Marine forces in Vietnam generally reported not to the MACV theater commander but to CINCPAC, who was 8,000 kilometers (5,000 miles) away from the war. COMUSMACV lacked authority over naval forces in South Vietnam and could not order air strikes against North Vietnam. This division of command responsibility between Saigon, Honolulu, and Washington greatly hampered the U.S. war effort in Vietnam. U.S. Army strategist Col. Harry Summers concluded that "the failure to establish a separate theater of war for Vietnam was a major strategic mistake."

BIBLIOGRAPHY

"Mr. Pacific." *Time,* 6 January 1961, 17–22.

SHARP, U. S. GRANT. *Strategy for Defeat: Vietnam in Retrospect.* 1978.

SUMMERS, HARRY G., JR. *Vietnam War Almanac.* 1985.

GLEN GENDZEL

COMMANDO HUNT. COMMANDO HUNT was the code name for U.S. air interdiction efforts against the Ho Chi Minh Trail from 1968 to 1973. It included five semiannual campaigns during the dry, northeast monsoon season, roughly October through April, focusing on chokepoints (places where terrain narrowed the Ho Chi Minh trail) and kill boxes (high-traffic areas selected for intense and repeated attack) south of the main passes crossing the Annamite Mountains into Laos: Nape, Mu Gia, Ban Karai, and Ban Raving. B-52 ARC LIGHT strikes were used for disruptive effect; fighter-bombers and night-flying AC-130 Spectre gunships hunted trucks and troops with targeting information from air-dropped seismic and acoustic sensors. COMMANDO HUNT exacted a heavy toll on communist troops and supplies but could not halt the supply and reinforcement of People's Army of Vietnam forces in the South.

BIBLIOGRAPHY

BALLARD, JACK S. *Development and Employment of Fixed-wing Gunships, 1962–1972.* 1982.

JOHN F. GUILMARTIN JR.

Commercial-Import Program.

Designed on the model of the post–World War II Marshall Plan for Europe, the Commercial-Import Program (CIP) was used by the United States to direct billions of dollars into South Vietnam from the late 1950s through the early 1970s. The U.S. Government financed Vietnamese importers with dollars through the Agency for International Development (AID); the importers in turn ordered foreign goods through the CIP, paying for them in South Vietnamese piasters. These piasters then went into a "counterpart fund" held by the National Bank of Vietnam, which the South Vietnamese government used to finance development projects and cover operating expenses.

The Commercial-Import Program demonstrated the failure of U.S. aid techniques in Vietnam. The CIP enabled the South Vietnamese economy to survive the first years after independence, and the program achieved some success covering South Vietnam's foreign exchange deficit and holding inflation in check. But the extensive patronage and corruption within the CIP prevented it from successfully promoting basic economic development. When the money did not go into the pockets of officials or merchants, importers ordered luxury consumer goods, which created an artificially high standard of living in the cities and contributed little to development in the countryside, where the bulk of the population lived.

BIBLIOGRAPHY

FITZGERALD, FRANCES. *Fire in the Lake: The Vietnamese and the Americans in Vietnam.* 1982.
GIBSON, JAMES WILLIAM. *The Perfect War: Technowar in Vietnam.* 1986.
KOLKO, GABRIEL. *Anatomy of a War: Vietnam, the United States, and the Modern Historical Experience.* 1985.

PAUL M. TAILLON

Conein, Lucien (fl. 1945–1963), French-born Office of Strategic Services (OSS) officer; agent for the Central Intelligence Agency (CIA) in Vietnam. Conein served in Hanoi in 1945 and returned to Vietnam to organize covert operations against the communists in North Vietnam in 1954, although with little success. He went to Saigon in 1962 as an adviser to the South Vietnamese Ministry of the Interior and in 1963 actively aided the coup that ousted Ngo Dinh Diem.

BIBLIOGRAPHY

HAMMER, ELLEN J. *A Death in November.* 1987.
KARNOW, STANLEY. *Vietnam: A History.* 1991.

SANDRA C. TAYLOR

Confucianism. Confucianism is a system of thought and belief based on the teachings of the Chinese philosopher Confucius, who lived during the sixth century B.C. His teachings emphasize ancestor worship and study of the past as the source of wisdom and power. Central to Confucianism are familial and social roles, obligations, and harmony, and the view that the state is an extension of the family. The Chinese introduced Confucianism to Vietnam when they annexed the region in 111 B.C. and, although Buddhism remained the dominant popular religion, Confucianism became the basis for politics, government, and formal education in Vietnam. Colonization of the region by the French in the nineteenth century enabled francophones and Catholics to gain political and social dominance, replacing the Confucian mandarins. Nevertheless, Confucianism remained a vibrant part of Vietnamese society, and scholars claim that the similarities between Confucian and communist precepts about the state, history, and social morality helped give political legitimacy to Ho Chi Minh and the Democratic Republic of Vietnam in the north.

BIBLIOGRAPHY

FITZGERALD, FRANCES. *Fire in the Lake: The Vietnamese and the Americans in Vietnam.* 1982.
JUMPER, ROY, and MARJORIE WEINER NORMAND. "Vietnam: The Historical Background." In *Vietnam and America: A Documented History,* edited by Marvin Gettleman, Jane Franklin, and H. Bruce Franklin, 1985.

JENNIFER FROST

Congressional Medal of Honor. *See* Medal of Honor.

Congress, U.S. Presidents from Harry Truman to Gerald Ford drove an interventionist policy in Vietnam in an attempt to contain communist expansionism in Southeast Asia. Congress acquiesced because it habitually deferred to the president in the realm of foreign policy throughout the Cold War, and because it shared the anticommunist ideology of the day.

Early U.S. Involvement. On occasion, though, Congress managed to play an influential role in shaping that policy. In the spring of 1954, a bloc of powerful Senate Democrats, led by Lyndon Johnson, fearing the prospect of a unilateral U.S. intervention in Indochina, persuaded President Dwight Eisenhower to consult with Winston Churchill's government in London before making a final decision about coming to the aid of the beleaguered French garrison at Dien Bien Phu. When Churchill refused to be drawn into the fray, the White House shelved plans to take military action, which had been recommended by some high officials in the administration, including Vice President Richard Nixon and some members of the Joint Chiefs of Staff (JCS).

After Vietnam was partitioned in 1954, France installed Ngo Dinh Diem's noncommunist government in power in South Vietnam. President Eisenhower and Congress, hoping to strengthen a useful ally in Southeast Asia, quickly provided South Vietnam with funds for military and economic purposes. In 1955, the Senate approved the Southeast Asian Treaty Organization (SEATO), which further committed the United States and its allies to defense of the region against possible future communist expansion. During the remaining Eisenhower years, Vietnam was not seen as a major problem, as Diem appeared to be effectively in charge and the prospects for "nation building" seemed good.

During the Kennedy years, informed members of Congress, led by the Senate Foreign Relations Committee, expressed concern about developments in South Vietnam. They focused on the growing unrest in the cities and a spreading grassroots insurgency in the countryside, fearing that without major reform of its prevailing social and economic institutions, South Vietnam would fall to forces under communist control. Other congressional voices were also beginning to be heard. Sen. George McGovern, speaking on 26 September 1963, suggested that the United States disengage from Vietnam and thereby avoid what he saw as a looming disaster.

The Johnson Years. In November 1963, Diem was murdered and his regime overthrown following a U.S.-backed military coup. President Kennedy was assassinated three weeks later, elevating Lyndon Johnson to the presidency. A former Senate majority leader, Johnson, like Kennedy, was determined to prevent a communist victory in South Vietnam, and he was prepared to use all of his Senate associations and political skills to muster support for that cause.

Johnson shrewdly secured passage of a congressional authorization to use military force in order to protect the independence of South Vietnam and to repel attacks on American military units. After responding with an air assault to an alleged North Vietnamese attack on U.S. destroyers in the Gulf of Tonkin, he pushed the Gulf of Tonkin Resolution through Congress in early August 1964 with the help of allies such as Senators J. William Fulbright and Richard B. Russell. Only Senators Wayne L. Morse and Ernest Gruening, who had already endorsed a U.S. withdrawal from Vietnam, voted against it, although some members of the Senate and others in the House felt uneasy about giving the president such a broad grant of power. They were concerned that the language of the resolution, which stated that the president had the authority to "take all necessary measures to repel any armed attack against the forces of the United States and to prevent further aggression," went too far.

By the summer of 1965, President Johnson, feeling that he had little choice, escalated the war by authorizing U.S. forces on the ground to engage in search-and-destroy missions. Congress, having given Johnson the authority to do this, was virtually powerless to halt the escalation once several hundred thousand U.S. troops had been committed to battle. For the next several years, a bipartisan majority in Congress, reflecting the public's mood, supported President Johnson's policy of avoiding either a pullout or an invasion of North Vietnam.

Only a few in Congress publicly disagreed with the president's policy. Led by Chairman Fulbright, who soon regretted his earlier support, members of the Senate Foreign Relations Committee expressed growing skepticism during public hearings in February 1966. But because that committee lacked the political influence to sway public opinion or to sway the president, the effect of the hearings was slight. Antiwar senators, supporting deescalation and negotiations, were seriously handicapped by the fact that a majority of Americans agreed that the war had to be fought to contain communist expansionism. Even after the Tet Offensive of February 1968, that same majority still did not want to lose the war, disagreeing more with Johnson's tactics than with his goal of keeping South Vietnam within America's orbit. This was the political context that prevailed during the Johnson years when Senate Majority Leader Mike Mansfield, Fulbright, Morse, and Frank Church, among others, dared to question and challenge, with little success, the war policies of their old friend and one-time Senate benefactor.

The Nixon Years. Facing a polity that wanted it both ways, President Richard Nixon initiated a diplomatic campaign on behalf of "peace with honor." Due in part to Vietnamization and to the ambivalence that many Americans still felt about the war, Nixon initially won the public relations battle with his critics in Congress, as there was no significant sentiment in Congress or in the country for a unilateral pullout from South Vietnam. Members of the Senate and House who were against the war had no politically acceptable strategy for ending it, but antiwar sentiment became more pronounced in the Senate than it had been during the Johnson years. Responding to growing middle-class involvement in the peace movement, the Senate passed the Cooper-Church amendment, which required the president to remove by 30 June 1970 those U.S. troops he had earlier dispatched to Cambodia. The Senate supported legislation favoring the withdrawal of all U.S. troops from Vietnam within a specific time period in exchange for North Vietnam's return of U.S. prisoners. The Senate also voted to repeal the Gulf of Tonkin Resolution. Furthermore, a substantial minority embraced the bipartisan McGovern-Hatfield amendment, which was designed to force the president to withdraw all U.S. troops from Vietnam by the end of 1971.

To the dismay of antiwar members of Congress, however, Nixon retained the loyalty of a more prowar House, where House Speaker John W. McCormack and his successor, Carl B. Albert, main-

SENATORIAL CRITICS OF THE VIETNAM WAR. George McGovern (D-S. Dak.), Alan Cranston (D-Calif.), Mark O. Hatfield (R-Oreg.), Charles E. Goodell (R-N.Y.), and Harold E. Hughes (D-Iowa), c. 1970. *Washington Star Collection, Washington Public Library*

tained support for administration policy. Also, the president commanded enough votes in the Senate to sustain any veto of antiwar legislation not to his liking. Nixon's ability to control Congress lasted until after his smashing victory in the 1972 election, when Congress, frustrated with the stalled peace talks in Paris, began to think seriously about legislating an end to the Vietnam War. Nixon's announcement on 23 January 1973 that the combatants had agreed to an armistice in South Vietnam temporarily undercut the strong antiwar feelings that had been steadily growing in Congress.

That peace agreement did not include a provision to end the fighting in Cambodia, however, and during the next several months, Nixon's struggles with Congress over his policy in Cambodia intensified, each side trying to impose its will on the other. Nixon sought to continue the bombing in Cambodia in an attempt to force North Vietnam to make a deal. Congress, on the other hand, hoped to end all U.S. military activity in the region, especially after North Vietnam had returned the U.S. prisoners of war. Initially, Nixon's bombing policy prevailed; but

by late spring in 1973, he had been so weakened politically by the Watergate scandal that Congress no longer feared to challenge and confront him. The stage was set for a decisive showdown between the two branches in the summer of 1973.

Congress forced Nixon to end the bombing of Cambodia by 15 August 1973, marking a major turning point in executive-legislative relations bearing on the Vietnam War. This was also the context for the passage of the War Powers Resolution, which survived a Nixon veto in November 1973. A direct outgrowth of the Vietnam War, the law attempted to restrict presidential warmaking powers by making the president more accountable to Congress. Senators Fulbright and Church, however, who voted for war powers legislation, believed that it was more symbolic than substantive in value.

After U.S. Withdrawal. The struggle over the direction of Vietnam policy continued with Gerald Ford, Nixon's successor. Ford asked Congress to authorize a substantial aid package for the faltering South Vietnamese government, but Congress refused to grant his request, reducing considerably the amount he believed necessary to keep South Vietnam viable. After the fall of Saigon in April 1975, the White House and Congress seemingly closed their books on the longest war in U.S. history, much to the relief of the American people.

Angered by the "loss" of South Vietnam, both Nixon and Ford held Congress responsible for the outcome. But they refused to acknowledge that the key to Congress's action in 1973–1974 was the state of public opinion. Once the American people had decided that enough blood had been spilled and treasure wasted on what was by then widely perceived as a lost cause, they supported legislation limiting or ending any further U.S. commitment to South Vietnam.

Yet, given the possibility that U.S. prisoners of war (POWs) were still being held by North Vietnam, or that North Vietnam had not fully disclosed what it knew about men still missing in action (MIA), the volatile political issue of POWs and MIAs precluded all efforts to effect a reconciliation between the United States and Vietnam for nearly two decades. Only after sixty-two senators, including Vietnam veterans such as John Kerry, Bob Kerrey, and John McCain, voted in favor of a nonbinding resolution to lift the U.S. trade embargo against Vietnam, was it possible to begin healing the wounds between the two countries. On 3 February 1994, President Bill Clinton formally removed that barrier, nearly thirty years after Congress had passed the Gulf of Tonkin Resolution.

BIBLIOGRAPHY

BERMAN, WILLIAM. *William Fulbright and the Vietnam War: The Dissent of a Political Realist.* 1988.

FRANCK, THOMAS, and EDWARD WEISBAND. *Foreign Policy by Congress.* 1979.

GIBBONS, WILLIAM. *The U.S. Government and the Vietnam War: Executive and Legislative Roles and Relationships.* 3 vols. 1984, 1986, 1989.

HALEY, P. EDWARD. *Congress and the Fall of Vietnam and Cambodia.* 1982.

KUTLER, STANLEY. *The Wars of Watergate.* 1990.

WILLIAM C. BERMAN

Conscientious Objectors. Conscientious objectors to the Vietnam War military draft were part of a broad grassroots antiwar movement that by 1972 had reached unprecedented proportions. Supported by local church groups and lawyers' organizations, conscientious objectors grew substantially as inductees took advantage of draft-resistance laws that were becoming more liberal. The growth of conscientious objector classification demoralized the Selective Service System and contributed to the repeal of the draft in 1973. In 1966 just over 6 citizens per 100 inductions received conscientious objector status. By 1970 the rate had increased to more than 25 per 100. In 1972 more draftees were given conscientious objector status than actually joined the services (130 per 100 inductees).

From 1968 to 1974, the federal courts dealt with numerous cases that tested and expanded the U.S. Supreme Court's conscientious objection doctrine. Traditionally, conscientious objection required a rejection of war on specific religious doctrinal grounds. In *United States v. Seegar* (380 U.S. 163 [1965]), the Supreme Court decided that religion did not have to be church-based to satisfy the statute's conditions for belief in a Supreme Being as grounds for conscientious objection.

The Court extended this broad interpretation in a Vietnam War–era case in 1970. Objections that stemmed from moral, ethical, or general religious beliefs were considered as valid as those originating in specific creeds (*Welsh v. United States,* 398 U.S. 333 [1970]). But in other Vietnam War–related cases, the Court refused to widen conscientious objection, denying, for example, "selective conscientious objection" to those who objected not to all wars, but specifically to the Vietnam War (*Gillette v. United States* and *Negre v. Larsen,* 401 U.S. 437 [1971]). Selective conscientious objection was a position that antiwar clergy increasingly supported as ethically valid.

More than 22,000 Americans were indicted for draft law violations between 1965 and 1975. Of this total, 8,756 were convicted of crimes, and 4,001 faced imprisonment.

BIBLIOGRAPHY

DEBENEDETTI, CHARLES. *An American Ordeal: The Antiwar Movement of the Vietnam Era.* 1990.

HALL, MITCHELL. *Because of Their Faith: CALCAV and Religious Opposition to the Vietnam War.* 1990.

KOHN, STEPHAN MARTIN. *Jailed for Peace: The History of American Draft Law Violaters, 1658–1985.* 1986.

VICTOR JEW AND ADAM LAND

Con Son. Originally a French colonial prison, Con Son Island was used by South Vietnam in the late 1960s and 1970s to jail political prisoners, Viet Cong guerrillas, and North Vietnamese prisoners of war. Con Son Island, which lies 80 kilometers (50 miles) off the coast of Vinh Binh province, became a center of controversy in 1970 when a U.S. congressional delegation visited the island and found that prisoners were living in inhumane conditions. Some were confined in "tiger cages," small cement cells in which they were chained and unable to move their legs, conditions that often resulted in paralysis. After the congressional visit Con Son Island became a topic of protest by the antiwar movement in the United States.

BIBLIOGRAPHY

EMERSON, GLORIA. "Americans Find Brutality in South Vietnam Jail." *New York Times,* 7 July 1970, A3.
NGUYEN TIEN HUNG and JERROLD L. SCHECTER. *The Palace File.* 1986.

KELLY EVANS-PFEIFER

Con Thien, village in Quang Tri province, located on the South Vietnamese side of the demilitarized zone (DMZ), which separated North Vietnam from South Vietnam. A U.S. Marine outpost in Con Thien was attacked by North Vietnamese Army (NVA) forces in September 1967, in a month-long pre–Tet Offensive siege. The NVA troops, equipped with the latest in new Soviet weapons, heavily bombarded the fire base with artillery and mortar fire. The marines, aided by U.S. air, naval, and artillery support, successfully defended the base, killing more than two thousand NVA soldiers. The battle served to distract U.S. forces' attention from South Vietnamese cities, which were about to be attacked in the surprise Tet Offensive.

BIBLIOGRAPHY

DAVIDSON, PHILLIP B. *Vietnam at War—The History: 1946–1975.* 1988.
KARNOW, STANLEY. *Vietnam: A History.* 1991.
TELFER, GARY L., LANE ROGERS, and V. KEITH FLEMING JR. *U.S. Marines in Vietnam: Fighting the North Vietnamese, 1967.* 1984.

ELLEN D. GOLDLUST

Cooper, Chester (1917–), Central Intelligence Agency (CIA) analyst, 1958–1964; senior member, U.S. National Security Council, 1964–1967; member, Institute for Defense Analysis, 1967. In 1965, as a member of the National Security Council, Cooper questioned the ability of the United States to win a guerrilla war. He also recognized that the U.S. government's idea of a political

solution actually required a North Vietnamese-negotiated surrender. In 1966 Cooper supported Operation Marigold, a diplomatic mission led by Polish diplomat Janusz Lewandowski, to negotiate with Hanoi. To this end he and Averell Harriman asked for a halt to the bombing of Hanoi. Robert McNamara agreed, but Dean Rusk and Walt Rostow opposed the request, and President Johnson refused to halt the bombing. Cooper later worked on Operation Sunflower, an abortive British diplomatic effort to encourage the Soviet Union to pressure the Democratic Republic of Vietnam (DRV) to compromise.

BIBLIOGRAPHY

KARNOW, STANLEY. *Vietnam: A History.* 1991.
KOLKO, GABRIEL. *Anatomy of a War: Vietnam, the United States, and the Modern Historical Experience.* 1985.
O'TOOLE, G. J. A. *Encyclopedia of American Intelligence and Espionage.* 1988.

ELLEN BAKER

Cooper, John Sherman (1901–1991), U.S. senator (R–Ky.), 1957–1973. Cooper doubted the wisdom of the war by 1964, though he voted in favor of the Gulf of Tonkin Resolution. A critic of U.S. involvement in Vietnam from the late 1960s on, Cooper unsuccessfully cosponsored the Cooper-Church amendment with Frank Church. The amendment, a response to the 1970 Cambodian incursion, called for the termination of funds for all military operations in Cambodia if U.S. troops were not withdrawn.

BIBLIOGRAPHY

HERRING, GEORGE C. *America's Longest War: The United States and Vietnam, 1950–1975.* 1986.
KARNOW, STANLEY. *Vietnam: A History.* 1991.

ELLEN D. GOLDLUST

CORDS. *See* Pacification.

COSVN. *See* Central Office for South Vietnam (COSVN).

Counterinsurgency. Counterinsurgency, or unconventional counterguerrilla warfare, appealed to U.S. strategic planners in the early 1960s as the appropriate response to Soviet support for guer-

ROUNDING UP SUSPECTS. During counterinsurgency operations, an ARVN soldier stands guard over villagers assembled for questioning about guerrilla activities. *U.S. Army*

rilla-based "wars of national liberation" in the developing world. The impetus came from Gen. Maxwell D. Taylor's *The Uncertain Trumpet* (1959), which cautioned against overreliance on nuclear weapons for defense and argued for the development of limited-war capability, including counterinsurgency. Guerrilla wars in distant lands required a new approach that emphasized winning the allegiance of civilians over defeating enemy forces in battle. President Kennedy strongly encouraged counterinsurgency doctrine and relieved top commanders such as Gen. George Decker, U.S. Army chief of staff until 1962, who clung to conventional firepower-and-mobility warfare. Kennedy expanded the U.S. Army Special Forces to fill the counterinsurgency role. Vietnam, according to Central Intelligence Agency (CIA) expert Douglas Blaufarb, "became the most serious, prolonged, and costly U.S. effort to realize the concepts and goals of counterinsurgency."

Under a variety of titles such as "population security" and "pacification," counterinsurgency became the "other war" in Vietnam—a vast American outpouring of agricultural experts, doctors, teachers, engineers, CIA agents, and civil advisers dedicated to "rooting out the Viet Cong infrastructure" and "winning the hearts and minds of the Vietnamese people." Diverse civilian aid projects and psychological-warfare campaigns came under unified command with the formation of Civil Operations and Revolutionary Development Support (CORDS) in 1967, headed by Robert W. Komer. His efforts culminated in the controversial Phoenix program, which led to the execution of about 20,000 suspected Viet Cong guerrillas. Some experts concluded that counterinsurgency failed in Vietnam because it never received sufficient support; others believed it distracted the United States from the main goal of defeating North Vietnam's forces in the field. Either way, unconventional warfare did not prevent a conventional victory by North Vietnamese and Viet Cong forces in 1975.

BIBLIOGRAPHY

BLAUFARB, DOUGLAS S. *The Counterinsurgency Era: U.S. Doctrine and Performance, 1950 to the Present.* 1977.

CABLE, LARRY. *Conflict of Myths: The Development of American Counterinsurgency Doctrine and the Vietnam War.* 1986.

GALULA, DAVID. *Counterinsurgency Warfare.* 1964.

MCCLINTOCK, MICHAEL. *Instruments of Statecraft: U.S. Guerrilla Warfare, Counterinsurgency, and Counter-Terrorism, 1940–1990.* 1992.

SHAFER, D. MICHAEL. *Deadly Paradigm: The Failure of U.S. Counterinsurgency Policy.* 1988.

GLEN GENDZEL

COWIN Report. In early 1971, a U.S. Army task force investigated whether Gen. William Westmoreland was personally culpable for war crimes. Its report, called the "Conduct of the War in Vietnam" (COWIN), found no basis for Westmoreland's guilt.

BIBLIOGRAPHY

LEWY, GUENTER. *America in Vietnam.* 1978.
WESTMORELAND, WILLIAM C. *A Soldier Reports.* 1976.

WILLIAM PAUL SCHUCK

Credibility Gap. A phrase used during the Johnson and Nixon administrations, *credibility gap* referred to the disparity between official pronouncements on the Vietnam War and actual policy and events. Reporter David Wise first wrote of a "credibility gap" in the *New York Herald Tribune* in 1965. President Johnson gave credence to the phrase when he spoke of peaceful intentions in Vietnam yet continued to bomb North Vietnam and to increase the number of U.S. troops there.

BIBLIOGRAPHY

KUTLER, STANLEY I. *The Wars of Watergate.* 1991.
TURNER, KATHLEEN J. *Lyndon Johnson's Dual War: Vietnam and the Press.* 1985.

JENNIFER FROST

Cronkite, Walter (1916–), CBS Evening News anchor, 1954–1981. Cronkite was one of the most respected and influential newsmen in the United States, and his coverage of the Vietnam War greatly concerned the Johnson administration. A consummate professional, Cronkite offered viewers a cautiously optimistic view of the war until the 1968 Tet Offensive, when he traveled to Saigon to assess first-hand the U.S. involvement and chances for success. In a special report on 27 February 1968, Cronkite concluded: "It seems now more certain than ever that the bloody experience of Vietnam is to end in stalemate." Sensing that Cronkite accurately reflected public opinion, Johnson reportedly remarked, "If I have lost Walter Cronkite, I have lost Mr. Average Citizen."

BIBLIOGRAPHY

KARNOW, STANLEY. *Vietnam: A History.* 1991
ZAROULIS, NANCY, and GERALD SULLIVAN. *Who Spoke Up?* 1984.

KELLY EVANS-PFEIFER

Cushman, Robert (1914–1985), commander of III Marine Amphibious Force (1967–1969), Central Intelligence Agency (CIA) deputy director (1969–1972). During his tour in Vietnam (1967–1969), Cushman oversaw the defense of Khe Sanh, the battle for Hue, and the overall I Corps counteroffensive against the Tet Offensive. As deputy director of the CIA, he became briefly enmeshed in allegations of CIA authorization of the burglary of Daniel Ellsberg's psychiatrist's office but was never formally charged. Cushman served as Marine Corps commandant from 1972 until his retirement in 1975, during which time he acted to end voluntary racial segregation in U.S. Marine facilities, although he resisted the post–Vietnam War movement within the armed forces for a more relaxed, less military image.

BIBLIOGRAPHY

Obituary. *New York Times,* 3 January 1985.
SIMMONS, EDWIN H. *The United States Marines.* 1974.

ELLEN D. GOLDLUST

D

Dak To, jungle region in the western Central Highlands near the Laotian and Cambodian borders. In October–November 1967, the North Vietnamese Army (NVA) launched a direct attack on U.S. forces in the area in one of the pre–Tet Offensive border battles. The North Vietnamese forces lost 1,600 men and were virtually destroyed. The extensive loss of forces by the NVA here and in other battles during this period convinced Giap to avoid future direct conflict with large U.S. forces.

BIBLIOGRAPHY

DAVIDSON, PHILLIP B. *Vietnam at War—The History: 1946–1975.* 1988.
HERRING, GEORGE C. *America's Longest War: The United States and Vietnam, 1950–1975.* 1986.
KARNOW, STANLEY. *Vietnam: A History.* 1991.

ELLEN D. GOLDLUST

Da Nang, South Vietnamese city, capital of Quang Nam province. The most important port in the Central Lowlands of Vietnam, Da Nang was a point of contention at the 1954 Geneva Conference. France insisted that the demarcation line between North and South Vietnam be set at the 17th parallel in order to include the city in South Vietnam. Da Nang in 1967 was the second largest urban area in South Vietnam, with a population of 143,910. During the Vietnam War, the social costs of the conflict were readily apparent in Da Nang, which developed an immense refugee problem as the rural peasantry fled their villages for the city. By 1970, the city's population had risen to 450,000. As a result of the decrease in food production in the countryside and the official corruption that hampered the delivery of food and medicine from the United States, the uprooted rural population lived at little more than subsistence level in makeshift camps on the outskirts of the city

To protect its air base at Da Nang, the United States landed two battalions of U.S. Marines there on 8 March 1965, beginning the U.S. commitment of ground forces in Vietnam. Da Nang was also the site of the headquarters of the Army of the Republic of Vietnam's (ARVN) I Corps and its 3d Division. A year later, Da Nang was the scene of the 1966 Buddhist "Struggle Movement" against Prime Minister Nguyen Cao Ky's government. When ARVN troops sided with the Buddhists, Ky declared the city under communist control (despite the presence of U.S. Marines stationed in Da Nang) and sent one thousand South Vietnamese marines to crush the uprising. In 1968, Da Nang was attacked by North Vietnamese Army (NVA) and Viet Cong forces during the Tet Offensive. During the NVA's Final Offensive in 1975, Da Nang fell within a matter of days. The city's defenses quickly disintegrated and the defending army and civilians fled in a disastrous retreat under heavy crossfire between the ARVN and the NVA. Da Nang was later a major port for the exodus of Vietnamese boat people.

BIBLIOGRAPHY

FITZGERALD, FRANCES. *Fire in the Lake: The Vietnamese and the Americans in Vietnam.* 1972.
KAHIN, GEORGE MCT. *Intervention: How America Became Involved in Vietnam.* 1986.

PAUL M. TAILLON

DANIEL BOONE Operations. DANIEL BOONE operations occurred in 1967 and 1968 when covert squads of U.S. Special Forces and South Vietnamese, dressed as peasants or in unrecognizable uniforms, undertook missions into Cambodia to gather intelligence or to sabotage communist installations at the southern end of the Ho Chi Minh Trail, despite U.S. law forbidding operations in countries not at war with the United States. The information gathered on these raids led to the 1969 secret bombing of Cambodia, Operation MENU, and to the 1970 invasion of Cambodia. DANIEL BOONE missions were renamed SALEM HOUSE in 1968 and THOT NOT three years later.

BIBLIOGRAPHY

KARNOW, STANLEY. *Vietnam: A History.* 1991.
SHAWCROSS, WILLIAM. *Sideshow: Kissinger, Nixon, and the Destruction of Cambodia.* 1979.
STANTON, SHELBY L. *The Green Berets at War: U.S. Army Special Forces in Southeast Asia, 1956–1985.* 1985.

ELLEN D. GOLDLUST

Dean, John Gunther (1926–), U.S. ambassador to Cambodia, 1974–1975. A career diplomat, Dean became ambassador to Cambodia after spending two years in the U.S. embassy in Laos (1972–1974). Dean's attempts to achieve a negotiated settlement of the war in Cambodia failed, partly because of conflicts with Secretary of State Henry Kissinger. As the Khmer Rouge prevailed over the U.S.-supported Lon Nol government in

April 1975, Dean supervised the evacuation of U.S. personnel from Cambodia.

BIBLIOGRAPHY

ISAACS, ARNOLD R. *Without Honor: Defeat in Vietnam and Cambodia.* 1983.
SHAWCROSS, WILLIAM. *Sideshow: Kissinger, Nixon and the Destruction of Cambodia.* 1979.

WILLIAM PAUL SCHUCK

Defense, Department of. Created by the National Security Act of 1947, which unified the War and Navy departments, the U.S. Department of Defense is a loose confederation of the military service branches. The U.S. Army, Navy, Air Force, and Marines each maintain separate staffs under their individual service chiefs, who report to the chairman of the Joint Chiefs of Staff (JCS). He in turn reports to the secretary of defense, who reports to the president and is part of the cabinet. The Defense Reorganization Act of 1958 removed the JCS from the direct chain of command, and Vietnam was the first war fought under this revised command system. Presidential directives were relayed through the secretary of defense to the Commander-in-Chief, Pacific (CINCPAC), excluding the top-ranking military advisers on the JCS, whose advice was seldom welcome at the White House. Interservice rivalry also obstructed communication between military commanders and civilian policymakers during the war. Each service branch tried to place its efforts in the best light and was reluctant to admit failure. The JCS never acknowledged that U.S. strategy was fundamentally flawed and incapable of achieving U.S. goals in Vietnam. The principal critics of Vietnam policy within the Defense Department were civilians, not generals.

Secretary of Defense Robert McNamara (1961–1968) grew to distrust the advice and information he received from the military. He created the civilian Office of Systems Analysis within the Defense Department to provide him with independent estimates. He staffed the office with young college graduates and RAND Corporation experts skilled in the advanced management techniques of systems analysis and operations research. Military commanders grew to loathe "McNamara's Whiz Kids," whom Gen. William Westmoreland called "self-appointed field marshals." While he was MACV commander, Westmoreland deeply resented civilian experts in the Defense Department who "constantly sought to alter strategy and tactics with naive, gratuitous advice." But

JOINT CHIEFS OF STAFF, 1973. The Joint Chiefs oversaw the United States' military withdrawal from Vietnam during one of the most turbulent periods in the history of America's armed forces. Left to right: General Creighton W. Abrams, army chief of staff; General John D. Ryan, air force chief of staff; Admiral Thomas H. Moorer, chairman, Joint Chiefs of Staff; Admiral Elmo R. Zumwalt Jr., chief of naval operations; General Robert E. Cushman, commandant of the Marine Corps. *National Archives*

Defense Department civilians were often more realistic about the progress of the war. Cost-benefit analysis of military troop requests suggested that the United States was failing massively by 1967, contributing to McNamara's disenchantment with the war and his resignation in 1968.

Secretary of Defense Clark Clifford (1968–1969) commissioned more civilian studies that recommended disengagement and shifting the combat burden to South Vietnam. Military commanders, including JCS Chairman Gen. Earle Wheeler, CINC-PAC Adm. Ulysses S. Grant Sharp, and General Westmoreland, demanded more troops and more bombing as the price of victory in Vietnam. But civilian opponents of escalation within the Defense Department, including Assistant Secretary of Defense Paul Warnke and Deputy Secretary of Defense Paul Nitze won out in March 1968, when President Johnson agreed to seek negotiations and not increase troop levels. When President Nixon stepped up the U.S. war effort by invading Cambodia in 1970 and bombing North Vietnam in 1972, he issued orders through the JCS with specific instructions not to inform Secretary of Defense Melvin Laird (1969–1973), an outspoken critic of escala-

tion. But opponents of the war within the Defense Department were usually too few and too powerless to halt the ponderous momentum behind the U.S. commitment. One exception was Daniel Ellsberg, a civilian analyst who leaked the top-secret Pentagon Papers and helped turn public opinion against the war in 1971.

BIBLIOGRAPHY

BORKLUND, C.W. *The Department of Defense.* 1968.

ENTHOVEN, ALAIN C., and K. WAYNE SMITH. *How Much Is Enough? Shaping the Defense Program, 1961–1969.* 1971.

GELB, LESLIE, and RICHARD BETTS. *The Irony of Vietnam: The System Worked.* 1979.

HOOPES, TOWNSEND. *The Limits of Intervention: An Inside Account of How the Johnson Policy of Escalation was Reversed.* 1969.

PALMER, GREGORY. *The McNamara Strategy and the Vietnam War.* 1978.

WESTMORELAND, WILLIAM C. *A Soldier Reports.* 1976.

GLEN GENDZEL

Defoliation. *See* Chemical Warfare; RANCH HAND.

De Gaulle, Charles. *See* Gaulle, Charles de.

Demilitarized Zone (DMZ).

At the 1954 Geneva Conference, the country of Vietnam was created from the former colony of French Indochina. It was temporarily divided into north and south along the Song Ben Hai River near the 17th parallel until national elections could be held. A 10-kilometer-wide (6-mile) buffer zone from which both sides agreed to withhold military forces surrounded this demarcation line. This demilitarized zone (DMZ) became the de facto border between North and South Vietnam. Early in the war, U.S. planners observed the sanctity of the DMZ, considered building a barrier to block infiltration through it, and expected North Vietnam to launch a conventional invasion across it. Instead, North Vietnamese Army (NVA) and Viet Cong units learned to seek refuge in the DMZ from U.S. planes and artillery. In response, the United States constructed a series of fire support bases along Route 9 just south of the DMZ in 1966–1967. From these positions U.S. artillery could reach enemy troop formations in the DMZ, and the NVA frequently attacked to suppress the shelling. NVA armor attacked and broke through the DMZ in the Easter Offensive of 1972, and again in the Spring Offensive in 1975—both conventional invasions.

BIBLIOGRAPHY

"Battle of the DMZ." *U.S. News and World Report,* 16 October 1967.

NICOLI, ROBERT V. "Fire Support Base Development." In *The Marines in Vietnam, 1954–1973.* 1974.

PEARSON, WILLARD. *The War in the Northern Provinces.* 1978.

PISOR, ROBERT. *The End of the Line: The Siege of Khe Sanh.* 1982.

GLEN GENDZEL

Democratic National Convention, 1968.

The 1968 Democratic National Convention took place in Chicago on 24–29 August. Ten thousand antiwar protesters gathered, and police and National Guard troops were mobilized to ensure order. In addition, U.S. military intelligence services and undercover Central Intelligence Agency (CIA) agents infiltrated the crowd, even though the CIA is prohibited by law from operating inside the United States.

On 28 August the demonstration erupted into violence when police and National Guard forces tried to prevent the protesters from marching on the International Amphitheater, where the convention met. A battle ensued, with the police using clubs, rifle butts, and tear gas, and the demonstrators responding with rocks and bottles. Hundreds of arrests resulted, but thousands of other protesters rallied the next day at Grant Park. That meeting also resulted in violence when law officers prevented a group led by comedian and activist Dick Gregory from marching to his house on the South Side. The demonstrators hurled objects at the police and troops, who retaliated with tear gas and beatings.

Inside the convention, the Democrats wrestled with the party platform on the war. Aides to Vice President Hubert Humphrey, the leading candidate for the party's presidential nomination, drafted a compromise that called for an end to U.S. air strikes against North Vietnam and for the shifting of more responsibility to the South Vietnamese. This platform appeared to satisfy the different Democratic factions, but the outgoing president, Lyndon Johnson, objected, believing that his party was undercutting his policy. Under this pressure, Humphrey scrapped his compromise and introduced a platform that agreed with Johnson's views. After three hours of debate that demonstrated the disagreement within the Democratic party on the issue, the convention finally adopted the Johnson plank by a narrow margin. The 1968 Democratic Convention highlighted the depth of the political divisions caused by the Vietnam War.

BIBLIOGRAPHY

KARNOW, STANLEY. *Vietnam: A History.* 1991.

MAILER, NORMAN. *Miami and the Siege of Chicago: An Informal History of the Republican and Democratic Conventions of 1968.* 1969.

WHITE, THEODORE. *The Making of the President, 1968.* 1969.

ZAROULIS, NANCY, and GERALD SULLIVAN. *Who Spoke Up? American Protest against the War in Vietnam, 1963–1975.* 1985.

ELLEN D. GOLDLUST

Democratic Party, U.S.

The domestic turmoil caused by U.S. involvement in Vietnam exposed deep divisions within the Democratic Party and contributed greatly to the breakup of the "New Deal coalition," which had carried the party to frequent presidential victories from Franklin D. Roosevelt's election in 1932 up through Lyndon Johnson's landslide in 1964. This coalition, bound primarily by economic concerns, had united disparate groups including ethnic minorities, blue-collar workers, farmers, southerners, big-city residents, and the educated upper-middle-class establishment. The coalition collapsed after the 1968 presidential election.

Presidents John F. Kennedy and Johnson and many within the Democratic establishment were strongly influenced by accusations that Democratic president Harry S. Truman had "lost" China to the communists. They believed they had to make a stand in Vietnam to prevent another such loss while the Democrats were in power. Fear of attacks from conservatives consequently held sway over the Democrats' Vietnam policy as much as did their belief in the domino theory and containment.

As the Vietnam War escalated with no end in sight, more liberal Democrats increasingly opposed the war. This wing believed that the war had disrupted the Great Society social agenda, and considered involvement in Vietnam contrary to U.S. interests and moreover immoral. Meanwhile, many blue-collar and rural Democrats felt increasingly alienated from the antiwar and civil rights movements, which they associated with the Democratic left wing. For many of these "middle Americans," whose sons were fighting and dying in Vietnam, their own concerns about the war were superseded by their hostility toward "privileged" student demonstrators.

The strains and stresses heightened during the 1968 Democratic presidential primaries and exploded at the national convention in Chicago. Robert F. Kennedy and Eugene J. McCarthy embodied the hopes of the antiwar Democrats, while Hubert Humphrey became the standard bearer for the administration's Vietnam policies when Johnson decided not to seek a second term and anointed Humphrey his heir apparent.

During the convention a bitter floor fight occurred over the party's Vietnam plank. Ultimately Humphrey, bullied by Johnson, succeeded in pushing through a plank that went along with the administration's policies and rejected calls for an immediate bombing halt and negotiations on withdrawal. Outside the convention hall, antiwar demonstrators clashed violently with Mayor Richard J. Daley's Chicago police, creating an embarrassing spectacle for the shocked national audience.

Republican nominee Richard Nixon appealed to those blue-collar Democrats with his themes of law and order and promises of an "honorable" settlement in Vietnam. This strategy worked again in 1972 against George McGovern, as the Democrats' more liberal elements dominated the party, which proved to be more isolated from the mainstream of political thought in the United States. Thus the Vietnam War, and the antiwar movement it created, contributed to a fundamental shift in allegiance away from the Democratic Party.

[*See also* Democratic National Convention, 1968.]

BIBLIOGRAPHY

DIONNE, E. J., JR. *Why Americans Hate Politics.* 1991.
OLSON, JAMES, and RANDY ROBERTS. *Where the Domino Fell.* 1991.
POWERS, THOMAS. *The War at Home.* 1973.

KELLY EVANS-PFEIFER

Democratic Republic of Vietnam (DRV).

See Vietnam, Democratic Republic of (DRV).

Depuy, William E.

(1919–1992), general, U.S. Army; chief of operations, Military Assistance Command, Vietnam (MACV), 1964–1966; assistant army vice chief of staff, 1969–1973. Gen. William Depuy devised the search-and-destroy strategy that pursued victory in Vietnam with "more bombs, more shells, more napalm," as he put it, "until the other side cracks and gives up." Depuy had absolute faith that U.S. firepower would prevail. "We are going to stomp them to death," he vowed. "I don't know any other way." After the war, Depuy helped devise the army's new "Airland Battle" doctrine, which prevailed in the Persian Gulf War.

BIBLIOGRAPHY

BROWNLEE, ROMIE L., and WILLIAM J. MULLEN III. *Changing an Army: An Oral History of General William E. Depuy.* 1988.

GLEN GENDZEL

Desertion.

The U.S. military defined desertion as being "absent with the intention to remain away permanently." Approximately 7,575,000 Americans served in the U.S. military between 1965 and 1973, and about 500,000 desertion incidents were reported. Of these deserters, however, only 93,250 remained away longer than thirty days. Few soldiers deserted from the field of battle or from Vietnam; 20,000 Americans deserted after they had finished their tour of duty in Vietnam.

During the Vietnam War, desertion rates reached an all-time high of 73.5 out of 1,000 soldiers in 1971, a 400 percent increase over the 1966 rate of desertion. In contrast, only 25 out of 1,000 soldiers deserted annually during the Korean War. Vietnam War deserters, in general, were younger than their fellow soldiers, poorly educated, and from low-income backgrounds. Of army deserters 75 percent were white, but an African American serviceman was twice as likely to desert. Navy deserters also were overwhelmingly white, while air force deserters tended to be African American and better educated. Soldiers were motivated to desert for a variety of reasons, including personal issues, family and financial problems, and antiwar sentiments. Many deserters, for example, cited difficulties with military life to explain their actions. The combination of desertion and the far more numerous absent without leave (AWOL) incidents cost the military about one million man-years of military service, almost half the total number of man-years spent by U.S. troops in Vietnam during the war.

For the 83,135 deserters who either returned or were found, the consequences of their actions were less-than-honorable discharges. Although such discharges were not "dishonorable," which required a court-martial conviction to prove intent to desert, they still were considered "bad paper." The approximately 9,000 deserters who evaded authorities were technically fugitives.

The clemency and amnesty policies of Presidents Gerald Ford and Jimmy Carter did little to improve the situation of deserters. Ford's program grouped together draft resisters and military deserters, offering both "clemency discharges" in return for two years of alternative service. The Carter administration gave blanket pardons to resisters, while demanding that deserters apply in person for a review and possible discharge upgrade. Due to these stringent requirements, application levels were low; only 19 percent and 9 percent of those eligible applied for the Ford and Carter programs, respectively. As a result, the vasty majority of deserters continued to be denied veterans' education and medical benefits and to be perceived by many Americans as traitors and cowards.

Desertion was also a problem for the other armies participating in the Vietnam War. In contrast to U.S. servicemen in Vietnam, Vietnamese deserters, from the Army of the Republic of Vietnam (ARVN), from the National Liberation Front (NLF), or from the North Vietnamese Army (NVA), could take refuge easily in the densely populated areas of South Vietnam. Between 1965 and 1972, the Republic of Vietnam Armed Forces (RVNAF) lost about 120,000 servicemen annually to desertion. The ARVN sustained the greatest losses, with

soldiers deserting at 2.5 times the overall RVNAF rate. South Vietnamese cited primarily low pay, homesickness, military corruption, and dangerous fighting, rather than political reasons, as motivations for desertion. Defection of RVNAF personnel to the NLF or NVA was rare. Desertion rates—officially considered defections—from the NLF and NVA were significantly lower than those for the RVNAF, averaging about 20,000 per year between 1967 and 1971. The ARVN Rangers, some of South Vietnam's best troops, were composed almost exclusively of NLF and NVA defectors. Scholars attribute the difference in desertion rates between South Vietnamese and North Vietnamese (including NLF) forces to the greater commitment and offensive, guerrilla fighting style of the NLF and NVA.

BIBLIOGRAPHY

BASKIR, LAWRENCE M., and WILLIAM A. STRAUSS. *Chance and Circumstance: The Draft, the War, and the Vietnam Generation.* 1978.
DONG VAN KHUYEN. *The Republic of Vietnam Armed Forces.* 1980.
LEWY, GUENTER. *America in Vietnam.* 1978.

JENNIFER FROST

DeSoto Missions. Since the 1950s, the U.S. Navy had conducted covert operations against the People's Republic of China (PRC), North Korea, and the Soviet Union. Code-named "DeSoto missions," these operations were conducted by intelligence-gathering destroyers that remained in international waters. In early 1964, President Johnson authorized covert operations against North Vietnam that included DeSoto missions and a program of clandestine warfare named OPLAN 34A. The DeSoto missions gathered information about North Vietnamese radar, charted and photographed the coast, monitored ship traffic, and recorded radio communications. A DeSoto mission, carried out by the destroyer *Maddox* on 2 August 1964, sparked the Gulf of Tonkin incident.

BIBLIOGRAPHY

HATCHER, PATRICK LLOYD. *Suicide of an Elite: American Internationalists and Vietnam.* 1990.
KARNOW, STANLEY. *Vietnam: A History.* 1991.

PAUL M. TAILLON

Détente. A French word meaning lessening of tension, *détente* is often used to denote the period from 1967 through 1976 when the United States and the Soviet Union sought to deescalate the cold war conflict between them. For the United States, détente represented a new tactic for carrying on the traditional policy of containment, albeit through limited cooperation and negotiation rather than confrontation. President Lyndon B. Johnson initially pursued détente when the United States commitment in Vietnam became too costly; he hoped that reducing tensions with the Soviet Union would help the United States extricate itself from Vietnam. The Soviets needed economic assistance and were willing to negotiate to a point, but not about Southeast Asia. Détente stalled until 1972, when, plagued by domestic troubles and bogged down in negotiations with the North Vietnamese, President Richard M. Nixon proposed economic aid to the Soviet Union. At the same time he opened talks with the People's Republic of China (PRC), exploiting the Sino-Soviet split to pressure the Soviets into negotiating in good faith at the Strategic Arms Limitation Talks and hoping to enlist the PRC's leverage with North Vietnam. Just before Nixon's May 1972 trip to Moscow, however, the North Vietnamese launched the Easter Offensive. While Nixon hoped to secure Soviet and Chinese cooperation in Southeast Asia, he believed that if the United States did not achieve "peace with honor," it would lose credibility and détente would fail. Therefore, despite fears that the Soviets might cancel the meeting if the United States launched a bombing campaign, Nixon responded to the offensive with Operation LINEBACKER. Nixon's gamble paid off: the Moscow summit was successful; both the Soviets and the Chinese responded to the U.S. bombing with only mild protests, and the North Vietnamese offensive ground to a halt.

BIBLIOGRAPHY

LaFeber, Walter. *America, Russia, and the Cold War, 1945–1990.* 1991.

Paterson, Thomas G. *Meeting the Communist Threat: Truman to Reagan.* 1988.

Paul M. Taillon

Diem, Ngo Dinh. *See* Ngo Dinh Diem.

Dien Bien Phu. Viet Minh forces, led by Gen. Vo Nguyen Giap, overran a French garrison at Dien Bien Phu (in northwestern Vietnam near the Laotian border) on 7 May 1954 after a bitterly contested two-month siege. In late 1953, French military commanders had aggressively dispatched a force to northwestern Vietnam, but they underestimated the Viet Minh, who successfully isolated and annihilated the outpost. The battle ended the eight-year Indochina War and brought formal French withdrawal from Indochina in July 1954. The Viet Minh, however, failed to gain a decisive political victory because they were forced to accept the country's partition at the Geneva peace talks. Nevertheless, the military victory at Dien Bien Phu represented a pivotal landmark in the demise of French and European colonialism.

The encounter at Dien Bien Phu took shape in late 1953, as the rival armies prepared for peace talks and adjusted to increases in U.S. aid for France. In November, French paratroopers occupied a small outpost along a 16-kilometer-long (10-mile) river valley near Laos. Gen. Henri Navarre, the French commander, hoped that such an aggressively positioned air head would disrupt the Viet Minh's rear operations and thwart raids into Laos. The French government, as Navarre knew, hoped for an "honorable settlement" to the conflict, and he strove to gain the military initiative before negotiations.

The Viet Minh forces surrounded the garrison during the winter. General Giap had purposely sent forces into Laos to overextend the French forces, and the isolated garrison provided him with an opportunity to strike a significant blow against the French. Viet Minh leaders strove to undermine French resolve before increased U.S. aid could change the fortunes of the war, and as did France, the Viet Minh hoped to bolster their posture in the looming negotiations at Geneva.

Military scholars credit the Viet Minh's success in the siege to their formidable logistical preparations. Because of the inaccessibility of the valley, French command expected a minimal assault on the base. The Viet Minh, however, mounted an extraordinary supply effort, supporting an eventual fifty thousand troops of the People's Army of Vietnam (PAVN) around Dien Bien Phu. "[H]undreds of thousand of men and women," as Giap noted, built new roads and transported food and war matériel. Laborers carried an estimated 250 heavy weapons, including 105 mm artillery and 37 mm antiaircraft weapons, through the rugged terrain. The extensive artillery, unexpected by the French, proved decisive during the battle. The French outpost depended on air transport for resupply, performed largely by an overtaxed fleet of U.S. C-47 transports. The Viet Minh's Chinese-supplied artillery, dug into the hills around Dien Bien Phu, disabled the French airstrip a few weeks into the siege, and subsequent Viet Minh antiaircraft fire hampered crucial airdrops, effectively strangling the garrison.

The Viet Minh attack on Dien Bien Phu began on 13 March 1954. The fifteen thousand defenders included some French soldiers, but most were Foreign Legion, Vietnamese, North African, and Tai montagnard forces. The garrison's defenses consisted of a central fortified area about 2,700 meters (3,000 yards) in diameter surrounding an airstrip and a former village. Limited supplies forced the garrison to dig earthen fortifications rather than construct more sturdy defenses. Giap initially attacked three defense outposts about 1.5 kilometers (1 mile) north of the central perimeter. An artillery barrage and human wave attacks captured the compounds within a week, though with heavy PAVN casualties. For subsequent attacks, the Viet Minh dug trenches so they could approach the French perimeter less dangerously. Inside the fortress, increasing resupply problems produced shortages and horrific conditions, particularly for casualties. By May only 3,000 effective troops, desperately low on ammunition, defended the central fortifications. The PAVN overran the fort on 7 May. An estimated 2,200 of the French garrison died in the siege, and 6,500 were taken prisoner. The Viet Minh suffered an estimated 23,000 casualties with 8,000 fatalities.

After the French realized the precarious situation of their forces in late March, the government asked President Eisenhower for U.S. air strikes to relieve the siege. Some administration figures favored intervention, including Secretary of State John Foster Dulles and Vice President Richard Nixon. Others expressed skepticism of such a raid's effectiveness and, led by Gen. Matthew Ridgeway, warned that intervention would draw U.S. ground forces into a protracted conflict. Congressional leaders, including Lyndon B. Johnson, also opposed air strikes. Later in April, Eisenhower expressed support for air raids if joined by Great Britain, but the British declined, sealing the fate of the garrison. The U.S. refusal to intervene at Dien Bien Phu, in light of its previous pressure on France to intensify the war effort and $3 billion in military aid, drew bitter responses from the French government.

The fall of Dien Bien Phu stunned the French public. The ruling French coalition fell, and a new government, led by Pierre Mendès-France, agreed to negotiate a withdrawal from Indochina. The Dien Bien Phu disaster, which fed public disillusionment with the government, contributed to the collapse of the Fourth Republic during the 1958 Algerian crisis. The defeat in Indochina hardened French resolve to stand firm in its North African colony; the Viet Minh victory, correspondingly, inspired Algerian nationalists, who perceived the vulnerability of the colonialists. The military success of the Viet Minh, however, did not transfer into a decisive political victory. The Geneva peace accords, concluded in July 1954, partitioned Vietnam at the 17th parallel with a vague promise for future national elections. The Viet Minh's allies, the People's Republic of China (PRC) and the Soviet Union, pressured them to accept the compromise peace terms. The PRC feared a unified Vietnamese power to the south, while the Soviet Union sought French support for European initiatives. The diplomatic failure, or the "betrayal," as the Vietnamese communists termed it, prepared the way for the next war.

BIBLIOGRAPHY

DAVIDSON, PHILIP. *Vietnam at War, 1946–1975*. 1988.

FALL, BERNARD. *Hell in a Very Small Place: The Siege of Dien Bien Phu*. 1966.

HERRING, GEORGE C. *America's Longest War: The United States and Vietnam, 1950–1975*. 1986.

ARTILLERY ON DIKES. Two coast defense 122 mm cannon emplaced on a dike near Thai Binh, North Vietnam, south of Haiphong, 22 July 1972. *Archive Photos*

RIOUX, JEAN-PIERRE. *The Fourth Republic, 1944–1958.* Translated by Godfrey Rogers. 1987.

ADAM LAND

Dikes. For two thousand years the Vietnamese people have constructed an elaborate network of dikes, dams, and ditches for irrigation and flood control. The most extensive system of dikes was in the Red River delta, a densely populated region of 3,000 square kilometers (1,800 square miles) that was the "rice bowl" of North Vietnam during the war. In 1966, Assistant Secretary of Defense John McNaughton proposed bombing the dikes in monsoon season to trigger floods and pressure the North Vietnamese government. U.S. strategic bombing doctrine, however, preferred industrial targets to rice paddies, and President Johnson feared a propaganda backlash if he induced famine. With few exceptions, U.S. pilots had strict orders to avoid bombing the Red River dikes, which then became favored sites for North Vietnamese antiaircraft batteries.

BIBLIOGRAPHY

CHALIAND, GERARD. *The Peasants of North Vietnam.* 1969.
CLODFELTER, MARK. *The Limits of Air Power: The American Bombing of North Vietnam.* 1989.
LARSEN, MARION R. *Agricultural Economy of North Vietnam.* 1965.
TRAN DANG KHOA. "Water Conservancy in North Vietnam." *Vietnamese Studies* 2 (1964).

GLEN GENDZEL

Diplomacy

Ends and Means
Diplomatic Shadowboxing
Fighting While Negotiating
The Persistence of Stalemate
Peace with Honor?

Diplomacy played a crucial role in the Vietnam War, secondary only to the application of military power but frequently subordinate to it. The major combatants did not have diplomatic relations with each other. Until the opening of negotiations in Paris in May 1968, they communicated, often awkwardly, through public pronouncements, private individuals, or third countries. Whatever the means of contact, they used peace moves and diplomacy to secure propaganda advantage, win support at home and internationally, and confuse and divide each other. Diplomacy was as much a means to achieve their respective goals as was military power.

Ends and Means. In April 1965, as North Vietnam and the United States were on the brink of full-scale war, each first publicly set forth its bargaining position. In a much-publicized speech at Johns Hopkins University on 7 April 1965, President Lyndon Baines Johnson reaffirmed the United States' long-standing commitment to the independence of South Vietnam, insisting that the United States would not be defeated and would not withdraw "either openly or under the cloak of a meaningless agreement." At the same time, he left open the door for a negotiated settlement with North Vietnam, proclaiming a willingness to engage in "unconditional discussions." As encouragement he promised a billion-dollar development project for Southeast Asia in which North Vietnam might participate.

One day later, North Vietnamese prime minister Pham Van Dong responded to Johnson's speech by outlining his nation's Four Points for a settlement. He insisted, first, that the United States must withdraw its forces from Vietnam and cease all acts of war. He called for the neutralization of both Vietnams pending

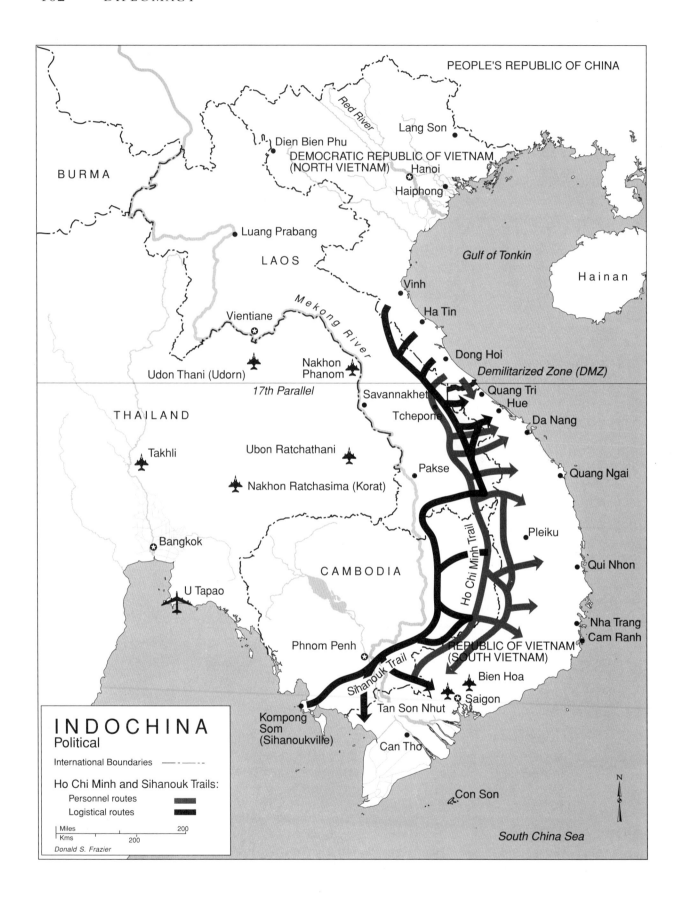

PEOPLE'S REPUBLIC OF CHINA

Red River

Lang Son

Dien Bien Phu
DEMOCRATIC REPUBLIC OF VIETNAM
(NORTH VIETNAM)

BURMA

Hanoi

Haiphong

Luang Prabang

LAOS

Gulf of Tonkin

Hainan

Vinh

Ha Tin

Mekong River

Vientiane

Dong Hoi

Demilitarized Zone (DMZ)

Udon Thani (Udorn)

Nakhon
Phanom

17th Parallel

Savannakhet

Quang Tri
Hue

THAILAND

Tchepone

Da Nang

Takhli

Ubon Ratchathani

Pakse

Quang Ngai

Nakhon Ratchasima (Korat)

Ho Chi Minh Trail

Pleiku

Bangkok

CAMBODIA

Qui Nhon

U Tapao

Nha Trang
Cam Ranh

Phnom Penh

REPUBLIC OF VIETNAM
(SOUTH VIETNAM)

Sihanouk Trail

Bien Hoa

Tan Son Nhut

Saigon

Kompong
Som
(Sihanoukville)

Can Tho

Con Son

South China Sea

N

INDOCHINA
Political

International Boundaries

Ho Chi Minh and Sihanouk Trails:
    Personnel routes
    Logistical routes

Miles   200
Kms
          200
Donald S. Frazier

unification of the country and proposed that the internal affairs of South Vietnam be settled in accordance with the program of the National Liberation Front (NLF). He affirmed, finally, that reunification of the country must be arranged by the Vietnamese people without outside interference.

The diplomatic language used by each of the adversaries only slightly obscured the longstanding goals they sought and the depth of their commitment. The North Vietnamese and their NLF allies had been fighting for more than three decades for unification of the country and freedom from outside interference. They had come very close to attaining these aims on several occasions, only to see them slip away. Since the early 1920s, North Vietnamese leader Ho Chi Minh had agitated for the independence of Vietnam from French colonialism. In the 1930s, his colleagues in the Indochina Communist Party had attempted an abortive revolution and had suffered imprisonment and other reprisals when they failed. In 1941, they formed the League for the Independence of Vietnam, or Viet Minh, to continue the struggle. They took advantage of the confusion at the end of World War II to proclaim Vietnam independent. France was not prepared to give up its Indochinese colonies without a struggle, however, and French-Vietnamese talks subsequently broke down on the key issues of unity and independence. In November 1946, the Viet Minh went to war with France to secure what they had been unable to achieve through negotiation.

Although they won the war militarily, the Viet Minh's goals of independence and unification were again frustrated at the conference table. After eight years of bloody conflict, culminating in the climactic French defeat in May 1954 at the remote fortress of Dien Bien Phu, the Viet Minh and France attempted to settle the conflict at an international conference in Geneva. For reasons of ideology and national interest, the Soviet Union and China had supported the Viet Minh war effort with money and supplies. Fearing possible U.S. intervention and a larger and much more costly war, however, the Viet Minh's allies compelled them at Geneva to accept a temporary partition of Vietnam at the 17th parallel pending elections to be held in 1956. Largely as a result of the subsequent political intervention by the United States in support of the South Vietnamese government headed by Ngo Dinh Diem, these elections were never held, Vietnam remained divided, and the Viet Minh goals were again thwarted.

In the late 1950s, the Viet Minh again resorted to military measures. Alarmed at the success of U.S.-backed South Vietnamese president Ngo Dinh Diem's repression campaign and buoyed by rising popular discontent with his government, Viet Minh "stay-behinds" in the South began to mobilize to defend themselves and to attract new adherents to the cause. North Vietnam subsequently sanctioned the insurgency and began to infiltrate men and supplies into South Vietnam, gradually increasing its support. In December 1960, the southern insurgents formally organized the National Liberation Front (NLF), and by early 1961 they posed a grave threat to the Saigon government. The insurgents and their North Vietnamese backers were not eager for a potentially destructive war with the United States, but they were determined to achieve, by force if necessary, the goals they had sought for so long.

To the United States, the insurgency threatened interests that had come to be considered vital. World War II had left the Soviet Union the most powerful nation in Europe and Asia, and Joseph Stalin's subjugation of Eastern Europe aroused growing fears among Americans that the USSR had broader, global designs. Between 1947 and 1949, the United States committed itself to the containment of communist expansion in Europe with the Truman Doctrine, the Marshall Plan, and the creation of the North Atlantic Treaty Organization (NATO). In 1950 it extended the policy to East Asia by intervening militarily in Korea.

The containment policy was also extended to Indochina in 1950. Because Ho Chi Minh and his top officers were communists and the Soviet Union and China supported the Viet Minh against France, U.S. officials came to view the revolution in Vietnam as part of the perceived Soviet drive for world domination. They also attached growing importance to holding the line in Vietnam. The fall of China to Mao Zedong's communists and the Soviet explosion of a nuclear weapon provoked near hysteria in the United States in 1949, persuading many Americans that the communist threat had assumed even more menacing proportions than that posed by the Axis powers a decade earlier. U.S. policymakers thus concluded that communist expansion had reached a point beyond which it must not be permitted to go. "Any substantial further extension of the area under the control of the Kremlin," warned a National Security Council study in 1950, "would raise the possibility that no coalition adequate to confront the Kremlin with greater strength could be assembled." In this context of a world seemingly divided into two hostile power blocs, an apparent zero-sum game in which any gain for communism was seen as a loss for the United States, areas that had been of marginal importance suddenly took on great significance.

There were other more specific reasons for the U.S. commitment. The so-called domino theory held that the fall of Vietnam to communism could cause the loss of all of Southeast Asia, denying the United States access to important raw materials and strategic waterways and threatening India to the west and the Philippines to the east. The possible loss of Southeast Asia had special implications for Japan. Should it be deprived of access to the raw materials and markets of Southeast Asia, U.S. policymakers reasoned, a crucial ally might be forced to come to terms with communism. In later years, the domino theory was supplanted by the notion of credibility, the belief that the United States must stand firm to demonstrate its determination to defend vital interests across the world. The United States also saw its commitment in Vietnam as a test of its willingness and ability to uphold world order. Across the globe, revolution seemed on the rise in the 1960s, and U.S. officials feared that if they could not contain wars of national liberation, the international system that had been so painstakingly constructed in the aftermath of World War II might crumble.

Vietnam thus became an integral part of the U.S. strategy of global containment of communism, and it absorbed a steadily growing commitment of resources. In 1950, the United States began to assist the French to suppress the Viet Minh revolution, and by 1954 it was paying nearly 80 percent of the cost of the war. When French defeat appeared inevitable, the United States tried to block a settlement at Geneva. That failing, it set out to construct in the southern half of Vietnam a bulwark against further communist penetration of Southeast Asia, and by the late 1950s the U.S. aid program in Vietnam was one of the largest in the world. When South Vietnam was subsequently threatened by the NLF insurgency, the United States responded by increasing its commitment of military assistance and advisers. When the strength of the insurgency and the weakness of the Saigon government threatened to bring about the collapse of South Vietnam in early 1965, the Johnson administration sought to uphold a longstanding and faltering commitment by bombing North Vietnam and then by sending U.S. ground forces into the war.

Although publicly committed in the Johns Hopkins speech to "unconditional discussions," Johnson was in large measure responding to domestic and international pressures for a peaceful settlement. The administration did not expect or want negotiations at that time and indeed it had not even formulated a negotiating position. It was prepared to accept nothing short of an independent, noncommunist South Vietnam and was confident that it could achieve its goals by military means. Fundamentally misunderstanding the depth of North Vietnam's commitment to its goals, Johnson hoped that his offer of massive financial aid might lure it into accepting the U.S. position.

Diplomatic Shadowboxing. Between 1965 and 1967, the United States and North Vietnam engaged in diplomatic shadowboxing. As the war escalated, for reasons as varied as the parties involved, the combatants, numerous private individuals, and a number of third countries launched peace initiatives. In May 1965 and again in January 1966, Johnson sponsored prolonged bombing pauses, and he accompanied the latter with a well-publicized "peace offensive," dispatching a host of dignitaries across the world to proclaim that the United States was prepared to negotiate without condition. World leaders such as French president Charles de Gaulle, U.N. secretary general U Thant, and Pope Paul VI used their influence in attempts to bring the combatants to the conference table, as did nonaligned nations and relatively obscure private individuals such as Florentine law professor Georgia La Pira and American peace activists Harry Ashmore and William Baggs. Such communist countries as Hungary, Poland, and Romania, U.S. allies Britain and Canada, and neutrals such as Sweden also tried to end the war. In all, U.S. officials counted as many as two thousand attempts to initiate peace talks in the years 1965–1967.

In several major instances, U.S. bungling appeared to undercut promising peace efforts. In late 1966, Polish diplomat Januscz Lewandowski had secured qualified U.S. and North Vietnamese agreement on the means to get negotiations started and a tentative agenda, and spokesmen for North Vietnam later claimed that a delegation was enroute to Warsaw for talks slated to begin in early December. Several days before the opening of the talks, however, U.S. aircraft struck railroad yards within eight kilometers (5 miles) of the center of Hanoi, causing heavy damage to residential areas and numerous civilian casualties. The North Vietnamese angrily broke off the contact and the initiative, code-named MARIGOLD, withered. Similarly, in early 1967, the United States failed to make clear to British prime minister Harold Wilson a major change in its position on a bombing halt, undermining Wilson's efforts to arrange talks through Soviet premier Alexei Kosygin.

It is doubtful that these or other initiatives would have succeeded, however, because each of the major combatants continued to rely on military means during these years and neither was prepared to negotiate except on terms that would have been tantamount to surrender for the other. The North Vietnamese could not appear indifferent to the various initiatives and often exploited them for propaganda advantage, but they counted on the American people to tire of the war and they remained certain they could achieve their goals if they persisted. North Vietnam adamantly refused to negotiate without first securing major concessions from the United States, most notably a complete and unconditional bombing halt.

A steadily widening rift between the Soviet Union and China worked to North Vietnam's advantage. It was able to play off its two allies against each other to secure growing commitments of military and economic aid. China at that time adamantly opposed negotiations and supported North Vietnam's diplomatic stance. The Soviet Union, which feared a wider war and especially a nuclear confrontation with the United States, on occasion privately urged negotiations, but for reasons of prestige it could not afford to appear too conciliatory and would not permit itself to be drawn into the role of mediator.

Johnson and his advisers also could not ignore the various proposals for negotiations, but they dismissed most of them as "Nobel Prize fever," doubted that anything would come of them, and suspected that Hanoi was expressing interest mainly to get the bombing stopped. Despite any firm evidence to support his conclusions, the president remained confident at least until 1967 that North Vietnam would eventually bend to U.S. pressure, and he feared that conciliatory moves would undercut his strategy. To defuse international and domestic criticism, Johnson repeatedly insisted that he was ready to negotiate, but he refused to make the concessions Hanoi demanded. As each side invested more in the struggle, the likelihood of serious negotiations diminished.

The bargaining positions assumed by each side left little room for compromise. The North Vietnamese denounced U.S. involvement in Vietnam as a blatant violation of the Geneva agreements, and, as a precondition to negotiations, insisted that the United States withdraw its troops, dismantle its bases, and stop all acts of war against their country. North Vietnam continued to demand that the internal affairs of South Vietnam be resolved by the South Vietnamese themselves "in accordance with the program of the National Liberation Front." The North Vietnamese were apparently flexible in regard to the timing and mechanism for political change in the South, but on the fundamental issues they were adamant. The "puppet" Saigon regime must be replaced by a government representative of the "people" in which the NLF would play a major role. Restating in emphatic language its longstanding goals, Hanoi officials made clear, moreover, that the "unity of our country is no more a matter for negotiations than our independence."

The United States' position was equally firm. Officials in Washington, D.C., indicated a willingness to stop the bombing, but only after North Vietnam took reciprocal steps of deescalation. U.S. troops would withdraw from South Vietnam, but only after a satisfactory political settlement had been reached. The Johnson administration accepted the principle that the future of South Vietnam must be decided by the South Vietnamese, but at the same time, it made clear that it would not admit the NLF to the government, going no further than to affirm that the NLF would "have no difficulty being represented," and this only after North Vietnam had "ceased its aggression." Beneath these ambiguous words rested a firm determination to maintain an independent, noncommunist South Vietnam.

Responding to international and—in the case of the United States—domestic pressures, the two sides edged away from their initial positions over the next two years. North Vietnam stopped insisting on acceptance of its four points, including a complete U.S. military withdrawal, as a precondition to substantive negotiations, demanding only that the bombing must be ended without condition. It also relaxed somewhat its terms for a settlement, indicating that reunification could take place over a long period of time. In early 1968, in a statement scrutinized with great care in the West, North Vietnamese foreign minister Nguyen Duy Trinh changed the verb *could* to *would* when indicating what would happen in terms of negotiations after the bombing stopped.

The United States also made concessions. It retreated from its original insistence that North Vietnam withdraw its forces from the South in return for cessation of the bombing, demanding merely that further infiltration must be stopped. In the so-called San Antonio formula, first conveyed secretly to the North Vietnamese by Harvard professor Henry Kissinger through French intermediaries, and then announced publicly by Johnson in a speech in San Antonio on 29 September 1967, the United States backed away from a firm prior agreement on mutual deescalation. It would stop the bombing "with the understanding" that "productive discussions" would follow promptly and would "assume" that North Vietnam would not "take advantage" of the cessation of air strikes. As later explained, this meant that it would not significantly increase the infiltration of men and supplies across the 17th parallel. In a move designed to split the NLF from its sponsor as well as to appease domestic and international critics, the administration in late 1967 also hinted at a willingness to admit the NLF to political participation in South Vietnam, a major step away from its earlier stance.

Despite these tactical moves, the two nations remained far apart on procedural and substantive issues. Each had met with frustration and had incurred heavy losses on the battlefield, but each still retained hope that it could force the other to accept its terms. Thus the two sides remained unwilling to compromise on the central issue—the future of South Vietnam—to the extent that their objectives would be jeopardized. The story of the 1965–1967 peace initiatives, political scientist Allan Goodman concluded, marks "one of the most fruitless chapters in U.S. diplomacy."

Fighting While Negotiating. The magnitude of the Tet Offensive of 1968 forced the belligerents to the conference table. Although the massive, tightly coordinated North Vietnamese and NLF 30 January 1968 attacks on urban areas in South Vietnam achieved nearly complete surprise, the United States and South Vietnam recovered quickly, repulsing the enemy thrusts and inflicting huge losses. Tet nonetheless had a tremendous psychological impact in the United States, giving the lie to the administration's year-end claims of progress, arousing grave doubts in many quarters that the nation could achieve its goals in Vietnam at an acceptable cost, and persuading some of the president's key advisers that the United States must extricate itself from the war as quickly and gracefully as possible. Responding to such pressures, Johnson, after nearly two months of soul-searching, announced in a dramatic speech on 31 March 1968 that the bombing henceforth would be limited to the area just north of the demilitarized zone, named W. Averell Harriman his personal representative for peace talks, and renewed earlier offers to negotiate. To facilitate the search for peace, he removed himself from the presidential race.

To the surprise of many U.S. officials, the North Vietnamese accepted the U.S. offer to negotiate. Badly hurt by the losses suffered during Tet, North Vietnam may have sought a respite from the bombing to rebuild for another offensive. The Tet attacks had fallen well short of their major goal of toppling the Saigon government; moreover, the North Vietnamese recognized the importance of their impact in the United States. Shifting to what they called *danh va dan, dam van danh* (fighting and talking, talking and fighting), a sophisticated, tightly integrated strategy coordinating military, diplomatic, and political moves and designed to stimulate internal conflicts within the U.S. and South Vietnamese camp, they viewed negotiations as a means of intensifying antiwar pressures in the United States and exacerbating differences between the United States and South Vietnam. To save face, they made clear they were establishing contact with the United States only as a means to secure the "unconditional cessation of U.S. bombing raids and all other acts of war so that talks may start."

The opening of formal talks in Paris on 13 May 1968, therefore, did not bring an end to the stalemate. Certain that the U.S. position in Vietnam was secure, and viewing negotiations mainly as a way to ease political pressures at home, the Johnson administration took a hard line. Backing away from the San Antonio formula, it agreed to stop the bombing, but only with assurances that North Vietnam would respect the demilitarized zone, refrain from further rocket attacks on Saigon and other cities, and initiate "prompt and serious" talks. Not eager for any substantive talks while the military balance was not in its favor, North Vietnam continued to reject the U.S. demand for reciprocity and refused any terms that limited its ability to support the war in the South while leaving the United States a free hand there. Deadlocked at the conference table, the two belligerents in the summer and fall of 1968 increased their military activities in South Vietnam.

In late 1968, each side sought to take advantage of the U.S. electoral calendar to achieve a settlement. Through Soviet intermediaries and then in private talks, North Vietnamese negotiators affirmed that serious negotiations would begin immediately after a bombing halt and made a major concession by indicating that the Saigon government could participate. Some of Johnson's advisers pressed him to do something dramatic to assist Hubert Humphrey's faltering presidential campaign, and the president may have been tempted by the prospect of ending the war before he left office. Thus on 31 October 1968, after close consultation with his top military and political advisers, he agreed to stop the bombing. To meet Hanoi's continuing objections to reciprocity, Harriman negotiated an understanding that the bombing would be stopped unilaterally but that the North Vietnamese would be expected to cease rocket and mortar attacks on South Vietnamese cities and limit the infiltration of men and supplies into South Vietnam. To circumvent the repeated refusals of Hanoi officials to negotiate directly with the "puppet" Saigon government and Saigon's refusal to participate in any negotiations to which the North Vietnamese were a party, Harriman devised an ingenious "our side, your side" formula. The negotiations would be two-sided, but each side would be free to work out its own composition and to interpret the makeup of the other as it chose. The NLF and Saigon government could thus take part in the preceedings without recognizing the other as an independent entity.

The South Vietnamese blocked the complex arrangements Harriman had negotiated with such care because they feared an American sellout. Republican leaders suspected a preelection gimmick to undercut Richard M. Nixon's campaign and encouraged their resistance. The government of Nguyen Van Thieu protested that the U.S.-arranged understanding was a clear admission of defeat and refused to meet with the NLF. South Vietnam took the position that Hanoi must issue formal assurances that it would deescalate the war and negotiate directly with Saigon.

Johnson eventually used a combination of threats and inducements to force the South Vietnamese to go along, but, once in Paris, they raised procedural objections that nullified any hope of a peace settlement. The United States had originally proposed that the delegations be seated at two long tables to emphasize the two-sided nature of the talks. When North Vietnam demanded a square table with one delegate on each side to give force to its contention that the NLF was a separate party, Harriman had proposed a round table and the North Vietnamese had acquiesced. Saigon officials again refused to go along. Thieu may have felt that the issue was of sufficient symbolic or even practical importance to merit resistance, or he may have seized upon it to stall the talks until a presumably more sympathetic Richard Nixon took office. Outraged at South Vietnamese obstinance, Harriman pressed Johnson to negotiate without them, and Secretary of Defense Clark Clifford even proposed beginning to withdraw U.S. troops. The president upheld South Vietnamese objections, however, and with the assistance of the Soviet Union persuaded North Vietnam to accept a compromise: two rectangular tables placed at opposite ends of a round table. By the time this so-called battle of the tables had ended, the Johnson administration was in its last days, and any chance of substantive negotiations had passed.

It seems unlikely that the intransigence of Saigon officials sabotaged an opportunity for peace. North Vietnam was more flexible on procedural issues in late 1968 than it had been before, perhaps to get the bombing stopped and possibly to try to extract a settlement before Johnson left office, but this flexibility did not extend to substantive issues. It would not have accepted anything less than a U.S. withdrawal and a coalition government, terms the United States was not prepared to offer. Although he had given in on a bombing halt and was deeply annoyed with Thieu, Johnson still clung to goals he had pursued since taking office. He had made clear to Thieu that he would not recognize the NLF or accept a coalition government. He seems to have felt that he could still achieve his original aim, and was convinced that he had the enemy on the ropes. Although it led to negotiations, Tet merely hardened the deadlock, and it took four more years of fighting while negotiating before it was finally broken.

The Persistence of Stalemate. The accession of Richard M. Nixon to the presidency in 1969 brought no fundamental change in U.S. policy. Nixon recognized that the war must be ended, but he and his national security adviser Henry Kissinger insisted that it must be ended honorably. This meant that the U.S. withdrawal must be conducted in a way that avoided any appearance of defeat. There must be no face-saving settlement designed merely to cover the U.S. exit from Vietnam. Nixon and Kissinger set as their optimum goal a "fair negotiated settlement that would preserve the independence of South Vietnam." At a minimum, they insisted on a settlement that would give South Vietnam a reasonable chance for survival.

Although this objective had eluded the United States for more than a decade, Nixon and Kissinger were certain they could succeed where their predecessors had failed. The Saigon government in 1969 appeared stronger than ever and with U.S. backing might hang on indefinitely. They also hoped to use leverage with the Soviet Union, gained through the prospect of trade and arms control agreements, to secure assistance in forcing North Vietnam to make major concessions. Comparing his situation with that of Eisenhower's with Korea in 1953, Nixon also concluded that the threat of massive retaliation might sway the North Vietnamese as he believed it had the North Koreans, and he counted on his image as a hard-line anticommunist to make it credible.

In the summer and fall of 1969, Nixon and Kissinger set out to end the war. Through intermediaries, they conveyed to the North Vietnamese their desire for peace and proposed the mutual withdrawal of their troops from South Vietnam and the restoration of the demilitarized zone. To signal that he meant business, Nixon ordered intensive, secret bombing attacks against North Vietnamese sanctuaries in neutral Cambodia. Publicly, he unveiled what he described as a "comprehensive peace plan," revealing the proposals he had made privately and then announcing the withdrawal of 25,000 U.S. troops. Through French and Soviet intermediaries Nixon also warned that if a settlement were not attained soon he would be compelled to employ "measures of great consequence and force."

Nixon's secret diplomacy and military threats failed to obtain concessions from North Vietnam. From the North Vietnamese standpoint, the president's proposals were no better than those of Johnson, and to accept them would be to abandon goals they had been pursuing for nearly twenty-five years. The North Vietnamese delegates to the peace talks publicly dismissed the U.S. offer as a "farce" and indicated that they were prepared to sit in Paris "until the chairs rot." They agreed to secret talks outside the formal Paris framework, but in both forums they continued to insist on the total and unconditional withdrawal of all U.S. forces from Vietnam and on the establishment of a provisional coalition government from which Thieu would be excluded. Still hurting from the losses suffered during the Tet Offensive, but stubbornly clinging to its goals, North Vietnam shifted in 1969 to a defensive, protracted war strategy, sharply curtailing the level of military activity in the South. Certain that American public opinion would eventually force Nixon to withdraw from Vietnam, it ignored his threats and prepared to wait him out, irrespective of the cost.

The deadlock persisted for more than two years. Frustrated in his inability to achieve his goals through diplomacy and threats, Nixon fell back on the Vietnamization policy introduced by Johnson. He hoped that if he could mobilize American opinion behind his policies, persuade North Vietnamese officials that he would not abandon Thieu, and intensify the buildup of South Vietnamese military strength, the North Vietnamese would conclude that it would be better to negotiate with him then, rather than with South Vietnam later, and he could salvage peace with honor. In part as a means of supporting Vietnamization, in part to pressure the North Vietnamese into concessions, in April 1970 he authorized an invasion of Cambodia.

Nixon's Cambodian venture backfired. From a military standpoint, it achieved only modest results, buying some time for Vietnamization. In the United States, the unexpected expansion of a war the president had promised to wind down enraged his critics and caused massive demonstrations across the country; the killing of six students at Kent State and Jackson State added to the uproar. The Cambodian venture also caused the most serious congressional challenge to presidential authority since the beginning of the war. And it merely hardened the diplomatic deadlock. North Vietnamese and NLF delegates boycotted the formal Paris talks until U.S. troops had been withdrawn from Cambodia, and the secret talks lapsed for months. North Vietnam was content to bide its time, and the massive protest in the United States reinforced North Vietnam's conviction that domestic pressures would eventually force a U.S. withdrawal.

After two years of continued heavy fighting, intensive secret diplomacy, and political maneuvering, Nixon's position was worse than it had been when he took office. The negotiations remained deadlocked, and a top-level study concluded that the United States could neither persuade nor force North Vietnam to remove its troops from the South. At home, Nixon barely managed to head off restrictions on his warmaking powers, but he faced hostile and even more determined opposition in Congress and the revival of an antiwar movement that had seemed moribund when he took office. Popular disillusionment with the war reached an all-time high—71 percent agreed that the United States had made a mistake sending troops to Vietnam and 58 percent regarded the war as immoral. War-weariness and demoralization were pervasive.

Nixon and Kissinger were sufficiently concerned by their plight in 1971 to try once again to break the stalemate in Paris. Nixon perceived that he needed peace to get reelected, but he hoped to get it far enough in advance of the election to avoid the appearance of blatant political maneuvering. Consequently, in May Kissinger secretly presented to the North Vietnamese the most comprehensive offer yet made by the United States. In exchange for release of U.S. prisoners of war, he pledged to withdraw all troops within seven months after an agreement had been signed. The United States also abandoned the concept of mutual withdrawal, insisting only that North Vietnam stop further infiltration in return for the removal of U.S. forces.

The U.S. proposal initiated the most intensive discussions since the beginning of the war. The North Vietnamese quickly rejected Kissinger's offer, believing that it required them to give up the prisoners of war, their major bargaining chip, stop fighting, and accept the Thieu regime in advance of a political settlement. They promptly made a counteroffer, however, agreeing to release the prisoners of war simultaneously with the withdrawal of U.S. forces, provided that the United States abandon Thieu prior to a political settlement.

The discussions eventually broke down on the future of the Thieu regime. From the start of the secret talks, the North Vietnamese had insisted on Thieu's removal as an essential precondition for any agreement. South Vietnamese elections were set for September, and North Vietnamese representative Le Duc Tho, Kissinger's counterpart in the secret talks, indicated that if the United States would withdraw its support from Thieu, permitting an open election, it could take the first step toward a settlement. Perhaps sensing such a deal, Thieu vastly complicated matters by forcing out the two opposition candidates. His blatant interference in the political process outraged U.S. officials and some even urged the president to disassociate himself from Thieu. Nixon and Kissinger refused to abandon him at this critical juncture, however, and thus rejected the North Vietnamese proposal and the recommendations of their own advisers.

After Thieu's reelection, Kissinger sought to revive the secret talks by proposing that elections be held within sixty days after a cease-fire and providing that Thieu would withdraw one month in advance. From North Vietnam's standpoint, this offer was an improvement, but it failed to guarantee that Thieu would not be a candidate or to prevent him from using the machinery of government to rig the election. North Vietnam promptly rejected the proposal. The secret talks once again broke off in late November, frustrating Kissinger.

Peace with Honor? Although the military stalemate remained unbroken, it became so costly for both sides in 1972 that each was forced to compromise. The negotiations of 1971 broke down for the same reason earlier efforts had failed. Having invested so much blood and treasure in a struggle of more than ten years' duration, neither combatant was willing to make the concessions necessary for peace. Perhaps more important, each still believed it could get what it wanted by other means. Since 1968, North Vietnam had built its resources and manpower for a final offensive to topple Thieu and force the United States from Vietnam. While attempting to keep Vietnam on the back burner in 1971, Nixon and Kissinger had concentrated on negotiating major changes in U.S. relations with the Soviet Union and China, ensuring the president's reelection and leaving North Vietnam isolated with no choice but to come to terms. Neither side achieved what it hoped with its dramatic moves of 1972 and each paid a high price trying. These moves did, however, bring the war into a final, devastating phase that would ultimately lead to a compromise settlement.

In March 1972, North Vietnam launched the Easter Offensive, a massive, conventional invasion of the South. North Vietnamese officials correctly assumed that domestic pressures would prevent Nixon from sending U.S. ground forces back into Vietnam. The invasion, like that of 1968, was also probably timed to coincide with the presidential campaign in hopes that, as before, a major escalation would produce irresistible pressures for peace in the United States. The North Vietnamese aimed the offensive at the ARVN main force units, hoping to discredit the Vietnamization policy and leave the countryside open for the NLF. In its first stages, the offensive was an unqualified success. North Vietnamese units advanced to Quang Tri in the north, Kontum in the Highlands, and An Loc, just 97 kilometers (60 miles) north of Saigon.

Although stunned by the swiftness and magnitude of the invasion, Nixon responded vigorously. Unwilling to send U.S. troops back to Vietnam, he nevertheless quickly approved B-52 strikes across the demilitarized zone and followed up with the most drastic escalation of the war since 1968, the mining of Haiphong harbor, a naval blockade of North Vietnam, and massive, sustained bombing attacks. The conventional military tactics employed by the North Vietnamese in the summer of 1972 required vast quantities of fuel and ammunition, and the bombing and blockade made resupply extremely difficult. Largely through U.S. airpower, the ARVN units stabilized their lines in front of Saigon and Hue and even mounted a small counteroffensive.

The furious campaigns of 1972 raised the longstanding stalemate to a new level of violence. Both sides suffered heavily, the North Vietnamese lost an estimated 100,000 men and South Vietnam 25,000, but neither emerged appreciably stronger than before. North Vietnam had demonstrated the ARVN's continued vulnerability and the NLF had scored some gains, but Thieu remained in power and Nixon had not given in. Despite heavy casualties and the massive damage from U.S. bombing, the North Vietnamese retained sizeable forces in the South, and U.S. intelligence reports indicated that they could continue to fight for at least two more years.

Thus by the fall of 1972 each side found compelling reasons to compromise. Nixon recognized that an indefinite continuation of the air war might cause serious problems at home for him politically. He was eager to uphold earlier promises to end the war, and he wanted a settlement before the election if it could be achieved without embarrassment. North Vietnam had suffered terribly from the latest round of U.S. bombing and also wanted peace if it could be attained without abandoning long-term goals. Nixon's strategy of détente with China and the Soviet Union was also paying dividends. Chinese aid to North Vietnam had dwindled and the Chinese pressed their ally to compromise. The Soviet Union continued to supply significant aid, but also urged a settlement. Battered, exhausted, and increasingly isolated from its allies, North Vietnam appears to have concluded that it might get better terms from Nixon before the election.

Both sides therefore moved cautiously toward a compromise. The United States had already made a major concession, agreeing to allow North Vietnamese troops to remain in the South after a cease-fire. It also retreated from its absolute commitment to Thieu by agreeing to a tripartite electoral commission that would arrange a political settlement after the cease-fire. In the meantime, the North Vietnamese dropped their insistence on the ouster of Thieu, accepting the principle of a cease-fire that would leave Thieu temporarily in control but would give the NLF status as a political entity in the south.

During three weeks of intensive negotiations in October, Kissinger and Le Duc Tho hammered out an agreement. Within sixty days after a cease-fire, the United States would withdraw its remaining troops and North Vietnam would return the U.S. prisoners of war. A political settlement would then be arranged by the tripartite National Council of Reconciliation and Concord, which would administer elections and assume responsibility for implementing the agreement. Tentative plans were made for Kissinger to travel to Hanoi to initial the treaty.

As in 1968, a desperate Thieu thwarted the U.S. plan. Certain that acceptance of the agreement would amount to signing his own death warrant, he bitterly protested that he had not been consulted and insisted that he would never accept an agreement that permitted North Vietnamese troops to remain in the South and accorded the NLF any measure of sovereignty. He brought to Kissinger's attention some notably careless phrasing that accorded the tripartite commission the status of a coalition government. He demanded wholesale changes in the text, apparently hoping to drive a wedge between the United States and North Vietnam, block the treaty, and continue the war.

Nixon and Kissinger used every instrument at their disposal to impose a crude and unworkable peace on the South Vietnamese. Nixon gave in to Thieu's demands to renegotiate some sixty points in the treaty, provoking the North Vietnamese to reopen a number of old issues, including their insistence on the ouster of Thieu. With the talks again deadlocked, Nixon used what Kissinger labelled "jugular diplomacy," unleashing what became known as the Christmas bombing against North Vietnam, the most intensive and devasting attacks yet mounted against

Hanoi. In the meantime, to entice Thieu to cooperate, the United States promised vast amounts of military hardware and Nixon gave him secret promises to respond "with full force" if North Vietnam violated the treaty. He added warnings that if South Vietnam refused to accept the best deal that could be negotiated the United States would go ahead on its own. This combination of threats and inducements, along with concessions on the part of the United States, finally worked, and on 23 January 1973, Kissinger and Le Duc Tho initialed the final peace agreement.

Only by the most narrow definition can it be said to have constituted "peace with honor." It permitted U.S. military extrication from the war and secured the return of the U.S. prisoners of war while leaving the Thieu government intact for the moment. On the other hand, 150,000 North Vietnamese troops remained in South Vietnam, and the NLF was accorded formal political status. The major question over which the war had been fought—the political future of South Vietnam—was left to be resolved later. The treaty of January 1973 presumed that it would be resolved by political means, but the mechanism established for that purpose was vague and inherently unworkable, and all parties perceived that it would ultimately be settled by force. "Peace with honor" represented merely another phase in the thirty-year struggle for control of Vietnam.

The final stage of the war began the instant that peace was proclaimed. Neither of the Vietnamese combatants had abandoned its goals, and each observed the agreements only to the extent that it was expedient. Thieu and the NLF sought to outdo each other in landgrabbing operations, and efforts to implement the political arrangements for South Vietnam achieved nothing. The United States continued to support the Thieu government, using various subterfuges to maintain a high level of military aid and using "civilian" advisers to replace the military advisers who had to be removed. In the meantime, the North Vietnamese quietly infiltrated troops and equipment into the south, built a system of modern highways linking staging areas to strategic zones, and constructed a pipeline to ensure adequate supplies of petroleum for its forces in the field.

By the end of 1973, Nixon was powerless to uphold the agreement he had negotiated at such great cost. A war-weary nation and Congress cut back military assistance for South Vietnam, blocked continued air operations in Indochina, and refused to appropriate the aid for North Vietnam called for in the Paris accords. Nixon's growing absorption with and implication in the Watergate scandals, themselves in many ways a product of his determination to maintain the U.S. position in Vietnam, increasingly crippled the White House and ultimately forced Nixon's resignation.

In 1975, Nixon's successor Gerald Ford was helpless to respond to the situation in Vietnam. North Vietnam, sensing that the United States could not respond and confident that the shaky Thieu regime could be toppled, launched a major and successful conventional military offensive early in the year. The Thieu government collapsed, and within fifty-five days Saigon had fallen. The United States could do nothing more than evacuate U.S. citizens and a small number of South Vietnamese who had worked with the United States.

For ten years, the combatants had carefully framed their negotiating positions, clinging stubbornly to their goals and using diplomacy to advance their position and weaken their opponents. The Tet Offensive forced them to the conference table in 1968, but the military balance remained essentially unchanged and negotiations were unproductive. Another major North Vietnamese offensive four years later forced a settlement that permitted U.S. extrication from what had become a quagmire but left the Vietnamese to settle the fundamental issues by other means. Peace finally came to Vietnam as a result of military force rather than diplomacy.

[*See also* Détente; Geneva Conference, 1954; Geneva Conference, 1962; International Commission for Supervision and Control; Paris Accords; Southeast Asia Treaty Organization (SEATO); *and individual countries mentioned herein.*]

BIBLIOGRAPHY

GOODMAN, ALLAN E. *The Lost Peace: America's Search for a Negotiated Settlement of the Vietnam War.* 1978.
HERRING, GEORGE C., ed. *The Secret Diplomacy of the Vietnam War: The Negotiating Volumes of the Pentagon Papers.* 1983.
KISSINGER, HENRY A. *White House Years.* 1978.
KRASLOW, DAVID, and STUART LOORY. *The Secret Search for Peace in Vietnam.* 1968.
NGUYEN TIEN HUNG, and JERROLD SCHECTER. *The Palace File.* 1986.
NIXON, RICHARD. *RN: The Memoirs of Richard Nixon.* 1978.
PORTER, GARETH. *A Peace Denied: The United States, Vietnam, and the Paris Agreements.* 1975.

GEORGE C. HERRING

Discipline. [*This entry includes three articles:*

People's Army of Vietnam (PAVN) and People's Liberation Armed Forces (PLAF)
Republic of Vietnam Armed Forces (RVNAF)
U.S. Military.]

People's Army of Vietnam (PAVN) and People's Liberation Armed Forces (PLAF)

Both the PAVN and the PLAF (commonly known as the Viet Cong) emphasized political indoctrination in their procedures for military discipline. The military, advised by Communist Party officials, addressed personnel problems with forced "education" designed to rehabilitate individuals for return to the war effort. On a unit level, self-criticism sessions among commanders and soldiers assessed individuals' performance and fostered coordinated, disciplined conduct. Serious personnel problems concerning lax combat duty, desertion, or theft brought incarceration. Disciplined soldiers faced manual labor in camps, accompanied by educational programs that stressed personal sacrifice and commitment to national and Communist Party goals. PAVN and Viet Cong security forces dealt harshly with crimes considered more serious, such as defecting while armed or performing espionage.

The PAVN and Viet Cong emphasis on ideological indoctrination reflected the Communist Party's concern with maintaining influence over the armed forces. Party elites feared the growth of an autonomous military during the wars for independence, and they established an institutional presence in the armed forces that included overseeing morale and military discipline matters. Political officers accompanied fighting units, though their uncertain advisory role often created tension with commanders. Military officers who offended political officers or who performed their duties poorly faced a purge from the party and an end to career advancement.

BIBLIOGRAPHY

LANNING, MICHAEL LEE, and DAN CRAGG. *Inside the VC and NVA: The Real Story of North Vietnam's Armed Forces.* 1992.
PIKE, DOUGLAS. *PAVN: People's Army of Vietnam.* 1986.

ADAM LAND

Republic of Vietnam Armed Forces (RVNAF)

The Republic of Vietnam Armed Forces (RVNAF) maintained a system of regular military and smaller field courts to try military discipline cases. After 1966, a military judicial police operated throughout South Vietnam, though the contingent was substantially understaffed. Infractions by RVNAF personnel, such as treating superiors with disrespect, dereliction of duty, or desertion, brought various punishments. Sentences ranged from demotion, fieldwork assignment, or incarceration at the notoriously harsh RVNAF military prisons. Disciplined officers generally received less severe punishment than enlisted personnel, at most restriction to quarters.

The RVNAF military discipline apparatus faced massive desertion of enlisted personnel during the war, estimated to have averaged about 120,000 per year between 1965 and 1972. Factors such as inadequate pay and food, inattentive commanders, and the unpopularity of the government fueled desertion rates. The RVNAF initiated several programs to improve soldiers' morale including increasing compensation and developing support activities. The RVNAF established field military courts to speed the processing of desertion cases, and increased punishment (the death penalty for third-time deserters). These policies failed to stem desertions, however, as soldiers continued to return to villages or blend into urban areas around Saigon with relative ease.

BIBLIOGRAPHY

DONG VAN KHUYEN. *The RVNAF.* 1980.

ADAM LAND

U.S. Military

Apparent erosion in discipline within the armed forces of the United States, particularly after 1967, was an important factor both during the war in Vietnam and in postwar reactions within the military to the events of the war.

Signs of the Erosion of Discipline. Evidence of a breakdown in self-control and respect for authority among individual service members was often highly subjective. Neglect of routine military courtesies, such as saluting, became commonplace. Individuals showed political dissent by decorating their clothing and equipment with graffiti and anti-war slogans. Some soldiers openly challenged authorities and customs. An army lieutenant carried an anti-Johnson placard on a local election day in El Paso, Texas, in 1965. A military doctor refused to teach medical procedures to Special Forces soldiers. Malingering became widespread. "Short-timer's fever," a neglect or refusal to perform assigned tasks, was common as soldiers neared the end of their tours in Vietnam. Drug use, particularly in Vietnam, became so common late in the war that officers and senior noncommissioned officers (NCOs) often ignored it. It was claimed that some men who received awards for bravery in combat were so heavily drugged that they simply did not know what they were doing. Desertion, defined as being absent without leave (AWOL) for more than thirty days, increased despite reluctance to report men as deserters: 27,000 in 1967; 29,234 in 1968; 56,608 in 1969; 65,643 in 1970. About 800 soldiers fled to other countries, notably Sweden. Deliberate errors in paperwork and other procedures sabotaged efficient administration. "Fragging"—violent attacks on superiors—alarmed the Pentagon as reported incidents increased from 96 incidents in 1969 to 363 in 1970. Troops in the 101st Airborne Division (Airmobile) even offered $10,000 to anyone who would kill the officer who ordered the bloody and pointless 1969 attack on Hamburger Hill. "Hero" came to mean someone who endangered others. Forty-three African American soldiers at Fort Hood refused to deploy to Chicago to suppress riots during the 1968 Democratic convention. In October 1968 twenty-seven prisoners at the U.S. Army's stockade in Oakland, California, refused to work for two hours to protest the shooting of a prisoner who had been trying to escape. There were also organized, explicit challenges to U.S. military authority. In Europe, where anti-Americanism created a supportive climate for resistance to the authority of the military, U.S. soldiers formed Resisters Inside the Army (RITA) in 1967. RITA claimed 50,000 members, published one of 245 unauthorized GI newspapers, and publicized the safest havens for deserters.

The Costs of Poor Discipline. Most military leaders associated discipline with basic military capability: discipline was vital to unit cohesion, which in turn was crucial to combat effectiveness. The priority placed on self-preservation during the Vietnam War spawned wholesale refusals to enter combat, such as the Alpha Company incident in August 1969, in which a "short-timer company" refused to return to battle. At the small-unit level, drug use seemed to threaten the safety as well as the aggressiveness of the group. Sentries who were "high" on drugs were less likely to be reliable. Commitment to tasks assigned differed sharply between "lifers"—career soldiers—and first-time enlistees and draftees. Lifers were more likely to push troops to achieve a mission, even if only to achieve promotion. The erosion of discipline also worried leaders because of its negative impact on public attitudes toward the military and possible influence thereby on future support for sustaining minimal capabilities to meet national needs.

The Causes of Indiscipline. Declining discipline could be linked to profound changes that stretched beyond the Vietnam experience. One focus was the shrinking ratio since World War II of the combat arms to total forces. This trend accompanied increasing demands for more skilled service members, which increased the burdens on recruiting and retention. Combat soldiers were most likely to be African Americans or lower-class, poorly educated whites, that is, those less equipped to acquire technical skills. The composition of the entire U.S. Army, especially of the combat troops, diverged from that of American society until 1968, when college draft deferments ended and more affluent and educated youth entered the manpower pool. Such trends raised concerns about the safety of a democratic society with a professional military, about social equity, and about the future value of the military in national policy.

Scrutiny of the factors underlying the decline in discipline revealed real dilemmas for the post–Vietnam War military. The values of career soldiers and conscripts conflicted. A 1970 study at Fort Polk, Louisiana, showed the lower-class origins of most deserters: two-thirds had not finished high school; most had volunteered "to get away from problems," "see what the army was like," "had nothing else to do," or were "forced by a judge." Unhappiness with the army and their particular military occupational specialty (MOS) motivated those who went AWOL. Most had used drugs before entering the army. Dissenters, however, were different; they were disproportionately college-educated and from wealthier regions of the country. African Americans dissented at about the same ratio in which they were found in the army as a whole—11 percent. The self-interest of service members reflected dominant values but contradicted the sacrifice that military duties could demand. Greater tolerance of dissent and a less rigid structure appealed to many, but career soldiers drew satisfaction from a highly organized and disciplined military. Many of the sources of discontent within the U.S. military disappeared upon the withdrawal of U.S. troops from Vietnam and the creation of the All-Volunteer Force (AVF), but difficulties in attracting high-quality recruits needed for the technical specialties plagued the military in the mid 1970s.

Indiscipline and Military Decline. Those who saw the decline in discipline as revealing causes of the U.S. failure in Vietnam fell into two camps. The first saw problems stemming from a social liberalism that undercut strong military authority. They believed that this trend began with leniency toward deserters in World War II and continued in Korea, where prisoners of war who had cooperated with military authorities had had their sentences drastically reduced. In Vietnam these critics saw military authority further undermined. In 1968 Congress passed a new Uniform Code of Military Justice (UCMJ) that guaranteed legal counsel before a court-martial. In June 1969 the Supreme Court, reversing the conviction of a sergeant for raping a civilian, restricted a court-martial to service-connected matters. Field commanders and senior NCOs were frustrated and confused when U.S. government officials set aside or reduced approved sentences, especially in highly publicized cases. The leaders of the U.S. Army warned commanders not to press cases that would make the chain of command look foolish.

Those in the second group, including many with long military service, believed that the disciplinary decline reflected a grievous decline in the quality of leadership, including at the highest levels. Convictions of the provost marshal general and the sergeant major of the army, who had used their positions for personal gain, illustrated that decline. Lavish awards of medals for valor, especially for general officers, seemed scandalous, because the nature of their positions and frequent rotations drastically reduced their exposure to dangers in combat. Units competed to see which received the most awards. Statistical measures such as body counts were falsified. There were glaring failures to prosecute war crimes; and brief rotations of officers to combat units to enhance their careers—"ticket-punching"—increased resentment among enlisted troops. A 1976 survey of students at the Command and General Staff College, who had been junior officers at the end of the U.S. involvement, considered the generalship of Vietnam "the dark ages in the Army's history."

Addressing Problems of Discipline. During the Vietnam War, military leaders began to address the disciplinary problems and the root causes within their immediate control. By the end of the war, the army had found ways to diffuse dissent. Command information programs, soldiers' councils, and chaplain and psychiatric services formed networks that addressed key concerns. Senior military leaders advocated innovations to replace customs that seemed demeaning. For example, the navy adopted the officer-type uniform for all rates and ranks and eliminated the liberty card required for junior enlisted men to prove permission to go ashore. The armed forces struck a balance between standards of discipline and dissent. Most of the military learned to accept dissent and understood that discipline did not require tyranny. The military also found ways to convey to most of its members that military support of national goals requires greater limits on individuality than is otherwise demanded in American society.

[*See also* Amnesty; Desertion.]

BIBLIOGRAPHY

CINCINNATUS. *Self-Destruction: the Disintegration and Decay of the United States Army during the Vietnam Era.* 1981.

GARDNER, FRED. *The Unlawful Concert: An Account of the Presidio Mutiny.* 1970.

RADINE, LAWRENCE B. *The Taming of the Troops: Social Control in the United States Army.* 1977.

SARKESIAN, SAM C., ed. *Combat Effectiveness: Cohesion, Stress, and the Volunteer Military.* 1980.

JAMES W. WILLIAMS

DMZ. *See* Demilitarized Zone (DMZ).

Dobrynin, Anatoly

(1919–), Soviet ambassador to the United States, 1962–1986. Dobrynin negotiated with Henry Kissinger to establish ground rules for the Brezhnev-Nixon summit in 1969. He maintained that the Soviets wanted to pursue improved relations with the United States separate from the Vietnam issue and he rejected the Kissinger-Nixon policy, which linked U.S.-USSR nuclear arms reduction agreement to Soviet cooperation in pushing the Democratic Republic of Vietnam for a peace settlement.

BIBLIOGRAPHY

KARNOW, STANLEY. *Vietnam: A History.* 1991.

KELLY EVANS-PFEIFFER

Domino Theory.

A political theory holding that the collapse of one country in a region to communism would lead to the collapse of the remaining countries, which would fall like dominoes. The domino theory originated with the Truman Doctrine in 1947. Communist activity in Greece and Turkey concerned U.S. policymakers who worried that fragile postwar Western Europe might be vulnerable to insurgency. They believed that a successful communist movement in one country would provide momentum and assistance for similar communist uprisings in neighboring countries. The fall of one country in a region would therefore produce a ripple effect. After China's "loss" to communism in 1949, U.S. policymakers applied the theory to Asia.

For Korea in 1950, President Harry S. Truman invoked the domino theory and the policy of containment, a commitment to preventing the spread of communism by all necessary measures. At the same time, Truman and then President Dwight D. Eisenhower and Secretary of State John Foster Dulles used the domino theory to justify U.S. aid for the French in Indochina. They believed that a communist victory in Vietnam would lead to a communist takeover of countries from the Philippines to Laos to India.

The domino theory served as the underpinning for the Vietnam policies of Democratic presidents John F. Kennedy and Lyndon Johnson, who were particularly sensitive to Republican charges that their party had allowed China to fall to the communists. In 1961, then–vice president Johnson invoked it to defend the presence of U.S. military advisers in Vietnam. Gen. Maxwell Taylor, chairman of the Joint Chiefs of Staff (JCS), encouraged Kennedy to increase U.S. military involvement, arguing: "If Vietnam goes, it will be exceedingly difficult, if not impossible, to hold Southeast Asia." As the war dragged on and the United States became entangled in a web of rapid escalation, the domino theory was repeatedly invoked to justify new troop requests.

Although the theory was occasionally revived—for example, by Ronald Reagan when he argued for aid to the Nicaraguan Contras—the Vietnam experience ended the domino theory's grip on U.S. foreign policy assumptions.

BIBLIOGRAPHY

KAHIN, GEORGE McT. *Intervention: How America Became Involved in Vietnam.* 1986.

KARNOW, STANLEY. *Vietnam: A History.* 1991.

KELLY EVANS-PFEIFER

Don, Tran Van. *See* Tran Van Don.

Dong, Pham Van. *See* Pham Van Dong.

Dong Xoai,

South Vietnamese town in Phuoc Long province, 83 kilometers (50 miles) north of Saigon. Site of a South Vietnamese government military headquarters and of a U.S. Special Forces camp, Dong Xoai was attacked on 10 June 1965 by Viet Cong troops, who decimated Army of the Republic of Vietnam (ARVN) forces over the next five days. To Gen. William Westmoreland the battle confirmed his assessment, made in the wake of the battle at Binh Gia on 29 May, that South Vietnamese troops could not defeat the Viet Cong forces without outside assistance.

BIBLIOGRAPHY

DAVIDSON, PHILLIP B. *Vietnam at War—The History: 1946–1975.* 1988.
KARNOW, STANLEY. *Vietnam: A History.* 1991.
WESTMORELAND, WILLIAM. *A Soldier Reports.* 1976.

ELLEN D. GOLDLUST

Donovan, William J.

Donovan, William J. (1883–1959), director, Office of Strategic Services (OSS), 1942–1945. As World War II neared its end, Maj. Gen. "Wild Bill" Donovan dispatched a United States OSS team to French Indochina to rescue downed aviators and provide intelligence about Japanese forces in the region. Ho Chi Minh had asked the United States to support the cause of Vietnamese independence; Donovan's OSS mission became the first U.S. involvement in Vietnam, as it worked briefly with Ho and the Viet Minh against the Japanese.

BIBLIOGRAPHY

BROWN, ANTHONY CAVE. *The Last Hero: Wild Bill Donovan.* 1982.

PAUL M. TAILLON

Doves.

Doves. *See* Hawks and Doves.

Draft.

Draft. *See* Conscientious Objectors; Selective Service.

Drugs and Drug Use.

Drugs and Drug Use. During the Vietnam War, the issue of drug abuse in the U.S. Army attracted a level of public and official concern without precedent in the country's military history. As with U.S. troops in all previous American wars, the troops sent to South Vietnam during the conflict's first phase, from 1965 to 1968, indulged in regular alcohol abuse without arousing any controversy. When great numbers of soldiers began using marijuana after 1968, however, the military command reacted with rigorous repression. As marijuana gave way to epidemic-level heroin use, the army became concerned about the combat effectiveness of its forces, and the public was aroused by the threat that addiction posed to their sons and society. In 1972, as America's military involvement in Vietnam was coming to a close, sociologist Dr. Clinton Sanders reviewed the literature and reported that "between 60 and 90 percent of enlisted men below the rank of E4 use one or more illicit drugs in the course of

their stay in Vietnam." Clearly, many drugs were used and abused by U.S. soldiers in Vietnam, but it was the heroin epidemic that served as the defining event in the history of this malaise.

The Growth of Drug Use. During the first three years of combat operations in Vietnam, most U.S. forces engaged in offensive operations that left little time for recreation of any sort. The military encouraged off-duty alcohol consumption by licensing service clubs on its rear-area bases and distributing beer to troops in frontline bunkers. The image of the "hard-drinking" GI matched the military's manly image, and tolerance of alcohol abuse was so ingrained within the army that off-duty drunkenness was even smiled upon. It was not until March 1972 that the Defense Department classified alcoholism as a treatable illness and launched a serious program to identify alcoholics in the services.

As the U.S. Army's combat role wound down after 1969, illicit drugs became a persistent problem in the ranks, reducing the readiness of some units and threatening public support for the war effort. Under the Nixon Doctrine, U.S. forces turned over all combat operations to forces of the Army of the Republic of Vietnam (ARVN) and began an intensified training of ARVN soldiers through the Vietnamization program. Although relieving U.S. troops of the ordeal of combat, this defensive posture required American conscripts to spend months in aimless, endless garrison duty—confined behind bunkers and concertina-wire cages in an alien land half a world away from home. In addition, the escalating antiwar protests in the United States robbed the war effort of its legitimacy and further eroded troop morale. Such circumstances created conditions inside the army conducive to a pandemic of drug abuse.

In 1969, a Defense Department study discovered that 25 percent of U.S. soldiers in Vietnam were using marijuana occasionally or frequently. By then, many units suffered an informal division between "the juicers," prowar career officers and noncommissioned officers (NCOs) who drank alcohol in their clubs, and "the heads," low-ranking draftees who were often antiwar or ambiguous about the war and who indulged in illegal drugs, particularly marijuana.

Disturbed by reports of widespread use, the military launched an aggressive campaign against marijuana use in Vietnam, assisted by the pungent aroma of the drug's smoke that made concealment virtually impossible. At the operation's peak in 1969, military police were arresting soldiers for marijuana possession at the rate of 1,000 per week. Under constant pressure from NCOs and junior officers, GIs found marijuana use risky and were forced to use it less frequently and more furtively. The military's suppression of marijuana use, however, inadvertently created a market for the powdery high-grade heroin, which soon began appearing for sale in Saigon, so pure that it could be smoked in an ordinary cigarette without any trace odor.

In mid 1970, heroin addiction spread with extraordinary speed through the ranks of the 450,000-strong U.S. military forces in South Vietnam. In May and June, the army had revived its antimarijuana campaign with a renewed burst of arrests and seizures that eliminated market competition for the incoming heroin. *The Senate Staff Report on Drug Abuse in the Military* (1971, p. 21) stated: "The upshot was that GIs who had been smoking only 'grass' turned to heroin, which was initially passed off to them as nonaddicting cocaine. They reasoned that the substance itself, heroin, and the smoking of it were more easily concealed from prying eyes and noses than marijuana." Thus, at all major U.S. military bases and social clubs, tiny plastic vials of 96-percent pure heroin became readily available for sale to U.S. soldiers for only $2.00 or $3.00 a dose, sold by Vietnamese civilians among others.

Subsequent survey research discovered an epidemic level of heroin use in the ranks. In September 1970, army medical officers questioned 3,103 soldiers of the American Division and found that 11.9 percent had used heroin since their arrival in Vietnam. In November, an army engineers battalion in the Mekong Delta reported that 14 percent of its troops were regular heroin users. In 1972, the White House Office for Drug Abuse Prevention interviewed 900 enlisted men who had returned from Vietnam in September 1971, the peak of the epidemic, and found that 44 percent had tried opiates while in Vietnam and 20 percent regarded themselves as having been "addicted." The full extent of the problem was not revealed until 1974 when the Office for Drug Abuse Prevention published later surveys showing that 34 percent of U.S. troops in Vietnam had "commonly used" heroin. If this figure is correct, then by mid 1971 there were more American heroin users in South Vietnam (81,300) than there were in the entire United States (68,000).

Attempts at a Solution. The causes underlying the GI drug epidemic were complex, but boredom and bad morale provided much of the motivation. Under President Nixon's Vietnamization program, launched in 1969, U.S. troops were confined to cantonments as a strategic reserve for the ARVN, and most units, without a clear mission, suffered a sharp decline in morale. Troops began using marijuana, and then heroin, to quench the boredom. With days stretching into months without event or ending, soldiers often used heroin to dull the psychological pain and accelerate the 365-day clock that marked the maximum tour of each soldier. "Drugs alter and enhance reality," wrote Dr. Sanders in a 1973 report of his interviews with Vietnam veterans. "They are a means of manipulating time—time which moves with such torturous slowness when not filled with copping drugs and using drugs and talking about drugs." Because most drug users in Vietnam sought the "tension-relieving effects" of a narcotic, Sanders and other researchers found that few soldiers took LSD (lysergic acid diethylamide) or other hallucinogens. These psychotropic drugs apparently heightened or intensified the very reality that soldiers were trying to escape.

On the whole, the army's attempts at education and eradication did little to stem the spread of addiction. Since illegal drugs became, in Sanders's words, "an effective, self-prescribed chemotherapy" for combat soldiers, drug users, or "heads," formed mutual-support networks that frustrated the military's antidrug efforts. Through interviews with veterans in 1971, the researchers David Bentel and David E. Smith argued that the majority of "fraggings," or murders, attempted against officers in Vietnam occurred "not because of racial strife or orders to move into combat, but because some 'gung ho' officer is 'hassling' drug users."

Not surprisingly, soldiers supported each other in efforts to frustrate the military's requirement, imposed in June 1971, that all GIs pass a drug urinalysis test before boarding their flight home. In testimony before Congress, the Defense Department announced that such a "mass screening effort . . . had never been attempted" and claimed that its procedures had "a much more rigorous sensitivity standard" than previous clinical prototypes. By 1973, the Defense Department was collecting 4 million urine specimens annually for worldwide screening of all U.S. troops in thirteen drug-testing laboratories. To defeat this new technology, the GI "heads" in Vietnam helped fellow drug users who were "short" through ad hoc detoxification schemes that included alcohol binges and induced vomiting, or provided a "clean" urine specimen from a buddy that could slipped into the sample vial during testing. Many veterans later reported that drug screening had been easy to defeat. Consequently, only 5.5 percent of troops departing Vietnam failed their first urinalysis and the bulk of those succeeded the second time after compulsory treatment.

Those who failed the second test were usually sent home for an immediate discharge without detoxification or treatment, a procedure that may have contributed to the rising domestic drug problem in the United States. At the start of the Vietnam heroin epidemic in 1970, there was great concern that veterans would return home with lasting heroin habits. But by 1974 it was clear that drug use in the war zone was largely a situational response to combat stress. The great majority of veterans who admitted to addiction in Vietnam did not continue to use the drug after they returned to the United States.

The Southeast Asian Context. When heroin use among U.S. soldiers in South Vietnam expanded in 1969–1970, its source was the subject of a great deal of speculation. At first, there were wild rumors among GIs of heroin cargoes being trucked down the Ho Chi Minh Trail or syringes strapped to the arms of dead North Vietnamese soldiers on the slopes of Khe Sanh. Gradually, however, U.S. intelligence work exposed the trafficking syndicates among America's Indochina allies. Significantly, these same investigations failed to detect any sign of communist involvement in drug trafficking.

Opium was a venerable vice in Indochina, but heroin, a chemical derivative, was a recent development. For nearly a century, the French colonial administration had permitted opium smoking, which provided as much as 16 percent of all tax revenues. In 1930, for example, French Indochina licensed 3,500 opium dens to supply the colony's 125,200 registered smokers. Under pressure from the United Nations, however, the French government finally abolished its opium monopoly in 1950. Instead of eradicating the vice, the French military transferred the drug trade informally to its intelligence service, whose commanders used it to finance their covert operations against the communist Viet Minh.

Although localized opium trading continued after the end of the Indochina War in 1954, large-scale heroin trafficking did not start until 1969, when a complex of seven laboratories opened in the Golden Triangle—a mountain region where Burma, Thailand, and Laos converge. Since the early 1950s, the region's drug merchants had been producing both smoking opium and crude, granular No. 3 heroin to service Chinese addicts in cities such as Bangkok and Hong Kong. Starting in 1969–1970, however, these syndicates used their opium supplies to manufacture the pure, powdery No. 4 heroin for U.S. troops then fighting in South Vietnam. Although these remote laboratories were operated by criminal chemists from Hong Kong,

their principals were all U.S. allies—notably the Nationalist Chinese irregulars based in northern Thailand and the commander in chief of the Royal Lao Army, Gen. Ouane Rattikone. In a June 1971 report on these laboratories, the Central Intelligence Agency (CIA) noted that their establishment "appears to be due to the sudden increase in demand by a large and relatively affluent market in South Vietnam"—U.S. combat troops.

Allied military forces in the Kingdom of Laos played a key role in the Indochina drug traffic. General Ouane owned the region's largest heroin laboratory, which processed, under its distinctive "Double U-O Globe Brand" label, some 100 kilograms per day of raw opium into heroin for export to U.S. soldiers in South Vietnam. While General Ouane used the troops and aircraft of the Royal Lao Army to transport his heroin, local commanders of the CIA's secret army, a force of some 30,000 Hmong highlanders, relied upon the agency's resources to market their opium. In villages scattered across the rugged mountains of northern Laos, Hmong farmers harvested their traditional crop of raw opium for sale to the new heroin refineries, and the CIA's contract airline, Air America, allowed the Hmong commanders, albeit on an informal basis, to transport opium on its aircraft.

Suffering from what might be called mission myopia, neither the CIA's station nor the U.S. embassy in Vientiane did anything to discourage its Laotian allies from exporting heroin to South Vietnam. In a 1972 investigation of the agency's Vientiane station, the CIA's inspector general explained the predicament of its covert-action operatives: "The past involvement of many of these [Lao Army] officers in drugs is well known, and the continued participation of many is suspected; yet their goodwill . . . considerably facilitates the military activities of Agency-supported irregulars." In a frank assessment of the CIA's de facto tolerance of drug trafficking by its Lao allies, the inspector general concluded: "The war has clearly been our overriding priority in Southeast Asia, and all other issues have taken second place in the scheme of things. It would be foolish to deny this, and we see no reason to do so."

Once the raw opium was processed into the powdery No. 4 heroin in the Golden Triangle's laboratories, elements within South Vietnam's ruling military factions secured the bulk of their heroin supplies through contacts in Laos. The structure of this traffic was exposed in 1970–1971 when seizures and subsequent investigations uncovered official involvement in South Vietnam's heroin trade. In 1971, the U.S. Army provost marshal reported that the "backers of the illicit drug traffic . . . may be high level, influential political figures, government leaders, or moneyed ethnic Chinese." In June, the director of the Public Safety Directorate for Civil Operations Revolutionary Development Support (CORDS) reported that "the father of General [Ngo]Dzu, MR [Military Region] II Commanding General, is trafficking in heroin." Allegations of official involvement gained substance in March when two national assembly representatives, both allied with President Nguyen Van Thieu, were arrested at Saigon's airport carrying 9.6 and 4.0 kilograms of Laotian Double U-O Globe Brand heroin. While President Thieu controlled the army and the assembly, another Saigon factional leader, Prime Minister Tran Thien Khiem, placed his close followers inside the customs unit. In February 1971, a U.S. customs adviser reported that the conditions at Saigon's main airport had "reached a point to where the Customs personnel of Vietnam are little more than lackeys to the smugglers."

In concert with other controversies in Vietnam such as the collapse of discipline, combat atrocities, and racial conflict, the GI heroin epidemic may well have contributed, in subtle but significant ways, to President Nixon's decision to accelerate troop withdrawals from Vietnam in 1970 and 1971. These withdrawals did little, however, to slow the region's rising heroin traffic. Even before the last GIs had left, criminal exporters, both Southeast Asian syndicates and U.S. veterans based in Bangkok, began shipping heroin to the United States. In November 1971, for example, a Filipino diplomat was arrested at the Lexington Hotel in New York City with 15.5 kilograms of Double U-O Globe Brand heroin that he had carried from Laos. By November 1972, the U.S. Bureau of Narcotics estimated that the Southeast Asia share of the heroin supply in the United States had increased from 5 to 30 percent.

After U.S. Withdrawal. After 1972, moreover, South Vietnam's heroin syndicates sought a new clientele among the unemployed youth, prostitutes, and street dealers within Saigon's camp-follower economy. By 1974, Saigon had an estimated 150,000 heroin addicts, a younger generation quite distinct from the aging opium smokers left by French colonialism. As South Vietnam spun into a crisis of corruption and economic collapse in 1974, a conservative priest, Father Tran Huu Thanh, launched the People's Anti-Corruption Movement with the support of Saigon's influential Catholic Church. In a series of public manifestos, Father Thanh charged

President Thieu with "undermining the nationalist cause for his own financial gain" and accused him of protecting the heroin traffic, now directed at the city's slum dwellers. Led by many of Saigon's prominent anticommunists, this movement represented a political revolt from within the ranks of the government's strongest supporters. Instead of reacting to the allegations with reforms, the Thieu government, supported by the U.S. embassy, ignored the charges and arrested many of its critics, effectively suppressing the protests.

In April 1975, the People's Army of Vietnam (PAV) captured Saigon, by then a city of 4 million people—including 300,000 unemployed, 150,000 heroin addicts, and 130,000 prostitutes. Within months, the socialist regime had established the New Youth College, a residential drug center with 1,200 beds and a treatment program combining acupuncture, martial arts, and indoctrination. With its small treatment facility overwhelmed by the massive scale of the problem, the new government's response to drug abuse was woefully inadequate. Although the year-long program established an 80-percent cure rate among the 8,000 addicts treated by 1981, this facility had beds for only about 5 percent of the overall addict population.

For over a decade the government had claimed that socialism was solving the problem, but Saigon still had a major narcotics traffic, and drug use was rampant among the city's youth gangs and prostitutes. The city's street life continued to trade in drugs, no longer No. 4 heroin but instead a low-grade processed opium that was smuggled into Vietnam from Thailand and socialist Laos by corrupt police, customs agents, and military officials. Although elements within the Lao People's Democratic Republic protected local heroin dealers during the 1980s, Vietnamese addicts could no longer afford the costly drug and Vientiane's traffickers now exported their heroin through Bangkok. Once gateway to the world market for Laos' heroin laboratories, Saigon had become a dead end in Southeast Asia's drug traffic.

When Vietnam opened to the world market in the early 1990s, Saigon's ailing economy soon revived from a surge of foreign investments in construction and tourism. As businesspeople, travelers, and heroin began arriving from Bangkok, an overlapping pattern of intravenous drug use and HIV infection, pronounced in nearby Thailand, appeared in Saigon. In March 1994, the city's Institute for the Rehabilitation of Drug Addicts found that 520 of the 780 opiate users tested were HIV positive—an infection rate of 66 percent. Significantly, simultaneous tests given to 500 Saigon prostitutes found less than 1 percent positive. One explanation for the difference is that Saigon's heroin and morphine users congregate in "shooting galleries," sharing needles and thus accelerating the spread of HIV. The Ministry of Health could document only 1,276 cases of HIV in Saigon, but social workers were still concerned that rising drug use might become the main vector for a rapid proliferation of the disease.

BIBLIOGRAPHY

BENTEL, DAVID, and DAVID E. SMITH. "Drug Abuse in Combat: The Crisis of Drugs and Addiction Among American Troops in Vietnam." *Journal of Psychedelic Drugs* 4, no. 1 (Fall 1971): 23–30.

CARON, HERBERT S., and VICTORIA BAY KNIGHT. "An Outreach Approach to Facilitating the Transition from Military to Civilian Life: A Critical Choice Point for the Drug Dependent." *Journal of Drug Issues* (Winter 1974): 52–60.

CRANSTON, ALAN. "Legislative Approaches to Addiction among Veterans: The Nation's Unmet Moral Responsibility." *Journal of Drug Issues* (Winter 1974): 1–10.

MCCOY, ALFRED W. *The Politics of Heroin: CIA Complicity in the Global Drug Trade.* 1991.

MOSS, GEORGE DONELSON. *Vietnam: An American Ordeal.* 1990.

ROBINS, LEE N. "A Follow-Up Study of Vietnam Veterans' Drug Use." *Journal of Drug Issues* (Winter 1974): 61–68.

ROHRBAUGH, MICHAEL, and SAMUEL PRESS. "The Army's War on Stateside Drug Use: A View from the Front." *Journal of Drug Issues* (Winter 1974): 32–43.

SANDERS, CLINTON R. "Doper's Wonderland: Functional Drug Use by Military Personnel in Vietnam." *Journal of Drug Issues* (Winter 1973): 65–78.

STANTON, MORRIS. "Drug Use in Vietnam." *Archives of General Psychiatry* 26 (March 1972): 279–286.

WILBUR, RICHARD S. "The Battle against Drug Dependency within the Military." *Journal of Drug Issues* (Winter 1974): 11–31.

ZINBERG, NORMAN E. "G.I.s and O.J.s in Vietnam." *New York Times Magazine,* 5 December 1971, pp. 37 ff.

ZINBERG, NORMAN E. "Heroin Use in Vietnam and the United States." *Archives of General Psychiatry* 26 (May 1972): 486–488.

ALFRED W. MCCOY

Dulles, Allen

Dulles, Allen (1893–1969), director, Central Intelligence Agency (CIA), 1953–1961, brother of John Foster Dulles. A supporter of Ngo Dinh Diem, Dulles urged President Dwight D. Eisenhower to bolster Diem's government during its first years. Later, Dulles also supported Diem's blocking of the 1955 elections, realizing that Ho Chi Minh would win them.

BIBLIOGRAPHY

OLSON, JAMES S., and RANDY ROBERTS. *Where the Domino Fell: America and Vietnam, 1945 to 1990.* 1991.

PAUL M. TAILLON

Dulles, John Foster

Dulles, John Foster (1888–1959), U.S. secretary of state, 1953–1959. John Foster Dulles believed that President Truman's containment policy was inadequate to deal with the threat of what he perceived as a monolithic communist bloc bent on world domination. Dulles regarded the Viet Minh as another instrument of communist aggression and argued that the fall of Indochina would lead to the loss of Southeast Asia with disastrous consequences for the United States. Yet Dulles was reluctant to commit U.S. combat troops to Southeast Asia, believing that France must bear that burden. Even when the French situation at Dien Bien Phu became critical in early 1954, Dulles remained unenthusiastic about U.S. air strikes or the use of nuclear weapons. Instead, he preferred his policy of "united action," a plan for the formation of a multinational coalition to guarantee the security of Southeast Asia. U.S. allies, however, particularly the British, were unwilling to support such a venture.

Dulles reluctantly participated in the Geneva Conference of 1954, instructing the U.S. delegation to act only as an "interested nation." When it became clear that the participants were progressing toward an agreement, however, Dulles endeavored to secure a settlement that would allow the United States to defend Southeast Asia after the conference. Later that year, Dulles brought his plan to fruition when he negotiated the Southeast Asia Treaty Organization (SEATO) treaty. Dulles enthusiastically supported Ngo Dinh Diem, encouraging him to break from the French and accept U.S. advisers and aid. Dulles apparently believed that Diem would survive if he received U.S. support. The secretary of state never saw the massive military intervention that followed—and failed—as he died of cancer in 1959.

BIBLIOGRAPHY

HERRING, GEORGE C. "'A Good Stout Effort': John Foster Dulles and the Indochina Crisis, 1954–1955." In *John Foster Dulles and the Diplomacy of the Cold War,* edited by Richard H. Immerman, 1990.

HOOPES, TOWNSEND. *The Devil and John Foster Dulles.* 1972.

PAUL M. TAILLON

ALLEN DULLES. On his way to the British Foreign Office, London, 16 June 1960. *Archive Photos*

Dung, Van Tien. *See* Van Tien Dung.

Duong Quynh Hoa (1930–), a top-ranking Viet Cong agent in Saigon, a founder of the National Liberation Front (NLF). Raised by an affluent family that collaborated with the French colonial regime, Duong Quynh Hoa attended medical school in Paris in the 1950s, where she joined the French Communist Party. After returning to Saigon, she worked covertly to undermine President Diem's regime while practicing medicine. In 1968, Hoa was secretly appointed health minister of the Viet Cong's Provisional Revolutionary Government in South Vietnam. She went into hiding after the Tet Offensive and traveled abroad on propaganda missions for North Vietnam. After the war, Hoa ran a children's hospital in Ho Chi Minh City and became a prominent critic of the communist government. In a 1981 interview, she spoke for many former Viet Cong guerrillas who were dismayed by North Vietnam's takeover: "They behave as if they had conquered us." A dozen years later, Hoa voiced a common complaint of Vietnamese discouraged by the long economic crisis under communist rule: "Our leaders don't have enough knowledge to run the country."

BIBLIOGRAPHY

DUONG QUYNH HOA. *Une Guerre larvée.* 1983.
KARNOW, STANLEY. *Vietnam: A History.* 1991.
HIEBERT, MURRAY. "Ex-Communist Official Turns into Vocal Critic." *Far Eastern Economic Review* 156 (2 December 1993).
TRUONG NHU TANG. *A Viet Cong Memoir.* 1985.

GLEN GENDZEL

Duong Van Minh (1916–), general, Army of the Republic of Vietnam (ARVN); chairman, Revolutionary Military Council, 1963–1964; president of South Vietnam, 1975. Known as Big Minh to Americans because of his size—six feet tall, two hundred pounds—Gen. Minh was born in the Mekong Delta town of My Tho. After receiving military training in France, he commanded Saigon's colonial garrison in the Indochina War. By suppressing the Hoa Hao uprising in 1955, Minh earned President Diem's favor and a promotion to major general, but Diem soon came to resent Minh's popularity and demoted him to "special adviser." After receiving assurances that the United States would "not thwart" a coup, Minh chaired the Revolutionary Military Council that overthrew Diem on 1 November 1963. Diem and his brother were assassinated the next day, and Minh briefly held power until his faction of older French-trained officers were overthrown on 30 January 1964 by the predominantly U.S.-trained faction known as the Young Turks. Minh went into exile for the next four years.

Out of power, Minh offered a noncommunist alternative to the Saigon regime. He tried to run for president of South Vietnam in 1966, but was disqualified as an exile. Returning to Vietnam in 1968, Minh tried again to run for president in 1971, but he withdrew under protest, complaining that the United States had meddled with the election. Never a hard-line anticommunist, Minh resurfaced during South Vietnam's final collapse as a compromise leader possibly acceptable to North Vietnam. As North Vietnamese Army (NVA) tanks closed in on Saigon, President Thieu resigned in favor of aged Vice President Tran Van Huong, who then appointed Minh as the new president on 28 April 1975. Two days later, however, NVA forces took the presidential palace and Minh was arrested. Imprisoned for years in communist reeducation camps, Minh emigrated to France in 1983.

BIBLIOGRAPHY

"Big Minh: The Patient Conciliator." *Time,* 5 May 1975.
DUONG VAN MINH. "Vietnam: A Question of Confidence." *Foreign Affairs,* October 1968.
KARNOW, STANLEY. "The Fall of the House of Ngo Dinh." *Saturday Evening Post,* 21–28 December 1963.
SHAPLEN, ROBERT. *The Lost Revolution: The U.S. in Vietnam, 1946–1966.* 1966.
TRAN VAN DON. *Our Endless War: Inside Vietnam.* 1978.

GLEN GENDZEL

Durbrow, Elbridge (1903–), U.S. ambassador to South Vietnam, 1957–1961. President Eisenhower appointed Durbrow, a career foreign service officer, U.S. envoy to Saigon in 1957. Durbrow sharply criticized official corruption and nepotism in President Diem's government. Clashing often with U.S. military advisers, Durbrow blamed official repression for driving the South Vietnamese people to support the Viet Cong guerrillas. Durbrow reluctantly backed Diem in the failed coup of 1960 but continued pressing him to build popular support for his regime with reforms and elections, which only annoyed Diem. U.S. ambassadorial criticism of Diem all but ceased when President Kennedy sent Frederick Nolting to replace Durbrow in 1961.

BIBLIOGRAPHY

MECKLIN, JOHN. *Mission in Torment: An Intimate Account of the U.S. Role in Vietnam.* 1965.
SPECTOR, RONALD H. *The United States Army in Vietnam, Advice and Support: The Early Years, 1941–1960.* 1983.
U.S. DEPARTMENT OF STATE. *Vietnam.* Vol. 1 of *Foreign Relations of the United States, 1958–1960.* 1986.

GLEN GENDZEL

E

Easter Offensive. In March 1972, North Vietnam launched the Easter Offensive, a massive attack designed to achieve a conventional military victory. 120,000 troops backed by armor and artillery struck South Vietnam on three fronts at a time when the dwindling U.S. combat troop strength was down to less than 100,000, of which only 5,000 were combat troops. Still in place, however, was the U.S. advisory network, which placed American advisers with each of the South Vietnamese combat divisions in order to facilitate training and air support.

Officials in Hanoi and Washington, D.C., viewed the event as a test of the U.S. policy of Vietnamization. North Vietnam sought a decisive battle because of its growing trepidation at the U.S. policy of détente with the Soviet Union and the People's Republic of China (PRC) and its desire to influence the coming presidential election in the United States.

Northern Offensive. The opening offensive began in I Corps, the northern five provinces of South Vietnam. At noon on 30 March the North Vietnamese Army (NVA) attacked the arc of South Vietnamese firebases along the demilitarized zone (DMZ) and the western border with Laos, raining artillery rounds on the surprised defenders. The

308th NVA Division plus two independent regiments moved south of the DMZ along the sandy coastal plains between the sea and Highway 1. They assaulted the "Alpha group" of firebases, known as the Ring of Steel, arranged in a loose arc just south of the DMZ. From the west, the *304th NVA Division,* including an armored regiment, rolled out of Laos along Highway 9, past Khe Sanh, and into the Quang Tri River Valley.

Realizing the seriousness of the situation, on 1 April Brig. Gen. Vu Van Giai, commander of the 3d ARVN Division, ordered his troops to withdraw and reorganize south of the Cua Viet River. The following morning South Vietnamese armor held off NVA tanks attempting to cross the river at Dong Ha, but some of the North Vietnamese crossed at the Cam Lo bridge, about 11 kilometers (7 miles) west.

Although natural barriers slowed the NVA assault from the north, the western approaches were completely exposed. Camp Carroll, a South Vietnamese base located halfway between the Laotian border and the coast, was strategic for both sides. For the South Vietnamese, its large artillery component was crucial because its 175 mm guns could provide support fire at ranges up to 32 kilometers (20 miles). For the NVA, Camp Carroll was the strongest obstacle before Quang Tri City. On 2 April Camp Carroll surrendered, and later that day, ARVN troops abandoned Mai Loc, its last western base, allowing the NVA almost unrestricted access to western Quang Tri province north of the Thach Han River.

The North Vietnamese advance slowed for three weeks, but on the morning of 28 April they attacked again, pushing to within about 1.5 kilometers (1 mile) of Quang Tri City. General Giai, with fewer than two thousand troops, intended to abandon the city and consolidate south of the Thach Han River, although this meant conceding most of Quang Tri province to the NVA. It was a sound decision and might have saved the remnants of the 3d Division had not I Corps Commander, Lt. Gen. Hoang Xuan Lam, a consummate bureaucrat, ordered Giai to "hold at all costs." General Lam allowed General Giai no flexibility to move any units without specific approval.

Bewildered by conflicting orders, South Vietnamese units splintered and virtually disappeared, abandoning most of the province north of the city. U.S. advisers in Quang Tri called for rescue helicopters, and on 1 May the U.S. Air Force evacuated 132 survivors from Quang Tri, 80 of them U.S. soldiers.

General Lam was relieved of command and given a position in the Ministry of Defense, but General Giai was stripped of his rank and imprisoned. Lt. Gen. Ngo Quang Truong, one of the best officers in the South Vietnamese army, took command of I Corps. His mission was to defend Hue, minimize further losses in northern I Corps, and recapture lost territory. Truong pushed the North Vietnamese from Quang Tri City in September, although much of the province remained in enemy hands.

The Central Region. In II Corps, South Vietnam's central region, the North Vietnamese tried to split South Vietnam from the rugged Central Highlands to the sea. Lt. Gen. Ngo Dzu, a timid commander, known for his involvement in drug smuggling and other corrupt activities, commanded II Corps. The negative effect of Dzu's presence was offset by his U.S. counterpart, John Paul Vann, one of the most experienced and effective advisers of the war.

Although the main objective of the North Vietnamese attack was the Central Highlands, the fighting began in coastal Binh Dinh province, long a stronghold of support for NVA and Viet Cong forces. The attacks in Binh Dinh province, which

succeeded in capturing a number of South Vietnamese firebases, was intended as a diversion to draw ARVN troops away from the Central Highlands. General Dzu almost fell into the trap, but Vann stopped him, ensuring that the 23d ARVN Division remained in the highlands to defend against the main thrust.

When the NVA realized its diversion had failed, it concentrated on the Central Highlands. During the second week in April elements of the *2d NVA Division* attacked two regiments of the 22d ARVN Division at the small district town of Tan Canh and nearby Dak To firebase. The South Vietnamese force quickly disintegrated, and with them went Vann's plan to inflict severe losses on the NVA as it moved south toward Kontum.

Vann faced a deteriorating situation by the end of April. Kontum lay exposed, with less than a single division of defenders. Still, Vann managed to find new troops while dealing with mounting personnel problems. Dzu became increasingly unable to make decisions, and personality conflicts among other South Vietnamese officers and their counterparts hampered progress.

The North Vietnamese inexplicably paused at Tan Canh and Dak To for almost three weeks, allowing the South Vietnamese time to reinforce Kontum. Had NVA forces moved down Highway 14, they would undoubtedly have taken Kontum in late April. Vann used massive B-52 strikes to hold the NVA at bay and to reduce the strength of its units before they could reach Kontum. On 14 May the North Vietnamese attacked Kontum in force.

Vann had been given the two tools he insisted he needed to win: time and B-52s, which enabled the South Vietnamese to hold Kontum despite heavy losses during a two-week battle. By early June, the NVA had faded away, and South Vietnamese patrols pushed out from the city to eliminate pockets of North Vietnamese resistance. John Paul Vann savored the victory in II Corps, but on 9 June he was killed in a helicopter crash.

An Loc. The third phase of the Easter Offensive occurred in III Corps just west of Saigon, around the town of An Loc. The area was a good site for a big battle as its open terrain was conducive to conventional warfare and three NVA divisions were stationed just over the border in Cambodia.

NVA troops feinted into neighboring Tay Ninh province, hoping to lure the South Vietnamese into believing that was the main attack. U.S. advisers with the 5th ARVN Division defending An Loc

T-54 MAIN BATTLE TANKS. Soviet-built T-54s burn near Dong Ha, 1972. *National Archives*

were not fooled, however. Col. William Miller, the division senior adviser, correctly predicted that An Loc was the real target.

NVA armor played a larger role at An Loc than at any other place during the Easter Offensive. NVA tanks entered the city on 13 April, but poor use of infantry in support of the armor, combined with the ARVN's effective use of handheld light antitank weapons (M72 LAWs) hampered the on-slaught. By 21 April, the attack had faltered and the North Vietnamese settled into a classic siege. Despite the danger of annihilation, the 5th ARVN Division commander, Brig. Gen. Le Van Hung, refused to launch offensive operations, relying instead on U.S. air power.

South Vietnamese military officials in Saigon planned to relieve the city by sending the 21st ARVN Division north from the Mekong Delta, but it never arrived. For three weeks the division crept north, often held at bay by much smaller NVA con-

tingents. Although the 21st ARVN Division never reached An Loc, its slow advance may have turned the tide of battle because it diverted almost a division of NVA troops.

On 11 May the North Vietnamese struck An Loc again in what U.S. advisers described later as "the fiercest attack." An Loc held, with terrible losses on both sides. North Vietnamese strength was spent. Although the NVA attempted limited attacks, the defenders sensed the NVA's weakness and launched a series of cautious counterattacks. South Vietnamese president Nguyen Van Thieu hailed the victory at An Loc as a triumph of democracy over communism, comparing it to the 1954 battle at Dien Bien Phu. The town of An Loc, however, was destroyed and much of the territory surrounding it remained in North Vietnamese hands for the re-mainder of the war. The area north of An Loc was eventually used as a staging point for the final NVA offensive in 1975.

Aftermath. Both sides claimed victory after the Easter Offensive, but neither gained much. North Vietnam never captured and held a provincial capital, and it did not decisively defeat the South Vietnamese army. Many ARVN units were rendered combat ineffective, and casualties were high (10,000 killed, 33,000 wounded, and 2,000 missing), but U.S. training and resupply brought them back to strength by early 1973. On the other hand, North Vietnam gained considerable territory along the Laotian and Cambodian borders as well as the area just south of the DMZ. While few people lived in these regions, the ground gained was used to advantage at the Paris negotiating table. Most important, Vietnamization was not conclusively tested because of the massive injection of U.S. air power; the real trial would come when South Vietnam had to stand and fight on its own.

For North Vietnam, the offensive had mixed results. Certainly, it had misjudged the effectiveness of American antiwar sentiment in preventing or minimizing the U.S. government's punishment of North Vietnam for its offensive, and it failed to anticipate the lack of response from the PRC and the Soviet Union. This was particularly apparent following the Nixon administration's decision in May 1972 to bomb North Vietnam, codenamed Operation LINE-BACKER, and mine Haiphong harbor in order to prevent resupply from Soviet and East Bloc ships. In December the United States increased the pressure once again with heavy bombing of Hanoi, LINE-BACKER II (the so-called Christmas bombings). In the end these campaigns temporarily destroyed North Vietnam's logistical system, but they had little effect on the Easter Offensive because Hanoi had stockpiled sufficient supplies near the battlefields in South Vietnam.

Strategically, the offensive was a military failure. Rather than concentrating its forces for a single strike, or perhaps two, North Vietnam attacked with virtually its entire army over three broad fronts and lacked the strength to prevail on any. In the end, the offensive significantly reduced NVA combat effectiveness for nearly two years.

U.S. air power was decisive. During the sieges of An Loc, Kontum, and to a lesser extent Quang Tri City, South Vietnamese troops had either lost or abandoned their artillery and relied almost exclusively on air strikes, without which the South Vietnamese would probably have lost on every front. Half of the estimated 100,000 NVA and Viet Cong soldiers killed and 450 tanks destroyed during the offensive were credited to air strikes.

From the American perspective, the failure of the Easter Offensive was evidence that Vietnamization was succeeding. North Vietnam was beaten badly enough to allow the United States a "decent interval" during which to bow out of Vietnam. Nevertheless, the North Vietnamese understood their failures, and corrected them before their final assault in April 1975. South Vietnam, on the other hand, could do little because when the United States departed in 1973, it dismantled the advisory structure and withdrew the air power that had been so effective during the Easter Offensive.

BIBLIOGRAPHY

ANDRADÉ, DALE. *Trial by Fire: The 1972 Easter Offensive, America's Last Vietnam Battle.* 1994.

DAVIDSON, PHILLIP B. *Vietnam at War: The History, 1946–1975.* 1988.

MELSON, CHARLES D., and CURTIS G. ARNOLD. *U.S. Marines in Vietnam: The War That Would Not End, 1971–1973.* 1991.

SHEEHAN, NEIL. *A Bright Shining Lie: John Paul Vann and America in Vietnam.* 1988.

TURLEY, G. H. *The Easter Offensive: The Last American Advisers, 1972.* 1985.

WILLBANKS, JAMES H. *Thiet Giap!: The Battle of An Loc, April 1972.* 1993.

DALE ANDRADÉ

Eden, Anthony (1897–1977), British foreign secretary, 1935–1938, 1951–1955; British prime minister, 1955–1957. Together with Soviet Foreign Minister Vyacheslav Molotov, Eden cochaired the 1954 Geneva Conference, which convened the day after Dien Bien Phu fell to the Viet Minh. Earlier, as Winston Churchill's foreign secretary, he opposed U.S. military intervention at Dien Bien Phu.

BIBLIOGRAPHY

JAMES, ROBERT RHODES. *Anthony Eden.* 1986.

PAUL M. TAILLON

Eisenhower, Dwight D. (1890–1969), U.S. president, 1953–1961. Eisenhower ("Ike") brought to the White House traits honed during an extraordinary military career: prudence, practical intelligence, and a knack for interpersonal diplomacy. Born in Texas and raised in Kansas, he graduated from West Point in 1915, mastered logistics during World War I, established himself as a promising junior officer in the stagnant interwar army, and rose rapidly during World War II, ultimately serving as

DWIGHT D. EISENHOWER. Addressing a joint session of Congress, 10 January 1957. *Library of Congress*

Allied Supreme Commander in Europe. Afterward he was in quick succession Army Chief of Staff, president of Columbia University, and commander of the North Atlantic Treaty Organization (NATO). Elected president as a Republican in 1952, Eisenhower achieved two of his major domestic goals: limiting growth of the welfare state without dismantling the New Deal and using his popular persona to calm national anxieties. Though a shrewd, flexible Cold War warrior, he accomplished less than he wanted to in foreign affairs. Mutual distrust (represented in the United States by fervent anticommunism) hampered Eisenhower's attempts to thaw the Cold War with the Soviet Union; Central Intelligence Agency (CIA) covert operations in the Third World tarnished his claim that he opposed colonialism; and the administration's strategic "New Look" military fueled an arms race and prompted criticism that Eisenhower brought the world closer to nuclear war.

Eisenhower's Indochina policy was his foreign policy in microcosm. Seeking to contain communism, he supported the French with money, arms, and a small contingent of technical personnel. As the French faltered in early 1954, he prudently considered larger-scale intervention. He believed that if Vietnam fell to communism, other Asian nations might collapse in turn according to the domino theory. Yet Eisenhower had slight faith in the

French, who refused to transform their colonial war into a broad anticommunist campaign, and he would not act without British assistance and congressional approval, neither of which was forthcoming.

By the time the French surrendered at Dien Bien Phu in May 1954, Eisenhower had reconciled himself to the partition of Vietnam and sought new ways to contain communism in Asia. The United States, he said, was neither a "party to" nor "bound by" the Geneva accords. Accordingly, his administration took the lead in creating the Southeast Asia Treaty Organization (SEATO) in order to join the noncommunist countries together, used CIA infiltrators to disrupt North Vietnam, and ensured Ngo Dinh Diem's consolidation of power in an independent South Vietnam. The Eisenhower administration provided $1 billion and in 1960 promised Diem that "the United States will continue to assist South Vietnam in the difficult yet hopeful struggle ahead." Subsequent presidents took Eisenhower's statement as a duty-bound commitment. Although exasperated by Diem's failure to democratize his regime, Eisenhower respected him and mourned his murder in later years.

While publicly supporting the Indochina policies of presidents Kennedy and Johnson, Eisenhower disliked the former's acceptance of a coalition government in Laos and grew increasingly disenchanted with the latter's failure to "swamp the enemy with overwhelming force." Eisenhower believed that senators who thought otherwise were wrong and that the activities of some demonstrators against the war verged on treason. When Johnson limited bombing raids and began negotiations in 1968, Eisenhower stopped offering advice and enthusiastically supported the presidential candidacy of his former vice president, Richard Nixon, who ultimately adopted a version of the forceful strategy that Eisenhower preferred. Ironically, while Eisenhower spent his last years as a proponent of the Vietnam War, liberal commentators began celebrating his refusal to intervene at Dien Bien Phu.

BIBLIOGRAPHY

AMBROSE, STEPHEN E. *Eisenhower: The President.* 1985.
BILLINGS-YUN, MELANIE. *Decision Against War: Eisenhower and Dien Bien Phu.* 1988.

LEO P. RIBUFFO

Elections, South Vietnam, 1955. The Geneva Conference of 1954 included a provision for reunification elections to be held in 1956 throughout Vietnam. At the end of the conference, the United States announced that it took note of the agreements and pledged not to interfere with them, but declined to endorse them. The State of Vietnam, the French puppet state under emperor Bao Dai, protested the provision for elections and refused to sign the accords. The North Vietnamese believed that Ho Chi Minh's popularity in the south and North Vietnam's larger population would allow them to win the elections and unify Vietnam under their banner. Both the U.S. and South Vietnamese governments also realized that truly free and open elections would probably result in a victory for the communists; Dwight D. Eisenhower later admitted that if elections had been held in 1956, "possibly 80 percent of the population would have voted for the Communist Ho Chi Minh as their leader."

In response to a North Vietnamese announcement that they were prepared to discuss elections, South Vietnamese president Ngo Dinh Diem declared in July 1955 that the State of Vietnam was not bound by the Geneva agreements. Instead, with U.S. support, he proposed a referendum to abolish the Bao Dai monarchy, ratify Diem's presidency, and proclaim a republic. Col. Edward Lansdale advised Diem against outright election fraud, but provided hints on how to manipulate the election machinery. For example, Diem's ballot, printed on red paper, symbolized good luck, while Bao Dai's appeared on "an uninspired shade of green." Massive fraud marked the October 1955 elections, which included a heavy police presence at the polls to intimidate voters to vote for Diem as well as unsupervised ballot-counting by Diem's men. According to Lansdale, Diem needed only a large majority to convince Americans of his mandate, but Diem recorded a landslide victory with 98.2 percent of the vote. One sample of electoral corruption: in Saigon, of a total of 450,000 registered voters, 605,025 voted for Diem.

BIBLIOGRAPHY

EDWARDS, HERMAN S., and FRANK BRODHEAD. *Demonstration Elections: U.S. Staged Elections in the Dominican Republic, Vietnam, and El Salvador.* 1984.
YOUNG, MARILYN B. *The Vietnam Wars, 1945–1990.* 1991.

PAUL M. TAILLON

Ellsberg, Daniel (1931–), senior liaison officer, U.S. embassy, South Vietnam, 1965–1966; assistant to the U.S. ambassador to South Vietnam, 1967. A Na-

tional Security Council operative and one of Secretary of Defense McNamara's renowned "whiz kids," Ellsberg turned from a stalwart war supporter to an antiwar activist. Ellsberg leaked parts of the Pentagon Papers to the *New York Times,* which in June 1971 began publishing excerpts of the classified study of U.S. policy in Vietnam. When the Nixon administration sought an injunction against the newspaper, the Supreme Court upheld the legality of the publications. Ellsberg was charged with conspiracy, theft, and violation of espionage statutes, but the presiding judge dismissed the case after evidence of government misconduct. Among other abuses, the Nixon administration had organized a clandestine unit, known as the "plumbers," to break into the home of Ellsberg's psychiatrist. The "plumbers" later became involved in the ill-fated Watergate burglary.

BIBLIOGRAPHY

ELLSBERG, DANIEL. *Papers of the War.* 1972.
KUTLER, STANLEY. *The Wars of Watergate.* 1990.

ADAM LAND

Ely, Paul (1897–1975), commander in chief of French armed forces in Indochina, 1954–1955. On 20 March 1954, the French government sent Ely to Washington, D.C., to request U.S. air support for the defense of Dien Bien Phu. During Ely's visit, Adm. Arthur W. Radford, chairman of the Joint Chiefs of Staff (JCS), advocated Operation VULTURE, a plan calling for U.S. air strikes against Viet Minh positions. Although the air force chief of staff, Gen. Nathan F. Twining, strongly supported the plan, the other members of the JCS opposed it. Ely's request was ultimately denied, and French forces surrendered Dien Bien Phu on 7 May 1954.

BIBLIOGRAPHY

BUTTINGER, JOSEPH. *Vietnam: A Dragon Embattled.* 1967.
HERRING, GEORGE C. *America's Longest War: The United States and Vietnam, 1950–1975.* 1986.
International Who's Who, 1964–1965. 1965.
Obituary. *New York Times,* 20 January 1975.

ELLEN D. GOLDLUST

Élysée Agreement. On 8 March 1949, former emperor Bao Dai and French president Vincent Auriol exchanged letters at the Élysée Palace in Paris that paved the way for Bao Dai to return to Vietnam as emperor and head the Associated State of Vietnam within the French Union. Vietnam's independent status within the French Union was designed to counter the Viet Minh's nationalist appeal, although French economic and political primacy would in fact remain unchanged.

BIBLIOGRAPHY

The Pentagon Papers: The Defense Department History of United States Decisionmaking on Vietnam. Senator Gravel Edition. Vol. 1. 1971.

VICTOR JEW

Embargo. In April 1975 after the fall of South Vietnam, the United States extended to all of Vietnam a trade embargo that had been in effect against the Democratic Republic of Vietnam (DRV) since 1964. Authorized under the 1917 Trading with the Enemy Act and the 1969 Export Administration Act, four U.S. presidents renewed the embargo annually, leaving it essentially unchanged until 1991. The embargo included a ban on commercial trade and financial transactions between the two countries, mandated a U.S. block on International Monetary Fund (IMF) and World Bank development aid, and froze Vietnam's assets in the United States. The United States allowed limited humanitarian aid from private American agencies and small-scale remittances by Vietnamese expatriates to their families. Together with Cambodia, North Korea, and Cuba, Vietnam faced the United States' most restrictive trade policy through the 1980s.

In the late 1980s, Vietnamese policy changes led to improved relations with the United States and a reconsideration of the embargo. In 1989, Vietnam began to move toward a market economy, scaling back state-subsidized industry and centralized planning. Reductions in Soviet foreign aid and the loss of protected Eastern bloc markets drove the new policies. Vietnam withdrew its forces from Cambodia in 1989 and in the early 1990s facilitated efforts to account for Americans still listed as missing in action (MIA). In addition, U.S. companies such as AT&T, Mobil, Caterpillar, and Boeing lobbied on Capitol Hill to allow participation in the Vietnamese market, citing the importance of U.S. economic competitiveness and noting that other countries, most prominently Japan, had begun investment and trade with Vietnam.

In 1991, President Bush lifted the ban on travel to Vietnam and authorized a $1 million aid package, the first official U.S. assistance for the country since

1975. In July 1993, President Clinton ended U.S. opposition to IMF and World Bank aid. After a symbolic Senate vote in support of a new trade policy, President Clinton repealed the embargo on 4 February 1994. Clinton's action did not affect Vietnam's frozen assets in the United States (estimated at $290 million in 1994). The resolution of the issue awaited negotiations over U.S. financial claims within former South Vietnam. Analysts estimated that U.S. investment and trade in Vietnam would increase to $2.6 billion by 1996.

BIBLIOGRAPHY

CHARNY, JOEL, and JOHN SPRAGENS JR. *Obstacles to Recovery in Vietnam and Kampuchea: U.S. Embargo of Humanitarian Aid.* 1984.
HEIBERT, MURRAY, and SUSUMU AWANAHORA. "Good Morning Vietnam: U.S. Declares Peace through Trade." *Far Eastern Economic Review* (17 February 1994).

ADAM LAND

Enclave Strategy. The enclave strategy, an alternative to search-and-destroy tactics, would have confined U.S. forces to coastal areas and bases. When the first U.S. combat troops arrived in Vietnam, civilian leaders debated whether they should statically defend installations or actively pursue the Viet Cong and North Vietnamese forces. Ambassador Maxwell Taylor and Gen. Harold Johnson proposed limiting U.S. forces to 80-kilometer (50-mile) zones around coastal base areas, and President Johnson initially approved this cautious enclave approach in April 1965. U.S. soldiers would thus be spared from fighting in unfamiliar terrain, while their presence would give South Vietnam time to build up its armed forces. The Army of the Republic of Vietnam (ARVN) would subsequently be able to bear the brunt of combat. But almost immediately, Gen. William Westmoreland, MACV commander, and Gen. Earle Wheeler, chairman of the Joint Chiefs of Staff (JCS), began pushing for a greater U.S. combat role. They denigrated the enclave strategy as timid, preferring aggressive search-and-destroy operations that would capitalize on superior U.S. firepower and mobility. "You must take the fight to the enemy," Gen. Wheeler advised President Johnson. "No one ever won a battle sitting on his ass."

Within a few months, U.S. troops left their enclaves and patrolled the hinterlands of South Vietnam. But as losses mounted, the enclave strategy enjoyed renewed attention because it offered potentially fewer casualties. James Gavin, a highly respected retired general, suggested returning to coastal enclaves in 1966, and Assistant Secretary of Defense Paul Warnke echoed the idea a year later. The enclave strategy seemed to offer a way to avoid continual troop escalations and a way to return the primary combat role to ARVN. But President Johnson sharply dismissed the idea: "We can't hunker down like a jackass in a hailstorm." Thus, U.S. troops pursued Viet Cong and North Vietnamese Army (NVA) troops throughout the country and waged an unsuccessful war of attrition until 1969, when Vietnamization again put ARVN in charge of offensive operations. Except for the invasion of Cambodia in 1970, U.S. soldiers returned to de facto enclaves as U.S. forces withdrew from Vietnam.

BIBLIOGRAPHY

GAVIN, JAMES M. "A Communication on Vietnam." *Harper's Magazine,* February 1966.
JOHNSON, HAROLD. "The Enclave Concept: A License to Hunt." *Army* (April 1968).
KREPINEVICH, ANDREW F. *The Army and Vietnam.* 1986.
PALMER, DAVE RICHARD. *Summons of the Trumpet: A History of the Vietnam War from a Military Man's Viewpoint.* 1978.
STENNIS, JOHN C. "The Enclave Theory." *Armed Forces Journal* 106 (12 July 1969).
TAYLOR, MAXWELL D. *Swords into Plowshares.* 1972.

GLEN GENDZEL

Enthoven, Alain

Enthoven, Alain (1930–), U.S. assistant secretary of Defense for systems analysis, 1968. Brought to the Pentagon as a McNamara "whiz kid" in the 1960s, Enthoven was an economist trained to spot trends in numerical data. From his weekly analysis of military activity, he punctured the military's estimates of victory. In a 20 March 1968 memorandum to incoming Secretary of Defense Clark Clifford, Enthoven debunked the notion that the United States could win the war by inflicting an unacceptable rate of casualties on Viet Cong and North Vietnamese Army forces. He maintained that they could control their casualty rate and outlast the Americans indefinitely.

BIBLIOGRAPHY

CLIFFORD, CLARK. *Counsel to the President.* 1991.
THAYER, THOMAS C. *War without Fronts: The American Experience in Vietnam.* 1985.

VICTOR JEW

European Defense Community

European Defense Community. The European Defense Community (EDC) was a treaty that attempted to create an integrated European army of German, French, Italian, and Benelux forces. Originally proposed by French premier René Pleven in 1950 to delay West German rearmament, the treaty took on a different nature when U.S. policymakers adopted it as the linchpin of their European strategy. They wished to integrate a resurgent West Germany into a defensive pact against the Soviet Union. The French subsequently tried to link possible ratification of the treaty with increased U.S. military aid for the French effort in Vietnam. The two issues became intertwined, leading to mutual recrimination and suspicion between the United States and France. In dealing with the Truman administration, France conditioned its support for the EDC on U.S. aid for the French war in Indochina, a connection that Secretary of State Acheson described as blackmail. The Eisenhower administration inherited this problem but nevertheless provided more than $1 billion in loans and grants in 1953 to the French efforts in Indochina.

Despite this largesse, French leaders refused to bring the EDC to a parliamentary vote until 30 August 1954, and Premier Pierre Mendès-France, alternately hostile and unenthusiastic about the measure, allowed it to be defeated on a predebate procedural motion in the National Assembly. The European allies eventually agreed on a substitute to the EDC: a rearmed West Germany would be admitted to the North Atlantic Treaty Organization (NATO) while forswearing nuclear and chemical weapons.

BIBLIOGRAPHY

HERRING, GEORGE C. *America's Longest War: The United States and Vietnam, 1950–1975.* 1986.
LE PRESTRE, P. "European Defense Community." In *Historical Dictionary of the French Fourth and Fifth Republics, 1946–1991.* Edited by Wayne Northcutt. 1992.
The Pentagon Papers: The Defense Department History of United States Decisionmaking on Vietnam. Senator Gravel Edition. Vol. 1. 1971.
WALL, IRWIN M. *The United States and the Making of Postwar France, 1945–1954.* 1991.

VICTOR JEW

F

Fall, Bernard (1926–1967), French-born associate professor at Howard University, Washington, D.C.; internationally known expert on Vietnam. Fall was the author of several books, including *The Two Viet-Nams* and *Viet-Nam Witness: 1953–1966,* and was a prominent critic of U.S. policy in Vietnam. He was killed by a Viet Cong booby trap in Hue in 1967.

BIBLIOGRAPHY

"Death of a Scholar." *Newsweek,* 6 March 1967.
FALL, BERNARD B. *Street without Joy.* 1961.
ZAROULIS, NANCY, and GERALD SULLIVAN. *Who Spoke Up?* 1985.

KELLY EVANS-PFEIFER

FANK, acronym for Forces Armées Nationales Khmères (Khmer National Armed Forces), the Cambodian national army. In 1970, FANK supported Lon Nol's overthrow of Prince Norodom Sihanouk's government, believing that the new pro-U.S. regime would mean the resumption of U.S. military aid to Cambodia. The Khmer Rouge defeated FANK in 1975.

BIBLIOGRAPHY

DOUGAN, CLARK, and DAVID FULGHUM. *The Vietnam Experience: The Fall of the South.* 1985.
SHAWCROSS, WILLIAM. *Sideshow: Kissinger, Nixon, and the Destruction of Cambodia.* 1979.

ELLEN D. GOLDLUST

Faure, Edgar (1908–1988), French prime minister, January 1952–February 1953, February 1955–January 1956. As prime minister in 1955–1956, Faure had a dramatic and decisive confrontation with U.S. Secretary of State John Foster Dulles over the course of Franco-American influence in Vietnam. The Eisenhower administration's support of Diem caused Faure to break sharply with the Americans. Faure rejected support for Diem, judging him to be incapable, and stated that France could "no longer take risks with him." This rupture between the United States and France created a clear path for unilateral U.S. action. Dulles proposed that France remain in Vietnam until the Vietnamese could exercise self determination through national elections; but he also told the French that the United States was going to pursue its own way without prior consultations with the French government. The French began to shift attention to their North African colonial troubles, and they abandoned their interest in Vietnam, concluding an imperial chapter that had begun in the eighteenth century. Meanwhile, the United States embarked on its independent course in Vietnam.

BIBLIOGRAPHY

HERRING, GEORGE C. *America's Longest War: The United States and Vietnam, 1950–1975.* 1986.

The Pentagon Papers: The Defense Department History of United States Decisionmaking on Vietnam. Senator Gravel Edition. Vol. 1. 1971.

VICTOR JEW

Federal Bureau of Investigation (FBI).

During the Vietnam War Presidents Lyndon Johnson and Richard Nixon used the FBI to undermine and harass domestic critics of the war. Both presidents believed that the increasingly vocal antiwar movement was a threat to their Vietnam policies and to domestic stability. Both also believed that North Vietnam and its allies influenced the movement. FBI director J. Edgar Hoover enthusiastically supported repressive policies against antiwar protestors. The FBI, created in 1908, is empowered to conduct domestic criminal investigations. As an organ of the federal government, operating under the Department of Justice, the FBI is to protect and respect citizens' civil liberties and is thus subject to general law enforcement restrictions, for example, strict conditions on the use of electronic surveillance. In its Vietnam War–related activities, however, the FBI often overstepped its bounds.

When Johnson faced opposition from liberal congressional Democrats over his Vietnam policies, Hoover offered to provide the administration with damaging information on Congress's most prominent antiwar members, including Senators J. William Fulbright and Wayne L. Morse. Beginning in 1967, Hoover, at Johnson's request, turned the FBI's attention toward the antiwar movement, particularly toward groups led by student radicals. Code-named Operation COINTELPRO, the FBI's campaign against the antiwar movement was two-pronged: it was to disrupt from the inside and intimidate from the outside. Agents of the FBI and agents of the Central Intelligence Agency (CIA) were directed to go undercover and infiltrate vari-

ous antiwar groups. This program, which was continued and expanded under President Richard Nixon, sought to keep the movement off guard and upset its activities. The disruptions included causing conflict within and among antiwar groups and cancelling reservations for antiwar rallies. In addition to the undercover program, FBI agents would show up at draft card burnings, rallies, and conventions held by Students for a Democratic Society (SDS), instilling paranoia and fear by their very presence. Internal FBI documents state that the purpose was "to get the point across that there is an FBI agent behind every mailbox." Under a program code-named VIDEM, FBI investigators attempted to discover links between movement leaders and the communist governments of North Vietnam, the People's Republic of China, and the Soviet Union. These investigations resulted in thousands of files but yielded no evidence of a connection.

Nixon's fear of the antiwar movement extended to those within his own administration. He directed the FBI to tap the phones of administration staff in an effort to uncover and plug leaks, and he tried to enlist the FBI in his illegal Huston Plan, which would allow the White House to control the domestic intelligence activities of agencies such as the FBI and CIA, but Hoover ultimately refused. Both Johnson's and Nixon's use of the FBI was unprecedented, but in Nixon's case it became part of the Watergate scandal and contributed to his eventual resignation.

BIBLIOGRAPHY

THEOHARIS, ATHAN G., and JOHN STUART COX. *The Boss: J. Edgar Hoover and the Great American Inquisition.* 1988.

ZAROULIS, NANCY, and GERALD SULLIVAN. *Who Spoke Up?* 1985.

KELLY EVANS-PFEIFER

Felt, Harry D.

(1902–), admiral, U.S. Navy; Commander-in-Chief, Pacific (CINCPAC), 1958–1964. A decorated naval aviator who served in Moscow during World War II, Adm. Harry "Don" Felt succeeded Adm. Felix Stump as CINCPAC in August 1958. An enthusiast of counterinsurgency warfare, Felt said of the U.S. role in Asia: "We are the fire brigade." More concerned with the communist threats in Korea, Taiwan, and Laos than with that in Vietnam, Felt in 1961 recommended against sending U.S. troops to South Vietnam, warning superiors that "if we go in, we can't pull out at will without damaging repercussions." He soon changed his position, however, and became a vocal supporter of intervention, predicting victory within three years. When journalists questioned his optimism, Felt's response typified the U.S. military approach to press relations in the Vietnam War: "Get on the team." The first reports of the insurrection against President Diem occurred while Felt was paying an official visit in November 1963, and he rushed out of the presidential palace just prior to the coup. Felt retired and was replaced by Adm. U.S. Grant Sharp Jr. in June 1964.

BIBLIOGRAPHY

"Big Man, Big Moment." *Time*, 9 June 1958.

MAROLDA, EDWARD J., and G. WESLEY PRYCE. *A Short History of the United States Navy and the Southeast Asian Conflict, 1950–1974.* 1984.

"Mr. Pacific." *Time*, 6 January 1961, 17–22.

"People of the Week: Admiral Harry D. Felt." *U.S. News and World Report*, 6 June 1958, 19.

GLEN GENDZEL

Film. *For discussion of the treatment of the Vietnam War in American film, see* Art and Literature.

Fishel, Wesley, political science professor, Michigan State University; head, Michigan State University Vietnam Advisory Group (MSUVAG), 1954–1961; chairman, American Friends of Vietnam. Fishel staunchly backed Ngo Dinh Diem and an anticommunist South Vietnam in the 1950s. He led the MSUVAG, which developed numerous institutions for the South Vietnamese government. As head of the American Friends of Vietnam, Fishel championed a large U.S. military commitment to preserve an independent South Vietnam.

BIBLIOGRAPHY

FISHEL, WESLEY, ed. *Vietnam: Anatomy of a Conflict.* 1968.

OLSON, JAMES, and RANDY ROBERTS. *Where the Domino Fell.* 1991.

KELLY EVANS-PFEIFER

Fishhook, a small strip of land in Cambodia's Mondolkiri province on the South Vietnamese border. The Fishhook area, 160 kilometers (100 miles) northwest of Saigon, was home to 1,640 people in thirteen villages. It was also a major supply base and sanctuary for Viet Cong guerrillas. President Nixon, believing the Central Office for South Vietnam (COSVN) headquarters of the Viet Cong was located there, ordered secret bombing of the Fishhook and other Cambodian sanctuaries in 1969–1970. Operation TOTAL VICTORY, the assault on the Fishhook by U.S. and Army of the Republic of Vietnam (ARVN) troops, was part of the invasion of Cambodia in May 1970. The invaders found deserted bunkers and tons of supplies, but few soldiers and no command post.

BIBLIOGRAPHY

"In Search of an Elusive Foe." *Time*, 18 May 1970.

"Sanitizing the Sanctuaries." *Time*, 11 May 1970.

SHAWCROSS, WILLIAM. *Sideshow: Kissinger, Nixon, and the Destruction of Cambodia.* 1979.

WHITAKER, DONALD P., et al. *Area Handbook for the Khmer Republic (Cambodia).* 1973.

GLEN GENDZEL

Five O'Clock Follies, nickname for the daily U.S. Information Agency press briefings on the progress of the war. Every day at 4:45 P.M. sharp, the U.S. Military Assistance Command Office of Information (MACOI) conducted official briefings for American and foreign journalists in Saigon. After 1966, these carefully choreographed performances were held at the Joint U.S. Public Affairs Office (JUSPAO) auditorium and directed by U.S. Information Agency officer Barry Zorthian. U.S. Army colonels trained in public relations passed out mimeographed body-count tallies and pointed to four-color overlay charts to impress journalists with the U.S. march toward victory. Military setbacks and operations by South Vietnamese forces received scant mention, while Viet Cong guerrilla and North Vietnamese losses were exaggerated. Fragmentary battle descriptions never gave reporters a sense of the overall U.S. war effort. When the briefings began, "the claims of victory presented there were taken most of the time at face value," according to media critic Daniel Hallin. Following the 1968 Tet Offensive, however, skeptical reporters lost faith in official pronouncements, and they derided the daily JUSPAO briefing as the "Five O'Clock Follies." Michael Herr of *Esquire* treated the Follies as the army's "psychological warfare" against the press, and instead he and other journalists pursued their own stories with the soldiers in the field.

BIBLIOGRAPHY

BRAESTRUP, PETER. *Big Story: How the American Press and Television Reported and Interpreted the Crisis of Tet 1968 in Vietnam and Washington.* 1977.
ELEGANT, ROBERT. "How to Lose a War." *Encounter* (August 1981).
HALLIN, DANIEL C. *The Uncensored War: The Media and Vietnam.* 1986.
HAMMOND, WILLIAM M. *Public Affairs: The Military and the Media, 1962–1968.* 1989.
HERR, MICHAEL. *Dispatches.* 1977.

GLEN GENDZEL

FLAMING DART. FLAMING DART, the successor to PIERCE ARROW, was the code name for February 1965 U.S. retaliatory air raids against North Vietnam. Triggered by the 6 February mortar attack on the U.S. air base at Pleiku, FLAMING DART was launched on 7 and 8 February from attack carriers *Coral Sea* and *Hancock* against barracks and port facilities in southern North Vietnam. FLAMING DART II was a response to the 10 February bombing of U.S. billets in Qui Nhon with strikes from *Coral Sea, Hancock,* and *Ranger.* The attack order specified the exact attack time to coincide with an evening prime-time address by President Lyndon Johnson and specified ingress and egress headings and ordnance carried. Three aircraft and one pilot were lost, but damage to the target was negligible.

BIBLIOGRAPHY

SCHLIGHT, JOHN. *The Years of the Offensive, 1965–1968.* 1985.

JOHN F. GUILMARTIN JR.

Flexible Response. Flexible response was a Cold War-era strategic doctrine founded on the principle that the United States should equip its armed forces to allow it to match any act of aggression from a communist nation with a reciprocal level of violence. In his book *The Uncertain Trumpet* (1959), retired general Maxwell Taylor suggested that a flexible response strategy should replace President Eisenhower's "New Look" defense policy of threatening massive nuclear retaliation in response to any threat from communist nations. Taylor cautioned that excessive reliance on air power and nuclear weapons left the United States unprepared to fight communism around the world. As he stated, "massive retaliation could offer only two choices: the initiation of general nuclear war or compromise and retreat." Instead, Taylor maintained that the United States should develop "a capability to react across the entire spectrum of possible challenges," from nuclear war to counterinsurgency operations. President Kennedy embraced flexible response and named Taylor his special military representative in 1961. Vietnam was to become a test of Kennedy's promise of "suitable, selective, swift and effective" response to aggression.

BIBLIOGRAPHY

ROSEN, STEPHEN P. "Vietnam and the American Theory of Limited War." *International Security* 7 (Fall 1982).
TAYLOR, MAXWELL D. "Our Changing Military Policy: Greater Flexibility." *Vital Speeches* 28 (15 March 1962).
TAYLOR, MAXWELL D. *The Uncertain Trumpet.* 1959.

GLEN GENDZEL

Fonda, Jane (1937–), actress; antiwar activist. Fonda spoke at numerous antiwar rallies beginning in 1969, and earned the nickname "Hanoi Jane." The State Department criticized her for a controversial trip to Hanoi in July 1972, during which she broadcast an appeal over Hanoi radio urging U.S. pilots to stop bombing North Vietnam.

BIBLIOGRAPHY

ZAROULIS, NANCY, and GERALD SULLIVAN. *Who Spoke Up?* 1985.

KELLY EVANS-PFEIFER

F-111. The F-111 is a U.S. Air Force low-altitude, all-weather strike fighter. Conceived by Secretary of Defense Robert McNamara as a multipurpose aircraft, it was produced by the TFX (tactical fighter experimental) program, which was intended to satisfy an air force requirement for a Europe-based nuclear strike aircraft and a navy requirement for a carrier-based, missile-armed, long-range fleet defense interceptor. The multiservice program was to achieve significant savings through a longer production run and common parts inventory; a variable-sweep, "switch-blade" wing, never before used in an operational aircraft, was to satisfy the disparate design requirements. In a controversial decision, McNamara overruled the services and selected General Dynamics rather than Boeing as contractor because the two

General Dynamics versions were closer in design. The navy F-111B proved badly overweight and was canceled. The air force version suffered from developmental problems, culminating in a disastrous premature deployment to Thailand in March 1968 in which three of eight aircraft were lost to unknown causes in fifty-five missions over North Vietnam. The aircraft's problems were ultimately resolved, and the F-111A proved itself in Operation LINEBACKER II on the basis of accurate radar bombing and high subsonic penetration speeds and low-altitude terrain-avoidance radar, which rendered it effectively immune to antiaircraft defenses. Attacking individually and with the advantage of surprise, F-111s played a major role in softening up North Vietnamese defenses and were particularly effective in attacking small, high-value targets such as radar sites, SAM sites, and airfields. The air force procured the F-111 in three significantly different versions, and the hoped-for savings were buried by cost overruns. Since the Vietnam War the F-111E and F served effectively in the 1991 Persian Gulf War.

BIBLIOGRAPHY

MORROCCO, JOHN. *Rain of Fire: Air War.* The Vietnam Experience, Vol. 14. 1985.

JOHN F. GUILMARTIN JR.

Fontainebleau Conference, a failed French-Vietnamese conference held at Fontainebleau on 6 July 1946. No agreement was reached on the key issues of the status of Cochinchina and Vietnam's role within the French Union. Even before the conference began, French high commissioner Georges Thierry d'Argenlieu undercut the Viet Minh by recognizing a French puppet state, led by former emperor Bao Dai, in Cochinchina. This action caused the Viet Minh to doubt French sincerity, and in the face of Argenlieu's unilateral actions, they left the meetings. Ho Chi Minh remained in France, however, to work out a modus vivendi with the French, thus salvaging something with which to placate the more extreme elements in the Viet Minh.

BIBLIOGRAPHY

HAMMER, ELLEN J. *The Struggle for Indochina.* 1954.

VICTOR JEW

Forces Armées Nationales Khmères (FANK). *See* FANK.

Ford, Gerald R., Jr. (1913–), U.S. president, 1974–1977. Ford, a pre–World War II isolationist turned Cold War internationalist, presided over the final U.S. withdrawal from Vietnam. He graduated from the University of Michigan and Yale Law School, where he was active in a group that later formed the nucleus of the America First Committee, the foremost nonintervention organization on the eve of U.S. entry into World War II. Moved by his service as a naval gunnery officer during the war, he converted to internationalism, defeated an isolationist incumbent in the Republican primary, and was elected to the U.S. House in 1948. A moderate Republican, he opposed most expansion of the welfare state and endorsed the liberation of Eastern Europe from Soviet rule. Chosen House minority leader in 1965, Ford criticized President Johnson for "pulling our best punches" in Vietnam. Subsequently he supported President Nixon's pursuit of détente with the Soviet Union, rapprochement with the People's Republic of China, and Vietnamization of the Vietnam War. Ford also defended Nixon against charges that he had covered up the Watergate scandal. Needing a well-liked Republi-

GERALD R. FORD JR. *Library of Congress*

can loyalist to replace Spiro Agnew, Nixon nominated Ford as vice president in 1973.

After succeeding Nixon in 1974, Ford worked to heal the domestic wounds of Watergate and Vietnam. In the latter case, he offered amnesty to draft evaders who performed alternative service. He also tried to bolster the sagging Cambodian and South Vietnamese governments. Except for the most stalwart conservatives, members of Congress were variously apathetic, hostile, or suspicious of presidential authority. They appropriated less than half of the $2 billion in aid for South Vietnam that Ford requested for fiscal year 1975. This decision, Ford believed, gravely impaired the chances of survival for South Vietnam. Facing major North Vietnamese and Khmer Rouge offensives in early 1975, Ford used discretionary funds to bring some two thousand South Vietnamese orphans to the United States (Operation Babylift) and made two unsuccessful efforts to secure emergency military assistance for the South Vietnamese government. The final request, made on 10 April, was motivated partly by a slim hope of preventing communist victories and partly by a desire to avoid blame if those victories occurred. Nonetheless, valuing national unity more than partisan advantage, Ford rejected Secretary of State Henry Kissinger's advice to accuse the Democratic Congress of losing the war. On 26 April, four days before Saigon surrendered, Ford told a cheering college audience that the war was "finished as far as America is concerned."

Yet responsibilities and consequences were not so easily evaded. Unwilling to admit that South Vietnam's collapse was imminent, Ford waited too long before starting to evacuate Americans and the ranking South Vietnamese who had served them. For the United States, this delay meant embarrassment; for many Vietnamese, it meant imprisonment or death. In May 1975 Ford responded with military action when Cambodia seized the U.S. merchant ship *Mayaguez*. Convinced by Kissinger that the United States was being tested by the new Khmer Rouge regime, he ordered air strikes on Cambodian bases and a rescue mission that cost the lives of forty-one Americans even as the *Mayaguez* crew was being released. Finally, the Vietnam conflict contributed to Ford's loss of the presidency in 1976. The American public, disgusted with how the Vietnam War had been handled, with political scandals such as Watergate, and with the political turmoil that had resulted, elected Democrat Jimmy Carter, who promised to restore morality to domestic and foreign policy.

BIBLIOGRAPHY

FORD, GERALD R. *A Time to Heal: The Autobiography of Gerald R. Ford.* 1979.
ISAACS, ARNOLD R. *Without Honor: Defeat in Vietnam and Cambodia.* 1984.

LEO P. RIBUFFO

Forrestal, Michael (1927–1989), National Security Council aide, 1962–1965. Forrestal visited Vietnam with Roger Hilsman at President Kennedy's request in January 1963. Their report presented a mixed assessment of the war, predicting a prolonged conflict but not recommending major policy changes. On 24 August 1963, Forrestal, Averell Harriman, George Ball, and Hilsman drafted a cable to Ambassador Henry Cabot Lodge that signaled the U.S. government's willingness to abandon Diem, and that ultimately led to the overthrow of the Diem government. The cable, drafted during a weekend, bypassed some U.S. officials and caused a rift among the president's advisers.

BIBLIOGRAPHY

HALBERSTAM, DAVID. *The Best and the Brightest.* 1992.
NEWMAN, JOHN M. *JFK and Vietnam: Deception, Intrigue and the Struggle for Power.* 1992.

WILLIAM PAUL SCHUCK

Fortas, Abe (1910–1982), U.S. Supreme Court Justice, 1965–1969. A trusted friend and unofficial adviser to President Johnson, Fortas played a significant behind-the-scenes role formulating Vietnam policy. Fortas strongly endorsed Johnson's escalation of the war and was virtually the only nonmilitary adviser to support further troop commitments after others had turned toward deescalation and withdrawal.

Fortas attended numerous 1965 policy meetings, vigorously advocating escalation and opposing any bombing halt prior to the new troop deployment. While many within the administration had changed their views on the war by 1967, Fortas urged Johnson to stay the course. As the number of those against escalation increased and included Defense Secretary Robert McNamara, Johnson relied increasingly on Fortas. The justice steadfastly sided with Johnson as the president became increasingly isolated. When newly appointed Defense Secretary Clark Clifford, who favored withdrawal, arranged a final "wise men" meeting for Johnson in 1968, Fortas joined the military men in dissenting from the recommendation to end the U.S. military role.

Fortas's advisory role was largely unpublicized, but when Johnson nominated him chief justice in 1968, critics charged that Fortas had improperly involved himself in executive branch decision making. That activity contributed directly to Fortas's failure to win Senate confirmation and indirectly to his forced resignation in 1969.

BIBLIOGRAPHY

KALMAN, LAURA. *Abe Fortas: A Biography*. 1990.
MURPHY, BRUCE ALLEN. *Fortas*. 1988.

KELLY EVANS-PFEIFER

Fort Hood Three. The Fort Hood Three—Private Dennis Mora, Private First Class James Johnson, and Private David Samas—refused orders to go to Vietnam after completing basic training at Fort Hood, Texas, in June 1966. They were court-martialed and served two years in prison. The antiwar movement widely publicized, and held demonstrations about, the case.

BIBLIOGRAPHY

ZAROULIS, NANCY, and GERALD SULLIVAN. *Who Spoke Up? American Protest against the War in Vietnam, 1963–1975*. 1985.

JENNIFER FROST

Four-Party Joint Military Commission. The Four-Party Joint Military Commission was created by the Paris peace accords of 1973 and included representatives from North Vietnam, the Provisional Revolutionary Government (formerly the National Liberation Front), South Vietnam, and the United States. From January to March 1973, the commission oversaw the pullout of more than fifty thousand troops—from Australia, New Zealand, South Korea, and the United States—from South Vietnam; arranged the return of prisoners-of-war, including almost six hundred Americans held by the North Vietnamese; and tried unsuccessfully to preserve the cease-fire. It was replaced on 29 March 1973 by the Four-Party Joint Military Team, with the same membership, which attempted in vain to resolve the issue of soldiers who were still listed as missing in action.

BIBLIOGRAPHY

DAWSON, ALAN. *55 Days: The Fall of South Vietnam*. 1977.
DILLARD, WALTER SCOTT. *Sixty Days to Peace: Implementing the Paris Peace Accords, Vietnam, 1973*. 1982.
HERRINGTON, STUART A. *Peace with Honor? An American Reports on Vietnam, 1973–1975*. 1984.

ELLEN D. GOLDLUST

Fragging, military slang for assassinating unpopular officers. Near the end of U.S. involvement in the Vietnam War, some U.S. troops became demoralized and mutinous. Symptoms included drug abuse, refusal to engage in combat, racial tension, and "fragging"—rolling fragmentation grenades into the tents of sleeping officers deemed incompetent or overzealous by their men. Because it left no traceable evidence, fragging was the preferred method for assassinating "hard chargers," officers eager for combat honors who exposed their men to undue risks. Fragging incidents began in 1969 and peaked in 1970–1971, even as U.S. troop strength declined rapidly. According to the Defense Department, 788 probable explosive-device assaults against officers and noncommissioned officers (NCOs) took place in Vietnam between 1969 and 1972, resulting in 86 dead and 714 wounded. Many more suspected fraggings were not investigated for lack of evidence, and "friendly fire" incidents, many of them suspicious, in general accounted for about 15 percent of U.S. casualties. Some units reportedly put cash bounties on the heads of their officers. The last years of war saw much rank-and-file hostility against careerist, medal-hungry, mostly white officers who ordered enlisted men (many of them nonwhite) to risk their lives for an unpopular cause. Fragging was the clearest sign that U.S. military discipline broke down in the Vietnam War.

BIBLIOGRAPHY

APPY, CHRISTIAN G. *Working-Class War: American Combat Soldiers and Vietnam*. 1993.
CINCINNATUS. [Cecil B. Curry]. *Self-Destruction: The Disintegration and Decay of the United States Army during the Vietnam Era*. 1978.
HEINL, ROBERT D. "The Collapse of the Armed Forces." *Armed Forces Journal* 108 (7 June 1971).
JOHNSON, HAYNES, and GEORGE C. WILSON. *An Army in Anguish*. 1971.
LINDEN, EUGENE. "Fragging and Other Withdrawal Symptoms." *Saturday Review*, 8 January 1972.

GLEN GENDZEL

FRENCH FOREIGN LEGIONNAIRE. A French Foreign Legion patrol during a sweep through communist-held areas in the Red River Delta. Note that the legionnaire has strapped his wrist watch to his shirt collar to avoid fungal skin infections on the wrist caused by tropical heat. Behind the legionnaire is a U.S. M-24 Chaffee tank, sent as aid to the French. *National Archives*

France. France established missionary and trade organizations in Vietnam in 1664 and consolidated its control throughout the eighteenth and nineteenth centuries. The French referred to the southern part of Vietnam, including the Mekong Delta and Saigon, as Cochinchina; the central third as Annam; and the northernmost section, including Hanoi, as Tonkin. In 1859 France conquered the Mekong Delta and in 1862 negotiated the Treaty of Saigon, which gave it control of Cochinchina. Between 1863 and 1893, France added Tonkin, Annam, Laos, and Cambodia as protectorates and in 1887 attempted to centralize control over the region by establishing the Union of Indochina under a single governor general. French control nevertheless remained decentralized; the French administered Cochinchina directly and the other areas only indirectly, through Vietnamese political institutions. The French levied taxes; controlled trade in rice, opium, and alcohol; confiscated land; and forced some peasants into labor on rubber plantations and in mines.

Armed resistance to French rule erupted in the 1930s. In an attempt to legitimize its control of the region, France in 1932 permitted the former emperor of Annam, Bao Dai, to return from France and assume governmental power in Vietnam. However, as with other indigenous leaders whose rule was reinstated by France, he was primarily a puppet. The Popular Front government in France was lenient toward the colony, but after its 1938 demise the French increased their repression of the independence movement. When France fell to Germany in 1940, it signed a treaty that allowed Japan to use military facilities in northern Vietnam. The French continued to staff the Japanese-controlled government, but the Viet Minh–led independence movement resisted both the French and the Japanese. In March 1945 the Japanese abolished French rule in the name of Asian nationalism and offered Bao Dai limited independence. Soon, however, the Japanese themselves had surrendered to the Allies, and by October, the French, with British and U.S. acquiescence, returned to Indochina.

In 1945 Ho Chi Minh declared Vietnam's independence and entered into negotiations with the French. In a 6 March 1946 treaty, France recognized Vietnam as a free state and Vietnam agreed to join the Indochinese Federation. This agreement was merely a truce as the two sides solidified their forces. France broke the treaty in November 1946 with attacks on Hanoi and Haiphong; the Viet Minh responded on 19 December with attacks on French barracks and residences.

From 1946 to 1954 France engaged in a protracted struggle to retain Vietnam. It installed a government under Emperor Bao Dai so that it could conclude a settlement with anticommunist Vietnamese; Bao Dai, however, made many of the same demands for independence as had Ho Chi Minh. France finally convinced Bao Dai to assume leadership of an anticommunist Vietnam in 1949 with only nominal independence from France.

The military struggle from 1947 to 1950 was marked by Viet Minh caution and refusal to engage in large-scale direct combat with the French. General Étienne Valluy began a campaign in 1947 to wipe out the Viet Minh but underestimated their strength and popular support. The French army of 30,000 could not penetrate mountainous and remote areas. French generals, beginning with Gen. Jean de Lattre de Tassigny in 1950, repeatedly requested the formation of a Vietnamese National Army, but this army never successfully freed the French expeditionary forces from their losing battle with the Viet Minh. Under Gen. Vo Nguyen Giap, the Viet Minh mounted repeated offensives beginning in 1952, culminating in the decisive battle and French defeat at Dien Bien Phu in March 1954. The 1954 Geneva Conference formalized the French withdrawal from northern Vietnam, although they remained in the South until March 1956, when their last troops departed after South Vietnamese President Diem expelled them. The French had backed numerous foes of Diem, and with U.S. support, he angrily turned on his former colonial masters. During the 1960s France opposed U.S. involvement; many of its leaders, such as General Charles de Gaulle, were convinced that the North Vietnamese were unlikely to lose and that Diem's government lacked popular support.

BIBLIOGRAPHY

BUTTINGER, JOSEPH. *Vietnam: A Political History.* 1968.
FITZGERALD, FRANCES. *Fire in the Lake: The Vietnamese and the Americans in Vietnam.* 1982.
KARNOW, STANLEY. *Vietnam: A History.* 1991.

ELLEN BAKER

Freedom Birds, nickname given by U.S. soldiers to the passenger airplanes that took them home from Vietnam. This quick return to the United States contributed to the development of post-traumatic stress syndrome in some returning soldiers by depriving them of a transitional period between the combat zone and civilian life.

BIBLIOGRAPHY

EILERT, RICK. *For Self and Country: For the Wounded in Vietnam the Journey Home Took More Courage Than Going into Battle.* 1983.

EMERSON, GLORIA. *Winners and Losers: Battles, Retreats, Gains, Losses, and Ruins from a Long War.* 1976.

WHEELER, JOHN. *Touched with Fire: The Future of the Vietnam Generation.* 1984.

ELLEN D. GOLDLUST

Free-Fire Zones.

Free-fire zones (FFZ) were areas in South Vietnam authorized for unrestricted U.S. attacks on North Vietnamese or Viet Cong forces. Free-fire zones were set up in accordance with procedures in the U.S. military's rules of engagement, which were designed to coordinate combat operations and minimize civilian injury. Province chiefs, appointed by the South Vietnamese government, authorized free-fire zones if National Liberation Front (NLF) forces were believed to control an area and civilians were not likely to be present. In practice, often without regard for the presence of civilians, South Vietnamese officials gave routine clearance at U.S. request. The U.S. military initially established free-fire zones during the early 1960s to authorize firepower around protected villages in the Strategic Hamlet program. In 1964, the military expanded their use, and they became a vital aspect of the strategy to direct massive firepower against the NLF insurgency.

After 1965, the Defense Department renamed the zones "specific strike zones," largely in response to the negative connotations of indiscriminate bombing that "free-fire zones" carried. The U.S. military's extensive use of the zones drew heated criticism from antiwar spokesmen. These figures, such as Daniel Ellsberg, decried the "large, semi-permanent" nature of free-fire areas and contended that their extensive use represented aspects of a "genocidal" strategy against the Vietnamese people. Even Gen. Bruce Palmer criticized the use of free-fire zones, claiming that they encouraged an excessive reliance on military force that revealed weaknesses in U.S. intelligence and communications.

BIBLIOGRAPHY

GIBSON, JAMES WILLIAM. *The Perfect War.* 1986.

LEWY, GUENTER. *America in Vietnam.* 1978.

PALMER, BRUCE, JR. *The 25-Year War: America's Military Role in Vietnam.* 1984.

ADAM LAND AND ELLEN BAKER

Free World,

term used to refer to the group of countries that assisted South Vietnam from 1959 to 1975. Six nations provided military aid: Australia, New Zealand, the Philippines, the Republic of China (Taiwan), the Republic of Korea (South Korea), and Thailand. More than thirty other nations provided technical and economic aid through the Free World Assistance Program, including Argentina, Belgium, Brazil, Canada, Costa Rica, Denmark, Ecuador, the Federal Republic of Germany, France, Greece, Guatemala, Honduras, Iran, Ireland, Israel, Italy, Japan, Laos, Liberia, Luxembourg, Malaysia, Morocco, the Netherlands, Norway, Pakistan, Spain, South Africa, Switzerland, Tunisia, Turkey, the United Kingdom, Uruguay, and Venezuela.

BIBLIOGRAPHY

LARSEN, STANLEY ROBERTS, and JAMES LAWTON COLLINS, JR. *Allied Participation in Vietnam.* 1975.

ELLEN D. GOLDLUST

Friendly Fire.

Friendly fire is the term for combat deaths or wounds accidentally caused by friendly forces. Estimates of casualties from friendly fire in the Vietnam War range from 2 percent to between 15 and 20 percent.

Friendly fire is a common aspect of battle in all wars. Accounts of friendly fire casualties span U.S. military actions from the French and Indian War in the 1750s through the 1991 Persian Gulf War. Friendly fire is caused by what military commanders refer to as the "fog of war," the confusion caused by smoke and noise from guns and artillery, faulty communications between troops and artillery and air forces, and the tension and fear of the combatants.

Friendly fire casualties most often result from artillery-to-ground, air-to-ground, and ground-to-ground fire. In Vietnam, casualties resulting from accidents in the first two categories were most often caused by the dense jungle fighting conditions and errors in calling in coordinates for artillery or air strikes. In Dak To in 1967, for example, 42 U.S. paratroopers were killed and 45 wounded when U.S. Air Force jets mistakenly bombed their position. Ground-to-ground friendly fire in Vietnam resulted from the war's pattern of guerrilla warfare. Marked by night patrols, ambushes, and a "shoot-first" survival mentality, this type of ground combat often created panic and confusion and sometimes led to attacks on friendly troops.

The national agony over the war and extensive media coverage heightened the American public's awareness of friendly fire casualties. C. D. B. Bryan's *New Yorker* article, his book, and a television adaptation of the friendly fire incident he described, particularly publicized the phenomenon.

BIBLIOGRAPHY

BRYAN, C. D. B. *Friendly Fire.* 1976.

HACKWORTH, DAVID H. "Killed by Their Comrades." *Newsweek,* 18 November 1991, 45–46.

SHRADER, CHARLES. *Amicide: The Problem of Friendly Fire in Modern War.* 1982.

KELLY EVANS-PFEIFER

Fulbright, J. William (1905–1995), U.S. senator (D-Ark.); chairman, Senate Foreign Relations Committee, 1959–1974. A committed globalist, Fulbright supported a continuing U.S. presence in South Vietnam during the Eisenhower and Kennedy administrations because he favored the containment of North Vietnam. In August 1964, as a result of his close friendship with President Lyndon Johnson and his concern about Sen. Barry Goldwater's presidential bid, Fulbright assumed floor leadership for the Gulf of Tonkin Resolution, which gave the president the legal authority to expand and Americanize the war. By mid 1965, however, Fulbright had second thoughts about Johnson's policy of escalation, fearing that it could undermine the possibility for improved relations with the Soviet Union and could precipitate a war with the People's Republic of China. Hence, he called for deescalation and a negotiated settlement of the conflict. After Johnson broke with him for giving a Senate speech that attacked the administration's April 1965 intervention in the Dominican Republic, Fulbright emerged as a major critic of Johnson's policy in Vietnam.

Having educated himself about the history of the war, especially the French phase, Fulbright then sought to inform the American public that the war was civil in character and not a threat to U.S. national interest. Thus, in early 1966 he directed the Senate Foreign Relations Committee in open hear-

J. WILLIAM FULBRIGHT. *Library of Congress*

ings on the administration's war policy, which gave moderate opponents of the war such as George Kennan a respectable platform inside the political system to disseminate their views. Fulbright's book *Arrogance of Power,* published in 1967, also helped legitimize domestic opposition to the Vietnam War, especially among college-educated liberals who shared his position that the war was corrupting democratic values at home, undermining the Great Society, and endangering world peace. Fulbright's intellectual dissent, which directly challenged the administration's case that Vietnam was of vital geopolitical interest to the United States, was a timely contribution to the growing debate about the war that swept across the United States during the late 1960s.

After Richard Nixon became president, Fulbright continued his staunch opposition to U.S. policy in Vietnam. He criticized Vietnamization, viewing it as an attempt by the administration to avoid serious negotiations with North Vietnam. He also joined many others in the Senate in denouncing Nixon's Cambodian incursion of April 1970 as an enlargement of the war, and he worked to obtain legislative enactment of the Cooper-Church amendment. Fulbright also was a major participant in the successful congressional fight of 1973 to force Nixon to end the bombing of Cambodia. At the same time, through publications, speeches, and committee work, Fulbright helped create a legislative climate in Congress that ultimately led to the passage of the War Powers Resolution of 1973, a direct challenge to the power of the president to commit troops to military action without the consent of Congress.

As a result of political events in the United States during and concerned with the Vietnam War, Fulbright viewed concentrated executive power, combined with an imperial outlook and behavior, as a grave threat to American democracy. He had thus arrived at the belief that a sound foreign policy protected the domestic liberties and the well-being of the American people.

BIBLIOGRAPHY

BERMAN, WILLIAM. *William Fulbright and the Vietnam War: The Dissent of a Political Realist*. 1988.
BROWN, EUGENE. *J. W. Fulbright: Advice and Dissent*. 1985.

WILLIAM C. BERMAN

G

Galbraith, John Kenneth (1908–), economist; U.S. ambassador to India, 1961–1963. Galbraith believed that the South Vietnamese government was hopelessly corrupt and that South Vietnam lacked the strategic or economic importance to justify U.S. military involvement. In 1967, he led the Negotiations Now! petition drive to get one million signatures calling for an end to the U.S. bombing of North Vietnam.

BIBLIOGRAPHY

OLSON, JAMES, and RANDY ROBERTS. *Where the Domino Fell.* 1991.
POWERS, THOMAS. *The War at Home.* 1973.

KELLY EVANS-PFEIFER

Gaulle, Charles de (1890–1970), Free French leader, 1940–1945; first president, Fifth Republic, 1958–1969. De Gaulle advanced different policies on Southeast Asia from 1945 through the 1960s. During World War II and in 1946, in the midst of the negotiations at Fontainebleau, de Gaulle supported continued French control of Indochina. He repeatedly advocated the use of military force wherever necessary to retain the overseas territories he believed were indispensable to the legitimacy of France as a world power.

As French president in the 1960s, however, de Gaulle sounded a different note. He warned President Kennedy to avoid entangling the United States in the "swamp" of Vietnam; he lectured President Johnson on U.S. involvement, admonishing him that a military solution would prove too costly and that peace must be made immediately. De Gaulle advocated neutrality for Southeast Asia, proposing that the United States, the Soviet Union, France, and China stay out of the region. To implement this peace, de Gaulle, on 23 July 1964, called for a conference of the same order and including the same participants as the Geneva conference of 1954. The United States showed no interest in neutrality or any other political compromise.

BIBLIOGRAPHY

HAMMER, ELLEN J. *The Struggle for Indochina.* 1954.
RASKIN, MARCUS G., and BERNARD B. FALL. *The Vietnam Reader: Articles and Documents on American Foreign Policy and the Viet-Nam Crisis.* 1965.

VICTOR JEW

Gavin, James M. (1907–1990), lieutenant general, U.S. Army; ambassador to France, 1961–1963. Always outspoken, James Gavin was a heavily decorated World War II hero who retired in 1957. Soon after U.S. combat troops arrived in Vietnam in 1965, Gavin became a sharp critic of U.S. intervention. He denounced the war as wasteful and without purpose, and in 1966 called for at least a return to the enclave strategy. After touring South Vietnam one year later, he wrote: "We are in a tragedy." Gavin enjoyed brief consideration as a presidential peace candidate in 1968.

BIBLIOGRAPHY

BIGGS, BRADLEY. *Gavin.* 1980.
BOOTH, T. MICHAEL, and DUNCAN SPENCER. *Paratrooper: The Life of Gen. James M. Gavin.* 1994.
GAVIN, JAMES M. "A Communication on Vietnam." *Harper's Magazine,* February 1966.
GAVIN, JAMES M. *Crisis Now.* 1968.
GAVIN, JAMES M. *On to Berlin.* 1978.
GAVIN, JAMES M. "We Can Get Out of Vietnam." *Saturday Evening Post,* 24 February 1968.

GLEN GENDZEL

Gayler, Noel (1915–), admiral, U.S. Navy; Commander-in-Chief, Pacific (CINCPAC), 1972–1976. An ace Navy fighter pilot in World War II, Noel Gayler headed the National Security Agency before being named as CINCPAC in September 1972, the last to hold that position during the Vietnam War. He planned Operation FREQUENT WIND, the last-minute helicopter evacuation of Americans and South Vietnamese from Saigon. Gayler repeatedly tried to persuade Ambassador Graham Martin to implement the plan, but afraid of touching off panic in the city, Martin demurred until it was almost too late. Gayler commanded the operation on 29–30 April 1975. In just eighteen hours, over six thousand people were flown "without a scratch" to safety aboard U.S. ships offshore. Gayler ended the evacuation when the U.S. embassy became "a bottomless pit of refugees," leaving many behind. "We really meant to help," he said of the U.S. failure in Vietnam, "but we went awry in a lot of ways."

BIBLIOGRAPHY

BUTLER, DAVID. *The Fall of Saigon.* 1985.
DAWSON, ALAN. *55 Days: The Fall of South Vietnam.* 1977.
GAYLOR, NOEL. "U.S. Strategy for Staying No. 1 Power in Asia." *U.S. News and World Report,* 25 March 1974.

SNEPP, FRANK. *Decent Interval: An Insider's Account of Saigon's Indecent End.* 1977.

GLEN GENDZEL

Gelb, Leslie (1937–), deputy director of Defense Department policy planning staff, 1967–1968. In June 1967 Secretary of Defense Robert McNamara asked Gelb to write a history of U.S. policy and involvement in Vietnam. He and thirty-five others labored for eighteen months to produce the 7,000-plus page history, which became known as the Pentagon Papers.

BIBLIOGRAPHY

OLSON, JAMES, and RANDY ROBERTS. *Where the Domino Fell.* 1991.

KELLY EVANS-PFEIFER

Geneva Conference, 1954. On 26 April 1954, the People's Republic of China (PRC), France, Great Britain, the Soviet Union, and the United States met in Geneva, Switzerland, to discuss issues relating to Berlin and Korea. On 8 May 1954, the day after the defeat of the French garrison at Dien Bien Phu, the principal delegations, plus representatives from Cambodia, Laos, the State of Vietnam, and the Viet Minh, turned to the issue of Indochina. The Viet Minh, who controlled most of Vietnam, desired a political settlement leading to the total withdrawal of French forces and the establishment of an independent government led by Ho Chi Minh. The French hoped to retain influence in the south, but could no longer pursue the war. U.S. Secretary of State John Foster Dulles, disappointed with the French refusal to continue the war and loath to negotiate with a communist country, instructed the U.S. delegation that the United States should participate only as an "interested nation." Great Britain and the Soviet Union cochaired the conference.

The talks proceeded slowly as the delegates pursued their individual goals in an atmosphere of tension and distrust. After two months of negotiating, and after China and the Soviet Union pressured the Viet Minh to compromise, the delegates reached an agreement. On 21 July 1954 France and the Viet Minh agreed to a temporary partition of Vietnam along the seventeenth parallel and a cease-fire throughout Vietnam. The accords provided for the peaceful withdrawal of French troops from the

GENEVA CONFERENCE, 1954. The opening session of the Geneva conference, 27 April 1954. Key delegates are identified by numbers as follows: (1) George Bidault; (2) John Foster Dulles; (3) Anthony Eden; (4) Zhou Enlai; (5) Nam Il of North Korea. *National Archives*

north and Viet Minh troops from the south within three hundred days, prohibited the introduction of new forces and the establishment of foreign military bases, and restricted future military alliances on the part of both zones. In addition, the agreement established a cease-fire and the removal of forces from Cambodia and Laos, and also prohibited those countries from entering into military alliances or permitting foreign bases on their soil. To unify Vietnam, the agreement provided for free elections in North and South Vietnam in 1956, supervised by an International Control Commission (ICC) composed of representatives from Canada, India, and Poland.

Only France, Great Britain, the People's Republic of China, and the Soviet Union endorsed the Geneva accords. The Viet Minh were bitter about

the partitioning and about the PRC's pressure on them to accept it, but they expected that the elections would bring about unification. The French hoped to retain authority in South Vietnam, but Ngo Dinh Diem, who became prime minister of the State of Vietnam, refused to sign the accords. Dulles likewise instructed the U.S. delegation not to sign. The Eisenhower administration pledged to abide by the Geneva agreement, and declared it would view any violation of the agreement "with grave concern." The United States later invoked this statement to justify intervention in Vietnam.

As a settlement that would end French influence in Vietnam became inevitable, the United States altered its policy and initiated plans for an active role in the defense of Southeast Asia. After the conference, the United States immediately provided support for the South Vietnamese government and developed the Southeast Asia Treaty Organization (SEATO). The Geneva accords ended the military war between the French and the Viet Minh but avoided the political question of who would govern all of Vietnam, setting the stage for future conflict.

BIBLIOGRAPHY

ISAACS, ARNOLD R. *Without Honor: Defeat in Vietnam and Cambodia.* 1983.
RANDLE, ROBERT F. *Geneva 1954: The Settlement of the Indochinese War.* 1969.
YOUNG, MARILYN B. *The Vietnam Wars, 1945–1990.* 1991.

PAUL M. TAILLON

Geneva Conference, 1962. The 1962 Geneva Conference met to resolve the Laotian civil war. In November 1957, the Royal Lao government and the Pathet Lao, as mandated by the 1954 Geneva Conference, agreed to create a neutralist coalition government under Prince Souvanna Phouma. Lao rightists within the government and military, however, ousted Phouma in July 1958. The Pathet Lao resumed fighting and civil war ensued, eventually involving North Vietnam and Thailand, backed by the Soviet Union and the United States.

Newly inaugurated President John F. Kennedy confronted the war in Laos in January 1961. Former president Dwight D. Eisenhower had advised Kennedy that it might be necessary to send U.S. troops to Laos to prevent a communist takeover, but after the Bay of Pigs fiasco in Cuba in April, Kennedy decided to seek a diplomatic rather than a military solution. In May, after British and Soviet mediation, a conference on Laos convened in Geneva, with Ambassador-at-Large W. Averell Harriman as the U.S. delegate.

The conference opened on 16 May 1961 with representatives of the major powers, members of the International Control Commission (ICC), and representatives of the nations of mainland Southeast Asia. While the discussions proceeded in Geneva, fighting continued sporadically in Laos, each faction hoping to gain territory and thus influence the outcome of the conference. Pathet Lao military successes and U.S. pressure on the Lao rightists led the Lao factions again to accept a coalition government under Souvanna Phouma. On 23 July 1962, the Geneva delegates formally signed the Declaration on the Neutrality of Laos and a related protocol

outlining provisions for Laotian neutrality in the Cold War.

The agreement provided for the withdrawal of foreign forces from Laos and reconciliation among the Lao factions. U.S. and Filipino personnel, who had been fighting on the side of the Royal Lao government, complied, but the North Vietnamese, who never admitted the presence of North Vietnamese Army (NVA) troops in Laos, did not. The Pathet Lao opposed international inspection and enforcement of neutralization, thus enabling NVA forces to cross freely into the communist-held areas of Laos, through which ran the Ho Chi Minh Trail.

Kennedy supported the Geneva agreement concerning Laos, but believing he had taken the "soft" option on Laos, he decided on a firm course for Vietnam. While the delegates met in Geneva, Kennedy sent hundreds of military advisers and Special Forces troops to South Vietnam, an act that violated the 1954 Geneva agreements.

BIBLIOGRAPHY

ISAACS, ARNOLD R. *Without Honor: Defeat in Vietnam and Cambodia.* 1983.
LANGER, PAUL F., and JOSEPH J. ZASLOFF. *North Vietnam and the Pathet Lao: Partners in the Struggle for Laos.* 1970.
TURLEY, WILLIAM S. *The Second Indochina War: A Short Political and Military History, 1954–1975.* 1986.

PAUL M. TAILLON

Germany, Federal Republic of (FRG). The Federal Republic of Germany officially supported U.S. policy in Vietnam. Its government provided economic and humanitarian aid to South Vietnam, averaging $7.5 million annually between 1966 and 1973, and including more than two hundred medical and technical personnel. Beginning in 1964, Chancellor Ludwig Erhart, a strong ally of President Johnson, agreed to purchase billions of dollars of U.S. military equipment to help finance U.S. policy, but continuing Johnson administration demands to step up payments and rising inflation rates from U.S. and FRG spending embarrassed Erhart's Christian Democratic/Free Democratic Party government and contributed to its collapse in 1966. U.S. preoccupation with Vietnam facilitated Chancellor Willy Brandt's 1969–1970 Ostpolitik diplomacy involving recognition of Eastern European states and normalization of ties with the USSR, which brought about renewed German influence within post–World War II Europe.

The Vietnam War attracted increasing opposition from the German public during the late 1960s. In response to widespread student demonstrations, the Bundestag passed emergency laws in 1967 that suspended some constitutional protections to stem disruptive activity. In the late 1960s, U.S. soldiers stationed at German bases began widespread antiwar agitation. A network of U.S. Army deserters formed Resist inside the Army (RITA), which staged demonstrations and published antiwar material throughout Europe. Starting in 1970, disgruntled U.S. soldiers sabotaged and firebombed U.S. Army property, protesting against the war and oppressive base conditions. The violence, sometimes led by black militants, peaked in mid 1971 and drew alarmed responses from military command. The United States moved to discharge many low-ranking soldiers in 1972 and staged a crackdown the following year.

BIBLIOGRAPHY

BARNET, RICHARD J. *The Alliance: America, Europe, Japan: Makers of the Postwar World.* 1983.
CORTRIGHT, DAVID. *Soldiers in Revolt: The American Military Today.* 1975.

ADAM LAND

Giap, Vo Nguyen. See *Vo Nguyen Giap.*

Goldberg, Arthur J. (1908–1990), secretary of labor, 1961–1962; associate justice of the Supreme Court, 1962–1965; ambassador to the United Nations (UN), 1965–1968. Arthur Goldberg, son of Russian Jewish immigrants, was raised in Chicago. A specialist in labor law, he eventually became general counsel to the Congress of Industrial Organizations (CIO). President Kennedy named him secretary of labor and, after nineteen months, nominated him to the Supreme Court, where he served for almost three years.

Upon the death of Adlai Stevenson in July 1965, President Johnson persuaded Goldberg to leave the Court and become ambassador to the United Nations. The president appealed to Goldberg's patriotism and vanity, assuring him that he would play an important role in bringing peace to Vietnam and in helping to formulate the foreign policies of the administration. Although Goldberg himself favored a halt to U.S. bombing and a negotiated withdrawal, his position forced him to defend official U.S.

policy. The *New York Times* commented that "his speeches at the United Nations have tended to set forth the United States position in the most diplomatically appealing manner, but always within the limits set by President Johnson and Secretary of State Dean Rusk." Pete Hamill in the *New York Post* was harsher: "The fact is that in public he was pushing the whole discredited line. If there ever were another War Crimes Tribunal, Goldberg would be in the dock, along with Rusk, Rostow, Humphrey and the rest of the Johnson claque."

By the start of 1968, Goldberg realized that he was being ignored by Johnson, and he regretted having left the Court. He resigned his position as UN ambassador in July and entered private life. In 1970 he reemerged as an unsuccessful candidate for governor of New York, endorsing the massive antiwar protests and claiming to have always favored deescalation and a negotiated settlement. He died in Washington, D.C., on 19 January 1990.

BIBLIOGRAPHY

GOLDBERG, DOROTHY. *A Private View of a Public Life.* 1975.
LASKY, VICTOR. *Arthur J. Goldberg: The Old and the New.* 1970.

DAVID W. LEVY

Goldman, Eric F. (1915–), American historian at Princeton University; "cultural ambassador" for the Johnson administration, 1963–1966. Goldman organized the White House Festival of the Arts in 1965 to enable Johnson to mingle with the nation's artistic community. But the event angered and embarrassed Johnson when several high-profile antiwar artists boycotted the event and others in attendance used the occasion to criticize the government's policy in Vietnam.

BIBLIOGRAPHY

POWERS, THOMAS. *The War at Home.* 1973.

KELLY EVANS-PFEIFER

Goldwater, Barry (1909–), U.S. senator (R-Ariz.), 1953–1965, 1969–1987; 1964 Republican presidential nominee. Goldwater was the central figure in the reorientation and revival of American conservatism. Born and raised in Arizona, he briefly attended the University of Arizona and then took over management of his family's department stores. During World War II, he flew cargo planes in the

BARRY GOLDWATER. *Library of Congress*

Asian theater and thereafter joined the U.S. Air Force Reserve, retiring as a general in 1967. After serving on the Phoenix city council, he was elected to the Senate in the Eisenhower landslide of 1952, but he soon criticized the president for acquiescing in the expansion of the welfare state and for negotiating with the Soviet Union. By 1960, he had emerged as the national leader of a growing conservative movement that uneasily united cultural traditionalists, economic libertarians, and fervent anticommunists. Along with most of his followers, Goldwater lacked the skepticism toward military intervention abroad that had characterized earlier, so-called isolationist conservatism. In 1963 and early 1964, he cited Johnson administration policy in Vietnam as yet another example of U.S. failure to seek "total victory" over communism. Specifically, he urged "carrying the war to North Vietnam" and ruminated about—without

actually endorsing—the use of nuclear weapons to defoliate infiltration routes.

In 1964 Goldwater became the first political outsider in modern times propelled to a presidential nomination by a grassroots insurgency, in this case the conservative movement that had been building for nearly a decade. In order to preserve a modicum of national unity, he and President Johnson privately agreed to say little about Vietnam during the campaign and both largely abided by the deal. Goldwater voted for the Gulf of Tonkin Resolution despite doubts about Johnson's account of the events at sea. Although Vietnam was not central to the campaign, Goldwater's earlier advocacy of escalation contributed to his image as a trigger-happy extremist. That image assured his overwhelming defeat: Goldwater garnered only 39 percent of the vote, to Johnson's 61 percent. Out of office during the next four years, he toured Southeast Asia twice, publicly promoted total conventional war instead of incremental escalation, and privately urged Johnson to fire Secretary of Defense Robert McNamara, whom he considered a chronic liar and architect of defeat.

Elected to the Senate again in 1968, Goldwater incongruously became a hero to liberals when he pressed President Richard Nixon to resign during the Watergate scandal in 1974. Yet, as his views on Vietnam illustrate, he never swerved from Cold War conservatism. Specifically, he urged Nixon to carry the war to North Vietnam, assailed liberals for promoting a "new isolationism" that strengthened the North Vietnamese during peace talks, opposed amnesty for "draft dodgers," and insisted that the war was lost "at home." His foremost political legacy was moving the Republican party to the right.

BIBLIOGRAPHY

GOLDWATER, BARRY M., with JACK CASSERLY. *Goldwater.* 1988.

WHITE, THEODORE H. *The Making of the President 1964.* 1965.

LEO P. RIBUFFO

Gravel, Mike (1930–), U.S. senator (D-Alaska), 1969–1981. In the 1968 Democratic senatorial primary, Gravel defeated Ernest Gruening, who had opposed U.S. involvement in Vietnam as early as 1964. Gravel soon became a vocal critic of the Vietnam War himself, however, and after an unsuccessful attempt to read the Pentagon Papers in the Senate chamber, he tearfully read from them in the Subcommittee on Buildings and Grounds, which he chaired, on 29 June 1971. He later published his own edition of the papers. The incident led to a Supreme Court case, *Gravel v. U.S.* The court held that the speech and debate clause of the Constitution, which protects legislative activity from prosecution, protected Senator Gravel's disclosure of the Pentagon Papers.

BIBLIOGRAPHY

Biographical Directory of the American Congress, 1789–1971. 1972.
ZAROULIS, NANCY, and GERALD SULLIVAN. *Who Spoke Up? American Protest against the War in Vietnam, 1963–1975.* 1985.

ELLEN D. GOLDLUST

Great Britain. After disarming the Japanese in Indochina at the end of World War II, Great Britain helped reestablish French power in Indochina and then withdrew in 1946. During the 1954 French crisis at Dien Bien Phu, President Dwight D. Eisenhower requested British support for a U.S. air strike to aid the beleaguered French forces. British foreign secretary Anthony Eden hinted that such support was possible, but Prime Minister Winston Churchill refused the request, believing that the Viet Minh's control over so much of Indochina had to be addressed diplomatically. Great Britain cochaired the 1954 Geneva Conference and supported the political division of Vietnam at the 17th parallel. Until 1962, the British government openly opposed military intervention in Vietnam, partly because it did not want to alienate Britain's important trading partners—Burma, Ceylon, and India.

From 1962 to 1968 Britain provided only moral support for the U.S. effort. Prime Minister Harold Wilson, in power from 1964 to 1970, prevented formal British participation in the war and did not contribute war matériel. Although both the Labour and Conservative parties supported the bombing of the Democratic Republic of Vietnam (DRV) following the Gulf of Tonkin incident, Wilson privately opposed continuation of the bombing and advocated a negotiated settlement. Great Britain supported the United States in part because it needed U.S. financial help to stabilize the British currency. Thus, in March 1965 Great Britain did not join the International Control Commission's con-

demnation of the U.S. bombing of the DRV. By December, however, Wilson strongly opposed such bombing and conveyed his position to President Lyndon B. Johnson.

Great Britain attempted three peace missions in 1965, all of which failed. Gordon Walker's April mission and Wilson's June Commonwealth Peace Mission failed because the DRV, the Soviet Union, and the People's Republic of China refused to receive it, although South Vietnam and the United States accepted it. An attempt in July to send a confidential envoy to Hanoi failed because of a press leak revealing the mission.

Great Britain acted as intermediary between the United States and the Soviet Union in an attempt to establish negotiations about Vietnam. Talks in February 1966 with Soviet prime minister Andrei Kosygin were unsuccessful. The Tet cease-fire of the following year, however, provided a better opportunity for U.S.-USSR cooperation, and Wilson worked closely with U.S. adviser Chester Cooper on Operation Sunflower to secure Kosygin's help in pressuring North Vietnamese officials to accept a U.S. offer: the United States would not resume bombing if the DRV made a secret assurance to stop infiltrating troops into the south. At the last minute, however, the U.S. Joint Chiefs of Staff substantially changed the proposal, requiring proof—not just a promise—of DRV compliance within twelve hours of accepting the offer. Kosygin submitted the altered proposal, but it was not satisfactory to North Vietnam.

In January 1968 Kosygin appealed to Wilson to convince the United States to respond to DRV foreign minister Nguyen Duy Trinh's assurance that a U.S. bombing halt would elicit a positive DRV response for negotiations. Johnson did not halt the bombings, however, until 31 March, when he announced that he would not run again for the presidential nomination.

The student movement in Britain opposed the Vietnam War and British complicity in the late 1960s. The government supported President Nixon's Vietnamization policy, the mining of North Vietnamese ports, and the continued bombing of the DRV. It refused to condemn the invasion of Cambodia despite sharp criticism from several members of Parliament, pushing instead for a new Geneva convention. For the entire duration of the Vietnam War, the British government walked a political tightrope, not wishing to alienate the United States, yet unconvinced of the war's necessity.

BIBLIOGRAPHY

CARLTON, DAVID. *Anthony Eden: A Biography.* 1981.

KARNOW, STANLEY. *Vietnam: A History.* 1991.

MACLEAN, DONALD. *British Foreign Policy: The Years since Suez.* 1970.

MORGAN, KENNETH O. *The People's Peace: British History, 1945–1989.* 1990.

WATT, D. C., and JAMES MAYALL, eds. *Current British Foreign Policy, 1970.* 1972.

WATT, D. C., and JAMES MAYALL, eds. *Current British Foreign Policy, 1972.* 1974.

WILSON, J. HAROLD. *A Personal Record: The Labour Government, 1964–1970.* 1971.

YOUNG, MARILYN B. *The Vietnam Wars.* 1991.

ELLEN BAKER

Great Society.

The Great Society was President Lyndon Johnson's ambitious plan, much of which was actually passed into law, to lift millions of Americans out of poverty and provide housing, health care, education, and equal opportunity to all. He later referred to the Great Society as "the woman I really loved" whom he lost because of "that bitch of a war on the other side of the world."

In 1949 Democratic president Harry S. Truman had been blamed for the "loss" of China to communism, and Johnson, faced with the prospect of being blamed by the right wing for another Democratic "loss" to communism, felt bound to preserve an anticommunist South Vietnam. He believed that the congressional and public support he would gain from his anticommunist stance on Vietnam would carry over into support for the passage and implementation of the Great Society. Johnson also, however, needed to retain support from antiwar Democratic members of Congress, and thus he walked a fine line, promising to pursue peace negotiations with North Vietnam in order to ensure antiwar Democrats' votes for the Great Society.

As the Vietnam War escalated, its costs skyrocketed, threatening the funding for domestic programs. Johnson's congressional allies and supporters around the country, people who had fought for the Great Society, turned against him because of the war. Martin Luther King Jr. said that "the Great Society has been shot down on the battlefield of Vietnam." The war so consumed Johnson that he had little time or energy for his domestic agenda. His hopelessness over the Vietnam War and his despair over the war's toll on the Great Society led Johnson to decide against seeking a second term.

BIBLIOGRAPHY

KEARNS, DORIS. *Lyndon Johnson and the American Dream.* 1976.

POWERS, THOMAS. *The War at Home.* 1973.

KELLY EVANS-PFEIFER

Green Berets.

See *Special Forces, U.S. Army.*

Greene, Wallace

(1907–), Marine Corps commandant, 1964–1968. Greene strongly supported John F. Kennedy's policy in Vietnam. In May 1965, he advocated an increased combat role for the U.S. Marines, stating that "You don't defend a place by sitting on your ditty box." Greene subsequently maintained an optimistic view of U.S. prospects in Vietnam, despite his prediction that pacification would take approximately ten years to accomplish. He retired in January 1968, just before the Tet Offensive.

BIBLIOGRAPHY

MILLETT, ALLEN R. *Semper Fidelis: The History of the United States Marine Corps.* 1980.

MOSKIN, J. ROBERT. *The U.S. Marine Corps Story.* 1982.

SHULIMSON, JACK, and CHARLES M. JOHNSON. *U.S. Marines in Vietnam: The Landing and the Buildup, 1965.* 1978.

ELLEN D. GOLDLUST

Group 559.

In May 1959, while officially claiming to respect the Geneva Conference ban on intervention, the leaders of North Vietnam ordered Maj. Vo Bam of the People's Army of Vietnam (PAVN) to create a logistical unit for supplying Viet Cong forces in the South. The top secret unit was code-named *Group 559.* Major Bam led a few hundred engineers and laborers into Laos to begin construction of the Ho Chi Minh Trail. "Walking without footprints, cooking without smoke, talking without sound" was their slogan. By 1960, tons of arms, ammunition, supplies, and trained cadres flowed along the trail into South Vietnam. Bam commanded five thousand troops and a regiment of engineers by 1963. Members of *Group 559* were trained to carry heavy loads of supplies on foot, bicycle, and truck. When U.S. bombing of the trail began in 1965, *Group 559* was reorganized as a special military zone under direct authority of North Vietnam's Communist Central Committee and commanded by Gen. Phan Trong Tue. The organization of *Group*

559 signaled North Vietnam's determination to support and control armed resistance to the government of South Vietnam.

BIBLIOGRAPHY

STEVENS, RICHARD L. *The Trail: A History of the Ho Chi Minh Trail and the Role of Nature in the War in Vietnam.* 1993.
TRUONG NHU TANG. *A Viet Cong Memoir.* 1985.
TURLEY, WILLIAM S. *The Second Indochina War.* 1986.
VO BAM. "Opening the Trail." *Vietnam Courier* 22 (May 1984).

GLEN GENDZEL

Gruening, Ernest (1887–1974), U.S. senator (D.-Alaska), 1959–1969. An early critic of U.S. involvement in Vietnam, he joined Sen. Wayne L. Morse in opposing the Gulf of Tonkin Resolution in 1964. He continued to criticize the war from the Senate floor, in public appearances, and in the media. Beginning in May 1965, he voted against every military appropriations bill. Partly because of his position on the war, Gruening was defeated by a slim margin in the 1968 Democratic Senate primary.

BIBLIOGRAPHY

GRUENING, ERNEST. *Many Battles: The Autobiography of Ernest Gruening.* 1973.
GRUENING, ERNEST, and HERBERT B. BEASER. *Vietnam Folly.* 1968.

JENNIFER FROST

Guam Conference. Held in March 1967, the Guam Conference was a largely symbolic meeting between President Lyndon Johnson and the leaders of South Vietnam, President Nguyen Van Thieu and Prime Minister Nguyen Cao Ky. In a display that was as much for the American media as it was for the Vietnamese, Johnson sought to demonstrate the continuing U.S. commitment to an independent, anticommunist South Vietnam. Nevertheless, the United States and South Vietnam had competing goals: During the conference Johnson pressed South Vietnam for a greater effort on their pacification program, while the South Vietnamese requested increased U.S. military commitment.

BIBLIOGRAPHY

FRANKEL, MAX. "Johnson, at Guam, Joins Ky in a Vow to Pursue Goals." *New York Times,* 20 March 1967, A1, A3.

KELLY EVANS-PFEIFER

Gulf of Tonkin Resolution. In early 1964, President Lyndon B. Johnson and members of his administration concluded that South Vietnam could survive only with massive support from the United States. But he hesitated to implement a full program of overt pressures against the North, fearing that expansion of the war would jeopardize his domestic programs and his reelection chances. Therefore, Johnson approved numerous covert operations against North Vietnam, including DeSoto missions, which were intelligence-gathering missions performed by specially equipped destroyers off the coast of the target country. By mid-summer, however, Viet Cong forces had become thoroughly entrenched throughout the South, and Sen. Barry Goldwater, the Republican presidential nominee, castigated Johnson for not pursuing the war more forcefully.

On the morning of 2 August 1964, North Vietnamese torpedo boats allegedly attacked the U.S. destroyer *Maddox,* which was conducting a DeSoto mission in the Gulf of Tonkin against North Vietnam. To assert U.S. claims to freedom of operations on the high seas and to avoid any appearance of weakness before the North Vietnamese, Lyndon Johnson ordered the *Maddox* to resume its offshore patrol accompanied by another destroyer, the *C. Turner Joy.* On the night of 4 August both destroyers reported hostile attacks, although the commander of the *Maddox* later conceded that this incident might in fact have resulted from the combined effects of bad weather and nervous radar and sonar operators.

Johnson, however, portrayed the incidents as "deliberate attacks" and "open aggression on the high seas," and immediately authorized retaliatory air strikes against four naval bases and an oil storage depot in North Vietnam. The same day, 5 August, he submitted to Congress a resolution that would authorize him to take "all necessary measures to repel any armed attacks against the forces of the United States and to prevent further aggression." A second section gave him authority to provide military assistance to any member state of the Southeast Asia Treaty Organization (SEATO). Congress approved the resolution, officially entitled *Joint Resolution to promote the maintenance of international peace and security in southeast Asia,* on 7 August; the only dissenting votes were cast by Senators Wayne L. Morse of Oregon and Ernest Gruening of Alaska. During the process, Johnson did not inform Congress about the circumstances of the incidents or of the covert operations the U.S. vessels had been conducting. In time, many members of Congress believed that Johnson and his advisers had misled them into supporting expansion of the war.

The Gulf of Tonkin Resolution gave Johnson broad authority to conduct the war in Vietnam, momentarily won him substantial popular support, and enabled him to refute Goldwater's criticisms. The resolution also committed the United States publicly to defending South Vietnam, and Johnson pointed to the resolution as evidence of congressional support for his military policies there. In 1970, Richard Nixon drew upon the resolution to justify the incursion into Cambodia; in the ensuing controversy, Congress repealed the resolution as of 30 December 1970.

BIBLIOGRAPHY

AUSTIN, ANTHONY. *The President's War: The Story of the Tonkin Gulf Resolution and How the Nation Was Trapped in Vietnam.* 1971.

KARNOW, STANLEY. *Vietnam: A History.* 1991.

WINDCHY, EUGENE G. *Tonkin Gulf.* 1971.

PAUL M. TAILLON

H

Habib, Philip (1920–1992), Foreign Service officer, 1949–1987; counselor for political affairs, U.S. embassy in Saigon, 1965–1967. In 1967 Habib led a State Department task force to examine Vietnam policy options. Pessimistic that the Saigon government could survive without U.S. military support, Habib advocated a bombing halt and peace negotiations. In 1968 Habib was the highest ranking career diplomat named to the U.S. negotiating team for the Paris peace talks. When President Nixon replaced head delegates Averell Harriman and Cyrus Vance with Henry Cabot Lodge and Lawrence Walsh, Habib retained his position. Lodge and Walsh resigned in November 1969 and Habib became acting head of the delegation. Nixon replaced him with David Bruce in July 1970.

BIBLIOGRAPHY

BERMAN, LARRY. *Lyndon Johnson's War: The Road to Stalemate in Vietnam.* 1989.
KARNOW, STANLEY. *Vietnam: A History.* 1991.
Current Biography Yearbook 1982.

WILLIAM PAUL SCHUCK

Hackworth, David H. (1931–), lieutenant colonel, U.S. Army. The U.S. Army's most highly decorated officer when he retired, David Hackworth spent four years in Vietnam and came to believe the U.S. had "badly botched" the war. Poor training and inappropriate tactics caused U.S. forces to suffer needless casualties from friendly fire and battlefield mistakes, while allowing communist forces to escape. Shortly before his retirement, Hackworth appeared on ABC's television program "Issues and Answers" on 27 June 1971, bitterly attacking his fellow officers for their ticket-punching careerism and for wasting the lives of their men in pursuit of combat honors so they could get promoted. Pentagon officials tried to delay his retirement and threatened Hackworth with court-martial, sending him to self-imposed exile in Australia for eighteen years. Hackworth considered himself a "regular soldier" devoted to the profession of "war-fighting," but he was thoroughly disillusioned by the Vietnam War: "I saw too much blood, too much waste and too much stupidity."

BIBLIOGRAPHY

FREEMAN, PATRICIA. "Self-Exiled after Vietnam, Army Hero David Hackworth is Finally Coming Home." *People Weekly,* 5 June 1989.
HACKWORTH, DAVID. "Our Advisors Must Pass the Ball." *Army* (May 1971).

HACKWORTH, DAVID. "The War without End." *Newsweek,* 22 November 1993.

HACKWORTH, DAVID. "When No One Wanted to Fight." *Newsweek,* 24 February 1992.

HACKWORTH, DAVID, with JULIE SHERMAN. *About Face.* 1989.

GLEN GENDZEL

Haig, Alexander M. (1924–), general, U.S. Army. Haig served in Vietnam for several months, beginning in July 1966. He was wounded while commanding the 1st Battalion, 26th Infantry, 1st Infantry Division, and later received the Distinguished Service Cross after the battle of Ap Gu. Haig became Henry Kissinger's military assistant at the National Security Council in 1971 and U.S. Army vice chief of staff in 1973. Nixon hastily appointed him White House chief of staff in April 1973 as the Watergate scandal unfolded. Nixon used Haig to persuade President Thieu to accept the Paris agreements. Haig has claimed that he challenged Kissinger's readiness to accept the DRV's terms and that he unsuccessfully encouraged the president to demand the removal of foreign troops from South Vietnam.

BIBLIOGRAPHY

HAIG, ALEXANDER M., JR. *Inner Circles.* 1992.

HERSH, SEYMOUR. *The Price of Power.* 1983.

KOLKO, GABRIEL. *Anatomy of a War: Vietnam, the United States, and the Modern Historical Experience.* 1985.

ELLEN BAKER

Haiphong. Haiphong was the primary port and a major industrial center in North Vietnam. The city stands along the Cua Cam River, roughly 48 kilometers (30 miles) inland from the Gulf of Tonkin. Railroads, rivers, and roads connect the city to Hanoi, 112 kilometers (70 miles) to the northwest. During the colonial period, the French developed

HAIPHONG. C. 1954. *Ngô Vĩnh Long*

the city as a seaport and railroad hub, and promoted industry using nearby coal and zinc mines. The Hanoi-Haiphong corridor was an economic center for the Democratic Republic of Vietnam (DRV) during the Vietnam War. Extensive aid from the Soviet Union and the People's Republic of China (PRC) developed heavy industry in the region, including a railyard and shipyard, phosphate plant, fish cannery, cement factory, and electric power plant. The city was the second largest in the DRV, with a population in 1960 of 369,000.

Haiphong was the site of extensive military hostilities beginning in World War II. In 1943, the Allies bombed the city, which was at the time occupied by the Japanese. In 1946 the French navy, after a dispute with the DRV over authority in Haiphong, opened fire on the native section of the city. The French naval bombardment, known as the Haiphong Incident, killed more than one thousand civilians and precipitated the slide toward war between the French and Viet Minh forces.

During the Vietnam War, Haiphong became a pivotal distribution hub for Soviet military aid. The U.S. military pressed for air strikes in the area and for operations to close the harbor. In September 1967, as part of Operation ROLLING THUNDER, President Johnson authorized air raids to disrupt transportation routes around the city, but they were only temporarily successful. In April 1972 President Nixon finally allowed extensive bombing of military installations and storage areas within the city. Nixon's authorization coincided with the Easter Offensive by North Vietnamese and Viet Cong forces in South Vietnam. Nixon approved the mining of Haiphong harbor on 8 May, another operation long advocated by the U.S. military. Later in 1972, Nixon ordered massive bombing of the Hanoi-Haiphong corridor. During the Christmas bombings of 18–29 December, U.S. planes dropped seventeen thousand tons of ordnance. Nixon initiated the strikes to pressure the DRV to negotiate accords formalizing U.S. withdrawal.

The 1972 bombing and mining of the harbor remains controversial. News accounts reported extensive civilian casualties from the Christmas Bombings. U.S. B-52s and fighter bombers, however, used laser-guided "smart bombs" that apparently limited nonmilitary damage. Official North Vietnamese estimates put civilian deaths at 1,300. Scholars remain divided over whether the 1972 military operations were decisive in advancing peace negotiations. Some contend that North Viet-

nam had developed road and rail links to the PRC that offset the mining of Haiphong harbor. Nonetheless, the DRV agreed to continue negotiations in late 1972 and accepted the Paris peace accords in January. After the signing of the Paris accords, the U.S. Navy helped clear the harbor of mines to reopen the port.

BIBLIOGRAPHY

DAVIDSON, PHILLIP B. *Vietnam at War: The History, 1946–1975.* 1988.

KARNOW, STANLEY. *Vietnam: A History.* 1991.

WHITFIELD, DANNY J. *Historical and Cultural Dictionary of Vietnam.* 1976.

ADAM LAND

Halberstam, David

Halberstam, David (1934–), *New York Times* Vietnam correspondent, 1962–1963. Halberstam exposed problems with the U.S. military effort and established a new tone for journalistic coverage of the war. His critical investigative pieces won him the enmity of the Kennedy administration and a Pulitzer Prize.

Halberstam was one of a handful of journalists in 1962 who recognized the instability and corruption of the Diem regime. Although he came to Vietnam believing in the basic aims of the American effort to preserve an independent South Vietnam, he eventually questioned American optimism for the South Vietnam regime and contended that Diem lacked popular support. In reporting problems within the Army of the Republic of Vietnam (ARVN) and the success of the Viet Cong forces in the Mekong Delta, Halberstam earned the ire of Secretary of State Dean Rusk, who accused him of trumpeting "communist propaganda."

The increasingly critical coverage by Halberstam and other journalists raised tensions between U.S. government and military officials in Saigon and the press corps. Halberstam's prominence as the *New York Times* correspondent led President Kennedy unsuccessfully to pressure the *Times*'s publisher to have Halberstam transferred out of Vietnam. Halberstam's determination to challenge the optimistic assertions of the U.S. military and policymakers about progress in Vietnam set the stage for perhaps the most open, uncensored war reporting in history.

BIBLIOGRAPHY

HALLIN, DANIEL C. *The Uncensored War: The Media and Vietnam.* 1986.

HAMMOND, WILLIAM M. *Public Affairs: The Military and the Media, 1962–1968.* 1989.

KELLY EVANS-PFEIFER

Halperin, Morton

Halperin, Morton (1938–), deputy assistant secretary of defense, 1966–1969; senior official, National Security Council (NSC), 1969–1970. A prominent young Nixon administration official, Halperin resigned from the NSC in protest over the 1970 invasion of Cambodia. From 1969 to 1971, President Nixon and Henry Kissinger ordered twenty-four-hour wire surveillance of Halperin's home as part of a campaign to investigate leaks from the White House. Halperin sued the government in 1972 over the wiretapping. After a twenty-year legal suit, he received a letter of apology from Kissinger. Nominated for the position of assistant secretary of defense for democracy and peacekeeping in 1993, Halperin faced significant opposition because of his outspoken criticism of Central Intelligence Agency (CIA) covert operations and U.S. interventionism abroad. The U.S. Senate refused to act on his nomination.

BIBLIOGRAPHY

BLUMENFELD, LAURA. "All That's Left of the Cold War." *Washington Post,* 19 November 1993.
FIALKA, JOHN. "Halperin Nomination to Defense Department Post Is Haunted by Ghosts of Ideological Battles Past." *Wall Street Journal,* 8 November 1993.

ADAM LAND

Hamburger Hill

Hamburger Hill. Soldiers coined the derisive term *Hamburger Hill* for the site of bloody fighting along the A Shau Valley near the Laotian border. In a ten-day battle in May 1969, the 101st Airborne Division successfully overtook a well-fortified North Vietnamese Army (NVA) position on Ap Bia Mountain. The U.S. Air Force delivered more than one million pounds of bombs to support the operation, including 152,000 pounds of napalm. The battle culminated with brutal bunker-to-bunker fighting. Fifty-six U.S. soldiers were killed, 420 were wounded; NVA losses were estimated at 505. The U.S. forces abandoned the hill soon after the fighting, and the North Vietnamese retook the position a month later. The battle received substantial media coverage. The negative reaction by the U.S. public to the seemingly senseless bloodletting increased pressure on President Nixon and the U.S. military to reduce U.S. combat casualties.

BIBLIOGRAPHY

ZAFFIRI, SAMUEL. *Hamburger Hill, May 11–20, 1969.* 1988.

ADAM LAND

Hanoi

Hanoi, northern Vietnamese city, capital of French protectorate of Tonkin (1884–1887), of French Indochina (1887–1946), of Democratic Republic of Vietnam (1954–1976), of Socialist Republic of Vietnam (1976–). Located 120 kilometers (70 miles) inland from the South China Sea at the center of the Red River Delta, with a metropolitan population of about 2.6 million, Hanoi is one of Vietnam's oldest cities. It first became a capital in the eleventh century A.D. French troops took the city in 1883, and French cultural influence had a lasting impact on Hanoi's architecture and ambience. Yet Hanoi was also the cradle of Vietnamese nationalist resistance to France beginning in the 1920s. Ho Chi Minh proclaimed Vietnam's independence in Hanoi in 1945, and the Indochina War started there one year later. Viet Minh forces reentered Hanoi in triumph when the French departed in 1954.

As the main industrial center and railroad hub of North Vietnam, Hanoi underwent periodic U.S. bombing after 1966. The bombing was heaviest during Operation ROLLING THUNDER in 1967 and Operations LINEBACKER and LINEBACKER II in 1972. Communist propaganda exaggerated the suffering of Hanoi civilians under U.S. air raids. The United States did not target nonmilitary installations such as schools, homes, and hospitals, but these nonetheless sustained considerable damage from accidental bomb strikes. About 1,300 people died in the Christmas bombings of December 1972, when U.S. warplanes dropped 17,000 tons of bombs on Hanoi in 12 days. Hanoi's wartime residents withstood air raids, drills, rationing, and shortages as well as "revolutionary zeal" campaigns, forced labor in underground factories, and compulsory evacuation to the countryside. Hanoi was not subjected, however, to the kind of saturation bombing that was inflicted on German and Japanese cities in World War II. Visitors to Hanoi since the end of the Vietnam War are often surprised at how few buildings were destroyed during the war and how many are crumbling from neglect.

BIBLIOGRAPHY

BARR, CAMERON W. "Once a War Zone, Now a Capitalist's Haven." *Christian Science Monitor,* 27 December 1994.
McCARTHY, MARY. *Hanoi.* 1968.

SALISBURY, HARRISON. *Behind the Lines: Hanoi, December 23, 1966–January 7, 1967.* 1967.

SMITH, HARVEY H., et al. *Area Handbook for North Vietnam.* 1967.

VAN DYKE, JON M. *North Vietnam's Strategy for Survival.* 1972.

GLEN GENDZEL

Hanoi Hannah, the collective nickname for the women who broadcasted propaganda into South Vietnam to destroy morale among soldiers there. Although most U.S. troops did not take her "news" seriously, her reports about the antiwar movement in the United States angered some soldiers, and her overstatements of casualties may have led some of them to question their participation in the war.

BIBLIOGRAPHY

HOWES, CRAIG. *Voices of the Vietnam POWs: Witnesses to Their Fight.* 1993.

MAITLAND, TERRENCE, and PETER MCINERNEY. *The Vietnam Experience: A Contagion of War.* 1983.

ELLEN D. GOLDLUST

Hanoi Hilton. Originally a French colonial jail, Hoa Lo prison was called the Hanoi Hilton by U.S. soldiers and airmen during the Vietnam War. Located near the center of Hanoi, it was the most renowned of the North Vietnamese prisons that together housed more than seven hundred U.S. prisoners-of-war (POWs) between 1964 and 1973. After the unsuccessful U.S. raid on the prison complex at Son Tay in 1970, North Vietnam concentrated its U.S. POWs in the Hanoi Hilton. The North Vietnamese insisted that the Hoa Lo captives were political internees rather than POWs, and therefore that they were not covered by the Geneva Conventions. As a result, conditions at Hoa Lo were horrendous, and prisoners were punished for anything that their captors considered a breach of rules.

BIBLIOGRAPHY

DENTON, JEREMIAH A. *When Hell Was in Session.* 1982.

HOWES, CRAIG. *Voices of the Vietnam POWs: Witnesses to Their Fight.* 1993.

SCHEMMER, BENJAMIN F. *The Raid.* 1976.

ELLEN D. GOLDLUST

Harassment-and-Interdiction Fire. Harassment-and-interdiction (H&I) fire consisted of the U.S. bombing and artillery shelling of probable

HOA LO PRISON. The "Hanoi Hilton," May 1973, where 352 POWs were concentrated after the abortive November 1970 U.S. raid on Son Tay prison camp. The prison was demolished in 1994 to make room for a luxury hotel. *National Archives*

concentrations of communist forces without direct observation of targeted sites. The U.S. military designed H&I fire to maximize the use of available firepower for disrupting suspected communist operations. A procedure for coordinating heavy weaponry in the U.S. military's rules of engagement, H&I fire required clearance from South Vietnamese officials, which was usually given on a routine basis. Because of its indiscriminate nature, the United States authorized H&I bombing or shelling mostly in remote areas. In 1966, nearly two-thirds of the total tonnage of U.S. ordnance consisted of H&I fire, much of which involved B-52 carpet bombing. Despite the massive amount of delivered firepower, H&I attacks had a negligible effect on North Vietnamese and Viet Cong resources while causing considerable civilian destruction and injury in Vietnam.

BIBLIOGRAPHY

GIBSON, JAMES WILLIAM. *The Perfect War.* 1986.

LEWY, GUENTER. *America in Vietnam.* 1978.

ADAM LAND

Hardhats. Officially known as the National Hard Hats of America, the Hardhats were a group of construction workers who organized to support the Vietnam War. The Hardhats supported President Nixon's Vietnam policies and conducted counter-demonstrations during antiwar protests, often clashing violently with opponents of the war. On 8 May

1970, two hundred New York City construction workers brutally attacked student demonstrators who were protesting the invasion of Cambodia, injuring seventy youths. White House sources suggest that the Nixon administration, working through the Teamsters Union, may have helped orchestrate Hardhat assaults on antiwar demonstrators during the early 1970s.

BIBLIOGRAPHY

WELLS, TOM. *The War Within: America's Battle over Vietnam.* 1994.

ADAM LAND AND KELLY EVANS-PFEIFER

Harkins, Paul D. (1904–1984), general, U.S. Army; MACV commander, 1962–1964. A cavalry officer and Gen. George Patton's protégé in World War II, Paul Harkins was the U.S. Eighth Army chief of staff in Korea, where he also commanded two infantry divisions. President Kennedy named Harkins the first commander of the U.S. Military Assistance Command, Vietnam (COMUSMACV) on 13 February 1962. "I am an optimist," Harkins announced, "and I am not going to allow my staff to be pessimistic." Harkins had built his career by pleasing superiors with tidy staff work, and for two years he sent positive reports to Washington, D.C., about President Diem's government and the war encouraging President Kennedy and his advisers to believe that victory was imminent. Harkins severely disciplined subordinates who criticized Diem, and he tailored the itineraries of visiting dignitaries to keep uncomplimentary facts well hidden. Harkins was "insulated from reality," according to journalist David Halberstam, but his self-deception spread from Saigon to Washington and helped prolong the Kennedy administration's commitment to Diem.

Harkins, who compared the Vietnam War to the American Revolution and Diem to George Washington, would not tolerate suggestions that South Vietnam was losing, because he never doubted that the United States would prevail. Harkins countered any pressure on Diem to liberalize his regime, promising continued U.S. support. Because the United States already backed Diem, Harkins believed all Americans had a patriotic duty to praise him. "You can't hurry the East," he told those anxious for more democracy in South Vietnam. Harkins worked well with U.S. ambassador Frederick Nolting, who shared his lofty estimation of Diem, but he

PAUL D. HARKINS. At right, with Earle G. Wheeler. *U.S. Army*

feuded constantly with Henry Cabot Lodge, who criticized Diem and encouraged the coup that killed him. Among reporters Harkins became "an object of ridicule," according to Neil Sheehan, because he typified the army's "professional arrogance, lack of imagination, and moral and intellectual insensitivity." Kennedy sent independent fact-finding missions to circumvent Harkins, who was finally replaced by his subordinate, General William Westmoreland, on 20 June 1964.

BIBLIOGRAPHY

HALBERSTAM, DAVID. *The Best and the Brightest.* 1992.

KAHIN, GEORGE McT. *Intervention: How America Became Involved in Vietnam.* 1986.

LODGE, HENRY CABOT. *The Storm Has Many Eyes.* 1973.

MECKLIN, JOHN. *Mission in Torment: An Intimate Account of the U.S. Role in Vietnam.* 1965.

NOLTING, FREDERICK. *From Trust to Tragedy.* 1988.

SHEEHAN, NEIL. *A Bright Shining Lie: John Paul Vann and America in Vietnam.* 1988.

"To Liberate from Oppression." *Time,* 11 May 1962.

GLEN GENDZEL

Harriman, W. Averell (1891–1986), assistant U.S. secretary of state for Far Eastern affairs, 1961–1963; undersecretary of state for political affairs, 1963–1965; ambassador-at-large, with responsibility for Southeast Asia, 1965–1969. Harriman consistently opposed a military solution in Vietnam, believing that a permanent settlement could be reached only through political and diplomatic means.

As chief U.S. representative at the 1962 Geneva Conference, Harriman negotiated a neutrality agreement for Laos. With the widening commitment to Vietnam, Harriman expressed doubts about the ability of President Ngo Dinh Diem to survive, warned that the United States should not stake its prestige on events in Vietnam, and urged a diplomatic settlement for Vietnam followed by a U.S. withdrawal. Harriman became increasingly critical of Diem, and in 1963 he collaborated with Roger Hilsman in drafting a cable that set in motion the coup against the South Vietnamese president.

Lyndon Johnson did not like Harriman's advocacy of a "political" solution to Vietnam and distrusted him because of his ties to the Kennedys. Still, in 1966 Johnson found use for Harriman's views and dispatched him on a worldwide tour to gather support for Johnson's "peace offensive." In 1968, Harriman, one of the "wise men," advised Johnson to deescalate the conflict in Vietnam. The president subsequently named Harriman to head the U.S. delegation at the Paris peace talks. Harriman urged a compromise with the North Vietnamese, but Johnson rejected his proposal. Harriman nevertheless worked to reach an understanding, but the talks dragged on inconclusively, and in 1969, Henry Cabot Lodge replaced him. Later that year Harriman endorsed the 15 October Moratorium protest organized by the antiwar movement.

BIBLIOGRAPHY

ABRAMSON, RUDY. *Spanning the Century: The Life of W. Averell Harriman, 1891–1986.* 1992.

ISAACSON, WALTER, and EVAN THOMAS. *The Wise Men: Six Friends and the World They Made: Acheson, Bohlen, Harriman, Kennan, Lovett, McCloy.* 1986.

PAUL M. TAILLON

Hawks and Doves. *Hawks* and *doves* were labels referring to supporters and opponents of U.S. involvement in Vietnam. Although first used during the Cuban Missile Crisis in 1960, the labels were used in the mid 1960s specifically to differentiate between groups of government policymakers who differed in their overall view on the war and to underscore divisions within the Johnson administration and Congress. More broadly, the labels identified segments of the American public. Generally, a dove favored ending the U.S. role in Vietnam, whereas a hawk was determined to see the United States win the conflict at all costs.

In the early stages of U.S. intervention, few officials opposed administration policy, and President Johnson was concerned primarily about hawks—Republicans and conservative Democrats—who would attack him if he "lost" South Vietnam to the communists. By mid 1967, however, the dove and hawk factions within the administration were discernable. The dove faction included George Ball and Averell Harriman at the State Department and Secretary of Defense Robert McNamara and his aides Paul Warnke, Townsend Hoopes, and John McNaughton. In addition to the Joint Chiefs of Staff (JCS), the hawk ranks included Secretary of State Dean Rusk, national security adviser Walt Rostow, and the leadership of the Central Intelligence Agency (CIA). Hawks and doves were also clearly defined in Congress, with dove Sen. J. William Fulbright of the Foreign Relations Committee and hawk Sen. John C. Stennis of the Armed Services Committee taking the lead for their respective positions.

The hawks in the administration and Congress subscribed to the domino theory and believed that the United States could not afford to lose in Vietnam. The doves, in turn, did not think that Vietnam was strategically significant and questioned whether the United States could win the war. Initially, the doves did not advocate disengagement but rather sought to block further troop deployments and pushed for a bombing halt. The Tet Offensive of 1968 caused most doves to support an end to U.S. involvement. Hawks reacted to the Tet Offensive by calling for more troops and bombing campaigns against North Vietnam. After Richard Nixon took office, the hawks in Congress pressed him to take aggressive action against North Vietnam if the Paris peace talks proved unproductive. The doves attacked Nixon's policies and called for a complete withdrawal of U.S. troops by late 1970. When Nixon ordered the mining of Haiphong harbor and increased bombing of North Vietnam in 1972, congressional doves reacted angrily, introducing resolutions designed to end U.S. participation in the war. Their most notable victory came in November 1973, when, over Nixon's veto, Congress successfully passed the War Powers Act, which limited the president's ability to carry out military action without congressional approval. Outside the government, the labels *hawk* and *dove* increasingly were used to describe popular sentiment and identify various public figures. Jane Fonda, Martin Luther King Jr., Norman Mailer, and Muhammad Ali, for example, were prominent doves. Beginning in 1967 Gallup polled citizens and asked them whether they considered themselves to be hawks or doves. After the Tet Offensive, respondents evenly split between dove and hawk, but as the war dragged on more and more considered themselves doves.

BIBLIOGRAPHY

HERRING, GEORGE C. *America's Longest War: The United States and Vietnam, 1950–1975.* 1986.
KARNOW, STANLEY. *Vietnam: A History.* 1991.

KELLY EVANS-PFEIFER

Heath, Donald (1894–1981), U.S. ambassador to Vietnam, Cambodia, and Laos, 1952–1954. A career Foreign Service officer, Heath became the first U.S. ambassador to Vietnam when the United States legation became an embassy. Stationed in Saigon, he also served as ambassador to Laos and Cambodia. Heath was sympathetic to the French and advocated a strong French role in Vietnam with minimal U.S. involvement. Despite early misgivings, Heath became a supporter of Ngo Dinh Diem and helped discourage a coup attempt by Gen. Nguyen Van Hinh in 1954. Gen. J. Lawton Collins replaced Heath in 1954.

BIBLIOGRAPHY

ARNOLD, JAMES A. *The First Domino: Eisenhower, The Military, and America's Intervention in Vietnam.* 1991.
COOPER, CHESTER L. *The Last Crusade: America in Vietnam.* 1970.

WILLIAM PAUL SCHUCK

Helicopters. Helicopters—rotary-winged, vertical takeoff and landing aircraft—came of age in U.S. hands as machines capable of combat. U.S. forces used helicopters to conduct rescues behind enemy lines in World War II and the Korean War; the French in Algeria and U.S. Marines in Korea used helicopters as battlefield transports; and the British conducted a helicopter assault in the 1956 Suez invasion. These, however, were small-scale operations, and the most important previous military use of helicopters was in evacuating U.S. battlefield casualties in Korea. Helicopters were used extensively in the Vietnam War for a wide variety of tasks previously performed by other means: for infantry assault, fire support, reconnaissance, and logistic support of troops in the field. The first combat use of U.S. helicopters in Vietnam was of piston-engine Army H-21s and Marine H-34s in assault operations with Army of the Republic of Vietnam (ARVN) troops from December 1961 and April 1962, respectively. The U.S. Army was by far the largest user of helicopters and fielded entire airmobile divisions with helicopter transport, reconnaissance, and fire support organic to the division. Most notable of these was the 1st Cavalry Division (Airmobile), which tested the airmobility concept in the pivotal Ia Drang Valley battles of mid-November 1965. U.S. helicopters were last used in Vietnam in the evacuation of Saigon by marine and air force helicopters on 29–30 April 1975.

The most important helicopter used in Vietnam was the turbine-engine UH-1 Huey, whose ubiquitous dipper-shaped silhouette and "whop-whop" rotor noise became symbols of the war. Modified Hueys carrying turreted machine guns, 40 mm grenade launchers, and rockets entered service in early 1962, and the AH-1G Cobra, which entered service in 1966, was the first helicopter gunship designed from the outset as such. Helicopter battlefield casualty evacuation was a salient feature of the war: specialized Huey-equipped U.S. Army aeromedical evacuation units rescued tens of thousands of U.S., ARVN, and communist wounded under fire, and the Marines used H-34s and CH-46s for the same purpose. Heavy-lift Army CH-54 "flying cranes," CH-47s, and Marine CH-53s were used to transport artillery pieces as large as 155 mm howitzers and heavy loads of ammunition using external cargo slings. Army H-13 and OH-6 light observation helicopters—the latter called "loaches" from the acronym LOH—became the eyes of the U.S. infantry in the field. The air force used HH-3Es and HH-53s, refueled in flight by HC-130 tankers, to rescue downed aviators deep in communist-held territory. The navy used carrier-based SH-3As for the same purpose. The navy and marines fielded RH-53 helicopter minesweepers.

UH-1 IROQUOIS "HUEY." Coming in with troopers of the U.S. 1st Cavalry Division (Airmobile) during Operation OREGON, April 1967. The troopers are balanced on the helicopter's skids to ensure they debark as quickly as possible, thus limiting the helicopter's exposure to ground fire while hovering. *U.S. Army*

The U.S. experience with helicopters in Vietnam had a profound impact on the theory and practice of war. The success of helicopter gunships prompted military establishments around the world to purchase or develop similar machines, notably the Soviet Mi-24 and the later U.S. AH-64. Helicopters have joined armored personnel carriers as preferred assault transports, and parachute assault has given way almost entirely to helicopter assault. Helicopters now supplement trucks in transporting soldiers and supplies in the battle area, and amphibious assault forces depend heavily on helicopters. Long-range rescue operations by air-refuelable helicopters, pioneered by the air force in

CH-54 TARHE "SKYCRANE." Capable of lifting up to 6,741 kg (18,000 lbs.) slung underneath the machine, the Skycrane was often used to transport cannon to fire bases being constructed. The helicopter shown carries a special detachable cargo module. *National Archives*

the November 1970 Son Tay raid, were demonstrated in the February 1991 Marine evacuation of the U.S. embassy in Mogadishu, Somalia.

BIBLIOGRAPHY

FAILS, WILLIAM R. *Marines and Helicopters. 1962–1973.* 1978.
YOUNG, WARREN R., et al. *The Helicopters.* 1982.

JOHN F. GUILMARTIN JR.

Helms, Richard M. (1913–), director, Central Intelligence Agency (CIA), 1966–1972. Helms served with the Office of Strategic Services (OSS) during World War II and worked his way up through the CIA to become the first career officer appointed Director of Central Intelligence (DCI). As director during most of the Vietnam War, Helms often had to provide two presidents the gloomy assessment of the war's progress. Helms spent most of his time dealing with internal dissension, shielding the CIA from outside attack, and resisting attempts to involve it in domestic politics. He maintained good relations with President Johnson, but less so with President Nixon. Still, Helms served as director longer than any other man, with the exception of Allen Dulles.

During the Johnson administration, Helms was at the center of a debate in 1966 over the appropriate level of U.S. bombing and the number of troops the United States should commit. Helms's position remained consistent throughout the war. The bombing, he believed, had not worked, neither breaking the resolve of the North Vietnamese, nor disrupting their supply lines to the south. Later, Helms became involved in a dispute with the Pentagon over the North Vietnamese Army's order of battle. Helms compromised with the military, but the incident put him in an awkward position and widened the already existing rift between the CIA and the Pentagon. In the late stages of the war, Helms came under attack from critics protesting covert CIA operations in Southeast Asia, and he appeared before a number of congressional hearings in the mid 1970s. Although never a Johnson intimate, Helms became part of the inner circle of advisers upon whom the president depended.

During the Nixon administration, however, Helms's relationship with the president deteriorated. Nixon pressured Helms into involving the CIA in Watergate; the director first agreed, but then disengaged the CIA from the cover-up. Helms believed that Nixon's personal use of the CIA made it vulnerable to congressional attacks in the 1970s.

Nixon subsequently dismissed Helms in November 1972, offering him an appointment as U.S. ambassador to Iran. In testimony before a Senate subcommittee in 1973, Helms denied CIA involvement in the overthrow of Chilean president Salvador Allende. He was subsequently indicted for perjury in November 1977 and given a fine and a suspended sentence.

BIBLIOGRAPHY

KUTLER, STANLEY. *The Wars of Watergate: The Last Crisis of Richard Nixon.* 1990.
POWERS, THOMAS. *The Man Who Kept the Secrets: Richard Helms and the CIA.* 1979.

PAUL M. TAILLON

Heng Samrin

Heng Samrin (1934–), president, Khmer People's Revolutionary Council, 1979–1991; general secretary, People's Revolutionary Party of Kampuchea, 1981–1991. A communist since 1959, Heng Samrin rose to political commissar and deputy commander of Cambodia's Eastern Zone under the Khmer Rouge. In 1978, after an unsuccessful coup attempt against Pol Pot, he fled to Vietnam and took charge of refugee Cambodians opposed to the Khmer Rouge. Samrin was named president of the People's Republic of Kampuchea when Vietnam occupied Cambodia in January 1979, and he replaced Pen Sovan as general secretary two years later. Widely regarded as Hanoi's puppet, Samrin ended the Khmer Rouge reign of terror, cultivated close ties with Moscow, and attempted economic reforms. Even after Vietnam's withdrawal from Cambodia in 1989, few countries recognized Samrin's regime, which depended on dwindling Soviet aid. In 1991, Samrin was replaced as party secretary by Chea Sim, and a few days later the party agreed to share power with other factions in Cambodia, including the Khmer Rouge. Prince Sihanouk returned from exile to replace Samrin as president in November 1991.

BIBLIOGRAPHY

CHANDLER, DAVID P. *A History of Cambodia.* 1992.
SHAPLEN, ROBERT. *Bitter Victory.* 1987.
SHAWCROSS, WILLIAM. *The Quality of Mercy: Cambodia, Holocaust and Modern Conscience.* 1984.
THU-HUONG NGUYEN-VO. *Khmer-Viet Relations and the Third Indochina Conflict.* 1992.
VICKERY, MICHAEL. *Kampuchea: Politics, Economics, and Society.* 1986.

ZHENG KANG KUN. "Vietnam in Cambodia." *World Press Review,* June 1986.

GLEN GENDZEL

Herbert, Anthony B.

Herbert, Anthony B. (1930–), lieutenant colonel, U.S. Army. A heavily decorated paratrooper, Herbert seized headlines in 1971 with sensational charges that his superior officers in Vietnam suppressed evidence of U.S. war crimes and harassed him into retirement. His claims were not confirmed, however, and CBS's television program "Sixty Minutes" later found that Herbert was relieved of command in 1969 because superiors considered him violently overzealous and "totally unfit to be an Army officer." Herbert's resulting libel suit against CBS News was dismissed in 1986.

BIBLIOGRAPHY

HERBERT, ANTHONY B. *Herbert—The Making of a Soldier.* 1982.
HERBERT, ANTHONY B., with JAMES T. WOOTEN. *Soldier.* 1973.
LANDO, BARRY. "The Herbert Affair." *Atlantic,* May 1973.
TOOBIN, JEFFREY R. "Enduring Insults." *New Republic,* 10 March 1986.
WOOTEN, JAMES T. "Army Officers' Accuser." *New York Times,* 13 March 1971.
WOOTEN, JAMES T. "How a Super-Soldier Was Fired from His Command." *New York Times Magazine,* 5 September 1971.

GLEN GENDZEL

Herbicides.

Herbicides. *See* Chemical Warfare; RANCH HAND.

Hersh, Seymour

Hersh, Seymour (1937–), winner of Pulitzer Prize for reporting the My Lai massacre. His report in 1969 led to a lengthy investigation of the incident. Writing for the *New York Times* in 1974, Hersh exposed the Central Intelligence Agency's (CIA) illegal domestic surveillance of opponents of the war.

BIBLIOGRAPHY

HERSH, SEYMOUR. *Cover-Up: The Army's Secret Investigation of the Massacre at My Lai 4.* 1972.
OLSON, JAMES, and RANDY ROBERTS. *Where the Domino Fell.* 1991.

KELLY EVANS-PFEIFER

Hilsman, Roger (1919–), director, U.S. Department of State, Bureau of Intelligence and Research, 1961–1963; assistant secretary of state for Far Eastern affairs, 1963–1964. Roger Hilsman influenced the direction of U.S. counterinsurgency programs in Vietnam in the early 1960s. Warning that military action alone could not win, he argued for building popular support and isolating the Viet Cong forces through the Strategic Hamlet program. In late 1962, Kennedy sent Hilsman and Michael Forrestal to Vietnam on a fact-finding mission. The resulting Hilsman-Forrestal report expressed reservations about U.S. policy in Vietnam, but concluded that it essentially was sound. The report, however, questioned the stability of Ngo Dinh Diem's regime. Following Diem's repression of Buddhists in 1963, Hilsman recommended that Kennedy encourage a coup against Diem. Together with Forrestal and W. Averell Harriman, Hilsman prepared a cable instructing Ambassador Henry Cabot Lodge to warn Diem that he had to reform or lose U.S. support. The cable also instructed Lodge to inform a group of South Vietnamese Army generals that the United States would not continue to support Diem if he refused to cooperate. Hilsman remained briefly as assistant secretary of state in the Johnson administration, although never as an insider, and he resigned in early 1964.

BIBLIOGRAPHY

HILSMAN, ROGER. *To Move a Nation: The Politics of Foreign Policy in the Administration of John F. Kennedy.* 1967.
KARNOW, STANLEY. *Vietnam: A History.* 1991.

PAUL M. TAILLON

Hmong. During the two decades of U.S. involvement in Indochina, the Hmong people of Laos remained a consistent U.S. ally. A migratory, highland tribe that practiced slash-and-burn farming on the region's highest ridges, the Hmong trace their origins to southern China. As the Chinese empire consolidated control over its borderlands during the eighteenth century, the Hmong launched abortive revolts and, in defeat, were forced southward into northern Vietnam and Laos. Indeed, the very term "Miao" or "Meo" used for the Hmong has strongly negative connotations and is a product of this long conflict between the Han Chinese state and this upland minority. After the French seized Laos in the 1890s, the Hmong achieved a tense accommodation with the French colonial administration punctuated by countless small conflicts and one major anticolonial revolt in 1919–1921. A disparate people fragmented by clan and family loyalties, the Hmong practiced a politics marked by intense internecine conflicts that allowed the French to rule them by playing upon personal and factional fissures.

Hmong involvement in the Indochina conflict began during World War II when French army commandos established a guerrilla maquis among the highland villages surrounding the Plain of Jars in northern Laos. Once several Hmong clans took up arms to aid a few French officers, the tribe became enmeshed, through internal conflicts and external alliances, as partisans in an expanding war. In prewar years, local Hmong leaders had competed intensely for the post of district officer, which, although a lowly office, still gave successful Hmong clans access to the comparatively vast material and coercive powers of the colonial state. In appointing Touby Lyfoung to the post before the war, and thereby disappointing his rival, Faydang Lo, the French gained both an ally and an enemy. In reestablishing control over the Plain of Jars at war's end, the French naturally sought the help of their loyal district official, Touby Lyfoung, who organized his followers into an ad hoc native militia. Simultaneously, Faydang Lo fled the territory into northern Vietnam, where he eventually made contact with the Viet Minh's anticolonial guerrillas. When Viet Minh forces attacked Laos in 1952, a majority of the Hmong clans, led by the district officer Touby Lyfoung, joined the French and later fought with them in the losing battle at Dien Bien Phu. Simultaneously, Faydang Lo led a minority of the Hmong clans into an alliance with the communist Pathet Lao.

After the French withdrawal, the U.S. Central Intelligence Agency (CIA) recruited Touby Lyfoung's clans to fight the Pathet Lao. By 1961, the CIA had eighteen U.S. agents working with 9,000 Hmong "equipped for guerrilla operations." Instead of dealing exclusively with Touby Lyfoung, the CIA found a new leader in Maj. Vang Pao, a Hmong officer who compensated for his lack of traditional status with a lust for combat. In only five years, Vang Pao used the CIA's arms and air support to recruit Hmong villagers into a secret army of thirty thousand tribal guerrillas.

When the Vietnam War spilled into Laos after 1965, the Hmong provided critical services for the U.S. effort—recovering downed pilots, blocking communist offensives, and, most important, guarding radar that guided the bombing of North Viet-

HMONG REFUGEES. Hmong refugees from the Plain of Jars receiving relief supplies at Sam Thong, Laos, c. 1964. *National Archives*

nam. After 1968, Gen. Vang Pao converted his Hmong partisans from guerrillas into ground troops, and—backed by CIA air logistics and U.S. Air Force bombing—mounted a series of hard-fought offensives against communist forces on the Plain of Jars. Supported by massive U.S. tactical bombardments, the Hmong guerrillas could capture portions of the Plain for a few weeks or months, but their limited, ill-trained forces could not hold the ground in combat against regular North Vietnamese and Pathet Lao infantry.

As the largest ethnic group in the secret army, the Hmong began to suffer casualties that strained their total population of only a quarter-million. According to a U.S. Air Force study: "By 1971, many families were down to the last surviving male (often a youth of 13 or 14), and survival of the tribe was becoming a major concern." Initially recruited into the secret army by clan loyalties and CIA rewards of arms and money, the Hmong found it impossible to extricate themselves as warfare swept across north-

ern Laos. With farms destroyed and many able-bodied male farmers killed in the fighting, the Hmong soon became dependent on the air drops of rice from the U.S. Agency for International Development (AID), which were delivered only with Gen. Vang Pao's approval. The few villages who tried to withhold their teenaged sons from the secret army soon faced a suspension of rice shipments and other AID relief supplies.

While the heavy U.S. bombing of Laos wound down between 1971 and 1973, the war turned against the secret army. In 1974, the last CIA operatives left Laos. A year later, as the Pathet Lao took power in Vientiane, Gen. Vang Pao and a thousand of his loyalists fled in a limited U.S. airlift. After migrating to the United States, Vang Pao paid a half-million dollars in cash for a 400-acre cattle ranch in Missoula, Montana—a considerable fortune for a man who had been born a poor peasant and had earned only a $100 per month as a Laotian general.

In postwar Laos, conflicts erupted between the Hmong and the new socialist government, eventually forcing over 100,000 to flee across the Mekong River into Thai refugee camps. In the late 1970s, Hmong families began migrating to the United States from the Thai camps, leaving behind a substantial refugee population facing an uncertain future.

Although initially scattered over much of the United States by the federal refugee program, the Hmong quickly concentrated themselves in small clusters across southern California and in communities lying between Minneapolis and Milwaukee. Under the Reagan administration's policy of global anticommunist resistance, Gen. Vang Pao emerged from retirement during the 1980s to organize an active anticommunist resistance inside Laos, collecting funds from Hmong families in the United States and arming Hmong guerrillas inside the Thai refugee camps. With the end of the Cold War and the subsequent end to his dream of liberating Laos, Vang Pao and the elderly Hmong veterans of the secret war were confronted with the reality of permanent exile just as their children and grandchildren faced the difficulties of becoming Hmong Americans.

BIBLIOGRAPHY

BRANFMAN, FRED. "Presidential War in Laos, 1964–1970." In *Laos: War and Revolution,* edited by Nina S. Adams and Alfred W. McCoy. 1970.

CASTLE, TIMOTHY N. *War in the Shadow of Vietnam: United States Military Aid to the Royal Lao Government, 1955–1975.* 1993.

HAMILTON-MERRITT, JANE. *Tragic Mountains: The Hmong, the Americans, and the Secret Wars for Laos, 1942–1992.* 1993.

MCCOY, ALFRED W. *The Politics of Heroin: CIA Complicity in the Global Heroin Trade.* 1991.

MCCOY, ALFRED W. "The Politics of the Poppy in Indochina: A Comparative Study of Patron-Client Relations under French and American Administration." In *Drugs, Politics, and Diplomacy: The International Connection,* edited by Luis R. S. Simmons and Abdul A. Said. 1974.

YANG DAO. *Hmong at the Turning Point.* 1993.

ALFRED W. MCCOY

Hoa, Duong Quynh. See *Duong Quynh Hoa.*

Hoa Hao.

The Hoa Hao was a Buddhist sect in South Vietnam whose private army opposed the Diem regime. Huynh Phu So founded the Hoa Hao, a reformist Buddhist group named for a village in the Mekong Delta, in 1919. He was a faith healer and was regarded as a prophet by the peasants. So based the sect on internal faith and simple prayers rather than on elaborate rituals in pagodas. Its doctrine was progressive and democratic, especially compared with that of the hierarchial Confucian worldview and animism of the villagers. In the 1940s, the French, fearing the sect would reduce French influence and encourage revolutionary activities, arrested So and committed him to an insane asylum. The Japanese invasion the next year thwarted French intentions to exile So. To undermine the French, who remained nominally in control until 1945, the Japanese armed the Hoa Hao, but So avoided being labeled a Japanese puppet when he prophesied the Japanese defeat. The sect turned anticommunist after the Viet Minh assassinated So in 1947; upon the death of their leader, the group split into three rival factions. Ngo Dinh Diem's pro-Catholic, anti-Buddhist stance, however, gave the three factions a common enemy. Col. Edward Lansdale bribed sect leaders in an attempt to gain their loyalty for Diem, but they joined the Binh Xuyen and Cao Dai armies in opposition. This coalition was defeated by Diem's forces in 1955, and the Hoa Hao sect was further crushed in 1956 when Ba Cut, one of its leaders, was publicly guillotined. Some Hoa Hao remnants then joined the National Liberation Front (NLF), but most took refuge near the Cambodian border, where they controlled An Giang province and passively avoided conflict during the last years of the South Vietnamese republic.

BIBLIOGRAPHY

HERRING, GEORGE C. *America's Longest War: The United States and Vietnam, 1950–1975.* 1986.

MOSS, GEORGE DONNEL. *Vietnam: An American Ordeal.* 1994.

NGUYEN VAN CANH. *Vietnam under Communism, 1975–1982.* 1983.

SANDRA C. TAYLOR

Hoang Duc Nha

(1941–), minister of information, Republic of Vietnam, 1973–1974. After attending universities in the United States, Hoang Duc Nha returned to South Vietnam in 1968 to become private secretary and later a prominent adviser to his older cousin, President Thieu. Nha also joined Thieu's cabinet as information minister in the early 1970s. In late 1972, Nha accompanied Thieu during meetings with Henry Kissinger concerning the conditions for U.S. withdrawal. Nha advised Thieu to reject the peace agreement arranged between Kissinger and Le Duc Tho because it maintained a North Vietnamese presence in the South. After receiving guarantees of continued U.S. military support and the threat of a cutoff of U.S. economic and military aid, Thieu agreed to the Paris peace accords in early 1973. After the war, Nha escaped to the United States, where he settled in New Jersey and later worked as an engineer for General Electric.

BIBLIOGRAPHY

NGUYEN TIEN HUNG and JERROLD L. SCHECTER. *The Palace File.* 1986.

ADAM LAND

Ho Chi Minh (1890–1969).

The founder of the Vietnamese Communist Party (1930) and the first president of the Democratic Republic of Vietnam (1945–1969), Ho is justly viewed as the father of the Vietnamese revolution and the most influential political figure in modern Vietnam.

Early Years. Ho Chi Minh was born Nguyen That Thanh in a small village in the central Vietnamese province of Nghe Tinh. His father, Nguyen Sinh Sac, was a Confucian scholar who had served as an official in the Vietnamese imperial bureaucracy but resigned his post in protest against French occupation of his country following the Treaty of Protectorate in 1884. Ho Chi Minh, educated at the prestigious National Academy (Quoc Hoc) in Hue, exhibited a fiercely patriotic spirit inherited from his

HO CHI MINH. At a hidden base in the Viet Bac area of northern Vietnam during the war with the French, 1946–1954. *Ngo Vinh Long*

father. After taking part in peasant tax protests in 1908, he signed on as a cook's helper with a French steamship company and went to Europe, apparently to discover the secret of Western success at its source.

After several years at sea followed by a short residence in London, Ho settled in Paris at the end of World War I and immediately became involved in socialist political circles. Using the name Nguyen Ai Quoc (Nguyen the Patriot), he gained instant renown within the local Vietnamese community by serving as coauthor of a petition to the Allied leaders gathered at Versailles to demand self-determination for all peoples under colonial rule. The petition was ignored, and in frustration Ho joined the French Communist Party at its founding congress in 1920.

Quickly gaining respect for his diligence and talent as a revolutionary organizer, in 1923 Ho Chi Minh was invited to Moscow to work at the headquarters of the Communist International (Comintern). At the end of the following year he was posted to the Comintern mission in Canton, with instructions to form a Marxist-Leninist revolutionary organization in French Indochina. Seeking adherents from radical nationalist elements living in south China, Ho formed the Vietnamese Revolutionary Youth League in 1925 as a training ground for a future communist party.

Reflecting Leninist strategy and the views that Ho Chi Minh had already formed regarding the key dynamic forces involved in the Vietnamese revolution, the program of the league emphasized the twin demands of national independence and social justice and made relatively little reference to Marxist ideology. But in 1928, Moscow shifted to a new policy that placed greater emphasis on class struggle and proletarian leadership in the revolution. The ideological shift split the league into rival factions.

The Indochinese Communist Party. Ho Chi Minh was not present at the time, having been forced to flee south China for the USSR in the aftermath of Chiang Kai-shek's crackdown on communist elements in Canton. In early 1930, he arrived in Hong Kong from Thailand, where he had been organizing the Vietnamese community in the Khorat Plateau, and presided over a "unity congress," which brought together the warring factions into a single Vietnamese Communist Party. The clear reference in the title to Vietnamese nationalism ran counter to official views in Moscow, however, and at a second meeting in October, the name of the new organization was changed to the In-dochinese Communist Party (ICP) to reflect the Comintern view that small countries could liberate themselves only by banding together in larger alliances.

In June 1931, Ho Chi Minh was arrested by British police in Hong Kong. Released on a legal technicality two years later, he fled to Moscow, where under suspicion from Stalin, who viewed independent-minded communists with hostility, he spent most of the remainder of the decade in virtual anonymity. In 1938, as the clouds of war thickened, he was granted permission to return to China to resume his activities as a Communist organizer in the field. After several months serving with communist Chinese forces in central and south China, in the spring of 1940 he finally resumed contact with leading elements of the ICP inside Vietnam. A few months later, the French colonial regime acceded to Tokyo's demands for access to economic resources and military installations inside Indochina.

In May 1941, under Ho Chi Minh's guidance, the ICP announced the formation of a broad nationalist alliance called the League for the Independence of Vietnam (Viet Minh). The new front, like the old league, downplayed ideological issues and emphasized anti-imperialism and land reform in order to win the support of moderate elements of all social classes against the twin enemies of French colonialism and Japanese fascism. The leading role of the ICP in the front was carefully disguised.

During World War II, the Viet Minh Front gradually strengthened its political and military base inside Vietnam. Its headquarters and the bulk of its guerrilla forces were in the mountains north of the Red River Delta, an area popularly known as the Viet Bac. Ho Chi Minh shuttled back and forth between Vietnam and China to build support for the movement. On one trip he was arrested and jailed by Chinese authorities, but was later released by his captors on the apparent premise that Ho's organizational talents could be useful in helping to defeat Japan. Ho also established contact with U.S. military units in south China and received some small arms and equipment in return for providing information on Japanese troop movements in Indochina.

The Democratic Republic of Vietnam. In August 1945, at the very moment the Japanese surrendered to the Allies, the Viet Minh occupied Hanoi and declared the formation of a provisional Democratic Republic of Vietnam (DRV). He adopted the pseudonym Ho Chi Minh ("He Who Enlightens"), apparently to appeal to moderate ele-

HO CHI MINH. Lt. Col. John Hemphill holds a banner of Ho Chi Minh captured by the 2d Battalion, U.S. 8th Cavalry, 3 March 1966. *National Archives*

ments who might have been repelled by a movement headed by the famous revolutionary Nguyen Ai Quoc, and became president of the new republic. During the next several months Ho maneuvered skillfully to placate Chinese occupation forces in the north, agreeing to guarantee seventy seats to representatives of the Viet Nam Quoc Dan Dang (VNQDD, the ICP's chief rival party) in the new national assembly to be elected in January 1946.

At the same time he carried on delicate negotiations with Jean Sainteny, the chief French representative in Indochina, to seek a peaceful resolution of the dispute over the future of Vietnam. In March 1946, a preliminary agreement was signed that provided for French recognition of Vietnam as a "free state" within the French Union. The status of the colony of Cochinchina was to be determined by a plebiscite. In return, the DRV agreed to guarantee that French economic and cultural interests would be protected throughout the country, and several thousand French troops were to be stationed in the north.

In June, formal negotiations with the French on a final settlement opened at Fontainebleau, near Paris. Ho Chi Minh attended as an observer and watched in dismay as talks broke down on the unwillingness of the French (a new and more conservative government having recently been installed in Paris) to honor their commitment to hold a plebiscite in the southern provinces. When DRV representatives adjourned the talks and returned home in protest, Ho remained in France and in September signed a modus vivendi that postponed a decision on the future of Vietnam until new talks could be held the following January. On his return to Hanoi, many members of the ICP were reportedly angry at Ho's decision to reach a compromise, but he apparently was able to persuade them that the DRV needed time to prepare for a possible future war.

The Indochina War. During the fall of 1946 Ho Chi Minh sought desperately to avoid hostilities, but differences between the Vietnamese and the French could not be resolved. After tensions between Vietnamese and French troops in North Vietnam increased dramatically in November, Ho Chi Minh and the Viet Minh high command began to prepare for war. In mid December, Vietnamese units attacked French government installations and residential areas in Hanoi and then withdrew to the Viet Bac. The first Indochina conflict had begun.

During the ensuing war against the French, Ho Chi Minh played an active part in the formulation of policy, although the role of chief military strategist largely fell to Gen. Vo Nguyen Giap. Ho appeared throughout liberated areas as a symbol of national resistance to the enemy and was primarily responsible for dealings with his country's chief allies, the Soviet Union and (after 1949) the People's Republic of China. Although Ho Chi Minh did not attend the Geneva Conference of 1954 as a member of the DRV delegation to the talks, he was active behind the scenes and may have been instrumental in the decision to accept a compromise peace settlement in July.

After the restoration of peace, Ho Chi Minh and his government returned to Hanoi in October. Ho Chi Minh was still in relatively good health, and during the next few years he played an active part in formulating policy and undoubtedly agreed with the decision to advance toward a socialist society. There are indications, however, that key decisions on domestic policy were at that time being made by others, such as General Secretary Truong Chinh. Ho

Chi Minh was still keenly interested in the issue of national reunification and reportedly took an active role in the decision to return to a policy of revolutionary war in the South in 1959.

Ho's Death. Ho Chi Minh's position as president of the DRV was confirmed in the Constitution of 1959, but his health was failing, and after the mid 1960s, his role in decision making was reportedly primarily ceremonial. He died in September 1969. In a testament that he dictated during his final days, he requested cremation and asked that taxes be lowered to reduce the burden of the war on people. Both requests were ignored. A mausoleum was erected on Ba Dinh Square in Hanoi, and Ho Chi Minh is officially revered as a revolutionary saint and the beloved "uncle Ho" of the Vietnamese people.

To the end of Ho Chi Minh's life and beyond, controversy has shrouded his career. To some, he was a heroic figure and the symbol of the struggle of the Vietnamese people for national independence and reunification. To others, he was a hardened revolutionary who disguised his commitment to proletarian internationalism behind a mask of patriotism. Was he primarily a nationalist or a communist? Was he a secret moderate surrounded by militant radicals, as some have alleged and he himself often implied?

The answer to these questions is not readily available from the evidence and is often obscured by emotion and political partisanship. In the judgment of most dispassionate observers, Ho Chi Minh was both an avid patriot and a convinced Marxist-Leninist, who saw no contradiction between those positions. He was capable of exuding great charm, and also of a ruthless determination to achieve his goals. Above all, he was a highly gifted leader, combining the talents of administrator, strategist, conciliator, and motivator in the cause of Vietnamese national independence.

BIBLIOGRAPHY

FALL, BERNARD B., ed. *Ho Chi Minh on Revolution: Selected Writings, 1920–1966.* 1967.
HALBERSTAM, DAVID. *Ho.* 1971.
HO CHI MINH. *Ho Chi Minh: Selected Writings.* 1977.
LACOUTURE, JEAN. *Ho Chi Minh: A Political Biography.* Translated by Peter Wiles. 1968.
NGUYEN KHAC HUYEN. *Vision Accomplished?* 1971.
TRAN DAN TIEN. *Glimpses of the Life of Ho Chi Minh.* 1958.
TRUONG CHINH. *President Ho Chi Minh.* 1966.

WILLIAM J. DUIKER

Ho Chi Minh Campaign. When U.S. troops withdrew from Vietnam in 1973, the Paris peace accords appeared to preclude a total communist victory; in actuality, North Vietnamese forces were allowed to remain in the South. When Congress slashed U.S. military assistance to South Vietnam one year later, however, the balance of forces tipped in favor of North Vietnam, and desertions reduced the ranks of the Army of the Republic of Vietnam (ARVN). North Vietnam equipped new armored divisions with the latest Soviet weaponry and built highways along the Ho Chi Minh Trail into the heart of South Vietnam. A probing attack was launched against the provincial capital of Phuoc Binh in the Central Highlands on 13 December 1974, serving notice that North Vietnam would not observe the Paris agreements. In the ensuing battle, the fall of Phuoc Long province exposed South Vietnam's military weakness and showed that the United States would not reintervene. Gen. Van Tien Dung of the People's Army of Vietnam (PAVN), second in command to Gen. Vo Nguyen Giap, then proposed a great offensive to capture all of the Central Highlands of South Vietnam in 1975. He expected to conquer Saigon the following year. Leaders in Hanoi approved Dung's plan and sent him south to take command.

Dung's offensive began on 10 March 1975 with a powerful armored assault against Ban Me Thuot in the Central Highlands. ARVN defenses quickly collapsed, and chaos erupted when President Nguyen Van Thieu ordered a withdrawal from the highlands and the northern provinces. Officers quietly boarded helicopters and flew away, leaving their men to save themselves. Vast columns of panicky South Vietnamese refugees, terrorized by PAVN artillery fire, clogged the roads and turned retreat into rout. In just ten days South Vietnamese forces lost six provinces and thousands of tons of equipment, while desperate soldiers and civilians jammed the seaports seeking transport to Saigon. Of the 160,000 ARVN troops defending the highlands and the northern provinces, only one in ten escaped. Realizing that victory was within reach, North Vietnam's rulers decided to commit the PAVN's entire armored reserves in a bid to take Saigon before the rainy season. Le Duc Tho and Pham Hung were sent to join Dung in the South and help plan the final offensive. To honor the father of the Vietnamese revolution, they called it the Ho Chi Minh Campaign.

Dung gave his men a slogan: "Lightning speed, daring, and more daring." Hundreds of new tanks and supply trucks raced south along the rebuilt Ho Chi Minh Trail, traveling day and night, free from fear of U.S. air strikes. Dung deployed thirteen armored divisions and hundreds of long-range artillery pieces in a circle around Saigon, "like a divine hammer held aloft." After decades of waging revolutionary guerrilla war against the French and the Americans, North Vietnamese forces now reached for victory with a full-scale conventional armored assault. In Washington, President Gerald Ford and Secretary of State Henry Kissinger asked for $722 million in emergency military aid to rescue South Vietnam, but Congress refused, pointing to the enormous stocks of U.S. tanks, planes, weapons, and ammunition already abandoned by retreating ARVN troops. Unlike 1972, when North Vietnam's Easter Offensive was turned back with U.S. air power, South Vietnam now faced a rejuvenated enemy alone.

The Ho Chi Minh Campaign began on 9 April 1975, with the shelling of Xuan Loc, sixty-five kilometers (forty miles) east of Saigon. ARVN's 18th Division and attached units held off the PAVN's *6th, 7th,* and *341st* divisions for several days of fierce fighting. After losing five thousand men, Dung finally captured Xuan Loc on 20 April, leaving the road to Saigon open. President Thieu resigned the next day, blaming the United States for abandoning South Vietnam. Dung received a message from Hanoi: "The opportunities facing us now demand that we act most quickly." On 26 April, from five directions at once, Dung's 120,000 men attacked the 30,000 disorganized and dispirited ARVN troops under Gen. Nguyen Van Minh. PAVN artillery and captured South Vietnamese air force bombers destroyed the former U.S. bases at Bien Hoa, Tan Son Nhut, and Long Binh. Dung threatened to do the same to Saigon as Americans frantically evacuated the city by helicopter on 29 April. North Vietnam, spurning South Vietnam's offers to negotiate, ordered Dung to "achieve complete victory for the campaign which bears the name of our great Uncle Ho."

Saigon's terrified populace watched in fear and fascination as PAVN tanks rolled into the city on the morning of 30 April 1975. ARVN soldiers shed their uniforms, dropped their weapons, and offered no resistance. The attackers cried "Giai Phong! Liberation!" and assured the residents they had nothing to fear. PAVN Col. Bui Tin drove *Tank No. 843* crashing through the gates of the Presidential Palace and accepted South Vietnam's surrender from President Duong Van Minh. In just three weeks, the Ho Chi Minh Campaign had ended a war that had lasted ten thousand days. "North and South are reunited under one roof," Le Duc Tho reported back to Hanoi. "Uncle Ho's dream has become reality." The war in Vietnam was over. Dung celebrated his birthday the next day.

BIBLIOGRAPHY

BUTLER, DAVID. *The Fall of Saigon.* 1985.

BUTTERFIELD, FOX. "How South Vietnam Died—By the Stab in the Front." *New York Times Magazine,* 25 May 1975.

CAO VAN VIEN. *The Final Collapse.* 1983.

CHANDA, NAYAN. "The Ho Chi Minh Campaign: How the South Was Won." *Far Eastern Economic Review* 89 (12 September 1975).

DAWSON, ALAN. *55 Days: The Fall of Saigon.* 1977.

HOSMER, STEPHEN T., et al. *The Fall of Saigon: Statements by Vietnamese Military and Civilian Leaders.* 1980.

ISAACS, ARNOLD R. *Without Honor: Defeat in Vietnam and Cambodia.* 1983.

LE GRO, WILLIAM E. *Vietnam from Cease-fire to Capitulation.* 1981.

SNEPP, FRANK. *Decent Interval: An Insider's Account of South Vietnam's Indecent End.* 1977.

TODD, OLIVER. *Cruel April: The Fall of Saigon.* 1990.

VAN TIEN DUNG. *Our Great Spring Victory: An Account of the Liberation of South Vietnam.* 1977.

GLEN GENDZEL

Ho Chi Minh City. See *Saigon.*

Ho Chi Minh Trail, the North Vietnamese infiltration and supply route and communication lifeline into the South Vietnamese Central Highlands through Laos and Cambodia. The trail, an intricate network of jungle paths not visible from the air, was used for centuries as a trade route before its use during the war against French and U.S. forces. In 1964 the North Vietnamese began to upgrade the trail into a modern transportation network. Engineers built roads and bridges and dug underground barracks, hospitals, and other facilities to withstand U.S. air attacks. By 1967 an estimated 20,000 or more North Vietnamese troops poured into South Vietnam via the trail each month, and Viet Cong guerrillas who had previously relied on old French or Japanese weapons, were supplied with modern Chinese and Soviet rocket launchers, AK-47 automatic rifles, and machine guns. Prior to 1974, the trail was defended by antiaircraft batter-

HO CHI MINH TRAIL. A unit of Viet Cong porters carry munitions and supplies to the South through the jungle on a prepared trail, 7 August 1965. *Archive Photos*

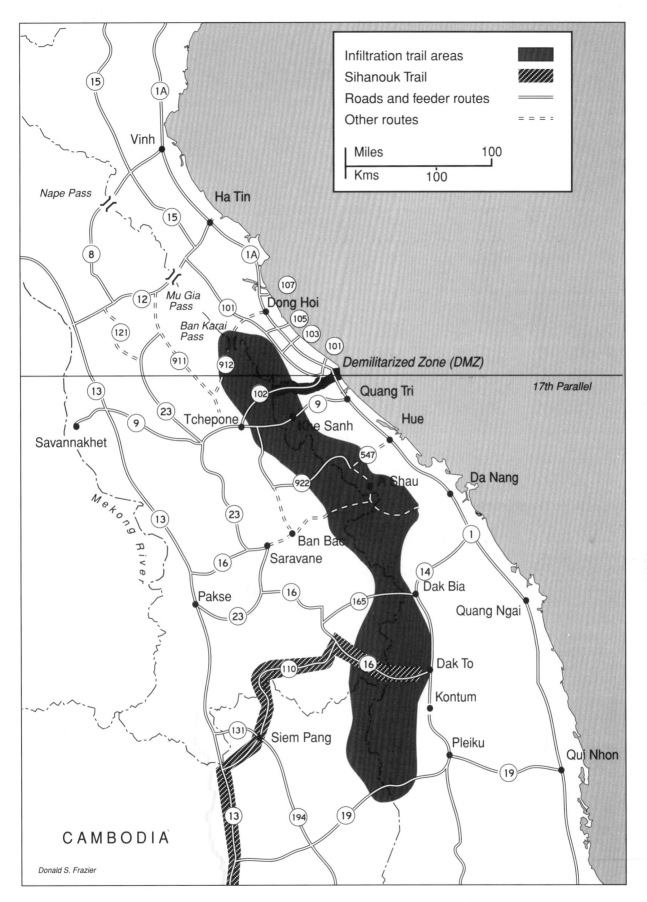

HO CHI MINH TRAIL.

ies, which made it difficult for U.S. warplanes to bomb effectively.

U.S. and South Vietnamese forces attempted several times to close the trail. During Operation ROLLING THUNDER in 1965–1968 U.S. aircraft bombed the trail daily, targeting areas based on electronic detection devices and intelligence gained by covert teams that infiltrated the area. These efforts, however, did little to slow the movement of troops or supplies southward along the trail. In 1971 LAM SON 719, a South Vietnamese army operation designed to sever the trail, also failed, although it disrupted traffic for some time and forced the North Vietnamese to use scarce resources to keep the trail open. By 1974 the trail had become a modern highway, with rest and service areas and protected by considerable antiaircraft weapons, that could be traveled by car.

BIBLIOGRAPHY

DAVIDSON, PHILLIP B. *Vietnam at War—The History: 1946–1975.* 1988.
KARNOW, STANLEY. *Vietnam: A History.* 1991.

ELLEN D. GOLDLUST

Honolulu Conferences. Between 1962 and 1967, a series of meetings were held in Honolulu to review the situation in South Vietnam, discuss strategy, and explore U.S. policy options. Various U.S. officials attended the conferences, including cabinet members, the ambassador to South Vietnam, and military leaders.

The most important conference was convened by President Johnson in February 1966, drawing attention away from Senate Foreign Relations Committee hearings critical of administration policy. Johnson, South Vietnam's prime minister Nguyen Cao Ky, and President Nguyen Van Thieu joined the U.S. officials. The conference focused on South Vietnam's social and economic development. The meeting appeared to signal full U.S. support for the Thieu-Ky government.

BIBLIOGRAPHY

FITZGERALD, FRANCES. *Fire in the Lake: The Vietnamese and the Americans in Vietnam.* 1972.
JOHNSON, LYNDON BAINES. *The Vantage Point: Perspectives of the Presidency 1963–1969.* 1971.

WILLIAM PAUL SCHUCK

Hoopes, Townsend (1922–), deputy assistant secretary of defense for international security affairs, 1965–1967; undersecretary of the U.S. Air Force 1967–1969. Although a self-described product of the Cold War, Hoopes was a leader of the faction within the Pentagon that opposed escalation of the Vietnam War. From the beginning of his tenure at the Defense Department, Hoopes was skeptical about U.S. involvement in Vietnam. In a 1965 memo to Assistant Secretary of Defense John McNaughton, Hoopes wrote that he believed continued bombing of North Vietnam would be counterproductive. He added that, "Similarly, I see no rewards or gains to be reaped by a further infusion of U.S. manpower." Hoopes suggested that the United States narrowly define victory as holding several key ports and cities. He also argued that the United States needed to regain a proper global perspective by ranking its commitment to Vietnam below more pressing relationships. By 1967, Hoopes and several other key officials, frustrated by the continuing escalation, sought to end the war and successfully influenced Secretary of Defense McNamara and his successor, Clark Clifford, to change their views. When the Joint Chiefs of Staff submitted another large troop request in the wake of the Tet Offensive, Hoopes and his cohorts urged the Ad Hoc Committee reviewing the request to turn it down. He sent two memos to Clifford outlining his views on U.S. involvement, concluding: "Judged against any rational scale of values, a military victory in Vietnam is therefore infeasible at any price consistent with U.S. interests." Hoopes reportedly also leaked the story of the request and the internal opposition to a *New York Times* reporter, incensing Johnson.

BIBLIOGRAPHY

HERRING, GEORGE C. *America's Longest War: The United States and Vietnam, 1950–1975.* 1986.
HOOPES, TOWNSEND. *The Limits of Intervention: An Inside Account of How the Johnson Policy of Escalation in Vietnam Was Reversed.* 1969.

KELLY EVANS-PFEIFER

Hue, South Vietnam's third-largest city, located 75 kilometers (45 miles) south of the demilitarized zone near the coast of Thua Thien province. The official population of 140,000 was swollen by refugees during the war. An old imperial capital widely considered Vietnam's most beautiful city, Hue was the center of Buddhist opposition to the Saigon regime. The city convulsed with protests against President Diem in May 1963 and against President Ky in March 1966, protests that were harshly suppressed by South Vietnamese armed forces. During the 1968 Tet Offensive North Vietnamese Army (NVA) and Viet Cong forces captured the city and held it for twenty-five days. Communist agents went house to house arresting civil servants, religious leaders, soldiers, educators, and anyone with American connections, who were summarily executed. U.S. Marines and ARVN troops fought desperate battles to retake Hue, which was largely destroyed, including the ancient inner city called the Citadel. Col. Dave Palmer entered Hue after the battle and found a "shattered, stinking hulk, its streets choked with rubble and rotting bodies." It took years to account for the nearly three thousand dead Vietnamese who had been executed by the North Vietnamese forces—a crime that Vietnam still officially denies. In March 1972, NVA shelling killed twenty thousand refugees fleeing toward Hue during the Easter Offensive. The city fell to North Vietnam's Spring Offensive in March 1975.

BIBLIOGRAPHY

ALEXANDER, DAVID. "Reviving Hue—Vietnam's Broken Heart on the River of Perfumes." *Smithsonian,* June 1986.

IRVING, FREDERICK F. "The Battle of Hue." *Military Review* 49 (January 1969).

NOLAN, KEITH W. *Battle of Hué: Tet 1968.* 1983.

OBERDORFER, DON. *Tet!* 1971.

SMITH, HARVEY H., et al. *Area Handbook for South Vietnam.* 1967.

VAN DINH TRAN. "Hue: My City, Myself." *National Geographic,* November 1989.

GLEN GENDZEL

Humphrey, Hubert H. (1911–1978), U.S. Senator (D-Minn.), 1948–1964, 1970–1978; vice president, 1964–1968; Democratic presidential nominee, 1968. Although Humphrey did not play a large role in the formulation of Vietnam policy as Johnson's vice president, his political career was inextricably bound to Vietnam whether he defended the administration, as he did at first, or tried to distance himself from it as the 1968 presidential nominee.

In the early 1960s Senator Humphrey favored a policy of providing only military training and sup-

plies to South Vietnam. But in 1964 he joined ninety-seven other senators to support the Gulf of Tonkin Resolution. As vice president, Humphrey at first opposed escalation of the conflict. Following the attack on the Pleiku air base in February 1965, Humphrey argued against bombing North Vietnam. His dissent angered Johnson, who expected Humphrey's loyalty, and prompted Johnson to exclude the vice president from all Vietnam policy deliberations for a year. Consequently, Humphrey did not participate in the decision to commit combat troops. During this "freeze out" period, Humphrey nevertheless publicly defended and backed Johnson's policies.

In the spring of 1966 Humphrey toured Southeast Asian capitals to solicit greater assistance in the fight against the Viet Cong and the North Vietnamese forces. A briefing in Saigon apparently convinced him that the escalation policy was correct and that the United States had to make a stand in Vietnam. Upon his return, the now-hardline Humphrey pas-

HUBERT H. HUMPHREY. *Library of Congress*

sionately defended Johnson's policies and participated in Vietnam deliberations. His conversion alienated many liberal supporters, setting the stage for the divisive 1968 Democratic presidential primaries.

When Johnson announced his intention to retire, Humphrey became the heir apparent. Although Humphrey anticipated campaigning in support of the Great Society and continuing the Kennedy-Johnson tradition of liberal domestic social policy, Vietnam was his dilemma. Humphrey could not afford to antagonize Johnson and was unwilling to break with the president. Yet, the popularity of antiwar candidates Robert Kennedy and Eugene J. McCarthy made Humphrey's position precarious. At the Democratic Convention in Chicago, internal splits on Vietnam erupted into a floor battle over the Vietnam platform plank. Humphrey proposed a halt in the bombing and an increase in South Vietnam's participation in the combat. This infuriated Johnson, and he bullied Humphrey into supporting a plank that more faithfully mirrored administration policies. Humphrey's inability to separate himself from Johnson on Vietnam haunted him throughout the rest of the campaign. Finally, on 31 October, one week before the election, Humphrey publicly called for a bombing halt, gradual U.S. disengagement, and a negotiated settlement. His stand came too late, and he lost to Nixon in the three-way race by less than 1 percent. Many historians believe that it was Humphrey's reluctance to establish his independence from Johnson's policies that doomed his presidential bid.

After failing in his quest for the presidency, Humphrey returned to Washington once more as a senator from Minnesota. He was denied his previous seat on the key Foreign Relations Committee, in part because of disputes he had had with the committee's more liberal members when he represented the Johnson administration as vice president. Humphrey generally sought to avoid involvement with the Vietnam issue in his second Senate career, although in 1972 he supported the Hatfield-McGovern amendment, which called for U.S.

troops to withdraw from Vietnam by the end of the year. Humphrey tried again for the presidency in 1972 but lost the Democratic nomination to George McGovern. During the Democratic primary season McGovern successfully used Humphrey's identification in the public mind with Johnson's Vietnam policies to undercut Humphrey's candidacy.

BIBLIOGRAPHY

KARNOW, STANLEY. *Vietnam: A History.* 1991.
SOLBERG, CARL. *Hubert Humphrey: A Biography.* 1984.
ZAROULIS, NANCY, and GERALD SULLIVAN. *Who Spoke Up?* 1985.

KELLY EVANS-PFEIFER

Huong, Tran Van.   See *Tran Van Huong.*

Huston Plan.   Designed with President Richard Nixon's knowledge by White House aide Tom Charles Huston, the Huston plan gave the White House control over the domestic intelligence activities of various agencies, including the Federal Bureau of Investigation (FBI), the Central Intelligence Agency (CIA), and U.S. Army intelligence. It authorized warrantless telephone taps, the opening of mail, break-ins, and other activities, all designed to harass and intimidate private citizens involved with the antiwar movement. The illegal and unconstitutional plan (the CIA is forbidden to conduct domestic operations under any circumstances) was blocked by objections from FBI director J. Edgar Hoover in a 1970 meeting with Nixon and top government officials, primarily because Hoover feared that the plan would decrease his own authority.

BIBLIOGRAPHY

KUTLER, STANLEY. *The Wars of Watergate.* 1990.
ZAROULIS, NANCY, and GERALD SULLIVAN. *Who Spoke Up?* 1984.

KELLY EVANS-PFEIFER

I

Ia Drang. In November 1965, U.S. soldiers engaged regulars of the People's Army of Vietnam (PAVN) in a fierce four-day battle near the Drang River in the Central Highlands. The combat marked the first military engagement between the armies as they escalated forces within South Vietnam. The 1st Cavalry Division (Airmobile) of the U.S. Army inflicted heavy casualties on the North Vietnamese (estimated at over 2,500), though the United States lost 234 dead and nearly 300 wounded. While signaling the onset of a destructive ground war in Vietnam, the battle at Ia Drang also proved a crucial test of the armies' combat tactics. For the Americans, the battle's apparent success validated General Westmoreland's "war of attrition," employing aggressive search-and-destroy missions. The PAVN commanders, on the other hand, developed tactics to counter massive U.S. firepower, though the costly failure also sparked debates on general strategy for defeating the United States.

On 14 November 1965, the 1st Battalion, 7th Cavalry, helicoptered into the Ia Drang valley 23 kilometers (14 miles) west of Plei Me. The 450-man unit pursued suspected North Vietnamese forces hidden in the mountainous area near the Laotian border. They landed within a few miles of two PAVN regiments with several thousand troops. A vicious battle ensued, in which U.S. soldiers desperately defended a perimeter only about 270 meters (300 yards) across. The PAVN nearly overran the U.S. position in a series of flanking operations, but the battalion held its position over the next seventy-two hours. U.S. troops fought courageously, led by a skilled officer, Lt. Col. Harold Moore, and numerous Korean War veterans who served as noncommissioned officers. Critical to the battle was the well-coordinated array of heavy U.S. firepower, which included aerial rocket artillery helicopters, attack aircraft, and B-52 bombers. Rapidly deployed 105 mm howitzers fired more than 33,000 rounds from an artillery support zone a few kilometers away.

By 16 November, the PAVN forces had withdrawn from the withering U.S. attack, but they suffered further casualties from Army of the Republic of Vietnam (ARVN) battalions helicoptered across their line of retreat. On 17 November, however, PAVN forces that had just arrived from Laos overran the 2d Battalion, 7th Cavalry, as it traveled on foot near the battle site, killing 155 U.S. soldiers.

The Ia Drang campaign previewed the tactics of U.S. ground forces in the war. The engagement rep-

239

resented the first time helicopters ferried large units into combat, a historically unprecedented battle scheme that would become the standard for U.S. forces in Vietnam. Even more crucial, the success of the main confrontation at the Ia Drang committed the United States to a "war of attrition," with its key instruments of search-and-destroy missions. The Ia Drang confirmed the effectiveness of this offensive-oriented tactic adopted in the summer of 1965 over rival plans such as an "enclave strategy" to protect populated coastal regions. As the United States expanded its forces, U.S. generals sought to repeat the Ia Drang engagement, where a search-and-destroy operation located PAVN or Viet Cong soldiers and, with superior weaponry and massive firepower, inflicted devastating casualties on North Vietnamese forces.

North Vietnamese commanders drew their own lessons from the Ia Drang. After the battle the PAVN forces generally did not fight head on against U.S. forces and rarely took the bait of ensuing search-and-destroy missions. When they did engage U.S. troops, the PAVN troops approached as closely as possible to the perimeter of U.S. forces, as soldiers did in attacks at the Ia Drang, to minimize their vulnerability to U.S. firepower, a maneuver termed "clinging to the belt." The battle also set off high-level debates in North Vietnam concerning military strategy for defeating U.S. forces. Some North Vietnamese commanders, led by General Vo Nguyen Giap, called for increased emphasis on guerrilla operations, citing the failure of conventional campaigns at the Ia Drang. These heated debates were not fully resolved until 1967, when the North largely abandoned conventional warfare in the Tet Offensive.

Military historians disagree on the effectiveness of Westmoreland's war of attrition. Some critics, such as Andrew Krepinevich, argue that with a non-confrontational strategy learned from the Ia Drang, the North Vietnamese kept U.S. forces on a "wild-goose chase" on the periphery of South Vietnam, while PAVN and Viet Cong forces successfully increased activity along populated coastal areas. Other scholars, such as Phillip Davidson, agree that search-and-destroy operations rarely matched the success of the Ia Drang, but they argue that the operations exacted a heavy toll on PAVN forces. With campaigns such as Operations ATTLEBORO (September–November 1966), CEDAR FALLS (January 1967), and JUNCTION CITY (February–May 1967), the U.S. military drove PAVN main forces into remote areas and undermined their combat capability. With high mobility, Davidson maintains, the United States could both attack effectively in the interior and defend coastal areas.

But even accepting the military value of the Ia Drang model of U.S. operations, several problems persisted with U.S. strategy. The United States confronted in the North Vietnamese and Viet Cong an enemy committed to protracted conflict and capable of mobilizing extensive national resources. Numerous U.S. tactical successes could never transfer into a decisive victory. The victory at the Ia Drang, while a testament to U.S. soldiers' fighting skills, was counterproductive because it offered the false promise for a military solution to the Vietnamese conflict. Beginning in 1965, the United States invested massive resources into an aggressive war. The U.S. military gave little support to pacification programs until the late 1960s and, convinced of its ability to win the war, slighted plans to improve the South Vietnamese army. These programs, while entailing their own problems, may have countered more effectively the protracted, political war that PAVN and Viet Cong forces waged in South Vietnam.

BIBLIOGRAPHY

DAVIDSON, PHILLIP B. *Vietnam at War: The History, 1946 – 1975.* 1988.

MOORE, HAROLD G., and JOSEPH L. GALLOWAY. *We Were Soldiers Once . . . and Young: Ia Drang—The Battle that Changed the War in Vietnam.* 1992.

KREPINEVICH, ANDREW F., JR. *The Army and Vietnam.* 1988.

ADAM LAND

India. Officially a nonaligned nation, India refused to join the Southeast Asia Treaty Organization (SEATO), even though the United States regarded the country as a "domino" threatened by Asian communism. India's own struggle against colonialism made it generally sympathetic to the Democratic Republic of Vietnam (DRV), but its conflicts with the DRV's ally, the People's Republic of China, caused India to tone down its support for the DRV. Public opinion in India supported the Vietnamese against the French and, throughout the 1960s, favored U.S. withdrawal. A 1965 report of the Ministry of External Affairs called for another "Geneva-type" conference, an end to the bombing of the DRV, a withdrawal of all troops from South Vietnam, and reunification of the two Vietnams. This report essentially dismissed the possibility of a military solution to the conflict. By 1970 India had moved closer to the DRV and Foreign Minister Swaran Singh demanded that U.S. troops begin to withdraw. In 1972 India improved its relations with the DRV by raising its consulate to the level of an embassy, while it maintained only a consulate in South Vietnam. Within hours of the fall of Saigon, India recognized the Provisional Revolutionary Government.

India joined the International Commission for Supervision and Control (ICSC) after the 1954 Geneva Conference. Because it was nonaligned, India chaired the ICSC and provided the vast majority of its personnel. By the mid 1960s the divisions within the ICSC were clear, with India generally siding with Poland against Canada; India withdrew from the ICSC in 1973.

BIBLIOGRAPHY

FitzGerald, Frances. *Fire in the Lake: The Vietnamese and the Americans in Vietnam.* 1972.
Thakur, Ramesh. *Peacekeeping in Vietnam: Canada, India, Poland, and the International Commission.* 1984.

ELLEN BAKER

Indochina War. *The term "Indochina War" refers to the war of Vietnamese independence against French colonial rule from the end of World War II to 1954. For discussion of the war and the French colonial period before 1954, see* Colonialism.

Indonesia. In 1947 Indonesia issued a joint appeal with the Democratic Republic of Vietnam (DRV) to the United Nations requesting recognition of their post-colonial independence. Although the United States considered Indonesia to be threatened by the spread of communism, Indonesia, like India, refused to join the Southeast Asia Treaty Organization (SEATO) and remained officially nonaligned. Under President Sukarno, Indonesia was critical of the U.S. war effort in Vietnam, but a bloody right-wing counter-coup in 1965 pushed the country more toward the United States under President Suharto. Indonesia replaced India on the 1973 International Commission for Control and Supervision (ICSC).

BIBLIOGRAPHY

FitzGerald, Frances. *Fire in the Lake: The Vietnamese and the Americans in Vietnam.* 1972.

Thakur, Ramesh. *Peacekeeping in Vietnam: Canada, India, Poland, and the International Commission.* 1984.

ELLEN BAKER

Insurgency. *See* Pacification.

International Commission for Supervision and Control. The International Commission for Supervision and Control (ICSC; also known as the International Control Commission [ICC] and later the International Commission for Control and Supervision [ICCS]) was established by the 1954 Geneva Conference on Indochina. Comprising three nations not directly involved in the military conflict—Canada, India, and Poland—the ICSC's mission was to supervise the cease-fire and political reunification of Vietnam. It was also charged with supervision of the 1956 elections, which never took place. The ICSC used mobile teams to investigate alleged treaty violations and established committees to evaluate the findings. Its broad mandate, combined with a lack of substantial enforcement powers and the requirement of unanimity on most issues, limited the commission's influence, particularly as the period of French withdrawal gave way to increased U.S. involvement.

The ICSC published eleven interim reports from 1954 through 1961 and three special reports from 1962 through 1965. These reports were increasingly pessimistic and criticized both sides for violating the Geneva agreement. Its 1962 special report was particularly critical of the Democratic Republic of Vietnam (DRV) for aggressive actions and of the military alliance between South Vietnam and the United States.

The members of the ICSC were divided along ideological lines and rarely reached unanimous decisions. Canada supported the United States and South Vietnam, Poland supported the Soviet Union and the DRV, and India tried to remain nonaligned, although it was generally more sympathetic toward the DRV. The 1965 special report, for example, included a majority report condemning the U.S. bombing and a Canadian minority report justifying it. An additional problem facing the ICSC was that it did not report to a political body, such as the United Nations. Instead, it directed its recommendations only toward the largely defunct Geneva Conference and toward the parties themselves. The ICSC's activities declined in the late 1960s.

The Paris Peace Accords of 1973 reconstituted the ICSC as the International Commission for Control and Supervision (ICCS), in which Hungary replaced Poland and Indonesia replaced India. Either the Four-Party Joint Military Commission or the Two-Party Joint Military Commission could request investigations of accord violations. Like its predecessor, the ICCS had no enforcement power: it merely reported its findings to all four parties to the Paris agreement, which were then supposed to resolve the conflict. Canada remained a member of the ICCS for only a few months, withdrawing because it believed that Hungary was undermining the ICCS's work. The commission became irrelevant after the North Vietnamese military victory in 1975.

BIBLIOGRAPHY

PORTER, GARETH. *A Peace Divided: The United States, Vietnam, and the Paris Agreement.* 1975.

THAKUR, RAMESH. *Peacekeeping in Vietnam: Canada, India, Poland, and the International Commission.* 1984.

YOUNG, MARILYN B. *The Vietnam Wars.* 1991.

ELLEN BAKER

International Reaction. In responding to the war in Vietnam, the world's nations were divided into three camps: capitalist countries sympathetic to the United States, socialist countries sympathetic to the Democratic Republic of Vietnam (DRV), and countries that wished to remain nonaligned.

The United States and South Vietnam waged war along with six official allies: Australia, New Zealand, the Philippines, the Republic of China (Taiwan), the Republic of Korea (South Korea), and Thailand. The leaders of these countries based their support on anticommunist ideology, a desire to strengthen ties to the United States, or both. The Free World Assistance Program provided nonmilitary aid to South Vietnam from thirty-two additional countries.

Many traditional U.S. allies, including Great Britain, France, and West Germany, expressed reservations about the U.S. policy. The bombing of the DRV, the mining of its ports, and the invasion of Cambodia were watershed events in stimulating opposition among citizens of allied nations. This opposition was apparent in the tentative criticism of the United States made, for example, by Canadian and British officials beginning in 1965.

All socialist countries opposed the U.S. presence in Vietnam but were not themselves united in their positions. The Soviet Union in the mid 1960s sought peaceful coexistence with the United States and, while continuing to provide military aid to the North Vietnamese, also acted as intermediary in several failed peace missions. The People's Republic of China (PRC), threatened by Soviet power, especially following the 1968 Soviet invasion of Czechoslovakia and subsequent attacks on the PRC's borders, refused to cooperate with Soviet policies in North Vietnam. The PRC viewed the National Liberation Front (NLF) and communist movements in neighboring countries as a counter to U.S. imperialism and thus supported them with material aid. North Vietnam played the Soviet Union and the PRC against each other in an attempt to increase the amount of aid it received, but it also suffered from the uncertainty of long-term commitments by the Soviet Union and PRC.

Nonaligned countries such as India remained officially neutral but generally called for a negotiated peace between the NLF and the South Vietnamese. Many of the nonaligned countries were themselves former colonies, and their citizens believed that the North Vietnamese and the NLF were resisting imperialism.

The United Nations was not officially involved in the conflict, but Secretary General U Thant tried to organize talks between U.S. and DRV officials in 1964, and by 1966 he called for a halt to the bombing of North Vietnam, negotiations that would include the NLF, and a reduction in military activities on all sides. The United Nations failed, however, to provide a resolution to the conflict because of the strongly divided camps.

BIBLIOGRAPHY

KARNOW, STANLEY. *Vietnam: A History.* 1991.

LARSEN, STANLEY ROBERT, and JAMES LAWTON COLLINS, JR. *Allied Participation in Vietnam.* 1975.

THAKUR, RAMESH. *Peacekeeping in Vietnam: Canada, India, Poland, and the International Commission.* 1984.

ELLEN BAKER

International Rescue Committee. Formed in 1942 to aid refugees from Nazi Germany, the International Rescue Committee is an American-sponsored, nonsectarian, volunteer organization. The committee first worked in Vietnam after the division of the country in 1954, when some 900,000 Vietnamese fled the north to relocate in the south. It provided emergency aid in the form of food, clothing, housing, and medical care for Vietnamese refugees and sponsored their permanent resettlement. After 1964, the committee organized refugee assistance for the millions of refugees within South Vietnam itself, displaced by the U.S. escalation of the war and, after the fall of South Vietnam in 1975, aided the final evacuation of Vietnamese refugees and their resettlement in the United States. The International Rescue Committee continues its work today.

BIBLIOGRAPHY

LEVENSTEIN, AARON. *Escape to Freedom: The Story of the International Rescue Committee.* 1983.

JENNIFER FROST

International War Crimes Tribunal.

Also known as the Russell tribunal, the International War Crimes Tribunal met in 1967 under the direction of the Bertrand Russell Peace Foundation, a private organization. Russell, an internationally known philosopher and mathematician who won the Nobel Prize for literature in 1950, was a longtime peace activist who opposed U.S. involvement in Vietnam. The tribunal declared that American treatment of prisoners, use of "experimental" weapons, and bombing of civilians constituted war crimes according to international law, particularly criticizing the use of napalm and cluster bombs against civilians. The testimony and findings were published by Russell in the book *Against the Crime of Silence* but had little impact on U.S. policy.

BIBLIOGRAPHY

RUSSELL, BERTRAND. *Autobiography.* 1969.
ZAROULIS, NANCY, and GERALD SULLIVAN. *Who Spoke Up?* 1984.

KELLY EVANS-PFEIFER

Iron Triangle.

Just 32 kilometers (20 miles) northwest of Saigon lay a major Viet Cong guerrilla base area known as the Iron Triangle, formed by the junction of the Saigon and Thi Tinh rivers between the villages of Ben Suc and Ben Cat. This heavily forested area concealed a vast underground tunnel complex containing 130 square kilometers (50 square miles) of guerrilla barracks, supply dumps, hospitals, and weapons factories. Operations CEDAR FALLS and JUNCTION CITY in January–February 1967 attacked this "human anthill" with bombs, shells, napalm, explosives, bulldozers, and 32,000 troops. The U.S. Army's historian considered it "the largest and most significant operation to this point in the war." Hundreds of tons of enemy supplies were captured, but most of the guerrillas escaped to Cambodia, and the Iron Triangle still served as the staging base for attacks on Saigon during the Tet Offensive just one year later. The Iron Triangle's underground bases were finally neutralized with delayed-fuse bombs dropped by B-52s in 1970.

BIBLIOGRAPHY

"After their Nests." *Time,* 27 January 1967.
"Destroying the Haven." *Time,* 3 March 1967.
MANGOLD, TOM, and JOHN PENNYCATE. *The Tunnels of Cu Chi.* 1985.
ROGERS, BERNARD WILLIAM. *Cedar Falls–Junction City: A Turning Point.* 1974.

GLEN GENDZEL

J

Jackson State College. On 14 May 1970, following several days of protests over the Vietnam War, racism, and local issues, police gunfire killed two students and wounded twelve others during a tumultuous protest at Jackson State College in Mississippi. The police claimed that they fired in response to an alleged sniper. The May events at Jackson State, the Kent State shootings, and protests on other college campuses contributed to the era's turmoil.

BIBLIOGRAPHY

PRESIDENT'S COMMISSION ON CAMPUS UNREST. *Report of the President's Commission on Campus Unrest.* 1970.

SPOFFORD, TIM. *Lynch Street: The May 1970 Slayings at Jackson State College.* 1988.

WILLIAM PAUL SCHUCK

Japan. During World War II, contrary to its pan-Asiatic rhetoric, Japan occupied Indochina (1940–1945), imposed de facto rule through the nominal control of French authorities, and exploited the Vietnamese. The Viet Minh, a communist-oriented nationalist force, resisted the occupation and proclaimed independence for Vietnam in 1945. Following the successful Chinese communist revolution in 1949, U.S. attention focused on Vietnam. The United States sought to contain the spread of communism and emerging nationalism and to provide a market to assist economic recovery in Japan.

Although not an official participant in the Vietnam War, Japan (and Okinawa) played a key role as an entrepôt for channeling U.S. military personnel and supplies from the United States to Vietnam. Japan hosted approximately 100,000 military-related Americans as well as some 50,000 troops in Okinawa, and provided a dozen major bases and more than 130 other military facilities. Meanwhile, Japan's rapid economic growth during this period offered an alternative noncommunist model for Southeast Asia.

Japan benefited greatly from the war. Between 1966 and 1971, the United States spent more than $150 billion for the war effort, of which at least $5 billion went to Japan for military procurement. Simultaneously, U.S. military personnel stationed in Japan and Okinawa and short-term visitors on R&R (rest and rehabilitation) consumed Japanese goods and used Japanese services, again to the benefit of the Japanese economy. Taking advantage of U.S. military protection, Japan spent less than 1 percent of its gross national product (GNP) on defense, devoting its efforts to domestic economic growth. Worldwide inflation during the war also strengthened Japanese international competitiveness. In addition, as the United States sent military and economic aid to other Asian countries to fend off communism, these countries in turn purchased goods from Japan. Consequently, the Japanese economy experienced an annual growth rate of approximately 10 percent during the Vietnam War era.

Following World War II, the Japanese government had two major aims: economic growth and the recovery of Okinawa. To realize these aims, the government employed a loose interpretation of the revised Japan–United States Security Treaty of 1960 to support U.S. policy in Vietnam. The Japanese government proclaimed that the United States could use its bases in Japan to take military actions if the Far East were endangered.

In contrast to this official attitude, an antiwar movement developed among far-left and moderate student groups, opposition political parties, and labor unions. Propelled by psychological and practical elements, some participants found themselves in an ambivalent position: although they preferred that Japan distance itself from the war, they felt compelled to collaborate with the United States because of treaty obligations. Consequently, they perceived themselves both as "victims" and "assailants," and their protests against the Vietnam War eased their consciences. In a more practical sense, they feared that intervention by the People's Republic of China could result in an attack on U.S. bases in Japan. There were several factors that kept the Japanese antiwar movement from becoming either effective or very radical. Japan sent no soldiers to Vietnam; economic prosperity created a broad middle class that favored conservative attitudes and disdained militant protests led by far-leftists; and—probably the most important factor—Vietnam was too far away, geographically and mentally, for ordinary citizens to pay serious attention to the war.

Although the protest movement had little direct effect on policy-making, it effectively set limits on the extent of Japan's involvement. The war-renunciation clauses of the Japanese constitution also limited Japan's participation. These limitations allowed the government to keep its involvement to a minimum while enjoying maximum benefits. The Japanese role ultimately proved advantageous—Japan regained Okinawa from the United States in 1972 and realized such immense economic prosperity that it became a keen economic competitor of the United States.

BIBLIOGRAPHY

HAVENS, THOMAS. *Fire across the Sea.* 1987.

KOSAI, YUTAKA, and YOSHITARO OGINO. *The Contemporary Japanese Economy.* 1984.

KUNO, OSAMU. "The Vietnam War and Japan," *Japan Quarterly* 20 (April–June 1973): pp. 143–150.

SHIBUSAWA, MASAHIDE. *Japan and the Asian Pacific Region.* 1984.

YONEYUKI SUGITA

Johns Hopkins Speech. On 7 April 1965 President Lyndon B. Johnson, in a speech at Johns Hopkins University in Baltimore, Maryland, stated that the United States was willing to take part in "unconditional discussions" about the prospect of peace in Vietnam. As a bargaining inducement for the North Vietnamese he proposed a massive economic development program for the Mekong River valley, in which North Vietnam could participate. Johnson made it clear, however, that these proposals did not change the U.S. commitment to an independent South Vietnam. The administration correctly believed that North Vietnam would not respond to this initiative because it was not accompanied by a pause in the U.S. bombing of North Vietnam and because Johnson offered no other tangible concessions. The speech represented the first significant example of the expanding antiwar movement's impact on U.S. foreign policy during the war.

BIBLIOGRAPHY

DEBENEDETTI, CHARLES. *An American Ordeal: The Antiwar Movement of the Vietnam Era.* 1990.

HERRING, GEORGE C. *America's Longest War: The United States and Vietnam, 1950–1975.* 1986.

JOHNSON, LYNDON BAINES. *The Vantage Point: Perspectives of the Presidency, 1963–1969.* 1971.

New York Times, 8 April 1965.

ELLEN D. GOLDLUST

Johnson, Harold K. (1912–1983), general, U.S. Army; U.S. Army chief of staff, 1964–1968. Survivor of the Bataan Death March and three year's imprisonment by the Japanese in World War II, Johnson was chosen over forty-three more senior generals to replace Gen. Earle Wheeler as chief of staff on 3 July 1964. President Lyndon B. Johnson sent him to South Vietnam in March 1965 with orders to "get things bubbling." Doubtful that bombing could win the war, General Johnson recommended sending the first U.S. combat troops. He came to regret his decision: "We act with ruthlessness, like a steamroller," he said of the U.S. war effort. Johnson retired and was replaced by Gen. William Westmoreland in 1968.

BIBLIOGRAPHY

BALDWIN, HANSON W. *Strategy for Tomorrow.* 1970.
HALBERSTAM, DAVID. *The Best and the Brightest.* 1992.
JOHNSON, HAROLD K. "End of Vietnam War in Sight?" *U.S. News and World Report,* 11 September 1967.
JOHNSON, HAROLD K. "Vietnam: Comparisons and Convictions." *Vital Speeches* 34 (1 January 1968).
KORB, LAWRENCE J. *The Joint Chiefs of Staff: The First Twenty-Five Years.* 1976.

GLEN GENDZEL

Johnson, Lyndon B. (1908–1973), U.S. representative (D-Tex.), 1937–1949; U.S. senator (D-Tex.), 1949–1961; Senate minority leader, 1953–1955; Senate majority leader, 1955–1961; vice president, 1961–1963; president, 1963–1969. Lyndon Baines Johnson, according to a 1988 Harris poll, is one of the least admired U.S. presidents since the Depression. The public's low opinion of Johnson is the result not only of the Vietnam War, which is remembered as the first defeat in U.S. history, but also of his overbearing personality and his deviousness as a behind-the-scenes operator who escalated the war in Vietnam without a national debate or consensus.

Johnson's manipulativeness as president was the product of his imperious personality and earlier political experience in Texas, where hidden political dealings were commonplace. Johnson was a larger-than-life character with a prodigious appetite for power and control. As president, he aimed to outstrip the achievements of all his predecessors in the office, including Franklin D. Roosevelt, his first mentor in Washington, and John F. Kennedy, his successful rival for the Democratic nomination in 1960.

LYNDON B. JOHNSON. Greeting U.S. troops in Vietnam, 1966. *National Archives*

LYNDON B. JOHNSON. At right, during the Honolulu conference, 1966. Left to right: William C. Westmoreland; Nguyen Van Thieu; Nguyen Cao Ky; unidentified; Johnson. Photo by Yoichi R. Okamoto. *National Archives*

Johnson's Early Experiences with Vietnam. Lyndon Johnson's first involvement with Vietnam occurred in 1954. As Democratic minority leader of the U.S. Senate, Johnson played a part in President Dwight D. Eisenhower's response to the impending defeat of French colonial forces by the Viet Minh. The president asked Johnson and other congressional leaders to support the use of U.S. air and sea power to help the French. Johnson helped persuade Eisenhower not to intervene, yet he later criticized the president for having lost part of Vietnam to the communists. The successful Viet Minh assault at Dien Bien Phu in 1954 led to the division of the country into North and South Vietnam.

In 1961, as vice president, Johnson traveled to Vietnam at President Kennedy's request to assure the government of Ngo Dinh Diem that the United States intended to protect South Vietnam from a communist takeover. Johnson promised Diem technical and financial aid and military supplies and

hinted at the possibility of sending U.S. combat troops. The latter proposal was only a gesture at that time, although the Kennedy administration stepped up other aid to South Vietnam, including an increase in the number of military advisers from 700 to 16,300.

Increased U.S. aid did not stabilize conditions in South Vietnam, however, where repressive measures against all dissidents by the government added to the instability. At odds with Johnson's judgment, the Kennedy administration endorsed a military coup that toppled Diem's government and took his life. Three weeks later, on 22 November 1963, the assassination of John Kennedy shifted the burden of responsibility for Vietnam to Johnson. Fearful that a communist victory in South Vietnam would open the rest of Southeast Asia to communist control, that it might embolden the Soviets and Chinese to actions that could lead to World War III, and that it could give the Republicans a compelling point of attack against his administration, Johnson determined at the start of his presidency not to "lose" South Vietnam.

Johnson as President. In following this policy, Johnson believed he was continuing Kennedy's intentions. Kennedy had remarked to various advisers in the last months of his life about getting out of Vietnam after the 1964 presidential election and had given indications of this shift by ordering one thousand troops home from Vietnam by the end of 1963. Despite this, Johnson had good reason to think that Kennedy would not have pulled out of Vietnam as long as there was a substantial risk of a communist takeover.

During 1964, Johnson's two principal concerns were his presidential election campaign against Barry Goldwater and the implementation of his Great Society, a domestic reform program enunciated in May at the University of Michigan. Fearing that a U.S. military buildup in Vietnam would jeopardize his chances for election and his domestic agenda, Johnson promised Americans that he would not send troops to Vietnam. At the same time, however, he quietly increased the number of advisers to 23,300 and increased economic assistance by $50 million.

Johnson also pressured North Vietnam to stop supporting Viet Cong insurgents in the South, and he appointed Gen. William Westmoreland commander of U.S. military operations in Vietnam. He also persuaded Congress to endorse administration freedom to combat what he and most Americans at the time viewed as communist aggression in Southeast Asia.

Gulf of Tonkin Incident and Resolution. On the night of 4 August 1964, two U.S. destroyers operating off the North Vietnamese coast in the Gulf of Tonkin reported that they were under attack. It was apparently the second North Vietnamese assault on U.S. ships in the gulf in two days. U.S. Navy commanders told Secretary of Defense Robert McNamara that unreliable radio and sonar contacts made it difficult for them to confirm the attack. Though he lacked conclusive evidence of an actual attack, Johnson nevertheless ordered retaliatory air strikes against North Vietnamese torpedo boat bases and oil storage depots. Moreover, though he later told Undersecretary of State George Ball that "those sailors out there may have been shooting at flying fish," Johnson asked Congress for a resolution that would allow him to repel future armed attacks and to prevent further aggression. The Gulf of

Tonkin Resolution, which won nearly unanimous congressional approval, stood as a symbol of national support for Johnson's foreign policy in Vietnam. In securing the resolution, Johnson misled Congress and the American people, failing to mention that the U.S. ships were engaged in electronic espionage and that the second "attack" on the 4th may not have occurred.

Toward the end of 1964, Johnson's advisers devised a plan to gradually intensify air attacks and to avert a collapse in South Vietnam. In November 1964, when a Viet Cong attack on a U.S. air base killed four servicemen, Johnson did not retaliate. But three months later, with Buddhist and student protests threatening to topple the South Vietnamese government and with North Vietnamese Army units entering South Vietnam, Johnson made further plans for an air assault on North Vietnam. After Viet Cong forces killed nine Americans on 6 February 1965 at Pleiku, Johnson ordered a series of reprisals. Most important, he initiated Operation ROLLING THUNDER, a sustained bombing campaign against North Vietnam.

Introduction of U.S. Troops. During the initial bombing campaign, Johnson maintained tight personal control over the war effort. Following the Pleiku incident, Westmoreland requested and Johnson approved the dispatch of two U.S. Marine battalions to protect the U.S. air base at Da Nang from Viet Cong attacks. Shortly after the first marines arrived, Johnson conferred with Secretary McNamara, Gen. Maxwell Taylor, and the Joint Chiefs of Staff in Honolulu. They agreed to send an additional 40,000 troops. Although this decision marked a major shift in policy, the president discouraged congressional and public debate on the issue. Johnson feared that a formal declaration of war might trigger a Soviet or Chinese response and was concerned that such a debate might interrupt passage of his Great Society program, which was then proceeding through Congress. Confident that Congress would defer to his will and that the Vietnamese could not resist U.S. power long enough to provoke significant antiwar opposition in the United States, Johnson deliberately misled the American public; the ground troops, he explained, were in Vietnam only to protect U.S. bases. Two months later, in April, the press revealed that U.S. forces had undertaken offensive operations.

At the same time, Johnson stated in a speech at Johns Hopkins University that the United States was prepared to discuss peace accords with North

Vietnam. The next month, partly in response to mounting public opposition to the expanding war in Vietnam, he approved a five-day bombing pause as a prelude to negotiations. The administration, however, was unwilling to accept anything less than an independent noncommunist South Vietnam, and North Vietnam, viewing Johnson's terms as unacceptable, continued its war against South Vietnam. Still no closer to peace, Johnson persuaded Congress to increase expenditures on Vietnam by $700 million.

Escalation. In July 1965, Secretary McNamara returned from Saigon with the warning that South Vietnam might soon collapse. Remembering the disastrous political consequence for Harry S. Truman of charges that he had "lost" China and had failed to gain victory in the Korean War, Johnson believed that the loss of Vietnam would destroy his presidency. On McNamara's recommendation, the president ordered the immediate deployment of 50,000 additional troops, with 50,000 more to follow later. Johnson also expanded their role, authorizing Westmoreland to use combat troops as he saw fit to strengthen the position of South Vietnamese forces. In addition, for the first time, Johnson approved saturation bombing of North Vietnamese strongholds in South Vietnam. Despite these dramatic changes in policy, the president explained his July decisions as little more than the continuation of past policy. In fact, his decisions to triple the number of U.S. soldiers and to expand the air campaign marked the beginning of an open-ended military commitment to preserve a noncommunist South Vietnam.

In early 1966 Johnson and South Vietnamese premier Nguyen Cao Ky met in Honolulu and agreed to a series of reforms designed to strengthen the South Vietnamese government. Through the Revolutionary Development Program, Johnson hoped to improve the standard of living of the South Vietnamese people, win greater support for U.S. military operations from the South Vietnamese, and undermine Viet Cong programs in rural areas. In June 1966, Johnson rejected suggestions by dissenting voices in his administration that he withdraw U.S. forces from Vietnam, approving instead General Westmoreland's request for a total of 431,000 troops, to be reached by mid 1967.

In December 1966, to counter growing domestic and international pressures for peace talks, Johnson halted the bombing campaign and sent Ambassador

Averell Harriman and Vice President Hubert Humphrey on missions to say that the United States was ready for negotiations. When North Vietnamese president Ho Chi Minh demanded a permanent halt to bombing as a condition of talks, Johnson refused. Instead, he resumed the bombing of North Vietnam. In response, Hanoi rebuffed a Polish-sponsored peace initiative and the fighting resumed.

Growth of Dissent. In 1967 Johnson came under increasing criticism at home and abroad for his handling of the war in Vietnam. Unwilling to unleash unrestrained use of U.S. power or to compromise the U.S. commitment to a noncommunist South Vietnam, Johnson was caught in the middle between right-wing "hawks" demanding further escalation and left-wing "doves" urging withdrawal from what they considered a Vietnamese civil war. Within his own administration, Johnson tried to balance conflicting points of view. He rejected the military's call for 200,000 more troops and mobilization of U.S. reserves, but at the same time he refused to back Secretary McNamara's proposals to halt the bombing, place a ceiling on U.S. troop levels, and limit ground operations. Instead, Johnson took a middle path, agreeing to an increase of 55,000 troops and lifting previous bombing restrictions.

Although Johnson publicly expressed confidence in the wisdom of his decisions, he was privately tormented by the growing domestic tensions over the war. Viewing himself as a great reform president who had advanced the causes of civil rights, education, medical care for the elderly, the environment, and the arts and humanities, he was deeply pained by attacks on him as a reactionary cold warrior more interested in imperial control for the United States than the freedom of Vietnam to choose its own destiny. Anguished by the increasing loss of U.S. and Vietnamese lives, Johnson took particular exception to chanting protesters asking: "Hey, hey, LBJ, how many kids did you kill today?" Yet Johnson's personal involvement in day-to-day operations of the war, including monitoring radio traffic of air-sea rescue attempts of downed aviators, extensive involvement in details of the Khe Sanh siege, and his personalization of the war as a conflict between himself and recalcitrant North Vietnamese leaders who rejected his overtures, blinded him to the larger issues of the war and U.S. involvement.

Throughout 1967 General Westmoreland issued a number of optimistic military reports that buoyed

Johnson and stiffened his resolve to continue the fighting despite the resignations of several important aides opposed to the war. To discredit war opponents outside of his administration, Johnson illegally used the Central Intelligence Agency (CIA) to investigate domestic antiwar groups that he believed were under the control of foreign communists. Johnson also created Vietnam Information Groups to win U.S. public opinion to his side in the debate over the war.

The Tet Offensive and Aftershocks. The February 1968 Tet Offensive, in which Viet Cong forces staged a concerted attack on the major cities of South Vietnam, discredited Johnson's and Westmoreland's optimistic assertions that the enemy had been severely crippled and that there was "light at the end of the tunnel." Although U.S. and South Vietnamese forces successfully repelled most of the assaults in a matter of days, images of Viet Cong troops infiltrating the U.S. embassy in Saigon and other U.S. strongholds around the country led a war-weary American public to conclude that the president had mismanaged the war or, at the very least, had misled the public about the capacity of the United States to win the conflict without great cost in blood and treasure. By the time of the Tet Offensive, more than 25,000 Americans had died in the fighting.

Shocked that after three years of steady escalation of force the Viet Cong and the North Vietnamese could still launch so bold an offensive, and deeply troubled by the erosion of public support for the war effort, Johnson rejected General Westmoreland's proposal to send 206,000 additional troops to Vietnam. Instead, he turned to new Secretary of Defense Clark Clifford for counsel and quickly accepted Clifford's recommendation that the United States limit its forces in Vietnam and that the South Vietnamese do more of the fighting.

Johnson's Role in the War Ends. In 1968, an election year, Johnson made several critical decisions that fundamentally altered the U.S. position in Vietnam. Opposed by Minnesota senator Eugene J. McCarthy, an antiwar candidate, in the presidential primaries, hurt by diminishing public approval, and convinced that South Vietnam was in a stronger position than before to defend itself, Johnson ended the policy of gradual escalation. On 31 March Johnson told the world that the bombing of North Vietnam would be reduced, that the United States was ready for talks, and that he would not run again for president.

Despite the start of formal peace talks in Paris later that year, the Johnson administration, like the North Vietnamese government, was unwilling to compromise on its goals with respect to the future of South Vietnam. During the talks, Johnson and his civilian advisers ordered military escalation to bolster their negotiating position, but that strategy had little effect on the continuing stalemate in Vietnam. A few weeks before the election, Johnson tried to help Hubert Humphrey, the Democratic nominee, by submitting new peace overtures, but the South Vietnamese, influenced by Richard Nixon's supporters, blocked the peace process.

Lyndon Johnson's escalation of the war in Vietnam divided Americans into warring camps, had cost 30,000 American lives by the time he left office, destroyed Johnson's presidency, and blocked further domestic reform, Johnson's principal goal. For Johnson, Vietnam was a tragedy that continues to affect his historical reputation.

BIBLIOGRAPHY

BORNET, VAUGHN DAVIS. *The Presidency of Lyndon Johnson.* 1983.

DALLEK, ROBERT. *Lone Star Rising: Lyndon Johnson and His Times, 1908–1960.* 1991.

JOHNSON, LYNDON B. *The Vantage Point: Perspectives of the Presidency, 1963–1969.* 1971.

KAHIN, GEORGE MCT. *Intervention: How America Became Involved in Vietnam.* 1988.

KEARNS, DORIS. *Lyndon Johnson and the American Dream.* 1976.

VANDEMARK, BRIAN. *Into the Quagmire: Lyndon Johnson and the Escalation of the Vietnam War.* 1991.

ROBERT DALLEK

Johnson, U. Alexis (1908–), U.S. Foreign Service officer, 1935–1977; deputy ambassador to South Vietnam in Saigon, 1964–1965. Johnson acted as the coordinator for the U.S. delegation to the Geneva Conference of 1954. During his stint in Saigon, he worked with Ambassador Maxwell Taylor to keep the South Vietnamese government intact.

BIBLIOGRAPHY

JOHNSON, U. ALEXIS, with JEF OLIVARIUS MCALLISTER. *The Right Hand of Power.* 1984.

PAUL M. TAILLON

Joint Chiefs of Staff. Created by the National Security Act of 1947, the U.S. Joint Chiefs of Staff (JCS) comprise the army chief of staff, the air force chief of staff, the chief of naval operations, and the commandant of the Marine Corps—plus a nonvoting chairman. The JCS advise the president on military matters and are responsible for strategic planning and review of major logistical and personnel requirements of the armed forces. Since the Defense Reorganization Act of 1958 removed the JCS from direct operational control over troops (the chain of command), they report directly to the secretary of defense and issue orders in his name. They meet in the Pentagon's Gold Room, known as "the Tank." During the Vietnam War, the JCS had six chairmen and thirty different members, which made for much discontinuity. Many of the members retired in frustration, feeling ignored or manipulated by civilian leaders. Lawrence Korb's postwar interviews noted that former JCS members harbored "unimaginable amounts and depths of resentment."

The JCS were not without fault in the Vietnam War, however. Interservice rivalry and bureaucratic intransigence often obstructed the flow of information between U.S. and South Vietnamese officials. Presidents Kennedy, Johnson, and Nixon all grew to distrust advice they received from the JCS. Top brass proved reluctant to offer realistic appraisals of the war's progress lest they appear disloyal or cast their service branch in a bad light. Most often the JCS voiced the military's dislike of political control over war strategy. They consistently advocated increased bombing of North Vietnam, greater U.S. troop commitments, and more aggressive tactics regardless of the costs. "Bomb, bomb, bomb, that's all you know," Johnson complained, but the entire JCS threatened to resign if he deescalated the war in 1967. When the JCS recommended calling up the reserves in 1968, President Johnson refused and sub-

JOINT CHIEFS OF STAFF, 1965. The Joint Chiefs oversaw the U.S. military's build-up in Vietnam. Seated, left to right: Admiral David L. McDonald, chief of naval operations; General Earl G. Wheeler, chairman, Joint Chiefs of Staff; General Harold K. Johnson, army chief of staff. Standing, left to right: General John P. McConnell, air force chief of staff; General Wallace M. Greene, commandant of the Marine Corps. *National Archives*

sequently withdrew from the presidential race. President Nixon promised to unleash the JCS from political constraints, but he found that "all they could think of was resuming the bombing of the North."

Throughout the war, the JCS was "unable to articulate an effective military strategy," according to Gen. Bruce Palmer, deputy commanding general, Military Assistance Command, Vietnam (MACV). In August 1965, the JCS officially recognized U.S. objectives in Vietnam: keep China out of the war, end North Vietnam's support for insurgency, and expand the authority of South Vietnam's government throughout the South. But the recommended means for achieving these political ends were entirely military: interdict communist supply routes, destroy communist forces, and improve the Army of the Republic of Vietnam (ARVN). Pacifying the countryside or rallying the people to support their government did not interest the generals. The JCS never grasped the political nature of the war, which they viewed as a military test of strength. Lawrence Korb's study concluded: "In Vietnam the JCS became advocates of a policy that continually widened the scope of the war and raised the stakes in a desperate attempt to achieve some form of victory, a policy that increasingly disenchanted larger and larger segments of the American public."

BIBLIOGRAPHY

BALDWIN, HANSON W. *Strategy for Tomorrow.* 1970.
KORB, LAWRENCE J. *The Joint Chiefs of Staff: The First Twenty-Five Years.* 1976.
PALMER, BRUCE, JR. *The 25-Year War: America's Military Role in Vietnam.* 1984.

GLEN GENDZEL

Joint General Staff.

South Vietnam's counterpart to the U.S. Joint Chiefs of Staff (JCS), the Joint General Staff (JGS) included the branch commanders of the Republic of Vietnam Armed Forces (RVNAF): the Army of the Republic of Vietnam (ARVN), the Republic of Vietnam Air Force (VNAF), and the Vietnamese Navy (VNN), which included the Vietnamese Marine Corp (VNMC). The JGS also had deputy chiefs of staff (all ARVN officers) for personnel, logistics, political warfare, and operations. Unlike the JCS, the JGS had direct operational control over troops, who often became pawns in personal and political intrigues among rival generals. The JGS had their own compound outside Saigon at Tan Son Nhut, close to the headquarters of the Military Assistance Command, Vietnam (MACV). Gen. William Westmoreland deluged the JGS with memos, advice, and personal emissaries. Considerable prodding was required to induce the JGS to enact military reforms, and when they acted, the JGS usually just transferred incompetent or thieving commanders. Army historian Lt. Col. Jeffrey Clarke considered the JGS "rife with corruption, and characterized by mismanagement and a general absence of command interest." Yet the United States never demanded "a complete overhaul" for fear it would be "too risky, too dangerous, too liable to upset the delicate political structure in Saigon," and too indicative of American control. Despite the JGS's supposed autonomy, longtime JGS chief of staff Gen. Cao Van Vien complained in 1969: "We Vietnamese have no military doctrine because the command of all operations in Vietnam is in the hands of the American side."

BIBLIOGRAPHY

CAO VAN VIEN and DONG VAN KHUYEN. *Reflections on the Vietnam War.* 1980.
CLARKE, JEFFREY J. *The United States Army in Vietnam, Advice and Support: The Final Years, 1965–1973.* 1988.
DONG VAN KHUYEN. *The RVNAF.* 1980.
GOODMAN, ALLAN E. *An Institutional Profile of the South Vietnamese Officer Corps.* 1970.
SMITH, HARVEY J., et al. *Area Handbook for South Vietnam.* 1967.
TRAN VAN DON. *Our Endless War: Inside Vietnam.* 1978.

GLEN GENDZEL

Jones, David C.

(1921–), general, U.S. Air Force; vice commander, Seventh Air Force, 1969; commander, Second Air Force, 1969–1971. A flight instructor in World War II and a bomber pilot in the Korean War, Jones served as vice commander and director of operations of the Seventh Air Force in Vietnam in 1969. He helped plan the secret bombing of Cambodia and kept it concealed from Congress under Operation MENU. Promoted to full general in 1971, he left Vietnam to command U.S. Air Forces in Europe. He succeeded Gen. George Brown as U.S. Air Force chief of staff in 1974, and as chairman of the Joint Chiefs of Staff in 1978. Jones retired in 1982.

BIBLIOGRAPHY

BERGER, CARL, ed. *The United States Air Force in Southeast Asia, 1961–1973.* 1977.
JONES, DAVID C. "America's Military Edge over Russia is Disappearing." *U.S. News and World Report,* 30 October 1978.

JONES, DAVID C. *Defense Challenges of the 1980s.* 1983.
"Team Player for the Joint Chiefs." *Time,* 17 April 1978.
WEINRAUB, BERNARD. "General Named Head of Chiefs."
    New York Times, 6 April 1978.

GLEN GENDZEL

Justice, Department of.

Justice, Department of. From 1965 to 1973, the U.S. Department of Justice confronted growing dissent and social unrest resulting from the Vietnam War. The agency's response reflected the different outlooks of its Democratic and Republican attorneys general under the Johnson and Nixon administrations. Johnson's appointees generally pursued restrained policies toward antiwar activities, while Republican officials tended toward more repressive measures. Despite differences, however, the department's policies displayed continuities over the course of the war. Both administrations sought to monitor and destabilize antiwar groups through infiltration and electronic surveillance. During the Johnson administration, the Federal Bureau of Investigation (FBI), the investigatory arm of the department, launched the COINTELPRO program of infiltration and disinformation of New Left activities, which continued through the Nixon era. The department similarly established intelligence surveillance of domestic antiwar groups beginning in the mid 1960s. Carried out by the FBI as well as by the U.S. Army, this campaign consisted primarily of covert infiltration and wiretapping.

As protests escalated in 1965, the department stepped up its activities, driven initially by concern over Communist Party infiltration of the antiwar movement. After the weekend of the International Days of Protests (15–16 October 1965), Attorney General Nicholas Katzenbach promised President Johnson a nationwide investigation of the antiwar movement. Citing statutes criminalizing interference with the draft and federal sedition laws, Katzenbach hinted that prosecutions might be forthcoming. Nevertheless, neither Katzenbach nor his successor, Ramsey Clark, agreed to carry out a prosecutorial witch-hunt; numerous department officials and others feared a reappearance of red-baiting and McCarthyism. To the dismay of conservative congressional critics, the department's prosecution record against draft resisters from 1965 to 1966 was almost nil, as it refused to equate antiwar dissent with treason or sedition. Nevertheless, Clark, perhaps reluctantly, agreed to prosecute the famed pediatrician Dr. Benjamin Spock for his antiwar activities.

Publicly, the administration upheld dissent as a right. For example, in 1966 Clark refused to endorse a bill sponsored by the House Committee on Un-American Activities to criminalize protests, and he opposed the Selective Service System's attempts to punish draft resisters by reclassifying their status to immediate service availability. Clark also chose not to prevent large-scale protests at the March on the Pentagon in 1967 and at the Democratic convention in 1968, despite having received intelligence that protesters intended to provoke clashes with police (and in the Pentagon march, even incite race riots in Washington, D.C.). Clark increased police preparations and contingency plans for potential violence, rather than canceling the marches under his authority to prevent civil disorders.

Under John Mitchell, the new attorney general in the Nixon administration, the Justice Department pursued a more confrontational policy toward antiwar activities. In 1969, Assistant Attorney General Richard Kleindienst inflamed an increasingly tense situation when he said that participants in the November 1969 march on Washington had reputations for violence and "we must assume that they may engage in violence here." In 1971, Assistant Attorney General William H. Rehnquist supported the suspension of normal arrest procedures in order to facilitate the detention of twelve thousand protesters in Washington, D. C. Nixon administration officials, who believed enemies were besieging the nation, found the Justice Department and the FBI to be too timid. In 1970, the White House proposed the Huston Plan for an interagency working group to practice a wide range of undermining activities such as mail openings, burglaries, wiretapping, break-ins, and infiltrations. The FBI balked at this riot of governmental illegality, but primarily out of concern for its image and for defending its own surveillance prerogatives.

The Justice Department still sought to find some constitutional cover for wiretaps deployed without judicial approval. Attorney General John Mitchell sought to bypass the Fourth Amendment with an appeal to an overarching exercise of presidential defense of national security. The Supreme Court rejected this argument in *United States v. U.S. District Court for the Eastern District of Michigan* (407 U.S. 297 [1972]).

Despite differences between the Johnson and Nixon Justice Departments, similarities can also be traced: both prosecuted high-profile antiwar figures and under both administrations, the department maintained electronic surveillance of antiwar groups and infiltrated these organizations.

[*See also* Federal Bureau of Investigation (FBI); Huston Plan.]

BIBLIOGRAPHY

ELLIFF, JOHN T. *Crime, Dissent, and the Attorney General: The Justice Department in the 1960s.* 1971.

ELLIFF, JOHN T. *The Reform of FBI Intelligence Operations.* 1979.

KUTLER, STANLEY. *The Wars of Watergate.* 1990.

VICTOR JEW AND ADAM LAND

K

Kampuchea. *See* Cambodia.

Katzenbach, Nicholas (1922–), U.S. attorney general, 1965–1966; undersecretary of state, 1966–1969. Katzenbach loyally supported the war effort. As attorney general in 1965, Katzenbach promised to investigate those who protested against the draft. As undersecretary of state, Katzenbach testified before the Senate Foreign Relations Committee on 17 August 1967, and offered a broad interpretation of presidential power to initiate military action. Congress's role, he said, was primarily to ratify the president's decisions. Katzenbach testified that congressional ratification of the Southeast Asia Treaty Organization (SEATO) treaty of 1954 and the passage of the Tonkin Gulf Resolution gave such authority to the president. Yet in 1973, Katzenbach charged that President Nixon had exceeded his constitutional powers, and Katzenbach supported the pending War Powers Resolution.

BIBLIOGRAPHY

ELLIFF, JOHN T. *Crime, Dissent, and the Attorney General: The Justice Department in the 1960's.* 1971.

WILLIAMS, WILLIAM APPLEMAN, et al. *America in Vietnam: A Documentary History.* 1985.

VICTOR JEW

Kennan, George (1904–), State Department official at the U.S. embassy in Moscow, 1933–1935 and 1944–1946; director of State Department policy planning staff, 1947; ambassador to the Soviet Union, 1942; ambassador to Yugoslavia, 1961–1963. Kennan formulated the policy of containment in 1947 that became the foundation for U.S. foreign policy for four decades. Containment was intended to prevent the spread of communism and was grounded in the belief that the Soviet Union, and later the People's Republic of China, would aggressively try to foster communism throughout the world. The policy of containment held that the United States and its Western allies must use all means necessary, including military force, to prevent the Soviet Union and China from building communist empires that would threaten democratic nations and U.S. economic interests. In numerous articles, speeches, and, most powerfully, in testimony before the Senate Foreign Relations Committee in

1966, Kennan, intellectual father of U.S. Cold War policy, criticized U.S. involvement in Vietnam, arguing that Vietnam had no strategic or economic significance and stating that he opposed the military effort. Kennan insisted that any further escalation would seriously reduce the chances for détente with the Soviet Union and China, imperiling relations that were far more important to U.S. interests than the future of Vietnam. His criticism of U.S. policy was a serious blow to the Johnson administration and a boost to the antiwar community.

BIBLIOGRAPHY

AMBROSE, STEPHEN E. *Rise to Globalism.* Rev. ed. 1988.
POWERS, THOMAS. *The War at Home.* 1973.

KELLY EVANS-PFEIFER

Kennedy, Edward M. (1932–), U.S. senator (D-Mass.), 1962–. During his first six years in office, Edward Kennedy focused primarily on domestic issues, although he offered limited support to Johnson's Vietnam policy in January 1966 by not opposing the bombing of North Vietnam. As chairman of the subcommittee on refugees, he visited

THE KENNEDY BROTHERS. Edward M. Kennedy, right, with Robert F. Kennedy on the steps of the U.S. Capitol, 1966. *National Archives*

South Vietnam in 1965 and in 1967 began to criticize America's failure to help the victims of war. Kennedy became openly outspoken against the war in Vietnam after the assassination of his brother, Robert, on 4 June 1968. On 21 August Kennedy outlined a four-point plan to end the war. This plan included an end to the bombing of North Vietnam, negotiations with North Vietnam to remove all foreign troops from South Vietnam, formation of a government in South Vietnam that could survive a U.S. departure, and a decrease in the U.S. military presence to begin in 1968. Along with Senators Eugene J. McCarthy (D-Minn.) and George McGovern (D-S. Dak.), Kennedy sponsored a similar plank at the 1968 Democratic convention, but the delegates voted against it, 1,567 ¾ to 1,041 ¼.

Kennedy continued as a vocal opponent of President Nixon's war policy. He denounced the battle for Ap Bia (Hamburger Hill), gave a speech at the Boston protest of 100,000 people in the 1969 moratorium (student strike and teach-ins against the war), criticized Nixon's apparent lack of a timetable for ending the war, and sharply condemned the invasion of Cambodia. In 1970 Kennedy demanded a withdrawal from Cambodia and Vietnam, and by 1973 he fully opposed the war in Vietnam.

BIBLIOGRAPHY

BURNER, DAVID, and THOMAS R. WEST. *The Torch Is Passed: The Kennedy Brothers and American Liberalism.* 1984.
GALLOWAY, JOHN, ed. *The Kennedys and Vietnam.* 1971.

ELLEN BAKER

Kennedy, John F. (1917–1963), U.S. representative (D-Mass.), 1947–1953; U.S. senator (D-Mass.), 1953–1960; U.S. president, 1961–1963. During the administration of John F. Kennedy, the United States substantially deepened its commitment to the South Vietnamese regime. In order to help the Diem government quell an increasingly effective communist insurgency, the president authorized an increase in U.S. advisers from just under 600 at the time that he assumed office to more than 16,000 by the end of 1963. In addition, he permitted those advisers to participate in combat operations; supported covert operations against North Vietnam; pronounced publicly America's unequivocal commitment to the preservation of a noncommunist South Vietnam; warned the Soviet Union to cease its support for the guerrillas; and encouraged the South Vietnamese military to assume power through ex-

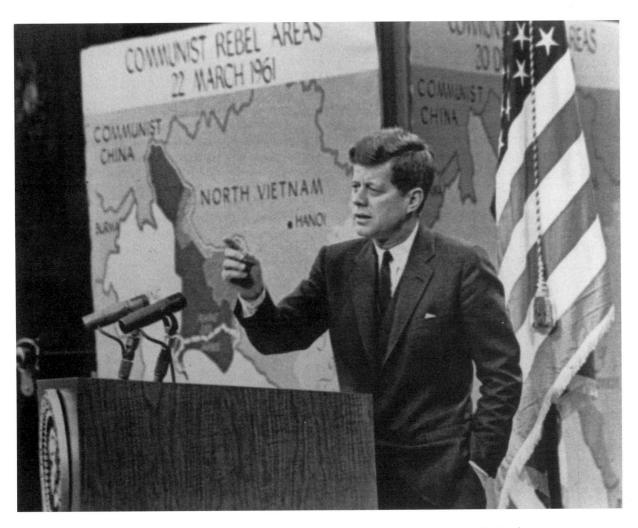

JOHN F. KENNEDY. Giving a press conference on the Laotian situation, 23 March 1961. *National Archives*

tra-legal means. Kennedy's assassination on 22 November 1963 leaves unresolvable questions about what path he would have followed had he lived.

Why Kennedy saw vital U.S. interests at stake in Vietnam has sparked less controversy. Scholars, journalists, and former associates agree that Vietnam served for Kennedy as a powerful symbol of America's commitment to contain communist advances in the developing world. As early as 1956, then-Senator Kennedy called South Vietnam "the cornerstone of the Free World in Southeast Asia," characterizing that struggling young nation as "a test of American responsibility and determination." Although he recognized that Vietnam's intrinsic economic and strategic importance to the United States was minimal, President Kennedy and his top foreign policy advisers believed that it held great symbolic value at a time of heightened Cold War tensions. He and his senior aides calculated that a communist victory in Vietnam would deal a severe blow to America's worldwide prestige and credibility, further embolden aggressive adversaries in the Soviet Union and the People's Republic of China, and lead its allies to doubt U.S. power and resolve. Kennedy also worried that a communist victory in Vietnam would spark an intensely divisive political debate at home, comparable to the "who lost China" inquisition that had damaged President Harry S. Truman a decade earlier. Thus, international and domestic factors impelled Kennedy toward ever-greater involvement in Southeast Asia during his three years in the White House.

Vietnam did not at first emerge as a major foreign policy crisis for the new president. Cuba, the Congo, and Berlin occupied far more of Kennedy's attention during his early months in office, as did another part of Indochina: Laos. In the spring of 1961 Kennedy sought a negotiated settlement of the Laotian civil war, a decision that led eventually to communist participation in a coalition government. The Laos compromise actually undermined the prospects for a similar compromise in Vietnam. Acutely conscious of images, and fearful of being judged weak by friends and foes in the wake of the Laos settlement and the Bay of Pigs debacle in Cuba, Kennedy determined to avoid any additional Cold War defeats or retreats. Consequently, in May 1961 he authorized a modest increase in the number of advisers attached to the U.S. Military Assistance Advisory Group (MAAG) in Vietnam, and also sent 400 Green Berets, members of U.S. Special Forces units, to Vietnam to help train the South Vietnamese military in counterinsurgency techniques.

That modest increase in U.S. support, however, did little to ease the panoply of problems facing South Vietnamese Premier Ngo Dinh Diem. In September 1961 Diem urgently requested a significant increase in U.S. economic assistance. In view of the growing strength and boldness of the Viet Cong guerrillas, who already controlled over 50 percent of the South Vietnamese countryside, Diem's request forced a painful set of decisions on the cautious Kennedy. Fearing that an allied government's very survival might be hanging in the balance, yet instinctively reluctant to permit open-ended expansion in the U.S. commitment, Kennedy dispatched his trusted military adviser Gen. Maxwell D. Taylor and National Security Council aide Walt W. Rostow to Saigon to provide him with a first-hand report.

The Taylor-Rostow assessment recommended the immediate dispatch of an 8,000-man logistical task force as a minimal step in order to ensure the survival of the Saigon regime, with the caveat that more drastic measures might be required in the near future. During the administration's extended deliberations about the Taylor-Rostow report, several advisers, including the Joint Chiefs of Staff (JCS), urged the dispatch of regular combat troops while others urged the president to seek a negotiated settlement similar to that concluded in Laos. Kennedy rejected the combat force option as "a last resort." He also staunchly opposed any neutralization scheme as a potentially dangerous sign of American

weakness. Instead, the president chose a middle course, opting to increase the number of U.S. advisers and the volume of U.S. aid in the hopes that those steps would bolster the South Vietnamese government sufficiently to preclude the need for regular U.S. combat units.

Kennedy's limited commitment of November 1961 postponed, but did not resolve, the core problems facing America's South Vietnamese ally. Over the next year, his middle course brought greater U.S. influence to bear on the conduct of military operations in Vietnam. U.S. equipment and expertise lent valuable assistance to the counterinsurgency campaign of the South Vietnamese army, enabling it to gain the initiative for the first time. Upon the urging of U.S. advisers, Diem's government also inaugurated the strategic hamlet program to separate and protect the peasantry from the Viet Cong guerrillas and their North Vietnamese allies, a program intended to serve as a political adjunct to the military effort. In tandem the new U.S.-aided initiatives appeared to yield at least modest progress throughout 1962, generating optimistic forecasts about the Diem government's prospects among many top U.S. experts.

That military-political progress soon proved illusory. Viet Cong forces had by early 1963 adapted effectively to the widespread utilization of helicopters by the South Vietnamese and U.S. armed forces, largely neutralizing that tactical innovation. The strategic hamlet program also faced severe limitations. With the local Self-Defense Corps and Provincial Civil Guard units of the Diem government increasingly unwilling to engage large and determined Viet Cong forces, government control over the strategic hamlets steadily eroded. The growing dependence of the Diem government on the United States, moreover, led to increased tension, resentment, and bitterness between the United States and South Vietnam.

Early in 1963, Kennedy sent Assistant Secretary of State Roger Hilsman and National Security Council staffer Michael Forrestal to South Vietnam to gauge the efficacy of the U.S. program. Upon their return, they sent Kennedy an appraisal that mixed frank criticism of the current situation with cautious optimism about the future. The Hilsman-Forrestal report questioned the effectiveness of the South Vietnamese army, the degree to which the strategic hamlet program was being successfully implemented, and the level of popular support for Diem. Although Hilsman and Forrestal concluded

VIETNAMESE MOURN KENNEDY. Students march through the streets of Saigon carrying banners mourning President Kennedy's death, November 1963. *National Archives*

that the United States and South Vietnam were "probably winning" the conflict, they cautioned that the war would "probably last longer than we would like" and "cost more in terms of both lives and money than we had anticipated." Although critical of the leadership and efficiency of the Diem regime, the Hilsman-Forrestal report gave Kennedy no hint of impending crisis. The president consequently saw no need to redirect or reassess U.S. policy; he viewed the conflict in Southeast Asia as primarily an operational problem.

The complacent assumptions undergirding Kennedy's approach to Vietnam were decisively shattered in the spring and summer of 1963. A series of demonstrations against Diem's dictatorial rule, led by Buddhists, students, and other disaffected groups within South Vietnam, crystallized for Kennedy and his foreign policy experts the depth of the internal opposition to the Diem regime. Diem's heavy-handed response to those protests, capped by brutal government-sanctioned raids on Buddhist pagodas in August, brought South Vietnamese society to the brink of chaos. Even more alarming, from Kennedy's perspective, were the indications that Diem was seriously considering opening negotiations with the Viet Cong.

A consensus soon developed among the president, most of his top national security aides in Washington, and U.S. Ambassador Henry Cabot Lodge in Saigon that Diem posed a fundamental obstacle to U.S. policy objectives in Vietnam. They remained deeply divided, however, on precisely how to deal with the problem. Some Kennedy administration officials insisted that the United States should cooperate with elements of the South Vietnamese military who were seeking to overthrow Diem. Others staunchly opposed so drastic a step, urging instead that the United States should apply selective political and economic sanctions on the Diem regime to force it to reform. Initially Kennedy leaned toward the first option. Thus in August 1963 he authorized Lodge to cooperate with a group of South Vietnamese officers who were plotting a coup against Diem. When that plot proved abortive, however, Kennedy decided to apply the "selective pressures" against Diem that Taylor and McNamara recommended after a brief trip to Saigon in October.

A month later another group of coup planners asked for U.S. backing. With his advisers once again at odds over how the United States should respond, Kennedy vacillated. Taking a characteristic middle course, he ordered U.S. representatives neither directly to encourage nor discourage the plotters. The anti-Diem generals almost certainly interpreted that ambiguous signal as a green light for their plans. On 1 November 1963, the military intriguers seized power, in the process murdering Diem and his brother, Ngo Dinh Nhu. The brutal double slaying greatly disturbed Kennedy, who doubtless accepted a degree of personal responsibility for the deaths. Three weeks later the president was murdered in Dallas.

How Kennedy would have responded to the mounting political turmoil and deepening security crisis that gripped post-coup South Vietnam has divided analysts of the Vietnam War ever since. Just before his fateful trip to Dallas, the president made a few statements that betrayed a growing skepticism about U.S. involvement in Vietnam; he even ordered a modest reduction in the number of U.S. advisers stationed there. On the other hand, there is no evidence that he had begun to reexamine the core assumption on which U.S. involvement had been based: namely, that the preservation of a noncommunist South Vietnam was vital to U.S. global interests. The fact that Kennedy's closest national security advisers were the same men whose advice President Johnson followed when he decided to commit U.S. combat forces in the spring of 1965 suggests the strong likelihood that Kennedy would have followed a similar course.

BIBLIOGRAPHY

BASSET, LAWRENCE J., and STEPHEN E. PELZ. "The Failed Search for Victory: Vietnam and the Politics of War." In *Kennedy's Search for Victory: American Foreign Policy, 1961–1963*, edited by Thomas G. Paterson. 1989.

HALBERSTAM, DAVID. *The Best and the Brightest*. 1992.

HAMMER, ELLEN J. *A Death in November: America in Vietnam, 1963*. 1987.

HERRING, GEORGE C. *America's Longest War: The United States and Vietnam, 1950–1975*. 1986.

NEWMAN, JOHN M. *JFK and Vietnam: Deception, Intrigue, and the Struggle for Power*. 1992.

PARMET, HERBERT S. *JFK: The Presidency of John F. Kennedy*. 1983.

RUST, WILLIAM J. *Kennedy in Vietnam*. 1985.

ROBERT J. MCMAHON

Kennedy, Robert F. (1925–1968), U.S. attorney general, 1961–1964; U.S. senator (D-N.Y.), 1964–1968. Robert F. Kennedy moved from un-

ROBERT F. KENNEDY. Speaking at a civil rights demonstration in Washington, D.C., outside the Department of Justice, June 1963. *Library of Congress*

conditional support for President John F. Kennedy's Vietnam policies to strong criticism of their continuation in the late 1960s. After his brother's assassination in 1963, Robert Kennedy remained in Johnson's cabinet as attorney general for several months. He resigned in 1964 and was elected to the U.S. Senate from New York. During the domestic debate over Vietnam policy in 1965, Kennedy supported Johnson, voting in May for a supplemental appropriations bill. At the same time, in his first major Senate speech on Vietnam, Kennedy articulated three possible policies that the United States could pursue: withdrawal, military escalation, or "honorable negotiations." By June 1965 Kennedy more clearly identified the need for political as well as military solutions to the conflict, and by the end of the year he expressed concern that the United States and South Vietnam had not developed political and economic strategies to establish a stable government in South Vietnam. Still he continued to support Johnson. Kennedy opposed resuming bombing of North Vietnam after the Christmas 1965 truce, but he refused to join fifteen senators in a letter condemning Johnson's action.

On 19 February 1966 Kennedy broke with the Johnson administration, calling for a coalition government in South Vietnam even without a complete North Vietnamese withdrawal from the south. Yet he dismissed any suggestion of a U.S. withdrawal. Johnson's press secretary, Bill Moyers, tried to diminish the difference between Kennedy and the president by stating that Johnson supported a coalition government after free elections. Kennedy neither endorsed nor condemned the bombing of Hanoi and Haiphong in June 1966, and for the rest of the year he remained silent on the war, even as domestic dissent escalated. During a Western European tour in January 1967, Kennedy received notice that North Vietnam would consider negotiations with the United States in return for an end to the bombings. The news was leaked and Johnson, believing that Kennedy intended to embarrass him, renewed his commitment to a military victory. Kennedy later denied receiving any peace message from North Vietnam.

Kennedy moved more decisively when he sharply criticized Johnson's resumption of bombing after the Tet truce in early 1967. On 2 March he blamed himself and his brother John F. Kennedy for having pursued the wrong policy. Kennedy continued his attacks on U.S. policy throughout 1967, although he never advocated a unilateral withdrawal of U.S. troops. After the 1968 Tet Offensive, Kennedy criticized the South Vietnamese government as an ineffective ally and advocated a political compromise. The United States, he believed, must eventually accept a political settlement with the National Liberation Front (NLF).

To some extent Kennedy's growing criticism of Johnson's war policies stemmed from his own presidential ambitions, which he declared openly on 16 March 1968. The political mantle that he inherited from his brother made him a serious threat to Johnson. In the campaign for the Democratic nomination he made the war the central issue, repeatedly advocating a negotiated solution. He differed from his strongest opponent, Sen. Eugene J. McCarthy (D-Minn.), in rejecting a coalition government for South Vietnam before negotiations took place. He was assassinated on 5 June 1968 in Los Angeles after winning the California primary.

BIBLIOGRAPHY

GALLOWAY, JOHN, ed. *The Kennedys and Vietnam.* 1971

KENNEDY, ROBERT F. *To Seek a Newer World.* 1967.

SCHLESINGER, ARTHUR M., JR. *Robert Kennedy and His Times.* 1978.

ELLEN BAKER

Kent State University. President Nixon's 30 April 1970 televised announcement that troops had invaded Cambodia to attack North Vietnamese and Viet Cong bases prompted student protests across the United States. Students at Kent State University in Ohio staged a demonstration that degenerated into a riot on 1 May. On 2 May, protesting students burned down the campus Reserve Officers' Training Corps (ROTC) building. In response, Governor James Rhodes called in the National Guard.

At midday on Monday, 4 May, students gathered to protest the Cambodian invasion and the presence of the National Guard on campus. National Guard soldiers moved in with tear gas to disperse the crowd and encountered heckling and rock throwing. Without warning, some of the soldiers fired upon the students, killing four and wounding at least nine. The protestors were not a serious threat to the lives of the National Guard soldiers; some victims were not even involved in the demonstration, but were merely walking through the area.

The Kent State shootings provoked protests on other, already turbulent, campuses. Hundreds of schools closed because of protests and the incident increased participation in the New Mobilization's (New Mobe) 9 May march in Washington, D.C.

A grand jury later exonerated the National Guard soldiers, while twenty-five protestors were indicted. Three were convicted of minor misdemeanors; all other charges were dropped or resulted in acquittals.

BIBLIOGRAPHY

DAVIES, PETER. *The Truth about Kent State: A Challenge to the American Conscience.* 1973.

PRESIDENT'S COMMITTEE ON CAMPUS UNREST. *Report of the President's Committee on Campus Unrest.* 1970.

WILLIAM PAUL SCHUCK

Khang, Le Nguyen. *See* Le Nguyen Khang.

Khanh, Nguyen. *See* Nguyen Khanh.

Khe Sanh. A Marine Corps base whose encirclement by elements of three North Vietnamese divisions in early 1968 marked one of the defining events of the Vietnam War. Located in the northwestern sector of South Vietnam, approximately 10 kilometers (6 miles) from the Laotian border and about 23 kilometers (14 miles) south of the DMZ, Khe Sanh was surrounded by tall, tree-canopied hills, some more than 1,000 meters (3,000 feet) in elevation. Khe Sanh overlooked Route 9, the main eastward entryway from Laos into South Vietnam's northern coastal region.

Establishing the Base. In August 1962, the Military Assistance Command, Vietnam (MACV), established a U.S. Army Special Forces camp for border surveillance near Khe Sanh, which was briefly reinforced by a Marine battalion in April 1966. A few months later, over the objections of the Marine command, Gen. William Westmoreland insisted that the Marines establish a base at Khe Sanh. Concerned over possible North Vietnamese infiltration, Westmoreland also viewed Khe Sanh as a possible staging area for an allied offensive into Laos. In October, the Marines built a one-battalion base just above the Special Forces camp. Reduced in strength for a time to that of one company, the garrison was reinforced by the III Marine Amphibious Force (MAF) to regimental strength in the spring of 1967. From 24 April through 12 May 1967, the 3d Marines engaged North Vietnamese regulars for a series of strategic hills, retaining the hills after heavy casualties on both sides. The 26th Marines replaced the 3d Marines, but kept only one battalion, its 1st at Khe Sanh.

By the end of 1967, U.S. intelligence indicated that elements of three North Vietnamese Army (NVA) divisions were in the Khe Sanh sector. Since the late summer or early fall, NVA forces had successfully cut Route 9 and the only means of resupply for the base was by air. The U.S. command reinforced Khe Sanh and by 24 January 1968, the 26th Marines' commander, Col. David E. Lownds, had one artillery and four infantry battalions under his operational control. With small detachments from the other services and the approximately 300-man South Vietnamese 37th ARVN Ranger battalion, the Khe Sanh defenders numbered more than 6,000 troops.

Fearful of a debacle similar to that of the French at Dien Bien Phu in 1954, President Lyndon B. Johnson sought repeated guarantees from Westmoreland and the Joint Chiefs of Staff (JCS) that Khe Sanh would

not be overrun. They reassured him that given the U.S. artillery and air support available to the Marines at Khe Sanh, the base could be defended indefinitely. Westmoreland had already instituted an all-out air assault including both tactical aircraft and B-52 bombers, Operation NIAGARA, against North Vietnamese troop positions. The MACV staff also studied the possible use of tactical nuclear weapons at Khe Sanh, but never seriously proposed their use. Despite the array of U.S. firepower, the specter of Dien Bien Phu was to haunt Johnson and his personal advisers throughout the siege, a fear reinforced by press analogies to the French experience.

The Battle Commences. On 21 January, forewarned by an NVA defector, the Marine outpost on Hill 861 beat back a determined assault by NVA infantry. While their ground forces were unable to capture any Marine positions, North Vietnamese artillery, which included Soviet-made 152 mm howitzers firing from positions in Laos, scored a direct hit on a Marine ammunition supply point, destroying about 1,500 tons of high explosive. Marine casualties for the day were 14 dead and 43 wounded. The battle for Khe Sanh had begun.

While the enemy launched occasional battalion-size ground attacks on exposed Marine positions, North Vietnamese forces confined most of their activity to small probing assaults and artillery, mortar, and rocket bombardment. Throughout the Tet Offensive launched shortly before the siege, the situation at Khe Sanh remained much the same. On 7 February a North Vietnamese division overran the U.S. Special Forces camp, manned by approximately 350 Brou Montagnards and 24 U.S. advisers, that had moved to Lang Vei, about 14 kilometers (9 miles) southwest of the Khe Sanh base. Fearing an ambush in the rugged terrain separating the two bases, Colonel Lownds refused to send a reaction force. Almost 300 of the Lang Vei garrison were killed, wounded, or missing, including 10 U.S. Special Forces soldiers killed or missing and 13 wounded. The heaviest loss to U.S. forces occurred on 25 February, when the North Vietnamese ambushed a Marine platoon, inflicting 48 casualties. Four nights later, on 29 February, NVA forces attempted to breach the South Vietnamese Ranger battalion's perimeter, but were repulsed with heavy losses when caught in the open by devastating artillery fire and a B-52 ARC LIGHT strike. The artillery and bombs killed more than 70 NVA soldiers, while the South Vietnamese Rangers suffered only 1 wounded.

From 22 January through 31 March 1968, U.S. aircraft conducted Operation NIAGARA in support of Khe Sanh. While B-52s and U.S. tactical aircraft dropped thousands of tons of high explosives on North Vietnamese positions, U.S. Air Force and Marine transport aircraft brought in food and ammunition. Although enemy antiaircraft fire and artillery kept large marine and air force transports from landing at the exposed Khe Sanh airfield, the air force devised several sophisticated parachute drop techniques to keep the base resupplied. The Marine Corps developed the "Super Gaggle," a mix of fixed-wing tactical aircraft and helicopters, to get supplies to the Khe Sanh hill outposts.

Relief and Aftermath. Using seismic and acoustic sensors closely coordinated with U.S. artillery and aviation, the Marines at Khe Sanh held the enemy at bay until the northeast monsoon weather broke and reinforcements arrived. By 15 April, in Operation PEGASUS, a relieving joint and combined Army-Marine and South Vietnamese Army task force, under the 1st Cavalry Division, had broken through and lifted the siege. General Westmoreland vetoed initial plans to raze the base, but after he relinquished command of MACV in June, his successor, Gen. Creighton W. Abrams, ordered the abandonment of Khe Sanh. On 5 July the Marines officially closed the base.

Controversy still surrounds the battle. It is not known if the North Vietnamese really intended to take Khe Sanh or if the attack was merely a feint to lure U.S. forces away from the cities. U.S. intelligence identified elements of one of the divisions supposedly at Khe Sanh taking part in the battle for Hue in February 1968. It is certain, however, that North Vietnamese troops surrounded the base and would have taken Khe Sanh if they had been able. It was the presence of U.S. troops on the ground supported by massive artillery and air bombardment that prevented North Vietnamese forces from doing so.

U.S. estimates of NVA soldiers killed ranged from 1,600 to more than 15,000 for the period from November 1967 through March 1968. Most of these casualties resulted from U.S. supporting arms, especially air force B-52 ARC LIGHT strikes, which dropped more than 60,000 tons of high explosives on North Vietnamese positions. During the same period, there were 200 U.S. troops killed and more than 1,600 wounded. Ironically, more than 400 U.S. soldiers were killed in the Khe Sanh sector following the siege through the month of June 1968.

BIBLIOGRAPHY

NALTY, BERNARD C. *Air Power and the Fight for Khe Sanh.* 1973.
PIDOR, ROBERT. *The End of the Line: The Siege of Khe Sanh.* 1982.
PRADOS, JOHN, and RAY W. STUBBE. *Valley of Decision: The Siege of Khe Sanh.* 1991.
SHORE, MOYERS S., II. *The Battle for Khe Sanh.* 1969.

JACK SHULIMSON

Khiem, Tran Thien. *See* Tran Thien Khiem.

Khmer Rouge. *Khmer Rouge* is the term Prince Sihanouk coined in the 1960s to describe Cambodia's heterogeneous communist-led dissidents, with whom he allied himself after he was overthrown in 1970. The Communist Party of Kampuchea (CPK) had grown out of the anti-French independence movement and was linked to Vietnam's communists. Its early leadership was rural, Buddhist-educated, and moderate, but by 1963, Pol Pot's younger group of urban, Paris-educated, anti-Vietnamese radicals had taken over the standing committee of the CPK Central Committee. They became known as the party "Center."

In the early 1970s, the Center, officially allied with North Vietnam in a war against the U.S.-backed Lon Nol government, quietly murdered nearly one thousand Vietnam-trained Khmer communists. The purges accelerated during the U.S. aerial bombardment of 1973. Other targets of the Center included those allied with Sihanouk, moderate indigenous communists, and such independent Marxists as Hou Yuon, a popular Paris-educated intellectual who disagreed with Pol Pot. The Center believed that dissident communist moderates who favored "a system of plenty" had been corrupted by "a little prosperity," were neglectful of ideology, and were "taken to pieces" by material things. Such CPK moderates remained concentrated in the Eastern Zone, and regional political differences became evident in the early and mid 1970s. But the Center slowly tightened its control. By 1978 half the members of the Central Committee, which had rarely if ever met, had been purged and executed.

The Khmer Rouge's activities following its 1975 victory over Lon Nol demonstrated the anti-urban sentiment that dominated the Khmer Rouge leadership. Khmer Rouge forces quickly emptied the cities of their 2 million inhabitants, who were forced to la-

VICTIMS OF THE KHMER ROUGE. Killed at Toul Sleng prison and unearthed from mass graves at Choeung Ek, near Phnom Penh; photo 13 May 1983. *AP/Wide World Photos*

bor in rural areas. Rural peasants initially supported the Khmer Rouge, but they too were soon forced into a life of unpaid collective labor. Rights to land, freedom of religion, and family life were prohibited; couples were separated, and youths were drafted into the work force, army, or militia. Many peasant children were trained to spy on their parents and to kill suspected "enemies" such as former city dwellers, "CIA" and "KGB" agents, and alleged malingerers. The Khmer Rouge also targeted ethnic minorities, who were removed from their homes and massacred, starved, or worked to death. The genocidal toll included 200,000 ethnic Chinese, 100,000 Cham Muslims, 20,000 Thais, and at least 10,000 ethnic Vietnamese. More were killed in cross-border raids, especially in Vietnam.

Most victims of the Khmer Rouge, however, were members of the majority Khmer population. On 10 May 1978, Phnom Penh radio broadcast a call not only to "exterminate the 50 million Vietnamese" but also to "purify the masses of the people" of Cambodia. The moderate Cambodian communists in the Eastern Zone rebelled two weeks later. Pol Pot's Khmer Rouge armies were unable to crush the rebellion quickly, but branded the 1.5 million easterners "Khmer bodies with Vietnamese minds." Between 100,000 and 250,000 were exterminated in six months, bringing the death toll in four years of Khmer Rouge rule to 1.5 million.

On 7 January 1979, the army of the Socialist Republic of Vietnam (SRV) captured Phnom Penh and drove the remaining Khmer Rouge forces into Thailand. Eastern Zone Khmer Rouge rebel commanders such as Hun Sen, who had defected to Vietnam in 1977, established a new regime. Sen became prime minister in 1985 and proceeded with liberalization. After the 1993 UN-organized elections, he was named second prime minister in a coalition with the Sihanouk party. But Pol Pot's remaining Khmer Rouge army of 10,000 troops, revived by assistance from the People's Republic of China and powerful Thai elements during the 1980s and still enjoying sanctuary in Thailand, posed a continuing threat on the western border.

BIBLIOGRAPHY

CHANDLER, DAVID P., and BEN KIERNAN, eds. *Revolution and Its Aftermath in Kampuchea: Eight Essays.* 1983.

KIERNAN, BEN, ed. *Genocide and Democracy in Cambodia: The Khmer Rouge, the United Nations, and the International Community.* 1993.

KIERNAN, BEN. *How Pol Pot Came to Power: A History of Communism in Kampuchea, 1930–1975.* 1987.

KIERNAN, BEN, and CHANTHOU BOUA, eds. *Peasants and Politics in Kampuchea, 1942–1981.* 1982.

VICKERY, MICHAEL. *Cambodia 1975–1982.* 1984.

BEN KIERNAN

Khrushchev, Nikita (1894–1971), secretary general of the Soviet Communist Party and leader of the USSR, 1958–1964. Khrushchev said that the Soviet Union would back nationalist movements, but he provided only lukewarm support for North Vietnamese and Viet Cong forces. Anxious to improve relations with the West, Khrushchev pressured the North Vietnamese government to negotiate with the United States in exchange for Soviet military aid. Ho Chi Minh distrusted him and wel-

NIKITA KHRUSHCHEV. *United Press International*

comed the more hard-line Leonid Brezhnev, who succeeded Khrushchev.

BIBLIOGRAPHY

HERRING, GEORGE C. *America's Longest War: The United States and Vietnam, 1950–1975.* 1986.

KAHIN, GEORGE McT. *Intervention: How America Became Involved in Vietnam.* 1986.

KELLY EVANS-PFEIFER

Kim, Le Van. *See* Le Van Kim.

King, Martin Luther, Jr. (1929–1968), civil rights leader; cochairman of Clergy and Laity Concerned About Vietnam, 1966–1968. King first broke with the Johnson administration over the Vietnam War in July 1965 in a speech opposing escalation of the conflict and calling for a negotiated settlement. He was the most prominent civil rights leader in the country, and his increasing opposition to the war between 1965 and his death in 1968 lent moral stature to the antiwar movement.

King's 1965 speech provoked harsh criticism from several quarters. President Johnson, recently allied with King to gain the passage of the Civil Rights Act of 1964 and the Voting Rights Act of 1965, felt betrayed by King's criticism of his Vietnam policy. The *New York Times* and other influential papers chastised King for linking the civil rights and antiwar movements, and the National Association for the Advancement of Colored People (NAACP) passed a resolution calling such linkage a "serious tactical mistake." Set back by such disapproval, King maintained a low profile on the war for the next year, but by late 1966 he decided he could no longer remain silent and became cochairman of Clergy and Laity Concerned About Vietnam.

King based his opposition to the Vietnam War on his belief in nonviolence, his concern about the war's cost and its effect on the Great Society, and the racial implications of the war as it became apparent that a disproportionate number of young black men were fighting and dying in Vietnam. King's criticism of the war became increasingly forceful throughout 1967. He explicitly aligned the civil rights movement with the antiwar movement, renewed his call for civil disobedience, and urged young men to seek conscientious objector status. In one speech King labeled the U.S. government "the greatest purveyor of violence in the world today."

MARTIN LUTHER KING JR. At center, with Lyndon B. Johnson, February 1964. *National Archives*

King's outspoken opposition radicalized his image from the "moderate" and "safe" civil rights leader of the early 1960s. But for many Americans, black and white, who respected and admired King, his articulate criticism of the war effectively stirred the national conscience.

BIBLIOGRAPHY

GARROW, DAVID J. *Bearing the Cross.* 1986.
KING, MARTIN LUTHER, JR. *Testament of Hope: The Essential Speeches and Writings of Martin Luther King, Jr.,* edited by James M. Washington. 1990.
ZAROULIS, NANCY, and GERALD SULLIVAN. *Who Spoke Up?* 1984.

KELLY EVANS-PFEIFER

Kissinger, Henry (1923–), national security adviser, 1969–1975; secretary of state, 1973–1977. Henry A. Kissinger played a prominent role in set-

ting U.S. policy in the Vietnam War in the administrations of Lyndon B. Johnson, Richard M. Nixon, and Gerald R. Ford. A German-born professor of international relations at Harvard University, Kissinger first undertook delicate negotiations regarding Vietnam on behalf of the Johnson administration. Generally supportive of Johnson's Vietnam policy during the period of escalation of the war, Kissinger came to believe by 1968 that the war in Vietnam had absorbed too much energy from the United States. Later he formed an unlikely partnership with Nixon, who selected him as his national security adviser. Kissinger wanted the war to end, but he believed that the way in which it ceased would determine U.S. credibility in world politics. From 1969 until the end of the war Kissinger directed often-secret negotiations over the future of Vietnam and advised Nixon and Ford about the military conduct of the war.

Kissinger's role in setting Vietnam policy began in the summer of 1967. Like many of the so-called realist analysts of U.S. foreign policy, he wanted the United States to redirect its foreign policy toward the more central issues of the management of relations with the Soviet Union. While still a professor at Harvard, he used personal contacts with French officials to open secret talks with representatives of North Vietnam on behalf of the Johnson administration. Code-named Pennsylvania, these talks foundered on the administration's refusal to announce an unconditional halt to the bombing of North Vietnam before the Democratic Republic of Vietnam (DRV) agreed to stop additional infiltration of troops to the south. Kissinger returned to Paris in 1968 to observe the preliminary public negotiations that began in May. He reported on the course of the talks to both the Democratic and Republican presidential nominees, Hubert Humphrey and Richard Nixon. He told Nixon of the administration's efforts to bring the talks to fruition before the election, and he helped the Republican nominee encourage the government of South Vietnamese President Nguyen Van Thieu to block progress on establishing formal peace talks before the U.S. presidential election on 5 November.

Negotiations. After the election, Nixon named Kissinger national security adviser, and together they developed strategies for diminishing the importance of the Vietnam War to the American public. For the next four years Kissinger played a complicated game of privately urging Nixon to take assertive military measures, while publicly cultivating the image of a conciliatory diplomat seeking a way to end the war. Kissinger and Nixon agreed that Vietnam had taken up too much foreign policy attention, and together the two developed relations with the People's Republic of China (PRC) and détente with the Soviet Union in order to minimize the significance of Vietnam. Kissinger supported the policy of Vietnamization. Inside the government, he backed Nixon's major escalations of the fighting in Southeast Asia—the 1969 bombing of Cambodia and the 1970 invasion of that country; the 1971 raid into Laos; and the bombing of North Vietnam in May and December 1972. A favorite with reporters and many academic foreign policy experts, Kissinger inaccurately indicated to them that he had dissented from some of the harsher military actions taken by the Nixon administration.

In the summer of 1969 Kissinger returned to Paris to commence secret negotiations with representatives of North Vietnam. These so-called backchannel talks, initially conducted without the knowledge of the official U.S. delegation to the peace negotiations, soon became the real venue for discussion. In three years of negotiations Kissinger offered to separate the military aspects from the political aspects of the war, a significant weakening of U.S. support for the South Vietnamese government. To balance that concession to the north, Kissinger sought to have the Soviet Union and the PRC, two communist countries whose relations with the United States had warmed, put pressure on the DRV. Neither the USSR nor the PRC, however, was willing or able to exert the sort of influence that Kissinger wanted.

Kissinger also believed that the United States had to continue to bomb the North to maintain U.S. credibility. In response to the Easter Offensive of the North Vietnamese in April 1972, Kissinger advocated Operation LINEBACKER, the intensive bombing of northern ports and cities. He and Nixon believed that LINEBACKER would not jeopardize the improving relations with the Soviet Union, and that the bombing would persuade the North Vietnamese to move forward in the talks. Little progress occurred, however, until the middle of the U.S. presidential campaign of 1972. At that time both the United States and North Vietnam had incentives to reach an agreement before election day. Nixon wanted a cease-fire as a foreign policy achievement, while the North Vietnamese expected that they would receive a better offer from Nixon before, rather than after, he was reelected.

Accord. On 26 October 1972 Kissinger announced that "peace is at hand." He claimed that he and North Vietnamese negotiator Le Duc Tho had reached an agreement that included the following points: a cease-fire in place; withdrawal of the remainder of U.S. forces within sixty days; exchange of prisoners of war; North Vietnamese troops could remain in the south but not have their numbers increased; continuation of the government of President Nguyen Van Thieu; the United States would replace South Vietnam's lost munitions and continue to train its soldiers; and Thieu's government would undertake to add coalition partners, including possibly the National Liberation Front (NLF). The agreement, however, was rejected by Thieu. In November Kissinger dispatched his deputy, Gen. Alexander Haig, to Saigon to threaten Thieu that the United States was prepared to sign an agreement without him. Should he agree to participate, however, the U.S. government would promise to reenter the war if the North violated the cease-fire. In Washington, Kissinger encouraged Nixon to go forward with the December bombing of the North, Operation LINEBACKER II, to show both South and North the extent of U.S. commitment to continue fighting. After twelve days of brutal bombing, North Vietnamese negotiators agreed to return to the talks in Paris. On 27 January 1973 Kissinger and North Vietnamese negotiator Le Duc Tho signed an agreement very similar to the one they had worked out in October.

Initially, Kissinger won praise for his negotiations, but his triumph was short-lived. Nixon named him secretary of state in September 1973, and he received the Nobel Peace prize jointly with Le Duc Tho, who refused to accept his share, saying that there was no peace. The cease-fire quickly began to unravel as both South Vietnamese and North Vietnamese forces staged intermittent attacks on one another's positions. U.S. attention was focused elsewhere in 1973 and 1974 as the Watergate scandal unfolded, the Yom Kippur War in Middle East demanded Kissinger's attention, and the domestic economy soured after the Organization of Petroleum Exporting Countries (OPEC) increased the price of oil by 400 percent. Congress passed the War Powers Resolution in November 1973, restricting the president's freedom to conduct military operations abroad. In early 1975, not long after Gerald Ford became president, the war resumed in earnest, and Kissinger urged Ford to reenter the fighting. The new president, realizing how unpopular that course would be, refused to resume the bombing or to contemplate sending more ground troops. Members of Congress of all points of view opposed renewed U.S. military participation in the war in Vietnam. Kissinger subsequently blamed both Watergate and Congress for the fall of South Vietnam, refusing to recognize that the United States was no longer committed to more war in Vietnam. In retrospect, Kissinger's direction of U.S. policy toward Vietnam must be judged a failure, despite moments of high diplomatic drama.

BIBLIOGRAPHY

KISSINGER, HENRY A. *Diplomacy.* 1994.
KISSINGER, HENRY A. *White House Years.* 1979.
KISSINGER, HENRY A. *Years of Upheaval.* 1982.
SCHULZINGER, ROBERT D. *Henry Kissinger: Doctor of Diplomacy.* 1989.

ROBERT D. SCHULZINGER

Knowland, William F. (1908–1974), U.S. senator (R-Calif.), 1945–1959; Senate majority leader, 1953–1955; minority leader, 1955–1959. Knowland consistently urged greater U.S. involvement in opposing communism in China, Korea, and Vietnam.

WILLIAM F. KNOWLAND. *Library of Congress*

He labeled the Geneva accords of 1954 a communist "victory," and he was an important congressional supporter of Ngo Dinh Diem.

BIBLIOGRAPHY

HERRING, GEORGE C. *America's Longest War: The United States and Vietnam, 1950–1975.* 1986.

JENNIFER FROST

Komer, Robert W. (1922–), deputy commander, U.S. Military Assistance Command, Vietnam (MACV), 1967–1968. A senior analyst for the Central Intelligence Agency (CIA), Robert Komer was deputy national security adviser when President Johnson named him special assistant for pacification in 1966. Sent to Saigon with ambassadorial rank a year later, Komer's official title was MACV Deputy Commander for Civil Operations and Revolutionary Development Support (CORDS). He took charge of diverse counterinsurgency programs that were operated by the military, the State Department, the U.S. Agency for International Development, and the CIA. Komer sent thousands of "pacification teams" into every district of South Vietnam with orders to "root out the Viet Cong infrastructure." CORDS lavished U.S. aid on friendly villages while "hostile" areas were forcibly evacuated to deprive Viet Cong forces of support. Komer's computerized Hamlet Evaluation Survey (HES) showed that the number of Viet Cong guerrillas was steadily decreasing—right up to the Tet Offensive. Komer then initiated the Phoenix program, which eventually led to assassinations of 20,000 Viet Cong suspects after his departure in 1968. Known as Blowtorch for his hard-driving style, Komer later regretted American destructiveness in Vietnam because it prevented the United States from winning popular support. "Military operations tend to alienate people as fast as the pacification operations are trying to help them," he wrote. Komer later served as President Carter's undersecretary of defense for policy and testified for William C. Westmoreland in his libel suit against CBS.

BIBLIOGRAPHY

KOMER, ROBERT W. *Bureaucracy at War.* 1986.
KOMER, ROBERT W. *Bureaucracy Does Its Thing.* 1972.
KOMER, ROBERT W. "Impact of Pacification on Insurgency in South Vietnam." *Journal of International Affairs* 25 (1971).

GLEN GENDZEL

Kong Le (c. 1934–), Laotian army captain. Kong Le led the August 1960 coup that overthrew the pro-U.S. regime and returned Prince Souvanna Phouma to the head of government. Souvanna Phouma led the Neutral Party of Laos, which sought to remain uninvolved in the Vietnamese conflict. Le's coup alarmed U.S. policymakers, who feared the spread of communism in Southeast Asia. By December, rightist Laotian forces supported by the U.S. Central Intelligence Agency (CIA) had defeated Kong Le's troops and retaken the capital city of Vientiane.

BIBLIOGRAPHY

THEE, MAREK. *Notes of a Witness: Laos and the Second Indochinese War.* 1973.

ADAM LAND

Korea, Republic of. Despite a constant North Korean military threat, the Republic of Korea (South Korea) committed large numbers of combat troops to South Vietnam's aid, a level of commitment second only to that of South Vietnam and of the United States. It did so in order to cement the South Korean alliance with the U.S. and thus help maintain the U.S. security presence in Asia.

The Republic of Korea deployed its first troops (known as ROKs) early in 1965 in conjunction with the first U.S. troops. The Republic of Korea Military Assistance Group, Vietnam (known as the "Dove Unit"), arrived in March 1965. Based in Bien Hoa province, it consisted of engineer, medical support, construction support, and security companies. In November 1965 South Korea also sent its Capital Infantry Division and 2d Marine Brigade to provide security for Cam Ranh Bay and Qui Nonh. Approximately 20,000 South Koreans served in Vietnam under Gen. Chae Myung-Shin during 1965, a number that more than doubled to 45,000 in 1966.

South Korea's domestic debate over its troop commitment threatened to stymie the U.S. request for additional Korean troops by July 1966. With leverage from this debate, the Koreans gained assurance from the United States that the war would not jeopardize the defense capabilities of South Korea, that the Koreans would not have to pay for the additional troop deployment, and that any economic benefits from the war—such as military contracts—would go first to South Korea. (South Korea ulti-

mately earned approximately $1 billion in military and insurance contracts between 1965 and 1973.) South Korea then deployed the 9th Division in September and October 1966, and in 1967, it sent a marine battalion.

The issue of command of Korean troops remained sensitive throughout the first few years of South Korea's involvement. Koreans served under the Free World Military Assistance Policy Council, but in 1965, as a result of the South Korean reputation for extreme brutality, they operated under special South Vietnamese restrictions—restrictions placed on no other Free World force. They were forbidden to fire unless attacked and forbidden to move outside specified areas. South Korea consequently demanded that its troops serve only under U.S. command. The United States eventually also agreed not to decrease the number of U.S. troops in South Vietnam as a result of the increase in the number of Korean troops, and the United States spent approximately $2 million each year to support the Korean military. General Westmoreland wanted the Dove Unit to assume a unified command over all Korean units while he retained control over noncombatants. The image, if not the reality, of Korean command independence was important both to South Korea's self-esteem and to the U.S. desire not to appear manipulative of other Asian countries.

South Korea was particularly interested in keeping its casualties at a very low level and consequently relied on extensive preparation and the use of what the United States viewed as excessive U.S. air support. South Korean troops engaged primarily in small unit operations. Troop deployment reached a high of 50,000 in 1968 and continued at approximately 48,000 during the following two years. As the United States reduced its troop levels in 1971, South Korea agreed to keep its Capital and 9th Infantry divisions in II Corps Tactical Zone until March 1973.

BIBLIOGRAPHY

BOK, LEE SUK. *The Impact of United States Forces in Korea.* 1987.

KOH, BYUNG CHUL. *The Foreign Policy Systems of North and South Korea.* 1984.

LARSEN, STANLEY ROBERT, and JAMES LAWTON COLLINS JR. *Allied Participation in Vietnam.* 1975.

LEWY GUENTER. *America in Vietnam.* 1978.

PALMER, BRUCE, JR. *The 25-Year War: America's Military Role in Vietnam.* 1984.

ELLEN BAKER

Korean War. The first application of the policy of containment in Asia, the Korean War served as a model for some U.S. policymakers during the Vietnam War. In Korea, the United States, leading a United Nations force, sought to contain the Chinese-backed communist North Korea north of the thirty-eighth parallel in order to preserve a democratic South Korea.

The Korean War began in 1950 and ended in a stalemate in July 1953. While the experience exhibited the difficulties of fighting a land war in Asia, it also contributed to the U.S. decision to enter the Vietnam conflict. First, the People's Republic of China's support of North Korea and later North Vietnam caused the United States to view events in Vietnam as communist expansionism rather than as an anticolonial or a nationalist movement. Second, U.S. intervention had allowed South Korea to remain a separate, anticommunist state, the same goal the U.S. government had for South Vietnam, convincing U.S. policymakers that a favorable outcome could be achieved. Third, the French secured U.S. aid for their struggle in Vietnam by emphasizing the similarities between the two conflicts. Finally, President Lyndon Johnson invoked the unhappy experience of stalemate in Korea as justification for an expanded effort in Vietnam. While some in Congress in 1953 said "no more Koreas," ironically the Korean War served as a prelude to U.S. involvement in Vietnam.

BIBLIOGRAPHY

DONOVAN, ROBERT. "The Korean War 40 Years Later: But at What Cost?" *New York Times,* 25 June 1990, p. A17.
KAHIN, GEORGE MCT. *Intervention: How America Became Involved in Vietnam.* 1986.

KELLY EVANS-PFEIFER

Kosygin, Alexei (1904–1980), prime minister of the Soviet Union, 1964–1980. Kosygin traveled to Hanoi in early 1965, before the increased U.S. combat troop commitment, to press North Vietnam for negotiations with the United States as a condition of Soviet aid. U.S. bombing of North Vietnam in retaliation for the Viet Cong guerrilla attack on the Pleiku air base ended Kosygin's trip and hardened his position on the conflict. Kosygin dropped the requirement for negotiations and approved unconditional Soviet military aid. Two years later, Kosygin informed British Prime Minister Harold Wilson that the Soviet Union was ready to pressure North Vietnam once again to come to the negotiating table.

BIBLIOGRAPHY

KAHIN, GEORGE MCT. *Intervention: How America Became Involved in Vietnam.* 1986.
KARNOW, STANLEY. *Vietnam: A History.* 1991.

KELLY EVANS-PFEIFER

Krulak, Victor (1931–), lieutenant general, U.S. Marine Corps. A 1934 Naval Academy graduate, Krulak had a distinguished combat record in World War II and the Korean War. Major General Krulak served as special assistant for counterinsurgency and special activities for the Joint Chiefs of Staff from February 1962 until January 1964. As such he was responsible for the development of counterinsurgency doctrine and policy, especially as it applied to Vietnam. Promoted to lieutenant general, Krulak

VICTOR H. "BRUTE" KRULAK. At right, with Lewis W. Walt, 1967. *National Archives*

commanded the Fleet Marine Force until his retirement in June 1968. In this capacity, he was responsible for the readiness and organization of all Marine units in the Pacific, including Vietnam. Although not in the operational chain of command, Krulak's forceful personality, his personal links with Secretary of Defense Robert S. McNamara, and his strategic location in Hawaii allowed him to strongly influence Marine strategy in the five northern provinces of South Vietnam. With his emphasis on pacification, he was a strong dissenting voice to the search-and-destroy tactics and attrition strategy pursued by the U.S. operational commander, Gen. William C. Westmoreland, Commander U.S. Military Assistance Command, Vietnam (COMUSMACV). In 1968, General Krulak, together with Lt. Gen. Lewis W. Walt, was a leading candidate for commandant of the Marine Corps. For various political and personal considerations, President Johnson instead selected Lt. Gen. Leonard A. Chapman, then assistant commandant. According to Lewis Sorley, the administration also toyed with the idea of making Krulak deputy commander to General Creighton Abrams when the later succeeded Westmoreland. Abrams and other army commanders objected, however, and the idea went no further.

BIBLIOGRAPHY

KRULAK, VICTOR H. *First to Fight: An Inside View of the U.S. Marine Corps.* 1984.
MILLET, ALLAN R. *Semper Fidelis: The History of the United States Marine Corps.* Rev. ed. 1991.
SIMMONS, EDWIN H. *The United States Marines: The First Two Hundred Years, 1775–1975.* 1976.
SORLEY, LEWIS. *Thunderbolt: General Creighton Abrams and the Army of his Times.* 1992.

JACK SHULIMSON

Ky, Nguyen Cao. *See* Nguyen Cao Ky.

L

Laird, Melvin R. (1922–), secretary of defense, 1969–1973. A longtime Republican party leader and Wisconsin congressman, Melvin Laird was President Nixon's choice for secretary of defense after Democratic senator Henry M. Jackson declined. During World War II, Laird served aboard the USS *Maddox*—the same destroyer supposedly attacked by North Vietnam in the Tonkin Gulf incident. In the Nixon administration, Laird pushed for timely disengagement from Vietnam, believing the American people were "fed up with the war." After visiting South Vietnam twice in 1969–1970, Laird urged President Nixon "to initiate the removal from Southeast Asia of some U.S. military personnel," and warned that victory was impossible "considering the restrictions with which we are compelled to operate." Unlike others in the Nixon administration, Laird harbored no illusions that the American public would stand for continued involvement in Vietnam or that the war could still be won.

Laird popularized the term *Vietnamization* to describe the Nixon administration's policy of shifting the burden of war-fighting from the United States to South Vietnam. Realizing that abandoning an ally would be as politically untenable as further escalation, Laird portrayed Vietnamization as "a cru-

cial test of the Nixon Doctrine," which relied on regional powers armed by the United States to preserve international stability. Laird also devised the term *protective reaction* to describe the newly cautious combat posture of U.S. forces in Vietnam, which was designed to minimize casualties by replacing search-and-destroy tactics. He consistently advocated lower draft calls, faster troop withdrawals, and reduction of U.S. expenditures in Vietnam. Laird was also the first U.S. official to condemn North Vietnam publicly for mistreating U.S. prisoners of war.

Laird wielded considerable clout early in the Nixon administration and was instrumental in convincing Nixon not to resume the bombing of North Vietnam. Presidential assistant Henry Kissinger, negotiating with Hanoi's representatives in Paris, resented Laird's disengagement policy for undercutting his bargaining position. Nixon, too, came to regard his secretary of defense as a "pusillanimous little nitpicker." As a result, Laird was not always informed of decisions made in the White House. During the secret bombing of Cambodia and the Christmas bombing of North Vietnam, both of which Laird opposed, President Nixon issued orders directly to the Joint Chiefs of Staff with explicit instructions not to inform Laird. As Laird's influence waned, he concentrated on dismantling the Selective Service and securing military aid for South Vietnam. Elliot Richardson replaced Laird in Nixon's second term after the Paris peace accords took effect in 1973. Laird served briefly as a White House assistant during Watergate but soon resigned because he had no faith in Nixon's honesty.

BIBLIOGRAPHY

CAMERON, JUAN. "A Political Pro at the Pentagon." *Fortune,* April 1969.
DUSCHA, JULIUS. "The Political Pro Who Runs Defense." *New York Times Magazine,* 13 June 1971.
KINNARD, DOUGLAS. *The Secretary of Defense.* 1980.
LAIRD, MELVIN. *A House Divided: America's Strategy Gap.* 1962.
LAIRD, MELVIN. *People, not Hardware—The Highest Defense Priority.* 1980.
SZULC, TAD. *The Illusion of Peace: Foreign Policy in the Nixon Years.* 1978.

GLEN GENDZEL

Lake, Anthony W. (1939–), U.S. vice consul, Saigon, 1964–1965; special assistant to the president for national security affairs, 1969–1970; national security adviser, 1993–. A Foreign Service officer who served in Vietnam and later as special assistant to Henry Kissinger, Lake resigned from the administration in 1970 in protest over the U.S. invasion of Cambodia. Initially a strong supporter of the war, Lake grew skeptical of the possibility of a military victory and urged a negotiated settlement to end the bloodshed. Kissinger ordered wire surveillance of his home two weeks after Lake's resignation. In 1989, Kissinger apologized for the action. In 1993, President Clinton named Lake his national security adviser.

BIBLIOGRAPHY

LAKE, ANTHONY. *The Vietnam Legacy: The War, American Society, and the Future of American Foreign Policy.* 1976.

ADAM LAND

LAM SON 719. Operation LAM SON 719 was a crucial test of Vietnamization that began on 8 February 1971. The United States provided air and artillery support for 16,000 elite troops from the Army of the Republic of Vietnam (ARVN) who crossed the border into Laos and raided the Ho Chi Minh Trail. Bad weather, command bungling, and North Vietnamese Army (NVA) counterattacks led to heavy losses on the withdrawal. There were more than 8,000 ARVN casualties and 1,462 U.S. casualties, and more than 100 helicopters and 150 tanks were left behind. ARVN morale was so devastated that observers doubted South Vietnam could defend itself. Nevertheless, President Nixon told Americans on 7 April 1971: "Tonight I can report that Vietnamization has succeeded." The North Vietnamese lost nearly 20,000 soldiers and enough equipment to set back the planned Easter Offensive until 1972.

BIBLIOGRAPHY

NGUYEN DUY HINH. *Lam Son 719.* 1981.
NOLAN, KEITH W. *Into Laos: The Story of Dewey Canyon II/Lam Son 719.* 1986.
SAAR, JOHN. "An Ignominious and Disorderly Retreat." *Life,* 2 April 1971.

GLEN GENDZEL

Land Reform. In the predominantly rural country of Vietnam, the land policies of the North and South Vietnamese governments served as crucial tools to shape social order. The Democratic Republic of Vietnam (DRV) and National Liberation Front (NLF) generally promoted the welfare of poorer and mid-level peasants in land reform schemes, while the Republic of Vietnam (RVN) until the late 1960s favored larger landlords. The DRV and RVN also used land policies to increase agricultural output and promote economic development. In the DRV, the effort entailed the collectivization of agriculture beginning in 1958, while RVN strategy relied on technologically advanced production practiced by wealthy peasants and landlords.

In 1946 as war erupted with the French, the communist-led Viet Minh began policies to mobilize peasants in support of the nationalist movement. In the late 1940s, the Viet Minh enforced a 25-percent rent reduction and redistributed the land of colonials and pro-French Vietnamese to the peasants. The policy particularly benefited peasants in the south, where 500,000 received the property of pro-French landlords. Communist Party elites wavered initially on whether to pursue confrontational policies against pro–Viet Minh landlords. In 1953, however, they initiated a broad program to eradicate the rich peasant and landlord class. Built upon Maoist political doctrine, the policy entailed

LAND REFORM: NORTH VIETNAM. A communist cadre planting a sign identifying a landless peasant, Nguyen Van Dinh, holding her child at a land reform rally. *Ngô Vĩnh Long*

massive land redistribution to poor and mid-level peasants. After initial success, the party accelerated the program in 1955, which led to extensive conflict within the countryside. Violence against landlords intensified, and many poor peasants faced imprisonment by abusive local tribunals. A People's Army of Vietnam (PAVN) division suppressed a peasant uprising in Nghe An, Ho Chi Minh's home province. An estimated 30,000–100,000 died in the turmoil before the government ended the program in 1956.

Beginning in 1958, the DRV attempted to collectivize agriculture by organizing peasants into large producer cooperatives. Party elites justified the program as a means to counter reemerging class hierarchy in villages. They also sought to increase production by implementing crop diversification and collective water technology such as canal building. Surplus output, they hoped, would help finance industrialization projects. The collectivization effort achieved considerable success; by 1960 86 percent of peasants were in cooperatives. Water programs also improved productivity, although farming remained nonmechanized. By 1959, production of

staple crops such as rice, corn, and potatoes had increased to 5.79 million metric tons, a 47-percent increase from 1955.

The Republic of Vietnam sponsored land policies largely favorable to landlords, as Ngo Dinh Diem had allied his government with this powerful group. Diem's land reform schemes did intend some benefits for poorer peasants and tenants. The 1955 program, Ordinance 2, established a moderate rent limit of 25 percent of crops. The policy, however, angered many peasants, who had paid no rent under the Viet Minh. The later Ordinance 57 promoted moderate redistribution and some limits on large landholdings. But Diem's vice president, Nguyen Ngoc Tho, a wealthy landlord, oversaw the program and enforced only minor reforms.

In the late 1960s, the U.S. government pressured President Thieu's government to instigate land redistribution. The United States had previously accepted rural inequality in the South as necessary to increase rice production to stimulate export-driven economic development. U.S. advisers had sought to modernize agricultural practices through seed technology, water pumps, and fertilizer purchased by

LAND REFORM: SOUTH VIETNAM. A refugee from North Vietnam receives the title to a parcel of land from the South Vietnamese secretary of state for agrarian reform, 1961. *National Archives*

wealthy peasants and landlords. The expected production boom, however, never materialized. Moreover, the 1968 Tet Offensive revealed extensive peasant support for the NLF forces. Beginning in 1969, the United States financed several Land-to-the-Tiller programs, which compensated landlords and gave 1–3 hectares (2.5–7.4 acres) of land to peasants. By 1972, the new policy had reduced tenancy from 60 to 34 percent, and benefited 400,000 Vietnamese. The program did suffer setbacks, as local South Vietnamese elites worked to thwart reform efforts through fraud and delay. Poorer laborers were also not likely to gain from the program.

The NLF land reform varied across regions under its control, although the insurgency generally pursued egalitarian policies that benefited poorer peasants. In a similar pattern to the DRV's land reform, the NLF did not challenge the landlord class until after 1963, when it had consolidated its political and military position. By 1964, an estimated 1.5 million hectares (3.8 million acres) of land had been redistributed by NLF policies.

BIBLIOGRAPHY

DUIKER, WILLIAM J. *The Communist Road to Power in Vietnam.* 1981.

WIEGERSMA, NANCY. *Vietnam: Peasant Land, Peasant Revolution.* 1988.

ADAM LAND

Laniel, Joseph (1889–1975), prime minister, French Fourth Republic, June 1953–June 1954. In June 1953, the new Laniel cabinet tried to placate the Eisenhower administration's demand for renewed military and political resolve by the French in Vietnam. Laniel's government promised a measure of independence for the Associated States, France's new name for its Indochinese colonies, and trumpeted the Navarre Plan, Gen. Henri Navarre's grand design to subdue the Viet Minh. Rather than victory, however, the Laniel government presided over Navarre's defeat at Dien Bien Phu. Immediately afterward, Laniel began negotiations to end the war, but his government was wracked with insurmountable internal divisions. Pierre Mendès-France replaced him, and with widespread public support, the new premier successfully concluded the Geneva peace agreement.

BIBLIOGRAPHY

HAMMER, ELLEN J. *The Struggle for Indochina.* 1954.

HERRING, GEORGE C. *America's Longest War: The United States and Vietnam, 1950–1975.* 1986.

VICTOR JEW

Lansdale, Edward G. (1908–1987), general, U.S. Air Force; assistant air attaché, U.S. embassy in Saigon, 1954–1956; special assistant to the U.S. ambassador, 1965–1968. Sometimes called "The Father of South Vietnam," Gen. Edward Lansdale was the model for Alden Pyle in Graham Greene's *The Quiet American* (1955) and Edwin Hillendale in William Lederer and Eugene Berdick's *The Ugly American* (1958). A former advertising man, Lansdale served with the Office of Strategic Services (OSS) in World War II. Working for the Central Intelligence Agency (CIA) from the time of its inception until 1956, he served with the CIA in the Philippines before arriving in South Vietnam on 1 June 1954—before the Geneva accords were signed. His mission for the CIA in Vietnam was to encourage emigration from North Vietnam and to shore up the government of South Vietnam. A colonel while in Vietnam, Lansdale organized the departure of nearly one million Catholic refugees from the north as the communists took over, and then he became an avid U.S. supporter of Ngo Dinh Diem. Diem won a rigged election with Lansdale's assistance, bought off opponents with CIA money, and followed Lansdale's advice in crushing rival sects before his American patron left in 1956. By then the United States was solidly committed to supporting Diem. From 1957 to 1963 Lansdale served as the deputy director of the Office of Special Operations of the Department of Defense.

President Kennedy sent Lansdale back to South Vietnam in 1961, and Lansdale recommended continued aid for Diem. In 1965, Lansdale returned to Saigon as special assistant to the U.S. ambassador. He tried to reorient the U.S. war effort toward counterinsurgency and pacification, but Lansdale's advice went unheeded by generals pursuing higher body counts. He became an isolated and forlorn figure in his Saigon villa, and returned to the United States in 1968. Lansdale's failure signaled the shift in U.S. priorities from building up South Vietnam to taking over the war, but Lansdale remained convinced that the United States could prevail against communism by "exporting the American way" and "winning the hearts and minds of the people" with economic and military aid to the developing nations.

BIBLIOGRAPHY

CURREY, CECIL B. *Edward Lansdale: The Unquiet American.* 1988.

LANSDALE, EDWARD G. *In the Midst of Wars: An American's Mission to Southeast Asia.* 1972.

LANSDALE, EDWARD G. "Two Steps to Get Us Out of Vietnam." *Look,* 4 March 1969.

LANSDALE, EDWARD G. "Vietnam: Do We Understand Revolution?" *Foreign Affairs* 43 (October 1964): 75–86.

LANSDALE, EDWARD G. "Vietnam: Still the Search for Goals." *Foreign Affairs* 47 (October 1968).

GLEN GENDZEL

Lao Dong. The Lao Dong Party (formally Dang Lao Dong Viet Nam, usually translated into English as the Vietnamese Workers' Party, or VWP) was created in February 1951 at a national congress held in Tuyen Quang, north of Hanoi. Nearly 160 delegates, representing 500,000 members, attended the congress.

The VWP was the lineal descendant of the Indochinese Communist Party (ICP), created in 1930. The ICP had been formally dissolved in November 1945 by its founder Ho Chi Minh to deflect suspicion about the communist nature of his new Democratic Republic of Vietnam (DRV), established in September 1945 in Hanoi. The party continued to exist as a clandestine organization directing the war of resistance against the French and resurfaced under its new name in 1951, perhaps as the result of pressure from the People's Republic of China (PRC) to adopt an ideological position that was more clear-cut to the Vietnamese people. The new name, however, indicated that party leaders were continuing, at least for the time being, to place primary emphasis on the struggle for national reunification rather than on imposing a socialist system within North Vietnam.

During the next quarter of a century, the VWP was the leading political party in the DRV and the guiding force in the struggle for the reunification of North and South Vietnam into a single country under a socialist system. Its organizational principles and its program were essentially Marxist-Leninist, and in the late 1950s it took initial steps to transform the DRV into a socialist society. That process, delayed by the resumption of revolutionary war in the South, resumed after the fall of Saigon in 1975.

In December 1976, at its Fourth National Congress, the VWP was renamed the Vietnamese Communist Party (Dang Cong San Viet Nam). The more than one thousand delegates at the congress represented more than 1.5 million party members.

BIBLIOGRAPHY

PIKE, DOUGLAS. *A History of Vietnamese Communism, 1925–1978.* 1978.

PIKE, DOUGLAS. *An Outline History of the Vietnam Workers' Party.* 1970.

WILLIAM J. DUIKER

Laos. Laos, until the Pathet Lao took over the government in December 1975, was ruled by a line of monarchs dating back more than six centuries to

LAOTIAN LEADERS. Souvanna Phouma, at left, with Phoumi Nosavan, Phnom Penh, Cambodia, 15 March 1961. *National Archives*

the ancient Lao kingdom of Lan Xang (Million Elephants). A mountainous and landlocked country slightly larger than the state of Utah (approximately 236,800 square kilometers, 91,428 square miles), Laos has a population of about 4 million. There are dozens of ethnic groups, in four primary divisions: the Lao Loum (lowland Lao), the Lao Tai (tribal Tai), the Lao Theung (mountainside Lao), and the Lao Sung (mountaintop Lao). The Lao Loum, predominantly Theravadan Buddhists, are the largest single group and have dominated commerce, government, and trade. The royal family and all but a few of the ruling elite during the Vietnam War were Lao Loum. The Lao Tai and Lao Theung are animists who practice subsistence farming in the upland valleys and on the mountainsides. Believed to have been the original inhabitants of Laos, the Lao Theung are sometimes referred to as the Kha, or "slave" people of Laos. The Lao Sung, also animists, traditionally have been called by outsiders the Meo (alternate spelling Miao), or "cat" people. The Lao Sung consider this term pejorative and today most people refer to them as the Hmong. Adept at raising opium poppies as a cash crop, the Hmong have a long tradition of self-sufficiency and fierce armed resistance to outside authority. During the Vietnam War the Hmong of northeastern Laos were sought after as guerrilla fighters by both the communist Pathet Lao/North Vietnamese alliance and the Royal Lao/American partnership.

Colonialism to Neutrality. In the late nineteenth century, France, already in control of Vietnam and Cambodia, pressured the Lao monarchy to accede to French domination. This sovereignty continued, except during the Japanese occupation of Indochina during World War II, until 1947, when France granted Laos limited independence and the country became a constitutional monarchy within the French Union. In 1953 Laos gained complete independence, but internal and external political factors battered the kingdom. The Pathet Lao (Lao Nation), a small communist movement nominally headed by Prince Souphanouvong, had been allied since the late 1940s with the powerful Viet Minh communist forces of Ho Chi Minh. Ho, recognizing the strategic importance of the long borders Laos shared with Cambodia, China, Thailand, and Vietnam, provided military equipment and advisers to the Pathet Lao. Moreover, Viet Minh units conducted large-scale military operations in Laos against French and Royal Lao government forces.

The 1954 Geneva agreements briefly halted the fighting as the international community pledged recognition of Laotian neutrality and called for the withdrawal from Laos of all foreign military forces. The French complied with the settlement, but communist-backed Vietnamese soldiers remained in Laos and continued their military support of the Pathet Lao. The agreements also created a Lao coalition government, but pressure from right-wing Laotian politicians and military officers quickly forced the Pathet Lao representatives to abandon any hope of a meaningful political accommodation. The Pathet Lao quit the coalition and, with assistance from North Vietnam, recommenced their insurrection against the central government. In August 1960 the political and military situation in Laos became even more fractured as royal army forces led by Captain Kong Le rebelled against the coalition government and seized control of Vientiane. Kong Le, intent on achieving true neutrality for Laos, handed over power to former prime minister Souvanna Phouma. Souvanna tried to form another coalition government, but because it included left-wing representation it was immediately rebuffed by the United States. The rebel government then turned to the Soviet Union for military and economic assistance and, much to the dismay of the U.S. government, the USSR responded with an airlift of supplies to Vientiane.

Civil War. Despite Soviet assistance, by December the coup had been put down by royal military units under the control of Gen. Phoumi Nosavan, a right-wing favorite of the U.S. Central Intelligence Agency (CIA). Unable to resist Nosavan, who was backed by U.S. military advisers and secret aerial resupply flights, Kong Le evacuated his forces north to the strategically located Plain of Jars. Isolated, but defiant, the Neutralists then entered an alliance with nearby Pathet Lao units. For the next eighteen months the Pathet Lao and Neutralist factions engaged in a loose state of conflict with the royal government. In June 1962, reacting to another international conference at Geneva, the Lao factions agreed to halt the fighting and formed a new coalition government headed by Souvanna Phouma. The coalition failed, however, and within a year the Pathet Lao had again allied with the communist North Vietnamese to effect an armed takeover of Laos. Despite international declarations of Laotian neutrality and numerous attempts by the Lao to settle their domestic political differences, the kingdom remained embroiled in external and internal political and military strife. Moreover, the escalating conflict between North and South Vietnam increased the likelihood that Laos would be drawn into a larger war. Laos, sharing lengthy and heavily forested borders with North Vietnam, South Vietnam, and Cambodia, became by geographic consequence a critical part of what has commonly been termed the Ho Chi Minh Trail. Not a single node, but thousands of paths, waterways, trails, and roads, the Ho Chi Minh Trail began in North Vietnam and latticed through northeastern and southern Laos to South Vietnam and Cambodia. The technically neutral kingdom of Laos became a critical, but unwilling, conduit for men and matériel destined to support communist operations in South Vietnam and Cambodia. In an effort to strangle North Vietnamese support to these operations, the United States and its Lao and South Vietnamese allies conducted a "secret war" against the Ho Chi Minh Trail in Laos.

Despite the knowledge that North Vietnamese forces remained in Laos, the U.S. government complied with the 1962 Geneva terms and ordered a complete withdrawal from Laos of the U.S. Military Assistance Advisory Group–Laos (MAAG–L). Within the year, however, the United States convinced Souvanna to allow the creation of a military assistance program to counter support by the USSR and the People's Republic of China of the Pathet Lao and Vietnamese communist forces in Laos. Because the 1962 Geneva agreements prohibited most military aid to Laos, the U.S. government developed a strategy that allowed the State Department, the Department of Defense, and the CIA to secretly supply military assistance to the technically neutral country.

The Secret War. This policy, the so-called secret war in Laos, involved six primary elements. First, it was a multi-billion-dollar aid program operating from Thailand under the auspices of a clandestine organization called Deputy Chief, Joint U.S. Military Assistance Group Thailand. This unit, more commonly known as DEPCHIEF, provided the Royal Lao military with military equipment and training. Second, in order to supplement the lackluster combat performance of the lowland Lao army, the United States actively recruited Hmong tribesmen as guerrilla fighters. Vang Pao, a charismatic Hmong officer in the Royal Lao army who had come to the attention of the CIA, was made commander of a strategic military region located in northeastern Laos. Vang Pao and his Hmong soldiers became expert at harassment raids and reconnaissance patrols against North Vietnamese and Pathet Lao forces operating along the Lao-Vietnamese border. Air America, Inc., the CIA's proprietary airline, was the third element: its vital role in Laos included the supply and movement of conventional and guerrilla troops, clandestine reconnaissance missions, and search-and-rescue operations for downed aviators. Under contract to the U.S. Agency for International Development (AID), Air America also relocated war refugees to safe areas and provided them with food and clothing. The fourth component was the CIA's extensive and unprecedented responsibilities for the management of military assistance to Laos. To provide operational and training advisers and to oversee specialized covert operations, the CIA established in Thailand the 4802d Joint Liaison Detachment (JLD), which worked closely with the fifth element of the U.S. strategy, the Royal Thai government. Thai cooperation was integral to the U.S. covert military aid program to Laos. In addition to providing land for U.S.-built and -operated air bases and army facilities supporting the Vietnam War, the Thais established a covert organization named "Headquarters 333," which assisted in the recruitment and training of Thai soldiers destined for duty in Laos. These Thai units, paid and directed by the CIA, eventually reached a strength in Laos of some 20,000 troops. Last, although the involvement in Laos of U.S. ground forces was minimal, U.S. aircraft waged an intense and long-term bombing campaign against military targets in Laos. From 1962 until 1973, these six elements constituted the U.S. government's nonattributable Lao policy.

End of the War in Laos. This covert paramilitary war in Laos of the early 1960s escalated into a conventional conflict that had enormous human and financial costs. By the end of the decade, the increased aggressiveness of the North Vietnamese forces' campaigns during the dry seasons, a new Republican administration in Washington, and a growing antiwar feeling in Congress brought change, albeit slowly, to U.S. activity in Laos. The Hmong, who for years had effectively served as guerrilla fighters, were regularly employed against sizable North Vietnamese forces. Marginally equipped and poorly suited for conventional combat, they suffered heavy casualties. The kingdom's defense began to depend almost entirely on massive aerial bombing and the infusion of additional CIA-directed Thai artillery and infantry units. Public revelations

about the true extent of U.S. involvement in the kingdom, however, brought about stiff congressionally mandated reductions in military aid to Laos. By late 1972, there was little question that the United States would soon disengage from the war in Vietnam and its secret conflict in Laos.

The February 1973 Vientiane Agreement ended U.S. bombing in Laos and, once a new Lao coalition government was formed, mandated the expulsion of Air America and the Thai military units. Although some U.S. government officials hoped that the new Lao government would allow a small U.S. military assistance program to continue, by August 1975 the Pathet Lao had gained control of the central government and the United States was forced to reduce the U.S. mission in Laos to fewer than twenty civilian personnel. A complete communist takeover occurred on 2 December 1975 when the Lao monarchy was abolished and the Lao People's Democratic Republic was established. Fearing for their lives, fully 10 percent of the Lao population, including most of the educated and business elite, fled to Thailand and other countries. The loss of this expertise, compounded by the devastation of the war, has left Laos one of the world's poorest and least developed countries.

[*See also* Hmong; Pathet Lao.]

BIBLIOGRAPHY

BROWN, MACALISTER, and JOSEPH J. ZASLOFF. *Apprentice Revolutionaries: The Communist Movement in Laos, 1930–1985.* 1986.

CASTLE, TIMOTHY N. *At War in the Shadow of Vietnam: United States Military Aid to the Royal Lao Government, 1955–1975.* 1993.

DOMMEN, ARTHUR J. *Conflict in Laos.* 2d ed. 1971.

GOLDSTEIN, MARTIN E. *American Policy Toward Laos.* 1973.

STEVENSON, CHARLES A. *The End of Nowhere: American Policy Toward Laos Since 1954.* 1972.

TOYE, HUGH. *Laos: Buffer State or Battlefield.* 2d ed. 1971.

TIMOTHY N. CASTLE

Lattre de Tassigny, Jean de (1889–1952), French high commissioner and commander in chief in Vietnam, 1950. The colorful and dynamic Lattre assumed political and military responsibility in the wake of humiliating French losses at Dong Khe, Cao Bang, and Lang Son in the fall of 1950. Instructed by the French government to revitalize the war effort, Lattre vigorously embraced this task as he exorcised defeatist attitudes with his personal

JEAN DE LATTRE DE TASSIGNY. At right, with Harry S. Truman, 1951. The general wears a black mourning band on his left arm in memory of his only child, Lt. Bernard de Lattre, killed 29 May 1951 at Ninh Binh, Vietnam. *National Archives*

Lattre himself actually resented the U.S. presence and activity in Southeast Asia, believing that U.S. missions in Vietnam undermined French interests. One U.S. official, Secretary of State Dean Acheson, was not impressed with the general, describing him as a "convinced egotist who has recently passed through a grave crisis carried away by enthusiasm after unexpected success." The "grave crisis" was the death of Lattre's son at the battle of Nam Dinh. General Lattre died of cancer three months after his visit to the United States, without having affected the course of events.

BIBLIOGRAPHY

HERRING, GEORGE C. *America's Longest War: The United States and Vietnam, 1950–1975.* 1986.
KARNOW, STANLEY. *Vietnam: A History.* 1991.
The Pentagon Papers: The Defense Department History of United States Decisionmaking on Vietnam. Senator Gravel Edition. Vol. 1. 1971.
WALL, IRWIN M. *The United States and the Making of Postwar France, 1945–1954.* 1991.

VICTOR JEW

brand of *dynamisme*. He brashly predicted victory within fifteen months of his arrival, and the French armed forces justified Lattre's optimism when they defeated a major Viet Minh offensive in the Red River delta in 1951.

Lattre tirelessly promoted visions of victory and brought his message to the United States in September 1951. Ostensibly invited by the U.S. Joint Chiefs of Staff (JCS) to Washington, D.C., to honor his World War II achievements, Lattre exploited the occasion to garner increased U.S. aid and improve the image of the war. His publicity campaign was a rousing success, with favorable appearances on television's "Meet the Press" as well as encomiums to the "fighting general" in *Time* and *Life* magazines.

Speaking at the Pentagon, he linked the French Indochina War to the geopolitical stakes of global anticommunism. Instead of waging a dirty colonial war, he argued that France was actually on a crusade and that its efforts were morally and strategically equivalent to those of the United Nations' war in Korea. Moreover, he claimed that the Gulf of Tonkin was the more important domino; if it fell, all of Southeast Asia would turn communist, India would "burn like a match," the Middle East and Africa would be lost, and Europe would be "outflanked." While the American press may have been taken in by the "General de Lattre show,"

Leclerc, Jacques Philippe (1902–1947), French military commander in Indochina, 1945–1946. "Jacques Philippe Leclerc" was the nom de guerre that Philippe de Hauteclocque adopted as a leader of the Resistance in France during World War II. Assigned to command French forces in Vietnam by Charles de Gaulle, Leclerc defeated the Viet Minh in southern Vietnam in 1945; nevertheless, he came to realize the futility of French military reconquest. He returned to Indochina on a fact-finding mission in 1946–1947, and recommended a political solution. He prophetically noted, "Anti-communism will be a useless tool as long as the problem of nationalism remains unresolved."

BIBLIOGRAPHY

HAMMER, ELLEN J. *The Struggle for Indochina.* 1954.
KARNOW, STANLEY. *Vietnam: A History.* 1991.
The Pentagon Papers: The Defense Department History of United States Decisionmaking on Vietnam. Senator Gravel Edition. Vol. 1. 1971.

VICTOR JEW

Le Duan (1908–1986), founding member of the Indochinese Communist Party (ICP); elected to Central Committee in 1939; leading member of the Vietnamese Workers' Party (VWP), 1951–1986;

named general secretary of VWP in 1957; remained general secretary of VWP (renamed the Vietnamese Communist Party, VCP in 1976) until his death in 1986. Born the son of a railway worker in Quang Tri province in central Vietnam, Le Duan joined Ho Chi Minh's Revolutionary Youth League in 1928 and became a founding member of the Indochinese Communist Party (the linear antecedent of the VWP) two years later. He became a member of the party's central committee in 1939 but spent most of World War II in the French jail on Con Son island.

After his release from Poulo Condore prison in 1945, Le Duan served under President Ho Chi Minh in Hanoi, and then in 1950 or 1951 was named the party's leading representative in the southern provinces. He remained in the South after the Geneva agreement of 1954 as secretary of the party's regional committee there and became a leading advocate of a more activist policy to promote the reunification of the two zones. His 1956 pamphlet, "The Path of Revolution in the South" ("Duong loi cach mang mien Nam"), is cited in official histories in Vietnam as a seminal work in the struggle for national liberation.

Summoned to Hanoi in late 1956, Le Duan was named acting general secretary of the VWP (with Ho Chi Minh nominally occupying the position) when Truong Chinh was removed from the post as a result of his mishandling of the land reform program in the DRV. At the party's Third National Congress in September 1960, Le Duan was formally elevated to the position. Under his guidance, the party in succeeding years unrelentingly pursued victory in the South, and Le Duan played an active part in propagating a Maoist strategy for a war of insurgency. His recommendation for a combined political-military approach, culminating in a general offensive and uprising, became the basis for the Tet Offensive in 1968.

After the end of the Vietnam War, Le Duan continued to serve as general secretary of the VWP (renamed the Vietnamese Communist Party in December 1976) until his death in June 1986. While lacking the personal charisma of his predecessor Ho Chi Minh, Le Duan possessed a talent for reconciling diverse views and strove to balance the growing split between ideologically conservative and pragmatic elements within the party leadership. At the same time he led his country into a more intimate relationship with the Soviet Union at the expense of ties with the People's Republic of China. After his death, the party discarded many of the classical principles of Marxism–Leninism in an effort to revitalize the economy and Vietnamese society as a whole.

BIBLIOGRAPHY

LE DUAN. *On the Right of Collective Mastery.* 1980.
LE DUAN. *The Vietnamese Revolution: Fundamental Problems, Essential Tasks.* 1971.

WILLIAM J. DUIKER

Le Duc Tho (1911–1990), born Phan Dinh Khai; secret negotiator for North Vietnam at the Paris peace talks, 1969–1973. The son of an official in the French colonial regime, Le Duc Tho helped found the Indochina Communist Party in 1930, for which he spent six years in Con Son prison. Ho Chi Minh placed Tho in charge of southern Viet Minh resistance to the French in the 1950s. Elected to the politburo in 1955, Tho supervised the war in the south from hidden jungle bases in the 1960s. In 1968, Xuan Thuy headed the first North Vietnamese delegation to the Paris peace talks, but Tho arrived soon thereafter as special adviser, becoming the real force behind the scenes in secret meetings with U.S. negotiator Henry Kissinger. Tho proved an implacable and tenacious adversary whom Kissinger remembered as "a dour, dedicated revolutionary" who "defended the position he represented with dedication." Knowing that the United States was under more pressure to end the war than was North Vietnam, Tho stonewalled for years with unconditional demands for U.S. withdrawal and President Thieu's resignation. A tentative agreement that allowed Thieu to remain in office was reached in October 1972, but both sides grew intransigent and President Nixon subsequently ordered the heaviest bombing of the war. Very little changed in the final peace accords signed in Paris by Tho and Kissinger on 25 January 1973. Co-recipient of the Nobel Peace Prize, Tho declined the award, stating that "peace has not yet really been established in Vietnam." The agreement soon broke down and Tho secretly returned to South Vietnam, where he joined Gen. Van Tien Dung in planning the Final Offensive of April 1975. Tho oversaw the Vietnamese invasion of Cambodia before resigning from the politburo in 1986.

BIBLIOGRAPHY

DILLARD, WALTER SCOTT. *Sixty Days to Peace.* 1982.
GOODMAN, ALLAN E. *The Lost Peace: America's Search for a Negotiated Settlement of the Vietnam War.* 1978.

LE DUC THO. C. 1972. *Archive Photos*

KISSINGER, HENRY. *The White House Years.* 1979.
QUINN-JUDGE, PAUL. "In Line for the Top." *Far Eastern Economic Review* 126 (13 December 1984).
Who's Who in North Vietnam. 1969.

GLEN GENDZEL

LeMay, Curtis (1906–), U.S. Air Force chief of staff, 1961–1965; George Wallace's vice presidential candidate, 1968. LeMay believed that air power could achieve most military aims. In late 1963 he advocated a massive bombing campaign against North Vietnam, gaining notoriety with his remark that the United States should "bomb them [the North Vietnamese] back to the Stone Age."

BIBLIOGRAPHY

KARNOW, STANLEY. *Vietnam: A History.* 1991.
POWERS, THOMAS. *The War at Home.* 1973.

KELLY EVANS-PFEIFER

Lemnitzer, Lyman (1899–1988), general, U.S. Army, commander in chief, Far East Command, 1955–1957; U.S. Army chief of staff, 1959–1960; chairman, Joint Chiefs of Staff, 1960–1962. Lyman Lemnitzer planned the first U.S. Military Assistance Advisory Group (MAAG) in Saigon, commanded the 7th Infantry Division in the Korean War, and supervised the rearming of Japan, gaining many years of military experience in Asia. As chairman of the Joint Chiefs of Staff, Lemnitzer toured South Vietnam in May 1961, returning to Washington unimpressed by the threat from Viet Cong guerrillas. The real danger, he believed, was a full-scale Korea-style invasion from the north. General Lemnitzer warned that Americans could not fight guerrilla wars, advising President Kennedy against intervention in Laos with anything less than 140,000 men and a willingness to use nuclear weapons if necessary. Lemnitzer's views clashed with President Kennedy's enthusiasm for limited war and counterinsurgency. Kennedy sent him to command NATO in 1962, and Lemnitzer retired in 1969.

CURTIS LEMAY. At right, with George Wallace, 3 October 1968. LeMay ran as Wallace's vice presidential running mate in the latter's independent bid for the U.S. presidency in 1968. *National Archives*

BIBLIOGRAPHY

HILSMAN, ROGER. *To Move a Nation: The Politics of Foreign Policy in the Administration of John F. Kennedy.* 1967.

KELLNER, KATHLEEN. "Broker of Power: General Lyman L. Lemnitzer." Ph.D. diss., Kent State University, 1987.

KORB, LAWRENCE J. *The Joint Chiefs of Staff: The First Twenty-Five Years.* 1976.

WALTON, RICHARD J. *Cold War and Counter-Revolution: The Foreign Policy of John F. Kennedy.* 1972.

GLEN GENDZEL

Le Nguyen Khang, (fl. 1954–1975) brigadier general, South Vietnamese armed forces; longest serving commandant of South Vietnam's marine corps. Born in Son Tay province, North Vietnam, Khang fled south after the Geneva accords of 1954. The first Vietnamese to graduate from the U.S. Marine Corps' Amphibious Warfare School, Khang was instrumental in the development of South Vietnam's Marine Brigade (later a division). A favorite of Diem, Khang did not participate in the coup that unseated Diem in 1963. The new government of Gen. Duong Van Minh, fearing his influence in the Army of the Republic of Vietnam (ARVN), quickly reassigned Khang to the Philippines in December 1963 as South Vietnam's military attaché. In February 1964 Gen. Nguyen Khanh, who toppled the Minh government, reinstated Khang to his former duties. Khang's competence and popularity among his troops, plus his carefully cultivated political connections, paved the way for new appointments. In 1968, in addition to his marine duties, Khang was commander of the Capital Military District, military governor of Saigon, commander of III Corps Tactical Zone (CTZ), governor-delegate for III CTZ, and a member of the National Leadership Committee. He relocated to the United States after South Vietnam collapsed on 30 April 1975.

BIBLIOGRAPHY

CANTWELL, THOMAS R. "The Army of South Vietnam: A Military and Political History, 1955–1975." Ph.D. diss., University of New South Wales, Sydney, Australia, 1989.

THOMAS R. CANTWELL

Le Van Kim (1918–), general, Army of the Republic of Vietnam (ARVN); born in Vietnam and raised in France, Gen. Le Van Kim was the top Vietnamese aide to Adm. Georges d'Argenlieu, French high commissioner of Indochina. Kim represented Vietnam's colonial army at Geneva in 1954. President Diem appointed him head of South Vietnam's military academy, but then fired him in 1960. Kim joined Duong Van Minh and Tran Van Don in the coup that killed Diem in November 1963. "The Americans told us to choose between Diem and American aid," he said. "We had no choice." Kim briefly became foreign minister and then chief of staff, but within days he and Don were arrested in Nguyen Khanh's coup of January 1964. Khanh accused them of conspiring with the French to create a neutral government in Vietnam. After a show trial, Kim was cleared and resumed command of the military academy. He retired in 1965 and founded an import-export business in Saigon.

BIBLIOGRAPHY

HAMMER, ELLEN J. *A Death in November: America in Vietnam.* 1987.

MACCLEAR, MICHAEL. *The Ten Thousand Day War.* 1981.

SMITH, HARVEY H., et al. *Area Handbook for South Vietnam.* 1967.

TRAN VAN DON. *Our Endless War.* 1978.

GLEN GENDZEL

Le Van Vien. *See* Bay Vien.

Levie, Howard S. (1907–), U.S. Army judge advocate, 1942–1963; professor of law emeritus, Washington University, St. Louis. A scholar of international law, Levie wrote extensively during the Vietnam War about the treatment and repatriation of prisoners of war and against U.S. use of tear gas, napalm, and defoliants.

BIBLIOGRAPHY

LEVIE, HOWARD S. "Maltreatment of Prisoners of War in Vietnam." *Boston University Law Review.* 1968.

LEVIE, HOWARD S. "Weapons of Warfare." In *Law and Responsibility in Warfare: The Vietnam Experience,* edited by Peter D. Trooboff. 1975.

JENNIFER FROST

Levy, Howard B. (1937–), physician, captain, U.S. Army. In 1967, after a long and widely publicized court-martial, Levy was convicted for refusing to train Special Forces medics bound for Vietnam and for speaking out against U.S. involvement in the Vietnam War to U.S. soldiers. He served twenty-seven months in prison before the Supreme Court ordered him released on bail in August 1969.

BIBLIOGRAPHY

"The Captain Who Refused an Order," *Newsweek* (12 April 1971).

JENNIFER FROST

LINEBACKER and LINEBACKER II. Two U.S. bombing campaigns, 10 May–23 October (LINE-BACKER) and 18–29 December 1972, (LINEBACKER II) against North Vietnam ordered by President Richard Nixon, were instrumental in bringing the Paris peace negotiations to a conclusion. Ordered in response to the 30 March 1972 Easter Offensive, LINEBACKER (the name reflected Nixon's fondness for football) was a resumption of the strategic bombing of North Vietnam, which had been dis-

continued since the cancellation of ROLLING THUN-DER. In contrast to the myriad of political and diplomatic rationales that underlay ROLLING THUN-DER, LINEBACKER's objectives were clear: to halt the invasion of South Vietnam by cutting the North Vietnamese Army's lines of supply and to force North Vietnam to resume peace negotiations. Consequently, unlike during ROLLING THUNDER, commanders were given wide latitude to achieve those goals. Air power was employed with full intensity from the outset; military commanders exercised full control of tactics and targeting within broad White House guidelines; B-52s were used extensively against North Vietnamese targets; precision-guided munitions (PGMs), notably laser-guided bombs, were available in quantity; and categories of targets previously off limits were attacked, notably airfields and Haiphong harbor, which was mined by Naval aircraft.

The operational burden of LINEBACKER was borne not only by B-52s, but also by U.S. Air Force

B-52 BOMBERS. At Anderson Air Force Base, Guam. *National Archives*

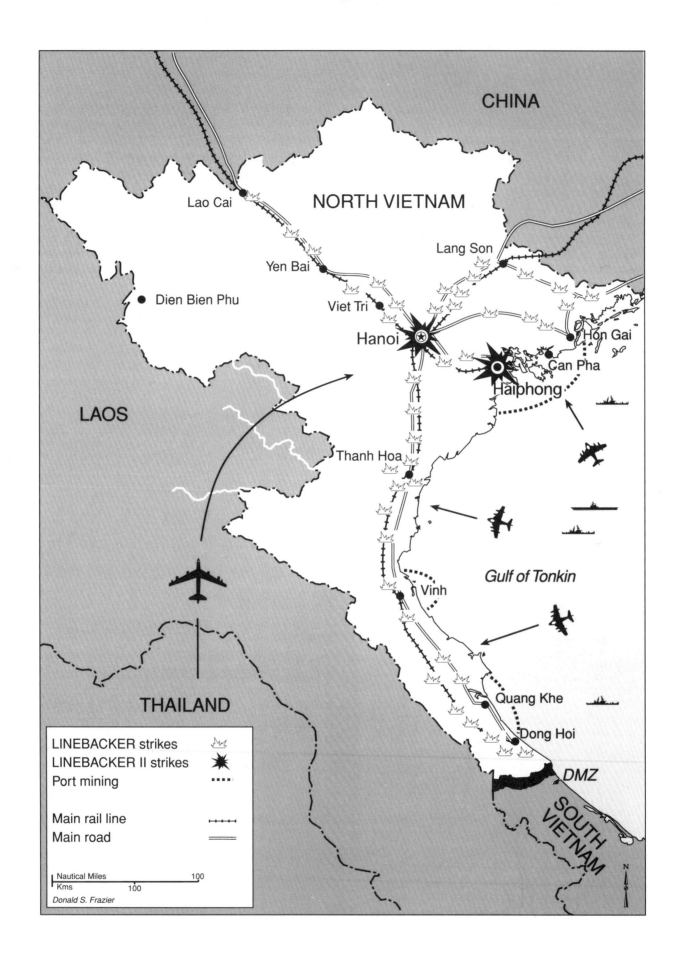

CHINA

NORTH VIETNAM

Lao Cai

Lang Son

Yen Bai

Dien Bien Phu

Viet Tri

Hanoi

Hon Gai

Can Pha

Haiphong

LAOS

Thanh Hoa

Gulf of Tonkin

Vinh

THAILAND

Quang Khe

Dong Hoi

DMZ

SOUTH VIETNAM

LINEBACKER strikes
LINEBACKER II strikes
Port mining

Main rail line
Main road

Nautical Miles   100
Kms   100

Donald S. Frazier

N

F-4 Phantom tactical fighter units and two-seater F-105G Thunderchief "Wild Weasel" surface-to-air missile (SAM) suppression aircraft based in South Vietnam and Thailand, and by U.S. Navy carrier-based F-4 Phantom, F-8 Crusader, A-6 Intruder, and A-7 Corsair fighter and attack squadrons. U.S. Air Force F-111s were also redeployed to Southeast Asia in September 1972, despite their disastrous operational debut in the final months of ROLLING THUNDER. After renewed "teething" problems, F-111s proved highly effective in precision low-altitude, night-radar bombing attacks during LINEBACKER II.

LINEBACKER was preceded by a massive redeployment of U.S. airpower and featured wide-ranging strikes on transportation, power-generation and petroleum production and storage targets and included mining harbors and rivers. Strikes were supported by attacks on airfields and SAM sites, chaff corridors (clouds of thin strips of aluminum foil), and radar jamming to block North Vietnamese radars, F-105G SAM-suppression patrols, and anti-MiG combat air patrols. PGMs proved particularly effective, notably in attacks on power plants and bridges. By mid-October, with war matériel depleted, the North's transportation net a shambles, and PAVN forces in the South feeling the pinch, North Vietnam communicated its readiness to negotiate, and LINEBACKER was terminated.

LINEBACKER II, the so-called Christmas bombings, was Nixon's response to diplomatic intransigence by the North Vietnamese, and it centered on B-52 attacks in the Hanoi and Haiphong areas. Strategic Air Command (SAC) headquarters dictated B-52 tactics, and for the first three nights of the operation the bombers attacked in three-ship cells at evenly spaced intervals using the same altitudes and ground tracks. B-52 losses to SAMs were

---

LINEBACKER AND LINEBACKER II.

May–December 1972. In Operation LINEBACKER, U.S. Air Force air strikes combined with U.S. Navy 7th Fleet carrier strikes and aerial mining of North Vietnamese ports severely hampered North Vietnam's ability to resupply its invasion forces in the South. During LINEBACKER II, in 729 sorties B-52s dropped approximately 14,000 tons of bombs on targets within Hanoi and Haiphong. Though denounced as "terror bombing," considering the weight of explosives expended, these massive strikes resulted in remarkably few civilian casualties: the North Vietnamese claimed to have sustained only between 1,300 and 1,600 casualties.

heavy and fell disproportionately on Guam-based B-52Gs, which had less capable electronics countermeasures suites. An aircrew mutiny protesting the rigid tactics resulted and made its point: B-52 raids were scaled back, but later resumed with full fury—and more intelligent tactics—after a two-day Christmas standdown. The attacks wreaked havoc on North Vietnam's economic and military infrastructure, forcing the North Vietnamese back to the peace table. Of a total of 206 B-52s deployed during LINEBACKER II, 15 were shot down by SAMs, 9 during the first three days. Despite the intensity of the attacks and over 20,000 tons of bombs dropped, the North Vietnamese claimed only 1,318 civilians killed. Air power advocates have cited LINEBACKER II as evidence that the war could have been won by air power alone, but the argument neglects the fact that Nixon's policy aims in 1972 were far more modest than Johnson's had been in 1965–1968.

BIBLIOGRAPHY

ESCHMANN, KARL J. *Linebacker: The Untold Story of the Raids over North Vietnam.* 1989.
PARKS, W. HAYS. "Linebacker and the Law of War." *Air University Review* 34, no. 2 (January–February 1983): 2–30.

JOHN F. GUILMARTIN JR.

Lippmann, Walter (1889–1974), Pulitzer Prize–winner and influential syndicated columnist for the New York *Herald Tribune.* Lippmann's opposition to escalating the war and his support for a negotiated settlement antagonized President Johnson. Johnson had courted Lippmann at the outset of his presidency, but reacted bitterly when Lippmann criticized his Vietnam policy. Particularly strong was his column of 3 February 1966, in which he wrote, "Gestures, propaganda, public relations and bombing and more bombing will not work."

BIBLIOGRAPHY

KARNOW, STANLEY. *Vietnam: A History.* 1991.
STEEL, RONALD. *Walter Lippmann and the American Century.* 1980.

KELLY EVANS-PFEIFER

Literature. *For discussion of the treatment of the Vietnam War in plays, poetry, memoirs, and novels, see* Art and Literature.

Loan, Nguyen Ngoc. *See* Nguyen Ngoc Loan.

Loc Ninh, South Vietnamese town, capital of Binh Long province, near Cambodian border, 117 kilometers (70 miles) north of Saigon. In one of the pre–Tet Offensive border battles, Viet Cong forces attacked the U.S. outpost at Loc Ninh on 29 October 1967. During ferocious fighting, U.S. forces inflicted heavy casualties on the Viet Cong forces and drove them back.

During the Easter Offensive of 1972, North Vietnamese Army (NVA) forces battled U.S. defenders successfully for the town on 4–6 April. Loc Ninh subsequently served as one of the NVA's main headquarters and communications centers, and was a key staging area for the 1975 Spring Offensive.

BIBLIOGRAPHY

CLARKE, JEFFREY J. *United States Army in Vietnam—Advice and Support: The Final Years, 1965–1973.* 1988.
DAVIDSON, PHILLIP B. *Vietnam at War—The History: 1946–1975.* 1988.
KARNOW, STANLEY. *Vietnam: A History.* 1991.

ELLEN D. GOLDLUST

Lodge, Henry Cabot, Jr. (1902–1985), U.S. ambassador to South Vietnam, 1963–1966. In 1963, Henry Cabot Lodge succeeded Frederick Nolting as ambassador to South Vietnam. Lodge arrived in Saigon in August during a crisis precipitated by President Ngo Dinh Diem's repression of Buddhists. Outraged by Diem's policy and convinced that the regime could not survive, Lodge notified U.S. officials in Washington, D.C., that a group of army generals sought U.S. support for a coup. He urged Kennedy to support the conspiracy, but when the generals appeared indecisive, Lodge advised the president that the coup would have to wait. In October the generals again planned a takeover, and Lodge was authorized to inform them that the United States would do nothing to "thwart a change of government." On 1 November, the army ousted and killed Diem and his brother, Nhu.

Lodge resigned in 1964 for a tentative run in the presidential election, but returned to Saigon as ambassador the following June. Attempting to revitalize U.S. pacification efforts, he outlined a program intended to create a base of popular support for the South Vietnamese government in the countryside.

In 1966, Lodge became involved in the conflict between Buddhists and Premier Nguyen Cao Ky when he provided Ky with U.S. airplanes to transport troops to quell the disturbance. As he left his post that year, Lodge remained pessimistic about the possibilities of democracy in South Vietnam, warning that national elections scheduled for 1967 should not be totally uncontrolled and thus provide a "vehicle for a Communist takeover."

As one of the "wise men" who met with Lyndon Johnson on 25 March 1968, Lodge recommended an end to search and destroy operations in the south and suggested that U.S. troops be used as a shield to protect South Vietnamese society. In early 1969, President Richard Nixon designated Lodge titular head of the U.S. delegation to the Paris Peace talks.

BIBLIOGRAPHY

HALBERSTAM, DAVID. *The Best and the Brightest.* 1992.
LODGE, HENRY CABOT. *The Storm Has Many Eyes.* 1973.
YOUNG, MARILYN. *The Vietnam Wars, 1945–1990.* 1991.

PAUL M. TAILLON

Long Binh, major U.S. military logistical and headquarters complex located just outside the city of Bien Hoa, about 32 kilometers (20 miles) north of Saigon. Headquarters of the II Field Force, Vietnam, and III ARVN Corps, on the base were surgical hospitals, restaurants, swimming pools, and movie theaters, among other facilities, with associated military equipment and support personnel. Long Binh served as a transit base where U.S. troops waited for transport while leaving or coming into country. The complex also included a U.S. Army jail known derisively as the LBJ, and on 29 August 1968 several hundred prisoners, almost all of them African Americans, rioted at the prison, the first widely publicized incident of the racial strife within the U.S. forces in Vietnam. Viet Cong forces unsuccessfully attacked Long Binh in 1968 as part of the Tet Offensive and later in 1969.

BIBLIOGRAPHY

CLARKE, JEFFREY J. *United States Army in Vietnam—Advice and Support: The Final Years, 1965–1973.* 1988.
SPECTOR, RONALD H. *After Tet: The Bloodiest Year in Vietnam.* 1993.
STANTON, SHELBY L. *The Rise and Fall of an American Army: U.S. Ground Forces in Vietnam, 1965–1973.* 1985.

ELLEN D. GOLDLUST

Lon Nol (1913–1985), general, Cambodian army; prime minister, Cambodia, 1966–1967, 1969; organizer of the coup that ousted Prince Sihanouk in March 1970; prime minister, 1970–1972; president, Khmer Republic, 1972–1975. Lon Nol, a promonarchist, authoritarian general in the Cambodian army, was born in Tay Ninh, Vietnam, was French-educated, and rose to power by preventing a coup against Sihanouk in 1959. He opposed infiltration by Viet Cong forces into eastern Cambodia, disliking both the Vietnamese and the Khmer Rouge. Dissatisfied with Sihanouk's neutrality, the United States encouraged a military coup against him in 1970 and supported Lon Nol's seizure of power. Lon Nol was nonetheless surprised by the U.S. invasion of Cambodia, announced on 30 April 1970. He tolerated the extensive U.S. bombing, which lasted throughout the next five years, in return for large amounts of military and economic aid. His poorly led forces suffered a string of defeats by the Khmer Rouge and by the North Vietnamese Army, and popular discontent against his regime mounted. By late 1972 North Vietnamese artillery, tank, and infantry attacks had broken Lon Nol's forces. Henry Kissinger attempted to persuade the Khmer Rouge to negotiate with Lon Nol, but they refused. After the United States signed the Paris peace accords with Vietnam on 30 January 1973, Lon Nol demanded that the Vietnamese communists withdraw from Cambodia, surrender their arms, and allow Cambodian government forces to occupy previously held communist territory. These demands, excessive given the weakness of Lon Nol's position, were not supported by the United States. Lon Nol apparently did not understand how tenuous was his control of Cambodia. After U.S. military involvement in Vietnam ended, U.S. forces continued to drop more than 257,000 tons of bombs in support of Lon Nol's forces in Cambodia, but this did not prevent a Khmer Rouge victory. The increasingly unpopular Lon Nol was allied in the popular mind with the United States; his regime, despite its corruption and inept and demoralized leadership, continued to receive U.S. support, but to no avail. Lon Nol escaped to Indonesia before the communist takeover on 17 April 1975.

BIBLIOGRAPHY

ISAACS, ARNOLD. *Without Honor: Defeat in Vietnam and Cambodia.* 1983.

KIERNAN, BEN, and CHANTHOU BOUA. *Peasants and Politics in Kampuchea, 1942–1981.* 1982.

KIERNAN, BEN. *How Pol Pot Came to Power.* 1985.

YOUNG, MARILYN. *The Vietnam Wars 1945–1990.* 1991.

SANDRA C. TAYLOR

M

McCain, John S., Jr. (1911–1981), admiral, U.S. Navy; Commander-in-Chief, Pacific (CINC-PAC), 1968–1972. A highly decorated submarine commander in World War II, Adm. John McCain Jr. was the first admiral's son to become a full admiral himself. He held important navy staff posts, including that of top congressional lobbyist, and he commanded amphibious landings in the Dominican Republic in 1965. McCain succeeded Adm. Ulysses S. Grant Sharp as CINCPAC on 31 July 1968. "The communists have chosen to make Vietnam the testing ground for their so-called wars of national liberation," he said. "We are there to prove to them that it won't work." McCain long advocated mining Haiphong harbor, which President Nixon approved in May 1972. McCain also called for increased bombing of Hanoi even though his son, a U.S. Navy aviator, was held prisoner there. Adm. Noel Gayler replaced McCain in September 1972.

BIBLIOGRAPHY

HUBBELL, JOHN G. "Sentinel of the Pacific." *Reader's Digest,* March 1970, 203–212.
McCAIN, JOHN S., JR. "Our Pacific Interests: An Interview." *Strategic Review* 1 (Spring 1973): 15–22.

GLEN GENDZEL

McCain, John S., III (1936–), lieutenant commander, U.S. Navy. The son and grandson of full admirals, Lt. Cmdr. John McCain III was a naval aviator aboard the USS *Forrestal* in the Vietnam War. Shot down over Hanoi on 26 October 1967, he suffered three broken limbs and was beaten and stabbed by angry mobs on the ground. McCain was denied medical attention and tortured for over three years in solitary confinement. "If you are going to make it," he said later, "you get tougher as time goes by." Released with other prisoners of war in 1973, McCain resumed his U.S. Navy career before retiring in 1981. He was elected as a Republican U.S. representative from Arizona in 1982 and U.S. senator in 1986.

BIBLIOGRAPHY

"Inside Vietnam: What a Former P.O.W. Found." *U.S. News and World Report,* 11 March 1985.
LEWIS, NEIL A. "An Ex-P.O.W. Leads Drive for Hanoi Ties." *New York Times,* 1 June 1988.
McCAIN, JOHN S., III. "How the POWs Fought Back." *U.S. News and World Report,* 14 May 1973, 44–52, 110–115.
"War Hero." *Time,* 17 November 1986.

GLEN GENDZEL

FATHER AND SON. John S. McCain III (on crutches) with his father John S. McCain Jr. shortly after his release as a POW, 1973. *National Archives*

McCarthy, Eugene J. (1916–), U.S. senator (D-Minn.), 1959–1971; member, Senate Foreign Relations Committee. A devout, cerebral Catholic, McCarthy invigorated the antiwar movement by challenging President Johnson's renomination in 1968. After graduating from St. John's College in Minnesota, serving in Army intelligence, and teaching high school and college, McCarthy was elected in 1948 to the House of Representatives, where he criticized Cold War anticommunist hysteria and helped to found the liberal Democratic Study Group. He moved to the Senate in 1958, attracted national attention with an eloquent nominating speech for Adlai Stevenson in 1960, and was widely mentioned as a vice presidential prospect in 1964. Bored by conventional politics, he remained conspicuously aloof from most of his colleagues.

Growing doubts about U.S. intervention in what he believed to be a Vietnamese civil war energized McCarthy in late 1965. In January 1966, he joined fourteen other senators in urging the continuation of a bombing pause. During the next eighteen months, he skeptically interrogated administration spokesmen as a member of the Foreign Relations Committee, ridiculed the argument that the defense of South Vietnam was necessary to contain the People's Republic of China, and spoke often against the war under the auspices of college groups and Clergy and Laity Concerned About Vietnam (CALCAV). Along with other antiwar members of Congress, McCarthy questioned the morality and constitutionality of the war, but he also ran for president in 1968 to reassert senatorial prerogative in foreign affairs, reverse the "personalization" of the presidency, restore hope to alienated youth, democratize the political process, and promote national reconciliation. Many students rallied to his cause and modified their demeanor to look "Clean for Gene" on the campaign trail. Still, McCarthy's deliberately low-key campaign looked inept until, following the Tet Offensive, he won 42 percent of the Democratic vote in the New Hampshire primary. Although Johnson won 48 percent of the vote, McCarthy's moral victory and an impending triumph in Wisconsin may have influenced his decision to retire. Subsequent bitter primary contests with Robert Kennedy (who defeated him everywhere except in Oregon) increased McCarthy's disdain for politics. Shocked by Kennedy's assassination and fearing violence in the streets, McCarthy warned his young supporters against attending the Democratic convention in Chicago. He continued to campaign himself primarily to influence the Democratic platform and to prod Hubert Humphrey, the likely nominee, in an antiwar direction. Both Humphrey and the convention majority rejected McCarthy's proposals for a bombing halt and negotiations to establish a coalition government in South Vietnam. When police beat antiwar demonstrators in the streets, McCarthy's ironic detachment gave way to seething anger. He refused to campaign for the Democratic ticket and offered only a grudging endorsement in late October, decisions that contributed to Humphrey's defeat.

McCarthy retired from the Senate in 1970 but thereafter wrote extensively on politics and occasionally conducted witty, idiosyncratic, and essentially symbolic campaigns for several offices, including the presidency. Democratic presidential aspirants were favorite targets of his barbs. By the late 1980s, McCarthy was lamenting that American politics had entered a state of entropy, yet he never acknowledged that his own flight from seriousness, partly a reaction to the disappointments of 1968, helped produce this condition.

BIBLIOGRAPHY

CHESTER, LEWIS, GEOFFREY HODGSON, and BRUCE PAGE. *An American Melodrama: The Presidential Campaign of 1968.* 1969.
MCCARTHY, EUGENE J. *The Year of the People.* 1969.

LEO P. RIBUFFO

McCloy, John (1895–1989), banker, civilian adviser to President Johnson, one of the "wise men." A firm adherent of the domino theory, McCloy told President Johnson in 1965 that Vietnam should be a "test case" for the U.S. policy of containment. In the crucial "wise men" meeting on 25 March 1968,

EUGENE J. MCCARTHY. At right, with J. William Fulbright, 3 October 1966. Photo by Yoichi R. Okamoto. *Lyndon Baines Johnson Library*

however, McCloy joined the majority in backing deescalation and the end of U.S. involvement in Vietnam.

BIBLIOGRAPHY

KAHIN, GEORGE McT. *Intervention: How America Became Involved in Vietnam.* 1986.

KELLY EVANS-PFEIFER

McCone, John (1902–1991), director, Central Intelligence Agency (CIA), 1961–1965. President John F. Kennedy appointed McCone, a conservative Republican millionaire, director of the CIA in September 1961. A fervent anticommunist, McCone believed that to be successful in Vietnam the United States must commit sufficient troops and resources to gain victory. A supporter of Ngo Dinh Diem, McCone unsuccessfully opposed the coup against the South Vietnamese president. In a late-1963 letter to President Lyndon B. Johnson, McCone maintained that South Vietnam lacked "an outstanding individual to lead" and had "no organized government." In September 1964, following the Gulf of Tonkin incident, McCone reported that the prospects for a stable government in South Vietnam remained slim and opposed counterstrikes against North Vietnam. McCone's influence in the Johnson administration subsequently declined, and he resigned in 1965.

BIBLIOGRAPHY

HATCHER, PATRICK LLOYD. *The Suicide of an Elite: American Internationalists and Vietnam.* 1990.
LAQUEUR, WALTER. *A World of Secrets: The Uses and Limits of Intelligence.* 1985.

PAUL M. TAILLON

McConnell, John P. (1908–1986), general, U.S. Air Force; chief of staff, 1965–1969. McConnell served as air adviser in India and China before he was named U.S. Air Force chief of staff in January 1965. During the Vietnam War, McConnell consistently advocated heavier bombing of a greater number targets in North Vietnam than President Johnson and his advisers were willing to accept for fear of provoking Chinese intervention and U.S. public disapproval. McConnell believed that ground forces alone could not defeat the enemy, but "a very severe application of air power" could win the war in a matter of days. He insisted that the air force could play a decisive role in limited wars through "strategic persuasion," but political restrictions on the exercise of air power in Vietnam left him frustrated. McConnell retired in 1969.

BIBLIOGRAPHY

BERGER, CARL, ed. *The United States Air Force in Southeast Asia, 1961–1973.* 1977.
"From LeMay to McConnell: A Change to the New Breed." *Newsweek,* 4 January 1965.
MCCONNELL, JOHN P. "Airpower Over North Vietnam." *Aviation Week,* 28 August 1967.
MCCONNELL, JOHN P. "The Lesson of Vietnam." *Vital Speeches* (1 January 1966).
MCCONNELL, JOHN P. "Role of Airpower in Viet-Nam." *Vital Speeches* (15 October 1965).
SCHLIGHT, JOHN. *The United States Air Force in Southeast Asia: The War in South Vietnam: The Years of the Offensive, 1965–1968.* 1988.
"USAF's Score in Limited War: Impressive." *Air Force and Space Digest* (September 1966).

GLEN GENDZEL

McGovern, George (1922–), U.S. senator (D-S. Dak.), 1963–1981; 1972 Democratic Party presidential nominee. McGovern, the most liberal major party presidential nominee in the twentieth century, tried to combine a critique of domestic and foreign policy from the left with a viable political strategy. Born in South Dakota in 1922, he served as a decorated bomber pilot during World War II but felt no thrill in combat. An early critic of the Cold War, he was a delegate to the left-of-center Progressive Party convention in 1948. Although McGovern abstained on election day, he later remembered the Progressive Party as an "idealistic" effort to improve relations with the Soviet Union. After receiving a Ph.D. in history from Northwestern University and briefly teaching college, McGovern was elected to the House of Representatives from South Dakota in 1956, served President Kennedy as director of Food for Peace, and won a Senate seat in 1962. Shrewd and ambitious beneath his mild-mannered demeanor, he contemplated a future presidential race while still in the House.

Although political realities required at least pro forma fealty to Cold War orthodoxy, McGovern was sufficiently skeptical to oppose the Eisenhower Doctrine, which committed the United States to containment of communism in the Middle East, and to question Kennedy's preoccupation with Cuba. In 1964 he reluctantly voted for the Gulf of

Tonkin Resolution in hopes of derailing Barry Goldwater's presidential campaign. Starting in early 1965, however, he steadily criticized U.S. participation in what he believed to be a Vietnamese civil war. Initially, McGovern opposed the bombing of North Vietnam and urged an enclave strategy; by 1970 he favored phased withdrawal and a congressional cut-off of funds, a position embodied in a Senate resolution he introduced with Mark Hatfield. While championing grassroots demonstrations, he tried to keep his distance from radicals and refused Daniel Ellsberg's offer of the purloined Pentagon Papers.

As the Democratic nominee in 1972, McGovern hoped to defeat President Richard Nixon by combining opposition to the war, support from party regulars, and appeals to "come home, America" through a domestic reform agenda. His campaign was unsuccessful, however. Vice presidential nominee Thomas Eagleton admitted a history of serious mental illness and was prodded into removing himself from the ticket. Both McGovern's choice of Ea-

GEORGE MCGOVERN. On 20 April 1971. *Library of Congress*

gleton and his decision to send Pierre Salinger to negotiate the release of U.S. prisoners of war with the North Vietnamese prompted questions about his judgment. Moreover, his politically or culturally radical supporters alienated many working-class Democrats; Republicans effectively stigmatized him as the candidate of "acid, abortion, and amnesty." At the same time, Nixon's policy of Vietnamization made the war seem less important than McGovern claimed, and the administration's temporary control of stagflation diminished the economy as a potent issue. Finally, McGovern's attacks on administration corruption, including the Watergate burglary, attracted little attention from the press and thus even less from the electorate.

After losing overwhelmingly to Nixon, McGovern in 1974 won reelection to the Senate, where he remained an effective critic of Cold War premises and prospective military interventions. McGovern's reputation as a radical, sealed in 1972, not only doomed his presidential ambitions but ultimately cost him his Senate seat in the conservative electorial sweep of 1980. In 1984, he conducted a thoughtful, quixotic campaign for the presidential nomination.

BIBLIOGRAPHY

ANSON, ROBERT SAM. *McGovern: A Biography.* 1972.
MCGOVERN, GEORGE S. *Grassroots: The Autobiography of George S. McGovern.* 1977.

LEO P. RIBUFFO

McNamara, Robert (1916–), U.S. secretary of defense, 1961–1968. The longest-serving Pentagon chief since World War II, Robert S. McNamara headed the Defense Department under presidents John F. Kennedy and Lyndon B. Johnson from January 1961 through February 1968—the period of deepening U.S. involvement in the Vietnam War. As defense secretary, McNamara shaped U.S. policy in Vietnam more than any other individual during these crucial years. His gradual disenchantment with the war powerfully symbolized America's own agony and disillusionment over Vietnam, and led to his departure from the Pentagon in a state of near emotional exhaustion.

Early Commitment. McNamara, who had been a brilliant corporate executive with the Ford Motor Company in the 1950s, entered the Pentagon in 1961 with vast faith in American goodness, American power, and his own ability. He shared the

ROBERT S. MCNAMARA. C. 1965. *National Archives*

assumptions of his time: that the United States led the "free world"; that it therefore had an obligation to resist "monolithic" communist expansion around the globe; and that it could do so anywhere, as in Vietnam, through the application of reason harnessed to superior and benevolent U.S. power. McNamara put great faith in empiricism as well. He approached the Vietnam War—as he did all issues—through a study of facts and figures, believing that objective analysis promised a solution to this and every problem.

Viewing the struggle in these terms, McNamara reasoned that the United States could prevail in Vietnam through its superior values and by committing its superior resources effectively—in this case, economic, political, and military support for the noncommunist South Vietnamese regime in its counterinsurgency war against the Viet Cong guerrillas aided by North Vietnam. McNamara believed that in this way the United States could stop communist-inspired "wars of liberation" short of a thermonuclear showdown with the Soviet Union or the People's Republic of China. He promoted this view throughout President Kennedy's years in office as he assumed greater day-to-day responsibility for the issue.

McNamara held to this view amid worsening political conditions in South Vietnam during the summer and fall of 1963. Although he steadfastly opposed a coup against South Vietnam's increasingly repressive leader, Ngo Dinh Diem, he advocated pressuring Diem to reform while expressing continued faith in the counterinsurgency program in a report to President Kennedy that October—even predicting that the bulk of U.S. military advisers could be withdrawn by the end of 1965.

Private Doubts. After Diem's death, however, South Vietnam's situation deteriorated rapidly, generating increasing pressure for direct U.S. intervention. A growing chorus of anxious critics began labeling the conflict "McNamara's War." While he maintained his public optimism that the Viet Cong and the North Vietnamese could be forced to abandon their war against the U.S.-backed South Vietnamese regime, McNamara began voicing private doubts to President Johnson about South Vietnam's political future. Because he still feared the international and domestic consequences of disengagement, McNamara continued to advocate steps to save the situation, including the sustained bombing of North Vietnam in February 1965 and U.S. combat troop deployments in July 1965.

By the fall of 1965, however, McNamara started to doubt the effectiveness of U.S. military operations—particularly air strikes against the North—and the likelihood of achieving a military solution in Vietnam at acceptable cost or acceptable risk. He pressed for construction of an anti-infiltration barrier system, which critics dubbed the "McNamara Line," and favored periodic bombing halts as an impetus to negotiations.

During 1966, McNamara's confidence eroded further. The war's increasing destructiveness, rising military and civilian casualties, mounting infiltration of troops from the North despite U.S. bombing, U.S. troop increases that failed to produce correspondingly large communist losses—all accelerated and deepened his anxiety, as did the growing disenchantment of his key Vietnam aide, John T. McNaughton. Running battles with the Joint Chiefs of Staff (JCS) over proper strategy and increasingly acrimonious domestic dissent on both the political left and right that was frequently aimed at him also took a toll.

McNamara's doubts crystallized in the spring of 1967 when he urged a radical change in policy: limiting the bombing of the North; capping U.S. troop deployments; lowering political objectives; and later, shifting war-fighting responsibility back to the South Vietnamese, with whom it had originated and with whom he now believed it belonged. Through these steps, McNamara sought to stabilize U.S. costs, buttress domestic support, and spark negotiations to end the war.

Johnson's Reaction. An increasingly embattled leader, President Johnson reacted coolly to McNamara's proposals. He viewed bombing halts skeptically, doubted North Vietnam's willingness to negotiate, and wanted to prevail. Frustrated and consumed by a war that had savaged both his popularity and political effectiveness, Johnson gradually lost confidence in his secretary of defense, whose growing differences with the JCS—culminating in the Stennis hearings of August 1967—and increasingly antiwar stance, coming after his earlier advocacy of escalation, rankled and embittered the president. He resisted McNamara's proposals and began to search for a replacement, believing that his able, conscientious, and loyal defense secretary had become a liability.

McNamara, exhausted and burdened by a costly and inconclusive war, commissioned the Pentagon Papers to enable future scholars to understand how and why things went wrong. He bluntly told President Johnson in late October 1967 that the U.S. strategy in Vietnam had become "dangerous, costly in lives, and unsatisfactory to the American people." Recognizing his deteriorating relationship with Johnson and increasingly at odds with the president, McNamara accepted Johnson's offer to head the World Bank in November 1967.

By this time, the pressures on McNamara had grown intense. Pained and disillusioned by a war for which he bore heavy responsibility, McNamara's normally tightly controlled exterior began to crack. At a farewell luncheon for him at the State Department in late February 1968, his anguished emotions came flooding out. A witness recalled the moment vividly: "He reeled off the familiar statistics—how we had dropped more bombs on Vietnam than on all of Europe during World War II. Then his voice broke, and there were tears in his eyes as he spoke of the futility, the crushing futility, of the air war. The rest of us sat silently. . . ."

McNamara remained silent about Vietnam for many years, both publicly and privately, except under legal compulsion in the CBS-Westmoreland trial in 1984. He finally published his memoir on the war, *In Retrospect,* in 1995.

BIBLIOGRAPHY

GRAVEL, MIKE, ed. *The Pentagon Papers: The Defense Department History of United States Decisionmaking on Vietnam.* 5 vols. 1971.

HALBERSTAM, DAVID. *The Best and the Brightest.* 1992.

MCNAMARA, ROBERT S., with BRIAN VANDEMARK. *In Retrospect: The Tragedy and Lessons of Vietnam.* 1995.

SHAPLEY, DEBORAH. *Promise and Power: The Life and Times of Robert McNamara.* 1993.

TREWHITT, HENRY L. *McNamara.* 1971.

BRIAN VANDEMARK

McNamara Line. *See* Barrier Concept.

McNaughton, John T. (1921–1967), assistant secretary of defense for international security affairs, 1964–1967. McNaughton strongly influenced Secretary of Defense Robert McNamara's Vietnam policy throughout McNamara's tenure.

In 1964, after Congress passed the Gulf of Tonkin Resolution, McNaughton advocated increased U.S. military involvement and endorsed bombing of North Vietnam. As a member of Assistant Secretary of State William Bundy's working group in 1964–1965 he supported the introduction of com-

bat troops and convinced McNamara to support the troop requests of the Joint Chiefs of Staff (JCS).

Deeply concerned about South Vietnam's ability and will to fight, by late 1966 McNaughton believed that the United States was primarily fighting to avoid defeat and humiliation, not because progress was being made in the war effort. As the American public became increasingly divided, McNaughton lost faith in the U.S. effort in Vietnam, telling McNamara, "we are trying to impose some U.S. image on distant peoples we cannot understand and . . . we are carrying the thing to absurd lengths." Involved in many aspects of the military effort, from strategic bombing planning to troop deployments, McNaughton was frustrated with the lack of military progress he saw. Further, by late 1966 he revised his earlier position that a communist Vietnam would threaten U.S. interests in Asia, from India to the Philippines to Korea. The domino theory, he now believed, did not apply to the Vietnam situation, and the loss of Vietnam would therefore be of no grave consequence for the United States.

McNaughton's change of view affected McNamara who, in turn, resisted further troop requests and called for disengagement before Johnson forced him out of the Defense Department. McNaughton, his wife, and one of his sons were killed in a plane crash in July 1967, just weeks before he was to assume the new post of secretary of the Navy.

BIBLIOGRAPHY

KAHIN, GEORGE MCT. *Intervention: How America Became Involved in Vietnam.* 1986.

KARNOW, STANLEY. *Vietnam: A History.* 1991.

KELLY EVANS-PFEIFER

McPherson, Harry (1929–), deputy secretary for international affairs, Defense Department, 1963–1964; special counsel and principal speech writer to President Johnson, 1965–1969. McPherson turned against the war after the Tet Offensive and subsequently worked with Defense Secretary Clark Clifford to influence Johnson to deescalate. In March 1968, McPherson drafted a presidential speech calling for an end to the bombing of North Vietnam; Johnson accepted the draft and added to it a statement of his decision not to seek a second presidential term.

BIBLIOGRAPHY

KARNOW, STANLEY. *Vietnam: A History.* 1991.

KELLY EVANS-PFEIFER

Madame Nhu. *See* Ngo Dinh Nhu (Madame Nhu).

Madman Strategy. During his 1968 campaign, Richard Nixon told aides that if the North Vietnamese believed that he would do anything to end the Vietnam War, including using nuclear weapons to annihilate them, then they would settle the war. Nixon borrowed the tactic from Dwight Eisenhower, who hinted during the Korean War that he would drop nuclear bombs on North Korea if they did not agree to an armistice. Describing the "Madman Theory" to his aide, Nixon said he wanted "the North Vietnamese to believe that I've reached the point where I might do anything to stop the war. We'll slip the word to them that . . . 'we can't restrain him [Nixon] when he's angry—and he has his hand on the nuclear button'—and Ho Chi Minh will be . . . begging for peace." No nuclear weapons were used, but Nixon firmly believed that massive bombing of the North eventually led to the signing of the Paris accords.

BIBLIOGRAPHY

KARNOW, STANLEY. *Vietnam: A History.* 1991.
KUTLER, STANLEY I. *The Wars of Watergate.* 1990.
NIXON, RICHARD M. *Memoirs.* 1978.

STANLEY I. KUTLER

Mailer, Norman (1923–), American author, anti–Vietnam War activist. Mailer was a frequent speaker at antiwar rallies and demonstrations. He also wrote *Why Are We in Vietnam?* (1967), an antiwar novel, and *The Armies of the Night* (1968), about the October 1967 march on the Pentagon.

BIBLIOGRAPHY

DeBENEDETTI, CHARLES. *An American Ordeal: The Antiwar Movement of the Vietnam Era.* 1990.

JENNIFER FROST

Malaysia. The Federation of Malaya was a British protectorate until 1957, when it became an independent state in the British Commonwealth. It joined the former British colony of Borneo to form the Federation of Malaysia in 1963. A communist insurrection, led by Malaya's Chinese population, began in 1946 and lasted sporadically until 1963. This long conflict marked Malaya as a potential "domino" and served as a model of guerrilla warfare for Western powers: Sir Robert Thompson, a British administrator in Malaya, developed a successful counterinsurgency program that later formed the basis for South Vietnam's Strategic Hamlet program.

Malaysia's official involvement in the Vietnam War was limited to training and the provision of equipment to South Vietnam. In 1964, Malaysia began training over three thousand South Vietnamese military and police officers in Malaysia and provided counterinsurgency equipment such as transport vehicles. Despite the relatively small amount of material support Malaysia gave to the South Vietnamese, the war nonetheless elicited popular opposition, even among anticommunists; demonstrations in several cities erupted in the late 1960s.

BIBLIOGRAPHY

GOULD, JAMES W. *The United States and Malaysia.* 1969.
LARSEN, STANLEY ROBERT, and JAMES LAWTON COLLINS JR. *Allied Participation in Vietnam.* 1975.
SMITH, R. B. *An International History of the Vietnam War.* 3 vols. 1983, 1985, 1991.

ELLEN BAKER

Manila Conference. The Manila Conference took place on 24–25 October 1966 and included representatives from Australia, New Zealand, the Philippines, South Korea, South Vietnam, Thailand, and the United States. The conference was called by Philippine president Ferdinand Marcos after consultation with the United States, in order to review the war and nonmilitary development programs and to consider the future of the region. The delegates issued a series of statements explaining their goals in Southeast Asia—peace, security, and an end to hunger, illiteracy, and disease—and setting forth the conditions under which U.S. and allied troops would withdraw from South Vietnam.

BIBLIOGRAPHY

BORNET, VAUGHN DAVIS. *The Presidency of Lyndon B. Johnson.* 1983.
JOHNSON, LYNDON BAINES. *The Vantage Point: Perspectives of the Presidency, 1963–1969.* 1971.
OLSON, JAMES S., and RANDY ROBERTS. *Where the Domino Fell: America and Vietnam, 1945–1990.* 1991.
SHULIMSON, JACK. *U.S. Marines in Vietnam: An Expanding War, 1966.* 1982.

ELLEN D. GOLDLUST

Mansfield, Mike (1903–), U.S. representative (D-Mont.), 1943–1953; U.S. senator (D-Mont.),

1953–1977; Senate majority leader, 1961–1977. A Catholic with an interest in Asian history, Michael J. Mansfield was an important early supporter of Ngo Dinh Diem and of the U.S. commitment to South Vietnam. By 1965, however, after several visits to Vietnam, he concluded that the South Vietnamese government enjoyed no popular support and that military action in Vietnam was doomed to failure. Mansfield urged President Johnson to pursue peace negotiations rather than escalate the war. When Johnson refused, Mansfield became an outspoken critic of the war, straining the relationship between the two men. As the war continued, Mansfield supported legislation to counter the precedent established by the Gulf of Tonkin Resolution and to reassert Congress's war powers. In 1969, he called for a cease-fire, and in June 1971, he sponsored an amendment to the Selective Service bill that required the withdrawal of U.S. troops within nine months. The amendment failed to pass in the House, but a provision was substituted that urged President Nixon to set a firm date for U.S. troop withdrawal; this was the first time Congress went on record in support of the withdrawal of troops from Vietnam. Mansfield later served Presidents Carter and Reagan as ambassador to Japan.

BIBLIOGRAPHY

BALDWIN, LOUIS. *Honorable Politician: Mike Mansfield of Montana.* 1979.

KARNOW, STANLEY. *Vietnam: A History.* 1991.

JENNIFER FROST

MIKE MANSFIELD. On 5 January 1967. *Library of Congress*

Mao Zedong (1893–1976), leader, Chinese Communist Party, 1935–1976; chairman, Central Committee of the Party, 1945–1976; president, People's Republic of China, 1949–1959. Mao was the final decision maker in China's support of the Vietnamese communists in their fight to end French colonialism and then against U.S. armed intervention. His ideological and strategic influence on the Vietnamese leaders can hardly be overestimated. Throughout most of the 1960s, Mao challenged the Soviet Union's Vietnam policy and advised the Vietnamese communists to insist on armed struggle (striving to overthrow South Vietnam by force) rather than to negotiate with the United States. Mao even turned down the USSR's proposal for "united action" by the socialist countries to aid North Vietnam against U.S. forces in Vietnam. In terms of strategy, he advocated protracted guerrilla war, or "people's war," based on his own revolutionary experience. Vietnamese leaders drew heavily on Maoist concepts of guerrilla war, but having a smaller population and less territory than the People's Republic of China, and confronting technologically superior U.S. forces, Ho Chi Minh and Vo Nguyen Giap made significant changes to Maoist doctrine to adapt it to the Vietnamese circumstances. The Vietnamese leaders placed less emphasis than Mao on self-reliance as opposed to external aid, rural areas as opposed to cities, guerilla war versus armed uprisings, and the preeminence of human beings and political actions over weapons and technological skills. With these modifications, Vietnamese communist leaders benefitted greatly from Mao's strategic ideas, including the three devices prescribed by Maoist doctrines as necessary for the triumph of the revolution—the party (whose role is to provide leadership for the revolution), the army (a tool to seize state power), and the united front (a means to win the support of the people).

BIBLIOGRAPHY

BROWN, T. LOUISE. *War and Aftermath in Vietnam.* 1991.
TAYLOR, JAY. *China and Southeast Asia: Peking's Relations with Revolutionary Movements.* 1976.

HAN TIE

Marines, U.S. The Vietnam War left the U.S. Marine corps an ambiguous legacy of valor, dedication, frustration, and a sense of guilt and defeat. The war demonstrated that the corps would fight with unparalleled courage, self-sacrifice, and skill in a conflict that offered little chance for national and institutional victory. Unlike its experience in the two world wars and the Korean War, the Marine Corps did not benefit from the Vietnam War in terms of public acclaim, increased size and funding, media approval, and organizational self-confidence. Marine veterans, especially those who served in Vietnam after the summer of 1969, remember the war for its corruption of marine standards of discipline and group cohesion. The last marines to die in the war zone did not perish until the fall of Saigon in April 1975 and the assault on the Cambodian island of Koh Tang the following month. Nevertheless, the Marine Corps was pulled out of the war in 1971, and its senior officers believed that the withdrawal had come none too soon.

The War's Toll on the Corps. The Vietnam War strained the Marine Corps to its very roots. It was the marines' longest war (seven years of major engagements) and its bloodiest; the war cost the corps 101,574 casualties, 4,000 more than it suffered in World War II. (Marine combat deaths from World War II, however, numbered 19,733 and for Vietnam 13,073 with an additional 1,748 deaths from all other causes in the war zone.) More marines served during the Vietnam War than during World War II 794,000 compared with 669,100. In 1968 more marines (85,755) were fighting in Vietnam than landed on either Iwo Jima or Okinawa. At

MAO ZEDONG. At right, welcoming Souvanna Phouma, c. 1956. *National Archives*

its wartime peak strength in 1969 the Marine Corps numbered 314,917, only 170,000 short of its World War II strength.

Such statistics only suggest the organizational strains the corps experienced: career officers and noncommissioned officers (NCO) exhausted and demoralized by multiple tours to the war zone, resignations and retirements of key personnel, the erosion of standards in the NCO ranks, the constant demands to rush ill-prepared youths to Vietnam as infantry replacements, and the growing shortages of equipment and supplies. As one veteran gunnery sergeant said: "First there was the Old Corps, then there was the New Corps. And now there's this goddamned thing!"

The Course of Marine Participation. Marine Corps participation in the Vietnam War followed the general pattern of the entire U.S. military commitment. The first period began in the waning days of the French war for Indochina and ended with the arrival of the 9th Marine Expeditionary Brigade at Da Nang in March 1965. The first marine adviser in Vietnam arrived in August 1954 to organize a Vietnamese riverine assault force that evolved into the marine corps of the Republic of Vietnam. As the Vietnamese marine corps grew from two battalions to a 6,000-man brigade in 1962, the number of U.S. Marines assigned as advisers also climbed, but only to about 20, while an additional 10 U.S. Marines helped staff the Military Assistance Command, Vietnam (MACV).

The Kennedy administration's decision to strengthen the faltering counterinsurgency war against the Viet Cong guerrillas soon brought additional marines to Vietnam. To support the direct use of U.S. aircraft and helicopters in the war, a marine radio intelligence detachment of 42 deployed in January 1962 to the Central Highlands as part of a larger U.S. Army communications unit. This commitment expanded in April with the arrival of a marine transport helicopter squadron in the Mekong Delta region. Reinforced, the marine aviation task unit eventually numbered about 500 officers and men, manning 24 CH-34 helicopters and 4 fixed-wing aircraft. The unit was maintained with personnel and equipment by the 1st Marine Aircraft Wing, based in Japan. From its first combat operation in April 1962, the marine helicopter task force moved to the I Corps Tactical Zone (the five northern provinces of South Vietnam) in September, where it set up its base at the Da Nang airfield. It remained

there until it became part of the larger marine aviation commitment in 1965.

As the Viet Cong and North Vietnamese Army (NVA) increased their offensive operations after the collapse of Ngo Dinh Diem's government in 1963, the aviation marines started operations in June 1964 with Marine Detachment, Advisory Team One, a group of radio intelligence experts and infantry deployed along the Laotian border in Quang Tri province. This unit soon grew too large to ensure its security and secrecy and returned to Okinawa and Hawaii in September. In the meantime, the ground support elements of the aviation group grew until the U.S. Marine Da Nang group numbered nearly 900. The ground support marines also received assistance from the Special Landing Force, a reinforced battalion and helicopter squadron aboard the amphibious force of the Seventh Fleet.

Escalation. Because the marines already had some advance elements in I Corps, Gen. Wallace M. Green Jr., commandant of the corps, and Lt. Gen. Victor H. Krulak, commander of Fleet Marine Force Pacific, agreed to send more marines to northern South Vietnam when the United States began active ground combat operations in 1965. The real offensive mission, however, went to the 1st Marine Aircraft Wing, assigned to participate in the U.S. air war. The first ground units from the 3d Marine Division assumed security duties around four aerial enclaves: Da Nang, Phu Bai, Chu Lai, and Qui Nhon. The marine command in I Corps became the III Marine Amphibious Force (III MAF), commanded by an accomplished veteran of World War II and the Korean War, Lt. Gen. Lewis W. Walt. Authorized to conduct counterattacks on the approaching NVA and Viet Cong forces, General Walt mixed conventional multibattalion operations with small-unit pacification and civic action patrols, as the latter activities were much favored by Krulak. He also instituted a program to place marine squads in villages with Vietnamese militiamen, which was labeled the Combined Action Program (CAP). Much of III MAF's war effort in 1965 and 1966, however, went into base development. Pacification operations along the densely populated coast and offensive operations into the NVA's mountain strongholds required air and helicopter support, which forced III MAF to construct a complex base system. III MAF, therefore, received substantial U.S. Navy and civilian engineering support to supplement its own five engineer battalions. Under the control of the Marine Force Logistics Command this support effort absorbed 40 percent of III MAF's manpower despite its best efforts.

Reinforced by the 1st Marine Division, which arrived from California in early 1966, III MAF followed a dual operational approach worked out by Greene, Krulak, and Walt. Large-unit offensive operations in the rugged backcountry or along the coastline would be conducted only when the marines could use helicopter assaults and close air support; the emphasis instead would be on pacification operations among the coastal population. Gen. William Westmoreland and activity by the North Vietnamese Army combined to weaken this pacification concept, which required patience and time, neither of which were available to the U.S. war effort.

Along the DMZ. After suffering heavy losses to U.S. Army divisions in II and III Corps in 1966 and 1967, the NVA retreated to its Cambodian and Laotian sanctuaries, but it remained aggressive along the Demilitarized Zone (DMZ) and the Laotian border, where it could use its artillery and rockets to greater effect. The ill-considered U.S. policy of respecting international borders added to III MAF's problems, complicated by Secretary of Defense Robert McNamara's obsession with building a fortified electronic barrier system along the 17th Parallel. From the first significant battles along the DMZ, which began in the summer of 1966, marines of the 3d Marine Division fought in places such as Khe Sanh, The Rockpile, Con Thien, Cam Lo, Gio Linh, and Dong Ha. In many ways the war along the DMZ resembled warfare on the western front in 1915–1918 and in Korea in 1952–1953. III MAF operations became a combination of big battles with the NVA along the northern and western approaches to Quang Tri province, supplemented by offensive operations into the western mountains and pacification activities conducted by the 1st Marine Division.

At the western flank of the DMZ, the combat base at Khe Sanh became a focus of national attention in the United States when, in late 1967, two NVA divisions closed around the marine regiment that held the base and the commanding hills to the north. Although marine commanders favored a temporary withdrawal, General Westmoreland ordered the post held, and III MAF reinforcements increased the strength of the garrison to 6,000 by January 1968. Poor weather and cautious U.S. operations forced the 26th Marines (Reinforced) to

hunker down in the base fortifications and the hill citadels from which it called in air strikes and artillery upon the besieging NVA. Aerial resupply ensured that the base would survive despite the anxiety of officials in Saigon and Washington. In March 1968, the Vietnamese withdrew after suffering approximately 10,000 casualties. The Khe Sanh force lost 205 killed in action and 800 wounded.

The Tet Offensive (January 1968) forced II MAF into battles with NVA forces to throw back attacks around Da Nang, and three marine battalions fought with Army of the Republic of Vietnam (ARVN) forces to recapture the ancient citadel of the city of Hue and much of its devastated downtown area. Attacking and counterattacking throughout 1968, the North Vietnamese and Viet Cong forces launched three distinct offensives against I Corps and lost 60,000 troops in the region. III MAF battalions drove deep into the border areas, attacking communist base camps and logistical centers. One regiment crossed into Laos and attacked a spur of the Ho Chi Minh Trail. While the 4,500 U.S. Marine fatalities in 1968 were dwarfed by communist losses, the North Vietnamese were able to quickly replace their casualties in quantity, if not in quality. In the summer of 1969, III MAF received direct orders to leave Vietnam as part of President Richard Nixon's Vietnamization program. The news was neither unexpected nor unwelcome.

Marine Withdrawal. For the next two years the marines withdrew from Vietnam, first turning over the DMZ area to the U.S. Army and the ARVN. The 3d Marine Division returned to Okinawa. The 1st Marine Division conducted operations with caution and reasonable success, supported by the 1st Marine Air Wing, which still flew most of its fighter-attack missions in the frustrating attempt to halt the North Vietnamese reinforcement and resupply effort. Nevertheless, battles in Quang Nam province (the Da Nang area) resulted in casualties. Drug abuse and war weariness plagued the 1st Division. Forty-seven "fraggings" occurred in the Marine Corps in 1970, and although that was significantly below the number in the U.S. Army, it was indicative of the declining morale in the corps. Racial violence added to the tension. Yet the remaining marines fought with skill and ardor, killing an estimated 5,000 North Vietnamese and Viet Cong troops at a cost of 403 dead in 1970.

Even after the 1st Marine Division and the 1st Marine Aircraft Wing completed their withdrawals in the summer of 1971, U.S. Marine advisers remained with the Vietnamese marines. Marine helicopters and aircraft stood offshore in the Special Landing Force, which had been available throughout the war for amphibious operations. Marine advisers and aviation supported the aborted ARVN raid into Laos in 1971 and battled throughout Quang Tri province to repel the Easter Offensive of 1972. When the Cambodian and Vietnamese armed forces collapsed in 1975, a marine expeditionary brigade conducted rescue and evacuation operations in both Phnom Penh and Saigon. The last two marines killed in Vietnam died during operations at the Tan Son Nhut military compound outside Saigon on 29 April 1975, thirteen years after the first marine deaths in Vietnam.

The Marines believed they had generally fought with valor and dedication. Nevertheless, the memory of the Vietnam War, passed down through the generations of the officer and NCO corps, will continue to frustrate the U.S. Marine Corps and make it skeptical of the media and foreign policy officials.

[*See also* Amphibious Landing Operations; Casualties; Combined Action Program; Project 100,000; Women, *article on* Women Marines (WM).]

BIBLIOGRAPHY

COSMAS, GRAHAM A., and TERRENCE P. MURRAY. *U.S. Marines in Vietnam: Vietnamization and Redeployment, 1970–1971.* 1986.

MILLETT, ALLAN R. *Semper Fidelis: The History of the United States Marine Corps.* 1980, rev. ed. 1990.

SHULIMSON, JACK. *U.S. Marines in Vietnam: An Expanding War, 1966.* 1982.

SHULIMSON, JACK, and CHARLES M. JOHNSON. *U.S. Marines in Vietnam: The Landing and the Buildup.* 1978.

SIMMONS, EDWIN H. *Marines in the Vietnam War.* 1987.

SIMMONS, EDWIN H., comp. *The Marines in Vietnam, 1954–1973: An Anthology and Annotated Bibliography.* 1974.

SMITH, CHARLES R. *U.S. Marines in Vietnam: High Mobility and Standdown, 1969.* 1988.

SOLIS, GARY D. *Marines and Military Law in Vietnam: Trial by Fire.* 1989.

TEFLER, GARY L., LANE ROGERS, and V. KEITH FLEMING. *U.S. Marines in Vietnam: Fighting the North Vietnamese, 1967.* 1984.

WALT, LEWIS W. *Strange War, Strange Strategy.* 1970.

WHITLOW, ROBERT H. *U.S. Marines in Vietnam: The Advisory and Combat Assistance Era, 1954–1964.* 1977.

ALLAN R. MILLETT

Martin, Graham A. (1912–1990), U.S. ambassador to South Vietnam, 1973–1975. A longtime diplomat and protégé of Averell Harriman, Martin was U.S. ambassador to Thailand (1963–1967) and Italy (1969–1973) before President Nixon appointed him the last U.S. envoy to South Vietnam. Arriving in Saigon after the Paris accords had raised fears of American abandonment, Martin concentrated on shoring up South Vietnamese faith in President Nixon's commitments of support and on lobbying Congress for increased military aid. Martin staunchly defended President Thieu against pressure to resign or negotiate with the communists until it was too late to form a coalition government. At the same time, Martin sent optimistic reports on the military situation back to his superiors in Washington, D.C., delaying the realization that the war was lost. To avoid creating panic during North Vietnam's Spring Offensive in April 1975, Martin declined to implement contingency plans for an orderly U.S. departure from Saigon. The last-minute helicopter evacuation of 29–30 April 1975 left behind piles of classified documents and thousands of South Vietnamese supporters of the U.S.-backed government, who were ruthlessly treated by the victorious communists. Martin himself, feverish from pneumonia and clutching the embassy flag, was among the last Americans to leave Saigon. Calling the evacuation "a hell of a good job," he blamed North Vietnam's victory on Congress's termination of military aid to South Vietnam. Martin served as special assistant to Secretary of State Henry Kissinger before retirement in 1977.

BIBLIOGRAPHY

BUTLER, DAVID. *The Fall of Saigon.* 1985.

"Graham Martin: Our Man in Saigon." *Time,* 21 April 1975.

"Graham Martin, 77, Dies." *New York Times,* 15 March 1990.

SNEPP, FRANK. *Decent Interval: An Insider's Account of Saigon's Indecent End.* 1977.

TIEN HUNG NGUYEN and JERROLD L. SCHECHTER. *The Palace File: The Remarkable Story of South Vietnam and the American Promises that Were Never Kept.* 1986.

GLEN GENDZEL

Mayaguez Incident. On 12 May 1975, the *Mayaguez,* a U.S.-registered container ship operating in the Gulf of Thailand near the Cambodian coast, was seized by Cambodian troops acting on local initiative, without the knowledge of the national government. President Gerald R. Ford decided that a military rescue of the ship and its crew was the proper response, but action was hampered by a lack of knowledge about the crew's location and by confusion stemming from the involvement of multiple branches of the U.S. armed forces. U.S. intelligence determined that the ship was being held off the coast of the Cambodian island of Koh Tang, and the rescue of the ship and crew was initiated on 15 May 1975. The USS *Holt* landed a boarding party on the *Mayaguez;* they found the ship abandoned. At the same time, U.S. Marines were landed by air force helicopters on Koh Tang, supported by U.S. Navy ships and aircraft and by air force aircraft. The marines encountered heavy fire from the Cambodians. Later in the day, the U.S. destroyer *Wilson* picked up the *Mayaguez's* crew, which was adrift at sea aboard a fishing boat. President Ford ordered four punitive air strikes against military targets on the Cambodian mainland near Kompong Som, including an oil depot, railroad yards, and an airfield at Ream, although only two strikes were carried out.

Underestimation of the number of Cambodian soldiers on Koh Tang, combined with poor coordination and communication among the branches of the U.S. armed forces, resulted in high U.S. casualties (eighteen men killed and fifty wounded) among the invading forces. Although the mission accomplished its goal, it did so at a high cost in terms of troops and equipment, and Ford's willingness to use force resulted in vigorous criticism from some members of Congress and the American media. The American public, however, generally supported the president's handling of the situation.

BIBLIOGRAPHY

DUNHAM, GEORGE R., and DAVID A. QUINLAN. *The U.S. Marines in Vietnam: The Bitter End, 1973–1975.* 1990.
FORD, GERALD R. *A Time to Heal: The Autobiography of Gerald R. Ford.* 1980.
ROWAN, ROY. *The Four Days of Mayaguez.* 1975.

ELLEN D. GOLDLUST

Mayday Tribe. The Mayday Tribe (or Mayday Collective), a group of mostly young antiwar activists, attempted to shut down the U.S. government from 3 May through 5 May 1971. Rennie Davis, a former leader of Students for a Democratic Society (SDS) and member of the Chicago Eight, led the group. They planned to use nonviolent direct ac-

tion, blocking bridges and street intersections, to interrupt traffic flow in Washington, D.C., and thus disrupt normal federal government activity by preventing federal employees from reporting to work. Washington, D.C., police, backed by federal troops, stopped the protest with mass arrests. More than twelve thousand people were arrested, some before the action began, the rest as they attempted to block traffic.

BIBLIOGRAPHY

DEBENEDETTI, CHARLES. *An American Ordeal: The Antiwar Movement of the Vietnam Era.* 1990.
ZAROULIS, NANCY, and SULLIVAN, GERALD. *Who Spoke Up? American Protest against the War in Vietnam, 1963–1975.* 1984.

WILLIAM PAUL SCHUCK

Mc-. *Names beginning with this prefix are alphabetized as if spelled Mac-.*

Meany, George (1894–1980), president of the American Federation of Labor–Congress of Industrial Organizations (AFL-CIO), 1955–1979. Meany, a staunch anticommunist, vigorously supported President Johnson's Vietnam policies. During the 1972 presidential campaign, Meany told the press that he refused to endorse either the pro-labor, antiwar George McGovern or Richard Nixon. After the election, Meany backed Nixon's Vietnamization plan. In 1974, in a television appearance on the Dick Cavett Show, Meany said that he had been wrong to support the war.

BIBLIOGRAPHY

ROBINSON, ARCHIE. *George Meany and His Times.* 1981.
ZAROULIS, NANCY, and GERALD SMITH. *Who Spoke Up?* 1984.

KELLY EVANS-PFEIFER

Medal of Honor. The Medal of Honor is the highest and most respected U.S. military decoration. Awarded by the president "in the name of the Congress of the United States," the medal is often erroneously called the Congressional Medal of Honor. Established during the Civil War as a decoration for the U.S. Navy and Marine Corps in 1861 and for the U.S. Army in 1862, the medal honors extraordinary bravery and valor on the battlefield.

POSTHUMOUS MEDAL OF HONOR. President Johnson presenting Mr. and Mrs. Jose Fernandez with their son's posthumous Medal of Honor, 6 April 1967. U.S. Army Specialist Daniel Fernandez died 18 February 1966 after throwing himself on a Viet Cong grenade to save the lives of four comrades. *National Archives*

Recipients are members of the armed forces who have distinguished themselves from their peers in battle by performing actions "beyond the call of duty" and at the risk of their own lives.

During the Vietnam War, 238 military personnel received the Medal of Honor, with 155 army, 57 Marine Corps, 14 navy, and 12 air force recipients. This was a higher proportion of awards to total military participants than in World War II. Capt. Roger Donlon received the first Medal of Honor for the Vietnam War from President Lyndon B. Johnson on 5 December 1964; prisoners of war Rear Adm. James Stockdale, Col. George Day, and Capt. Lance J. Sijan (who died in captivity) received the last medals of the war from President Gerald R. Ford in 1976. Presidents Johnson and Nixon regularly held public ceremonies to award the medal, using the occasion as an opportunity to spark support for the war, while President Ford held the last ceremony quietly, at a time when Americans wished to forget the Vietnam War.

BIBLIOGRAPHY

U.S. SENATE. COMMITTEE ON VETERANS' AFFAIRS. *Medal of Honor Recipients, 1863–1978.* 96th Cong., 1st sess., 1979. S. Committee Print No. 3.

JENNIFER FROST

Media and the War

Neither the media nor U.S. government officials anticipated the controversies that developed between the military and the news media when the United States embarked upon its commitment to South Vietnam. Although the two had often opposed one another during the nineteenth century, most notably during the American Civil War, their relationship had been relatively even during the twentieth, especially during World War II, when both had agreed that cooperation held more benefits for all concerned than open confrontation. (The opinions presented in this essay are those of the author and do not necessarily represent the positions of either the Department of the Army or the Department of Defense.)

Difficulties did arise during the conflict in Korea, when the fragile consensus supporting that war disintegrated in the United States, but the sense of compromise developed during World War II generally held firm. A reporter inadvertently announced the landing at Inchon almost ten hours before it occurred, *Newsweek* published the order of battle for the entire U.S. Eighth Army, and other lapses in security occurred. Even so, the military delayed for months before imposing censorship, despite advice from a number of newsmen that the expedient would eliminate cutthroat competition between rival media outlets. In general, if mistakes occurred on both sides, the military provided the press with reasonable access to events and reporters took steps to safeguard legitimate military interests.

The Early Years of the War. The military and the news media began the war in Vietnam in much the same spirit. During the early years of the conflict, between 1961 and 1963, such reporters as Neil Sheehan and Peter Arnett of the Associated Press and David Halberstam of the *New York Times* questioned assertions of progress that flowed liberally from the U.S. mission in Saigon. All, however, showed great sympathy for the U.S. soldiers advising the South Vietnamese. Indeed, even though Homer Bigart of the *New York Times* predicted accurately that U.S. intervention would lead to a major military commitment for the United States at a cost of untold lives, most reporters never penetrated much beneath the surface of events. Failing to question either the decision to become involved in the war or the goals of the United States, they argued instead for efficiency. The United States, they said, should push the inept government of South Vietnamese president Ngo Dinh Diem aside and give the U.S. military a free hand in running the war. That would bring the conflict to a swift, favorable conclusion. David Halberstam asserted in his best-selling 1964 book, *The Making of a Quagmire,* that South Vietnam was one of the five or six nations in the world truly vital to the interests of the United States. In that sense, he believed it might well be worth a larger U.S. commitment: "We do have something to offer these emerging nations. We can get things done."

With Diem receiving lukewarm support from conservatives in the United States and with major newspapers such as the *New York Times* and the *Washington Post* underscoring the increasing ambivalence of officials within the administration of President John F. Kennedy toward Diem's government, it was, perhaps, inevitable that the opinions of on-the-scene, anti-Diem reporters such as Halberstam would carry significant weight within the U.S. policy-making establishment. Convinced that Diem was the only alternative to chaos, the president's American supporters in South Vietnam, especially U.S. Ambassador Frederick Nolting and commander of the U.S. Military Assistance Command, Vietnam (MACV), Gen. Paul Harkins, attempted to refute the reporters' pessimistic appraisals. Diem and his spokesmen, however, heightened the effect of those allegations by baiting their political opponents in public and by unabashedly violating the civil rights of those they considered enemies. In the end, Kennedy sided with the press and Diem fell in a coup d'état condoned by the United States.

As the war progressed and the U.S. commitment in South Vietnam increased, reporters continued to criticize the U.S. approach to the war. Many officers bridled at the complaints reporters leveled against U.S. commanders and their tactics but few in positions of authority either in South Vietnam or the United States were inclined to retaliate with vigor. It was a matter of principle for some; whatever their differences with the news media, they had grown up in the United States and subscribed to the concept of a free press. The attitude of Nolting provides a case in point. Subject to strong criticism himself in the press, the ambassador still opposed efforts to cut reporters off from the war. There could be no defense for erroneous, discourteous journalism, he told the State Department privately in 1962, but he would uphold the right of the press to practice it. The best defense, he said, was not repression but success against the enemy.

In addition to idealism, however, there was also an element of self-interest in the approach. As the U.S. commitment to South Vietnam increased, policy makers recognized that the war was controversial and that American public support was fragile. In that light, they understood that any attempt to impose severe restrictions upon the press might be viewed by those inclined to question the war as an effort to manipulate American public opinion. If that occurred, the outcry that resulted might make it more difficult for the president to achieve his ends in Southeast Asia.

Whatever the problems the press caused, the presence of an uncensored corps of correspondents in South Vietnam also had benefits for the U.S. government. Individual reporters and media outlets could be used from time to time to signal U.S. intentions to the North Vietnamese or to present alternatives for public reaction without directly identifying the government with those ideas. Meanwhile, caustic, uncensored news dispatches from the field contradicted by their very existence enemy claims that the U.S. government was luring its citizens into an unwanted war. They also refuted in a highly credible manner North Vietnamese statements that communist forces were killing far more Americans than U.S. officials were willing to admit. In that sense, they were an important source of comfort to an American public that grew increasingly sensitive to casualties as the war progressed.

With time, as U.S. aircraft struck deeper into North Vietnam and U.S. ground forces entered combat in the south, it became apparent that the military would still have to exercise some control over what the press reported, if only to ensure the safety of the troops. Concerned that the South Vietnamese government would become involved in any attempt at formal censorship and that its officials would inevitably impair relations with the news media by attempting to repress

OVAL OFFICE PRESS CONFERENCE. Reporters gather around Lyndon B. Johnson's desk during an impromptu press conference, 1964. *National Archives*

legitimate commentary on the war, the administration of President Lyndon Baines Johnson opted in 1965 for a system of voluntary guidelines for the press that promised to preserve military security without infringing upon the rights of reporters.

A quid pro quo came into being. Correspondents agreed to withhold broad categories of strictly military information such as future plans, operations, or air strikes; rules of engagement; the quantities of fuel and ammunition on hand in support and combat units; unit designations; future troop movements and tactical deployments; the methods, activities, and locations of intelligence units; the exact number and type of casualties suffered in specific actions by friendly forces; the number of aircraft damaged or destroyed by enemy antiaircraft batteries; altitudes, courses, speeds, or the angles of attack of striking aircraft; and information on efforts to recover downed airmen while search-and-rescue operations remained in progress. The television networks agreed to refrain from broadcasting recognizable pictures of American dead in order to keep relatives from learning of a loved one's death in combat from an evening news program rather than through an official notification. In return, the U.S. command in South Vietnam instituted a system of broad support for the press. Although reporters who infringed upon the rules faced the loss of their privileges, usually for a period of thirty days, those who cooperated obtained the right to use post exchange facilities, access to daily news conferences and press releases, admission at subsidized rates to special press camps located at strategic locations in South Vietnam, and permission to ride on military aircraft and other vehicles when traveling into the field. The U.S. command even allowed reporters access, on a space available basis, to seats on the small, scheduled airline that flew to South Vietnam's main cities and military bases each day.

The Reporters. Over the years that followed, the number of correspondents covering the war on a regular basis increased from fewer than 10 in 1960 to 464 in January 1968. One hundred and seventy-nine of those present on that later date were Americans, 114 South Vietnamese, and 171 other nationalities. They represented more than 130 journalistic enterprises from almost every nation of consequence in the world: *Joon-Gang Ilbo* of South Korea, *Mainichi Shimbun* of Japan, the *Times of London, Stern* of West Germany, the Associated Press, United Press International, Agence France-Presse, *Time, Life, Newsweek, U.S. News & World Report,* and the American and European television networks. The number of correspondents surged to 648 during the Tet Offensive of 1968 but dropped to the earlier level when tensions subsided later in the year. There were other surges—during the invasions of Cambodia and Laos during 1970 and 1971 and the Easter Offensive of 1972—but in general the number held steady until the final two years of the war, when the U.S. role in combat diminished and the corps of correspondents in South Vietnam shrank to between 300 and 400. In all, according to U.S. Army records, close to 6,000 individuals were accredited at one time or another to cover the conflict.

It might seem from the numbers involved that the war and the controversies surrounding it claimed the preponderant attention of the American news media. In fact, the reality was far different. Oriented toward their local markets, most newspapers in the United States relied upon such services as the Associated Press (AP) and United Press International (UPI) for the news they carried and refrained from assigning full-time reporters to South Vietnam on a consistent basis. At the beginning of 1968, for example, the 31 Gannett papers, the 22 Newhouse papers, the 6 Knight papers, the *Chicago Tribune,* the *Chicago Sun Times,* and the *St. Louis Post Dispatch* all declined to spend the large sums necessary to maintain reporters in the field. When they found it necessary to supplement the work of the news services, they relied upon stringers (independent reporters who sold their work by the piece to various agencies) or dispatched reporters to South Vietnam on brief tours of duty.

Even those newspapers and news syndicates that employed reporters in the field were frugal. The AP and UPI each carried eight reporters in the field at the height of the war in January 1968. Reuters had four and Agence France-Presse three. The *New York Times,* which prided itself on its foreign coverage, increased its staff in South Vietnam from one to three reporters only in 1965, when U.S. ground forces entered full-scale combat. By 1968 it had four in its Saigon bureau. The *Washington Post* meanwhile generally carried only two reporters on its Saigon roster. At the beginning of 1968, the Scripps-Howard chain and newspapers and magazines of the stature of the *Wall Street Journal,* the *Christian Science Monitor,* the *Baltimore Sun, U.S. News & World Report,* and *Long Island Newsday* maintained only one reporter each.

The news magazines and the television networks were somewhat more expansive. *Time Magazine* used six full-time reporters in 1968 while *Newsweek* employed two full-timers and two stringers. CBS and NBC each carried six reporters and ABC four. On any given date, the networks also employed a number of television soundmen and cameramen, some of whom were Vietnamese nationals.

WAR FOR THE CAMERAS. An ABC television cameraman films ARVN soldiers for the American news audience. *National Archives*

Of the reporters present in any given month, fewer than one-third were true working correspondents. Of the rest, some were the wives of reporters who had taken accreditation in order to share in their husbands' post exchange privileges; others were camera operators, soundmen, stenographers, translators, secretaries, and other media support personnel. The average age of all was thirty-five.

Normally, according to military public affairs officers, only about forty reporters were in the field on a given day. Many of those represented the television networks, which required the color and action that only cameras on location could provide. Others worked for the press associations (Reuters, AP, UPI) that provided mainstay coverage for the news media of the world or for the relatively few major newspapers prosperous enough to keep more than one or two reporters on the scene. Writers of feature articles also tended to be present because they had the luxury of long lead times and the ability to stay out of touch with their employers for extended periods.

The other reporters covering the war were either members of very small news bureaus or the sole representatives of their agencies. They had to stay in touch with their home offices and produce a news dispatch every day. Because communications were poor throughout South Vietnam, they had no choice but to congregate in the country's capital city, Saigon, where cable and telephone lines were at least adequate and where the U.S. command's office of information held daily briefings. Only in that way could they satisfy the demands of their employers.

Perspectives of Journalists. Opponents of the press in the military have long contended that if more of those reporters had gone into the field and seen the excellent job U.S. forces were doing they might have been much less inclined to criticize official policy. In fact, the reverse appears to have been the case. There were exceptions, but reporters who spent a large amount of time in the field—for example, Peter Arnett of the AP and Craig Whitney of the *New York Times*—tended to encounter more problems and to be more critical than those who rarely left Saigon.

The reason for this can be found in the way the news media work. Few editors are interested in their reporters' opinions; they want eyewitness accounts or stories based on the word of sources, the higher the better. Influenced by those of their associates who visited the field regularly or by carefully cultivated contacts, reporters based in Saigon were capable of asking penetrating questions. Often, however, if only because of their insatiable need for information, they tended to replicate the word of the sources most available to them; that is, officials of the U.S. mission in Saigon, military spokesmen, and the senior officers that regularly briefed the press. Much the same thing happened in the United States, where the press took many of its cues from the policy makers and establishment figures who always had news to release or comments to make. As a result, as one of the U.S. Army's most experienced public affairs officers during the war, Maj. Gen. Winant Sidle, would later attest, if some notable exceptions occurred, most reporting of the war was either advantageous to government policy or, given the errors of fact that often accompanied the transmission of fast-breaking news, a reasonable approximation of what was happening in the field.

Throughout much of the war, the American news media thus tended to give both their government and the U.S. soldier the benefit of the doubt. Until Harrison Salisbury of the *New York Times* revealed in 1966, for example, that U.S. bombing had caused major damage to civilian facilities and structures in North Vietnam, the print and broadcast media in the United States paid little attention to the story, even though European newspapers such as *Le Monde* covered it in detail. In that case, while unwilling to accept at face value statements by the U.S. military that U.S. bombs were dropped with pinpoint accuracy, they appear to have been just as unwilling to spread what they considered North Vietnamese propaganda. In the same way, during 1966 and 1967, editors and producers in the United States failed to cover with any consistency controversies that developed over defects in the M16 rifle. Although stories appeared from time to time by such reporters as Don Webster of CBS News and Bob Erlandson of the *Baltimore Sun,* most reporters, out of good will for the military, appear either to have accepted the official line that the weapon functioned properly or to have been unwilling to say anything that might undermine the confidence of the soldier in his basic weapon.

Much the same thing happened during 1969, when the news media were much more critical than they had been earlier of the U.S. effort in South Vietnam. It took nearly six months from the time the first allegations appeared for the press to show much interest in the story that U.S. soldiers had massacred more than three hundred defenseless civilians in My Lai, a village in South Vietnam. That the Defense Department at first held the story close and released few details was certainly part of the reason for the delay, but more than enough information was available at least to prompt questions. None came. Instead, reporters and editors once more appear either to have discounted the allegation as North Vietnamese propaganda or to have doubted the motives and veracity of those making the charge. Once the full dimensions of the atrocity were confirmed by Seymour Hersh, the press turned the incident into a cause célèbre. Yet Hersh himself at first had difficulty interesting the major media in his efforts. Both *Life* and *Look* turned him down before the less well-known, antiwar Dispatch News Service agreed to support his investigation.

Television Coverage. Critics of the media often assert that Vietnam was the first war to appear on television and that the effects of television coverage on public opinion were particularly negative because of the violence it portrayed. In fact, until at least 1968, television was lopsidedly favorable to U.S. policy. Television reporters often described attacks by U.S. forces with enthusiasm, and most of the stories they presented were devoid of the blood and gore that might have dismayed viewers. As the media historian Lawrence Lichty noted, between 1965 and 1970 less than 5 percent of all evening news film reports showed real violence—actual combat close up with casualties.

The effect was partly the product of the war itself and partly the result of the requirements television imposed upon the news. The war, on the one hand, was difficult for camera teams to cover. It moved in fits and starts, with moments of intense action interspersed among days and weeks of stultifying boredom. During one month in 1968, for example, U.S. military units conducted more than fifteen thousand small-unit operations but only seven hundred made contact with the enemy, often at night, when cameras were virtually useless. It took a great deal of luck, in other words, for one of the few television news teams operating in Vietnam to be present when real fighting occurred. The result, as *New Yorker* television critic Michael Arlen noted, was that television viewers received a "distanced overview of disjointed conflict . . . composed mainly of scenes of helicopters landing, tall grasses blowing in the helicopter wind, American soldiers fanning out across a hillside on foot, rifles at the ready, with now and then [on the soundtrack] a far off ping or two, and now and then a column of dark, billowing smoke a half mile away."

On top of that, there was no such thing as live coverage of the war. Most of the film the networks played was flown by jet from South Vietnam to the United States, where it was developed and edited. By the time it arrived in New York, it was often several days old and suitable mainly for news segments that dealt with undated generalities rather than specific events. Indeed, television reporters often composed their stories with that thought in mind, filming segments on, for example, the condition of the morale of U.S. troops or the South Vietnamese black market that could fit into any news program at any time. The situation improved in 1967 with the introduction of satellite transmission coverage of that year's Winter Olympics in Sapporo, Japan. From then on, the networks flew film of particularly important Vietnam stories to Japan for developing and instant transmission to New York. Even then, however, the procedure was so expensive that most stories continued to travel by the old method.

Television coverage of the war was also heavily conditioned by the networks' desire to keep viewers from changing channels at the dinner hour by offending as few as possible. Producers and directors presented strikingly savage reports when the overriding importance of an event seemed to require it—for example, NBC's depiction of South Vietnamese general Nguyen Ngoc Loan executing a Viet Cong captive on a Saigon street—but they generally shielded their audiences from the horrors that war produced. U.S. casualties were particularly sacrosanct.

STREET PRESS CONFERENCE. Maxwell D. Taylor (left) and William C.
Westmoreland briefing reporters. *National Archives*

By agreement with the U.S. command in South Vietnam, the networks never
showed the pictures of American dead and wounded, lest the families involved
learn of a loved one's misfortune from a television report rather than an official
notification.

Johnson's Strategy. Although the net effect of such reporting worked to
the advantage of the official point of view, there were contradictions at the root
of the war that prompted doubts on the part of some within the press from the
very beginning. The strategy President Johnson adopted in 1965 for fighting the
war was the reason. The president believed the conflict was necessary but suspected that the American public and Congress lacked the will to carry it to a successful conclusion. He also considered himself a social reformer and wanted to
keep within definite limits whatever war occurred, in order to retain room for
the domestic programs he hoped to inaugurate. The way to do that, he decided,
was gradually to increase the U.S. commitment to South Vietnam by adopting a
policy of gradually increasing pressures against North Vietnam. That would minimize public relations problems in the United States and retain leeway for his social programs. It would also reduce the possibility of a major confrontation with

North Vietnam's allies, the Soviet Union and the People's Republic of China (PRC); give the U.S. military the time it needed to prepare a proper base for future action in South Vietnam; and cut off the objections of prowar advocates in Congress who might otherwise gain the upper hand and force the United States into a larger war.

The system worked to the extent that Johnson succeeded in committing the United States to war on his terms, but it also harmed official credibility. By postponing some unpopular decisions and making others only after weighing how the press and public would react, the president filled the public record with so many inconsistencies and contradictions that the phrase *credibility gap* became a fixture in media coverage of the war. As Charles Roberts put it in *Newsweek* during December 1966, the record of the Johnson administration's "concealments and misleading denials" seemed "almost as long as its impressive list of achievements."

Once U.S. troops became heavily committed to battle, other problems brought on by the president's strategy added to the effect. Concerned more than ever that the war might escalate out of control or that the PRC might choose to enter the conflict on the side of North Vietnam much as it had allied itself with North Korea during the Korean War, Johnson adopted limited goals in South Vietnam. There would be no extension of ground combat into North Vietnam and no attempt by ground forces to cut North Vietnamese supply lines in neighboring Cambodia and Laos. Although the approach once again succeeded in achieving the president's aims by containing the war in South Vietnam, it once more also engendered contradictions. Unable to strike at supply lines, the U.S. military had little choice but to surrender the initiative to the North Vietnamese and Viet Cong forces. They could choose when and where to fight, and, if they suffered a defeat, could withdraw into their Cambodian and Laotian sanctuaries to regroup. Meanwhile, their allies in South Vietnam could hide among that nation's people, subvert its institutions, and wait for the day when the Americans would inevitably grow tired and withdraw.

Under the circumstances, Johnson had few choices. He could either convince North Vietnam that further conflict would be counterproductive or persuade the American people that South Vietnam was worth a prolonged war of attrition and all the suffering that it would cause. With the Soviet Union and the PRC replacing the matériel that North Vietnamese forces expended in the field, however, and more men coming of age each year in North Vietnam than U.S. forces could ever conceivably kill or wound in combat, the North Vietnamese had the ability to endure indefinitely. As for South Vietnam, the political immaturity of its government, the obvious corruption of its leaders, and the willingness of its armed forces to allow Americans to do the bulk of the fighting, did little to endear its cause to the American people. The Johnson administration argued that every developing country experienced the same problems and that even the United States during its early years had been less than responsive to its allies, but those arguments had little effect. Reporters in the field told of battles fought time and again over the same territory that seemed to settle nothing, of South Vietnamese military units more interested in stealing chickens than in fighting, of pervasive political corruption that allowed smugglers and black marketeers to milk millions of dollars out of South Vietnam's economy every year, of programs to win the hearts and minds of the South Vietnamese people that seemed somehow never to achieve their goals, and of the terrible wounds that the U.S. war machine sometimes inflicted upon South Vietnam's long-suffering peasantry.

Expectations and Reality. Those stories were sometimes lost among the large number of reports that continued to replicate the official point of view, but they had an effect. Beginning in 1966, but increasingly in 1967, some officials within the U.S. government responsible for planning the war combined the stories with information they alone possessed to conclude that the conflict was falling into a stalemate. Claims began to rise within the State and Defense Departments that the military used dubious statistics to justify its assertions of progress, especially the "body count" of enemy dead. Secretary of Defense Robert McNamara himself caused a sensation during August 1967, when word leaked to the press that he had stated in closed testimony before Congress that the air campaign against North Vietnam's infiltration routes in Laos was incapable of cutting off the small amount of supplies—a mere fifteen tons per day—communist forces needed to continue the war indefinitely. The amount was so insignificant, McNamara said, that it could slip through even the most devastating bombing campaign.

Concerned that talk of stalemate might sap support for the war, the president responded with public relations campaigns designed to demonstrate to the American people that the South Vietnamese armed forces were competent, American programs were achieving their ends, and sufficient progress was occurring on all fronts to justify optimism for the future. Similar campaigns had occurred during earlier conflicts, but on those occasions the president himself and his politically appointed spokesmen had conducted them. As the Vietnam War escalated, Johnson and his appointees spoke out, but they also drew the military into the process. As a result, by late 1967, the generals conducting the war and their subordinates were sometimes as much involved in explaining and justifying the conflict as the president and his advisers themselves.

For a time, the president's public relations strategy once more seemed to work. When the U.S. commander in South Vietnam, Gen. William C. Westmoreland, asserted in a speech at the National Press Club in November 1967 that North Vietnamese and Viet Cong forces were so beaten down they had not won a major battle in more than a year and could use their large units only at the edges of the Laotian and Cambodian sanctuaries, the press gave the statement wide and generally favorable coverage. The mood passed rapidly, however. Within two months, North Vietnam rebutted the general's assertions by launching the Tet Offensive, a series of coordinated, simultaneous assaults against South Vietnam's five largest cities and its main provincial and district capitals.

The attack stunned both the Saigon correspondents and their editors in the United States. Already doubtful about the Johnson administration's claims of progress, they concluded that the president and the military had been less than honest in their descriptions of the war and rejected out of hand military assertions, later verified, that communist forces had suffered a stunning setback. Fixing, instead, upon a comment Johnson had made that the communists would attempt to inflict a psychological defeat upon the American people, they made that point themselves and played the attack as a disaster for the United States. Then, focusing upon the enemy's siege of the U.S. base at Khe Sanh, located in South Vietnam's northernmost sector near the Laotian border, they exaggerated that event into a possible repeat of the 1954 battle of Dien Bien Phu, when Viet Minh forces had destroyed both a major French colonial force and the will of the French people and government to continue the Indochina War. In fact, the enormous firepower U.S. forces could bring to bear ensured that the U.S. Marines defending Khe Sanh were never in danger of annihilation. A case can be made, indeed, that the attack on the base was merely a feint designed to draw U.S. forces into the countryside, away from South Vietnam's cities, where the main assault was to occur.

CHARLES ARNOT. ABC foreign news correspondent making a filmed report for American television news, Saigon, 1966. *National Archives*

The pessimism of the press had little effect upon American public opinion, which rallied aggressively to the side of the president. According to Gallup polls, the percentage of Americans who considered themselves prowar "hawks" rose from 56 percent prior to the offensive to 61 percent after its start. Meanwhile, despite the news media's questioning of military claims of progress, the number of those who expressed confidence in U.S. military policies in Vietnam rose from 61 to 74 percent.

Reinforcing Doubts. If media coverage had little effect upon the American people, it still reinforced the doubts about the war that were already circulating within both the Johnson administration and Congress. Former supporters of the war who had already begun to waver compared what was appearing in the press with their own reservations and concluded that U.S. entry into the conflict had been a mistake. As presidential speech writer Harry McPherson observed, "I put aside my own interior access to confidential information and was more persuaded by what I saw on the tube and in the newspapers. . . . I was fed up with the 'light at the end of the tunnel' stuff. I was fed up with the optimism that seemed to flow without stopping from Saigon."

The most prominent spokesman for the war, President Johnson, contributed to the effect by failing to exercise effective leadership as the crisis developed. Although he made a few comments to the press shortly after the start of the offensive, he left most public statements to his aides and made little personal effort to marshal support for his policies. The impression of indecision that resulted affected Congress, where, in the absence of a firm presidential hand, doubters felt free to speak out. Looking to the White House for leadership and perceiving little forward motion, the public also began to waver. Although its mood of aggressiveness remained high, polls indicated by the end of February that public disapproval of the president's handling of the war had risen drastically, from 47 to 63 percent. In the month that followed, lacking any further direction from the

White House, the public's fighting spirit also began to drain away. The percentage of Americans expressing confidence in U.S. military policies in Vietnam fell in the polls from 74 to 54 percent.

During that time, McNamara's replacement as secretary of defense, Clark Clifford, at Johnson's behest conducted a broad-ranging reevaluation of U.S. policy in Vietnam. He concluded that the war was hurting the United States. "We must look at our own economic stability," he told the president, "our other problems in the world, our other problems at home; we must consider whether or not this thing is tying us down so that we cannot do some of the other things we should be doing." Although unwilling to disengage from the war, Johnson decided a fresh approach was necessary. On 31 March he announced a bombing halt in North Vietnam above 20 degrees north latitude and then stunned the nation by declaring that he would not run for a second full term in office in order to devote himself entirely to the search for peace.

Johnson's decision had profound effects. By setting up an expectation in the country that realistic negotiations would shortly occur and that the war would end within a reasonable period of time, it cut off many of the options Johnson's successor, Richard M. Nixon, might have exercised. Nixon thus had little choice during the election campaign but to hint that he had a plan to end the war. Once in office, rather than escalate the conflict, he had to begin withdrawing U.S. forces. He possessed some room for maneuver at first, but as Secretary of Defense Melvin Laird continually stressed, time was short.

During 1969, public opinion polls told the story. Although few Americans advocated a precipitate U.S. withdrawal from South Vietnam and 52 percent during October said they were willing to support an escalation to achieve victory, 43 percent also considered the draft unfair because, according to the pollster Louis Harris, "it made young men fight in a war they didn't believe in." In April, 44 percent approved of Nixon's handling of the war; by the end of September, only 35 percent approved.

The expectations that Johnson's decision had fostered and the shift in public opinion it had helped to bring about also affected the way the news media covered the war. With President Nixon publicly committed to the search for peace, the slightest seeming deviation from that end became the source of criticism by antiwar advocates both in Congress and among the nation's elite. Taking their cues, as always, from newsmakers, reporters covered the broadening of debate and the tone of their reporting began to change. According to Daniel Hallin, the effect was particularly apparent in the case of television. Describing the results of a content analysis he conducted of television news programs over the course of the war, Hallin noted that between 1965 and 1968 spokesmen for the war predominated over critics on evening news programs by a heavily disproportionate ratio of 26.3 to 4.5 percent. After the Tet Offensive and the change in consensus in the United States that accompanied Johnson's decision to explore the possibility of a negotiated settlement, the two figures achieved a rough parity, going from 26.1 for the critics to 28.4 for supporters. Although value judgments were certainly involved, the change came less because television executives had made some arbitrary decision to promote the opposition than because the sources the news media followed in the nation's establishment had begun to switch sides. Forty-nine percent of all domestic criticism of the war on television, according to Hallin, thus came from public officials, while only 16 percent originated in the commentaries and interpretations of reporters. As Max Frankel of the *New York Times* would later note, the press is an establishment institution and tends to reflect the attitudes of its constituency. When opposition to the war moved from the fringes of society to the nation's elite, that fact "naturally picked up coverage. And then naturally the tone of the coverage changed."

Changes in the Media. Alterations occurring within the press itself added to the effect. Through normal processes of promotion and retirement, senior editors and commentators who had earlier shared the official viewpoint on the war moved up or out. Their successors, reflecting the changing climate of opinion, were sometimes less sympathetic to the official viewpoint. For example, when the director of the *Washington Post*'s editorial page, Russell Wiggins, left that newspaper to become U.S. ambassador to the United Nations, and Phillip Geyelin, who had a more negative view of the war, took his place, the *Post*'s editorials became less supportive of official policy.

In the same way, many of the reporters who had covered the war's early years in South Vietnam and who had accepted the status quo moved on, to be replaced by younger people more sympathetic to the antiwar sentiments of their contemporaries in the United States. Although most of the new reporters considered themselves professionals and conscientiously attempted to cover both sides of every issue, their opinions of necessity colored the choices they made. The support of most correspondents for the U.S. soldier thus remained strong, but many reporters were more than ever inclined to question the motives and sincerity of the higher officers who were responsible for the continued conduct of the war. Also, whereas prior to the Tet Offensive reporters had paid hardly any attention to the medals and awards bestowed upon departing generals, after Tet they suggested on a number of occasions that some generals had received their awards more as a formality than on merit.

Although changes in personnel were less apparent at the television networks, similar events happened there. As debate over the war broadened, so did the attitudes of network anchormen and journalists. Earlier in the war, Walter Cronkite of CBS News had referred often to the North Vietnamese and Viet Cong forces as "the Communists," but in the years following Tet he did so rarely. In the same way, according to Hallin, many television journalists prior to Tet had cast the war in terms of "our side" versus "their side" and had made frequent references to communist aggression and the fight for democracy in South Vietnam. Those terms disappeared after the offensive.

As U.S. withdrawal began and President Nixon instructed U.S. commanders in South Vietnam to lower the tempo of the fighting, changes also occurred in the amount of attention the press paid to the conflict. Between 1966 and 1968, for example, the *New York Times,* according to Edward Jay Epstein, averaged 130 editorials per year on the war. Between 1969 and 1971 that number fell to fewer than 70 per year. The same thing occurred on television. According to surveys by the media analyst George Bailey, between August and November 1968 evening network television news programs covered the war 91 percent of days. After Nixon's election and the advent of an administration pledged to the search for peace, that number dropped to 61 percent. From then on, television coverage fluctuated in relation to events. Overall, if it rose during the U.S. and South Vietnamese invasions of Laos and Cambodia and the Easter Offensive of 1972, it remained 20 percent below what it had been in earlier years.

By the beginning of 1969, the news media were also paying less attention than ever to the fighting, in part because the subject seemed stale and in part because both reporters and their sources were preoccupied with the peace negotiations, which had begun after the Tet Offensive. During March, the executive producer of the ABC Evening News, Av Westin, thus instructed his correspondents in South Vietnam to shift their attention away from the battlefield to subjects more

CRONKITE DURING TET. On 20 February 1968, Walter Cronkite, the CBS news anchor, interviews a battalion commander of the 1st Marines in Hue. *U.S. Marine Corps*

in tune with the possibility that some sort of settlement was in the offing. Did South Vietnamese president Nguyen Van Thieu's political opposition have much chance in a truly free election? Did the government's treatment of civilians build loyalty among the people or destroy it? Was South Vietnam's bureaucracy as corrupt as in the past or had the presence of American money and advice made it more equitable and efficient?

Executives at NBC sent out similar instructions. Whereas during most of 1968 that network's evening news program had run three or four combat stories a week, during the final two months of the year it played a total of only three. The effect may have been the product of expectations produced by President Johnson's announcement, just prior to the U.S. presidential election in November, of a halt to the bombing of North Vietnam. But, as the executive producer of NBC's Huntley-Brinkley Report, Robert J. Northshield, later explained, by that time producers and editors had also become fatigued with the war. "The trend," said Northshield, "was away from Vietnam."

The Nixon Years. That circumstance was, at first, much to the advantage of President Nixon. He took steps to reinforce the mood by publicizing the effort to turn the war over to the South Vietnamese, the so-called Vietnamization program, and by beginning the withdrawal of U.S. forces. By the end of 1969, as a result, he had so preempted the issues that antiwar activists relied upon that the movement to end the war seemed to have lost much of its momentum.

There were, nevertheless, contradictions at the root of Nixon's approach to the war as profound as those that had dogged Lyndon Johnson, and as certain to gain heavy play in the press. Nixon, for example, had little choice but to reduce the number of U.S. forces in South Vietnam, but he still hoped to maintain an appearance of resolution and success in hopes of convincing North Vietnam to negotiate a settlement favorable to American ends. When he and his spokesmen thus proclaimed the success of Vietnamization, reporters duly repeated the assertion, but they also began to investigate the issue. They came away with the realization that if some South Vietnamese military units were indeed highly trained and capable, others were not. U.S. advisers and B-52 bombers were thus often all that stood between victory and defeat for South Vietnamese forces in battle. In the same way, when Nixon decided to buy time for his policies to work by invading the sanctuaries in Cambodia, some reporters asserted that the attack was long overdue but many more reacted with anger. How, they asked, could the United States withdraw from the war while sponsoring a major escalation? Reporters in the field meanwhile noted—as had General Westmoreland in a private conversation with Nixon—that the operation was too short and too limited in scope to have much more than a temporary effect.

The Cambodian incursion revived the antiwar movement in the United States by throwing Nixon's credibility into question. Protests ensued on the nation's college campuses, and many newspapers and magazines that had thus far held back turned forthrightly against the war. Congress adopted the Cooper-Church amendment, a measure that from then on prohibited the president from committing U.S. ground forces to combat in Laos and Cambodia.

Already angry at the news media's coverage of his administration and disposed to see the worst, Nixon came increasingly to view the press as his enemy. Inclined to equate opposition to the war with disloyalty to the United States, he indulged those journalists who agreed with his point of view but employed his vice president, Spiro Agnew, to wage verbal war on the rest. The barrage Agnew launched—accompanied by threats of lawsuits, license challenges, tax audits, and investigations by official commissions—appears to have had little effect on the print media, which were secure in their First Amendment freedoms. It may, however, have succeeded in the case of the television networks because they were subject to Federal control over broadcast licensing and more subject to intimidation. Over the years that followed Agnew's attack, according to Marvin Kalb, the director of the Joan Schorenstein Barone Center on Press, Politics, and Public Policy at Harvard University, the spirit Agnew set in motion permanently dampened political commentary on network news programs. Instant analyses gradually disappeared, to be replaced by "brief, highly produced minidocumentaries" in which commentators received advance notice of the kinds of questions they would be asked to answer. The appearance of a freewheeling exchange of ideas remained, but the candor that sometimes springs from spontaneity was gone.

Whatever the effects of Agnew's criticisms, if the news media disagreed with the direction Nixon had given the war, they were hardly as radical as he presumed. During the Cambodian incursion, for example, AP correspondent Peter Arnett described how a U.S. military unit had looted the small Cambodian town of Snoul. The reporter's story played in full around the world but the section on the looting never appeared in the United States. Arnett's employers deleted those paragraphs because, as AP Managing Editor Wes Gallagher later observed, the nation seemed to be coming apart and he had little wish to publish a story that might contribute further to the chaos. Although the press was critical of the war, it still remained much more protective of the status quo than either Nixon or Agnew was willing at the time to concede.

As the U.S. drawdown proceeded, the troops serving in South Vietnam suffered a decline in morale that created further problems with the press. Aware that war weariness was spreading at home and that no U.S. soldier wanted to be the last to die in Vietnam, reporters contended—occasionally in tones that showed little sympathy for the many soldiers who did their jobs and caused no problems—that drug abuse, interracial tensions, attacks upon officers, and the refusal to obey lawful orders in combat had become common occurrences. The military protested that those conclusions were far too extreme but their rebuttals had little effect. Reporters could see for themselves. Many soldiers no longer bothered to trim their hair to regulation lengths and had allowed it to grow long. Those stationed in rear areas often wore only the barest of uniforms and often appeared during duty hours wearing peace symbols and love beads. Drug abuse was so widespread that the empty vials that had contained heroin and other narcotic drugs crunched continually under foot on some military bases.

Although most reporters attempted conscientiously to cover the military's point of view, their stories were still at times so pointed that they alienated professional military men. Some generals, as a result, refused to deal with the press and some commanders in the field began to require escorts for reporters visiting their units. Although most officers remained correct in their dealings with the media, a few retaliated by declining to provide transportation for reporters covering combat, delaying the release of information until deadlines had passed, and neglecting to provide timely briefings. Those actions damaged official credibility and drove the press further into opposition.

The South Vietnamese added to the effect. With U.S. forces withdrawing, they of necessity assumed a larger and larger portion of the burden in handling the press. Lacking a tradition of free speech and inclined to view the news media as propaganda organs, they considered any reporter who disagreed with them an "enemy sympathizer." When South Vietnamese forces invaded Laos in 1971, newsmen had little difficulty reaching the border on U.S. aircraft but found their way into the combat zone barred on instructions from South Vietnamese commanders. Although the U.S. command managed to gain permission for a few correspondents to fly into Laos on one-day tours of the battlefield, most had to content themselves with the barest information supplied by the harried U.S. helicopter pilots who flew support for the operation.

In the end, the problems encountered by the press in covering the Laotian operation worked to the disadvantage of the South Vietnamese. When the attack went sour and the force in Laos began to withdraw, sometimes in panic, the credibility of government spokesmen was so low that no amount of explanation could convince reporters that the operation had been anything less than an unmitigated disaster.

By December 1972, the press had lost much of its remaining confidence in the Nixon administration, and the president himself was resolved to forge ahead without any regard for the media. As a result, when Nixon during December decided to force North Vietnam to sign a peace treaty by launching a massive bombing campaign against Hanoi, he cut the press off completely. Official spokesmen released little if any information of substance on the attacks, in part to shield Nixon's intentions from North Vietnam but mainly because the president believed he had nothing to lose where the press was concerned.

The result once more worked to the advantage of North Vietnam. The North Vietnamese and their sympathizers filled the vacuum, alleging that Nixon had caused many civilian casualties by indulging in the indiscriminate bombing of

TELEVISION AS POLITICAL FORUM. Robert F. Kennedy is interviewed on the CBS simulcast radio-television program "Face the Nation," Washington, D.C., 26 November 1967. *National Archives*

Hanoi and its environs. Lacking solid information to counter those assertions and disposed to believe the worst, the press repeated those stories. The image of the United States fell around the world.

The effect was unfortunate. Nixon and his spokesmen would have had little difficulty showing that U.S. airmen had sometimes put their own lives at risk in order to bomb strictly military targets while preserving civilian lives and facilities in North Vietnam. If noncombatants had inevitably suffered (1,318 were killed by North Vietnamese count, and 1,261 were wounded), the toll was the product of stray bombs directed against legitimate military targets and nowhere near what it would have been if the United States had intended to wage the sort of unrestricted campaign North Vietnam had alleged. Although Nixon suffered needless blows to his credibility, however, he still achieved his goal. On the tenth day of the attacks, the North Vietnamese ran out of the antiaircraft missiles they needed to defend themselves and signaled that they were ready to deal. They concluded a treaty of peace that postponed the final demise of South Vietnam for two years and allowed the United States to save a measure of face.

The Legacy of Vietnam. The residue of Nixon's conflict with the press remained, to surface over the years that followed, whenever the United States attempted a major military operation. As late as 1991, when U.S. forces went to war in the Persian Gulf, many reporters arrived at the scene of conflict prepared to encounter all of the problems that had flourished in Vietnam. While there were exceptions, especially among the Marines, some within the military were just as hostile. Convinced that unfavorable, biased news reporting had turned the American public and Congress against the Vietnam War, they attempted to insulate themselves from the press.

If the expectations of reporters, in that case, were unrealistic—the force in the gulf proved to be one of the best the United States had ever fielded—the reaction of the military was equally unfounded. Although many officers blamed the news media for the loss in Vietnam, questions can legitimately be raised as to whether press coverage of that conflict had all that much effect upon public opinion in the United States. Indeed, evidence exists that from the beginning the American people had gone their own way, allowing the press to highlight the issues but thinking their own thoughts. While the news media thus turned against the war only belatedly, when the ruling establishment from which reporters and editors took their cues began to turn, public opinion dropped steadily, in step with American losses.

By 1973, public patience both with the government and the news media had run out. According to Harris Polls, Americans not only rejected Nixon's bombing of Hanoi by a margin of 51 to 37 percent, an even more emphatic 67 percent rejected the claims appearing in the press that hospitals and residential areas had been hit. The reason they gave for repudiating the attacks was simple. By a margin of 55 to 30 percent they asserted that they were no longer willing to bear the expense. During the raids, they told interviewers, "we lost many American lives and B-52's." "The fat is on the fire," Nixon told Thieu shortly thereafter. If no final settlement were forthcoming, the American people, through their representatives in Congress, would force the abandonment of South Vietnam. At the end of the war as throughout its course, the American people had followed their own course, and, by finally rejecting the claims of both the government and the press, had quietly shown their contempt for all those who had attempted to manipulate them over the years. It was a lesson for policymakers, generals, and reporters alike to consider whenever the United States prepares to go to war.

BIBLIOGRAPHY

ARLEN, MICHAEL. "The Air: The Falklands, Vietnam, and Our Collective Memory." *New Yorker*, 16 August 1982.

BAGDIKIAN, BEN. "The Fruits of Agnewism." *Columbia Journalism Review* 11 (January 1973).

BAILEY, GEORGE A. *The Vietnam War According to Chet, David, Walter, Harry, Peter, Bob, Howard, and Frank.* 1973.

BRAESTRUP, PETER. *Battle Lines: Report of the Twentieth Century Fund Task Force on the Military and the Media.* 1985.

BRAESTRUP, PETER. *Big Story: How the American Press and TV Reported and Interpreted the Crisis of Tet in Vietnam and Washington.* 2 vols. 1977.

BRAESTRUP, PETER, ed. *Vietnam as History: Ten Years after the Paris Peace Accords.* 1984.

DONOVAN, ROBERT J., and RAY SCHERER. *Unsilent Revolution: Television News and American Public Life.* 1992.

EPSTEIN, EDWARD JAY. *News from Nowhere. 1973.*

EPSTEIN, EDWARD JAY. "What Happened vs. What We Saw." *TV Guide,* 29 September 1973.

GANS, HERBERT J. *Deciding What's News.* 1979.

GITLIN, TODD. *The Whole World Is Watching: Mass Media in the Making and Unmaking of the New Left.* 1980.

HALBERSTAM, DAVID. *The Making of a Quagmire.* 1964, 1965.

HALLIN, DANIEL. *The Uncensored War: The Media and Vietnam.* 1986.

HAMMOND, WILLIAM M. *The U.S. Army in Vietnam: Public Affairs, The Military and the Media, 1962–1968.* 1988.

HAMMOND, WILLIAM M. *The U.S. Army in Vietnam: Public Affairs, The Military, and the Media, 1968–1973.* Forthcoming.

HAMMOND, WILLIAM M. "The Press in Vietnam as Agent of Defeat: A Critical Examination." *Reviews in American History* (June 1989).

KERN, MONTAGUE, PATRICIA W. LEVERING, and RALPH B. LEVERING. *The Kennedy Crises: The Press, the Presidency, and Foreign Policy.* 1983.

LICHTY, LAWRENCE W., and EDWARD FOUHY. "Television Reporting of the Vietnam War." *The World and I* (April 1987).

MUELLER, JOHN. *War, Presidents, and Public Opinion.* 1973.

SIGAL, LEON V. *Reporters and Officials: The Organization and Politics of News Making.* 1973.

WILLIAMS, ALDEN. "TV's First War: Unbiased Study of Television News Bias." *Journal of Communication* 25 (Autumn 1975): 190.

WILLIAM M. HAMMOND

Medical Support. *[This entry includes four articles:*

People's Army of Vietnam (PAVN)
People's Liberation Armed Forces (PLAF)
Republic of Vietnam Armed Forces (RVNAF)
U.S. Military.

People's Army of Vietnam (PAVN)

Compared with those of its U.S. adversaries, the North Vietnamese People's Army of Vietnam (PAVN) had crude medical facilities. While helicopter ambulances provided rapid evacuation for U.S. troops, casualties in the PAVN were moved by foot, boat, or, occasionally, vehicle. But the North Vietnamese medical operations received considerable resources and successfully maintained force levels despite staggering, ongoing losses. A medical brigade accompanied each PAVN division and constructed field hospitals, often in underground tunnels to protect them against U.S. air power or artillery. The North Vietnamese established larger medical facilities away from combat areas, such as hospitals with extensive underground operating rooms situated along the Ho Chi Minh Trail.

North Vietnamese medical personnel resorted frequently to limb amputations for the treatment of combat casualties. They often found unorthodox sources for surgical material; medical equipment and bandages, for instance, were recycled from ammunition shells and parachutes, and sterilized nylon thread was used in all surgeries. In their treatments, medical personnel often combined formal Western medical procedures with traditional Asian herbal techniques. Hemoglobin serum, for instance, was obtained from water buffalo or pigs; an extract from the placenta of newborn buffalo calves provided some relief from malaria; powdered tiger bones, liquefied and combined with selected tree bark, acted as a stimulant when drunk by troops suffering from acute exhaustion.

North Vietnamese soldiers typically suffered from malnourishment. In 1965, the daily combat ration of a PAVN soldier consisted of rice (250 g, 8.75 oz) and vegetables (300 g, 10.5 oz). If available, supplementary foods were issued to all soldiers based on strict rationing: salt (25 g, 0.875 oz), salted fish (18 g, 0.63 oz), bean curd/sesame (9 g, 0.315 oz), meat or fish (8 g, 0.28 oz), and coconut oil (6 g, 0.21 oz). These infrequent extras, however, did not meet the basic nutritional standard required of combat troops. Therefore foraging was a necessity, and most

fauna were targeted, including snakes, monkeys, tigers, wild dogs, and elephants.

North Vietnamese soldiers also faced health problems associated with prolonged exposure to jungle conditions. Snake bites and, more critically, malaria were constant problems. In 1971 Dr. Pham Ngoc Thach, Hanoi's health minister, journeyed south to assess how PAVN and Viet Cong troops were handling increased rates of malaria; while there he succumbed to the disease and died.

The North Vietnamese manufactured many antibiotics and other medicines and purchased items on the black market. They also received medical supplies from Eastern bloc countries as well as from neutral European nations. During the war, the government constructed a rural medical network in the North, staffed by an informally trained medical cadre, to treat civilians injured during the U.S. bombing campaigns. Conservative estimates put civilian deaths from U.S. bombing in the North at 65,000. An estimated 670,000 North Vietnamese and Viet Cong soldiers died in combat between 1965 and the end of the war.

BIBLIOGRAPHY

LANNING, MICHAEL LEE, and DAN CRAGG. *Inside the VC and the NVA: The Real Story of North Vietnam's Armed Forces.* 1992.
LEWY, GUENTER. *America in Vietnam.* 1978.
VAN DYKE, JON M. *North Vietnam's Strategy for Survival.* 1972.

THOMAS R. CANTWELL AND ADAM LAND

People's Liberation Armed Forces (PLAF)

The PLAF (commonly known as the Viet Cong), developed a crude but effective medical care system for soldiers in South Vietnam. First aid cadre members, usually women, maintained medical stations at combat hamlets within sympathetic territory. Medical personnel, although often informally trained, accompanied small fighting groups, while medical contingents were incorporated into larger units. Viet Cong personnel utilized a combination of indigenous, Asian medical treatments and Western medical procedures. The Viet Cong forces created elaborate facilities, occasionally staffed with doctors from the North, at fixed installations throughout South Vietnam. These facilities were often located in underground tunnels. Severe casualties were sometimes transferred to North Vietnamese facilities. During the Vietnam War, Viet Cong soldiers frequently suffered from malnourishment as well as from tropical diseases such as malaria.

The Viet Cong guerrillas obtained much of their medical supplies from North Vietnam or international sources. They also acquired medical material from the South Vietnamese army through raids or illicit purchases from corrupt officials. In addition, the Viet Cong personnel used found war material (e.g., parachutes and artillery shells) to manufacture medical equipment or produced indigenous medicines from local plants and animals. Viet Cong forces also occasionally abducted South Vietnamese doctors temporarily for treatment of prominent National Liberation Front (NLF) officials.

BIBLIOGRAPHY

LANNING, MICHAEL LEE, and DAN CRAGG. *Inside the VC and the NVA: The Real Story of North Vietnam's Armed Forces.* 1992.

PIKE, DOUGLAS. *Viet Cong: The Organization and Techniques of the National Liberation Front of South Vietnam.* 1966.

THOMAS R. CANTWELL AND ADAM LAND

Republic of Vietnam Armed Forces (RVNAF)

Although subsidized and overseen by the United States, the Republic of Vietnam Armed Forces' (RVNAF) medical operations were largely inadequate during the war, and the poor quality of medical care contributed to high desertion rates and poor morale within the Army of the Republic of Vietnam (ARVN). At the height of the war, the RVNAF maintained several dozen military hospitals and a few convalescent centers for recuperating soldiers. Though in general South Vietnamese personnel treated South Vietnamese wounded, the United States supervised operations and provided nearly all medical supplies. In addition, U.S. Army helicopters performed combat casualty evacuations until late in the war, because the ARVN did not have an air command and the South Vietnam Air Force (VNAF) was reluctant to commit resources to assist ground troops.

Chronic shortages of medical personnel, supplies, and facilities undermined RVNAF medical operations during the war. In 1966 the nation had approximately one thousand doctors, many of whom shunned demanding military duties or assignments in rural areas. The RVNAF did not establish a nursing corps until 1971. Medical facilities were also inadequate for extensive combat casualties. In 1968, the South Vietnamese military had 21,000 hospital beds, yet the ARVN averaged 16,595 casualties per month in that year. Near the end of the war, RVNAF medical operations struggled to address a rising level of casualties, but cutbacks in U.S. aid during the early 1970s exacerbated shortages. In 1975, the RVNAF surgeon general reported that 548 of 865 essential medical drugs were unavailable, contributing to a rise in death-from-injury rates above 10 percent.

South Vietnamese soldiers suffered from malnutrition during the war, as did the North Vietnamese and Viet Cong troops. In 1972, the RVNAF's surgeon general reported that 78 percent of the diet of combat soldiers came from white rice devoid of fiber. Consequently, most soldiers suffered from deficiencies in iron, folic acid, and vitamins A, C, and the B-complex group. These imbalances resulted in excessive fatigue, dysentery, disorientation, and optical problems, compounded in many cases by skin infections and malaria.

The South Vietnamese government's ministry of health maintained a network of provincial hospitals for civilians throughout the country. These facilities were often meager, though after 1965 the United States committed military medical personnel to staff clinics. An estimated 300,000 civilians died in the war after 1965. Between 1955 and 1975, approximately 250,000 RVNAF personnel died in combat, and a further 300,000 suffered injuries. ARVN combat units accounted for 85 percent of all military casualties. The ARVN's casualty rate was five to six times greater than that of its U.S. ally.

BIBLIOGRAPHY

DONG VAN KHUYEN. *The RVNAF.* 1980.

LEWY, GUENTER. *America in Vietnam.* 1978.

THOMAS R. CANTWELL AND ADAM LAND

U.S. Military

When the U.S. military entered the Vietnam conflict, its system of medical care was prepared for a conventional war in which most casualties would occur at an obvious front. The military had designed mobile medical facilities intended to follow front-line troops. But the Vietnam War confounded these expectations. Instead of casualties occurring near the front and flowing through battalion aid stations, division clearing stations, surgical hospitals, and then, if necessary, to an evacuation hospital, casualties in this unconventional war could occur anywhere in South Vietnam.

In response, both the army and the navy modified their medical operations, creating a system in which a hospital supported a given geographic area

COMBAT FIRST AID. After treating two wounded Vietnamese paratroopers, an ARVN medic repacks his kit. *Center of Military History*

of the country, regardless of the units that operated within it. When coupled with the ability of helicopters to move patients long distances rapidly, this area support concept made mobile large facilities unnecessary. Military hospitals replaced austere field equipment with permanent, more sophisticated technology, and buildings on concrete slabs replaced tents. As a result, the wounded in the Vietnam War under U.S. care were treated in clean, comfortable surroundings in which medical personnel rarely wanted for equipment or supplies.

The U.S. military relied critically upon helicopter evacuation to support its area-based medical operations. Although the military became interested in aeromedical evacuation between the two world wars, advances in helicopter design made this rapid transport mission feasible. The U.S. Army deployed its first helicopter ambulance units during the Korean War, and in the Vietnam conflict, medical evacuations by helicopter, or "dustoffs," became the norm. Helicopter evacuation teams carried critically wounded soldiers directly to military hospitals, replacing the intermediate aid stations that had previously stabilized casualties.

The Army Medical Service adapted the UH-1 "Huey," developed initially as an evacuation helicopter, to become its first effective air ambulance. The Huey had the size and lift capacity to carry multiple patients and a crew to fly the aircraft and care for patients in flight. Each model, from the "B" (introduced in 1964) through the "H" (adopted in 1967), increased medical evacuation capability. Beginning in April 1966 the 44th Medical Brigade operated most army medical helicopters. At the height of the war, the brigade controlled 116 air ambulances that transported casualties to the several dozen army hospitals in South Vietnam. In the Central Highlands the 1st Cavalry Division and the 101st Airborne Division maintained their own evacuation helicopters (because of the vast distances, these divisions also maintained clearing stations to stabilize casualties, unlike other units).

The U.S. Navy, which oversaw medical services for U.S. Marines in the I Corps Tactical Zone in northern South Vietnam, similarly relied on helicopters to transport casualties to large, sophisticated facilities. The U.S. Navy, however, never utilized single-mission air ambulances as did the army. Navy and marine helicopters moved the wounded to either the 600-bed navy hospital in Da Nang or to the hospital ships USS *Repose* and USS *Sanctuary*. Smaller battalion and regimental aid stations treated less severe casualties and provided routine services for marines in the tactical zone. Navy medical detachments also supported marine and navy coastal and riverine operations, such as campaigns in the Mekong Delta beginning in 1967. More extensive casualties in these operations were transported by helicopter to nearby army hospitals.

The U.S. Air Force (USAF) provided additional medical support, transporting severe casualties by plane both inside Vietnam and to hospitals in Asia and the United States. Soldiers requiring treatment unavailable in Vietnam (or if recovery would take longer than sixty days) were moved by modified USAF transport planes, usually to Clark Air Force Base in the Philippines before transfer. The USAF maintained limited medical facilities on its air bases in Vietnam and Thailand. Serious air force casualties were treated at navy or army hospitals or transported outside the combat area.

Ultimately, the extensive U.S. medical operations achieved some success in minimizing U.S. fatalities. U.S. Army studies estimate that, between 1965 and 1975, 19 percent of U.S. casualties died from their

WOUNDED MARINE. A U.S. Marine, wounded near Dong Ha during Operation HASTINGS, waits to be evacuated. *National Archives*

wounds in Vietnam, compared with 26 percent in Korea and 29 percent during World War II.

Besides casualties from combat, the U.S. military confronted medical problems resulting from tropical fevers, parasitic diseases, and, most critically, malaria. Early in the war, the Military Assistance Command, Vietnam (MACV), established malaria control procedures, recognizing the potential havoc from the disease. The medical services initially had difficulty treating the malaria strain (*falciparum*) encountered in Vietnam, which was resistant to common drugs. A new preventive, Dapsone, proved partially effective against the strain. Preventive measures within each unit remained the key to malaria control. Unless commanders enforced procedures, such as ensuring that soldiers took medicines or rolled their sleeves down to minimize insect bites, the incidence of malaria would rise. The constant turnover in troops and leaders resulted in repeated cycles of discipline breakdown. Beginning in 1968, commanders used a urinary test for chloroquinea, the standard preventive medicine, to maintain malaria discipline among troops. Though remaining

a serious medical problem, malaria never became a military liability.

During the war the United States also committed medical resources to civic programs for the South Vietnamese. These policies were designed to gain civilian political support, though such goodwill efforts were undermined by the U.S. military's reliance on heavy firepower which caused significant destruction and civilian injury in South Vietnam. Beginning in the early 1960s, the U.S. Agency for International Development (USAID) funded the construction of numerous hospitals and several hundred smaller medical dispensaries. During the war, the military also integrated civilian casualties into the helicopter evacuation system. In response to President Johnson's directives in 1966, military personnel increased medical and dental care programs for civilians, often establishing clinics in rural villages. During lulls in combat, U.S. Army physicians trained Vietnamese medical personnel or served in provincial hospitals. In northeast Thailand, USAF medical teams similarly treated civilians in politically sensitive areas.

In the late 1960s, the military medical services faced a sharp rise in drug use among U.S. servicemen. Drug-production laboratories in the Golden Triangle (Burma, Thailand, and Laos) gained increasing technical sophistication during the war, and the Cambodian incursion in 1970 enabled corrupt South Vietnamese officers to enter the drug trade. Furthermore, the U.S. military's tactical shift from active combat to an enclave strategy gave soldiers significant unstructured free time within protected bases. The combination of cheap, pure heroin and troops available to use it created a drug problem unparalleled in U.S. military history. The issue received intense press and congressional attention, and the prevalent, but erroneous, belief that heroin users remained addicted for life fueled public fears. The military reacted with a program that included testing, treatment, and amnesties for drug use.

During the war, military medical services had little problem with instances of combat exhaustion (also known as shell shock or battle fatigue). The combination of frequent rest and the one-year rotation policy resulted in psychiatric morbidity rates little higher than those in peacetime. While combat neurosis may have been low, many Vietnam veterans suffered lingering trauma from the war. Beginning in the 1970s, veteran activists and mental health professionals agitated for recognition of the psychiatric difficulties facing many veterans. Allied with sympathetic politicians, these activists successfully lobbied in 1979 for a federal program, the Vietnam Veterans Outreach Program, to fund counseling clinics for Vietnam veterans nationwide. In 1980, these activists pressured the American Psychiatric Association into recognizing post-traumatic stress syndrome (PTSS) as a mental illness that affected many veterans. A Veterans Administration study, released in 1988, estimated that 15 percent of Vietnam veterans suffered from PTSS.

[*See also* Women, U.S. Military, *article on* Nurses.]

BIBLIOGRAPHY

DORLAND, PETER, and JAMES NANNY. *Dust Off: Aeromedical Evacuation in Vietnam.* 1982.
MCCLENDON, FRANK O. "Doctor and Dentists, Nurses and Corpsman." In *Vietnam: The Naval Story.* 1986.
NEEL, SPURGEON. *Medical Support of the U.S. Army in Vietnam, 1965–1970.* 1973.
SCOTT, WILBUR. *The Politics of Readjustment: Vietnam Veterans since the War.* 1993.

ADAM LAND AND JEFFREY GREENHUT

Mekong River and Delta. The Mekong River originates in China and runs through Burma, Laos, Thailand, and Cambodia before entering southern Vietnam, where it forms the Mekong Delta and empties into the South China Sea. A fertile region (including Saigon) laced with canals and irrigation ditches, it constitutes just less than one-quarter of the total area of South Vietnam, although the delta was home to 40 percent of the population in 1963. Travel in the region was difficult, except by

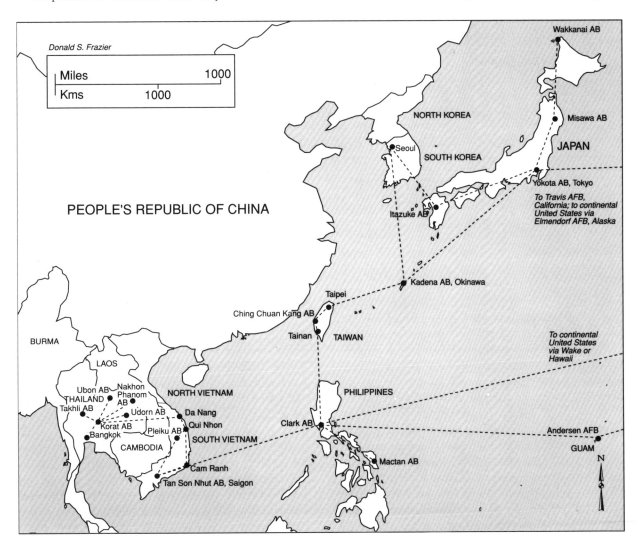

MAJOR U.S. MEDICAL EVACUATION AIR ROUTES.

SWAMP TERRAIN. U.S. soldiers carry a wounded comrade through a landscape typical of the Mekong Delta. *National Archives*

boat or helicopter, because the terrain consisted largely of water, mud, and nearly impenetrable tropical foliage. To combat these conditions, the French, during their colonial rule, constructed a road system and expanded the canal system, which played a vital role in the Vietnamese and Cambodian economies.

As early as 1954, pro-independence guerrillas established bases in the delta, where the thick jungles provided cover for operatives in their campaign to oust the French by attacking the region's inhabitants and commerce. South Vietnamese government forces countered with pacification programs designed to destroy guerrilla influence in certain areas. These efforts, with U.S. Marine assistance, reduced Viet Cong guerrilla activity to minor levels by 1964.

In 1962 the Diem government created a series of strategic farming hamlets throughout the region to isolate peasant farmers from Viet Cong guerrillas. These hamlets were extremely unpopular with the Vietnamese people because the program uprooted them from the lands their ancestors had inhabited for centuries. Regional support for the South Vietnamese government dwindled as a result of this spreading discontent. During the 1968 Tet Offensive, much of the fighting occurred in the delta, and the North Vietnam–backed guerrillas expected the peasants to rise against Diem's government. Instead, because the guerrilla-initiated fighting caused further disruption and suffering for the people, their support for the South Vietnamese government increased.

Although most of the fighting during the 1972 Easter Offensive occurred outside the delta region, the guerrillas took a number of settlements in the area because President Nguyen Van Thieu was forced to move South Vietnamese army units out of the delta to combat North Vietnamese troops in other areas; Viet Cong guerrillas quickly filled the vacuum left by the redeployment. By the summer of 1973, North Vietnam controlled enough of South Vietnam to begin construction of a major highway from Quang Tri province to the delta, which when completed enabled the North Vietnamese to move large-scale weaponry and troops into position for an attack on Saigon. The delta highway was an important route in the 1975 Spring Offensive.

BIBLIOGRAPHY

DAVIDSON, PHILLIP B. *Vietnam at War—The History: 1946–1975.* 1988.
FUTRELL, ROBERT F. *The United States Air Force in Southeast Asia: The Advisory Years to 1965.* 1981.
KARNOW, STANLEY. *Vietnam: A History.* 1991.
MELSON, CHARLES D., and CURTIS G. ARNOLD. *The U.S. Marines in Vietnam: The War That Would Not End, 1971–1973.* 1991.

ELLEN D. GOLDLUST

Mendenhall, Joseph (1920–), Foreign Service officer, 1946–1975. President Kennedy sent Mendenhall, who had been stationed in Saigon, and Gen. Victor Krulak to Vietnam on an investigative trip in September 1963. Mendenhall, who visited Vietnamese and U.S. civilian officials, reported that the Diem government could not win the war. Krulak, who visited U.S. military advisers, concluded that South Vietnam was winning the war. Kennedy reportedly responded by asking if the men had visited the same country. These conflicting reports reflected the split over Vietnam policy among the president's advisers.

BIBLIOGRAPHY

NEWMAN, JOHN. *JFK and Vietnam: Deception, Intrigue, and the Struggle for Power.* 1992.
RUST, WILLIAM J. *Kennedy in Vietnam.* 1985.

WILLIAM PAUL SCHUCK

Mendès-France, Pierre (1907–1982), French prime minister, June 1954–February 1955; foreign minister, 1954–1955. In "seven months and seventeen days" Mendès-France, as premier and foreign

PIERRE MENDÈS-FRANCE. At center, meeting with Richard M. Nixon and John Foster Dulles, November 1954. *National Archives*

minister, achieved the end of the French Indochina War. Mendès-France prepared for this role as an outspoken critic of post–World War II French foreign policy. As a maverick deputy, he electrified the French National Assembly in 1950 with a speech that unmasked the costs of the Indochina War and exposed French policy as a sham. His election as premier on 18 June 1954 came amid a two-month stalemate at the Geneva Conference. He was the one major politician willing to end the war. His dramatic vow, "I promise to resign if, one month from now, on July 20, I have failed to obtain a cease fire in Indochina," underscored his commitment and convinced wavering deputies to entrust him with the government.

Mendès-France, sensing public support for ending hostilities, was more willing than previous premiers to pursue every effort toward achieving a reasonable settlement; however, privately, previous French negotiators were already toying with options such as Vietnamese partition. Last-minute negotiations among Mendès-France, Pham Van Dong, Zhou Enlai, and Vyacheslav Molotov broke the conference deadlock; the latter two abandoned communist unity with the Viet Minh to pursue their respective geopolitical goals. Zhou and Molotov pressured Pham Van Dong to retreat from the strong positions won by the Viet Minh on the battlefield and to accept partition and late elections. With this assistance, Mendès-France met his deadline and secured a settlement that pleased most of France. As the Pentagon Papers noted, "Paris had extracted itself from *la sale guerre* [the dirty war] with honor, yet had also retained a foothold in South Vietnam. . . . French military power would have to be surrendered . . . but French influence could (and did) remain." In sum, Mendès-France extricated France militarily from a lost war and won much for France by negotiation, while denying the Viet Minh the victor's spoils.

BIBLIOGRAPHY

DEVILLERS, PHILLIPE, and JEAN LACOUTURE. *End of a War: Indochina, 1954.* 1969.

KARNOW, STANLEY. *Vietnam: A History.* 1991.

The Pentagon Papers: The Defense Department History of United States Decisionmaking on Vietnam. Senator Gravel Edition. Vol. 1. 1971.

WALL, IRWIN M. *The United States and the Making of Postwar France, 1945–1954.* 1991.

VICTOR JEW

MENU. MENU, the code name for President Richard Nixon's secret bombing of Cambodia, was an early manifestation of Nixon's penchant for secrecy. The MENU raids, so-called because they were named for meals, reflected Nixon's policy of covering the withdrawal of U.S. ground forces with sharp military escalations. Intended to destroy communist Vietnamese sanctuaries in Neutral Cambodia, the raids were prompted by Gen. Creighton Abrams's intimation that U.S. intelligence had located COSVN (Central Office for South Vietnam), the communist military headquarters in the south, just over the Cambodian border. Overriding Secretary of State William Rogers's opposition and Secretary of Defense Melvin Laird's reservations, Nixon determined to keep secret the extension of ARC LIGHT strikes to then-neutral Cambodia. To this end, selected B-52 crews were called aside after permission briefings and told that they would be diverted in flight by the Skyspot radar at Bien Hoa air base. They were to bomb on the radar site's instructions and report that they had struck their originally briefed targets. "Breakfast" was launched on 18 March 1969; "Lunch," "Dinner," "Snack," "Supper," and "Dessert" followed over the next fourteen months, amounting to 3,630 B-52 sorties, more than 100,000 tons of bombs, and resulting in substantial Cambodian civilian loss of life. The targets were all within 8 kilometers (5 miles) of the border, so the diversions were not apparent from flight times. Aside from Nixon and Secretary of State Henry Kissinger, only the colonel who devised the system, representing the Strategic Air Command (SAC) on the Joint Chiefs of Staff, his immediate superiors, and the major commanding the Skyspot site knew that the actual targets were in Cambodia. Word eventually leaked out, prompting a series of news stories, beginning in the 9 May *New York Times,* and sparking heated debate about the legality and morality of the raids. Nixon responded by ordering taps on the phones of reporters and officials, beginning the spiral of illegal activity, secrecy, and cover-up that ultimately forced his resignation. After the May 1970 ground invasion of Cambodia the MENU bombings continued openly until Congress cut off funds for Cambodian operations in August 1973.

BIBLIOGRAPHY

MOROCCO, JOHN, et al. *Rain of Fire: Air War.* Vol. 14 of *The Vietnam Experience.* 1985.

SHAWCROSS, WILLIAM. *Slideshow: Kissinger, Nixon, and the Destruction of Cambodia.* 1979.

JOHN F. GUILMARTIN JR.

Meo. *See* Hmong.

MIA. *See* POW/MIA Controversy.

Michigan State University Vietnam Advisory Group (MSUVAG).

An advisory group of scholars and public administration experts, the Michigan State University Vietnam Advisory Group was created to draft recommendations for U.S. policy and to help the South Vietnamese government establish democratic institutions. Granted a contract by the U.S. Operations Mission, a government relief organization, MSUVAG was led by Michigan State professor Wesley Fishel and operated under the auspices of the university. The group worked from 1954 to 1961 to train Vietnamese civil servants and set up an internal security force of civil guard and police units in South Vietnam.

The MSUVAG had difficulties overcoming South Vietnam's authoritarian style of governance and faced particular problems over the civil guard issue. President Ngo Dinh Diem believed the guard should be a heavily armed auxiliary military unit whereas the American advisers pressed for a more traditional police force with light weapons. The U.S. government backed the MSUVAG in the dispute, and the civil guard soon became a "dumping ground" for poorly trained personnel from the Army of the Republic of Vietnam (ARVN). Outfitted with nightsticks and whistles, the guard was unprepared to deal with guerrillas armed with machine guns and grenades, leading some to argue that the MSUVAG failed to appreciate the specific training needs of the guard's assignment. Conflicts between the South Vietnamese government and the MSUVAG reached a boiling point in 1961 when several returning advisers, including Milton C. Taylor, wrote articles in the American media highly critical of Diem, who subsequently ordered the MSUVAG contract dissolved.

BIBLIOGRAPHY

FITZGERALD, FRANCES. *Fire in the Lake: The Vietnamese and the Americans in Vietnam.* 1972.

HERRING, GEORGE C. *America's Longest War: The United States and Vietnam, 1950–1975.* 1986.

KELLY EVANS-PFEIFER

Midway Island Conference.

The Midway Island Conference took place on 8 June 1969. President Richard Nixon met for six hours with his South Vietnamese counterpart, Nguyen Van Thieu, to discuss the Paris peace talks, the battlefield situation, and South Vietnam's assuming a larger share of the fighting. Thieu probably would not have attended if he had known Nixon's true purpose. At the meeting, Nixon announced Vietnamization, a policy he had already settled upon privately, despite objections from Thieu and General Creighton Abrams, commander of the Military Assistance Command, Vietnam (MACV).

BIBLIOGRAPHY

AMBROSE, STEPHEN E. *Nixon.* Volume 2: *The Triumph of a Politician, 1962–1972.* 1989.

"Nixon Off to Meet with Thieu Today on Course of War," *New York Times,* 8 June 1969.

ELLEN D. GOLDLUST

Military Assistance Advisory Group–Vietnam (MAAG-V).

Fearing a communist takeover of Indochina in 1955, the Eisenhower administration rushed to provide the Republic of South Vietnam with direct military assistance. On 1 November 1955 the Military Assistance Advisory Group–Vietnam (MAAG-V), was activated in Saigon. It replaced the Military Assistance Advisory Group–Indochina (MAAG-I), which had been created by President Truman in September 1950 to funnel military aid to the French, who were fighting to retain their colonial empire in Indochina.

MAAG-V, until deactivated on 15 May 1964, directed U.S. military advisory efforts in South Vietnam. Primarily concerned with the development of the Army of the Republic of South Vietnam (ARVN), MAAG-V advisers organized and trained ARVN soldiers in the image of the U.S. Army. They focused on preparing to repel a conventional invasion by communist North Vietnam and until the early 1960s, failed to recognize the threat of the Viet Cong insurgency.

Early in 1962, the Kennedy administration expanded the U.S. military's role in South Vietnam and established the Military Assistance Command,

Vietnam (MACV), to oversee logistical and operational support for the South Vietnamese military. MAAG-V continued to operate as an independent entity, but its overall importance declined. Although the total number of MAAG-V advisers increased from 900 in 1961 to more than 3,400 at the beginning of 1963, it was only a small proportion of the nearly 16,000 U.S. military personnel on duty in South Vietnam. In May 1964 MAAG-V transferred its advisory functions to MACV and was dissolved.

Commanders, MAAG-I

Brig. Gen. Francis G. Brink (October 1950–August 1952)
Maj. Gen. Thomas J. H. Trapnell (August 1952–April 1954)
Lt. Gen. John W. O'Daniel (April 1954–November 1955)

Commanders, MAAG-V

Lt. Gen. Samuel T. Williams (November 1955–September 1960
Lt. Gen. Lionel C. McGarr (September 1960–July 1962)
Lt. Gen. Charles J. Timmes (July 1962–May 1964)

[*See also* Military Assistance Command, Vietnam (MACV).]

BIBLIOGRAPHY

PALMER, BRUCE, JR. *The 25-Year War: America's Role in Vietnam.* 1984.
STANTON, SHELBY L. *Order of Battle: U.S. Army and Allied Ground Forces in Vietnam.* 1981.

DANIEL T. BAILEY

Military Assistance Command, Vietnam (MACV).

By late 1961 the Kennedy administration had become increasingly concerned about the military situation in the Republic of South Vietnam. Pressure from North Vietnam combined with a growing communist insurgency threatened the stability of the pro-Western government. Despite serious misgivings about deepening U.S. involvement in Southeast Asia, President Kennedy concluded that increased U.S. military aid to South Vietnam was necessary to prevent a communist takeover of the country. To oversee the expanded U.S. effort, the Joint Chiefs of Staff (JCS) recommended the establishment of a new military command in South Vietnam.

Activated on 8 February 1962, the Military Assistance Command, Vietnam (MACV), became responsible for directing the activities of U.S. military units being deployed to provide the South Vietnamese with logistical and operational support. General Paul D. Harkins was the first of four officers to hold the title of commander of the U.S. Military Assistance Command, Vietnam (COMUSMACV). MACV's authority extended to most U.S. military operations in South Vietnam, including air operations along both sides of the demilitarized zone (DMZ).

Throughout its existence, MACV suffered from serious flaws in the U.S. command structure. Although MACV was a joint service headquarters with responsibility for a specific battle zone, the Pentagon refused to declare MACV a full-fledged theater command, and placed its operational jurisdiction under very tight restrictions. COMUSMACV reported to the commander-in-chief, Pacific (CINCPAC), who received his orders from the JCS. The senior military officer in South Vietnam, therefore, was not directly responsible to the top U.S. military and political leadership, but to CINCPAC. The U.S. secretary of defense confused the situation by ordering CINCPAC to forward all MACV communications to the Pentagon undiluted.

MACV operated under strict geographic limitations as well. For example, military operations in North Vietnam and Laos, which had a significant impact on the military situation in South Vietnam, were technically outside the geographic boundaries of the COMUSMACV's authority. Special permission was required from Washington for such operations, and CINCPAC generally conducted them through other subordinate commands. MACV had no control and little input. The continued independent existence of the Military Assistance Advisory Group–Vietnam (MAAG-V), for more than two years after the creation of MACV also complicated the command situation. The lack of unified direction and undivided responsibility for the U.S. military effort became a growing problem as the number of U.S. troops in South Vietnam increased to nearly 16,000 by the end of 1963.

General Harkins and his replacement, General William D. Westmoreland, pressured CINCPAC and the JCS to allow them to centralize command and control in South Vietnam. The most significant change came in May 1964 with the abolishment of MAAG-V and the transfer of its functions to MACV. The task of advising and training the Army of the Republic of Vietnam (ARVN) then became MACV's responsibility. Although it made sense to centralize control of all U.S. military activities under a single headquarters, responsibility for ARVN's development was dispersed among the MACV headquarters staff and senior advisers in each of the corps tactical zones. The advisory effort soon became a low-priority item, and the ARVN's poor battlefield performance reflected the lack of U.S. interest in the ARVN's development.

In an effort to centralize MACV control further, General Westmoreland refused to establish a U.S. Army field headquarters in South Vietnam. He completely ignored the Korean War experience in which the Eighth Army focused exclusively on the ground war and operated under the direction of a separate theater headquarters. Westmoreland wanted MACV to serve as both a joint service and a field army headquarters with a single staff handling all military issues. In addition to holding the title of COMUSMACV, he became commanding general, U.S. Army, Vietnam (USARV), as well. This command arrangement broadened MACV's area of responsibility to include field operations, assistance and advisory efforts, various politico-military issues, and numerous other activities. It was too much for one headquarters and one commanding officer, and the execution of U.S. military operations in South Vietnam suffered accordingly.

The military command structure remained relatively unchanged after the summer of 1964. MACV directed the U.S. war effort until it was dissolved on 29 March 1973. MACV's inability to be a completely effective headquarters was only one factor in the United States' failure to achieve its goals.

[See also Military Assistance Advisory Command–Vietnam (MAAG-V).]

Commanders, MACV

General Paul D. Harkins (February 1962–June 1964)
General William D. Westmoreland (June 1964–July 1968)
General Creighton W. Abrams (July 1968–June 1972)
General Frederick C. Weyand (June 1972–March 1973)

BIBLIOGRAPHY

KREPINEVICH, ANDREW F., JR. *The Army and Vietnam.* 1986.
PALMER, BRUCE, JR. *The 25-Year War: America's Role in Vietnam.* 1984.
STANTON, SHELBY L. *Order of Battle: U.S. Army and Allied Ground Forces in Vietnam.* 1981.

DANIEL T. BAILEY

Military Revolutionary Council. The Military Revolutionary Council (MRC) was the junta that governed South Vietnam after it assassinated President Diem in November 1963. MRC members were convinced that South Vietnamese support for the National Liberation Front (NLF) grew essentially out of disaffection with Diem rather than out of the NLF's positive appeal. The MRC declared itself to be noncommunist rather than anticommunist and consciously sought some sort of "neutralization" of Vietnam and an eventual reconciliation with the Democratic Republic of Vietnam (DRV) and the NLF. The MRC freed jailed Buddhists in an effort to build domestic political support. Seeking the ultimate disengagement of foreigners, the MRC opposed the U.S. bombing of the DRV and the entry of U.S. personnel into villages, maintaining that this degree of intervention would serve only to solidify opposition to the South Vietnamese government.

The MRC was divided; some members sought improved relations with the DRV, but its officers lacked vital political experience and a clear, coherent program. The MRC was shortlived; President Johnson was not interested in negotiating with the DRV, and a pro-U.S. faction within the MRC, led by Gen. Nguyen Khanh, helped depose Gen. Duong Van Minh, who headed the junta, in January 1964. Khanh's plans were known to U.S. officials, but they did nothing to prevent it.

BIBLIOGRAPHY

HERRING, GEORGE C. *America's Longest War: The United States and Vietnam, 1950–1975.* 1986.
YOUNG, MARILYN B. *The Vietnam Wars.* 1991.

ELLEN BAKER

Mine Warfare. [*This entry includes two articles:*

Land Mine Warfare
Naval Mine Warfare.]

Land Mine Warfare

The military forces in the Vietnam conflict relied heavily upon land mines in their tactical warfare. U.S. ground forces widely used the small, powerful M18A1 Claymore mine. When detonated by trip wire or hand-held device, the Claymore exploded, firing several hundred steel balls in a cone-shaped spiral with a devastating impact up to 50 meters (55 yards). The U.S. military used Claymores to protect air and fire bases. Army and marine fighting units deployed the mine to defend positions or to ambush Viet Cong and North Vietnamese troops. The U.S. military also used aircraft-delivered mines in campaigns to close enemy supply routes in southern Laos along the Ho Chi Minh Trail. In operations over Laos beginning in 1967, U.S. Air Force attack aircraft, and later Hercules transport planes, dropped gravel mines designed to disable vehicles. The mine-laying strategy, part of an interdiction effort that included electronic sensors and air strikes, had limited success at slowing transport along the supply corridor.

North Vietnamese and Viet Cong forces used land mines effectively against U.S. ground operations. Mines accounted for approximately 75 percent of the losses of U.S. tanks and armored personnel carriers during the war. Along with booby traps, mines served as deadly and effective weapons against U.S. soldiers on patrols and sweeps. The North Vietnamese and Viet Cong troops often deployed Claymore-style mines manufactured in the North or in the People's Republic of China, though they also used recovered U.S. mines. In addition, they constructed mines with undetonated bombs from U.S. air raids and artillery.

BIBLIOGRAPHY

BERGERUD, ERIC M. *Red Thunder, Tropic Lightning: The World of a Combat Division in Vietnam.* 1993.
STAAVEREN, JACOB VAN. *Interdiction in Southern Laos, 1960–1968.* 1993.
THOMPSON, LEROY. *The U.S. Army in Vietnam.* 1990.

ADAM LAND

Naval Mine Warfare

The mining of ports was both a controversial and important military tactic for the belligerents during the Vietnam War. During the war, Viet Cong guerrillas repeatedly mined the Saigon harbor and river channel, in addition to other rivers, and the U.S. Navy aided the South Vietnamese navy with regular mine sweeps beginning in 1961.

The U.S. and South Vietnamese military leadership gave priority to the interdiction of North Vietnamese supplies to Viet Cong forces in the south. To that end, the U.S. Navy proposed as early as 1961 a naval blockade and aerial mining of North Vietnamese ports, especially Haiphong harbor, and continued to urge the adoption of this tactic throughout the war. The Kennedy and Johnson ad-

ministrations both rejected these proposals, first because the United States was not officially at war with North Vietnam and, later, because Johnson feared that such strong measures against North Vietnam would provoke overt conflict with the People's Republic of China (PRC) and a wider war. In addition, U.S. military leaders were divided over how much North Vietnam used the sea to transport supplies. As a result, U.S. naval policy during the Vietnam War sought to halt the flow of war material into South Vietnam through Operation MARKET TIME, a much more difficult task than halting the flow of material out of North Vietnam. In 1972, President Richard M. Nixon ordered the mining of Haiphong harbor as part of the U.S. response to North Vietnam's Easter Offensive. The administration's goals were to stabilize the military situation in the south, bring about a cease-fire, and force the North Vietnamese into peace negotiations. Some scholars believe the tactic helped achieve these goals.

BIBLIOGRAPHY

MAROLDA, EDWARD J., and OSCAR P. FITZGERALD. *The United States Navy and the Vietnam Conflict.* Vol. 2: *From Military Assistance to Combat, 1959–1963.* 1986.
SCHREADLEY, R. L. *From the Rivers to the Sea: The United States Navy in Vietnam.* 1992.

JENNIFER FROST

Minh, Duong Van. *See* Duong Van Minh.

Missing in Action. *See* POW/MIA Controversy.

Mitchell, John (1913–1988), U.S. attorney general, 1969–1972; chairman, Committee for the Reelection of the President (derogatorily known as CREEP), 1972. As President Nixon's point man in his legal campaign against the antiwar movement, Mitchell pushed the Justice Department to initiate numerous conspiracy trials against such groups as Vietnam Veterans against the War and the Chicago Eight. Although many government efforts never resulted in indictments, they intimidated and undermined some of Nixon's war critics. Mitchell also pursued draft evaders and deserters, directed the Federal Bureau of Investigation (FBI) to infiltrate and disrupt antiwar groups, and ordered massive numbers of illegal wiretaps. When the *New York*

Times printed the Pentagon Papers, Mitchell directed the effort for an injunction to block further publication. In 1975 he was convicted for his role in Watergate and subsequently served eighteen months in prison.

BIBLIOGRAPHY

KUTLER, STANLEY. *The Wars of Watergate.* 1990.
ZAROULIS, NANCY, and GERALD SULLIVAN. *Who Spoke Up?* 1984.

KELLY EVANS-PFEIFER

Molotov, Vyacheslav

Molotov, Vyacheslav (1890–1986), commissar for foreign affairs, USSR, 1939–1949, 1953–1956. As Russian foreign minister, Molotov, with British prime minister Anthony Eden, cochaired the 1954 Geneva Conference, which negotiated the cessation of hostilities for the Indochina war. Along with the representative from China, the other major communist power, Molotov pressured the Viet Minh to accept unfavorable peace terms despite their clear military victory against the French. The Viet Minh were forced to accept partition of the country and failed to gain international recognition for their communist allies in Cambodia and Laos.

BIBLIOGRAPHY

LACOUTURE, JEAN. *Vietnam between Two Truces.* 1966.

ADAM LAND

Momyer, William W.

Momyer, William W. (1916–), general, U.S. Air Force; commander, Seventh Air Force, and deputy commander, U.S. Military Assistance Command, Vietnam (MACV), 1966–1968. An ace fighter pilot in World War II, "Spike" Momyer succeeded Gen. Joseph H. Moore as commander of the Seventh Air Force in Vietnam in July 1966. Momyer directed extensive bombing campaigns against North Vietnam during Operation ROLLING THUNDER and in south Vietnam during Operation NIAGARA. He opposed target restrictions that undercut the impact of U.S. air power, and he complained that bombing halts signaled "weakness and lack of resolve" to Hanoi. After the war Momyer wrote that victory could have been attained with "airpower applied in full strength against the heart of North Vietnam." He left Vietnam to lead the Tactical Air Command in August 1968 and retired in 1973.

BIBLIOGRAPHY

MOMYER, WILLIAM W. *Airpower in Three Wars.* 1978.
MOMYER, WILLIAM W. *The Vietnamese Air Force, 1951–1975.* 1975.
"Rolling the Thunder." *Time,* 29 December 1967.
"Rolling Thunder: William W. Momyer, the Man Who is Running the Air War." *Time,* 10 April 1967.
SCHLIGHT, JON. *The United States Air Force in Southeast Asia: The War in South Vietnam: The Years of the Offensive, 1965–1968.* 1988.

GLEN GENDZEL

Monsoon

Monsoon. Semiannual periods of heavy rain and inclement weather, monsoons dominate the climate and agricultural economy of Southeast Asia and historically have determined the timing and often the outcome of military operations.

The southwest monsoon, which lasts from about mid-May to mid-October, drenches the entire region with heavy rain, with the exception of the coastal strip of central Vietnam east of the Annamite Mountains. It inundates the Mekong Delta and Southeast Asia west of the Annamite Mountains before moving into the Tonkin Highlands and the Red River Delta.

The northeast monsoon occupies the balance of the year save for a month or so of unsettled weather at each end. It reverses the wet/dry cycle over the area, bringing clear skies and dry weather to Thailand, Laos, and the Mekong Delta, but depositing rain on the Red River Delta and the coastal strip of Vietnam south to Nha Trang between mid-September and mid- to late-December.

The southwest monsoon renders unimproved roads impassable; both monsoons feature poor flying weather in which visual bombing is often impossible. Weather favorable to military campaigns is generally limited to the relatively dry mid-October to mid-May "winter-spring" period, and many of the pivotal battles of Vietnamese history have occurred during this season. The communist forces adapted well to the monsoon cycle, launching virtually all of their major offensives during this period. Conversely, U.S. decision-makers were curiously insensitive to the weather, launching a high proportion of major bombing escalations into the teeth of one or the other of the wet monsoons, including ROLLING THUNDER and LINEBACKER II. Operations in such adverse weather conditions caused inordinate numbers of jettisoned bombs, aborted missions, and missed targets.

BIBLIOGRAPHY

DAVIDSON, PHILLIP B. *Vietnam at War: The History, 1946–1975.* 1988.

BATES, CHARLES C., and JOHN F. FULLER. *America's Weather Warriors, 1814–1985.* 1986.

JOHN F. GUILMARTIN JR.

Montagnards. The montagnards consisted of thirty-three tribes, estimated at 800,000 to 1 million people, living in the southern half of the Annamite mountain range, from the 17th Parallel southward to Bien Hoa. Ethnically distinct from the Vietnamese, they never considered themselves Vietnamese, and they rejected Vietnamese political authority, which in turn led to centuries of Vietnamese discrimination against them. Given the strategic importance of the Central Highlands, forces of both the National Liberation Front (NLF) and the Army of the Republic of Vietnam (ARVN) sought montagnard support during the Vietnam War. In the early 1960s the montagnards made up much of the Civilian Irregular Defense Groups (CIDG), organized by the Central Intelligence Agency (CIA) in conjunction with U.S. Special Forces. The montagnards cooperated with U.S. advisers and welcomed them as an alternative to the disdainful Vietnamese. ARVN forces continued to alienate the montagnards by taking their animals and destroying their crops and houses; in response, montagnards organized themselves into the Front Unifié pour la Lutte des Races Opprimées (FULRO), which by 1966 was in open revolt against South Vietnam. Nevertheless, in the late 1960s the montagnards were transferred from the CIDG to the ARVN, although the South Vietnamese doubted montagnard loyalty. By 1971 large numbers of montagnards had defected from the ARVN; those who remained rebelled against the army in February. In March 1975, montagnards did not report to ARVN officials the movements of North Vietnamese troops around Ban Me Thuot, thus contributing to the North Vietnamese and victory.

Approximately 200,000 montagnards died during the Vietnam War, and 85 percent were displaced from their original homes. After 1975 many continued their fight against the Vietnamese. FULRO was decimated by 1979, forcing some montagnards to seek asylum in the United States while others moved their bases into Cambodia.

MONTAGNARD MOTHER AND CHILD, 1964. *National Archives*

BIBLIOGRAPHY

FITZGERALD, FRANCES. *Fire in the Lake: The Vietnamese and the Americans in Vietnam.* 1972.

HICKEY, GERALD. *Free in the Forest: An Ethnohistory of the Vietnamese Central Highlands, 1954–1976.* 1982.

KOLKO, GABRIEL. *Anatomy of a War: Vietnam, the United States, and the Modern Historical Experience.* 1985.

MOLE, ROBERT L. *The Montagnards of Vietnam: A Study of Nine Tribes.* 1970.

THAYER, NATE. "The Forgotten Army." *Far Eastern Economic Review* (10 September 1992): 16–18.

ELLEN BAKER

Montgomery Committee. Officially titled the House Select Committee to Study the Problem of United States Servicemen Missing in Action in Southeast Asia, the Montgomery Committee was known by the name of its chairman, G. V. "Sonny" Montgomery, a Mississippi Democrat. Established on 11 September 1975, the committee was formed to determine if any Americans listed as prisoners of war (POWs) or missing in action (MIAs) were being held by the Vietnamese government. At the outset, Representative Montgomery had insisted that Vietnam still held U.S. prisoners, but after fifteen months of investigation, the committee concluded that "no Americans are still being held alive as prisoners in Indochina, or elsewhere, as a result of the war in Indochina." The committee conceded that some deserters probably remained in Southeast Asia. The National League of Families of American Prisoners and Missing in Southeast Asia denounced the committee and its conclusions and increased its own political activities and demands for Vietnamese accountability. Ronald Reagan and other political leaders supported the families' claims and undermined the Montgomery Committee's credibility. The committee was terminated on 3 January 1977.

BIBLIOGRAPHY

FRANKLIN, H. BRUCE. *M.I.A. or Mythmaking in America.* 1992.

KEATING, SUSAN KATZ. *Prisoners of Hope: Exploiting the POW/MIA Myth in America.* 1994.

STANLEY I. KUTLER

Moorer, Thomas H.

Moorer, Thomas H. (1912–), admiral, U.S. Navy; commander in chief, Pacific Fleet, 1964–1965; chief of naval operations, 1967–1970; chairman, Joint Chiefs of Staff, 1970–1974. President Nixon appointed Thomas Moorer chairman of the Joint Chiefs of Staff in July 1970, just after the invasion of Cambodia. Moorer planned the mining of Haiphong harbor and the Vietnamization policy. After peace talks broke down in December 1972, President Nixon told him: "This is your chance to use military power to win this war, and if you don't, I'll consider you responsible." The result was Operation LINEBACKER II, which dropped over 36,000 tons of bombs on Hanoi in twelve days. After retiring in 1974, Moorer said the United States should have invaded North Vietnam, "where you don't have to worry whether or not you are shooting friendly civilians."

BIBLIOGRAPHY

BEECHER, WILLIAM. "U.S. Moves Toward New Strategy as Admiral Moorer Becomes JCS Chairman." *Navy* 13 (June 1970).

KORB, LAWRENCE J. *The Joint Chiefs of Staff: The First Twenty-Five Years.* 1976.

MAROLDA, EDWARD J., and G. WESLEY PRYCE. *A Short History of the United States Navy and the Southeast Asian Conflict.* 1984.

GLEN GENDZEL

Morse, Wayne L.

Morse, Wayne L. (1900–1974), U.S. senator (R, D-Oreg.), 1945–1969. Morse was an early, outspoken opponent of U.S. participation in the Vietnam War. With Sen. Ernest Gruening, he voted against the Gulf of Tonkin Resolution in 1964, arguing that it violated the Constitution; three years later, he unsuccessfully fought to repeal the resolution. Divisions among Oregon Democrats over the war and local issues led to Morse's defeat for reelection in 1968.

BIBLIOGRAPHY

MORSE, WAYNE. "Analysis." In *Report of the U.S. Senate Hearings: The Truth of Vietnam,* edited by Frank M. Robinson and Earl Kemp. 1966.

WILKINS, LEE. *Wayne Morse: A Bio-Bibliography.* 1985.

JENNIFER FROST

Movies

Movies. *For discussion of the treatment of the Vietnam War in American film, see* Art and Literature.

Munich Analogy

Munich Analogy. An analogy drawn by U.S. policymakers between the British response to an expansionist Nazi Germany and the perceived threat of the expansion of international communism, the Munich analogy refers to British prime minister Neville Chamberlin's attempt in September 1938 to appease Adolf Hitler on the eve of World War II. In an effort to avert world war, Chamberlin acquiesced to nearly all of Hitler's demands, ceding him the Sudetenland region of Czechoslovakia and leaving the rest of that nation defenseless. When Hitler invaded Czechoslovakia and then Poland the following year, Chamberlin was reviled as an appeaser.

Presidents John F. Kennedy and Lyndon Johnson and their advisers, civilian and military, were strongly affected by the events of World War II. Their foreign policy philosophies were grounded in the lessons of that war and then shaped by containment policy and the domino theory. The Munich analogy convinced them that if they allowed North Vietnam to take over the anticommunist South, North Vietnam's aggression would turn toward neighboring countries such as Cambodia and Laos. The Munich analogy also affected the U.S. negotiations with the North Vietnamese, influencing the United States to take a hard line in the peace talks. A few months before he committed the first U.S.

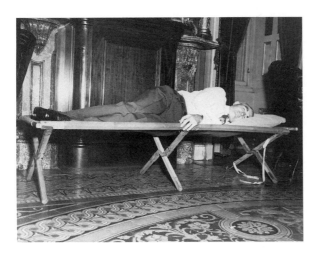

WAYNE L. MORSE. Resting during a Senate debate. *Library of Congress*

combat troops, Johnson said that "the appetite of aggression is never satisfied." He later expressed the logic behind the Munich analogy as, "If you let a bully come into your front yard one day, the next day he'll be on your porch, and the day after that he'll rape your wife in your own bed."

BIBLIOGRAPHY

KAHIN, GEORGE MCT. *Intervention: How America Became Involved in Vietnam.* 1986.
KARNOW, STANLEY. *Vietnam: A History.* 1991.

KELLY EVANS-PFEIFER

Murphy, Robert D. (1894–1978), Foreign Service officer, 1921–1959. Murphy was a member of Lyndon Johnson's informal group of senior foreign policy advisers called "the wise men." At meetings of the group in 1967 and 1968, Murphy persistently advocated vigorous pursuit of the Vietnam War despite growing pessimism among Johnson's advisers and the public.

BIBLIOGRAPHY

BERMAN, LARRY. *Lyndon Johnson's War: The Road to Stalemate in Vietnam.* 1989.

WILLIAM PAUL SCHUCK

Muste, A. J. (1885–1967), important American radical pacifist leader from the 1940s through the 1960s. An early leader of the anti–Vietnam War movement, Muste served as chair of the 1966 Mobilization Committee and conducted private peace missions to South and North Vietnam in 1966 and 1967.

BIBLIOGRAPHY

ISSERMAN, MAURICE. *If I Had a Hammer . . . The Death of the Old Left and the Birth of the New Left.* 1987.
ROBINSON, JO ANN. *Abraham Went Out: A Biography of A. J. Muste.* 1981.

JENNIFER FROST

My Lai. Hamlet in Quang Ngai province, South Vietnam. On 16 March 1968, during what was supposed to be a routine search-and-destroy mission in My Lai 4—so-called because it was one of several hamlets of Song My village—Company C, 1st Battalion 20th Infantry, part of Task Force Barker of the 23d Infantry (American) Division, went on a rampage. The soldiers killed between 175 and 400 unresisting, unarmed Vietnamese men, women, and children, committed several rapes, and engaged in unauthorized destruction of dwellings, livestock, and other property.

The causes of this atrocity were various. They included weak company and platoon leadership, inadequate training and lack of combat experience among the troops, and hatred of the Vietnamese because of recent booby trap casualties inflicted on U.S. soldiers in the area. Intelligence and planning for the operation were also inadequate. The men of Company C had been told that an enemy local force battalion was occupying the hamlet and that no civilians would be present; they received no instructions for dealing with civilians if encountered. Some soldiers in Company C nevertheless refused to participate in the massacre, and the pilot of one supporting helicopter, Hugh C. Thompson Jr., protected a group of Vietnamese by threatening their would-be killers with his machine guns.

Later investigations revealed that the task force and company plans and orders for this action violated Military Assistance Command, Vietnam (MACV), and American Division rules of engagement and operating procedures. The responsible officers, from Capt. Ernest Medina of Company C through the division commander, Maj. Gen. Samuel Koster, took no corrective or punitive measures although they either observed during the action or learned subsequently from reports that the operation had gone terribly wrong. By omission and commission, they suppressed reports of the incident and submitted false or misleading accounts to higher headquarters.

The crime came to light early in 1969 through a letter from a Vietnam veteran, Ronald Ridenhour, to the chairman of the House Armed Services Committee. Informed of the allegations, Secretary of the Army Stanley Resor and Chief of Staff General William Westmoreland initiated an army investigation. The investigation determined that a major atrocity had occurred and secured sufficient evidence to begin indictments, the first of which was of Lt. William Calley, whose platoon had done much of the killing. The army's low-key public announcement of Lieutenant Calley's indictment in September initially drew little attention from the news media, but Seymour Hersh, a free-lance investigative reporter, followed up on the army announcement. In November 1969 he published the first full story of the massacre. Hersh's articles set off an outcry in the media and by the public. As the controversy expanded, the army appointed a special board, headed by Lt. Gen. William R. Peers, to look into the Americal Division's cover-up of the incident. Simultaneously, the House Armed Services Committee conducted its own inquiry.

These investigations eventually led to indictments against 25 officers and enlisted men on various charges—13, including Calley, for war crimes and 12, including General Koster, for offenses connected with the cover-up. Of these, only Lieutenant Calley was convicted by military court-martial of murder and sentenced to life imprisonment. Charges against General Koster were dismissed, but the army reduced him in rank and issued a letter of censure, effectively terminating his hitherto promising military career. The other My Lai cases ended either in acquittals or in the dropping of charges on various technicalities.

The case of Lieutenant Calley, the only officer convicted, dragged on for years. After his conviction on 29 March 1971, his defense carried appeals through both military and civilian courts. The conviction, coupled with the dropping of charges against higher-ranking defendants, resulted in much public sympathy for Calley, whom many viewed as either a hero or a scapegoat. President Richard Nixon, attempting to capitalize politically on the issue, intervened on Calley's behalf. He transferred Calley from the Fort Benning, Georgia, army stockade to house arrest and then promised to make a final review of Calley's sentence once all legal appeals had been exhausted. Nixon's actions drew criticism as unwarranted interference with military justice. Even as appeals proceeded, the commanding general at Fort Benning used his prerogative as the officer convening the court-martial to reduce Calley's life sentence to twenty years, which the secretary of the Army subsequently reduced to ten. President Nixon, by then deep in the Watergate scandal, approved without demur. Calley, his case still under review in the courts, entered federal prison early in 1974, but he was eligible for parole in six months because of time already spent in confinement. He had been released by the time a federal district court, on 10 September 1975, finally upheld his conviction.

Revelation of the My Lai massacre and its attendant derelictions of duty by higher commanders set off a wave of self-analysis and reform within the army. In response to the My Lai incident, the service intensified its training of all its personnel in the law of war and military professional ethics. Nevertheless, the atrocity, and the failure of the army judicial system to punish more of those involved, left a permanent stain on the reputation of the service.

BIBLIOGRAPHY

Bilton, Michael, and Kevin Sim. *Four Hours in My Lai.* 1992.

Hammond, William M. *The United States Army in Vietnam: Public Affairs, the Military and the Media, 1968–1973.* 1995.

Hersh, Seymour. *My Lai 4.* 1970.

Peers, William R. *The My Lai Inquiry.* 1979.

Graham A. Cosmas

N

Napalm. Napalm, an incendiary weapon developed during World War II, is a gasoline-based compound that burns at about 2,000 degrees Fahrenheit. In Vietnam, U.S. forces used napalm, mostly in aerial bombs, for defoliation, tactical bombing, and, most commonly, close air support against North Vietnamese and Viet Cong forces. Napalm kills by burning or by asphyxiation; its burning causes massive deoxygenation and produces lethal amounts of carbon monoxide.

While an effective weapon, napalm is indiscriminate, and it will burn anyone it contacts. Aerial bombs splatter it over a considerable area. As a result, civilian casualties occurred in Vietnam despite restrictive rules of engagement. During the war, publications as diverse as *Ramparts* and *Ladies Home Journal* described napalm and the disfiguring injuries it can cause, generating public concern about the cruelty of its use. As early as 1966, protestors picketed the New York offices of the main napalm manufacturer, the Dow Chemical Company, calling for a production halt. Later, Dow facilities in California, Michigan, and Washington, D.C., were picketed or even attacked. In February 1967, students at the University of Wisconsin–Madison protested when Dow recruiters tried to interview job applicants on campus. Similar protests against Dow recruitment, often organized by the Students for a Democratic Society (SDS), occurred on many college campuses in the next year.

Americans' perceptions of napalm were especially shaped by a June 1972 photograph of a naked Vietnamese girl screaming as she ran down a road after a napalm attack. The photograph appeared in numerous publications and is one of the most enduring images of the Vietnam War. Despite the public outcry against it, napalm continued to be used throughout the war.

BIBLIOGRAPHY

DUFFETT, JOHN, ed. *Against the Crime of Silence: Proceedings of the International War Crimes Tribunal.* 1968.

STOCKHOLM INTERNATIONAL PEACE RESEARCH INSTITUTE. *Incendiary Weapons.* 1975.

ZAROULIS, NANCY, and SULLIVAN, GERALD. *Who Spoke Up? American Protest against the War in Vietnam, 1963–1975.* 1984.

WILLIAM PAUL SCHUCK

National Assembly Law 10/59. On 6 May 1959, Ngo Dinh Diem's government enacted Law 10/59, a measure that stiffened penalties for those with communist affiliations and provided for special military tribunals to try the accused. Although Diem had instituted the Anti-Communist Denunciation Campaign in 1955 to conduct ideological warfare against communist activists, the measures in Law 10/59 were aimed at more than communists, as they suppressed dissenters in general. In 1956, by presidential order, anyone "deemed dangerous to the safety of the state" could be arrested. Armed with Law 10/59 and supplemental decrees issued in October 1961 and May 1962, Diem expanded the number of military courts and wielded state-of-emergency powers to suspend the application of laws in any part of the country. By the time of Diem's death in 1963, more than 75,000 people had been jailed, the majority of whom were neither communists nor procommunists. According to a U.S. intelligence report in 1960, such repression resulted in an "attitude of apathy or resentment" toward the government among the South Vietnamese people. Law 10/59 apparently remained in use until the collapse of South Vietnam in 1975. In any event, Diem's successors continued his repressive measures.

BIBLIOGRAPHY

HERRING, GEORGE. *America's Longest War: The United States and Vietnam, 1950–1975.* 1986.
The Pentagon Papers: The Defense Department History of United States Decisionmaking on Vietnam. Senator Gravel Edition. Vol. 1. 1971.
SCIGLIANO, ROBERT. *South Vietnam: Nation Under Stress.* 1963.

VICTOR JEW

National Bank of Vietnam.

North Vietnam's official state monopoly on revenue, currency, and foreign aid was called the National Bank of Vietnam. Established by the Viet Minh in 1951, the bank issued unconvertible banknotes called *dong*, for which all North Vietnamese had to exchange their money in 1954. Private businesses in North Vietnam paid heavy taxes and interest on National Bank loans, while state enterprises received subsidies. All foreign currency and business profits were deposited with the National Bank after 1960. Within five years, 95 percent of North Vietnam's economy was state-owned.

In South Vietnam, President Diem created his own National Bank of Vietnam in 1955 and put his brother in charge. Local merchants paid national currency called *piasters* into the bank's "counterpart fund" for U.S. imports. U.S. foreign aid dollars then bought the goods and shipped them to South Vietnam under the Commercial Import Program, which channeled $1.9 billion in economic aid to South Vietnam by 1964. Most of the imports were luxury consumer goods for the Saigon elite and contributed little to economic development.

In 1975, after the fall of Saigon, the North Vietnamese bank assumed control of South Vietnam's economy by requiring residents to exchange their *piasters* for *dong* at the rate of 500 to 1. Runaway inflation and hoarding of gold plagued Vietnam until the National Bank floated the *dong* in 1989.

BIBLIOGRAPHY

DAVIES, S. GETHYN. *Central Banking in South and East Asia.* 1960.
HONEY, P. J. *Communism in North Vietnam.* 1963.
NGO VINH HAI. "Postwar Vietnam: Political Economy." In *Coming to Terms: Indochina, the United States, and the War.* Edited by Douglas Allen and Ngô Viñh Long. 1991.
PIKE, DOUGLAS. *History of Vietnamese Communism, 1925–1976.* 1978.
SMITH, HARVEY H., et al. *Area Handbook for North Vietnam.* 1967.
TAYLOR, MILTON C. "South Vietnam: Lavish Aid, Limited Progress." *Pacific Affairs* 34 (1961).

GLEN GENDZEL

National Committee for Peace and Freedom in Vietnam,

a bipartisan group of legislators and private citizens formed in 1967 with the active encouragement of Johnson administration officials. The organization, headed by Sen. Paul Douglas, strongly endorsed U.S. activities in Vietnam and claimed that the United States' "silent center" supported Johnson's policies.

BIBLIOGRAPHY

BERMAN, LARRY. *Lyndon Johnson's War: The Road to Stalemate in Vietnam.* 1989.
SMALL, MELVIN. *Johnson, Nixon, and the Doves.* 1988.

WILLIAM PAUL SCHUCK

National Council of Reconciliation and Concord.

The 1973 Paris Peace Accords provided for the establishment of a council to administer elections and promote the implementation of the peace agreement in Vietnam. The tripartite council, which included representatives from the

Democratic Republic of Vietnam (DRV), the Republic of Vietnam, and the Provisional Revolutionary Government of South Vietnam, was the center of great contention throughout the peace process. The council was never effectively organized, and the military resolution of the war made it irrelevant.

BIBLIOGRAPHY

GOODMAN, ALLAN E. *The Lost Peace: America's Search for a Negotiated Settlement of the Vietnam War.* 1978.

PORTER, GARETH. *A Peace Denied: The United States, Vietnam, and the Paris Peace Agreement.* 1975.

WILLIAM PAUL SCHUCK

National Liberation Front. The National Liberation Front (Mat Tran Dan Toc Giai Phong Mien Nam, literally, the National Front for the Liberation of South Vietnam, but usually known simply as the NLF) was created at a secret meeting somewhere in South Vietnam on 31 December 1960. Established as a result of decisions reached at the Third National Congress of the Vietnamese Workers' Party (VWP) in Hanoi in September, it was designed as a broad national front organization to attract support from various classes in South Vietnam in a struggle to overthrow the government of Ngo Dinh Diem and to reunify the country under communist rule.

The NLF was the immediate successor of the Fatherland Front (Mat Tran To Quoc), a national front that had been established in Hanoi in 1955 to represent the interests of all Vietnamese, north and south, and that continued to function in North Vietnam after 1960. But the spiritual ancestor of the NLF was the League for the Independence of Vietnam, popularly known as the Viet Minh Front, which had been established in May 1941. Like the Viet Minh Front, the NLF disguised the communist character of its leadership, and its program stressed widely shared objectives such as national independence, social justice, and democratic reforms as a means of appealing to a broad audience. Unlike the Viet Minh Front, the NLF was designed to appeal to regional sentiment in the south, not throughout the entire country. For that reason, the NLF's direct link to the party leadership in North Vietnam was concealed, and its program stated only that reunification would take place gradually and by peaceful means.

VICTORY CELEBRATION. President of the Democratic Republic of Vietnam Ton Duc Thang reads a speech at a victory celebration in Ho Chi Minh City on 17 May 1975. Standing to Thang's left are (in foreground, left to right) in dark shirt, Nguyen Huu Tho, chairman of the National Liberation Front; applauding, Le Duc Tho, who had been North Vietnam's representative at the Paris peace talks; and Huynh Tan Phat, vice chairman of the Provisional Revolutionary Government of South Vietnam. *Ngô Viñh Long*

The organizational structure of the NLF was similar to that of the Viet Minh Front. At the apex was an elected central committee and a presidium. The chairman of the presidium was Nguyen Huu Tho, a lawyer who had been involved in resistance activities since the late 1940s. Similar committees existed at the provincial and district levels. At the heart of the NLF were the functional liberation associations, grassroots organizations designed to appeal to specific constituencies such as peasants, workers, women, students, writers and artists, and the ethnic and religious minorities.

Such associations served as the initial contact point between the NLF leadership and the masses and provided a vehicle for channeling local aspirations into mobilizing support for the programs of the movement. Talented and dedicated members of such organizations could then be enlisted into higher levels of the NLF, into the People's Liberation Armed Forces (PLAF, popularly known in the West as the Viet Cong), or into the People's Revolutionary Party, a branch in the South of the Vietnam Workers' Party.

During the next several years, the NLF served as the organizational focus for the revolutionary movement in South Vietnam, with a membership in its various organizations reportedly numbering in the millions. In 1969 its role was superseded somewhat by the Provisional Revolutionary Government (PRG), which was designed to provide a legal counterpart to the government in Saigon, but the NLF continued to exist as a nongovernmental national front until the end of the war. The NLF suffered heavy losses during the final years of the Vietnam War, and in December 1976, to the dismay of many of its leading members, it was merged into the Fatherland Front, its counterpart in the North.

[See also People's Liberation Armed Forces (PLAF); Provisional Revolutionary Government (PRG).]

BIBLIOGRAPHY

South Viet Nam National Front for Liberation: Documents. 1968.
PIKE, DOUGLAS. *Viet Cong: The Organization and Techniques of the National Liberation Front of South Vietnam.* 1966.

WILLIAM J. DUIKER

National Security Action Memorandum (NSAM) 263.

Issued 11 October 1963 by the National Security Council, NSAM 263 outlined a plan to withdraw one thousand U.S. military advisers from South Vietnam by December 1963, with all remaining forces to be withdrawn by late 1965, when the communist insurgency was expected to be fully suppressed. After President Kennedy's death, President Johnson reiterated this policy in NSAM 273.

BIBLIOGRAPHY

NEWMAN, JOHN M. *JFK and Vietnam.* 1992.

KELLY EVANS-PFEIFER

National Security Action Memorandum (NSAM) 288.

NSAM 288 was drafted by national security adviser McGeorge Bundy in March 1964, prior to the Tonkin Gulf incidents and Resolution. The document called for increased U.S. military and economic aid for South Vietnam to put the Army of the Republic of Vietnam (ARVN) in a position to fight Viet Cong and North Vietnamese Army (NVA) forces effectively and established the United States's commitment to a noncommunist South Vietnam. NSAM 288 also advocated increased bombing of strategic targets in North Vietnam in retaliation for Viet Cong guerrilla attacks in the South. Bundy argued for a congressional resolution supporting such actions to ensure an independent, anticommunist South Vietnam.

BIBLIOGRAPHY

OLSON, JAMES, and RANDY ROBERTS. *Where the Domino Fell.* 1991.

KELLY EVANS-PFEIFER

National Security Council.

Established by the National Security Act of 1947, the National Security Council (NSC) evaluated intelligence and advised the president on the integration of foreign and military policy relating to national security. The NSC was composed of the president, the vice president, and the secretaries of State and Defense, with the director of central intelligence (DCI) and the Joint Chiefs of Staff (JCS) acting as statutory advisers. Two important additions to the NSC not officially mandated by law were the NSC staff and the assistant to the president for national security affairs, known as the national security adviser.

The NSC played an important role in the formation of U.S. policy in Vietnam. Beginning in 1949, the National Security Council warned of the possibility of communism sweeping Southeast Asia; in 1952, it issued a formal statement of U.S. objectives in Indochina, emphasizing support of the French against the Viet Minh. Following the 1954 Geneva Conference, the council recommended U.S. efforts to weaken the communist-dominated Viet Minh government in northern Vietnam and support for the creation of a non-communist South Vietnam. Although the NSC's influence declined under Presidents Kennedy and Johnson, national security advisers McGeorge Bundy and Walt Rostow remained among the closest and most influential presidential counselors. In 1964, Bundy formulated a program of gradually increasing the bombing of North Vietnam and the deployment of twenty thousand U.S. troops to Vietnam in 1965. Rostow helped persuade Johnson to expand the war effort. In 1969, Richard Nixon and his national security adviser Henry Kissinger revitalized the NSC as a policymaking body. By 1970, however, the NSC concluded that the United States could not force North Vietnam to remove its troops from the south, in effect anticipating the U.S. withdrawal.

BIBLIOGRAPHY

BRADFORD, JAMES. *The Puzzle Palace: A Report on America's Most Secret Agency.* 1982.

HERRING, GEORGE C. *America's Longest War: The United States and Vietnam, 1950–1975.* 1986.

PRADOS, JOHN. *Keepers of the Keys: A History of the National Security Council from Truman to Bush.* 1991.

PAUL M. TAILLON

Navarre, Henri (1898–1983), French commander in chief, Combined Forces, Indochina, 1953–1954. A career soldier, Navarre shared the colonial-military background of his post–World War II peers: service in Syria and French Morocco in the 1920s and 1930s. He also distinguished himself as a Resistance leader from 1943 to 1945, earning a promotion to brigadier general. In 1953 Navarre was named to replace Raoul Salan as commander in chief of French forces in Vietnam, thus satisfying one of the U.S. government's conditions—an inspirational leader for French forces—of continued aid to the French. Navarre was optimistic in public, forecasting victory in a manner shunned by Salan and recalling the dynamic General Lattre de Tassigny. Privately, however, Navarre was distant and detached; one contemporary described him as "physically and morally feline." Navarre lent his name to the Navarre plan, the purported blueprint for victory that Eisenhower administration officials demanded as another condition of continued U.S. aid. Ultimately, Navarre's forces were defeated in Vietnam because he underestimated the Viet Minh. A French War College assessment of Dien Bien Phu faulted Navarre for disregarding evidence that belied his opinion of his Asian foe. The report noted that Navarre and his staff "substituted their preconceived idea of the Vietminh for the facts," thus belittling Giap and the fighting capacity of his army, and lending bitter irony to the oft-cited Navarre remark: "Now we can see it clearly—like light at the end of the tunnel."

BIBLIOGRAPHY

HERRING, GEORGE C. *America's Longest War: The United States and Vietnam, 1950–1975.* 1986.

KARNOW, STANLEY. *Vietnam: A History.* 1991.

VICTOR JEW

Navarre Plan. The Navarre plan was the supposed blueprint for French victory in Indochina, yet its primary objective was not the defeat of the Viet Minh. The plan's real work was to placate the French government's patron in Vietnam, the Eisenhower administration, and to assure the United States that the French had "larger perspectives than simply the maintenance of a sterile and costly status quo." Given this evidence of "larger perspectives" of victory, the United States would continue to supply funding. The imperative to produce the Navarre plan stemmed from U.S. insistence in March 1953 that the French design a proposal to win the war within twenty-four months. The French felt compelled to tell the U.S. government something that would ensure increased U.S. aid. Jean Letourneau, France's minister of overseas territories, improvised a quick scheme: secure the south with Vietnamese forces and then win a decisive battle in the north, all to be accomplished by 1955.

In early May 1953, the French government responded to increasing U.S. demands for aggressive warmaking by appointing Gen. Henri Navarre commander of French forces in Vietnam. Navarre was portrayed by the French government as forceful and strong and this satisfied the U.S. government. In June 1953 the new Laniel government promised to "perfect" the independence of the Associated States, the former French colonies in Southeast Asia, by granting them responsibilities formerly exercised by France. Finally, the Laniel government offered its strategy for victory: the Navarre plan. Adhering closely to U.S. specifications, the plan proposed an enlarged Vietnamese National Army of at least 200,000 men, all of whom would benefit from a new training program especially established for this army of nationals. The overall strength of the anti–Viet Minh effort would be reinforced by nine battalions of French regulars. Strategically, the plan called for concentrating existing French forces and wielding them as an offensive scythe to destroy Viet Minh strength in the Red River delta area.

Publicly, the plan was courageous, but privately both General Navarre and the Laniel government were dubious about the possibilities for a French victory. Even the U.S. armed forces' Joint Chiefs of Staff were skeptical, but France and the United States were so entangled in mutual commitments that the plan went forward. In September 1953 the United States agreed to supply more military assistance, totaling $385 million, conditioned by French promises to aggressively implement the Navarre plan. Ironically, General Navarre was forced to dismantle the grand scheme in the fall of 1953, when Gen. Vo Nguyen Giap's offensive opened simultaneously on many fronts in central and southern Laos, thus forcing the French to disperse the forces they had concentrated for their own "win the war" push.

BIBLIOGRAPHY

HERRING, GEORGE C. *America's Longest War: The United States and Vietnam, 1950–1975*. 1986.

WALL, IRWIN. *The United States and the Making of Postwar France, 1945–1954*. 1991.

VICTOR JEW

Navy, U.S. The U.S. Navy's ability to fight an enemy ashore in Southeast Asia, dominate the waters of the western Pacific, and sustain a major overseas military conflict ensured its heavy involvement in the Vietnam War. The physical geography of the combat theater, marked by the South China Sea, with its long coastlines, myriad islands, and thousands of nautical miles of rivers and canals, also called for a major commitment of naval forces.

The Chain of Command. During the Vietnam War, the U.S. Navy was one of many components of the U.S. national security establishment. U.S. naval units functioned in different chains of command. The commander of the Seventh Fleet took direction from the Commander-in-Chief, U.S. Pacific Fleet (CINCPACFLT), who received his orders from the Commander-in-Chief, U.S. Pacific Command (CINCPAC). Thus, the Hawaii-based CINCPAC, an admiral, controlled the navy's carrier and other forces involved in combat operations outside South Vietnam. In theory, CINCPAC also directed the Commander, U.S. Military Assistance Command, Vietnam (COMUSMACV), and

the latter's naval subordinates, Commander, U.S. Naval Forces, Vietnam (COMNAVFORV), and Commanding General, III Marine Amphibious Force (III MAF), but in practice COMUSCMACV exercised independent command. Accordingly, the Saigon-headquartered COMUSMACV, a U.S. Army general, controlled the operations of III MAF and the U.S. Navy's coastal, river, SEAL, advisory, and logistical units in South Vietnam. In general, the naval service carried out policies and strategies that normally were established in Saigon, Pearl Harbor, or Washington, D.C.

This was especially true of the Tonkin Gulf Incidents of 1964. Frustrated by the deteriorating political and military situation in South Vietnam that year, President Lyndon B. Johnson applied military pressure against North Vietnam hoping to compel that nation to cease its support of the Viet Cong insurgents. Naval force was the primary instrument of that policy. The navy provided U.S.- and Norwegian-built fast patrol boats (PTF) to the Republic of Vietnam Navy, trained the South Vietnamese crews, and repaired the craft at a facility in Da Nang. In covert Operation (OPLAN) 34A missions, these PTFs sortied into North Vietnam's territorial waters to land saboteurs and bombard coastal targets. The operations of this boat force soon revealed the need for intelligence on North Vietnamese patrol units, naval bases, and coastal radar sites.

Via the military chain of command, U.S. government officials in Washington directed the navy to focus its longstanding Desoto Patrol intelligence collection program on North Vietnam. In early August 1964, the U.S. destroyer *Maddox* steamed along the Tonkin Gulf coast gathering information. This occurred soon after the OPLAN-34A force had shelled targets further south.

Instead of buckling under this pressure, however, North Vietnam retaliated. On the afternoon of 2 August, three North Vietnamese motor torpedo boats unsuccessfully attacked the *Maddox* with torpedoes and gunfire. Determined not to back down from this unexpected challenge, the Johnson administration reinforced the patrol with the destroyer *Turner Joy*. In the middle of the Gulf of Tonkin on the night of 4 August, the two U.S. ships reported fighting a running battle with a number of hostile patrol craft. To this day, it is not certain that this second attack took place, but U.S. officials at the time were convinced by special intelligence and other information that it did. At the president's direction, on 5 August the navy's carrier forces bombed coastal patrol bases in North Vietnam. Of greater significance, on 7 August the U.S. Congress overwhelmingly passed the so-called Gulf of Tonkin Resolution, which enabled Johnson to expand an increasingly unpopular war.

Strategy and Success. Although the navy was often compromised at the strategic level by civilian political decisions, it achieved notable tactical successes in the Vietnam War. The Seventh Fleet aircraft carriers of Task Force 77 operated from Yankee Station in the Gulf of Tonkin and, for a time, at Dixie Station southeast of Cam Ranh Bay. Carrier squadrons carried out day and night bombing of fuel and supply facilities, power plants, bridges, and railroads in Laos, North Vietnam, and after 1970, in Cambodia. The air campaigns were indecisive and cost the navy 881 pilots and other aircrew killed and captured and 900 aircraft. Nonetheless, they made North Vietnam's resupply efforts costly and delayed and weakened North Vietnamese Army (NVA) and

Viet Cong ground offensives in South Vietnam. The combined navy–air force LINEBACKER campaigns and the navy's simultaneous mining of North Vietnam's ports during 1972 and 1973 were instrumental in ending the long U.S. involvement in Southeast Asia. Sea-based aircraft also provided vital close air support to U.S. and allied units locked in battle with NVA and Viet Cong forces in South Vietnam. Search-and-rescue (SAR) helicopters operating from navy aircraft carriers plucked hundreds of U.S. aviators from the sea and, with the help of navy and air force combat planes, saved many others whose aircraft were shot down in Laos and North Vietnam.

The battleship *New Jersey,* as well as numerous cruisers, destroyers, and other surface vessels that steamed off North Vietnam rained high-explosive shells on North Vietnam's bridges, railway lines, radar sites, artillery batteries, and coastal craft. These same ships also ranged the 1,900-kilometer (1,200-

ON YANKEE STATION. The USS *Kitty Hawk,* its deck crowded with A-4 Skyhawks, operates in the Gulf of Tonkin, 1967. *National Archives*

OPERATION MARKET TIME. U.S. advisers and crewmen of the South Vietnamese coastal naval force check civilian junks for smuggled weapons and supplies intended for the Viet Cong, 1966. *National Archives*

mile) littoral of South Vietnam bombarding NVA and Viet Cong troops, fortifications, and supply caches. Much ordnance was wasted on relatively unproductive "harassment and interdiction" fire missions against unobserved targets. During the Easter Offensive of 1972, however, naval gunfire support ships devastated North Vietnamese armor and infantry units advancing along the coast toward the South Vietnamese city of Hue.

The U.S. Navy–Marine Corps amphibious team took advantage of the fleet's mobility and flexibility to launch large-scale assaults, smaller combat raids, and intelligence forays along the coast between the Gulf of Thailand in the south and the Demilitarized Zone (DMZ) in the north. Early in the war U.S. Marines, debouching from landing craft and helicopters, linked up with allied group troops to encircle and destroy NVA and Viet Cong forces. In Operation STARLITE of August 1965, for instance, U.S. and South Vietnamese units wiped out the Viet Cong 1st Regiment. Subsequently, Viet Cong units generally declined combat with amphibious forces by avoiding open coastal areas. The marines, however, suffered increasing losses from booby traps and

snipers. Adjusting to the situation, naval leaders employed the amphibious force as a floating reserve that could rapidly pump fresh reinforcements ashore. This was especially valuable during the World War II–like set-piece battles along the DMZ in 1967 and 1968, when the shore-based III MAF command needed extensive support.

The U.S. Naval Forces, Vietnam (NAVFORV), command also exploited the thousands of rivers, canals, and other waterways in South Vietnam, especially in the Mekong Delta region, to deploy combat forces deep into the midst of NVA and Viet Cong forces. The river patrol boats and SEAL commandos of NAVFORV's River Patrol Force, in Operation GAME WARDEN, hindered supply traffic on the main rivers. An Army-Navy Mobile Riverine Force (MRF) composed of heavily armed and armored monitors (similar to the joint Union force that battled its way down the Mississippi River in the American Civil War) also was a mainstay of the allied inland effort. The primary goal of this force was to find and destroy large NVA or Viet Cong ground units, and both the patrol force and the riverine force enjoyed successes. This prompted the Viet Cong forces to divert their sampans and other supply craft to smaller rivers and canals and to avoid combat with the powerful MRF units.

In response, the commander of NAVFORV, Vice Adm. Elmo R. Zumwalt Jr. adopted a new strategic approach, which he labeled SEALORDS (Southeast Asia Lake, Ocean, River, Delta Strategy). In a major campaign, which lasted from 1968 to 1972, U.S. and Vietnamese river forces regained the initiative by establishing patrol boat barriers along the Cambodian border and by penetrating the traditional swampland strongholds of the NVA and Viet Cong forces in the Mekong Delta, the IV CTZ area of South Vietnam. As a result of the navy's success in the delta, the enemy forces were unable to mount a major attack there during the Easter Offensive, as they did in the other three corps areas of South Vietnam.

The Vietnamese navy's performance during the SEALORDS campaign and the invasion of Cambodia in 1970 was creditable, which reflected not only the abilities of the Vietnamese but also decades of effort by U.S. naval advisers. U.S. advisers since 1950 had been training Vietnamese sailors and supplying them with ships, craft, and weapons. The Vietnamese navy, with 1,500 vessels and 42,000 men in 1972, was the fifth largest in the world. Although it showed potential, poor leadership, inadequate training, high desertion rates, and low operational readiness of combat units were endemic.

Control of the Sea and Air. In addition to projecting power ashore, the U.S. Navy established and then preserved control of the sea off Vietnam and the air space above it. The powerful carrier forces, with their fighter, attack, early warning, and electronic warfare aircraft, surface-to-air missiles, deck guns, antisubmarine weapons, and escorting submarines successfully deterred the North Vietnamese from risking more than a few of their over one hundred combat aircraft and forty high-speed gunboats and torpedo boats at sea. In August 1964 and July 1966, when motor torpedo boats of the North Vietnamese navy sortied into the Gulf of Tonkin, the units were promptly sunk, heavily damaged, or driven off by the U.S. Seventh Fleet. Moreover, although the People's Republic of China (PRC) deployed fifty thousand military "volunteers" to North Vietnam to man antiaircraft weapons and repair damaged roads, railways, and bridges, it did not use its thousands of ships and coastal combatants to interfere with U.S. naval operations offshore.

Employing destroyers, mine warfare ships, Coast Guard cutters, gunboats, patrol vessels, shore-based aircraft, and high-powered radars, U.S. and allied naval forces mounted a coordinated effort, Operation MARKET TIME, to limit North Vietnamese seaborne infiltration of supplies into South Vietnam. All but two of the fifty steel-hulled trawlers discovered heading for the South Vietnamese coast between 1965 and 1972 were destroyed or forced to abort their missions by the patrol force. MARKET TIME compelled the North Vietnamese to supply their forces in the South, at greater cost in lives, resources, and time, through the Cambodian port of Sihanoukville and the Ho Chi Minh Trail.

The Johnson administration, however, fearful of provoking intervention by the PRC or the Soviet Union, prohibited the fleet from taking full advantage of its superiority at sea to halt the shipment of war matériel into the ports of Cambodia or North Vietnam. Merchant ships from many nations, communist and noncommunist, steamed brazenly through the offshore armada to deliver fuel, ammunition, vehicles, and supplies for the use of North Vietnamese and Viet Cong forces ashore.

Logistical Operation. The North Vietnamese resupply effort paled in comparison to that of the U.S. Navy's seaborne logistic operation, which sustained a huge coalition army on the Asian continent from supply bases all over the Pacific Ocean. The merchant ships of the navy's Military Sealift Command delivered 95 percent of the vehicles, ammunition, fuel, equipment, and other military supplies that entered the ports of South Vietnam. Navy Seabee construction units built enormous logistic support bases at Da Nang and Saigon to supply all navy-marine forces in the field and some air force and army units. The military effort did not fail from lack of logistic support.

In fact, the full development of the logistic pipeline led to an embarassment of riches. The ready availability in Vietnam of beer, stereo equipment, air conditioners, and tens of thousands of tons of other nonessential material fueled a black market, corrupted Vietnamese and U.S. officials, and alienated combat troops, who resented the comforts enjoyed by their rear-area comrades.

The Cost of the War for the Navy. The ten years of heavy commitment to the Vietnam War, which ended on 30 April 1975, cost the navy dearly. Of the 1,842,000 navy men and women who served in Southeast Asia, 2,600 were killed and 10,000 suffered wounds. Not unlike the other armed forces and American society in general, the navy was faced with serious morale, drug abuse, disciplinary, and race relations problems. Racial conflict caused the disruption of operations on board two Pacific Fleet carriers, *Kitty Hawk* and *Constellation*.

Equally serious was the obsolescence of many of the navy's World War II–era surface ships. The war's high operating costs limited the funds available for needed repairs and for the design and construction of new, more capable ships. In addition, to help pay for the war, the Ford and Carter administrations reduced the navy's Vietnam-era fleet of 769 ships to just over 450 vessels.

From the crucible of war, however, the Navy emerged in some ways stronger. The Vietnam War, as had the Korean War, reaffirmed the vital importance of naval forces to the conduct of warfare far from the United States. The navy fought as part of an integrated team that included U.S. and allied ground, air, and naval forces. Furthermore, the Vietnam War educated a whole generation of mid-level naval officers, many of whom became key leaders in the years thereafter, about the limitations of U.S. military power. Their stress on the judicious and appropriate use of force would hold great weight when successive U.S. administrations contemplated actions in Central America, Africa, and the Middle East. In many ways, the Vietnam War marked a watershed in the navy's post–World War II history.

[*See also* Coast Guard, U.S.; Commander-in-Chief, Pacific (CINCPAC); Discipline, *article on*

U.S. Military; Marines, U.S.; SEALs; Seabees; Women, U.S. Military, *article on* Women Accepted for Voluntary Emergency Service (WAVES).]

BIBLIOGRAPHY

CUTLER, THOMAS J. *Brown Water, Black Berets: Coastal and Riverine Warfare in Vietnam.* 1988.
MAROLDA, EDWARD J. *By Sea, Air, and Land: An Illustrated History of the U.S. Navy and the War in Southeast Asia.* 1994.
MAROLDA, EDWARD J., and OSCAR P. FITZGERALD. *The United States Navy and the Vietnam Conflict.* Vol. 2: *From Military Assistance to Combat, 1959–1965.* 1986.
MERSKY, PETER, and NORMAN POLMAR. *The Naval Air War in Vietnam, 1965–1975.* 1981.
SCHREADLEY, RICHARD L. *From the Rivers to the Sea: The United States Navy in Vietnam.* 1992.

EDWARD J. MAROLDA

New Left. Sociologist C. Wright Mills termed the leftist youth movement that emerged in the early 1960s the "new left" to differentiate it from the "old left"—Marxists and socialists whose roots lay in the activism of the 1930s. The new left was disillusioned with both Soviet communism and the West and viewed the established left as excessively focused on international affairs. Members of the new left, largely affluent middle-class urban and suburban college students, were cynical about the American culture of their 1950s childhoods and were inspired by the civil rights movement to become politically active. The movement included such groups as Students for a Democratic Society (SDS), the Revolutionary Youth Movement, the Progressive Labor Party, and the Worker-Student Alliance.

By the mid 1960s the new left had turned its attentions to the Vietnam War, although the various groups debated whether the war should be their sole issue. Ultimately, disagreements on this question and on tactics led to a split within the movement. Militancy increased and many, such as the Revolutionary Youth Movement, advocated violence, while others were content with peaceful demonstrations and community activism. The most notorious of the radical new left groups was the Weathermen, which was formed to wage a war at home against the U.S. government.

BIBLIOGRAPHY

GITLIN, TODD. *The Sixties: Years of Hope, Days of Rage.* 1987.
POWERS, THOMAS. *The War at Home.* 1973.

ZAROULIS, NANCY, and GERALD SULLIVAN. *Who Spoke Up?* 1984.

KELLY EVANS-PFEIFER

New Mobe. Socialists, communists, Trotskyites, religious pacifists, union organizers, and older antiwar activists including Benjamin Spock, William Sloane Coffin, and Dave Dellinger formed the New Mobilization Committee to End the War in Vietnam (New Mobe) in July 1969. The main organizers were Sidney Lens, Douglas Dowd, Stewart Meacham, Sidney Peck, and Cora Weiss. Student activists on the Vietnam Moratorium Committee lent some cooperation after Moratorium Day in October 1969. Denounced by antiwar radicals as "an attempt by Establishment liberals to co-opt the student movement," dismissed by conservatives as a communist front, the New Mobe sponsored the largest protest in U.S. history on 15 November 1969. An estimated 700,000 marchers in Washington, D.C., and another 250,000 in San Francisco carried signs, listened to antiwar speeches, and sang "Give Peace a Chance." A handful of radicals fought with police in Washington after the rally. President Nixon spent the day barricaded in the White House watching football on television to dramatize his indifference. New Mobe organizers then returned to their churches, unions, and party work.

BIBLIOGRAPHY

DEBENEDETTI, CHARLES. *An American Ordeal: The Antiwar Movement of the Vietnam Era.* 1990.
GOODMAN, WILLIAM. "The New Mobe." *New York Times Magazine,* 30 November 1969.
GRAY, FRANCINE DU PLESSIX. "The Moratorium and the New Mobe." *New Yorker,* 3 January 1970.
HALSTEAD, FRED. *Out Now! A Participant's Account of the American Movement against the Vietnam War.* 1978.
ZAROULIS, NANCY, and GERALD SULLIVAN. *Who Spoke Up? American Protest against the War in Vietnam, 1963–1975.* 1984.

GLEN GENDZEL

New York Times v. United States. *See* Pentagon Papers; Supreme Court, U.S.

New Zealand. New Zealand entered the war in Vietnam less out of fear of communism than from the desire to maintain and strengthen its ties to the United States and Australia, ties that had been first cemented in the 1951 ANZUS (Australia–New Zealand–U.S.) pact. New Zealand coordinated its deployment and withdrawal of troops with Australia, but its commitment never approached the level of Australia's troop commitment. In 1964, New Zealand sent engineers and medical personnel, totaling 20 people. In 1965 New Zealand replaced them with combat troops—the 161st Battery of the Royal New Zealand Artillery—whose mission was to support Australians in Phuoc Thuy province.

New Zealand's political parties sharply disagreed over the war. The National party, in power from 1960 to 1972, supported the U.S. effort to halt communism. The Labour party was equally anticommunist but grew increasingly critical of the war, drawing on widespread and often noncommunist popular criticism of U.S. aggression. Nonetheless, in 1966 the New Zealand government augmented its artillery forces and medical team in Qui Nhon. The National party's election victory that year was viewed as a mandate for the government to continue its war effort. After lengthy discussions with the U.S. Military Assistance Command, Vietnam (MACV), New Zealand sent another medical team, two rifle companies, and a platoon of New Zealand Special Air Services personnel to South Vietnam in 1967. The two rifle companies joined Australians to form an ANZAC battalion. In 1968 New Zealand arranged with the MACV to reimburse the United States for U.S. logistical support of ANZAC forces. New Zealand maintained its troop strength at the same level from 1967 to 1969; it began to withdraw its troops in 1970, and withdrew all combat troops in 1971.

BIBLIOGRAPHY

BALL, DESMOND, ed. *The ANZAC Connection.* 1985.
LARSEN, STANLEY ROBERT, and JAMES LAWTON COLLINS JR. *Allied Participation in Vietnam.* 1975.
MCKINNON, MALCOLM. *Independence and Foreign Policy: New Zealand in the World since 1935.* 1993.

ELLEN BAKER

Ngo Dinh Can

Ngo Dinh Can (d. 1963), administrator of Hue and environs. After his brother, Ngo Dinh Diem, came to power in July 1954, Ngo Dinh Can controlled the northern provinces around Hue. Although he never held an official post, his familial ties permitted him to direct the shipping and cinnamon trade in the region. He controlled a private police force whose aim was to kill any person with ties to the Viet Cong guerrillas. He was the only family member to advocate conciliation during Diem's 1963 Buddhist crisis. After Diem's fall in 1963, Can was tried and executed in a public square in Saigon.

BIBLIOGRAPHY

BUTTINGER, JOSEPH. *Vietnam: A Political History.* 1968.
FALL, BERNARD B. *The Two Viet-Nams: A Political and Military Analysis.* 1963.
FITZGERALD, FRANCES. *Fire in the Lake: The Vietnamese and the Americans in Vietnam.* 1972.
KOLKO, GABRIEL. *Anatomy of a War: Vietnam, the United States, and the Modern Historical Experience.* 1985.

ELLEN BAKER

Ngo Dinh Diem

Ngo Dinh Diem (1901–1963), prime minister and president, Republic of Vietnam, 1954–1963. Ngo Dinh Diem was born in Hue on 3 January 1901 to a family that had been converted to Catholicism as early as the seventeenth century. His grandparents had been poor peasants and fishermen in the province of Quang Binh. But at the time of his birth Diem's father, Ngo Dinh Kha, had become a high mandarin at court, thanks to the French colonial conquest that had helped Christian Vietnamese climb quickly up the ladder of success. Third in a family of eight children, Diem attended Le Lycéum Pellerin, a Catholic secondary school in Hue. After graduating, Diem enrolled in the French school of administration, Collège Hâu Bô, taught by a group of French schoolteachers appointed by the French Resident of Annam.

With his French and Catholic training, in a short period of only ten years after his graduation, Diem bypassed many officials to become minister of the interior under Emperor Bao Dai in 1933 at the relatively young age of thirty-two. In this capacity Diem would have become prime minister if the French had fulfilled their promise to liberalize the colonial administrative structure. According to Diem, he told the French that they had to "transform the country in order to fight Communism," but when they refused to accede to his demand for reforms, he resigned in protest.

Diem's anticommunist and anti-French attitude thereafter made him appear as a credible nationalist figure to many in Vietnam and in the West. In the eyes of others, however, his nationalist credentials had been tarnished by his willingness to work with the Japanese. In March 1945 he negotiated with

NGO DINH DIEM. Officiating at the opening of a farming project in southern South Vietnam. *Center of Military History*

them to become prime minister in the client government with which they planned to replace the French, but they did not reach an agreement before the end of the war. Ironically, his nationalist stature was reestablished when he refused an offer of a high position in Ho Chi Minh's government in late 1945, partly because he regarded the Viet Minh as ultimately responsible for the assassination of his brother Ngo Dinh Khoi, governor of Quang Ngai province.

From 1950 to 1954 Diem lived quietly in Europe and the United States, missing the fiercest years of anticolonial struggle in Vietnam. During a 1951–1953 stay at a Maryknoll seminary in New Jersey, Diem was introduced to numerous influential American religious and political leaders, including Francis Cardinal Spellman and Senators John F. Kennedy and Mike Mansfield. They, in turn, promoted him in Washington. Diem's opportunity came after the French surrendered at Dien Bien Phu on 7 May 1954. The United States pressured Emperor Bao Dai to appoint Diem prime minister in June 1954, and on 7 July Diem returned to Saigon to formally take over the government.

After he dethroned Bao Dai in 1955, Diem quickly made his family the core of the political structure. Of the nine cabinet ministries, he himself held the three most important; Tran Van Chuong, the father-in-law of his brother Ngo Dinh Nhu, held another; Tran Van Don, Madame Nhu's uncle, was foreign minister; and another relative was minister of education. Diem's brother, Ngo Dinh Can, ran the northern provinces around Hue; and loyal supporters from this region were given the most sensitive and important jobs in the regime. Bishop Ngo Dinh Thuc, Diem's older brother, ran the Catholic Church, which was composed largely of northern refugees who gave the regime its only appearance of mass support. And Diem rewarded Catholics handsomely. In a country that was more than 90 percent non-Catholic, the majority of high officials in the government were members of the Church. Ngo Dinh Nhu was Diem's chief political adviser and, by 1956, the creator and chief of the Can Lao party, which also served as a secret police. Membership in the party was a prerequisite for advancement to higher posts in the administration and military. Nhu and his wife, who headed the Women's Solidarity Movement, were from the beginning the regime's famous *éminences grises,* exercising enormous influence over Diem and power over the government and the country.

Diem's nepotism and favoritism resulted in grave administrative inefficiency and widespread resentment. In an effort to consolidate power and stabilize the regime, Diem mounted a repressive campaign against all potential political opposition in the urban area and a merciless pacification program against the countryside. According to the regime's statistics, by May 1956 more than 94,000 former Viet Minh cadres had "rallied to the government," with an additional 5,613 having surrendered. In addition, thousands had been jailed, executed, or sent to so-called reeducation camps. As part of pacification, Diem instituted a so-called land reform program that in effect allowed landlords to reclaim lands the revolution had parceled out to the peasants and to collect land rents for as many years back as the landlords could claim. When peasants reacted with fierce struggles, the Diem regime blamed the unrest in the countryside on the Viet Cong guerrillas, or literally, "Vietnamese Communists." With the help of U.S. and British experts, in 1959 Diem began a wholesale resettlement program that forced the resident population into so-called agrovilles—and later on, strategic hamlets—in an effort to weed out the communists and control the population.

Despite the deaths and suffering the North Vietnamese government denied repeated appeals from antigovernment forces in the South for permission to carry out armed struggles against Diem's government. Only after the insurrection of January 1960 in Ben Tre, which resulted in the takeover of nearly the entire province by former Viet Minh cadres and caused a chain reaction throughout the Mekong Delta, did North Vietnam finally approve the shift to armed struggle in the South at the Third Congress of the Lao Dong party in September. (North Vietnam had grudgingly allowed cadres who had evacuated to the North to return to the South with limited arms supplies in spring 1959.) With North Vietnam's blessing, on 20 December some twenty organizations, opposed to the United States and the Diem regime, merged with the former southern

RALLY FOR DIEM. A group of children carry banners displaying the picture of President Diem, Binh Dinh, 1955. *National Archives*

Viet Minh revolutionaries into the National Front for Liberation (NLF), whose program included the overthrow of the Diem regime, the establishment of a national coalition government, and a foreign policy of peace and neutrality. From then on the NLF dealt the Diem regime repeated military and pacification setbacks and the urban opposition created such turmoil and instability that the United States became convinced that Diem was no longer equal to his task.

When South Vietnamese troops killed nine Buddhist marchers in Hue on the 2,527th birthday of the Buddha on 8 May 1963, tensions between Diem and the United States reached a crisis. By mid-June the United States was threatening to break with Diem over the issue of Buddhist repression. At that point Nhu privately, through the French government, contacted both the Democratic Republic of Vietnam (DRV) and the NLF to seek a negotiated settlement. It is still unclear whether these contacts were in earnest or whether they were meant to blackmail the United States. Nevertheless, the United States was convinced that Diem should be removed. In October 1963, U.S. ambassador to South Vietnam, Henry Cabot Lodge, secretly informed a group of South Vietnamese military officers plotting a coup against Diem that the U.S. government would not oppose a change in leadership in the South. On 2 November 1963, Diem and his brother were ousted and murdered, and Duong Van Minh became the leader of South Vietnam.

BIBLIOGRAPHY

BUTTINGER, JOSEPH. *Vietnam: The Unforgettable Tragedy.* 1977.
HAMMER, ELLEN J. *A Death in November: America in Vietnam.* 1987.
KAHIN, GEORGE McT. *Intervention: How America Became Involved in Vietnam.* 1987.
YOUNG, MARILYN. *The Vietnam Wars, 1945–1990.* 1991.

NGÔ VĨNH LONG

Ngo Dinh Luyen, youngest brother of Ngo Dinh Diem; South Vietnam's ambassador to Great Britain, early 1960s. Earlier, Luyen had worked for Diem in the Parisian Vietnamese community as Diem prepared to challenge Bao Dai's leadership. Luyen nevertheless served in Bao Dai's delegation to the Geneva Conference in 1954 where he had significant contact with Zhou Enlai. Interestingly, Luyen failed to interest the American delegates in his brother. Luyen's service reflected Diem's nepotism and extensive exploitation of his family and kin

contacts. Diem particularly used Luyen to gain support from European nations.

BIBLIOGRAPHY

FITZGERALD, FRANCES. *Fire in the Lake: The Vietnamese and the Americans in Vietnam.* 1972.
KARNOW, STANLEY. *Vietnam: A History.* 1991.

STANLEY I. KUTLER

Ngo Dinh Nhu (1910–1963), chief adviser to Ngo Dinh Diem; chief of the Can Lao party; head of the various police services, Republic of Vietnam.

Ngo Dinh Nhu, Ngo Dinh Diem's immediate younger brother, was born on 7 October 1910 in Hue. He was the first Vietnamese admitted to the elite French archivist school, the École des Chartes. Graduating with a degree of paleography at the age of twenty-eight, he worked at the archives of the governor general of Indochina in Hanoi from 1938 to 1943. In 1943, he became chief of the archive of the French Residence in Hue and directed a commission to catalog the records of the Nguyen dynasty.

Nhu first gained prominence in 1953 as an organizer of the Vietnamese Federation of Christian Workers, which was modeled after France's Force Ouvrière and affiliated with the International Federation of Christian Workers. His real talent, however, was behind-the-scenes political manipulations, which manifested itself in the summer of 1953 when he organized the National Union for Independence and Peace, in support of a new government to be headed by his brother. The union, composed of diverse religious groups and political leaders, was subsequently used in September 1953 to undermine the positions of former emperor Bao Dai and the French and to promote Diem's cause.

After Diem gained power in 1954, Nhu served as the regime's ideologue and directed the various secret and police services in his capacity as Diem's chief political adviser and minister of the Interior. In fact, Nhu wielded far greater power than Diem himself, partly because he also headed his own semi-secret Can Lao party (Can Lao Nhan Vi Cach Mang Dang, or Revolutionary Personalist Diligent Labor party), which he created in 1956 along with the uniformed Republic Youth and Special Forces.

The Can Lao party comprised roughly 16,000 secret members in 1959 (although Nhu claimed that it had 70,000), consisting chiefly of civil servants and army officials in key positions in the South Vietnamese government and military. It was a combination of private political machine and mafia, and membership in it was a prerequisite for advancement to higher posts in the government and the military. Can Lao members of the army were at times able to give orders to their nominal superiors. Nhu used the Can Lao to obtain intelligence on suspect members of the government, military officers, and private citizens; and he allowed it to take over much of the criminal activity in South Vietnam in order to expand its coffers. Nhu's Republic Youth and Special Forces, meanwhile, were used for popular control and for repression; their tactics have been likened by Joseph Buttinger, one of the regime's early staunch supporters, to those of Nazi storm troopers.

A cynical and devious man who resorted to all kinds of tactics—including systematic use of corruption and terror—to maintain political power for the regime, Nhu discreetly explored the possibility of a political settlement with the National Liberation Front (NLF) and the Democratic Republic of Vietnam (DRV) in the spring of 1963 in face of mounting opposition to the regime. In August 1963, he ordered elite U.S.-trained troops to raid pagodas throughout South Vietnam, brutally expelling and arresting resident monks who protested the regime's policies. Vietnamese of all political persuasions were appalled. Madame Nhu's father and mother resigned, respectively, as Saigon's ambassador to the United States and observer to the United Nations. U.S. officials repeatedly told Diem that Nhu and his wife had to be removed, but Diem refused. In late August, in cables between the White House and Saigon, Ambassador Henry Cabot Lodge and President John F. Kennedy both agreed that a coup against Diem remained the best hope if the war was to be won. On 27 October 1963, Undersecretary of State George Ball signed a "green light" cable for the coup. On 2 November Nhu and Diem were dead.

BIBLIOGRAPHY

BUTTINGER, JOSEPH. *Vietnam: A Political History.* 1968.
KAHIN, GEORGE McT. *Intervention: How America Became Involved in Vietnam.* 1987.

NGO VINH LONG

Ngo Dinh Nhu (Madame Nhu) (1924–),
wife of Ngo Dinh Nhu; "first lady" of the Diem regime. Caricatured in the West as the "Dragon Lady" and the "woman who ruled the men who ruled Vietnam," Madame Nhu (maiden name Tran Le Xuan) was born into an upper-class family whose grandfathers on both sides had been high court mandarins. In 1943, after graduating from a *lycée* in Hanoi, she married Ngo Dinh Nhu and converted from Buddhism to Catholicism.

A woman of exceptional intelligence and immense energy, Madame Nhu wielded enormous direct power under the Diem regime. This was partly because of her influence on Diem and her husband, Diem's most trusted adviser and chief of the nation's security forces, and partly because of her organizational skills. She organized and headed an anticommunist paramilitary organization called the Vietnamese Women's Solidarity Movement—the directing committees of which consisted largely of the wives of government officials from the central level down to the various local levels—and used it to lobby the various branches of the government. She was able, for example, to push through the National Assembly the Family Code and the Law for the Protection of Morality, which, among other things, outlawed polygamy, divorce, dancing, beauty contests, gambling, fortune-telling, cockfighting, use of contraceptives, marital infidelity, and prostitution. Although female high school and university students were pressured to join the movement, many did so willingly because of the feminism, moralism, idealism, and power that it exhibited.

A charming and beautiful woman, Madame Nhu was not known for her grace and tact. When asked in August 1963 about the self-immolation of Buddhist monks to protest the repression by the Diem regime, Madame Nhu said: "I would clap hands at seeing another monk barbecue show." This and other uncharitable remarks made her a political liability and officials in Washington, D.C., pressured Diem many times to send her and her husband abroad. Diem steadfastly refused, however, because they were very useful to him. Consequently, Madame Nhu was blamed for the fall of the regime and has not been regarded as a sympathetic figure on either side of the Pacific. Having lost her husband, her parents (who were murdered by her brother in Washington, D.C.), and her four children, she is a lonely and bitter person living out her remaining days in a Rome neighborhood.

BIBLIOGRAPHY

LACOUTURE, JEAN. *Vietnam: Between Two Truces.* 1966.
YOUNG, MARILYN. *The Vietnam Wars 1945–1990.* 1991.

NGÓ VIÑH LONG

Ngo Dinh Thuc (1897–1984), Roman Catholic archbishop of Hue. As eldest male in the Ngo family, Thuc exercised formidable influence in the regime of his brother Ngo Dinh Diem, whose ruling circle consisted of Ngo family members. An anticommunist and nationalist Catholic priest, and later archbishop of Hue, Thuc served as a liaison to South Vietnam's 1.2-million-member Catholic community, from which the government drew crucial support. Some Catholics resented the church's affiliation with the regime, but Catholic refugees from the North strongly backed the Ngo brothers. Diem lobbied for Thuc's appointment as archbishop of Saigon, but the Vatican refused because it would appear as a public endorsement by the Vatican of Diem's government. Archbishop Thuc was in Rome at the time Diem was overthrown. The Vatican later twice excommunicated Thuc for illegal consecrations of bishops and he died in the United States in 1984.

BIBLIOGRAPHY

LACOUTURE, JEAN. *Vietnam: Between Two Truces.* 1966.

ADAM LAND

Ngo Quang Truong (1929–), general, Army of the Republic of Vietnam (ARVN); commander, I Corps Tactical Zone (CTZ), 1972–1975; commander, IV CTZ, 1970–1972. Born in Cochinchina, General Truong was one of the most competent commanders in the ARVN, possibly its best field officer. In May 1972 Truong, then IV CTZ commander, was sent to Hue to replace Gen. Hoang Xuan Lam. Lam and Gen. Vu Van Giai had incompetently managed the ARVN's northern defense networks during the Easter Offensive, resulting in the collapse of its 3d Division. Truong, through resourcefulness and the respect of his men, managed to regain lost territory and save the ARVN's reputation. Much of his success, however, was also based on unlimited U.S. air support plus the fact that North Vietnamese units were overextended and undersupplied. In March 1975 Truong, the incumbent commander of I CTZ, faced his greatest challenge after the ARVN's position in the Central Highlands collapsed. After a week-long debate with President Thieu and senior military staff, highlighted by accusations, vague orders, or impossible suggestions, Truong was told to evacuate all ARVN forces from I CTZ. This Herculean task failed, but Truong should not bear the blame for failure in such a difficult situation. A small number of troops from the Central Highlands did eventually reach safety in Saigon, but the army had fallen apart. General Truong relocated to the United States after South Vietnam collapsed on 30 April 1975.

BIBLIOGRAPHY

ANDRADÉ, DALE. *Trial by Fire: The 1972 Easter Offensive, America's Last Vietnam Battle.* 1995.

THOMAS R. CANTWELL

Nguyen Cao Ky (1930–), prime minister, Republic of Vietnam, 1965–1967; vice president, 1967–1971. Nguyen Cao Ky was born in Son Tay province, northwest of Hanoi. After graduation from junior high school he joined the French air force as a corporal. A short tour of training in France and a French wife helped him rise quickly through the ranks. Although officially only vice air marshall during the coup against Diem in November 1963, the absence of the air force chief and the personal loyalty of the men toward him gave Ky effective control of the air force and hence considerable leverage over other military leaders.

Ky felt, however, that he was not sufficiently rewarded, and accused the coup leader, Gen. Duong Van "Big" Minh, of being soft on communism. In January 1964 Ky joined Gen. Nguyen Khanh in a coup against Minh's government. In February, after General Khanh became premier at U.S. secretary of state Dean Rusk's suggestion, Ky was appointed "aspirant brigadier general" and head of the air force. On 21 July Ky attracted worldwide attention when he disclosed that his planes had been ferrying combat teams on sabotage missions "inside North Vietnam," adding that he thought it was time for systematic bombing of the North. "We are ready," he said; "we could go this afternoon; I cannot assure you that all of North Vietnam would be destroyed, but Hanoi would certainly." After General Khanh purportedly sought secret negotiations with the National Liberation Front (NLF), in February 1965, Gen. Maxwell Taylor and Gen. William Westmoreland relied on Ky to urge the Armed Forces Council to remove Khanh from his position of commander in chief. On 24 February Khanh left South Vietnam as "roving ambassador" and Ky's fortune rose. In June 1965 Ky accused the new premier, the U.S.-sponsored Phan Huy Quat, of being a weakling and joined forces with Gen. Nguyen Van Thieu and Gen. Nguyen Chanh Thi to oust Quat.

The U.S. mission judged that among the triumvirate Ky, a nominal Buddhist, would be the safest bet to be the new prime minister.

Ironically, Ky became the most effective destroyer of the Buddhists. On 3 April 1966, with the approval of both Ambassador Henry Cabot Lodge and General Westmoreland, Ky announced that the Buddhist movement had fallen into communist hands and requested U.S. aid in shuttling loyal troops to Da Nang. The Buddhist movement had attracted the loyalty of key units of the army, led by Gen. Nguyen Chanh Thi. In early May, Ky flew heavy troops in and launched his attack. Aided by U.S. Marines, Ky brutally crushed the Buddhists and their supporters. In June, Ky turned against the city of Hue and, once more, aided by U.S. troops, succeeded in ending that opposition. Remnants of the movement in Saigon were similarly crushed.

In 1967 Ky effectively used his protégés, including Gen. Nguyen Ngoc Loan, head of South Vietnam's police and intelligence services, and Gen. Le Nguyen Khang, commander of the 3d Army Division, to rig the presidential election and intimidate the National Assembly into ratifying the results that allowed him and Thieu to become vice president and president, respectively. During the 1968 Tet Offensive, six of Ky's military comrades were killed in a bombing accident, which Ky's supporters publicly accused Thieu of having ordered. Relations between the two men deteriorated after that. In 1971 Thieu sought to contain Ky's power by having him disqualified as a presidential candidate. Rebuffed by his military cohorts, Ky retired from politics, yet maintained a public presence. Just prior to the fall of Saigon in 1975, Ky led a well-publicized demonstration in front of the U.S. embassy and publicly promised, with four hundred other officers, never to leave Vietnam. But a few days later, Ky and many of these officers fled with the Americans, vowing to return to liberate the country from communism. Ky is now a businessman in the United States.

BIBLIOGRAPHY

HARRISON, JAMES PINCKLNEY. *The Endless War: Vietnam's Struggle for Independence.* 1982.

KAHIN, GEORGE MCT. *Intervention: How America Became Involved in Vietnam.* 1987.

NGÓ VĨNH LONG

Nguyen Chanh Thi (1923–), general, Army of the Republic of Vietnam (ARVN). A devout Bud-

dhist, Col. Nguyen Chanh Thi helped President Diem subdue the Binh Xuyen gangsters in 1955. Rising to paratroop commander, Thi came to resent Diem's favoritism toward Catholics. After leading rebel paratroopers in an abortive coup against Diem in 1960, he fled to temporary exile in Cambodia. Four years later, after the fall of Diem, he joined the so-called Young Turks, who overthrew Duong Van Minh's Military Revolutionary Council. Numerous coups ensued until U.S. ambassador Maxwell Taylor called Thi and other top generals together in December 1964. Taylor offered to send more U.S. troops and start bombing North Vietnam if the generals would stabilize the Saigon government and institute democratic reforms. But a few days later, Thi helped stage yet another coup. Thi rose to virtual warlord status in Central Vietnam until President Nguyen Cao Ky tried to relieve him in March 1966. Thi and his ally Tri Quang then led a major revolt among Buddhists and students opposed to the Saigon regime. Thi's loyal troops joined the Struggle Movement, as it was called, and manned barricades in defiance of Ky. They denounced the United States and demanded elections to restore civilian government. Hundreds of Thi's followers perished in Danang when Ky's government forces attacked on 14 May 1966. Thi was arrested and exiled to the United States, ending hopes of a noncommunist alternative to the Saigon regime. Thi predicted that the communists would win because "the Americans never listened to the people of Vietnam."

BIBLIOGRAPHY

FITZGERALD, FRANCES. *Fire in the Lake: The Vietnamese and the Americans in Vietnam.* 1972.

KARNOW, STANLEY. "Diem Defeats His Own Best Generals." *The Reporter,* 19 January 1961, 24–29.

NGUYEN CAO KY. *Twenty Years and Twenty Days.* 1976.

NGUYEN CHANH THI. *Viet Nam, Mot Tri Tams.* 1987.

SHAPLEN, ROBERT. *The Lost Revolution: The U.S. in Vietnam, 1946–1966.* Rev. ed., 1966.

GLEN GENDZEL

Nguyen Chi Thanh (1914–1967), general, North Vietnamese commander of operations in South Vietnam, 1965–1967. In 1965 General Thanh infiltrated into South Vietnam to take control of North Vietnamese and Viet Cong troop movements. He sought a quick victory using conventional tactics, and as a consequence his forces sustained heavy losses when U.S. troops were de-

NGUYEN CHI THANH. A general in the People's Army of Vietnam, Thanh was a member of both North Vietnam's politburo and its national defense council as well as of the secretariat of the Lao Dong Party. As head of the Central Office for South Vietnam (COSVN), Thanh commanded the People's Liberation Armed Forces—the Viet Cong. The photo, believed to have been taken in South Vietnam, was discovered by U.S. forces during Operation JUNCTION CITY in War Zone "C," Tay Ninh province, March 1967. Note the black-and-white checked scarf in the background, an identifying symbol of the Viet Cong guerrilla. *National Archives*

ployed in 1965–1966. Gen. Vo Nguyen Giap opposed Thanh's use of conventional methods, and when Thanh was killed in a U.S. bombing raid in July 1967, the communists switched to an emphasis on guerrilla operations and an eventual political victory.

BIBLIOGRAPHY

DAVIDSON, PHILLIP B. *Vietnam at War—The History: 1946–1975.* 1988.
Obituary. *New York Times,* 9 July 1967.

ELLEN D. GOLDLUST

Nguyen Co Thach (1928–), one of North Vietnam's negotiators in the Paris peace talks; foreign minister of the Socialist Republic of Vietnam (SRV), 1975–. Thach, leader of the liberal wing of the Vietnamese Communist Party, sought to normalize relations with the United States after the war. His efforts were, however, unsuccessful: the United States rejected the SRV's demand for war reparations and opposed the 1977 Vietnamese invasion of Cambodia.

BIBLIOGRAPHY

KARNOW, STANLEY. *Vietnam: A History.* 1991.
NGUYEN VAN CANH. *Vietnam under Communism, 1975–1982.* 1983.

KELLY EVANS-PFEIFER

Nguyen Huu Tho (1910–), chairman, National Liberation Front (NLF), 1960–1976. A French-trained Saigon lawyer, Tho was active in the anti-French movement and was later jailed by the Diem government. He became chairman of the NLF when it was formed in December 1960. A noncommunist, Tho was chosen for his broad public appeal, but he was a figurehead without significant power.

BIBLIOGRAPHY

FALL, BERNARD B. "Viet-Cong—the Unseen Enemy in Viet-Nam." In *The Viet-Nam Reader,* Marcus G. Raskin and Bernard B. Fall, eds. 1965.
PIKE, DOUGLAS. *Viet Cong: The Organization and Techniques of the National Liberation Front of South Vietnam.* 1966.

WILLIAM PAUL SCHUCK

Nguyen Khanh (1927–), general, Army of the Republic of Vietnam (ARVN); prime minister, South Vietnam, 1964–1965; president, South Vietnam, 1965. South Vietnam's flamboyant Nguyen Khanh ran away from his wealthy, well-connected family at the age of 16, joined the Viet Minh and fought the French for a year before he was dismissed for poor discipline. Khanh then switched sides, attended a French officers' school, and led colonial troops against the Viet Minh. Rising through the elite ranks of the *gardes mobiles,* Khanh always wore the paratrooper's red beret. As deputy chief of staff, Khanh joined the coup that killed President Diem in November 1963. Two months later, Khanh led the so-called Young Turks faction of junior officers who overthrew Duong Van Minh's Revolutionary Military Council. Khanh then named himself prime minister, explaining to his U.S. patrons that Minh had failed "to respond to the exigencies of the struggle against the communists" and vowing to "fight communism to the final victory." Swaggering and blustery, Khanh never won over his own people, and he alarmed U.S. advisers by jeopardizing the war effort with repeated attempts to establish a dictatorship. His purging of the ARVN officer corps turned Khanh's fellow generals against him while stepped-up draft calls angered the populace. Playing Catholics and Buddhists against each other, he quickly earned the enmity of both groups.

Amid rising protests against his rule, Khanh used the Tonkin Gulf incident to proclaim a state of emergency on 7 August 1964. A week later he proclaimed himself president, but angry mobs in Saigon forced him to resign on 25 August. Khanh returned to power on 27 August as a member of the Provisional Leadership Committee, which reappointed him prime minister on 3 September. He foiled a coup attempt by Catholic officers on 13 September, and appointed a civilian council to draw up a new constitution. Tran Van Huong was named prime minister of the new government on 4 November, but Khanh retained supreme command of the military. He led the Armed Forces Council in yet another coup on 20 December. Ambassador Maxwell Taylor then suspended U.S. military aid in hopes of forcing Khanh to resign, but a month later, Khanh dismissed the rest of the Armed Forces Council and assumed dictatorial powers. Khanh's erstwhile supporters Gen. Nguyen Van Thieu, Gen. Nguyen Van Cao, and Air Marshal Nguyen Cao Ky finally deposed him for the last time on 21 February 1965. U.S. officials were greatly relieved when Khanh left the next day to become South Vietnam's "roving ambassador." He spent the rest of the war in France and eventually became a restaurateur in West Palm Beach, Florida.

BIBLIOGRAPHY

KARNOW, STANLEY. *Vietnam: A History*. Rev. ed., 1991.
"The Quiet Coup: And Now General Khanh." *Newsweek,* 10 February 1964.
SHAPLEN, ROBERT. *The Lost Revolution: The U.S. in Vietnam, 1946–1966*. Rev. ed., 1966.
SMITH, HARVEY H., et al. *Area Handbook for South Vietnam.* 1967.
TRAN VAN DON. *Our Endless War: Inside Vietnam.* 1978.

GLEN GENDZEL

Nguyen Ngoc Loan, general, Army of the Republic of Vietnam (ARVN). A colonel with a reputation for ruthlessness, Loan, Saigon's chief of police, in 1966 was given the job of eliminating South Vietnamese president Nguyen Cao Ky's opponents in Da Nang. He performed so well that he was assigned to crush the dissident Buddhist movement in Hue several months later. Loan's performance earned him a promotion to general and to chief of South Vietnam's national police. During the Tet Offensive in 1968, an Associated Press photographer snapped a picture of Loan summarily executing a Viet Cong suspect in Saigon. The photograph, widely circulated in the United States, increased Americans' disgust with the war. In 1975, Loan fled to the United States, where he operated a restaurant in the Washington, D.C., suburbs.

BIBLIOGRAPHY

FITZGERALD, FRANCES. *Fire in the Lake: The Vietnamese and the Americans in Vietnam.* 1972.
KARNOW, STANLEY. *Vietnam: A History.* 1991.
"Obscurity Now Cloaks Thieu Aides," *New York Times,* 2 May 1976.

ELLEN D. GOLDLUST

Nguyen Thi Binh (1927–), minister of foreign affairs, People's Revolutionary Government (PRG), chief delegate, National Liberation Front (NLF) at Paris peace talks, 1969–1973. Born near Saigon, Madame Binh was a granddaughter of the patriot Phan Chau Trinh, advocate of Vietnamese independence in the 1920s. From a civil servant's family, French-educated, Madame Binh joined the revolution against the French as a schoolgirl and participated in the August Revolution (1945) against the Japanese and the resurgent French, becoming a leader of student-intellectual resistance. In 1950 she was arrested for participating in a Saigon demonstration against U.S. aid to France and was jailed from 1951 to 1954. After the Geneva Conference in 1954, she returned to political activism and married, but she kept her husband's name secret to protect him from the police.

A vigorous opponent of U.S. intervention in the Vietnam War, Binh was elected to the NLF central committee and also served as vice president of the South Vietnam Women's Union for Liberation. She led numerous delegations abroad for both, participated in the third Afro-Asian People's Solidarity Conference in Cairo in 1963, and attended meetings in Moscow, Beijing, and many other locations. She commanded considerable respect, which she attributed not to her gender but to her cause, stating that any woman of her generation would have done the same.

Binh was named foreign minister of the PRG, which she represented at the Paris peace talks, ranking second only to politburo member Le Duc Tho. Kissinger regarded her as a party hack who presented indefensible proposals and lacked any real importance in the negotiating team. He felt justified in his assessment when Binh underwent a brief postwar fall from power. Binh found Kissinger "vain."

In 1975, Madame Binh became minister of education in the Socialist Republic of Vietnam (SRV), one of the highest positions to be held by a member of the PRG and the highest held by a woman. She considered this appointment more important than her work in the PRG because in this new role she served in the government of a united Vietnam. She continued to work for peace and served in the National Assembly. She participated in Aspen Institute dialogues on normalization of U.S.-SRV relations held in Bali (1991) and Fiji (1992), and she visited the United States for the first time in 1992. In 1993 she was elected vice president of Vietnam, a largely symbolic office.

BIBLIOGRAPHY

EISEN, ARLENE. *Women and Revolution in Vietnam.* 1984.
FITZGERALD, FRANCES. *Fire in the Lake: The Vietnamese and Americans in Vietnam.* 1972.
HERRING, GEORGE C. *America's Longest War: The United States and Vietnam, 1950–1975.* 2d ed. 1986.
KARNOW, STANLEY. *Vietnam: A History.* 1991.
KISSINGER, HENRY. *White House Years.* 1979.
NGUYEN THI BINH. Personal interview with contributor, 23 June 1992, Salt Lake City, Utah.

SANDRA C. TAYLOR

Nguyen Thi Dinh (1920–1992), a leading woman revolutionary leader in southern Vietnam, 1940s–1975. Dinh, from a peasant family in Ben Tre province, joined the revolution against the French while still in her teens. Ngo Dinh Diem's campaign to eliminate Viet Cong guerrillas was carried out with extreme harshness in the countryside, solidifying in her a desire for independence from exploitive rule that had been kindled by the war against the French. Dinh married a fellow revolutionary who was imprisoned shortly after the birth of their son, and who was killed on Con Dao island. Dinh was jailed from 1940 to 1943, but helped lead an insurrection that seized power in Ben Tre in 1945. Leader of the women's association in the province, in 1946 she persuaded Ho Chi Minh to provide weapons for the province and successfully smuggled them past the French naval blockade. In 1960 she led an uprising of women in Ben Tre province in which the women wielded wooden replicas of guns and children set off firecrackers, frightening Army of the Republic of Vietnam (ARVN) forces into running away and enabling the Viet Cong to seize power there. This was the first concerted uprising of peasants against the Saigon regime, and it began a form of protest in which women (the so-called long-haired warriors) demanded from government officials the cessation of atrocities committed against their people.

Dinh believed that she and other peasants had literally "no other road to take"; that they had to oppose U.S. troops and the abusive Saigon government by taking up arms. She remained a leading figure in the National Liberation Front, which she helped to organize in Ben Tre province, and was a member of the Presidium Central Committee in 1964. In 1965 she became chair of the South Vietnam Women's Liberation Association, a group with which she had been associated since her release from prison. Also in 1965 she was appointed deputy commander of the South Vietnam Liberation Armed Forces, the highest ranking combat position held by a woman during the war. She continued to be active in the Women's Union, which she subsequently headed, and in the party and was probably its best-known female revolutionary in Vietnam until her death.

BIBLIOGRAPHY

EISEN, ARLENE. *Women and Revolution in Vietnam.* 1984.
ELLIOTT, MAI V., trans. *No Other Road to Take: Memoir of Mrs. Nguyen Thi Dinh.* 1976.
Exhibits in Women's Museum, Ho Chi Minh City.

SANDRA C. TAYLOR

Nguyen Van Thieu (1923–), president, Republic of Vietnam, 1967–1973. Nguyen Van Thieu was born on 5 April 1923 to a relatively prosperous family of farmers and fishermen near the town of Phan Rang in Ninh Thuan province, central Vietnam. In 1948 he graduated from the French-founded Dalat Military Academy. As the United States pushed for a new Vietnamese army to replace French forces, Thieu was brought to the United States in 1957 and 1960 for training. Although born a Buddhist, in 1958 he converted to Catholicism, principally because Diem consistently favored Catholics in promotions.

During the coup against Diem in 1963 Colonel Thieu led Gen. Ton That Dinh's 5th Division—supported by artillery, tanks, and air power—against the

NGUYEN VAN THIEU. At center, during the Honolulu conference, 26 October 1966. Left to right: Lyndon B. Johnson; William C. Westmoreland; Thieu; unidentified; Nguyen Cao Ky. Photo by Yoichi R. Okamoto. *Lyndon Baines Johnson Library*

presidential palace. Gen. Duong Van ("Big") Minh, leader of the new government, rewarded Thieu by making him a brigadier and member of the twelve-man Military Revolutionary Council, which was the major repository of government power. Thieu did not feel that he had been sufficiently rewarded, however, and became one of Maj. Gen. Nguyen Khanh's chief allies in the coup of 20 January 1964 against Minh. Khanh made Thieu commander of the IV Corps and promoted many young colonels who supported him, including Nguyen Cao Ky, to the new rank of "aspirant brigadier general." They were collectively referred to by the U.S. embassy as the "Young Turks." On 21 December Gen. Maxwell Taylor, with the approval of the U.S. government, told Khanh to resign and leave the country. On 19 January 1965 Taylor prevailed upon Prime Minister Tran Van Huong to add four Young Turks to his cabinet, including General Thieu as second deputy prime minister.

Thieu forcefully advocated expanding the war to the North and adamantly opposed the Buddhists'

demands for a negotiated settlement. His growing prominence led to his appointment as deputy prime minister and minister of defense on 14 February 1965. The new prime minister, Phan Huy Quat, on 1 March responded to pressure from the U.S. embassy and the Young Turks and announced that there could be no peace until "the Communists end the war they have provoked and stop infiltration." This was the signal for U.S. escalation of its own war effort. The next day U.S. warplanes launched their first air attacks on the North. In June, General Thieu became chief of state and chairman of the powerful military junta, the National Leadership Committee, and Gen. Nguyen Cao Ky was installed as prime minister. A few days after his inauguration, Ky ordered a full-scale mobilization of all able-bodied men and declared that the country needed a leader like Adolf Hitler. Meanwhile, on 16 July Thieu urged that the U.S. expeditionary force be increased to 200,000 men.

Because Ky could not explain away his Hitler statement and because he mercilessly repressed the

Buddhists in the central part of Vietnam in 1966, the junta selected Thieu as the "official" candidate and forced Ky to withdraw his already-declared presidential candidacy and join Thieu as vice presidential nominee for the September 1967 presidential election. Although this election was designed to give the regime respectability, according to daily Saigon papers (*Than Chung,* 16 August 1967; *Chanh Dao,* 26 September and 3 October 1967) and detailed testimonies by U.S. observers, the regime blatantly engaged in election violations and harshly repressed protestors. Thieu and Ky used troops and police to force people to vote for their ticket in the provinces. The Special Election Committee of the National Assembly found that 5,105 polling stations experienced numerous procedural and voting violations. On 1 October combat police surrounded the National Assembly and Gen. Le Nguyen Khang brought the 3d Infantry Division into Saigon. The next day, Gen. Nguyen Ngoc Loan, head of the national police and security forces, walked into the National Assembly with armed guards and watched until the deputies agreed to ratify Thieu and Ky as the "legitimate" president and vice president of the "Second Republic." Thieu was reelected president in another rigged election in 1971.

During the post–Paris agreement period of 1973–1975 Thieu persistently ordered attacks on the areas controlled by the Provisional Revolutionary Government (PRG) and suppressed any alternative elements in a publicly stated effort to prevent the formation of a coalition government as stipulated by the Paris accords. Lavish U.S. military aid, dispatched by President Nixon as part of his Vietnamization strategy, encouraged Thieu's bellicose stance. A study by the U.S. Defense Attaché Office in conjunction with the Vietnamese Joint General Staff and the U.S. Pacific Command revealed in May 1974 that

the countryside ratio of the number of rounds fired by South Vietnamese forces [since the signing of the Paris agreement] to that fired by the Communist forces was about 16 to 1. In Military Regions II and III, where South Vietnamese commanders have consistently been the most aggressive and where some U.S. officials said that random 'harassment and interdiction' fire against Communist-controlled areas was still common, the ratio was on the order of 50 to 1.

In addition to the shellings, an average of 15,000 bombs were dropped and 10,000 military operations were conducted into the countryside every month.

The military attacks coupled with Thieu's "economic blockade" of the countryside so disrupted food production and economic activities that, according to reports by Saigon deputies and Catholic priests, up to 60 percent of the population in the central provinces was reduced to eating bark, cacti, banana roots, and the bulbs of wild grass by mid 1974. In some villages, in central Vietnam, deaths from starvation reached 1–2 percent of the total population each month (*Dai Dan Toc,* 30 August 1974). In the once rice-rich Mekong Delta, acute rice shortages became commonplace (*Dien Tin,* 20, 22, and 24 September 1974). Hunger was so widespread that even in the wealthiest section of Saigon, the Tan Dinh district, a poll conducted by Catholic students in late summer 1974 disclosed that only 22 percent of the families had enough to eat. Half of the families could only afford a meal of steamed rice and a meal of gruel per day (*Chinh Luan,* 5 November 1974).

The suffering inflicted upon the general population made the Thieu regime so unpopular that when PRG and Democratic Republic of Vietnam (DRV) forces launched the Ho Chi Minh Offensive in spring 1975, one province after another fell with hardly a fight. At first, Thieu ordered his troops to abandon the northern areas as part of his strategy of "lightening the top and keeping the bottom." When North Vietnamese forces rapidly advanced, Thieu directed South Vietnamese army forces to fight, but officers and men readily deserted or laid down their arms to the North Vietnamese. On 20 April Ambassador Graham Martin asked Thieu if he would resign for the good of the country. On 21 April Thieu gave a three-hour radio and television address to the nation, denouncing the United States for having sealed the fate of South Vietnam by signing the Paris agreement. Five days later, Thieu flew into exile in a U.S. transport plane loaded with fifteen tons of baggage. Since the early 1980s he has lived in a Boston suburb, reportedly a billionaire several times over. In 1992, in a prominent front-page *Boston Globe* interview, Thieu said that he was ready to return to Vietnam to lead the country again.

BIBLIOGRAPHY

CRAIGHILL, FRANCIS H. III, and ROBERT C. ZELNICK. "Ballots or Bullets: What the 1967 Elections Could Mean." In *Vietnam: Matters for the Agenda.* 1967.

ISAACS, ARNOLD R. *Without Honor: Defeat in Vietnam & Cambodia.* 1984.

KAHIN, GEORGE McT. *Intervention: How America Became Involved in Vietnam.* 1987.

WERNER, JAYNE and LUU DOAN HUYNH, eds. *The Vietnam War: Vietnamese and American Perspectives.* 1993.

YOUNG, MARILYN. *The Vietnam Wars 1945–1990.* 1991.

NGÓ VĨNH LONG

Nha, Hoang Duc. *See* Hoang Duc Nha.

Nhu, Madame. *See* Ngo Dinh Nhu (Madame Nhu).

Nhu, Ngo Dinh. *See* Ngo Dinh Nhu.

NIAGARA. NIAGARA was the code name for the 18 January–31 March 1968 aerial bombing of the People's Army of Vietnam (PAVN) forces besieging the U.S. marine base at Khe Sanh. The bombing, the most concentrated use of air power in tactical support of ground forces in history, was a combined service effort under Seventh Air Force commander Gen. William Momyer. Under the "single manager" concept, Gen. William Westmoreland gave Momyer direct authority over all U.S. air force and naval air strikes used in the defense of Khe Sanh; the marines, however, retained control over their own close support sorties. The PAVN divisions were decimated by the more than 100,000 tons of bombs dropped, which included B-52 ARC LIGHT strikes as close as 900 meters (3,000 feet) from defending forces.

BIBLIOGRAPHY

DAVIDSON, PHILLIP B. *Vietnam at War: The History, 1946–1975.* 1988.

JOHN F. GUILMARTIN JR.

Nitze, Paul (1907–), assistant secretary of defense for international affairs, 1961–1963; secretary of the Navy, 1963–1967; deputy secretary of defense, 1967–1969. A protégé of Dean Acheson in the 1940s, Paul H. Nitze held many key government posts in the Roosevelt and Truman administrations. He was instrumental in creating the North Atlantic Treaty Organization (NATO), the Marshall Plan, and the containment policy. President Kennedy brought Nitze back into government service in

1961 after Nitze chaired the Kennedy campaign task force on national defense. Nitze was the only high-level dissenter from the Kennedy administration's policy to commit ground troops to South Vietnam in 1962. As President Johnson's secretary of the Navy at the peak of the Vietnam War, Nitze was one of the most prominent opponents of escalation within the administration. He helped to draft the San Antonio Formula, which offered to halt bombing in exchange for negotiations in 1967. Nitze served on the Ad Hoc Task Force on Vietnam in 1968, and he dissented from its recommendation that President Johnson call up the reserves and send more troops to Vietnam, which Nitze denounced as "reinforcing weakness." To him the Vietnam War was "the American Dien Bien Phu." After the war, Nitze was a top U.S. arms control negotiator and founded the Paul H. Nitze School of Advanced International Studies at Johns Hopkins University.

BIBLIOGRAPHY

CALLAHAN, DAVID. *Dangerous Capabilities: Paul Nitze and the Cold War.* 1990.

HOOPES, TOWNSEND. *The Limits of Intervention: An Inside Account of How the Johnson Policy of Escalation in Vietnam Was Reversed.* 1969.

ISAACSON, WALTER, and EVAN THOMAS. *The Wise Men.* 1986.

NITZE, PAUL H. *From Hiroshima to Glasnost.* 1989.

NITZE, PAUL H. *Tension between Opposites: Reflections on the Practice and Theory of Politics.* 1993.

GLEN GENDZEL

Nixon, Richard M. (1913–1994), U.S. vice president, 1953–1961; president, 1969–1974. Richard M. Nixon played a prominent and sometimes dominant role in setting U.S. policy toward Vietnam from 1953 to 1974. As vice president he advocated deeper U.S. involvement in the Vietnam War. Out of office from 1961 to 1968, Nixon supported forceful military intervention by the United States, exploiting widespread public dissatisfaction with the conduct of the war to win the presidential election of 1968. As president he directed public attention away from Vietnam with his Vietnamization policy, gradually withdrawing U.S. ground forces and turning more of the conduct of the war over to the Army of the Republic of Vietnam (ARVN), at the same time ordering more intensive bombing of North Vietnam. A secretive, insecure man, Nixon came to fear the power of the antiwar movement in

RICHARD M. NIXON. With U.S. troops in Vietnam, July 1969. *National Archives*

the United States. Worried that critics of his Vietnam policy might jeopardize his foreign policy, Nixon authorized a series of illegal actions against dissenters. He directed negotiations with the North Vietnamese and the National Liberation Front, leading to the Paris peace agreement of January 1973, which ended direct U.S. involvement in the war. Despite the high hopes engendered by the Paris accords, the cease-fire did not hold. The North Vietnamese triumphed in Vietnam less than eight months after Nixon had resigned the presidency in disgrace on 9 August 1974.

Vice President and Beyond. As vice president, Nixon, who had been an ardent anticommunist member of the House of Representatives and later the Senate from 1947 to 1953, became one of the most forceful advocates of direct U.S. involvement in the war in Vietnam. He visited Vietnam twice, each time praising the efforts of anticommunist forces—in 1953 the French and in 1955 the government of President Ngo Dinh Diem—and promising additional U.S. aid in their struggle against communism. During the Dien Bien Phu crisis of April 1954, he consistently recommended deeper U.S. military involvement than President Eisenhower wanted to provide. He advocated U.S. air strikes, including possibly the use of tactical nuclear weapons, to relieve the embattled French, and later suggested introducing U.S. forces into the war should the French pull out. Each time Eisenhower decided that U.S. military participation should not go as far as Nixon wanted, and the vice president loyally supported the lesser, but still highly entangling, U.S. commitment to South Vietnam.

Nixon remained active in Republican politics after losing the presidency to Democrat John F. Kennedy in 1960, publicly supporting the initial stages of U.S. escalation in Vietnam from 1963 to 1965. By 1966, however, the war and domestic political upheaval had exacted a heavy toll on President Lyndon B. Johnson's domestic popularity, and Nixon prepared for another try at the White House in 1968. Nixon distanced himself from Johnson's policies by attacking the conduct of the war in Vietnam from two directions. He complained that the war had not been won quickly enough because gradual escalation had not forced the north to capitulate. He also claimed that U.S. preoccupation with the war had diverted attention from the more important foreign policy goals of managing the direct relationship between the United States and the Soviet Union.

Election of 1968. The Vietnam War played a significant role in Nixon's successful 1968 presidential campaign against Democrat Hubert H. Humphrey and independent candidate George C. Wallace. During the campaign Nixon assailed the Johnson administration for letting the war grind on indefinitely without a clear victory for South Vietnam and the United States. He agreed to a reporter's characterization that he had a "secret plan" to end the fighting, but said that he would not reveal its contents in order not to jeopardize the negotiations that were going on in Paris. Privately, Nixon's campaign tried to thwart Humphrey's opportunity to capitalize on progress at the bargaining table by secretly sabotaging the negotiations. Nixon's representatives, most prominently Anna Chennault, persuaded South Vietnamese President Nguyen Van Thieu to withhold his support for ongoing negotiations until the very last minute before the U.S. election, in the expectation that a Nixon presidency would prove more supportive of the south than a Humphrey administration.

After his inauguration as president, Nixon tried to make the war seem less important to Americans. "I'm not going to end up like Lyndon Johnson," he promised his chief of staff. "Holed up in the White House, afraid to show my face on the street. I'm going to end that war fast." His strategy for doing so involved pressing forward with Vietnamization, a policy developed at the end of the Johnson administration of turning the ground fighting over to the South Vietnamese. In the summer of 1969 Nixon announced a gradual reduction in the number of U.S. ground troops, promising to lower the level by 25,000 by the end of the year. He also announced a new policy for the United States to follow toward Vietnam-style conflicts after the Vietnam War ended. Quickly characterized by journalists as the Nixon Doctrine, this formula promised U.S. equipment, munitions, and training, but not troops or pilots, to governments threatened by domestic communist insurrections. At the same time Nixon expanded the air war. In spring of 1969 he acceded to the perennial requests from the Joint Chiefs of Staff (JCS) for bombing of Cambodia to stop infiltration along the Ho Chi Minh Trail. Until the middle of 1970, B-52s flew more than 3,600 sorties and dropped more than 100,000 tons of explosives over Cambodia. The air raids were kept secret.

Cambodian Incursion. The gradual reduction in the number of U.S. ground forces temporarily calmed public demands for a speedy end to the war, but there were still huge antiwar demonstrations in Washington in the fall of 1969. Nixon authorized White House aides to infiltrate antiwar groups and disrupt their activities. In March 1970 Nixon announced that another 150,000 soldiers would return home by the end of the year. But the antiwar movement revived in the spring after Nixon ordered the invasion of Cambodia. He did so to demonstrate continued U.S. support for the South Vietnamese as the withdrawal of ground forces went forward. The invasion produced little of military value other than buying some additional time for Vietnamization. It signally failed to find the headquarters of the North Vietnamese operations as promised by Nixon and the generals planning the operation, and it ignited some of the most intensive antiwar demonstrations of the Vietnam era. Hundreds of college campuses were shut down by student strikes after National Guard troops shot dead four demonstrators at Kent State University in Ohio. More than 100,000 young people spontaneously converged on Washington to protest the war. One morning before dawn at the Lincoln Memorial Nixon met with a group of them to explain his policies. He persuaded few, yet came away from the encounter convinced that the future success of his presidency depended on ending the war before the 1972 election. The publication of the Pentagon Papers by the *New York Times* in June 1971 reinforced Nixon's belief that public discussion of Vietnam could threaten his chances for reelection in 1972. Immediately after the publication of the Pentagon Papers, White House officials created the "plumbers" unit of secret operatives who would plug leaks of government documents.

Meanwhile the Paris peace talks continued along two tracks. Publicly, Ambassador David Bruce met weekly with counterparts from the Democratic Republic of Vietnam (DRV) and the National Liberation Front (NLF). However, the more significant work at Paris occurred in secret meetings, begun in August 1969, between Henry Kissinger, Nixon's national security adviser, and two negotiators from North Vietnam, Xuan Thuy and Le Duc Tho. These talks made little progress for over two years because the United States refused to end its support for the government of President Thieu or to promise to remove all of its troops. The North Vietnamese, for their part, refused the U.S. demand to acknowledge that South Vietnam was a separate country and that they had troops fighting there. In 1971 Nixon and Kissinger adopted a strategy of threatening the North with more ferocious bombing, while at the same time demanding that the South make greater concessions. By the beginning of 1972 Nixon told Kissinger that he felt "terrible pressure" to end the war before the presidential election.

The Easter Offensive. Vietnam faded from public view at the beginning of 1972, overshadowed by Nixon's dramatic trip to the People's Republic of China in February. In March, however, 120,000 North Vietnamese troops launched the full-scale Easter Offensive invasion of the south. They encountered little resistance as they approached to within 100 kilometers (60 miles) of Saigon. Only 6,000 of the 95,000 remaining U.S. troops were combat soldiers, so ARVN forces faced the North Vietnamese on their own. The military situation deteriorated until 8 May, when Nixon ordered the largest U.S. escalation of the war since 1968. "Those bastards are going to be bombed like they've never been bombed before," he said. In Operation LINEBACKER, B-52s bombed targets in Hanoi and U.S. Navy planes mined Haiphong harbor. Antiwar politicians castigated Nixon, but opposition from the general public was far less than two years previously, upon the invasion of Cambodia.

Peace talks finally moved forward in August 1972. Kissinger told North Vietnamese representative Le Duc Tho that public opinion polls put Nixon 30 percentage points ahead of Sen. George McGovern, the Democratic nominee who campaigned as an ardent opponent of continued U.S. involvement in the war. Kissinger explained that the DRV would receive the best possible offer from the Americans if they reached an agreement before the fall election. In October the two sides developed the outline of a settlement. The United States would remove its remaining troops within sixty days of a cease-fire and the North would return U.S. and South Vietnamese prisoners of war. The government of President Thieu would remain in place, but it would make a good faith effort to create a coalition with other factions, including the NLF. The United States would limit its military aid to Thieu to training and the replacement of expended munitions. The DRV would keep forces in the south, but not increase the numbers. On 26 October, two weeks before the election, Kissinger announced that "peace is at hand."

The announcement clinched Nixon's victory, but it did not bring an end to the war. President Thieu felt betrayed and refused to go along with the agreement before the election, just as he had done in 1968. Over the next two months, Nixon and Kissinger cajoled and threatened South Vietnamese leaders to drop their objections. Kissinger dispatched his deputy, Gen. Alexander Haig, to Saigon with word that Nixon would "go ahead [and sign the agreements] regardless of anything" Thieu did. If Thieu continued to resist, the U.S. would abandon him. Should the South Vietnamese government acquiesce, however, Washington promised increased military aid, including the resumption of direct U.S. involvement in the event of a breakdown of the cease-fire. In December Nixon showed what kind of military actions he had in mind. He ordered massive B-52 bombings of North Vietnam in Operation LINEBACKER II. For twelve days, beginning on December 22 U.S. planes dropped 36,000 tons of explosives over the North, more bombs than in the period from 1969 to 1971.

Peace accords. In early January 1973, the South Vietnamese government announced that it had dropped its objections to the October formula and North Vietnam offered to return to the bar-

gaining table at Paris. Nixon ordered the cessation of LINEBACKER II and Kissinger and Le Duc Tho made a few minor changes to their earlier agreement. On 27 January they signed the Paris accords, bringing a cease-fire to Vietnam and an end to direct U.S. military involvement.

Initially the Paris accords drew praise for Nixon. In retrospect, however, the achievements were illusory. The peace Nixon promised in 1968 was long in coming and it differed little from what the DRV was willing to offer the Johnson administration. The four years from 1969 to 1972 saw some of the heaviest fight of the war. An additional 20,553 U.S. soldiers lost their lives. Approximately 107,000 ARVN troops and another 500,000 North Vietnamese and Viet Cong fighters also lost their lives. The number of civilian casualties will never be known, but most estimates place the dead at about one million for the period. The cease-fire lasted barely two years, and South Vietnam was conquered in April 1975.

Nixon later claimed that congressional interference, the passage of the War Powers Resolution in

THE PRESIDENT'S MEN. Left to right: Richard M. Helms, Henry Kissinger, William P. Rogers, Nixon, Melvin R. Laird, Thomas H. Moorer, Alexander M. Haig. *Richard Nixon Library*

November 1973 two weeks after he fired Archibald Cox (the special prosecutor investigating Watergate) in the so-called "Saturday Night Massacre," and his own preoccupation with defending himself against impeachment, prevented him and his successor, Gerald R. Ford, from providing the military aid to South Vietnam promised at the time of the Paris Accords. That assertion cannot be tested, but it is almost undoubtedly incorrect. Heartily sick of the war, the American public would not have tolerated a resumption of U.S. participation in the fighting, especially if it resulted in additional casualties or prisoners of war, even if Watergate had never occurred.

BIBLIOGRAPHY

AMBROSE, STEPHEN E. *Nixon.* 3 vols. 1986, 1989, 1991.

KUTLER, STANLEY I. *The Wars of Watergate.* 1990.

NIXON, RICHARD M. *In the Arena.* 1990.

NGUYEN TIEN HUNG and JERROLD SCHECTER. *The Palace File.* 1986.

SMALL, MELVIN. *Johnson, Nixon and the Doves.* 1988.

SZULC, TAD. *The Illusion of Peace: Foreign Policy in the Nixon Years.* 1978.

ROBERT D. SCHULZINGER

FREDERICK NOLTING. At right, entertaining Ngo Dinh Diem at the U.S. embassy in Saigon, 1962. *National Archives*

Nolting, Frederick E.

(1911–1989), U.S. ambassador to South Vietnam, 1961–1963. Frederick "Fritz" Nolting was a North Atlantic Treaty Organization (NATO) diplomat with no experience in Asia when President Kennedy sent him to Saigon. Nolting believed that President Diem's anticommunist stance made him worthy of unqualified U.S. support despite his repressive rule. Diem promised democratic reforms in exchange for more U.S. advisers, whose numbers increased from 2,000 to 16,000 during Nolting's tenure. The reforms never materialized, but Nolting nevertheless continued to praise Diem. He chided critics of the regime for looking at "the hole in the donut." Nolting became "more Diem's envoy to the United States than vice versa," according to journalist David Halberstam. When Nolting left South Vietnam in August 1963, Diem sent troops on bloody raids against Buddhist temples only days after assuring Nolting he would respect Buddhist rights. *Time* magazine accused Diem of "flagrant abrogation of his solemn last word to this fine man who had staked his career on the regime's defense." Yet Nolting's devotion to Diem never wavered, and he left government service in disgust over the U.S.-approved coup that killed Diem in November 1963. Nolting's memoirs praised Diem as "an honest and dedicated man" who was "very much concerned with the welfare of his people," and berated Kennedy administration officials for "disgraceful" connivance in his murder.

BIBLIOGRAPHY

NEWMAN, JOHN M. *JFK and Vietnam: Deception, Intrigue, and the Struggle for Power.* 1992.

NOLTING, FREDERICK E., JR. *From Trust to Tragedy: The Political Memoirs of Frederick Nolting, Kennedy's Ambassador to Diem's Vietnam.* 1988.

GLEN GENDZEL

Normalization.

After expending 58,000 lives and $150 billion dollars in Vietnam, the United States spurned the Democratic Republic of Vietnam's (DRV's) request for normal relations in 1975. Outrage over the DRV's violations of the Paris agreements and questions about the 2,238 Americans missing in action (MIA) left the U.S. in no mood to fulfill President Nixon's secret promise of $3.25 billion in postwar reconstruction aid. Instead, President Ford demanded a full accounting of MIAs, vetoed Vietnam's entry into the United Nations (UN) and imposed a trade embargo. In 1978, President Carter allowed Vietnam to join the UN after gaining some new MIA information, and Vietnam dropped demands for reparations in 1979. But the American public's sympathy for families of MIAs and for Vietnamese refugees kept pressure on the U.S. government to delay normalization of relations between the two nations. Official hostility intensified when the United States renewed ties with the People's Republic of China while the DRV joined the Soviet trade bloc and invited the Soviet Union to establish military bases in Vietnam. All hopes for normalization disappeared when the DRV invaded Cambodia in 1979.

In the 1980s, the Reagan administration adamantly refused to normalize relations as long as the DRV occupied Cambodia and withheld MIA information. Under the U.S. trade embargo, the DRV became one of the world's poorest countries while the Soviet military presence grew. The DRV sporadically returned remains of dead Americans and permitted joint U.S.-DRV investigation of wartime crash sites. President Reagan sent Gen. John Vessey to Hanoi as official MIA liaison in 1987, but polls still showed that only 37 percent of Americans favored normalization.

The United States agreed to permit private charitable donations to Vietnam, and in response the DRV loosened emigration restrictions in 1988. The trade embargo continued, however, and when Soviet aid ended in 1989–1990, the DRV's already weak economy collapsed. In desperation the DRV withdrew its troops from Cambodia and began high-level talks with the U.S. government.

In April 1991, the Bush administration announced that the United States would move toward lifting the trade embargo if the DRV complied with the U.N. peace plan for Cambodia and provided "the fullest possible accounting" of MIAs. Progress toward normalization continued slowly and delicately despite renewed allegations that Vietnam retained American prisoners after the war. President Bush promised to "run down every single lead" on MIAs, and as Vietnamese cooperation improved, he allowed sales of food and medicine and permitted United States companies to sign contracts and open offices in Vietnam in 1992. President-elect Bill Clinton vowed to deny normalization if the DRV withheld MIA information, and despite expanding investments in Vietnam by Japanese and European companies, the U.S. trade embargo remained in place.

On 3 February 1994, President Clinton ended the nineteen-year U.S. trade embargo against the DRV, citing satisfactory Vietnamese cooperation in locating MIAs. Vietnam veterans groups protested the decision, which nonetheless had the backing of retired general William C. Westmoreland and prominent veterans in Congress. Not among them was Sen. Bob Dole (R-Kans.), who called lifting the embargo "the wrong decision at the wrong time for the wrong reason." On 28 January 1995, the United States and the DRV agreed to exchange diplomats and open liaison offices in each other's capitals, another step toward normalization, while reaching new accords that ended wartime disputes over frozen assets and seized property. U.S. investors scrambled to open businesses in the DRV, but twenty years after the war's end, total U.S. commitments totaled only $270 million out of $10 billion in foreign capital invested in Vietnam. The United States formally recognized Vietnam on 11 July 1995.

BIBLIOGRAPHY

APPLE, R.W., JR., and FREDERICK Z. BROWN. *Second Chance: The United States and Indochina in the 1990s.* 1989.

COOPER, MATTHEW. "Give Trade a Chance." *U.S. News & World Report,* 14 February 1994.

ENGARDIO, PETE. "Champing at the Bit in Vietnam." *Business Week,* 26 July 1993.

JEHL, DOUGLAS. "Clinton Drops 19-Year Ban on U.S. Trade with Vietnam." *New York Times,* 4 February 1994.

LAKE, TONY. "Dealing with Hanoi: What Washington Can Do." *Indochina Issues* (August 1984).

LEBOUTILLIER, JOHN. *Vietnam Now: A Case for Normalizing Relations with Hanoi.* 1989.

PIKE, DOUGLAS. "American-Vietnam Relations." *Parameters* (Autumn 1984).

RICHBURG, KEITH. "Back to Vietnam." *Foreign Affairs* (Fall 1991).

GLEN GENDZEL

North Vietnam. *See* Vietnam, Democratic Republic of (DRV).

North Vietnamese Army (NVA). *See* People's Army of Vietnam (PAVN).

Nuclear Weapons. The United States was the only nuclear-capable country directly engaged in the Vietnam War, and although it never deployed nuclear weapons in the conflict, it did consider using them on several occasions. In 1954, U.S. Air Force Chief of Staff Nathan Twining and chairman of the Joint Chiefs of Staff Adm. Arthur Radford proposed dropping three tactical nuclear bombs to assist the French forces at Dien Bien Phu. Vice President Richard Nixon supported this idea, but President Dwight D. Eisenhower and U.S. Army Chief of Staff Matthew Ridgeway opposed it; Secretary of State Allen Dulles appeared ambivalent. Nevertheless, the administration did allow Col. Edward Lansdale to spread a rumor in Indochina of possible U.S. nuclear involvement.

In the mid 1960s, Walt Rostow, President Johnson's national security adviser, reportedly considered the possible utilization of nuclear weapons in the Vietnam War. In a private interview in 1965, Secretary of Defense Robert McNamara stated that the United States had never ruled out the use of tactical nuclear weapons in Vietnam, although at that time such use would not serve U.S. interests. In 1968, while planning the defense of besieged Khe Sanh, Gen. William Westmoreland began preparations for nuclear deployment, but congressional apprehension after a press leak in early February pressured Gen. Earl Wheeler to halt any such plans. In the 1968 meeting of the "wise men," McGeorge Bundy stated that using nuclear weapons was "unthinkable." President Nixon reportedly considered the use of nuclear weapons several times.

BIBLIOGRAPHY

GOOLD-ADAMS, RICHARD. *John Foster Dulles: A Reappraisal.* 1962.

PISOR, ROBERT. *The End of the Line: The Siege of Khe Sanh.* 1982.

SHAWCROSS, WILLIAM *Sideshow: Kissinger, Nixon, and the Destruction of Cambodia.* 1979.

WILLIAMS, WILLIAM APPLEMAN, et al., eds. *America in Vietnam: A Documentary History.* 1985.

YOUNG, MARILYN B. *The Vietnam Wars.* 1991.

ELLEN BAKER

Nurses. *See* Women, U.S. Military: Nurses.

O

O'Daniel, John W. (1894–1975), lieutenant general, U.S. Army; chief of U.S. Military Assistance Advisory Group-Indochina (MAAG–I), 1954–1956. A veteran of three wars, Lt. Gen. John "Iron Mike" O'Daniel had trained South Korea's army and was U.S. Army commander in the Pacific when President Eisenhower sent him to Vietnam to assess French military needs in 1953. A year later, he returned to head the first U.S. MAAG in Indochina. O'Daniel expressed confidence that first the French and then President Diem would win against the communists. He trained South Vietnam's military to repel a Korea-style conventional invasion, but not to counter a guerrilla war. O'Daniel departed Vietnam in October 1955, retired, and cofounded the American Friends of Vietnam.

BIBLIOGRAPHY

O'DANIEL, JOHN W. *The Nation that Refused to Starve.* 1960.
SPECTOR, RONALD H. *The United States Army in Vietnam, Advice and Support: The Early Years, 1941–1960.* 1983.
U.S. DEPARTMENT OF STATE. Part 1 of *Indochina.* Vol. 13 of *Foreign Relations in the United States, 1952–1954.* 1982.
U.S. DEPARTMENT OF STATE. *Vietnam.* Vol 1 of *Foreign Relations in the United States, 1955–1957.* 1985.

GLEN GENDZEL

Office of Strategic Services. Established in 1942, the Office of Strategic Services (OSS) was the precursor to the Central Intelligence Agency (CIA). Headed by William J. Donovan, the organization collected intelligence, disseminated propaganda, subverted foreign governments, conducted paramilitary operations, and supported resistance groups.

Toward the end of World War II, the OSS involved itself in Indochina, relying on Viet Minh networks for intelligence and help in rescuing downed airmen. The OSS also supported Ho Chi Minh against the Japanese in early 1945 by parachuting an advisory team into northern Vietnam. Supplying the Viet Minh with rifles, mortars, and ammunition, the team trained them to use the weapons and taught them how to train other partisans. Hoping to enlist the United States against the reestablishment of French rule over Vietnam, Ho Chi Minh received OSS officers warmly and earned an official appointment as OSS Agent 19. Many OSS officers favored self-rule for the Vietnamese, including Maj. Archimedes Patti, who helped Ho draft his declaration of independence. The Truman administration, however, was unsympathetic to this idea and supported the French and British effort to crush an independence movement in Saigon in September 1945. An

375

WILLIAM J. DONOVAN. *National Archives*

OSS team found itself caught in the struggle, and its leader, Lt. Col. A. Peter Dewey, became the first American casualty in Vietnam when he was killed in an ambush. While the OSS experience in Vietnam represented the beginning of U.S. involvement in Indochina, Donovan and his organization lacked the resources to promote postwar U.S. influence in the region successfully.

BIBLIOGRAPHY

KARNOW, STANLEY. *Vietnam: A History.* 1991.
SMITH, BRADLEY F. *The Shadow Warriors: O.S.S. and the Origins of the C.I.A.* 1983.

PAUL M. TAILLON

ORDER OF BATTLE. [*This entry includes three articles:*

Army of the Republic of Vietnam (ARVN)
People's Army of Vietnam (PAVN) and People's Liberation Armed Force (PLAF)
U.S. Military.]

Army of the Republic of Vietnam (ARVN)

[As with the order of battle for communist forces, data for ARVN commanders' names, ranks, and dates of service are often incomplete or inconclusive. The following lists give the date an officer was officially appointed to command a unit, or, whenever possible, the date he actually assumed command; *c.* indicates that the officer in question held the position at the date noted. Ranks given are the highest known rank attained by the officer while in command of a specific entity. Province names are those in official RVN use during the war; see map at *Vietnam, Republic of.*]

The origins of the Army of the Republic of Vietnam (ARVN) can be traced to the Vietnamese colonial units organized by the French to fight the Viet Minh. After the French defeat, a number of these units were turned over to the noncommunist State of Vietnam. When incorporated into the armed forces of the new state, these units usually retained the designations of their French antecedents to retain a link with their pasts. With the creation of the Republic of Vietnam on 26 October 1955, the ARVN went through a number of reorganizations. The result is a complex organizational history, in which unit designations change repeatedly. Light divisions, created on 1 August 1955, were redesignated four months later on 1 November and abolished during the first half of 1959. Numerous units were created, converted, or merged. The following article provides an overview of the complex thirty-year history of the ARVN's corps and divisions.

The ARVN was the largest combat component of the Republic of Vietnam Armed Forces (RVNAF). At its height, it consisted of eleven regular infantry divisions, each assigned to one of the four corps commands, or Corps Tactical Zones (CTZ), that divided the country. The airborne and marine divisions, under semi-independent command, served as South Vietnam's general reserve at the dis-

ARVN DIVISIONS, DECEMBER 1972. The map shows ARVN divisional headquarters as located after the Easter Offensive. Note that the Airborne and Marine divisions, though headquartered in Saigon, were operating in and around Quang Tri City, which was retaken in the closing stages of the offensive. (Map adapted from William E. Le Gro, *Vietnam from Cease-Fire to Capitulation.* Center of Military History, 1981.)

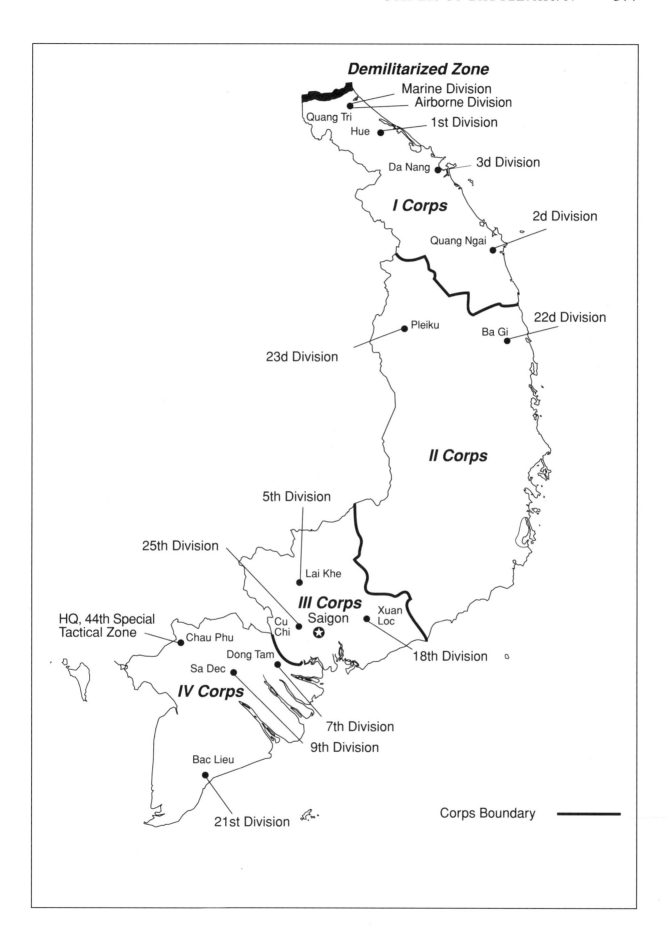

cretion of the president. Armor, artillery, and ranger units, nominally part of separate commands, were allocated to the various corps and operated under the control of corps commanders. Also under the control of corps commanders were local militia units, most importantly the Regional Forces and Popular Forces (RF/PF). A number of semi-autonomous Special Tactical Zones (STZ) existed within the CTZs, created to concentrate military resources in key areas.

Corps Commands

I Corps. Organized 1 June 1957, I Corps, directly south of the DMZ, consisted of the five northern provinces of the Republic of Vietnam: Quang Tri, Thua Thien, Quang Nam, Quang Tin, and Quang Ngai (transferred from II Corps in November 1963). The semiautonomous Quang Da Special Zone coordinated the security of the area around Da Nang.

Commanding Officers, I Corps

Lt. Gen. Tran Van Don	15 October 1957
Maj. Gen. Le Van Nghiem	7 December 1962
Maj. Gen. Do Cao Tri	21 August 1963
Lt. Gen. Nguyen Khanh	11 December 1963
Maj. Gen. Ton That Xung	30 January 1964
Lt. Gen. Nguyen Chanh Thi	14 November 1964
Maj. Gen. Nguyen Van Chuan	14 March 1966
Lt. Gen. Ton That Dinh	9 April 1966
Maj. Gen. Huynh Van Cao	15 May 1966
Gen. Tran Thanh Phong★	20 May 1966
Lt. Gen. Hoang Xuan Lam	30 May 1966
Lt. Gen. Ngo Quang Truong	3 May 1972 to 30 April 1975

★Acting commander

II Corps. Organized 1 October 1957, II Corps, the largest in geographical area of all the corps, encompassed much of the Central Highlands as well as South Vietnam's narrow coastal plain. It consisted of the following provinces: Kontum, Binh Dinh, Pleiku, Phu Bon, Phu Yen, Darlac, Khanh Hoa, Quang Duc, Tuyen Duc, Ninh Thuan, Lam Dong, and Binh Thuan. The semiautonomous 24th Special Tactical Zone, to which the independent 42d Regiment was assigned, covered areas of heavy communist infiltration along the Laotian border. Established July 1966 and located in Kontum province in the Central Highlands, the 24th STZ was abolished 30 April 1970.

During the 1975 Ho Chi Minh Campaign, the fall of Ban Me Thuot on 12 March impelled President Nguyen Van Thieu to abandon I and II Corps. The disastrous withdrawal of II Corps forces down Route 7B from Pleiku to Tuy Hoa, mishandled by corps commander Maj. Gen. Pham Van Phu, marked the beginning of the end for the Republic of Vietnam.

Commanding Officers, II Corps

Maj. Gen. Tran Ngoc Tam	1 October 1957
Maj. Gen. Ton That Dinh	13 August 1958
Lt. Gen. Nguyen Khanh	20 December 1962
Lt. Gen. Do Cao Tri	12 December 1963
Maj. Gen. Nguyen Huu Co	15 September 1964
Lt. Gen. Vinh Loc	25 June 1965
Lt. Gen. Lu Lan	28 February 1968
Lt. Gen. Ngo Dzu	28 August 1970
Maj. Gen. Nguyen Van Toan	10 May 1972
Maj. Gen. Pham Van Phu	30 October 1974 to 1 April 1975

III Corps. Provisionally organized 1 March 1959 and permanently organized 20 May 1960, III Corps consisted of the following provinces: Phuoc Long, Long Khanh, Binh Tuy, Binh Long, Binh Duong, Bien Hoa, Phuoc Tuy, Tay Ninh, Hau Nghia, and Long An. Saigon, with neighboring Gia Dinh province, formed the semiautonomous Capital Military District (CMD), which also had a political dimension: it was intended as much to protect Saigon from coup attempts by ambitious corps commanders as from attack by communist forces. The Rung Sat Special Zone, an area of intense Viet Cong activity at the mouth of the Dong Nai River, protected the river approaches to Saigon.

Commanding Officers, III Corps

Lt. Gen. Thai Quang Hoang	1 March 1959
Lt. Gen. Nguyen Ngoc Le	11 October 1959
Maj. Gen. Le Van Nghiem	5 May 1960
Maj. Gen. Ton That Dinh	7 December 1962
Lt. Gen. Tran Thien Khiem	5 January 1964
Maj. Gen. Lam Van Phat	2 February 1964
Lt. Col. Tran Ngoc Tam	4 April 1964
Maj. Gen. Cao Van Vien	12 October 1964
Maj. Gen. Nguyen Bac Tri	11 October 1965
Lt. Gen. Le Nguyen Khang	9 June 1966
Lt. Gen. Do Cao Tri★	5 August 1968
Lt. Gen. Nguyen Van Minh	23 February 1971
Lt. Gen. Pham Quoc Thuan	29 October 1973
Lt. Gen. Du Quoc Dong	30 October 1974
Lt. Gen. Nguyen Van Toan	January 1975 to 25 April 1975

★Killed in a helicopter crash 23 February 1971.

IV Corps. Organized 1 January 1963, IV Corps, which encompassed the Mekong Delta, contained more than half of both the nation's population and cultivated land. It consisted of the following provinces: Go Cong, Kien Tuong, Dinh Tuong, Kien Hoa, Kien Phong, Sa Dec, Vinh Long, Vinh Binh, Chau Doc, An Giang, Phong Dinh, Ba Xuyen, Kien Giang, Chuong Thien, Bac Lieu, and An Xuyen. The semiautonomous 44th Special Tactical Zone coordinated ARVN military operations and security in the northwestern delta along the Cambodian border until late 1973. After a string of tactical successes that eliminated communist main-force units in the area, the STZ was abolished, its Ranger battalions deactivated, and their personnel sent to battalions further north. However, since the units had been recruited from the delta area, many personnel deserted rather than leave their home region.

Commanding Officers, IV Corps

Maj. Gen. Huynh Van Cao★	1 January 1963
Maj. Gen. Nguyen Huu Co	4 November 1963
Maj. Gen. Duong Van Duc★★	4 March 1964
Maj. Gen. Nguyen Van Thieu	15 September 1964
Lt. Col. Dang Van Quang	20 January 1965
Maj. Gen. Nguyen Van Manh	23 November 1966
Lt. Gen. Nguyen Duc Thang	29 February 1968
Lt. Gen. Nguyen Viet Thanh★★★	1 July 1968
Maj. Gen. Ngo Dzu	1 May 1970
Lt. Gen. Ngo Quang Truong	21 August 1970
Maj. Gen. Nguyen Vinh Nghi	4 May 1972
Maj. Gen. Nguyen Khoa Nam	30 October 1974

★Relieved in aftermath of 1 November 1963 coup.
★★Attempted unsuccessful coup 13 September 1964.
★★★Killed in a helicopter crash 23 February 1971.

Divisions. The ARVN's divisions tended to develop local attachments, as they were usually based in the same locales for years, even decades, and often were formed with units and personnel drawn from the area around their base. Military dependents of division personnel naturally lived in the vicinity as well. Such ties contributed to the general immobility and inertia of the ARVN, and had a significant impact on unit performance. For example, during the 1975 Ho Chi Minh Campaign, the 1st, 2d, and 3d divisions all collapsed as I Corps was overrun, partly because soldiers deserted in droves to protect their families. On the other hand, the 18th Division fought tenaciously in defense of its home base, Xuan Loc.

1st Division. Organized 1 January 1955, the 1st Division had its origins in the 21st Mobile Group, established by the French 1 September 1953 and raised in Thua Thien and Quang Tri provinces. The 21st Mobile Group provided the nucleus for the 21st Infantry Division, redesignated on 1 August 1955 as the 21st Field Division. Renumbered on 1 November 1955 as the 1st Field Division, the unit became the 1st Infantry Division in January 1959.

Considered to be one of the best units in the ARVN, the 1st Division conducted operations in Quang Tri, Thua Thien, Quang Nam, and Quang Ngai provinces throughout the war. The 1st also took part in Operation LAM SON 719, the South Vietnamese invasion of Laos in late January–March 1971. The division, headquartered at or near Hue throughout its history, supported the Buddhist-led Struggle Movement in Hue during the 1966 uprisings in I Corps. During the 1975 Ho Chi Minh Campaign, the 1st Division disintegrated during the fighting to cover the evacuation of Hue. The remnants of the division, two officers and forty men, were evacuated to Ba Ria, Phuoc Tuy province, captured 27 March.

Commanding Officers, 1st Division

Lt. Col. Le Van Nghiem★	1 January 1955
Gen. Do Cao Tri	c. 1963
Gen. Nguyen Chanh Thi	c. 1964
Maj. Gen. Nguyen Van Chuan	c. 1965 to 1966
Gen. Pham Xuan Nhuan	12 March 1966
Lt. Gen. Ngo Quang Truong	June 1966
Maj. Gen. Pham Van Phu	21 August 1970
Brig. Gen. Le Van Than	c. 1973
Maj. Gen. Nguyen Van Diem	31 October 1974 to 30 April 1975

★Information on units commanders between 1955 and 1963 is unavailable.

2d Division. Organized 1 February 1955, the 2d Division was created from the 32d Mobile Group, established by the French 3 November 1953 in the Red River Delta of North Vietnam. After the 1954 Geneva agreements, the group was transported to Da Nang from Haiphong and reorganized as the 32d Infantry Division; the commander of the 32d Mobile Group became the new division's first commander. The unit was redesignated on 1 August 1955 as the 32d Field Division. Renumbered on 1 November 1955 as the 2d Field Division, the unit became the 2d Infantry Division in January 1959.

The 2d Division conducted operations in Quang Nam, Quang Tin, and Quang Ngai provinces throughout the war. First headquartered at Da Nang, the 2d Division alternated its headquarters between Da Nang and Quang Ngai before settling at Quang Ngai in May 1965. In early 1972, the 2d shifted its headquarters to the former U.S. base camp at Chu Lai, Quang Tin province. During the 1975 Ho Chi Minh Campaign, the 2d held Tam Ky until 24 March. The division was almost destroyed in the fighting, and its remnants were withdrawn to Da Nang and evacuated by sea. Reconstituted at Ham Tan, the 2d Division held Phan Rang until 16 April 1975, when the city and its defenders were overrun.

Commanding Officers, 2d Division

Col. Ton That Dinh	1 January 1955
Lt. Col. Dang Van Son	22 November 1956
Lt. Col. Le Quang Trong	14 June 1957
Col. Duong Ngoc Lam	23 August 1958
Col. Lam Van Phat	8 June 1961
Col. Truong Van Chuong	18 June 1963
Brig. Gen. Ton That Xung	6 December 1963
Brig. Gen. Ngo Dzu	30 January 1964
Col. Nguyen Thanh Sang	29 July 1964
Maj. Gen. Hoang Xuan Lam★	15 October 1964
Maj. Gen. Nguyen Van Toan	10 January 1967
Brig. Gen. Pham Hoa Hiep	22 January 1972
Brig. Gen. Tran Van Nhut	27 August 1972 to 30 April 1975

★Concurrently commander of I Corps from 30 May 1966.

3d Division. Organized 1 October 1971, the 3d Division was established to make up for the withdrawal of U.S. forces from the heavily contested northern area of I Corps along the DMZ. The new division was formed from the newly raised 56th and 57th regiments and from the 2d Regiment, transferred from the 1st Division. First headquartered at Ai Tu, near Quang Tri City, the division had barely become fully operational when it was struck by the initial thrusts of the 1972 Easter Offensive. The division disintegrated, allowing Quang Tri to be overrun by communist forces. Reconstituted at Da Nang, the 3d operated in Quang Nam and Quang Tin provinces for the remainder of the war, with the defense of Da Nang as its primary responsibility. During the 1975 Ho Chi Minh Campaign, the bulk of the division was overrun and Da Nang captured on 30 March 1975.

Commanding Officers, 3d Division

Brig. Gen. Vu Van Giai★	1 October 1971
Maj. Gen. Nguyen Duy Hinh	9 June 1972 to 30 April 1975

★Relieved of command 3 May 1972.

5th Division. Organized 1 February 1955, the division was formed from Nung veterans of French service against the Viet Minh transported south after the 1954 Geneva accords. Many Nung, members of an ethnically Chinese minority group, had fled China to escape the 1948 communist takeover. The unit, at first exclusively made up of Nung, was purposefully diluted with ethnic Vietnamese by President Ngo Dinh Diem. However, the division retained a number of Nung personnel throughout the war.

Originally designated the 6th Infantry Division, the unit was redesignated on 1 August 1955 as the 6th Field Division and on 1 September 1955 was renumbered as the 41st Field Division. Renumbered on 1 November 1955 as the 3d Field Division, the unit became the 5th Infantry Division in January 1959.

First headquartered at Song Mao in Binh Thuan province, the 5th was moved to Bien Hoa in May 1961. Troops of the division, directed by Col. Nguyen Van Thieu, participated in the 1 November 1963 coup that overthrew President Ngo Dinh Diem. Moved to Binh Duong province in July 1964, the 5th was first headquartered at Phu Loi and moved to Lai Khe in February 1970. The 5th, which operated in the northern provinces of III Corps, participated in cross-border operations into Cambodia in 1970 and 1971. During the 1972 Easter Offensive, the 5th successfully held the city of An Loc, besieged for more than two months. During the 1975 Ho Chi Minh Campaign, the 5th Division formed part of Saigon's defenses north of the city near Ben Cat on Route 13 until the city fell on 30 April.

Commanding Officers, 5th Division

Col. Vong A Sang	1 March 1955
Col. Pham Van Dong	25 October 1956
Lt. Col. Nguyen Quang Thong★	18 March 1958
Col. Ton That Xung	16 September 1958
Lt. Col. Dang Van Son	19 November 1958
Col. Nguyen Van Chuan	3 August 1959
Brig. Gen. Tran Ngoc Tam	20 May 1961
Col. Nguyen Duc Thang	16 October 1961

Col. Nguyen Van Thieu	20 December 1962
Brig. Gen. Dang Thanh Liem	2 February 1964
Brig. Gen. Cao Hao Hoa	5 June 1964
Brig. Gen. Tran Thanh Phong	21 October 1964
Maj. Gen. Pham Quoc Thuan	19 July 1965
Maj. Gen. Nguyen Van Hieu	15 August 1969
Brig. Gen. Le Van Hung	14 June 1971
Brig. Gen. Tran Quoc Lich	4 September 1972
Col. Le Nguyen Vy	7 November 1973 to 30 April 1975

*Acting commander

7th Division. Organized 1 January 1955, the 7th Division traced its origins back to the 7th Mobile Group, raised by the French in the Red River Delta of North Vietnam. The unit was later redesignated as the 2d and then, on 1 September 1953, as the 31st Mobile Group. After the 1954 Geneva agreements, the group was transported to Da Nang from Haiphong and reorganized 1 January 1955 as the 31st Infantry Division; the commander of the 31st Mobile Group became the new division's first commander. Based initially at Tam Ky, the 31st was moved south during the summer of 1955. On 1 August 1955, it was redesignated as the 31st Field Division. It was redesignated only a few weeks later as the 11th Field Division and redesignated again on 1 November as the 4th Field Division. The 4th established its headquarters at Bien Hoa 11 November 1955. The 4th Field Division fought in early 1956 against the Hoa Hao military forces commanded by Ba Cut (Le Quang Vinh), operating in the Mekong Delta in an area that later became part of Chau Doc province. The 4th was redesignated as the 7th Infantry Division on 1 January 1959. The 7th moved its headquarters from Bien Hoa to My Tho, Dinh Tuong province, 20 May 1961; the 5th Division moved to Bien Hoa at the same time. On 1 September 1969, the division moved to Dong Tam, near My Tho. The former base camp of the 9th U.S. Infantry Division, Dong Tam was an island built by U.S. engineers from earth dredged from the My Tho branch of the Mekong.

The 7th Division conducted operations in the heavily populated provinces of Long An, Go Cong, Kien Tuong, Dinh Tuong, Kien Hoa, Kien Phong, Sa Dec, Vinh Long, Vinh Binh, An Giang, and Phong Dinh throughout the war. The 7th participated in cross-border operations into Cambodia in 1970 and 1971. In June during the 1972 Easter Offensive, the 7th fought in the Cambodian border area known as the Elephant's Foot, north of Moc Hoa, Kien Tuong province. In November, it fought in Kien Phong province. During the 1975 Ho Chi Minh Campaign, the 7th Division, fighting in the northern Mekong Delta, reinforced the defenders of Tan An with a regiment, the 12th Infantry. Tan An, southwest of Saigon in Long An province, formed part of the capital's defenses and held out until the capitulation of the Republic of Vietnam.

Commanding Officers, 7th Division

Lt. Col. Nguyen Huu Co	1 January 1955
Col. Ton That Xung	15 June 1955
Lt. Col. Ngo Dzu	27 April 1957
Col. Tran Thien Khiem	17 March 1958
Col. Huynh Van Cao	30 March 1959
Col. Bui Dinh Dam	22 December 1962
Brig. Gen. Nguyen Huu Co	1 November 1963
Col. Pham Van Dong	5 November 1963
Brig. Gen. Lam Van Phat	2 December 1963
Col. Bui Huu Nhon	2 February 1964
Col. Huynh Van Ton	7 March 1964
Brig. Gen. Nguyen Bao Tri	16 September 1964
Brig. Gen. Nguyen Viet Thanh	9 October 1965
Brig. Gen. Nguyen Thanh Hoang	3 July 1968
Maj. Gen. Nguyen Khoa Nam	16 January 1970
Gen. Tran Van Hai	30 October 1974 to 30 April 1975

9th Division. Organized 1 January 1962, the 9th Division was created, along with the 25th Division, as part of a program to increase the strength of the ARVN by 30,000 personnel. Its first headquarters were at Phu Thanh, Binh Dinh province, near Qui Nhon. The 25th operated in Binh Dinh, Phu Bon, and Phu Yen provinces until 20 September 1963, when it transferred its headquarters to Sa Dec, in IV Corps. On 5 April 1972, the division moved its headquarters to the former U.S. base at the town of Vinh Long.

The 9th operated in nearly every province of IV Corps, acting as the mobile force for the corps from 1969 on. During the 1963 coup that overthrew President Ngo Dinh Diem, the 9th, controlled by Diem loyalists, was blocked from moving to Diem's aid: one of the conspirators, Col. Nguyen Huu Co, took control of the 7th Division at My Tho and used it to seize the ferries that crossed the Mekong River. The 9th participated in cross-border operations into Cambodia in 1970 and 1971. During the Easter Offensive, the 9th Division detached a regiment, the 15th Infantry, to assist in an abortive attempt in May 1972 to relieve the besieged 5th Division at An Loc. During the 1975 Ho Chi Minh Campaign, the 9th Division fought in the northern Mekong Delta until the capitulation of the Republic of Vietnam.

Commanding Officers, 9th Division

Col. Bui Dzinh★	1 January 1962
Col. Doan Van Quang	7 November 1963
Brig. Gen. Vinh Loc	9 February 1964
Brig. Gen. Lam Quang Thi	29 May 1965
Maj. Gen. Tran Ba Di	3 July 1968
Brig. Gen. Huynh Van Lac	26 October 1973 to 30 April 1975

★Relieved in aftermath of 1 November 1963 coup.

18th Division. Provisionally organized 16 May 1965 and permanently organized August 1965, the 18th Division was formed at Xuan Loc, Long Khanh province, which served as its main headquarters throughout its existence. First designated as the 10th Division, it was redesignated on 1 January 1967 as the 18th because of the inauspicious connotations of the original name: "number 10" in both Vietnamese and American military slang meant "the worst."

The 18th, considered to be perhaps the worst division in the ARVN, generally operated in eastern III Corps throughout the war. During the 1972 Easter Offensive, elements of the 18th Division was moved to Binh Long province and fought at An Loc. During the 1975 Ho Chi Minh Campaign, the 18th Division held Xuan Loc from 17 March to 16 April, enduring repeated assaults as well as some of the heaviest artillery bombardment of the war. The battle proved to be the last stand of the Army of the Republic of Vietnam.

Commanding Officers, 18th Division

Col. Nguyen Van Manh	5 June 1965
Brig. Gen. Lu Lan	20 August 1965
Brig. Gen. Do Ke Giai	16 September 1966
Maj. Gen. Lam Quang Tho	20 August 1969
Brig. Gen. Le Minh Dao	4 April 1972 to 30 April 1975

21st Division. Organized 1 June 1959, the 21st Division traced its origins back to the 1st and the 3d Light Divisions. The 1st, formed at Long Xuyen but soon moved to Sa Dec, was redesignated the 11th Light Division on 1 November 1955. The 3d, formed at Thu Dau Mot (later Phu Cuong), was moved shortly afterward to Ben Keo, Tay Ninh, establishing itself in the former headquarters of the Cao Dai armed forces. The unit was also redesignated on 1 November, becoming the 13th Light Division. Both divisions fought against Hoa Hao military forces in the Mekong Delta in 1955 and 1956. The two units were officially combined as the 21st Infantry Division on 1 June 1959. The commander of the 11th was the new division's first commander and the Sa Dec headquarters of the 11th became the 21st Division's main headquarters. The 21st was dispersed throughout southern South Vietnam by late 1960, operating around Tay Ninh, Long An, Kien Tuong and Kien Phong, and Ca Mau in An Xuyen province. The division was later concentrated in IV Corps in the southern Mekong Delta, transferring its headquarters from Sa Dec to Bac Lieu.

The 21st, under Col. Tranh Thien Khiem, helped put down the 11 November 1960 coup attempt against President Ngo Dinh Diem, led by Col. Nguyen Chanh Thi, commander of the Airborne Division. The division fought in the U Minh forest in Kien Giang province in 1970 and 1971. During the 1972 Easter Offensive, much of the division was temporarily moved to Binh Dinh province. The 21st, along with the 25th Division, participated in an abortive attempt in May 1972 to relieve the besieged 5th Division at An Loc. During the 1975 Ho Chi Minh Campaign, the 21st Division fought in the southern Mekong Delta until the capitulation of the Republic of Vietnam.

Commanding Officers, 21st Division

Lt. Col. Nguyen Bao Tri★	1 June 1959
Lt. Col. Tran Thanh Chieu	8 September 1959
Col. Tranh Thien Khiem	2 February 1960
Col. Bui Huu Nhon	December 1962
Col. Cao Hao Hon	November 1963
Brig. Gen. Dang Van Quang	1 June 1964
Col. Nguyen Van Phuoc★★	20 January 1965
Brig. Gen. Nguyen Van Minh	21 March 1965
Maj. Gen. Nguyen Vinh Nghi	13 June 1968
Brig. Gen. Ho Trung Hau	3 May 1972
Brig. Gen. Chuong Dzanh Quay	21 August 1972
Brig. Gen. Le Van Hung	9 June 1973

★Lt. Col. Tri became commander of the 11th Light Division, the predecessor of the 21st Division, on 16 October 1957.
★★Acting commander.

22d Division. Organized 1 April 1959, the 22d Division traced its origins back to the 4th and the 2d Light Divisions. The 2d, formed at Kontum but manned almost entirely by troops from the Mekong

Delta, was redesignated the 12th Light Division 1 November 1955. The troops of the 4th, formed at Ban Me Thuot, originally were overwhelmingly montagnards. The 4th was redesignated the 14th Light Division 1 November. Transferred to Qui Nhon, the 14th fought in early 1956 against the Hoa Hao military forces commanded by Ba Cut (Le Quang Vinh) in the Mekong Delta. Later moved to Kontum, the 14th Light Division was redesignated as the 22d Infantry Division on 1 April 1959; the personnel of the 2d, which was disbanded the day before, were transferred into the new unit.

The 22d was responsible throughout most of the war for the five northern provinces of II Corps (Binh Dinh, Phu Bon, Phu Yen, and Kontum and Pleiku in the Central Highlands). Originally at Kontum, the 22d's headquarters were moved to Ba Gi, Binh Dinh province, in March 1965. During the Easter Offensive, the division, responsible for defending both Kontum and the coast, disintegrated 24 April 1972 at Tan Canh; the 23d Division had to be rushed in to hold the city. Later in 1972, the division, reconstituted in Binh Dinh, reopened coastal highway Route 1. During the 1975 Ho Chi Minh Campaign, the 22d Division held Binh Dinh province until cut off by the collapse of ARVN forces in the Central Highlands at Binh Khe. It broke through to Qui Nhon and was evacuated by sea to Vung Tau. Reconstituted, the 22d held out at Tan An and Ben Luc, southwest of Saigon in Long An province, until the capitulation of South Vietnam.

Commanding Officers, 22d Division

Lt. Col. Tran Thanh Chieu★	1 April 1959
Lt. Col. Nguyen Bao Tri	8 September 1959
Col. Nguyen Thanh Sang	5 November 1963
Brig. Gen. Linh Quang Vien	5 February 1964
Col. Nguyen Van Hieu	7 September 1964
Brig. Gen. Nguyen Xuan Thinh	24 October 1964
Brig. Gen. Nguyen Thanh Sang	1 March 1965
Brig. Gen. Nguyen Van Hieu	28 June 1966
Brig. Gen. Le Ngoc Trien	11 August 1969
Col. Le Dac Dat★★	1 March 1972
Brig. Gen. Phan Dinh Niem	28 April 1972 to 30 April 1975

★Lt. Col. Chieu became commander of the 14th Light Division, the predecessor of the 22d Division, on 28 March 1958.
★★Missing in action, April 1972.

23d Division. Organized 1 April 1959, the 23d Division had its origins in the 5th Light Division, established at Nha Trang and redesignated the 15th Light Division 1 November 1955. From January to May 1956, the 15th fought in the Nguyen Hue campaign launched by President Ngo Dinh Diem to suppress the Hoa Hao and Cao Dai religious armies. The division operated throughout the upper Mekong Delta in the Dong Thap Muoi area (later divided into Kien Tuong and Kien Phong provinces), as well as Tay Ninh and the areas that later became Long An, Hau Nghia, and An Giang provinces. After the campaign, the 15th returned to Nha Trang, but was moved to Duc My, Khanh Hoa province, 14 August 1956. On 1 April 1959, the 15th Light Division became the 23rd Infantry Division. The 23d was moved into the Central Highlands beginning in late 1960, transferring its headquarters to Ban Me Thuot, Darlac province, by June 1961.

The 23d operated throughout central South Vietnam from 1958 to 1969, both in the Central Highlands and along the coast from Quang Ngai to Binh Tuy, although the division's area of responsibility consisted of the seven southern provinces of II Corps (Darlac, Khanh Hoa, Quang Duc, Tuyen Duc, Ninh Thuan, Lam Dong, and Binh Thuan). Part of the 23d participated in cross-border operations into Cambodia in 1970 and 1971. In May 1972 during the Easter Offensive, the 23d, rushed to defend Kontum City after the defending 22d Division crumbled, held the city despite heavy communist artillery bombardment and repeated assaults. In 1975, the 23d attempted to retake the captured town of Ban Me Thuot but failed and was shattered in the attempt. The remnants of the division were evacuated by air to Camh Ranh, 21 March 1975, and then to Long Hai, Phuoc Tuy province, captured 27 March.

Commanding Officers, 23d Division

Lt. Col. Tran Thanh Phong	19 May 1959
Col. Le Quang Trong	17 May 1963
Brig. Gen. Hoang Xuan Lam	14 December 1963
Brig. Gen. Lu Lan	14 October 1964
Brig. Gen. Nguyen Van Manh	20 August 1965
Brig. Gen. Truong Quang An★	24 November 1966
Brig. Gen. Vo Van Canh	9 September 1968
Brig. Gen. Ly Tong Ba	25 January 1972
Brig. Gen. Tran Van Cam	20 October 1972
Brig. Gen. Le Trung Tuong★★	24 November 1973 to 10 March 1975

★Killed in action in a helicopter crash.
★★Slightly wounded on 10 March 1975, Brig. Gen. Tuong had himself evacuated.

25th Division. Organized 1 July 1962, the 25th Division was created, along with the 9th Division, as part of a program to increase the strength of the ARVN by 30,000 personnel. It was formed in Quang Ngai province, with its first headquarters at Thuan Hoa, near Quang Ngai City. The 25th operated in Quang Ngai and Binh Dinh provinces until 28 October 1964, when it was transferred to Cay Diep, Gia Dinh province, near Saigon, and moved again 23 December 1964 to Duc Hoa, Hau Nghia province. On 13 December 1970, the division moved to Cu Chi, the former base camp of the 25th U.S. Infantry Division, also in Hau Nghia.

The 25th operated in the western provinces of III Corps throughout the war. Units of the 25th took part in the cross-border operations into Cambodia that began in April 1970, attacking down Route 1 into the "Parrot's Beak" area and advancing through Svay Rieng as far as Kampong Trabek. Other units of the 25th pushed into Krek and Chup along Route 7. During the Easter Offensive, the 25th, along with the 21st Division, participated in an abortive attempt in May 1972 to relieve the besieged 5th Division at An Loc. During the Ho Chi Minh Campaign, in April 1975 the 25th Division defended Tay Ninh City and Go Dau Ha, both along Route 22 west of Saigon, as part of the capital's defenses until the capitulation of the Republic of Vietnam.

Commanding Officers, 25th Division

Col. Nguyen Van Chuen	July 1962
Col. Lu Lan	28 December 1962
Col. Nguyen Viet Dam	19 March 1964
Brig. Gen. Nguyen Thanh Sang	December 1964
Brig. Gen. Phan Trong Chinh	16 March 1965
Lt. Gen. Nguyen Xuan Thinh	10 January 1968
Brig. Gen. Le Van Tu	25 January 1972
Col. Nguyen Huu Toan	7 November 1973
Brig. Gen. Ly Tong Ba	to 30 April 1975

Airborne Division. Organized 1 May 1955, the Airborne Division traced its origins back to the 1st Airborne Battalion, formed by the French with Vietnamese members of the airborne Troupes Aeroportées en Indochine, 1 August 1951. This unit was combined with several other Vietnamese-manned units to form Groupement Aeroporte 3 (G.A.P. 3; equivalent to an airborne regimental combat team) on 1 May 1954, under the command of a Vietnamese officer, then-major Do Cao Tri. After the Geneva agreements, Lt. Col. Tri was named commander of airborne troops of the armed forces of the State of Vietnam, 1 March 1955; G.A.P. 3 was transformed into the Airborne Group, 1 May 1955, at Tan Son Nhut. It was expanded to a brigade on 1 December 1959 and to a division on 1 December 1965.

An independent command under the direct control of the JGS, the Airborne Division was headquartered at Tan Son Nhut throughout the war, where it also had its training base. Considered one of the best units in the RVNAF, its ranks were filled exclusively by volunteers. Many airborne officers went on to command infantry divisions and corps, among them Nguyen Chanh Thi, Ngo Quang Truong, and Do Cao Tri. As part of South Vietnam's general reserve, the Airborne Division operated throughout the country as reinforcement for ARVN units. It also took part in the cross-border operations into Cambodia in 1970 and 1971 as well as in Operation LAM SON 719. The division operated in I Corps from the 1972 Easter Offensive on, maintaining a forward headquarters in the area. During the 1975 Ho Chi Minh Campaign, the Airborne Division was withdrawn from I Corps, a move that helped precipitate the collapse of ARVN forces in the region. The division's 3d Brigade, rushed to the defense of Nha Trang, was virtually destroyed 30–31 March. The 2d Brigade, sent to reinforce the defenders of Phan Rang 9 April, was badly battered and later relieved by the 2d Division. The 1st Brigade attempted to break through to the 18th Division at Xuan Loc. Failing in the attempt, the brigade retreated to Ba Ria, Phuoc Tuy province, where it held out until the capitulation of the Republic of Vietnam.

Commanding Officers, Airborne Division

Lt. Col. Do Cao Tri	1 March 1955
Col. Nguyen Chanh Thi	1 September 1956
Col. Cao Van Vien	12 November 1960
Lt. Gen. Du Quoc Dong	19 December 1964
Brig. Gen. Le Quang Luong	11 November 1972

Marine Division. Organized 1 October 1954, the Vietnamese Marine Corps (VNMC) was descended from the French-organized 1st and 2d Bataillons de Marche. The 1st Bataillon, raised in North Vietnam, was moved south following the July 1954 Geneva agreements, and both units were transferred by the French to the armed forces of the State of Vietnam 1 January 1954. The combat element of the VNMC, first designated as the Marine Infantry, was expanded to a group on 16 April 1956, to a brigade on 1 January 1962, and to a division on 1 October 1968. The VNMC, which essentially consisted of the Marine Division, was officially part of the Vietnamese Navy. In actual practice, however, the VNMC was an independent command under the direct control of the JGS and headquartered in Saigon.

All South Vietnamese marines were volunteers, and the Marine Division was considered one of the best units in the RVNAF. As part of South Vietnam's general reserve, the Marine Division operated throughout the country in support of ARVN units. It also took part in the cross-border operations into Cambodia in 1970 and 1971 as well as in Operation LAM SON 719. The Marine Division operated in I Corps from the 1972 Easter Offensive on, recapturing Quang Tri City 16 September 1972 after the 3d Division was driven out of the city in May. During the 1975 Ho Chi Minh Campaign, the remnant of the Marine Division was the last body of organized troops to leave Da Nang before the city fell 30 March 1975. Reconstituted in Vung Tau under their commander, Brig. Gen. Bui The Lan, the Marine Division held the city until the capitulation of the Republic of Vietnam. Many of the marines and their dependents were evacuated by U.S. forces with the country's collapse.

Commanding Officers, Marine Division

Lt. Col. Le Quang Trong	1 October 1954
Maj. Pham Van Lieu	16 January 1956
Capt. Bui Pho Chi★	31 July 1956
Maj. Le Nhu Hung	30 September 1956
Maj. Le Nguyen Khang	7 May 1960
Lt. Col. Nguyen Ba Lien	16 December 1963
Lt. Gen. Le Nguyen Khang	26 February 1964
Brig. Gen. Bui The Lan	5 May 1972 to 30 April 1975

★Acting commander.

BIBLIOGRAPHY

ANDRADÉ, DALE. *Trial by Fire: The 1972 Easter Offensive, America's Last Vietnam Battle.* 1995.

CLARKE, JEFFREY J. *Advice and Support: The Final Years, 1965–1973.* 1988.

ISAACS, ARNOLD R. *Without Honor: Defeat in Vietnam and Cambodia.* 1983.

LE GRO, WILLIAM E. *Vietnam from Cease-Fire to Capitulation.* 1981.

U.S. DEPARTMENT OF STATE. "Command Histories and Historical Sketches of RVNAF Divisions," typed memorandum. 6 February 1974.

STEVEN J. TIRONE

People's Army of Vietnam (PAVN) and People's Liberation Armed Force (PLAF)

[The available sources for this order of battle provide too little information on some units to make useful description possible. They also are sometimes imprecise, incomplete, or mute about commanders' names, ranks, and service dates. In the lists below, the word *before* signifies that service began or ended at an indeterminate time before the date; the word *after* signifies that service began or ended at an indeterminate time after the date; and *c.* (circa) indicates a date based on inference rather than specific mention in a source. Ranks are those that officers held at some time during the period of service. Province names are those in official use during the war; see map at *Vietnam, Republic of.*]

People's Army of Vietnam (PAVN). The PAVN High Command (Bo Tong tu lenh) consisted after January 1950 of a General Staff (Bo Tong tham muu), Political General Directorate (Tong cuc chinh tri), and Supply (Rear Services) General Directorate (Tong cuc hau can). Each directorate had a chain of command running from the center to regions and on down to basic units. A second major reorganization during 1958–1960, facilitated by assistance from the Soviet Union (USSR) and the People's Republic of China (PRC), created new technical services and branches, established universal military service, professionalized the officer corps, and introduced formal insignia of rank. Air and naval forces developed as integral parts of the army rather than as separate services.

The Military Affairs Party Committee (MAPC), composed of civilian and military members of the party central committee, wielded the party's authority over the high command. The party further exercised control through the membership of military personnel in party committees at all echelons. Nearly all officers were members of the party and subject to supervision by their unit committees.

Following standard communist practice, units had both a military commander and a political officer. Formally they had equal authority but separate responsibilities. Military commanders were responsible for unit administration and combat, political officers for motivation, morale, and liaison with civilian organizations. Although military commanders tended to enjoy precedence in the field, political officers had sufficient military training to take over a command when necessary. In a few instances a single individual held both positions simultaneously.

In March 1965 the central committee directed certain divisions to leave skeleton staffs in the North as "frame" units when the divisions left for the South. Frame units trained replacements while providing reserves for defense of the North. Replacement units received the designation of the frame unit that had created them plus a letter (e.g. *Division 325B, Regiment 95D*). The purpose was to reproduce the PAVN's oldest units, giving new units an instant lineage and troops a sense of continuity with the armed resistance against French colonialism during the 1946–1954 Indochina War. Further confusing the system of designations, units often took cover numbers upon entering the South and frequently changed numbers when moving to a different theater.

At the end of the Vietnam War in 1975, the entire military establishment of the Democratic Republic of Vietnam (DRV) consisted of 685,000 regular army troops organized into twenty-four divisions (plus three training divisions), one artillery command of ten regiments, ten independent infantry regiments, fifteen surface-to-air (SAM) missile regiments, and forty antiaircraft artillery (AAA) regiments; 3,000 troops in the navy; 12,000 troops in the air force organized into one light bomber squadron, four MiG-21 interceptor squadrons, two MiG-19 interceptor squadrons, six MiG-15/17 fighter-bomber squadrons, and support units; 50,000 troops of the *Frontier, Coast Security,* and *People's Armed Security Forces;* and militia numbering about 1,500,000. These figures excluded forces recruited in the South under the party's auspices.

From 1945 to February 1980 the combined office of commander in chief and minister of national defense was held by Gen. Vo Nguyen Giap. Two chiefs of staff served under General Giap: Maj. Gen. Hoang Van Thai from December 1945 to 1953 and Col. Gen. Van Tien Dung from 1953 to 1980.

People's Liberation Armed Force of South Vietnam (PLAF). The People's Liberation Armed Force, formally established on 15 February 1961, was nominally the armed wing of the National Liberation Front (NLF) in the South, but it operated as a theater force of the PAVN under the direct command of the Central Office for South Vietnam (COSVN) regional headquarters. Although the distinction between the PAVN and PLAF was more formal than real at the top command level, PLAF personnel were distinctly different from their PAVN comrades. In order to lend plausibility to Hanoi's claim of noninvolvement with the PLAF, the PLAF had to rely initially on troops recruited locally and on southern "regroupees" returning from the North after 1959. PAVN fillers who began arriving in the B2 theater (see Southern Regional Headquarters, below) in 1965 joined existing PLAF units or fleshed out new ones. PLAF-designated units composed largely of southern troops carried the burden of combat until losses in the 1968 Tet Offensive led to greatly expanded use of entire former PAVN units that had been recruited and trained in the North. The PAVN formally absorbed the PLAF in June 1976.

Political General Directorate. A PAVN political department was first established in 1946. In 1950 it became a formal part of the high command with the assignment to assist the communist party to implement and administer political work and the party committee system in the army. Political officers installed in all units down to company level reported to this directorate.

Commanding Officers, Political General Directorate

Gen. Nguyen Chi Thanh, director	June 1950 to 1961
Lt. Gen. Song Hao, director	1961 to after December 1975
Sen. Gen. Chu Huy Man, director	before April 1977 to after October 1984

Rear Services General Directorate. Established in January 1950, the General Supply Directorate later evolved into the Rear Services General Directorate, with the primary functions of supporting units in the field, managing base and medical facilities, and providing construction services. The Rear Services General Directorate advised *Group 559* and the rear services department of Southern Regional Headquarters, which organized logistics within the B2 theater.

Commanding Officers, Rear Services General Directorate

Maj. Gen. Dinh Duc Thien, director	April 1971 to April 1975
Lt. Gen. Bui Phung, director	April 1975 to before June 1984

Technical General Directorate. This directorate was created in September 1974 to take over machine maintenance, defense industries, technical research and training, personnel management, and cartography from the General Rear Services Directorate.

Commanding Officers, General Technical Directorate

Maj. Gen. Le Van Tri, director   before September 1977 to
                                   after March 1988

Transportation Groups

Military Transportation Group 559. A directive dated 19 May 1959 established *Group 559* to move troops, weapons, and matériel from the North to the South and to maintain support facilities at way stations (*binh tram*) en route. In 1962 the group's force level was 6,000 troops organized into two regiments and several smaller units equipped with 1,000 bicycles and a few trucks. Within a year the force level grew to 24,400 troops and six motorized transport battalions plus engineering, antiaircraft, and security elements. In 1965 *Group 559* moved a volume of supplies nearly equal to the total volume of the preceding five years. Increased PAVN involvement in the war and U.S. interdiction of *Group 759's* transportation activities at sea sharply increased dependence on the group's overland route. In 1965, *Group 559* acquired the status of a military region reporting directly to the MAPC and the General Staff, with three subordinate commands for the supply corridors through Laos.

Preparations for large-scale main force offensives after the U.S. withdrawal sharply increased logistical requirements. In July 1973 the group, redesignated the *Truong Son Command,* converted sectoral (*khu vuc*) and way station (*binh tram*) forces into divisions or regiments and established five additional regiments. By late 1974 forces under its command included *AAA Division 377, Transportation Division 571, Engineering Division 473, Infantry Division 968,* the sectoral divisions *470, 471* and *472,* plus fourteen regiments and various repair facilities and hospitals with total personnel of 100,495.

Commanding Officers, Military Transportation Group 559/Truong Son Command

Sen. Col. Vo Bam, commander	May 1959 to 1965
Maj. Gen. Phan Trong Tue, commander	1965 to 1967
Sen. Col. Dong Sy Nguyen, commander	1967 to c. March 1975
Maj. Gen. Hoang The Thien, political officer	to before March 1975

Military Transportation Group 759. Group 759 originated in the assignment of several general staff officers in July 1959 to consider supporting forces in the South by sea. The group was formally activated on 23 October 1961 and for some time provided the only practical means of moving weapons, supplies, and high-ranking cadres to distant southern points such as the Mekong Delta. From 1962 to 1965, up to 70 percent of supplies from the North moved by sea.

The navy took over responsibility for the group in August 1963 and redesignated it *Group 125.* In the year prior to February 1965, when the U.S. Navy captured one of its ships in Phu Yen province, the group's twenty junks and trawlers delivered 4,000 tons of weapons to the South. Interdiction by the U.S. Navy's Operation MARKET TIME forced the North to depend more on the land route, and the group suspended activities in 1973.

Commanding Officers, Military Transportation Group 759/125

Doan Hoang Phuoc, commander	October 1961 on
Vo Huy Phuc, political officer	October 1961 on

Military Transportation Group 100/959. The Vietnamese communists advised and supported the Pathet Lao insurgency in Sam Neua and Phong Saly provinces after 1954 through *Transportation Group 100.* This group became *Group 959* on 9 September 1959, when it acquired the additional duty of commanding PAVN "volunteer" units in Sam Neua, Xieng Khoang, and Vientiane. The group, though not its activities, came to an end with the signing of a cease-fire with Laos in 1973.

Regional Commands

Military Region 1. Military Region 1 corresponded to the colonial resistance-era Viet Bac region of mountainous provinces on the border with the PRC. At the height of the air war, up to 100,000 Chinese troops and laborers helped the DRV keep road and rail links open through this region.

Military Region 2. Military Region 2 included the resistance-era Tay Bac region, from the Laotian border to the Red River northwest of Hanoi.

Commanding Officers, Military Region 2

Lt. Gen. Vu Lap, commander	before April 1979 to after December 1982

Military Region 3. This region initially encompassed the "right bank" area south and east of Hanoi, including the southern half of the Red

River Delta, and by 1970 included parts of the "left bank" and coastal Dong Bac military regions.

Commanding Officers, Military Region 3

Maj. Gen. Hoang Sam, commander	before 1965 on
Sen. Col. Nguyen Quyet, political officer	before 1965 to after May 1979

Military Region 4. North Vietnam's panhandle region came under exceptionally heavy U.S. bombardment because it was the staging area for the movement of reinforcements and supplies by *Group 559* into Laos and the South. The bombing grew so severe that in October 1968 the political general directorate set up a special Command Headquarters 500 under major generals Nguyen Don and Le Quang Dao and reinforced the region with the antiaircraft artillery divisions *367, 377,* and *368* to provide security for transportation and communications. PAVN units deployed from this region into the Route 9–Tri Thien Front remained under the region's command.

Commanding Officers, Military Region 4

Maj. Gen. Tran Van Quang, commander	1965 to 1974
Lt. Gen. Dam Quang Trung, commander	c. December 1975
Lt. Gen. Le Quang Hoa, commander/ political officer	before December 1977 to after June 1979

Military Region 5. Military Region 5 covered the northern half of South Vietnam from 1954 until April 1966, when Quang Tri and Thua Thien provinces were split off to form the Tri-Thien-Hue Military Region. Throughout the war Military Region 5 coordinated two fronts, one for the Tay Nguyen highlands (B3 theater), the other for the lowlands stretching from Da Nang to Nha Trang (B1 theater). The region's strategic mission was to coordinate the varied forms of armed action in the densely populated lowlands with the main force offensives launched from the highlands, linking the two during general offensives to isolate ARVN forces farther north.

The region acquired a command headquarters in July 1961 and, with the first resources supplied to the South by *Transportation Group 559,* it organized regiments *1, 2,* and *3* during 1962. *Regiment 1* (minus a battalion) battled U.S. Marines in U.S. Operation STARLITE, the first major offensive operation by U.S. forces in the war, on the Batangan Peninsula in Quang Ngai province in August 1965. In the fall of

that year the region consolidated forces to form divisions *2* and *3* and *Regiment 10* in the coastal provinces.

In January 1966 Region 5 organized a front command for Binh Dinh province under Sen. Col. Giap Van Cuong to coordinate resistance against U.S., South Korean, and ARVN forces. In 1968 the region strengthened this command with the appointment of Doan Khue as commander and set up another command for Quang Ngai province under Lu Giang. To direct attacks on Da Nang in 1968, it also set up Front 4 (Quang Da Front), which became the Quang Nam–Da Nang Front under the command of Le Trong Tan and Chu Huy Man on 25 March 1975.

Commanding Officers, Military Region 5

Maj. Gen. Nguyen Don, commander	1961 on
Lt. Gen. Hoang Van Thai, commander/political officer	August 1966 to June 1967
Lt. Gen. Chu Huy Man, commander	before late 1970 to after September 1975
Lt. Gen. Doan Khue, commander/political officer	before May 1977 to after April 1981

Tay Nguyen Front. This subordinate zone of Military Region 5, set up on 1 May 1964, became a front command in September. It covered the Central Highlands parallel to the Ho Chi Minh Trail in southern Laos and northeastern Cambodia. Control of the area would have allowed communist forces to link the trail with roads inside the South and increase the scale of offensives in the lowlands. This front comprised the B3 theater.

U.S. and communist forces struggled for control of the highlands in fierce battles at Pleime, Pleiku, and Ia Drang Valley, the first major clashes between U.S. forces and PAVN regulars, during 1965. In spring 1966 the Tay Nguyen Front received reinforcements of three regiments from divisions *304, 308,* and *325B,* plus one regiment and two battalions of artillery. But insufficient logistical support prevented the front from consolidating forces until spring 1972, when U.S. withdrawals and successful PAVN assaults on the outposts at Dak To and Tan Canh presented an opportunity to organize *Division 10.* In February 1975 the front command set up a campaign headquarters under Maj. Gen. Hoang Minh Thao with the objective of seizing Ban Me Thuot.

Commanding Officers, Tay Nguyen Front

Sen. Col. Nguyen Chanh, commander	May 1964 to July 1965
Sen. Col. Doan Khue, political officer	May 1964 to July 1965
Maj. Gen. Chu Huy Man, commander/political officer	July 1965 on
Maj. Gen. Hoang Minh Thao, commander	June 1967 to
Sen. Col. Tran The Mon, political officer	June 1967 to
Nguyen Hiep, political officer	c. 1975

Tri-Thien-Hue Military Region. This region was carved out of Military Region 5 in April 1966. The PAVN command attached special importance to the area, perceiving control of it as crucial to the defense of both the North and the PAVN's lines of communication through Laos. Two front commands set up in June 1966—the Route 9 front known as theater B5 and the rest known as theater B4—corresponded to the distinction between the conventional war of main forces near the Demilitarized Zone (DMZ) and the emphasis on the "people's war" in the rest of Quang Tri and Thua Thien provinces. The strategy was to divide U.S. and ARVN forces between the main force war on Route 9 and the people's war in the lowlands, intensifying one or the other as circumstances required.

For a few months after June 1968 the region unified command over all the forces of B4 and B5, thus becoming the Tri-Thien Front, but the attempt proved premature and was abandoned. The regional leadership made the attempt again in March 1972 in order to sustain the momentum of the Easter Offensive, which also proved unsuccessful. The main forces were organized under the region's command as *2d Corps* in May 1974.

Commanding Officers, Tri-Thien-Hue Military Region

Maj. Gen. Le Chuong, commander	April 1966 to June 1967
Maj. Gen. Le Chuong, political officer	April 1966 to after April 1968
Maj. Gen. Tran Van Quang, commander	June 1967 on

Commanding Officers, Tri Thien Front Command

Le Trong Tan, commander	March 1972 on
Le Quang Dao, political officer	March 1972 on

Southern Regional Headquarters. The communist party central committee set up the Central Office for South Vietnam (COSVN) in 1961 as a forward element of its operations in South Vietnam. The early COSVN contained a Military Committee (Ban quan su) which doubled as the Military Affairs Committee of the National Liberation Front and the command of the People's Liberation Armed Force (PLAF). The first head of COSVN's Military Committee, Maj. Gen. Tran Luong (aka Tran Nam Trung), a deputy director of the PAVN General Political Directorate, was also chairman of the Military Affairs Committee of the NLF and, after June 1969, minister of defense of the Provisional Revolutionary Government (PRG). Luong had come south in May 1961 with five hundred PAVN cadres to help set up the command headquarters at COSVN and its subordinate regions, military regions 6, 7, 8, 9 and the Saigon–Gia Dinh Special Zone, known collectively as the B2 theater.

In October 1963 COSVN organized the Military Affairs Party Committee (Quan uy) and Regional Military Headquarters (Bo tu lenh Mien). COSVN first secretary Nguyen Van Linh served concurrently as secretary of the MAPC, while Col. Gen. Tran Van Tra became commander of the Regional Military Headquarters. Other PAVN officers who took key posts in Southern Regional Headquarters at this time were Maj. Gen. Le Trong Tan, Maj. Gen. Tran Do, and Sen. Col. Hoang Cam. Gen. Nguyen Chi Thanh, a member of the party political bureau, arrived at COSVN later in 1963 or early 1964 to serve as Southern regional political officer and was the dominant figure until his death in 1967. This regional command structure reported through Thanh to the PAVN general staff in Hanoi. When Pham Hung replaced Thanh as the political bureau's representative, he also became first secretary of COSVN and of the MAPC.

The headquarters' jurisdiction covered communist military regions 6 through 9 and the special zones within them. On the eve of the 1968 Tet Offensive, it directly controlled three infantry divisions and one artillery division. Two forward command centers, one for main forces operating northeast of Saigon, and one for forces entering the city from the south and west, coordinated the attacks. In spring 1972, the region directed attacks by divisions *5, 7,* and *9* northeast of Saigon, drawing the *21st* ARVN Division out of the Mekong Delta so that guerrillas and four main force regiments could disrupt the pacification program. For the final offensive of the war, it organized these forces under two corps-level commands, the *4th Corps* and *Group 232*.

First Secretaries, COSVN Military Committee

Maj. Gen. Tran Luong, first secretary	May 1961 to October 1963

First Secretaries, COSVN Military Affairs Party Committee

Nguyen Van Linh	October 1963 to 1964
Sen. Gen. Nguyen Chi Thanh	1964 to June 1967
Pham Hung	June 1967 to May 1975

Commanding Officers, Southern Regional Military Headquarters

Col. Gen. Tran Van Tra, commander	October 1963 to January 1967
Lt. Gen. Hoang Van Thai, commander	January 1967 to 1973
Col. Gen. Tran Van Tra, commander	1973 to May 1975

Military Region 6. This region covered the southern part of central Vietnam, including Quang Duc, Tuyen Duc, Ninh Thuan, Binh Thuan, Lam Dong, and Binh Tuy provinces.

Commanding Officers, Military Region 6

Sen. Col. Nguyen Trong Xuyen, commander	c. January 1975

Military Region 7. This region, more commonly known as the Eastern Nam Bo Region, comprised Phuoc Long, Long Khanh, Phuoc Tuy, Binh Long, Binh Duong, Bien Hoa, Tay Ninh, and Hau Nghia provinces. The Ho Chi Minh Trail brought forces and supplies close to Saigon in this region, which absorbed the Saigon–Gia Dinh Special Zone in October 1967 for the Tet Offensive.

Commanding Officers, Eastern Nam Bo Military Region

Nguyen Van Xuyen, commander	c. 1946 to 1960
Col. Le Van Ngoc, commander	before Jan 1975 to after April 1975
Col. Gen. Tran Van Tra, commander/political officer	before 1976 to March 1978
Maj. Gen. Duong Cu Tam, political officer	before December 1978

Military Region 8. This region lay southwest of Saigon, stretching from Cambodia to the South China Sea and including Long An, Kien Tuong, Sa Dec, Dinh Tuong, Go Cong, and Kien Hoa provinces. The boundary between regions 8 and 9 bisected the Mekong Delta.

Commanding Officers, Military Region 8

Tran Van Tra, commander	c. 1946 on

Military Region 9. Military Region 9 covered the southern tip of Vietnam, including Chau Doc, An Giang, Vinh Long, Vinh Binh, Phong Dinh, Ba Xuyen, Kien Giang, Bac Lieu, and An Xuyen provinces.

Commanding Officers, Military Region 9

Le Duc Anh, commander	c. December 1965 on
Pham Ngoc Hung, commander	before 1975 to after January 1983

Route 9–Northern Quang Tri Front. The Route 9 or B5 Front was established in June 1966 to command forces just south of the Demilitarized Zone (DMZ). Short supply lines from the North made it possible for the PAVN to wage set-piece battles with U.S. forces on this front. Until late 1967, the front reported to the command of Military Region 4, which lay north of the DMZ; after that it reported to Tri-Thien-Hue Military Region command. In the 1966–1967 dry season, the front organized attacks on strongpoints south of the DMZ with PAVN divisions *325C* and *324,* and infantry regiments *27* and *31.* In December 1967 elements of the PAVN divisions *304* and *320* joined the front for assaults on outposts along Route 9 to distract U.S. and ARVN attention from preparations for attacks against the cities. A western sector commanded *304* and *325C,* and an eastern sector commanded *320* and *324.* The region combined the commands of B4 and B5 theaters in November 1972.

Commanding Officers, Route 9–Northern Quang Tri Front

Sen. Col. Vu Nam Long, commander	June 1966 to December 1967
Maj. Gen. Nguyen Xuan Hoang, political officer	June 1966 to December 1967
Maj. Gen. Tran Quy Hai, commander	December 1967 on
Maj. Gen. Le Quang Dao, political officer	December 1967 on

Saigon–Gia Dinh Special Zone. This region organized intelligence and "special activity" operations inside the South's largest urban area. In 1965 this special zone had two "security" units under its command, and later its special action units coordinated with sappers (infiltration and demolition commandos) in the Rung Sat Special Zone to attack shipping in the Long Tau river and harass Tan Son Nhut airfield and the U.S. and ARVN base at Long Binh. In October 1967 it merged with Military Region 7 to form part of the Main Target Region (Khu trong diem) for the Tet Offensive.

Military Branches

Air Defense–Air Force Branch. The establishment on 3 March 1955 of an Airfield Studies Committee to advise the General Staff marked the beginning of a North Vietnamese air force. The committee had responsibility for civil as well as military aviation and received its first aircraft (five Soviet and Czech transports donated by China) in early 1956. It also organized the dispatch of personnel for training in the PRC and the USSR. The committee was upgraded to a department and given command of *Military Air Transport Regiment 919* in January 1959.

Meanwhile, the PAVN's antiaircraft artillery forces had grown to about 7,500 men organized into six antiaircraft and two radar regiments. On 22 October 1963 these forces were combined with the air force to form the Air Defense–Air Force Branch (Quan chung Phong khong–Khong quan). Soviet training, advice, and equipment were crucial to development of both forces. In August 1964, the branch organized troops who had returned from training abroad into *Air Force Regiment 921*. A year later it established *Regiment 923*. The first Il-28 bombers (Ilyushin-28) and MiG-21 fighters arrived about the same time. In mid 1965 the branch also deployed the first two antiaircraft missile regiments, raising in one year the total of personnel under its command from 22,500 to 52,700.

In June 1966, the branch organized the air defense units into "strategic" divisions *361, 363, 365,* and *369* and "mobile" *Division 367* to improve coordination of antiaircraft and air force operations. Air, missile, and radar forces became separate services with their own commanders reporting to the branch in March 1967. Air force regiments *921* and *923* combined to form *Air Force Division 371*. *Regiment 925* emerged in February 1969, *Regiment 927* in February 1972. The force organized a bomber unit equipped with eight IL-28s in October 1968, but it had no mission until October 1972, when two of its planes carried out a single strike near the Laotian border. In general, antiaircraft artillery and ground-to-air missiles posed a much greater threat than did MiGs to U.S. aircraft. The PAVN air force's main role in spring 1975 was to take over the airfields and equipment abandoned by the ARVN. The Air and Air Defense forces became separate branches on 6 May 1977.

Commanding Officers, Airfield Studies Committee/Air Force Department

Sen. Col. Dang Tinh, commander	September 1955 to October 1963
Col. Hoang The Thien, political officer	September 1956 to October 1963

Commanding Officers, Air Defense–Air Force Branch

Sen. Col. Phung The Tai, commander	October 1963 on
Sen. Col. Dang Tinh, political officer	October 1963 to April 1970
Sen. Col. Le Van Tri, commander	April 1973 to May 1977
Hoang Phuong, political officer	before April 1975 to May 1977

Commanding Officers, Air Force

Col. Nguyen Van Tien, commander	March 1967 on
Col. Phan Khac Hy, political officer	March 1967 on
Col. Dao Dinh Luyen, commander	
Lt. Col. Do Long, political officer	
Sen. Col. Dao Dinh Luyen, commander/political officer	May 1977 to after March 1984

Commanding Officers, Air Defense Force

Maj. Gen. Hoang Van Khanh, commander	before December 1979 to before October 1983
Maj. Gen. Nguyen Xuan Mau, political officer	before December 1979 to before July 1981

Armored Branch. The PAVN's first tank regiment, *202,* was commissioned on 5 October 1959, though the armored service did not achieve branch status until 22 June 1965. *Regiment 202* and its sibling unit, *203,* developed into brigades, and *203* in particular fought extensively in the South from January 1968 onward. Two tanks of *Regiment 203,* numbers 390 and 843, broke into the grounds of Saigon's presidential palace on 30 April 1975.

Commanding Officers, Armored Branch

Dao Huy Vu, deputy commander/commander	June 1965 to after September 1984

Artillery Branch. The PAVN established an artillery force on 29 June 1946 to defend Hanoi from the returning French. In 1955 artillery regiments of the "heavy" *Division 351* were redesignated as divisions *675, 45,* and *349* and placed under a new Artillery Command. By 1960 this command had organized 17,500 men into artillery brigades *364, 368, 374,* and *378;* four long-range artillery regiments; and four antiaircraft regiments.

Commanding Officers, Artillery Branch

Maj. Gen. Le Thiet Hung, commander	1955 on
Maj. Gen. Doan Tue, commander	before June 1972 to after April 1975
Sen. Col. Nam Thang, commander	February 1978 to before September 1979

Engineer Branch. The Communications Bureau in the General Staff commanded engineering regiments *333, 444, 555,* and *506* in 1955. Forces of about 4,500 were assembled into construction regiments *229, 239, 219,* and *249* during the reorganization of the PAVN in 1958–1960.

Commanding Officers, Engineer Branch

Maj. Gen. Tran Va Dang, commander	before December 1979 to after July 1984
Maj. Gen. Nguyen Huan, political officer	before March 1981 on

Navy Branch. The PAVN established a Coastal Defense Department on 7 May 1955 to train officers and technical personnel for the North's tiny fleet of patrol boats and motorized junks. Renamed the Navy Department in January 1959, with Soviet help it began developing patrol boat bases, mobile coastal artillery, and radar stations. The Ministry of Defense renamed it the Navy Branch on 3 January 1964.

At 9:15 P.M. on 1 August 1964 the navy received orders from the General Staff to attack ships that radar had detected repeatedly entering the North's territorial waters. The orders apparently made no distinction between ARVN commando and naval activities and maneuvers by U.S. warships in the same general area. The execution of these orders by three PAVN torpedo boats against the U.S. destroyer *Maddox* constituted what Americans came to know as the Gulf of Tonkin Incident.

U.S. air and naval dominance subsequently left the PAVN navy little role at sea. In spring 1967 the Ministry of Defense attached the naval command to the Northeast Military Region (MR 3) and reassigned one-third of the navy's personnel. In 1972 the PAVN captured Cua Viet, a village port just south of the DMZ, allowing the navy to ferry men and supplies directly into Quang Tri province from then until the war's end.

Commanding Officers, Navy Department/Branch

Sen. Col. Ta Xuan Thu, commander/political officer	January 1959 to January 1964
Maj. Gen. Ta Xuan Thu, commander/political officer	January 1964 to March 1967

Sen. Col. Nguyen Ba Phat, commander	March 1967 to late 1974
Sen. Col. Doan Phung, political officer	March 1967 to April 1970
Hoang Tra, political officer	April 1970 to late 1974
Sen. Col. Doan Ba Khanh, commander	late 1974 to March 1977
Sen. Col. Tran Van Giang, political officer	late 1974 to March 1977

Sapper Branch. Sappers (*dac cong*) consisting of small teams and units, attached to political or military commands, developed early during the war with France. A subcategory of sappers known as special activities (*biet dong*) forces operated in towns and cities. Several hundred sappers (infiltration and demolition commandos) from the South who regrouped in the North formed two battalions attached to *Division 338* and Military Region 4. Some of these men began returning to the South in small numbers to gather intelligence as early as August 1955. Military regions in the South began developing their own sapper companies and battalions in 1961, and the General Staff organized a uniform sapper training program in July 1962.

The special training requirements and role that sappers were to play in the Tet Offensive were recognized with the establishment of the Sapper Branch (Binh chung Dac cong) on 19 March 1967, with direct control over the *Brigade 305, Regiment 426,* (naval) *Group 126,* and nine battalions. The branch primarily trained sappers for attachment to other PAVN commands and units. In its first year it trained and dispatched over 2,500 sapper officers and troops to the South, and it doubled this output within two years.

Southern Regional Headquarters maintained its own sapper department, known as J16, and for a time it trained as many sappers as the branch. In 1973 B2 controlled eight sapper "groups" equivalent to regiments, including one in Cambodia. On the eve of the 1975 Spring Offensive, 12 sapper regiments or their equivalents, 36 battalions, 121 companies, 15 groups of *biet dong,* and hundreds of squads, teams, and cells were scattered across the South. The entire *dac cong–biet dong* "brigade" *316* was operating inside Saigon or its outskirts by war's end.

Commanding Officers, Sapper Branch

Sen. Col. Nguyen Chi Diem, commander	March 1967 to after March 1975
Sen. Col. Vu Chi Dao, political officer	March 1967 to after May 1973

Signals Branch. This branch traced its origins to an army signals office set up on 9 September 1945 and later absorbed into a signals department of the high command. Many of the department's personnel received training abroad to prepare for the PAVN's modernization. In 1958 the department organized the PAVN's first signals regiment, the *205* (initially designated the *303*). One of this regiment's missions was to maintain a station for radio communications with the South, known as B18. *Regiment 205* also maintained the link with the groups *559, 759, 959* and other transportation groups supplying PAVN forces in distant theaters.

The department's radios often provided the North's only working communications during the air war. The department commander was himself killed while traveling to Military Region 4. The increased demand for communications led to the establishment of *Regiment 26* in February 1965 specifically to serve air and antiaircraft defense forces and to the creation by August 1966 of two more signals regiments (*132* and *134*) and four battalions under the department's direct command. The Ministry of Defense elevated the department to a branch on 31 January 1968.

Commanding Officers, Signals Branch

Hoang Dao Thuy, commander	June 1949 to 1962
Hoang Buu Dong, political officer	before October 1954 on
Nguyen Anh Bao, commander	1962 to August 1965
Hoang Niem, commander (acting)	August 1965 to January 1969
Le Cu, political officer	before 1965 on
Col. Ta Dinh Hieu, commander	January 1969 to mid 1973
Pham Nien, commander	mid 1973 on
Sen. Col. Nguyen Duy Lac, political officer	before December 1976 on

Main Force Combat Units

1st Military Corps (Quyet Thang Corps). The *1st Corps* was established in the North on 24 October 1973 to command infantry divisions *308, 312,* and *320B, Antiaircraft Division 367, Artillery Brigade 45, Tank Brigade 202, Engineer Brigade 299,* and *Signal Regiment 140.* In March 1975 the corps was building dikes in the North when the PAVN overran the Central Highlands. Ordered into the fighting on 25 March, it traveled 1,700 kilometers to reach South Vietnam just in time for the final push on Saigon.

Commanding Officers, 1st Corps

Maj. Gen. Le Trong Tan, commander	October 1973 on
Maj. Gen. Le Quang Hoa, political officer	October 1973 on
Maj. Gen. Nguyen Hoa, commander	before March 1975 on
Maj. Gen. Hoang Minh Thi, political officer	before March 1975 on

2d Military Corps. The *2d Corps* was established on 17 May 1974 in the Tri Thien Front area in preparation for the final offensive of the war. Forces under its command included infantry divisions *304, 324,* and *325, Antiaircraft Division 367, Tank Brigade 203, Artillery Brigade 164, Engineering Brigade 219,* and *Signals Regiment 463.* Following success in Quang Tri and Hue, the *2d Corps* seized Da Nang, and a branch of the corps under Lt. Gen. Le Trong Tan, commander, and Lt. Gen. Le Quang Hoa, political officer, proceeded down the coast, taking Phan Rang and Phan Thiet on the way.

Commanding Officers, 2d Corps

Lt. Gen. Hoang Van Thai, commander	October 1973 on
Maj. Gen. Le Linh, political officer	October 1973 to after March 1975
Maj. Gen. Nguyen Huu An	c. 1974 to after March 1975

3d Military Corps (Tay Nguyen Corps). The command staff of the Tay Nguyen Front became the staff of the *3d Corps* on 26 March 1975. The corps supervised infantry divisions *10, 320,* and *316,* artillery regiments *40* and *675,* antiaircraft regiments *234* and *593, Tank Regiment 273, Engineer Regiment 7,* and *Signal Regiment 29* during their approach to Saigon through eastern South Vietnam in the final offensive of the war. In June 1976 the corps returned to Military Region 5 and established headquarters in Nha Trang.

Commanding Officers, 3d Corps

Vu Lang, commander	March 1975 on
Dang Vu Hiep, political officer	March 1975 on

4th Military Corps (Cuu Long Corps). Southern Regional Headquarters began forming its first regiments (*1* and *2*) in 1962. Further growth in forces allowed the region to organize divisions *5, 9,* and *7* in 1965–1966. In March 1971 the region placed these and other forces under the command of *Group 301,* which became the nucleus of the *4th Corps* at its founding on 20 July 1974. The corps grouped divisions *5, 9,* and *7, Mobile Artillery Regiment 24, Anti-*

aircraft Artillery Regiment 71, Engineer Regiment 25, Sapper Regiment 429, Signals Regiment 69, and support elements, consisting altogether of 35,000 officers and men.

In late December 1974, *1st Corps* moved to seize Route 14 in Phuoc Long province. The accomplishment of this aim in early January allowed forces and supplies to move swiftly toward Saigon. *Division 341* reinforced the corps for the drive on Saigon from the northwest, while *Division 5* was reassigned to *Group 232*. Divisions *341, 7,* and *9* remained the main units of the corps after war's end.

Commanding Officers, 4th Corps

Maj. Gen. Hoang Cam, commander	July 1974 to c. May 1975
Maj. Gen. Hoang The Thien, political officer	March 1975 on

70th Military Corps. The *70th Military Corps* appeared in October 1970 to coordinate the operations of divisions *304, 308, 320,* and several regiments along Route 9 and in Laos.

Group 232. Group 232 was set up in February 1975 to serve as a forward element of Southern Regional Headquarters during the final phase of the war. Equivalent to a corps command, it organized the attacks by divisions *3* and *5* west and southwest of Saigon in coordination with *4th Corps.*

Commanding Officers, Group 232

Le Duc Anh, commander	February 1975 to March 1975
Le Van Tuong, political officer	February 1975 to March 1975
Maj. Gen. Nguyen Minh Chau, commander	March 1975 on
Maj. Gen. Tran Van Phac, political officer	March 1975 on

Group 301. Established on 18 March 1971, this group incorporated divisions *5, 7,* and *9* plus *Artillery Regiment 28.* Essentially a campaign headquarters, it coordinated the regroupment and counterattack of COSVN's main forces against ARVN operations in Cambodia. The group served as the nucleus for the formation of *4th Corps* in 1974.

Commanding Officers, Group 301

Tran Van Tra, commander	March 1971 on
Tran Do, political officer	March 1971 on

Division 1. The Tay Nguyen Front command formed *Division 1* on 20 December 1965 with regiments *33, 320,* and *66,* which had taken heavy ca-

sualties in fighting for control of the Central Highlands. Most of these forces had entered the South as elements of other units, principally *Division 325A,* in early 1965. *Regiment 33* later operated independently and was replaced in the division by *Regiment 88,* which left Tay Nguyen to reinforce B2 theater in late 1967.

Division 2. This division, activated on 20 October 1965 in Quang Nam province, was based on PLAF *Regiment 1,* PAVN *Regiment 21,* and *Battalion 70. Regiment 1* had originated in Military Region 5 in the early 1960s, *Regiment 21* had recently arrived from the North, and *Battalion 70* consisted mainly of regroupees. PAVN *Regiment 31* joined the division in 1966.

Division 2 was supposed to complement guerrilla and political action in the lowlands, thwarting "pacification" and tying down ARVN forces. Under increasing pressure after the introduction of U.S. and South Korean troops, it did not mount division-level operations until August 1967. Devastating strikes by helicopter gunships killed many of the division's top officers in December, and it went into the Tet Offensive under the command of officers dispatched from region headquarters.

The division retreated to Laos in mid 1970, received PAVN *Regiment 141* to replace the *21st,* and fought in Laos until early March 1971. In spring 1972 it fought in the Tay Nguyen highlands, after which it returned to Quang Ngai and incorporated *Regiment 52* from *Division 320.* The divisional command suffered a second decimation when a B-52 strike scored a direct hit on its headquarters in September 1972.

A major reorganization of Military Region 5 forces in mid 1973 transformed *Regiment 52* into a brigade and left *Division 2* with regiments *141, 31,* and *38,* and some remnants from the disbanding of *Division 711.* Strengthened by the addition of the PAVN's *Infantry Regiment 36* and *Artillery Regiment 368* in late 1974, the division participated in the capture of Da Nang on 29 March 1975. It subsequently participated in the defense of the western border and intervention in Cambodia.

Commanding Officers, Division 2

Nguyen Nang, commander	October 1965 to before August 1967
Nguyen Minh Duc, political officer	October 1965 to December 1967
Le Huu Tru, commander	before August 1967 to December 1967
Giap Van Cuong, commander	December 1967 to before February 1969

Nguyen Ngoc Son, political officer	December 1967 to before February 1969
Le Kich, commander (acting)	before February 1969 to August 1969
Ho Xuan Anh, commander	August 1969 to before March 1971
Nguyen Huy Chuong, political officer	October 1969 to before April 1972
Nguyen Chon, commander	before March 1971 to June 1972
Le Dinh Yen, political officer	before April 1972 on
Duong Ba Loi, commander (acting)	June 1972 to September 1972
Nguyen Viet Son, commander June 1973	September 1972 to
Nguyen Chon, commander	June 1973 on
Mai Thuan, political officer (acting)	before March 1975 on

Division 3. Infantry regiments *2, 12,* and *22* plus mortar, antiaircraft, engineers, and signals battalions formed the *Sao Vang (Gold Star) Division* on September 2, 1965, the National Day of the DRV. *Regiment 2* had been organized in Quang Nai province in 1962, *Regiment 12* (formerly *18* of PAVN *Division 312*) had come from the North in February 1965, while *Regiment 22* had come into existence in summer 1965 by combining troops from the North with local forces from Military Region 5. The division's primary mission was to tie down ARVN forces in Quang Ngai, Binh Dinh, and Phu Yen provinces while the PAVN built offensive capability in the highlands.

U.S. occupation of the highlands blocked that strategy until late in the war. In the 1968 Tet Offensive the *3d* played mostly a support role for provincial and local forces that attacked the towns but had to disperse its forces until mid 1971. Regrouped in June (with *Regiment 21* replacing the *22d*), it participated in the capture of several district capitals in Binh Dinh during spring 1972. PAVN *Regiment 141* replaced the *21st* in the *3d* during a reorganization of Military Region 5 forces in June 1973. In spring 1975 the division participated in the capture of Phan Rang and Vung Tau, joining *2d Corps* on April 18.

In mid 1976 the division moved to Military Region 3, and in July 1978 to Lang Son in Military Region 1, where it met the Chinese attack in February 1979.

Commanding Officers, Division 3

Sen. Col. Giap Van Cuong, commander	September 1965 on
Dang Hoa, political officer	September 1965 on

Lu Giang, commander	before May 1968 to July 1970
Nguyen Nam Khanh, political officer	before May 1968 to July 1970
Huynh Huu Anh, commander	July 1970 to before June 1974
Mai Tan, political officer	June 1971 on
Tran Trong Son, commander (acting)	before June 1974 on
Do Quang Hung, commander	before March 1975 on
Tran Van Khue, commander	before April 1975 on

Division 4. This unit appeared in Military Region 9 during the 1975 Spring Offensive. It returned to region 9 from "internationalist duty" in Cambodia in 1989.

Division 5. PLAF *Infantry Division 5* was formed in Ba Ria base area on 23 November 1965 by combining the *Dong Nai* (4th) *Regiment* of Military Region 7 with *Regiment 5,* which had been assembled from regional units in Nam Bo. The division operated only at regimental level for some years. Two regiments of this division coordinated with regional forces to attack Route 15 and the U.S. base at Vung Tau in 1966. In March 1971 it became part of *Group 301* for operations in Cambodia. It was a major component of the forces that attacked Route 13 and Loc Ninh in spring 1972.

Commanding Officers, Division 5

Bui Thanh Van, commander	before April 1972 on
Nguyen Van Cuc, political officer	before April 1972 on
Tran Thanh Van, commander	c. 1975
Vu Van Thuoc, commander	c. 1975
Nguyen Xuan On, political officer	c. 1975

Division 6. This unit appeared in Military Region 6 during the Spring Offensive.

Commanding Officers, Division 6

Dang Ngoc Si, commander	August 1974 on

Division 7. Southern Regional Headquarters established PLAF *Division 7* on 13 June 1966 in the area of Phuoc Lon, Eastern Nam Bo (South Vietnam). The *7th's* first regiments were the *16th,* formerly the *101A* of PAVN *Division 325;* the *141st,* formerly of PAVN *Division 312;* and the *165th,* also of PAVN *Division 312. Regiment 52* of PAVN *Division 320* soon replaced the *16th.*

In spring 1967 the division moved to Tay Ninh province to resist the joint U.S./ARVN Operation JUNCTION CITY. For the Tet Offensive, the *7th's* mission was to distract attention from Saigon with attacks in Tay Ninh and Binh Long provinces, helping assault forces achieve surprise in the city. While that mission was successful, the division suffered heavy casualties in the counteroffensive that followed. After reorganization in late 1968, the *7th* was composed of three regiments descended from PAVN *Division 312*. Units of the *7th* took the brunt of the U.S./ARVN "incursion" into Cambodia in spring 1970, *Regiment 141* seeing particularly heavy action around Snoul and Mimot. In March 1971 the *7th* joined *Group 301* for the spring 1972 attacks in Binh Long province that seized Loc Ninh and nearly overran An Loc. *Regiment 209* of the *7th* took the brunt of the B-52 and tactical airstrikes while serving as the main blocking force south of An Loc.

Division 7 joined *4th Corps* in Eastern Nam Bo in July 1974 and participated in the 1975 Spring Offensive in Phuoc Long province. Regiments *141* and *165* of the *7th* entered the provincial capital on January 6, and a large part of the division assisted in overcoming the last major ARVN resistance at Xuan Loc on April 20.

The division redeployed from Saigon to the border with Cambodia in mid 1977 and entered Cambodia with the rest of *4th Corps* on 1 January 1979. The division returned to Vietnam in May 1983.

Commanding Officers, Division 7

Nguyen Hoa, commander	June 1966 on
Duong Thanh, political officer	June 1966 on
Nguyen The Bon, commander	1967 to c. 1970
Vuong The Hiep, political officer	1967 to c. 1970
Dam Van Nguy, commander	c. 1970 to September 1972
Le Thanh, political officer	c. 1970 to after 1972
Le Nam Phong, commander	September 1972 to 1977
Tu Vinh, political officer	before July 1974 on
Phan Liem, political officer	before March 1975 to 1977

Division 8. This unit appeared in Military Region 8 during the 1975 Spring Offensive.

Commanding Officers, Division 8

Sen. Col. Huynh Van Nhiem, commander	August 1974 on

Division 9. PLAF *Division 9* had its origins in two battalions organized by regroupee officers in 1961. These battalions became PLAF regiments *1* and *2* in 1963. With RPG-2 rocket launchers, 82 mm mortars, and recoilless rifles supplied by *Group 759*, elements of these regiments defeated a larger ARVN force at the pivotal battle of Binh Gia village in December 1964. These regiments plus a third received formal commissioning as *Division 9* on 2 September 1965. The *9th* was the first communist main force division formed entirely in the South under COSVN's supervision.

Attempting to maintain a case close to Saigon, the division had its first engagement with U.S. forces at the strategic hamlet of Bau Bang in December 1965. Elements of the division took heavy casualties but emerged intact from the U.S.-led search-and-destroy operations ATTLEBORO and CEDAR FALLS in 1966 and 1967. Plagued by shortages of supply, weapons, and manpower, it regrouped in Tay Ninh province, closer to the Cambodian border.

The division's assignment at the beginning of the 1968 Tet Offensive was to distract U.S. and ARVN posts on the outskirts of Saigon while sappers and special forces attacked inside the city. This limited success led to the use of elements from two *Division 9* regiments in direct attacks on the city in May, with disastrous results. One 500-man battalion retreated with only 43 troops not dead or wounded.

Replenishment the following year brought in *Regiment 95C* of *Division 325C* (redesignated *Regiment 3*) to replace *Regiment 3B* (formerly *Regiment 88* of *Division 308*). The U.S./ARVN "incursion" in 1970 pushed the division deep into Cambodia, where in March 1971 as part of *Group 301* it helped defeat the Phnom Penh government's Operation CHEN-LA 2. Elements of the division returned to battle inside Vietnam in spring 1972 along Route 13 near Loc Ninh and An Loc. Reinforced with infantry and both ground and antiaircraft artillery, *Division 9* became a component of the *4th Corps* in July 1974 and participated in the seizure of Phuoc Long province in January 1975. The division's intervention in Cambodia after 1978 corroded the morale of the new southern recruits who composed it.

Commanding Officers, Division 9

Sen. Lt. Col. Hoang Cam, commander	September 1965 to 1967
Sen. Col. Le Van Tuong, political officer	September 1965 to 1967
Ta Minh Kham, commander	1967 to 1969
Nguyen Van Tong, political officer	1967 to 1969
Le Van Nho, commander	1969 to c. 1969
Nguyen Thoi Bung, commander	c. 1969 to c. 1972

Nguyen Van Quang, political officer	c. 1969 to c. 1972
Vo Van Dan, commander	c. 1972 on
Pham Xuan Tung, political officer	c. 1972 on
Tam Tung, political officer	before July 1974 on

Division 10. This division emerged from the concentration of forces in the Tay Nguyen Front for the 1972 Easter Offensive. An "Eastern Command Staff" set up to supervise regiments *28, 66,* and *95* in attacks in northern Tay Nguyen in February became the command of *Division 10* upon activation on 20 September 1972. The division incorporated *Regiment 24* in spring 1973. Along with elements of *Division 320* the *10th* pushed ARVN forces out of areas near Pleiku and Ban Me Thuot in 1974. In spring 1975, the *10th* participated in the final assault on Ban Me Thuot, and *Regiment 95B* transferred from the *10th* to *Division 320* for the pursuit of ARVN forces down Route 7 to Nha Trang. The division became a part of the *3d Military Corps* upon the corps' formation on 26 March 1975 and fought as part of that corps in Eastern Nam Bo during the final stage of the war, reaching Tan Son Nhut airbase on the outskirts of Saigon on April 30.

Following the war the division moved to Lam Dong province, where it concentrated on economic reconstruction, the suppression of remnant montagnard dissidence, and defense of the border against Khmer Rouge attacks in 1977. It participated in the intervention in Cambodia in December 1978, and its units were among the first to enter Phnom Penh.

Commanding Officers, Division 10

Nguyen Manh Quan, commander	September 1972 to May 1973
Sen. Col. Dang Vu Hiep, political officer	September 1972 to May 1973
Do Duc Gia, commander	May 1973 to mid 1974
La Ngoc Chau, political officer	May 1973 to 1975
Ho De, commander	mid 1974 to April 1975
Hong Son, commander	April 1975 to September 1976
Luu Quy Ngu, political officer	1975 to March 1979
Sen. Col. Phung Ba Thuong, commander	September 1976 on

Division 303. Southern Regional Headquarters organized *Division 303* to prepare for the final offensive of the war. Briefly designated *Division 3* after establishment on 19 August 1974, the division comprised PLAF infantry regiments *201, 205,* and *271,* and PAVN *Artillery Regiment 262.*

The division's first assignment was to cut Route 14 and isolate Phuoc Long province, which it accomplished by March 1975. With the ARVN falling back more rapidly than communist strategists had expected, the *303d* advanced almost immediately into Tay Nih province and the Plain of Reeds, and in April it was attached to *Group 232* for the attack on Saigon.

Following the war the bulk of the division returned to Phuoc Long province, where it worked in economic reconstruction as the Phuoc Long Unified Economic Group. It was reconstituted in August 1978 for the intervention in Cambodia and redeployed a year later to defend the Red River Delta in the brief border war with China.

Commanding Officers, Division 303

Do Quang Huong, commander	August 1974 on
Sen. Col. Tran Hai Phung, commander	1977 to September 1977
Col. Cao Hoai Sai, commander	September 1977 to August 1978

Division 304. The *304th,* the second of six infantry divisions organized during the resistance against France, was commissioned on 4 January 1950 in Thanh Hoa province. During the resistance against the French it fought in the Red River Delta and also saw action in Laos and Dien Bien Phu. The division received orders in August 1965 to march south, and regiments *24* and *66* entered the Tay Nguyen Front around the end of the year while *Regiment 9* served briefly in Laos. The *304th* was picked in September 1967 as one of four PAVN divisions to support the Tet Offensive. *Regiment 24* helped to overrun the U.S. Special Forces camp at Lang Vei in February 1968, while *Regiment 9* joined the attack on Hue and *Regiment 66* participated in the siege of Khe Sanh.

Gravely depleted, the division returned in June 1968 to the North. In October 1970 it was attached to the newly formed *70th Military Corps* of the Route 9 Front and Laos and participated in the counterattack on ARVN Operation LAM SON 719 in spring 1971. In 1972 it participated in the capture of Quang Tri province and the following year became part of the *1st Military Corps.* In the final offensive of the war it traveled down the coast from Hue as part of the *2d Army Corps,* and elements of *Infantry Regiment 66* and *Tank Brigade 203* under its command seized the presidential palace in Saigon.

At the same time that the *304th* departed for the South, Military Region 3 received orders to organize the "second" *304th*, designated the *304B*. This division entered the fighting in early 1968 around the western end of Route 9 including Khe Sanh.

Commanding Officers, Division 304

Hoang Minh Thao, commander	February 1950 to November 1953
Tran Van Quang, political officer	February 1950 to 1951
Hoang Sam, commander	November 1953 to late 1955
Le Chuong, political officer	1951 to late 1955
Nam Long, commander	late 1955 on
Truong Cong Can, political officer	late 1955 on
Ngo Ngoc Duong, commander	to March 1965
Tran Huy, political officer	to March 1965
Mai Hien, commander (acting)	March 1965 to August 1965
Hoang Kien, commander	August 1965 to c. 1967
Truong Cong Can, political officer	August 1965 to January 1968
Thai Dung, commander	1967 to June 1968
Tran Nguyen Do, political officer	January 1968 to June 1968
Hoang Dan, commander	June 1968 on
Hoang The Thien, political officer	June 1968 on
Le Cong Phe, commander	c. 1973 on
Nguyen An, commander (acting)	c. 1974 on

Commanding Officers, Division 304B

Nguyen Thai Dung, commander	September 1967 on

Division 308. The *308th*, the first of six infantry divisions organized during the resistance, was established in August 1949. Significantly upgraded with artillery, tanks, engineers, and communications in 1961–1962, the *308th* contributed one of three battalions in late 1964 that formed *Regiment 320,* which then infiltrated the Tay Nguyen Front, followed in 1966 by *Regiment 88.* In September 1967, the *308th* was picked as one of four PAVN divisions that would participate in the Tet Offensive. *Regiment 36* joined the Quang Da Front in Military Region 5 while regiments *102* and *88* entered the Route 9 Front in 1968 and saw action at Khe Sanh.

Commanding Officers, Division 308

Vuong Thua Vu, commander	August 1949 on
Song Hao, political officer	August 1949 on

Thai Dung, commander	June 1968 on
Nguyen Huu An, commander	c. 1972

Division 312. The *Chien Thang* (Victorious) *Division,* established 27 October 1950, fought at Dien Bien Phu. A battalion of the *312th* crossed the Ben Hai river into Quang Tri province in spring 1963, and a year later a second battalion entered Military Region 5, where it participated in the early fighting with U.S. forces on the Batangan peninsula in August 1965. Regiments *141* and *165* were dispatched to the B2 Front in 1966 to serve as the nucleus of PLAF *Division 7.* In September 1967, the *312th* was picked as one of four PAVN divisions that would participate in the Tet Offensive. From 1963 through 1968 the *312th* supplied a total of four regiments, nine battalions, and numerous teams of officers to the fighting in the South.

Regrouped near Hanoi after the Tet Offensive, regiments *141, 165,* and *209* finally fought as a single unit when sent to enlarge the PAVN's logistical corridor through Laos in 1969–1970. In late 1971 it fought in Laos, supported, for the first time, by T-34 tanks and 130 mm long-range artillery. The *312th*'s regiments entered the Tri Thien Front in July 1972 as attachments of divisions *325, 308,* and *304* and later replaced the *308th* and *304th* as the defense force south of the Thach Han river. Stationed in the North when the 1975 Spring Offensive began, the *312th* was among the forces that the high command ordered into the South in late March to sustain the offensive's momentum.

Commanding Officers, Division 312

Le Trong Tan, commander	October 1950 to 1954
Sen. Col. Hoang Cam, commander	1954 to 1964
Tran Do, political officer	before 1954 to after July 1958
Nguyen Nang, commander	before September 1969 to October 1971
Le Chieu, political officer	before September 1969 to October 1971
La Thai Hoa, commander	October 1971 to July 1972
Pham Sinh, political officer	October 1971 to July 1972
Nguyen Chuong, commander	before April 1975 to after December 1977
Nguyen Xuyen, political officer	before April 1975 on

Division 316. Nearly half of the troops in *Division 316* at the time of its founding were from ethnic minorities of the Viet Bac region near Vietnam's border with China. The division was formally estab-

lished on 1 May 1951 with regiments *98, 174,* and *176.* One regiment operated in the Tay Nguyen highlands in 1967, and two of them helped expand the Pathet Lao zone of control in December 1968. But for most of the war the *316th* was a light infantry division that fought in Laos. It joined the *3d Corps* for the attack on Ban Me Thuot in spring 1975, returned to the North after the war, and was among the forces stationed on the border when China attacked in February 1979.

Commanding Officers, Division 316

Chu Huy Man, deputy political officer	May 1951 to after 1953
Le Quang Ba, commander	1953 to 1958
Lt. Gen. Vu Lap, commander	
Sen. Col. Dam Van Nguy, commander	before March 1975 on
Col. Ha Quoc Toan, political officer	before March 1975 on

Division 320. Division 320, the *Dong Bang* (Delta, or Plains) *Division,* was organized in the delta region south of the Red River on 16 January 1951. The division sent its *Antiaircraft Battalion 14* to Laos in late 1964, and in August 1965 one of its mortar battalions entered the South to form the core of a PLAF artillery unit in the Eastern Nam Bo Region. In February 1966 *Regiment 64* went into combat in Quang Ngai and Quang Nam provinces, and later in the year *Regiment 52* reinforced the B2 Front. In September 1967, the *320th* was one of four PAVN divisions picked to participate in the Tet Offensive. Under the Route 9–Northern Quang Tri Front Command (B5), it attacked along Route 9 in coordination with assaults by divisions *304* and *325* on Lang Vei and Khe Sanh. It withdrew to the North in October 1968, returned to action in October 1970, and part of it joined the *70th Corps* to fight around Route 9 and in southern Laos in 1971. After another period of regroupment in the North, the division moved to the Tay Nguyen Front, arriving there in January 1972. In spring 1975, it pursued ARVN remnants down Route 7 toward the coast, became part of the *3d Corps* in March, and moved entirely by truck to Tay Ninh for the final push on Saigon.

The *320th's* frame unit trained 153,000 men from 1965 through 1970, sending many to the South in battalion strength. However, because of the force requirements of the 1972 Easter Offensive,

regiments of *Division 320B* were sent into combat as integral units. The *320B* withdrew to the North's Thanh Hoa province in September 1973 and became part of the newly formed *1st Military Corps* in October. *Regiment 48* of the *320B,* then a training unit, participated in the defense of the northern border against the attack by China in February 1979. The *320B* was officially redesignated *Division 390* on 4 May 1979.

Commanding Officers, Division 320

Van Tien Dung, commander/political officer	January 1951 on
Sung Lam, commander	c. 1967 to c. 1971
Sen. Col. Luong Tuan Khang, political officer	c. 1965 to c. 1971
Kim Tuan, commander	c. 1971 to March 1975
Phi Trieu Ham, political officer	c. 1971 to March 1975
Bui Dinh Hoe, commander	March 1975 on
Col. Bui Huy Bong, political officer	March 1975 on

Commanding Officers, Division 320B

Pham Thanh Son, commander	September 1965 to early 1966
Nguyen Duy Tuong, political officer	September 1965 to early 1966
Bui Sinh, commander	early 1966 to 1969
Nguyen Huan, political officer	early 1966 to 1969
Ha Vi Tung, commander	mid 1969 to c. 1973
Tran Ngoc Kien, political officer	mid 1969 to c. 1973
Sen. Col. Luu Ba Xao, commander	c. 1973 to c. 1976

Division 324. Formed with regroupees from the South in June 1955, *Division 324* trained specially to attack fortified strongpoints. In late 1966 it moved to the Route 9 Front, where its artillery supported assaults on U.S. Marine outposts. *Regiment 3* of the *324th* participated in fighting in Hue during the Tet Offensive. In spring 1975 the division fought as part of the *2d Corps* in the Tri Thien Front but remained in Hue and Da Nang to provide security while the rest of the corps proceeded to Saigon.

Commanding Officers, Division 324

Nguyen Don, commander	c. 1955
Duy Son, commander	c. 1975
Nguyen Trong Dan, political officer	c. 1975

Division 325. Activated on 11 March 1951, the *325th* was the only resistance-era division organized

in what was to become South Vietnam after 1954. In 1961, elements of this division expanded Pathet Lao control around Tchepone, permitting easier passage by *Group 559* through southern Laos. In November 1964 regiments *95* and *101* of the *325th* left the North to enter Military Region 5 while *Regiment 18* went to the Tay Nguyen Front. The division took the designation *325A* as the skeleton staff it had left behind began to build *Division 325B*, and later divisions *325C* and *325D*, regiments *95B*, *95C*, *95D*, and so forth.

Division 325B entered the South in spring 1966. Two regiments of this division, the *95B* and *101B*, reinforced the Tay Nguyen Front, where the *95B* pushed U.S. Special Forces out of the A Shau valley during March. Heavy losses, however, forced regiments *101B* and *101C* to combine as *Regiment 33*. The *33d, 24th,* and *95B* operated for a time as independent regiments in Kontum, Gia Lai, and Quang Duc provinces. *Regiment 33* moved to Eastern Nam Bo in late 1968, while the *95B* remained in Tay Nguyen until the end of the war.

Division 325C comprising regiments *101D*, *95C*, and *18C* began entering the Route 9–Tri Thien Front in late 1966, and the *95C* and a battalion of the *18C* fought around Khe Sanh a year later. *Regiment 18C* spearheaded the attack on Hue while elements of regiments *95C* and *101D* participated in attacks on Lang Vei and around Khe Sanh in February 1968. The *95C* and *101D* were redeployed farther south following the Tet Offensive, while divisional headquarters returned to the North to build *Division 325D*.

Division 325D was built around three regiments raised in Military Region 3. Although the *325D* sent *Regiment 18D* to help *Group 559* expand supply routes through Laos and sent *Regiment 95D* to Route 9 in early 1969, it was essentially a training and reserve unit until the 1972 Easter Offensive. The *325D* played a large role in the seizure of Quang Tri province, and from that time on—other offspring of the *325th* having disappeared or merged into new units—it dropped the "D" from its designation. In May 1974 the *325th* became part of the *2d Corps,* and in spring 1975 it helped take Hue and Da Nang before joining the assault on Saigon. Most of the division moved down the coast, taking Phan Rang, Phan Thiet, Long Thanh, and Long Trach along the way. Elements of the division were stationed in Laos until 1977 and saw action on the border with Cambodia in 1978–1979.

Commanding Officers, Division 325

Tran Quy Hai, commander	c. 1953 on
Chu Van Bien, political officer	c. 1951 to 1955
Hoang Van Thai, political officer	1955 on
Quach Si Kha, political officer	1961 to 1964
Maj. Gen. Nguyen Huu An, commander	1964 to May 1964
Nguyen Minh Duc, political officer	1964 to May 1964

Commanding Officers, Division 325B

Vuong Tuan Kiet, commander	c. 1964 on
Quoc Tuan, political officer	c. 1964 on

Commanding Officers, Division 325C

Chu Phuong Doi, commander	c. 1965 on
Nguyen Cong Trang, political officer	c. 1965 on

Commanding Officers, Division 325D

Thang Binh, commander	1968 to c. 1971
Vu Duc Thai, political officer	1968 to c. 1971
Le Kich, commander	c. 1971 to May 1974
Sen. Col. Nguyen Cong Trang, political officer	c. 1971 to May 1974
Col. Pham Minh Tam, commander	May 1974 on
Col. Le Van Duong, political officer	May 1974 on

Division 330. Infantry Division 330 was formed in January 1955, partly with regroupees from the South's eastern, central, and Mekong Delta regions, and served for a time after 1959 as a training unit for troops preparing for operations in the South's populated lowland areas.

Commanding Officers, Division 330

Maj. Gen. Tran Van Tra, commander	before 1958 on

Division 338. This division at its founding on 12 December 1956 consisted largely of troops who regrouped from Nam Bo to the North in 1954. From 1959 to 1963 it was the main training unit for troops, cadres, and officers preparing to enter the South, especially for assignment in their native provinces of Western Nam Bo.

Division 341. Brigade 341 of Military Region 4 became *Light Infantry Division 341* in February 1962. It was disbanded when several of its units left for the South, reconstituted in March 1965, disbanded again in late 1966, and finally established with some permanence in November 1972. In January 1975 five hundred trucks of *Transportation Di-*

vision *571* moved the entire division from its base in Nghe Tinh province to Eastern Nam Bo to reinforce the *4th Corps* for the attack on Saigon.

Commanding Officers, Division 341

| Tran Van Tran, commander | c. January 1977 |
| Tran Nguyen Do, political officer | c. January 1975 |

Antiaircraft Artillery Division 361. The *361st* "Hanoi Air Defense Division" was founded on 19 May 1965 and designated a "strategic" or fixed site division in June 1966 to defend the capital.

Antiaircraft Artillery Division 363. Division *363* was a "strategic" antiaircraft artillery division established in June 1966 and provided the main antiaircraft defense of Haiphong.

Antiaircraft Artillery Division 365. Division *365* was a fixed site antiaircraft artillery division established in June 1966.

Antiaircraft Artillery Division 367. The *367th*, established in 1955, was the nucleus of what would become the PAVN's Air Defense–Air Force Branch. A "mobile" air defense division consisting of four regiments of antiaircraft artillery and one of missiles (added in June 1966), the *367th* was assigned to Military Region 4 in 1968 to bolster defenses against intensified U.S. bombardment.

Antiaircraft Artillery Division 368. Division *368*, its date of establishment not known, was assigned to Military Region 4 in 1968 to bolster defenses against intensified U.S. bombardment.

Antiaircraft Artillery Division 369. Division *369* was a fixed site antiaircraft artillery division established in June 1966.

Antiaircraft Artillery Division 371. Air force regiments *921* and *923* were combined on 24 March 1967 to form *Air Force Division 371* when the air force became a separate command within the Air Defense–Air Force Branch.

Antiaircraft Artillery Division 377. Division *377* was formed with three regiments taken from fixed site divisions in 1968 for the purpose of bolstering antiaircraft defenses in Military Region 4.

Divisions 470, 471, 472, 473 (of Group 559). Group *559* organized these divisions to administer key segments of the Ho Chi Minh Trail complex. The *470th*, for example, came into existence in spring 1970 to organize an alternative source of supply for units in Cambodia and Nam Bo when the PAVN lost use of the Cambodian port of Sihanoukville. The *470th*, *471st*, and *472d* were "sectoral" or "areal" (*khu vuc*) divisions until late 1974, when the *470th* and *472d* were designated engineering divisions and the *471st* became a transportation division modeled on the *571st*. The *473d* was an engineering division from the time of its establishment. The *471st* was abolished after the war.

Transportation Division 571. The expansion and reorganization of *Group 559* to meet the increased logistical requirements of corps level operations included the establishment of the PAVN's first motorized transportation division on 12 July 1973. The division had been a sectoral command of the Ho Chi Minh Trail known as the Rear Service Command 571 after October 1972.

The main duty of the *571st* was long distance hauling to trail termini where other units took over distribution to the field. In mid 1974 it had 2,600 vehicles and 8,500 officers, men, and women. The division's trucks operated on roads running through southern Laos to Stung Treng in Cambodia and over parts of Route 14 in South Vietnam. After PAVN victories in Phuoc Long province and the Central Highlands in early 1975, the division's mission shifted to the deployment and direct support of troops in battle.

The *571st* avoided being decommissioned after the war by becoming, under the command of the Rear Services General Directorate, a conduit of assistance and trade with Laos as well as of logistical support for PAVN "volunteers" there.

Commanding Officers, Division 571

Col. Nguyen Dam, commander	August 1973 to November 1973
Hoang Tra, commander (acting)	November 1973 to 1975
Col. Phan Huu Dai, political officer	August 1973 on
Sen. Col. Phan Huu Dai, commander/political officer	1975 on

Division 711. Military Region 5 organized *Division 711* on 29 June 1971 in Binh Dinh province. The region decommissioned the division in late June 1973 during a general reorganization of Military Region 5 main forces, forming *Brigade 52* out of its remnants.

Commanding Officers, Division 711

| Nguyen Chon, commander | June 1972 to June 1973 |

Tank Brigade 202. Upon being commissioned 5 October 1959 under officers who had trained abroad,

Tank Regiment 202 consisted of two battalions equipped with World War II–vintage T-34s and one battalion of self-propelled artillery. The *202d's* main combat role in 1965–1968 was to support air defenses aroundVinh Linh. In 1969 a thirty-man team patched up half a dozen PT-76 amphibious tanks to form *Group 195,* which helped push the Hmong warlord Vang Pao and Thai mercenaries out of the Plain of Jars. A year later, *Battalion 397* saw action in the counterattack on ARVN Operation LAM SON 719.

Regrouped near Vinh Linh in March 1972, the regiment crossed the Ben Hai River to support attacks by *Division 308* on Dong Ha and *Division 320B* on Cua Viet. The *202d* was officially designated an "armored and tank brigade" on 25 October 1973. In December it became a part of *1st Corps.* After a period of recovery in the North and the acquisition of T-59 tanks, the *202d* joined the 1975 Spring Offensive in late March. With the ARVN's collapse, tanks were able to move freely over the South's roads for the first time and arrived with *Division 320B* at the ARVN General Staff compound on 27 April.

Commanding Officers, Tank Brigade 202

Dao Huy Vu, commander	October 1959 to June 1965
Dang Quang Long, political officer	October 1959 to June 1965
Le Xuan Kien, commander	June 1965 to November 1971
Vo Ngoc Hai, political officer	June 1965 to November 1971
Nguyen Van Lang, commander	November 1971 to 1972
Vo Ngoc Hai, political officer	November 1971 to 1972
Do Phuong Ngu, commander	1972 to 1980
Hoang Khoai, political officer	1972 to 1980

Tank Brigade 203. The PAVN's first tank brigade gave birth to its second, the *203d,* sometimes before June 1965. Battalions *297* and *198* of the *203d* saw action against Operation LAM SON 719 in early 1971. The brigade participated in the 1975 Spring Offensive under Tri Thien Front command as part of *2d Corps.*

[*See also entries on individual communist military services.*]

BIBLIOGRAPHY

The main sources of information for this order of battle are some thirty histories of PAVN units and commands written by People's Army historians and memoirs by PAVN generals published in the Vietnamese language since the end of the Vietnam War. They include, for example, histories of specific divisions and services such as the air force, navy, and sappers, as well as a two-volume general history of the PAVN. Many of these books can be found in the Library of Congress and in the Southeast Asia collections of libraries at Harvard University, Cornell University, the University of Hawaii, the University of California, and the University of Washington. The Vietnamese were continuing to publish such works; not all of those which had been published were available at the time this entry was written. Sources in English include:

FOREIGN BROADCAST INFORMATION SERVICE. *Daily Report: Asia and Pacific.* U.S. Department of Commerce.

FOREIGN BROADCAST INFORMATION SERVICE. *Daily Report: East Asia.* U.S. Department of Commerce.

NATIONAL FOREIGN ASSESSMENT CENTER. *Directory of Officials of the Socialist Republic of Vietnam: A Reference Aid.* Central Intelligence Agency. December 1980.

TRAN VAN TRA. *Concluding the 30-Years War.* Vol. 5 of *Vietnam: History of the Bulwark B2 Theater.* Translated by the Joint Publications Research Service. Foreign Broadcast Information Service, Southeast Asia Report No. 1247. 2 February 1983.

U.S. MILITARY ASSISTANCE COMMAND, VIETNAM. Office of the Assistant Chief of Staff–J2. *Order of Battle: Viet Cong Forces, Republic of Vietnam.* 1 October 1962, 15 March 1963, and 1 October 1963.

U.S. MILITARY ASSISTANCE COMMAND, VIETNAM. Office of the Assistant Chief of Staff–J2. *North Vietnam Personnel Infiltration into the Republic of Vietnam.* CICV ST 70-05. 16 December 1970.

U.S. MILITARY ASSISTANCE COMMAND, VIETNAM. Office of the Assistant Chief of Staff–J2. *Order of Battle Study ST 67-023, Command and Control.* CICV OBS 67-028. 6 January 1967.

U.S. EMBASSY, SAIGON. *Viet-Nam Documents and Research Notes.* [See especially nos. 23 (March 1968), 40 (August 1968), and 41 (August 1968).]

VAN TIEN DUNG. *Our Great Spring Victory.* Translated by John Spragens Jr. 1977.

WAR EXPERIENCES RECAPITULATION COMMITTEE OF THE HIGH-LEVEL MILITARY INSTITUTE. *The Anti-U.S. Resistance War for National Salvation 1954–1975: Military Events.* Translated by the Joint Publications Research Service. Foreign Broadcast Information Service, JPRS No. 80968. 3 June 1982.

WILLIAM S. TURLEY

U.S. Military

[This article is not intended to be a complete order of battle of U.S. military forces in the Vietnam War. It is only a brief overview of the major commands.

For more detailed information, see the sources cited in the bibliography.]

Service/Field Headquarters

Military Assistance Command, Vietnam. Formed on 8 February 1962, the Military Assistance Command, Vietnam (MACV), was the joint service headquarters for U.S. military forces in Vietnam. The commanding general of the U.S. Military Assistance Command, Vietnam (COMUSMACV), reported to the Commander-in-Chief, Pacific (CINCPAC) located in Hawaii. COMUSMACV's authority was limited to U.S. operations within South Vietnam and along its immediate borders. Therefore, CINCPAC attempted to coordinate military operations throughout Southeast Asia through MACV, the Seventh Fleet, and a confusing chain of command for air operations.

The complex command structure within South Vietnam also seriously complicated military matters. In May 1964 MACV absorbed the responsibilities of the Military Assistance and Advisory Group–Vietnam (MAAG-V), which had been advising the South Vietnamese military since September 1950. With the deactivation of MAAG-V, the advisory effort lost its central direction. MACV also played a dual role as both a joint service headquarters and the U.S. Army's field headquarters in Vietnam. Finally, the South Vietnamese armed forces remained independent of U.S. control. Such a decentralized and disorganized command arrangement seriously undermined MACV's effectiveness.

The following elements fell under MACV's direct authority: Field Advisory Element, MACV; U.S. Army, Vietnam (USARV); Naval Forces Vietnam; Seventh Air Force; III Marine Amphibious Force; I Field Force; II Field Force; XXIV Corps; and 5th Special Forces Group. A wide range of political and civil projects existed as well. MACV departed South Vietnam on 29 March 1973.

Commanding Generals, U.S. Military Assistance Command, Vietnam

General Paul D. Harkins	February 1962–June 1964
General William C. Westmoreland	June 1964–July 1968
General Creighton W. Abrams	July 1968–June 1972
General Frederick C. Weyand	June 1972–March 1973

U.S. Air Force

2d Air Division. Reporting to MACV, the 2d Air Division controlled U.S. air operations in South Vietnam between 8 October 1962 and the establishment of the Seventh Air Force on 1 April 1966. Until the rapid U.S. military buildup began in 1965, the 2d Division relied on propeller-driven aircraft to provide air support for the Army of the Republic of Vietnam (ARVN). Jet fighters arrived in the spring of 1965, and by the end of the year the United States had deployed nearly 500 U.S. combat aircraft in South Vietnam. When eventually transformed into the Seventh Air Force, the 2d Division consisted of nearly 1,000 aircraft and roughly 30,000 personnel.

Commanding Generals, 2d Air Division

Brig. Gen. Rollen H. Anthis	October–December 1962
Brig. Gen. Robert R. Rowland	December 1962–December 1963
Brig. Gen. Milton B. Adams	December 1963–January 1964
Lt. Gen. Joseph H. Moore	January 1964–March 1966

Seventh Air Force. Organized on 1 April 1966 to replace the 2d Air Division, the Seventh Air Force was responsible for U.S. air operations in Southeast Asia until its departure in March 1973. Headquartered at Tan Son Nhut Air Base near Saigon, the Seventh Air Force took its orders from the COMUSMACV for missions conducted within South Vietnam, along its immediate borders, and in southern Laos. The commander of the Seventh Air Force also served as the deputy COMUSMACV for air.

For air operations against targets in northern Laos and North Vietnam, however, the commanding general of the Seventh Air Force reported to the Commander-in-Chief of the Pacific Air Force (CINCPACAF), who reported to CINCPAC. Under CINCPACAF's direction, the Seventh Air Force and the Thirteenth Air Force in the Philippines also shared a joint command in Udorn, Thailand—the Seventh/Thirteenth Air Force. To further confuse the situation, the Strategic Air Command (SAC) retained direct control of its B-52 bombers deployed against targets in Southeast Asia. The lack of a single headquarters for all air operations seriously handicapped efforts for effective coordination.

Subordinate commands of the Seventh Air Force included: the 3d Tactical Fighter Wing in the III Corps Tactical Zone (CTZ); the 12th, 31st, and 35th Tactical Fighter Wings in the II CTZ; the 366th Tactical Fighter Wing in the I CTZ; the 834th Air Division; and the Air Force Advisory Group.

Commanding Generals, Seventh Air Force

Lt. Gen. Joseph H. Moore	April–June 1966
General William W. Momyer	June 1966–July 1968
General George S. Brown	August 1968–August 1970
General Lucius D. Clay Jr.	September 1970–July 1971
General John D. Lavelle	August 1971–April 1972
General John W. Vogt Jr.	April 1972–September 1973

Seventh/Thirteenth Air Force. Stationed in Udorn, Thailand, the Seventh/Thirteenth Air Force was organized on 6 January 1966. It was an independent air division taking orders from two different commands. The commander of the Seventh/Thirteenth Air Force reported to the Seventh Air Force on operational matters and to the Thirteenth Air Force on logistical and administrative matters.

At its peak in 1968, the Seventh/Thirteenth Air Force numbered 35,000 personnel and 600 aircraft. Its major combat units included the 8th Tactical Fighter Wing, the 355th Tactical Fighter Wing, the 388th Tactical Fighter Wing, the 432d Tactical Reconnaissance Wing, the 553d Tactical Reconnaissance Wing, and the 56th Special Operations Wing.

Commanding Generals, Seventh/Thirteenth Air Force

Maj. Gen. Charles R. Bond	January 1966–May 1967
Maj. Gen. William C. Lindley Jr.	June 1967–May 1968
Maj. Gen. Louis T. Seith	June 1968–May 1969
Maj. Gen. Robert L. Petit	June 1969–March 1970
Maj. Gen. James F. Kirkendall	March 1970–October 1970
Maj. Gen. Andrew Evans Jr.	October 1970–June 1971
Maj. Gen. DeWitt R. Searles	July 1971–September 1972
Maj. Gen. James D. Hughes	September 1972–April 1973

Strategic Air Command. The Strategic Air Command (SAC) retained direct control of its strategic bombers employed against targets in Southeast Asia. The B-52 strategic bomber was the mainstay of U.S. strategic forces in the 1960s and 1970s and was used extensively during the Vietnam War for tactical and strategic missions. B-52 strikes began on 18 June 1965 and ended on 23 January 1973. Between 1965 and 1973, B-52s flew more than 126,000 sorties in Southeast Asia.

SAC initially controlled the employment of B-52 bombers via the 3d Air Division in Guam, but after July 1970 the Eighth Air Force assumed responsibility. Widely scattered subordinate units included the 4133d Bombardment Wing out of Guam, 4258th Strategic Air Wing (later designated the 307th Strategic Air Wing), which began flying out of Thailand in 1967, and the 4252d Strategic Air Wing out of Okinawa.

Military Airlift Command. The Military Airlift Command (MAC) transported a large percentage of the supplies, equipment, and personnel deployed to South Vietnam. MAC's resupply missions to Southeast Asia totaled 340 million kilometers (210 million miles) in 1967 and accounted for nearly 348,000 passengers. This airlift included the transportation of the entire 25th Infantry Division in 1965 and the 101st Airborne Division in 1967. Equally significant was the transport of more than 400,000 medical evacuees flown to the United States between 1963 and 1973.

Prior to 1973 the MAC and the Tactical Air Command divided airlift responsibilities. To further complicate matters, MAC retained direct control of its aircraft rather than turning them over to the operational control of area air commanders. The result was a divided airlift effort with duplicate responsibilities and functions and intense competition for limited ramp space, fuel, and ground crews.

Tactical Air Command. The Tactical Air Command (TAC) was responsible for meeting the U.S. Air Force's tactical airlift needs in the Vietnam War. Tactical airlift delivered more than 7 million tons of passengers and cargo within South Vietnam between 1962 and 1972. Unlike the MAC, TAC placed its aircraft under the operational control of units in the combat theater. The 834th Air Division handled tactical airlift within South Vietnam and reported directly to the Seventh Air Force. It received support from the 315th Air Division stationed in Japan.

834th Air Division. Organized on 25 October 1966 and placed under the Seventh Air Force, the 834th Air Division provided centralized control for tactical airlift within South Vietnam until its departure in November 1970. Its duties included logistical airlift, airborne operations, and medical evacuations. Subordinate units included the 315th Special Operations Wing, the 483d Tactical Airlift Wing, and the Airlift Control Center (ALCC). The ALCC was a flexible headquarters that controlled transport aircraft rotated into South Vietnam by the 315th Air Division.

315th Air Division. The 315th Air Division was activated at Tachikawa Air Base in Japan on 25 January 1951 and reported to the Thirteenth Air Force stationed at Clark Air Base in the Philippines. Subordinate units of the 315th Air Division included the 374th Troop Carrier Wing in Taiwan and the 463d Troop Carrier Wing at Clark. The division was deactivated on 15 April 1969.

U.S. Army

I. Support and Advisory Elements

Field Advisory Element, Military Assistance Command, Vietnam. Following the deactivation of MAAG-V in May 1964, the advising and training of the ARVN became the primary function of the Field Advisory Element, MACV. No single individual coordinated the training and advising effort; central direction came from diverse elements within the MACV staff and from senior advisers in the CTZs. This arrangement left the advisory effort virtually ignored for several years, and the development of the South Vietnamese military suffered accordingly. It was not until after the Tet Offensive of 1968 that the ARVN's combat capabilities became a fundamental concern. The selection and training of advisory teams subsequently received a higher priority and reached a broader array of defense forces. Despite these changes, the inability to make wholesale changes in the ARVN command structure doomed the advisory program to failure.

U.S. Army, Vietnam. Established on 20 July 1965, the U.S. Army, Vietnam (USARV), was intended to be the field headquarters for the U.S. Army's combat units in Vietnam, but MACV retained direct operational control of those forces. Without a combat role, USARV developed into an administrative and logistical support command and played a pivotal role in the U.S. buildup. Although the commanding general of MACV was technically the commander of USARV as well, in reality his deputy exercised that responsibility. Units under USARV control included the 1st Logistical Command, 1st Aviation Brigade, 18th Military Police Brigade, 34th General Support Group, 525th Military Intelligence Group, and a wide variety of other commands. USARV was dissolved on 15 May 1972.

Deputy Commanding Generals, MACV

Maj. Gen. John Norton	July 1965–January 1966
Lt. Gen. Jean E. Engler	January 1966–July 1967
Lt. Gen. Bruce Palmer Jr.	July 1967–June 1968
Lt. Gen. Frank T. Mildren	June 1968–July 1970
Lt. Gen. William J. McCaffrey	July 1970–September 1972
Maj. Gen. Morgan C. Roseborough	September 1972–March 1973

II. Tactical Corps Headquarters

I Field Force, Vietnam. Headquartered at Nha Trang, the I Field Force, Vietnam (I FFV), exercised operational control over U.S. Army and allied units in the II CTZ from 15 November 1965 to 30 April 1971. Originally it was called Field Force, Vietnam, but the name change became necessary in March 1966 with the formation of II Field Force, Vietnam. The U.S. Army employed the designation of Field Force to denote the command's flexibility as a tactical organization and to avoid confusion with the geographically defined corps tactical zones established by South Vietnam. Each field force was an army corps headquarters.

Major combat units that served under the control of the I FFV included the 1st Cavalry Division, 4th Infantry Division, 25th Infantry Division, 101st Airborne Division, and 173d Airborne Brigade.

Commanding Generals, I Field Force

Lt. Gen. Stanley R. Larson	November 1965–March 1968
Lt. Gen. William R. Peers	March 1968–March 1969
Lt. Gen. Charles A. Corcoran	March 1969–March 1970
Lt. Gen. Arthur S. Collins Jr.	March 1970–January 1971
Maj. Gen. Charles P. Brown	January–April 1971

II Field Force, Vietnam. Organized on 15 March 1966, the II Field Force, Vietnam (II FFV), exercised operational control over U.S. and allied units in the III CTZ. A significant U.S. presence was required in the region to protect Saigon and the vast number of key military installations. Headquartered at Bien Hoa and later Long Binh, the II FFV became the largest U.S. Army field element in South Vietnam. It frequently conducted multidivisional operations against North Vietnamese and Viet Cong strongholds in War Zones C and D and in the Iron Triangle. In May 1970 the commanding general of the II FFV organized and executed the invasion of Cambodia.

Major combat units that served with the II FFV included the 1st, 4th, 9th, and 25th Infantry Divisions, the 1st Cavalry Division, the 101st Airborne Division, the 3d Brigade of the 82d Airborne Division, the 196th and 199th Infantry Brigades, and the 173d Airborne Brigade. The II FFV was deactivated on 2 May 1971.

Commanding Generals, II Field Force

Lt. Gen. Jonathan O. Seaman	March 1966–March 1967
Lt. Gen. Bruce Palmer Jr.	March 1967–July 1967
Maj. Gen. Frederick C. Weyand	July 1967–August 1968

Maj. Gen. Walter T. Kerwin Jr.	August 1968–April 1969
Lt. Gen. Julian J. Ewell	April 1969–April 1970
Lt. Gen. Michael S. Davison	April 1970–May 1971

XXIV Corps. In February 1968, General William C. Westmoreland temporarily sent MACV's forward headquarters to the I CTZ to exercise control over the substantial number of army units recently deployed there. He eventually transformed the headquarters into the U.S. Army Provisional Corps, Vietnam. Finally, on 15 August 1968, MACV activated the XXIV Corps to replace the Provisional Corps. Since the III Marine Amphibious Force directed U.S. operations in the I CTZ, the XXIV Corps came under its command.

The XXIV Corps conducted operations along the demilitarized zone (DMZ) and the Laotian border in conjunction with U.S. Marine units. By March 1970 the U.S. Army's maneuver elements in the I CTZ outnumbered the marines three to one, and the XXIV Corps became the senior U.S. headquarters in the region. Major combat units that served with the XXIV Corps included the 23d (American) Infantry Division, 1st Cavalry Division, 101st Airborne Division, several separate infantry brigades, and Marine Corps units. The XXIV Corps departed Vietnam on 20 June 1972.

Commanding Generals, XXIV Corps

Lt. Gen. William B. Rosson	February–July 1968
Lt. Gen. Richard G. Stilwell	July 1968–June 1969
Lt. Gen. Melvin Zais	June 1969–June 1970
Lt. Gen. James W. Sutherland Jr.	June 1970–June 1971
Lt. Gen. Welborn G. Dolvin	June 1971–June 1972

III. Combat Divisions

1st Cavalry Division (Airmobile). The 1st Cavalry Division (Airmobile) was the first U.S. Army division to enter combat in South Vietnam. It arrived on 11 September 1965 and was immediately sent to the II CTZ to stem a growing North Vietnamese Army (NVA) threat in the critical Central Highlands. The 1st Cavalry Division relied totally on helicopters for mobility. It established headquarters at An Khe and proceeded to challenge the NVA for control of the Ia Drang Valley. Although the division's mobility and firepower resulted in a tactical victory, that success masked fundamental weaknesses in U.S. strategy and doctrine. The division served throughout South Vietnam and participated in the 1970 invasion of Cambodia. It earned a reputation for aggressive and successful combat op-

erations. The bulk of the 1st Cavalry Division withdrew on 29 April 1971, but a brigade task force remained until June 1972.

Commanding Generals, 1st Cavalry Division

Maj. Gen. Harry W. B. Kinnard	July 1965–May 1966
Maj. Gen. John Norton	May 1966–April 1967
Maj. Gen. John J. Tolson III	April 1967–July 1968
Maj. Gen. George I. Forsythe	July 1968–May 1969
Maj. Gen. Elvy B. Roberts	May 1969–May 1970
Maj. Gen. George W. Casey	May–July 1970
Maj. Gen. George W. Putnam Jr.	July 1970–April 1971

1st Infantry Division. The oldest of the U.S. Army's combat divisions, the 1st Infantry Division arrived in South Vietnam on 2 October 1965 and established headquarters at Bien Hoa in the III CTZ. Under the control of the II FFV, the division participated in some of the largest combat operations of the Vietnam War including operations AT-TLEBORO, CEDAR FALLS, and JUNCTION CITY. The 1st Infantry Division developed a reputation for relying on a preponderance of firepower to overwhelm the opposition. Although this kept casualties low, the doctrine was not well suited for maintaining contact with elusive NVA and Viet Cong forces in the jungle. The division withdrew from South Vietnam on 15 April 1970.

Commanding Generals, 1st Infantry Division

Maj. Gen. Jonathan O. Seaman	October 1965–March 1966
Maj. Gen. William E. DePuy	March 1966–February 1967
Maj. Gen. John H. Hay Jr.	February 1967–March 1968
Maj. Gen. Keith L. Ware	March–September 1968
Maj. Gen. Orwin C. Talbott	September 1968–August 1969
Maj. Gen. Albert E. Milloy	August 1969–March 1970
Brig. Gen. John Q. Herrion	March–April 1970

4th Infantry Division. Arriving in South Vietnam on 25 September 1966, the 4th Infantry Division established headquarters at Pleiku in the II CTZ. A significant portion of the division, however, never reached Pleiku. The division's 3d Brigade and supporting armor were ordered to the II CTZ and were later exchanged for elements of the 25th Infantry Division. The 4th Division spent the next four years in the Central Highlands and earned a reputation for steadfast dependability. In June 1970, when the 4th Division was on the coast awaiting shipment home, it received orders to participate in the invasion of Cambodia. The division took less than three days to move to the border and launch the operation. It departed Vietnam on 7 December 1970.

Commanding Generals, 4th Infantry Division

Maj. Gen. Arthur S. Collins Jr.	September 1966–January 1967
Maj. Gen. William R. Peers	January 1967–January 1968
Maj. Gen. Charles P. Stone	January–December 1968
Maj. Gen. Donn R. Pepke	December 1968–November 1969
Maj. Gen. Glenn D. Walker	November 1969–July 1970.
Maj. Gen. William A. Burke	July–December 1970

9th Infantry Division. The 9th Infantry Division landed in South Vietnam on 16 December 1966, only eleven months after being activated. Sent to the III CTZ, the division established headquarters at Bear Cat, south of Saigon. In June 1967 the 9th Division lost its 2d Brigade to the Mobile Riverine Force (MRF) in the IV CTZ. The MRF was a joint U.S. Army-Navy operation designed to deny the Viet Cong control of the waterways of the Mekong River. The force employed river gunboats and amphibious assault forces to patrol the region and attack Viet Cong strongholds. The 9th Infantry Division returned to the United States on 27 August 1969, but its 3d Brigade remained in the III CTZ until October 1970.

Commanding Generals, 9th Infantry Division

Maj. Gen. George C. Eckhart	December 1966–June 1967
Maj. Gen. George C. O'Connor	June 1967–February 1968
Maj. Gen. Julian J. Ewell	February 1968–April 1969
Maj. Gen. Harris W. Hollis	April–August 1969

23d (American) Infantry Division. Reactivated in Vietnam on 25 September 1967, the 23d (American) Infantry Division was the brainchild of General William C. Westmoreland. Early in 1967 the Marine Corps was stretched to its limit in the I CTZ and needed urgent reinforcement. Westmoreland decided to send a collection of U.S. Army infantry brigades to the region and placed them under a division-size headquarters named Task Force Oregon. The task force was transformed into the 23d (American) Division, first raised on New Caledonia during World War II. Consisting of the 11th, 196th, and 198th Infantry Brigades plus other supporting units, the division handled security for Quang Nam and Quang Tri provinces. Intense NVA and guerrilla activity provided a serious challenge, and the American Division suffered from weak leadership and low morale. Deactivated on 29 November 1971, the division is probably best known for the My Lai massacre.

Commanding Generals, 23d (American) Infantry Division

Maj. Gen. Samuel W. Koster	September 1967–June 1968
Maj. Gen. Charles M. Gettys	June 1968–June 1969
Maj. Gen. Lloyd B. Ramsey	June 1969–March 1970
Maj. Gen. Albert E. Milloy	March–November 1970
Maj. Gen. James L. Baldwin	November 1970–July 1971
Maj. Gen. Frederick J. Kroesen Jr.	July–November 1971

25th Infantry Division. Initially stationed in Hawaii as the ready-reserve for the Pacific, the 25th Infantry Division moved to Vietnam in several stages. Its 3d Brigade arrived late in 1965 and went to the II CTZ. The 2d Brigade landed in January 1966 and went to Cu Chi in the III CTZ; the rest of the division followed in March. The 25th Division remained in the III CTZ and eventually exchanged its 3d Brigade for elements of the 4th Division. It took part in Operation JUNCTION CITY and participated in the 1970 invasion of Cambodia. The bulk of the 25th Division withdrew from Vietnam on 8 December 1970, but the 2d Brigade remained until April 1971.

Commanding Generals, 25th Infantry Division

Maj. Gen. Frederick C. Weyand	March 1966–March 1967
Maj. Gen. John C. F. Tillson III	March–August 1967
Maj. Gen. Fillmore K. Mearns	August 1967–August 1968
Maj. Gen. Ellis W. Williamson	August 1968–September 1969
Maj. Gen. Edward Baultz Jr.	September 1969–December 1970

101st Airborne Division (Airmobile). The 1st Brigade of the famed 101st Airborne Division (Airmobile) arrived in Vietnam on 29 July 1965 and began operating in the II CTZ. It later temporarily joined Task Force Oregon. The bulk of the division arrived on 19 November 1967 and established its headquarters at Bien Hoa in the III CTZ. Initially earmarked for conversion to an elite airmobile division, the 101st Airborne Division arrived short of trained personnel and aviation assets, which forced

MACV to postpone the conversion until mid 1969. During the 1968 Tet Offensive, the division shifted north to the city of Hue and remained in the I CTZ. In 1970 and 1971, it took part in Operation JEFFERSON GLENN—the last major U.S. ground operation of the war. The division began to withdraw from Vietnam in December 1971 and completed the process by 10 March 1972.

Commanding Generals, 101st Airborne Division

Maj. Gen. Olinto M. Barsanti	November 1967–July 1968
Maj. Gen. Melvin Zais	July 1968–May 1969
Maj. Gen. John M. Wright Jr.	May 1969–May 1970
Maj. Gen. John J. Hennessey	May 1970–January 1971
Maj. Gen. Thomas M. Tarpley	January 1971–March 1972

Task Force Oregon. Activated in the I CTZ on 12 April 1967, Task Force Oregon was a provisional division deployed to support the U.S. Marines in the northern provinces. Its combat elements consisted of the 3d Brigade, 25th Infantry Division, the 1st Brigade, 101st Airborne Division, and the 196th Infantry Brigade. The task force was replaced by the American Division on 22 September 1967.

Commanding Generals, Task Force Oregon

Maj. Gen. William B. Rosson	April–June 1967
Maj. Gen. Richard T. Knowles	June–September 1967

IV. Independent Combat Brigades

1st Aviation Brigade. Activated in Vietnam on 25 May 1966, the 1st Aviation Brigade flew helicopter air support for U.S. and allied forces throughout the four corps tactical zones. At peak strength it consisted of more than 24,000 personnel and 4,000 combat and support helicopters. Headquartered at Tan Son Nhut and Long Binh, the 1st Brigade departed Vietnam on 28 March 1973.

11th Infantry Brigade (Light). The 11th Infantry Brigade (Light) arrived in Vietnam on 19 December 1967 and joined the American Division. Stationed in Hawaii since 1966 as the strategic reserve for the Pacific, the division was completely unprepared for combat deployment. Poor leadership and lack of training earned the 11th Brigade an unenviable reputation during the war for its morale problems and brutality, including its involvement in the massacre at My Lai. The brigade departed Vietnam on 13 November 1971.

173d Airborne Division. Specially trained for warfare in Southeast Asia, the 173d Airborne Brigade was the first major combat unit sent to Vietnam. It arrived on 7 May 1965 and began providing security for the extensive military facility at Bien Hoa. Although intended for short-term deployment, the brigade remained in Vietnam until 25 August 1971. Generally considered one of the most elite units to serve in the Vietnam War, the 173d Brigade won acclaim for its parachute jump into Tay Ninh province during Operation JUNCTION CITY in February 1967. In November of that same year the brigade won a Presidential Unit Citation for its conduct during the Battle of Dak To.

196th Infantry Brigade (Light). Originally slated for duty in the Dominican Republic, the 196th Infantry Brigade (Light) was the first "light infantry" brigade formed by the U.S. Army. Activated in September 1965, the brigade suffered from shortages of training cadre and of experienced noncommissioned officers. It arrived in Vietnam on 26 August 1966 unprepared for combat.

The 196th Brigade was initially assigned to the III CTZ but moved north to the I CTZ in the spring of 1967 to form Task Force Oregon. On 25 September 1967 it became part of the American Division and remained part of the division until 29 November 1971. The brigade remained in Vietnam until June 1972 providing security for the region surrounding Da Nang.

198th Infantry Brigade (Light). Activated to man the proposed "McNamara Line" infiltration barrier along the DMZ, the 198th Infantry Brigade (Light) was sent to Vietnam several months ahead of schedule and arrived on 21 October 1967. It immediately joined the American Division in the I CTZ. Because the barrier never materialized, the brigade remained with the division until it departed Vietnam on 13 November 1971. Hampered by a hurried training schedule and poor leadership, the 198th Brigade suffered from lack of discipline and low morale throughout the war.

199th Infantry Brigade (Light). To provide badly needed ground support in the III CTZ, the 199th Infantry Brigade (Light) was rushed to Vietnam in December 1966 after an abbreviated training period. The brigade, however, overcame its initial shortcomings and participated in one of the most intense battles of the Tet Offensive in 1968, successfully defending the vast U.S. military installation at Long Binh, outside Saigon, from an attack by the *275th Viet Cong Regiment*. One battalion was sent by helicopter into Saigon as well to help regain control of key areas of the city. The 199th Brigade returned to the United States on 11 October 1970.

1st Brigade, 5th Infantry Division (Mechanized). The 1st Brigade, 5th Infantry Division (Mechanized), arrived in Vietnam on 25 July 1968 as an emergency deployment to meet MACV's dire need for combat units. Sent to the I CTZ to serve with the Marine Corps, the brigade's heavy firepower and mechanized mobility provided the capabilities necessary to combat the regular units of the NVA encountered along the DMZ. It also supported South Vietnamese forces during the January 1971 invasion of Laos. The 1st Brigade, 5th Division, withdrew from Vietnam on 27 August 1971.

3d Brigade, 82d Airborne Division. Arriving in Vietnam on 18 February 1968, the 3d Brigade, 82d Airborne Division, provided emergency reinforcement during the Tet Offensive. A massive airlift of more than 140 aircraft flew the brigade to Vietnam from Fort Bragg, North Carolina, in only four days. The brigade, initially sent to Hue to provide security, was shifted to Saigon in September and remained there before returning to the United States on 11 December 1969.

The 82d Airborne Division was the only combat-ready division in the U.S. Army's reserve, and the option of deploying the entire division to Vietnam was considered and rejected as too risky. Still, deploying a single brigade severely reduced the effectiveness of the entire division.

V. Special Forces

U.S. Army Special Forces, Vietnam (Provisional). Formed in Saigon in September 1962, the U.S. Army Special Forces, Vietnam (Provisional), supervised Special Forces activities in South Vietnam. Its mission was to assist in the development of the Civilian Irregular Defense Group (CIDG) forces. The South Vietnamese government and counterinsurgency experts hoped CIDG forces would provide adequate local security to permit the regular army to embark on large-scale operations. Popularly known as the Green Berets, the Special Forces were the U.S. Army's elite counterinsurgency branch. Detachments from various Special Forces groups went to Vietnam on a rotating basis. The provisional group was replaced by the 5th Special Forces Group (Airborne) on 1 October 1964.

5th Special Forces Group (Airborne), 1st Special Forces. The 5th Special Forces Group (Airborne), 1st Special Forces, arrived from Fort Bragg, North Carolina, on 1 October 1965 and established headquarters at Nha Trang in the II CTZ. The group consisted of five companies, each consisting of a number of detachments. The command operations of each company were handled by a C-detachment,

which directed a number of B-detachments; each B-detachment commanded several A-teams.

Company A was stationed at Bien Hoa in the III CTZ and consisted of 5 B-detachments and 23 A-teams. Company B established its headquarters in the II CTZ at Pleiku and deployed 4 B-detachments and 34 A-teams. The I CTZ was served by Company C headquartered at Da Nang with 2 B-detachments and 9 A-teams. Serving in the IV CTZ with headquarters at Can Tho, Company D consisted of 5 B-detachments and 20 A-teams. Company E was employed for special operations by MACV and included 7 B-detachments and a fluctuating number of A-teams.

Before departing Vietnam on 13 November 1971, the 5th Special Forces Group won a Presidential Unit Citation and the Meritorious Unit Citation for its exceptional service in the Vietnam War. Thirteen members of the group won Medals of Honor and seventy-five won Distinguished Service Crosses.

U.S. Coast Guard

Commander Coast Guard Activities, Vietnam. The U.S. Coast Guard arrived in South Vietnam in the summer of 1965. The position of Commander Coast Guard Activities, Vietnam, was established on 3 February 1967 to provide central direction to the growing Coast Guard presence. This officer commanded Coast Guard Squadron One, Coast Guard Squadron Three, and various detachments that provided port security, handled the unloading of ammunition and other explosive cargo, and flew search-and-rescue missions. Nearly fifty different Coast Guard vessels served in Vietnam, participating in more than 5,000 combat support missions and boarding nearly 250,000 Vietnamese vessels. Beginning in May 1969 and continuing until August 1972, the Coast Guard transferred its assets to the South Vietnamese navy.

Coast Guard Squadron One. Formed in May 1965 for deployment to Vietnam, Coast Guard Squadron One arrived in July 1965 with seventeen 25-meter (82-foot) patrol boats; another nine arrived in February 1966. The squadron served with the U.S. Navy's Task Force 115 and provided coastal surveillance patrols as part of Operation MARKET TIME.

Squadron One consisted of three separate commands. Coast Guard Division 11 was stationed at An Thoi in the IV CTZ with nine patrol boats. Division 12 with eight patrol boats established its headquarters at Da Nang in the I CTZ. Based at Cat Lo in the II CTZ, Division 13 consisted of nine patrol boats.

Before departing Vietnam on 15 August 1970, the squadron had cruised more than 6.5 million kilometers (4 million miles) and transferred its twenty-six patrol boats to the South Vietnamese navy.

Coast Guard Squadron Three. The continued demand for coastal surveillance vessels resulted in a request for high-endurance cutters, and Coast Guard Squadron Three arrived in South Vietnam in May 1967. The squadron consisted of five heavily armed cutters whose shallow draft allowed them to cruise the Gulf of Thailand. Besides patrolling coastal waters, Squadron Three conducted fire support missions for ground forces and often provided logistical services to smaller vessels involved in Operation MARKET TIME.

Coast Guard cutters typically spent six to nine months on duty with the squadron before being sent back to the United States. By the spring of 1970, the number of cutters on patrol had been reduced to three. Squadron Three officially departed South Vietnam on 21 December 1971.

U.S. Marine Corps

III Marine Amphibious Force. Formed on 7 May 1965 in Vietnam, the III Marine Amphibious Force (MAF) was a corps-level headquarters based at Da Nang with responsibility for U.S. combat operations in the I CTZ. Marines were initially deployed in South Vietnam in March 1965 to provide security for the Da Nang airfield. It quickly became apparent, however, that the military situation in the northern provinces required a much larger commitment of ground forces. The lack of port facilities in the region meant the burden fell to the Marine Corps, and the 3d Marine Division arrived in May 1965.

The III MAF became involved in some of the largest battles of the Vietnam War. The most notable occasion was the extensive fighting at Khe Sanh that began in 1967 and lasted well into 1968. At its peak in late 1968, the III MAF had command of the U.S. Army's XXIV Corps, the 1st and 3d Marine Divisions, the 1st Marine Air Wing, and two Marine Corps regimental combat teams. The Marine Corps began to withdraw from Vietnam in 1969, and in April 1970, the overwhelming preponderance of U.S. Army personnel in the I CTZ required the III MAF to relinquish control of operations in the region to the XXIV Corps. The III MAF left South Vietnam on 14 April 1971.

Commanding Generals, III Marine Amphibious Force

Maj. Gen. William R. Collins	May–June 1965
Maj. Gen. Lewis W. Walt	June 1965–February 1966

Maj. Gen. Keith B. McCutcheon	February–March 1966
Lt. Gen. Lewis W. Walt	March 1966–June 1967
Lt. Gen. Robert E. Cushman	June 1967–March 1969
Lt. Gen. Herman Nickerson Jr.	March 1969–March 1970
Lt. Gen. Keith B. McCutcheon	March–December 1970
Lt. Gen. Donn J. Robertson	December 1970–April 1971

1st Marine Air Wing. Although a Marine Corps helicopter squadron arrived in South Vietnam as early as April 1962, it was not until May 1965 that the 1st Marine Air Wing (MAW) established headquarters at Da Nang and began operations. The 1st MAW provided tactical air support for ground forces in the I CTZ and took its orders from the III MAF. The independent command of Marine Corps aviation was an irritant for the Seventh Air Force.

The 1st MAW, at its peak strength, consisted of six Marine Air Groups—three helicopter groups and three fighter-bomber or attack aircraft groups. This amounted to approximately 225 helicopters and 250 fixed-wing aircraft. Although one Marine Corps air wing typically supported each Marine Corps division, the 1st MAW was reinforced to provide support for the entire III MAF. The air wing departed Vietnam on 14 April 1971.

Commanding Generals, 1st Marine Air Wing

Maj. Gen. Paul J. Fontana	May–June 1965
Maj. Gen. Keith B. McCutcheon	June 1965–May 1966
Maj. Gen. Louis B. Robertshaw	May 1966–June 1967
Maj. Gen. Norman J. Anderson	June 1967–June 1968
Maj. Gen. Charles J. Quilter	June 1968–July 1969
Maj. Gen. William G. Thrash	July 1969–July 1970
Maj. Gen. Alan J. Armstrong	July 1970–April 1971

1st Marine Division. The 1st Marine Division arrived in Vietnam in February 1966 and established headquarters at Chu Lai in the I CTZ before shifting north to Da Nang in November. The division initially conducted operations against NVA and Viet Cong forces in the southern provinces of Quang Tin and Quang Ngai. During the Tet Offensive in 1968, it assisted South Vietnamese forces in recapturing Hue. The departure of the 3rd Marine Division in 1969 left the 1st Marine Division with sole responsibility for defending Da Nang and the surrounding provinces. The division withdrew from Vietnam in April 1971.

A powerful combat force, the 1st Marine Division at its peak consisted of four infantry regiments—the 1st, 5th, and 7th Marine Regiments, and beginning in February 1968, the 27th Marine Regiment detached from the 5th Marine Division. Its other combat elements included an artillery regiment consisting of six battalions, a battalion of tanks, an antitank battalion, and a reconnaissance battalion. On two separate occasions the division received a Presidential Unit Citation for gallantry in action.

Commanding Generals, 1st Marine Division

Maj. Gen. Lewis J. Fields	February–October 1966
Maj. Gen. Herman Nickerson Jr.	October 1966–October 1967
Maj. Gen. Donn J. Robertson	October 1967–June 1968
Maj. Gen. Ormond R. Simpson	December 1968–December 1969
Maj. Gen. Edwin B. Wheeler	December 1969–April 1970
Maj. Gen. Charles F. Widdecke	April 1970–April 1971

3d Marine Division. Forward elements of the 3d Marine Division first landed in the I CTZ in March 1965, initially assigned to the defense of Da Nang and Quang Nam province. In October 1966 it moved north and deployed in the northern provinces and along the DMZ. Beginning in late 1967, elements of the 3d Marine Division successfully defended Khe Sanh against repeated assaults.

The 3d Marine Division was a heavily armed combat force of four infantry regiments—the 3d, 4th, and 9th Marine Regiments, and by April 1967, the 26th Marine Regiment detached from the 5th Marine Division. The division's artillery regiment controlled eight battalions, and at one point in 1967, had three army battalions attached as well. Other combat elements included a tank battalion, an antitank battalion, a reconnaissance battalion, and an amphibious tractor battalion. The 3d Marine Division departed Vietnam on 30 November 1969 having been awarded a Presidential Unit Citation for gallantry in action.

Commanding Generals, 3d Marine Division

Maj. Gen. William R. Collins	March–June 1965
Maj. Gen. Lewis Walt	June 1965–March 1966
Maj. Gen. Wood B. Kyle	March 1966–March 1967
Maj. Gen. Bruno A. Hochmuth	March–November 1967
Maj. Gen. Rathvon McC. Tompkins	November 1967–May 1968
Maj. Gen. Raymond G. Davis	May 1968–April 1969
Maj. Gen. William K. Jones	April–November 1969

U.S. Navy

Seventh Fleet. Subordinate to the Commander-in-Chief, Pacific Fleet (CINCPACFLT), the Seventh Fleet was stationed in Japan and deployed elements in the waters off Southeast Asia. It had responsibility for most naval operations in the western Pacific, but after 1 April 1966, Naval Forces, Vietnam, reporting directly to MACV, controlled naval activities deemed internal to the conflict in South Vietnam. Although both MACV and CINCPACFLT reported to CINCPAC in Honolulu, naval activities in the combat area lacked unity of command and direction.

Seventh Fleet task forces conducted a variety of missions to support the war effort. Carrier-based aircraft from Task Force 77 launched air strikes against targets throughout Southeast Asia. Cruisers and destroyers of Task Group 70.8 attacked enemy shipping and bombarded inland targets. Task Force 73 provided logistical support at sea for naval warships operating off Vietnam, while amphibious assault forces under Task Force 76 cruised the coast.

As early as 1961 the Seventh Fleet began to maintain a presence off the coast of Vietnam. This presence increased tremendously in 1965 and became fairly permanent until mid-1973.

Commanding Officers, Seventh Fleet

Vice Admiral Roy L. Johnson	June 1964–March 1965
Vice Admiral Paul P. Blackburn Jr	March–October 1965
Rear Admiral Joseph W. Williams	October–December 1965
Vice Admiral John J. Hyland	December 1965–November 1967
Vice Admiral William F. Bringle	November 1967–March 1970
Vice Admiral Maurice F. Weisner	March 1970–June 1971
Vice Admiral William P. Mack	June 1971–May 1972
Vice Admiral James L. Holloway III	May 1972–July 1973

Task Force 77. The Seventh Fleet's Attack Carrier Striking Force was Task Force 77. Before May 1966, the task force generally consisted of two to three attack carriers supported by escorts and deployed southeast of Cam Ranh Bay at a staging area called Dixie Station. From that vantage point, naval aircraft consistently supported ground operations throughout South Vietnam. By the summer of 1966, Task Force 77 had shifted northward to Yankee Station, a staging point just north of the 17th parallel. This placed the carriers in a better position to conduct operations against North Vietnam, Laos, and the Ho Chi Minh Trail. Three to four attack carriers typically operated from Yankee Station, each holding 70 to 100 combat aircraft.

Task Force 77 did not rely on air power alone; as part of Operation SEA DRAGON, cruisers, destroyers, and other warships from the task force conducted operations against shipping in the coastal waters off North Vietnam. These vessels also participated in search-and-rescue missions and provided naval gunfire support as part of Task Group 70.8.

After 1968 the strength of Task Force 77 decreased to two carriers, and the number of monthly sorties decreased from a peak of 6,000 to less than 2,500 by 1971. The task force briefly swelled to five carriers during the North Vietnamese Easter Offensive of 1972, but combat operations gradually halted in 1973.

Task Force 73. Task Force 73—technically Service Squadron 3, Service Force, U.S. Pacific Fleet—was the Seventh Fleet's logistical support element. Specifically designed for flexibility and versatility, the task force resupplied and repaired the fleet while at sea. More than 70 percent of the Seventh Fleet's supply requirements were satisfied in this fashion. The hospital ships *Sanctuary* and *Repose* were also part of Task Force 73. Located 50 kilometers (30 miles) off the coast of the I CTZ, the ships had modern medical facilities and nearly 300 doctors, nurses, and corpsmen aboard and saved thousands of American lives.

Task Force 76. Task Force 76, the Seventh Fleet's Amphibious Task Force, initially consisted of a Marine Corps Special Landing Force (SLF) and several vessels of an Amphibious Ready Group (ARG). The task force conducted amphibious landings along the coast of South Vietnam beginning with the initial landing at Da Nang on 8 March 1965. A second ARG/SLF joined Task Force 76 in April 1967, and the two were designated ALPHA and BRAVO.

Beginning in the fall of 1966, Task Force 76 was stationed off the DMZ in a position to flank the North Vietnamese Army. When NVA units launched strikes across the border, the task force countered with rear area raids or simply augmented existing ground forces in I CTZ. In early 1969 Task Force 76 conducted the largest amphibious operation of the Vietnam War—Operation BOLD MARINER. Working in conjunction with the Americal Division, the task force sealed off Batangan Peninsula and conducted a massive search-and-destroy mission. Despite the size of the operation, the results were less than desired. Task Force 76 withdrew from the waters off Vietnam later in 1969.

Task Group 70.8. Task Group 70.8 was the Seventh Fleet's Cruiser-Destroyer Group. Elements of the task group participated in Operation SEA DRAGON—attacking enemy shipping and bombarding military targets along the coast of North Vietnam. The Naval Gunfire Support Unit (Task Unit 70.8.9) was subordinate to Task Group 70.8 and operated in conjunction with MACV to provide gunfire support to allied ground forces in South Vietnam. In addition to the cruisers and destroyers from Task Group 70.8, the Naval Gunfire Support Unit relied on warships from the Royal Australian Navy, escorts from the carrier groups, and the battleship *New Jersey,* which had 16-inch guns.

Naval gunfire support began in May 1965 and ranged along the entire coast of Vietnam, but the highest concentration of activity was in the I CTZ where nearly one-third of the available targets were within range. Although typically consisting of one cruiser, four destroyers, and three smaller vessels, the Naval Gunfire Support Unit peaked at twenty-two warships during the Tet Offensive.

After early 1969, Task Group 70.8 played an increasingly smaller role in the war effort. Missions into North Vietnamese waters were restricted and gunfire support in the I CTZ was reduced. Targets near Haiphong, however, were hit sharply by naval vessels as part of Operation LINEBACKER in the spring of 1972.

Naval Forces, Vietnam. Advisers from the U.S. Navy had been in South Vietnam since 1950. The increasing role of naval operations in 1966 required the creation of a separate headquarters under MACV's control. On 1 April 1966, Naval Forces, Vietnam (NAVFORV), was established and assumed control of all naval activities in the II, III, and IV CTZs and along the coast of South Vietnam. The III Marine Amphibious Force had basic responsibility for naval operations in the I CTZ; the Seventh Fleet handled operations beyond the immediate coastal waters.

NAVFORV's major combat elements consisted of the Costal Surveillance Force (Task Force 115), the River Patrol Force (Task Force 116), and the Riverine Assault Force (Task Force 117). Other organizations under its command included the Naval Advisory Group, the 3d Naval Construction Brigade (Seabees), the Military Sea Transportation Service Office, Vietnam, and the Coast Guard Command, Vietnam. NAVFORV was deactivated on 29 March 1973.

Total U.S. Military Personnel in South Vietnam

DATE	ARMY	NAVY	MARINE CORPS	AIR FORCE	COAST GUARD	TOTAL
31 Dec. 1960★	800	15	2	68	—	About 900
31 Dec. 1961	2,100	100	5	1,000	—	3,205
30 June 1962	5,900	300	700	2,100	—	9,000
31 Dec. 1962	7,900	500	500	2,400	—	11,300
30 June 1963	10,200	600	600	4,000	—	15,400
31 Dec. 1963	10,100	800	800	4,600	—	16,300
30 June 1964	9,900	1,000	600	5,000	—	16,500
31 Dec. 1964	14,700	1,100	900	6,600	—	23,300
30 June 1965	27,300	3,800	18,100	10,700	—	59,900
31 Dec. 1965	116,800	8,400	38,200	20,600	300	184,300
30 June 1966	160,000	17,000	53,700	36,400	400	267,500
31 Dec. 1966	239,400	23,300	69,200	52,900	500	385,300
30 June 1967	285,700	28,500	78,400	55,700	500	448,800
31 Dec. 1967	319,500	31,700	78,000	55,900	500	485,600
30 June 1968	354,300	35,600	83,600	60,700	500	534,700
31 Dec. 1968	359,800	36,100	81,400	58,400	400	536,100
30 April 1969	363,300	36,500	81,800	61,400	400	543,400★★
30 June 1969	360,500	35,800	81,500	60,500	400	538,700
31 Dec. 1969	331,100	30,200	55,100	58,400	400	475,200
30 June 1970	298,600	25,700	39,900	50,500	200	414,900
31 Dec. 1970	249,600	16,700	25,100	43,100	100	334,600
30 June 1971	190,500	10,700	500	37,400	100	239,200
31 Dec. 1971	119,700	7,600	600	28,800	100	156,800
30 June 1972	31,800	2,200	1,400	11,500	100	47,000
31 Dec. 1972	13,800	1,500	1,200	7,600	100	24,200
30 June 1973	★★★	★★★	★★★	★★★	★★★	★★★

SOURCE: U.S. Department of Defense, OASD (Comptroller), Directorate for Information Operations, Mar. 19, 1974.

★Between 1954 and 1960, U.S. military strength averaged about 650 advisers.

★★Peak strength.

★★★Totals for all five services less than 250.

Commanding Officers, Naval Forces, Vietnam

Rear Admiral Norvell G. Ward	April 1966–April 1967
Rear Admiral Kenneth L. Veth	April 1967–September 1968
Vice Admiral Elmo R. Zumwalt	September 1968–May 1970
Vice Admiral Jerome H. King	May 1970–April 1971
Rear Admiral Robert S. Salzer	April 1971–June 1972
Rear Admiral Arthur W. Price Jr.	June–August 1972
Rear Admiral James B. Wilson	August 1972–March 1973

Military Sea Transportation Service. Responsible for the line of communication and supply to Southeast Asia, the Military Sea Transportation Service (MSTS) was an independent service command. By mid 1967, it controlled more than 500 supply vessels that served the 11,000-kilometer (7,000-mile) transoceanic lifeline between the United States and U.S. forces in Vietnam. With its Far East headquarters in Japan, the MSTS established an office in South Vietnam, operationally under the control of Naval Forces, Vietnam.

More than 99 percent of the ammunition and fuel and 95 percent of other supplies used by U.S. forces in the theater arrived by means of MSTS, which also shuttled cargo along the coast. During the evacuation of the northern provinces in 1975, MSTS elements from the Seventh Fleet transported 130,000 refugees to Saigon.

Task Force 115. Task Force 115, the U.S. Navy's Coastal Surveillance Force, attempted to cut the flow of seaborne supplies from North Vietnam to NVA and Viet Cong forces in the South. Organized on 11 March 1965 under the code name Operation MARKET TIME, Task Force 115 initially reported to the Seventh Fleet but later came under the authority of the Naval Advisory Group in July 1965 and then Naval Forces, Vietnam. Its original headquarters was in Saigon, but it was transferred to Cam Ranh Bay in July 1967.

Nine patrol sections divided the 2,000-kilometer (1,200-mile) coast of South Vietnam. Each sector relied on a diverse collection of airplanes, warships, and small patrol boats to cover three different zones. The zone farthest out—160–240 kilometers (100–150 miles) offshore—was covered by air surveillance; the middle zone was patrolled by destroyer escorts, minesweepers, and Coast Guard cutters; and the zone closest to the coast relied on small, fast U.S. patrol boats and South Vietnamese navy coastal junks.

By the summer of 1967, Task Force 115 nearly succeeded in halting seaborne infiltration altogether. At its peak the Coastal Surveillance Force employed 81 fast patrol boats, 24 Coast Guard cutters, and 39 other vessels. The South Vietnamese navy assumed a larger role in 1969 and assumed responsibility for the inner zone in September 1970. One year later it had complete control of the operation.

Task Force 116. Formed on 18 December 1965, Task Force 116, the U.S. Navy's River Patrol Force, reported to Naval Forces, Vietnam, and directed naval units involved in Operation GAME WARDEN. The operation focused on denying the Viet Cong use of the critical waterways in the country, especially in the Mekong Delta region. It also attempted to make navigation safe for friendly vessels.

River Patrol Squadron 5 served under Task Force 116 and commanded the patrol boats used on the rivers. The squadron was divided into five divisions—four in the IV CTZ and one at Da Nang. Each consisted of two ten-boat sections and a base ship, often a converted Landing Ship, Tank (LST). A crew of four manned the 8.5-meter (28-foot) patrol boats, which carried a variety of machine guns and a grenade launcher. Crews required several months of training, and full-scale operations did not begin until March 1966.

Task Force 116 also employed direct air support. Initially the task force relied on U.S. Army helicopters, but by August 1966 the U.S. Navy's Helicopter Squadron 1 was assigned to it. Helicopter Squadron 1 was replaced by Helicopter Attack (Light) Squadron 3 on 1 April 1967.

Additional firepower came from other sources. A dozen or so small minesweepers from Mine Division 112 were attached to the task force to scour the inland waterways for mines. Task Force 116 also received assistance from highly trained Navy SEALs. By mid 1968, the Pacific Fleet's SEAL Team 1 had deployed four or five 14-man platoons to South Vietnam. Three platoons generally served under the task force commander and conducted reconnaissance patrols, ambushes, and special intelligence operations.

Task Force 116 managed to keep the major waterways open and forced the Viet Cong to divert significant resources to maintain their water communications in the IV CTZ. The patrol boats also played a critical role during the Tet Offensive in assisting villages under siege. In 1969 Task Force 116 began to turn over its resources and responsibilities to the South Vietnamese navy and was deactivated in December 1970.

Task Force 117. Task Force 117 was the Riverine Assault Force, and the U.S. Navy's component of the joint U.S. Army-Navy Mobile Riverine Force. Activated on 28 February 1967 and stationed in the Mekong Delta, it consisted of four river assault squadrons. Each 400-man squadron manned a variety of vessels to support operations of the army's 9th Infantry Division. Armored troop carriers shuttled infantry along the waterways and heavily armed monitors provided critical fire support. The armor-plated monitors carried 40 mm and 20 mm cannons, grenade launchers, machine guns, and 81 mm mortars.

The task force also included a floating base, which consisted of barracks ships, LSTs, repair ships, and other support vessels. One or two infantry battalions were held in reserve as well.

The Mobile Riverine Force played a key role in breaking up NVA and Viet Cong troop concentrations in the Mekong Delta and in recapturing cities taken by the Viet Cong forces in the first days of the Tet Offensive. Task Force 117 was the first major U.S. Navy command to turn over its responsibilities to the South Vietnamese navy. It was deactivated on 25 August 1969.

BIBLIOGRAPHY

BERGER, CARL, ed. *The United States Air Force in Southeast Asia, 1961–1973.* 1977.

DAVIDSON, PHILLIP A. *Vietnam at War: The History, 1946–1975.* 1988.

MAROLDA, EDWARD J. *A Short History of the United States Navy and the Southeast Asian Conflict, 1950–1973.* 1984.

MILLETT, ALAN R. *Semper Fidelis: The History of the U.S. Marine Corps.* 1980.

PALMER, BRUCE, JR. *The 25-Year War: America's Role in Vietnam.* 1984.

SCHLIGHT, JOHN. *The War in South Vietnam: The Years of the Offensive, 1965–1968.* 1988.

STANTON, SHELBY L. *Order of Battle: U.S. Army and Allied Ground Forces in Vietnam.* 1981.

STANTON, SHELBY L. *The Rise and Fall of an American Army: U.S. Ground Forces in Vietnam, 1965–1973.* 1985.

TULICH, EUGENE. *The United States Coast Guard in South East Asia During the Vietnam Conflict.* 1975.

U.S. MARINE CORPS. *The Marines in Vietnam, 1954–1973: An Anthology and Annotated Bibliography.* 1985.

DANIEL T. BAILEY

PQ

Pacification. Twenty years after the end of U.S. military involvement in Vietnam, historians and analysts remain divided on the essential nature of the war. Was it a conventional invasion by North Vietnam, or did the United States fail there because it did not recognize the basic insurgent nature of the war in South Vietnam? The answer is in dispute, but whatever conclusions are reached, one is indisputable: a coherent strategy for pacification came too late in the war, and it was often relegated to a minor role by the military, which concerned itself with a fruitless war of attrition.

In its basic form, pacification is the process by which a government extends its influence into an area beset by insurgency. This includes aid programs to distribute food and medical supplies to poor villagers as well as more lasting reforms such as land redistribution. But since guerrillas inevitably resist such efforts, the core of pacification is bringing security to the countryside. Inevitably, this means developing new military methods to cope with the insurgency. Although pacification was often described by the U.S. military as "low-level conflict" and often derisively called "the other war," to the guerrillas and to the rural citizens caught up in it, the insurgency was total. To Americans, total war

means huge armies, weapons of mass destruction, and carpet bombing of cities. But to the developing world, insurgent total war simply means involving the entire population in the struggle. Nothing can be more total than a conflict that involves each and every person.

The Viet Cong followed the Chinese Maoist model of guerrilla war, establishing secret political cadres in the countryside and forming "front" organizations. Fundamental to this system was the intimidation and assassination of government officials ranging from province administrators to village schoolteachers. In short, the insurgents sought to replace rural government with one of their own. Between 1956 and the introduction of U.S. combat troops in 1965, the Viet Cong managed to penetrate virtually every level of Vietnamese rural life, from the province down to the smallest hamlet.

Insurgency, as practiced by the Vietnamese communists, entailed three phases. The first consisted of limited hit-and-run attacks against the government's presence in the countryside. The second phase included development of mobile warfare aimed at wearing down the U.S. and South Vietnamese forces, and the final phase was all-out conventional war aimed at the complete destruction of

VIET CONG SUSPECTS. South Vietnamese soldiers prepare to question two women captured near Ap La Chi, 25 August 1965. The woman in the foreground was caught carrying the Soviet-made rifle slung around her neck. *National Archives*

these forces. Crucial to this evolution was a shift from rural targets in the early phase to urban targets in the final phase. If pacification were to be successful, it had to begin while the insurgency was still in the countryside.

Agrovilles and Strategic Hamlets. The earliest pacification program established with American advice was the Agroville program, launched in 1959 by the U.S. Military Assistance and Advisory Group–Vietnam (MAAG-V) and the South Vietnamese government. Borrowed from a similar British concept used in Malaya, "Agrovilles" were communities built by the government as a means of protection from the insurgents. Peasants, however, resented being uprooted, and worst of all, the government forced them to build the Agrovilles themselves in exchange for vague promises of schools, farm aid, and land. The South Vietnamese government mandated that eighty Agrovilles be built, but in 1960, peasant resistance and insurgent attacks led to the program's abandonment.

In 1961, the government launched a new version of the Agrovilles. Called the Strategic Hamlet pro-

gram, villages were surrounded by barbed wire and other defenses and the villagers were armed and trained in basic defense. Hamlets were to be transformed into "antiguerrilla bastions" and thereby to confront the Viet Cong guerrillas with a network of fortified hamlets organized into a "crisscrossed line of defense." But unlike the Agroville program, strategic hamlets received better government support, though they remained unpopular with the peasants. By the end of 1962, 3,235 strategic hamlets were built, leading South Vietnamese officials to claim that 34 percent of the population lived under government control. In reality, the Viet Cong concentrated their forces at will and destroyed individual strategic hamlets with overwhelming force.

A series of crises in 1963 led to the dissolution of the strategic hamlets and the development of a new pacification system. Internal opposition to the South Vietnamese government eventually resulted in the ouster and murder of Ngo Dinh Diem on 2 November. Less than three weeks later, U.S. president John F. Kennedy was also assassinated. Buddhist uprisings in Da Nang and Hue, as well as a series of debilitating coups, turned attention away from the countryside and focused on the population centers, which were traditionally threats to the power structure in South Vietnam. As Saigon looked inward the Viet Cong guerrillas again infiltrated the countryside.

Pacification Strategies. Although U.S. officials agreed on the importance of pacification, there was no consensus on how to implement it. Not until President Lyndon Johnson personally intervened was the issue of implementing a single pacification strategy undertaken. Johnson viewed pacification as a counterbalance to Gen. William C. Westmoreland's (commander of the Military Assistance Command, Vietnam [MACV]) military emphasis, which was increasingly criticized for ignoring the political dimensions of the conflict.

In February 1966 U.S. and South Vietnamese officials conferred in Honolulu. The South Vietnamese agreed to place special emphasis on pacification, the most notable being the creation of mobile 59-man teams called Revolutionary Development Cadres. These teams were charged with improving the lives of rural villagers, both with new programs and by emulating the "three withs" espoused by the guerrillas: eat with, sleep with, and work with the peasants.

The Revolutionary Development (RD) program was the first step in a hands-on pacification program, but if it were to be more successful than the earlier strategic hamlets, RD teams had to be protected from retribution by Viet Cong guerrillas. The Army of the Republic of Vietnam (ARVN) was hesitant to do this, reasoning that placing regular troops within the pacification chain of command would dilute the power and authority of military commanders. Always mindful of possible coups launched by disgruntled military commanders, President Thieu balked. General Westmoreland supported him, arguing that confining the ARVN to a pacification role undermined the flexibility of the big-unit war.

The Honolulu conference ended without a consensus on the RD debate, or on pacification in general. Both U.S. and South Vietnamese troops participated in operations aimed at pacifying rural areas, but that mission remained secondary to pursuing North Vietnamese and Viet Cong regulars. By 1967, however, the situation in the countryside continued to deteriorate, prompting the United States to send more soldiers. Increasingly, U.S. troops fought the war while the ARVN had responsibility for maintaining security in the countryside.

On the American side pacification continued to be regarded as a political problem best handled by civilians. But the U.S. embassy in Saigon—the central clearinghouse for all pacification programs—failed to find a successful formula. The operating concept was that of a "country team," headed by the ambassador, his deputy, and the heads of the Central Intelligence Agency (CIA), the Agency for International Development (AID), and the U.S. Information Service (USIS). But the war had outpaced the standard State Department system. By the beginning of 1967 more than 250,000 U.S. soldiers were in South Vietnam and economic assistance was more than $500 million per year. Determined to halt the mounting bureaucratic inertia of the civilian pacification system, President Johnson appointed Robert Komer, a trusted adviser, to study the problem. The result was a conference held in Guam on 20 March 1967 at which President Johnson announced that pacification would be placed under General Westmoreland's authority. The civilian agencies would maintain their autonomy, but the military would exert overall control. This was an important step for two reasons: first, the existing

CIVIL OPERATIONS. A U.S. Army medic swabs a sore on the arm of a montagnard boy in a Central Highlands village, 4 March 1966. *National Archives*

SPECIAL FORCES ADVISERS. Inspecting punji stakes surrounding a strategic hamlet in An Giang province. *National Archives*

MACV system provided a sound command-and-control structure; second, MACV's money, manpower, and material assets were vital for projecting pacification into the countryside.

The program was called Civil Operations and Revolutionary Development Support (CORDS) and Komer was its civilian chief. He answered directly to General Westmoreland and was equal in status and authority to Gen. Creighton Abrams, Westmoreland's military deputy. Formation of CORDS progressed rapidly. The placement of CORDS within the military chain of command demonstrated that U.S. planners had come to recognize three basic facts. First, no matter how successful big-unit operations were, they would never solve the war in the countryside as long as the Viet Cong had influence there; second, U.S. economic and social programs had to be better coordinated with U.S. and South Vietnamese military efforts; and, third, no pacification program could succeed without providing permanent security within the villages.

Security was a thorny issue for pacification officials, particularly when the North Vietnamese Army (NVA) forces and Viet Cong guerrillas could bring overwhelming conventional force to bear, as exemplified by the 1968 Tet Offensive. Although the Tet Offensive's nationwide series of assaults dealt a severe blow to pacification, they also provided the U.S. and South Vietnamese with some surprising benefits. Although Viet Cong forces eliminated much of the government's limited control in the countryside, it cost the Viet Cong thousands of its political and military cadres when they attacked the better-defended urban targets. The Viet Cong never fully recovered from the massive casualties, making it difficult for them ever again to dominate the countryside. In addition, the ferocity of the Tet Offensive convinced the South Vietnamese government that pacification needed to be made a top priority.

In the wake of the communists' military defeat in the Tet Offensive, Komer suggested that President Thieu send his forces into the countryside to provide security and government services and to fill the vacuum left by the substantial infrastructure and personnel losses suffered by the Viet Cong. Still new to the presidency, Thieu was reluctant to dilute his strength in Saigon, and he feared that the Viet Cong might still have the ability to launch another offensive. But Komer persisted and in August he received the backing of the new MACV commander, Gen. Creighton Abrams, for a revamped pacification campaign closely coordinated with U.S. military operations. The plan was not implemented until October, when Thieu was finally convinced that the Viet Cong lacked the ability to launch another offensive.

The Accelerated Pacification Campaign (APC), as it was called, began on 1 November 1968 and ran for three months in an attempt to take advantage of the Viet Cong's heavy losses. Although Komer planned the program, it was carried out by his successor, former CIA official William Colby. APC was intended to improve existing security in contested hamlets throughout South Vietnam by coordinating military operations and pacification teams, and to deny the Viet Cong guerrillas their traditional access to the countryside. By the end of the campaign, 1,100 formerly contested hamlets were considered secure, and communist control reportedly dropped from 17 percent to 12 percent.

Colby initiated a number of other reforms that aided the progress of pacification. Most important, he bolstered the existing rural militia, known as the Regional Forces and Popular Forces (RF/PF), by providing more U.S. advisers and upgraded weapons. By 1970 over 90 percent of the RF/PF were armed with M16 rifles. The RF/PF allowed villagers to enlist in units from their own villages and kept men close to their families. Although not always militarily effective, the RF/PF kept pressure on the Viet Cong and provided a constant security presence within the villages.

Colby also helped form the People's Self-Defense Force (PSDF), an informal militia designed to give the government an armed presence in even the most remote villages. The PSDF was neither well trained nor well armed, but in Colby's words, "the Viet Cong could no longer walk into villages unopposed." By the end of 1970 more than 3.5 million villagers—young and old, men and women—had joined the PSDF.

The Phoenix Program. Perhaps the most controversial, and one of the most important, programs of pacification was the Phoenix program. Phoenix was designed to counter the most basic aspect of an insurgency—the political underground, known as the Viet Cong Infrastructure (VCI). As long as a viable infrastructure existed, the insurgency could not be defeated. Phoenix was designed to coordinate intelligence gathering as well as paramilitary efforts aimed at rooting out the VCI. The South Vietnamese called the program Phung Hoang, after the mythical Vietnamese bird that heralded peace and prosperity; Americans called it Phoenix, the closest Western mythological comparison they could imagine.

Phoenix officially began in July 1968, though a preliminary program, known as Intelligence Coordination and Exploitation (ICEX), had been in place since mid 1967. Phoenix emphasized four as-

STRATEGIC HAMLET. On fire after a night attack by the Viet Cong, 1964. *National Archives*

pects in its attack on the VCI. First, it decentralized its command process by placing most of the responsibility in the provinces and districts. This included building intelligence-gathering and interrogation centers in regions where the Viet Cong operated. Second, Phoenix established a reporting system of files and dossiers on suspects and concentrated on "neutralizing"—capturing, converting, or killing—members of the Viet Cong Infrastructure. Third, the system established rules by which suspected VCI could be tried and imprisoned. Finally, Phoenix emphasized the police, rather than the armed forces, as the main operational arm of the program.

Phoenix was meant to be a South Vietnamese project with U.S. advisers. Roughly, Phung Hoang was the actual intelligence and operations side and Phoenix was the U.S. advisory effort that paralleled Phung Hoang. The Phoenix program proposed to share intelligence and focus it on the single goal of eliminating the VCI, but that priority did not always make sense to the South Vietnamese officials in Saigon, who were uncomfortable with the idea of decentralizing authority and intelligence to the provincial and district levels.

The Phoenix program implied that regular military forces were unable to combat the VCI. The new emphasis was placed on existing forces that could be tailored for anti-infrastructure operations. In addition to the RF/PF, these included the National Police and the Provincial Reconnaissance Units (PRU). The RF/PF were territorial forces recruited from local areas and used as civil guard units. Part of their responsibilities included reacting to information sent from the District Intelligence and Operations Coordinating Center (DIOCC; PIOCC at the provincial level). The National Police included two subsections, the Police Special Branch (PSB—the intelligence branch) and the National Police Field Force (NPFF—the paramilitary component). For the most part, the National Police performed their anti-VCI tasks poorly, although there were exceptions. The PRU, a largely CIA-operated paramilitary unit, were considered the best "action arm" available to the Phoenix program, and most of the stories that came out of Vietnam about brutality and assassination pointed to the PRU. Established in 1966, the PRU never numbered more than 4,000 throughout South Vietnam, and its members were charged with other missions besides the Phoenix program. Despite their reputation, the PRU were responsible for only a small percentage of Phoenix "neutralizations."

Each DIOCC was led by a Vietnamese Phung Hoang chief, who was aided by a U.S. Phoenix adviser. The Phoenix adviser had no authority to order operations; his only real input was advice. The DIOCC was answerable to the district chief who in turn reported to the province chief. DIOCC personnel compiled intelligence on VCI in the district and made blacklists that included all the available data on members of the VCI. An accusation brought against a suspected member had to be accompanied by at least three separate reports of communist activities to corroborate the other evidence. When the whereabouts of a person on the blacklist was discovered, an operation was planned, and one of the groups—RF/PF, PRU, or NPFF—went to capture the target. After capture, the prisoner was taken to the DIOCC and interrogated for information that might lead to other VIC members. The prisoner was then sent to the province center for further interrogation and trial. If the evidence against the suspect was strong enough, he or she was sentenced. High-ranking VCI members received up to two-year sentences, which could be extended if the government thought it appropriate, which it usually did if the prisoner were a high-ranking cadre.

Operations against specifically targeted VCI members were supposed to be the cutting edge of the Phoenix program, but the reality was often quite different. Many DIOCC's did little work, taking months to establish even the most rudimentary of blacklists. In many cases the Phung Hoang chief was the most incompetent officer in the district, put there by a district chief who only wanted the man out of the way. Some districts ran very few Phoenix operations, relying instead on standard military sweeps performed by U.S. or South Vietnamese troops in the area. When it came to trial and sentencing, some suspected VCI members were released because they bribed government officials or because the officials feared retribution by the Viet Cong. Some districts released as many as 60 percent of VCI suspects.

Abuses and corruption plagued the Phoenix program. Some prisoners were tortured; Americans were required to report such incidents, which they frequently did. Other suspects were arrested because local officials had a quarrel with them or because rich relatives could be blackmailed into paying a ransom for their release. On the whole, such abuse was the exception. More serious was the Phoenix program's bureaucratic shortcomings, which were never completely worked out of the system.

The U.S. advisory side of the program was also beset by problems and criticism throughout its existence. The first affected the entire U.S. military in Vietnam: the one-year tour. Combat units found their fighting cohesion hindered when infantrymen and officers moved out after twelve-month tours. In the Phoenix program the negative effect of this constant rotation was magnified because advisers worked on a one-to-one basis with their Vietnamese counterparts. Thus, the trust, understanding, and general rapport established were lost when the adviser returned to the United States. Lack of experienced personnel was an additional factor.

The Phoenix program had an undeniable impact on the Viet Cong. Captured documents testified that countless political cadres were identified and captured or killed. But there were negative aspects as well. Some officials used Phoenix to settle old scores and many operations undoubtedly netted innocent people. By the end of 1972 "neutralization" figures for Phoenix were 81,740, with 26,369 prisoners killed.

The End of Pacification. By late 1969 pacification seemed to have turned the tide against Viet Cong forces and influence, and for the remainder of U.S. involvement in Vietnam government control over the countryside steadily increased. Two factors nullified pacification's hard-won gains. First, President Thieu's tight control of the South Vietnamese government did not allow the systemic political and economic reforms that were necessary to reinforce pacification's gains in the countryside. Second, because North Vietnam controlled the tempo of the war, its forces were able to shift unopposed from guerrilla warfare to conventional conflict, a strategy that ultimately conquered South Vietnam. Pacification could not survive while the Republic of Vietnam was being crushed by the concerted efforts of massive conventional attacks.

In 1973 the U.S. military departed Vietnam, leaving pacification to the South Vietnamese. But the war had changed since North Vietnam's Easter Offensive of 1972, and pacification was no longer paramount. Instead, the war had become conventional, with an emphasis on the destruction of military forces and the seizure of territory. While South Vietnam continued to maintain limited pacification programs at the province and district levels, most attention was necessarily focused on battling North Vietnamese units, which continued to cross into South Vietnam despite the Paris Peace Accords signed in January 1973. During 1974 pacification

became less important to South Vietnam as U.S. supplies diminished and the South Vietnamese military found itself pressed on all fronts. When the war ended in 1975, pacification had become irrelevant.

[*See also* Civilian Irregular Defense Groups (CIDG); Counterinsurgency; Provisional Reconnaissance Units (PRU); Regional Forces/Popular Forces; Special Forces, U.S.; Special Forces, ARVN.]

BIBLIOGRAPHY

ANDRADÉ, DALE. *Ashes to Ashes: The Phoenix Program and the Vietnam War.* 1990.
COLBY, WILLIAM E. *Lost Victory.* 1989.
DONOVAN, DAVID. *Once a Warrior King: Memories of an Officer in Vietnam.* 1985.
DOYLE, EDWARD, SAMUEL LIPSMAN, et al. *The Vietnam Experience: America Takes Over.* 1982.
GRANT, ZALIN. *Facing the Phoenix: The CIA and the Political Defeat of the United States in Vietnam.* 1991.
KOMER, ROBERT W. *Bureaucracy at War: U.S. Performance during the Vietnam Conflict.* 1986.
LIPSMAN, SAMUEL, EDWARD DOYLE, et al. *The Vietnam Experience: Fighting for Time.* 1983.
RACE, JEFFREY. *War Comes to Long An: A Revolutionary Conflict in a Vietnamese Province.* 1972.
SCOVILLE, THOMAS W. *Reorganizing for Pacification Support.* 1982.
TRAN DINH THO. *Pacification.* 1984.
WEST, F. J. *The Village.* 1972.

DALE ANDRADÉ

Palmer, Bruce, Jr. (1913–), commanding general II Field Force, Vietnam, 1967–1968; vice chief of staff, U.S. Army, 1968–1972; chief of staff, U.S. Army, 1972–1974. General Bruce Palmer served in Washington and in Vietnam during the war. As assistant and then deputy chief of staff of military operations from 1963 to 1965, Palmer witnessed the deliberations of the Joint Chiefs of Staff (JCS) prior to the massive escalation of U.S. troop levels. In 1967 and 1968 he commanded the II Field Force, Vietnam, and served as deputy commanding general of the U.S. Army, Vietnam (USARV). From 1968 to 1972 he was vice chief of staff of the U.S. Army, became chief of staff in 1972, and retired from the military in 1974. In his book *The 25-Year War* (1984) Palmer blames both U.S. civilian leadership and military leadership for the failure of Vietnam policy. U.S. political leaders did not adequately mobilize public support, Palmer charges, and established ambiguous combat goals for the military. Senior U.S. military leaders, even though they recognized that "U.S. strategy was not working and over time would probably fail to achieve stated U.S. objectives," failed to make their realization that "the strategy was fatally flawed" clear to the president and the secretary of defense. Palmer believes that the United States should have blockaded northern ports and invaded Laos to destroy the Ho Chi Minh Trail, but these actions were prevented by civilian restrictions on the military.

BIBLIOGRAPHY

PALMER, BRUCE, JR. *The 25-Year War: America's Military Role in Vietnam.* 1984.

ADAM LAND

Paris Accords. After nearly five years of negotiations between the United States and North Vietnam, the Paris peace accords were signed on 25 January 1973. Essentially the same agreement had been reached three months earlier, but intransigence over details and South Vietnam's refusal to cooperate delayed the treaty. In December 1972, President Nixon ordered the heaviest bombing of the war to intimidate North Vietnam and to reassure South Vietnam. Another week of talks between Henry Kissinger and Le Duc Tho finally resulted in an agreement in which both sides accepted a cease-fire under international supervision and obtained their key demands. North Vietnam retained control over large areas of the south, left its troops in place there, and continued to receive Soviet and Chinese aid. The United States gained a "decent interval" to withdraw its troops and obtain the release of prisoners of war. South Vietnam received promises from North Vietnam not to invade and U.S. promises of reintervention if the agreement broke down. "We have finally achieved peace with honor," Nixon told the American public. Within sixty days the last U.S. troops departed, and military aid to South Vietnam was cut off entirely.

President Thieu strongly opposed the Paris accords initially, but Nixon warned him to decide "whether you desire to continue our alliance or whether you want me to seek a settlement with the enemy which serves U.S. interests alone." Thieu had no choice but to agree, although no one doubted that war would break out again. Tho and Kissinger jointly received the Nobel Peace Prize, but Tho declined, stating that "Peace has not yet really been

PARIS PEACE TALKS. White House adviser Henry Kissinger (left) and the DRV's senior representative Le Duc Tho (right) with Tho's interpreter (center), 23 November 1972. *National Archives*

established in Vietnam." Differences between communist and noncommunist members of the International Commission of Control and Supervision (ICCS) and the Four-Party Joint Military commission (FPJMC) hampered peace efforts right from the start. These multilateral organizations were supposed to oversee implementation of the accords, but fighting continued sporadically as both sides sought to enlarge their control over South Vietnamese territory and blamed each other for violating the cease-fire.

North Vietnam vowed to unify the country by force if necessary, and Nixon promised to resume bombing and military aid if South Vietnam were attacked. But Congress refused to send more aid or permit bombing, and the Watergate scandal forced Nixon from office. After two years, North Vietnam broke the Paris accords with a massive conventional invasion that ended the war in 1975. "The peace treaty did nothing for Saigon," admitted John Negroponte, Kissinger's deputy in Paris. "We got our prisoners back; we were able to end our direct military involvement. But there were no ostensible benefits for Saigon to justify all of the enormous effort and bloodshed of the previous years."

BIBLIOGRAPHY

DILLARD, WALTER SCOTT. *Sixty Days to Peace.* 1982.

GOODMAN, ALLEN E. *The Lost Peace: America's Search for a Negotiated Settlement of the Vietnam War.* 1978.

HERRINGTON, STUART A. *Peace with Honor?* 1983.

PORTER, GARETH. *A Peace Denied: The United States, Vietnam, and the Paris Peace Agreements.* 1975.

SZULC, TAD. *The Illusion of Peace: Foreign Policy in the Nixon Years.* 1978.

TIEN HUNG NGUYEN and JERROLD L. SCHECHTER. *The Palace File: The Remarkable Story of South Vietnam and the American Promises that Were Never Kept.* 1986.

GLEN GENDZEL

Parrot's Beak. A region of mostly uninhabited jungle in the southeastern Cambodian province of Svay Rieng, the Parrot's Beak juts into South Vietnam sixty-five kilometers (forty miles) west of Saigon. The Parrot's Beak was an area in which Prince Norodom Sihanouk, the ruler of Cambodia, permitted Vietnamese communist forces to establish base camps, beginning in 1965. U.S. military commanders requested permission for massive retaliation against these sanctuaries. Denied by Lyndon Johnson, they conducted illicit clandestine fo-

rays into Cambodia. In February 1969, President Richard Nixon ordered the bombing of the Parrot's Beak, and the following year he endorsed a proposal that South Vietnamese and U.S. forces attack sanctuaries there. The invasion failed to end the communists' use of the area as a sanctuary.

BIBLIOGRAPHY

SHAWCROSS, WILLIAM. *Sideshow: Kissinger, Nixon, and the Destruction of Cambodia.* 1979.

PAUL M. TAILLON

Pathet Lao. *Pathet Lao* (Lao Nation) was a generic term first coined in 1950 to describe Lao nationalists agitating against French colonial rule. The Pathet Lao was largely created by two men: Prince Souphanouvong, a French-trained member of the royal family, and Kaysone Phomvihan, a member of the Indochina Communist Party (ICP), who had studied law in Hanoi. Both men had observed the modest rise of the Lao Seri (Free Lao), a small band of nationalist sympathizers led by Prince Phetsarath, who in August 1945 had proclaimed a neutralist buffer zone around the kingdom of Luang Prabang following Japan's capitulation in the region. Phetsarath's activities resulted in censure by the monarch and Phetsarath's loss of rank, but, undeterred, he created a rebel government called the Lao Issara (Free Lao) two months later, which stimulated Souphanouvong's and Phomvihan's nationalist sympathies.

In August 1950, Souphanouvong convened a Lao national assembly, which created a new freedom front based on Marxist-Leninist concepts. For the next five years Lao cadres were organized, trained, and supplied by the Viet Minh, which enabled them to establish modest operational areas along the eastern borders of Laos. The withdrawal of all French forces from Indochina by 1955 gave the Pathet Lao room to maneuver. At Sam Neua on 22 March 1955, the Lao People's Revolutionary Party (LPRP), sometimes referred to as the People's Party of Laos (Phak Pasason Lao), was created. Ten months later, in January 1956, the party established a covert wing—the Lao Patriotic Front (Neo Lao Hak Sat)—and expanded the Lao People's Liberation Army (LPLA) with North Vietnam's support.

In the field, Pathet Lao (PL) cadres established cells and people's action committees identical to those used by the Viet Minh. The party's political platform focused on social and agricultural reforms, eradication of the corruption of elite business groups, and the expulsion of growing Western interests in Laos. The direct interference of the United States in Lao politics during the late 1950s was the greatest single influence stimulating the Pathet Lao's growth. In 1957 Souphanouvong, in conjunction with his half brother, Prince Souvanna Phouma, attempted to create a new coalition government, which was contested in an election by representatives from all political parties. The conservatives, led by Souvanna Phouma and Prime Minister Phoui Sanaikone, were alarmed by the election's results: PL cadres seemed to have won 13 of 21 eligible seats even though all parties were guilty of ballot stuffing and electioneering characterized by excessive graft and corruption. A reconciliation was attempted, but failed when Sanaikone arrested PL leaders and attempted to disarm 1,500 LPLA troops monitoring the election at Vientiane. The LPLA troops escaped, and the PL withdrew to jungle sanctuaries.

In 1957 the U.S. government, absorbed with the Cold War, identified the PL as a communist menace and exerted pressure on Souvanna Phouma to nullify his half brother's growing influence. Despite enormous U.S. aid, Souvanna Phouma failed to censure or placate all interest groups, which strengthened the position of his critics within the U.S. government. The United States proceeded to sponsor an alternative army of Lao and Thai forces led by Gen. Phoumi Nosavan, which toppled Souvanna Phouma in 1959 and attempted to destroy the Pathet Lao. By December 1960, two regimes existed: Souvanna Phouma's neutralist government set up headquarters in the Plain of Jars; an alternative right-wing faction, led by Nosavan, remained in Vientiane. The Pathet Lao again withdrew to its mountain sanctuaries. Within a year, a point of no return was reached: Souphanouvong and Souvanna Phouma joined forces against Nosavan, which sparked the Laotian crisis of 1961. The Geneva Convention of 1962 reinstated Phouma and gave the Pathet Lao a minor voice in government, which prompted the United States to expand its covert operations in Laos, especially against Pathet Lao forces.

The Lao People's Liberation Army (Kongthap Potpoi Pasason Lao), the Pathet Lao's military wing, grew from 5,000 in 1956 to nearly 50,000 by 1970. It was composed of dissident Lao nationals, aspiring communists, highland tribesmen, half-castes, and deserters from Phouma's Royal Lao Army (RLA). Soldiers, like political cadres, were trained and equipped by the Viet Minh between 1950 and 1954; after that, the People's Army of Vietnam (PAVN) assumed sole patronage of LPLA activities and operations, albeit with mixed results due to Lao sociocultural traditions. The Lao people did not have a military heritage similar to that of the Vietnamese; rather, a contemplative gentleness, highlighted by a Buddhist-inspired acceptance of everyday life, set the tone for family and community relationships. PAVN officers often criticized the LPLA for its lack of aggressiveness, but overall their relationship was harmonious.

Any comparison of the LPLA with the PAVN would be faulty, although Pathet Lao forces became relatively competent guerrilla fighters whose primary value was to assist PAVN units operating within Laos or along its borders. The rugged Laotian terrain, a combination of dense jungles and remote mountains, defined the size and mission of Pathet Lao guerrilla forces. Regiments of 1,500 troops existed, but most day-to-day operations were carried out by smaller units—battalions of 500 troops and companies of 100 troops. Soldiers wore green utility uniforms of Soviet or Chinese manufacture but rarely displayed insignias of rank. Mao-style caps or brimmed hats were commonplace, often adorned with a round, white sun badge surrounded by red and blue stripes trimmed with gold. The LPLA's greatest contribution was its assistance in building and maintaining the Laotian segments of the Ho Chi Minh Trail, plus a labyrinth of supply bases, underground field hospitals, and staging depots where PAVN-LPLA forces regrouped and retrained.

As the Vietnam War intensified after 1965, the United States embarked on one of the most secret covert operations in contemporary military history. Operation BARREL ROLL, conceived in 1964 and designed to destroy the Ho Chi Minh Trail and PAVN-LPLA bases, intensified to a point at which thousands of hectares of Laotian soil were laid waste by U.S. bombers. On the ground, a variety of armies clashed to contest territory and, most importantly, to control the lucrative opium trade. Phouma's Royal Lao Army (RLA) top heavy with ineffective generals and light on talent, avoided confrontations with PAVN-LPLA forces if at all possible. Alternatively, the Central Intelligence Agency (CIA) funded a 40,000-strong Meo-Hmong army, led by "General" Vang Pao, which attacked and harassed PAVN-LPLA units at every opportunity in order to disrupt the Ho Chi Minh Trail and maintain the steady flow of raw opium out of the Laotian sector of the Golden Triangle via Air America, the CIA's airline. Opium was a profitable business and its sale, through Saigon and other outlets, helped to pay for the U.S. government's covert operations. North Vietnam and the Pathet Lao also recognized the value of opium and sold it, through their own connections, to purchase essential war materials.

The LPLA developed a strong rapport with the Lao people as CIA–Meo–Hmong activities increased. Grassroots-oriented politics, carefully interwoven with communist doctrine, enabled the Pathet Lao to increase its popular support. Lao tribal minorities were not forgotten: the Kha, a highland group with historical animosity toward the lowland Lao, became targets for PL propaganda. Sithone Komadam, titular chief of the Kha, was appointed a minister in Souphanouvong's alternative government. An anti–United States Meo resistance league, led by Phay Dong, was also added to the Pathet Lao's infrastructure.

A cease-fire was proclaimed in February 1973, but in actuality the covert war continued through April 1975. By then the Pathet Lao dominated Laos's coalition government. Souvanna Phouma's downfall, like that of the CIA's tribal armies, was caused by the withdrawal of U.S. resources from Laos. Tens of thousands of loyal irregulars were abandoned, although Vang Pao and a considerable number of his followers were later relocated in Montana through American connections. Phouma's RLA, whose last commanding officer before his flight was Maj. Gen. Oudone Sananikone, surrendered to the Pathet Lao on 8 May 1975, one week after the collapse of Saigon. On 2 December 1975, the Lao People's Democratic Republic was declared: Souphanouvong emerged as president, and Kaysone Phomvihane was appointed secretary of the Lao People's Revolutionary Party (Phak Pasason Pativat Lao) and prime minister. In September 1986, Souphanouvong fell victim to a stroke and was replaced by Phoumi Vongvichit. Five years later, Phomvihane took charge of the nation until his death in December 1992. He was succeeded by Nouhak Phoumsavane, the current president.

BIBLIOGRAPHY

ADAMS, NINA S., and ALFRED W. MCCOY, eds. *Laos: War and Revolution*. 1970.

BROWN, MACALISTER, and JOSEPH J. ZASLOFF. *Apprentice Revolutionaries: The Communist Movement in Laos, 1930–1985*. 1986.

DEUVE, JEAN. *Le Royaume du Laos, 1949–1965: Histoire événementielle de l'indépendance à la guerre américaine*. 1986.

DOMMEN, ARTHUR J. *Conflict in Laos: The Politics of Neutralization*. 1971.

ROBBINS, CHRISTOPHER. *The Ravens: Pilots of the Secret War in Laos*. 1989.

TOYE, HUGH. *Laos: Buffer State or Battleground?* 1968.

THOMAS R. CANTWELL

Pathfinders, U.S. Army combat aircraft–control crews. Known as the black hats because of the black baseball caps they wore, the pathfinders were landed by helicopter or parachuted into territory that was held by North Vietnamese or Viet Cong forces to direct air traffic. Because so much of the U.S. effort involved planes and helicopters, the pathfinders played a pivotal role in the Vietnam War, with responsibility for coordinating aircraft flights, identifying drop and landing zones for helicopters, assisting in navigation, and targeting and coordinating artillery fire and aircraft bombardment.

BIBLIOGRAPHY

ROGERS, BERNARD W. *Cedar Falls–Junction City: A Turning Point*. 1974.

STANTON, SHELBY L. *The Green Berets at War: U.S. Army Special Forces in Southeast Asia, 1956–1985*. 1985.

TOLSON, JOHN J. *Airmobility, 1961–1971*. 1973.

ELLEN D. GOLDLUST

Paul VI (1897–1978), born Giovanni Battista Montini; pope, Roman Catholic Church, 1963–1973. Known as Paul VI, he became an important spokesman for world peace, social reform, and human rights after assuming office in 1963. He viewed the Catholic Church as a global mediator in the era of nuclear weapons and maintained an independent diplomatic position on the Vietnam War. In 1965, in a speech before the United Nations General Assembly, Paul VI issued a fervent call for peace: "No more war! War never again." He consistently pressed for a cease-fire and for negotiations to end the conflict in Vietnam.

BIBLIOGRAPHY

HANSON, ERIC O. *The Catholic Church in World Politics*. 1987.

JENNIFER FROST

Pearson, Lester (1897–1972), Canadian prime minister, 1963–1968. Initially, Pearson supported the United States' entry into the war, but by 1965 the left wing of his own Liberal Party had gained influence and Pearson could not afford to ignore their criticism of the war. On 2 April 1965 he delivered a speech at Temple University in Philadelphia calling for a cease-fire and a suspension of U.S. bombing, a speech that drew sharp criticism from President Johnson. Pearson approved two Canadian missions to Hanoi in June 1964 and March 1966; the first informed North Vietnam of the U.S. intention to escalate the war, and the second, not fully supported by the United States, sought an opening for negotiations.

BIBLIOGRAPHY

ENGLISH, JOHN. *The Worldly Years: The Life of Lester Pearson.* Vol. 2. 1992.
PEARSON, LESTER B. *Mike: The Memoirs of the Right Honourable Lester B. Pearson.* Vol. 3. 1975.
STURSBERG, PETER. *Lester Pearson and the American Dilemma.* 1980.

ELLEN BAKER

Pentagon Papers. The Pentagon Papers were a document written secretly by Pentagon officials between 1967 and 1969 at the instruction of Secretary of Defense Robert McNamara, who wanted a thorough history of U.S. policy in Vietnam. In 1971, the papers became public and controversial when they were leaked to the national media and President Richard Nixon sought to block their publication.

Thirty-six Defense Department aides, including Daniel Ellsberg and Leslie Gelb, worked on the 47-volume, 7,000-page archive, which chronicled U.S. actions in Vietnam from 1945 to 1968. The Pentagon Papers included both "official policy" statements and "unofficial" Defense Department memos and touched upon various subjects, from the coup against Ngo Dinh Diem, to problems with American public opinion and tactics for peace negotiations. The papers do not provide much information on President Lyndon Johnson's role in the decision to send U.S. combat troops and the subsequent escalation, for they do not include White House memoranda. Nevertheless, antiwar critics believed that the papers established a "credibility gap" and demonstrated that the administration had deceived Congress and the public to justify and expand U.S. involvement in Vietnam.

Daniel Ellsberg, who had served as an aide to both McGeorge Bundy and John McNaughton, had turned against the war after he worked on the archive. He secretly copied the Pentagon Papers,

LESTER PEARSON. At right, with Lyndon B. Johnson at the LBJ Ranch, Johnson City, Texas, January 1965. *National Archives*

and in February 1971 he turned the documents over to *New York Times* reporter Neil Sheehan. The *Times* began publication on 13 June 1971. President Nixon was enraged. Although the papers primarily embarrassed his predecessors, John F. Kennedy and Johnson, Nixon believed the document would undermine his ability to make policy in Vietnam and pressed for a court order to block further publication on national security grounds. The Justice Department succeeded in obtaining a temporary court order against the *Times*, but by this time both the *Washington Post* and the *Boston Globe* were printing the papers. Also, in June, Sen. Mike Gravel of Alaska read portions of the papers into the public record during a subcommittee hearing. He was later held immune from prosecution by the Supreme Court in *Gravel v. U.S.* On 30 June the Supreme Court, citing the First Amendment freedom of the press clause, ruled that the *Times* had the constitutional right to publish the documents.

The day before the Supreme Court order, Ellsberg was indicted for his role in leaking the papers. The Nixon administration, not content to wait for the Ellsberg trial to work its way through the justice system, organized the "Plumbers," a secret White House group, to investigate and discredit Ellsberg.

They broke into the office of Ellsberg's psychiatrist, Dr. Lewis Fielding, looking for damaging information. Several of the Plumbers and their administration supervisors, including Egil Krogh, Charles Colson, John Erlichman, and G. Gordon Liddy, pled or were found guilty in the Fielding break-in. In 1973 Ellsberg's case was declared a mistrial because of the Plumbers' activities, and the indictment was dropped. The Pentagon Papers were thus significant both in exposing government policy and in prompting the Plumbers break-in, a harbinger for the Watergate scandal.

BIBLIOGRAPHY

KAHIN, GEORGE McT. *Intervention: How America Became Involved in Vietnam.* 1986.

KUTLER, STANLEY I. *The Wars of Watergate.* 1990.

ZAROULIS, NANCY, and GERALD SULLIVAN. *Who Spoke Up?* 1984.

KELLY EVANS-PFEIFER

People's Army of Vietnam (PAVN).

The People's Army of Vietnam (PAVN) was best known to Americans during the Vietnam War as the North Vietnamese Army, so called because it was the army of the Democratic Republic of Vietnam (DRV), which lay north of the demilitarized zone (DMZ). Before that war, however, it had fought the French in all parts of the country. The basic structure of the military establishment was a pyramid consisting of a main force of regular or mobile troops, a regional force of full-time troops responsible for territorial security and support of the main force, and a popular self-defense force of part-time militia in the villages.

Origins. The PAVN's official history claims antecedents in the "self-defense teams" (*doi tu ve*) organized by Communist Party members during the abortive peasant rebellion in Nghe An and Ha Tinh provinces in 1930. Brutally suppressed in the aftermath of that rebellion, the party in 1935 nonetheless adopted guidelines for the future organization of armed forces on the Soviet model. Chinese communist resistance to Japan's invasion in 1937 attracted Vietnamese attention to the military writings of Chinese strategists, including Mao Zedong.

The opportunity for the Vietnamese to attempt armed struggle did not arise until Japan occupied Indochina in 1940. The communists organized a guerrilla movement in the mountains near Vietnam's northern border in May 1941 and named it the Viet-nam Doc-lap Dong-minh (Vietnam Independence League), or Viet Minh for short. On 22 December 1944 the party commissioned 31 men and 3 women from this movement to form the Vietnam Propaganda and Liberation Unit under the command of Vo Nguyen Giap. The unit combined with other bands to form the Vietnam Liberation Army of about one thousand troops in May 1945. Youthful urban nationalists as well as peasants swelled the Liberation Army's ranks to a few thousand by the August Revolution later in 1945, after which it was renamed the National Defense Army and later still, in 1950, the People's Army of Vietnam.

Development in the First War. The DRV moved swiftly after declaring independence on 2 September 1945 to expand its nascent forces. On the eve of war with France in December 1946, the total force level was about 100,000 troops armed with 80,000 weapons. By 1950, the main force alone had 130,000 troops and was capable of manufacturing recoilless rifles and mortars in its own machine shops. Although most of the manpower came from the poor peasantry, the sons of middle and higher peasant families could better afford the absence from home, knew how to read, and so tended to fill the cadre ranks. Officers came at first from among the handful of party members who had attended short courses in the People's Republic of China (PRC) or had gained experience in the Liberation Army before the August Revolution. After 1945 they gained experience in primitive "academies" located in the mountains, in some cases with help from Japanese defectors. All top-ranked commanders such as Giap were party members who had begun their revolutionary careers as political activists; none of them were military professionals.

Though capable of defending revolutionary base areas, the PAVN lacked a centralized command structure and operated in small units until the late 1940s. The first division, the *308th,* was commissioned in August 1949 in Viet Bac, near the border with the PRC. A second, the *304th,* emerged in northern central Vietnam in March 1950. The commander in chief's office was divided into a general staff, political directorate, and supply directorate. Four more divisions, bringing the total to six (four in the northern provinces, two in the center), took shape by late 1952.

Successful attacks on French outposts along the northern border opened up access to the PRC in fall 1950. China set up training centers for the PAVN at six locations on its side of the border, and the volume of Chinese material assistance increased slowly to 1,500 tons per month at the beginning of the battle of Dien Bien Phu. But Chinese aid never constituted more than 20 percent of the PAVN's total requirements, whereas U.S. aid exceeded 70 percent of French needs by war's end. Moreover, the PAVN's lack of mechanized transport required it to depend heavily on its own manpower and civilian laborers to move weapons, equipment, and supplies to battle. Forty thousand porters were needed to support one division on a simple operation, and 260,000 porters supplied PAVN siege forces at Dien Bien Phu.

The party did not have to be as concerned as its Soviet, Eastern European, or even Chinese counterparts about officer loyalty because very few of the officers had served with the colonial auxiliaries. The party installed a political apparatus in the army mainly to motivate peasant recruits, provide political instruction on nationalist themes, and manage liaison with the civilian population. Although the party assigned political officers to some units as early as 1945, with authority to veto military orders, a formal system of these officers from company through regional levels and a parallel hierarchy of party committees was not fully in place until 1949. A party decision in 1951 to place more emphasis on social revolution, perhaps in response to Chinese advice, led to a tightening of ideological criteria in the promotion of officers, a commensurate tightening of political supervision, and some defections.

The Vietnamese mimicked a great deal of Chinese tactical doctrine and organizational structure, but they had to adapt Chinese strategy to Vietnam's much smaller territory and population. There could be no Long March or completely secure rear base in Vietnam. Mao's concept of three-stage war thus became, in Vietnam's "unique military art," a metaphor for different balances between armed and political struggle, and guerrilla and positional warfare, depending on opportunities across time and space. The concept of a front acquired more of a social than spatial definition, reflecting the overlap of liberated populations with the enemy's rear, in the image of interlocking teeth (*cai rang luoc.*). The Vietnamese also tapped their own history and that of the Soviet October Revolution for models of general offensive and uprising and the coordination of action in rural and urban areas. Communist strategists in Vietnam, as they put it in their formulaic phrase, had to find ways for "the few to defeat many, quality to defeat quantity, and weakness to defeat strength."

Modernization. The PAVN emerged from its war with France a quasi-modern force composed overwhelmingly of infantry. It had captured nearly 70 percent of its weaponry, and its officers wore no insignia of rank. Eighty-seven percent of officers above the level of platoon leader were party members, but 90 percent were in the infantry and of these only 10 percent had graduated from an officer training school. The army's first tasks after the 1954 Geneva agreements were to consolidate its many scattered elements into larger units and absorb some of the 87,000 combatants and recruits from the South who regrouped in the North. Many units were assigned tasks in internal security, land reform, and economic reconstruction, and subsequently combat readiness declined.

Modernization did not begin until 1957. Over the objections of "old resistance cadres" wedded to purist notions of "people's war," the modernization program centralized authority, imposed uniform criteria for recruitment and promotion, and established formal ranks with insignia. Chinese and Soviet advisers helped establish a central main force officers' academy with a three-year curriculum that mixed studies of conventional tactics, modern technologies, and people's war. Two (later three) years of compulsory military service became law in 1960.

The return of 2,400 officers who studied abroad between 1955 and 1960 enabled the PAVN to update its equipment and structure. Ground combat forces were organized into infantry, air defense, artillery, engineering, and communications branches. The first units of an air force, navy, and small armored, transportation, and chemical elements also appeared. The infantry was organized into seven divisions, six brigades, and twelve independent regiments. The standard division had 8,690 soldiers organized into three regiments, one battalion (later a regiment) of artillery, one battalion of antiaircraft, plus support elements; brigades had about 3,500 men each. Both the Soviet Union and the PRC supplied assistance, in which a small quantity of T-34 medium tanks and transport aircraft facilitated the establishment of the armored and air units. In 1960, the PAVN main force had 160,000 soldiers of which three-quarters (including 93,000 infantry) were assigned to ground combat.

Role in the Second War. The party's decision in January 1959 to support armed struggle in the South led to the formation in May of the PAVN *559th Transportation Group* to begin infiltrating troops and supplies overland. *Group 759* was commissioned later to move supplies by sea, and *Group 959* to sup-

PEOPLE'S ARMY OF VIETNAM. PAVN soldiers parade in Hanoi, 1966. *National Archives*

port the Pathet Lao and PAVN "volunteers" in Laos. Training intensified for "regroupee" units, composed of southern Vietnamese who went to North Vietnam for indoctrination and training after the Geneva agreements in autumn 1954. The *559th* infiltrated 3,500 officers and technical personnel from this pool into the South by early 1960. Regroupees, of whom 44,000 would go South by 1964, formed the backbone of a "South Vietnam Liberation Army," which, according to its commission, was "an element of the People's Army of Vietnam, created, built, trained, and led by the Party." In February 1961 it provided the main force of the People's Liberation Armed Forces of South Vietnam (PLAF), nominally under the authority of the National Liberation Front (NLF).

The communists in 1950 had divided the entire country into nine zones, or military regions, plus a special zone for the Saigon area, and North Vietnam commanded revolutionary armed forces in the South through this structure with minor changes in the second war. A military commission attached to the Central Office for South Vietnam (COSVN), a detachment of the party central committee, had overall command in Regions Six through Nine, which encompassed the area from the southern Central Highlands through the Mekong Delta. This area also was known as the B2 Front. The military commission and staff for Region Five, which encompassed the area from the southern central provinces to the Demilitarized Zone (DMZ), reported directly to North Vietnamese officials in Hanoi. Separate "front commands" were set up in later stages of the war for Quang Tri and Thua Thien provinces (B4), the central coast (B1), and the western highlands (B3). The PAVN major generals who first headed the COSVN and Region Five military commissions in the early 1960s, Tran Luong and Nugyen Don, were members of the central committee.

Against a background of increasing U.S. support for South Vietnam and a dwindling supply of regroupees to send south, the ninth plenum of the central committee approved plans to increase support for the southern revolution in December 1963. The first whole unit of northern-born PAVN regulars entered the South one year later. By mid 1966, an estimated 46,300 of these troops were fighting in the South. The PAVN's early mission was to wage mobile warfare in the thinly settled Central Highlands and along Route 9 just south of the demilitarized zone, permitting PLAF and guerrilla forces to operate in the densely populated lowlands. The strategy was to emphasize armed struggle in the mountains, a balance of armed and political struggle in the lowlands, and political struggle in the cities until, and if necessary, a general offensive including attacks on cities could be coordinated with an uprising of the urban population.

That moment came in the Tet Offensive of 1968, to which the PAVN contributed by drawing U.S. forces out of the lowlands with diversionary attacks at Khe Sanh and other points just south of the DMZ. With few exceptions PAVN forces stayed out of the cities. The decimation of southern regional and guerrilla forces that attacked the cities led to a compensatory increase in PAVN forces in the South to eighty or ninety thousand and reinforcement of PLAF units with northern troops. Lowland forces in particular, under pressure from "pacification" and small-unit patrolling by U.S. forces, sometimes found it necessary in 1969–1971 to disperse and operate as guerrillas. The main factors laying the basis for an expanded PAVN role, however, were a massive influx of Soviet T-54 tanks, armed personnel carriers, 57mm antiaircraft batteries, SA-7 handheld surface-to-air missiles (SAMs), 130 mm long-range field artillery, and the reduction of U.S. forces. The expansion of conventional capability allowed the PAVN to organize fifteen infantry divisions of about 12,000 men each, while U.S. withdrawal lowered the risk of maneuvering in large units.

Five PAVN divisions, each with integral artillery, tank, antiaircraft, and missile units, spearheaded frontal assaults on South Vietnamese positions in spring 1972. The attacking forces seized all former U.S. Marine bases just south of the DMZ, occupied the capital of Quang Tri province, and overran a number of South

Vietnamese outposts in the Central Highlands and Mekong Delta. The South Vietnamese forces beat back the attacks but needed the support of U.S. air power to do so.

The PAVN launched its final offensive of the war in January 1975. Total main forces by then numbered 685,000 organized into twenty-four divisions, a separate artillery command of ten regiments, ten independent infantry regiments, fifteen SAM regiments, and forty antiaircraft regiments. The PAVN had begun gathering some of these forces into army corps in October 1973, establishing four by war's end. Its weapons included nine hundred T-34, T-54, and T-59 Soviet-made medium tanks and eight hundred field guns in sizes from 85 mm to 152 mm. While these total resources were roughly equal to those of the South Vietnamese army, the thirteen divisions with 150,000 soldiers (plus 30,000 PLAF troops and 50,000 guerrillas) and six hundred tanks that the PAVN deployed in the South at the beginning of the offensive constituted the smaller theater force. It was the overextension of South Vietnamese forces that allowed the PAVN to concentrate overwhelming might against exposed positions and caused the disintegration of South Vietnamese forces that ended the war on 30 April 1975.

Logistics and Infiltration. Geography, distance, and chance determined how the North delivered troops and supplies south. While *Group 559* was developing the Ho Chi Minh Trail to support commands in the northern and highlands provinces, *Group 759* was established in October 1961 to supply by sea the more distant provinces that were under COSVN's jurisdiction. The group's small ships and junks carried arms into the river mouths and mangrove swamps of Ca Mau, Tra Vinh, Ben Tre, and Ba Ria provinces until U.S. and South Vietnamese naval forces discovered them in early 1965. Search for an alternate route led to an arrangement with Prince Sihanouk of Cambodia in 1966 that permitted trucking supplies overland from the port of Sihanoukville to bases on Cambodia's side of the border. Supplies reached Sihanoukville on board commercial cargo ships, and two private Cambodian companies hauled them to the bases in COSVN's rear. The Sihanouk Trail ceased operation in 1969 as a result of opposition from Sihanouk's republican rivals.

The vulnerability of external routes, as well as need of access to the Central Highlands, forced the PAVN to develop the interior route. This was the Ho Chi Minh Trail through the Truong Son Moun-

SUICIDE VOLUNTEER. Carrying an antitank mine. *Ngô Vĩnh Long*

tain range, which divided the three countries of Indochina. Initially a network of footpaths, dirt roads, and waterways that had served as communications links between revolutionary bases in the war against the French, the trail improved after PAVN and Pathet Lao troops captured roads in southern Laos in 1961 and engineering regiments attached to the *559th Transportation Group* began work. From the staging area in Vinh City, Nghe An province, the route climbed toward the mountains, split into three different routes to cross into Laos, and then headed south into Cambodia, branching back into Vietnam at points along the way. A fourth route passed through the western end of the DMZ. Porters carrying 25 kilograms (55 pounds) on their backs or 68 kilograms (150 pounds) on bicycles provided, along with oxcarts, the principal means of conveyance in the beginning. But engineers soon developed some of the paths into narrow dirt roads; redundant routes helped avoid bottlenecks and detection. *Group 559* moved forty times as much tonnage in 1964 as in all previous years, half of it by truck.

Troops moved mostly on foot, resting at fifty commo-liaison stations (logistical support bases)

scattered throughout the trail complex. The trip took three weeks to make the short hook through the Demilitarized Zone, three months to cover 1,000 kilometers (620 miles) to the most distant destinations. U.S. intelligence estimated that over 15 percent of troops fell behind their units because of malaria, beriberi, dysentery, or other ailments.

The trail terminated in bases on Vietnam's borders with Laos and Cambodia, where *Group 559* turned over troops and supplies to the rear service units of commands inside South Vietnam. There, the shortage of motorized transport until the last stages of the war made it necessary to pre-position supplies clandestinely for all but the simplest of operations. Even main forces had to obtain a considerable amount of their food locally and arrange for local manufacture of such items as uniforms.

The number of PAVN troops stationed in Laos by the late 1960s fluctuated around 40,000, of which most guarded the trail. U.S. bombardment limited the volume of troops and supplies moving down the trail but could not decrease it. A thrust into Laos by South Vietnamese forces in March–February 1971 to disrupt the trail collapsed into a rout when the

PAVN counterattacked. The trail became obsolete when much of the Central Highlands fell under communist control in 1974, permitting 30,000 workers to construct Corridor 613 on Vietnam's side of the border with Laos. By early 1975 ten thousand trucks were operating over this two-lane gravel road running from Route 9 to the edge of the Mekong Delta.

Tactics and Techniques. The basic problem for the PAVN most of the time was overcoming material discrepancies. This meant that its units had to be trained in techniques associated with guerrilla warfare, such as ambush and placing booby traps, although these were the specialty of forces-in-place. Conditions permitting, PAVN main forces concentrated on "big unit" mobile warfare. Attempting to wage such warfare, particularly against far more powerful U.S. units, had important implications for PAVN tactics and techniques. The PAVN attempted to nullify the enormous advantage that air mobility and air and artillery support gave to U.S. units, for example, by concentrating fire on helicopter landing zones, engaging at close quarters, and attacking strong points at night.

All communist forces typically planned operations far in advance and rehearsed until troops had memorized their movements. This procedure limited flexibility, but it helped compensate for inadequate communications. Unable to modify operations in progress, standard practice was to keep strong forces in reserve to cover withdrawal or seize unexpected opportunities. By such means the PAVN was able to stay in the field against superior forces even if it could not overcome them.

In rear areas the PAVN sometimes dug tunnels and deep underground bunkers for concealment, storage, medical facilities, and protection from bombardment by B-52s. The most spectacular of these complexes, stretching from the Cu Chi district northwest of Saigon to the Iron Triangle, was the work of various forces going back to the war with France. From 50 kilometers (30 miles) in 1954, the tunnels were extended to over 300 kilometers (200 miles) in length by the time of the Tet Offensive, after which U.S. forces succeeded in collapsing some of them with heavy bombs and rendering the area useless with chemical defoliants.

Matériel inferiority was the main justification also for the PAVN's extensive use of sappers (*dac cong*), or specialists in the use of explosives to breach defenses, sabotage airfields, mine roads and waterways, lead assaults, and conduct clandestine operations in cities and towns. The PAVN's first sappers, including a unit composed of women, grew out of an effort by the Saigon Communist Party committee to oppose the return of French forces in 1946. Compared with large maneuver forces, sappers were highly cost-effective and were among the first troops infiltrated into the South. Sapper training added six months to basic training and had the highest priority of the PAVN's special training programs. Communist forces relied particularly heavily on sappers after 1968 to help conserve other forces. In 1973 sappers were organized into four regiments, thirty-five battalions, and two special groups.

Motivation, Morale, and Political Work. More than one observer has commented on the extraordinary resilience of the PAVN infantry. The typical recruit, steeped from childhood in traditions of resistance to foreign rule and liberation from colonialism, genuinely believed the war was a defense of the homeland and a crusade for its unity. It took no feat of indoctrination to persuade PAVN troops of the justness of their cause and, therefore, of their eventual victory.

A "political work" system employing a quarter of all cadres in the armed forces reinforced these beliefs and provided emotional sustenance. The resources of this system were concentrated at company level, where "political sections" consisting of a political officer plus assistants supervised the company party chapter (*chi bo*), youth group, and military council. Party membership offered status and advancement; the youth group was the recruitment pool for the party; and the military council was a meeting of officers and men that permitted troops to air grievances and make suggestions. The political officers used these organizations to lead discussion on political topics, explain party policies, and develop a sense of participation. They also organized the surges of activity known as emulation campaigns in which troops who met fixed criteria could win recognition and sometimes promotion. Both political and military officers interacted with the men on a frequent and friendly basis. Finally, soldiers were grouped into three-man cells that took collective responsibility for each member, and they were expected to lay bare worries and feelings in weekly sessions of criticism and self-criticism (*phe binh* or, for party members, *kiem thao*). Whether such techniques worked because they appealed to recruits' patriotism or because family-like practices strengthened interpersonal bonds, American analysts concluded that PAVN soldiers' morale could not be broken short of their units' physical destruction, surrender, or disintegration. Setbacks did sometimes produce "wavering," most notably for a couple of years following the Tet Offensive, but the number of prisoners and deserters was small considering the incredibly adverse conditions under which the PAVN often had to fight.

Defense of the North. Until the U.S. withdrawal in 1973, the PAVN was forced to devote a large part of its resources to the defense of the "strategic rear" in the North. Aside from maintaining the bulk of its forces there, it helped to organize civilian support of the war effort and to train local militia of forces of around 2 million, or 10 percent of the population. Had the United States sent ground combat forces into the North, they would have had to contend with a nation-at-arms as well as the PAVN reserve.

The PAVN also had responsibility for the North's air and sea defenses against U.S. bombardment. Naval, air force, and air defense commands were components of the PAVN and subordinate to its general staff. In 1973 the 3,250-man navy had 56 small coastal escorts, gunboats, torpedo boats, and patrol boats, and the 10,000-man air force possessed 178 combat aircraft (rising to 268 in 1975) including forty MiG-21s and thirty MiG-19s. As there was no way these forces could match U.S. resources, however, the main effort went into constructing the world's densest defense network of radar-directed SAMs and antiaircraft guns ranging in size from 37mm to 100 mm. The latter weapons accounted for most of the U.S. aircraft shot down over the North.

The PAVN after 1975. Because regional tensions continued after 1975, the PAVN delayed demobilization. PAVN intervention in Cambodia in December 1978 to remove the Khmer Rouge government by force provoked a punitive strike across Vietnam's northern border by Chinese forces in February–March 1979. The PAVN force level in the early 1980s peaked at 1.2 million, making it the world's fourth largest army. But the ongoing economic crisis, a program of domestic reform adopted in 1986, and declining Soviet military assistance (terminated in 1991) forced cuts in spending, undermined morale, and led to the demobilization of 600,000 soldiers, including 200,000 officers, specialists, and workers in defense industries.

[*See also* Central Office for South Vietnam (COSVN); Group 559; Ho Chi Minh Trail.]

BIBLIOGRAPHY

LOCKHART, GREG. *Nation in Arms: The Origins of the People's Army of Vietnam.* 1989.
PIKE, DOUGLAS. *PAVN: People's Army of Vietnam.* 1986.
TURLEY, WILLIAM S. *The Second Indochina War: A Short Political and Military History, 1954–1975.* 1986.

WILLIAM S. TURLEY

People's Liberation Armed Forces. The People's Liberation Armed Forces (PLAF), popularly known to the outside world as the Viet Cong (VC), was the military arm of the National Liberation Front (NLF). Formally established at a meeting of insurgent leaders in early 1961, the PLAF was created as the result of a decision by North Vietnamese communist leaders to escalate the level of armed struggle in South Vietnam. Like its antecedent, the Viet Minh, which had fought successfully against the French during the late 1940s and early 1950s, the PLAF was organized at three levels: (1) regular forces operating under the command of the southern leadership, usually known as the Central Office for South Vietnam (COSVN), (2) full-time guerrillas organized in companies and serving under provincial or district leadership, and (3) a part-time self-defense militia, composed of units organized in squads and platoons and used primarily for village defense.

During the early and mid 1960s, the PLAF grew rapidly in strength and numbers, reaching an estimated 30,000 by the summer of 1964. Some of its leading cadres and officers were infiltrated from North Vietnam to the South along the Ho Chi Minh Trail, but the majority were recruited from villages or urban areas inside South Vietnam. Beginning in the early 1960s, the PLAF launched periodic hit-and-run attacks on government installations, military outposts, convoys, strategic hamlets, and even district towns throughout the Republic of Vietnam. Its most celebrated victory was at the village of Ap Bac in early January 1963, when Viet Cong guerrillas engaged South Vietnamese regular forces flown in by U.S. helicopters. The all-day battle resulted in heavy casualties for the South Vietnamese units, and was widely reported as a defeat for the South Vietnamese government.

After the introduction of U.S. combat troops in 1965, the role of the PLAF was gradually superseded by regular forces of the People's Army of Vietnam (PAVN), who were being infiltrated in increasing numbers from the North. Whereas the PAVN bore the brunt of the fighting with U.S. troops, PLAF units were most commonly used against lightly armed South Vietnamese units. The PLAF, however, assumed the primary role in the Tet Offensive, launched in early February 1968. Viet

Cong troops attacked villages, towns, and cities throughout the Republic of Vietnam. Although the offensive had a major impact on the course of the war, the attackers suffered over 30,000 casualties in the process, and as a result the PLAF, which had numbered by some estimates over 200,000 on the eve of Tet, declined as a major factor on the battlefield for the remainder of the war. Some have speculated that the communist leadership in the North deliberately ordered PLAF units into the fighting to reduce southern influence within the movement, but there is little evidence to support this assertion. In any case, the PLAF played little role in the 1975 offensive that led to the fall of South Vietnam. After the end of the war, PLAF units were disbanded or integrated with the PAVN.

BIBLIOGRAPHY

PIKE, DOUGLAS. *Viet Cong: The Organization and Techniques of the National Liberation Front of South Vietnam.* 1966.

TRUONG NHU TANG. *A Viet Cong Memoir: An Inside Account of the Vietnam War and Its Aftermath.* 1985.

WILLIAM J. DUIKER

Perot, H. Ross (1930–), businessman; self-proclaimed champion of American prisoners of war (POWs). Between 1969 and 1973, Perot sought to publicize the plight of American prisoners held in Vietnam. He attempted to deliver Christmas presents to them and conducted meetings (illegal under U.S. law) with North Vietnamese officials, offering to rebuild schools and clinics in exchange for the release of POWs. Since 1973 he has continued his efforts on behalf of those still listed as missing in action, contending that the federal government knowingly left Americans behind in 1973 and that servicemen remain alive in Southeast Asia. Although he has financed his own investigations of this alleged conspiracy as well as private, armed missions to rescue U.S. servicemen, none of his efforts has produced evidence of a cover-up or proof that prisoners still exist. Perot's running mate in his unsuccessful 1992 independent presidential campaign was former POW Adm. James B. Stockdale, who was awarded the Medal of Honor for his heroic resistance to years of torture in Hoa Lo prison.

BIBLIOGRAPHY

MASON, TODD. *Perot: An Unauthorized Biography.* 1990.

ELLEN D. GOLDLUST

H. ROSS PEROT. At right, with Yu Thien, the North Vietnamese chargé d'affaires in Laos, Vientiane, December 1969. Perot had been refused permission to enter North Vietnam with Christmas packages for U.S. prisoners of war. *National Archives*

Pham Hung (1912–1988), commander, Central Office of South Vietnam (COSVN), 1967–1975; deputy premier, Democratic Republic of Vietnam (DRV), 1976–1980; interior minister, DRV, 1980–1986; premier, DRV, 1987–1988. Born Pham Van Thien in the Mekong Delta region of southern Vietnam, Pham Hung was expelled from school at age 16 for anti-French agitation. He joined the newly formed Indochinese Communist party in 1930, and after he was arrested for murdering a French official, Hung spent fourteen years in colonial prisons. Upon his release in 1945, Hung was a key party leader in the Indochina War. He became Pham Van Dong's protégé and the highest-ranking party official from southern Vietnam, elected to the politburo in 1956. Nine years later, Hung secretly returned to his native South Vietnam to take charge of the Viet Cong insurgency. As COSVN commander he oversaw the Tet Offensive in 1968 and later served as political commissar for Gen. Van Tien Dung's Spring Offensive in 1975. After the war, Hung rose through several DRV posts to premier in 1987, but he died less than a year later.

BIBLIOGRAPHY

CHANDA, NAYAN. "Man in the Limelight." *Far Eastern Economic Review* (11 June 1976).

PIKE, DOUGLAS. *History of Vietnamese Communism, 1925–1976.* 1978.

TRUONG NHU TRANG. *A Viet Cong Memoir.* 1985.

"Vietnam's Phan Hung Is Dead." *New York Times,* 12 March 1988.

Who's Who in North Vietnam. 1969.

GLEN GENDZEL

Pham Van Dong (1906–), premier, North Vietnam, 1955–1975; premier, Socialist Republic of Vietnam, 1975–1986. Pham Van Dong, one of North Vietnam's ruling triumvirate along with Ho Chi Minh and Gen. Vo Nguyen Giap, was born a mandarin's son. His father was chief secretary to Emperor Duy Tan. Dong attended the finest French colonial schools and was a classmate of Ngo Dinh Diem, future president of South Vietnam. Dong entered the University of Hanoi in 1925, organized a student strike against the French, and fled to China to join the Indochina Communist Party in 1930. Sent back to Vietnam, Dong spent six years in the Con Son prison before resuming his exile in China in 1939. He cofounded the Viet Minh and helped organize resistance to Japan in World War II, becoming finance minister after the war. Ho Chi Minh dismissed Dong from the Viet Minh leadership in 1947, hoping to attract noncommunist support, but already Dong was known as Ho's esteemed "best nephew" and "other self." Never far from power, Dong won election to the politburo in 1951.

During the Indochina War, Dong commanded Viet Minh forces in his home province of Quang Ngai. Ho named him foreign minister and sent him to the Geneva peace conference in 1954. A year later, Dong became North Vietnam's first premier. He guided the communist takeover of North Vietnam's economy in the 1950s and gradually assumed more power as Ho faded from view in the 1960s. After Ho's death in 1969, Dong took charge of North Vietnam's war for national unification. Witty, urbane, yet resolute, Dong welcomed press interviews, which he conducted in impeccable French. Playing on American fears of prolonged involvement in Vietnam, Dong told reporters that "you Westerners" would never comprehend "the force of the people's will to resist, and to continue." He taunted Harrison Salisbury of the *New York Times* in 1966: "And how long do you Americans want to fight, Mr. Salisbury? One year? Two years? Five years? Ten years? Twenty years? We will be glad to accommodate you."

Bowing to pressure from Moscow, Dong accepted a cease-fire and U.S. withdrawal in 1973, but resumed the war against South Vietnam a year later

PHAM VAN DONG. C. 1972. *Archive Photos*

in violation of the Paris peace accords. Dong approved the victorious Ho Chi Minh Offensive in April 1975, then supervised the communist takeover of the south where 400,000 people were sent to "reeducation camps." Nearly a million refugees left Vietnam in the next five years as the economy collapsed, which Dong blamed on the United States for reneging on promises of reconstruction aid. In 1979, Vietnam's invasion of Cambodia and border clashes with China sapped precious resources, and Dong was forced to reintroduce capitalist incentives in 1981, especially in the south. "Yes, we defeated the United States," he said. "But now we are plagued by problems." Dong admitted that "waging a war is simple, but running a country is very difficult." Aged, ill, and discredited, he resigned the premiership in December 1986.

BIBLIOGRAPHY

"An Interview with Pham Van Dong." *Time,* 11 November 1985.

MORGANTHAU, TOM. "Vietnam: Sending Some Signals." *Newsweek,* 14 May 1984.

PHAM VAN DONG. *Selected Writings*. 1977.

PHAM VAN DONG. *Twenty Five Years of National Struggle*. 1970.

GLEN GENDZEL

Phan Huy Quat (1901–1975), prime minister, South Vietnam, 1965. Phan Huy Quat, a physician from Hanoi, enjoyed brief support from the United States as a possible replacement for President Diem in 1955. A longtime nationalist, he formed a fragile government at the request of Gen. Nguyen Khanh, president and de facto dictator during the chaotic months from February to June 1965. Quat was surprised by the initial U.S. commitment of combat troops during his presidency because no one had informed him. His government fell to a military coup led by Air Marshal Nguyen Cao Ky. Quat was arrested and executed by the communists in 1975.

BIBLIOGRAPHY

SHAPLEN, ROBERT. *The Lost Revolution: The U.S. in Vietnam, 1946–1966*. Rev. ed., 1966.

SMITH, HARVEY H., et al. *Area Handbook for South Vietnam*. 1967.

GLEN GENDZEL

Philippines. Throughout the Vietnam War, the Philippines was a strategic rear area that provided a vast array of critical support services for the war effort. Most important were the U.S. Navy base at Subic Bay and the U.S. Air Force base at Clark Field, which were located directly across the South China Sea from Vietnam. Moreover, as a former U.S. colony and close U.S. ally, the Republic of the Philippines remained a staunch supporter of the U.S. position in Vietnam.

After 1965, when the United States intervened directly in Vietnam, the Philippines provided significant support for the war effort. The U.S. Thirteenth Air Force based at Clark Field, north of Manila, used its Philippine facilities to support the bombing campaigns against North Vietnam. Similarly, the U.S. Seventh Fleet operating in the Tonkin Gulf had its home port at nearby Subic Bay. Moreover, the Philippines provided all U.S. forces in Vietnam with a nearby site for logistic support, medical evacuation, and recreation.

As a signatory of the Southeast Asia Treaty Organization (SEATO) in 1955, the Philippine government firmly supported U.S. policy in Vietnam from the outset. When President Lyndon Johnson asked for allied troops in 1965, Philippine president Ferdinand Marcos dispatched 2,000 combat engineers in February 1966. Evidently reluctant to commit troops, Marcos had agreed only after considerable diplomatic pressure by the United States, and even then negotiated privately for special payments totaling $39 million. In addition to this extraordinary subsidy, Marcos won lucrative contracts for Filipino firms as third-country nationals providing civilian support services in Vietnam. In October 1966, Marcos hosted a Manila summit of all allied nations fighting in Vietnam, an ambitious diplomatic overture that fell flat. As student and nationalist opposition to Philippine involvement intensified, however, Marcos withdrew Filipino forces in October 1969, only one month before the end of his campaign for reelection as president. During his second term, Marcos focused on rising domestic problems and largely ignored the Vietnam War.

BIBLIOGRAPHY

BONNER, RAYMOND. *Waltzing with a Dictator: The Marcoses and the Making of American Policy*. 1967.

ALFRED W. MCCOY

Phnom Penh, capital of Cambodia since the fall of the ancient Angkor kingdom. The city of Phnom Penh, considered the most beautiful in France's Indochina empire, escaped the direct effects of the Vietnam War. When Lon Nol governed, the city prospered from the effects of U.S. aid, but when President Richard Nixon ordered the secret bombing of the Cambodia-Vietnam border area, the resulting air war forced refugees west into the city or into the ranks of the Khmer Rouge. By 1970 civil war was widespread, the result of the overthrow of Prince Sihanouk, his replacement by Lon Nol, and the increase in the numbers of the Khmer Rouge. The war widened as U.S. and Army of the Republic of Vietnam (ARVN) forces invaded in pursuit of North Vietnamese and Viet Cong troops and the Central Office for South Vietnam (COSVN), the supposed communist command post for operations in South Vietnam. After U.S. forces left, the Vietnamese soldiers continued to fight.

Phnom Penh was besieged by the Khmer Rouge in April 1975, but many citizens welcomed the revolutionaries, seeing relief from governmental corruption and the war, which had spread throughout the countryside. With the defeat of the Lon Nol regime on 17 April, the Khmer Rouge, which disdained city life, equating it with decadence and the evils of the West, ordered evacuation of the population on the pretext that the United States intended to bomb the city. Thousands of city dwellers died of starvation, malnourishment, and lack of medical care as they fled and were resettled in the countryside. Intellectuals, doctors, and other professionals were systematically killed by the Khmer Rouge, and many others were separated from family members. Phnom Penh became a virtual ghost town. On 7 January 1979 forces of the Socialist Republic of Vietnam (SRV) captured Phnom Penh and gradually began restoring services in the city. Heng Samrin, a former member of the Khmer Rouge, was installed to head a new pro-Vietnam government. Gradually some of the former population returned; new inhabitants, brought in by the Khmer Rouge and unaccustomed to city life, essentially camped there for a decade. The city returned to a semblance of its former elegance when a truce was signed in 1991 between the factions of the civil war. By 1993 the long war seemed ended; foreign capital financed the rebuilding of hotels and restaurants, and tourism began again.

BIBLIOGRAPHY

Indochina Digest, 1990–1994.
ISAACS, ARNOLD. *Without Honor: Defeat in Vietnam and Cambodia.* 1993.
KIERNAN, BEN. *How Pol Pot Came to Power.* 1985.

SANDRA C. TAYLOR

Phoenix Program. *See* Pacification; Provincial Reconnaissance Units (PRU); Regional Forces/Popular Forces.

Phoumi Nosavan (1920–1985), deputy prime minister of Laos, minister of defense, chief of the Lao general staff. A right-wing officer, Nosavan rose to power via the U.S. Central Intelligence Agency–supported Committee for Defense of National Interests (CDNI). Despite considerable U.S. aid in the late 1950s, Phoumi was unable to develop an effective national army.

BIBLIOGRAPHY

CASTLE, TIMOTHY N. *At War in the Shadow of Vietnam: United States Military Aid to the Royal Lao Government, 1955–1975.* 1993.
DOMMEN, ARTHUR J. *Conflict in Laos.* 2d ed. 1971.

TIMOTHY N. CASTLE

PIERCE ARROW. PIERCE ARROW, code name for the 5 August 1964 retaliatory air raid against North Vietnam, was the first U.S. air attack on North Vietnam and the precursor to Operations FLAMING DART and ROLLING THUNDER. In response to the Gulf of Tonkin incidents, aircraft from the U.S. aircraft carriers *Ticonderoga* and *Constellation* attacked torpedo boat bases and petroleum storage facilities in southern North Vietnam. Four aircraft were lost, one pilot was killed, and one, Lt. (jg) Everett Alvarez, became the first U.S. prisoner of war (and the longest held, for eight years) in North Vietnam.

BIBLIOGRAPHY

DAVIDSON, PHILLIP B. *Vietnam at War: The History, 1946–1975.* 1988.

JOHN F. GUILMARTIN

Pike, Douglas (1924–), State Department Foreign Service officer, 1958–1982; expert on Vietnamese communism and its political-military strategies. Pike spent considerable time in Saigon and Washington, D.C., advising policymakers on the communists' insurgency. He intensively studied the writings of leading Vietnamese communists and wrote books on the People's Army of Vietnam and the Viet Cong, stressing the communists' tactic of close coordination of military struggle (*dau tranh vu trang*) and political action (*dau tranh chinh tri*). Describing the Vietnamese concept of "revolutionary war," Pike said that "there is no proven counterstrategy." He also credited North Vietnamese propaganda and political activities for the success of the antiwar movement in the United States. Pike retired from government service in 1982 and became director of the Indochina Studies Program at the University of California, Berkeley.

BIBLIOGRAPHY

PIKE, DOUGLAS. *PAVN: People's Army of Vietnam.* 1986.
PIKE, DOUGLAS. *War, Peace, and the Viet Cong.* 1969.

STANLEY I. KUTLER

Pleiku, South Vietnamese city, capital of Pleiku province, located in the Central Highlands. Pleiku City is a market town and was the site of a small French garrison during the Indochina War between the French and the Viet Minh. During the Vietnam War, the city served as the headquarters of the South Vietnamese Army's II Corps, which directed patrols against communist infiltration routes from Cambodia and Laos. After 1965, with the arrival of U.S. troops, Pleiku became an important U.S. command center.

On the morning of 7 February 1965, a Viet Cong company attacked a U.S. helicopter base and army barracks housing specialists and military advisers in Pleiku. Killing eight Americans and destroying ten aircraft, the attack, with another on Qui Nhon, provided the Johnson administration with the rationale to initiate reprisal air strikes against North Vietnam, code-named Operation FLAMING DART. Johnson quickly upgraded the strikes into the sustained bombing campaign ROLLING THUNDER.

In 1975, during the North Vietnamese Spring Offensive, President Nguyen Van Thieu of South Vietnam ordered regular army troops withdrawn from the Central Highlands, including Pleiku. Military commanders did not inform civilian officials, and when the panicked population fled, the ensuing chaos and attacks by the North Vietnamese Army upon the line of retreat turned the withdrawal into a rout. Part of the "Convoy of Tears," the retreat signalled the beginning of the collapse of the Army of the Republic of Vietnam (ARVN).

BIBLIOGRAPHY

ISAACS, ARNOLD R. *Without Honor: Defeat in Vietnam and Cambodia.* 1983.
KAHIN, GEORGE McT. *Intervention: How America Became Involved in Vietnam.* 1986.

PAUL M. TAILLON

Plumbers. A secret group of political operatives formed in 1971 to plug leaks to the press within President Nixon's administration, the Plumbers were authorized to use legal or illegal methods to accomplish that aim. The Plumbers were led by White House aides David Young—who gave the group its comical name—and Egil "Bud" Krogh, and it operated under the supervision of White House Counsel John Ehrlichman; its operatives included key Watergate figures E. Howard Hunt and G. Gordon Liddy. The group reflected Nixon's paranoia toward the antiwar movement and his obsession with preventing leaks from his staff. Krogh once said "Anyone who opposes us, we'll destroy."

The Plumbers were formed initially to investigate Daniel Ellsberg and the Pentagon Papers leak. After publication of the papers in June 1971, the Plumbers installed dozens of illegal wiretaps on the phones of administration staff and in September 1971 broke into the office of Ellsberg's psychiatrist, Dr. Lewis Fielding, to find material to discredit Ellsberg. Ehrlichman and several of the Plumbers pled guilty or were found guilty of perjury or of violating Fielding's rights. The Plumbers' activities were included as part of the impeachment articles charging Nixon with "abuse of power" and thus contributed to the downfall of his presidency.

BIBLIOGRAPHY

KUTLER, STANLEY. *The Wars of Watergate.* 1990.
ZAROULIS, NANCY, and GERALD SULLIVAN. *Who Spoke Up?* 1984.

KELLY EVANS-PFEIFER

Poland. A member of the International Control Commission (ICC), Poland as a socialist-bloc country generally supported the Democratic Republic of Vietnam (DRV). Its delegate, Janusz Lewandowski, participated in the Marigold negotiations in June 1966, which resulted in the DRV dropping its demand that South Vietnam become a neutral state and that the United States withdraw all its troops. Poland agreed to host a DRV-U.S. meeting in Warsaw in November 1966, but North Vietnam canceled the meeting in December when President Johnson refused to halt U.S. bombing of the DRV, despite the urging of Averell Harriman and Chester Cooper.

BIBLIOGRAPHY

KARNOW, STANLEY. *Vietnam: A History.* 1991.

ELLEN BAKER

Pol Pot (1928–), head of the Khmer Rouge; secretary, Communist Party of Kampuchea (CPK), 1962–; prime minister, Democratic Kampuchea (Cambodia), 1976–1979. Pol Pot was born Saloth Sar in Kompong Thom province, Cambodia. His parents were landowners and had royal connections. Sar was sent to Phnom Penh at the age of six to join his brother Loth Suong, who worked in the palace as an administrator. Sar's upbringing was strict, and he was isolated from Cambodia's vernacular culture. Following one year in the royal monastery he spent six in an elite Catholic school. The palace compound was closeted and conservative, and Sar had little contact with Phnom Penh's 100,000 inhabitants, who were mostly Chinese shopkeepers and Vietnamese workers.

In 1948, Sar received a scholarship to study radioelectricity in Paris, where he joined the Cambodian section of the French Communist Party. Most of Sar's Paris student friends, such as Khieu Samphan, Ieng Sary, and Son Sen, remain in his circle in the 1990s. He stood out in his choice of a nom de plume: Pol Pot means "the original Cambodian." Self-effacing and charming, he kept company with Khieu Ponnary, the first Cambodian woman to receive a *baccalauréat* degree, and when the couple married in Cambodia in 1956, they chose Bastille Day for their wedding.

His scholarship ended after he failed his course three years in a row, and he arrived home in January 1953, just after King Sihanouk had declared martial law to suppress Cambodia's independence movement, which was becoming radicalized in response to French colonial repression. Sar and his closest brother joined the Cambodian and Vietnamese communists. Following independence in 1954, Sar rose within the Cambodian communist movement, becoming party leader in 1962 after his predecessor, a former Buddhist monk, was killed. Sar criticized North Vietnam and Cambodians who supported Sihanouk's neutrality.

In Pol Pot's view, Cambodia did not need to learn or import anything from its neighbors. Rather, he believed that under his rule Cambodia would recover its pre-Buddhist glory by rebuilding the powerful economy of the medieval Angkor kingdom and regaining ancient territory from Vietnam and Thailand. Pol Pot's group treasured the Cambodian "race," not individuals, and believed that impurities included the foreign-educated (himself and his colleagues excepted) and "hereditary enemies," especially Vietnamese. To return Cambodians to their imagined origins, Pol Pot saw the need for war and for secrecy as "the basis of the revolution." Pol Pot did not trust the grassroots, pragmatic Cambodian communists to implement such plans, and so he kept his plans secret, just as he kept his identity as Saloth Sar a secret.

Sar first visited China in 1964–1965. In 1966 he returned to Cambodia, and he and the Cambodian communists whom he led, dubbed the Khmer Rouge by Sihanouk, began planning an uprising against Sihanouk. Beginning in 1970, a second civil war tore Cambodia apart, and Lon Nol deposed Sihanouk, who ironically became the powerless titular head of the Khmer Rouge. After defeating the U.S.-backed general Lon Nol in 1975, Pol Pot became prime minister, claiming a "*clean victory . . . without* any foreign connection." He had the Khmer Rouge evacuate Cambodia's cities amid continuing warfare, now against Vietnam. A true nationalist chauvinist, Pol Pot could not see Cambodia living in peace with its neighbors in a community of nations. "When we are strong they are weak, when they are weak we are strong." He shared the traditional Khmer elite's racism and grandiose designs on "lost territories." Raids on Laos, Thailand, and Vietnam began simultaneously in 1977.

Pol Pot claimed to be "four to ten years ahead" of the other Asian communist states, adding: "We have no model in building up our new society." This disguised the influence of Maoism in the call for a "Super Great Leap Forward," of Stalinism, and even of the French revolution, copied by introducing the ten-day working week (with one-day weekends).

Agricultural products were exported to China for weapons. Imposing these policies by force caused the deaths of 1.5 million Cambodians. In his administration, Pol Pot was honorifically known as "the Organization"—one that made speeches, watched movies, was sometimes "busy working," but could be asked favors if one dared. His wife, Khieu Ponnary, reputedly went mad. They had no children. His identity as Saloth Sar was realized in late 1978, when his brother, Loth Suong, recognized him in a poster. Two months later the Pol Pot regime was overthrown by the invading army of the Socialist Republic of Vietnam.

In a secret 1988 briefing to his commanders in Thailand, Pol Pot blamed most of his regime's killings on "Vietnamese agents." But he defended having massacred the defeated Lon Nol government's officers, soldiers, and officials. "This strata of the imperialists had to be totally destroyed," he insisted. Ironically, U.S. policies since 1978 had assisted the Khmer Rouge to rebuild its strength after defeat by Vietnam. The United States also legitimized Khmer Rouge participation in the 1991 Paris agreement, which readmitted the movement to Cambodian political life. But the Khmer Rouge opposed the 1993 U.N.-organized elections, which produced a new government. Pol Pot, still leading the Khmer Rouge army, continued to wage war from the jungles on the Thai border.

[*See also* Cambodia.]

BIBLIOGRAPHY

CHANDLER, D. P. *Brother Number One: A Political Biography of Pol Pot.* 1992.

CHANDLER, D. P., BEN KIERNAN, and CHANTHOU BOUA, eds. *Pol Pot Plans the Future: Confidential Leadership Documents from Democratic Kampuchea, 1976–1977.* 1988.

KIERNAN, BEN. *How Pol Pot Came to Power: A History of Communism in Kampuchea, 1930–1975*. 1985. Reprint 1987.
KIERNAN, BEN, ed. *Genocide and Democracy in Cambodia: The Khmer Rouge, the United Nations, and the International Community*. 1993.

BEN KIERNAN

Porter, William J.

Porter, William J. (1914–1988), U.S. deputy ambassador to South Vietnam; supporter of the war; delegate to the Paris peace talks. For eighteen months beginning in 1965, Porter was responsible for coordinating the ongoing pacification programs of various U.S. government agencies in South Vietnam. Porter also served as an adviser to Lyndon B. Johnson and as a negotiator at the Paris peace talks.

BIBLIOGRAPHY

Current Biography Yearbook. 1974.
International Who's Who, 1983–1984. 1983.
"Talking Tough in Paris." *Time*, 17 January 1972, 26–27.

ELLEN D. GOLDLUST

Post-traumatic Stress Disorder (PTSD).

Post-traumatic stress disorder (PTSD), currently known as post-traumatic stress syndrome (PTSS), is a condition marked by feelings of anxiety, depression, thoughts of suicide, recurring nightmares, and sudden outbursts of violence. Traumatic events such as natural disasters or accidents can trigger PTSD, and it is quite common among combat veterans. In World War I, PTSD was called shell-shock, in World War II, combat fatigue. Several unique aspects of the Vietnam experience, however, contributed to greater incidence of PTSD: the one-year individual tour of duty, as opposed to rotations of entire platoons, which made combat an individual, rather than a shared group, experience; the uncertain and unpredictable nature of guerrilla combat in the jungle in which booby traps and ambushes were used extensively; the moral ambiguities surrounding the war; and the treatment veterans received upon returning home. Many veterans felt unable to talk about Vietnam, and they often vividly reexperienced traumatic combat memories when they heard a helicopter or a car backfire.

It has been estimated that between 500,000 and 700,000 Vietnam veterans, about one-fourth of all who served, suffer from PTSD. The veterans administration (VA) was slow to recognize and treat PTSD, maintaining that psychological problems experienced by veterans had existed prior to their ser-

vice in Vietnam. By the 1980s, however, most VA facilities offered counseling and group therapy sessions for veterans with PTSD.

BIBLIOGRAPHY

MACPHERSON, MYRA. *Long Time Passing*. 1984.

KELLY EVANS-PFEIFER

POW/MIA Controversy.

POW/MIA Controversy. Two decades after all U.S. troops were withdrawn from Vietnam the issue of Americans still listed as prisoners of war (POWs) or missing in action (MIAs) remained controversial and unresolved. A 1991 public opinion poll indicated that more than 70 percent of Americans believed that POWs were left behind after the war and may still be held captive today; three-fourths of those believed that the U.S. government was not doing enough to secure their release. The issue has significantly shaped United States–Vietnam relations since the war. Some contend that those who insist that Americans are alive and being held in Vietnam and Laos are cynically playing upon the hopes and emotions of POW families for political reasons. Those who believe that Americans are alive in Indochina advance "live sightings" of alleged Americans as proof and argue that the Vietnamese government could clear up all questions if pressed hard enough. The POW/MIA issue, given new momentum by President Reagan in the early 1980s, reemerged in 1992 when the Senate Select Committee on POW/MIA Affairs began an investigation into the possibility that some Americans were not returned in 1973.

Nixon and the POW Issue. President Richard Nixon, in his "Go Public" campaign, used the POW issue to counter the antiwar movement beginning in 1969 and insisted on a satisfactory settlement of that issue in the Paris negotiations. One of the key agreements of the Paris peace accords of 1973 was that all American POWs be returned to the United States within sixty days of complete U.S. troop withdrawal. In March 1973, 591 POWs were released. The returning men were given the only official "welcome home" tribute—dubbed "Operation Homecoming"—of the war and were hailed as heroes. The Nixon administration, eager to put Vietnam behind it, maintained that all Americans were now returned. However, family members of unaccounted for soldiers, Vietnam veterans, and others, including H. Ross Perot, did not accept that conclusion and formed support groups, the main organization being the National

POW AS PROPAGANDA. U.S. Air Force Colonel J. L. Hughes is paraded through the streets of Hanoi after capture, June 1969. *National Archives*

League of Families of American Prisoners and Missing in Southeast Asia, to lobby for further efforts on the POW issue. POW/MIA organizations raised millions of dollars in an effort to keep the issue before the American public and to lobby the government.

Assessing the Numbers of POWs and MIAs. In no previous war has there been full accounting for the dead and missing. Nearly 80,000 troops were unaccounted for after World War II, and more than 8,000 after the Korean War. Of the 2,273 troops in Vietnam listed as unaccounted for (roughly 4 percent of the total Vietnam dead), half are known to have died, but their bodies were not recovered. These were primarily aviators who were shot down in remote jungle areas and were not seen parachuting to safety. Many pilots reported their comrades as MIA in order to maintain the flow of benefits to the families of downed pilots. The remaining missing, 1,172 men, were lumped into a POW/MIA category, even though the POW designation had formerly been used only for known prisoners and even though in nearly all cases the missing men were believed to have been killed, al-

though their deaths were not witnessed. Some also were known to be deserters or defectors.

An investigation in 1975–1976 by the House Select Committee on Missing Persons in Southeast Asia (Montgomery Committee), supported by an independent National Defense University study, concluded that "no Americans are still being held alive as prisoners in Indochina, or elsewhere, as a result of the war in Indochina." Despite that pronouncement, which agreed with internal Defense Department investigations, the POW/MIA issue persisted.

Resurgence of the Issue. The flood of refugees from Vietnam in the late 1970s and early 1980s brought reports of "live sightings" of POWs. These reports, investigated by the Defense Intelligence Agency (DIA) and often solicited by organizations such as the Joint Casualty Resolution Center, which maintains open files on all MIA cases, fueled the POW movement in the United States. Of the 1,053 sightings reports on file at the DIA as of 1988, the vast majority have been explained or discredited and only a few dozen remain unresolved. These live sightings reports prompted President Reagan to triple the budget of

FREEDOM FLIGHT. POWs released by North Vietnam lift off from Hanoi, March 1973. *National Archives*

the DIA and establish the POW/MIA Interagency Working Group. He also allegedly gave private sanction to the efforts of mercenaries such as former Special Forces lieutenant colonel "Bo" Gritz, who planned two ill-fated POW rescue attempts into Laos in the early 1980s. Reagan frequently said he believed that many Americans could still be alive as POWs in Southeast Asia, and he promised renewed attention to the issue. Both the Reagan and Bush administrations publicly operated on the assumption that "at least some Americans are still held captive."

The POW/MIA Issue in the 1990s. In 1992 former Reagan and Nixon aides testified before the Senate Select Committee that Nixon and Kissinger were told in 1973 that as many as 135 troops who were thought to be prisoners were not returned and may have been alive at the time. No hard evidence has been uncovered to suggest that these men have survived in captivity to this day, but the testimony gave support to those who allege a massive govern-

ment betrayal and cover-up of the POW issue. The Reagan and Bush administrations' publicly declared sympathy with this view was the major barrier to normalizing relations with Vietnam because the United States demanded the "fullest possible accounting" for American POW/MIAs.

Since 1973, Vietnam has insisted that all POWs had been released according to the terms of the Paris peace accords. It refused, however, to provide detailed information on MIAs, maintaining that the United States had failed to implement the peace agreement's provisions for U.S. payment for war damages. In 1992, Vietnam began new efforts to cooperate in resolving the MIA question and the next year released the "Blue Book," a detailed archival record involving the wartime fate of U.S. pilots or soldiers who died in combat or captivity. In response, the Clinton administration took the first steps toward normalization of relations, including lifting the trade embargo. As government officials sift through the millions of Vietnamese documents, it is clear that there are no American POWs. Still, it is likely that charlatans and political opportunists will continue to exploit the issue and leave many Americans believing that U.S. soldiers remain captive in Southeast Asia.

[*See also* Montgomery Committee.]

BIBLIOGRAPHY

COLVIN, ROD. *First Heroes: The P.O.W.s Left Behind in Vietnam.* 1987.
FRANKLIN, H. BRUCE. *M.I.A. or Mythmaking in America.* 1992.
KEATING, SUSAN KATZ. *Prisoners of Hope.* 1994.
MCCONNELL, MALCOLM. *Inside Hanoi's Secret Archives.* 1995.
OLSON, JAMES, and RANDY ROBERTS. *Where the Domino Fell.* 1991.

KELLY EVANS-PFEIFER AND STANLEY I. KUTLER

Prelude to U.S. Combat Intervention

The United States in Vietnam, 1945–1965

U.S. Policy after World War II
The Cold War Perspective
Defeat of the French
Support of Diem
Policy under Kennedy
The Failure of Early Efforts
The Coup against Diem
Policy under Johnson
Bombing North Vietnam

When most Americans thought about the world in the fall of 1945, they thought about the recent war with Germany and Japan. They worried about the Soviet Union, whose troops had liberated Eastern Europe, or about Europe itself, exhausted by six years of war. Some may have contemplated the fate of postwar China, the disposition of British India, or the future of relations with Latin America. Few thought about events in Indochina, a small and distant place that had briefly seized the spotlight in the early 1940s as a target of Japanese expansionism, and then receded into obscurity for the duration of the war. Hanoi might have been a city in Zanzibar; Ho Chi Minh was perhaps a Chinese general or a river in the Himalayas.

U.S. Policy after World War II. Within the departments of the U.S. government, however, there were men and women whose jobs were to monitor the situation in Southeast Asia and make recommendations to the secretary of state and the president about actions that should be taken. These people knew that Indochina was made up of three states, Vietnam, Laos, and Cambodia, and that the French had ruled all three until the Japanese usurped them in early 1945. They knew that in Vietnam in particular the Japanese takeover had encouraged the growth of nationalism among the Vietnamese people, and that in September 1945 the leaders of the nationalist movement, or Viet Minh, had declared Vietnam an independent nation. Ho Chi Minh, leader of the Viet Minh, was a communist of long standing, but in his declaration of independence he had quoted passages from the U.S. Declaration of Independence and had in other ways made it clear that he would welcome U.S. help in getting the new nation established. The U.S. experts also knew that France intended to reassert its control over Indochina. Vietnam in particular was too valuable to the French, materially and psychologically, to be surrendered to the Vietnamese nationalists, regarded by the French as a group of ragged peasants quoting Marx and Lenin.

Thus, the U.S. experts in the State Department, the Department of War, the Office of Strategic Services (OSS, the predecessor of the Central Intelligence Agency [CIA]), and in the White House were faced with a choice: Should they support Vietnamese independence in the hope of gaining influence over a nationalist revolution that might otherwise turn for help to the Soviet Union? Or should they endorse French efforts to return Indochina to colonial status, believing that France needed its colonies in order to repair its wartorn economy and restore its battered pride?

The U.S. president in the fall of 1945 was Harry S. Truman, who had come to the office the preceding April when Franklin D. Roosevelt had died. Truman was a plainspoken and earthy Missourian whose direct style of governing contrasted sharply with that of the patrician and ruminative Roosevelt. Truman, because he was relatively inexperienced in foreign policy–making, was at first willing to follow Roosevelt's lead on issues he considered beyond his ken. Indochina policy fell into this category. Roosevelt had opposed the return of France's colonial possessions. At least, he thought, what he called the "brown people" of the world deserved to have their countries placed under the tutelage of responsible great powers (not France), which would restore order, teach the lessons of democracy and capitalism, then usher in a brave new world of independent states that would remain forever grateful to their instructors. But toward the end of his life, Roosevelt appeared to change his mind. Yielding to objections from the French, the British (who despite Roosevelt's assurances worried that they too might be shorn of their colonies), and many of his own advisers, the president told a close friend that if France promised to behave as a trustee he "would agree to France retaining these colonies [Indochina] with the proviso that independence was the ultimate goal." This was the somewhat ambiguous policy inherited by Harry Truman.

While Truman was inclined to follow Roosevelt's lead on Indochina and other foreign policy issues, there was one important matter on which he decisively toughened his predecessor's stance. Throughout the war, Roosevelt had maintained an uneasy understanding with Soviet dictator Joseph Stalin. In return for Soviet cooperation in Asia, Roosevelt seems to have conceded the Russians a tacit sphere of influence in Eastern Europe. Truman could not accept this, believing that Soviet control of a country meant slavery for its inhabitants, its isolation from trade and investment, and potential military danger to its neighbors. To prevent what it believed would be the expansion of Soviet communism, the Truman administration implemented a series of measures designed to shore up the noncommunist nations of Western Europe. The Truman Doctrine speech of March 1947 offered U.S. aid to Greece and Turkey, two bastions of autocracy, and more broadly divided the world into two camps: the children of light and the children of darkness, as a prominent theologian put it. The Marshall Plan, which followed just three months later, extended millions of dollars in economic assistance to those Western European states judged most essential to the economic recovery of the noncommunist world and most vulnerable to Soviet subversion. The strength of this emerging coalition came from the North Atlantic Treaty, signed in the spring of 1949 by the United States, Canada, and a number of European nations. The treaty stipulated that an attack against one signatory would be considered an attack against them all, making an alliance that was aimed pointedly at the Soviet Union.

The Cold War Perspective. The division of the world into two armed camps solidified the so-called Cold War, and that conflict had clear implications for U.S. policy in Vietnam: Ho Chi Minh was a communist; communists were the children of darkness so one did not negotiate with them; therefore, there could be no question of helping Ho in his quest for independence. U.S. policymakers occasionally complained about the slow pace of reform in French Indochina, and they objected periodically to the French refusal to promise eventual independence for Vietnam. But in the end the Truman administration stood by while the French moved back into Vietnam, did not act when war broke out between the French and Vietnamese in late 1946, and muffled its concerns when the French tried to outflank Ho Chi Minh by appointing the former Vietnamese emperor (and collaborator with the Japanese) Bao Dai to the presidency of a Vietnamese state "within the French Union." Policymakers discounted Ho Chi Minh's manifest popularity and nationalism. As Secretary of State Dean Acheson wrote in May 1949, in the clipped phrasing of the absolutely certain, the "question [of] whether Ho [is] as much nationalist as Commie is irrelevant. All Stalinists in colonial areas are nationalists."

To the administration, Ho Chi Minh's communism linked him to a worldwide movement to subvert liberty and prosperity. By late spring of 1949, when Acheson rendered his judgment on nationalists, the United States seemed to be losing ground in the Cold War. Germany was divided; its western half, controlled by the United States, Great Britain, and France, remained economically impotent and militarily vulnerable, excluded from the North Atlantic alliance because of French reservations. France was still mired in postwar stagnation, the victim of its own determination to remain a colonial power without the means to do so. Angry French workers turned increasingly to communism, but little could be done for the working class while France continued with its expensive project to "save" Vietnam. In Great Britain, there was more distressing news. Although U.S. assistance provided under the Marshall Plan had helped the British economy rebound in 1948, a brief recession in the United States reversed this progress, and

U.S. ADVISERS. With Vietnamese troop leaders, during Operation DAN CHI, 1964. *National Archives*

the British pleaded for more U.S. help. Meanwhile, communists throughout the world seemed to be flourishing. In late summer of 1949 the Soviets detonated an atomic bomb, and on 1 October the Chinese Communist leader Mao Zedong raised the flag of the People's Republic of China (PRC). (Mao's adversary, Generalissimo Chiang Kai-shek, fled to Taiwan a few months later.)

Just at this critical juncture, the French requested U.S. aid for their ongoing efforts in Vietnam. They needed economic aid for their man Bao Dai, and they needed jeeps, planes, and guns to fight the Viet Minh. Because their postwar economy was so fragile the French could not provide these things themselves. It was time, they said, for the Americans to shoulder some of the burden of fighting communism in Southeast Asia.

Reeling from its Cold War setbacks, the Truman administration decided to honor the French request. In May 1950, the president announced that the United States would provide French-backed Vietnam with $10 million in military aid and a small amount of economic assistance to bolster the country against communism. The decision addressed a host of problems. Protecting Vietnam from communism would protect Southeast Asian markets for the rebuilding Japanese, keeping the recent imperialists prosperous and hopefully peaceful. A U.S. presence in Indochina would reassure the British, who acknowledged that their return to economic stability was closely linked to the success of the tin and rubber industries in their lucrative Malayan colony. With help in Vietnam the French could concentrate on the important business of reviving their own economy. Once relieved of their military obligations in Vietnam (following victory, of course), they could bring their troops home to Europe, where they could be used to keep a watch on a rearmed West Germany. It was in many ways a logical step and a neat scheme, but it was too much to expect of a mere $10 million.

Truman's decision to aid the French-supported government in Vietnam marked a critical turning point in U.S. policy. Years later, U.S. presidents would argue that the United States had to stay on in Vietnam in order to honor its commitment there. Few remembered when the commitment had first been made, or why.

The stakes rose in Southeast Asia in late June 1950, when communist North Korea invaded U.S.-backed South Korea. Under United Nations auspices the United States rushed troops into Korea, stopped the North Korean offensive, and then reversed it. Surprised at the speed with which the North Korean army crumbled and tempted by the prospect of liberating a communist country, the United States followed its South Korean allies across the 38th parallel that divided the peninsula with visions of total victory. Instead, in late autumn of 1950 the Chinese intervened in force and drove the Americans out of North Korea. After two and a half more years of bloody stalemate and frustrating negotiations, the two sides reached an armistice in 1953.

Defeat of the French.   The Korean War had a major impact on events in Vietnam. The Americans came to believe that Vietnam was next on the communist agenda, and that the Chinese would likely cross the border in force. The United States therefore increased its financial commitment to the Bao Dai government, so that by 1952 it was paying almost one-third of the cost of the war. While the French were pleased to have the assistance, they were wary of U.S. efforts to displace them altogether. The war in Vietnam had become *la salle guerre,* the dirty war. In the fall of 1950 the French sustained a series of stunning defeats, administered by Viet Minh general Vo Nguyen Giap. Hoping to gain the upper hand, the French military decided to concentrate its forces in the valley of Dien Bien Phu, in northwest Vietnam. If all went as planned, the Viet Minh would be lured into fighting a set-piece battle with the French, in which the allegedly superior French forces would prevail. "If he [the Viet Minh] comes down, we've got him," explained the French colonel in charge of the garrison.

It took only a few months for Giap to prove the French wrong. By early 1954, the French at Dien Bien Phu were surrounded and subject to daily artillery barrages of remarkable effectiveness. As panic set in, the possibility of negotiation loomed. The French decided to place the Indochina problem on the agenda of the upcoming Geneva conference, called to consider Asian issues. They also requested more U.S. aid. This time they sought U.S. military intervention at Dien Bien Phu, at minimum air strikes against Viet Minh positions.

The new U.S. president was Republican Dwight D. Eisenhower, elected in 1952. A World War II military hero, Eisenhower had considerable experience with combat and respected its limitations. While he took seriously the French plea for military help at Dien Bien Phu, he was skeptical of its chances for success. He listened to those in the administration who supported the air strike plan. One advocate, Adm. Arthur Radford, chairman of the Joint Chiefs of Staff, called for the use of atomic bombs against the Viet Minh. The president went so far as to

BOMBED U.S. OFFICER'S QUARTERS. Four Vietnamese and three Americans were killed and dozens of buildings were heavily damaged by a Viet Cong bomb attack against a U.S. officers billet in Saigon. The bomb was believed to be a 250-pound charge carried by truck. *National Archives*

suggest that if an air strike were carried out the planes should be painted with the French tricolor, "so we could deny it forever." Vice President Richard Nixon declared his support for military involvement. Ultimately, Eisenhower decided to make U.S. intervention contingent on three conditions: acceptance of the plan by Congress, military collaboration with the British, and a French agreement to set a date for Vietnamese independence. Several historians have pointed out that Eisenhower knew that satisfaction of all three conditions was impossible, that he had willingly tied his own hands. As Eisenhower later wrote, "I was convinced that no military victory was possible in that type of theater."

It is unclear if U.S. help would have made a difference in the outcome of Dien Bien Phu. As it was, the French garrison collapsed in early May, and the French turned to the talks at Geneva, hoping that their position in Indochina could be salvaged. Despite the grave situation on the battlefield, the French came out of the conference with their presence in Vietnam intact. Ho Chi Minh's allies, the Soviet Union and the PRC, wanted to limit U.S. involvement in Southeast Asia, so they forced the Viet Minh to compromise and yield some of its military advantage. Under the terms of the Geneva agreements, signed in July 1954, a cease-fire was to take hold throughout Indochina. Vietnam was divided at the 17th Parallel: the northern part was controlled by the Viet Minh and the southern part by Bai Dai and the French. The two zones were to be reunited by elections scheduled for the summer of 1956. While some Viet Minh officials complained that their allies (the PRC and the Soviet Union) had sold them out, most were optimistic that the reunification election would produce an overwhelming victory for Ho Chi Minh. In the streets of Hanoi, Ho's supporters greeted each other with fin-

MCNAMARA IN SAIGON. At left, being welcomed by South Vietnamese general Nguyen Huu Co. U.S. deputy ambassador to Vietnam U. Alexis Johnson is at center. *National Archives*

gers raised in a V: "Two more years!" Viet Minh soldiers laid down their arms and waited.

Support of Diem. The U.S. government did not find the Geneva agreements satisfactory, and refused to sign them. Ignoring the realities of Vietnam's political situation, Eisenhower's secretary of state, John Foster Dulles, characterized the accords as "something to gag about" and set about to undermine them. The United States snubbed Bao Dai, circumvented the French, and, at the urging of a creative CIA operative named Edward Lansdale, annointed Ngo Dinh Diem to lead southern Vietnam down the path to anticommunist stability. Secretive and fundamentally undemocratic—Diem's sister-in-law Madame Ngo Dinh Nhu once said, "if we open the window not only sunlight but many bad things will fly in also"—Diem was a Catholic in a Buddhist country seeking a Confucian "Mandate of Heaven" to validate his control. He crushed his opposition with what the U.S. government regarded as admirable decisiveness. Within two years the French were gone and the Americans were involved in a "nation building" exercise in the South. Most significantly, Diem indefinitely postponed the 1956 reunification elections, using the argument that communists did not respect the democratic process.

While the Eisenhower administration avoided direct military involvement with Diem's regime, it took other steps to support and encourage the Vietnamese leader. Dulles tied South Vietnam to a defense pact called the Southeast Asia Treaty Organization (SEATO). The administration substantially increased aid to Diem, so that by 1961 it totaled $1 billion. U.S. officers proffered advice to the South Vietnamese military, and the CIA, led by Lansdale, undertook subversive operations against the Vietnamese communists and their supporters. The Americans and their Vietnamese trainees spread phony information designed to frighten the populace away from communism, contaminated the oil supply of the Hanoi bus company, and provided transport south for those seeking refuge from the authoritarianism of the North. In 1960, Eisenhower promised Diem that "so long as our strength can be useful, the United States will continue to assist Viet-Nam in the difficult yet hopeful struggle ahead."

The Viet Minh were not merely patriots interested in the liberation of the Vietnamese people from foreign tyranny. Ho Chi Minh and his lieutenants were communists, for which they made no apology. The Viet Minh were quite capable of committing their own dirty tricks, and worse. The most obvious example of outrageous communist behavior was the brutal land reform campaign of 1955 and 1956, in which thousands of landlords and others were killed. But while Ho was willing to fight for a unified Vietnam, he preferred to rely on elections. He was enormously popular; as Eisenhower later admitted, "If the elections had been held in 1956, Ho Chi Minh would have won 80% of the vote."

Diem's refusal to abide by the Geneva accords was accompanied, beginning in the mid 1950s, by his increasing repression of alleged political enemies in the South. Diem campaigned zealously to eliminate dissent in any form, harassing, detaining, torturing, and frequently murdering those he suspected of opposing him. One historian estimated that the southern chapter of the Communist Party, for example, lost two-thirds of its members to arrest and murder during 1957–1958. When the beleaguered southern Viet Minh asked Ho Chi Minh for help, they were at first rebuffed. The southerners therefore took matters into their own hands, assassinating Diem's agents and corrupt village officials. In early 1959, Ho agreed to reinfiltrate into the South anti-Diem southerners who had come north in 1954. They were to begin the armed struggle, this time against the South Vietnamese government and its U.S. sponsors. The following year saw the formation of the National Liberation Front (NLF), an organization made up of dissatisfied peasants and former religious cultists formed around a Communist Party core. Diem derisively called the front the Viet Cong, or "Vietnamese Commies."

Policy under Kennedy. These important events at first made little impression on U.S. policymakers. In early 1961 Dwight Eisenhower was succeeded by Democrat John F. Kennedy, who had beaten Republican Richard Nixon in a close election. While Vietnam had not been a campaign issue, Kennedy had struck hard at what he called Republican inaction around the globe. The communist government officials in Moscow and Beijing, Kennedy claimed, strutted arrogantly in a world made vulnerable by U.S. complacency. The Soviets had more nuclear missiles than the United States; the communist Fidel Castro thumbed his nose at the United States from Cuba; the forces of nationalism in the so-called Third World admired communism and scorned the bloated and passive United States. Revolution, so honorable when undertaken by the Americans and the French in the eighteenth century, was viewed by Kennedy's men as the carrier of a lethal virus. All in all, Kennedy said, it was time to get the country moving again.

Movement, of course, need not be directed; a country that moves backward or lashes out wildly is still moving. In the early months of the Kennedy administration it looked as if the president and his advisers relished movement for its own sake, never mind the consequences. The administration blundered colossally in Cuba, when a group of anti-Castro Cubans, trained by the CIA and supported by a U.S. air strike, were utterly defeated by Castro's forces at the Bay of Pigs. The "missile gap" charge (i.e., that the Soviet Union had built more intercontinental ballistic missiles than the United States) that Kennedy had used to good effect during the campaign proved groundless. When the new secretary of defense, Robert McNamara, admitted as much, he was quickly silenced by the administration.

The president had another opportunity to prove his vigor in Laos, Vietnam's northeastern neighbor. In early 1961 the political and military situation in Laos was so complicated that most American observers had difficulty keeping straight the loyalties of the various protagonists. The United States championed the current head of government, a reactionary general named Phoumi Nosavan. Arrayed against Phoumi was a broad coalition, led by the moderate Prince Souvanna Phouma, and Prince Souphanouvong, who admired Ho Chi Minh. Despite massive aid from the CIA, which operated the country's airline, Phoumi's government was in imminent danger of collapse. "Your chief of staff couldn't lead a platoon around the corner to buy a newspaper," a U.S. official told Phoumi. "I know," replied the general, "but he's loyal."

Some in the Kennedy administration clamored for action to save Laos from coalition. Robert McNamara called for air strikes. The Joint Chiefs of Staff urged that the United States invade Laos with a quarter million men, with tactical nuclear strikes held in reserve. In March, Kennedy placed 5,000 U.S. troops in Thailand. U.S. military intervention in Laos was a real possibility in the spring of 1961. In the end, stung by the Bay of Pigs fiasco and unsure whether military action was sensible, Kennedy drew back. He allowed "roving ambassador" W. Averell Harriman to negotiate a deal with Phoumi's opponents. In July 1962, a new Geneva agreement called for the creation of a compromise government headed by Souvanna Phouma. Other nations, including the United States and North Vietnam, were to stay out of Laos, but neither side kept the agreement. The Americans created an anticommunist army out of Hmong tribals, while the North Vietnamese encouraged the communist Pathet Lao to seek power and violated Laotian neutrality by stationing their own troops on the Laotian side of the border.

In Vietnam, the formation of the NLF and its increasingly violent activity in the countryside had made Diem's position more precarious, although the South Vietnamese president was loath to admit it. Kennedy concluded that the United States must act. He decided on a response that would convey U.S. concern without fully committing American prestige. He sent in more military advisers; he recalled Ambassador Elbridge Durbrow and replaced him with Frederick Nolting, a staunch supporter of Diem; and most importantly, he secretly dispatched four hundred Green Berets to Vietnam to teach the South Vietnamese how to fight what was called "counterinsurgency warfare." The Green Berets, specially trained in jungle fighting, were supposed to live among the people they were trying to protect, speaking the local dialect, respecting local customs, and eating what the natives ate.

The Failure of Early Efforts.   Years later, U.S. policymakers who attempted to understand the failure of these early efforts to save South Vietnam puzzled over the inability of the Green Berets and other U.S. advisory groups to strengthen the will to fight of Diem's soldiers and win the hearts and minds of the Vietnamese people. The Americans offered the soldiers the best training and increasingly sophisticated weapons, yet most South Vietnamese soldiers (and especially their officers) were reluctant to fight, even when the odds favored them. To the peasants the Americans brought strategic hamlets, instant villages with brand-new houses made of bricks and concrete, not mud and thatch. But the peasants often ran away from the hamlets, and those who remained proved highly susceptible to recruitment by the NLF. Supposedly the best and the brightest of their generation, Kennedy's advisers could not win in Vietnam. What went wrong?

One problem was that U.S. policymakers persistently underestimated the tenacity and popularity of the North Vietnamese and Viet Cong. Those who ruled North Vietnam had been fighting for many years, and their experience in jungle warfare was of incalculable value. The communism espoused by the North Vietnamese and the cadres, or core workers, of the NLF, often appealed to peasants who had been heavily taxed or denied land by the colonialists and their Vietnamese collaborators. When the NLF called for higher wages for workers and civil servants and redistribution of rice-growing lands, it found supporters in the cities and the countryside. The Soviet Union and the PRC, seeking to counter the anticommunist efforts of the United States and hoping to outdo each other as

OLD U.S. EMBASSY. The Viet Cong bombing of the original U.S. Embassy in Saigon in 1965 led the construction of a more secure embassy, the building overrun by Viet Cong sappers during the Tet Offensive in 1968. *National Archives*

a loyal friend of nationalism in developing countries, competed to provide North Vietnam with assistance. Most significant was the NLF's ability to convince ordinary Vietnamese that the mantle of nationalism rested on them. The communists were popular because they behaved better than Diem's officials. They treated villagers with respect, did not loot, and made themselves part of the community; they became "the children of the people." And they pointed out that the South Vietnamese government that asked for the people's loyalty was totally dependent on the United States for sustenance.

Another reason the United States failed in Vietnam was that South Vietnamese officials themselves were in a certain sense foreigners. It could be said of the South Vietnamese government, as Gertrude Stein said of Oakland, that there was no there there. Diem's men could not be the children of the Vietnamese people because they wore U.S.-made uniforms, carried U.S. weapons, had U.S. canned rations clanking at their belts, and often showed up in villages with U.S. advisers. It was evident that if the United States withdrew its support the South Vietnamese government would not last long. Many South Vietnamese officials ruled their districts like fiefs, routinely exacting bribes from villagers in exchange for protection from the South Vietnamese army. U.S. commanders who tried to train the South Vietnamese found corruption deeply embedded in the military; for example, a South Vietnamese general was afraid to move against the Viet Cong forces because defeat in battle might enrage Diem and result in the general's dismissal, or because victory might make Diem jealous and achieve the same result. Over the years, American expressions of enthusiasm for various South Vietnamese governments were like the compliments of an undertaker describing a corpse.

In the final analysis, the Americans failed in Vietnam because they were fighting against a culture they did not understand. Of course, it is unlikely that Americans understood Japanese culture in 1945 or Iraqi culture in 1991, but in Vietnam culture significantly affected the way war was waged. By being dependent on the people, the NLF associated itself intimately with those whose loyalties were the object of the struggle. On the other hand, the Americans and the

South Vietnamese alienated the people. When they relocated people to strategic hamlets, they forced them to leave the lands of their ancestors and thus ruptured the Gordian knot of Vietnamese culture. When U.S. planes bombed and strafed the countryside, the Americans killed not only innocent people but also the animals on which the peasants relied. U.S. soldiers tramped on planted rice fields; as one historian wrote, "Rice cultivation . . . simply did not register with the troops." "Maybe," a fictional U.S. soldier mused, "the gooks have it backwards. Maybe they cry when they're happy and laugh when they're sad."

The Coup against Diem. Among the Americans there were dissenters, those who warned that the country was becoming enmeshed in a dangerous war that it could not win. The most prominent dissenter, Undersecretary of State George Ball, was allowed to remain within the administration, but his advice was never heeded. Nevertheless, by early 1963, with U.S. aid and advisers continuing to flow to the South Vietnamese government, there were signs that Diem's regime was deteriorating. Rather than interpret this as an indication that South Vietnam itself was rotten, Kennedy's men concluded that Diem and his family had corrupted a system that was essentially sound and that could be restored to health with the right leadership.

It was a crisis involving South Vietnam's Buddhists that sealed Diem's fate. On 8 May 1963 government troops opened fire on a group of Buddhists who had gathered for a rally in the city of Hue. When Diem was unrepentant, the Buddhists raised the stakes. In June, a Buddhist monk burned himself to death at a busy Saigon intersection in protest against Diem's repressive policies. The Diem government barely stirred, except for Madame Nhu, who offered to supply matches for the next "barbecue," as she put it. There were more immolations, and Buddhist protests escalated. In August, Diem and his brother, Ngo Dinh Nhu, cracked down, raiding pagodas throughout the country, killing and jailing protestors.

Now even Diem's defenders in the Kennedy administration agreed that something must be done, although they were not clear what it should be. Some thought it would be enough if Diem got rid of Nhu and his wife, who were bad influences on Diem. One official suggested that Diem, a notoriously compulsive talker, should be given a teaching position at Harvard. Following the pagoda raids, Kennedy made a critical decision: he recalled Ambassador Frederick Nolting and sent in his place the prominent Republican Henry Cabot Lodge. Lodge was experienced and tough, and he had no sympathy for Diem. Soon after arriving in Saigon, he reported that "there is no possibility that the war can be won under a Diem administration"; the man Frances FitzGerald called "the sovereign of discord" would have to be overthrown.

The agents of the coup against Diem and Nhu were several South Vietnamese officers who were disgruntled with Diem's leadership and thought their troops would fight harder for the right government. Led by Duong Van ("Big") Minh, the conspirators proved to be a cautious group. On the verge of a coup they drew back, unsure of U.S. support and fearful that without it they would fail. The Kennedy administration then signaled its support by tightening the aid conduit to Diem. Thus reassured, Minh and the others staged their coup on 1 November. Diem and Nhu were captured in a church, then murdered in the back of a personnel carrier. Big Minh claimed the brothers had committed suicide, but as a CIA agent told him, "There's a one-in-a-million chance that people will believe your story."

Just three weeks later, Kennedy was assassinated. In the years since his death, some of Kennedy's admirers have argued that he had seen the folly of Vietnam

END OF THE PRELUDE. A Vietnamese woman welcomes an American soldier of the 25th Infantry Division, Vung Tau, 18 January 1966. *National Archives*

by he fall of 1963 and was preparing to withdraw all U.S. forces from Vietnam. It has even been alleged that Kennedy was killed by conspirators who wanted the war to continue and thought there was a better chance that it would if Kennedy were eliminated. The evidence for the claim that Kennedy was preparing to withdraw is skimpy and contradictory. Most often cited is a White House policy statement of 2 October 1963, which included a recommendation that the United States withdraw 1,000 troops from Vietnam by the end of the year and bring the bulk of the troops home by the end of 1965. The statement, however, made it clear that the "overriding objective" of the United States was to keep South Vietnam out of communist hands. The claim that Kennedy was assassinated by prowar "hawks" is the product of disillusionment and overexcited imaginations. Americans know that Kennedy's successor, Lyndon Baines Johnson, retaining most of Kennedy's foreign policy advisers, increased the U.S. commitment. It is also known that when Kennedy was killed the United States had more than 16,000 "advisers" in Vietnam and had suffered more than 100 dead.

Policy under Johnson. "I'm one powerful sonofabitch," Lyndon Johnson had crowed in 1958, when he was Senate majority leader. Johnson relished power, and he spent most of his life seeking it. He had risen through the ranks of Texas politics, prevaricating, pandering, and otherwise doing what was necessary to win elections. He had been a congressional aide, a representative, a senator, and Kennedy's vice president, and now he was president, though not under the best circumstances. In his first address to Congress following Kennedy's assassination, Johnson said, "All I have, I would have given gladly not to be standing here today." Indeed, Lyndon Johnson entered the presidency an insecure man. He reacted violently to criticism, sometimes calling television newscasters during commercial breaks to "correct" unflattering comments they had made about him. He hated to be alone or understimulated, so he surrounded himself with televisions, spent hours on the phone, and even briefed embarrassed aides while he sat on the toilet. Johnson also felt the natural insecurity of someone who succeeds a martyr.

Johnson had been to Vietnam in 1961 and had returned from the trip convinced that U.S. security depended on victory over the Viet Cong. Like his predecessors, he despised communism and believed in the U.S. commitment to Vietnam for its own sake: the United States had given its word to defend South Vietnam, and it could not rescind that commitment without suffering a loss of credibility throughout the world. Johnson also looked upon Vietnam as a test of manhood for him. He compared the war to a hunt, an important rite of passage for southern men. "We've got to nail that coonskin to the wall," Johnson used to say about winning in Vietnam. There was even an element of sexual conquest involved: Johnson frequently likened Vietnam (or Ho Chi Minh) to a woman. "I'm going up her [North Vietnam's] leg an inch at a time," the president told George McGovern, describing his policy of gradual escalation. "I'll get to the snatch before they know what's happening."

While Johnson's considerable political skills served him well on the domestic front, they were of limited use in Vietnam. The Kennedy administration's hope that getting rid of Diem and Nhu would bring stability to South Vietnam proved empty. Chaos followed the coup by Big Minh, and the NLF forces and their North Vietnamese allies took advantage of the situation by escalating the military campaign in the South. Increasing numbers of North Vietnamese regulars infiltrated across the border, and they usually bloodied any South Vietnamese military units they encountered. By late 1964, U.S. officials estimated that NVA and Viet Cong forces controlled 50 percent of the population and 40 percent of the territory of South Vietnam. Big Minh's regime soon gave way to a government led by Gen. Nguyen Khanh. The Americans were briefly infatuated with Khanh. Johnson called him "my American boy" and convinced him to give his people fireside chats, like Franklin Roosevelt—a novel idea for a tropical country. It was soon apparent to U.S. officials, however, that Khanh, like Diem, had a penchant for secrecy and repression.

The problems in the South tempted Johnson and his advisers to seek a military solution north of the 17th Parallel. With North Vietnamese forces increasingly involved in the fighting, the administration concluded that the war could be won if it could inflict pain on North Vietnam to persuade the northerners to cease their support of the NLF. In early summer of 1964, Johnson's military advisers devised plans to bomb North Vietnam, but the plans would work only if Congress granted the president liberal discretionary power to determine where and when bombing raids were needed. To receive such power from Congress, Johnson required evidence of belligerent conduct by the North Vietnamese. His opportunity came in early August, when two U.S. destroyers and North Vietnamese patrol boats apparently clashed in the Gulf of Tonkin, off the east coast of Vietnam. What actually happened in the Gulf was not clear. A sonar operator thought he detected patrol boats, and a U.S. sailor thought he saw North Vietnamese torpedoes in the water. The U.S. ships opened fire. In the aftermath of the "clash," however, there was considerable doubt that the North Vietnamese had been there at all. A U.S. pilot aloft during the episode saw "nothing but the black sea and American firepower." The commander of one of the destroyers radioed his doubts about the "engagement," and admitted that no one on board had actually seen North Vietnamese vessels.

Johnson ignored the doubts about the incident; it was the pretext he needed to seize control of Vietnam policy. Within twenty-four hours the president had placed before Congress a resolution permitting him to take "all necessary measures to repel any armed attacks against the forces of the United States and to prevent further aggression." The Gulf of Tonkin Resolution passed the Senate by a vote of 88 to 2 and was approved unanimously by the House. The resolution has been called a functional declaration of war, and it gave the commander in chief the authority to prosecute the war as he chose. Congress thus abdicated its power to restrict U.S. escalation.

Bombing North Vietnam. Johnson did not immediately take advantage of his new authority. Bombing North Vietnam was a dramatic step that promised to change the nature of U.S. involvement in the war, and he did not want to be labeled a warmonger, especially just prior to the 1964 election. Once the election was safely past—Johnson won a tremendous victory, in part because he depicted his opponent, Barry Goldwater, as a warmonger—the president acted. Nguyen Khanh's government still seemed to be a bigger problem than North Vietnamese infiltration, but Johnson believed that U.S. bombing of the North would stiffen the resolve of the South Vietnamese forces. In early February 1965, NLF fighters killed 9 Americans in an attack on a military installation at Pleiku. Johnson quickly ordered retaliatory air strikes against targets in North Vietnam, and four days later, on 10 February, approved a program of systematic bombing of the North. This decision made bombing an integral and ongoing part of the U.S. war effort. The administration believed the bombing would succeed because, as Johnson's adviser Walt Rostow put it, "Ho Chi Minh has an industrial complex to protect." Or, as Henry Kissinger would later say, "every nation has a breaking point."

The bombing had an impact on the war, but it was not always what the United States sought. It was tremendously destructive. North Vietnamese officials spoke of it scornfully, but U.S. bombing, especially by the B-52s, damaged North Vietnamese industry and brought great pain to those who lost family members and ancestral homes. On the other hand, the bombing never found the North Vietnamese breaking point. When bridges, roads, and vital buildings were destroyed, the Vietnamese quickly reconstructed them. The Hanoi leadership also decentralized the economy, moving factories and shops out of the capital and reassembling them in the countryside. Well camouflaged, these establishments, vital to the North Vietnamese war effort, were difficult for the bombers to target. Ironically, U.S. intelligence had predicted in 1965 that bombing North Vietnam's economic infrastructure would not bring a halt to its attempts to reunify the country. Perhaps Johnson disbelieved this, but others claim that given the type of war the United States was prepared to fight, the president simply saw no other choice but to bomb.

For many years, U.S. policymakers had subscribed to the domino theory in Vietnam. The theory held that if one nation in Southeast Asia fell to communism, all contiguous nations would fall too, like dominoes lined up on end. As the Americans applied it, the domino theory was dubious, but in an interesting way it described U.S. military involvement in Vietnam. First came military advisers. The advisers found it frustrating to work with untrained and frequently unmotivated South Vietnamese troops, so they asked for more Americans. With American lives then at greater risk, military officials pleaded for bombing north of the 17th Parallel, which would supposedly stop the flow of communist troops moving south. Some of the planes used for the bombing would be stationed in South Vietnam, and these newly expanded air bases required U.S. troops to protect them. In fact, this was precisely the argument used by the U.S. commander in Vietnam, William Westmoreland, to justify a request for combat troops, a request granted by Lyndon Johnson in February 1965.

On 8 March, 3,500 U.S. Marines waded ashore near the air base at Da Nang. They were not advisers or support troops—they were combat soldiers who were there to kill Viet Cong guerrillas. As the story is often told, the wary marines were greeted on the beach by the mayor of Da Nang, who read a welcoming speech, and a group of schoolgirls, who smiled and placed wreaths around the soldiers' necks. It was a suitably surreal beginning to what would become an unimaginable disaster.

[*See also* American Friends of Vietnam; Domino Theory; Military Assistance Advisory Group–Vietnam (MAAG-V); Munich Analogy.]

BIBLIOGRAPHY

BERMAN, LARRY. *Lyndon Johnson's War: The Road to Stalemate in Vietnam.* 1989.
FITZGERALD, FRANCES. *Fire in the Lake: The Vietnamese and the Americans in Vietnam.* 1972.
GARDNER, LLOYD. *Approaching Vietnam: From World War II through Dienbienphu.* 1988.
HAMMER, ELLEN. *A Death in November: America in Vietnam 1963.* 1987.
HERRING, GEORGE C. *America's Longest War: The United States and Vietnam, 1950–1975.* 2d ed. 1986.
RACE, JEFFREY. *War Comes to Long An: Revolutionary Conflict in a Vietnamese Province.* 1972.
ROTTER, ANDREW. *The Path to Vietnam: Origins of the American Commitment to Southeast Asia.* 1987.
SHEEHAN, NEIL. *A Bright Shining Lie: John Paul Vann and America in Vietnam.* 1988.
TRUONG NHU TANG. *A Viet Cong Memoir: An Inside Account of the Vietnam War and Its Aftermath.* 1986.
YOUNG, MARILYN. *The Vietnam Wars, 1945–1990.* 1991.

ANDREW J. ROTTER

Prisoners of War. *See* POW/MIA Controversy.

Project 100,000, a controversial plan to provide remedial training within the U.S. military to men with poor academic skills, with the ultimate goal of better equipping them as members of society. As a part of this plan, the armed services also accepted a considerable number of men who previously would have been rejected for service because of their low scores on military aptitude tests. Project 100,000 has been interpreted by some commentators as a scheme to shunt disadvantaged minorities into ground combat and by others as the source of the rampant disciplinary problems within the military of the late Vietnam War period.

Background. U.S. political leaders had shown interest in military remedial training as a form of social engineering from the end of World War II on.

Moreover, wartime experience had shown that full mobilization required the armed services to take large numbers of illiterate and poorly educated men and thus had fostered a similar interest within the military in the development of effective remedial training programs. In 1945 the Truman administration proposed a universal military training program intended to correct both physical and educational shortcomings among America's young men (a program supported by then-senator Lyndon B. Johnson). Congressional opposition prevented any large-scale program, but a few small experiments were conducted within the armed forces. Interest in remedial training waned among both military and political leaders during the Eisenhower administration.

In 1963, President Kennedy again suggested using the military to provide remedial training to disadvantaged men, charging the Task Force on

Manpower Conservation, among its other duties, to examine the military's experience with "special training units for illiterates." In 1964 the U.S. Army, with the enthusiastic backing of Secretary of Defense Robert S. McNamara, proposed the Special Training and Enlistment Program, which over three years would train a total of 60,000 men with low aptitude scores. The army was interested in developing a training program to be used in the event of full mobilization. McNamara was interested in the potential for providing remedial literacy and vocational training to improve the trainees' ultimate socioeconomic status. Congress, however, refused to fund the program.

In the summer of 1966 McNamara learned that for over a decade the Marine Corps had used part of its normal training funds to run Special Training Branches at its recruit training camps, providing remedial training to those recruits who required it. McNamara realized that by expanding this program to all services, the military could provide remedial training to men with low scores without congressional authorization.

Establishment and Operation. On 23 August 1966 Secretary McNamara announced Project 100,000, declaring that the military would "salvage tens of thousands of these men each year, first to productive military careers and later for productive roles in society." The armed forces would take 40,000 disadvantaged youths the first year and 100,000 every year thereafter, hence the name.

In addition to its remedial aspects, McNamara acknowledged that Project 100,000 also addressed the services' need for recruits. In fact, to meet the growing manpower demands of the Vietnam War, the army and Marine Corps had already lowered their entry standards a number of times before McNamara's announcement.

Project 100,000 lasted from October 1966 to December 1971, when Congress ended quotas based on aptitude-test-score results. During this period, Defense Department quotas required that one-fifth of all recruits be drawn from those whose scores placed them in Mental Group IV, the lowest-scoring group legally eligible for service, and one-tenth of all recruits be so-called New Standards men, who did not meet the entry standards in effect before October 1966. The year prior to the implementation of Project 100,000, just over 16 percent of all recruits had scored in Mental Group IV. During World War II and the Korean War, far higher percentages of men with low scores served, includ-

ing many who would not have been accepted during Project 100,000.

The armed forces accepted roughly 354,000 New Standards men over the course of Project 100,000. The bulk of these men had low scores on military aptitude tests, although just over 30,000 of them were volunteers who had easily correctable physical shortcomings. New Standards men were generally poorly educated and from disadvantaged backgrounds, a natural consequence of the fact that this group was defined by its members' extremely low test scores on standardized tests. Roughly 37 percent of all New Standards men were African American. More than 157,000 of the New Standards men were draftees, but they made up only one-tenth of all draftees. Similarly, New Standards volunteers made up one-tenth of all volunteers. New Standards volunteers did help to reduce draft pressure because these volunteers filled positions that otherwise would have been filled by draftees.

Three-quarters of the New Standards men served in the army or Marine Corps. Because their low test scores prevented most New Standards men from qualifying for technical jobs, just over a third received ground combat assignments, compared to only a quarter of non–New Standards men. New Standards men therefore were more likely to be killed or wounded than servicemen in general, but were no more likely to be casualties than other men in the combat arms. Nearly 2,100 New Standards men died in the Vietnam War.

Evaluation. Project 100,000 actually had little effect on the military. Even if McNamara had not launched this program, the manpower demands of the Vietnam War almost certainly would have forced the army and Marine Corps to continue lowering entry standards anyway, as they had before October 1966. Since the cost of the Vietnam War meant that there was little time or money available for remedial training, most New Standards men passed through exactly the same training regimen as other recruits, indistinguishable from their comrades. Early in the program, the services used a variety of methods to identify New Standards men. In some cases, soldiers in the field figured out the system. To avoid stigmatizing the New Standards men, all services soon developed methods for tracking these men without clearly identifying them to their peers or superiors.

Since most New Standards men did not receive special training, they received only the same benefits from military service as other men: veterans' benefits, self-discipline, the G.I. Bill, and so forth.

They also experienced the same hardships as other veterans: the risks of combat, post-traumatic stress, and rejection by an indifferent public. Some studies have found that military service benefited most New Standards men. Others have found that New Standards men fared less well than men with similar backgrounds who did not serve. Studies also disagree on whether military service benefited or harmed soldiers in general. Military service undoubtedly placed many hardships on New Standards men, but there is no evidence to suggest that military service hurt New Standards men more than other veterans.

After the Vietnam War, senior military officers, including General William Westmoreland, unjustly blamed the rampant disciplinary problems of the late Vietnam period on the New Standards men. These officers ignored the fact that the men who served in Vietnam, including the New Standards men, had the highest average test scores and educational attainments of any force the United States had ever sent to fight a major war.

BIBLIOGRAPHY

LAURENCE, JANICE H., and PETER F. RAMSBERGER. *Low-Aptitude Men in the Military: Who Profits, Who Pays?* 1991.
STICHT, THOMAS G., WILLIAM B. ARMSTRONG, DANIEL T. HICKEY, and JOHN S. CAYLOR. *Cast-Off Youth: Policy and Training Methods from the Military Experience.* 1987.

DAVID A. DAWSON

Prostitution. Prostitution was officially illegal in South Vietnam but, by the time Saigon fell in 1975, approximately 400,000 Vietnamese women worked as prostitutes. Women had worked as prostitutes under the French regime also, but the increase in the number of U.S. troops and the refugee problem dramatically increased prostitution in South Vietnam. The majority of the prostitutes were in Saigon, although many worked in the other major cities. Never viewed merely as an economic activity, prostitution meant severe and permanent ostracism from Vietnamese society. Documents left in the U.S. embassy after the North Vietnamese victory revealed high-level South Vietnamese governmental sponsorship of brothels, called "centers of leisure." Women who worked in these brothels received one day a week off and could not leave the brothel for more than ten hours.

Women were by no means limited to the government-controlled establishments, but they were seldom independent of male or female pimps. In addition, women often combined their sexual services for U.S. soldiers with domestic services; a soldier could, for example, rent a so-called wife for a specified period of time, a practice amounting to sexual slavery for many Vietnamese women. Prostitution was closely associated with sexually transmitted diseases and with drug addiction. There is also some evidence that prostitutes infiltrated U.S. army bases and gained information for North Vietnamese or National Liberation Front (NLF) forces.

North Vietnam banned prostitution and after reunification systematically rehabilitated prostitutes by offering food, housing, and job training. This rehabilitation was especially significant in countering traditional prejudice against "fallen women." Ho Chi Minh City, however, continues to have a high number of prostitutes.

BIBLIOGRAPHY

EISEN, ARLENE. *Women and Revolution in Vietnam.* 1984.

ELLEN BAKER

Provincial Reconnaissance Units (PRU). The destruction of the Viet Cong Infrastructure (VCI)—the clandestine organization of spies, intelligence agents, and political commissars of the National Liberation Front (NLF)—was a challenge that continually frustrated the U.S. and South Vietnamese intelligence communities. The VCI was estimated to be 70,000 strong. The largest and most controversial program aimed at eliminating the VCI surfaced in June 1968 with the name Phuong Hoang (Phoenix). Provincial Reconnaissance Units (PRUs) were the enforcement branch of this program. Originally called Counter-Terror Units in 1965, PRUs obtained their new name one year later because it seemed more politically acceptable. The basic mission, however, to destroy the VCI by sabotage, kidnapping, and assassination, remained unchanged. The Central Intelligence Agency (CIA) funded the program.

PRU members were Vietnamese mercenaries who performed any duty for a price. They were paid 15,000 piasters monthly, or nearly four times the equivalent wage of a private in the Army of the Republic of Vietnam (ARVN). Bounties also existed: 10,000 piasters (US$85) per prisoner. In 1969, PRU strength was approximately 4,454 men. The force was organized into 18-man units; each unit had 3 teams of 6 men each. A minority of South Vietnamese volunteered for PRU service. The majority of the PRU's members were murderers, rapists, extortionists, and social outcasts from local jails who were given the option of PRU duties in lieu of life imprisonment. A considerable number were Viet Cong or North Vietnamese defectors who rallied under the Chieu Hoi (Open Arms) program, a risky experiment that ultimately failed because it relied too heavily on the honesty and loyalty of its members. Once recruited, this colorful assortment of questionable men underwent basic training at My Tho, the PRU headquarters in the Mekong Delta, supervised by U.S. military and intelligence personnel.

In the field, PRU teams often worked with Military Assistance Command, Vietnam–Studies and Observations Group (MACV-SOG), U.S. Navy SEAL teams, or South Vietnam's Lien Doi Nguoi Nhai (underwater demolition teams/frogmen), usually at night. Considerable controversy surrounds the Phoenix-PRU experiment. The use of sodium pentothal or scopolamine on prisoners is often mentioned. Likewise, electric shock treatment, incarceration in bamboo cages, and assassination by being thrown out of a helicopter over the South China Sea appears in the literature.

Archival reports on Phoenix activities in 1969 note that 8,515 Viet Cong had been captured, 4,832 converted, and 6,187 murdered by PRU units. These figures are conservative; others claim that there were 25,000 assassinations by 1971. The Phoenix program has thus often been labeled "Murder Incorporated."

Although there were reports of widespread inefficiency and corruption within the Phoenix program, high-ranking North Vietnamese and Viet Cong officials interviewed after the war stated that the program was highly effective and that it severely damaged the VCI.

BIBLIOGRAPHY

KARNOW, STANLEY. *Vietnam: A History.* 1983.
KUNEN, JAMES S. *Standard Operating Procedure.* 1971.
VALENTINE, DOUGLAS. *The Phoenix Program.* 1990.

THOMAS R. CANTWELL

Provisional Revolutionary Government.
The Provisional Revolutionary Government (PRG) was established at a congress of resistance leaders convened near the border of Cambodia and South Vietnam in June 1969. Largely superseding the governmental role of the National Liberation Front (NLF) in the South, the PRG was created at the order of the communist government in North Vietnam as a means of providing a legal alternative to the

Republic of Vietnam in the peace talks. Huynh Tan Phat was chosen as chairman of the organization, and Madame Nguyen Thi Binh was named foreign minister.

The PRG was eventually recognized as the legal government of South Vietnam by the Democratic Republic of Vietnam (DRV) and a number of other socialist countries, and it became an active participant in the Paris negotiations as North Vietnam's counterpart to the Republic of Vietnam. Madame Binh served as the chief PRG representative in the talks. The PRG was one of the four signatories of the Paris agreement, and was granted legal recognition as an equal participant with the government of President Nguyen Van Thieu in the National Council for Reconciliation and Concord that was created as a result of the accords.

The programs of the National Liberation Front (NLF) and the DRV had indicated that after the restoration of peace, the people of South Vietnam would form their own independent government, which would in due time engage in discussions with the DRV to achieve the reunification of the entire country. After the fall of Saigon in 1975, however, the PRG was rapidly brushed aside by ambitious northern leaders, and in early July 1976 the two zones were reunited into the Socialist Republic of Vietnam, with its capital in Hanoi.

BIBLIOGRAPHY

PORTER, GARETH. *A Peace Denied: The United States, Vietnam, and the Paris Agreement.* 1975.
TRUONG NHU TANG. *A Viet Cong Memoir: An Inside Account of the Vietnam War and Its Aftermath.* 1985.

WILLIAM J. DUIKER

Public Opinion, American. Public opinion about the Vietnam War in many ways followed the predictable patterns of public opinion about any war. But the war's excessive length, its lack of clear progress toward a U.S. victory, and the accompanying domestic turmoil made this war different from earlier wars. Ultimately the government failed to sustain supportive public opinion, and some have argued that public opinion undermined the government's ability to stay the course in Vietnam. President Lyndon Johnson once said, "The weakest link in our armor is American public opinion." Others have suggested that if the war had been grounded in sound policies from the start then public support would have followed.

In the early stages of the conflict, before U.S. combat troops were deployed, few Americans had an opinion on Vietnam. By late 1964, however, many viewed North Vietnam as a puppet of the People's Republic of China and supported active assistance for South Vietnam. This feeling increased after the attack on the Pleiku air base in February 1965. Harris and Gallup polls indicated that a majority of Americans favored bombing of North Vietnam in retaliation and sending U.S. combat troops. A majority of those polled believed the Vietnam conflict would result in a U.S. victory or, at worst, in a stalemate as in Korea. This climate enabled the Johnson administration to send the first U.S. combat troops into Vietnam with solid public support. Such supportive poll numbers are typical of the "rally 'round the flag" phenomenon that occurs when a president takes military action as commander in chief. At the same time, in response to polls indicating that most Americans wanted a settle-

THE PEACE SIGN. Students flash the peace sign during a demonstration at Columbia University, New York, 30 April 1968. *National Archives*

ment, the Johnson administration publicly advocated negotiations to end the war.

By mid 1966 three-fourths of the public expected that the war would be long. This realization prompted the biggest decline in support for the U.S. involvement until it bottomed out between 45 and 50 percent. A 1966 Gallup poll found that 35 percent viewed U.S. involvement as a mistake. That figure jumped to 48 percent in 1967 and 52 percent in 1969. This disillusionment was prompted by the increasing number of war casualties, lack of progress, and concern for the war's divisive effect on the United States itself. The media may have also played a role, as coverage of the conflict and editorial opinions became increasingly critical.

Although a majority of Americans opposed U.S. involvement by 1969, there was little consensus about what action to take. Indeed, many who viewed U.S. entry as a mistake also believed that, once begun, the war must be vigorously prosecuted. For example, in a 1969 Gallup poll, while a majority labeled U.S. involvement a mistake, 51 percent of that majority believed U.S. forces should remain in Vietnam and that the United States should either escalate (32 percent) or continue the present policy (19 percent). Forty-five percent either advocated a withdrawal (26 percent) or called for the United States to end the war as soon as possible (19 percent).

President Richard Nixon in 1969 appealed to those who believed U.S. involvement in Vietnam should continue in his "Silent Majority" speech, urging support for his "peace with honor" Vietnam proposals, but he was too late to reverse the tide of public opinion. In 1971 public opinion in support

PRO-JOHNSON DEMONSTRATION. Organized labor rallies to support President Johnson's Vietnam policies, 23 July 1966. *Lyndon Baines Johnson Library*

of the war continued to slip dramatically. Sixty-one percent called U.S. involvement a mistake and 58 percent said they believed the war was "immoral." Increasingly, a majority wanted a settlement to end the war even if it led to a communist takeover of South Vietnam. In 1972 and 1973 public opinion polls indicated support for Nixon's Vietnamization policy and for peace negotiations. When the last U.S. troops were withdrawn, few Americans believed that the United States should have kept fighting. When North Vietnam launched its Spring Offensive against the south, which culminated in the fall of Saigon in 1975, most Americans opposed increasing military aid to the south, let alone renewing active military involvement. Americans were resigned to the fall of South Vietnam and were anxious to close the book on U.S. involvement.

BIBLIOGRAPHY

KARNOW, STANLEY. *Vietnam: A History.* 1991.
LOVELL, MARK, and CHARLES KELLEY, JR. *Casualties, Public Opinion, and Presidential Policy during the Vietnam War.* 1985.
MUELLER, JOHN E. *War, Presidents, and Public Opinion.* 1973.

KELLY EVANS-PFEIFER

Pueblo Incident. The USS *Pueblo,* an intelligence-gathering ship, was seized by North Korea on 23 January 1968. Because nearly all available U.S. forces were committed to Vietnam, more than fourteen thousand U.S. Navy and Air Force reserves were mobilized in case troops had to be sent into North Korea. North Korea claimed that the ship had violated its territorial waters, but the crew and U.S. radio locators placed the ship well outside the twelve-mile limit. The incident combined with cold war tensions in Berlin and the Tet Offensive to heighten strains in the Johnson administration. The *Pueblo* crew remained captive until December 1968, when all 82 were released.

BIBLIOGRAPHY

JOHNSON, LYNDON BAINES. *The Vantage Point: Perspectives of the Presidency, 1963–1969.* 1971.
LISTON, ROBERT A. *The Pueblo Surrender: A Covert Action by the National Security Agency.* 1988.

ELLEN D. GOLDLUST

Quang Tri, South Vietnamese city, capital of Quang Tri province. As the capital of the province that bordered the demilitarized zone (DMZ) with North Vietnam, Quang Tri was a key point for control of the northern sector of South Vietnam. The city was attacked by North Vietnamese Army (NVA) forces in April 1972 as part of the northernmost prong of the Easter Offensive. On 1 May, troops of the Army of the Republic of Vietnam (ARVN) panicked and abandoned the city, fleeing with their families and other refugees to the south. Fire from ARVN and NVA forces and U.S. aircraft and ships resulted in the death of as many as twenty thousand soldiers and civilians. At the end of June, ARVN troops began a counterattack with the aid of U.S. air support, and the city was retaken on 16 September.

BIBLIOGRAPHY

CLARKE, JEFFREY J. *United States Army in Vietnam—Advice and Support: The Final Years, 1965–1973.* 1988.
DAVIDSON, PHILLIP B. *Vietnam at War—The History: 1946–1975.* 1988.
KARNOW, STANLEY. *Vietnam: A History.* 1991.

ELLEN D. GOLDLUST

Quat, Phan Huy. *See* Phan Huy Quat.

Qui Nhon. South Vietnamese coastal city located in Binh Dinh province, 677 kilometers (420 miles) north of Saigon. Beginning in August 1965, the U.S. military used Qui Nhon as a major supply base and transportation terminal, eventually providing support service for nearly 100,000 troops. The bombing of U.S. enlisted personnel's quarters at Qui Nhon on 10 February 1965 led to retaliatory U.S. naval air strikes of North Vietnam, code-named FLAMING DART II, and helped Johnson decide to launch Operation ROLLING THUNDER. Qui Nhon was one of five coastal surveillance centers supporting Operation MARKET TIME, the U.S. naval interdiction of seaborne infiltration of supplies and personnel from North Vietnam to South Vietnam.

BIBLIOGRAPHY

DUNN, CARROLL H. *Base Development in South Vietnam, 1965–1970.* 1972.

JENNIFER FROST

R

Racial Epithets, American. Americans in Vietnam often used racial denunciations during the Vietnam War, such as *gooks, dinks, slopes, slants, running dogs, yellow people, little people,* or *zips* to characterize the Vietnamese. In wartime, soldiers from all countries have employed such derogatory language to dehumanize the enemy and to justify violence. Some Americans in Vietnam directed these terms toward the entire local population, not just toward the North Vietnamese or Viet Cong troops. Several factors contributed to the racial atmosphere of the war. In Vietnam, Americans confronted an impoverished and largely rural society with unfamiliar practices in food, sanitation, and sexual mores. Furthermore, the guerrilla warfare practiced by the North Vietnamese (NVA) and Viet Cong forces fueled American fear and hostility toward the local population. U.S. soldiers suffered extensive casualties from mines and booby traps, often near South Vietnamese villages. Thus, unable to distinguish between combatants and neutral civilians, soldiers expressed their anger and vengeance toward the Vietnamese as a whole.

American racial epithets drew from a tradition of negative American and European stereotypes concerning Asians. U.S. military conflicts in Asia over the previous century contributed to the formation of this racialized language. U.S. soldiers first used the epithet *gook* for the Filipino guerrilla soldiers fighting the U.S. occupation of the Philippines at the turn of the century (the word is derived from the Filipino language). During World War II and the Korean War, U.S. personnel in the Pacific used the epithet extensively. *Dink* emerged from the 1920s Australian term for the Chinese. The epithets *slants* and *slopes* date from at the least the 1930s and also were used extensively by U.S. soldiers in the Pacific during World War II.

BIBLIOGRAPHY

BARITZ, LOREN. *Backfire: A History of How American Culture Led Us into Vietnam and Made Us Fight the Way We Did.* 1985.

DOWER, JOHN. *War without Mercy: Race and Power in the Pacific War.* 1986.

LEWY, GUENTER. *America in Vietnam.* 1978.

New Dictionary of American Slang. Edited by Robert L. Chapman. 1986.

Oxford English Dictionary. 2d ed. Prepared by J. A. Simpson and E. S. C. Weiner. 1989.

ADAM LAND

Radford, Arthur W. (1896–1973), admiral, U.S. Navy; chairman, Joint Chiefs of Staff (JCS), 1953–1957. A veteran of three wars, Adm. Arthur Radford helped devise President Eisenhower's "New Look" defense policy in the 1950s. Radford believed that nuclear weapons coupled with superior U.S. air power would guarantee U.S. security, and that ground forces were practically superfluous in modern warfare. The first test of Radford's faith came in March 1954, when the French appealed for U.S. assistance during the siege of Dien Bien Phu. After meeting with Gen. Paul Ely, the French chief of staff, Radford proposed massive U.S. air strikes—possibly including nuclear weapons—against the Viet Minh forces surrounding Dien Bien Phu. Operation VULTURE would have involved sixty B-29 heavy bombers based in the Philippines plus fighter escorts from U.S. carriers of the Seventh Fleet. Most of Radford's own JCS balked at the plan. Army chief of staff Gen. Matthew Ridgway predicted that air strikes would lead to troop commitments and authored a JCS report critical of Radford's plan. President Eisenhower rejected Operation VULTURE as "politically impossible" after Congress and the European allies refused their support.

BIBLIOGRAPHY

ARNOLD, JAMES R. *The First Domino: Eisenhower, the Military, and America's Intervention in Vietnam.* 1991.

PRADOS, JOHN. *The Sky Would Fall: Operation Vulture.* 1983.

RADFORD, ARTHUR W. *From Pearl Harbor to Vietnam: The Memoirs of Admiral Arthur W. Radford.* 1980.

ROBERTS, CHALMERS M. "The Day We Didn't Go to War." *Reporter* 11 (14 September 1954): 31–35.

U.S. DEPARTMENT OF STATE. Part 1 of *Indochina.* Vol. 13 of *Foreign Relations of the United States, 1952–1954.* 1982.

GLEN GENDZEL

Rainy Season. *See* Monsoon.

RANCH HAND. The U.S. Air Force aerial defoliation program, code-named Operation RANCH HAND, sprayed roughly 19 million gallons of herbicides over 2.5 million hectares (6 million acres) in South Vietnam from January 1962 to February 1971, and 400,000 gallons over 66,000 hectares (163,000 acres) in Laos from December 1965 to September 1969. Conceived as a means to deprive North Vietnamese and Viet Cong forces of cover and concealment along roads and canals, RANCH HAND was expanded to encompass the destruction of forests and crops in areas controlled by these forces. Spraying was done by air commandos, never more than a squadron strong, flying C-123 transports fitted with tanks of herbicide, pumps, and spray bars. The herbicides were based on widely used commercial products, principally Agent Orange and related chlorinated phenoxy acid–based agents with low soil persistence, though persistent picloram-based Agent White comprised about 14 percent of the total. Although these agents were considered nontoxic to humans and animals except in very large doses, mounting evidence implicated dioxin, an impurity in Agent Orange, as the cause of debilitating illnesses, rashes, tumors, and birth defects.

Operation RANCH HAND achieved notoriety in early 1963 when Richard Dudman, in the *St. Louis Post–Dispatch,* accused U.S. forces of "spraying the land with poison." The Kennedy administration denied that "poison" was being used and maintained that food denial was a "wholly normal" warfare tactic. Operations continued despite criticism, though trucks and helicopters were increasingly used as spray vehicles to reduce public visibility. While defoliation along roads and canals and around base perimeters sharply reduced casualties from attacks, the success of deforestation and crop destruction operations was equivocal. Long-term effects included the destruction of coastal mangrove forests and claims of widespread health problems by Vietnamese authorities and U.S. veterans, who successfully sued the Veterans Administration for recognition of Agent Orange–related disabilities. The balance of scientific opinion holds that dioxin poses serious long-term health risks, although the mechanism is unclear.

BIBLIOGRAPHY

BUCKINGHAM, WILLIAM A., JR. *Operation RANCH HAND: The Air Force and Herbicides in Southeast Asia, 1961–1971.* 1982.

JOHN F. GUILMARTIN JR.

RAND Corporation. Founded in 1948 with grants from the U.S. Air Force and the Ford Foundation, the RAND (an acronym for Research and Development) Corporation was the first private, nonprofit, federally funded think tank. It conducts classified research on defense and security issues at its headquarters in Santa Monica, California. RAND helped devise the U.S. strategic doctrine of nuclear deterrence in the 1950s and provided systems analysis experts to carry out Secretary of Defense Robert McNamara's military reforms in the 1960s. During the Vietnam War, RAND produced hundreds of reports on topics ranging from bomb damage assessment to counterinsurgency warfare. Early studies suggested that the Viet Cong guerrillas were dedicated patriots who would not be deterred by U.S. power, but this view was not welcome at the Pentagon. RAND experts then tailored their assessments to assure their air force clients that bombing North Vietnam would help defeat the guerrillas in South Vietnam. This became the logic behind Operations FLAMING DART and ROLLING THUNDER, which dropped thousands of tons of bombs on North Vietnam with little effect on the Viet Cong, as the Tet Offensive revealed. RAND's most famous defense expert was Daniel Ellsberg, who leaked the top-secret Pentagon Papers to the media in 1971.

BIBLIOGRAPHY

FRIEDMAN, SAUL. "The RAND Corporation and Our Policy Makers." *Atlantic Monthly,* September 1963.
LANDAU, DAVID. "Behind the Policy Makers: RAND and the Vietnam War." *Ramparts* (November 1972).
MARINE, GENE. "Think Factory De Luxe." *Nation,* 14 February 1959.
MITCHELL, EDWARD J. *Land Tenure and Rebellion.* 1967.
RAND Vietnam Interview Series. 1972.
RUSSO, ANTHONY. "Looking Backward: RAND and Vietnam in Retrospect." *Ramparts* (November 1972).
SMITH, BRUCE L. R. *The RAND Corporation.* 1966.
ZASLOFF, JOSEPH J. *Political Motivation of the Viet Cong.* 1968.

GLEN GENDZEL

R&R. U.S. Army and Marine soldiers in the field received a five-day rest and recuperation (R&R) leave during their service in Vietnam. The program provided service personnel with transportation to a "liberty" town in an Asian country friendly to the United States. The U.S. government paid Pan American World Airways nearly $24 million per year during the war to assist the program. The military provided soldiers with information on reliable hotels, local currency (if necessary), and precautions against venereal disease. Married service personnel frequently met their spouses in Honolulu, and many soldiers used the leave to buy cheap Asian consumer products. R&R destinations included Hong Kong, Japan, Manila, Seoul, Singapore, Sydney, and Taipei. The military viewed the R&R policy as an important asset to maintain soldiers' morale, working in conjunction with recreation and entertainment facilities at bases within Vietnam. The U.S. command occasionally rewarded fighting units for high body counts with extra R&R, and officers disciplined soldiers with its cancellation.

BIBLIOGRAPHY

APPY, CHRISTIAN G. *Working-Class War.* 1993.
GOLDMAN, PETER, and TONY FULLER. *Charlie Company.* 1983.

ADAM LAND

Read, Benjamin (1925–1993), executive secretary and special assistant to Secretary of State Dean Rusk, 1963–1969. By 1968 Read was opposed to U.S. involvement in Vietnam. As a powerful behind-the-scenes influence, Read convinced Rusk to support peace negotiations and served as a liaison channeling to the U.S. government in Washington information from the preliminary Paris talks between the United States and North Vietnam. Read ensured that his ally, Defense Secretary Clark Clifford, was kept informed of progress in negotiations, contrary to the wishes of National Security Adviser Walt Rostow, who sought to exclude Clifford. Read also was the point man in Washington aiding Ambassador Ellsworth Bunker, who was working to bring South Vietnam to the negotiating table.

BIBLIOGRAPHY

CLIFFORD, CLARK. *Counsel to the President: A Memoir.* 1991.

KELLY EVANS-PFEIFER

Reagan, Ronald (1911–), governor of California, 1966–1974; U.S. president 1981–1989. Reagan viewed the Vietnam War as a "noble cause" that failed because politicians in Washington did not let the military do its job. The antiwar movement was active in California during Reagan's campaign for governor in 1966. Despite an initial conservative isolationist stance, by late 1965 Reagan staunchly supported the war. He criticized student protestors and promised to "clean up the mess at Berkeley." Once elected, Reagan used the pulpit of the governorship to support U.S. involvement in Vietnam and to condemn those who opposed that involvement. His political success owed much to the backlash against the civil rights and antiwar movements of the 1960s.

Reagan's 1980 presidential campaign relied in part on a theme of restoring American pride and self-confidence, which he felt was lost because of

RONALD W. REAGAN. *Library of Congress*

the Vietnam War. He blamed the government for the war's failure, telling veterans groups that "we will never again ask young men to fight and possibly die in a war our government is afraid to win," and he repeatedly invoked the phrase "No more Vietnams." As president, Reagan opposed normalizing relations with Vietnam and spoke often in support of full resolution of the MIA/POW issue.

BIBLIOGRAPHY

CANNON, LOU. *Reagan.* 1982.

KELLY EVANS-PFEIFER

Reeducation Camps. Established after the fall of Saigon in 1975, reeducation camps were intended to punish former South Vietnamese citizens and dissident former Viet Cong guerrillas and suppress political dissent, all in the name of indoctrination of communist philosophy and *cai tao* (thought reform).

Estimates of the number of people sent to the camps range from the official SRV figure of 50,000 to more than 350,000. After the communist takeover of the country, entire classes of South Vietnamese citizens were ordered to report to the camps. These included former Army of the Republic of Vietnam (ARVN) officers, civil servants, teachers, the native Catholic clergy, journalists, doctors, engineers, and political activists. Typically a person was told to report for ten days of classes but was in fact sent to a reeducation camp for as long as several years.

The time required for reeducation could be a few months, but most were held for three to five years, and some refugees reported that camps operated well into the 1980s. The prisoners regarded as most threatening to the SRV government were held in the camps farthest north and were reportedly subjected to hard labor under conditions not unlike those of Nazi concentration camps. Camp inmates were forced to dig canals, build dams, clear jungles, and, in a few cases, build more camps. Most of the reeducation camps were located in the mountains and jungles away from population centers. The United States had evidence of fifty camps, which held an average of four thousand prisoners each. The reeducation process involved lectures and readings on American imperialism, Vietnamese nationalism, and socialism. Prisoners were forced to write regular reports detailing their "crimes."

The reeducation camps, in addition to punishment for the South Vietnamese, also served as a useful internal security tool. Peasants who were not working hard enough and those people who disagreed with the government could be threatened with being sent to the camps. In addition, the camps held political dissidents from North Vietnam and many former Viet Cong guerrillas—called Hoi Chanh—who had turned against North Vietnam toward the end of the war. Some reports suggest that reeducation camps had been operating in North Vietnam since 1954. Many believe the camps failed in their ultimate purpose of uniform indoctrination because the black market and Western pop culture flourish on the streets of Hanoi and Ho Chi Minh City. Numerous camp inmates died from starvation and disease although the number who died in the camps is undetermined. Many who were released from the camps immigrated to the United States where they were given priority for political asylum.

BIBLIOGRAPHY

NGUYEN VAN CANH. *Vietnam under Communism, 1975–1982.* 1983.

REEDUCATION CAMP PRISONERS. Former officers of the Army of the Republic of Vietnam (ARVN) at work in a reeducation camp, Tay Ninh, 1977. *National Archives*

OLSON, JAMES, and RANDY ROBERTS. *Where the Domino Fell.* 1991.

SANTOLI, AL. *To Bear Any Burden.* 1985.

KELLY EVANS-PFEIFER

Refugees. The problem of refugees displaced by military and political conflict in Vietnam, and later in Cambodia and Laos, from 1954 to the 1980s became a significant issue for the governments of Vietnam and the United States and for the international community. An "internal refugee" problem in Vietnam emerged during the French Indochina War and became more severe after the Geneva accords of 1954 and the division of the country at the 17th Parallel. The agreement provided for a period of 300 days during which Vietnamese were free to move and resettle in either North or South Vietnam. An estimated 80,000 to 120,000 Vietnamese in the South, mainly Viet Minh guerrillas, relocated to the North; more than 900,000 northerners, including an estimated 700,000 Roman Catholics, moved to South Vietnam. By mid 1957, the government of South Vietnam, with the assistance of the United States and private volunteer organizations, had established "refugee villages" for some 605,000 refugees; the remaining 300,000 refugees resettled themselves in both urban and rural areas. The large number of Catholic refugees from the North created an important anticommunist constituency in the South, which strongly supported the government of Ngo Dinh Diem. Some of these refugees also joined the political and military leadership of South Vietnam.

Between 1955 and 1963, Diem's government implemented rural resettlement programs, including the Strategic Hamlet program, which displaced 1.3 million Vietnamese from their villages. To achieve primarily political-military aims, such as cutting the links between the Viet Cong guerrillas and South Vietnamese villagers, these programs moved peasants into areas ostensibly controlled and defended by the government of South Vietnam. The vast majority of the peasants were moved involuntarily. These programs failed to achieve their objectives, and were abandoned by 1964; their greatest legacy was the creation of an alienated and resentful relocated population who were insecure in their new homes and villages. Many later joined the flood of refugees fleeing rural Vietnam for the urban areas.

The deployment of U.S. troops and the escalation of the Vietnam War in 1965 intensified the problem of internal refugees. Ground combat, widespread bombing, forcible relocation, and offen-

REFUGEES FROM COMMUNISM. South China Sea, 1975. *National Archives*

sives by North Vietnamese Army (NVA) and Viet Cong forces displaced some 4 million South Vietnamese between 1964 and 1969. For much of this period, the U.S. military strategy against the Viet Cong guerrillas included search-and-destroy missions and the use of massive firepower. In many areas, the rural population was moved to create free fire zones and to prevent Viet Cong guerrillas from gaining influence among the peasantry. During the Tet Offensive of 1968, NVA and Viet Cong military forces concentrated their assaults on the cities of South Vietnam, which resulted in the first significant number of urban refugees (over 800,000) in the South. Most refugees moved into crowded, dismal refugee camps or relocated themselves to urban slums. South Vietnam's poor treatment of refugees contributed to their hostility toward, or at least to their lack of support for, the government and the war effort. Scholars estimate that by 1975 nearly 12 million South Vietnamese civilians had fled, or had been displaced or relocated, from their homes; this number represented half of the country's population.

With the defeat of South Vietnam and the fall of Saigon in 1975, many Vietnamese became international refugees. First, there was an immediate evacuation of 140,000 Vietnamese with ties to the defeated government and to the United States. This was followed by about 983,000 refugees, many of whom were ethnic Chinese, from Vietnam to other countries over the next thirteen years. Some of the latter group were called boat people because they left Vietnam by sea. Fleeing by boat became an especially risky undertaking after 1978, when the neighboring countries of Malaysia and Thailand began turning away refugees and incidents of piracy against the refugee boats increased. Tens of thousands of boat people were lost at sea; it is estimated that 10–50 percent of the refugees who attempted the ocean passage drowned.

The acceptance and resettlement of the boat people and other refugees became an international political issue. From 1975 into the 1980s, between 1.5 million and 2 million refugees fled the communist-led Socialist Republic of Vietnam (SRV), Cambodia, and Laos because of political instability and military conflict. Many ethnic Chinese from Vietnam settled in the People's Republic of China (PRC), while other nations opened their doors to small numbers of refugees. More than half of the Cambodian, Laotian, and Vietnamese refugees, however, came to the United States. In 1978, one of the U.S. preconditions for normalization of relations with the SRV was that measures be taken to stem the flood of refugees to the United States. Still, the early consensus among the American population and in the government was that the United States had an obligation to aid refugees from the Vietnam War. As a result, President Jimmy Carter in June 1979 used his executive authority to raise quotas for immigrants from communist countries and Southeast Asia to a high of fourteen thousand per month. The resulting stream of refugees led to antagonism from some Americans and a number of anti-immigrant incidents in the late 1970s. A considerable number of former South Vietnamese officials and soldiers released from Vietnamese "reeducation" camps also immigrated to the United States. For many refugees of the Vietnam War, in the United States and elsewhere, racism and economic resentment accompanied the process of resettlement.

BIBLIOGRAPHY

GRANT, BRUCE. *The Boat People: An "Age" Investigation.* 1979.
LEVENSTEIN, AARON. *Escape to Freedom: The Story of the International Rescue Committee.* 1983.
WIESNER, LOUIS A. *Victims and Survivors: Displaced Persons and Other War Victims in Viet-Nam, 1954–1975.* 1988.

JENNIFER FROST

Regional Forces/Popular Forces.

Between 1886 and 1953, the French colonial government in Indochina created a variety of part-time militia and full-time police forces to help consolidate and enforce colonial rule. These forces included the Garde Indigène (Native Guard), established at Hue in 1886, and the Garde Civile de la Cochinchine (Civil Guard of Cochinchina), founded in Saigon the same year. Partisan troops, mostly tribal minorities from the Tonkin region, were also included in this security network, which was expanded or reduced in size according to needs. On 1 January 1953, a new entity, designated Regional Forces and Provincial Forces (RF/PF), was added to assist pacification teams called Les Groupements Administratifs Mobiles Opérationnels

(GAMOS), a combined civilian and military group aimed at securing popular support during a time when French control of Vietnam was weakening.

Regional Forces were organized into 120-man companies of 3 platoons (40 troops each), plus 10 officers. Provincial Forces operated in 40-man platoons supervised by 2 noncommissioned officers (NCOs). All RF/PF units were subordinate to senior French army officers who shared responsibilities for their development and deployment with three French pacification commissioners appointed by the French colonial governors of Annam, Tonkin, and Cochinchina. Because no central nationwide pacification directorate existed, clashes developed between military and civilian colonial authorities who used RF/PF units as they saw fit. Theoretically the mission of RF/PF forces—to assist the French with hamlet control, supply, and propaganda via a decentralized militia—was sound, but it was initiated too late to provide much help to the French in holding on to their colonial empire. The RF/PF network (Territorials) was the largest indigenous army controlled by France; by 1 January 1954, it numbered some 144,150 men, while the Vietnamese National Army (VNA) numbered only 123,800 troops.

Following the defeat of the French at Dien Bien Phu in 1954, the French forces were withdrawn from Indochina, and the country was divided into North and South Vietnam at the Geneva Conference. In 1955, the U.S. Military Assistance Advisory Group–Vietnam (MAAG-V) assumed control of the training and development of the Army of the Republic of Vietnam (ARVN), organized out of the VNA. MAAG-V advisers, however, largely ignored the former Territorial network. Funding presented a problem: the U.S. government desired an ARVN of about 100,000 troops but was loath to finance in addition an irregular Territorial army of equivalent size. Strategic issues were also at stake; the U.S. government's initial plans for the ARVN included its possible use in a general engagement against the People's Republic of China (PRC). MAAG-V advisers believed it would be easy to transform the fragmented VNA into the ARVN, a force that would satisfy the U.S. government's needs, but they had little experience working with thousands of irregular militia—the essence of the RF/PF concept. President Ngo Dinh Diem was not satisfied with the U.S. government's priorities. Rather, he wanted to transform the RF/PF network into a new unit called the Civil Guard (CG), responsible only to the

PEOPLE'S SELF-DEFENSE FORCE. Members from Hue. *National Archives*

president, which he could use to offset the growing power of the ARVN's officer corps.

Diem eventually prevailed, but for the next five years MAAG-V, the U.S. State Department, and the U.S. military staff argued about how these forces were to be used and who should control them. Initially the Civil Guard was funded by the U.S. Operations Mission (a State Department agency) and trained by the Michigan State University Advisory Group (MSUAG), which had contracts with the South Vietnamese and U.S. governments to develop police forces in South Vietnam. In 1956 Diem divided the Civil Guard, now 14,000 strong, in half, creating a new entity, the People's Self-Defense Force (PSDF), as yet another alternative to the ARVN, which exacerbated already serious problems of command and control, accountability, and plan-

ning. Fully disgusted with the situation, MSUAG was ejected from South Vietnam by Diem in 1959, leaving the fate of these forces to Diem and Gen. Samuel T. Williams, commander of MAAG-V.

Williams, a career military officer, opposed State Department (a civilian agency) control over a military force in South Vietnam. He believed that the CG/PSDF network should be incorporated into South Vietnam's Defense Ministry and be accountable only to the U.S. Joint Chiefs of Staff (JCS) along a chain of command similar to that of the ARVN. Diem, thanks to Williams' support, finally got his way in December 1960. The CG/PSDF network was included in the nation's defense budget and within twelve months had grown to a combined strength of nearly 100,000 troops. Despite its size, this force suffered from problems identical to those of the ARVN: all commanders were Diem loyalists with little, if any, practical military experience. Reflecting Diem's policy of rotating, promoting, or demoting his senior staff to win friends or neutralize political enemies, the CG had five different senior commanders between 1955 and 1958. Members of the Joint General Staff (JGS) of the Republic of Vietnam Armed Forces (RVNAF), often unsure of their own responsibilities, added to the problem; collectively they resented the potential threat that the Civil Guard represented as an alternative army controlled by the president.

The Civil Guard was supposed to be a full-time, regional force operating in company-size (approximately 150-man) units scattered throughout South Vietnam's forty-four provinces, but in reality only one-third reported for duty while the remaining two-thirds pursued other activities assigned by the province chiefs who controlled them. Frequently CG units harvested rice, fish, or plantation fruits, missions totally outside their prescribed duties. Accountability in the PSDF, which operated in platoon-size (30-man) formations in thousands of hamlets, was worse. Both the CG and the PSDF forces suffered serious morale problems because the ARVN was always given first priority. The Territorials' weapons were hand-me-downs or castoffs, some dating from World War I, and for five years (1955–1960) the Territorial forces had no MAAG-V advisers or formal training. A crude logistical system was set up to support them in 1960, but it rapidly collapsed because of inefficiency and corruption. In 1964 the Civil Guard was renamed the Regional Forces (RF); the PSDF became known as the Popular Forces (PF).

Despite poor pay—an RF colonel earned US$1,922 per annum while privates could expect no more than US$413 per year in 1968—there was never a lack of volunteers because service in either branch allowed them to remain closer to home, a morale-boosting consideration not extended to the ARVN's draftees. In 1968, South Vietnam declared nationwide mobilization, which embraced all males aged 16–50 in some form of military service. Not unexpectedly, competition for positions in an RF/PF unit intensified. Corruption was widespread: men destined for service in the ARVN bribed province chiefs, who controlled all Territorial forces, for placement with a local unit. Consequently, some provinces had more than ten times the prescribed number of militia troops, which drained resources and placed further burdens on lo-

cal training centers. In 1969 two Regional Force training centers and fifteen Popular Force training centers, with a combined capacity of 27,400 billets, were expected to transform recruits into RF/PF soldiers in a five-week basic training course prior to their four-year assignment in the RF/PF. The degree of success anticipated, however, did not materialize. Those fortunate enough to complete basic training were not fully qualified soldiers because of inadequate resources, inexperienced teaching staff, and the army's continual need for replacements, factors that often reduced basic training to one or two weeks.

In 1968 the combined strength of the RF (152,549) and PF (151,945) made it slightly smaller than the ARVN's ten divisions (324,637), but the Territorials carried more of the war effort, had a lower desertion rate, and were more cost efficient than the ARVN. As Andrew Krepinovich (1986) notes, the RF/PF consumed only 2–4 percent of the total annual cost of the war yet inflicted 12–30 percent of all VC and NVA combat deaths. Like the French, the U.S. advisers (at this time part of the Military Assistance Command, Vietnam [MACV]) did not recognize the potential value of the Territorial forces until too late. Even in 1966, only 4 percent of the U.S. advisers were involved in the training of RF/PF units, some eleven years after MAAG-V had restructured the ARVN. The status of all Territorial forces began to improve in 1967 as they received new weapons, more equipment, and more advisers, but these measures were insufficient and were introduced too late to significantly alter the course of the war. By that time North Vietnamese Army (NVA) and Viet Cong forces had established nearly impregnable areas of operation and command centers that the U.S. and ARVN units had been unable to eliminate on a permanent basis.

Cooperation between the ARVN and RF/PF units was unpredictable. Some Territorial units refused to support ARVN forces because of the ARVN's condescending attitude toward hamlet militias. The ARVN forces were often pessimistic and overly conservative when confronted by NVA and Viet Cong forces, while the RF/PF network preferred to avoid combat entirely if possible. This was largely because the RF/PF lived in the vicinity of, or within, areas controlled by the NVA and Viet Cong forces.

The degree to which the RF/PF network supported the government of South Vietnam varied from indifference to silent defiance. Political ideologies did not play as significant a role as might be expected among the rural Vietnamese, who were merely trying to maintain a degree of normalcy in their lives while surrounded by hostilities they did not start and could not control. Defining the "enemy" was especially difficult; some families had members of opposing armies living under the same roof. Under these circumstances, compliance and cooperation were facts of life, which helps to explain why the ARVN never realistically controlled vast amounts of countryside even though RF/PF units resided on the periphery of contested zones.

After 1967 RF/PF units sometimes assisted, or were actually a part of, new pacification and security groups created or adapted to destroy the Viet Cong Infrastructure (VCI). Funded by the Central Intelligence Agency (CIA), these groups included People's Action Teams (PATs) and the People's Self-Defense Force (PSDF), the latter name copied from French precedents. In retrospect the Territorial forces were a potentially important component in the Vietnam conflict, but they were largely ignored, by both the French and the Americans, because their command structure was decentralized to the grassroots level. If U.S. strategists had recognized their potential earlier in the war, the Republic of Vietnam Armed Forces (RVNAF) might have been more successful after the United States withdrew.

BIBLIOGRAPHY

CANTWELL, THOMAS R. "The Army of South Vietnam: A Military and Political History, 1955–75." Ph.D. diss., University of New South Wales, Sydney, Australia, 1989.

THOMAS R. CANTWELL

Republican Party, U.S.

Members of the Republican Party did not have a united monolithic position on the Vietnam War, but nearly all Republican political leaders and officeholders supported U.S. involvement. In addition, the Republican Party benefited greatly from the Vietnam War, both by blaming President Lyndon Johnson's administration for not pursuing winnable policies in the conflict and from the public backlash against the antiwar movement. The net result, which analyst Kevin Philips labeled "the emerging Republican majority," was that the Republican Party enjoyed two decades of electoral success on the presidential level, despite the Democrats' continued strength in congressional, state, and local elections, until the election reversals of 1994.

Ironically, fear of Republican criticism contributed to Johnson's decision to commit U.S. forces to Vietnam. During his 1964 campaign against the conservative Republican nominee Senator Barry Goldwater, Johnson was wary of compromising in Vietnam because he thought Goldwater would accuse him of being "soft on communism." Goldwater had in fact promised to escalate the war drastically if elected. After Johnson's victory and the initial commitment of U.S. troops it was the Republicans in Congress, more than the Democrats, who supported further escalation and backed Johnson's requests for more money for the war effort. Although Cold War foreign policy throughout the 1950s and early 1960s had been conducted on a largely bipartisan basis, the Vietnam conflict revealed fissures. At times Johnson enlisted the support of congressional Republicans to refute arguments against his Vietnam policies by antiwar Democrats.

By 1967, when most Americans were discontented with Vietnam policies, Republicans tended to favor large-scale military escalation, including an intensified bombing campaign against North Vietnam, while many Democrats had begun calling for reduced U.S. involvement and eventual withdrawal. The Tet Offensive of 1968 exacerbated this philosophical split. With Johnson out of the 1968 presidential race and the Democratic nominee, Hubert H. Humphrey, trying desperately in the last phase of the campaign to soften his stance on the conflict, Richard Nixon and the Republicans promised to deliver an "honorable" peace, implying that the Democrats would "sell out" the South Vietnamese to the communists.

The Republicans, sensing the distaste of America's conservative middle class for the antiwar movement and particularly for its radical student leaders, scored heavily with a law-and-order theme expressing abhorrence of the counterculture. Nixon succeeded in wooing a significant Democratic voting bloc away from its roots, forging a new Republican coalition in presidential elections. In the 1972 campaign, the Republicans again campaigned on their policies of "peace with honor" and painted Democratic nominee George McGovern as a dangerous antiwar liberal.

As president, Nixon enjoyed broad support from his party in conducting his Vietnam policies. Although a few moderate Republicans such as Jacob Javits of New York and John Sherman Cooper of Kentucky increasingly challenged those policies, they were in the minority. The Republicans in

REPUBLICAN STATE CONVENTION. Barry Goldwater (left) watches Texas
Republicans demonstrate before he speaks, Dallas, 16 June 1964. *National Archives*

Congress were unable, however, to prevent the passage, over Nixon's veto, of the War Powers Act in 1973.

The themes of the Democrats' weak resolve in the face of communism and their approval of a "permissive" counterculture that emerged from the Vietnam War era became the stock-in-trade of the Republican Party. Ronald Reagan repeated these themes often, arguing that Democratic policymakers had not let the U.S. military win in Vietnam.

BIBLIOGRAPHY

DIETZ, TERRY. *Republicans and Vietnam 1961–1968.* 1986.
KAHIN, GEORGE MCT. *Intervention: How America Became Involved in Vietnam.* 1986.
ZAROULIS, NANCY, and GERALD SULLIVAN. *Who Spoke Up?* 1984.

KELLY EVANS-PFEIFER

Republic of Vietnam (RVN). *See* Vietnam, Republic of (RVN).

Revolutionary Development Cadres. *See* Pacification.

Revolutionary War. *See* Pacification.

Rheault, Robert (1925–), commander, U.S. Army Fifth Special Forces Group, May–July 1969. Rheault was accused of ordering the June 1969 execution of a suspected Viet Cong double agent who was working for the Special Forces. The Central Intelligence Agency (CIA) refused to release classified information because of the secret nature of the project on which the double agent was working, and the case against Rheault was dropped, but he resigned from the army the same year. Like the My Lai massacre, the incident raised moral questions about U.S. conduct of the war.

BIBLIOGRAPHY

DAVIDSON, PHILLIP B. *Vietnam at War—The History: 1946–1975.* 1988.
"Green Beret Colonel: Robert Bradley Rheault," *New York Times,* 7 August 1969.
SIMPSON, CHARLES M., III. *Inside the Green Berets: The First Thirty Years, a History of the U.S. Army Special Forces.* 1983.

ELLEN D. GOLDLUST

Richardson, Elliot (1920–), secretary of defense, 1973; attorney general, 1973. Richardson had little influence on Vietnam policy during his four-month tenure as secretary of defense, although he had hoped to provide an alternative voice to that of Henry Kissinger. His time at the Pentagon ended abruptly when President Nixon appointed Richardson to the Justice Department after the Watergate-related resignation of Attorney General Richard Kleindienst. Nixon believed that Richardson's liberal credentials would ensure Senate confirmation. As attorney general, Richardson believed there was no distinction between the "plumbers" break-in of Dr. Fielding's office in the Pentagon Papers case and Watergate, and he favored prompt disclosure of the former, although he hesitated at first when he realized the plumbers' trail led to the White House.

BIBLIOGRAPHY

KUTLER, STANLEY. *The Wars of Watergate.* 1990.
RICHARDSON, ELLIOT. *The Creative Balance: Government, Politics, and the Individual.* 1976.

KELLY EVANS-PFEIFER

Richardson, John H. (1913–), Central Intelligence Agency (CIA) station chief, Saigon, 1962–1963. Like his predecessors, Richardson had close ties to the Diem regime, particularly to Ngo Dinh Nhu. Ambassador Henry Cabot Lodge had Richardson recalled on 5 October 1963 because of his links to the Ngo family, reflecting the Kennedy administration's growing disillusionment with Diem's government.

BIBLIOGRAPHY

COLBY, WILLIAM, and PETER FORBATH, *Honorable Men: My Life in the CIA.* 1978.
RUST, WILLIAM J. *Kennedy in Vietnam.* 1985.

WILLIAM PAUL SCHUCK

Ridgway, Matthew B. (1895–1993), general, U.S. Army; supreme commander, North Atlantic Treaty Organization (NATO), 1952–1953; U.S. Army chief of staff, 1953–1955. Gen. Matthew Ridgway, the architect of U.S. Army airborne forces, concluded after Korea that the United States must never fight another Asian war. By his own estimation, his opposition to U.S. intervention in support of the French at Dien Bien Phu "played a considerable, perhaps decisive part in persuading our government not to embark on that tragic adventure." Ridgway dismissed Adm. Arthur Radford's proposal to end the siege with air strikes as a delusion "that we could do things the cheap and easy way," warning that it would draw the United States into further commitments. As one of the "wise men," Ridgway helped persuade President Johnson to deescalate the Vietnam War in 1968. He considered Vietnam "the most egregious mistake any U.S. Government has ever made."

BIBLIOGRAPHY

ALBERTS, ROBERT C. "Profile of a Soldier: Matthew B. Ridgway." *American Heritage* 27 (February 1976): 4–7, 73–82.
RIDGWAY, MATTHEW B. "Indochina: Disengaging." *Foreign Affairs* 49 (1971).
RIDGWAY, MATTHEW B. *Soldier: The Memoirs of Matthew B. Ridgway.* 1956.

GLEN GENDZEL

Riot Control Agents (RCA). *See* Chemical Warfare.

Rogers, William P. (1913–), secretary of state, 1969–1973. Appointed by President Nixon, Rogers had little experience with foreign policy. This served Nixon's intention of weakening State Department influence and allowing the White House to directly control international affairs. Vietnam policy was formulated by Nixon and National Security Adviser Henry Kissinger with little input from Rogers. It is unclear whether Rogers was deliberately kept uninformed or whether he deceived Congress when he testified in 1970 that the United States would not infringe on Cambodia's neutrality at the same time that U.S. helicopters carrying ARVN troops were invading Cambodia. Rogers strongly opposed Nixon's bombing and invasion of Cambodia, while he strongly supported Nixon's Vietnamization program. In 1973, Kissinger replaced him as secretary of state.

BIBLIOGRAPHY

KARNOW, STANLEY. *Vietnam: A History.* 1991.
OLSON, JAMES, and RANDY ROBERTS. *Where the Domino Fell.* 1991.

KELLY EVANS-PFEIFER

ROLLING THUNDER. ROLLING THUNDER was the code name for President Lyndon Johnson's aerial bombing campaign against North Vietnam from 2 March 1965 to 31 October 1968. ROLLING THUNDER was intended by President Johnson and Secretary of Defense Robert McNamara as an incremental application of force designed to induce North Vietnam to come to the negotiating table. The operation was also used by the Joint Chiefs of Staff (JCS), the Commander-in-Chief, Pacific (CINCPAC), and air force and navy air commanders as an interdiction campaign against communist supply lines; by Gen. William Westmoreland to justify additional U.S. ground troops in South Vietnam for air base security; and by presidential adviser McGeorge Bundy as a means to bolster South Vietnamese resolve. The majority of Operation ROLLING THUNDER missions were carried out by U.S. Air Force F-105 and F-4 tactical fighter units based in South Vietnam and Thailand and by U.S. Navy carrier-based F-4, F-8, A-4, and A-6 fighter and attack squadrons. Pilots and weapon systems operators from these units suffered a disproportionately high share of their services' combat losses. Of the 655 U.S. military prisoners of war (POWs) returned by North Vietnam, 457 were aviators downed over the North, most during ROLLING THUNDER.

The campaign was marked by conflict between senior military commanders, who argued for a brief, intensive campaign to isolate North Vietnam from external sources of supply and destroy its ability to produce and move war matériel south, and Johnson and McNamara, who alternated escalation with bombing halts in hope of inducing the North Vietnamese to negotiate. Johnson and McNamara also insisted on detailed tactical control, dictating the numbers and types of aircraft, kinds of ordnance, timing, and tactics to be used against specific targets. Targets were chosen by Johnson, McNamara, Secretary of State Dean Rusk, White House press secretary George Reedy, and the current presidential assistant for national security affairs (McGeorge Bundy, later Walt Rostow) at Tuesday White House luncheons. The targets chosen came from a short list selected by McNamara's staff from among targets nominated by the Seventh Air Force and the U.S. Navy's Task Force-77 (TF-77) that had been approved by CINCPAC and the State Department.

RAIL TARGET. An example of the problems faced by ROLLING THUNDER: a bombed railroad bridge lies in the riverbed next to the ad hoc replacement bridge speedily constructed by North Vietnamese work gangs. *Ngô Vĩnh Long*

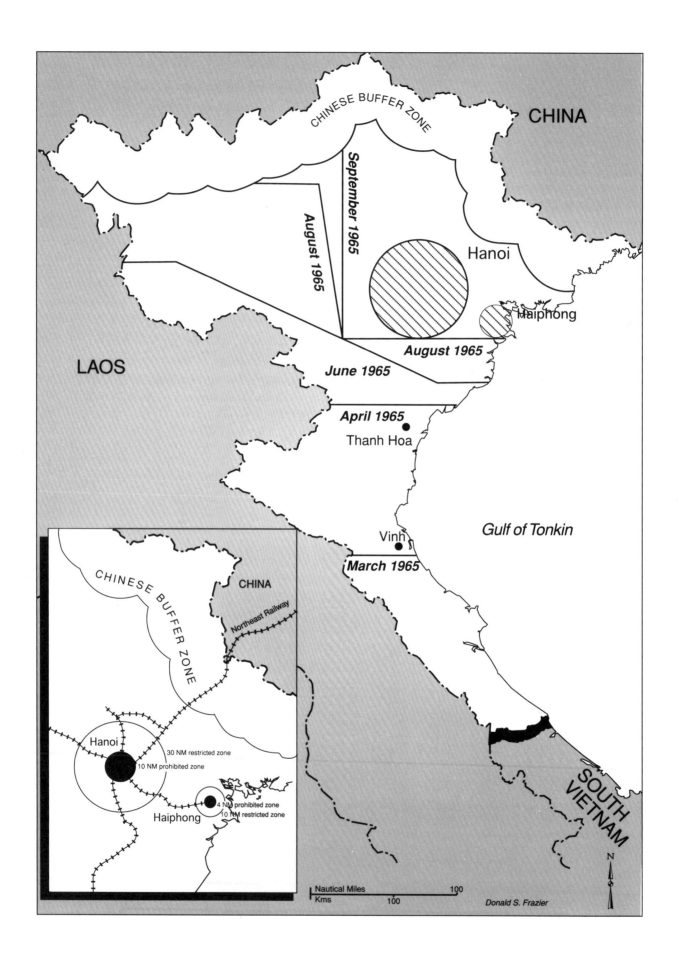

CHINESE BUFFER ZONE

CHINA

September 1965

August 1965

Hanoi

Haiphong

August 1965

June 1965

LAOS

April 1965

Thanh Hoa

Gulf of Tonkin

Vinh

March 1965

CHINESE BUFFER ZONE

CHINA

Northeast Railway

Hanoi

30 NM restricted zone

10 NM prohibited zone

4 NM prohibited zone

10 NM restricted zone

Haiphong

SOUTH VIETNAM

Nautical Miles   100

Kms   100

Donald S. Frazier

N

For much of the campaign, high-value targets such as POL (petroleum, oil, lubricants) storage facilities, electric power generation plants, and airfields were off-limits and many aviators considered the approved targets hardly worth hitting. This judgment was implicitly endorsed by commanders, who made no objection to the essentially unlimited diversion of strike sorties from assigned targets to search-and-rescue (SAR) missions to recover aviators downed in communist territory. The campaign generated political controversy as well, notably in the wake of Harrison Salisbury's reports from North Vietnam, published in the *New York Times* on 25 and 27 December 1966, that the United States was deliberately targeting the civilian populace. The accusation was hotly denied by the Pentagon but drew public expressions of regret from President Johnson.

ROLLING THUNDER strikes were initially restricted to southern North Vietnam above the DMZ. The northernmost boundary of operations was the so-called bomb line, above which attacks were forbidden. It was imposed from the White House and was based primarily on political and diplomatic and not military considerations. After initial attacks south of the city of Vinh, the bomb line was moved progressively northward, reaching lines 48 kilometers (30 miles) south and west of Hanoi by September 1965, and by July 1966 encompassing all of North Vietnam except for prohibited areas around Hanoi and Haiphong and a buffer zone along North Vietnam's border with the People's Republic of China (PRC). Meanwhile, the North Vietnamese had deployed Soviet-supplied SA-2 Guideline surface-to-air missiles (SAMs) and radar-controlled antiaircraft artillery in the Hanoi and Haiphong areas: when targets there came under attack, U.S. aviators encountered the densest and most sophisticated defenses in the history of aerial warfare. ROLLING THUNDER's climax came between August and October 1967 when Johnson, bowing to military pressure, ordered attacks on critical petroleum storage, electrical power generation, and transportation targets in the Hanoi and Haiphong areas.

Though British chargé d'affaires to Hanoi John Colvin estimated that U.S. air power came close to breaking North Vietnam's war economy in the autumn of 1967, judgments about ROLLING THUNDER's military value remain speculative. The campaign was never coordinated with U.S. ground operations in the South, and after six separate phases, seven bombing halts, and inconclusive results, ROLLING THUNDER was cancelled by President Johnson in the wake of the 1968 New Hampshire primary, a clear strategic and political failure.

BIBLIOGRAPHY

COLVIN, JOHN. "Hanoi in My Time." *Washington Quarterly* 4(1981): 138–156.

MORROCCO, JOHN, et al. *Thunder from Above: Air War.* Vol. 9 of *The Vietnam Experience.* 1984.

PARKS, W. HAYS. "Rolling Thunder and the Law of War." *Air University Review* 33, no. 2 (January–February 1982): 2–23.

TILFORD, EARL H., JR. *Setup: What the Air Force Did in Vietnam and Why.* 1991.

JOHN F. GUILMARTIN JR.

THE BOMB LINE. Imposed from the White House, the "bomb line" was the northernmost limit of ROLLING THUNDER bombing operations. As part of a "slow squeeze" strategy, the area of operations was extended as the bombing failed to deter the North Vietnamese. The approximate operational boundaries as of the end of the months noted are shown. Strikes were not automatically approved even within these authorized target areas. Moreover, operations were strictly forbidden within a 30-nautical-mile buffer zone along the Chinese border, and restricted and prohibited zones were also established around Hanoi and Haiphong.

Inset: No air strikes were permitted within prohibited zones unless personally approved by President Johnson; except for attacks on transportation links, strikes in restricted zones required Pentagon or White House approval. Note that the Chinese buffer zone contracted to 25 nautical miles approximately within the area shown within the inset. During the 1972 Christmas bombings, the prohibited zones were eliminated and the Hanoi restricted zone was reduced to a radius of 10 nautical miles. (Map adapted from Barrett Tillman and John B. Nichols, *On Yankee Station.* Naval Institute Press, 1987.)

Romney, George (1907–1995), governor of Michigan, 1963–1969. Romney was the early front-runner for the 1968 Republican presidential nomination. Nelson Rockefeller and moderate Republicans supported him, but Romney's indecisive stand on Vietnam—he vaguely hinted that he would end it—hurt his candidacy. A September 1967 statement that U.S. officials in Vietnam had "brainwashed" him further weakened his reputation. He ended his campaign on 28 February 1968 because of poor showings in the polls.

BIBLIOGRAPHY

MOLLENHOFF, CLARK R. *George Romney: Mormon in Politics.* 1968.

WHITE, THEODORE H. *The Making of the President 1968.* 1969.

WILLIAM PAUL SCHUCK

Roosevelt, Franklin Delano (1882–1945),

U.S. president, 1933–1945. President Roosevelt followed an ambivalent policy toward Indochina from 1942 to 1945. He envisioned international trusteeships for colonies after the end of World War II: an apprenticeship for dependencies such as Indochina to lead them to independence. Despite his remarks that the French had milked the area for one hundred years and that the Indochinese were "entitled to something better than that," by 1945 Roosevelt had allowed the demands of war to overshadow any desire for the trusteeship concept. When he died in 1945, the United States had no overall plan to deal with a concerted effort to reimpose French rule.

BIBLIOGRAPHY

DALLEK, ROBERT. *Franklin D. Roosevelt and American Foreign Policy, 1932–1945.* 1979.

Memorandum by Roosevelt to Secretary of State Cordell Hull, 24 January 1944. In *Vietnam: The Definitive Documentation of Human Decisions,* edited by Gareth Porter. Vol. 1. 1979.

The Pentagon Papers: The Defense Department History of United States Decisionmaking on Vietnam. Senator Gravel Edition. Vol. 1. 1971.

VICTOR JEW

Rostow, Eugene V. (1913–), undersecretary of

state, 1966–1969. Rostow, innovative dean of Yale Law School from 1955 to 1965, held several U.S. government and United Nations posts before President Johnson appointed him undersecretary of state for political affairs in 1966. Rostow joined his brother Walt Rostow, national security adviser, among the Johnson administration's decision-making elite at the peak of the Vietnam War. Rostow believed the war was necessary if the United States was to uphold its commitments to defend allies and contain communism, and he steadfastly supported administration policy in Vietnam. Rostow supervised the "Marigold" initiative and other secret peace offers in which the U.S. offered to cease bombing North Vietnam in exchange for an end to guerrilla infiltra-

tion into South Vietnam. He came to believe that these initiatives were a "sign of weakness" after North Vietnam rejected them. Rostow's principal regret about Vietnam was that politics interfered with strategy and public opinion weakened the U.S. war effort. After 1969, he was one of the few high-ranking members of the previous administration who still defended former president Johnson's policies in Vietnam. He returned to Yale Law School and later served as director of the Arms Control and Disarmament Agency under President Reagan.

BIBLIOGRAPHY

BARRETT, DAVID M. *Uncertain Warriors: Lyndon Johnson and his Vietnam Advisers.* 1993.

BROWNSTEIN, RONALD, and NINA EASTON. *Reagan's Ruling Class.* 1982.

ROSTOW, EUGENE. *Law, Power, and the Pursuit of Peace.* 1968.

ROSTOW, EUGENE. *Peace in the Balance: The Future of American Foreign Policy.* 1972.

ROSTOW, EUGENE. *Toward Managed Peace: The National Security Interests of the United States.* 1993.

WHITWORTH, WILLIAM. *Naive Questions about War and Peace.* 1970.

GLEN GENDZEL

Rostow, Walt Whitman (1916–), special assis-

tant for national security affairs, 1961–1966; national security adviser, 1966–1969. An affable professor of economics from Massachusetts Institute of Technology (M.I.T.), Walt Rostow was perhaps the most consistent and influential proponent of escalation in the Vietnam War. He worked for the Kennedy presidential campaign in 1960, coining the New Frontier slogan. Rostow was rewarded with appointments as special assistant for national security affairs and chairman of the State Department's policy planning staff. Rostow firmly believed that the United States should meet the global challenge of communism with military intervention and economic aid. A key member of President Kennedy's "brain trust," Rostow considered Southeast Asia "the last great confrontation" with communism. Rostow accompanied Gen. Maxwell Taylor to Vietnam in October 1961, and their report led to the first commitments of U.S. ground troops. Rostow's experience choosing bombing targets in World War II left him supremely confident in U.S. air power. As the Viet Cong insurgency grew, Rostow suggested bombing the north to defeat guerrillas in the south, for he firmly believed that the Viet Cong were controlled from the

Democratic Republic of Vietnam. Kennedy rejected the idea, but President Johnson approved it in 1965. When bombing of North Vietnam began in earnest in 1966, Rostow was promoted to national security adviser.

At the peak of the war, Rostow regularly attended the Tuesday strategy luncheons at the White House, and for years he predicted imminent victory. As public opinion turned against the war, President Johnson relied heavily on Rostow's optimism and perseverance. He appreciated that Rostow would not "turn tail and run" like other advisers who grew disenchanted with the war and resigned. Rostow stood by Johnson, shielding him from unfavorable press reports and discouraging intelligence estimates. After the Tet Offensive, Rostow served on both the Ad Hoc Task Force in February 1968 and the Senior Advisory Group (more commonly known as the "wise men") in March 1968 that reassessed Vietnam policy and recommended against further escalation. Rostow, however, approved military requests for intensifying the bombing, mobilizing the reserves, and sending more troops to Vietnam. Johnson finally decided to ignore Rostow's advice and stopped escalating the war in March 1968. Out of office a year later, Rostow found himself no longer welcome at M.I.T., and so he become professor of economics at the University of Texas. Of his role in the war, Rostow has said, "History will salute us."

BIBLIOGRAPHY

BARRETT, DAVID M. *Uncertain Warriors: Lyndon Johnson and his Vietnam Advisers.* 1993.

CAMPBELL, ALEX. "Walt Whitman Rostow." *New Republic,* 4 November 1967.

GRAFF, HENRY. *The Tuesday Cabinet: Deliberation and Decision on Peace and War under Lyndon B. Johnson.* 1970.

HALBERSTAM, DAVID. *The Best and the Brightest.* 1972.

ROSTOW, WALT. *The Diffusion of Power: An Essay in Recent History.* 1972.

ROSTOW, WALT. *Essays on a Half-Century: Ideas, Policies, and Action.* 1988.

GLEN GENDZEL

Rules of Engagement.

The rules of engagement (ROEs) were the formal authorizations for U.S. ground, air, and naval combat operations in Southeast Asia. Although the Joint Chiefs of Staff (JCS) and the Military Assistance Command, Vietnam (MACV), formed many ROEs, the White House exercised final authority in their development. ROEs changed frequently during the war and affected numerous combat contingencies. They generally worked, however, to prevent geographical expansion of the war and to limit civilian casualties. The Vietnam War ROEs remain highly controversial as some spokesmen, particularly military analysts, contend that they undermined U.S. ability to bring decisive force against the enemy. As Sen. Barry Goldwater declared in 1985, "the Armed Forces did not suffer a military defeat in any sense of the term. Rather, it was civilian managers of the U.S. Government who denied our military forces a victory by imposing a complex and lengthy set of restrictions." Current debates reveal, however, wide disagreement over the ROEs' contribution to the U.S. military setbacks in Vietnam.

The ROEs established strict territorial limits on U.S. military operations during the war. The directives forbade ground operations outside South Vietnam (except for the 1970 incursion into Cambodia) and established complex restraints on air power in Cambodia, Laos, and North Vietnam. President Lyndon Johnson established the territorial contours of the ROEs in 1965, choosing a strategy of "limited war" for the emerging conflict. The concept, popularized by academic theorists in the 1950s, proposed a gradual escalation of military force to gain a favorable negotiated settlement. The strategy and restrictive ROEs reflected administration concern that provocative military activities in the region would trigger a confrontation with the Soviet Union or the People's Republic of China (PRC). The gradualist approach also revealed Johnson's initial desire to limit U.S. intervention, fearing a political backlash against an expensive war and extensive reserve call-up. Johnson and key advisers judged that carefully directed and contained military power could stem the communist war against South Vietnam.

Criticisms of ROEs. Critics of the Vietnam ROEs contend that a determined initial use of U.S. military power may have deterred the North Vietnamese Army (NVA) and Viet Cong. Johnson's gradualist approach failed to draw diplomatic concessions. Moreover, despite superior military capabilities, the administration never delivered a decisive blow to North Vietnam's war machine, allowing its forces to adapt to U.S. military intervention. In particular, analysts challenge the air war begun over the North in February 1965. Johnson and his civilian advisers viewed Operation ROLLING THUNDER as a key instrument of limited war escalation and exercised detailed oversight of the air strikes. The administration gradually expanded the list of targets within North Vietnam, but by July 1966 ROEs still prohibited strikes near the PRC border and on key industrial and logistics centers around Hanoi and Haiphong. Directives forbade the bombing of prominent infrastructure sites and attacks on shipping along the coast. Critics note that President Nixon's massive 1972 bombing of the Hanoi-Haiphong corridor and the naval blockade forced concessions at the peace negotiations in Paris, unlike Johnson's restrained policies.

Military analysts, such as army colonel Harry G. Summers, assail U.S. failure to aggressively threaten NVA and Viet Cong bases and supply routes in Cambodia and Laos. ROEs placed the Cambodian sanctuaries off-limits to any U.S. strikes until the 1969 bombing campaign and the 1970 incursion. These bases provided NVA and Viet Cong forces with ready supplies and refuge and allowed them to dictate the site and timing of battles, critics charge. Gen. William Westmoreland even developed plans for a ground invasion into Laos to block the Ho Chi Minh Trail but the ROEs precluded such a U.S. operation. An air interdiction campaign, begun in 1967, proved unable to disrupt the key supply corridor.

Many military personnel also contend that ROEs produced a confusing and even dangerous regulatory oversight of day-to-day operations. ROEs changed rapidly, reflecting in part ongoing pressure from field commanders to adapt directives. Other complex combat rules revealed institutional tensions over responsibility for military policy, particularly in the air war. Air targets in Laos required approval from the U.S. ambassador in Vientiane, which caused significant delays. Some ROEs developed by the administration put U.S. aviators at risk, drawing fierce objections from the military. Directives forced U.S. pilots on bombing missions over North Vietnam to approach targets at low altitude for visual verification, increasing their vulnerability to antiaircraft fire. Furthermore, North Vietnam used some U.S. ROEs to its advantage; for example, by placing antiaircraft artillery on dikes, which were off limits to U.S. bombers.

Such criticisms of the Vietnam ROEs have received a sympathetic hearing among the American public. A 1990 *Time* magazine poll noted that more than half of the respondents expressed resentment that the government did not fight the war more aggressively (even though studies show an overwhelming majority of Americans still believe intervention was a "mistake"). In a 1990 Gallup poll, 53 percent of respondents agreed that the United States could have won the war with "a stronger military effort." Among the armed forces, one study found that a startling 82 percent of Vietnam veterans believed that ROEs prevented the United States from winning the war. Enduring military resentment yielded new policies during the Persian Gulf War, in which the Bush administration reduced civilian oversight of operations and simplified ROEs. Furthermore, unlike in Vietnam, the United States successfully brought overwhelming military power, both in the air and on the ground, to bear against Iraq.

Support for ROEs. Even accepting the flawed "limited war" escalation and the bureaucratic tension over combat policies, however, the restrictive Vietnam ROEs appear not to have decisively undermined the war effort. The administration's cautious territorial and air war restraints did successfully avoid a superpower confrontation in Vietnam, which was certainly not a foreordained result. Fifteen years earlier, in Korea, Gen. Douglas MacArthur's aggressive but ill-fated march to the Yalu River had drawn the PRC into the Korean War, and there is evidence that in 1966 the PRC threatened to intervene if the United States invaded North Vietnam or struck the Red River dikes, North Vietnam's most vulnerable infrastructure. Even so, some critics, such as Phillip Davidson, cite directives protecting the dikes to demonstrate the weakness of Operation ROLLING THUNDER.

Other commentators question the value of U.S. ground invasions into Cambodia and Laos. Even without foreign intervention, an expanding ground war in Southeast Asia would have created substantial new problems. A U.S. attack on the sanctuaries may have required occupation of eastern Cambodia to disrupt NVA and Viet Cong bases permanently, involving enormous resources. As shown during the 1970 incursion, NVA and Viet Cong forces could effectively move their bases into the interior of Cambodia. Similarly, an invasion of Laos to block the Ho Chi Minh Trail may have resulted in exorbitant numbers of casualties as U.S. soldiers attempted to hold interdiction lines. Moreover, the determined North Vietnamese supply efforts may have simply been rerouted through Thailand, around U.S. forces.

Andrew Krepinevich, in *The Army in Vietnam*, charged that traditional U.S. military emphasis on conventional warfare, rather than the restrictive civilian oversight, was at the root of the U.S. failure in Vietnam. A 1967 Central Intelligence Agency (CIA) report confirmed that the bulk of supplies for the Viet Cong guerrillas and their recruits came from the local populations. Aggressive U.S. operations to block the Ho Chi Minh Trail or to disrupt logistical operations in the North could never address the indigenous sources of the armed struggle in South Vietnam. In opposition to many military analysts, Krepinevich suggested that their preoccupation with ROEs stems from the flawed belief that unrestricted and overpowering conventional warfare could have succeeded in a counterinsurgency conflict. Moreover, the focus shows the military's inability to conceive creative strategies that could foster the political and social aspects of pacification. As Krepinevich declared, the U.S. military's fixation on the restraints on conventional warfare reveal that "in spite of its anguish in Vietnam, the Army has learned little of value."

ROEs and the Civilian Population. Government and military leaders also designed extensive ROEs to minimize civilian injury and property loss from U.S. combat operations inside South Vietnam. The directives were seen as crucial to gain South Vietnamese support for U.S. intervention and the anticommunist South Vietnamese government. ROEs addressed such matters as the positive identification of NVA and Viet Cong forces, clearance procedures for air and artillery fire, and handling of civilian refugees. Most commentators agree that the directives failed, however, to prevent significant civilian casualties within South Vietnam. The attrition strategy pursued by U.S. forces, which relied on aggressive search-and-destroy missions and heavy firepower, caused tremendous destruction in the country and alienated many South Vietnamese.

U.S. tactics in the ground war in South Vietnam involved the extensive use of U.S. firepower (e.g., air raids, naval and land artillery, and helicopter gunships) against North Vietnamese and Viet Cong resources. MACV designed certain ROEs to limit the use of destructive firepower, though such directives frequently had a negligible effect. For instance, directives called for the use of napalm to be "avoided unless absolutely necessary" during attacks on villages. In practice, napalm was used extensively, and an estimated 400,000 tons of napalm bombs were

delivered in South Vietnam over the course of the war. ROE procedures for assessing civilians' presence in areas subject to bombing or shelling were also flawed. For example, the South Vietnamese officials who provided clearance for unrestrained shelling in "free-fire zones" often showed little concern for civilian casualties.

ROEs also proved inadequate to address the uncertain and volatile environment created by the Viet Cong guerrilla warfare and aggressive U.S. sweeps of rural Vietnam. ROEs called for soldiers to carefully distinguish neutral civilians from Viet Cong forces. U.S. fighting units, however, suffered extensive casualties from mines and booby traps near South Vietnamese villages, which contributed to tense and hostile confrontations with local populations. U.S. units in the field developed crude, and often arbitrary, means for identifying Viet Cong guerrillas, including checking for specific clothes or physical markings. Other "tests" represented more disturbing abuses of ROEs; U.S. Army helicopter crews, for instance, were known to fire on South Vietnamese who ran from their aircraft, citing their fleeing as evidence of loyalty to the Viet Cong guerrillas.

Extensive controversy has arisen from the failure of U.S. policies to prevent civilian casualties within Vietnam. The My Lai massacre in March 1968, in particular, sparked domestic and international outrage. Antiwar critics charged the United States with war crimes in violation of the 1949 Geneva conventions. In response to this incident, in which more than three hundred South Vietnamese, most of them women, children, or elderly, were killed by U.S. soldiers, MACV intensified its training for military personnel in ROE directives. Vietnam War scholars remain divided over whether civilian atrocities such as the My Lai incident occurred frequently during the war.

BIBLIOGRAPHY

DAVIDSON, PHILLIP B. *Vietnam at War: The History, 1946–1975.* 1988.

DRAKE, RICKY JAMES. *The Rules of Defeat: The Impact of Aerial Rules of Engagement on USAF Operations in North Vietnam, 1965–1968.* 1993.

HERRING, GEORGE C. *LBJ and Vietnam: A Different Kind of War.* 1994.

KREPINEVICH, ANDREW F., JR. *The Army and Vietnam.* 1986.

LEWY, GUENTER. *America in Vietnam.* 1978.

SUMMERS, HARRY G., JR. *On Strategy: The Vietnam War in Context.* 1981.

ADAM LAND

Rusk, Dean (1909–1994), assistant U.S. secretary of state for Far Eastern affairs, 1950–1953; secretary of state, 1961–1969. As one of the leading foreign policy advisers to both presidents John F. Kennedy and Lyndon B. Johnson, Rusk fully supported and helped implement Kennedy's and Johnson's decisions to escalate the U.S. commitment in Vietnam. "I thought the principal decisions made by President Kennedy and President Johnson were the right decisions at the time they were made," he reflected in his 1990 memoir, *As I Saw It*. "I supported their decisions."

A former Rhodes scholar, Rusk served as chief of staff to Gen. Joseph Stilwell in the China-Burma-India theater during World War II. At the end of the war, he joined the State Department, developing expertise in United Nations and East Asian affairs. Rusk proved more sensitive than many of his diplomatic colleagues to the postwar stirrings of Asian nationalism, particularly when that nationalism assumed a moderate cast. He played a crucial role, for example, in moving the Truman administration to support Indonesian independence in 1949. At the same time, Rusk's anticolonial inclinations were tempered and in some cases eclipsed by his vigorous anticommunism. As Truman's assistant secretary of state for Far Eastern affairs, he backed the adminis-

tration's decision in the spring of 1950 to begin providing military assistance to French authorities in Indochina. Rusk was convinced that the communist-led Viet Minh insurgency formed part of a broader communist challenge to Western interests in Asia, a threat that appeared increasingly ominous to him with the victory of the Chinese communists in 1949 and the onset of the Korean War the next year. Southeast Asia represented for Rusk and other leading State and Defense Department officials a critical arena in the global Cold War struggle between the United States and the Soviet Union.

Rusk continued to view developments in Vietnam through that Cold War lens when, after a long stint as president of the Rockefeller Foundation, he returned to government service in 1961. As Kennedy's secretary of state, Rusk had responsibility for a wide range of foreign policy issues, which left little time for sustained attention to Vietnam. Only when the Diem regime began to unravel in the spring and summer of 1963 did Rusk fully focus upon the issue. His advice to Kennedy, however, remained clear-cut and straightforward throughout this period. Rusk argued with conviction and consistency that U.S. global interests required the preservation of a noncommunist South Vietnam. America's treaty obligations under the Southeast

DEAN RUSK. Speaking before the Senate Foreign Relations Committee, February 1966. *Library of Congress*

Asia Treaty Organization, its prestige as a world power, the credibility of its commitments, and its ability and willingness to deter aggression—all vital issues—were in Rusk's view being tested and challenged in Vietnam. For Rusk there was no debating the ultimate objective of U.S. policy; what he invariably characterized as external communist aggression simply had to be contained, much as the Nazi challenge had had to be quelled in an earlier era. The most difficult issues for the secretary of state concerned not ends but means. Rusk characteristically favored moderation and gradualism, and advocated the policy of incremental escalation that Kennedy ultimately followed. Although he prized Rusk's experience and loyalty, Kennedy considered the Georgian plodding and unimaginative. Some of Kennedy's aides contend that the president would have replaced him as secretary of state had there been a second Kennedy administration. After Kennedy's death brought Lyndon Johnson to the White House, Rusk gradually played a more prominent policy role. Johnson, a fellow southerner, valued Rusk's counsel far more than Kennedy had.

With the steady deterioration of the political and security situation within South Vietnam throughout 1964 and early 1965, Rusk abandoned his earlier opposition to the introduction of U.S. combat forces and joined Secretary of Defense Robert S. McNamara and national security adviser McGeorge Bundy to urge Johnson to do whatever was necessary to prevent a North Vietnamese victory. In a rare private memorandum to Johnson in July 1965, Rusk laid out the overarching issue as he saw it. "The central objective of the United States in South Vietnam must be to insure that North Vietnam not succeed in taking over or determining the future of South Vietnam by force," Rusk argued. "The integrity of the U.S. commitment is the principal pillar of peace throughout the world. If that commitment becomes unreliable, the communist world would draw conclusions that would lead to our ruin and almost certainly to a catastrophic war." That core assumption shaped Rusk's views toward the war and his policy recommendations to Johnson through the very end of the administration. Even when the 1968 Tet Offensive turned some of the president's advisers against escalation, Rusk continued to insist upon the inviolability of the U.S. commitment to South Vietnam.

The memory of Chinese intervention in the Korean War inclined Rusk to oppose any military actions against North Vietnam that might be construed as excessively provocative in the People's Republic of China or the Soviet Union. During the bitter debates within the administration in 1966 and 1967 about the proper targets of U.S. bombing, for example, he consistently argued against bombing Hanoi and Haiphong. The characteristically cautious Rusk feared that aerial attacks on those cities might spark Chinese intervention. During that same period, the secretary of state also pursued several abortive peace initiatives with North Vietnam, including Operation Marigold. Rusk remained firm in his conviction that a negotiated settlement offered the United States the most promising avenue for an honorable exit from Vietnam—provided that Hanoi made the concessions that he considered essential for the survival of a noncommunist South Vietnam.

Rusk left office deeply scarred by the Vietnam War. The passions unleashed by that divisive conflict took a heavy personal toll on a man long renowned for his unflappability. But the consistency of principle that stands as one of the hallmarks of Rusk's career—what critics would term a stubborn inflexibility—remained intact. He continued to believe that U.S. intervention was justified and that the war could have been won—"if we could have maintained solidarity on the home front and if we could have accepted 'winning' as defined by the Kennedy and Johnson administrations: preventing North Vietnam's takeover of South Vietnam by force."

Rusk's conviction that the U.S. cause in Vietnam was righteous—the defense of peace against aggression, of democracy and freedom against communist tyranny—has never wavered. "I have not apologized for my role in Vietnam," the former secretary of state asserted in his memoir, "for the simple reason that I believe in the principles that underlay our commitment to South Vietnam and why we fought that war." By the late 1960s, that uncompromising stance made the colorless and taciturn Rusk a major target for antiwar protestors. Upon his retirement from public life, he was probably one of the nation's most controversial—and vilified—figures. Leaving Washington, he returned to his native Georgia in 1970, where he spent the next two decades as a law professor at the University of Georgia, proudly unrepentant about his role in the Vietnam War.

BIBLIOGRAPHY

COHEN, WARREN I. *Dean Rusk*. 1980.
HALBERSTAM, DAVID. *The Best and the Brightest*. 1972.
RUSK, DEAN, as told to Richard Rusk. *As I Saw It*. 1990.

RICHARD B. RUSSELL. *Library of Congress*

SCHOENBAUM, THOMAS J. *Waging Peace and War: Dean Rusk in the Truman, Kennedy, and Johnson Years.* 1988.

ROBERT J. MCMAHON

Russell, Richard B. (1897–1971), U.S. senator (D-Ga.), 1933–1971; chairman, Senate Armed Services Committee, 1951–1969; chairman, Senate Appropriations Committee, 1969–1971. By virtue of his chairmanships, Russell greatly influenced military appropriations and policy. He initially opposed U.S. involvement in Vietnam because he did not consider North Vietnam a threat to U.S. interests. Once U.S. troops were committed, however, Russell supported the war as a point of national honor, although he remained a critic of U.S. strategy and conduct of the war. After the Tet Offensive in 1968, he rejected the piecemeal escalation of the ground war and called for full-scale bombing of North Vietnam.

BIBLIOGRAPHY

FITE, GILBERT C. *Richard B. Russell, Jr., Senator from Georgia.* 1991.
HOOPES, TOWNSEND. *The Limits of Intervention.* 1973.

JENNIFER FROST

S

Saigon. Saigon, the largest city in Indochina, was the capital of South Vietnam (1954–1975) and is located 75 kilometers (45 miles) from the coast of the South China Sea on the Sai Gon River. Tree-lined streets, sidewalk cafés, grand hotels, and elegant villas graced the "Paris of the Orient" after many years of French rule. Adm. Léonard Victor Joseph Charner first conquered Saigon for France in 1861. Emperor Tu Duc then ceded the surrounding provinces to form Cochinchina, the first colony of French Indochina. Saigon became a thriving commercial center of the Mekong Delta and the home to rich Vietnamese planters, French aristocrats, and Chinese merchants. The struggle against French rule in the south began when Saigon workers went on strike in September 1945 following the withdrawal of Japanese occupation forces. French troops, rearmed by the British, assassinated Viet Minh leaders, and in retaliation French settlers were massacred. But the Viet Minh never enjoyed much support in Saigon during the Indochina War.

Saigon became the capital of South Vietnam when the country was divided in 1954. Binh Xuyen gangsters controlled the city until Ngo Dinh Diem subdued them in 1955, signaling his rise to power. Buddhist-led protests in Saigon and in Hue against the repressive South Vietnamese government hastened Diem's downfall in 1963. Saigon's official population of 1.5 million nearly doubled during the next decade as war refugees streamed into squalid shantytowns. The sudden and gigantic influx of U.S. troops and dollars rapidly transformed the Asian capital into a carnival of Western decadence. Saigon swarmed with thieves, beggars, prostitutes, drug dealers, and black market peddlers. "Saigon has become an American brothel," Sen. J. William Fulbright complained in 1967. This process took place with official connivance as rampant corruption stole away U.S. aid intended to make Saigon a showplace of U.S. generosity. Antiwar critics often cited the corruption and chaos in Saigon as justification for U.S. withdrawal.

The U.S. war effort flowed through Saigon, the port of entry for 136,000 metric tons (150,000 tons) per month of U.S. cargo. Huge U.S. bases sprawled nearby at Tan Son Nhut, Bien Hoa, and Long Binh. Saigon abounded with offices, apartments, and barracks erected for U.S. personnel. Yet even apart from the notorious pickpockets, Americans were never safe there—notably when Viet Cong guerrillas blew up the U.S. officers' billet at the Brinks Hotel in 1964 and attacked the U.S. em-

SAIGON. The city's old financial quarter, dominated by buildings built under French colonial rule, along the Kinh Ben Nghe waterfront of the Sai Gon River. *Center of Military History*

bassy in 1968 during the Tet Offensive. Nor were the Saigon regime's corrupt and conniving generals accorded much respect in the rest of the country. Saigon became a symbol of how the United States ruined a nation that it meant to save. After North Vietnamese Army (NVA) tanks rolled into the city on 30 April 1975, the communists opened "reeducation camps" for 400,000 government officials, military officers, petty criminals, and anyone with U.S. connections. Saigon was renamed Ho Chi Minh City, but visitors in the mid 1990s reported that communist rule had not stamped out the city's hustling spirit.

BIBLIOGRAPHY

BARR, CAMERON W. "Renovating Everything but Communist Rule." *Christian Science Monitor,* 30 December 1994.

BUTLER, DAVID. *The Fall of Saigon.* 1985.

DAWSON, ALAN. *55 Days: The Fall of Saigon.* 1977.

FITZGERALD, FRANCES. *Fire in the Lake: The Vietnamese and the Americans in Vietnam.* 1972.

HASSLER, ALFRED. *Saigon, U.S.A.* 1970.

SHEEHAN, NEIL. *After the War Was Over: Hanoi and Saigon.* 1992.

WHITE, PETER T. "Saigon: Fourteen Years After." *National Geographic,* November 1989.

GLEN GENDZEL

Sainteny, Jean (1907–1978), French diplomat. A former Hanoi banker, Jean Sainteny represented the French government during negotiations with Ho Chi Minh in March 1946. Sainteny and Ho agreed to accords in which France recognized Vietnam as a free state within the French Union. The agreement broke down by December, igniting the eight-year Indochina War. Largely because of his personal friendship with Ho, Sainteny represented the French on three later diplomatic missions, including a 1966 peace effort. In 1969, Sainteny brokered correspondence between Kissinger and the

North Vietnamese leader. Sainteny also arranged the 1972 secret meetings between Kissinger and Le Duc Tho in Paris.

BIBLIOGRAPHY

LACOUTURE, JEAN. *Ho Chi Minh: A Political Biography.* Translated by Peter Wiles. 1968.

ADAM LAND

Salan, Raoul (1899–1984), commander in chief, French forces in Vietnam, 1952–1953. Salan brought a lifetime of highly decorated military experience to his Vietnam command: he fought in World War I, was wounded in the Levant in 1921, served in Indochina in 1924, and undertook intelligence and subversion operations against the Italians in North Africa in 1942–1943. Succeeding the dynamic General Lattre de Tassigny in Vietnam in 1952, Raoul Salan chose a different strategy for pursuing the Indochina War. He favored a defensive war and refused to predict imminent victory. The same year he took command, Salan was forced to withdraw his forces from Hao Binh, an important position southeast of Hanoi. In 1953, the Eisenhower administration, dissatisfied with Salan's leadership, sent Gen. John O'Daniel to interview the French commander and instruct him on how to win the war. Salan refused the American's advice and especially denied the parallels O'Daniel drew between the Korean conflict and the Indochina War. Furthermore, Salan was tepid on the politico-military solution of employing more Vietnamese in the French effort, claiming that the Vietnamese lacked the training to be officers. The Eisenhower administration's frustration with Salan, its insistence on dynamic leadership, and the French government's willingness to placate the U.S. government's desire for a winning outlook led to Salan's replacement by Navarre, to the Navarre Plan, and, eventually, to the French military defeat at Dien Bien Phu.

BIBLIOGRAPHY

HERRING, GEORGE C. *America's Longest War: The United States and Vietnam, 1950–1975.* 1979.

WALL, IRWIN M. *The United States and the Making of Postwar France, 1945–1954.* 1991.

VICTOR JEW

SAM Missiles. The SA-2 Guideline, the latest Soviet-made surface-to-air missile (SAM), appeared in the skies above North Vietnam in 1965. A two-stage, supersonic radar-guided missile measuring 10.6 meters (35 feet) long with a 1.8-meter (6-foot) wing span, the SA-2 carried a 130-kilogram (285-pound) warhead and was effective up to 26,000 meters (85,000 feet). U.S. pilots described the SA-2's appearance as a "flying telephone pole" and quickly devised evasive maneuvers, but multiple or undetected SAM launches could bring down even the best pilots. "If you can see Sam, you can usually escape," wrote pilot Jack Broughton about the "soul-searing" experience of dodging SAMs. North Vietnam fired nearly 6,000 SAMs before the bombing halt in 1968. Improved tactics reduced the kill rate from 5.7 percent in 1965 to 0.9 percent in 1968. When the bombing of North Vietnam resumed in 1972, the United States further minimized losses with electronic counter-measures (ECMs) and "Wild Weasel" aircraft equipped with radar-homing missiles that destroyed SAM sites on the ground. But SAMs still took such a heavy toll on B-52 bombers during Operation LINEBACKER II that pilots nearly mutinied before flight tactics were altered to avoid the missiles. After 1972, a new Soviet-made portable SAM, the shoulder-fired, heat-seeking SA-7 Strella (or Grail), inflicted frightful losses on low-flying strike aircraft and helicopters. U.S. Army Hawk missiles, the mainstay of U.S. air defense, were deployed around base areas but never used because North Vietnam made no air attacks on South Vietnam until the Spring Offensive of 1975.

BIBLIOGRAPHY

BEARDEN, THOMAS E. "What Really Happened in the Air Defense Battle of North Vietnam?" *Air Defense Magazine* (April–June 1976).

BROUGHTON, JACK. *Going Downtown: The War against Hanoi and Washington.* 1988.

BROUGHTON, JACK. *Thud Ridge.* 1985.

CLODFELTER, MARK. *The Limits of Air Power: The American Bombing of North Vietnam.* 1989.

DAVIS, LARRY. *Wild Weasel: The SAM Suppression Story.* 1986.

FOX, ROGER P. *Air Base Defense in the Republic of Vietnam, 1961–1973. 1979.*

NORDEEN, LON O., JR. *Air Warfare in the Missile Age.* 1985.

WERRELL, KENNETH P. *Archie, Flak, AAA, and SAM.* 1988.

GLEN GENDZEL

San Antonio Formula. In August 1967, the U.S. government secretly offered to stop bombing North Vietnam if the North Vietnamese agreed to enter productive peace negotiations immediately and not take advantage of the cessation. Henry Kissinger, then a private citizen, carried the message to the North Vietnamese. President Lyndon Johnson publicly announced the plan in San Antonio on 29 September. The North Vietnamese rejected the offer, because it did not promise a concrete role for the National Liberation Front (NLF) in peace negotiations.

BIBLIOGRAPHY

GOODMAN, ALLAN E. *The Lost Peace: America's Search for a Negotiated Settlement of the Vietnam War.* 1978.
PORTER, GARETH. *A Peace Denied: The United States, Vietnam, and the Paris Agreement.* 1975.

WILLIAM PAUL SCHUCK

Schlesinger, Arthur M., Jr. (1917–), special assistant to the president, 1961–1964. A historian and educator, Schlesinger was primarily involved in Latin American, European, and United Nations issues. He cautiously supported President Kennedy's involvement in South Vietnam, but he broke with President Johnson in 1965 and spoke out against the war, which Schlesinger blamed for "the ebbing away of belief in the American government" at home and abroad. Schlesinger's *The Bitter Heritage* (1966) criticized U.S. policy in the war. He later wrote antiwar speeches for Sen. Robert F. Kennedy and helped persuade him to run for president in 1968.

BIBLIOGRAPHY

SCHLESINGER, ARTHUR M., JR. *The Bitter Heritage: Vietnam and American Democracy.* 1966.
SCHLESINGER, ARTHUR M., JR. *The Crisis of Confidence: Ideas, Power and Violence in America.* 1969.
SCHLESINGER, ARTHUR M., JR. "A Middle Way out of Vietnam." *New York Times Magazine,* 18 September 1966.
SCHLESINGER, ARTHUR M., JR. *Robert Kennedy and His Times.* 1978.
SCHLESINGER, ARTHUR M., JR. *A Thousand Days: John F. Kennedy in the White House.* 1965.

GLEN GENDZEL

Schlesinger, James (1929–), director of the Central Intelligence Agency (CIA), 1973; secretary of Defense, 1973–1975. Schlesinger testified at the Watergate hearings that the CIA's involvement in the Pentagon Papers–related break-in of Daniel Ellsberg's psychiatrist's office was "ill advised." While he was secretary of defense, Schlesinger, like his predecessor Elliot Richardson and like William Rogers at the State Department, was largely by-passed in Vietnam policy-making by Henry Kissinger and Defense Secretary Melvin Laird. Schlesinger was considered a hard-liner and as secretary of defense made several speeches defending the bombing of Cambodia in 1969–1970. Schlesinger was unaware that President Nixon and Kissinger secretly promised Nguyen Van Thieu in 1973 that if North Vietnam violated the Paris peace accords, the United States would grant South Vietnam "full economic and military aid." When he learned of that promise a decade later, he was furious because he believed disclosing Nixon's pledge of aid at the time might have forced Congress to follow through. Moreover, he realized that the Nixon administration had deliberately deceived the government of South Vietnam.

By 1975, Schlesinger realized the United States could do little to change the course of events in Vietnam, and accordingly, he sought to downplay U.S. strategic interests and the dangers of a full-scale invasion by North Vietnam in violation of the peace agreement. In a January 1975 press conference he commented "I am not at this time anticipating a major country-wide offensive of the type of 1972." Schlesinger, who often disagreed with Kissinger, was fired in June 1975 in a shake-up of President Ford's defense and foreign policy team.

BIBLIOGRAPHY

HUNG NGUYEN TIEN and JERROLD L. SCHECHTER. *The Palace File.* 1986.
KUTLER, STANLEY. *The Wars of Watergate.* 1990.
OLSON, JAMES, and RANDY ROBERTS. *Where the Domino Fell.* 1991.

KELLY EVANS-PFEIFER

Seabees. Navy construction engineers, called Seabees—their name derived from the initials C. B., for Construction Battalion—were present in Vietnam from the onset of U.S. intervention in 1954. Most belonged to the 3d and 32d Naval Construction Regiments with headquarters in Saigon, later moved to Da Nang in 1967. Seabees built port facilities, air strips, roads, bridges, dams, warehouses, barracks, schools, hospitals, and refugee camps. Some of the more notable Seabee projects were the sprawling port at Cam Ranh Bay, the fortified Special Forces camps in the Central Highlands, the 6,000-meter (2,000-foot) Liberty Bridge over the Thu Bon River, and the U.S. Navy hospital at Da Nang.

In 1966, Seabee construction mechanic third class Marvin G. Shields received the navy's first Medal of Honor of the war. It was awarded posthumously for heroism in defense of the Civilian Irregular Defense Group (CIDG) camp at Dong Xoai on 9 June 1965.

BIBLIOGRAPHY

DUNN, CARROLL H. *Base Development in South Vietnam, 1965–1970*. 1972.

MAROLDA, EDWARD J., and G. WESLEY PRYCE III. *A Short History of the United States Navy and the Southeast Asian Conflict, 1950–1975*. 1984.

MERDINGER, CHARLES J. "Civil Engineers, Seabees, and Bases in Vietnam." *U.S. Naval Institute Naval Review* 96 (1970).

MIDDLETON, WILLIAM D. "Seabees in Vietnam." *U.S. Naval Institute Naval Proceedings* 93 (1967).

TREGASKIS, RICHARD. *Southeast Asia: Building the Bases: The History of Construction in Southeast Asia*. 1975.

GLEN GENDZEL

SEALs. Sea, Air, Land (SEAL) teams of the U.S. Navy are highly trained commandos who can attack the enemy from underwater as frogmen, from small speedboats, from helicopters, by high-altitude parachute drop, or by silent overland infiltration. Among the most elite of U.S. armed forces, SEALs first arrived in Vietnam in 1966, reaching a peak strength of about one hundred men in 1968. They typically operated in six-man squads and their training was well-suited to South Vietnam's jungle swamps and winding rivers. Most SEALs were attached to Task Force 116, the River Patrol Force stationed in the Mekong Delta and the Rung Sat Special Area. SEAL missions emphasized the element of surprise—night ambushes, reconnaissance patrols, underwater sabotage, and daring commando raids on Viet Cong guerrilla bases. SEALs took part in Operation GAME WARDEN (1965–1968) and Operation SEALORDS (1968–1969), which cut Viet Cong river supply lines from Cambodia. Some SEALs also performed top secret intelligence missions as part of the U.S. Military Assistance Command's Studies and Observation Group (SOG). "Mobile, versatile, and extremely effective in their dangerous work," the U.S. Navy's official history records, "the SEALs were a valuable resource in the riverine environment of Vietnam." SEALs themselves, who lost forty-three men killed in action, were most proud that not a single member of their team was captured or missing in Vietnam.

BIBLIOGRAPHY

BOSILJEVAC, T. L. *SEALs: UDT/SEAL Operations in Vietnam*. 1990.

MAROLDA, EDWARD J., and G. WESLEY PRYCE III. *A Short History of the United States Navy and the Southeast Asian Conflict, 1950–1975*. 1984.

U.S. NAVY. *Riverine Warfare: The Navy's Operations on Inland Waterways*. 1968.

WATSON, JAMES, and KEVIN DOCKERY. *Point Man: Inside the Toughest and Most Deadly Unit in Vietnam by a Founding Member of the Elite Navy SEALs*. 1993.

YOUNG, DARRYL. *The Element of Surprise: Navy Seals in Vietnam*. 1990.

GLEN GENDZEL

Search and Destroy. Search and destroy was the tactical implementation of the attrition strategy, which guided U.S. military efforts in the Vietnam War. The tactical role of U.S. troops in South Vietnam was unclear when they first arrived. Would they stay in coastal enclaves? Would they create secure areas for the population? Or would they pursue Viet Cong guerrillas in the countryside? The latter approach, dubbed "search and destroy," became the U.S. strategy for winning the Vietnam War. U.S. troops aggressively pursued enemy force concentrations and sought to initiate battles in hopes of inflicting decisive losses. Building a secure ally, bolstering the government, or protecting the population were deemed less important than killing Viet Cong forces; the former tasks were left to South Vietnamese forces. President Johnson approved the tactic in July 1965 after Gen. William Westmoreland and the Joint Chiefs of Staff predicted success with it. By mid 1967, more than 80 percent of U.S. battalion-size operations used search-and-destroy tactics. Westmoreland decided that only the inelegant and unpopular phrase, not the tactic, was flawed. "There was no alternative to 'search and destroy' type operations," he wrote in his memoirs, "except, of course, a different name for them." Later renamed "reconnaissance-in-force" and "pre-emptive operations," the strategy was used by U.S. forces until 1969. Then search and destroy was turned over to ARVN troops.

BIBLIOGRAPHY

KREPINEVICH, ANDREW F., JR. *The Army and Vietnam*. 1986.

LEWY, GUENTER. *America in Vietnam*. 1978.

PALMER, DAVE RICHARD. *Summons of the Trumpet: A History of the Vietnam War from a Military Man's Viewpoint*. 1978.

WESTMORELAND, WILLIAM C. *A Soldier Reports*. 1976.

GLEN GENDZEL

SEARCH AND DESTROY MISSION. Members of the 2d Platoon, Company D, 2d Battalion, 7th Cavalry, 1st U.S. Cavalry Division (Airmobile), on a search-and-destroy mission during Operation JEB STUART, 9 March 1968. Search-and-destroy missions were characterized by some who participated in them as "hours of boredom punctuated by moments of sheer terror." *U.S. Army*

Search and Rescue. Search-and-rescue (SAR) operations plucked more than 3,800 downed U.S. airmen from the swamps, jungles, hilltops, and open seas of Southeast Asia. Battle-proven in Korea, the U.S. Air Rescue Service (part of the U.S. Air Force) flew missions for the French in the 1950s, but no squadrons were stationed in Vietnam at the start of U.S. intervention. Official reluctance to admit growing U.S. involvement in the war slowed the development of SAR capability. Before the Third Aerospace Rescue and Recovery Group was formed in 1966, SAR operations relied on borrowed helicopters and Central Intelligence Agency (CIA) contract pilots. SAR units eventually operated out of air bases at Tan Son Nhut, Da Nang, and Tuy Hoa in South Vietnam, and at Udorn in Thailand. The key to successful SAR

in Vietnam was the advent of long-range helicopters—the H-3 Jolly Green Giant in 1965 and the HH-53 Super Jolly Green Giant in 1967. F-4 jets warded off North Vietnamese aircraft, A-1 Skyraiders flew close air support, and C-130 transport planes served as SAR airborne command posts. Navy ships at "Yankee Station" in the Gulf of Tonkin kept UH-2 Sea Sprite and SH-3 Sea King helicopters on SAR duty around the clock. Despite hazardous weather and terrain, SAR units rescued more than one-third of downed U.S. airmen, many of them critically wounded. They officially claimed 3,883 personnel rescued. "That Others May Live" was the motto of the Aerospace Rescue and Recovery Service (renamed in 1966). SAR personnel sometimes suffered heavy losses themselves because distress signals from downed pilots also attracted Viet Cong guerrillas, who deployed "flak traps" around crash sites and opened fire on vulnerable rescue helicopters.

BIBLIOGRAPHY

ANDERSON, WILLIAM C. *BAT 21.* 1983.

GLINES, CARROLL V., and JIMMY W. KILBOURNE, eds. *Escape and Evasion: 17 True Stories of Downed Pilots Who Made It Back.* 1973.

SHERSHUN, CARROLL S. "It's the Greatest Mission of Them All." *Aerospace Historian* 14 (1969).

TILFORD, EARL H., JR. *Search and Rescue in Southeast Asia, 1961–1975.* 1980.

GLEN GENDZEL

SEATO. *See* Southeast Asia Treaty Organization (SEATO).

Secret War. *See* Hmong; Laos; Thailand.

Selective Service. Created by the Selective Service Act of 1948, the Selective Service was a U.S. federal agency that drafted male citizens and residents aged eighteen to twenty-six to serve in the armed forces. If they met certain criteria, draft-age men could avoid induction into the armed services by qualifying for deferments of or exceptions from the draft obligation. Gen. Lewis B. Hershey, director of the agency from 1948 to 1969, advocated using deferments and exceptions for social engineering purposes. Rather than draft men randomly from all walks of life, Hershey preferred "channelling" them with "pressurized guidance." He believed that the draft—much like the tax code—could be used to encourage socially useful behavior: Hardship deferments would keep families clothed and fed; student deferments would keep young men in college; occupational exemptions would channel them into vital jobs as doctors, engineers, and scientists, or encourage them to join the National Guard, the Coast Guard, or the reserves. Hershey proclaimed that the Selective Service was "developing more effective human beings in the national interest," not just inducting young men into the military. Prior to the Vietnam War the main criticism of the Selective Service was that stringent mental and physical re-

RESCUE AT SEA. A U.S. Air Force HH-3 "Jolly Green Giant" picks up a downed pilot in Vietnamese waters. *National Archives*

quirements deprived unqualified men of the "benefits" of military life. But when draft calls increased from less than 10,000 to more than 30,000 per month in 1966, the Selective Service soon became extremely unpopular, and a lightning rod for antiwar protest.

The first outcry erupted over the capricious policies of local draft boards. Although nine out of ten Selective Service officials were military officers, Hershey insisted on civilian control at the local level. The four thousand decentralized draft boards consisted almost entirely of white middle-class war veterans. Often elderly, they were part-time unpaid volunteers with virtually no training, no staff help, and no sympathy for "misfits." Young men who appeared before them routinely were asked questions about their moral conduct and views on the war. Draft boards expected that military service would "rehabilitate" nonconformists and "punish" antiwar protestors. Hershey himself encouraged draft boards to threaten antiwar college students with the "club of induction" by stripping away their deferments. Carefully prepared draftees, however, could avoid service by feigning ailments, filing appeals, switching locales, or otherwise bending the rules. Local draft board policies were so inconsistent and arbitrary that legal challenges almost ground the system to a halt by the late 1960s. Draft counselors and attorneys became adept at postponing or preventing the induction of anyone who could afford their services. "If you got the dough," ran a popular slogan, "you don't have to go."

A second and more disturbing criticism of the Selective Service did not arise until near the end of the Vietnam War, when race and class discrimination became apparent in casualty figures. African Americans, for example, made up 11 percent of the U.S. male draft-age population, but 31 percent of combat troops in Vietnam—and 24 percent of U.S. Army combat deaths before 1970. Poor men of all races filled the draft rolls because relatively few of them went to college, escaped to Canada, or landed exempt jobs, and many inherited strong traditions of military service. Poor families could not hire draft lawyers, conscientious-objector counselors, sympathetic doctors, and others who might arrange exemptions for their sons. "Going to Vietnam was the penalty for those who lacked the wherewithal to avoid it," wrote draft researchers Lawrence Baskir and William Strauss. "The draftees who fought in Vietnam were primarily society's 'losers,' the same

men who get left behind in schools, jobs, and other forms of social competition." In 1965–1966, for example, only 2 percent of all draftees were college graduates. Hershey's hopes for social engineering through the draft turned into a Darwinian nightmare that sentenced the poor and uneducated to die in Asian jungles while affluent, privileged, or connected young men stayed home.

Out of 26.8 million draftable men who came of age during the Vietnam War, only 2.2 million were inducted by the Selective Service; 8.7 million enlisted voluntarily. Almost 16 million men, or over 60 percent of those eligible for the draft, avoided military service entirely during the Vietnam War—by legal means. Only 8,750 of an estimated 570,000 draft offenders were ever convicted. Such widespread draft evasion, combined with rampant inequality and an unpopular war, eventually discredited General Hershey's Selective Service. Dr. Curtis Tarr replaced Hershey in 1969 and introduced a random lottery, while sharply curtailing the controversial deferment policy. President Nixon revoked student deferments in 1971, by which time draft calls had fallen to insignificant levels anyway, and bid for public support by ending the draft completely on 27 January 1973. As the Selective Service was dismantled, defense experts warned that an all-volunteer force would be even more class-bound and professionally isolated from the rest of society. Since 1980, young men have been required to register with the federal government, raising the possibility of a renewed draft at any time.

BIBLIOGRAPHY

BASKIR, LAWRENCE M., and WILLIAM A. STRAUSS. *Chance and Circumstance: The Draft, the War, and the Vietnam Generation.* 1978.
DAVID, JAMES W., and KENNETH M. DOLBEARE. *Little Groups of Neighbors: The Selective Service System.* 1968.
GERHARDT, ROGER W., ed. *The Draft and Public Policy.* 1971.
GOTTLIEB, SHERRY GERSHON. *Hell No, We Won't Go: Resisting the Draft during the Vietnam War.* 1991.
KERLEY, GILLAM. "Do You Feel a Draft?" *The Progressive* 49 (March 1985).
MARMION, HARRY A. *Selective Service: Conflict and Compromise.* 1968.

GLEN GENDZEL

Sharp, Ulysses S. Grant, Jr.

Sharp, Ulysses S. Grant, Jr. (1906–), admiral, U.S. Navy; Commander-in-Chief, Pacific (CINCPAC), 1964–1968. "Oley" Sharp was one of the most hard-line proponents of the Vietnam War, which he supported as necessary to "stop communist-supported aggression." He succeeded Adm. Harry Felt as CINCPAC in June 1964, and after the Tonkin Gulf incident six weeks later, President Johnson approved Sharp's plan for immediate retaliatory airstrikes, the first U.S. bombing of North Vietnam. Sharp believed the war could be won "by keeping the pressure on North Vietnam through air attacks," and he often argued against bombing halts or target restrictions. Sharp insisted that "toughness" was "the only policy the communists understand." He retired in 1968, and a decade later, Sharp's memoirs voiced the popular "stab in the back" thesis about Vietnam: "The war was lost in Washington, not on the battlefield."

BIBLIOGRAPHY

"Imperturbable Admiral." *Time,* 21 December 1970.

SCHLIGHT, JON. *The United States Air Force in Southeast Asia: The War in South Vietnam: The Years of the Offensive, 1965–1968.* 1988.

SHARP, U. S. GRANT, JR. "Air Power Could Have Won in Vietnam." *Air Force Magazine* 54 (September 1971).

SHARP, ULYSSES S. GRANT, JR. "How to Win the War in South Vietnam." *U.S. News and World Report,* 28 March 1966.

SHARP, U. S. GRANT, JR. *Strategy for Defeat: Vietnam in Retrospect.* 1978.

SHARP, U. S. GRANT, JR., and WILLIAM C. WESTMORELAND. *Report on the War in Vietnam.* 1968.

"The Thinking Man's Admiral." *Life,* 28 March 1966.

GLEN GENDZEL

Sheehan, Neil (1936–), United Press International correspondent and Saigon bureau chief, 1962–1964; *New York Times* reporter. Early in the war, Sheehan exposed problems with the U.S. effort in Vietnam and the corruption of the Diem regime. In 1968, Sheehan broke the story of the large troop request by the Joint Chiefs of Staff following the Tet Offensive. Daniel Ellsberg later leaked the Pentagon Papers to Sheehan, who published them in the *Times.*

BIBLIOGRAPHY

HAMMOND, WILLIAM W. *Public Affairs: The Military and the Media 1962–1968.* 1989.

KARNOW, STANLEY. *Vietnam: A History.* 1991.

KELLY EVANS-PFEIFER

Short-timer, slang term for a U.S. soldier with relatively little time left on his 365-day tour of duty in Vietnam. In previous conflicts, U.S. soldiers had been assigned to combat duty for the duration of

SHORT-TIMER. A U.S. marine, his thirteen-month tour about to end, identifies his status with the plea "STOP!!! DON'T SHOOT I'M SHORT." *U.S. Marine Corps*

the war. However, in the Vietnam War, soldiers served for fixed periods of time. Consequently, they knew exactly how long they had to serve and could count the number of days until their assignment ended. Short-timers often became more reluctant to fight, and on occasion even refused to enter combat.

BIBLIOGRAPHY

SANTOLI, AL. *Everything We Had: An Oral History of the Vietnam War by Thirty-three American Soldiers Who Fought It.* 1981.

ELLEN D. GOLDLUST

Shoup, David M. (1904–1983), general, U.S. Marine Corps.

General Shoup was probably the highest ranking military officer to publicly oppose U.S. participation in the Vietnam War. Shoup entered the Marine Corps as a second lieutenant in July 1926. With pre–World War II service in China and Iceland, then-colonel Shoup commanded the 2d Marines, the spearhead regiment, in the assault on Tarawa in November 1943 and was awarded the Medal of Honor. On 1 January 1960, he became the twenty-second commandant of the Marine Corps. While commandant, Shoup counseled against U.S. involvement in Vietnam, but never openly questioned policy. He retired in 1963.

With the commitment of U.S. troops and an expanding war, General Shoup went public with his criticism. In May 1966, in a speech at Pierce College in California, he declared: "I don't think the whole of Southeast Asia . . . is worth the life and limb of a single American." After remaining relatively quiet for a period, in December 1967 Shoup stated in a radio interview that President Johnson's contention that the war was vital to U.S. interests was "pure, unadulterated poppycock." Finally, in April 1969 he charged in the *Atlantic Monthly* that "America has become a militaristic and aggressive nation."

BIBLIOGRAPHY

MILLETT, ALLAN R. *Semper Fidelis: The History of the United States Marine Corps.* Rev. ed., 1991.
SHOUP, DAVID M., and JAMES A. DONOVAN. "The New American Militarism." *Atlantic Monthly,* April 1969.

JACK SHULIMSON

SIGMA.

SIGMA was the codename for a series of highly detailed political and strategical war games played in the early 1960s to forecast potential outcomes of an expanded U.S. involvement in the conflict in Vietnam. The games were given top priority by the Johnson administration, and key administration figures participated as players, among them McGeorge Bundy, John T. McNaughton, and generals Curtis LeMay and Earle Wheeler.

Conducted by the U.S. Joint Chiefs of Staff, the games were designed and umpired by the RAND Corporation to ensure neutrality. During SIGMA I, played in late fall 1963, John McCone controlled the blue team, which represented the United States and the Republic of Vietnam. Maxwell D. Taylor headed the red team, which represented the Democratic Republic of Vietnam (DRV) and the Viet Cong, with William H. Sullivan as his deputy. SIGMA I resulted in a clear victory for the red team; despite the deployment of more than 500,000 U.S. troops, the communists controlled most of South Vietnam and Laos. The game indicated that the DRV could rapidly match U.S. deployments by infiltrating increased numbers of troops into the South and that U.S. bombing of the industrially undeveloped, predominantly rural DRV would have little deterrent effect on the North's policymakers. The game also forecast widespread U.S. domestic unrest.

Reaction among the players to the game's predictions was mixed. William Sullivan claims that John McCone found its results convincing and that "the experiences of that game made him a dove on Vietnam then and forever more." The outcome outraged General LeMay, then chief of staff of the air force, who claimed that the rules discounted the capabilities of air power. SIGMA II-64 was played in mid-September 1964 to forecast the impact of a U.S. air offensive against the DRV.

The second game essentially confirmed the results of SIGMA I, although changes in players led to a better outcome for the blue team. SIGMA II-65, played in August 1965, confirmed the results of the previous games, predicting that communist guerrilla tactics would pose serious difficulties for U.S. forces and that bombing the DRV would have fundamentally little impact. Robert McNamara claims to have been greatly disturbed by the results of SIGMA II-65; however, the games, though ultimately prophetic, had little influence on U.S. policy.

BIBLIOGRAPHY

HALBERSTAM, DAVID. *The Best and the Brightest.* 1992.

KREPINEVICH, ANDREW F., JR. *The Army and Vietnam.* 1986.

MCNAMARA, ROBERT S., and BRIAN VANDEMARK. *In Retrospect: The Tragedy and Lessons of Vietnam.* 1995.

SULLIVAN, WILLIAM H. *Obbligato: Notes on a Foreign Service Career.* 1984.

STEVEN J. TIRONE

Sihanouk, Norodom (1923–), ruling monarch of Cambodia, 1941–1955; premier, Cambodia, 1955–1970; Cambodian head of state, 1993. Sihanouk, while in his last year at the French lycée in Saigon, succeeded his great grandfather, King Sisowath Monivong, in 1941. Sihanouk received a French education and acquired a taste for French culture and language that he never lost.

Sihanouk and his people passively submitted to first Vichy French and then Japanese rule during World War II. When the Japanese overthrew the Vichy regime in Indochina on 10 March 1945, the French informed Sihanouk that his country was independent. Two days later, the prince proclaimed independence himself. When the French returned after the defeat of the Japanese, they attempted to reassert control by using measures designed to lessen Sihanouk's influence. The French decided to establish a parliamentary government, urging the promulgation of a constitution and permitting political parties. Sihanouk soon realized that only by championing real independence from France could he maintain his popularity and power. A charismatic leader, when he entered self-imposed exile after the outbreak of war against the French, he was widely loved despite his petulance and idiosyncracies.

The 1954 Geneva Conference proclaimed Cambodia's independence and neutrality and called for free elections. Sihanouk then abdicated his throne in favor of his father to form his own political party, which took as its theme loyalty to monarchy, Buddhism, and nation. Immensely popular among the peasantry, Sihanouk strongly championed neutrality and his continued leadership was assured. Only the communists, the intelligentsia, and politicians excluded from power opposed him.

With great political skill, he kept Cambodia out of the Vietnam War until 1969, despite North Vietnamese incursions, the Viet Cong forces' use of the eastern zone as a sanctuary, U.S. bombing raids, and cross-border operations on both sides. An army

NORODOM SIHANOUK. C. 1968. *National Archives*

coup in 1970 ousted him while he was visiting Paris, an event Sihanouk blamed on the Central Intelligence Agency. He lived in exile in Beijing and allied himself with the Khmer Rouge, even though they had killed members of his family. Cambodian prime minister Lon Nol allowed Sihanouk occasional visits to Cambodia.

During the Vietnamese invasion of Cambodia in 1978, Sihanouk headed a faction that attempted, without much success, to form a coalition with the Khmer Rouge and noncommunist groups to establish a government to end the war. After the Vietnamese withdrew in 1989, Sihanouk returned briefly as symbolic head of state in 1993 following U.N.-supervised elections, but left when violence resumed and Hun Sen took power. Even as his health declined, Sihanouk resumed the symbolic role of monarch.

BIBLIOGRAPHY

BECKER, ELIZABETH. *When the War Was Over.* 1986.

CHANDA, NAYAN. *Brother Enemy.* 1986.

KARNOW, STANLEY. *Vietnam: A History.* 1991.

KIERNAN, BENEDICT. *How Pol Pot Came to Power.* 1985.

SANDRA C. TAYLOR

Sihanouk Trail. *See* People's Army of Vietnam (PAVN).

"Silent Majority" Speech. President Richard Nixon delivered his "silent majority" speech on 3 November 1969. The speech followed large antiwar protests on 15 October and preceded large protests scheduled for 15 November. Some believed that Nixon would announce an accelerated withdrawal of troops from Vietnam to stem the protests.

Instead, Nixon vowed to continue the Paris peace negotiations and his policy of gradual withdrawal, called Vietnamization. More important, Nixon called on "the great silent majority" of Americans to support him and used conservative, patriotic rhetoric to attack antiwar protestors as cowardly, spoiled students and leftist agitators. The speech revealed Nixon's strategy to shift public focus away from the unpopular war by attacking protestors and his intentions to aggressively defy his opponents. It also generated, albeit temporarily, public support for Nixon's policies.

BIBLIOGRAPHY

AMBROSE, STEPHEN E. *Nixon: The Triumph of a Politician 1962–1972.* 1989.
NIXON, RICHARD M. *RN: The Memoirs of Richard Nixon.* 1978.

WILLIAM PAUL SCHUCK

Smart Bombs, weapons with some ability to direct themselves to a designated target using laser beams, television cameras, and computers (and, in later years, infrared detectors). These bombs were used beginning in 1967 to combat the increasing effectiveness of North Vietnamese antiaircraft defenses by reducing the importance of the initial aim while increasing the accuracy rate.

BIBLIOGRAPHY

DOLEMAN, EDGAR C., JR. *The Vietnam Experience: Tools of War.* 1984.
SHAFRITZ, JAY M., TODD J. A. SHAFRITZ, and DAVID B. ROBERTSON. *The Facts on File Dictionary of Military Science.* 1989.

ELLEN D. GOLDLUST

Smith, Walter Bedell (1895–1961), director, Central Intelligence Agency (CIA), 1950–1953; undersecretary of state, 1953–1954. Smith was head of the U.S. delegation to the Geneva Conference of 1954. Despite Secretary of State John Foster Dulles's instructions to play a passive role in the open negotiations, Smith worked behind the scenes to arrange a settlement preventing all of Vietnam from coming under communist control, by partitioning the country at the 17th parallel.

BIBLIOGRAPHY

CROSSWELL, D. K. R. *The Chief of Staff: The Military Career of General Walter Bedell Smith.* 1991.

PAUL M. TAILLON

Socialist Republic of Vietnam (SRV). *See* Vietnam; Vietnam, Democratic Republic of (DRV).

Song Be, South Vietnamese city; capital of Phuoc Long province, about 80 kilometers (50 miles) north of Saigon, near the Cambodian border. Viet Cong forces attacked and overran the town, a U.S. forces outpost, on 11 May 1965, inflicting severe casualties on the defenders, U.S. advisers and South Vietnamese troops. The Viet Cong forces withdrew after holding the town overnight. Attacked again by Viet Cong and NVA troops on 27 October 1967 in one of the pre–Tet Offensive border battles, Song Be was successfully defended by South Vietnamese troops aided by U.S. air support.

BIBLIOGRAPHY

DAVIDSON, PHILLIP B. *Vietnam at War—The History: 1946–1975.*
KARNOW, STANLEY. *Vietnam: A History.* 1991.

ELLEN D. GOLDLUST

Son Tay Raid. The largest and most celebrated of many U.S. prisoner-of-war (POW) rescue efforts in the Vietnam War was Operation KINGPIN, a joint U.S. Army–Air Force raid on the Son Tay prison camp outside Hanoi. The original plan, devised by Brig. Gen. Donald D. Blackburn and approved by President Nixon, was to stage a quick helicopter raid deep inside North Vietnam to free Americans believed held in Son Tay. Gen. Leroy J. Manor of the air force was overall task force commander and Col. Arthur D. "Bull" Simons took charge of the fifty-six Special Forces volunteers who trained secretly for three months in Florida. Despite last-minute intelligence reports that the prisoners had been moved, the operation went ahead on the night of 21 November 1970. Most of the assault force crash-landed in the wrong compound and no Americans were found in Son Tay. But the raiders killed scores of surprised defenders and returned without losing a single man. General Manor declared that the operation was "a complete success with the exception that no prisoners were rescued." Admiration for what President Nixon called the "incomparable bravery" of Colonel Simons and his raiders tempered criticism of the intelligence failure that led to raiding an empty camp. Only after the war did Americans learn that the Son Tay raid buoyed prisoner morale and forced North Vietnam to pool the scattered POWs together in Hanoi, where they felt less isolated and could support each other. In that sense, the Son Tay raid was quite successful in improving conditions for American POWs.

BIBLIOGRAPHY

"Freeing POWs." *New Republic,* 12 December 1970.
HARRIS, RICHARD. "Raid at Son Tay." *American History Illustrated* 25 (March/April 1990).
HUBBELL, JOHN G. *P.O.W.: A Definitive History of the American Prisoner-of-War Experience in Vietnam, 1964–1973.* 1976.
RUHL, ROBERT K. "Raid at Son Tay." *Airman* (August 1975).
SCHEMMER, BENJAMIN F. *The Raid.* 1976.

GLEN GENDZEL

Souphanouvong (1909–1995), titular head of the wartime Pathet Lao (Lao Nation) communist movement; deputy premier, minister of planning, and minister of reconstruction; first president of the Lao People's Democratic Republic (LPDR), 1975–1986. Prince Souphanouvong was a member of the Laotian royal family (Luang Prabang branch) and the younger half-brother of long-time Laotian prime minister Prince Souvanna Phouma. A leader in the post–World War II Lao Issara (Free Laos) independence movement, the prince became disenchanted with the group's political policies and sought

assistance from the Viet Minh. Souphanouvong became a close associate of Ho Chi Minh and a leader in the Viet Minh–supported Pathet Lao. Souphanouvong's decision to join the communists, despite his aristocratic origins, caused some journalists during the Vietnam War period to refer to him as the "Red Prince." The prince was by far the most visible member of the secretive Pathet Lao hierarchy and in 1957 and 1962 served in coalition governments, respectively, as minister of planning, and deputy premier and minister of reconstruction. Under strong right-wing and U.S. pressure, Pathet Lao participation in both governments was short-lived and Souphanouvong was eventually dropped from the government. Along with most of the Pathet Lao leadership, Souphanouvong spent much of the war in a cave complex in northeastern Laos. Following the U.S. withdrawal from Vietnam, the prince returned to the Lao capital and in mid 1974 joined the new coalition government as president of the newly formed National Political Consultative Council. This final royal Lao government, without U.S. support, was unable to resist Pathet Lao domination and eventually collapsed. In December 1975 the communists established the Lao People's Democratic Republic and Souphanouvong became its first president.

BIBLIOGRAPHY

BROWN, MACALISTER, and JOSEPH J. ZASLOFF. *Apprentice Revolutionaries: The Communist Movement in Laos, 1930–1985.* 1986.
CASTLE, TIMOTHY N. *At War in the Shadow of Vietnam: United States Military Aid to the Royal Lao Government, 1955–1975.* 1993.
DOMMEN, ARTHUR J. *Conflict in Laos.* 2d ed. 1971.
GOLDSTEIN, MARTIN E. *American Policy toward Laos.* 1973.
STEVENSON, CHARLES A. *The End of Nowhere: American Policy toward Laos since 1954.* 1972.
TOYE, HUGH. *Laos: Buffer State or Battlefield.* 2d ed. 1971.

TIMOTHY N. CASTLE

Southeast Asia Treaty Organization (SEATO). Following the 1954 Geneva Conference, U.S. Secretary of State John Foster Dulles negotiated the creation of a regional defense system for Southeast Asia paralleling that of the North Atlantic Treaty Organization (NATO). Signed in September 1954 (entered into force on 19 February 1955) as part of the Manila Pact, the SEATO pact included Australia, New Zealand, Pakistan, the Philippines, and Thailand, in addition to the western powers France, Great Britain, and the United States. Taiwan was excluded from the treaty because the treaty's definition of Southeast Asia did not include countries north of 21 degrees, 30 minutes north latitude. The neutral countries of India, Burma, and Indonesia refused to join, and because of restrictions imposed by the Geneva accords, Cambodia, Laos, and southern Vietnam could not participate.

The treaty established a council to provide for consultation among the signatories but did not include a unified military command as did the NATO agreement. Nevertheless, Dulles believed that the existence of the alliance would deter the expansion of communism in Southeast Asia. In the treaty's centerpiece, Article IV, the signatories agreed that in the event of "aggression by means of armed attack in the treaty area against any of the Parties or territory which the Parties by unanimous agreement may hereafter designate," they would "act to meet the common danger." They also agreed that "if the inviolability or the integrity of the territory or the sovereignty or political independence of any Party . . . is threatened . . . other than by armed attack," they would "consult immediately . . . for the common defense." A separate protocol specified Cambodia, Laos, and southern Vietnam as areas vital to the security of the signatories. This protocol, as Dulles explained, extended an "umbrella" to those countries.

In 1964, the pact provided President Lyndon Johnson with justification for U.S. military intervention to defend an anticommunist state in South Vietnam following the Gulf of Tonkin incident, even though he never consulted with SEATO allies. In 1969, President Richard Nixon, seeking to bring the war and domestic protest under control, initiated his policy of Vietnamization and denied that membership in SEATO guaranteed a commitment of U.S. troops. In the 1970s, differences appeared among the SEATO countries as they questioned the United States' conduct of the war in Vietnam. These divisions undermined SEATO's effectiveness, and the alliance disbanded in 1977.

BIBLIOGRAPHY

LaFeber, Walter. *America, Russia, and the Cold War, 1945–1990.* 1991.
Williams, William Appleman, Thomas McCormick, Lloyd Gardner, and Walter LaFeber, eds. *America in Vietnam: A Documentary History.* 1985.

Paul M. Taillon

South Vietnam. *See* Vietnam, Republic of (RVN).

Souvanna Phouma (1901–1984), prime minister of Laos, 1951–1954, 1956–1958, August–December 1960, 1962–1975. A member of the Laotian royal family (Luang Prabang branch) and older half-brother of Prince Souphanouvong, Souvanna Phouma was titular head of the wartime Pathet Lao (Lao Nation) communist movement. A proclaimed neutralist for most of his life, Souvanna was often called upon to head the politically fractured government of Laos. However, the prince was never able to bring conflicting pressures from North Vietnam and the United States sufficiently into balance to avoid Laotian entanglement in the Vietnam War. His willingness in the 1950s to allow participation in the central government by members of the Pathet Lao led to charges by right-wing Lao officials and the United States government that Laos would be taken over by communist agents. After 1962, Souvanna, acquiescing to pressure from the Lao right wing and the U.S. government, abandoned inclusion of the Pathet Lao in a coalition government. From 1963 until the 1973 American withdrawal from South Vietnam, Souvanna's government publicly declared a neutral policy with regard to the war in neighboring North Vietnam, South Vietnam, and Cambodia. In reality, however, the prime minister allowed the United States to conduct large-scale bombing and reconnaissance campaigns against communist supply routes in Laos and supported U.S. efforts to use Laotian hill tribes in ground and air operations against Pathet Lao and North Vietnamese military forces operating in Laos. Upon the December 1975 communist takeover of Laos, Souvanna was named special adviser to the president of the Lao People's Democratic Republic (LPDR).

BIBLIOGRAPHY

Brown, MacAlister, and Joseph J. Zasloff. *Apprentice Revolutionaries: The Communist Movement in Laos, 1930–1985.* 1986.
Castle, Timothy N. *At War in the Shadow of Vietnam: United States Military Aid to the Royal Lao Government, 1955–1975.* 1993.
Dommen, Arthur J. *Conflict in Laos.* 2d ed. 1971.
Goldstein, Martin E. *American Policy toward Laos.* 1973.
Stevenson, Charles A. *The End of Nowhere: American Policy toward Laos since 1954.* 1972.
Toye, Hugh. *Laos: Buffer State or Battlefield.* 2d ed. 1971.

Timothy N. Castle

SOUVANNA PHOUMA. At left, conferring with President Lyndon B. Johnson in the Rose Garden of the White House, Washington, D.C., 20 October 1967. *National Archives*

Special Forces, ARVN. One of South Vietnam's earliest attempts at clandestine warfare against North Vietnam began in February 1956 when a select group consisting of Nung tribal mercenaries, Vietnamese previously trained by French intelligence authorities, defectors from North Vietnam, and volunteers from Ngo Dinh Diem's security guards became the nucleus of the 1st Observation Group (1st O.G.). Funded by the U.S. Military Assistance Program (MAP) and organized by the Central Intelligence Agency (CIA), the 1st O.G.'s primary mission was to reduce North Vietnam's capacity to subvert the South Vietnamese government. Accordingly, some 300 men (20 15-man teams) began training supervised by U.S. Army Special Forces (USASF) and U.S. Ranger advisers at 1st O.G.'s Nha Trang headquarters. During the next seven years insertion teams of the 77th Group (1st O.G.'s later designation and a companion unit, the 31st Group, carried out kidnappings, assassinations, intelligence gathering, and sabotage inside Cambodia, Laos, and North Vietnam, usually accompanied by U.S. personnel.

Operations inside North Vietnam were generally unsuccessful, and the exact number of personnel lost, killed, or captured north of the 17th Parallel remains obscure. Success rates in Cambodia and Laos were higher. As Viet Cong activities increased in South Vietnam after 1960, the role of the 77th and 31st groups was altered. For the next three years, both groups spent most of their time performing covert duties within South Vietnam against the National Liberation Front (NLF) and against noncommunist groups in order to protect Diem's unstable government. On 15 March 1963, the 31st and 77th groups were renamed the Luc Luong Dac Biet (LLDB, South Vietnamese Special Forces) and, like its predecessors, remained outside the chain of command of the Army of the Republic of Vietnam (ARVN). Instead, the LLDB's groups were operational components within the Presidential Liaison Office (PLO) and were accountable only to Diem and his brother Nhu, which rapidly polarized this force from the ARVN's Joint General Staff (JGS).

The LLDB, in conjunction with South Vietnam's Central Intelligence Organization (CIO, founded in

May 1961 with a staff of 1,400), monitored the activities of the Can Lao Nhan Vi Cach Mang Dang (Revolutionary Personalist Labor Party) and its members. Created by Diem and Nhu in 1954, the Can Lao offered political careers and business connections to Ngo family loyalists, who were carefully investigated before selection. Commanded by Col. Le Quang Tung, a 45-year-old Annamese Catholic who had trained for the priesthood, the LLDB also worked closely with Nhu's secret police, headed by Dr. Tran Kim Tuyen. Together they recruited and trained the Cong Hoa (Republican) Youth, a sociopolitical organization of nearly 1 million adolescents in forty-three chapters nationwide. The Cong Hoa's largest unit (6,000 members) was in Saigon, and it, in conjunction with Madam Nhu's Women's Solidarity Movement, whose members were young women aged 12–25 years, acted as the eyes and ears of the government in the streets. Not unexpectedly, the LLDB's close association with the CIO, secret police, Can Lao, and Cong Hoa Youth made its members a target after the November 1963 coup that resulted in Diem's and Nhu's deaths.

During the coup Colonel Tung and his brother, Maj. Le Quang Trieu, the LLDB's deputy commander, were also killed. For the next five months army officials debated the LLDB's future as a nonpolitical unit within the ARVN. On 1 April 1964 the LLDB, now commanded by Gen. Doan Can Quang, was attached to the ARVN's Ranger and Reconnaissance Command as an independent unit, but its activities were carefully monitored by the JGS. LLDB soldiers participated in many projects, some highly classified, including the Phoenix program, the Civilian Irregular Defense Group (CIDG) network, and covert missions initiated by the Military Assistance Command, Vietnam–Studies and Observations Group (MACV-SOG). The LLDB's largest, and least successful, operation occurred with the CIDGs, an immense network of ethnic minorities and montagnards funded and trained with CIA-USASF resources. Historically, the South Vietnamese considered such minorities inferior, especially the semi-primitive mountain tribes, and this diminished effective cooperation and a mutual sense of purpose between the LLDB and its Central Highland militia. Command and control was frequently strained, a factor that contributed to an unsuccessful rebellion in September 1964 by tribal groups loyal to the Front Unifié de Lutte de la Race Opprimée (FULRO).

The degree to which the tribal minorities influenced the war cannot be underestimated; they provided intelligence, acted as scouts, and in many cases became effective guerrilla soldiers. Thus, the South Vietnamese, despite their racist attitudes, needed the assistance they received from the montagnards, and USASF and Australian Special Air Service (SAS) advisers acted as intermediaries when clashes occurred between the LLDB and the montagnards. Ultimately, however, the advisers could not exercise complete jurisdiction because the South Vietnamese were technically, though not realistically, in charge of these programs. During the period of Vietnamization (1969–1972), the number of U.S. advisers was reduced, then eliminated, which forced the LLDB to assume complete control over tens of thousands of ethnic troops, which the ethnic troops resented.

The attitude of the South Vietnamese, combined with drastic U.S. financial cutbacks, effectively ended these special programs. Without U.S. assistance, tribal groups attempted to resume traditional life-styles, but their prior support for U.S. and South Vietnamese activities made neutrality difficult, if not impossible, as North Vietnamese Army (NVA) and Viet Cong forces threatened retribution if they did not support North Vietnam's war effort. As the montagnard network dissolved, the South Vietnamese lost a valuable ally. LLDB units were withdrawn and reassigned to the ARVN Ranger and Reconnaissance units along with their comrades who had previously worked with MACV-SOG. By 1975, all large-scale covert operations by the LLDB had ceased.

The degree to which the LLDB force, at most 3,000 officers and men, can be considered "Special Forces" remains controversial. Critics point out that this designation is not applicable when its training, duties, and responsibilities are compared with those of similarly named units in other countries. However, South Vietnam's Special Forces, like the ARVN, did fight with determined professionalism on many occasions, although their accumulated internal shortcomings gradually wore both forces down. Observed as a whole, the degree of psychological fortitude ingrained within NVA and Viet Cong forces was not present in the ARVN on a long-term basis, despite the efforts of many.

BIBLIOGRAPHY

KELLY, FRANCIS J. *U.S. Army Special Forces, 1961–1971.* 1973.
RESKE, CHARLES F. *MACV-SOG Command History, Annex B. Vols. 1 and 2.* 1990.
SIMPSON, CHARLES M., III. *Inside the Green Berets.* 1983.
STANTON, SHELBY. *Green Berets at War.* 1985.

THOMAS R. CANTWELL

Special Forces, U.S. Army. Known as the Green Berets for their distinctive headgear, the U.S. Army Special Forces were organized in 1952. Their original mission was to wage guerrilla war and organize resistance behind enemy lines. In the early 1960s, President Kennedy made the Special Forces the centerpiece of his counterinsurgency strategy for combating "wars of national liberation" in developing countries. Kennedy expanded the Special Forces from 2,500 to 10,000 members and emphasized counterguerilla tactics in their training. At the Special Warfare Center in Ft. Bragg, North Carolina, the Green Berets learned how to beat guerrillas at their own game of unconventional warfare by combining civic action with political subversion and psychological operations. The first test of their new counterinsurgency mission came in Operation WHITE STAR, during which Green Berets trained local militias to resist the communist Pathet Lao in Laos in 1962.

Most of the Green Berets who served in Vietnam belonged to the 5th Special Forces Group, with headquarters in Nha Trang. Members of the 1st and 7th Special Forces Groups also served. Some were assigned to the U.S. Military Assistance Command's Studies and Observation Group (SOG) for top secret intelligence operations, and many helped train the South Vietnamese special forces of Luc Luong Dac Biet (LLDB). But most Green Berets fought a lonely and perilous war from desolate hilltops accessible only by helicopter. They took over a Central Intelligence Agency (CIA) operation that organized Civilian Irregular Defense Groups (CIDGs) among the montagnard tribesmen of the Central Highlands in 1963. A chain of forts manned by CIDG local self-defense forces and Green Beret advisers screened South Vietnam's border from infiltration from the North. After 1965, mixed teams of Green Berets and LLDB conducted long-range reconnaissance missions into Laos and directed air strikes against the Ho Chi Minh Trail. Although quite effective at defending their villages, the CIDGs were never popular with high-level U.S. commanders, who considered them a manpower drain outside the overall war effort. Gen. Harold Johnson, U.S. Army chief of staff, toured the CIDG camps and complained that Green Berets had "buried themselves in concrete" and become "fugitives from responsibility," who resisted military discipline. CIDGs were even less popular with South Vietnam's government, which accused the Special Forces of fomenting montagnard separatism and ended the program in 1968. As a result, the achieve-

KENNEDY'S INTEREST IN SPECIAL FORCES. The president confers with Brig. Gen. William P. Yarborough, a Green Beret, at the U.S. Army Special Warfare Center, Fort Bragg, October 1961. *U.S. Army*

ments of 2,500 members of the Special Forces who raised an army of 40,000 tribesmen in remote and hostile territory were often overlooked. Green Berets earned seventeen Medals of Honor and eighty-eight Distinguished Service Crosses in the Vietnam War.

BIBLIOGRAPHY

KELLY, FRANCIS J. *U.S. Army Special Forces, 1961–1971.* 1973.
SIMPSON, CHARLES M. *Inside the Green Berets: The First Thirty Years.* 1983.
STANTON, SHELBY L. *The Green Berets at War.* 1986.
STARR, MARK. "Green Grow the Green Berets." *Newsweek,* 10 October 1983.

GLEN GENDZEL

Spellman, Francis Joseph (1889–1967), cardinal (1946–); Roman Catholic archbishop of New York (1939–). Spellman was an active, influential promoter of the Catholic Ngo Dinh Diem regime in South Vietnam. In keeping with the Catholic Church's view of communism as inherently evil and the opinion of some American Catholics that the Cold War was a moral crusade, Spellman consistently supported U.S. military intervention in Vietnam.

BIBLIOGRAPHY

MECONIS, CHARLES A. *With Clumsy Grace: The American Catholic Left, 1961–1975.* 1979.

JENNIFER FROST

Spock, Benjamin (1903–), author; pediatrician. Dr. Spock's trusted reputation as America's preeminent child care authority earned him a leading role in U.S. domestic opposition to the Vietnam War. He first became known as a peace activist when he joined the National Committee for Sane Nuclear Policy in 1962. As the United States became involved in the Vietnam War, Spock, an active speaker and participant in numerous protests, attempted to unite moderate and radical antiwar groups. He published an antiwar treatise, *Dr. Spock on Vietnam,* written with Mitchell Zimmerman, in 1968. In January 1968, Spock was indicted for conspiring to aid and encourage resistance to the draft. He was convicted, but the verdict was overturned on appeal and the charges were eventually dropped.

BIBLIOGRAPHY

MITFORD, JESSICA. *The Trial of Dr. Spock, The Rev. William Sloane Coffin, Jr., Michael Ferber, Mitchell Goodman, and Marcus Raskin.* 1969.

SPOCK, BENJAMIN, M.D., and MARY MORGAN. *Spock on Spock: A Memoir of Growing Up with the Century.* 1989.

WILLIAM PAUL SCHUCK

State, Department of. U.S. State Department officials often offered advice on the proper course of action for the United States to follow during the Vietnam War, but theirs was not the dominant voice in decision making, especially during the period of escalation in the middle 1960s and during the negotiations arranging a cease-fire in the early 1970s. With several significant exceptions, representatives from the Department of Defense or the Central Intelligence Agency (CIA) and the presidents' personal representatives had more influence over the course of U.S. policy toward Vietnam than did the State Department. The State Department's subordinate role resulted from three factors: early differences of opinion within the department between representatives in Vietnam, who favored accommodation with Ho Chi Minh, and higher officers in Washington, who perceived events in Southeast Asia as part of a global struggle with communism; the legacy of Sen. Joseph McCarthy's accusations of communist sympathies among Foreign Service officers; and the dominant influence of the Pentagon and the commanders of the Military Assistance Command, Vietnam (MACV) in Saigon once the United States escalated the war.

The pattern began at the very end of World War II when the War Department persuaded President Harry S. Truman not to follow the advice of Assistant Secretary of State Abbott Low Moffat, who recommended a U.S. overture to Ho Chi Minh. In the late 1940s Foreign Service officers in Southeast Asia recommended that the U.S. government distance itself from France and pursue better relations with Ho. Secretary of State Dean Acheson and other high State Department officials concerned with European affairs overruled the U.S. consuls in Hanoi and Saigon. These higher officials persuaded Truman that maintaining good relations with France at a time of Cold War competition with the Soviet Union took precedence over establishing cordial relations with the Democratic Republic of Vietnam (DRV). A few years later, McCarthy made his wild charges about communist infiltration of the State Department, and Foreign Service officers became reluctant to express opinions that might be construed as sympathetic to communist movements or governments. Secretary of State John Foster Dulles played a more significant role in supporting the South Vietnamese government of Prime Minister, later President, Ngo Dinh Diem. Dulles resisted U.S. participation in the Geneva Conference of 1954 because he believed that the United States could exert its influence through Diem. To do so, however, Dulles overruled Gen. J. Lawton Collins, the State Department's representative in Vietnam, and followed the suggestions of the CIA's Gen. Edward Lansdale.

As the U.S. military presence in Vietnam increased in the early 1960s, a variety of U.S. agencies in Washington and Saigon competed for preeminence. During the Kennedy administration, Secretary of Defense Robert McNamara overshadowed Secretary of State Dean Rusk in setting policy toward Vietnam. In Saigon, generals Paul Harkins, William Westmoreland, and Creighton Abrams often had more influence than did the U.S. ambassador, despite Kennedy's directive that the chief of mission was to coordinate all U.S. activities in Vietnam. Kennedy believed that ambassadors Elbridge

U.S. AID. Vietnamese peasant women ferry sacks of rice, part of U.S. food aid distributed by State Department programs. *National Archives*

Durbrow and Frederick Nolting did not forcefully represent U.S. positions to Diem. In late spring 1963, the Kennedy administration appointed Henry Cabot Lodge, a prominent Republican, U.S. ambassador to South Vietnam. Lodge's appointment augmented the State Department's influence. In late summer and fall of 1963, Lodge, working with the local CIA chief and staff members of the national security council, assisted dissident South Vietnamese generals in two plots to overthrow the Nhu family. The State Department also became more important in the administration of President Lyndon B. Johnson. From late 1963 until early 1966 both Secretary of State Rusk and Secretary of Defense McNamara agreed that the United States should escalate the war. During these years Rusk saw little room for diplomatic initiatives to end the war, and he did not visit South Vietnam. Until mid 1966, McNamara continued to dominate the timing of escalation, but he then expressed misgivings about the course the United States was following in Vietnam. By late 1967 McNamara had changed his mind about the effectiveness of bombing North

Vietnam, and Johnson subsequently relied more on advice from prowar Rusk in the latter stages of his presidency.

The secretary of state convinced Johnson that the North Vietnamese did not seriously want negotiations on any terms other than what Johnson would consider a surrender of the U.S. position. Yet Johnson, in opposition to Rusk's views, announced on 31 March 1968 that he was stopping the bombing above the nineteenth parallel and opening negotiations with North Vietnam. The influence of the State Department fell to its lowest level during the administration of Richard Nixon. While State Department officials David Bruce and Philip Habib conducted the formal talks with North Vietnamese representatives in Paris, Henry Kissinger, the president's national security adviser, undertook the real negotiations that led to the Paris accords of 1973. Kissinger was secretary of state as well as national security adviser at the end of the war. Graham Martin, the last U.S. ambassador to South Vietnam, advised him and President Gerald Ford to provide additional aid to the South Vietnamese government, but political realities and public opinion in the United States made it impossible. Throughout the war the State Department's role was often to confirm decisions made elsewhere. Rarely did the State Department exercise decisive influence over Vietnam policy.

[*See also* Agency for International Development (AID); United States Information Agency (USIA).]

BIBLIOGRAPHY

KAHIN, GEORGE MCT. *Intervention: How America Became Involved in Vietnam.* 1986.
KARNOW, STANLEY. *Vietnam: A History.* 2d ed. 1991.
RUSK, DEAN. *As I Saw It.* 1990.

ROBERT D. SCHULZINGER

Stevenson, Adlai E., III (1900–1965), U.S. ambassador to the United Nations, 1961–1965. In 1964 Stevenson discussed with U.N. Secretary General U Thant the prospects for secret United States–North Vietnam negotiations. Stevenson passed the information on to Secretary of State Dean Rusk, but the administration, allegedly suspicious of North Vietnam's intentions and preferring to wait until after the 1964 election, did not respond. Although he believed that military intervention should be a last resort after all diplomatic efforts have been exhausted, Stevenson consistently defended U.S. policy in Vietnam, including in an interview on the BBC in London the evening before his death in 1965.

BIBLIOGRAPHY

KAHIN, GEORGE MCT. *Intervention: How America Became Involved in Vietnam.* 1986.
MARTIN, JOHN BARTLOW. *Adlai Stevenson and the World: The Life of Adlai E. Stevenson.* 1977.

KELLY EVANS-PFEIFER

Stilwell, Richard G. (1917–1991), general, U.S. Army; chief of staff, U.S. Military Assistance Command, Vietnam (MACV), 1964–1965. General Stilwell was a respected military intellectual with years of service with the Central Intelligence Agency (CIA) when he went to Saigon in 1963. Gen. Paul Harkins made him chief of operations and promoted him to chief of staff a year later. He commanded a field corps in Vietnam and United Nations forces in Korea before retiring in 1976.

BIBLIOGRAPHY

HALBERSTAM, DAVID. *The Best and the Brightest.* 1972.
STILWELL, RICHARD G. "Evolution in Tactics: The Vietnam Experience." *Army* 20 (February 1970).

GLEN GENDZEL

Stockdale, James B. (1923–), vice admiral, U.S. Navy. A wing commander aboard the USS *Oriskany,* Vice Adm. James Stockdale was shot down on his two-hundredth mission over North Vietnam on 9 September 1965. Hanoi tried to turn Stockdale into a propaganda tool as the highest-ranking prisoner of war (POW), but he defied his captors despite nearly eight years of torture and solitary confinement. Instead, through messages tapped out on prison walls, Stockdale encouraged other POWs to resist. His wife Sybil Stockdale founded the League of Wives of American Vietnam POWs. Promoted after his release in 1973, Stockdale received the Medal of Honor in 1976. He ran for the vice presidency with independent presidential candidate H. Ross Perot in 1992.

BIBLIOGRAPHY

ROSENBAUM, DAVID E. "Eager to Face the Test: James Bond Stockdale." *New York Times,* 2 October 1992.
STOCKDALE, JAMES. *A Vietnam Experience.* 1985.
STOCKDALE, JAMES, and SYBIL STOCKDALE. *In Love and War.* 1984. Rev. ed., 1990.

GLEN GENDZEL

Strategic Hamlet Program. *See* Free-fire Zones; Pacification; Rules of Engagement.

Strategy and Tactics

By 1963, the United States' involvement in the Republic of South Vietnam's (RVN) struggle against indigenous and externally supported insurgents was well-grounded in the Cold War policy of containment. The U.S. military assistance program, limited in 1963 to advising, training, and supporting the Republic of Vietnam Armed Forces (RVNAF), was part of a global strategy designed to strengthen the military forces of noncommunist nations on the rim of the communist bloc to deter communist expansion and to cope with internal subversion. Between 1963 and 1975, as military success eluded the U.S. and its allies in the Vietnam War, U.S. strategy and tactics evolved through several phases.

Counterinsurgency, 1963–1965. Having initially nurtured the RVNAF to resist a conventional invasion by its communist neighbor to the north—the Democratic Republic of Vietnam (DRV)—U.S. military assistance by 1963 had begun to devote its efforts to strengthening South Vietnam's counterinsurgency program against the Viet Cong insurgents. Spurred by President John F. Kennedy's interest in developing a U.S. strategy to oppose communist wars of national liberation, military counterinsurgency became part of the repertoire of military strategies subsumed under the strategy of flexible response to address sub-limited, unconventional forms of conflict. The war in South Vietnam became its principal testing ground.

In 1963, the insurgents were in the first, or guerrilla warfare, phase of a three-phase strategy of protracted revolutionary war that the DRV's leaders espoused. Subsequent phases consisted of a combination of guerrilla and conventional warfare, a transitional phase, moving in the last phase to conventional military operations. Although numerically inferior and equipped with few modern weapons, the Viet Cong guerrilla movement had grown stronger since 1961. Among the guerrillas' most important strategic assets were the reservoir of support among the rural population of South Vietnam and the virtually uninhibited support from the DRV through infiltration. For the most part, they enjoyed the tactical advantage of choosing the time and place to engage the South Vietnamese military, thereby creating the maximum opportunity for success. Their strategic objective, however, was not the defeat of the Army of the Republic of Vietnam (ARVN), but to translate military success into political advantage by increasing their control over the rural population and undermining the political will of its opponents through military actions.

The Viet Cong forces' military challenge of a strong ARVN force at the village of Ap Bac in the opening days of 1963 was an inauspicious sign for South Vietnam's counterinsurgency efforts. At Ap Bac the Viet Cong forces demonstrated a potential to mount conventional multibattalion operations and to execute effective countermeasures against U.S. helicopters, whose introduction during 1961–1962 had initially thrown the insurgents off balance. Despite their success

INFANTRYMAN. A soldier of the 1st Platoon, Company A, 9th U.S. Infantry Division eats his C-rations in the platoon's night camp, December 1968. *Department of Defense*

at Ap Bac, which presaged a change in military strategy in the South, the insurgents assiduously sought to undermine South Vietnam's principal effort to pacify rural areas, the Strategic Hamlet program. Most of the newly constructed hamlets were vulnerable to Viet Cong depredations, and the inability of the South Vietnamese government to provide security and to follow through with promised economic and social reforms led to popular disaffection with the program. President Ngo Dinh Diem's preoccupation with Buddhist demonstrations in the summer of 1963 further contributed to the neglect of the strategic hamlets and to a general reduction in the RVNAF's activities.

The Viet Cong insurgents quickly filled the vacuum created in the countryside by the reduction of counterinsurgency operations by South Vietnam in the summer and fall of 1963. The Viet Cong guerrillas' newly gained access to the rural population enabled them to improve their strategic position by obtaining new recruits, supplies, and money through contributions and taxes. In many rural areas, the Viet Cong shadow government, or infrastructure, was the only viable political presence. The United States was not aware of the extent of the deterioration of rural security until after the coup that led to Diem's downfall in November 1963.

Reassessing the situation in South Vietnam in the wake of that coup and the assassination of President Kennedy later in November, some Americans questioned the efficacy of a strategy limited to advice and support, which had prevailed since 1955. Despite the mobility and firepower provided by U.S. Army and Marine helicopters, the use of fixed-wing U.S. Air Force fighters for close air support and interdiction, the introduction of armored personnel carriers to enhance cross-country mobility, an improved communication system, and an infusion of advisers and U.S. Army Special Forces, the RVNAF was unable to translate this assistance into tactical advantage. The RVNAF's operations were stereotyped and predictable; its commanders were predisposed to conducting large sweeps or search-and-destroy operations that alerted the insurgents, precluded contact, and minimized casualties. Such operations posed little threat to the Viet Cong forces and contributed little to the counterinsurgency effort, particularly to the problem of separating the insurgents from the population. The more austerely armed and equipped paramilitary forces, the Regional and Popular Forces, absorbed the brunt of the Viet Cong forces' onslaught against South Vietnam's counterinsurgency programs.

Searching for ways to improve the RVNAF's performance and to revive South Vietnam's flagging pacification efforts, the United States was slow to change its strategy. The United States dispatched advisers to lower echelons of the RVNAF and to the district level to improve the tactical effectiveness and to better assist the South Vietnamese in coordinating military and political operations in support of pacification and provided more helicopters, naval craft, and aircraft to support South Vietnamese military efforts. Additional U.S. Special Forces were sent to work among the montagnard tribal groups of the Central Highlands. The Viet Cong insurgents, continuing to grow in strength and size, convincingly demonstrated their capacity for conventional military operations by amassing a multiregimental (or perhaps division-size) force that defeated RVNAF units at the village of Binh Gia in December 1964.

Expanding the War, 1965. Frustrated by the lack of progress in the counterinsurgency effort in the South, U.S. policymakers, on the assumption that North Vietnam exercised control over the Viet Cong forces in the South, increasingly shifted the focus of their military strategy to North Vietnam. Through a strategy of gradually increasing military pressures against military and economic targets in North Vietnam and the Ho Chi Minh Trail in Laos, U.S. officials hoped to reduce and eventually end North Vietnamese support of the Viet Cong forces and to attain a political settlement that preserved South Vietnam's independence. As a corollary to this strategy, U.S. policymakers also assumed that if South Vietnam fully mobilized its counterinsurgency efforts, it could quell the insurgency once the insurgents had been denied external aid. Given North Vietnam's long-held strategic goal of unifying Vietnam, however, North Vietnamese leaders were unlikely to capitulate to such pressures. A more realistic goal was that mounting military pressure might induce North Vietnam to enter negotiations.

The extension of the war to the North began in 1964 in the form of covert cross-border operations and maritime raids. These served a demonstrative purpose at best, signaling that North Vietnam was no longer immune from attack. This message was accented by punitive retaliatory air strikes by carrier-based aircraft in August 1964 following North Vietnam's attack on U.S. destroyers in the Gulf of Tonkin. Near the end of 1964, U.S. air and naval aircraft began interdiction attacks against the Ho Chi Minh Trail in Laos in Operation BARREL ROLL. Following additional retaliatory air strikes against North Vietnam in February 1965 in the wake of attacks on U.S. facilities at Pleiku and Qui Nhon, the United States, on 2 March, launched Operation ROLLING THUNDER, a program of sustained air strikes against North Vietnam. At about the same time, the U.S. Navy instituted Operation MARKET TIME to stop infiltration by sea from the North into the South.

By overtly expanding the war to North Vietnam, ROLLING THUNDER represented a major departure for U.S. strategy. As the principal military means of exerting pressure against the DRV, ROLLING THUNDER was tied to a strategic concept of gradually increasing military pressure, which allowed U.S. national leaders to limit or increase the intensity of the air campaign by their choice of targets. Hobbled by rules of engagement designed to avoid provoking the People's Republic of China (PRC) and to minimize damage to Hanoi and Haiphong, ROLLING THUNDER initially lacked the force necessary to compel North Vietnam's leaders to alter their policy and the military effectiveness to interdict the flow of men and matériel from the North. It was also punctuated by intermittent pauses to test the DRV's willingness to negotiate, adding further ambiguity to ROLLING THUNDER's strategic purposes.

As the onset of direct air attacks against the North changed the Vietnam War from a largely counterinsurgency effort to a limited war, the quickening of Viet Cong guerrilla activity and the infiltration of regular North Vietnamese Army (NVA) units into the South changed the strategic contours of the war in the South. The uncertainty of the DRV's response to U.S. bombing, a buildup of Viet Cong and NVA forces in the South, and South Vietnam's precarious military and political situation spurred interest among U.S. government and military officials in the introduction and future role of U.S. ground combat forces.

Westmoreland's Strategy. The first U.S. ground combat forces to be deployed to South Vietnam in March 1965, had a defensive mission, the security of air bases in the South from which operations against North Vietnam were launched. Except for releasing some RVNAF units from static security duties for operations against Viet Cong forces, these initial deployments were devoid of any strategic concept that related U.S. ground forces to the larger concerns of counterinsurgency in the South. The lodgment of Marines at Da Nang and Chu Lai and a U.S. Army brigade at Bien Hoa and Vung Tau between March and early May nevertheless implied a more permanent commitment of U.S. military forces

THE U.S. ADVISORY EFFORT. Sgt. Stanley Harold and Capt. Robert Lopez, both Green Berets, instruct ARVN soldiers in marksmanship using live ammunition, 1965. Note the World War II–era M1 rifles the soldiers have been issued. *National Archives*

to the war than did the sporadic air strikes against the North, which could be stopped on short notice.

Lyndon B. Johnson, who succeeded to the presidency after Kennedy was assassinated and was elected in his own right one year later, approached the use of ground forces in the South with the same caution that he had used when developing his strategy for the application of air power in the North. He rejected the recommendations of Army Chief of Staff Gen. Harold K. Johnson to send two U.S. divisions to South Vietnam's Central Highlands or to extend a multidivision force across the Laotian panhandle to interdict the Ho Chi Minh Trail. In April 1965, the president sanctioned a change in the Marines' mission from a strictly defensive one to one that included a phase-in of offensive counterinsurgency operations. The conversion from defensive to offensive operations was to proceed in measured increments, moving outward from the secure perimeters of established coastal enclaves over a period of about three months. Despite the addition of an offensive mission, ground forces remained tied to an operational concept rooted in defensive, albeit expanded, enclaves.

To move U.S. ground forces into a more offensive military posture, Gen. William C. Westmoreland, Commander, U.S. Military Assistance Command, Vietnam (COMUSMACV), obtained permission to use Marine and army ground forces in South Vietnam as reserve/reaction forces in acute situations anywhere in the South. This so-called fire brigade concept together with the establishment of enclaves was the dominant U.S. ground war strategy during the initial stages of the buildup. Given the limited number of U.S. ground units in South Vietnam in the spring and summer of 1965, Westmoreland had little choice but to embrace these operational concepts as essentially economy-of-force measures, and neither concept embodied a truly offensive operational strategy.

The Three-phase Strategy. President Johnson's decision on 28 July to increase the number of U.S. ground forces in South Vietnam from 75,000 to 175,000 by the end of 1965, prompted COMUSMACV to formulate a comprehensive three-phase strategic concept to defeat Viet Cong and NVA forces in South Vietnam. The strategy required an infusion of large numbers of U.S. ground combat forces, a revitalization of South Vietnam's military forces and pacification programs, and the success of air and naval efforts throughout Southeast Asia to stem infiltration from the North. Phase I, which was already being implemented, entailed the development of coastal enclaves and bases and the use of U.S. units in a reserve/reaction role. Its objective was to secure population centers and strategic military bases and to stabilize the military situation by halting the Viet Cong and NVA's string of successes, thus laying the foundation for a further buildup of U.S. military forces and the development of a logistical support base.

In Phase II, as more ground forces arrived, COMUSMACV planned to take the offensive to locate and destroy Viet Cong and NVA main force units and bases and to begin the crucial efforts of separating the insurgents from their base of support among the rural population, thereby eroding the Viet Cong forces' fighting strength. Driven into sparsely settled hinterlands, Viet Cong units would be attacked by the superior air and ground firepower of U.S. forces. Of equal importance to reducing Viet Cong combat strength was refurbishing the RVNAF to enable it to assume a more active combat role in support of pacification in areas cleared of larger Viet Cong units by U.S. forces.

The third phase of Westmoreland's strategy entailed concerted attacks to destroy the remnants of main force units forced to seek haven in remote bases and a nationwide effort to eliminate the Viet Cong shadow government in every hamlet and village. While the former might entail ground attacks into Laos or even North Vietnam, the latter would fall largely to the RVNAF, which would gradually assume full responsibility for defense of South Vietnam.

The three phases overlapped one another, and each would be repeated as the strategy was applied in new areas of the South as additional forces became available. Other aspects of the overall strategy, the U.S. advisory and support efforts, for example, would persist through all three phases and, indeed, would require strengthening if the Viet Cong Infrastructure were to be eliminated. COMUSMACV's strategy was broadly similar to that adopted earlier by the French. Reluctant to attach a firm timetable to the fulfillment of his strategy, Westmoreland thought that the situation envisioned in Phase III could be attained in three to five years if the ground, air, and naval elements of U.S. strategy were successful and if South Vietnam fully mobilized its counterinsurgency efforts.

Conditions for Success. As initially envisioned, Westmoreland's strategy sought to exploit U.S. military advantages in overwhelming firepower and mobility to avert the pitfalls of a war of attrition, a protracted conflict, the slow erosion of the Viet Cong and NVA's military strength, and the likelihood of greater American

THE BASE BUILD-UP. Aerial view of a part of the 25th U.S. Infantry Division base camp at Cu Chi, 19 November 1970. A significant portion of all U.S. personnel in Vietnam were logistical troops devoted to building and maintaining such installations. *Department of Defense*

casualties. To avoid these dangers, Westmoreland had to wrest the tactical initiative from the Viet Cong and NVA forces and curb infiltration. Failure to accomplish these goals would reduce the benefits of firepower and mobility on which Westmoreland's strategy rested by allowing the Viet Cong and NVA forces to regulate their rate of casualties and to replace and increase manpower. Westmoreland's campaign strategy already was handicapped by rules of engagement that prevented U.S. ground forces from pursuing forces into Cambodia, Laos, or North Vietnam, thus providing Viet Cong and NVA forces with inviolate sanctuaries where they could hide to reduce casualties and refurbish forces.

Success in the South also depended on the effectiveness of air and naval operations in North Vietnam and Laos over which COMUSMACV had no control. The overall U.S. strategy, moreover, labored under the disadvantage of a lack of unity of command, effort, and sometimes purpose. Operation ROLLING THUNDER, in particular, followed a muddled strategy that wavered between attaining military objectives and inducing negotiations. The expansion of North Vietnam's air defense system to formidable proportions, including the use of Soviet-made surface-to-air missiles (SAMs), raised the cost of interdiction and armed reconnaissance north of the demilitarized zone (DMZ) and necessitated the introduction of new tactics to evade both SAMs and MiG jet interceptors.

Perhaps more important to the realization of Westmoreland's strategy in the South was the speed with which U.S. officials made available additional ground forces. Forgoing even a partial mobilization of reserve forces in the summer of

1965, the army and Marines were limited to meeting troop requirements for South Vietnam by using already existing forces, resorting to the use of strategic reserves, or activating new units from scratch. While the services met all of Westmoreland's early force requirements, his ground strategy was held hostage to the pace at which they could organize and deploy additional units. Relying solely on active forces, the administration was compelled to adopt an incremental strategy for the prosecution of the ground war, and by its decision not to mobilize the reserves, it sapped both its policy and military strategy of an element of resoluteness and public backing.

The Ground War, 1965–1967. As the buildup progressed two divergent operational strategies emerged for the conduct of the ground war.

Two Operational Strategies. While all ground forces that deployed to South Vietnam needed secure bases from which to operate, the enclave concept as the core of an operational strategy was embraced most extensively by the Marines in the I Corps Tactical Zone (I CTZ). Retired army general James M. Gavin also championed it. Operating within the enclave and slowly expanding its perimeters entailed close coordination with and participation in the pacification efforts of the RVNAF. Search-and-clear and clear-and-hold operations were preeminent. Their objective was to provide a tactical security shield for areas undergoing pacification, thereby enabling the pacification zone to expand in the manner of a spreading inkblot. To enhance antiguerrilla operations in support of pacification, Marine forces organized combined action platoons consisting of Marine and Popular Force elements and engaged in civic action and psychological operations. When required, Marine forces ventured beyond the enclave as a reaction force. The enclave concept, in short, constituted the Marines' concept of a "balanced strategy." In contrast, many U.S. Army commanders, including Westmoreland, opted for an operational strategy that was less defensive-minded and that took advantage of the superiority in firepower and mobility, especially air mobility afforded by helicopters, that U.S. Army forces possessed. To some extent, the Marines were constrained from adopting a more offensive strategy because they had fewer helicopters, lacked heavy artillery, and depended on seaward logistical support. Rather than concentrating U.S. Army forces in populated zones, army leaders believed that ground units could be used more effectively to locate and engage the Viet Cong and NVA regular forces in remote, sparsely populated regions as they infiltrated into South Vietnam or emerged from their hidden bases. While such offensive operations, usually characterized as search-and-destroy or reconnaissance-in-force operations, served indirectly as a shield for areas undergoing pacification, the objective of army operations was the destruction of Viet Cong and NVA combat power rather than population security, as was the case in the enclave concept. A third strategic concept also had particular appeal within the U.S. Army. It sought to use U.S. ground forces to directly interdict infiltration through the Laotian panhandle. Made impossible by military problems and restrictive rules of engagement based on political considerations, this approach was not tried until later in the war, and then primarily by the RVNAF.

In practice, the two major operational strategies were not mutually exclusive or strictly confined to one or the other service. Marine forces, in operations STARLITE, UTAH, and TEXAS, were called on to operate beyond the confines of their enclaves to pursue forces or to retake important outposts. The forces in such operations, however, did not stray far from the coastal lowlands. Army units, their bases usually farther inland, conducted intensive operations in the vicinity of their bases to improve local security and enhance pacification.

AIRMOBILE SUPPORT. Massed U.S. UH-1 Iroquois helicopters, commonly known as Hueys, wait on the ground and in the air to refuel at a temporary refueling station set up along a roadside northeast of Saigon. The fuel is being pumped from large rubber bladders (foreground). These helicopters are operating in support of the 173d U.S. Airborne Brigade. *National Archives*

Mobile Offensive Operations. The pattern of deployments and operations by U.S. Army units in the III CTZ and in the II CTZ revealed Westmoreland's preference for mobile offensive operations. In III CTZ, as the buildup progressed, Westmoreland placed three U.S. Army divisions and several separate brigades in a defensive arc around Saigon. The 1st and 25th Infantry Divisions, north and northwest of Saigon, were located along the most likely invasion routes to the capital. The 9th Infantry Division, with its units to the west and south of the capital, completed the security belt around Saigon upon its arrival in South Vietnam in 1966. One of its brigades, moreover, was deployed to the northern delta of the IV CTZ, the only U.S. ground unit to conduct sustained operations in that zone. Trained as a riverine force, the brigade and its naval components used the delta's numerous estuaries to attain mobility. The riverine force, in addition, complemented the U.S. Navy's brown-water GAME WARDEN program, which sought to interdict the Viet Cong guerrillas' use of intercoastal and interior waterways.

Centered on the defense of Saigon, Westmoreland's strategy in III CTZ had a clarity of design and purpose that was not found in U.S. operations in other regions of South Vietnam. Once base camps were established, army units began to secure important routes and conducted forays into the Viet Cong forces' base areas north and northwest of the capital. During 1966 and 1967, the pace of U.S.

operations quickened to disrupt the Viet Cong and NVA forces' use of the Iron Triangle, War Zone D, and War Zone C.

Large search-and-destroy operations such as ATTLEBORO, CEDAR FALLS, and JUNCTION CITY followed a common pattern. Airmobile assaults, often in the wake of B-52 ARC LIGHT bombing strikes, were followed by helicopter and ground sweeps that usually made episodic contact with Viet Cong and NVA forces. Americans often uncovered evidence of hasty departure—abandoned camps, vacated tunnels, caches of food and supplies—indicating that the communist forces had been alerted by the preparations for large search-and-destroy operations. When contact was made, usually at the initiative of Viet Cong or NVA forces, it was in the form of an ambush, sometimes followed by a second ambush against the U.S. reaction force. Mines and booby traps were often used in connection with ambushes but also were frequently placed randomly and ingeniously on roads and trails. For the Viet Cong and NVA forces, mine warfare assumed prodigious proportions, supplying firepower to substitute for the artillery that they lacked and serving as an economy-of-force measure.

In response to any contact—ambush or meeting engagement—U.S. Army forces sought to pin down Viet Cong and NVA forces through maneuver and firepower to prevent their escape. Holding them in place, U.S. forces "piled on" air and artillery fire to destroy them, tactics that not only exploited the U.S. advantage in firepower and mobility, but also served as an economy of force to minimize American casualties. To reduce the effectiveness of these tactics Viet Cong and NVA units tried to force U.S. units into tight defensive perimeters in which close combat ensued, trying to "hug" U.S. units to prevent the delivery of supporting air and artillery fire. The Viet Cong and NVA forces usually disengaged under the cover of darkness, dividing into small elements to disperse into the countryside or withdraw into Cambodia, only to return to the base areas after U.S. forces withdrew. To detect their return, U.S. forces used small stay-behind elements of Special Forces or Rangers. However, because U.S. forces were unable to remain in the base areas for extended periods of time, U.S. operations caused only temporary disruptions in Viet Cong and NVA activity, necessitating repeated forays into the base areas.

The Highlands War. As U.S. ground forces arrived in South Vietnam in 1965, the most critical military situation was in the Central Highlands (II CTZ), where the Viet Cong guerrillas and recently infiltrated NVA units mounted a strong summer offensive, overrunning border camps and besieging some district towns, while other Viet Cong units ravaged coastal communities. Westmoreland believed that these units intended to link the forces in the Central Highlands with those on the coast to cut South Vietnam in two and thus isolate the northern provinces closest to North Vietnam from the rest of the country. This estimate of North Vietnamese intentions exerted a strong influence on COMUSMACV's strategy and concept of operations in II CTZ. The short-term goal of the North Vietnamese, however, was to dominate the Highlands, establishing a strategic base area there from which to mount or reinforce operations in other areas of II CTZ and in III CTZ. For communist strategists, the Highlands constituted a strategic fulcrum for operations elsewhere, as well as a "killing zone" where communist forces, at times and under conditions advantageous to them, could mass and challenge U.S. and South Vietnamese forces. Hoping to achieve quick, salient victories by engaging U.S. units, they believed that such actions might deter a further buildup of U.S. combat forces and weaken the U.S. government's resolve to continue the war.

To counter that strategy, Westmoreland proposed sending the army's newly organized 1st Cavalry Division (Airmobile), with its large contingent of helicopters, to the Highlands to establish an operational base from which it could interdict NVA units as they infiltrated from Cambodia and Laos, thereby precluding their penetration into the lowlands. Westmoreland's superiors, however, believing that a U.S. unit in an exposed inland position might be cut off from the sea and suffer a fate similar to that of the French at Dien Bien Phu, opposed this concept, preferring instead to establish a secure, less vulnerable coastal base of operations. Contending that the deployment of the airmobile division to a coastal enclave made poor use of its mobility, COMUSMACV and his superiors compromised and established a base camp at An Khe, halfway between the highland town of Pleiku and the coastal town of Qui Nhon.

The confrontation that the NVA sought occurred in October 1965, approximately one month after the airmobile division deployed to II CTZ. Entering South Vietnam from Cambodia, three NVA regiments attacked ARVN and Special Forces camps in the vicinity of Pleiku. U.S. Army units were quickly committed and engaged each of the NVA regiments before they withdrew into Cambodia. The rapid insertion and extraction of U.S. Army units by helicopter and the use of air cavalry helicopter gunships for fire support became hallmarks of army airmobile operations throughout South Vietnam. As the first large-scale combat of Americans against NVA regulars, the battle assumed a larger strategic importance than the tactical defeat of NVA forces. It reinforced Westmoreland's conviction of the necessity to screen the border and confront Viet Cong and NVA forces as far forward as possible to establish a security shield for more densely populated coastal regions. The NVA's setback in the Highlands dashed North Vietnamese hopes for an early decisive victory that might forestall the dispatch of more U.S. ground forces to South Vietnam. Throughout 1966 and 1967 each side pursued a strategy of military confrontation in the Highlands, but as U.S. combat strength increased, North Vietnam's hope of obtaining a decisive victory became more remote. The efficacy of U.S. strategy was compromised by (1) restrictive rules of engagement that provided Viet Cong and NVA forces with safe havens, (2) continued infiltration from the north, and (3) a failure by the United States to seize the tactical initiative from the Viet Cong and NVA forces. For both sides, the war in the Central Highlands quickly evolved into a war of attrition, each side seeking to weaken the opposing side's forces and will to fight.

From their Highland bases, U.S. and RVNAF units protected the few key roads that traversed the Highlands, screened the border, and reinforced border posts and tribal camps attacked by the NVA. Occupied by Civilian Irregular Defense Group (CIDG) units and army Special Forces teams, outposts and camps were usually located along known infiltration routes or near base areas to detect Viet Cong and NVA activity. By threatening or attacking these outposts, NVA forces sought to eradicate them and to lure U.S. and RVNAF relief units into ambushes. Such bases were established at Dak To, Plei Djering, Duc Co, Pleime, Dak Seang, Dak Pek, and other sites in the Central Highlands.

Army operations such as PAUL REVERE, FRANCIS MARION, SAM HOUSTON, and MACARTHUR during 1966 and 1967 involved a continual search for tactical concepts and techniques to compensate for the constraints of distance, difficult terrain, an inviolable border, and a limited number of forces. Locating Viet Cong and NVA forces was the most difficult problem. Many U.S. Army operations entailed days of futile searching punctuated by sporadic but intense battles, usually fought at the initiative of Viet Cong or NVA units. Tactical concepts such as the "checkerboard" technique divided a vast area into small squares, with each square methodically searched for Viet Cong or NVA troops. Patrols often operated for days without resupply to avoid having helicopters reveal their location. After several days in one square, the patrols leapfrogged by helicopter to another. To provide the firepower needed to attack opposing forces, Americans established fire support bases. Bristling with artillery and mortars and serving as a base for patrols, the fire support base became a ubiquitous feature of the ground war throughout the south.

Operations in the Highlands usually followed a pattern of air assaults and establishing fire bases, although occasionally they entailed efforts to dislodge Viet Cong or NVA forces from fortified positions in the high ground. While supported by massive air and artillery fire support, such engagements often became a slow grueling infantry assault that was reminiscent of the hill battles of the Korean War. Once the NVA forces disengaged, blocking forces and fires were brought to bear to renew contact and to prevent their escape.

The Lowlands War. In II CTZ, as in other military regions, Westmoreland faced two major threats. His strategy in the Highlands entailed interdiction, confrontation, and attrition. In the coastal lowlands of II CTZ, he confronted a different threat and adopted a different operational strategy, which emerged in early 1966. In the heavily populated coastal region, army forces encountered local and main force Viet Cong units that had long flourished among the lowland population. For Westmoreland's lowland strategy to succeed, U.S. Army and RVNAF operations had to uproot guerrilla units that lived among the population and had to eradicate base areas in the piedmont from which main force units made forays into the lowlands. From the outset, this concept was flawed because COMUS-MACV lacked sufficient U.S. forces in II CTZ to sustain operations in either the Highlands or coastal plain. U.S. units that might be committed to support pacification on the coast would also have to be used to meet emergencies in the Highlands. This factor was apparent to NVA commanders, who manipulated the military threat between coast and Highlands. North Vietnamese strategists were thus able to keep U.S. forces in II Corps off balance, using threats in the Highlands to divert Americans from pacification support and relieve pressure on local and guerrilla forces that operated in those areas. Weaker, less aggressive RVNAF forces that remained in areas vacated by the Americans were unable to prevent guerrilla forces from returning and reasserting their military and political influence.

In operations such as IRVING, PERSHING, and THAYER, U.S. Army forces in northern II CTZ fought Viet Cong and NVA forces in the coastal plain of Binh Dinh province in what came to be known as the Binh Dinh Pacification Campaign. In contrast to operations in the Highlands or the large sweeps through the base areas of III CTZ, U.S. Army operations along the central coast were more closely attuned to the support of local pacification, although army units did not become as intimately involved in pacification as the Marines. Army units were generally used to flush out Viet Cong and NVA units from the nearby piedmont. In a typical operation, U.S. Army units would be inserted into an upland valley to seek out and drive opposing forces toward the coast, where U.S., RVNAF, and South Korean forces would block their path along the coast. Thus trapped, these Viet Cong and NVA forces would be attacked by ground, naval, and air forces. In this tactical scheme, known as the "hammer and anvil," the coastal plain and the natural barrier formed by the sea constituted the anvil or killing zone.

Army units also adopted techniques to support pacification, such as "County Fair" operations, which had been pioneered by the Marines. These were essentially cordon-and-search operations in which U.S. forces surrounded a hamlet or

SEARCH AND DESTROY. U.S. soldier dumping confiscated rice, 1966. U.S. units routinely destroyed Vietnamese peasants' food caches that might have gone to support Viet Cong forces. *National Archives*

village at dawn to prevent the escape of local guerrillas or cadres, while South Vietnamese forces and various government cadres undertook a house-to-house search. Specially trained cadres took a census, interrogated suspected Viet Cong guerrillas, instituted, with U.S. support, a variety of civic action and psychological operations, and put in place the rudiments of local government and social services. Army units also used "checkpoint and snatch" operations to conduct surprise roadblocks to inspect traffic on roads frequented by insurgents. In other operations, army units protected seasonal rice harvests, furnished security for provincial elections, and conducted a variety of population and resource control measures.

Returning to Binh Dinh province repeatedly over the course of two years, U.S. Army forces tended to operate over similar ground. Each time they found conditions differing little from those they had first encountered. For the most part, Viet Cong and NVA units had refurbished themselves and continued to operate in the area. The lack of a permanent U.S. military presence and the lackluster performance of the South Vietnamese government in following up with security and services caused pacification to languish and in some areas allowed the Viet Cong guerrillas to maintain a dominant position. The most dubious success was the creation of hundreds of thousands of refugees who fled to coastal cities to escape the effects of the war. The most significant factor that militated against the success of pacification support, however, was the threat in the border area, which continually frustrated Westmoreland's search for a comprehensive strategy for II CTZ.

The DMZ. While Marine units in I CTZ expanded their coastal enclaves north and south of Da Nang, North Vietnam intensified its military threat along the DMZ to draw U.S. forces away from populated areas. Increasingly in 1966 and 1967, Marines were compelled to reinforce the DMZ by the transfer of forces from southern I CTZ. In operations such as HASTINGS and PRAIRIE the Marines withstood NVA artillery attacks and ground assaults across the DMZ. The NVA's continued presence in the vicinity of the DMZ and Khe Sanh necessitated the construction or reinforcement of a string of fire bases just south of the DMZ—Con Thien, Gio Linh, Camp Carroll, and Dong Ha. To prevent breaches of the DMZ, the United States created the so-called McNamara Line, which combined electronic sensors and other detection devices with manned strongpoints. Although its purpose was to reduce the large investment of manpower that the Marines had committed to protect the DMZ, the McNamara Line instead forced the Marines into a somewhat static defense of large tracts of barren territory. By the spring of 1967, North Vietnamese strategy had tied down a major portion of the Marine force in Vietnam in the vulnerable border area along the DMZ and around Khe Sanh. Supported by massed counterbattery fire by Marine and army artillery, naval gunfire support, and constant air strikes, including B-52 bombardment, the Marines, in such operations as CIMMARON, BUFFALO, HICKORY II, KINGFISHER, and KENTUCKY, repelled repeated NVA attacks in combat that frequently resembled World War I trench warfare rather than counterinsurgency. Areas vacated by the Marines in southern I CTZ were occupied by U.S. Army and South Korean forces who had been moved from II and III CTZs. Their transfer, however, reduced the military support for ongoing pacification programs, especially in coastal II CTZ.

Strategic Stalemate. As 1968 approached, the war in Vietnam had reached a strategic equilibrium. For both sides, the war had become a contest of strategies of attrition; neither side faced imminent defeat or victory. While Westmoreland's strategy had denied North Vietnamese forces a significant tactical success, it fell short of attaining the level of attrition needed to diminish North Vietnam's abilities to wage its own war of attrition against U.S. forces. In the context of his three-phase campaign strategy, Westmoreland had succeeded in stabilizing the military situation and undertaking offensive operations as called for in Phase II. But while U.S. forces achieved many tactical victories, Westmoreland was unable to transcend the strategic defense that he was forced to assume by the constraints placed on U.S. ground and air operations and the incremental buildup of military forces in the south. Although U.S. forces frequently assumed the tactical offensive, Westmoreland generally was unable to deny the tactical initiative to Viet Cong or NVA forces. ROLLING THUNDER and other air and naval actions against North Vietnam and the Ho Chi Minh Trail, moreover, neither stopped infiltration nor achieved the strategic goal of changing North Vietnam's policy. In the "other war," South Vietnam's pacification efforts, only marginal progress had been made since 1965, despite the fact that nearly 50 percent of the ARVN and all paramilitary forces were dedicated to this effort.

Unswerving in their strategic goal of unification, North Vietnam's leaders recognized that the strategy of military confrontation they had pursued in the south for over two years had also failed. To maintain its strategic position in the south, North Vietnam had matched the U.S. military buildup; the number of NVA divisions increased from one in early 1965 to nine at the start of 1968. Guerrilla forces in the south, however, retained a strong foothold in many rural areas. North Vietnam also retained other important advantages, among them use of cross-border base areas, the ability to continue infiltration under arduous conditions, continued external support from communist bloc nations, a society in the north mobilized for war, and a large untapped pool of manpower.

To carry out his campaign strategy, Westmoreland needed additional forces. He had requested additional ground forces in 1967 to reinforce those already in place, to compensate in part for the diversion of forces from other corps areas into I CTZ, and to extend operations into Laos and possibly North Vietnam. The U.S. government's rejection of his request had serious strategic implications because, in effect, it placed a troop ceiling on U.S. strength in South Vietnam and, for the time being, confined Westmoreland's strategic options to South Vietnam. Still confident of success, Westmoreland acknowledged that the realization of Phase III of his initial strategic concept would be set back two to three years without additional reinforcements.

The Tet Offensive, 1968. Although a strategic stalemate prevailed at the start of 1968, the initiative was taken by the communists when they launched the Tet Offensive of January–February 1968. The offensive was a strategic watershed of the Vietnam War, marking a unique stage in North Vietnam's strategy of revolutionary war. In a brilliant stroke of strategy, North Vietnam altered the conflict from primarily a battlefield confrontation to one that encompassed both negotiating and fighting. Violent, widespread, simultaneous military actions in rural and urban areas throughout the south represented the general offensive. Attacking the RVNAF and the populace rather than U.S. forces, North Vietnam sought to undermine the morale and will of the RVNAF and, by its collapse, to subvert popular confidence in South Vietnam's ability to prosecute the war. Anticipating a crescendo of popular protest against the South Vietnamese government that would lead to a general uprising, North Vietnam expected the fighting to end and some form of political accommodation to occur, with the likelihood that Americans would leave the south. To some extent, the Tet Offensive was an admission by North Vietnam that it was unable to defeat U.S. combat units and that the NVA's own large unit war had failed.

In a formidable display of military prowess and coordination, communist forces, primarily Viet Cong units, struck 36 of 44 provincial capitals and 64 of 242 district towns, as well as 5 of South Vietnam's 6 autonomous cities, including Saigon. NVA forces, meanwhile, had massed in border areas adjacent to III CTZ and I CTZ, ready to exploit local successes. Except in I CTZ, the NVA, as a rule, was not committed to the Tet Offensive. In the northern CTZ, formidable NVA forces massed around the Marine base at Khe Sanh. Some Americans likened the situation to that of Dien Bien Phu in 1954. Khe Sanh preoccupied Westmoreland even before the Tet Offensive began, raising questions of whether Khe Sanh was a diversion or the NVA's main effort. In I CTZ, officials debated whether Khe Sanh or Hue, the latter being attacked and occupied by NVA forces, was the main focus of the offensive. With the NVA tenaciously maintaining a foothold in Hue, Khe Sanh's defense assumed strategic importance. Its loss or abandonment would allow NVA units to reinforce Hue and outflank U.S. forces along the DMZ, thus jeopardizing all of Quang Tri, South Vietnam's northernmost province.

Khe Sanh and Hue were linked in North Vietnam's strategy. By threatening and finally attacking Khe Sanh, the NVA sought to siphon U.S. military forces from the defense of Hue and elsewhere in the coastal lowlands. Recognizing that his military options were limited and that he could not afford to defend both Hue and Khe Sanh with the forces available in I CTZ, Westmoreland decided that Khe Sanh would be defended by the forces already there and by massive firepower delivered by all available means. Hue's recapture by U.S. Army, Marines, and South Vietnamese forces after almost a month of fighting, which included the only extended urban warfare of the war, greatly reduced Khe Sanh's significance for North Vietnam. Suffering heavy losses from massive air and artillery bombardments, NVA forces in the vicinity of Khe Sanh began to disperse.

Although all of the NVA attacks were defeated, the magnitude of the Tet Offensive profoundly affected U.S. policy and strategy. Despite Westmoreland's insistence that the Viet Cong and North Vietnamese forces had suffered a major defeat that should be exploited, U.S. officials denied his request for 206,000 additional troops. President Johnson's decision again foreclosed operations that Westmoreland had envisioned in the last phase of his campaign strategy. Limited to making the best possible use of existing U.S. forces, the decision meant that the RVNAF would have to shoulder a larger share of the war effort. Johnson also profoundly altered the strategy of the air war against North Vietnam by curtailing air strikes north of the twentieth parallel to induce negotiations in March 1968, and stopping the bombing entirely at the end of October.

These decisions reflected the deep psychological repercussions that the Tet Offensive registered on American policy and public opinion, crystallizing a view that previous strategies had failed and that the war was not winnable. For North Vietnam, this was the most important strategic outcome of the offensive, even though communist forces had suffered a major military defeat. The Viet Cong forces, in particular, lost thousands of combatants and seasoned cadres, which severely weakened the insurgents' base in the south. North Vietnam nevertheless achieved its strategic goal of nudging U.S. policy toward military disengagement. Following "mini-Tet" offensives in May and August 1968, the last gasps of North Vietnam's strategy of a general offensive/general uprising, Viet Cong and NVA forces dispersed to avoid contact with U.S. forces; only when conditions were favorable did they pursue a war of attrition against U.S. and South Vietnamese forces.

Vietnamization, 1968–1973. Under an overarching policy called Vietnamization, which began in the waning days of the Johnson administration under Clark M. Clifford, who had replaced Robert McNamara as secretary of defense in early 1968, U.S. strategy and operations entered a new phase. The two main objectives of Vietnamization were the withdrawal of U.S. forces and creation of a stronger, largely self-reliant South Vietnamese military force. While the latter was an ongoing goal of U.S. advisory and support efforts, past efforts to strengthen and modernize the RVNAF had been conducted without the pressure of diminishing U.S. support, the prospect of large-scale conventional combat, or the presence of strong NVA forces in the south.

The military aspect of Vietnamization consisted of three overlapping phases: the redeployment of U.S. units and the RVNAF's assumption of their combat and support roles; measures to improve the RVNAF's combat and support capabilities, especially firepower and mobility, through training and the transfer of equipment; and the retention of a residual U.S. presence in the form of an advisory group. An additional aspect of Vietnamization was the fostering of political, social, and economic reforms to create a vibrant political and social foundation to bolster the South Vietnamese government's political stature. The success of this aspect was closely tied to progress in the pacification program.

Abrams's Strategy. The task of implementing Vietnamization and its supporting military strategy fell to Gen. Creighton Abrams, who replaced General Westmoreland as COMUSMACV in June 1968. Abrams was under pressure from U.S. officials to minimize American casualties and to conduct operations with an eye toward leaving South Vietnam in the strongest possible military position after U.S. forces withdrew. Adjusting his strategy to a new military situation, Abrams took advantage of the weakened condition of Viet Cong forces to promote and

AIR ASSAULT. Cavalrymen of Troop B, 1st Reconnaissance Squadron, 9th Cavalry, 1st U.S. Cavalry Division (Airmobile) jump from an UH–1B Iroquois ("Huey") in search of a suspected Viet Cong outpost during Operation OREGON, a search-and-destroy mission underway three kilometers (two miles) west of Duc Pho, Quang Ngai province, 24 April 1967. *Department of Defense/U.S. Army*

accelerate efforts to restore rural security and enhance pacification. He stressed the importance of small unit tactics in the context of clear-and-hold operations instead of large search-and-destroy operations. To improve the RVNAF's effectiveness, he encouraged the conduct of more combined operations. As Viet Cong and NVA forces dispersed across South Vietnam's borders into Laos and Cambodia after the Tet Offensive, Abrams increased military pressure against their logistical support system in lieu of the attrition of combat forces. At the same time, the reduction in air operations over North Vietnam allowed for a more concentrated air effort against the Ho Chi Minh Trail in Laos, thus complementing Abrams' logistical offensive.

At the completion of Vietnamization Abrams envisioned the RVNAF assuming the majority of combat, its operations shifting to the border to assume a role of a defensive shield similar to that performed by U.S. forces. In turn, paramilitary forces were to take over the ARVN's role in area security and pacification support. The newly organized People's Self-Defense Force would assume responsibilities for village and hamlet defenses. To help the South Vietnamese government carry out its pacification programs, Abrams accorded a high priority to the U.S. advisory effort and initiated new efforts, such as the Phoenix program, to eradicate the Viet Cong infrastructure. Stressing the importance of subsuming and coordinating all operations under a unified strategy, Abrams propounded the concept of "one war" in contrast to the dichotomy of the big unit war and the "other war," or pacification, that had defined U.S. operational strategies before the Tet Offensive.

Abrams' strategy, however, retained elements of continuity with Westmoreland's. Operations in War Zones C and D in III CTZ were similar to those launched by U.S. Army units in 1966 and 1967. As part of a post–Tet Offensive, Abrams also sought to disrupt and reduce the bases from which communist forces could again threaten the Saigon region. Rather than large sweeps, U.S. Army and RVNAF forces scoured the base areas with numerous small unit operations, frequently resweeping areas, and established a more effective screen along the Cambodian border to prevent Viet Cong and NVA forces from regaining access to their bases. The communist forces, as an economy-of-force measure, resorted to a "high point" strategy that entailed occasional rocket attacks against Saigon and other cities. Such attacks incurred little risk to their forces and were a violent reminder of their presence and the South Vietnamese government's inability to protect the population. The attacks also distracted U.S. and allied forces from other tasks in order to periodically clear the "rocket belts" that were established around nearly every urban center in South Vietnam.

Abrams' Strategy in Action. Until all U.S. Army forces withdrew from the Highlands in 1971, the war there changed little under Abrams' tenure. Army units continued a war of attrition, with combat focusing on the defense of border posts and Special Forces camps. Viet Cong and NVA attacks against such targets along the entire border attested to their ability to seize the tactical initiative. Many camps—Ben Het, Thien Phuoc, Thuong Duc, Bu Prang, Dak Saeng, Dak Pek, Katum, Bu Dop, and Tong Le Chon—attacked earlier because of their proximity to communist bases and infiltration routes were attacked anew. With the departure of U.S. Special Forces in March 1971, and the conversion of CIDG units to Regional Forces, the future of some camps was in doubt. The departure of the Special Forces brought to an end any significant U.S. Army role in the Highlands.

Army and Marine operations in the northern provinces were emblematic of Abrams' strategy. While continuing to support pacification along the coast, U.S. and RVNAF units began a series of forays into long-neglected communist base areas. Operations such as DELAWARE and DEWEY CANYON in the A Shau valley along the Laotian border were part of COMUSMACV's logistical offensive. The operation in the A Shau produced some of the bloodiest combat of the war, such as that at Hamburger Hill in May 1969. Like Westmoreland's search-and-destroy operations, the effects of such operations were transient. As the number of U.S. forces dwindled, few of the major base areas could be reentered or permanently occupied. Military operations on the coast, where the pacification effort had made some modest gains, would likewise feel the effects of diminished support as Marines and army units withdrew.

With most U.S. combat units slated to leave South Vietnam in 1970 and 1971, time was critical for the success of Vietnamization. Although Abrams' logistical offensive helped reduce the level of Viet Cong and NVA activity in the south, NVA forces, command centers, logistical depots, training camps, and other facilities remained across the border in Cambodia and Laos. These forces still posed a

ARVN SOLDIERS UNDER FIRE. The ARVN fought on alone for three years after the U.S. withdrawal, albeit with massive U.S. air support during the 1972 Easter Offensive. *Department of Defense/U.S. Army*

threat to Vietnamization and pacification. To reduce this threat and to give the South Vietnamese government more time to consolidate its strength and pacify the country, Abrams proposed large-scale sweeps into base areas in Cambodia and Laos.

Cambodia and Laos. Because of their proximity to Saigon, bases in Cambodia were accorded first priority. Beginning in late April 1970, RVNAF and U.S. Army units cut a broad swath through communist bases in Cambodia, but encountered few Viet Cong or NVA forces, which moved deeper into the interior. Initially underestimating the adverse American reaction against widening the war, President Richard M. Nixon quickly imposed both geographical and time limits on the operation, thus circumscribing its strategic import and allowing the communist forces to move beyond the reach of U.S. forces. Although their command and logistical facilities were disrupted, the communist forces merely shifted their bases deeper into Cambodia. RVNAF units, unaffected by Nixon's limitations, remained in Cambodia, where they became bogged down in combat against Cambodian communist guerrillas and NVA forces. Having sought to gain time to strengthen the RVNAF and pacification in South Vietnam, the Cambodian incursion instead distracted the RVNAF from its missions in South Vietnam. The eruption of a civil war in Cambodia in the wake of the incursion transformed what was once a quiescent "sideshow" into a major combat area. The events in Cambodia brought into sharp focus what many Americans had only dimly perceived, namely that for North Vietnam all of former French Indochina was a single strategic theater of operations.

The second major cross-border incursion occurred in February 1971 against the Ho Chi Minh Trail in Laos. The incursion was launched in response to a buildup of NVA forces in the Laotian border area, which presaged an NVA spring offensive in the northern provinces in 1971. Like the Cambodian incursion, Americans viewed the Laotian invasion as a benefit to Vietnamization, with a bonus of spoiling a prospective offensive. Unlike the thrust into Cambodia, no U.S. forces entered Laos. Called Operation LAM SON 719, its objective was the town of Tchepone, a logistical center on the Ho Chi Minh Trail approximately 40 kilometers (25 miles) from the border with South Vietnam. Almost from the outset, the RVNAF encountered stiff resistance, and many South Vietnamese forces did not perform well. Only U.S. air strikes, including B-52 strikes, and the use of U.S. Army helicopters to rescue the beleaguered RVNAF, who were withdrawing from Laos in disarray, prevented LAM SON 719 from becoming a total disaster. As tests of the Vietnamization effort, both the Cambodian and Laotian incursions revealed numerous weaknesses in the RVNAF's leadership and tactical competency. Both cross-border attacks indicated that the RVNAF was ill-prepared to hold its own without the firepower and mobility furnished by U.S. air support. Although LAM SON 719 failed to interdict the Ho Chi Minh Trail and the lackluster performance of the RVNAF indicated that Vietnamization was not progressing as hoped, it did forestall the NVA's 1971 spring offensive.

The Easter Offensive. As U.S. forces withdrew, the RVNAF lost a large portion of the U.S. artillery, air, and naval support on which it had come to depend. Some operations, such as the U.S. Navy's MARKET TIME and GAME WARDEN, were turned over to the South Vietnamese. When the U.S. Army's riverine brigade and its naval component were withdrawn from the upper Mekong Delta, NVA units infiltrated into the delta for the first time. The transfer of tanks, artillery, and other equipment to the RVNAF was insufficient to offset reductions in U.S. combat strength. In mid 1969, there had been an aggregate of 56 allied combat battalions present in South Vietnam's two northern provinces; that number had dwindled to 30 battalions by 1972. Artillery strength alone had declined from approximately 400 guns to 169 during the same period. Similar reductions occurred in every region of South Vietnam, with a concomitant diminution of RVNAF mobility, firepower, intelligence support, and air support.

By 1972 nearly all U.S. ground combat forces had left South Vietnam. North Vietnam's military leaders regarded the strategic situation in the south as advantageous for a resumption of major operations. Despite Vietnamization they sensed an opportunity to hasten the RVNAF's collapse and to gain an edge in any revival of the stalled negotiations in Paris. In its strategic objectives, the *Nguyen-Hue* campaign, or Easter Offensive, of 1972 resembled the 1968 Tet Offensive. The offensive was carried out countrywide, and included a major effort in the northern provinces and Highlands and a significant military thrust toward Saigon. It differed in that the NVA rather than the Viet Cong guerrillas bore the brunt of combat.

The job of countering the offensive on the ground fell almost exclusively to the RVNAF. Attacking on three fronts, the NVA crossed the DMZ and struck from Laos to capture Quang Tri, the northernmost province in South Vietnam. In the Central Highlands, NVA units moved into Kontum province, forcing the South Vietnamese to relinquish several border posts before the offensive was contained. In early April, the NVA opened a third front, attacking Loc Ninh, just south of the Cambodian border on Highway 13, and advanced to An Loc along one of the main invasion routes toward Saigon. A two-month battle ensued until the NVA forces were driven from An Loc and forced to disperse to Cambodia. By late summer, the Easter Offensive had run its course. In a slow, cautious counteroffensive, the RVNAF recaptured Quang Tri City and most of the lost province. The margin of victory or defeat, however, often rested with the supporting firepower provided by U.S. fighters, bombers, and helicopter gunships. In response to the NVA attacks, the United States, in Operation LINEBACKER, resumed bombing North Vietnam for the duration of the offensive and mined North Vietnamese harbors.

North Vietnam's strategic blunder in the Easter Offensive was underestimating the U.S. response. Nevertheless, the NVA's operations and tactics indicated that North Vietnam was ready to enter a final stage of the war, which would be characterized by conventional operations against the RVNAF. During the Easter Offensive, the NVA made increasing use of armor and artillery and introduced the Soviet SA-7 Strella handheld antiaircraft missiles, effective against low-flying helicopters and tactical aircraft. The U.S. Army's Cobra helicopter with its antitank missiles, which had supported the RVNAF during the Easter Offensive, were soon withdrawn from the South, leaving South Vietnamese forces with only a limited antitank capability. U.S. air and naval operations against North Vietnam were also discontinued, only to be resumed in late 1972 and early 1973 in LINEBACKER II. As the most intense strategic bombing of North Vietnam, that final air campaign was designed to bring communist negotiators back to the peace talks to conclude an armistice and peace treaty.

The Final Years, 1972–1975. The long-awaited accord was signed in January 1973. Although South Vietnam's leaders were encouraged by the massive U.S. bombardment of North Vietnam in LINEBACKER II, they were discouraged by the cease-fire provisions that allowed NVA forces to remain in the south, a distinct strategic disadvantage to South Vietnam. After March 1973, when all U.S. military forces and advisers left South Vietnam, RVNAF forces were increasingly dispersed throughout the south. Stretched thin, their disposition resembled that of the RVNAF in the period before U.S. ground forces had been introduced in 1965. Taking advantage of this situation, communist forces in the Mekong Delta attacked lightly defended outposts and hamlets and regained control over portions of the rural population that only years before had been under the South Vietnamese government's control.

Between 1973 and 1975 South Vietnam's military security further declined. Seeking to preserve its diminishing assets, the RVNAF reverted to a static force, reluctant or unable to react to a growing number of attacks that eroded rural security and undermined the fragile pacification program. In the United States, congressionally mandated reductions in U.S. aid reduced the delivery of repair parts, fuel, and ammunition, exacerbating the plight of the RVNAF. U.S. air operations in Cambodia and Laos, which had continued after the cease-fire in South Vietnam had gone into effect, ended in 1973 after Congress cut off funds. The RVNAF, which had been organized, trained, equipped, and supported in the image of its U.S. counterparts, now had to do without U.S. largesse. South Vietnam's president, Nguyen Van Thieu, said that his country faced the prospect of fighting a "poor man's war."

By 1975 North Vietnam enjoyed every strategic advantage. In the absence of air attacks and cross-border operations, it had vastly improved its logistical support systems adjacent to South Vietnam. Its troops were refurbished and located in secure bases. Most of all it retained the strategic initiative, not only in South Vietnam but throughout Indochina. Although still uncertain of how the United States would respond to renewed hostilities, North Vietnam began planning a limited offensive in the south. Proceeding cautiously, the NVA overran Phuoc Long province, north of Saigon. When the United States failed to respond militarily and the South Vietnamese ceded the province without concerted opposition, North Vietnamese strategists launched an offensive in the Central Highlands. What started as a limited offensive to gain a foothold in the Highlands evolved into an all-out campaign to conquer South Vietnam. Reacting promptly to the surprising collapse of RVNAF resistance, NVA forces moved quickly to cut South Vietnam in two. Still husbanding its military assets, South Vietnamese leaders chose to retreat rather than to reinforce the Highlands or the northern provinces, which the NVA had isolated. As NVA forces moved north and south along the coast, additional NVA units crossed the DMZ and came out of Laos to create an untenable situation in the northern provinces, eventually capturing Hue and Da Nang. At the same time, the NVA mounted a major assault on several fronts to capture Saigon. Hurriedly established defense lines north of Saigon failed to stop the offensive. As South Vietnam's leaders pleaded in vain for U.S. assistance, Saigon fell to the communists on 29 April 1975, ending the Vietnam War.

[*See also* Atrocities; Attrition Strategy; Barrier Concept; Body Count; Chemical Warfare; Clear and Hold; Counterinsurgency; Enclave Strategy; Flexible Response; Free-fire Zones; Harrassment and Interdiction Fire; Rules of Engagement; Search and Destroy; Vietnamization; Weapons; *and entries on individual U.S. and foreign military services.*]

BIBLIOGRAPHY

CABLE, LARRY. *Unholy Grail: The US and the Wars in Vietnam, 1965–1968.* 1991.

CLODFELTER, MARK. *The Limits of Airpower: The American Bombing of North Vietnam.* 1989.

COLLINS, JAMES LAWTON, JR. *The Development and Training of the South Vietnamese Army, 1950–1972.* 1975.

DAVIDSON, PHILLIP B. *Secrets of the Vietnam War.* 1990.

KREPINEVICH, ANDREW F., JR. *The Army and Vietnam.* 1986.

MAROLDA, EDWARD J., and G. WESLEY PRYCE III. *A Short History of the United States Navy and the Southeast Asian Conflict, 1950–1975.* 1984.

MILLETT, ALLAN R. "The Longest War: The Marines in Vietnam, 1965–1975." In *Semper Fidelis: The History of the United States Marine Corps.* 1980.

PALMER, BRUCE, JR. *The 25-Year War: America's Military Role in Vietnam.* 1984.

SCHLIGHT, JOHN. *The War in South Vietnam: The Years of the Offensive, 1965–1968.* 1988.

SPECTOR, RONALD. *After Tet: The Bloodiest Year in Vietnam.* 1993.

STANTON, SHELBY L. *The Rise and Fall of an American Army: The U.S. Ground Forces in Vietnam, 1965–1973.* 1985.

TILFORD, EARL H., JR. *Setup: What the Air Force Did in Vietnam and Why.* 1991.

VINCENT H. DEMMA

Students for a Democratic Society (SDS). Founded in 1960 by a group of University of Michigan students and inspired by the civil rights movement, Students for a Democratic Society (SDS) developed a broad agenda concerned with racism, poverty, and social justice. In 1962 Tom Hayden and other SDS leaders issued the Port Huron Statement, outlining their views.

After the start of Operation ROLLING THUNDER, the bombing campaign of North Vietnam in 1965, as the United States stood poised on the brink of major escalation, SDS sponsored the first anti–Vietnam War march on Washington on 17 April 1965. By this time there were SDS chapters across the country, most on college campuses. At the annual SDS convention delegates debated whether the

SDS should focus exclusively on the Vietnam War on a national level or whether local chapters should work independently toward social justice and "stopping the seventh war from now." The majority favored local community organization, a decision that prevented the SDS from becoming the leading national voice for youth against the war. Still, local SDS groups organized against the war, protesting campus visits by administration officials and military research at universities.

Although the SDS failed to assume a national leadership role in the antiwar movement, by 1968 many members had become more militant and had adopted radical Marxist doctrine. Eventually the group fragmented and some broke off to form the terrorist group known as the Weathermen. Although the SDS sponsored another march on Washington in 1969, the split within the movement marked the end of its national profile.

BIBLIOGRAPHY

POWERS, THOMAS. *The War at Home.* 1973.
ZAROULIS, NANCY, and GERALD SULLIVAN. *Who Spoke Up?* 1984.

KELLY EVANS-PFEIFER

Sullivan, William H.

Sullivan, William H. (1922–), U.S. ambassador to Laos, Foreign Service officer. A career diplomat, Sullivan served as deputy U.S. representative to the 1962 Geneva Conference. In 1964, President Lyndon B. Johnson appointed Sullivan as ambassador to Laos, and from this office he directed the secret U.S. bombing campaign in Laos. At the Vietnam peace talks in 1972, Sullivan was Henry Kissinger's chief deputy; throughout he staunchly supported President Richard Nixon's Southeast Asia policy.

BIBLIOGRAPHY

MORITZ, CHARLES, ed. *Current Biography Yearbook.* 1979.
SULLIVAN, WILLIAM H. *Obbligato, 1939–1979: Notes on a Foreign Service Career.* 1984.

PAUL M. TAILLON

Summers, Harry G., Jr.

Summers, Harry G., Jr. (1932–), instructor, U.S. Army War College. Considered a leading analyst of the Vietnam War, Summers served two tours of duty in Vietnam, including service with the Four-Party Joint Military Team, which investigated the status of U.S. soldiers still listed as missing-in-action (MIA) after 1973. Summers criticized Gen. William Westmoreland's war of attrition strategy as a misapplication of U.S. resources. He believed that the South Vietnamese army should have countered the Viet Cong political insurgency and that the United States should have invaded Laos to the Mekong River to cut communist supply routes. This strategy, Summers contends, would have reduced U.S. casualties and the U.S. military burden. Summers also criticized the Johnson administration for its failure to summon public support for intervention. Summers reportedly commented to a PAVN colonel that North Vietnam "never defeated us on the battlefield." The communist officer trenchantly replied, "That may be so, but it is also irrelevant."

BIBLIOGRAPHY

KARNOW, STANLEY. *Vietnam: A History.* 1983.
SUMMERS, HARRY G., JR. *On Strategy: The Vietnam War in Context.* 1981.

ADAM LAND

Supreme Court, U.S.

Supreme Court, U.S. The nation's highest tribunal dealt with the Vietnam War mainly through cases involving First Amendment rights. The Court also dealt with draft resistance and conscientious objection, as well as broad governmental claims to national security. The justices consistently refused, however, to decide whether the war, never officially declared, was constitutional.

Dissent and Publication. From 1967 to 1974, the Court disapproved of government efforts to punish dissent, limit protest, or prevent newspaper publication of embarrassing historical disclosures of the war's origins. In *Bond v. Floyd* (385 U.S. 116 [1966]), the Court invalidated the Georgia state legislature's refusal to seat a newly elected representative, Julian Bond, because of his antiwar statements. In *Tinker v. Des Moines Independent Community School District* (393 U.S. 503 [1969]) the Court held that school administrators could not infringe on the First Amendment right to symbolic expression, such as when schoolchildren wore black armbands to bear silent witness for peace. Similarly, the Court upheld the rights of an antiwar group in Baltimore against Maryland's public disturbance law (*Bachellar v. Maryland,* 397 U.S. 564 [1970]), and defended antiwar sentiment, even when expressed in language offensive to many, including the justices themselves (*Cohen v. California*, 403 U.S. 15 [1971]).

When the Nixon administration tried to prevent the *New York Times* and the *Washington Post* from publishing excerpts from the Pentagon Papers, the Defense Department's classified history of the war, the Court rejected on First Amendment grounds the government's national security plea for prior restraint (government authority to prohibit or restrict publication) in *New York Times Co. v. United States* (403 U.S. 713 [1971]).

Similarly, the Court rejected the Nixon administration's national security claims in *United States v. United States District Court for the Eastern District of Michigan* (407 U.S. 297 [1972]). The government argued that the president had "inherent powers" for wiretapping antiwar activities because he needed to defend the nation against "the attempts of domestic organizations to attack and subvert the existing structure of Government." The Court disagreed, holding that that duty was circumscribed in "a manner compatible" with the Constitution.

While the Court disappointed the administration in these cases, it provided some significant victories for the Johnson and Nixon administrations. For example, the Court did not fully protect Sen. Mike Gravel of Alaska when he arranged to have the Pentagon Papers published in book form. The Court found that Gravel's act was not shielded from a grand jury's inquiry. As such, the Court narrowly read the debate clause immunity granted to members of Congress.

Draft Resistance. From 1968 to 1974, the Supreme Court heard several draft resistance cases, and held that the First Amendment did not protect all forms of antiwar expression. In *United States v. O'Brien* (391 U.S. 367 [1968]), Chief Justice Earl Warren declared the government's interest in raising and supporting armies compelling enough to incidentally limit First Amendment freedoms, in this case, the asserted symbolic act of burning a draft card. Justice Thurgood Marshall also did not support draft resistance if it was brazen and openly contemptuous of the procedures regulated by the Selective Service System (*McGee v. United States*, 402 U.S. 479 [1971]). But the Court protected those whom the Selective Service System tried to punish with punitive reclassifications, finding the First Amendment broad enough to defend young men against reprisals for expressing their antiwar defi-

ance (*Gutknecht v. United States*, 396 U.S. 295 [1970]). Still, more often than not the Court refused to interfere judicially with the draft process, specifically in cases where young men sought to challenge their induction through the courts (*Fein v. Selective Service System Local Board No. 7*, 405 U.S. 365 [1972]).

Constitutional Issues. For the Supreme Court, the Vietnam War was best dealt with indirectly, and it sidestepped the war's essential constitutional problem: its undeclared nature. But the lower courts struggled with the issue as various litigants challenged presidential authority to initiate and conduct the Vietnam War. From 1966 to 1973, federal district and appellate court judges considered the problems of standing (a litigant's qualification to bring a suit before the courts) and justiciability (a case's status as being appropriate for judgment by a court). Various judges had to decide whether the Vietnam War was foreclosed to judicial inquiry because it was a political question. As opposition to the war intensified, some judges entered this political thicket and began to question if the executive had acted in conflict with either the expressed or implied will of Congress.

The Supreme Court generally refused to hear constitutional challenges to the war, deferring to the political questions doctrine, which states that questions that involve politics are best left to the political branches of government (the executive and the legislative), and denying these cases the writ of certiorari (an order from a higher court instructing a lower court to forward the record of a case for review). Justice William O. Douglas, however, urged his colleagues to consider the war's constitutionality, admonishing them that "[t]he question of an unconstitutional war is neither academic nor 'political.' . . . It should be settled here and now" (*Massachusetts v. Laird, cert. denied*, 400 U.S. 886 [1970]).

While the war's constitutionality was avoided, the justices found themselves personally embroiled with the war. Justice Abe Fortas operated as a personal adviser to President Johnson. The bombing of Cambodia in 1973 ruffled judicial relations when the justices breached decorum and courtesy in overturning one another's decisions regarding a lower federal court's injunction to halt that bombing (order stayed, *Schlesinger v. Holtzman*, 414 U.S. 1321 [1973], *cert. denied*, 416 U.S. 936 [1973]).

In its long history, the Supreme Court has witnessed many wars. The Vietnam conflict, being an

Supreme Court Cases Related to the Vietnam War

Selective Service Cases

Oestereich v. Selective Service System Local Board No. 11, 393 U.S. 233 (1968).

Gutknecht v. U.S., 396 U.S. 295 (1970)

Welsh v. U.S., 398 U.S. 333 (1970)

Toussie v. U.S., 397 U.S. 112 (1970)

Breen v. Selective Service Board, 396 U.S. 460 (1970)

Mully v. U.S., 398 U.S. 410 (1970)

U.S. v. Sisson, 399 U.S. 267 (1970)

Gillette v. U.S., 401 U.S. 437 (1971)

Ehlert v. U.S., 402 U.S. 99 (1971)

McGee v. U.S., 402 U.S. 479 (1971)

Clay aka Ali v. U.S., 403 U.S. 698 (1971)

Fein v. Selective Service System Local Board No. 7, 405 U.S. 365 (1972)

Musser v. U.S., 414 U.S. 31 (1974)

First Amendment and Fourth Amendment Issues

Bond v. Floyd, 385 U.S. 116 (1966)

U.S. v. O'Brien, 391 U.S. 367 (1968)

Tinker v. Des Moines Independent Community School District, 393 U.S. 503 (1969)

Bachellar v. Maryland, 397 U.S. 564 (1970)

Schact v. U.S., 398 U.S. 58 (1970)

Cohen v. California, 403 U.S. 15 (1971)

New York Times Co. v. U.S., 403 U.S. 713 (1971)

U.S. v. U.S. District Court for the Eastern District of Michigan, 407 U.S. 297 (1972)

Parker v. Levy, 417 U.S. 733 (1974)

Certiorari Denied on the Constitutionality of the War

Holmes v. U.S., cert. denied, 391 U.S. 936 (1968)

Kalish v. U.S., cert. denied, 396 U.S. 835 (1969)

Massachusetts v. Laird, cert. denied, 400 U.S. 886 (1970)

Velvel v. Nixon, cert. denied, 396 U.S. 1042 (1970)

Standing-to-Sue Issues

Schlesinger v. Reservists to Stop the War, 418 U.S. 208 (1974)

undeclared war, presented unusual pressures and challenges. With respect to the government, the Court refused to hand down sympathetic decisions in the Pentagon Papers case and in *United States v. U.S. District Court for the Eastern District of Michigan.* Yet the Court did not obstruct the government's war-making capabilities, and it did not disrupt the Selective Service System, choosing to support the legitimacy of the government's wartime manpower demands. With respect to individual rights, the Court often defended brittle First Amendment liberties. Yet here too, the justices did not offer unqualified approval to all forms of antiwar resistance. Finally, on the one issue that spoke directly to the war's constitutionality, the Court abstained from judgment and left unclear the ambiguous relations between the executive and legislative branches during times of undeclared war.

[See also Conscientious Objectors.]

BIBLIOGRAPHY

KALVEN, HARRY, JR. "Even When a Nation Is at War." *Harvard Law Review* 85 (November 1971).

KEYNES, EDWARD. *Undeclared War: Twilight Zone of Constitutional Power.* 1982.

KUTLER, STANLEY I. *The Wars of Watergate.* 1990.

WORMUTH, FRANCIS D., and EDWIN B. FIRMAGE. *To Chain the Dog of War: The War Power of Congress in History and Law.* 1986.

VICTOR JEW

T

Taiwan. *See* China, Republic of (Taiwan).

Tan Son Nhut. Located on the outskirts of Saigon, Tan Son Nhut air base was the headquarters of the South Vietnamese air force. Throughout the Vietnam War, the base handled most of South Vietnam's commercial and military air traffic. After 1962, it served as headquarters for the U.S. 2d Air Division, which directed all U.S. air operations in the country, and after 1967 it served as the headquarters for the Military Assistance Command, Vietnam (MACV), as well. In 1975, following the evacuation of several thousand Americans and Vietnamese, MACV headquarters was destroyed by the departing troops on 29 April. The airport was later repaired and rebuilt to serve Ho Chi Minh City, formerly Saigon.

BIBLIOGRAPHY

CLARKE, JEFFREY J. *United States Army in Vietnam—Advice and Support: The Final Years, 1965–1973.* 1988.
SMITH, HARVEY, et al. *Area Handbook for South Vietnam.* 1967.
TOBIN, THOMAS G. *Last Flight from Saigon.* 1978.

ELLEN D. GOLDLUST

Taylor, Maxwell D. (1901–1987), general, U.S. Army; U.S. Army chief of staff, 1955–1959; special military representative, 1961–1962; chairman, Joint Chiefs of Staff (JCS), 1962–1964; ambassador to South Vietnam, 1964–1965. Extremely talented, ambitious, handsome, and multilingual, Gen. Maxwell Taylor capped a brilliant military career in World War II and Korea by publishing *The Uncertain Trumpet* (1959) upon his retirement. The book cautioned against excessive reliance on nuclear weapons and argued for a limited-war capability that would give U.S. leaders more options for responding to communist aggression. President Kennedy adopted Taylor's "flexible response" doctrine and named him special military representative. In October 1961, Kennedy sent Taylor and White House aide Walt Rostow to South Vietnam to assess the military situation. The Taylor-Rostow report downplayed the risks of U.S. intervention and led to Kennedy's commitment of the first U.S. ground troops. Kennedy then brought Taylor back into military service by appointing him chairman of the JCS in 1962.

A leading exponent of counterinsurgency warfare, Taylor believed that the U.S. had to prevent a communist takeover of South Vietnam, and he si-

MAXWELL D. TAYLOR. *National Archives*

lenced any doubters at the Pentagon. Kennedy sent Taylor to South Vietnam on another fact-finding mission with Secretary of Defense Robert McNamara in September 1963. The Taylor-McNamara report stressed "great progress" in the war, but recommended support for "alternative leadership" in Saigon. President Diem was overthrown a few weeks later. In 1964, President Johnson sent Taylor back to Saigon to manage the American war effort as U.S. ambassador. While there, Taylor developed new doubts about the wisdom of taking over the war—and about the ability of U.S. troops to fight it. Taylor reversed his earlier positions and advocated bombing North Vietnam instead of committing U.S. combat troops. When Johnson sent troops anyway, Taylor lobbied hard to keep them in coastal enclaves. He lost out to Gen. William Westmoreland and others who insisted on search-and-destroy operations. Taylor rightly predicted that it would be impossible to "hold the line" against further troop

commitments once the U.S. took charge of the war effort.

As U.S. ambassador, Taylor despaired over the continual coup-plotting in Saigon, scolding South Vietnam's generals for their squabbling: "We cannot carry you forever if you do things like this." At the end of his tour Taylor was virtually thrown out of the country by President Ky, who resented Taylor's high-handed meddling. Taylor returned to Washington as a special White House consultant, now calling for more troops and escalated bombing of North Vietnam. In Taylor's view the consequences of failure outweighed the costs of continued involvement, and he never quite understood how the communists could persist in the face of U.S. power. Taylor was prominent among the "wise men" who advised Johnson on the war, but he dissented from the Senior Advisory Group's recommendation that the United States disengage from Vietnam in 1968. After the war, Taylor humbly decided that "we'd better keep out of this dirty kind of business" in the future.

BIBLIOGRAPHY

HALBERSTAM, DAVID. *The Best and the Brightest.* 1972.
KARNOW, STANLEY. "A Soldier of Quality." *New York Times Book Review,* 25 June 1989.
KINNARD, DOUGLAS. *The Certain Trumpet: Maxwell Taylor and the American Experience in Vietnam.* 1991.
TAYLOR, JOHN. *General Maxwell Taylor: The Sword and the Pen.* 1989.
TAYLOR, MAXWELL D. *Precarious Security.* 1976.
TAYLOR, MAXWELL D. *Swords and Plowshares.* 1972.
TAYLOR, MAXWELL D. *The Uncertain Trumpet.* 1959.

GLEN GENDZEL

Taylor-McNamara Report. President Kennedy, having lost faith in the glowing reports he received from Gen. Paul Harkins about President Diem and the Strategic Hamlet program, sent Gen. Maxwell Taylor, chairman of the Joint Chiefs of Staff (JCS), and Secretary of Defense Robert McNamara to South Vietnam on a ten-day fact-finding mission in September 1963. Harkins set the Taylor-McNamara itinerary, steering them away from U.S. advisers skeptical of South Vietnam's military, but they also interviewed Ambassador Henry Cabot Lodge, a stern critic of Diem. The Taylor-McNamara report of 2 October 1963 mixed Harkins's optimism about the military situation with Lodge's pessimism about the political outlook:

The report found "great progress" in the war against the Viet Cong guerrillas, particularly in the strategic hamlets, but cautioned that Diem faced a "crisis of confidence" in South Vietnam. It recommended that the United States encourage "alternative leadership" while pressuring Diem to make his regime more democratic and more effective in fighting Viet Cong forces. President Kennedy approved the recommendations, and Ambassador Lodge's overtures to coup-plotting generals in Saigon may have contributed to Diem's overthrow a few weeks later.

BIBLIOGRAPHY

HILSMAN, ROGER. *To Move a Nation: The Politics of Foreign Policy in the Administration of John F. Kennedy.* 1967.
KAHIN, GEORGE McT. *Intervention: How America Became Involved in Vietnam.* 1986.
KINNARD, DOUGLAS. *The Certain Trumpet: Maxwell Taylor and the American Experience in Vietnam.* 1991.
NEWMAN, JOHN M. *JFK and Vietnam: Deception, Intrigue, and the Struggle for Power.* 1992.
SHAPLEY, DEBORAH. *Promise and Power: The Life and Times of Robert McNamara.* 1993.
TAYLOR, MAXWELL D. *Swords and Plowshares.* 1972.
U.S. DEPARTMENT OF STATE. *Vietnam, August–December 1963.* Vol. 4 of *Foreign Relations of the United States, 1961–1963.* 1991.

GLEN GENDZEL

Taylor-Rostow Report. In October 1961, President Kennedy sent his aides Maxwell Taylor and Walt Rostow on a fact-finding mission to South Vietnam. Unconnected to the State and Defense department bureaucracies, both men favored granting President Diem's request for U.S. troops. Their report, dated 3 November 1961, portrayed the Viet Cong insurgency as part of the global communist threat in the Cold War. They warned that communism would spread across Southeast Asia if unchecked by a "hard U.S. commitment on the ground" to shore up Diem's regime. The risk of a protracted war was "not impressive," assured Taylor and Rostow, and Americans would find Vietnam "not an excessively difficult or unpleasant place to operate." Taylor and Rostow recommended sending 8,000 troops immediately to reassure President Diem and to intimidate the Viet Cong guerrillas. Secretary of Defense Robert McNamara added to the report his warning that up to 205,000 troops might eventually be needed. Kennedy made the first sizeable commitment of advisers in accordance with the Taylor-Rostow recommendations. The number of U.S. troops in Vietnam increased from 600 to 15,000 within one year.

BIBLIOGRAPHY

HILSMAN, ROGER. *To Move a Nation: The Politics of Foreign Policy in the Administration of John F. Kennedy.* 1967.
KAHIN, GEORGE McT. *Intervention: How America Became Involved in Vietnam.* 1986.
KINNARD, DOUGLAS. *The Certain Trumpet: Maxwell Taylor and the American Experience in Vietnam.* 1991.
NEWMAN, JOHN M. *JFK and Vietnam: Deception, Intrigue, and the Struggle for Power.* 1992.
TAYLOR, MAXWELL D. *Swords and Plowshares.* 1972.
U.S. DEPARTMENT OF STATE. *Vietnam, 1961.* Vol. 1 of *Foreign Relations of the United States, 1961–1963.* 1988.

GLEN GENDZEL

Teach-Ins. The first teach-in took place at the University of Michigan on 24 March 1965. A group of faculty members who opposed increasing U.S. involvement in Vietnam organized the session in response to Lyndon Johnson's ordering of three thousand Marines into Da Nang, the first deployment of U.S. combat troops. The professors debated the war with three thousand students who attended the all-night session. The gatherings quickly spread to other universities throughout the country, where they continued for the rest of the war. The forum sought to educate people about the conflict rather than to recruit protesters into the antiwar movement, although the process did turn many students against the policies of the Johnson administration.

In May 1965 the State Department launched a "truth team" to visit campuses in the Midwest and counter the teach-ins, but the government officials received hostile responses and had little success. On 15 May 1965, a special radio link connected 122 campuses nationwide for a national teach-in, and participants included both pro- and antiwar speakers. This phenomenon was extended to the military through the "Free the Army" campaign, led by Tom Hayden (one of the founders of Students for a Democratic Society [SDS]) and Jane Fonda, which modified the teach-in format, using less formal meetings and holding them at sites near military installations so they could more easily include soldiers. Teach-ins continued to be held at various locations until Saigon was taken by the North Vietnamese in 1975.

BIBLIOGRAPHY

POWERS, THOMAS. *Vietnam, the War at Home: Vietnam and the American People, 1964–1968.* 1984.

WATERHOUSE, LARRY, and MARIANN WIZARD. *Turning the Guns Around: Notes on the GI Movement.* 1971.

ZAROULIS, NANCY, and GERALD SULLIVAN. *Who Spoke Up? American Protest against the War in Vietnam, 1963–1975.* 1984.

ELLEN D. GOLDLUST

Television.

For discussion of the treatment of the Vietnam War on American television, see Art and Literature; Media and the War.

Ten-Pin Theory.

Widely embraced by French leaders between 1946 and 1954, the ten-pin theory held that the loss of France's colony in Vietnam would encourage nationalist independence movements in other parts of the French empire such as Algeria. Unlike the image suggested by the domino theory of neat rows of contiguous lands toppling one-by-one in Asia, the ten-pin theory envisioned a more explosive spreading effect. The effect of toppling one "head pin" country would scatter in random directions, overthrowing French control in noncontiguous lands in all parts of the worldwide French empire—in Africa as well as in Asia. By the 1960s, U.S. policymakers embraced a similar random effect theory, believing that the fall of Vietnam threatened more than the Southeast Asian "dominoes" of Laos, Cambodia, Thailand, Indonesia, the Philippines, and beyond to Japan. In the context of the Castro revolution in Cuba and the rise of radical nationalism throughout Latin America, the U.S. government feared that a victory by North Vietnamese and National Liberation Front forces in Vietnam would embolden similar movements within the United States's traditional sphere of influence, Latin America.

BIBLIOGRAPHY

HEARDEN, PATRICK J. *The Tragedy of Vietnam.* 1991.

THOMAS J. MCCORMICK

Tet Offensive.

The 1968 Tet Offensive, a surprise North Vietnamese Army (NVA) and National Liberation Front (NLF) attack launched on the Vietnamese New Year, represented the decisive battle of the Vietnam War. On 30–31 January, during the holiday cease-fire, nearly 84,000 NLF and NVA soldiers attacked South Vietnamese military and government installations throughout the country.

The offensive's aim was to topple the South Vietnamese government, but the expected popular uprising in the South in support of communist forces failed to materialize. Though it was a substantial military failure and political miscalculation, the broad offensive shocked the American public, which had been assured that a U.S. victory was imminent. The Tet Offensive convinced many Americans that the war could not be won, setting in motion the process of eventual U.S. withdrawal and tilting public opinion in favor of ending combat intervention.

Planning the Campaign. North Vietnamese military leadership conceived the Tet Offensive to regain the initiative in the war. NVA and NLF forces had suffered extensive losses in conventional warfare against U.S. forces during 1965–1966. General Vo Nguyen Giap developed the strategy called the "General Offensive, General Uprising," which coordinated political, military, and diplomatic initiatives. Its crucial aspect entailed attacks on South Vietnamese government and military sites on the Tet holiday to spur defections within the Army of the Republic of Vietnam (ARVN) and a public revolt in the cities. Preparatory military and diplomatic maneuvers would separate the South's "puppet" regime from U.S. military resources. North Vietnam set in motion Giap's "General Offensive, General Uprising" in mid 1967. The military replenished NLF guerrilla ranks with People's Army of Vietnam (PAVN) soldiers and armed the insurgents with improved weaponry, including AK-47 rifles and B-40 rocket launchers (obtained from the USSR and China). NLF personnel infiltrated cities and secured weapons caches. Motivational campaigns among soldiers and civilians were begun in the fall of 1967 to prepare for the "total victory."

In summer 1967 General Giap also initiated conventional military campaigns to draw U.S. forces into the interior and thus away from South Vietnam's populated areas, which were generally near the coast. PAVN forces attacked U.S. and ARVN positions beginning in July at Con Thien near the demilitarized zone (DMZ) and continued until November at Dak To in Kontum province. During these campaigns, termed the "border battles," the PAVN forces suffered heavy casualties as its ranks were exposed to the superior U.S. firepower. But combined with later operations against the U.S. Marine base at Khe Sanh begun in late 1967, the attacks succeeded in drawing U.S. forces into remote areas. By the Tet holiday, more than half of U.S.

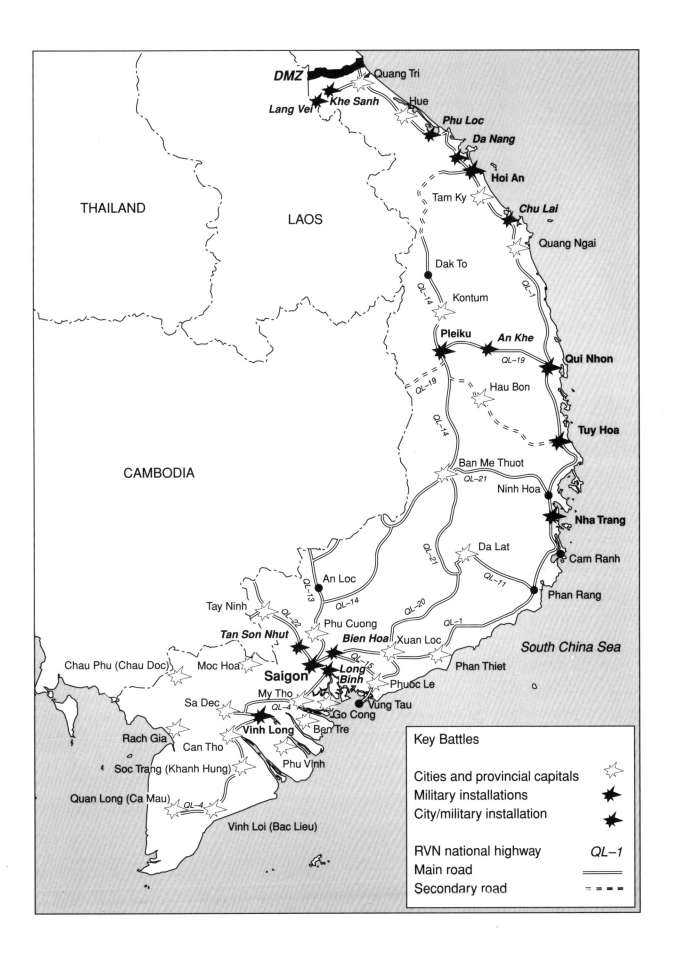

THAILAND

LAOS

CAMBODIA

DMZ
Quang Tri
Lang Vei   Khe Sanh   Hue
Phu Loc
Da Nang
Hoi An
Tam Ky   Chu Lai
Quang Ngai
Dak To
Kontum
Pleiku   An Khe   Qui Nhon
Hau Bon
Tuy Hoa
Ban Me Thuot
Ninh Hoa
Nha Trang
Da Lat
Cam Ranh
An Loc
Phan Rang
Tay Ninh
Phu Cuong
Tan Son Nhut   Bien Hoa   Xuan Loc
Chau Phu (Chau Doc)   Moc Hoa
Saigon   Long Binh   Phuoc Le
My Tho   Phan Thiet
Sa Dec   Go Cong   Vung Tau
Rach Gia   Ben Tre
Can Tho   Vinh Long
Soc Trang (Khanh Hung)   Phu Vinh
Quan Long (Ca Mau)
Vinh Loi (Bac Lieu)

South China Sea

QL-1
QL-14
QL-19
QL-21
QL-11
QL-20
QL-13
QL-22
QL-4
QL-15

Key Battles	
Cities and provincial capitals	☆
Military installations	★
City/military installation	✦
RVN national highway	QL-1
Main road	——
Secondary road	– – –

STREET EXECUTION. South Vietnam's chief of the national police, Brig. Gen. Nguyen Ngoc Loan, executing a Viet Cong officer in Saigon, 1 February 1968. The photo, in tandem with an NBC film of the execution, turned many in America and around the world against the Vietnam War. Photo by Eddie Adams of the Associated Press. *Associated Press/World Wide Photos*

combat battalions had been moved into the I Corps Tactical Zone (CTZ) to counter the siege of Khe Sanh.

North Vietnam also began diplomatic initiatives intended to create tension in the U.S.–South Vietnamese alliance. In late 1967, the North agreed to participate in peace negotiations if the United States would end the bombing campaigns. The appeal was intended to sow distrust among the South Vietnamese concerning U.S. resolve to continue the war.

The Offensive Begins. Under the cover of the Tet celebrations—a traditional time for a cease-fire—PAVN and NLF forces massed around cities.

Attacks were initially planned for 30 January, but officials delayed the offensive by twenty-four hours. Many units did not receive the new orders and fighting began prematurely in six cities. By the next night, 27 of South Vietnam's 44 provincial capitals, 5 of 6 autonomous cities, 58 of 245 district towns, and more than 50 hamlets were under fire. NLF battalions and commando teams led the offensive, while PAVN forces usually remained in reserve. The attacks targeted South Vietnamese government installations, military sites, and communication centers, and bypassed U.S. forces except for jointly held air bases and high-profile sites such as the U.S. embassy. The NLF guerrillas exhorted southerners at roadblocks and with leaflets to revolt against the government; but the insurgency received very little support from the South Vietnamese.

Though at half strength because of the holidays, ARVN units with U.S. assistance fought valiantly in defense of their homes and families. Most attacking forces failed to penetrate cities, although fighting continued for several days in Ban Me Thuot, Ben Tre, Can Tho, and Kontum. Protracted fighting in Saigon continued for more than a week, and in Hue until early March. In Saigon, NLF forces attacked the presidential palace, police headquarters, and radio station while a sapper team penetrated the U.S.

embassy for a few hours on 31 January. Fifteen U.S. battalions, which had recently been moved to Saigon by III CTZ commander Gen. Frederick Weyand, were critical in reclaiming the capital. At Hue, a PAVN division with NLF forces and prisoners from local jails held the old imperial city. Three U.S. Marine battalions, along with ARVN troops, recaptured the city in bloody house-to-house fighting.

Failing to spark revolts, the Tet Offensive was a costly military failure. Without a public uprising, most attacks were little more than suicidal raids because of the small number of troops. The broad of-

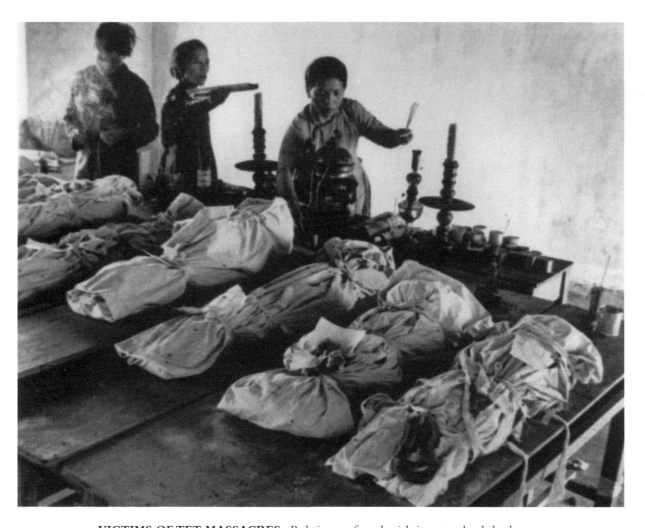

VICTIMS OF TET MASSACRES. Relatives perform burial rites over the skeletal remains of civilians killed during the 1968 Tet Offensive, Trung Thien, South Vietnam, 1971. The bodies were discovered in shallow graves north of Hue on 6 April. The bodies of thousands of civilian victims of mass executions by communist forces were discovered for several years after Tet. *National Archives*

fensive also lacked plans for retreat, which led to further casualties. PAVN and NLF losses were estimated at 45,000, of an 84,000-member attack force; South Vietnamese losses were 2,300 while the United States suffered 1,100 combat fatalities.

Gen. William Westmoreland, his staff, and his intelligence group did not anticipate the Tet Offensive. The U.S. command had ascertained that the North had developed a new strategy but determined that the decisive confrontation would be at Khe Sanh. It failed to consider the possibility of bold, unorthodox attacks by PAVN and NLF forces. U.S. military commanders believed they held the initiative in the war, and they expected North Vietnamese tactics to be in response to U.S. operations. Ironically, their decisions prompted Giap's deceptive intention. The siege at Khe Sanh was viewed by Westmoreland as a preemptive strike against plans to interdict the Ho Chi Minh Trail from the U.S. Marine base at Khe Sanh. Earlier border battles were interpreted as showing the effectiveness of "shield" operations by U.S. forces on the periphery of South Vietnam.

U.S. Reactions. While the Tet Offensive surprised the U.S. military, it stunned the American public. Citing the erosion of North Vietnamese and NLF forces, Westmoreland had recently contended that "we have turned the corner," part of a successful effort by President Johnson to bolster public support. The Tet Offensive shattered these assurances. Near-record American audiences watched television coverage of the urban warfare, which showed fighting seemingly spiraling out of control. Events challenged the justifications and coherence of the U.S. war effort. Widespread assaults throughout Vietnam cast doubt on whether the United States could foster a stable South Vietnamese regime. The determined communist offensive, following supposed U.S. military successes, confounded the U.S. government's and Americans' expectations for a final victory.

The Tet Offensive created an atmosphere of gloom and uncertainty within the United States's halls of power. Elected politicians, government bureaucrats, and business leaders expressed pessimism about achieving U.S. war aims. Reflecting frustration with the apparent "credibility gap" of the administration, media coverage turned negative. Reporting ranged from "disaster" scenarios of a supposed major Tet defeat and an impending Khe Sanh "bloodbath," to more balanced appraisals of persisting "stalemate."

Among the wider public, the Tet Offensive had a complex though less pivotal effect, ultimately continuing a decline in support that began in 1967. In February 1968, Gallup polls noted that public confidence in the war actually increased to 74 percent, reflecting a rally of support typical during an international crisis (by March, this figure had dropped to 54 percent). On one key gauge, the Tet Offensive had a decisive impact, as the number of self-proclaimed proponents of the war declined to 41 percent of the population in March, well below the pre–Tet Offensive figure. But in an overall measure of whether the Vietnam intervention was a "mistake," negative sentiments increased gradually to 49 percent in March, reflecting a rise in frustration with the war that began in early 1967 and that would continue to increase. Public frustration grew as U.S. casualties mounted in the massive military commitment that now appeared uncertain of victory. President Johnson's recent public relations effort had attempted to address this rising ambivalence, although his efforts ironically contributed to the shock of the Tet Offensive.

Consequences of Tet. With influential Americans turning against the war, and uncertain public support, President Johnson struggled to recapture political momentum. Johnson ended the buildup of forces in Vietnam, denying Westmoreland's request for more troops and recalling the general to Washington. But Johnson's leadership had been discredited. His approval ratings sank to 24 percent in March, and he nearly lost the New Hampshire primary to the relatively obscure antiwar candidate Eugene J. McCarthy. The New Hampshire result showed no clear mandate against the war, however, because more than half of McCarthy's supporters were prowar. Voters blamed Johnson, as did many Americans, for the war's setbacks and the social discord of the era. On 31 March, Johnson told the nation he would not seek reelection and would pursue peace negotiations with North Vietnam.

The North Vietnamese continued under the design of Giap's General Offensive with smaller "mini–Tet Offensives" in several cities during May 1968, but the assaults were equally costly. The Tet Offensive failed disastrously in its intended objectives. The attacks decimated the NLF combatants and resulted in growing morale problems among the armed forces. Moreover, the southern insurgency lost many of its veteran leaders. The North Vietnamese eventually replaced these seasoned combatants with PAVN officers, but the absence of local officers impaired NLF organization and guerrilla operations for years. But Giap's plan, despite the costs, had regained the initiative of the war, though by unanticipated means. North Vietnam had not targeted the American domestic audience in its strategy, but the Tet Offensive had unexpectedly fractured the U.S. consensus for the war.

BIBLIOGRAPHY

Braestrup, Peter. *Big Story.* 1977.
Davidson, Phillip. *Vietnam at War.* 1988.
Karnow, Stanley. *Vietnam: A History.* 1991.
Hammond, William M. *Public Affairs: The Military and the Media, 1962–1968.* 1988.
Oberdorfer, Don. *Tet! The Turning Point in the Vietnam War.* 1984.
Wirtz, James J. *The Tet Offensive: Intelligence Failure in War.* 1991.

Adam Land

Thach, Nguyen Co. *See* Nguyen Co Thach.

Thailand. Thailand and Vietnam have been traditional rivals contesting for domination over Laos and Cambodia since the early nineteenth century. After the Viet Minh defeated the French at Dien Bien Phu in 1954, the Thai state was alarmed by the possible threat from the coupling of Vietnamese nationalism and communism. The anti-communist paranoia of the Thai military governments perfectly served the containment policy of the United States, and throughout the Vietnam War, Thailand proved to be the best ally of the United States.

Thailand and the United States have had a special relationship, beginning with agreements for non-military cooperation in 1950, and continuing later with the commitment of Thai forces during the Korean War. The Viet Minh victory prompted the United States to create the Southeast Asia Treaty Organization (SEATO) in 1954, and Thailand was one of only two Southeast Asian countries to join it.

The conflicts within Laos that erupted into violent fighting and eventually a coup by a leftist military officer in 1960, and the advance of communist forces in 1960–1961, became the first test of SEATO. Nearly 10,000 U.S. Marines from the SEATO military exercise at the time were sent to the Thai-Laotian border, but the empty show of force exposed the inadequacy of SEATO. Its members could not agree on any measure, apart from a warning, to contain the communist Lao, or to guarantee Thailand's security. The Thai government demanded a more concrete commitment. Thus, in 1962 the United States announced the Rusk-Thanat Agreement, guaranteeing Thai security against any external threat or even internal insurgency, and this became the basis for the U.S. military presence in Thailand throughout the Vietnam War.

U.S. military assistance to Thailand rapidly increased to prepare the country against possible foreign aggression and to establish supply bases for the U.S. troops in Vietnam. As the U.S. intervention in Vietnam escalated after 1964, Thailand's strategic significance increased. The stability of Thai politics under the military regime and the relative lack of serious insurgency made Thailand the ideal staging site for the U.S. operation in Vietnam.

U.S. military commands and headquarters were established, military air bases built, and the first group of U.S. personnel were stationed in Thailand in 1964. Thai military leaders personally and verbally approved the U.S. presence. The number of U.S. soldiers in Thailand increased from 6,000 in 1964 to a peak of 49,000 in 1969. The United States had seven major air bases, which it used for logistical supplies and also for launching air attacks over Vietnam. Three of these air bases were less than 80 kilometers (50 miles) from the Thai-Laotian borders, and only a 30–40 minute flight from Hanoi. The $200-million U Tapao air base, one of the largest in Asia at the time, was built for B-52 operations and was capable of docking about eighty warplanes. There were also numerous radar and other telecommunication centers, several camps for the U.S. Special Forces, a Central Intelligence Agency (CIA) operation command, and several counterinsurgency training camps. As the Vietnamization of the war developed after 1969, air operations from Thailand were intensified in an attempt to reduce U.S. casualties. After the war the significance of the U.S. bases and the place of Thailand in U.S. strategic needs gradually diminished, and in 1976 the United States turned the bases over to the Thai government.

Thailand was the first Asian country to send troops to Vietnam, in 1964. Three years later, in response to a Pentagon request, it committed its best combat units of 11,000 soldiers (14 percent of the Thai force at the time) to the front lines. The United States paid all expenses for the Thai troops for training, ammunition, and wages.

With U.S. funding, Thailand also conducted a secret war in Laos against the Pathet Lao, the communist Laotian insurgency. Beginning in 1965, under a

SARIT THANARAT. Prime minister of Thailand, with Laotian rightist leader Boun Oum, Bangkok, 1962. *National Archives*

special command of the Thai army, highly paid mercenaries joined the Hmong force under Vang Pao to operate deep inside the Pathet Lao's areas. At its peak, there were about 16,500 Thai and other ethnic "volunteer" soldiers in Laotian territory. The United States also funded at least six counterinsurgency training camps for Hmong and right-wing Laotian forces.

The Vietnam War benefited the Thai economy enormously. The United States provided $936 million in military assistance to the Thai armed forces between 1951 and 1971, nearly 60 percent of Thailand's total military budget. This sum did not include several hundred million dollars in operating costs, the investment in construction of air bases and roads, and the funding of Thai troops in Vietnam

and Laos. Nonmilitary assistance increased from $111.9 million in the 1960–1964 period to $256.7 million during 1965–1970. The infusion of this capital into the Thai economy had an enormous impact on the construction and other war-related industries in the emerging urban areas and around the bases, and in transportation and communication infrastructures. The U.S. presence in Thailand created an estimated 150,000 jobs, including 44,000 in construction alone. Moreover, approximately 6,000 U.S. soldiers per month came to Thailand for rest and recreation, resulting in an expansion of related services around the bases. Overall, this war-supported economy contributed approximately $800 million to the Thai economy between 1964 and 1969, nearly 50 percent of the country's gross domestic product (GDP). These developments served as the foundation for Thailand's rapid industrialization in the following decades.

Yet, as the Thai economy benefited from the U.S. presence, the scaling down of U.S. military activities after 1972 caused significant upheaval. The U.S. withdrawal affected domestic politics as the rapidly growing middle class increasingly challenged the military rule. The presence of U.S. bases and military operations on Thai soil became a focal point of the radical movement after the student uprising in 1973. The end of the war in 1975, however, frightened the Thai state, and intensified the fear of communism within the military and the public alike. Cambodia, Laos, and Vietnam in particular, remained Thailand's primary enemies. Anticommunist propaganda and an extreme right-wing movement targeted both external and internal enemies. The political polarization eventually ended with the return of the military regime and the massacre of radical students in Bangkok in 1976 to protect the country from falling into communist hands.

Finally, Thailand found itself flooded with refugees from the Vietnam War from 1975 onward, but particularly as a result of the continuing conflict in Cambodia after 1978. At its peak, "temporary" camps housed more than 250,000 refugees, with separate camps for each nationality and for the different factions in the case of Cambodians. Some of the camps trained insurgents and guerrillas, including the Khmer Rouge.

BIBLIOGRAPHY

ANDERSON, BENEDICT. "Withdrawal Symptoms: Social and Cultural Aspects of the October 8 Coup." *Bulletin of Concerned Asian Scholars* 9:13–30.

GIRLING, JOHN S. *Thailand: Politics and Society.* 1981.

MORELL, DAVID, and CHAI-ANAN SAMUTVANIJA. *Political Conflicts in Thailand.* 1981.

NUMNONDA, THAMSOOK. *Kanthut thai sami rattanakosin* (Thai diplomacy in the Bangkok period). 1985.

RANDOLPH, SEAN. "Diplomacy and National Interests: Thai-American Security Cooperation in the Vietnam Era." Ph.D. diss., Fletcher School of Law and Diplomacy, 1978.

THONGCHAI WINICHAKUL

Thanh, Nguyen Chi. *See* Nguyen Chi Thanh.

Thi, Nguyen Chanh. *See* Nguyen Chanh Thi.

Thieu, Nguyen Van. *See* Nguyen Van Thieu.

Thompson, Robert G. K. (1916–), British expert on counterinsurgency; unofficial adviser to President Nixon. Based on his experience as a British colonial administrator in Malaya, Sir Robert G. K. Thompson developed the Strategic Hamlet program. Begun in Vietnam in 1962, this program relocated Vietnamese villagers into stockaded hamlets ostensibly for their better protection, and was intended to force the North Vietnamese and Viet Cong forces to fight in the open. Later in the 1960s Thompson served as key unofficial adviser to President Nixon, endorsing the Vietnamization strategy recommended by former Secretary of Defense Clark Clifford.

BIBLIOGRAPHY

HERRING, GEORGE C. *America's Longest War: The United States and Vietnam, 1950–1975.* 1986.

KOLKO, GABRIEL. *Anatomy of a War: Vietnam, the United States, and the Modern Historical Experience.* 1985.

ELLEN BAKER

Thuc, Ngo Dinh. *See* Ngo Dinh Thuc.

Ticket Punching. *Ticket punching* is a U.S. military slang term referring to careerism in the armed forces. Many officers were more concerned with doing whatever was necessary to be promoted, to get their "ticket punched," than they were with leading troops to success in combat. Officers hoping to attain the rank of general needed an "outstanding" mark in their six-month tour of duty in Vietnam. Critics of careerism in the military have argued that ticket punching yielded officers who inflated body counts and provided poor leadership to their men, as evidenced by the high incidence of drug abuse and fragging.

BIBLIOGRAPHY

HACKWORTH, DAVID L., and JULIE SHERMAN. *About Face: The Odyssey of an American Warrior.* 1989.

KINNARD, DOUGLAS. *The War Managers.* 1985.

KELLY EVANS-PFEIFER

Tiger Cages. The "tiger cages" were five feet by nine feet cement cells located at Con Son prison in South Vietnam. Built by the French in the 1940s, the tiger cages were used in the 1960s by the Thieu government to hold political prisoners and prisoners of war. The cells were uncovered in a 1970 U.S. congressional visit to Con Son prison and were subsequently cited by the International Red Cross as a violation of the Geneva Convention. In 1974, antiwar groups conducted a vigil at the U.S. Capitol demanding pressure on Thieu to release the dissidents confined in the tiger cages.

BIBLIOGRAPHY

NGUYEN TIEN HUNG and JERROLD L. SCHECTER. *The Palace File.* 1986.
ZAROULIS, NANCY, and GERALD SULLIVAN. *Who Spoke Up?* 1984.

KELLY EVANS-PFEIFER

Tonkin Gulf Resolution. *See* Gulf of Tonkin Resolution.

Tra, Tran Van. *See* Tran Van Tra.

Tran Do (1922–), North Vietnamese commander. A North Vietnamese soldier of near-mythic reputation, General Tran Do moved south in 1964 to become deputy commander of National Liberation Front (NLF) and North Vietnamese Army (NVA) forces in South Vietnam. In the mid 1960s, Tran Do increased the number of North Vietnamese commanders, political officers, and technical experts within the NLF to ensure the North's oversight and control of the expanding insurgency force. Tran Do was an architect of the 1968 Tet Offensive. He later acknowledged that the operation failed in its main goal of igniting uprisings across the South, although it had the unintended result of turning American public opinion against the war, which in his words was a "fortunate result."

BIBLIOGRAPHY

KARNOW, STANLEY. *Vietnam: A History.* 1991.

ADAM LAND

Trang Sup. Early on the morning of 26 January 1960, about two hundred Viet Cong guerrillas attacked the headquarters of the South Vietnamese Army's 32d Regiment in the village of Trang Sup, northeast of Saigon in Tay Ninh province. They overran the base, blew up the barracks, inflicted heavy casualties, and seized large stores of U.S.-supplied arms and ammunition. Lt. Gen. Samuel Williams, commander of the U.S. Military Assistance Advisory Group-Vietnam (MAAG-V) called the Trang Sup attack "a severe blow to the prestige of the Vietnamese Army and [an] indication of the VC ability to stage large-size well-planned attacks. Williams recommended military reforms but did not call for more U.S. troops. The attack showed that South Vietnam faced not a full-scale Korea-style invasion, but rather a protracted guerrilla war, and it revealed the weakness of Ngo Dinh Diem's poorly organized forces.

BIBLIOGRAPHY

RACE, JEFFREY. *War Comes to Long An: Revolutionary Conflict in a Vietnamese Province.* 1972.
SPECTOR, RONALD H. *The United States Army in Vietnam, Advice and Support: The Early Years, 1941–1960.* 1985.

GLEN GENDZEL

Tran Thien Khiem (1925–), general, Army of the Republic of Vietnam (ARVN). Gen. Tran Thien Khiem was chief of staff when he helped overthrow President Diem in November 1963. He then held many offices in South Vietnam's government: defense minister (1964) under Gen. Khanh, ambassador to Taiwan (1964–1965) and to the United States (1965–1968) under President Ky, and prime minister (1969–1975) under President Thieu. Khiem grew wealthy in office and was suspected of drug dealing and working for the Central Intelligence Agency (CIA). He escaped to Taiwan in April 1975, and from there to France.

BIBLIOGRAPHY

"Limiting the Leadership." *Time,* 29 August 1969.
SHAPLEN, ROBERT. *The Lost Revolution: The U.S. in Vietnam, 1946–1966.* Rev. ed., 1966.
TRAN VAN DON. *Our Endless War: Inside Vietnam.* 1978.

GLEN GENDZEL

Tran Van Don (1917–), South Vietnamese commander. Born and educated in France, General Don was one of the four South Vietnamese generals who orchestrated the November 1963 coup against Ngo Dinh Diem. As chief of staff for the Army of the Republic of Vietnam (ARVN), Don established the crucial liaison with a U.S. Central Intelligence Agency (CIA) operative through which the generals ascertained U.S. support for the coup. Don reportedly opposed the murder of Diem, which was ordered by his coconspirator General Minh. A personal colleague of President Nguyen Van Thieu, Don served as deputy prime minister, army chief of staff, and roving ambassador over the course of Thieu's administration. He escaped to the United States in 1975 and subsequently worked as a real estate broker and travel agent.

BIBLIOGRAPHY

KARNOW, STANLEY. *Vietnam: A History.* 1991.

ADAM LAND

Tran Van Huong (1903–), South Vietnamese prime minister, 1964–1965, 1968–1969, 1975; vice president, 1971–1975. Tran Van Huong was the mayor of Saigon and, although a critic of the Diem regime, was widely perceived as senile and inept. Gen. Nguyen Khanh, after overthrowing the Military Revolutionary Council in January 1964, established a civilian government led by President Phan Khac Suu, with Huong as prime minister. Huong served in this capacity from October 1964 through January 1965, when Khanh took over completely. After another brief stint as prime minister in 1968–1969, Huong served Thieu as vice president from 1971 through 1975, but largely as a figurehead. When Thieu fled Saigon on 25 April 1975, ahead of advancing NVA forces, he appointed Huong president. Huong resigned and transferred his authority to Gen. Duong Van Minh on 28 April, two days before the final collapse of the Republic of Vietnam.

BIBLIOGRAPHY

HERRING, GEORGE C. *America's Longest War: The United States and Vietnam, 1950–1975.* 1986.
KOLKO, GABRIEL. *Anatomy of a War: Vietnam, the United States, and the Modern Historical Experience.* 1985.

ELLEN BAKER

Tran Van Tra (1918–), military leader of National Liberation Front (NLF); member, Central Committee of Lao Dong Party; lieutenant general, North Vietnamese Army (NVA); chairman, Military Affairs Committee of the Central Office of South Vietnam (COSVN), 1964–1976; minister of defense, Provisional Military Government (PRG), 1969–1976). Tran Van Tra fought with the Viet Minh against the French from 1946 to 1954. Born in Quang Ngai Province in southern Vietnam, he became lieutenant general of the North Vietnamese Army in 1961 and commanded B2 region, the southern half of South Vietnam. Tra's upbringing in the south made him especially suited to this role. From 1964 to 1976, he served as chairman of COSVN and coordinated the guerrilla movement against South Vietnam, including the assault on Saigon in the 1968 Tet Offensive. While minister of defense for the Provisional Military Government of South Vietnam, as the NLF was renamed after the Tet Offensive, he advocated a national military campaign in 1974–1975 in order to prevent the Army of the Republic of Vietnam (ARVN) from deploying its forces region by region. His strategy for the final push—in which he served as deputy commander—was an attack on Route 14 across Phuoc Long province and a quick assault on Saigon from five directions. In 1982 Tran Van Tra was purged from the Vietnamese Communist party because his written account of that offensive, *Vietnam: History of Bulwark B2 Theatre,* volume 5, criticized the North Vietnamese communists and admitted that the Tet Offensive was poorly planned and executed.

BIBLIOGRAPHY

KARNOW, STANLEY. *Vietnam: A History.* 1991.
SUMMERS, HARRY G., JR. *Vietnam War Almanac.* 1985.

ELLEN BAKER

Tri Quang (1922–), prominent Buddhist monk and noncommunist dissident in South Vietnam. Devout and ascetic and a great admirer of Gandhi, Tri Quang insisted that Vietnam must find a Buddhist "middle way" between communism and Western influence. Tri Quang originally sided with the Viet Minh against the French in the 1950s, but he broke with the communists and entered the Dieude Temple monastery in the ancient capital of Hue. Speaking from the back of a sound truck, Tri Quang incited Buddhist protests against President Diem's repressive regime and favoritism toward Catholics in 1963. His speeches exhorting Vietnamese to embrace traditional culture and reject foreign influences were electrifying. Buddhist monks set themselves aflame in the streets of Saigon to protest the government's policies. Diem was overthrown a few months later.

In 1966, when President Nguyen Cao Ky refused to call elections, Tri Quang and Gen. Nguyen

HARRY S. TRUMAN. At left, with president-elect Dwight D. Eisenhower, 1952. *National Archives*

Chanh Thi led the so-called Struggle Movement that staged a rising series of protests against the U.S.-backed regime in Saigon. South Vietnam plunged into virtual civil war as government troops fought Buddhists, radical students, and rebel soldiers in Danang and Hue. With heavy military force, President Ky crushed the rebellion in May 1966, and Tri Quang was arrested. "I am merely a monk," he told a reporter who asked what sort of government he wanted for South Vietnam. "Those are questions for politicians." After almost starving to death on a hunger strike, Tri Quang withdrew to the Saigon monastery of An Quang and abstained from politics after 1966. Placed under house arrest soon after the communist takeover, Tri Quang was jailed in 1982.

BIBLIOGRAPHY

FITZGERALD, FRANCES. *Fire in the Lake: The Vietnamese and the Americans in Vietnam.* 1982.

KARNOW, STANLEY. *Vietnam: A History.* 1991.

MIRSKY, JONATHAN. "Conversation with a Monk." *Nation* 205 (25 December 1967).

NGUYEN TAI THU, ed. *History of Buddhism in Vietnam.* 1992.

SHAPLEN, ROBERT. *The Lost Revolution: The U.S. in Vietnam, 1946–1966.* Rev. ed., 1966.

WULFF, ERICH. "The Buddhist Revolt." *New Republic,* 31 August 1963.

GLEN GENDZEL

Truman, Harry S. (1884–1972), U.S. senator (D-Mo.), 1934–1944; vice president, 1944; president, 1944–1952. Truman reversed President Franklin D. Roosevelt's tentative policy of abandoning support for a continued French presence in Indochina. Beginning in 1948 Truman viewed Vietnam as one of the possible "points of contact" where "a Soviet-controlled Communist world might choose to attack." He viewed Ho Chi Minh's revolutionary force as a communist puppet in the global Cold War and frequently invoked the domino theory and the policy of containment in discussing his policy in Indochina. At one point he remarked that communist activity in Vietnam marked a pattern of communist challenges to the West in general and to the United States in particular.

In his 1950 speech announcing the decision to send U.S. troops to Korea, Truman also called for aid to the beleaguered French in Vietnam. Truman saw Vietnam in a broader Asian context and feared that the whole region could be lost to communism. With Truman's urging, Congress appropriated funds for the French war in Indochina, a policy continued by President Eisenhower until the French defeat at Dien Bien Phu in 1954. Truman said the aid was "designed to reinforce areas exposed to Communist pressure." His financial commitment to fighting the communists in Vietnam was significant in establishing U.S. interests in the country, but his ideological constructs were even more fundamental. In viewing Ho Chi Minh's forces as communist tools in the Cold War and in his repeated references to containment and the domino theory, Truman established the ideological framework within which the conflict would be viewed for the next two decades. In the 1960s, President Lyndon Johnson made several attempts to persuade Truman to back his Vietnam policies, but Truman refused to make any public statement about the war.

BIBLIOGRAPHY

KARNOW, STANLEY. *Vietnam: A History.* 1991.

TRUMAN, HARRY S. *Memoirs by Harry S. Truman: Years of Trial and Hope.* 1956.

KELLY EVANS-PFEIFER

Truong Chinh (1907–1988), general secretary, Indochinese Communist party, 1941–1956; president, national assembly, Democratic Republic of Vietnam (DRV), 1960–1976; co-president, DRV, 1981–1987; general secretary, Vietnamese Communist Party, 1986. Born Dan Xuan Khu, Chinh was the leader of North Vietnam's pro-Chinese faction, adopting a name that meant "Long March" to show his dedication to Mao Zedong. He helped co-found the Indochinese Communist party in 1930, and for the next twenty-six years, Chinh ranked second only to Ho Chi Minh on the politburo. In 1956, acknowledging "serious mistakes" in his disastrous land reform program, Chinh resigned as general secretary, but he remained the party's top ideologist. Chinh advocated reunifying Vietnam by supporting guerrillas in the South, but he was eventually overruled in favor of conventional invasion. Although long opposed to capitalist reforms, Chinh invited the reintroduction of private enterprise when he served again as general secretary for five months in 1986.

BIBLIOGRAPHY

HIEBERT, MURRAY. "A New Gerontocracy." *Far Eastern Economic Review* (1 January 1987).

HIEBERT, MURRAY. "Veteran Ideologue." *Far Eastern Economic Review* (13 October 1988).

PIKE, DOUGLAS. *History of Vietnamese Communism, 1925–1976.* 1978.

TRUONG CHINH. *Primer for Revolt: The Communist Takeover in Vietnam.* 1963.

TRUONG CHINH. *Selected Writings.* 1977.

Who's Who in North Vietnam. 1969.

GLEN GENDZEL

Truong Dinh Dzu. A Buddhist Saigon lawyer, Dzu ran against Nguyen Van Thieu in South Vietnam's 1967 presidential election. Despite Dzu's questionable reputation, the Central Intelligence Agency (CIA) purportedly supported him as a last-minute opposition candidate to avoid any appearance of a rigged election. The election laws barred "peace" candidates, but once on the ballot, Dzu called for a bombing pause and negotiations with the National Liberation Front (NLF). He captured 17 percent of the vote, nearly half of Thieu's total of 35 percent. Contemporaries interpreted the results as a protest against the military rule, but they may instead have reflected the early disenchantment of the South Vietnam populace with the war. Thieu was angered and embarrassed by Dzu's strong showing, and after the election, Dzu was arrested for illegal currency dealings, a widespread practice at the time. For many of the South Vietnamese, the election was further proof that Thieu maintained power only because of his U.S. support.

TRUONG DINH DZU. Greeting the crowd at an election campaign rally, Qui Nhon, 1967. *National Archives*

Dzu was released from prison in 1973. His son, David Truong, lived in the United States during the war and was a prominent figure in the antiwar movement. In a controversial 1978 trial, David Truong was convicted of performing espionage in the United States for the Socialist Republic of Vietnam (SRV), and he spent four years in a U.S. federal prison during the early 1980s.

BIBLIOGRAPHY

HERRING, GEORGE C. *America's Longest War: The United States and Vietnam, 1950–1975.* 2d ed. 1986.

KARNOW, STANLEY. *Vietnam: A History.* 1991.

STANLEY I. KUTLER

Truong, Ngo Quang. *See* Ngo Quang Truong.

Tunnels. A prime tourist attraction in the Socialist Republic of Vietnam is an underground tunnel complex on the outskirts of Ho Chi Minh City (formerly Saigon). This national museum at Cu Chi is a tribute to the Viet Cong guerrillas' extensive use of tunnels, a traditional tactic used against the French, Japanese, and Chinese invaders in earlier wars. South Vietnam contained numerous underground guerrilla bases, built and supplied with forced labor from nearby villages. The largest tunnel

TUNNEL RAT. Australian 2d Lt. Peter Vincent emerges from searching a Viet Cong tunnel, 8 March 1968. He hands out Chinese-made grenades that were part of the defenders' arsenal. *Archive Photos*

complexes were in the Iron Triangle region and nearby at Cu Chi. Together these underground installations contained about 200 kilometers (125 miles) of tunnels, 1 meter (3 feet) high by 0.75 meters (2.5 feet) wide, dug in dense laterite clay strata, which set as hard as concrete. The tunnels zigzagged to confuse intruders and to isolate the effects of gas or explosives. Four levels of tunnels were connected by hidden trapdoors and tiny air shafts. Viet Cong fighters spent their days safely underground and emerged at night for raids on Saigon or to attack unsuspecting U.S. and South Vietnamese troops, often camped right on top of them.

The U.S. Army's 1st Infantry Division discovered the Cu Chi tunnels during Operation CRIMP in January 1966. After taking casualties for days from invisible snipers within secured perimeters, the soldiers painstakingly searched the jungle floor to find concealed entrances that were the outer works of the Phy My Hung tunnel complex. Further exploration uncovered barracks, armories, supply dumps, and hospitals—as well as kitchens, air-raid shelters, classrooms, conference centers, graveyards, printing presses, factories, and holding pens for water buffalo. The volunteers who entered these tunnels often surprised resting Viet Cong fighters and engaged in furious hand-to-hand combat. They became the first Tunnel Rats—specially trained underground commandos chosen for their steel nerves, small stature, good night vision, and lack of claustrophobia. They entered the tunnels armed only with hand grenades, a flashlight, and a pistol to do battle with snipers, booby traps, rats, bats, scorpions, and snakes. "There were no bad days," recalled

Capt. Herbert Thornton, who founded the Tunnel Rats. "They were all good days if you got through them." Tunnel Rats received extra hazard pay and most served no longer than four months.

Gen. William Westmoreland, calling the Viet Cong guerrillas "an army of moles," launched Operation CEDAR FALLS to destroy the Iron Triangle tunnels in February 1967. More than thirty thousand U.S. and South Vietnamese troops evacuated the local villagers and created a 156-square-kilometer (60-square-mile) free fire zone. The area was bombed, shelled, defoliated, napalmed, and crushed by bulldozers with deep-cutting Rome plows called hog jaws. Tons of guerrilla supplies were captured. Despite the success of Operation CEDAR FALLS, the underground bases again served as the staging ground for guerrilla raids on Saigon in the Tet Offensive one year later. In 1970, B-52s dropped thousands of delayed-fuse bombs that buried deep in the ground before exploding. The resulting 9-meter (30-foot) craters finally drove the Viet Cong forces out of the Iron Triangle tunnels. In North Vietnam, extensive tunnels were also dug for protection from U.S. bombing raids.

BIBLIOGRAPHY

MANGOLD, TOM, and JOHN PENNYCATE. *The Tunnels of Cu Chi.* 1985.

ROGERS, BERNARD WILLIAM. *Cedar Falls–Junction City: A Turning Point.* 1974.

GLEN GENDZEL

Twining, Nathan F. (1897–1982), general, U.S. Air Force; chief of staff, 1953–1957; chairman, Joint Chiefs of Staff (JCS), 1957–1960. Commander of the unit that dropped atomic bombs on Japan, Twining was the only member of the JCS to approve Adm. Arthur Radford's plan for air strikes to save the French at Dien Bien Phu in 1954. Twining recommended using one to three small atomic weapons against Viet Minh positions to demonstrate U.S. resolve in fighting communism. After retirement Twining entered Republican politics. He advised Sen. Barry Goldwater's presidential campaign in 1964 and lost his own New Hampshire senate race in 1966.

BIBLIOGRAPHY

ARNOLD, JAMES R. *The First Domino: Eisenhower, the Military, and America's Intervention in Vietnam.* 1991.

BLAIR, CLAY, JR. "The General Everybody Loves." *Saturday Evening Post,* 17 August 1957.

MROZEK, DONALD J. "Nathan F. Twining: New Dimensions, a New Look." In J. L. Frisbee, ed., *Makers of the United States Air Force.* 1989.

TWINING, NATHAN F. *Neither Liberty nor Safety.* 1966.

GLEN GENDZEL

U

Union of Soviet Socialist Republics (USSR). The Soviet Union was, with the People's Republic of China (PRC), the most important military and economic supporter of the Democratic Republic of Vietnam (DRV) during the Vietnam War. Although the Soviet Union had provided military aid to the Viet Minh in the early 1950s, it chose not to publicize the assistance for fear of jeopardizing the success of diplomatic maneuvers with France and intruding on its ally's (the PRC) special relationship with the DRV. Soviet aid during the Indochina War included trucks, artillery, and communications equipment, estimated to have a total value of $1 billion. At the 1954 Geneva Conference, the USSR advocated terms relatively favorable to the French and pressured the Viet Minh to accept partition of Vietnam. Considered a betrayal by the DRV, the USSR's actions reportedly reflected an effort to encourage France to forestall the rearming of Germany, a central concern of Soviet foreign policy.

In the early 1960s Khrushchev's policy of disengagement from Cold War rivalries, sparked by the Sino-Soviet rift, negatively affected Soviet relations with the DRV. Khrushchev chose to pursue conciliatory policies with the West on Vietnam, rather than support his ally, the PRC. But Leonid Brezh-

nev, his successor, changed Soviet policy in 1964, aggressively aiding North Vietnam. He hoped to counter the PRC's influence in the region, and the Soviet military saw an opportunity to expand its international influence. The DRV, with its limited industrial and economic base, depended upon foreign assistance to support its reunification effort, and the Soviet Union provided the military resources to sustain warfare against the South. Shipping most material through Haiphong, the Soviets provided such equipment as high-technology surface-to-air missiles, planes, artillery, tanks, fuel, and ammunition. Nearly three thousand military technicians trained North Vietnamese personnel and maintained advanced equipment. The USSR also provided commodities such as food, fertilizer, and cement to support the domestic economy. Total military aid is estimated at $5–8 billion between 1965 and 1975.

In the late 1960s, under pressure from the United States, the Soviet Union attempted to exert influence on the DRV to pursue peace negotiations. President Nixon and Henry Kissinger explicitly linked U.S.–USSR talks on a number of issues, including arms control, to Soviet assistance in bringing North Vietnam to the bargaining table. Some

INTERNATIONAL COMMUNISM. Communist leaders view a military parade from atop Lenin's mausoleum during the celebration of the 46th anniversary of the establishment of the communist state in Russia, 7 November 1961. Left to right: Blas Roca, Cuban delegate to Soviet Communist Party Congress; Ho Chi Minh, president of North Vietnam; Soviet premier Nikita Khrushchev; Hungarian Communist Party leader Janos Kadar; Soviet president Leonid Brezhnev; Soviet deputy premier Frel Koslov; Soviet presidium member Mikhail Suslov; first deputy premier Anastas Mikoyan. *National Archives*

Soviet leaders also hoped to reduce the extensive cost of their military aid to North Vietnam, which assisted the DRV war effort in the South. North Vietnamese leaders, however, ignored the Soviet initiative, which embarrassed Soviet diplomats and created tension in the relationship of the communist allies. In 1972, the USSR declined to cancel a superpower summit despite the U.S. Christmas bombings of Hanoi and Haiphong and the mining of Haiphong harbor.

After unification in the late 1970s, Vietnam moved firmly into the Soviet Union's political and economic orbit, particularly as Vietnam's relations with China deteriorated. On 29 June 1978, Vietnam joined the communist common market, COMECON, and launched a massive economic integration with the Soviet Union. Soviet economic aid increased to more than $1 billion annually, financing joint projects in mining, oil and gas, industry, agriculture, and education. The two countries also tightened their military alliance, signing the Treaty of Friendship and Cooperation on 2 November 1978. The Soviets moved into former U.S. air and naval bases such as the prized Cam Ranh Bay naval base. After the Vietnamese invasion of Cambodia, Soviet military aid also rose to over $1 billion a year, and included high-technology MIG fighters, tanks, and warships. During Vietnam's invasion of Kampuchea, Soviet cargo and transport planes, piloted by Russians, provided extensive logistical support for PAVN operations within the former Cambodia.

BIBLIOGRAPHY

PIKE, DOUGLAS. *Vietnam and the Soviet Union.* 1987.

ADAM LAND

United Nations.

The United Nations did not play a significant role in settling the Vietnamese conflict, primarily because the major Western players, first France and then the United States, both members of the U.N. Security Council, could veto resolutions unfavorable to their position. In addition, the 1954 Geneva peace accords provided no role for the United Nations, and neither the Democratic Republic of Vietnam (North Vietnam) nor the Republic of Vietnam (South Vietnam) was a member of that international organization. As the war intensified in the mid 1960s, the U.N. General Assembly did become a forum for heated rhetoric between communist-bloc countries and U.S. supporters. After the war, the United States initially blocked the unified nation's entry into the United Nations, protesting the lack of progress on information about U.S. servicemen missing in action (MIA). After U.S. intransigence receded, the Socialist Republic of Vietnam (SRV) joined the international body in 1977.

During the war, the U.N. secretary general, neutralist Burmese diplomat U Thant, made several attempts to initiate peace negotiations. In 1964, he sought to arrange secret talks between the United States and North Vietnam. Using the Soviet Union as a go-between, he secured North Vietnam's agreement to participate in bilateral discussions, but after President Johnson's landslide victory and several months of delay, the United States declined to participate. The U.S. refusal infuriated U Thant, who criticized the U.S. intransigence, but his public rebuke also increased U.S. distrust of the secretary general. In 1968, U Thant urged the United States to agree to a unilateral cease-fire, arguing that North Vietnamese and Viet Cong forces would follow suit. The United States again rejected U Thant's proposal, refusing to take unilateral action. In 1970, the secretary general made a final peace initiative,

proposing an international conference to mediate the dispute, but this proposal also failed.

The secretary general did, however, successfully challenge certain aspects of U.S. military policy in Vietnam. In the late 1960s, U Thant sought to ban the use of herbicides used to defoliate jungle (Agent Orange and Agent Blue), arguing that the provisions of the 1925 Geneva conventions outlawing chemical warfare applied to the weapons. His pressure, combined with domestic and international criticism, brought about the Nixon administration's renunciation of herbicide first use in 1969. It also led to an April 1972 international treaty outlawing the production of biological weapons.

U.N. institutions played a critical role in addressing the dislocation and turmoil caused by the war. U.N. programs facilitated the emigration of several hundred Amerasian children from Vietnam in the mid 1980s. The U.N. high commissioner on refugees also began initiatives to address the problem of the Vietnamese boat people, who left Vietnam in a massive exodus of more than 1.5 million refugees between 1975 and 1992. In 1979, the United Nations established an alternative Orderly Departure Program within Vietnam and in 1982 began patrolling the Gulf of Thailand to protect refugees from piracy. It also coordinated Southeast Asian countries' efforts to repatriate boat people. Following Vietnam's 1979 invasion of Kampuchea (former Cambodia), the United Nations managed refugee camps for the hundreds of thousands fleeing the Khmer Rouge and the pro-Vietnam regime. It also coordinated food shipments to address famine conditions in the country until 1982. Throughout the decade, U.N. diplomacy attempted to broker political stability among warring national and foreign parties within Kampuchea.

BIBLIOGRAPHY

EVANS, GRANT, and KELVIN ROWLEY. *Red Brotherhood at War: Indochina since the Fall of Saigon.* 1984.
KARNOW, STANLEY. *Vietnam: A History.* 1991.
LEWY, GUENTER. *America in Vietnam.* 1978.

ADAM LAND AND KELLY EVANS-PFEIFER

United States Information Service.

The United States Information Service (USIS) was the overseas component of the United States Information Agency (USIA). Organized in 1953, the USIA was intended to foster a sympathetic understanding of American culture abroad and to build public support for U.S. foreign policy in other nations. The USIA planned government-sponsored cultural and information activities while the USIS implemented those initiatives. Conceived of during the height of the Cold War, the content of USIA and USIS informational materials was stridently anticommunist; to counter Soviet propaganda, the USIA engaged in a worldwide campaign to explain and justify U.S. policy in Indochina. The demands upon the USIS in Vietnam expanded greatly in the early 1960s when Lyndon Johnson delegated responsibility for all psychological action (with the exception of military operations) in Vietnam to the USIA. The USIA established a Joint U.S. Public Affairs Office (JUSPAO) in Saigon, which directed propaganda at the South Vietnamese people, Viet Cong guerrillas, and the North Vietnamese through radio, leaflet drops, and airborne loudspeakers. The purpose, according to a RAND Corporation report, was to convince the Vietnamese people that the Saigon regime was the legitimate government of South Vietnam and to enlist nationalistic sentiment on the side of that government. By 1967 this counterinsurgency effort involved 12 to 14 percent of all USIA foreign service officers. Throughout the remainder of the Vietnam War, the USIA maintained information centers and libraries, which often became the targets of guerrilla attacks.

BIBLIOGRAPHY

BOGART, LEO. *Premises for Propaganda: The United States Information Agency's Operating Assumptions in the Cold War.* 1976.

ELDER, ROBERT E. *The United States Information Agency and American Foreign Policy.* 1968.

PAUL M. TAILLON

United States of America.

The U.S. intervention in Vietnam, the longest war in U.S. history, exposed the limitations and costs of the nation's international power. Beginning in the late 1940s, U.S. leaders committed extensive resources and prestige to create a pro-Western, anticommunist regime in French Indochina. The United States supported French efforts to maintain its Far Eastern colonial empire, and after the French defeat in 1954, pursued a continued policy of economic aid, and finally military intervention to promote the Republic of Vietnam. After a nearly thirty-year conflict, the North Vietnamese triumph in April 1975 marked a disorienting and painful setback for U.S. Cold War policies. The Vietnam War created stark divisions within American society and intensified a global overextension of resources that damaged the domestic economy. The crises forced a broad reconsideration of U.S. diplomatic and military policies and, ultimately, left a bitterness that pervaded American life for decades.

The Early Years. In the late 1940s, Southeast Asia emerged as a critical site of U.S. efforts to reshape world economic and political structures in the post–World War II era. The United States supported the policies of Great Britain and France, nations severely weakened by World War II, to revitalize their political and economic interests within Southeast Asia. U.S. leaders also hoped to restore Japan's regional economic influence, which had relied on Indochina's raw materials and markets. The Korean War and 1949 triumph of the Chinese communists sharpened U.S. determination to contain communist expansionism in Asia and to support the beleaguered French in Indochina. Despite unease with French colonialism, the United States began direct assistance in 1949 and expended $3 billion in military support (nearly 80 percent of the total cost of the conflict) for France's war against the Viet Minh. But when the French military faltered at the siege of Dien Bien Phu in 1954, President Dwight D. Eisenhower rejected French requests for a U.S. military air strike, despite support from Vice President Richard Nixon and several members of the Joint Chiefs of Staff (JCS).

After the French withdrawal and the 1954 Geneva Convention, which partitioned Vietnam, the United States extended wide assistance to the newly created Republic of Vietnam in the south. U.S. officials deemed South Vietnam a "showcase" for third-world state building and provided technical expertise and more than $2 billion in economic and military aid through 1961. But South Vietnamese president Ngo Dinh Diem's repressive tactics, his widespread nepotism, and the government's inadequate land reform programs weakened public support for his government. In the late 1950s, former Viet Minh soldiers who participated in the war against the French, joined by many noncommunists, initiated an insurgency movement against Diem's government. In 1960, North Vietnam lent direct support to the insurgency, now named the National Liberation Front, which ignited open military hostilities. In the face of mounting threats to the South Vietnamese government, President John F. Kennedy authorized the deployment of U.S. mili-

ANTIWAR PROTEST. Vietnam veterans protest the war at the U.S. Capitol, 19 April 1971. *Library of Congress*

tary advisers to the region in 1961; by 1963 they numbered sixteen thousand. After losing faith in Diem's ability to govern effectively, the United States tacitly supported his overthrow in 1963, although the military coup failed to stabilize the country.

As shown during the initial military commitment, U.S. policymakers had difficulty assessing the Vietnamese communists' conception of "revolutionary war," one that combined political and military tactics and involved the entire society's sacrifice for "national liberation." U.S. advisers did not accurately gauge the North Vietnamese and NLF organization and commitment, misled in part by Western racism and an arrogance about the effectiveness of overwhelming U.S. resources. When Gen. Lyman Lemnitzer, chairman of the JCS, visited Saigon in 1961, a foreign service officer told him that the French had inflicted more than a million

casualties on the Viet Minh. Lemnitzer replied: "Didn't kill enough then. We'll teach 'em to kill more."

Faced with the continued weakness of the South Vietnamese government and military successes by the NLF, President Lyndon Johnson committed U.S. combat forces to Vietnam in 1964. The need to ensure the credibility of U.S. global commitments drove the military intervention—an issue magnified by the substantial U.S. support for South Vietnam. Johnson also feared conservative political reprisals at home if South Vietnam collapsed, similar to the McCarthy era recriminations of the 1950s over "who lost China." Johnson gained near-unanimous congressional support with the Gulf of Tonkin Resolution in August 1964, which gave him broad authority to expand the war in an effort to curtail communist "aggression." In retaliation for the Gulf of Tonkin incident, the United States bombed North Vietnam in 1964, and after NLF attacks on U.S. military installations, the U.S. ground presence was significantly escalated in July 1965.

U.S. Strategy in Vietnam. In shaping U.S. military policy, President Johnson pursued a strategy of "limited war" in the region. Confident in U.S. military capability, Johnson sought to limit U.S. intervention both to curtail domestic social costs and to avoid a superpower confrontation. U.S. policy called for gradual escalation of military pressure to force a disarming of the insurgency and an end to North Vietnam's military support. This escalating combat presence, however, failed to achieve U.S. objectives. The number of U.S. military personnel in Vietnam increased from 185,000 in December 1965 to 385,000 one year later and peaked at 585,000 in early 1968. The U.S. field commander, Gen. William Westmoreland, pursued an attrition strategy that entailed aggressive search-and-destroy missions and heavy use of U.S. firepower. U.S. forces successfully hindered NLF and North Vietnamese Army (NVA) operations, but this conventional style of warfare failed to stem or destroy the insurgency, despite staggering losses by the NLF and NVA forces. In the face of mounting antiwar protests and U.S. casualties (more than 15,000 fatalities by December 1967), American public opinion wavered. In October 1967, polls noted that a near-majority of Americans believed intervention had been a mistake, beginning an ominous erosion of once-solid public support for the war.

The Tet Offensive in January 1968 marked the turning point of U.S. policy in Vietnam and the beginning of U.S. disengagement. Although NLF and NVA forces suffered heavy losses in the campaign, the widespread, spectacular attacks convinced many Americans that the United States could never foster a stable, noncommunist regime in South Vietnam. In March 1968, the Johnson administration capped U.S. escalation and openly pursued peace negotiations. In 1969, President Richard Nixon continued U.S. troop withdrawals and inaugurated a policy of Vietnamization, transferring military responsibility to South Vietnam. The U.S. government intensified pacification efforts in rural Vietnam and funded land reform programs, but the programs proved to be too little and too late to coalesce solid peasant support for the South Vietnamese government. The 1973 Paris peace accords resulted in the withdrawal of U.S. military forces but allowed North Vietnamese troops to remain in the South. Congressional mandates, against the backdrop of the emerging Watergate scandal and firm antiwar sentiment, sharply reduced military and economic aid to South Vietnam. In 1975, North Vietnam launched its massive Spring Offensive, and Saigon fell to communist forces on 30 April 1975. The frantic, final scenes of U.S. helicopters evacuating the U.S. embassy in Saigon provided a telling counterpoint to an earlier confidence in U.S. policy.

Under the banner of a Cold War crusade to challenge communist expansionism and maintain a global economy, the United States expended massive resources during a twenty-five year engagement in Indochina. But despite 58,000 American war dead, 23,000 permanently disabled veterans, and $170 billion, the United States failed to shape a viable anticommunist state in Vietnam. During the war, Henry Kissinger, Nixon's national security adviser, derided Vietnamese communists as a "fourth-rate power," but even the full weight of U.S. power could not deter North Vietnam or the NLF. For Vietnam, the costs were extraordinary: more than two million were killed during its wars for liberation, and social and economic upheaval continue in the postwar era. Within the United States, the war sparked a tide of social and economic discord, tensions that tore at a social consensus built in part on anticommunism and the global role of the United States. The war eroded confidence in public institutions and contributed to wide challenges to social order and authority in the 1960s.

Domestic Consequences. Beginning in 1965, student groups organized antiwar protests, often building upon the tactics of the civil rights move-

ment. Student activism also grew out of an older peace movement that had contested U.S. international policies since the 1940s. The Students for a Democratic Society (SDS), most notably, challenged intervention as "imperialistic" and questioned the nation's sacrifice for a corrupt, unpopular South Vietnamese government. Many activists' defiance of traditional authority troubled other citizens, as did the disruptive nature of protest demonstrations, but protesters eventually succeeded in forcing many Americans to confront and analyze the justifications of the war. The antiwar movement gained increasing grassroots support, evolving to include numerous religious, labor, and professional groups. Major protests occurred at the 1967 March on the Pentagon and during the 1968 Democratic Convention in Chicago. The Tet Offensive, in particular, energized demonstrators and contributed to President Johnson's decision not to run for president in the 1968 election. Unprecedented upheaval followed the May 1970 Cambodian invasion during Nixon's presidency, resulting in tragic student deaths at Kent State and Jackson State universities. Antiwar sentiment stymied Johnson's and Nixon's attempts to pursue the war and ultimately forced the withdrawal of U.S. forces from Vietnam.

The Vietnam War also heightened class tensions in the United States. Of the 2.5 million U.S. personnel in Vietnam, 80 percent were from working-class or poor backgrounds. The Selective Service provided draft deferments for college students, and many university students effectively manipulated the system to avoid combat duty. The National Guard, especially, served as a refuge for young elites; only fifteen thousand National Guard troops were called to duty in Vietnam. To meet global personnel needs, the government pursued such policies as "Project 100,000," which drafted 354,000 poor and less-educated Americans under the guise of a social welfare program. Many U.S. soldiers in Vietnam and their families expressed bitter resentment toward the college-centered peace movement. Among African Americans in particular, who had a disproportionately high representation in the combat arms in Vietnam, support for the war declined significantly over the course of the conflict.

U.S. fiscal policies to support Vietnam policy exacerbated larger economic problems arising from Cold War military commitments. Choosing to limit public sacrifice, the Johnson administration ran budget deficits to fund the war and refused to restrain an overheated economy. Johnson hoped to maintain domestic government programs, confident that U.S. resources could finance both "guns and butter." But his inflationary policies combined with larger structural flaws that arose from the international role of the United States. Since 1945, the United States had spurred world economic growth largely through military spending around the globe. The nation's extensive military production also brought about disproportionate investment in noncommercial industries, impairing U.S. industrial competitiveness against the growing Asian and European economies. U.S. global spending and its declining business strength created a chronic balance-of-payments deficit, which was intensified by wartime inflation. The resulting international weakness of the dollar led the United States to abandon the gold standard in 1971, after which the United States effectively lost control of international financial policy. The monetary crises contributed to and symbolized the larger decline of the nation's economy, which brought heightened inflation and a stagnation in real wages to post–Vietnam War America.

Richard Nixon's administration intensified domestic divisions, and his presidency ultimately foundered in the social turmoil of the era. His administration's rhetoric appealed to law-and-order themes, tapping public ambivalence toward the peace movement and the civil rights movement and addressing wider concerns over social order. Heated administration rhetoric equated war protesters with Nazi storm troopers or dismissed them as "bums," language that fueled violence against activists. Antiwar activities, among other reasons, also led the administration to establish an illicit intelligence unit within the White House. The group, known as the "plumbers," performed espionage and conducted smear campaigns against such war opponents as Daniel Ellsberg, the former national security official who leaked the Pentagon Papers. The unit helped orchestrate the ill-fated Watergate burglary in June 1972. The administration's concern about public disclosure of plumber activities triggered a wide, illegal cover-up that resulted in President Nixon's resignation in 1974, after the U.S. House of Representatives had initiated impeachment proceedings. The upheaval and crises of authority surrounding the Vietnam War was at the root of the Watergate debacle.

Policy Consequences. The Vietnam crises forced U.S. policymakers to reformulate U.S. military and international policies. By 1970, U.S. military leaders faced an unprecedented collapse of morale and discipline in the ranks of the armed forces. The erosion of public support in the late 1960s and the decision gradually to withdraw all U.S. forces from Vietnam removed incentive for soldiers to risk their lives in Vietnam. Racial disturbances reflected the growing racial tensions in the United States and African American soldiers' challenges to military discrimination on bases worldwide. The turbulence within the ranks of the military along with public antiwar sentiment led President Nixon to end the military draft in 1973, a new policy supported by many military leaders. Among various policies to spur recruitment for their personnel needs, the U.S. military's volunteer services increased training and career opportunities for women soldiers. Women's representation in the armed forces grew from 1.9 percent of total personnel in 1972 to 8.4 percent in 1980 and reached 11.6 percent in 1994.

After the war, U.S. military strategists were determined to avoid another Vietnam "quagmire." Military policymakers abandoned preparations for Vietnam War–style counterinsurgency warfare, which had been developed in the late 1950s, and instead developed tactics and weaponry for a model of European land warfare. In addition, U.S. military leadership pressured political leaders to forsake the "limited war" strategy that U.S. policymakers had implemented in Vietnam. Military leaders blamed their setbacks in Vietnam in part on the gradual escalation of U.S. military power during the war. In a future conflict, U.S. military leadership planned to seek the establishment of clear military objectives as well as permission to use overwhelming military power. They also planned to pressure political leaders to seek assurances of strong public support for military action, such as a declaration of war or its equivalent. U.S. policy in the Persian Gulf War was to incorporate all these elements. After the Gulf War the commander of U.S. forces, General Norman Schwarzkopf, exclaimed, "I measure everything in my life from Vietnam."

During the 1980s U.S. leaders attempted to reassert U.S. global prestige and influence, but though the nation retained enormous resources, its diminished economic leverage and the emergence of European and Asian centers of power placed sharp limits on U.S. power. In the 1970s, after the Vietnam War, the United States reshaped its foreign policy commitments and pursued détente with the USSR and the People's Republic of China (PRC). But after the 1979 Soviet invasion of Afghanistan, President Carter assumed a new, aggressive worldwide posture and initiated a buildup of military forces, which was continued during the Reagan and Bush administrations. In addition to the comparative decline in U.S. power, American public opinion also restricted the use of military force. Twenty years after the fall of Saigon, Americans remained highly suspicious of military actions that would risk U.S. lives and resources. After the Persian Gulf War, President Bush claimed that the country had "kicked the Vietnam Syndrome," but he recognized the need to limit U.S. involvement and casualties to maintain public support for the war.

Social Consequences. Veterans have remained at the center of the nation's effort to assess the American experience in Vietnam, and the continuing toll of the war. The Vietnam War Memorial, organized by a veterans group, became a focal point for national reconciliation after its unveiling in 1982. The memorial in Washington D.C. drew nearly 30 million visitors by 1992, becoming the most visited monument in the country. Vietnam veterans have contributed noted literary and artistic works about their experiences, such as the writings of W. D. Erhart and Tim O'Brien, and films of director Oliver Stone. Other veteran issues have drawn attention to the difficult readjustment for many soldiers from their war service. The lasting trauma experienced by many combatants brought medical recognition in 1980 of Post Traumatic Stress Syndrome (PTSS), which affected an estimated 15% of Vietnam veterans. A 1984 court settlement awarded $180 million to U.S. soldiers who suffered health ailments from exposure to Agent Orange, the U.S. military herbicide used in Vietnam.

But the war continues to divide American society. In the 1992 presidential campaign, Bill Clinton came under fire for his avoidance of Vietnam service, his record similar to that of many college students in the 1960s. Studies from the early 1990s suggest that a majority of Americans believe that restrictions placed upon the U.S. armed forces by political leaders prevented a military victory in the war and that U.S. soldiers still listed as missing in action (MIA) in Vietnam are being held in Southeast Asia. These sentiments, felt by so many, reflect the deep distrust by the American public of their government in recent U.S. politics. In larger terms, the Vietnam War ended an era of growing domestic prosperity and destabilized a social consensus and government authority based on an anticommunist mission at home and abroad. World War II taught many Americans that the nation's global role was benevolent, a responsibility and belief that continued in the Cold War. But the Vietnam War's destructiveness, portrayed nightly on television sets across the nation, and its divisive and wasteful toll on American society undermined that vision. The war sparked a difficult, evolving reconsideration of the nation's common purpose and identity, a debate that still echoed two decades after the U.S. guns in Vietnam fell silent.

BIBLIOGRAPHY

APPY, CHRISTIAN G. *Working-Class War: American Combat Soldiers and Vietnam.* 1994.

DAVIDSON, PHILLIP B. *Vietnam at War: The History, 1946–1975.* 1988.

HERRING, GEORGE C. *LBJ and Vietnam: A Different Kind of War.* 1994.

KUTLER, STANLEY I. *The Wars of Watergate: The Last Crisis of Richard Nixon.* 1990.

MCCORMICK, THOMAS J. *America's Half-Century: United States Foreign Policy in the Cold War.* 1989.

OLSON, JAMES S., and RANDY ROBERTS. *Where the Domino Fell: America and Vietnam, 1945–1990.* 1991.

WELLS, TOM. *The War Within: America's Battle over Vietnam.* 1994.

ADAM LAND

University of Wisconsin Bombing. At 3:42 A.M. on 24 August 1970, a bomb blast ripped apart the Army Mathematics Research Center (AMRC) in Sterling Hall on the University of Wisconsin Madison campus. Local police were alerted by a phone call just prior to the blast but did not have enough time to warn the building's occupants; postgraduate researcher Robert Fassnacht was killed and three others were injured. The building and the research materials were destroyed or badly damaged. The "New Year's Gang" took credit for the bombing, contending that the AMRC research contributed to weapons development for the Vietnam War. The AMRC was in fact funded by a grant from the U.S. Army and devoted half its work to "militarily applicable" research, including determining casualty statistics for various weapons. The bombers were Karl and Dwight Armstrong, two Madison residents, and university students David Fine and Leo Burt. They fled to Canada after the Federal Bureau of Investigation (FBI) launched an extensive manhunt. Between 1972 and 1976 all except Burt were caught. In 1973 Karl Armstrong was tried, convicted, and sentenced to twenty-three years in prison. His sentence was later reduced to ten years after his younger brother Dwight and David Fine pleaded guilty to second- and third-degree murder, respectively, and received seven-year sentences. Burt remains at large.

BIBLIOGRAPHY

BATES, TOM. *Rads: The 1970 Bombing of the Army Math Research Center at the University of Wisconsin and Its Aftermath.* 1992.

"Rise of the Dynamite Radicals." *Time,* 7 September 1970.

KELLY EVANS-PFEIFER

V

Vance, Cyrus R. (1917–), U.S. secretary of the army, 1962–1963; deputy secretary of defense, 1964–1967. Vance was one of many top Pentagon officials who supported the war in its early years but later regarded U.S. involvement in Vietnam as futile. As an aide to Secretary of Defense McNamara, Vance was involved in the initial decision to send U.S. combat troops to Vietnam, participating in White House meetings on the escalation policy and supporting General Westmoreland's request for troops. By late 1967, however, Vance's view of the war had changed. He was one of the "wise men" who, at a pivotal post–Tet Offensive meeting with Johnson in 1968, advocated American disengagement from Vietnam. Vance took the lead in a 1968 initiative to set up peace talks in Paris, but his efforts failed when South Vietnam pulled out of the planned meeting just days before it was to have begun in November 1968.

In 1969 Henry Kissinger asked Vance, who was not in government service at the time, to approach the Soviets with an arms reduction deal linked to Soviet agreement to pressure North Vietnam to negotiate an end to the war. Vance never had the opportunity to carry forth Kissinger's mission because the Soviets refused to hold any discussions involving linkage of U.S.–USSR relations and the Vietnam conflict. As Jimmy Carter's secretary of state in 1977, Vance worked to normalize relations with Vietnam, but the U.S. government's rejection of Vietnam's demand for $3 billion in war reparations thwarted his efforts.

BIBLIOGRAPHY

KAHIN, GEORGE McT. *Intervention: How America Became Involved in Vietnam*. 1986.

KARNOW, STANLEY. *Vietnam: A History*. 1991.

KELLY EVANS-PFEIFER

Vang Pao (1929–), Hmong military officer. Vang Pao worked with the French against the Viet Minh and then commanded Hmong troops against the North Vietnamese and the Pathet Lao. The Central Intelligence Agency (CIA) recruited Major Vang Pao as leader of the Hmong in 1961, bypassing the Hmong's nominal leader, Touby Lyfoung. By mid-decade Vang Pao had used CIA matériel and monetary support to recruit a Hmong army of 30,000 troops. Ruthless in his domination of Hmong villagers, Vang Pao used his CIA connections to make them dependent upon his support for rice supplies.

He withheld shipments of U.S. aid from villages that tried to keep their sons from entering his army. He also was notoriously corrupt. When the Pathet Lao overran his army in 1975, Vang Pao escaped to the United States with millions of dollars and several thousand Hmong followers. Settling in California, Vang Pao became a leader of the Hmong community within the United States.

BIBLIOGRAPHY

CASTLE, TIMOTHY N. *War in the Shadow of Vietnam: United States Military Aid to the Royal Lao Government, 1955–1975.* 1993.

HAMILTON-MERRITT, JANE. *Tragic Mountains: the Hmong, the Americans, and the Secret Wars.* 1993.

O'TOOLE, G. J. A. *Encyclopedia of American Intelligence and Espionage.* 1988.

STANLEY I. KUTLER

Vann, John Paul (1924–1972), lieutenant colonel, U.S. Army. As a senior adviser to the Army of the Republic of Vietnam (ARVN) in 1962–1963, John Paul Vann concluded that President Diem was more interested in collecting U.S. aid than in fighting communism. Vann charged that ARVN commanders were corrupt, incompetent, and cowardly, an accusation that brought a stern rebuke from his superiors. Vann retired in 1963, then returned to Saigon as a U.S. Agency for International Development officer in 1965. He became Military Assistance Command, Vietnam (MACV) Civil Operations and Revolutionary Development Support (CORDS) adviser for the entire area around Saigon. Vann's intense dedication made him "one of the legendary Americans in Vietnam," according to the Washington Post. In 1971, Gen. Creighton Abrams appointed Vann, still a civilian, to command all U.S. forces (through ranking military aides) in II Corps. This unprecedented experiment in civil-military relations ended when Vann died in a helicopter crash near Kontum during the North Vietnamese Army's Easter Offensive in June 1972. Vann carefully cultivated journalists to enhance his reputation; his criticism of U.S. military decisions appealed to many of them. "My entire involvement here," he said, "has been to try to bring some reason and justice to our effort."

BIBLIOGRAPHY

BRANCH, TAYLOR. "A Soldier's Story." *Washington Monthly,* October 1988.

"Death of a Perfectionist." *Time,* 19 June 1972.

HALBERSTAM, DAVID. *The Best and the Brightest.* 1972.

HILSMAN, ROGER. *To Move a Nation: The Politics of Foreign Policy in the Administration of John F. Kennedy.* 1967.

SHEEHAN, NEIL. *A Bright Shining Lie: John Paul Vann and America in Vietnam.* 1988.

ZUCKERMAN, LAURENCE. "A Flawed Hero in a Flawed War." *Time,* 17 October 1988.

GLEN GENDZEL

Van Tien Dung (1917–), general, People's Army of Vietnam (PAVN); PAVN chief of staff, 1954–1974; PAVN commander in chief, 1974–1980; Socialist Republic of Vietnam defense minister, 1980–1986. Gen. Van Tien Dung was North Vietnam's only high-level communist of peasant origin. He joined the party in 1936, escaped from a French prison in 1944, and fought against the Japanese in World War II. During the Indochina War, Dung rose through the Viet Minh ranks to become Gen. Vo Nguyen Giap's chief of staff during the victorious siege of Dien Bien Phu in 1954. For the next twenty years, Dung's military reputation in North Vietnam was second only to Giap's—even after expensive debacles in the Tet Offensive of 1968 and the Easter Offensive of 1972, which Giap commanded. Giap's close identification with Ho Chi Minh, the victory over France, and guerrilla war doctrine kept him firmly in charge until North Vietnam shifted from insurgency to conventional warfare in pursuit of victory. Dung replaced Giap as PAVN commander in chief in 1974, signaling North Vietnam's final acceptance of the need for an all-out conventional invasion of South Vietnam. Giap's guerrilla war would give way to Dung's armored columns and regular infantry.

While planning North Vietnam's final offensive in 1975, Dung assured his superiors that the Americans would not reintervene: "Having withdrawn from Vietnam," he told them, "the U.S. could hardly return." When South Vietnam's defenses collapsed, he shrewdly committed PAVN reserves and captured Saigon on 30 April 1975. Dung also directed Vietnam's invasion of Cambodia and the border war with China in 1979. Dung became defense minister in 1980, again replacing Giap, but he was removed during the politburo shakeup of 1986.

BIBLIOGRAPHY

PIKE, DOUGLAS. *History of Vietnamese Communism, 1925–1976.* 1978.

VAN TIEN DUNG. *Our Great Spring Victory: An Account of the Liberation of South Vietnam.* 1977.
Who's Who in North Vietnam. 1969.

GLEN GENDZEL

Veterans. [*This entry includes two articles:*

American Veterans
Vietnamese Veterans.]

American Veterans

Because of the many unique aspects of the Vietnam War, veterans had a postwar experience different from that of veterans of earlier wars. The challenges U.S. Vietnam veterans faced included the often cool welcome they received upon return, the general hostile attitude of the public toward the war, and their difficulty making the transition back to civilian life.

Throughout the roughly ten-year period of U.S. military involvement, 27 million men were of draft age, and just over 10 percent of that group served in some capacity in Vietnam. Vietnam veterans were thus from the outset different from veterans of earlier conflicts such as World War II, in which a majority of the draft-age population participated in the war. Furthermore, rather than being sent to and from Vietnam as a unit, troops went on individual one-year tours of duty, which undermined group cohesion and caused feelings of isolation upon return. The Defense Department failed to provide comprehensive readjustment programs so it was not uncommon for a soldier to be in a jungle firefight one day, on a plane the next, and home in the United States and out of the military the day after that.

After their return to the United States, many veterans complained that there were no victory parades, no recognition, no thanks for their service. Americans were so bitterly divided over the war that their frustrations sometimes focused on the returning soldiers. In a few extreme cases, war protestors spat on veterans or called them "murderers" or "baby-killers." Without a united country offering its thanks and support, Vietnam veterans often found it difficult to rationalize their experience. World War II veterans, for example, could justify all they had seen and done because they were told that they had fought the "good war." They were treated like heroes, whereas Vietnam veterans fought a morally ambiguous war that the United States lost.

The GI Bill provided Vietnam veterans with only about half the benefits it had provided to World War II veterans. Despite this lack of government support, the majority of Vietnam veterans adjusted without significant problems, experiencing various levels of post-traumatic stress disorder (PTSD), but finding jobs and establishing families. Among the more than 6,400 women who served in Vietnam (primarily as nurses), numerous cases of PTSD have occurred. But most of the women veterans, like the men, did not have major problems with their lives when they returned. Yet a substantial number of men veterans faced severe psychological problems, drug addiction, and employment troubles. Because draftees had come disproportionately from the ranks of poor rural and inner-city men who had little job training and education prior to their service in Vietnam, many were ill-equipped to handle the problems they faced upon return. Disabled and minority veterans have been disproportionately unemployed and homeless and many continue to experience severe PTSD.

The existence of troubled veterans has at times caused problems for those who made a successful transition to civilian life. Vietnam veterans as a group have been stereotyped as violence-prone drug addicts who cannot function in the real world. Beginning in the mid 1980s, and in the wake of such films as *Platoon,* an effort has been made to distinguish the veterans from the war itself. Memorials were built around the country and belated "welcome home" tributes were held as part of this national healing process. While Vietnam veterans were pleased by these events, many remain concerned about the ongoing problems of homelessness and drug abuse, as well as Agent Orange–related health problems, which still plague many veterans. They have been assisted over the years by several veterans' organizations, including the United Vietnam Veterans Organization, Veterans of Foreign Wars, Vietnam Veterans of America, and Vietnam Veterans against the War.

BIBLIOGRAPHY

BASKIR, LAWRENCE, and WILLIAM A. STRAUSS. *Chance and Circumstance.* 1978.
FIGLEY, CHARLES R., and SEYMOUR LEVENTMAN, eds. *Strangers at Home: Vietnam Veterans since the War.* 1980.
MACPHERSON, MYRA. *Long Time Passing.* 1984.

KELLY EVANS-PFEIFER

Vietnamese Veterans

When the Vietnam War ended in 1975 there were at least eight million Vietnamese veterans from all sides out of a total population of less than 40 million. Precise figures are unavailable, but in 1993 the Ministry of Defense of the Socialist Republic of Vietnam (SRV) disclosed that approximately 3.5 million had been inducted into the northern army and the southern revolutionary forces during the war years. Of these, about a half million had been killed and another half million wounded. The U.S. government estimated the number of communist casualties at about 1 million. As the war ended, the South Vietnamese government forces included 1.1 million men in the regular army (Army of the Republic of Vietnam, ARVN), nearly 4 million in the Regional and Popular Forces (RF/PF), and at least a half million disabled veterans. With the war's end, the South Vietnamese armed forces totally disintegrated. The North Vietnamese government, meanwhile, disbanded southern revolutionary (National Liberation Front, NLF) forces, although its high-ranking officers were given the option of joining the People's Army of Vietnam (PAVN), which by late 1975 was reduced to about 350,000 because most North Vietnamese soldiers fighting in the South, in Laos, and in Cambodia had been allowed to go home.

According to U.S. statistics, 33 percent of the 145,000 refugees who left Vietnam in 1975 were ARVN or RF/PF veterans. Many of these veterans and their families have been successful in the United States, thanks in part to subsidies and support by U.S. federal, state, and local governments and by private organizations. South Vietnamese veterans who remained in Vietnam after 1975, however, suffered great hardship.

More than 80 percent of all Vietnamese veterans came from peasant backgrounds. Those with families or family connections in the villages quickly returned to them and attempted to reintegrate into village life. Those from the south—both NLF and South Vietnamese veterans—fared much better than their northern counterparts, although more of the economic and social life in the south had been disrupted. Southern veterans had kept in closer touch with their families and villages during the war, and the political and economic structures in southern villages were more open and flexible than those in the north. Many northern veterans had been absent from their villages for nearly the duration of the war, and when they returned home they could not—and were often forbidden by local officials to—participate in the economic and political life of the villages. Until recently, they were given meager subsidies—in most cases about 10 kilograms (22 pounds) of rice, a few packs of cigarettes, and a couple of kilograms of fish and meat per month—by the central government and the villages. According to SRV officials, in 1993 more than 30 percent of northern war veterans were either homeless or living in dilapidated housing that was beyond their physical and financial capabilities to repair. Among the illiterate or least educated youngsters, 39 to 52 percent belonged to households of veterans or of soldiers killed during the war.

Veterans from displaced peasant background and their families generally suffered most. During the war, the bulk of the half million prostitutes and bar girls in southern cities were wives, sisters, and mothers of these veterans. After the war, veterans of the South Vietnamese forces from this background and their families made up nearly one-half of the estimated 1 million people who were sent to the New Economic Zones (NEZs) in an effort to cultivate fallow lands in mosquito-infested areas. Many died of malaria and other diseases; others returned to the cities after the supplies they had been given (usually enough only for one-half year) ran out. Many became cyclo (pedicab) drivers, as did many former NLF soldiers and PAVN deserters. Children of cyclo drivers with NLF or PAVN backgrounds were entitled to attend universities if they qualified. Many veterans, including former PAVN and NLF soldiers, became "boat people" during the exodus from Vietnam during the late 1970s and early 1980s. About one hundred thousand South Vietnamese veterans arrived in the United States in this manner, although many others died at sea. Those who remained in Vietnam have fared better of late, thanks in part to the improved economic situation since the late 1980s and in part to the fact that many of their daughters are among the several hundred thousand prostitutes taking advantage of the new "market economy."

The final group of veterans were former South Vietnamese officers considered dangerous by the new regime. They were among the 100,000 persons incarcerated in "reeducation camps" created after 1975. These were labor camps where the internees attended regular indoctrination classes. They were normally given the same food rations as their guards, although family members regularly brought them food and gifts, some of which were given to the guards. These family members endured great hardship because they had to support themselves as well as make long trips to the camps. In 1989 the last reeducation camp detainees were released. Many of them and members of their families—approximately 60,000—arrived in the United States through the "orderly departure program" reserved for former South Vietnamese officers and officials. They reportedly remain bitter, accusing former South Vietnamese and U.S. officials of having let them down and also because of what they regard as inadequate financial support after arriving in the United States.

A sense of the war's futility and its bitter aftermath runs through Vietnamese society as it does through U.S. society. A substantial number of veterans have turned to alcohol or drugs to deal with their memories of the war and their resulting personal problems. These feelings have been described in graphic detail in hundreds of short stories and novels by northern and southern veterans. Bao Ninh's *The Sorrow of War,* Nguyen Khac Truong's *A Land Full of People and Teeming with Ghosts,* and Nguyen Huy Thiep's *The Retired General* are some of the most haunting and disturbing accounts.

BIBLIOGRAPHY

HY VAN LUONG. *Revolution in the Village.* 1993.
MARR, DAVID G., and CHRISTINE P. WHITE, eds. *Postwar Vietnam.* 1988.
PORTER, GARETH. *Vietnam: The Politics of Bureaucratic Socialism.* 1993.

NGÓ VIÑH LONG

Viet Cong. *See* National Liberation Front (NLF); People's Liberation Armed Forces (PLAF); Provisional Revolutionary Government (PRG).

Viet Minh. Ho Chi Minh and his communist followers founded the Viet Nam Doc Lap Dong Minh (League for Vietnamese Independence) in 1941, inviting "patriots of all ages and all types" to join a united front against French colonial rule. Gen. Vo Nguyen Giap raised an army for the Viet Minh that fought the Japanese in Vietnam during World War II and occupied Hanoi in 1945. In 1946, when the French returned, fighting broke out between Viet Minh troops and the French, touching off the Indochina War. Ho and Giap withdrew the Viet Minh to mountain strongholds and appealed for broad support by ostensibly disbanding the Communist Party and emphasizing antiimperialism. New names—Lien Viet (United Vietnam Nationalist Front) and Mat Tran To Quoc Viet Nam (Vietnam Fatherland Front)—were adopted in the 1950s. But the communists, bolstered with aid from China, never surrendered control of the Viet Minh. When the French left Vietnam in 1954, the communists took power in the north—while in the south, where the Viet Minh was never very strong because of a more pronounced French colonial influence there, President Diem's noncommunist regime received U.S. support. By 1960, southern cadres of the old Viet Minh had reorganized as the National Liberation Front, nicknamed the Viet Cong, and launched a communist-led guerrilla war against South Vietnam.

BIBLIOGRAPHY

BUTTINGER, JOSEPH. *Vietnam: A Dragon Embattled.* 1967.
FALL, BERNARD B. *Street without Joy: Indochina at War, 1946–1954.* 1961.
FALL, BERNARD B. *The Two Viet-Nams: A Political and Military Analysis.* Rev. ed., 1964.
FALL, BARNARD B. *The Viet Minh Regime.* 1956.
HAMMER, ELLEN. *The Struggle for Indochina, 1940–1955.* 1966.
HUONG VAN CHI. *From Colonialism to Communism.* 1965.
TURNER, ROBERT F. *Vietnamese Communism: Its Origins and Development.* 1975.

GLEN GENDZEL

Vietnam

The state of Vietnam, formerly known as the Socialist Republic of Vietnam (SRV), is shaped like the letter S and extends along the eastern coast of mainland Southeast Asia from the border with the People's Republic of China (PRC) to the Gulf of Thailand. The country measures more than 1,600 kilometers (1,000 miles) from north to south, while the distance from east to west is often less than 160 kilometers (100 miles). The western border is formed by a string of mountains known to the Vietnamese as the Truong Son, or Central Mountains. Beyond the Truong Son are Vietnam's immediate neighbors, Laos and Cambodia. To the east is the South China Sea. The entire country is situated approximately within the tropical zone, stretching from 8 degrees to 23 degrees north latitude. It is a region of dense jungles, swamps, and lush rice paddies. In the northern region of the country, the temperature occasionally falls to 10–15°C (50–60°F); in the south the temperature rarely drops below 15°C (60°F), and in the daytime usually averages between 25°C (80°F) and 35°C (95°F).

The population of the SRV in the early 1990s was nearly 70 million, the second largest in Southeast Asia, after the Republic of Indonesia. The vast majority of the people are ethnic Vietnamese. Nevertheless, as in the region as a whole, Vietnam has a number of ethnic minorities, including Khmer (Cambodians), Cham (Malayo-Polynesian), overseas Chinese, and nearly sixty tribal minority groups. Even the ethnic Vietnamese are divided by religion. Although the vast majority are nominally Buddhist, there are over 2 million Roman Catholics and an equal number belong to two other sects, the Cao Dai and the Hoa Hao.

Early History. The modern Socialist Republic of Vietnam is a vastly expanded version of the original Vietnamese state. The historical homeland of the Vietnamese people was in the Red River Delta, surrounding the present-day capital of Hanoi. Calling themselves the "Lac," the early Vietnamese were probably related to Austro-Asiatic–speaking peoples who had been living throughout much of southern China and mainland Southeast Asia since prehistoric times. In grammar and syntax, the Vietnamese language bears close resemblance to Mon-Khmer, a member of the Austro-Asiatic family of languages spoken by the present-day peoples of Cambodia and lower Burma.

According to legend, the Vietnamese people were governed in early times by a series of extremely long-lived rulers called the Hung Kings. While such accounts are apocryphal, there is no doubt that an advanced Bronze Age civilization, known historically as the kingdom of Van Lang or in archeological terms the Dong Son era, had emerged in the Red River Delta by the early seventh century B.C.

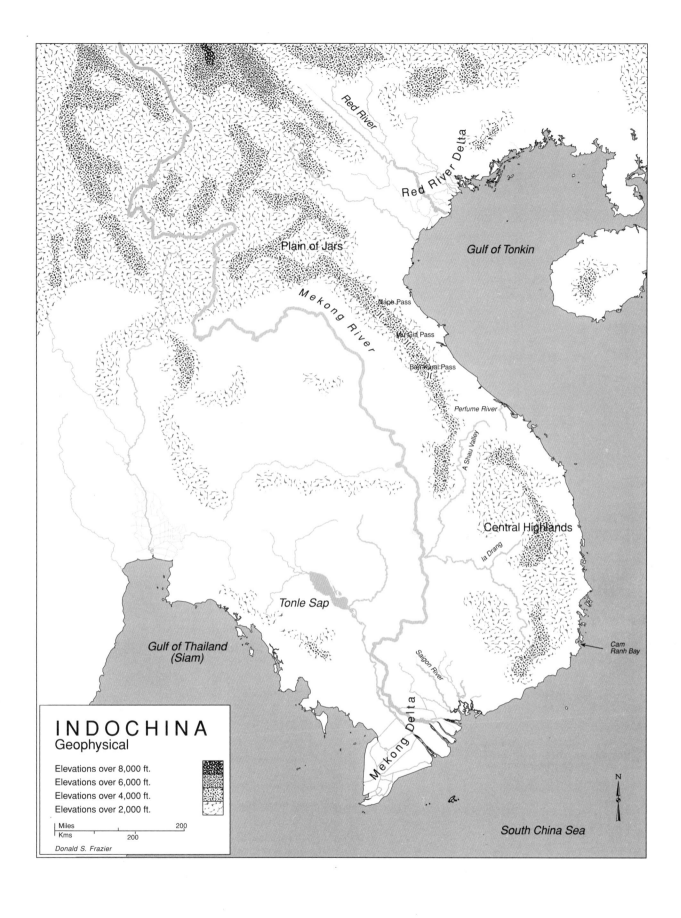

Red River

Red River Delta

Gulf of Tonkin

Plain of Jars

Nape Pass

Mekong River

Mu Gia Pass

Ban Karai Pass

Perfume River

A Shau Valley

Central Highlands

Ia Drang

Tonle Sap

Gulf of Thailand
(Siam)

Cam
Ranh Bay

Saigon River

Mekong Delta

N

INDOCHINA
Geophysical

Elevations over 8,000 ft.
Elevations over 6,000 ft.
Elevations over 4,000 ft.
Elevations over 2,000 ft.

Miles   200
Kms   200

Donald S. Frazier

South China Sea

While few reliable accounts of this period exist, the available evidence suggests that these early peoples were primarily rice farmers ruled by a hereditary aristocracy known as the "Lac lords." Although this embryonic Vietnamese state was originally restricted to the swampy lowland regions of the Red River Delta, it eventually expanded into the neighboring mountains and integrated the peoples there (known to the Vietnamese as the Au) into a new state called Au Lac. Vietnamese mythology chronicles this momentous unification of the lowland and upland peoples in the legend of Lac Long Quan, a lord of the sea whose marriage to the wife of a lord of the mountains produced the ancestors of the Vietnamese race.

Chinese Rule. By the third century B.C., the kingdom of Au Lac had become a well-organized state, but at the end of the century Chao T'o (in Vietnamese, Trieu Da), a military commander of the Qin dynasty in China, conquered the state and renamed it Nam Viet, or Southern Viet. *Viet* (in Chinese *Yueh*) was an ancient kingdom in southern China and a Chinese term for all the proto-Chinese peoples living along the coast south of the Yangtze River. Thereafter it was applied by the Vietnamese to themselves.

The kingdom of Nam Viet was relatively shortlived. In 111 B.C. it fell to the powerful Han Dynasty, which had replaced the Qin after the death of Qin Shihuangdi in 206. The Han placed the Red River Delta under Chinese military jurisdiction and administered the entire area through the indigenous Lac lords. Although the Han made little effort to assimilate the area directly into the Chinese empire, their occupation aroused resistance from the indigenous aristocracy, and in A.D. 39 a tax rebellion led by the famous Trung sisters (the Trung sisters were wives of local aristocrats who had been put to death by the Chinese for resisting Han rule) broke out. The rebellion was suppressed, but the two sisters would later be revered as patriots who led the fight for Vietnamese independence against foreign rule.

The immediate consequences of the Trung sisters' rebellion were unfortunate. Undoubtedly shaken by the strength of anti-Chinese sentiment among local elites, the Han instituted direct rule over their dependency and placed it under Chinese administration. Chinese officials were posted to the area and the Han assimilated the Vietnamese into the Chinese empire. Over the next several centuries, Chinese institutions and values strongly influenced Vietnamese society. Chinese political institutions, social customs, literature and art, and even the Chinese written language, were introduced and became interwoven with native forms of expression and behavior. Out of this process a new Vietnamese ruling elite emerged, one strongly influenced by Chinese civilization. But that same elite also took on an increasingly strong sense of local identity, and during succeeding centuries, periodic rebellions against Chinese rule took place in times of dynastic weakness in the north. Finally, in the tenth century A.D. a local aristocrat, Ngo Quyen, took advantage of the collapse of the Tang Dynasty and declared the independence of a new kingdom called Nam Viet.

Traditional Vietnam. At first, internal factionalism plagued the new state, but in the early eleventh century a powerful figure called Ly Thai To emerged through court intrigue and seized power. Making liberal use of Chinese institutions and organizational principles, the Ly Dynasty stabilized the country and ruled it effectively for two hundred years. At the same time, the Ly competed with the neighboring kingdom of Champa along the coast to the south. The Cham were a Malay-speaking people ethnically distinct from the Vietnamese who had been converted to Islam because of frequent contact with Muslim

KHAI DINH. The emperor of Annam (Vietnam) from 1916 to 1925 at his capital, Hue, 1923. *Archive Photos*

traders in the area. The kingdom of Champa was an active participant in the regional trade patterns passing through the area en route to the Indian Ocean and the South China Sea. During the next centuries, periodic conflicts broke out between Champa and Vietnam and the border shifted back and forth in response to the vicissitudes of the relationship. The Cham occasionally seized the Vietnamese capital of Thang Long (today known as Hanoi), while Vietnamese armies sometimes penetrated deep into Cham territory.

The Ly Dynasty declined in the early thirteenth century, and in 1225 the Tran, a dynamic new ruling house, replaced it and consolidated the internal development of the Vietnamese state despite ongoing conflicts with the kingdom of Champa. The Tran also clashed repeatedly with the Khmer state of Angkor, then the most powerful kingdom in mainland Southeast Asia. But the primary threat to Tran rule came from the north, where the conquest of China by the Mongols in the late thirteenth century placed a new and aggressive enemy along the northern border. In 1279 the Mongols asked the Tran for permission to pass through Vietnam to invade Champa. When the Tran ruler refused, a Mongol army invaded the Red River Delta. Under the inspired leadership of the Vietnamese commander Tran Hung Dao, the Vietnamese inflicted a major defeat on the Mongol army, forcing it to withdraw. The Mongols returned a few years later, but the Tran again resisted and destroyed the Mongol fleet in the Bach Dang River, ending their dreams of conquest.

Like the Ly, the Tran Dynasty lost its vigor in later years, and in the early fifteenth century a new Chinese dynasty, the Ming, took advantage of court intrigue inside Vietnam and restored Vietnam to Chinese rule. Chinese occupation once again sparked internal resistance, this time under the leadership of Le Loi, the son of a wealthy landowner. With the aid of the brilliant strategist Nguyen Trai, Le Loi won a major victory over the Ming army in 1426 and forced it to evacuate. After the Chinese withdrawal, Le Loi founded a new dynasty, the Le.

The Le Dynasty continued the tradition of cohesive rule established by its two predecessors. Under its most competent ruler, Le Thanh Tong (1460–1497), the Le further consolidated the territory of the Vietnamese state, while expanding steadily southward and reducing rival Champa to the status of a vassal. During the seventeenth century, the Vietnamese "march to the South" (as the process is labeled by Vietnamese historians) had extended into the Mekong River Delta. This hot and marshy region had long been under the rule of the Angkor empire, once the most powerful state on the Southeast Asian mainland and the predecessor of the modern-day kingdom of Cambodia. Defeated by the Thai in the fifteenth century, the Angkor state rapidly declined and lost territory to the neighboring states of Thailand to the west and Vietnam to the northeast. By 1800 the entire region of the Mekong Delta and the Ca Mau peninsula to the south had been conquered by the Vietnamese.

The integration of these new territories into the Le empire was facilitated by the arrival of Vietnamese settlers into the area. Many were former soldiers who were assigned farmlands in agricultural settlements under the command of their military officers. Once the area came under cultivation it was reorganized as a village or a hamlet under the state administration. There was little settlement of Vietnamese into the mountainous Central Highlands, however, an area inhabited by a wide variety of non-Vietnamese tribal peoples. Other parts of the Mekong River Delta were still farmed by their original inhabitants, known as the Khmer, the ancestors of the modern-day Cambodians. There are an estimated 300,000 Khmer living in southern Vietnam today.

As it expanded, the Le state also engaged in a major program of nation-building. Confucianism was adopted as the state ideology, and a new law code was introduced, based on the Chinese model, but which paid deference to local tradition by assigning greater legal rights to women.

At the height of its rule, the Le Dynasty might be considered the apogee of traditional Vietnamese civilization, but the Le were unable to avoid the fate of their predecessors. By the end of the sixteenth century, the once powerful state had been reduced to impotence by court intrigue, and rival noble families competed for power and influence. Imperial expansion turned into a disadvantage as the Vietnamese empire divided into two separate administrations, one in the north and one in the south, ruled by two princely families, the Trinh and the Nguyen, respectively.

Arrival of the West. Direct contact with the West also began in the sixteenth century. The Portuguese arrived in about 1540. A Portuguese fleet commanded by Adm. Alfonso de Albuquerque had seized the Muslim sultanate of Malacca in 1511 as a way station en route to the Spice Islands. A few decades later, a Portuguese ship appeared at the harbor of Da Nang, and shortly after a Portuguese trading fort was set up at Fai Fo (today Hoi An) on the central coast. During the next century, European merchants and Christian missionaries from several countries established their presence in Vietnam, competing for converts and profits.

Although the Portuguese were the first to arrive, the French demonstrated the most sustained interest in the area. French influence was sparked by the ambitions of the Jesuit priest Alexander of Rhodes, who spent several years as a missionary

VIETNAMESE TRADITIONAL AGRICULTURE. *National Archives*

in Vietnam while devising a transliteration of the Vietnamese spoken language in the Roman alphabet (known as *quoc ngu,* or the national tongue), which remains in use in Vietnam.

At first, the Vietnamese expressed a mild interest in commercial contacts with the Europeans, and thousands were converted to Christianity. But by the end of the seventeenth century the relationship had soured, as Vietnamese officials increasingly feared the effect of Christian influence on Confucian teachings and the tendency of the Europeans to intervene in local politics. European merchants gradually lost interest in the area because it provided relatively few profits, and in the early seventeenth century, only the Portuguese, along with a few French priests, remained.

During most of the eighteenth century, Vietnam was left alone, while rural unrest, some of it erupting among the Cham and the tribal peoples in the Central Highlands, ravaged the now defunct empire. Finally, in the 1770s a major peasant revolt led by the so-called Tay Son brothers (from the name of their native village in southern Vietnam) unseated the Nguyen family in the south and then conquered the north. The Tay Son had revolted in the name of the Le emperor, but following their victory, Nguyen Hue, the leading Tay Son brother, unseated the Le and established his own Nguyen Dynasty.

Ruling under the imperial title of Quang Trung, Nguyen Hue was a powerful personality and even launched an attack on neighboring China. After his death, however, his dynasty rapidly disintegrated, and in 1802 Nguyen Anh, a scion of the princely Nguyen family in the south, defeated the remnants of the Tay Son kingdom and established a new Nguyen Dynasty. As a demonstration of his intention to reunite the country under his authority, he placed his imperial capital in the central Vietnamese city of Hue.

Nguyen Anh had been assisted in seizing power by Pigneau de Béhaine, a French missionary-adventurer who hoped that his aid to Nguyen Anh would restore French influence in the area. As emperor, the latter was sufficiently grateful to his benefactor to provide him with privileges at the Nguyen court, but he was suspicious of French activities and limited their influence in his kingdom. His son and successor, Minh Mang, was even more hostile to foreign influence, and attempted to drive out French missionaries, while persecuting their local converts.

The French Conquest. By the late 1850s, agitation by mercantile and missionary interests in France for intervention in Vietnam had intensified, spurring the government of Napoleon III to action. Concerned with British advances in Burma and determined to establish a French presence in Southeast Asia, Napoleon ordered a French fleet (with token participation by Spain) to launch a naval attack on Da Nang harbor. French troops under the command of Adm. Rigault de Genouilly, advanced toward the imperial capital of Hue but, hampered by local resistance and the ravages of disease, abandoned the effort. Genouilly then sailed south to the region north of the Mekong Delta, where under new leadership French troops defeated imperial forces and occupied the area of modern-day Saigon (Ho Chi Minh City).

In 1862, a dispirited Emperor Tu Duc, discouraged by the failure of his troops to launch effective resistance, signed the Treaty of Saigon, which ceded three provinces in the south to the French. Two years later, three additional provinces were added, and France transformed its new possessions into the colony of Cochinchina. At the same time, the French declared a protectorate over neighboring Cambodia, which had been in a state of decline since the collapse of the Angkor empire in the fifteenth century, and had recently fallen under the joint control of Vietnam and Thailand.

The French had hoped that control over the mouth of the Mekong River would provide access to the potentially rich market of southern China, but discovered that the river was not navigable to the Chinese border. After an abortive effort in the 1870s, the French succeeded in extending their influence over the remnant of the Vietnamese empire. In 1884 the Vietnamese court signed a treaty granting the French a protectorate over the remaining part of the empire, reducing the Nguyen emperor to a figurehead.

For the remainder of the century, the French consolidated their position, dividing Vietnam into two regions—Tonkin in the north and Annam in the center—and establishing a protectorate over Laos in 1893. In 1896, the entire area was integrated into a single Indochinese Union to provide overall administrative control. The minority peoples in the mountains, however, were ruled separately, as were those in the overseas Chinese communities, most of whom were engaged in manufacturing or commerce in the major cities.

The "Civilizing Mission." In later years, defenders of the French colonial enterprise were fond of declaring that France had come to Southeast Asia to perform a *mission civilisatrice* (civilizing mission) for the backward peoples of In-

NUOC MAM. Bui Van Luyen checks her store of fermenting *nuoc mam,* a sauce made from fish that is a traditional Vietnamese dietary staple. Binh Thuan province, 1970. *National Archives*

dochina. French objectives were actually much more self-serving and involved a complicated amalgam of national grandeur and private profit. Like all industrializing nations, France desired a source of cheap raw materials and markets for its manufactured goods. It found both in Indochina. The French exported rice, rubber, tea, and other tropical products from the area, while turning it into a monopoly for the importation of French manufactured goods.

French official propaganda declared that with the aid of French economic activities, the peoples of Indochina would eventually be brought into the international capitalist marketplace and introduced to modern means of production, transport, and communications. Indeed, the French built roads and railroads in Indochina and drained the swamps of the Mekong River Delta to increase rice production. They opened thousands of new acres of land along the Cambodian border to the cultivation of rubber trees, and established tea and rubber plantations in the Central Highlands. French rule also led to the creation of a small commercial and manufacturing sector in such urban centers as Hanoi, Haiphong, Da Nang (known to the French as Tourane), and Saigon.

For millions of Vietnamese, however, the price for French tutelage was steep. Although new lands opened for rice cultivation, most were offered for sale to the highest bidder, creating a new class of absentee landlords. The average farmer saw only increased taxes, forcing many into tenancy or seeking employment as workers in the rubber and tea plantations. Life was no better in the cities. While French rule provided an improved life-style for a small urban bourgeoisie, the modern heavy industry sector (e.g., coal, steel, railroads) was dominated by European and overseas Chinese interests, while manufacturing for domestic consumption was depressed because of the government's determination to preserve the area as a market for French goods. The colonial system also created a growing class of factory workers and coal miners who often worked in abysmal conditions for long hours and low wages.

One element in the French program was the promise to introduce the peoples of Indochina to Western democratic values and attitudes through the introduction of representative institutions and a new educational system. The French established a new Franco-Vietnamese school system, but only a minority of students attended beyond the elementary level, and higher education was primarily for the elite. As for the commitment to political reform, the French soon recognized that the extension of democratic liberties could only lead to demands for an end to colonial rule. Legislative assemblies were eventually established on the local level, but they had only advisory powers, and the franchise was limited to French residents and a handful of wealthy natives.

Whether French colonial policies were more repressive or more enlightened than those of other Western powers in the area is a matter of debate. For the small number of Vietnamese merchants and landowners who collaborated with the colonial authorities, the advantages were apparent. But for most Vietnamese, for whom the benefits of the colonial experience were less apparent, subjugation to foreign authority was galling and humiliating.

At first, the reaction of many had been to resist French rule while defending traditional institutions. Vietnamese resistance to the French began even before the completion of French conquest, when some members of the traditional civilian and military elite, despite a lack of guidance from the royal court, attempted to organize guerrilla operations in the mountains against foreign-held territory along the coast. Lacking modern weapons and effective coordination at the national level, such groups were suppressed with relative ease by the French, who contemptuously labeled them "pirates."

At the beginning of the twentieth century, a more complex attitude began to take shape, as the desire for self-determination intermingled with admiration for Western culture and a sense of a new world emerging. The first to act were members of the traditional elite class who had been educated under the old system but lived as adults under colonial authority. By this time, most educated Vietnamese recognized that their country must change in order to survive, but early efforts to institute changes had little success. Phan Boi Chau, sometimes called Vietnam's first modern nationalist, promoted the idea of violent resistance to be followed by the establishment of a republic on the Western model, but he was driven into exile, captured in China, and eventually returned for trial in Hanoi, where he lived the remainder of his life under house arrest. Phan Chu Trinh, who argued that reform was preferable to revolt, was betrayed by the reluctance of the French to heed his appeal to fulfill their civilizing mission. Arrested for allegedly supporting rural protests in central Vietnam, he spent most of the remainder of his life in exile in France.

After World War I, a new wave of anticolonialist ferment arose in the big cities. Ironically, it had been provoked in part by the French themselves, as young graduates of the new Franco-Vietnamese school system, attracted to the allure of European freedom and material affluence, realized that they did not possess such benefits. During the 1920s, political parties were founded in all three regions of

SAIGON TRAFFIC, 1955. *National Archives*

the country. Some, such as the Constitutionalist Party based in Saigon, were essentially reformist in nature, promoting dominion status and a larger role for indigenous elements within the colonial political system. Others, including the Nationalist Party (Viet Nam Quoc Dan Dang, VNQDD), sought the eviction of the French by violent means and the establishment of an independent republic on the capitalist model.

The Birth of Vietnamese Communism. The Vietnamese communist movement emerged from the nationalist agitation of the 1920s. Marxist ideas became familiar to Vietnamese workers and intellectuals living in France during and after World War I and gradually penetrated into Vietnam during the years immediately following the war. But the true founder of the party was a young revolutionary who had taken the name Nguyen Ai Quoc (Nguyen the Patriot), later known to the world as Ho Chi Minh.

The son of a member of the Confucian scholar-gentry in central Vietnam, Ho Chi Minh traveled to Europe in 1911 and settled in Paris after World War I, where he became a founding member of the French Communist Party. Sent by the Comintern (Communist International) to southern China in late 1924, he established a proto-Marxist political organization called the Revolutionary Youth League among radical Vietnamese elements living in China. Five years later, the league was transformed into a formal Indochinese Communist Party (ICP).

In the summer and fall of 1930, taking advantage of rural unrest and an abortive revolt launched by the VNQDD, the ICP sought to organize peasant dissatisfaction into a full-scale revolt against colonial rule. Success proved elusive, however, and in the bloody French suppression the ICP was almost entirely destroyed. Still, the party managed to revive, and when French repressive efforts relaxed in the latter half of the 1930s, the ICP gradually reemerged as a major force within the anticolonialist movement.

The onset of World War II shook French authority in Indochina to its foundations and provided anticolonial elements with a golden opportunity, to which the communists responded effectively. In the fall of 1940, Vichy France and a weakened colonial regime acceded to Japan's demands and permitted the Japanese to use military facilities in Indochina. Operating under the guise of a multiparty nationalist alliance called the Viet Minh Front, the ICP organized guerrilla resistance forces in the mountains north of the Red River Delta, and when Japanese occupation authorities deposed the French colonial administration in March 1945, the Viet Minh gradually seized control of rural areas throughout the northern part of the country. Immediately following the Japanese surrender in mid August, the Viet Minh occupied Hanoi and other major urban centers throughout the country and declared the creation of a provisional democratic republic.

Ho Chi Minh hoped to provide arriving Allied occupation forces (the Nationalist Chinese in the north, the British in the south), with a fait accompli. The strategy succeeded in the north, where Ho placated the Chinese by agreeing to form a multiparty government with VNQDD and other noncommunist elements in Hanoi. But the British commander in the south, Douglas Gracey, refused Ho's requests and returned power to the French in Saigon. During the next several months, the Viet Minh government (known formally as the Democratic Republic of Vietnam, or DRV) and the French engaged in delicate negotiations to seek a compromise settlement. In March, Ho Chi Minh and French representative Jean Sainteny signed a preliminary agreement calling for Vietnamese autonomy in a so-called free state within the French Union. A plebiscite was to be held in each region to determine whether it wished to join the new state.

During formal negotiations at Fontainebleau, France, in the summer of 1946, however, negotiations broke down when the French refused to hold such a plebiscite in Cochinchina. After tension increased between French and Viet Minh armed forces inside Vietnam, war erupted in December when Viet Minh units attacked French installations in Hanoi and other cities in the north. The bulk of the Vietnamese forces then retreated to prepared positions in the countryside to wage a guerrilla resistance against French positions in major populated areas.

The Franco–Viet Minh War. The French hoped for a quick victory, but Viet Minh forces, assisted by a political program that emphasized national independence and land to the poor, gradually increased in strength, despite a French effort to undercut the DRV by forming a puppet government under former emperor Bao Dai. The Viet Minh received additional encouragement when the Communist Party came to power in China in 1949 and provided them with military training and equipment. In desperation, the French turned for assistance to the United States, which after 1949 was increasingly concerned about the possibility of communist expansionism in Southeast Asia. Also anxious to ensure French cooperation for European security, the United States provided military assistance to anticommunist forces in Indochina beginning in early 1950.

As the war turned into a stalemate on the battlefield, French public support for the war effort steadily weakened. In the spring of 1954, France agreed to discuss a peace settlement at Geneva. Negotiations opened on 7 May, immediately after the Viet Minh achieved a major victory by overrunning the French base at Dien Bien Phu, in the far northwest. In July, an agreement was signed providing

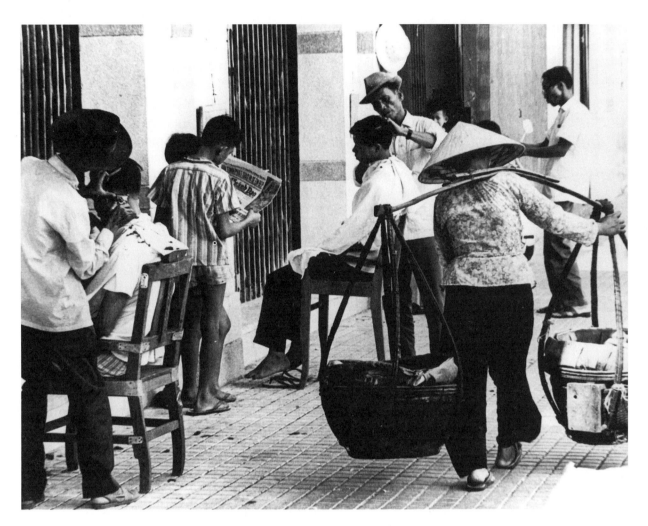

SIDEWALK BARBERS, SAIGON, 1966. *National Archives*

for a cease-fire on the battlefield and the creation of regroupment zones for each side, the DRV in the north and the French and the Bao Dai government and their supporters in the south. A demilitarization line at the 17th Parallel separated the two zones, and the agreement established a tripartite International Control Commission composed of representatives from Canada, India, and Poland to enforce it. A political declaration drafted at Geneva and approved by representatives of all attending countries except the Bao Dai government and the United States called for national elections to be held in the two zones in 1956 in order to create a united Vietnamese government.

The Diem Regime. After the Geneva settlement, communist leaders returned to Hanoi to build a socialist society in the North. Ho Chi Minh hoped that national elections would result in the reunification of the country under communist rule, but in Saigon a new government led by the anticommunist prime minister Ngo Dinh Diem refused to hold consultations on such elections and persecuted pro–Viet Minh elements remaining in the South. Convinced that the communists would win majority support in such elections, President Dwight D. Eisenhower's administration supported Diem in his decision, while seeking to persuade him to adopt political and economic reforms to broaden the popular base of his support in the South.

Ngo Dinh Diem faced an intimidating challenge in forging a new nation. The population in the southern provinces was more diverse than that in the North. In addition to 10 million ethnic Vietnamese, there were nearly 1 million overseas Chinese (most of them in Saigon's commercial sister city of Cholon) and an approximately equal number of tribal minorities in the Central Highlands. Nearly one-half million ethnic Khmer—the remnants of the old Angkor empire—lived in the lower Mekong Delta. Even the Vietnamese population was fragmented, with 2 million Roman Catholics (nearly half of them refugees from the North who arrived after the cease-fire), and several hundred thousand members of two religious sects—the Cao Dai and the Hoa Hao—that had been formed in the region of the delta during the pre–World War II era.

Ngo Dinh Diem bowed to U.S. requests to draft a new constitution and establish a democratic republic based on the Western model. But his governing instincts were authoritarian, and the base of his political support lay among educated Catholics (he himself was a devout Catholic) and affluent members of the rural landed gentry. Diem's efforts to suppress all opposition to his authority (he was elected president of the new Republic of Vietnam, or RVN, in 1957) alienated intellectuals and leading elements of many of the ethnic and religious minority groups in the country, while his failure to carry through on an implicit promise to equalize landholdings in the country (less than 3 percent of the population owned over 50 percent of the cultivated land in the South) convinced many peasants that the government's interests lay with the rural landed class.

Following the restoration of peace, party leaders in Hanoi had decided to trust to the political process established at the Geneva Conference. But Diem's determined effort to root out all support for the communists in the South, combined with growing opposition to his rule in urban and rural areas in the RVN, convinced the communists by early 1959 that only a return to revolutionary war would reunite the two zones under their authority. Under North Vietnamese guidance, the National Front for the Liberation of South Vietnam (NLFSVN, or NLF) was created in December 1960, and a small number of political and military cadres (many of them southerners who had been trained in the North) were infiltrated into the South to provide cadres for the new organization, which, like its predecessor the Viet Minh, was under secret Communist Party leadership.

At first, party strategists, fearful of direct U.S. intervention in the conflict, hoped that victory could be achieved without a return to full-scale war. But as insurgent forces in the South—popularly known as the Viet Cong, or Vietnamese communists—had increasing success in igniting discontent against the South Vietnamese government, President John F. Kennedy responded by increasing U.S. military and economic assistance to the RVN. When anger among Buddhists at Diem's alleged favoritism toward Catholics led to urban riots in the spring and summer of 1963, the White House, exasperated at Diem's stubborn refusal to agree to broaden his base of support, acquiesced in a military coup that overthrew Diem in early November. Diem and his widely detested brother, Ngo Dinh Nhu, were killed in the coup.

The Vietnam War. Policymakers in the U.S. government hoped that a new government in South Vietnam could reverse the deteriorating situation in the RVN. But the military regime that rose to power after the overthrow of Diem lacked competent leadership and a sense of direction, and the insurgency continued to gain strength as political chaos reigned in Saigon. In early 1965, faced with intelligence reports that the Viet Cong guerrillas could attain power in the South

BURNING VILLAGE. Montagnard village destroyed by the Viet Cong, 1964. *National Archives*

within a year, President Lyndon B. Johnson introduced U.S. combat forces into South Vietnam and announced a bombing campaign in the North to persuade North Vietnam to reduce its support for the insurgency.

North Vietnam responded in kind. In November 1965, party leaders increased the rate of infiltration of regular forces of the North Vietnamese Army (known formally as the People's Army of Vietnam, or PAVN) into the RVN in an all-out effort to achieve victory. By the summer of 1966, the United States had committed more than 200,000 troops into the South, while a new military government in Saigon under President Nguyen Van Thieu promulgated a new constitution to broaden its popular support.

During the next two years, the conflict increasingly became a conventional war, as U.S. troops under the command of Gen. William C. Westmoreland engaged in massive search-and-destroy missions to root out the communist infrastructure from rural areas and reduce infiltration from the DRV. Party strategists in North Vietnam gambled that heavy U.S. casualties would erode popular support for the war in the United States and force the White House to withdraw on their terms.

In February 1968, communist forces launched the Tet Offensive and uprising throughout the South. Suicide squads occupied RVN government installations in Saigon and seized the ground floor of the U.S. embassy, while Viet Cong forces assaulted government-held villages in rural areas. In the northern provinces, PAVN units seized the old imperial capital of Hue, holding it for nearly three weeks until driven out by a heavy counterattack.

The Tet Offensive resulted in heavy casualties for the insurgent forces—nearly 40,000 by U.S. estimates—and it failed to ignite the general uprising against the South Vietnamese government that party leaders in the North had expected. Nevertheless, it led the Johnson administration to halt the bombing of the North in return for peace talks with representatives of the DRV. Under President Nixon, peace talks continued in Paris, while under his direction U.S. combat troops were gradually withdrawn from South Vietnam. North Vietnam had demanded the resignation of the Thieu government as a condition for peace, a demand that the Nixon administration firmly rejected. Party leaders clearly hoped that as U.S. forces withdrew, further communist gains on the battlefield would force the United States to accept North Vietnam's terms. But when a major offensive launched by North Vietnamese regular units during the Easter holidays in 1972 failed to force the collapse of the Thieu regime, DRV negotiators in Paris finally agreed to peace terms that left President Nguyen Van Thieu in office.

According to the terms of the agreement signed in Paris in January 1973, all U.S. military forces were to be withdrawn from South Vietnam, while nothing was said about the presence of over 100,000 North Vietnamese troops in the RVN. To provide the framework for a future political settlement between the two Vietnams, a subgovernmental National Council of Reconciliation and Concord consisting of NLF, RVN, and neutralist elements was to be formed to work out arrangements for future national elections.

Like the Geneva Agreement of 1954, the Paris treaty rapidly lost its practical significance. President Thieu had disliked the terms of the agreement and flatly refused to carry out its provisions. South Vietnamese troops attacked Viet Cong–held areas throughout the country, attempting to dislodge them from their positions. The communists meanwhile strengthened their military forces in the South in preparation for a decisive confrontation. When it became clear that President Thieu had no intention of permitting NLF elements to play a political role in the RVN, North Vietnam planned a major new offensive to be launched in the early months of 1975.

Party strategists did not anticipate a rapid victory in their new offensive, and they watched carefully to observe the reaction from the United States. Richard Nixon (who had promised Thieu that he would respond firmly to any provocative action by the North) had been forced to resign from office because of the Watergate scandal in August 1974, and President Gerald Ford realized that the American people strongly opposed any new intervention. When North Vietnamese regular forces won stunning victories in the Central Highlands and along the northern coast in March 1975, the Ford administration half-heartedly requested an increase in U.S. military aid for the Thieu government. When Congress rejected the request, the White House announced that Vietnam was "a war that is finished."

With his armed forces weakened by declining U.S. military assistance and psychologically shaken by the U.S. failure to respond to North Vietnam's offensive, President Thieu resigned from office and fled the country. A successor government failed to negotiate a peace settlement and on 30 April North Vietnamese troops entered Saigon and occupied the presidential palace. The long Vietnam War was indeed "a war that was finished."

After the War. After the end of the war, Vietnamese leaders set forth three major goals: to unify the two zones into a single nation, to lead the entire Vietnamese people to socialism, and to ensure the national security of the state in a still dangerous world.

The regime had more success with the first objective than with the other two. In July 1976, a new Socialist Republic of Vietnam (SRV) was created, with its capital in Hanoi. The leadership of the Communist Party and the government remained the same, although a number of leading political figures from the southern provinces were assigned senior positions in the governmental bureaucracy. Although there was some grumbling among southerners that these decisions had been made without their consent, unification took place with a minimum of violence, although thousands were sent to reeducation camps for indoctrination or punishment.

The government encountered greater difficulty achieving its goal of building an advanced socialist society throughout the country. Part of the problem can be ascribed to excessive zeal on the part of the veteran party leadership. Despite the reality of heavy wartime damage, lack of capital investment, and the challenge of integrating the southern provinces into the socialist northern half of the country, the government launched an ambitious program of socialist transformation in the south. In early 1978 all industry and commerce above the family level was nationalized, while private farmers in the south were urged to join low-level collective farms.

The results were disastrous. Thousands of Vietnamese, many of them ethnic Chinese who saw the new regulations as directed at reducing their own economic livelihood, fled the country by sea or across the northern border into the PRC. Industrial and farm production declined drastically and unrest appeared among key sectors of society, including the Catholics, the sects, and the mountain minorities.

One of the factors in the country's continuing economic difficulties was the deterioration in relations with neighboring Cambodia and the PRC. Border clashes on both frontiers broke out in 1975. The new revolutionary government in Phnom Penh also refused the SRV's proposal to form a militant alliance of the three Indochinese countries under Vietnamese guidance. Vietnamese troops occupied Cambodia in December 1978, and the PRC responded with a brief but bloody invasion of northern Vietnam in February 1979. When Vietnamese forces created a new pro-Vietnam government in Phnom Penh, the PRC joined other countries, including the United States, in supporting resistance forces in Cambodia and imposing an economic embargo on the SRV.

In 1986, the Sixth National Congress of the Vietnamese Communist Party elected a new leadership with Nguyen Van Linh as party chief. The government announced major reforms similar to those of Mikhail Gorbachev's program of *perestroika* and *glasnost* in the Soviet Union and signaled a willingness to withdraw its troops from Cambodia in preparation for the installation of a coalition government in Phnom Penh. Vietnam also made a number of gestures signaling a desire to improve relations with the PRC and the United States.

In the years since the Sixth Congress, the Vietnamese economy, spurred by a more tolerant official attitude toward private sector activities, has shown modest signs of improvement. Wary of repeating the experience of other communist regimes, the party has been less receptive to political reform and jealously guards its total power over the governmental apparatus. In the meantime, Vietnam continues to improve its relations with the United States. As a result of Vietnamese cooperation in resolving the issue of MIAs, the Clinton administration announced an end to the economic embargo on trade with Vietnam in January 1994, and the United States normalized relations with the Socialist Republic of Vietnam on 11 July 1995. Two decades after the end of the Vietnam War, the legacy of that bitter conflict is finally being erased.

[*See also* Montagnards; National Liberation Front (NLF); Provisional Revolutionary Government (PRG); Reeducation Camps; Refugees; Veterans, *article on Vietnamese Veterans;* Viet Minh; Vietnam, Democratic Republic of (DRV); Vietnam, Republic of (RVN); Vietnamese Perspectives; *entries on individual Vietnamese military services, and entries on religious groups mentioned herein.*]

BIBLIOGRAPHY

BUTTINGER, JOSEPH. *The Dragon Embattled.* 2 vols. 1967.
BUTTINGER, JOSEPH. *The Smaller Dragon.* 1958.
DUIKER, WILLIAM J. *Vietnam: Nation in Revolution.* 1983.
HAMMER, ELLEN J. *Vietnam Yesterday and Today.* 1966.
HODGKIN, THOMAS. *Vietnam: The Revolutionary Path.* 1981.
KARNOW, STANLEY. *Vietnam: A History.* Rev. ed. 1991.
SMITH, RALPH B. *Vietnam and the West.* 1968.

WILLIAM J. DUIKER

Vietnam, Democratic Republic of (DRV).

In August 1945, at the end of World War II, the communist-led nationalist movement in Vietnam, popularly known as the Viet Minh, seized power in Hanoi, Hue, and Saigon. The Viet Minh had developed a military force and popular base during the Japanese occupation, and it moved to secure political authority in the country before the arrival of Allied powers. Emperor Bao Dai, the Japanese puppet, abdicated in late August. On 2 September 1945, Viet Minh leader Ho Chi Minh declared Vietnam's independence as the Democratic Republic of Vietnam (DRV), quoting from the U.S. Declaration of Independence and the French Declaration of Rights of Man. Allied and contending Vietnamese political groups quickly challenged the DRV in southern Vietnam. British forces, dispatched to accept the Japanese surrender under the Potsdam agreement, refused to recognize the DRV, but in northern Vietnam the occupying Kuomintang (Nationalist Chinese) army acceded to Ho's government after receiving payments from the Viet Minh.

Establishing the DRV, 1945–1954. In November 1945, hoping for U.S. support for the DRV and trying to appease moderate Vietnamese nationalists, Ho dissolved the Vietnamese Communist Party and formed a coalition government with rival political parties. The disciplined communist organization, however, still maintained primary influence. National elections were held in January 1946 and a state constitution based on a U.S. and French parliamentary model was promulgated in November. The constitution established a unicameral legislative body, and provided nominal protection for civil liberties of speech, religion, and habeas corpus. Western nations, however, deferred to French officials who were intent on reclaiming their Asian colonies. In March 1946, Viet Minh and French negotiators reached accords proposing self-determination for Vietnam within the French Union, but French colonial interests, eager to regain their previous authority, sabotaged the treaty. French–Viet Minh hostilities broke out in November 1946, and the DRV and its forces fled to the mountainous region in northwest Vietnam.

Between 1946 and 1954, the DRV remained a skeleton government-in-exile. Real power belonged to the Communist Party, which consolidated its position within the Viet Minh through a violent campaign against noncommunist nationalists. Communist Party policies to alleviate famine conditions in the countryside and to redistribute French-owned land to Vietnamese peasants helped the Viet Minh expand its popular base. With ample military aid from communist allies and an effective national mobilization, Ho and his key advisers directed the war effort that defeated the French, climaxing in the battle of Dien Bien Phu. After the 1954 Geneva peace accords partitioned Vietnam at the 17th Parallel, Ho Chi Minh triumphantly returned to Hanoi and reestablished the Democratic Republic of Vietnam.

The State Structure. The Democratic Republic of Vietnam consisted of four political and social components: party, state, mass organization, and military. The Communist Party's top decision-making bodies, the central committee and politburo, held preeminent authority in the country. Party elites pursued a political administrative scheme termed *parallel hierarchies* for governing the country. The strategy emerged in the war years and facilitated communist hegemony even in areas occupied by the French. Under the system, the party regimented citizens into organizations (such as for youths, farmers, workers, veterans) and constructed a formal political structure at the village, regional, and national levels. The Communist Party, itself organized hierarchically from the village cadre member to governing committees, infiltrated and oversaw the social and political apparatus.

Communists also relied upon proselytizing campaigns to elicit mass support. In the 1940s, indoctrination teams stressed nationalist themes such as anticolonialism and Vietnamese emancipation to garner Vietnamese support for the regime. As the party consolidated its position, organizers also emphasized communist doctrine drawn from Marx, Engels, Lenin, and Mao Zedong. The Communist Party, known from 1951 to 1976 as the Vietnam Workers' Party, claimed 525,000 members in 1960; in 1975, just prior to reunification, membership stood at 1.2 million in a nation of 25 million.

From 1954 until 1959 the DRV state structure ostensibly reflected the 1946 state constitution, which was replaced by a more orthodox socialist constitution in 1960. The new constitution en-

WELCOMING THE NEW ORDER. Residents of Haiphong hold banners to welcome Viet Minh forces, 17 May 1955. The Viet Minh, by prearrangement, occupied the city 12 May in the wake of withdrawing French troops. *National Archives*

THE AIR WAR. North Vietnamese ferrying fragments of a shot-down U.S. aircraft. *Ngô Vĩnh Long*

were provided for peasants, workers, women, and youths as well as for such "special interest" groups as artists, journalists, intellectuals, and ethnic groups. The Vietnam Fatherland Front, a huge umbrella organization, oversaw the mass organizations, and the party, in turn, controlled and directed the front. The front served as a crucial vehicle for steering public activities and sentiments toward support of communist goals. The front encompassed practically every social movement in society, including nearly all adult North Vietnamese. Through the front organizations, the party communicated its principles and objectives to citizens.

The party also maintained oversight of the armed forces, known as the People's Army of Vietnam (PAVN). Political officers accompanied PAVN units, and party committees assisted military command. The National Defense Council, headed by Ho, served as the nation's military administrative center. In 1959 the state made conscription universal and most adult Vietnamese men served in the armed forces.

Socialist Reform. After assuming state power in 1954, the Communist Party moved to organize the economy along socialist lines. This effort entailed the development of large-scale industry and the collectivization of agriculture in which large, egalitarian cooperatives replaced village and family-oriented production. In this campaign, the state promoted centralized economic planning in place of a market economy. The process of economic development can be divided into four distinct periods: land reform, socialist construction, "air war," and resumption of building socialism.

In 1954–1955 the party conducted a Chinese communist–inspired land reform that redistributed land from landlords and rich peasants to poor peasants and the landless. The campaign against "feudal interests," however, brought extensive violence in the countryside. Zealous local tribunals imprisoned and executed thousands, often on arbitrary grounds. A division of PAVN troops suppressed a peasant uprising in Ho's home province, Nghe An, that had been sparked by the reform. In all, an estimated 30,000–100,000 Vietnamese were killed in the redistribution turmoil. In October 1956, the regime ended the program and launched a "rectification of errors," including the imprisonment of 12,000 accused "exploiters," and dismissed the party officials deemed responsible.

In the late 1950s, when stability had returned to the countryside, the party commenced a period of

shrined the leading role of the party and communist ideals and established a state structure borrowed from Chinese and Soviet constitutional practice. The executive, legislative, and judicial powers were combined into a unitary state structure. The State Planning Commission exercised rigid central control of the economy.

The National Assembly, nominally the highest organ of state power, met infrequently and was in practice a rubber stamp body. Its first members were selected in direct elections beginning in May 1960, though few seats were contested. Smaller standing committees, such as the Committee for Current Affairs, exercised extensive power in the DRV government apparatus. These committees, directed by party members, had legislative authority in the frequent recess periods of the National Assembly. Government ministries also had substantial influence, particularly agencies that directed the planned economy such as the Ministry of Agriculture and Ministries of Heavy and Light Industry. Politburo members led important, large ministries including the National Defense and Interior ministries.

To monitor and direct public activity, the party created mass organizations for citizens. Associations intensive socialist reform. In 1958, it launched a campaign to collectivize agriculture. Organized by party cadre members at the village level, the campaign steered peasants into producers' cooperatives. The communal nature of Vietnamese villages facilitated the process, and the program achieved near total success by the early 1960s, as 90 percent of Vietnam's peasants had joined cooperatives. The DRV also placed priority on developing an industrial base, an emphasis reflected in Vietnam's First Three-Year Plan (1958–1960) and First Five-Year Plan (1961–1965). The program included the nationalization of former French-owned industries and the state-directed development of mining enterprises and hydroelectric power sources. Assisted by large-scale Chinese and Soviet aid, Vietnam's industrialization had initial success. Industrial workers doubled to 40,000 from 1958 to 1960, and industrial output expanded by 20 percent in each of the first few years of the 1960s. But in September 1960, the party's Third National Congress committed the North to a "war of national liberation" in the South, aimed at reunification—a decision that ultimately siphoned significant resources away from economic development.

War in the South. Guerrilla warfare, supported by the North, intensified in the early 1960s in its effort to topple the U.S.-supported Republic of Vietnam, and in 1965 a full-scale ground war began against U.S. forces and the South Vietnamese government. In retaliation, the United States launched bombing campaigns against northern military installations, industry, and infrastructure, disrupting the DRV's political and social institutions. During the "air war" period (1965–1968), the National Assembly was suspended. Major cities were partially evacuated, and when possible, industry was dismantled and dispersed. The exigencies of the war resulted in the delay of party goals for collectivizing agriculture and promoting industrialization. Family-based agricultural production came to the fore, and leaders encouraged provincial autarky in place of centralized planning. Women took men's positions in economic and village administrative roles. On the industrial front, Vietnam eschewed long-term programs for development, preferring to fi-

INDEPENDENCE CELEBRATION, 2 SEPTEMBER 1975. *Ngô Vĩnh Long*

nance annual economic plans and the war with large-scale foreign assistance.

Despite the deprivations, the North Vietnamese government successfully mobilized its citizens for the war effort. The North suffered tremendous casualties (estimated at more than 800,000 deaths) and emerged from the war as one of the poorest countries in Asia. To manage social problems, the party intensified its oversight of government activities and security efforts against "counterrevolutionaries." But North Vietnamese citizens proved willing to make great sacrifices, testimony to the strength of nationalist ideals embedded in the Vietnamese culture. The party drew upon the legacy of its anti-imperial struggle against the Chinese and French for its war propaganda.

After the end of the air war, DRV government and social institutions gradually resumed their normal functions. Party elites attempted to reimpose suspended economic programs, renewed efforts were made to collectivize the peasantry, and the party prepared a five-year plan to be initiated in 1976. But until the cessation of hostilities, national resources were committed to the campaigns in the South. In 1975, Vietnam was reunited under communist rule, and in April 1976 nationwide elections were held. The new National Assembly, which met in July 1976, adopted the 1960 DRV constitution for the nation, now officially called the Socialist Republic of Vietnam.

[See also Land Reform; Lao Dong; entries on individual military services, and entries on individual countries mentioned herein.]

BIBLIOGRAPHY

FALL, BERNARD B. The Two Viet-Nams: A Political and Military Analysis. 2d rev. ed. 1967.
FFORD, ADAM, and SUZANNE H. PAINE. The Limits of National Liberation: Problems of Economic Management in the Democratic Republic of Vietnam. 1987.
PIKE, DOUGLAS. History of Vietnamese Communism. 1978.
WIEGERSMA, NANCY. Vietnam: Peasant Land, Peasant Revolution. 1988.

ADAM LAND AND CARLYLE A. THAYER

Vietnam, Republic of. The Republic of Vietnam (RVN), formally promulgated on 26 October 1955, consisted of the territories included in the southern regroupment zone, south of the 17th parallel, created by the Geneva Agreement in July 1954. The capital was located in Saigon.

The RVN's origins can be traced to the period of France's war with the Viet Minh, when the French began to conceive various ways of dealing with the challenge presented by Ho Chi Minh's protocommunist Democratic Republic of Vietnam (DRV), which had been established immediately following World War II. French officials first attempted to create a separate Cochinchinese Republic consisting of those territories originally included in the French colony of Cochinchina, in the southern part of Vietnam. Then, in March 1949, the so-called Élysée Accords created the Associated State of Vietnam (ASV), with former emperor Bao Dai as chief of state. The ASV consisted of all the territory included in the Vietnamese Empire, which in the late nineteenth century had been divided by the French into three separate regions, the colony of Cochinchina and the protectorates of Tonkin and Annam.

The Élysée Accords were formally ratified by the French National Assembly in February 1950, and diplomatic recognition by the United States and several other countries followed shortly after. During the remainder of the Franco–Viet Minh conflict, the ASV under chief-of-state Bao Dai collaborated with the French in seeking to prevent a communist victory in Vietnam.

The Geneva agreement of 21 July 1954 divided Vietnam into two cease-fire zones in the north and the south, separated by the Demilitarized Zone (DMZ) at the 17th Parallel. A political declaration drafted at the conference called for reunification elections in both zones in 1956, but in the south, the prime minister of the former Associated State of Vietnam, Ngo Dinh Diem, refused to hold consultations on elections and established a separate state.

At first, the new state was known to its supporters as "Free Vietnam," but in October 1955, Prime Minister Diem held a referendum between himself and chief-of-state Bao Dai to determine the future leadership of the country. Diem received nearly 95 percent of the total vote (Bao Dai had gone to live in France and did not contest the election), and on 26 October 1955, Diem formally established the Republic of Vietnam.

During the next few months, Diem filled out the structure of the new republic, and a 123-member national assembly was elected in March 1956. One of its first duties was to ratify a new constitution, which had been drafted by a presidential commission the previous fall. The new charter was formally promulgated on 26 October 1956, based roughly on

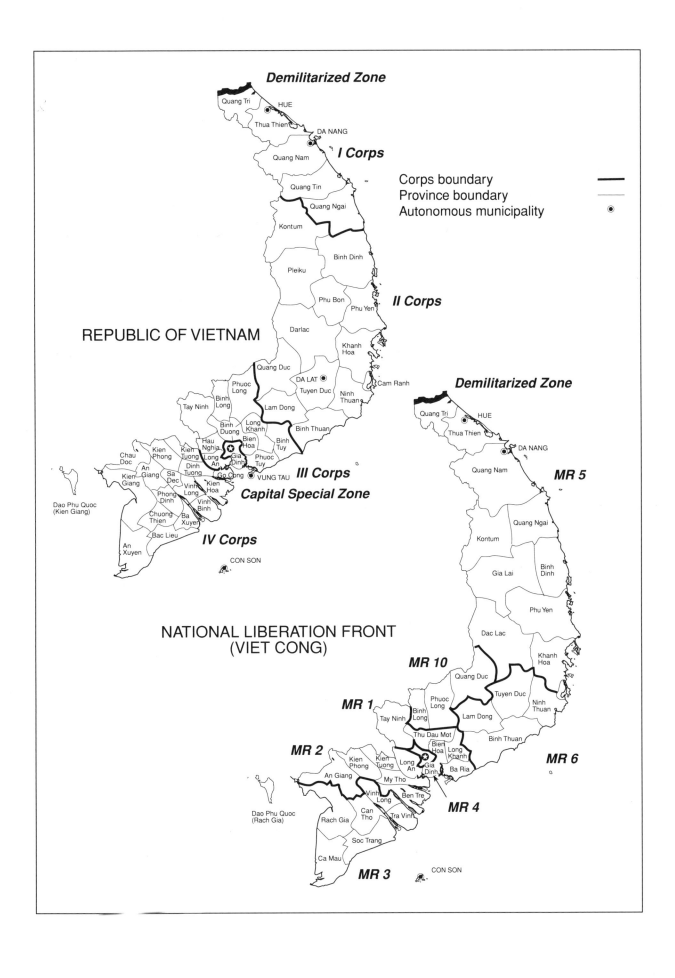

Demilitarized Zone

I Corps

Corps boundary
Province boundary
Autonomous municipality

REPUBLIC OF VIETNAM

II Corps

Demilitarized Zone

III Corps

Capital Special Zone

IV Corps

NATIONAL LIBERATION FRONT
(VIET CONG)

MR 5

MR 10

MR 1

MR 2

MR 6

MR 4

MR 3

ESTABLISHMENT OF THE REPUBLIC. Crowds in Saigon celebrate the proclamation of the new republic, 1955. *National Archives*

the U.S. Constitution, with a strong president, operating within a tripartite system consisting of executive, legislative, and judicial branches. At the local level, the country was divided into forty-one provinces, each in turn subdivided into districts and villages.

In practice, the system was highly centralized. President Diem possessed strong executive powers, and the National Assembly became a virtual rubber stamp to ratify his decisions. Autocratic by inclination, he suppressed all dissent to his rule, communist or noncommunist. Although Diem had indicated to U.S. advisers that he had no intention of creating a progovernment political party, he agreed to the formation of an elite organization called the Personalist Labor Party (often called the Can Lao Party) under his brother, Ngo Dinh Nhu. The government also created a broad nationalist front called the National Revolutionary Movement.

Diem's autocratic methods were not much different from those of his counterparts elsewhere in the region; democratic political institutions were ignored or toppled with regularity throughout the re-

gion during the 1950s and 1960s. Diem, however, appeared almost systematically to undermine the scope of his popularity by alienating the various interest groups in the RVN and relying almost exclusively on Catholics and the affluent landed class for support. As his popularity waned, rural unrest increased and rumors of potential coup attempts spread rapidly in the cities. One such effort, in November 1960, nearly brought an end to Diem's rule.

In 1963, Diem's favoritism toward Catholics provoked nationwide Buddhist demonstrations against the regime. Exasperated at Diem's chronic failure to resolve his domestic difficulties, the Kennedy administration secretly approved a military coup that overthrew the Diem regime in early November. Diem and his brother Nhu were killed during the coup, and the so-called Military Revolutionary Council chaired by the popular general Duong Van "Big" Minh took power.

Contrary to the hopes of policymakers in Washington, D.C., the toppling of the Diem regime ushered in an era of political instability in Saigon. Military governments, lacking any semblance of legitimacy, replaced each other with bewildering frequency. In several instances, civilians were placed in positions of authority to placate the United States, but the military continued to rule behind the scenes as the strength of the communist-led insurgency in the rural areas rapidly increased. In early 1965, to prevent a total collapse of the Saigon government, the Johnson administration introduced the first U.S. combat troops into South Vietnam and initiated a bombing campaign against the DRV in the North.

In June, a new group of "young Turks" took power, led by two ambitious young RVN military officers, Nguyen Cao Ky and Nguyen Van Thieu. Contrary to expectations, Ky and Thieu managed to consolidate power and bring a measure of stability to the political situation in Saigon, although unrest—marked in part by tensions between Buddhists and Catholics—continued to simmer beneath the surface. Convinced that the Ky-Thieu regime, ruled

by an armed forces council and a ten-member directorate, was the best hope for political stability in South Vietnam, the United States firmly supported the new government and pressed it to initiate political reforms to enhance its legitimacy among the Vietnamese people and abroad.

In September 1966, a 117-member constituent assembly was elected to draft a new constitution. The final version, approved in April 1967, created a new presidential system based on a bicameral legislature. The president, who served a four-year term and was eligible for reelection once, had considerable authority to promulgate laws and initiate legislation. He also served as the commander in chief of the republic's armed forces. The constitution also provided for a prime minister appointed by the president to assist him in his duties.

The two-house legislature, which consisted of a lower national assembly and a senate, was to be elected by universal suffrage and secret ballot. The

END OF THE REPUBLIC. The Vietnamese pilot of a Huey helicopter deliberately ditches his craft near the USS *Blue Ridge* as one of the ship's boats stands by. The helicopter was one of fifteen that landed aboard or ditched near the ship on 29 April 1975 carrying Vietnamese military personnel and their families. All the helicopters that landed aboard the ship were pushed overboard to make room on deck. *U.S. Navy*

judiciary, in theory, was independent. Political parties were permitted to exist, although an article in the constitution prohibited the promotion or practice of communism "in any form." In elections held in September, Nguyen Van Thieu was elected president, with Nguyen Cao Ky as his vice president.

Like Diem, Thieu ruled autocraticly, arresting active opponents of his regime and vigorously prosecuting the war against the communists. But Thieu was more sensitive than Diem had been to the concerns of the various religious and ethnic groups in the RVN such as the sects, the montagnards, and the Buddhists. He also recognized, as Diem had not, the importance of appealing to the rural masses and in 1969 promulgated a new "Land to the Tiller" law that effectively turned land ownership over to the previous tenants, bringing to an end one of the primary economic sources of rural discontent.

Nguyen Van Thieu's tight control over the political system was vividly demonstrated during the presidential elections of 1971, when he was able to neutralize all political opposition, including that of rivals Nguyen Cao Ky and Duong Van Minh, and win easy reelection to a second term. Thieu's electoral success, however, did not disguise the fact that South Vietnamese society was beset by a number of serious problems, in the social and economic as well as in the political realms. Years of civil strife had eroded the morale of the populace and brought a widespread yearning for peace, while a high level of official corruption had alienated much of the population from the regime in Saigon. Despite U.S. economic largesse, the economy was in a shambles, as the fighting in the countryside had driven millions of peasants to abandon their homesteads in the countryside and flee into fetid refugee camps on the edges of major cities.

The ultimate threat to Nguyen Van Thieu and the RVN, however, came from the communists. To Thieu's dismay, the Nixon administration negotiated a peace settlement with North Vietnam in January 1973 that called for the withdrawal of U.S. troops without a corresponding departure of North Vietnamese forces from the South. In the months that followed, Thieu tried to sabotage the agreement by refusing to deal with the communists or to permit them to take part in political activities in the RVN. His armed forces also attempted to dislodge them from areas assigned to them by the Paris agreement.

In early 1975, North Vietnam launched a major offensive to topple the Saigon regime and unify the country under communist rule. Faced with declining material and diplomatic support from the United States, President Thieu abandoned the northern provinces of the country and attempted to consolidate his authority in the area south of the Central Highlands. The effort failed, and in mid-April Thieu resigned as president to provide an opening for a compromise settlement. The North Vietnamese government was not interested, and as North Vietnamese tanks broke through onto the grassy lawn of the presidential palace in Saigon on 30 April 1975, the Republic of Vietnam came to its tragic end.

[*See also* Commercial-Import Program; Elections, South Vietnam, 1955; Geneva Conference, 1954; Land Reform; Military Revolutionary Council; Montagnards; Pacification; Refugees; Viet Minh; *entries on individual military services, and entries on religious groups mentioned herein.*]

BIBLIOGRAPHY

BUI DIEM, with DAVID CHANOFF. *In the Jaws of History.* 1987.
FALL, BERNARD B. *The Two Vietnams.* 1967.
GOODMAN, ALLAN E. *Politics in War: The Bases of Political Community in South Vietnam.* 1973.
HALBERSTAM, DAVID. *The Making of a Quagmire.* 1965.
LINDHOLD, RICHARD W., ed. *Viet-Nam: The First Five Years.* 1957.
NGUYEN TIEN HUNG and JERROLD L. SCHECTER. *The Palace File.* 1986.
RACE, JEFFREY. *War Comes to Long An.* 1972.
SCIGLIANO, ROBERT. *South Vietnam: Nation under Stress.* 1963.

WILLIAM J. DUIKER

Vietnam, Socialist Republic of (SRV).

See Vietnam; Vietnam, Democratic Republic of (DRV).

Vietnamese National Army (VNA).

In December 1950, France formed the Vietnamese National Army (VNA), officially titled the Armed Forces of the Associated State of Vietnam, to assist in the French war against the Viet Minh. Bao Dai, leader of the Associated State of Vietnam, served as commander in chief and authorized limited national conscription in July 1951. French commanders, beginning with Gen. Jean de Lattre de Tassigny, envisioned the VNA as a crucial auxiliary force to perform defensive, territorial responsibilities, freeing the French Expeditionary Force for offensive operations. The United States viewed the

VNA as an important step toward independence and pressured French authorities to allow U.S. officers to train the army. Although it had 300,000 troops by 1954, the VNA never became an effective fighting force. The Vietnamese public resented the French-dominated Bao Dai government, and educated Vietnamese declined to join the VNA's officers' ranks. Following the 1954 Geneva Conference, the VNA became the Army of the Republic of Vietnam (ARVN).

BIBLIOGRAPHY

BUTTINGER, JOSEPH. *A Dragon Embattled.* 1967.

ADAM LAND

Vietnamese Perspectives

Hamlets and Refugees
Vietnamese Traditions
    Ancestors and Tombs
    The House
    The Nation and the Land
Revolutionary Strategy
Interpreting the Tet Offensive
The Effects of War
Opposition in the South
The End in the South
The War in the North
Response in the North
The Political Response
Legacies of the War
Structural Changes in the 1980s

The war in Vietnam primarily—and most heavily—affected the Vietnamese people, north and south. The number of casualties—civilian and military—was enormous. According to conservative estimates, about 4 million Vietnamese on all sides were killed, wounded, or missing during the 1965–1975 period alone. The Pentagon's final estimate of civilian casualties for the South, a nation of about 18 million in 1972, was as high as 1,225,000 for the period between 1965 and 1972. A U.S. Senate subcommittee report estimated 1,350,000 civilian casualties, including 415,000 killed, for the same period. "Enemy soldiers" killed were at least 850,000, according to both estimates. A substantial number of these "enemy soldiers," however, were civilians whom the U.S. military defined as "enemy" because they were within free-fire zones, areas controlled by the National Liberation Front (NLF). Estimates of casualties suffered by the Republic of Vietnam Armed Forces (RVNAF) ran from 300,000 to 500,000. During the "postwar war" of 1973–1975, another half a million Vietnamese were killed and wounded—340,000 of them civilians—according to U.S. and South Vietnamese estimates.

Hamlets and Refugees. The war also vitally affected the land and native institutions and traditions in both parts of the country. Vietnam is less than 1/25th the area of the United States; Cambodia, Laos, and Vietnam combined have about the same area as France. Between 1965 and 1973, the United States used more than 14 million tons of air- and artillery-delivered high explosives on the area. The bombing alone accounted for about 7 million tons, or more than three times the tonnage used during World War II. Most of the bombs and artillery shells, and virtually all the defoliants (nearly 12 million tons), fell on the southern half of the country. The purpose was to destroy the National Liberation Front revolutionaries' infrastructure and to deprive them of popular support in the south by driving the population into areas controlled by the South Vietnamese government. In congressional testimony in January 1966, Secretary of Defense Robert McNamara introduced evidence on the success of air and artillery attacks, including "the most devastating and frightening" B-52 raids, in forcing the villagers "to move where they will be safe from such attacks . . . regardless of their attitude to the GVN." This, McNamara continued, not only disrupted Viet Cong guerrillas' activities but also threatened "a major deterioration of their economic base."

The effect, however, was to destroy nearly one-third of the cropland and more than one-half of the hamlets. By 1972, according to a U.S. Senate subcommittee report, U.S. air and artillery attacks were responsible for the great bulk of the 10 million refugees and most of the civilian casualties.

"Refugee-generation," in fact, became a central goal of the U.S. war efforts in Vietnam. In April 1967 Robert Komer, who directed the pacification program—officially called "The Other War: The War to Win the Hearts and Minds of the People"—recommended that the United States must "*step up refugee programs deliberately aimed at depriving the VC of a recruiting base*" [his emphasis]. In actuality, by the beginning of 1967, some 40,000 "pacification cadres," about 10 percent of all U.S. troops and 90 percent of South Vietnamese regular armed forces, were already being used exclusively for pacification efforts, which included the destruction of villages and wholesale resettlement of the rural population into "New Life Hamlets" in order to "secure" them. The program created enormous resentment, and consequently resistance, from the Vietnamese so that by mid 1967 U.S. Operation Mission (USOM) data on loyalties of the hamlets reported that only 168 hamlets out of a total of 12,537 in South Vietnam were controlled by the government. On the other hand, the NLF controlled 3,978. The remainder were listed as "contested" or partially controlled by both sides.

The contested hamlets were in areas variously referred to as "leopard spots" by the Americans, "rice and beans regions" (*vung xoi dau*) by most South Vietnamese, and "adjoining combs positions" (*the cai luoc*) by the southern revolutionaries. RVNAF forces conducted almost daily military operations against these areas in order to expand the territories under their control. The process was clear. "Security guards" and "civil guards"—two types of local military forces—were dispatched to occupy newly erected forts in each village and hamlet, presumably to provide protection and security for inhabitants. Barbed-wire fences and spiked moats were built around each village or hamlet to guard against communist infiltration and terrorism. Next, teams of "pacification cadres" distributed medicine, construction materials, and aid money so that the inhabitants could presumably have a "new life." Finally, as evidence that a certain village or hamlet was truly under the control of the South Vietnamese government, a village or hamlet administration was established.

In reality, however, such villages and hamlets were controlled by the government only during the day; the NLF controlled them by night, largely because the villagers politically supported the revolutionaries. The villagers had been organized into various secret and semisecret mass organizations and the revolutionaries had infiltrated the ranks of the local South Vietnamese armed forces and administrations. While most village headmen and other officials received their monthly pay and supplies from the South Vietnamese administration, they carried out the orders of the revolutionary side. Significantly, the official U.S. "Hamlet Evaluation System" (HES) admitted in an overall analysis of the 1967 pacification results that to a large extent the NLF dominated the countryside.

STRUGGLING TO SURVIVE. Villagers crouch in the muddy water of an irrigation ditch as they take refuge during an intense firefight at Bao Trai, South Vietnam, January 1966. Behind them are soldiers of the 173d U.S. Airborne Brigade. *National Archives*

Vietnamese Traditions. There were many reasons the United States and South Vietnam failed to "win hearts and minds." To begin with, their strategies and tactics conflicted with traditional Vietnamese customs and beliefs. To provide the Western reader with insight into this very pertinent issue, which has hardly been touched upon in English-language sources, it is necessary to describe three items: the concepts of the "tomb and graveyard" (*mo ma*), the house (*nha*), and the land—and what their destruction meant to Vietnamese in all regions of Vietnam, north and south. Although the concepts of the tomb and graveyard and the land bear some resemblances to the practices during the Shang and Zhou periods in China and the later Confucian ethics, the mixture is believed to be uniquely Vietnamese.

Ancestors and Tombs. Because most Vietnamese—irrespective of their religious affiliation and political persuasion—consider reverence for their ancestors a religious obligation, they believe that "people live on the tombs and graveyards, and no one lives on rice alone" (*Song ve mo ma, ai song ve ca bat com*). Tombs are houses for the dead; but in fact, no one is ever "dead." When a person passes away, his or her soul lives on and is never destroyed. The dead and the living are believed to exist in the same world, only in different forms, and are in communication with each other. Therefore, ancestors participate in the daily activities of their descendants and protect them, sometimes warning them in dreams or through certain signs of possible dangers. Because the souls of the ancestors are so important for the destiny and welfare of their descendants, filial behavior requires that the descendants provide for them. They must see to it that their ancestors lack nothing. In life one's parents are one's foremost benefactors, and therefore it is everyone's duty to provide for his or her parents when they grow old. When one's parents have passed away, one must give offerings and perform rituals to one's ancestors (usually not more than three generations back), on the anniversaries of their marriages and deaths as well as on many other holy days. This is considered a family reunion of sorts.

Those who shirk their ritual duties are the most unfilial of all, for thus they turn the souls of their ancestors into hungry, wandering, forsaken spirits. The result of such ill behavior would be misfortunate not only for themselves and their descendants but also for society at large since these wandering spirits would be forced to commit destructive acts. Thus it is of the utmost importance that Vietnamese behave correctly toward their ancestors; and the first requirement is the upkeep of the tombs and graveyards.

Should the graveyards of the ancestors be destroyed, the Vietnamese feel that they must avenge the souls of the dead. Otherwise, they and all their children will succeed in nothing throughout their entire lives. Even verbal slighting of parents and ancestors is not tolerated in Vietnam. If in the course of a heated argument one of the disputants should run out of words and pronounce the simple phrase *bo me may* or *to cha may*—"your father and your mother" or "your ancestors"— his opponent is left with no choice but to avenge the violated honor of his parents and ancestors by force. This belief thus made it all the more difficult for Vietnamese to tolerate the desecration and destruction of their ancestors' tombs and graveyards when a village was bombed or razed during a pacification operation.

The House. The Vietnamese house is next in importance to the tombs and graveyards. It is the central sanctuary for altars honoring the ancestors and, in most cases, the Spirit of the Soil (*tho than*). The Vietnamese express their feelings about house and tomb in the oft-quoted saying, "When alive, one must live in a house; when dead, one must have a tomb." To a Vietnamese, the construction of a house is one of the most important activities of his life and an act that might greatly influence the future of the family for good or bad. For this reason, he must wait until he reaches a certain age and must choose a good orientation that ensures great advantages (*coi huong dai loi*) before he starts building his house. A geomancer is thus needed to search for a "propitious location" that meets the requirements of a basic set of taboos and sanctions. For instance, a house preferably should face south; other permitted directions are east, northeast, or southeast, while west and northwest should be avoided. A house should never face another house, nor should it be constructed on a site where three roads meet.

Apart from its religious significance, in Vietnam a house is also a place of emotional attachment. Husbands and wives refer to each other as *nha toi,* or literally, my house. Also, because houses are frequently handed down from one generation to the next, they usually carry with them all the characteristics associated with the ancestors, especially in a society where ancestor worship is widespread. The destruction of a Vietnamese house is thus regarded as an unpardonable crime. In fact, mere desecration of a single house in a village may be regarded as having an impact on the village as a whole.

The Nation and the Land. The concept of the *nha* is uniquely Vietnamese and can also be synonymous with "nation" or "country," as can be seen in oft-quoted proverbs such as "*giac den nha, dan ba phai danh.*" (When the invaders come into

FORCED LABOR. Peasants were required by the South Vietnamese government to build strategic hamlets. This and other forced-labor programs alienated and embittered much of the rural population. *Agency for International Development*

the house/nation, women must fight.) Indeed greater significance is attached when *nha* is combined with *nuoc* (water), for example. *Nuoc nha* (water and house) means "nation" and *nha nuoc* (house and water) means "government," because for thousands of years the Vietnamese have been wet rice cultivators and most households (*nha*) had to cooperate to control water, which was their common priority, by building dikes, canals, and irrigation ditches. Therefore *nuoc* must be placed before *nha* in the case of "nation," and hence by itself *nuoc* acquired the meaning of "nation." The importance of this can be seen in the proverb "*nuoc mat, nha tan.*" (When the nation/water is lost, the households disintegrate.) Hence, it is in everyone's interest and duty to defend the nation, which explains the incredible outpouring of Vietnamese patriotism (*yeu nuoc,* love of water/nation) whenever Vietnam is threatened by outsiders. In the concept of government, however, the *nha* gains precedence over *nuoc* because the foremost duty of each and every government is to give support to and protect the welfare of the households, or the national community. Historically, any regime that violated this tradition did not last for an extended period.

The land itself is considered precious in the extreme because the livelihood of the vast majority of the people has traditionally depended on rice cultivation. As a Vietnamese saying suggests, an inch of land is an inch of gold. The Vietnamese peasants also worship the land, making offerings to the Spirit of the Soil on the anniversaries of ancestors, on the days of marriages or funerals, and on many other occasions and holy days. When people repair their family tombs they must request from the Spirit of the Soil permission to disturb the earth. Moreover, since many Vietnamese live on the same piece of land that their parents, grandparents, and great-grandparents before them had tilled, it becomes an emotional attachment. Even those who in the course of their lives move away from the place of birth feel that, as a matter of principle, they should return there, if at all possible, when the time of their death is near.

Vietnamese call their native village *que cha, que me*, or *dat to* (birthplace of the father, the mother, or the land of the ancestors, respectively). These terms also have a wider meaning analogous to the terms *fatherland* or *motherland* in English. Also, because the tombs of their forefathers are on the same piece of land occupied by their houses and fields, the scorched-earth tactic applied during the pacification campaigns of villages in Vietnam was even more serious than the desecration of a church in the Western sense.

Revolutionary Strategy.   To capitalize on the resentment against the Americans and the South Vietnamese government, however, the revolutionaries had to apply skillfully their "three-prong coordinated offensive" (*ba mui giap cong*)—the standard strategy, which involved a symbiotic relationship between political struggle, military struggle, and *binh van* ("proselytization among enemy military troops"). An appropriate mix of these three factors in a particular area—which depended on the political consciousness and creativity of the inhabitants as well as on the political experience and organizing ability of the revolutionary leaders there—was necessary to maintain or extend revolutionary control. Political struggle occurred in a wide variety of forms on a daily basis in thousands of villages and hamlets throughout the southern part of Vietnam. Different locations—whether government- or NLF-controlled, or a contested area—and different U.S. and South Vietnamese activities dictated different forms of political struggle to be employed. Sometimes in a single village various forms of political struggle could be used simultaneously on a particular day.

Political activists also used different kinds of *binh van* techniques and activities—ranging from one-on-one personal contacts to massive psychological warfare—to gain the sympathy and support of RVNAF soldiers. The overall result was that, combined with political struggle and military struggle, *binh van* activities induced many RVNAF soldiers in forts and base camps to become "fifth columns" for the NLF or to take their arms and join the NLF when the latter needed them. Throughout the war years the average yearly desertion rate from the RVNAF was nearly 20 percent.

Although political struggle and *binh van* were necessary for the development and maintenance of revolutionary control and power, popular support systems could be maintained or increased only with the aid of adequate military forces, especially the regular provincial units. This was apparent in Long An province, which lies immediately south of Saigon and was the gateway to the Mekong delta. South Vietnamese and U.S. advisers regarded the area as of utmost importance and therefore devoted more men, more dollars, and other means to pacify it than any other province in South Vietnam. The U.S. 25th Infantry Division, the ARVN 25th Division, and hosts of other military and paramilitary forces were stationed in the province. Hundreds of U.S. and RVNAF patrol boats were deployed on the waterways there, and warplanes bombed it on a daily basis. Yet the senior U.S. adviser in Long An province was forced to admit in March 1967 that these forces could control only 4 percent of the province in the daytime and only 1 percent during the night.

Interpreting the Tet Offensive.   By 1967 the U.S. "war of attrition" and its "pacification program" had failed miserably in Vietnam, allowing the NLF to control most of the countryside in the south. Confronted by the deteriorating situation in the south the United States stepped up its air war against the north to unprecedented levels throughout 1967 in the hope that North Vietnam would call off the NLF attacks in exchange for a bombing halt. It was under these cir-

MOURNING HIS LOSS. Farmer with his eight-year-old daughter, who was killed by sniper fire, Binh Dinh province, 1964. *National Archives*

cumstances that the Central Committee in the north decided in October 1967 to carry out a series of widespread offensives against the urban areas in the south to remind the United States that its main enemies and problems were in the south and not in the north. The attacks, it was believed, might induce the United States to call off the bombing against the north and to participate in negotiations. The attacks began during the Vietnamese New Year in 1968—and hence were dubbed the Tet Offensive in the West—and consisted of three phases, lasting until October of that year.

The Tet Offensive and its aftermath have been seriously misinterpreted and misrepresented in both official North Vietnamese and U.S. conservative sources, each for their own ideological and political reasons. American sources, which primarily focus on the first phase of Tet, from the end of January to the beginning of March, contend that Tet not only represented a major military defeat for the revolutionaries but also practically destroyed the NLF as a political organization in the south. After the spring of 1968, they claim, the war in Vietnam became a conventional war between the main force units of the North Vietnamese and those of the United States and South Vietnam. Had the American press, the peace movement in the United States, and Congress not prevented the U.S. administration from going all out against the north, the United States could have won the war. These sources also add that since there were no "general uprisings" during Tet, there was really no popular support for the NLF.

Meanwhile, postwar Hanoi sources have stated that Tet was only a partial setback for the revolutionary side because regular North Vietnamese forces were never fully committed, except for about 1,000 persons in Hue. They claim that whenever regular forces were used—such as in Laos in 1971, during the Easter Offensive of 1972, and during the Spring Offensive of 1975—great results were achieved. This argument has been used by officials in Hanoi to justify North Vietnam's taking the lion's share of state power after the war, short of an all-out coup d'état. But by overemphasizing the roles of northern forces and leaders and denigrating the achievements of the southern revolutionaries—both rural and urban—Vietnamese officials have ironically reinforced the viewpoints of American conservatives.

Fortunately, this convergence of official statements has been effectively countered by scholars on both sides of the Pacific in recent years. For example, hundreds of thousands of people provided the NLF forces with the necessary logistical support to enable them to attack almost simultaneously all major South Vietnamese cities, 36 of the 44 provincial capitals, and 64 of the 242 district towns. Planned "uprisings" in the form of demonstrations or taking over of administrative offices by civilians were called off partly because the main force units were never committed—for unexplained reasons that are still hotly debated today—to occupy key target areas as they were supposed to and partly because there was no point in doing so when U.S. firepower was reducing 30 to 80 percent of most cities to rubble. NLF casualties were also relatively light partly because not that many people were involved. In Saigon, the main target of the offensive, only 1,000 armed personnel engaged over 11,000 U.S. and Army of the Republic of Vietnam (ARVN) troops and police for three weeks. Most of the casualties in Hue and Khe Sanh were North Vietnamese regulars.

Out of the Tet Offensive also came the story of the "Hue massacre," which was used by the West as evidence of the unpopularity of the NLF and the supposedly inevitable bloodbath that would follow a communist victory. The fear created and perpetuated by this event contributed to the initial mass exodus from Vietnam in 1975. Many scholarly sources agree that what happened in Hue was an unusual occurrence that took place in an extremely charged atmosphere. The revolutionaries did execute people in Hue as they were withdrawing from the city, but there is still considerable disagreement about who actually did the killing—NVA troops or local NLF forces—and the number of people killed. U.S. official figures vary from a low of 2,800 to 5,700, although some independent American scholarly estimates put the number between 300 and 400. Most agree, however, that both before and after Hue the NLF was very selective in its political killings, being careful to execute or assassinate only those rural officials who were widely considered local despots by the resident population. Before each killing, the NLF often either held a "people's court" or distributed leaflets listing the purported crimes of the victim. In this way, the NLF often gained popular support, partly because they appealed to the tradition of the legendary Vietnamese knight errants, the *dung si* ("brave scholars").

NLF troops suffered heavy casualties only after the politburo in North Vietnam decided to mount the second and third phases of the offensive, leaving the revolutionary units too long in forward positions around the urban areas where they were subjected to heavy air and artillery strikes. In addition, after the third phase was mounted, U.S. and ARVN troops "leapfrogged" over the revolutionary forces who were still massing around the urban areas to attack them from the rear as well as to take over liberated areas. Caught in this way in the outskirts of the urban areas the revolutionary units not only suffered heavy casualties from late 1968 on but also were unable to return to the countryside in time to provide the necessary protection to NLF political cadres and the rural population, who were then exposed to various pacification programs such as the Phoenix Program and the Accelerated Pacification Program. Compounding this, the Vietnamese leadership in Hanoi, in one of its biggest errors of the war, ordered the remnants of the revolutionary units in the south to retreat to the border areas of Cambodia and Laos for rebuilding. This was tantamount to surrendering NLF-controlled areas of the south to the U.S. and South Vietnamese forces without a fight. When NLF units later returned to the villages to rebuild the revolutionary infrastructure, they suffered untold sacrifices. In addition, northern units sent into the south during 1969 and 1970 could not operate effectively and were killed in large numbers because they did not have the necessary tactical grassroots support. In the views of most southern revolutionary fighters, 1969 and 1970 were the two most difficult years in the entire war. Initiative was reclaimed only after the southern revolutionaries rebuilt connections between villagers and fighters in 1971 and 1972. This rebuilding process was done mainly through the tactic of *bam tru* ("clinging to the post," or figuratively, to the people), although the U.S. and South Vietnamese invasions of Cambodia and Laos in 1970 and 1971 and the urban struggles during the same years diverted U.S. and South Vietnamese troops from the rural areas of the south and thus gave the NLF forces extra space and time to recover.

The use of northern tanks and regular troops in Quang Tri province during the Easter Offensive of 1972 and the Spring Offensive of 1975 grabbed headlines in the Western press, but in reality all the northern tanks were destroyed by U.S. air power after only one week into the Easter Offensive. Had it not been for the timely decision of the southern revolutionary fighters to "share firepower" (chia lua) by mounting attacks against U.S. and South Vietnamese forces in many provinces, the northern troops also would have been obliterated. In 1975 northern regulars did create the initial shocks and contributed to the unraveling of the South Vietnamese forces, but most areas, including many of the largest cities, had already been taken over by local revolutionaries long before the first northern troops arrived. In fact, the South Vietnamese government had become increasingly unpopular during the early 1970s, and eventually would have fallen of its own weight.

The Effects of War. The indiscriminate bombing and strafing from the air of urban areas during Tet by U.S. planes made it almost impossible for U.S. officials to argue convincingly that they were "winning hearts and minds." Nor was there any further mention of gaining territory. Henry Kissinger, for example, wrote in an article, which appeared in the January 1969 issue of *Foreign Affairs*, that the crux of the pacification program was to get more people and not to gain more territory. This was done through the so-called Accelerated Pacification Program, which involved increased punishment of the rural areas through massive B-52 bombings, artillery shelling, chemical spraying, and "mop-up" operations. During the first three years of the Nixon administration 6 million tons of high explosives, or the equivalent of about two and one-half times the tonnage of bombs dropped on all fronts during World War II, were expended on South Vietnam alone. About 3 million tons were delivered by artillery strikes, which in many cases caused more systematic damage than bombardment.

The most noticeable results of the air and artillery strikes were the destruction of dams, dikes, and canals, and huge areas of paddyfields pockmarked with large craters, which filled with stagnant water and provided breeding places for malarial mosquitoes. These results, combined with the effects of chemical spraying (which the Pentagon admitted in 1969 was limited only by the ability of the United States to produce the chemicals), had by the end of 1970, according to official sources in South Vietnam, destroyed nearly half the crops in South Vietnam. About 12 million hectares (30 million acres) of forests and covered hills (six times the total cropland of the south) had been destroyed, and the resulting runoff and erosion during the monsoon seasons caused disastrous floods (which still occur) each year that destroyed food crops.

During the war, South Vietnam consequently had to import an average of 1 million metric tons of rice annually—much of it rice from the United States under the "Food for Peace" program—while before the war it had been one of the largest rice exporters in the world. Although this huge importation of rice was enough to provide 5 million people, or about one-fourth the population of the south, with 440 pounds of rice each per year, Saigon newspapers frequently reported widespread hunger and starvation, especially in the central provinces, from 1970 to the end of 1974. In districts in the central area many had to eat banana roots, leaves, and cacti to satisfy their hunger.

Worse still, during the first three years of the Nixon administration, 60,000 "mop-up" operations—each involving more than a battalion of U.S. or allied troops—were directed against inhabited areas of South Vietnam. The South Vietnamese government claimed in early 1972 that there were an average of 300 mop-up operations daily. The net result was more than 3,000 hamlets destroyed, about 25 percent of the total, during Nixon's first three years in the White House.

The human costs of the combined U.S.–South Vietnamese operations during the Nixon years were staggering. Statistics from Long An province are illustrative. According to U.S. and South Vietnamese sources, the population of Long An province in 1968 was about 350,000. A 1987 classified report by the Long An Military Command revealed that from 1954 to 1975, 84,000 revolutionary fighters and active supporters who lived in the province were killed. Officially, 18,000 families in Long An were listed as having one or more family members killed as combatants; many families had from three to eight. The report stressed that the vast majority of the 84,000 were killed during the period 1969–1972. It is important to note that these figures do not include the province's civilian casualties or the 5,000 revolutionary soldiers from other provinces and regular DRV troops who were killed during the war.

To escape the effects of combat and bombing in the rural areas tens of thousands of peasants fled into district and provincial towns or Saigon. Others were taken to the "camps for refugees fleeing from Communism." Thus, although more than 90 percent of the population of South Vietnam had lived in the countryside before the arrival of the Americans, by 1972 about 60 percent of the total population had become "urbanized." Harvard professor Samuel P. Huntington, chief foreign policy adviser to Vice President Hubert H. Humphrey during the 1968 presidential election, referred to this process as "forced-draft urbanization" and optimistically argued that time favored the South Vietnamese government.

Life became increasingly hard for most people in the urban areas of South Vietnam. By 1972 approximately 800,000 orphans were roaming the streets of Saigon and some other cities begging, shining shoes, washing cars, picking pockets, and pimping for their sisters or mothers. There were reportedly some

CAUGHT IN THE MIDDLE. Civilian survivors of Dong Xoai after a pitched battle fought in the village by Viet Cong and ARVN forces, 11 June 1965. Nearly half the inhabitants of the village were killed or wounded. *National Archives*

500,000 bargirls and prostitutes, many of whom were wives of South Vietnamese soldiers who participated in these activities to supplement their husbands' salaries, which were usually inadequate to buy enough rice to feed one person. In addition, there were about 2 to 3 million persons, many of them older people or disabled RVNAF veterans, who could not find work at all. By 1974 hunger had become so widespread that, according to a poll conducted by Catholic students, even in the wealthiest section of Saigon, the Tan Dinh district, only one-fifth of the families had enough to eat. Half of the families could afford only one meal of steamed rice and one meal of gruel per day; the remainder went hungry. Hunger and unemployment resulted in an increase in crime, suicides, and demonstrations throughout the areas under South Vietnamese control. It is important to note that these were not spontaneous demonstrations by desperate people, but rather were well-organized demonstrations conducted by the urban opposition of non-aligned "neutralists" or "third force" organizations. This group was later officially recognized by the January 1973 Paris Agreement as one of the three equal political segments of a coalition government called the National Council of National Reconciliation and Concord.

Opposition in the South. The urban opposition to the U.S.-supported South Vietnamese government came into being after the Tet Offensive of 1968, when U.S. bombs destroyed from 30 to 90 percent of most of the urban areas attacked and occupied by NLF forces. Fierce protests, however, did not begin until after President Richard Nixon announced his Vietnamization program in November 1969. Part of this program was to increase the size of the South Vietnamese army and the various local military forces, which the Americans called "Oriental Minutemen," so that the Vietnamese could take over the combat duties. This not only saved American lives but also American dollars. It cost the United States $38,000 to send an American to Vietnam to fight for one year, but it cost only $400 per year to hire an Asian mercenary. The money saved enabled the United States to keep about 50,000 South Korean troops in Vietnam and to increase the size of the South Vietnamese regular army to 1.1 million men and the local forces to about 4 million by 1971.

The Vietnamization program was opposed by most Vietnamese as soon as Nixon announced it, and the first wave of protests was spearheaded by students with wide support among urban inhabitants. The response of the South Vietnamese government and U.S. military was increased repression. U.S. military police and Vietnamese combat and service police rounded up hundreds of students and their leaders, detaining them for "investigations" of possible Viet Cong guerrilla connections; many of the students were tortured during the investigations. On 25 June 1970 *Tin Sang*, a Catholic daily in Saigon, reported that 124 trade unions representing 100,000 workers in the greater Saigon area called a general strike to show their support for the students. Other trade unions, the Disabled Veterans Movement, the An Quang Unified Buddhist Church, and several other organizations issued statements praising the strike and pledging their support. The National Student Congress distributed a resolution that included the following points: (1) an immediate end to the war; (2) an immediate and total withdrawal of all U.S. and allied troops from Vietnam and the return of independence to the country; (3) the extension of the university age limit and abandonment of all military training programs.

President Nguyen Van Thieu was furious. The 16 July 1970 issue of the *New York Times* reported that on 15 July Thieu declared, "I am ready to smash all movements calling for peace at any price. . . . We will beat to death the people who demand an immediate peace." On the same day, the national police chief, Brig. Gen. Tran Van Hai, told his police chiefs to use "strong measures, including bayonets and bullets" to smash all demonstrations "at any price." Despite these threats, on 25 July 1970 the Women's Movement for the Right to Life came into being. At a meeting attended by 1,000 women representatives from all walks of life, the group's president, Columbia University–trained lawyer Ngo Ba Thanh, read a four-point manifesto, declaring: (1) the dignity of Vietnamese in general, and that the dignity of Vietnamese women in particular should be respected and protected; (2) women will struggle for peace and the right to life; (3) all U.S. soldiers must be withdrawn from Vietnam as a necessary condition to end the war; and (4) a coalition government should be formed to represent the Vietnamese people.

At this meeting, women from various parts of the country testified about the wanton killing, raping, and other criminal acts committed by Americans everywhere. Consequently, hundreds of members of the Women's Movement were arrested and tortured. Standard tortures included "chain raping," electric shocks administered by attaching electrodes to the reproductive organs, insertion of live nonpoisonous snakes, soft drink bottles, sticks, and electric bulbs into the vagina, branding and burning of the inner thighs or the vulva with lighted cigarettes or heated irons, and hanging by the thumbs or toes.

Despite this repression, the women's movement grew stronger, working closely with other groups, including student groups. The close cooperation among various groups led to the formation of the People's Front in Struggle for Peace on 7 October 1970. The majority of civic organizations in Vietnam participated in this group, and on 11 October 1970 the Front issued a ten-point platform headed by a demand "that the Americans and their allies withdraw completely from Vietnam as the most important precondition for an end to the war." From this point on antigovernment activities in urban areas in Vietnam were well-coordinated and a strategy for continual struggle was developed. This invited more repression by the Thieu government. In 1972 the Committee for the Reform of the Prison System in South Vietnam, an organization headed by South Vietnamese Catholic priests and intellectuals, claimed that the government held 350,000 political prisoners. Political prisoners were, according to the government's definition, anyone who was suspected of having an antiwar or neutralist position or who was a relative of such a person. On 10 November 1972 the *Washington Post* reported that 40,000 new political prisoners had been picked up in the first two weeks after the final draft of the Paris Agreement was announced.

The End in the South. The Paris Agreement, which was signed on 17 January 1973, virtually unchanged from its October version after the United States had carried out the Christmas bombing and had demanded 126 substantial changes, established two parallel and equal parties in South Vietnam—the South Vietnamese government and the Provisional Revolutionary Government (PRG)—and stipulated that a National Council of National Reconcilication and Concord would be created with "three equal segments." The third segment was supposed to be composed of nonaligned "neutralists" or the "third force" as it was known. But as soon as the Paris Agreement was signed, Thieu ruled out any political role for the PRG or the third segment by reiterating his Four No's policy: no recognition of the enemy, no coalition government, no neutralization of the southern region of Vietnam, and no concession of territory.

Encouraged by increased U.S. military and economic aid, Thieu increased repression against the third force and immediately carried out so-called military operations to saturate the national territory (hanh quan tran ngap lanh tho) through indiscriminate bombings and shellings as well as ground assaults on PRG-controlled areas. The 16 February 1974 issue of the *Washington Post* quoted Pentagon sources as saying that Thieu's armed forces were "firing blindly into free zones [i.e., PRG-controlled areas] because they knew full well they would get all the replacement supplies they needed from the United States." The South Vietnamese government's military aggressiveness not only caused death and suffering among the civilian population but also exposed its own armed forces to danger. As early as 30 August 1973 the French newspaper *Le Monde* reported that the South Vietnamese high command had stated that about 41,000 of its troops had been killed and 4,000 were missing since the signing of the Paris Agreement. The casualty rate climbed steadily as Thieu increased his attacks on rural areas.

Thieu's military attacks and his "economic blockades" also caused massive hunger and starvation in the countryside and created a major economic depression in the urban areas. Hatred of the Thieu regime among the general population intensified and demonstrations multiplied. The intensity of the urban struggles is illustrated by the following examples taken from the Saigon daily,

Dien Tin, in September 1974. On 19 September, 116 trade unions in Saigon and Cholon met to demand food and clothes and an end to mistreatment and unwarranted layoffs (*Dien Tin*, 20 September). Two days later, the entire work force of Saigon, Cholon, and Gia-dinh demonstrated for food, clothes, and temporary relief (*Dien Tin*, 22 September). While this was going on, huge numbers of workers in Da Nang, the second largest city in South Vietnam, marched in the streets and then went on a mass hunger strike (*Dien Tin*, 22 and 24 September).

The government met the demonstrators with selective, but extremely harsh, repression. In a demonstration in the Chanh Tam district of Saigon on 3 November 1974, for example, Thieu's police forces fired into the crowd, killing one person and wounding many others. These forces also burned houses and destroyed religious shrines. When the people of the area and religious leaders protested, the government claimed to be conducting a regular military operation against the communists in the area (*Song Than, Dong Phuong*, and *Chinh Luan*, 7 November 1974).

The Thieu government's harsh repression severely weakened public support for the government. When the U.S. Congress authorized an increased aid package to South Vietnam on 17–18 December 1974, the PRG interpreted this action as a renewed commitment to the South Vietnamese government. In response, the PRG increased its counterattacks and by early January 1975, it controlled eight districts and one province. The White House and South Vietnamese officials then accused Congress of having weakened the South Vietnamese military by its reduction of the increased aid requests and clamored for supplemental appropriations. But it was already clear even to the most conservative and anticommunist public opinion makers in South Vietnam that there was no longer any mood for a military confrontation. Huynh Trung Chanh, a deputy in the Lower House, wrote the following in an editorial in the 17 January 1975 issue of *Dien Tin*: "The leaders of the Republic of Vietnam are now spreading the view that the present deteriorating situation is due to the lack of aid. But the reality of the situation is that the difficulty is not because of a lack of aid but because of *lack of support of the people* [emphasis in original]." Even Father Nguyen Quang Lam, an ultraconservative Catholic priest, admitted, in the 10 February issue of *Dai Dan Toc*, "Yesterday I wrote that whether there is an additional $300 million or $3,000 million in aid, South Vietnam will still not be able to avoid collapse. . . . In the afternoon, a reader called me up and said that I should have put it more strongly. I must say that the more the aid, the quicker the collapse of South Vietnam. . . . Come to think of it, the reader has a point there."

By late 1974 and early 1975 most South Vietnamese believed that the massive infusions of American dollars into the body politic of South Vietnam had so sickened it that its collapse was inevitable. The stampede in March and April 1975 as one province after another fell with hardly a fight further proved the correct nature of their observations. As it turned out, North Vietnamese troops were sent rushing into the south to snatch political power not from the South Vietnamese government but from the southern revolutionaries.

The War in the North. In North Vietnam U.S. air and artillery attacks also exacted a heavy toll. About 1 million tons of bombs were dropped on the Democratic Republic of Vietnam (DRV), 1.5 million on Laos (the greater bulk on the Ho Chi Minh Trail where troops and supplies from the north moved south), and more than 0.5 million on Cambodia (most on the border area where the Viet Cong guerrillas' sanctuaries were supposedly situated). About 900,000 artillery shells were delivered on the DRV from the Seventh Fleet and from below the demilitarized zone (DMZ), which separated the two halves of the country.

AMONG THE RUINS. Woman holds onto the only part of her home left standing after a Viet Cong raid on the village of Dai Loc, 14 November 1967. *National Archives*

When President Lyndon B. Johnson first ordered the bombing of the DRV in 1964 he said that the aim was "to save the South." After the United States introduced ground forces into South Vietnam in March 1965, ostensibly to contain "North Vietnamese aggression" (although not until six weeks later was a small contingent of North Vietnamese troops spotted by U.S. intelligence), the Joint Chiefs of Staff consistently argued that the primary purpose of the bombing of the north was to break "the will of the regime." During Operation ROLLING THUNDER from 1965 to 1968, an average of 800 tons of bombs per day were dropped on the north. According to the Pentagon, these sorties were directed primarily against industrial areas and communications facilities of the DRV. Over 70 percent of all large and medium industrial enterprises in the DRV was severely damaged; its roads and railroads were hit numerous times over, with an average of more than two dozen bombs per kilometer. The effect on North Vietnam's fledgling industrial sector was devastating; industries were forced to decentralize and were moved to remote rural areas or reestablished in mountain caves, thus causing considerable loss to the economy. The index of real output value fell to only 92 percent of its 1964 level in 1967 and physical output declined by 40 to 60 percent for most major industrial products. Massive destruction of communications and transport networks also hampered the ability of industry to obtain raw materials. Money also had to be invested for the repair and rebuilding of the infrastructure, including railways and bridges. The overall impact would have been much greater had it not been for a yearly average of about US$400 million of foreign aid from the People's Republic of China (PRC), the Soviet Union, and Eastern European countries during the 1965–1975 period.

The U.S. military's efforts were intended to make it more difficult for northerners to aid their compatriots in the south. Admiral Ulysess S. Grant Sharp, Jr., reported that in the north 8,304 buildings were destroyed and damaged in 1966 and 3,547 in 1967. He estimated that the principal benefit of the bombing was "to force Hanoi to engage from 500,000 to 600,000 civilians in full-time and part-time war-related activities, in particular for air defense and repair of LOCs [lines of communication.]" Gen. William W. Momyer, chief of staff of the U.S. Air Force during the war, later estimated in a 1978 book that "[t]he labor devoted to the maintenance of both rail and road systems included 500,000 troops and civilian militia plus another 175,000 committed to the country's air defense system. These were troops who could have been in combat units if not diverted to this task." Yet the U.S. air war never achieved its intended military aim; the movement of troops and supplies into the south flowed at a steady pace. For example, the United States estimated in August 1967 that the DRV only had about 50,000 troops in the south, the same figure as in 1966. This level was maintained partly because the NLF had most of the material and human resources available for its own needs in the south and partly because it usually took another whole year to make a northern soldier ready for battle in the south.

U.S. air attacks damaged 4,000 of North Vietnam's 5,788 villages, and also damaged graveyards, schools, temples, churches, and medical facilities. The World Health Organization (WHO) reported at its March 1976 meeting in Manila that the medical facilities that had been destroyed cost over US$1 billion. In human terms, despite the preparedness of the North Vietnamese population, which included underground bomb shelters and tunnels in many villages, the 643,000 tons of U.S. bombs dropped by ROLLING THUNDER killed 52,000 civilians and injured several hundred thousand others.

After the Tet Offensive of 1968 the United States agreed to a cessation of bombing over the north in order to initiate peace talks. But under the new category of "protective reaction strikes," the United States continued to bomb the north intermittently to maintain pressure. In 1969, for example, U.S. planes flew 37,000 sorties against targets in the DRV, which were selected to exact the maximum damage with the minimum public outcry. In 1972, U.S. bombing of the north resumed with an intensity greater than that during the 1965–1968 period—culminating in the "Christmas" bombing, in which 40,000 tons of bombs were dropped on Hanoi and 15,000 tons on Haiphong. Due to prior evacuation of the two cities as well as ingenious air defense systems and tactics, only about 1,600 people were killed and several thousand wounded.

Response in the North. The bombing of the north did not directly affect agricultural output very much, although the dikes protecting the cropland in the Red River delta from floods were frequently bombed, and intentionally so during the Nixon years. Only 162,000 hectares (5.6 percent) of northern cropland was destroyed by U.S. bombs. The indirect effects of the bombing were signifi-

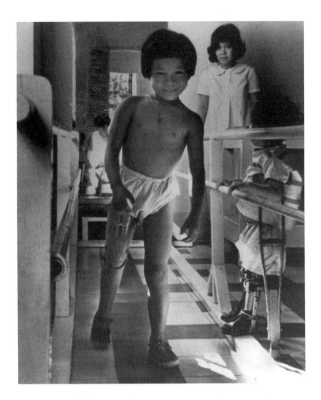

VIETNAMESE ORPHAN. Nguyen Thi Ky, with artificial leg, walks for the first time without the assistance of crutches at Regina Pacis orphanage, Saigon, 1966. *National Archives*

cant, however, in part because about 500,000 persons were diverted from agricultural production to maintain the several thousand kilometers of dikes and in part because the North Vietnamese government was forced to place the rural economy on a war footing. This meant consolidating hamlet-level cooperatives, which comprised only one-fourth or one-fifth of the households in an average village, into "high-level cooperatives," which included entire village populations, in an attempt to channel human and material resources for the war effort. By the beginning of 1970 some large cooperatives included several villages, and nearly 80 percent of the agricultural workers were females.

Paddyfields were reshaped, new irrigation systems were put in place, and reservoirs, warehouses, seed nurseries, machine shops, and drying yards were built. These activities necessitated a new division of labor, and in response work units were developed that specialized in, for example, soil preparation, irrigation, production of seedlings, formulation and application of fertilizers, plant protection, and so on. These specialized units existed side-by-side with the basic production brigades (composed mostly of women), which performed all other tasks until the crops were gathered. The cooperatives, after formulating economic and technical yardsticks for each type of work, contracted out certain jobs to specialized units and paid them work points based on the quantity and quality of work performed. The tasks performed by the basic production brigades, however, were paid for according to the system of "three contracts": a "product contract" between the cooperative and each brigade to deliver at the end of each harvest or each year a given quantity of product at an agreed standard of quality based on the fertility of the assigned cultivated surface; a "production-costs contract" that provided brigades with fixed amounts of seeds, fertilizers, and fuel, for example, to grow certain quantities of food; and a "piece-work contract" that fixed the number of work days for each task based on past experience.

Although this complicated system minimized the effect of the labor shortage, it bred irresponsibility, inequity, and inefficiency, which together contributed to a significant decrease in agricultural production in the north from 1966 to 1972. Production of staple foods, soybeans, and sugar production decreased by 3.4 percent (182,000 metric tons), 18 percent, and 15 percent, respectively. Total agricultural output levels stagnated at an annual average of 6.7 million metric tons in the 1965–1968 period and 6.2 million metric tons in the 1969–1971 period. Meanwhile, the population increased more than 2 percent per year.

The Political Response. Despite the production problems, the DRV government mounted a campaign called "All for the Brotherly South" (*Tat Ca Cho Mien Nam Ruot Thit*) as soon as the bombing against the north started. This was partly because—just as in the south—the destruction of the land, houses, and graveyards had deep cultural meanings. It is the tradition of the Vietnamese people, for example, to fight those who "bring elephants home to stamp out the graveyards of their ancestors" (*dem voi ve day ma to*)—or who bring foreigners in to destroy the fatherland. *Fatherland* in Vietnamese is *dat to* (land of the ancestors), and it was clear to most Vietnamese who the "elephants" were and who had brought them in to trample the country. In addition, because the Vietnamese considered the Red River delta region—the site of the famous Dong Son culture and of thousands of pagodas, temples, and historical structures—the cradle of their civilization, and because the United States tried to bomb it "back into the Stone Age" as U.S. Air Force general Curtis LeMay had advocated, most Vietnamese were ready to sacrifice everything to rid their country of the "elephants."

Perhaps more important than the appeal to Vietnamese cultural traditions were the efforts by the party and government of the DRV to promote participatory democracy and social mobility in order to mobilize the population. In 1965 the party embarked on a "mass line" to transform itself from an inherently elitist Leninist organization into one more representative of the people and their opinion. Party membership tripled to nearly 1.6 million over the next decade, and new members were supposedly selected from among the best candidates, while incompetent ones were removed. The "mass line" was also a means to urgently decentralize power and responsibility in an attempt to maximize the efficiency and effectiveness of the war effort. Party secretary general Le Duan introduced the concept of "the people as the collective masters" (*nhan dan lam chu tap the*) to mobilize the masses for war and to put a check on party members who might abuse their power and become local despots. The head of the Party Propaganda and Education Department, To Huu, issued a directive in April 1966 stating that the revolution was not the monopoly of the party, but "primarily a matter concerning the laboring masses." Party members therefore had to know how to listen to the people, stress the people's mastery of their situation, aid them, and rely on the progressive elements among them.

Also crucial to wartime challenges—as well as the needs of postwar reconstruction in later years—was the creation of technically competent personnel. From 1960 to 1972 the DRV created a large work force of over 1 million in the technical fields—370,000 cadres with university and technical school education, and over 670,000 technical workers. Because most of these people were recruited from the peasantry, their upward mobility not only made them deeply committed to the society that had provided them with such opportunities but also helped rally others to the cause of the revolution. At the same time, expansion of the entire education system continued. By 1974 one of every three inhabitants of the north attended school, often in three shifts a day because of a severe shortage of classrooms caused by the American bombing destruction. In the 1974–1975 school year, 5.3 million students were attending school for a general education and about 120,000 were attending universities and technical schools. As for health care, by 1974 there were 439 general hospitals, 646 infirmaries, and 5,683 medical stations, with 120,500 sickbeds. The number of doctors and specialists was 28 times that of 1939, the peak year under French rule.

Legacies of the War. The government of North Vietnam successfully mobilized the masses to respond to the needs of the nation in wartime. It was the legacies of the Vietnam War, however, that have troubled and weakened the Vietnamese government for the last two decades. Before the war ended, for example, the areas under the control of the South Vietnamese government had about 4 million unemployed people. The 1 million South Vietnamese soldiers and their families (5 million people) lived completely off U.S. aid. This created a false sense of prosperity, a consumer mentality, and a widespread attitude of complacency and dependency, which continues to plague the southern urban areas. By the time of liberation, the disintegration of the Thieu government and its armed forces added more than 1.5 million to the ranks of the unemployed. In the effort to feed the urban population the new government distributed free food and sold rice and other foodstuffs at below market costs for the next ten years. This huge subsidy program plus the large defense outlay for the war with the Khmer Rouge and the prolonged conflict with the People's Republic of China (PRC) created a large budgetary deficit, which in turn caused hyperinflation that reached 600 percent per year by 1986.

The economic difficulties and the conflict with the Khmer Rouge and the PRC, ironically, strengthened the position of the Maoist factions in the Vietnamese government and enabled them to legislate a series of policies and programs that further exacerbated the country's economic and political problems. Two such programs were the rural cooperativization program and the related campaign to "eradicate commercial capitalists."

The cooperativization program was first announced in 1977 but, for at least two reasons, was not stressed until mid 1978. One was to exact the necessary material and human resources to fight the war against the Khmer Rouge as the cooperativization program in the north had proven so useful in this respect during the war with the United States. The second aim was to make the land more productive through mass mobilization for land reclamation and irrigation, for example. At the time of liberation, the entire country had less than 5 million hectares of cropland (pockmarked with some 30 million craters and some 25 million pounds of unexploded mines and ammunition), which produced slightly more than 10 million metric tons of paddy rice for a total population of about 55 million. Each Vietnamese thus had less than 0.1 hectares of cultivated land and 200 kilograms of paddy rice per year. In contrast the per capita availability of paddyfields and rice to each person in Thailand was 2.45 hectares and about 5 metric tons, respectively. The collectivization efforts backfired, however, and caused the agricultural sector to stagnate and government food procurement to decrease.

The purported aim of the campaign to "eradicate commercial capitalists" was to prevent the Cholon-based rice merchants (mostly Chinese) from undermining the government's rice purchase policy and cooperativization efforts. This campaign merely drove the private economy underground and broadened the problem of bribery. Worse still, along with the continuing conflict with the PRC, it raised fears of a government-induced campaign against Chinese merchants, in particular, and all traders in general, thereby creating a second wave of exodus out of Vietnam from 1978 to 1980—and with it a loss of capital and technically skilled personnel.

The Vietnamese conflict with the Khmer Rouge and the PRC, especially with the public support given to the PRC by the Carter administration in this "proxy war" against Soviet expansionism, created paranoia among some government officials in Vietnam. For example, some high officials argued that the release of former South Vietnamese officials from the "re-education camps" after the maximum term of five years promised at the time of liberation would endanger the security of the nation because these people might participate in antigovernment activities. Adding to this paranoia were periodic commando raids by Vietnamese into Vietnam in the early 1980s, some of which were organized and directed from the United States. The end result was the continued imprisonment of many former South Vietnamese officials for nearly two decades and the creation of more "boat people."

Structural Changes in the 1980s. In response, the government initiated a series of structural changes in 1986 and more far-reaching reforms along the "socialist market economy" line in 1988. At the same time, it sought solutions for the Cambodian situation and the conflict with the PRC, realizing that economic, social, and political stability required a peaceful environment. The overall economic results have been promising. Average gross domestic product (GDP) increased 5 percent during 1986–1990 and 7 percent during 1991–1993. From 1989 to 1993 agriculture increased by 22 percent and industry by 50 percent. Agricultural production has become almost totally privatized and represented about 32 percent of the GDP during the 1991–1993 period. Grain production reached 22, 24.2, and 25 million metric tons in rice equivalents in 1991, 1992, and 1993, respectively, allowing Vietnam to become the third largest rice exporter in the world—after Thailand and the United States—three years in a row.

Confidence in the economic performance of Vietnam can be seen in the fact that foreign investment in 1993 equaled 40 percent of total investment in the entire country. This was about the same percentage as in Singapore, the most open economy in Asia; twice that of Hong Kong; three times that of Malaysia, and 15–20 times that of the PRC and South Korea. Since the World Bank predicted in mid 1993 that Vietnam's economy would expand by at least 8 percent annually until the year 2000, foreign investment has continued to pour in. This indicates, however, that domestic investment must be actively promoted if Vietnam does not want to replace its dependence on the former Eastern bloc with dependence on capitalist countries. What was encouraging in 1993 was that domestic savings represented 10–15 percent of GDP. Even at 10 percent, this was equal to US$1.1 billion, a significant increase over the average of about 7 percent during the 1989–1992 period. This meant that there was more domestic money available for investment. The government borrowed US$200 million from its citizens and $600 million from abroad for its budgetary outlay, enabling it to keep the budget deficit down to 7 percent for GDP and inflation to only 5 percent. Vietnamese working overseas sent nearly US$0.5 billion in remittances.

The overall political and economic climate resulted in the U.S. government's lifting its two-decade-long trade embargo against Vietnam in early February 1994, thereby opening a new chapter in relations between the two countries. Pepsi Cola and Coca Cola celebrated the event by covering Hanoi and Ho Chi

Minh City with red advertisement banners and passing out free samples of their soft drinks to smiling crowds.

[*See also* Pacification; Prostitution; Reeducation Camps; Refugees; Vietnam; Women, Vietnamese.]

BIBLIOGRAPHY

ALLEN, DOUGLAS, and NGO VINH LONG, eds. *Coming to Terms: Indochina, the United States, and the War.* 1991.

BERGERUD, ERIC M. *The Dynamics of Defeat: The Vietnam War in Hau Nghia Province.* 1991.

CLODFELTER, MARK. *The Limits of Air Power: The American Bombing of North Vietnam.* 1989.

KOLKO, GABRIEL. *Anatomy of a War: Vietnam, the United States, and the Modern Historical Experience.* 1985.

GIBSON, JAMES W. *The Perfect War: Technowar in Vietnam.* 1986.

TRUONG NHU TANG. *A Viet Cong Memoir: An Inside Account of the Vietnam War and Its Aftermath.* 1986.

U.S. Senate, Committee on Foreign Relations. *Bombing as a Policy Tool in Vietnam: Effectiveness.* Staff Study No. 5. 12 October 1972.

WERNER, JAYNE, and DAVID HUNT, eds. *The American War in Vietnam.* 1993.

WERNER, JAYNE, and LUU DOAN HUYNH, eds. *The Vietnam War: Vietnamese and American Perspectives.* 1993.

NGÔ VĨNH LONG

Vietnam Information Group. In response to press criticism of President Lyndon Johnson's Vietnam policies, the White House formed the Public Affairs Policy Committee for Vietnam in August 1965. Later renamed the Vietnam Information Group, its task was to centralize all administration public relations activities concerning Vietnam in order to receive more favorable press coverage.

BIBLIOGRAPHY

SMALL, MELVIN. *Johnson, Nixon, and the Doves.* 1988.

WILLIAM PAUL SCHUCK

Vietnamization, the U.S policy, initiated by President Nixon in 1969, of phasing out U.S. forces and turning the war responsibilities over to the South Vietnamese. Vietnamization included maximizing U.S. military materiel assistance to strengthen South Vietnam and intensifying ongoing pacification programs. By strengthening the government's control over the population and improving the Army of the Republic of Vietnam's (ARVN) military capabilities, largely by expanding and reorganizing the army's force structure, U.S. strategists hoped that South Vietnam could successfully oppose the North Vietnamese and Viet Cong forces without U.S. support. President Nixon announced this policy at the Midway Island Conference on 8 June 1969 without consulting the South Vietnamese government of President Nguyen Van Thieu, which raised questions about the motives behind the policy and the extent of U.S. commitment to the war. In essence, Vietnamization, designed to extricate the United States from Vietnam, was a political decision based on the collapse of support among U.S. decision makers and among the American public. As orchestrated by Secretary of Defense Melvin Laird, the first priority of the U.S. effort became the success of the policy, rather than winning the war. Although U.S. leaders hoped South Vietnam could be prepared to defend itself, that goal was secondary to getting out of the war with "honor," as Nixon characterized it.

Nixon announced the program's success on 7 April 1971 following Operation LAM SON 719, an ARVN offensive intended to cut the Ho Chi Minh Trail and to occupy and demolish North Vietnamese and Viet Cong base areas in southern Laos. In reality, however, the failure of that operation demonstrated the failure of Vietnamization, and

VIETNAMIZATION. Moments before the U.S. flag is replaced by the Vietnamese flag, Vietnamese Air Force crewmen line up before one of the 62 UH-1 "Huey" helicopters turned over to them along with command of the Soc Trang airfield, 4 November 1970. *National Archives*

U.S. advisers began trying to remedy those defects that they thought might be cured. Among the American public, support for the war continued to erode because, although the policy's aim was the withdrawal of U.S. troops, American losses continued. Throughout 1972, U.S. officials proclaimed the success of Vietnamization, but continued North Vietnamese military victories, particularly during the Easter Offensive, demonstrated that Vietnamization had failed.

BIBLIOGRAPHY

AMBROSE, STEPHEN E. *Nixon.* Volume 2: *The Triumph of a Politician, 1962–1972.* 1989.

DAVIDSON, PHILLIP B. *Vietnam at War—The History: 1946–1975.* 1988.

KARNOW, STANLEY. *Vietnam: A History.* 1983.

SCHULZINGER, ROBERT D. *Henry Kissinger: The Doctor of Diplomacy.* 1989.

ELLEN D. GOLDLUST

Vietnam Moratorium Committee. In the spring of 1969, a group led by antiwar activists Sam Brown, David Hawks, David Mixner, and Marge Sklencar organized the Vietnam Moratorium Committee (VMC) to arrange a nationwide strike to protest U.S. involvement in Vietnam. The VMC planned to stage a moratorium each month, the first on 15 October, with each protest becoming progressively longer until the United States withdrew from the war.

A moderate organization, the VMC successfully appealed to the American mainstream. Supporters included the Americans for Democratic Action (ADA), the Teamsters, the United Auto Workers, Averell Harriman, John Kenneth Galbraith, and twenty-four U.S. senators, as well as many students across the country. By October, the VMC had an office in Washington, D.C., 31 full-time staffers, and 7,500 field organizers.

The 15 October moratorium was the largest nationwide protest in U.S. history. Activities included rallies, teach-ins, and memorial services. But moratorium's success prompted President Nixon's "silent majority" strategy of attacking antiwar protestors in order to shift focus from the increasingly unpopular war.

The second moratorium coincided with the New Mobe's (New Mobilization) 15 November rallies in Washington and San Francisco. The two groups allied for these protests despite fundamental differences: the New Mobe was radical, while the VMC was moderate to liberal. The alliance did not last. The November protests, while successful, were not as large as those in October.

Participation in the December moratorium was poor due to declining funds and the growing divisions within the antiwar movement. The VMC's final moratorium, in April 1970, was about as successful as the November protest. Frustrated and divided into factions, the VMC disbanded on 19 April 1970.

BIBLIOGRAPHY

DEBENEDETTI, CHARLES. *An American Ordeal: The Antiwar Movement of the Vietnam Era.* 1990.

JURMA, WILLIAM E. "Moderate Movement Leadership and the Vietnam Moratorium Committee." *Quarterly Journal of Speech* 68 (August 1968): 262–272.

WILLIAM PAUL SCHUCK

Viet Nam Quoc Dan Dang (VNQDD). In 1927, Vietnamese admirers of the Chinese

Kuomintang founded the Viet Nam Quoc Dan Dang, or Vietnamese Nationalist Party. Their leader was Nguyen Thai Hoc, a young teacher in Hanoi. The VNQDD preached modernization, anticommunism, and resistance against French rule. After staging the Yen Bay uprising in 1930, Hoc and other leaders were arrested and executed, although a few escaped to China. When Kuomintang troops occupied Hanoi in 1945, the VNQDD briefly held power, but they were viewed as Chinese puppets. So, most nationalist support went to the Viet Minh. The VNQDD protested violently when the Chinese sponsored elections that the Viet Minh were certain to win. The VNQDD kidnapped Vo Nguyen Giap, releasing him only when Ho Chi Minh agreed to grant the VNQDD equal status in his government. When the French returned in 1946, most VNQDD members joined the Viet Minh, though a few were still active in South Vietnam in the 1960s.

BIBLIOGRAPHY

BUTTINGER, JOSEPH. *Vietnam: A Dragon Embattled.* 1967.
HAMMER, ELLEN. *The Struggle for Indochina.* 1954.
MCALISTER, JOHN T., JR. *Vietnam: The Origins of a Revolution.* 1969.
MARR, DAVID G. *Vietnamese Anticolonialism.* 1971.
PATTI, ARCHIMEDES. *Why Vietnam?* 1980.

GLEN GENDZEL

Vietnam Syndrome.

The term *Vietnam syndrome* refers in general to the lingering effects of Vietnam on the U.S. national conscience and specifically to the American public's reluctance to support military actions abroad. A year after the fall of Saigon, *Washington Post* columnist David Broder wrote that "Vietnam has left a rancid aftertaste that clings to almost every mention of direct military intervention." This observation remained accurate up to the Persian Gulf War in 1991, which somewhat dissipated the effects of the Vietnam syndrome.

While the War Powers Act put limits on the president's ability to wage war without congressional consent, the real restraint upon executive action was the public mood. Americans after the Vietnam War were very reluctant to have U.S. troops committed for anything but the literal defense of U.S. territory. This mood limited President Jimmy Carter's options in dealing with the Iran hostage crisis and prevented Ronald Reagan from aggressively aiding the Nicaraguan Contras. The American public did not support military involvement in Nicaragua, and that opposition was in large part rooted in fears of an-

other Vietnam. Reagan repeatedly said there would be "no more Vietnams," a phrase that meant different things to different people. For Reagan and the military establishment, the phrase meant that military commitments would be backed by a political commitment to provide the resources necessary to ensure victory. But all realized that Vietnam syndrome made it all but impossible for a president to commit troops without popular support, particularly in potentially long conflicts pursued to prevent the spread of communism.

Prior to the Persian Gulf War, President George Bush had to contend with Vietnam syndrome in building public backing for the war. Bush succeeded in whipping up widespread public approval of U.S. military intervention in the Middle East—the largest effort since Vietnam—and was able to sustain that support throughout the relatively brief air and land war. He equated support for the over 500,000 U.S. troops deployed to the Middle East with support for his policies and minimized U.S. casualties through extensive use of air power. After the war, Bush and others argued that the "ghost of Vietnam" had been put to rest. While Americans may be more likely to support strategic action given the success in the Middle East, Vietnam still remains in the minds of policymakers and the public. The prolonged indecisiveness regarding U.S. policy toward the civil wars in Bosnia and Somalia is illustrative. The end of the Cold War has changed the context in which the United States considers international intervention, yet fears of another protracted involvement abroad with murky objectives remains an underlying concern.

BIBLIOGRAPHY

HERRING, GEORGE C. *America's Longest War: The United States and Vietnam, 1950–1975.* 2d ed. 1986.

KELLY EVANS-PFEIFER

Vietnam Veterans against the War.

In 1967, six Vietnam veterans met at a protest march in New York City and organized the Vietnam Veterans against the War (VVAW). The VVAW had only six hundred members by April 1970, but attracted thousands in the next few years.

On 31 January 1971 the VVAW launched its three-day Winter Soldier Investigation in a Detroit motel as the Calley court-martial took place. During these hearings, more than one hundred witnesses testified that they had committed or witnessed acts of brutality or war crimes in Vietnam. The investigation attempted to demonstrate that the atrocities at My Lai were not an isolated incident in order to protest continued U.S. involvement in the war.

In April 1971 the organization drew national attention with "Operation Dewey Canyon III." Named after Operation DEWEY CANYON II, the U.S. part of Operation LAM SON 919, the ARVN invasion of Laos in February–March, it was a week-long encampment in Washington to protest the war and to lobby Congress. The protest began on 19 April when veterans and mothers of soldiers killed in Vietnam marched to Arlington National Cemetery. Veteran John Kerry (later a senator from Massachusetts) spoke against the war at Senate Foreign Relations Committee hearings. During the week, veterans performed "guerrilla theater," simulating attacks on "civilians" played by actors. Approximately sixty men tried to surrender themselves to the Pentagon for committing war crimes. They were turned away. On the last day, 23 April, seven hundred veterans threw their medals and ribbons over a barricade onto the Capitol steps.

In December 1971 VVAW members occupied the Betsy Ross House in Philadelphia and the Statue of Liberty in New York to protest the bombing of North Vietnam. In the summer of 1972, they demonstrated at the Republican National Convention in Miami. As the war ended, the group called for universal amnesty for deserters and draft resisters.

BIBLIOGRAPHY

KERRY, JOHN, and VIETNAM VETERANS AGAINST THE WAR. *The New Soldier.* 1971.

ZAROULIS, NANCY, and GERALD SULLIVAN. *Who Spoke Up? American Protest against the War in Vietnam 1963–1975.* 1984.

WILLIAM PAUL SCHUCK

Vietnam Veterans Memorial.

The Vietnam Veterans Memorial, popularly known as the Wall, is a powerful nonpolitical tribute to the men and women who died in the Vietnam War. Like the war itself, the memorial's history was controversial.

The brainchild of veteran Jan Scruggs, the Vietnam Veterans Memorial was dedicated on Veterans Day, 13 November 1982. The effort to build it, however, had begun in 1979 when Scruggs and fellow veterans Robert Doubek and John Wheeler established a fund to raise the money necessary for construction. Sen. Charles Mathias Jr. of Maryland sponsored a bill in Congress to set aside land between the Washington Monument and the Lincoln Memorial for the Vietnam Veterans Memorial. The agreement between the federal government and Scruggs's organization provided that the memorial be paid for entirely by private funds, and in the end 650,000 people contributed more than $5 million for its construction.

The memorial's design competition attracted more than 1,400 entries, and they were judged by a panel of architects and sculptors. The guidelines stipulated that the memorial must contain the names of all the American dead, it must not make a political statement, and it must complement its location. Maya Lin, a twenty-one-year-old Yale architecture student, submitted the winning design. Her plan consisted of a 150-meter (500-foot) V-shaped wall of polished black granite set into the ground. The names of the men and women killed in Vietnam were listed chronologically, from 1959 to 1975, along 140 panels on the wall, which was 20 centimeters (8 inches) high at each end and 3 meters (10 feet) high in the center.

While many believed the design offered a moving tribute to the dead in Vietnam, others strongly objected, calling it "unheroic" and "a black gash of shame." Some attacked Lin, a Chinese American, in thinly veiled racist undertones. Opponents of the design, including some veterans, conservative politicians, and public figures such as H. Ross Perot, forced a compromise by blocking funds for construction and persuading Interior Secretary James Watt to withhold the construction permit. Despite Lin's objections, authorities finally agreed to install a statue of American soldiers near the Wall. Sculptor Frederick Hart designed a bronze statue that portrays three U.S. soldiers in Vietnam. On Veterans Day in 1993, sculptor Glenna Goodacre's bronze statue of three women nurses attending a wounded U.S. soldier, was unveiled. The women's memorial was promoted by Vietnam nurse Diane Carlson Evans, who wanted to honor the 11,500 women who served in Vietnam. The Vietnam Veterans Memorial is the most-visited monument in Washington, D.C. Despite the earlier controversy, most agree that it is a powerful and appropriate monument to the veterans of the war and the more than 58,000 Americans who never came home. Families and friends of the dead often leave letters, flowers, photographs, or other mementos at the base of the Wall, and veterans maintain a constant vigil at the site.

BIBLIOGRAPHY

ASHABRANNER, BRENT. *Always to Remember.* 1988.
OLSON, JAMES, and RANDY ROBERTS. *Where the Domino Fell.* 1991.

KELLY EVANS-PFEIFER

Vietnam War. *The term "Vietnam War" refers to the period of direct U.S. military intervention in Southeast Asia and its aftermath from 1965 to 1975. For discussion of the French colonial period before 1954, see* Colonialism. *For discussion of the United States and the Republic of Vietnam prior to 1965, see* Prelude to U.S. Intervention. *For discussion of the military aspects of the Vietnam War, see* Pacification; Strategy and Tactics; *and entries on individual U.S. and foreign military services. For discussion of the diplomatic aspects of the Vietnam War, see* Diplomacy.

Vogt, John W., Jr. (1920–), general, U.S. Air Force; commander, Seventh Air Force, 1972–1973. Vogt commanded the U.S. Air Force during some of the heaviest bombing of the Vietnam War: Operation FREEDOM TRAIN, which blunted the Easter Offensive of the People's Army of Vietnam (PAVN), and operations LINEBACKER and LINEBACKER II against North Vietnam. Vogt also supervised the U.S. Air Force's withdrawal from South Vietnam in 1973, transferring his command to Nakhon Phanom Air Base in Thailand. Vogt later commanded U.S. air forces in the Pacific and in Europe before retiring in 1975.

BIBLIOGRAPHY

BERGER, CARL, ed. *The United States Air Force in Southeast Asia, 1961–1973.* 1977.
CLODFELTER, MARK. *The Limits of Air Power: The American Bombing of North Vietnam.* 19889.

GLEN GENDZEL

Vo Nguyen Giap (1911–), general and commander, People's Army of Vietnam (PAVN), (1946–1972); member of the politburo, Vietnam Communist Party (1951–1976); minister of National Defense (1946–1980). In the 1940s, Giap organized the incipient Vietnamese armed forces and later directed Viet Minh forces in their successful war against the French. In the 1960s, Giap was a central military official and elite Communist Party figure, though his opposition to an aggressive, conventional war in the South made him a controversial figure within politburo debates. Nevertheless, he continued to be the preeminent military strategist for North Vietnam throughout its war to unify Vietnam.

The Early Years. Born in impoverished Quan Bin province from a family with fervent anti-French sentiments, Giap became an underground member of the Communist Party in his mid-teens, influenced by the writings of Ho Chi Minh. French authorities imprisoned him for political activities at age sixteen. An excellent student, Giap attended a lycée in Hue that offered a mixed Western and Vietnamese education. In 1933, he entered the country's premier university in Hanoi, where he obtained a bachelor of law degree. At the university, Giap tutored students and studied communism, history, and military strategy. In this period, he also began writing political tracts, coauthoring with Truong Chinh in 1938 *The Peasant Problem,* a study that became a key work for Viet Minh planning on agriculture. The next year Giap wrote *The Question of National Liberation in Indochina,* which stressed the importance of protracted war for defeating a powerful foreign adversary.

After the French banned the Communist Party in 1939, Giap fled to China, where he became a key deputy to Ho Chi Minh. He entrusted Giap with the command of the fledgling Viet Minh guerrilla forces, who fought the Japanese occupying Vietnam from 1940 to 1945. Begun as a small armed band, the insurgency grew rapidly, benefiting from the communists' skill at recruiting support among villagers. During the political vacuum following World War II, the communists seized power in northern Vietnam in the 1945 August Revolution, and Giap became a top figure in the new government, serving as minister of interior in Ho's cabinet and a negotiator with the French in 1946.

While organizing the insurgency in 1954, Giap learned that his wife, a party activist, had died in a French prison in Hanoi. The event deeply embittered Giap, and he reportedly grew increasingly tempestuous over the course of his career, becoming arrogant and highly sensitive to slights. His outbursts earned him the nickname Nue Lau (Volcano under the Snow).

Commander and Military Theorist. During the war with the French, Giap shaped the People's Army of Vietnam (PAVN) into a potent fighting force. His talent for organization and the Democratic Republic of Vietnam's (DRV) ability to mobilize national resources facilitated the process, although substantial Chinese and Soviet military aid was also crucial. Drawing on a Chinese communist model, Giap and elite communist planners constructed a three-tier system for the armed forces, with regular troops as well as regional and local forces. Giap also initiated a political indoctrination and education program, credited with developing the highly motivated PAVN soldiers. The proselytizing program, stressed in basic training and by political officers accompanying units, extolled sacrifice to nationalist and communist ideals. By 1952, the PAVN had more than 250,000 troops and nearly two million local militia that assisted and scouted for main regiments.

Giap envisioned the war for independence as a complex, political conflict. The "people's war," as Giap termed it, demanded the nation's total resources and incorporated military, diplomatic, psychological, and economic dimensions. Conceived with Ho and Truong Chinh, Giap's warfare blurred the distinction between civilians and combatants, merging the political and armed *dau tranh* (struggle) for national emancipation. In accordance with Mao Zedong's original theory of revolution, Giap saw revolutionary war as composed of three stages, each requiring a distinct balance of military and political activity: (1) guerrilla warfare and building of political support; (2) mixed guerrilla and conventional warfare; and (3) a decisive conventional offensive leading to political revolution.

Giap's skill as a tactician did not match his organizational genius, but over the course of the Indochina War he learned from his defeats at the hands of the French. In 1951, he blundered with a general counteroffensive, losing 20,000 men in campaigns in the Red River delta. Giap had formulated an all-out conventional attack, desiring a decisive "third-stage" communist victory, but the general directed troops poorly and did not properly gauge French air and naval power. After the offensive, Giap realized that his commitment to conventional attacks was premature. He subsequently resisted set-piece battles with the French, seeking to overextend and frustrate their forces.

Giap's historical reputation results from his victory at Dien Bien Phu in May 1954. PAVN feints into Laos led the French commander, Gen. Henri Navarre, to position a vulnerable 14,000-troop garrison near the border. Using siege tactics, Giap defeated the French with an extraordinary logistical buildup and effective use of well-protected artillery. Giap achieved the garrison's surrender just days before the beginning of the 1954 Geneva Conference, which would negotiate the French withdrawal from Vietnam but would also leave the country partitioned.

Political Battles over Strategy. In the late 1950s and 1960s, Giap remained a key military figure in the DRV, but he became embroiled in fierce debate over strategy for reunification. Details of the struggle within the politburo remain uncertain, but Giap's faction apparently supported pursuing a political solution in the South while developing North Vietnam's socialist economy. But a rival politburo faction emerged, intent on an aggressive military effort for reunification. This group, including such southern Vietnam–born party elites as Le Duan and Nguyen Chi Thanh, gained Ho Chi Minh's favor in the late 1950s. After national elections mandated by the Geneva accords failed to occur and Diem's southern government gained support in rural areas, Ho committed northern resources to arm the National Liberation Front (NLF) guerrilla forces.

As a major land war erupted in the mid 1960s, Giap remained on the losing side of politburo debates over tactics. Echoing lessons from the 1950s, Giap expressed skepticism that PAVN forces could succeed in conventional war against formidable U.S. military power, advocating instead guerrilla warfare and the advancement of a communist political base in the South. Siding again with the southern Vietnamese faction, however, Ho supported aggressive, conventional warfare and ignored Giap's pleas. As revealed in party deliberations, Giap (joined by Truong Chinh) argued for first-phase revolutionary warfare—guerrilla attacks and political organizing—whereas the militant faction, led by Nguyen Chi Thanh, favored second-phase tactics evolving quickly into a decisive offensive.

The power struggle resulted in unprecedented assaults on Giap's standing in the early 1960s. The party demoted Giap's politburo rank (from fourth to sixth) in 1960. Adversaries ridiculed Giap's and Chinh's protracted, political warfare as old-fashioned and criticized the general's supposedly ostentatious lifestyle. In the early 1960s, Ho designated NLF forces in the South. Giap weathered the crisis, retaining his position as head of the armed forces.

VO NGUYEN GIAP. With enlisted men of the People's Army of Vietnam, September 1968. *Archive Photos*

Giap remained a member of the entrenched, old-guard politburo elite and with his twenty-year leadership of the military, had the continued and crucial support of the armed forces.

Architect of the Tet Offensive. Giap's tactical concerns were largely validated after PAVN forces suffered extensive defeats to U.S. forces in 1965–1966. With Thanh's death in mid 1967, Giap reassumed command of North Vietnamese strategy. Later that year, Giap designed the Tet Offensive, co-ordinating political and military initiatives in the distinctive style of "people's" warfare. The offensive collapsed, however, when the expected popular up-rising in support of communist forces failed to de-velop, resulting in heavy losses to the NLF. Between 1968 and 1972, Giap directed the small-unit guer-rilla warfare that frustrated the U.S. and South Viet-

namese armies and doubled U.S. combat casualties. In the early 1970s, Giap finally advocated a conven-tional offensive to take advantage of the apparent weakness of the Army of the Republic of Vietnam (ARVN) and the North's new Soviet high-technol-ogy weaponry. The resultant 1972 Easter Offensive failed, however, because of the PAVN's inability to coordinate its various attacks and because of deci-sive U.S. air and naval power.

Retirement. In 1973, Giap stepped down from direct command of the armed forces. The immedi-ate cause of the demotion is uncertain, although Giap reportedly suffered from Hodgkin's disease. Giap resigned as minister of defense in 1980 and lost his seat on the politburo in 1982, when he became chief of the Science and Technology Commission. Despite his waning power in the party and government hierarchy, Giap remained popular among the Vietnamese public, and in July 1992 he was awarded the Gold Star Order, Vietnam's highest decoration, "for his services to the revolutionary cause of party and nation."

BIBLIOGRAPHY

DAVIDSON, PHILLIP B. *Vietnam at War: The History, 1946–1975.* 1988.

MACDONALD, PETER. *Giap: The Victor in Vietnam.* 1993.

VO NGUYEN GIAP. *The Military Art of a People's War.* Edited by Russell Stetler. 1970.

ADAM LAND

W–Z

Walt, Lewis W. (1913–1989), general, U.S. Marine Corps. After graduation from Colorado State University, Walt became a Marine Corps second lieutenant in July 1936 and proved an outstanding combat leader in World War II and the Korean War. Lieutenant General Walt commanded the III Marine Amphibious Force (III MAF) in Vietnam from June 1965 until June 1967, with responsibility for the I Corps sector, the five northern provinces of South Vietnam. Walt initiated what U.S. Marine leaders called a balanced campaign of small unit patrolling, large unit operations, and an innovative pacification program that consisted of both civic action and the formation of U.S. Marine Combined Action Platoons (CAP) operating in conjunction with local Vietnamese militia in the countryside. Marine civic action in Vietnam consisted of assistance to South Vietnamese villagers in the III MAF area of operations in several self-help projects to raise the local standard of living. These included the construction of schools and hospitals, instruction in more efficient farming techniques, and visits by marines and doctors to the various hamlets to treat minor illnesses and to teach better health practices.

While similar in many respects to Military Assistance Command, Vietnam (MACV) operational concepts, the marine campaign placed more emphasis on small unit operations and pacification than did General Westmoreland's concentration on large communist units and search and destroy operations.

In 1968 President Johnson considered both Walt and Lt. Gen. Victor H. Krulak for the position of commandant of the Marine Corps. While there was little difference between Walt and Krulak on most policy matters, both enjoyed powerful support within the administration and Congress and among the officer corps for appointment to the commandancy. Faced with the personal rivalry between the two leading contenders, President Johnson selected the well-respected assistant commandant, Lt. Gen. Leonard A. Chapman, as the new commandant to retain harmony within the Marine Corps. Walt replaced Chapman as assistant commandant in January 1968 and was promoted to full general in June 1969, retiring in February 1971.

BIBLIOGRAPHY

U.S. MARINE CORPS. Historical and Museum Division. *U.S. Marines in Vietnam, 1965: The Landing and the Buildup.* 1978

U.S. MARINE CORPS. Historical and Museum Division. *U.S. Marines in Vietnam, 1966: An Expanding War.* 1982.

619

U.S. MARINE CORPS. Historical and Museum Division. *U.S. Marines in Vietnam, 1967: Fighting the North Vietnamese.* 1984.

WALT, LEWIS W. *Strange War, Strange Strategy.* 1970.

JACK SHULIMSON

Warnke, Paul (1920–), general counsel at the Defense Department, 1966–1967; assistant secretary of defense for international security affairs, 1967–1969. Warnke became one of the leading proponents of deescalation in the Defense Department, influencing both Secretaries Robert McNamara and Clark Clifford. When General Westmoreland requested an additional 206,000 troops in 1968, Warnke seized the opportunity to prepare a critical assessment of Vietnam policy. He argued that more troop deployments would lead to increased casualties and that it was time to reduce U.S. involvement. Warnke's analysis helped to sway Clifford, especially when the Joint Chiefs of Staff failed adequately to address Clifford's concerns about further troop requests and the uncertain length of the war.

BIBLIOGRAPHY

KAHIN, GEORGE MCT. *Intervention: How America Became Involved in Vietnam.* 1986.

KARNOW, STANLEY. *Vietnam: A History.* 1991.

KELLY EVANS-PFEIFER

War Powers Resolution. Passed over Richard Nixon's veto on 7 November 1973, the War Powers Resolution (87 Stat. 555–560) was an attempt to establish congressional coordination with the executive branch over deployment of combat troops abroad. (Officially a joint resolution, it has the same legal force as an act of Congress, and thus is often referred to as the War Powers Act.) The resolution reflected five years of growing congressional resistance to the Vietnam War. In 1970 Congress repealed the Tonkin Gulf Resolution, and by 1973 it had imposed deadlines on U.S. involvement in Vietnam through ten major laws. Nixon's Watergate entanglement substantially weakened his bargaining power with Congress, thus contributing to the resolution's passage.

The resolution's purpose, as stated in Section 2(a), is to ensure that the "collective judgment of both the Congress and the President" be applied to the introduction of U.S. armed forces into hostilities or "situations where imminent involvement in hos-

tilities is clearly indicated by the circumstances." This collective judgment is also to be applied to the continued use of such forces. Ironically, while seeking to ensure such collective judgment, the War Powers Resolution actually sanctions executive-initiated warmaking. It provides for situations "in the absence of a declaration of war." Under conditions of undeclared war in which U.S. armed forces are introduced into hostilities or situations threatening hostilities, the president is required by Section 4(a)(1) to submit within forty-eight hours a report to the Speaker of the House of Representatives and to the president pro tempore of the Senate. The president is to explain in writing the circumstances necessitating the introduction of U.S. armed forces; the constitutional and legislative authority under which such introduction took place; and the estimated scope and duration of the hostilities or involvement. The submission of the report under Section 4(a)(1) starts the War Powers Resolution "clock." Within sixty calendar days after the report is submitted or "is required to be submitted," the War Powers Resolution orders the president to terminate any use of U.S. military forces unless Congress has declared war; has acted specifically to authorize the use of U.S. armed forces; has extended by law the sixty-day period; or is physically unable to meet as a result of an armed attack on the United States. If the clock is started and the president does not receive congressional authorization to continue the use of U.S. armed forces, the president may extend the sixty-day period for an additional thirty days. This extension is allowed only under written presidential certification to Congress that "the safety of the United States Armed Forces" necessitates continued deployment to implement the "prompt removal of such forces." For its part, Congress may withhold authorization during the sixty-to-ninety-day period or it can pass a concurrent resolution to order the president to remove U.S. armed forces from hostilities or situations threatening hostilities.

The War Powers Resolution, ostensibly promulgated to ensure congressional counsel and collaboration, actually delegates some warmaking power to the executive as it tacitly approves presidential intervention in armed conflicts. As one U.S. senator complained, the law gave the president an "undated ninety day declaration of war."

Since 1973, presidents have proved adept at avoiding the reporting requirements of Section 4(a)(1). From 1973 to 1993, presidents have filed approximately two dozen reports "consistent" with the resolution but not under Section 4(a)(1). Presidents have invoked the commander-in-chief clause of the Constitution or have cited the exigencies of the situation to justify their use of military force. Congress's power to terminate military action by concurrent resolution has been cast into doubt by the U.S. Supreme Court's decision in *Immigration and Naturalization Service v. Chadha* (1983), which held legislative vetoes unconstitutional. While the War Powers Resolution provides a framework for possible interbranch negotiation, its history since 1973 has shown little promise of involving Congress with the executive in collective judgment on warmaking.

BIBLIOGRAPHY

ELY, JOHN HART. *War and Responsibility. Constitutional Lessons of Vietnam and Its Aftermath.* 1993.
SCHLESINGER, ARTHUR M., JR. *The Imperial Presidency.* 1974.
WORMUTH, FRANCIS D., and EDWIN B. FIRMAGE. *To Chain the Dog of War: The War Power of Congress in History and Law.* 1986.

VICTOR JEW

Watergate. Watergate is the generic term for the scandal that engulfed President Richard Nixon from 17 June 1972, when the Committee to Reelect the President (often referred to derogatorially by the unofficial acronym CREEP) authorized a break-in of the Democratic National Committee headquarters in the Watergate office complex in Washington, D.C., until the president's unprecedented resignation on 9 August 1974.

The causes of the Watergate break-in were deeply rooted in the Vietnam War. Antiwar and congressional critics had profoundly disturbed the president, national security adviser Henry Kissinger, and others in the administration, and they reacted with stern and illegal methods to repress that criticism. Attorney General John Mitchell later described the "White House Horrors" of Nixon's first term (1969–1973), events that involved intimidation and harassment of those who opposed Nixon's Vietnam policy. These included sponsorship of the Huston Plan to centralize surveillance and domestic intelligence activities; the use of the Federal Bureau of Investigation (FBI), Central Intelligence Agency (CIA), and U.S. Army personnel and resources to spy on antiwar protest groups; the creation of an "enemies list" to exclude and intimidate opponents,

using such measures as income tax audits; and most notably, the creation of the "plumbers," a clandestine group that used illegal methods to gain compromising information on antiwar foes. Daniel Ellsberg's leaking of the Pentagon Papers in June 1971 was the immediate occasion for creating the plumbers. The president's chief domestic adviser, John Ehrlichman, authorized them to break in to Ellsberg's psychiatrist's office to find embarrassing material on Ellsberg, an act that the president rationalized as a necessary national security measure. Actions such as these led to the impeachment charge of "abuse of power," one of three charges brought by the House Committee on the Judiciary in July 1974, and eventually forced Nixon's resignation.

Nixon's power declined precipitously after the Saturday Night Massacre, in which he dismissed Special Prosecutor Archibald Cox in October 1973. Several weeks later, in a vote indicative of Nixon's weakness, Congress passed the War Powers Resolution over his veto.

Nixon and Kissinger blamed the Watergate imbroglio for Nixon's inability to carry out his commitment to defend South Vietnam. Such reasoning is fallacious, however, because in the Paris accords of 1973, Nixon tacitly accepted that the struggle in Vietnam would continue after the withdrawal of U.S. troops, for North Vietnamese troops were allowed to remain in South Vietnam. Quite simply, even had there been no Watergate scandal, the American public and Congress would not have countenanced renewed U.S. involvement. Thus Watergate is a tenuous, improbable scapegoat for what Nixon and Kissinger knew was a foreordained end for the war.

[See also Plumbers.]

BIBLIOGRAPHY

KUTLER, STANLEY I. *The Wars of Watergate.* 1992.
NIXON, RICHARD M. *RN: The Memoirs of Richard Nixon.* 1978.

STANLEY I. KUTLER

Weapons. [*This entry includes three articles:*

Almost every form of modern warfare short of the use of nuclear weapons occurred during the three decades of conflict in Vietnam, ranging from

M16 AUTOMATIC RIFLE. An American adviser holds an M16 during riverine operations, 1964. Note that his ARVN companions are equipped with World War II–era M1 rifles. *National Archives*

low-level insurgency to full-blown conventional war. The belligerents used a bewildering variety of weapons, from crude home-made bombs to bombers designed for nuclear warfare. The United States armed itself and the military of its client, the Republic of Vietnam, with most of the weapons in its arsenal. The Soviet Union, the People's Republic of China, and several Warsaw Pact nations supplied the People's Army of Vietnam (PAVN) and the Viet Cong (VC) with a broad spectrum of weaponry. The following articles provide an overview of some of the most common weapons used in the Vietnam conflict.]

Infantry Weapons

The Vietnam conflict, a political war, was fought over the control of the Vietnamese people. As a result, for most of its duration the war was fought primarily by infantry.

United States. For the bulk of the war, the main infantry weapon for U.S. and ARVN forces was the 5.56 mm M16 automatic rifle, which entered widespread service by 1966. Early M16s frequently jammed in combat, leading to the deaths of many U.S. servicemen. The problem was so common that a U.S. House of Representatives subcommittee, the Ichord committee (named after its chair, Rep. Richard H. Ichord), was formed to investigate. Modifications and revised maintenance procedures largely solved the problem by late 1966 and early 1967.

The first U.S. troops deployed to Vietnam were armed with the 7.62 mm V14 automatic rifle. The lengthy and heavy rifle, difficult to carry, was nearly impossible to control when fired on full automatic. As a result, soldiers generally used only the M14's semiautomatic setting. Hundreds of thousands of ARVN troops and South Vietnamese militia were equipped with M14s as well as World War II–era M1 Garands and M2 carbines.

The standard U.S. general purpose machine gun was the 7.62 mm M60 light machine gun. Rather heavy at 10.4 kg, the bipod-mounted, belt-fed M60 fired 600 rounds per minute and had a range of 900 meters. It served as the basic infantry platoon automatic weapon and was also mounted on a number of vehicles, including helicopters. Heavier fire was provided by .30-inch and .50-inch Browning machine guns, which were used for base defense or as vehicle-mounted weapons.

The 66 mm M72 light antitank weapon (LAW) provided instant firepower for infantry, proving especially useful against bunkers. A telescoping, self-contained rocket launcher, the M72 fired an unguided high-explosive antitank (HEAT) missile from a disposable launch tube. The weapon's light weight (2.1 kg) and compact size (65.3 cm long collapsed; 89 cm in firing position) allowed infantrymen to carry several at a time.

The primary U.S. grenade launcher was the 40 mm M79, a single-shot breech-loading weapon resembling a break-open shotgun. The M79 lobbed grenades up to 400 meters, but was dangerous to use at close range, as its explosive projectiles were potentially lethal to the user. As this left grenadiers defenseless at short range, the M203 grenade launcher was developed, which attached directly to the M16 rifle.

A wide variety of U.S. hand grenades were issued in Vietnam, including the Mk2 cast-iron "pineapple" grenade of World War II fame, M26 and M61 fragmentation grenades, white phosphorous grenades, CS (tear gas) grenades, illumination grenades, and smoke grenades.

U.S. and ARVN forces used many types of pistols. The most common were the .45 pistol, often issued to M79 grenadiers for personal protection, and the .38 revolver.

The M2A17 portable flamethrower, which was carried and fired by one soldier, was often used by so-called "zippo squads" to destroy buildings, most notoriously village huts (or "hootches") during search-and-destroy missions.

Large numbers of conventional U.S. antipersonnel and antitank mines were used for base defense in

M72 LIGHT ANTITANK WEAPON. Members of Company A, 2d Battalion, 35th Infantry, fire M72 light antitank weapons at Viet Cong positions during Operation OREGON, a search-and-destroy mission conducted by elements of the 3d Brigade Task Force, 25th U.S. Infantry Division, near Duc Pho, Quang Ngai province, 23–26 April 1967. *Department of Defense*

Vietnam. However, the most common explosive antipersonnel device in U.S. and ARVN service was the tripod-mounted M18A1 Claymore. Developed to provide an area defense against mass attack, the

Common Rifles of the Vietnam War

	M16	*M14*	*M1 Garand*	*M2 carbine*	*AK47*	*SKS carbine*
Caliber	5.56 mm	7.62 mm	.30-inch	.30-inch	7.62 mm	7.62 mm
Length	98 cm	112 cm	110.7 cm	90.4 cm	86.8 cm	102.1 cm
Weight	2.9 kg	3.9 kg	4.3 kg	2.5 kg	4.3 kg	3.5 kg
Effective Range	400 m	550 m	550 m	300 m	400 m	450 m
Magazine	20/30 rounds, detachable	20 rounds, detachable	8-round clip	15/30 rounds, detachable	30 rounds, detachable	10 rounds, nondetachable
Rate of Fire	650–800 rpm*	750 rpm	semiautomatic	semiautomatic	600 rpm	semiautomatic

Source: Owen, J. I. H., ed. *Brassey's Infantry Weapons of the World.* 1975.

*Rounds per minute.

U.S. INFANTRY WEAPONS. U.S. military advisers, armed with M16 rifles, accompany a Vietnamese patrol searching for Viet Cong, 22 August 1963. The ARVN soldier at left holds an M72 grenade launcher. The adviser behind him, at center, holds a .45 caliber pistol and wears a smoke grenade; the last man holds a .38 revolver as well as his rifle. *National Archives*

Claymore projected 700 steel balls in a 60 degree arc when triggered, which were lethal out to 50 meters. M18A1s often were used to defend the night camps of patrolling infantry. Unlike conventional buried mines, unused Claymores could be removed and reused with ease. This fact was not lost on the Viet Cong, who often surreptitiously removed the devices or even turned them around to point back at the defenders. As a result, U.S. and ARVN troops often booby-trapped Claymores when emplacing them and left them in place when moving on.

Infantry units were provided with heavy direct support weapons, such as 90 mm and 106 mm recoilless rifles and 81 mm and 4.2-inch mortars. Given the ready availability of air strikes and artillery support, however, these weapons were usually left at base camp during patrols, where they served as part of the camp defense. A number of these weapons were also mounted on vehicles. In addition, U.S. Marines used the officially obsolescent but lightweight and portable 60 mm M19 mortar, which was unofficially adopted by many U.S. Army units as well.

U.S. and ARVN units called in fire support using a number of types of two-way radios, most notably the backpack-carried AN/PRC10 and AN/PRC25 portable command radios.

ANTIAIRCRAFT FIRE. Viet Cong soldiers fire a Soviet-made SG43 Goryunov machine gun against attacking U.S. aircraft, 4 September 1969. The soldier at left has an AK47 slung over his shoulder. *Archive Photos*

RPG-2 ROCKET-PROPELLED GRENADE LAUNCHER. Carried by communist soldier Pham Trung Than, July 1970. *Archive Photos*

Communist. The main infantry weapon of Vietnamese communist forces was the Soviet-made 7.62 mm AK47 automatic rifle (and its Chinese-made version, the Type 56), extremely rugged, mechanically simple, reliable, and with a high rate of fire. Another common rifle was the Soviet-made 7.62 mm SKS carbine (and its Chinese-made version, the Carbine Model 56), which used the same ammunition as the AK47 and thus reduced problems of supply.

A number of the machine guns commonly used by the PAVN and the VC also shared the same 7.62 mm ammunition, most notably the Soviet-made RDP and RPK light machine guns. These weapons had a range of 800 meters and a rate of fire of 150 rounds per minute.

A common medium machine gun in communist service was the Soviet-made 7.62 SG43 Goryunov, with a 1,500-meter range and a rate of fire of 600–700 rounds per minute. The Soviet-made 12.7 mm DShK 38/46 heavy machine gun (and its Chinese-made variant, the Type 54), a common heavy machine gun, had a range of 2,000 meters and a rate of fire of 540–600 rounds per minute. Both guns proved extremely effective against aircraft.

Several types of pistols were carried by communist officers, less as a weapon than as a symbol of authority. The most common pistols in use were the 7.62 mm Soviet-made Tokarev TT33 (and its Chinese-made variants, the Types 51 and 54) and the 9 mm Makarov PM (and its Chinese-made variant, the Type 59).

The Soviet-made 40 mm RPG2 light antitank weapon (and its variants, the Chinese-made types 56 and 69 and the Czech-made P27) provided instant firepower for infantry and proved especially useful against bunkers and armored vehicles. Known in Vietnam as the B40, the RPG2 fired unguided 82 mm HEAT missiles (whose 40 mm tail booms were inserted into the muzzle of the launcher) to a range of 100 meters. An improved version of the RPG2, the RPG7, was introduced in 1962 but both weapons remained in Vietnamese service. During the 1972 Easter Offensive, the Soviet-made AT-3 Sagger wire-guided antitank missile was also introduced. Both types of weapon took a heavy toll of ARVN armor during both the 1972 offensive and the 1975 Ho Chi Minh Campaign.

Communist forces, which were forced to operate without artillery support for much of the war, also relied on a number of easily portable light and medium mortars and recoilless rifles for heavy firepower in the field. Typical mortars include the 60 mm Chinese-made Type 63 light mortar, which had

BOOBY TRAPS. Despite the danger, Viet Cong troops cannibalize unexploded U.S. shells for explosives. Such attempts frequently proved fatal, yet dud munitions fired by U.S. and ARVN artillery provided the matériel for many communist-made booby traps. *Ngô Vĩnh Long*

SOVIET-MADE 12.7 MM DSHK 38/46 HEAVY MACHINE GUN. Captured from the Viet Cong by ARVN soldiers, 1965. *National Archives*

a range of 1,530 meters, and the 82 mm Soviet-made M1937 medium mortar, which had a range of 3,000 meters, and which could fire U.S. 81 mm mortar rounds. Typical recoilless rifles include the Chinese-made 75 mm Type 56 antitank gun and the Soviet-made 107 mm B11 antitank gun. Additionally, PAVN forces used Soviet- and Chinese-made towed heavy mortars (often transported by pack animal), ranging in caliber from 107 mm to 160 mm.

The Soviet-made SA7 Strella antiaircraft missile launcher proved effective against helicopters and ground-attack aircraft. Carried by one soldier and fired from the shoulder, the SA7 launched a heat-seeking, supersonic high-explosive (HE) rocket out to a range of 3,700 meters.

Communist forces employed a wide variety of hand grenades, including World War II–era F1 and RG42 cast-iron "pineapple" grenades, RDG33

FLYING MACE. Australian journalist Wilfred Burchett, a supporter of the Vietnamese communists, examines a Viet Cong booby trap, the "flying mace," 3 October 1964. The hidden flying mace, suspended from vines, swings down when triggered and sweeps back and forth over jungle trails within a few inches of the ground. It is made from wicker baskets packed with clay and laced through with sharp bamboo spears. *National Archives*

stick grenades, RKG3 antitank grenades, and RDG1 and RDG2 smoke grenades. These were often used in booby traps. Soviet- and Chinese-made antitank and antipersonnel mines were used against U.S. and ARVN forces, as were captured U.S. mines and grenades; volunteers even dug up emplaced mines for reuse. Other devices were made in local workshops with explosives extracted from unexploded U.S. bombs and shells. Guerrilla units also used a number of primitive traps, including hidden crossbows triggered by tripwires and boards embedded with nails hidden in river beds at fords. Punji sticks, sharpened bamboo spears often smeared with human excrement to cause infection, were placed at the bottom of concealed pits.

Throughout the war, a significant portion of VC forces were armed with weapons captured from U.S. and ARVN units.

BIBLIOGRAPHY

HOGG, IAN V., and JOHN WEEKS. *Military Small Arms of the 20th Century.* 1985.

OWEN, J. I. H., ed. *Brassey's Infantry Weapons of the World.* 1975.

ROSSER-OWEN, DAVID. *Vietnam Weapons Handbook.* 1986.

STANTON, SHELBY L. *Vietnam Order of Battle.* 1981.

STEVENS, R. BLAKE, and EDWARD C. EZELL. *The Black Rifle: M16 Retrospective.* 1987.

STEVEN J. TIRONE

Artillery and Air Defense

U.S. logistical and matériel superiority largely determined the patterns of use of artillery and air defense by both sides throughout the Vietnam conflict.

United States. Tactically, U.S. and ARVN forces depended on artillery. Towed howitzers frequently were lifted by helicopter into landing zones within range of units engaged in combat. Riverine operations were often supported by cannon mounted on barges. Moreover, hundreds of fire support bases were established throughout South Vietnam. Self-contained strongholds relying on helicopters for supply, they provided fire on call to patrolling units and served as bases for infantry operations. They were positioned within range of one another to provide mutual support as well as to ensure that the fire from at least one and usually two or more bases could hit any point within the area of operations. Their guns could deliver accurate, concentrated fire even in weather that grounded aircraft, important given Vietnam's monsoons. Additional fire support for U.S. and ARVN ground forces was provided by naval gunfire, air strikes, and aerial rocket artillery fired from helicopters.

The mainstay of U.S. and ARVN artillery was the 105 mm towed light howitzer. The M101A1 model, first produced in 1939, was light enough at 2,258 kg to be deployed by a variety of helicopters, including the ubiquitous Huey. It had a range of 11,000 meters and a rate of fire of 8 rounds per minute. The M102, which entered service in 1966, gradually replaced the M101A1. It was lighter (1,450 kg), had a greater range (12,800 meters), and fired more quickly (10 rounds per minute). Additionally, the M102's carriage had a built-in turntable that allowed the gun to be rotated quickly through 360 degrees. Both models fired high-explosive (HE), high-explosive antitank (HEAT), and smoke shells, including incendiary white phosphorous rounds. Both required a crew of eight.

The M114A1 155 mm towed medium howitzer, which dated back to 1939, provided heavier support. Weighing 5,800 kg, it could be deployed by the CH-54 Tarhe heavy-lift helicopter. Served by a crew of eleven, it fired 4 HE shells per minute to a

FIRE BASE. Engineers of the 8th Engineer Battalion, attached to the 1st U.S. Cavalry Division (Airmobile), build a battalion fire base in support of Operation PEGASUS, the effort to relieve the besieged marine garrison at Khe Sanh, April 1968. They dig an ammunition bunker for an M102 105 mm howitzer, at right. Note that the M102 is resting on its turntable, with its wheels in the air, to allow it to be rapidly rotated through 360 degrees. *Department of Defense/U.S. Army*

range of 16,600 meters. The M109, the self-propelled gun version of the M114A1, was also deployed to Vietnam.

The heaviest guns in the U.S. and ARVN inventory were the M107 175 mm self-propelled gun (for flat-trajectory direct fire) and the M110 8-inch (203.2 mm) self-propelled howitzer (for high-arc, plunging indirect fire). Both used the same carrier vehicle, which allowed artillery units to adapt themselves to differing missions by simply swapping weapons, a common practice in Vietnam. The M107 gun fired HE shells to a range of 32,600 meters, while the M110 howitzer had a range of 16,800

meters. Both fired at a rate of 1 round per 2 minutes, and both were served by a crew of eight.

Given the relative weakness of the PAVN air arm, air defense was essentially unnecessary for U.S. and ARVN forces. Indeed, most of the air-defense weapons deployed were used as antipersonnel weapons. Most notable were the M55 quad .50-caliber antiaircraft weapon, which mounted four heavy machine guns firing in tandem, and the M42 "Duster" self-propelled gun, which mounted twin 40 mm cannon.

Communist. Communist forces employed a wide assortment of artillery throughout the war.

However, until the U.S. withdrawal, U.S. dominance in air power, artillery support, and airmobility forced the PAVN and the VC to depend primarily on infantry and guerrilla tactics. Up to the 1972 Easter Offensive, communist forces used artillery sparingly. Guerrilla units used a variety of highly portable but extremely inaccurate rocket artillery launchers to create "rocket belts" around South Vietnam's cities and bases, from which they struck randomly for psychological effect. Often single tubes stripped from multiple rocket launchers, these weapons ranged in caliber from 102 mm to 140 mm and fired unguided HE rockets.

PAVN field guns ranged from the Soviet-made M1942 ZIS3 towed 76 mm field gun to the Soviet-made M46 towed 130 mm field gun (and their Chinese-manufactured counterparts). The M46, which fired HE shells to a range of 31,000 meters, comfortably outranged any U.S. artillery piece deployed to Vietnam and was often used to batter U.S. and ARVN fire support bases from the safety of positions in Laos and North Vietnam. The weapon had a rate of fire of 6 rounds per minute and a crew of nine. One of the best cannon of the war, the M46 (and its Chinese variants, the types 59 and 59-1) was a mainstay of communist artillery. It commonly was used as mobile artillery from the Easter Offensive on.

PAVN howitzers ranged from the Soviet-made M1938 towed 122 mm howitzer to the Soviet-made towed D20 152 mm gun-howitzer (and their Chinese-manufactured counterparts). A representative weapon was the Soviet-made D30 towed 122 mm howitzer, which fired HE shells to a range of 15,300 meters. The D30 had a rate of fire of 8 rounds per minute and required a crew of seven.

During the various offensives, the PAVN also deployed a number of Soviet-made BM14 140 mm, BM21 122 mm, and Chinese-made Type 63 107 mm vehicle-mounted multiple rocket artillery launchers.

Given U.S. and South Vietnamese strength in helicopters and aircraft, air defense was of primary importance to the PAVN. North Vietnam itself was defended by interlocking layers of surface-to-air missiles (SAMs) and antiaircraft artillery (AAA) ranging from ZPU 14.5 mm antiaircraft machine guns to the KS30 130 mm AA gun. Many of the same weapons also served in the field. The most important field weapon was the Soviet-made S60 57 mm towed or vehicle-mounted antiaircraft gun. The S60 had a horizontal range of 12,000 meters, a

vertical range of 8,800 meters, a rate of fire of 70 rounds per minute, and a crew of seven.

The SA2 Guideline SAM, carried by ZIL-157 cross-country semi-trailer transporters and fired from separate rotating launchers, provided high-altitude antiaircraft coverage. The missile, 10.7 meters long and with a 130 kg warhead, was guided by ground radar to the target. The SA2 had a ceiling of 18,000 meters (59,000 feet).

BIBLIOGRAPHY

FOSS, CHRISTOPHER F. *Artillery of the World.* 1974.
FOSS, CHRISTOPHER F. *Jane's World Armoured Fighting Vehicles.* 1976.
OWEN, J. I. H., ed. *Brassey's Infantry Weapons of the World.* 1975.
ROSSER-OWEN, DAVID. *Vietnam Weapons Handbook.* 1986.
STANTON, SHELBY L. *Vietnam Order of Battle.* 1981.

STEVEN J. TIRONE

Armored Vehicles and Transport

U.S. logistical and matériel superiority largely determined the patterns of use of armor and transport by both sides throughout the Vietnam conflict.

United States. As communist forces rarely used armor in combat until the closing stages of the U.S. withdrawal, U.S. and ARVN armor was relegated to a supporting role throughout much of the Vietnam conflict. Armored vehicles escorted convoys on South Vietnam's contested highways, and were used as "jungle busters," breaking through undergrowth in support of infantry patrols. Conventional tank-to-tank battles occurred between ARVN and PAVN forces during both the 1972 and the 1975 offensives.

ARVN armored units relied on the M41 Walker Bulldog light tank throughout the war. The M41, which dated back to 1949, had a crew of four. It was armed with a 76 mm cannon with a coaxial .30-inch machine gun and an externally mounted .50-inch machine gun.

The M48 main battle tank was the heaviest tank in general use by U.S. and ARVN units during the war. The M48, with a crew of four, was armed with a 90 mm cannon with a coaxial .30-inch machine gun and an externally mounted .50-inch machine gun. In the closing years of the war, the ARVN was equipped with a number of M60 tanks, improved versions of the M48 armed with 105 mm cannon.

U.S. forces were also equipped with the M551 Sheridan armored reconnaissance assault vehicle. The Sheridan, with a crew of four, was armed with a

M48 MAIN BATTLE TANK. *Department of Defense*

152 mm combination gun–missile launcher with a coaxial M60 7.62 mm machine gun and an externally mounted .50-inch machine gun. Designed to be portable by aircraft, the Sheridan was fitted with lightweight aluminum hull armor and special caseless ammunition for its main gun. As a result, the vehicle was vulnerable to mines and missiles; moreover, when hit, the Sheridan's ammunition frequently caught fire, incinerating the vehicle and its crew.

The most common U.S. and ARVN armored vehicle was the M113 armored personnel carrier. The M113 had numerous variants, including a number created by modifications made in the field. M113s were fitted to carry .30- and .50-inch heavy machine guns, 90 mm and 106 mm recoilless rifles, 81 mm and 4.2-inch mortars, flamethrowers, 20 mm XM163 Vulcan cannon, or TOW (XM-71A) wire-guided antitank missiles. M113s also served as com-mand posts, recovery vehicles, bridgelayers, and bulldozers.

Highly mechanized U.S. and ARVN forces relied on a wide variety of support vehicles, ranging from the Jeep-like M151 4 2 4 ¼-ton utility truck to the XM8002 6 2 6 16-ton containerized cargo transporter. A representative vehicle was the M35 6 2 6 2 ½-ton cargo truck. The M35 could carry 4,693 kg on roads and 2,462 kg cross-country, or tow 4,563 kg on roads and 2,722 kg cross-country. Modified M35s were used as fuel or water carriers, wreckers, shop vans, and troop carriers.

Communist. Given U.S. dominance in artillery and aircraft, the PAVN used armor sparingly before the 1972 Easter Offensive, after the bulk of U.S. forces had withdrawn from South Vietnam. Even so, U.S. air power decimated PAVN tank units and played a significant part in halting the offensive. PAVN armor was instrumental in the 1975 com-

M113 ARMORED PERSONNEL CARRIER. An Australian M113 of the 4/19th Prince of Wales Light Horse, operating in support of the 1st Battalion, Royal Australian Regiment, near Bien Hoa, 17 December 1965. The radio operator at center wears a AN/PRC10 command radio. *Department of Defense*

munist victory. The PAVN relied on three models of tank: the PT-76, the T-54, and the T-34.

The Soviet-made PT-76 amphibious tank first appeared in combat during the Tet Offensive, when five PT-76s of the PAVN *Division 304* overran the U.S. Special Forces camp at Lang Vei, near Khe Sanh, on 7 February 1968. The thinly armored PT-76, with a crew of three, was armed with a 76.2 mm cannon with a coaxial 7.62 mm machine gun.

The Soviet-made T-54 main battle tank, the heaviest tank in the PAVN armory, made its first appearance at the battle for the South Vietnamese provincial capital of An Loc during the 1972 Easter Offensive. The T-54, with a crew of four, was armed with a 100 mm cannon with a coaxial 7.62 mm machine gun, a bow-mounted 7.62 mm machine gun,

and an externally mounted 12.7 machine gun. The PAVN also deployed the T-55, an improved version of the T-54, as well as the Chinese-made variant, the T-59.

The World War II–vintage Soviet-made T-34/85 medium tank, with a crew of five, was armed with an 85 mm cannon with a coaxial 7.62 mm machine gun and a bow-mounted 7.62 mm machine gun.

PAVN forces were also equipped with a variety of armored vehicles, including Soviet-made BTR-152, BTR-40, BTR-50, and BTR-60 armored personnel carriers, BRDM-2 armored reconnaissance vehicles, and Chinese-made K-63 amphibious cargo carriers.

Many types of trucks were used in the immense logistical effort that supplied communist forces in the South. Soviet-made ZIL trucks were among the most commonly used; a representative type was the ZIL-151 62 6 2 ⅒-ton truck. The ZIL-151 could carry 4,500 kg on roads, 2,500 kg cross-country, and tow 3,600 kg. Communist forces also relied on bicycles, carts, pack animals, and human porters for transport throughout the war.

BIBLIOGRAPHY

Foss, Christopher F. *Jane's World Armoured Fighting Vehicles.* 1976.
Foss, Christopher F. *Military Vehicles of the World.* 1976.
Rosser-Owen, David. *Vietnam Weapons Handbook.* 1986.
Stanton, Shelby L. *Vietnam Order of Battle.* 1981.

Steven J. Tirone

Weathermen. A violent radical group led by Bernadine Dohrn and Mark Rudd, the Weathermen split off from Students for a Democratic Society (SDS) and the Revolutionary Youth Movement in 1969. Taking their name from a line in the Bob Dylan song, "Subterranean Homesick Blues," the Weathermen sought to bring the war home to the streets of the United States through violent protest and guerrilla attacks. After a spree of vandalism and attacks on police, the Weathermen formed small cells and went underground, surfacing occasionally to plant bombs at corporate, military, and government targets. They caused several fatalities and many injuries, including the death of three of their own members when they accidentally blew up their Greenwich Village townhouse in 1970. Most of the Weathermen were arrested or had surrendered by the early 1980s.

BIBLIOGRAPHY

Zaroulis, Nancy, and Gerald Sullivan. *Who Spoke Up?* 1984.

Kelly Evans-Pfeifer

T54 MAIN BATTLE TANKS. In front of Saigon's Presidential Palace, 1975. *Ngô Vĩnh Long*

Weinberger Doctrine.

The Weinberger doctrine offered an official reflection of the "Vietnam Syndrome," for it involved the reluctance to use force following the failure of U.S. intervention in Vietnam. Secretary of Defense Caspar Weinberger, in a 28 November 1984 speech, announced a six-point doctrine stating that (1) U.S. forces would only be committed on behalf of a "vital national interest," (2) troops would be committed only with the "clear intention of winning," (3) political and military objectives must be clearly defined in advance, (4) the relationship between objectives and forces committed must be "continually reassessed and readjusted if necessary," (5) troop commitments must be made with the assurance of support from Congress and the people, and (6) commitment of troops should only be a last resort. Secretary of State George Shultz adamantly opposed Weinberger's policy, believing that it applied the wrong lessons from Vietnam and threatened to prevent U.S. military power from combating terrorism. Another critic sarcastically called it "The Capgun Doctrine."

BIBLIOGRAPHY

SHULTZ, GEORGE P. *Turmoil and Triumph: My Years as Secretary of State.* 1993.

WEINBERGER, CASPAR. *Fighting for Peace: Seven Critical Years in the Pentagon.* 1990.

STANLEY I. KUTLER

Westmoreland–CBS Libel Suit.

William Westmoreland's libel suit against the Columbia Broadcasting System (CBS) resulted from a documentary aired on the network on 23 January 1982. The program charged that in 1967, prior to the Tet Offensive, Gen. William C. Westmoreland had directed a conspiracy to underreport the strength of North Vietnamese and Viet Cong forces. Westmoreland sued CBS for libel, and although the case went to trial, a settlement was reached before the jury began deliberations. CBS issued a statement that said, in part, that the network "never intended to assert, and does not believe, that General Westmoreland was unpatriotic or disloyal in performing his duties as he saw them." Both Westmoreland and CBS stood by their charges and claimed victory.

BIBLIOGRAPHY

ADLER, RENATA. *Reckless Disregard.* 1986.

BREWIN, BOB, and SYDNEY SHAW. *Vietnam on Trial: Westmoreland vs. CBS.* 1987.

DAVIDSON, PHILLIP B. *Vietnam at War—The History: 1946–1975.* 1988.

KARNOW, STANLEY. *Vietnam: A History.* 1983.

ELLEN D. GOLDLUST

Westmoreland, William

(1914–), general, U.S. Army; commander, U.S. Military Assistance Command, Vietnam (COMUSMACV), 1964–1968; U.S. Army chief of staff, 1968–1972. William C. Westmoreland was first captain (in effect, commander of the Corps of Cadets) in the West Point class of 1936. Commissioned in the field artillery, Westmoreland served with distinction in World War II, commanding an artillery battalion during the North African campaign and serving as chief of staff of the 9th Division in the final assault against Germany.

After holding many of the most visible and important positions in the U.S. Army, Westmoreland became superintendent of the U.S. Military Academy at West Point in 1960. As superintendent, he impressed President Kennedy and Vice President Johnson with his abilities, and was subsequently selected to replace Gen. Paul Harkins as COMUS-MACV.

In Vietnam. Taking command in Vietnam in June 1964 after six months as Harkin's deputy, Westmoreland began to lay the groundwork for an expanded U.S. role in Vietnam. In 1965, when North Vietnamese regulars threatened to cut through the country in the Central Highlands, President Johnson, acting upon the advice of Westmoreland and the Joint Chiefs of Staff (JCS), increased the level of U.S. combat forces in South Vietnam to more than 100,000.

From 1965 to 1967 U.S. and Army of the Republic of Vietnam (ARVN) soldiers waged a war of attrition against Viet Cong and North Vietnamese forces. During this period, Westmoreland was instrumental in raising the level of U.S. forces committed to South Vietnam and in developing the military strategy for the ground war. He has been faulted for undue reliance on U.S. combat forces, for excessive use of helicopters, and for lack of attention to counterinsurgency. Westmoreland believed, however, that U.S. forces were necessary to counter the forces of the People's Army of Vietnam (PAVN); that the mobility provided by helicopters compensated for the limits on numbers of U.S. forces committed and the difficulties of terrain, especially in the Central Highlands; and that the

FACING THE PRESS. General Westmoreland points to map of Vietnam at a news briefing at the Pentagon, 1968. *National Archives*

counterinsurgency mission properly belonged to the ARVN.

Partly from worries over successes of U.S. and ARVN forces in the south, North Vietnam launched the Tet Offensive in 1968. Westmoreland's command, although taken by surprise, reacted quickly and wrought devastating losses on the attackers. Interpreting his success as an opportunity, and encouraged by the chairman of the JCS, Gen. Earle Wheeler, Westmoreland proposed a new strategy that called for operations outside South Vietnam and for the commitment of an additional 200,000 troops. Opposed to a further widening of the war and the economic costs that such an expansion would entail, President Johnson refused the military's recommendations and re-

called Westmoreland to be chief of staff of the U.S. Army.

As chief of staff, Westmoreland's major challenges dealt with the withdrawal of U.S. forces from Vietnam; restoring the army's readiness to function in other theaters (a capability that had dwindled during the war years); mitigating the army's racial tensions; bringing drug use in the army under control; and making the transition to a volunteer army—all in the climate of powerful antimilitary sentiment in U.S. politics and society. He was probably most successful at improving the army's readiness, and laying the foundation for his successors to solve the other problems.

Westmoreland retired in 1972 but remained a major figure in the debate over the Vietnam War. He vigorously defended his conduct of the war in his 1976 memoir, *A Soldier Reports,* and in public statements and appearances. In the mid 1980s he sued the Columbia Broadcasting System over a television program that alleged his participation in a conspiracy to manipulate estimates of the number of Viet Cong and North Vietnamese troops he faced. The suit was settled out of court, and both sides claimed victory.

Evaluation. Westmoreland has been called "the inevitable general" and his achievements before the Vietnam War were substantial. History will judge him, however, on the basis of that war. Westmoreland's strategy in the war was threefold: first, halt the losing trend of South Vietnamese forces by the end of 1965; second, conduct offensive operations to defeat major Viet Cong and PAVN units and restore pacification programs; and third, secure and destroy enemy base areas. Concurrently, he sought to modernize and improve the ARVN—important ingredients for what was later termed Vietnamization. Implicit in the defeat of enemy units and base areas was cutting logistic support of North Vietnam to the south, which Westmoreland intended to do when ground troops were available to operate against the Ho Chi Minh Trail in Laos and Cambodia.

Some critics charge that Westmoreland's strategy could never have prevailed in Vietnam without far higher troop levels than President Johnson was willing to provide, and that Westmoreland knew this. Westmoreland repeatedly asked for more combat units than the administration was willing to give, and he consistently predicted that the war would go on for a longer time. It is possible that Westmoreland thought that in time the constraints on troop levels would be removed.

Some of Westmoreland's problems in the Vietnam War resulted from a flawed articulation of his policies. The operational concept dubbed "search and destroy" was never explained clearly to the American people. Although Westmoreland envisioned operations that would search for enemy units, base areas, and logistic support services to destroy them, images of soldiers burning thatched huts translated for many Americans into a policy of destroying Vietnam itself. From 1964 to 1967, Westmoreland's press coverage was positive to mixed; following the Tet Offensive, it was almost uniformly negative. A forceful public speaker, Westmoreland persisted in giving press conferences, seeming to believe that if he could explain his policies in enough detail, reporters would understand and approve of them. While this may have worked early in the U.S. involvement, the media's later hostility toward him and toward the war made his courting of the press counterproductive. Some facets of Westmoreland's personality undoubtedly contributed to his problems with the press and the public. A courtly southern gentleman—handsome, ramrod erect, immaculate, and somewhat aloof—he often appeared at odds with the culture of the 1960s.

Whether Westmoreland's strategy could ever have won the war will never be known. Certainly victory would probably have required many things he did not have—more troops, more time, more political will, and reform of the ARVN, to name a few. Additionally, Westmoreland operated under constraints that U.S. commanders had not experienced in either World War II or Korea: he did not control the air war against North Vietnam, and he did not exercise command over the military forces of the allied nation. The Tet Offensive proved a military defeat for Viet Cong and PAVN forces, yet a psychological coup for them on the American home front. In the aftermath of Tet, as key policymakers and the press concluded that the war could not be won at acceptable costs, political support for the strategy that had become identified with Westmoreland crumbled, and negotiations and withdrawal became U.S. policy.

BIBLIOGRAPHY

DAVIDSON, PHILLIP B. *Vietnam at War: The History 1946–1975.* 1988.

HALBERSTAM, DAVID. *The Best and The Brightest.* 1972.

JOHNSON, LYNDON B. *The Vantage Point: Perspectives of the Presidency, 1963–1969.* 1971.

WESTMORELAND, WILLIAM C. *A Soldier Reports.* 1976.

K. E. HAMBURGER

Weyand, Frederick C. (1916–), general, U.S. Army; commander, U.S. Military Assistance Command, Vietnam (MACV), 1972–1973; U.S. Army chief of staff, 1974–1976. The last MACV commander, Gen. Frederick Weyand had previously commanded the 25th Infantry Division and the II Field Force in Vietnam before replacing Gen. Creighton Abrams in June 1972. Weyand supervised the final withdrawal of U.S. forces. In his last report, Weyand warned that "we will be faced with the difficult decision of U.S. reinvolvement" if the cease-fire broke down. He insisted that South Vietnam's future secu-

FREDERICK C. WEYAND. *National Archives*

rity depended entirely on "the continuation of adequate levels of U.S. military and economic assistance." President Ford sent him to assess South Vietnam's military needs in April 1975, but Weyand's recommendation for $722 million in emergency military aid went unheeded by Congress, and Saigon fell a few days later.

BIBLIOGRAPHY

CLARKE, JEFFREY J. *The United States Army in Vietnam, Advice and Support: The Final Years, 1965–1973.* 1988.
"New Star In Vietnam." *Newsweek,* 16 November 1970.
WEYAND, FRED C. "Vietnam Myths and American Military Realities." *Commander's Call* (July–August 1976).

GLEN GENDZEL

Wheeler, Earle G. (1908–1975), general, U.S. Army; chief of staff, 1962–1964; chairman, Joint Chiefs of Staff (JCS), 1964–1970. Gen. Earle "Bus" Wheeler was a lifelong staff officer with no combat experience when President Kennedy appointed him U.S. Army chief of staff in 1962. He shared Kennedy's enthusiasm for counterinsurgency warfare and Secretary of Defense Robert McNamara's penchant for statistics, having taught mathematics at West Point. For his support of the controversial Limited Test Ban Treaty, Wheeler was appointed chairman of the JCS in 1964. Soon he began promising success in Vietnam through further escalation. Wheeler personified the U.S. military's incomprehension of communist determination and resiliency in Vietnam. "The essence of the problem in Vietnam is military," he often asserted. A regular participant in President Johnson's Tuesday luncheons at which war strategy was planned, Wheeler never doubted that more troops and more bombing would prevail. He resented Johnson's reluctance to unleash the full might of U.S. power against North Vietnam—yet he also feared the war undermined U.S. security commitments around the globe. For that reason, Wheeler encouraged Gen. William Westmoreland's increased troop requests after the Tet Offensive in hopes of forcing Johnson to expand overall troop levels in 1968. With half a million U.S. troops already in Vietnam, Wheeler advised Johnson to call up the reserves and send another 200,000 men. Instead, Johnson withdrew from the 1968 presidential race; President Nixon began withdrawing U.S. troops from Vietnam a year later. After serving longer than any other JCS chairman, Wheeler retired in 1970.

BIBLIOGRAPHY

BARRETT, DAVID M. *Uncertain Warriors: Lyndon Johnson and His Vietnam Advisers.* 1993.
GELB, LESLIE H., with RICHARD K. BETTS. *The Irony of Vietnam: The System Worked.* 1979.
HALBERSTAM, DAVID. *The Best and the Brightest.* 1972.
KORB, LAWRENCE J. *The Joint Chiefs of Staff: The First Twenty-five Years.* 1976.
VAN DE MARK, BRIAN. *Into the Quagmire: Lyndon Johnson and the Escalation of the Vietnam War.* 1991.
WHEELER, EARLE G. "The Challenge Came in Vietnam." *Vital Speeches* 33 (15 December 1966).
WHEELER, EARLE G. "Vietnam." *Vital Speeches* 34 (1 August 1968).

GLEN GENDZEL

Williams, Samuel T. (1897–1984), lieutenant general, U.S. Army; commander, U.S. Military Assistance Advisory Group, Vietnam, 1955–1960. A strict disciplinarian known as "Hanging Sam," Williams was a veteran of both world wars and Korea. He continued the U.S. policy of training South Vietnamese troops to repel a Korea-style conventional invasion from the north. Williams dismissed the Viet Cong guerrilla threat and regarded their attacks as diversionary tactics. He cultivated close relations with President Diem while feuding constantly with Ambassador Elbridge Durbrow. Williams retired in 1960.

BIBLIOGRAPHY

ARNOLD, JAMES R. *The First Domino: Eisenhower, the Military, and America's Intervention in Vietnam.* 1991.

MEYER, HAROLD J. *Hanging Sam: A Military Biography of General Samuel T. Williams.* 1990.

SPECTOR, RONALD H. *The United States Army in Vietnam, Advice and Support: The Early Years, 1941–1960.* 1983.

GLEN GENDZEL

Wilson, Harold (1916–1995), British prime minister, 1964–1970. Wilson received numerous requests from the United States for military aid in Vietnam, but he refused them all. Although he never officially opposed the U.S. war effort, Wilson repeatedly criticized the U.S. bombing of North Vietnam and privately called for negotiations. He was central to the Operation SUNFLOWER negotiations in 1967, but his efforts to encourage Soviet prime minister Alexei Kosygin to pressure North Vietnam to negotiate failed when President Johnson adopted a tougher negotiating stance.

BIBLIOGRAPHY

KARNOW, STANLEY. *Vietnam: A History.* 1983.

WILSON, J. HAROLD. *A Personal Record: The Labour Government, 1964–1970.* 1971.

ELLEN BAKER

Winter Soldier Investigation. Sponsored by the Vietnam Veterans against the War, the Winter Soldier Investigation was a meeting intended to demonstrate the widespread incidence of war crimes and atrocities committed by U.S. troops in Vietnam. For three days, 31 January–2 February 1971, in a Detroit motel, more than one hundred veterans and sixteen civilians presented testimony about crimes they claimed to have committed or witnessed. Discussions were also held on such topics as racism and the effect of the war experience on soldiers. Although the media paid little attention to the investigation, Sen. Mark O. Hatfield (R-Oreg.) entered the testimony in the *Congressional Record* and urged that official hearings be held about the conduct of U.S. forces in Vietnam.

BIBLIOGRAPHY

LEWY, GUENTER. *America in Vietnam.* 1978.

VIETNAM VETERANS AGAINST THE WAR. *The Winter Soldier Investigation: An Inquiry into American War Crimes.* 1972.

JENNIFER FROST

Wisconsin Bombing. *See* University of Wisconsin Bombing.

Wise Men. The "wise men" was a nickname given to a group of elder statesmen who met periodically from 1965 to 1968 to advise President Lyndon Johnson. Drawing upon their vast collective experience in government and the military, Johnson relied upon the "wise men" for insightful analysis of the Vietnam situation and policy options.

The group variously included former secretary of state Dean Acheson, New York banker John McCloy, Clark Clifford, Ambassador Robert Murphy, U.N. Ambassador Arthur Goldberg, former undersecretary of State George Ball, former national security adviser McGeorge Bundy, former ambassador Henry Cabot Lodge, Supreme Court justice Abe Fortas, banker and former ambassador Douglas Dillon, Gen. Maxwell Taylor, former assistant secretary of defense Cyrus Vance, and retired generals Omar Bradley and Mathew Ridgway.

The "wise men" first met in July 1965 to consider Secretary of Defense Robert McNamara's proposal for escalation, including the deployment of forty-four U.S. combat battalions. They endorsed the escalation and Johnson's determination to make a stand against communism in Vietnam. The "wise men" met again in November 1967 and, with the exception of George Ball, continued to back Johnson's Vietnam policies.

But after the Tet Offensive of 1968, Clark Clifford, at the time secretary of Defense, sensed that many in the group had determined that the United States should prepare to disengage. Clifford recognized the "wise men's" influence with Johnson, and he convened a meeting for 25 March 1968. The group was briefed on the current military situation and the outlook for further escalation and issued their assessment the next day. With McGeorge Bundy as spokesman, the "wise men" told Johnson he "must begin to take steps to disengage." Only Fortas, Murphy, and Generals Taylor and Bradley dissented. The change of opinion from this gener-

WISE MEN. Left to right: George Ball, Dean Acheson, Dean Rusk, with Johnson and aides, 16 March 1968. *Lyndon Baines Johnson Library*

ally prowar group profoundly affected Johnson, as Clifford had hoped.

BIBLIOGRAPHY

Isaacson, Walter, and Evan Thomas. *The Wise Men: Six Friends and the World They Made.* 1988.
Karnow, Stanley. *Vietnam: A History.* 1991.
Olson, James, and Randy Roberts. *Where the Domino Fell.* 1991.

KELLY EVANS-PFEIFER

Women, U.S. Military. [*This entry includes five articles:*

Nurses
Women's Army Corps (WAC)
Women in the Air Force (WAF)
Women Accepted for Voluntary Emergency Service (WAVES)
Women Marines (WM)

Unlike Vietnamese women, American women who pursued a military career during the Vietnam War-era were segregated into separate women's branches of the U.S. armed forces. American women were excluded from combat, again unlike their Vietnamese counterparts, who served in a variety of military roles throughout the Vietnam conflict. Career opportunities for women in the U.S. military were therefore restricted to administrative fields and, particularly, nursing and health services; although large numbers of men served as nurses, the majority of U.S. military nurses during the Vietnam War were women.

Although American women were not conscripted, the elimination of the draft in 1973 paradoxically improved the position of women in the U.S. military. The personnel shortage caused by the end of the draft led the military to abolish separate women's service branches and expand career possibilities for women in the U.S. armed forces.]

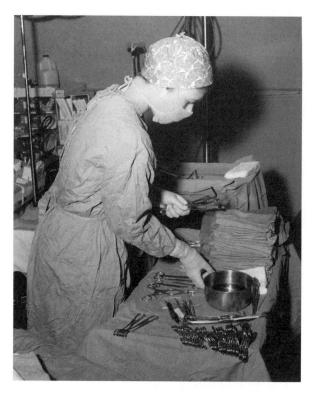

PREPPING FOR SURGERY. An operating room at Long Binh hospital, 1969. *National Archives*

Nurses

Most of the women who served in the U.S. military in Vietnam were military nurses. The department of defense estimates that 7,465 women served in the military in Vietnam, of whom 80 percent were in the army, air force, and navy nurse corps, with the vast majority (6,250) army nurses. Official records indicate that eight female and two male military nurses died from injury or illness in the Vietnam War; only one nurse, Sharon Lane, died as a result of hostile fire.

Unlike doctors, many of whom were drafted into the military, the vast majority of nurses were volunteers. Volunteers were necessary to meet the military's demand for nurses after the escalation of the Vietnam War. In 1963, the U.S. Army's nurse corps numbered only 2,928 nurses, but by 1965 the army began extensive recruiting of civilian volunteers. The nurses, who had to be at least twenty-one years old, were all commissioned officers and generally served one-year tours in Vietnam. Many served in Vietnam after being recruited into student nurse programs, whereby the army, air force, or navy paid for their final years of education in return for service. Before being assigned to Vietnam, army nurses

had to attend basic training for eight weeks, navy nurses were required to serve two years in the nurse corps, and air force nurses received flight training for two months. Despite these preparations, military nurses were generally inexperienced. Anna Mae Hayes, assistant chief of the army nurse corps, reported that 60 percent of the army nurses in Vietnam had less than two years of nursing experience, and 60 percent of these had less than six months.

In Vietnam, army nurses were stationed in hospitals throughout South Vietnam and often cared for North Vietnamese Army or Viet Cong prisoners of war (POWs) and Vietnamese civilians. Navy nurses were assigned to hospital ships off the coast, such as the USS *Repose* and USS *Sanctuary,* and to the Naval Support Activity unit in Da Nang. Air force nurses cared for patients on evacuation flights within and outside of the country and at casualty staging facilities. By the time of the Vietnam War, the military had developed medical evacuation ("medevac") techniques, using helicopters to evacuate casualties from the combat zone to medical installations at military bases that primarily handled battle casualties. During major actions, nurses and other medical personnel treated a steady flow of severely wounded soldiers. They worked long and grueling shifts that sometimes lasted forty-eight–seventy-two hours. Often, nurses were responsible for "triage"; that is, deciding which soldiers should be given medical attention first, which could wait, and which were beyond medical aid. These physical and emotional pressures led to exhaustion among nurses. As Juddy Marron wrote of her experience as a nurse in Vietnam, "It was a war zone. . . . There were days when the stress and strain and blood and guts almost had to equal . . . the frontlines."

Although nurses shared similar war experiences with their male nurse colleagues, they faced other difficulties as women. Nurses were expected to provide emotional comfort and care to their patients as well as medical treatment. Women experienced a great deal of sexual pressure from the men they encountered. Some men assumed that nurses were available for dating and sex, and nurse veterans reported incidents of rape as well. The sexual double standard existed in Vietnam as it did in the United States. Women who had sexual relationships often found their reputations slandered, which could reflect on all women in the military, reinforcing the long-held myth that women interested in military service had lower moral standards than did civilian women. Nurse veteran Lynda Van Devanter recalled a meeting, called by the chief nurse at the 71st Evacuation Hospital in Pleiku, to reprimand the nurses for their sexual behavior and curfew violations and to urge them to "act like ladies." Although not reflected in official records, nurse veterans report that a few nurses, overwhelmed by work, emotional, or sexual pressures, committed suicide in Vietnam.

After returning to the United States, some nurse veterans, like many Vietnam veterans, suffered from serious problems such as depression, anger, anxiety, recurring nightmares, and feelings of alienation, symptoms often diagnosed as Post-Traumatic Stress Disorder (PTSD). At first, women received no public recognition for their military service and were excluded from veterans organizations. The Veterans Administration (VA) did not extend support services to women and rarely publicized information about educational and financial benefits for women veterans. Women were ignored in Agent Orange studies, even though the health hazards of dioxin, such as cancer and birth defects, were considered greater for women.

In response, nurse veterans organized to bring more attention to the issues and problems they faced. In 1979, Van Devanter helped launch the Vietnam Veterans Association Women's Project and became the project's first spokeswoman. Extensive publicity about women veterans sparked congressional hearings in 1983 to investigate the VA for lack of services and outreach to women. Nurse veterans also commissioned and raised funds for a memorial to recognize the service and contributions of women in the military during the Vietnam War era. A bronze statue of three women and a wounded soldier, designed by Glenna Goodacre, was dedicated on Veteran's Day 1993 on the Mall in Washington, D.C.

BIBLIOGRAPHY

MARSHALL, KATHRYN. *In the Combat Zone: An Oral History of American Women in Vietnam, 1966–1975.* 1987.

NORMAN, ELIZABETH. *Women at War: The Story of Fifty Military Nurses Who Served in Vietnam.* 1990.

PALMER, LAURA. "The Nurses of Vietnam, Still Wounded." *New York Times Magazine,* 7 November 1993.

VAN DEVANTER, LYNDA, with CHRISTOPHER MORGAN. *Home before Morning: The Story of an Army Nurse in Vietnam.* 1983.

JENNIFER FROST

Women's Army Corps (WAC)

The Women's Army Corps (WAC) operated in Vietnam between 1964 and 1973. The WAC was formed during World War II "for the purpose of making available to the national defense the knowledge, skills, and special training of the women of the nation." Approximately 700 WACs served in Vietnam during the war, reaching a peak strength of 20 officers and 139 enlisted women in January 1970. A sizable WAC attachment was also in Japan to accommodate the needs of hospitals for trained medical specialists. Many of the enlisted women in Vietnam were nineteen to twenty-three years of age, with little more than a year of service with the WAC. Many WACs received service awards for their contributions to the war effort; Sheron L. Green received a Purple Heart. No WACs died in the Vietnam War.

WAC advisers were initially brought to Vietnam to aid the government of South Vietnam with the planning and development of the Women's Armed Forces Corps (WAFC). WACs advised the WAFC on organization, recruitment, training, and administration. For additional training, WAFC officer candidates traveled to the United States and attended courses at the WAC school. WAC officers and enlisted women later were assigned to clerical and administrative positions in the headquarters of the Military Assistance Command, Vietnam (MACV), in Saigon; in the headquarters of the U.S. Army, Vietnam, at Tan Son Nhut Air Base; and in the U.S. Army Central Support Command at Qui Nhon and Cam Ranh Bay. Enlisted women primarily worked as stenographers and clerk-typists, while officers held jobs in such areas as personnel, public information, logistics, and military justice.

Although WAC personnel, as well as members of the other separate women's units in the military, remained generally in desk jobs while serving in Vietnam, the war set in motion forces that helped transform women's military roles during the 1970s. The demands of mobilization created new opportunities for women in the U.S. military worldwide. Furthermore, the abolition of the draft in 1973, largely as a result of antiwar sentiment, forced the services to utilize more effectively the skills of volunteer servicewomen. These dynamics were augmented by the growing women's movement and federal court rulings barring sexual discrimination in the military. In the 1970s, women soldiers gained increased opportunities in education and training and in the field. The proportional numbers of women in the military increased from less than 2 percent in 1972 to over 8 percent by 1980. As part of this transformation, the separate women units of the U.S. services, including the WAC, were disbanded during the 1970s.

BIBLIOGRAPHY

HOLM, JEANNE. *Women in the Military: An Unfinished Revolution.* 1982.

MORDEN, BETTIEN J. *The Women's Army Corps, 1945–1978.* 1990.

JENNIFER FROST AND ADAM LAND

Women in the Air Force (WAF)

More than five hundred Women in the Air Force (WAFs) served in Southeast Asia between 1967 and 1973. Members of this separate unit of the U.S. Air Force provided administrative and technical support for the Seventh Air Force (Vietnam) and the Thirteenth Air Force (Thailand). They also served with the Military Assistance Command, Vietnam (MACV) and the corresponding operational hub in Thailand (MACTHAI). Enlisted WAFs generally performed secretarial and clerical work while officers performed technical duties in fields such as communications, logistics, and information service. Air force officials' concern over the propriety of women's presence in a combat area initially kept members of the unit out of Southeast Asia even after escalation in 1965. Demands on personnel resulting from mobilization, however, as well as directives from the Department of Defense overcame initial reluctance. Resistance to women's presence, however, persisted in the Seventh Air Force, which until 1970 maintained a ceiling on the number of WAF officers allowed and restricted enlisted assignments exclusively to Saigon. A new Seventh Air Force command relaxed restrictions on WAF postings in the latter stages of the war. As part of the changing gender composition of the U.S. military in the post–Vietnam War era, the WAF was fully incorporated into the U.S. Air Force in 1976.

BIBLIOGRAPHY

HOLM, JEANNE. *Women in the Military: An Unfinished Revolution.* 1982.

ADAM LAND

Women Accepted for Voluntary Emergency Service (WAVES)

Nine WAVES served in Vietnam during the war, all officers; no uncommissioned WAVES served in Vietnam. Most were assigned to the Military Assistance Command, Vietnam (MACV), in Saigon with either the commander of naval forces or the Communications Information Center. A few WAVES also served at Cam Ranh Bay with the Naval Support Activity unit. From 1972 to 1973, Commander Elizabeth Barrett served as ranking officer for 450 enlisted men in the naval advisory group in Saigon. High-ranking naval officers, including the woman director of the WAVES, had serious reservations about the appropriateness of the living and working environment in Vietnam for women. Their objections erected obstacles for WAVES eager to volunteer for service in Vietnam and kept the number of WAVES present in Southeast Asia to a minimum. The separate support structure for servicewomen in the U.S. Navy was disbanded in 1972.

BIBLIOGRAPHY

EBBERT, JEAN, and MARIE-BETH HALL. *Crossed Currents: Navy Women from WWI to Tailhook.* 1993.

ADAM LAND

Women Marines (WM)

A total of thirty-six Women Marines (WMs) served in Vietnam between 1967 and 1973. The WM contingent usually consisted of a few officers and six to ten enlisted women serving with the Military Assistance Command, Vietnam (MACV), in Saigon. WMs served specifically in the Marine Corps personnel section on the staff of the Commander of Naval Forces, which provided administrative support for U.S. Marines in Vietnam. Resistance to a WM presence in Vietnam by marine officers initially prevented members of the unit from being assigned to Vietnam, but new policies in 1967 brought WMs assignments at MACV. In 1966, the Marine Corps' efforts to free male marines for service in Vietnam led to the stationing of WMs in bases in the western Pacific, including the Marine Air Corps Station in Iwakuni, Japan, and Camp Butler and the Air Station Futema in Okinawa. The position of Director of Women Marines was abolished in 1977 as the number of women in the U.S. Marines rapidly expanded.

BIBLIOGRAPHY

STREMLOW, MARY V. *A History of Women Marines, 1946–1977.* 1986.

ADAM LAND

Women, Vietnamese.

South Vietnamese women played a minimal role in the war. Madame Ngo Dinh Nhu organized the Women's Solidarity

Movement, which was used to spy for Diem's government and drum up public support for official policy, and whose younger members dressed as female militia, mainly for show. Others, particularly Catholics and the middle class, supported the South Vietnamese government in more passive ways, as secretaries, maids, and servants for the government of Vietnam and the Americans. In contrast, women in North Vietnam and those fighting for the communist cause in South Vietnam took a very active role in the conflict, filling diverse roles from those of farmers to nurses to guerrilla fighters. And unofficially, many women on both sides of the Vietnam War worked as prostitutes.

Women in what is now Vietnam have participated in wars for independence from the earliest years, building upon traditional legends of heroines such as the Trung sisters, who fought in a war against China nearly 2,000 years ago. Ho Chi Minh, leader of the Viet Minh's nationalist movement against the French in the 1950s, emphasized women's equality with men. In a land where polygamy and Confucian submission of women was traditional, his promise of equality and an end to polygamy found ready acceptance among women, despite the strong, countervailing neo-Confucian legacy. The communist-supported Viet Minh organized The Women's Unions to spread propaganda and organize support for the Indochina War. Women served with the Viet Minh during the French war, with the Viet Cong guerrillas in the South during the Vietnam War, and virtually all North Vietnamese women were extensively involved in resistance to the southern government and the Americans on some level. Women eagerly worked to end foreign exploitation of their country, for as laborers they had suffered colonial oppression, just as had the men. In an effort to mobilize the entire population of North Vietnam, Ho Chi Minh announced "three responsibilities" for women to adhere to: care for their families; take charge of production, taking the place of men in the fields and factories; and be prepared to fight if necessary—with a "rifle on one shoulder, a hoe on the other." They were also to be prepared to sacrifice husbands and sons to the cause, bearing children for the war and keeping an extra kilo of rice in reserve, so that fighters would never go hungry. Women's Unions helped stir up anger against the United States and South Vietnam, but the U.S. bombing was responsible for recruiting most to the cause.

Since no one could escape the ravages of war, some younger women actually joined the fighting forces, marching with men to form artillery battalions on the Ho Chi Minh Trail. They acted as nurses and served in repair crews, keeping the intermeshing trails open and repairing bomb damage. Even Buddhist nuns were active in the war effort.

The intensive bombing of the North brought women other duties. Many learned to fire the antiaircraft weapons that defended Hanoi from U.S. bombers. Other women took groups of children to live in the countryside to escape the bombings, continuing their education, instructing them in the principles of revolution, acting as surrogate mothers, and nursing and comforting those who had lost parents or siblings.

In the South, women actively served with the Viet Cong, in some places accounting for one-third of its membership. They joined the fight in the South to protest Ngo Dinh Diem's harsh policies

NGUYEN KIM OANH. A North Vietnamese traffic regulator at a frequently bombed ferry in Nghe An province. *Ngô Vĩnh Long*

MILITIA. South Vietnamese women are sworn in as volunteer soldiers at a graduation ceremony at a military training center for women after completing a month-long course, Saigon, 1962. *National Archives*

and suppression of traditional religious beliefs. Some achieved renown organizing the National Liberation Front (NLF) and serving in the Provisional Revolutionary Government (PRG).

Women were most useful as couriers and liaisons because they could go from one area to another under the guise of peasants bringing goods to market and were less suspect than men. They transported weapons, food, and clothing, and were especially active in the tunnel area of Cu Chi, where they served as nurses, entertainers, cooks, and construction workers, and carried weapons and information to and from Saigon. They operated as spies in the cities, infiltrating the government as well as U.S. bases and brothels. Women also fought, forming units of so-called long-haired warriors, who bore arms against the Army of the Republic of Vietnam (ARVN) and U.S. forces, as regular combatants or snipers. When captured, they suffered torture and imprisonment as did the men.

Postwar Vietnam has been slow to acknowledge the role of its women warriors, although the Women's Union, organized in the 1930s and active today in health, education, family planning, and propaganda is building museums to honor the heroines of the past. Streets in Ho Chi Minh City bear female heroines' names: Vo Thi Sau, a martyr of the French war, and Nguyen Thi Minh Khai, the wife of Ho Chi Minh from 1940 to 1941, when she was executed by the French. Statues of heroic women dot the cities and countryside. However, traditional roles for women never ceased, and women must manage home and family, although most also work as farmers, saleswomen, traders, or professionals. Few have achieved fame in politics, and they are no longer active in the military. There is a long tradition of legendary Vietnamese women warriors and heroines, but the active participation of women in the military struggles of twentieth-century Vietnam came from ideological persuasion and the necessity of resistance. It was the result of the mobilization of an entire population in a conflict pursued along the lines of a communist model, but reflective of Vietnam's unique heritage.

[*See also* Prostitution.]

BIBLIOGRAPHY

EISEN, ARLENE. *Women of Vietnam.* 1978.
FITZGERALD, FRANCES. *Fire in the Lake: The Vietnamese and the Americans in Vietnam.* 1972.
MAI THI TU and LE THI NHAM TUYET. *Women of Vietnam.* 1978.
MANGOLD, TOM, and JOHN PENNYCATE. *The Tunnels of Cu Chi.* 1986.
Mountain Trail: Tales of Women Fighting with the Viet Cong. 1970.
TRUONG NHU TANG. *A Viet Cong Memoir.* 1985.
TÉTRAULT, MARY ANN. "Vietnam," in M. A. Tétrault, ed. *Women and Revolution in Africa, Asia, and the New World.* 1994.

SANDRA C. TAYLOR

Xuan Loc. South Vietnamese city, located 60 kilometers (37 miles) northeast of Saigon. The site of a South Vietnamese command center vital for protecting the air base at Bien Hoa, Xuan Loc was attacked on 9 April 1975 by overwhelming numbers of North Vietnamese Army (NVA) troops and artillery. Army of the Republic of Vietnam (ARVN) forces fought back in their last effective action, aided by air support from the South Vietnamese air force that included the dropping of cluster bombs. Although the defenders inflicted severe casualties on the NVA troops, the ARVN forces were forced to withdraw on 22 April. One week later, on 30 April 1975, the Republic of Vietnam officially surrendered.

BIBLIOGRAPHY

DAVIDSON, PHILLIP B. *Vietnam at War—The History: 1946–1975.* 1988.
KARNOW, STANLEY. *Vietnam: A History.* 1983.

ELLEN D. GOLDLUST

Xuan Thuy (1912–1985), foreign minister, Democratic Republic of Vietnam (DRV), 1963–1965; chief delegate, Paris peace talks, 1968–1970. The son of a Confucian scholar, Xuan Thuy was arrested by the French colonial police for nationalist activity while still a teenager. He joined the Indochina Communist party in 1938 and spent World War II in prison. Upon his release in 1945, Thuy edited *Cuu Quoc,* the official Viet Minh newspaper, and he traveled widely in Europe during the Indochina War to publicize the nationalist cause. Because he was considered too pro-Soviet, Thuy never joined the politburo, and he served only briefly as foreign minister. But he resurfaced as the DRV's chief delegate to the Paris peace talks in 1968. Thuy shared the conviction of other communist leaders that they had been duped in earlier negotiations with western powers, so he stonewalled the peace talks with non-negotiable demands that the U.S. withdraw immediately and that President Thieu resign. By 1970, the real negotiations were taking place in secret between Le Duc Tho and Henry Kissinger, while Thuy issued unyielding propaganda for public consumption. Averell Harriman, a veteran of diplomatic negotiations with Thuy, described him as "a dreadful fellow to face across the table day after day."

BIBLIOGRAPHY

DILLARD, WALTER SCOTT. *Sixty Days to Peace.* 1982.
GOODMAN, ALLAN E. *The Lost Peace: America's Search for a Negotiated Settlement of the Vietnam War.* 1978.
KISSINGER, HENRY. *White House Years.* 1979.
PIKE, DOUGLAS. *History of Vietnamese Communism, 1925–1976.* 1978.
Who's Who in North Vietnam. 1969.
"Xuan Thuy, Hanoi's Negotiator at Paris Peace Talks, Dies at 73." *New York Times,* 21 June 1985.

GLEN GENDZEL

Yankee Station. An area of the South China Sea located in international waters off the coast of North Vietnam, "Yankee Station" was an operations area for Task Force 77, an aircraft carrier strike group of the U.S. Navy's Seventh Fleet. From this staging point, the navy launched air operations against North Vietnam. For strikes over Cambodia, Laos, and South Vietnam, Task Force 77 carriers operated at "Dixie Station," southeast of Cam Ranh Bay.

BIBLIOGRAPHY

MERSKY, PETER B., and NORMAN POLMAR. *The Naval Air War in Vietnam.* 1981.
NICHOLS, JOHN B., and BARRETT TILLMAN. *On Yankee Station: The Naval Air War over Vietnam* 1988.

PAUL M. TAILLON

ZHOU ENLAI. 29 April 1954. *National Archives*

Zhou Enlai (1898–1976), premier, People's Republic of China, 1949–1976. At the 1954 Geneva Conference, Zhou broke the deadlock between the French and the Viet Minh and successfully brokered a compromise that resulted in the partition of Vietnam. Although Zhou and Ho Chi Minh had reached a prior agreement on the compromise, some in the Viet Minh believed Zhou had negated their battlefield victory. "He has double-crossed us," Pham Van Dong, the head of the Viet Minh delegation, privately complained. But the Viet Minh could not afford to alienate its ally. When hostilities resumed in Vietnam, Zhou supported the Vietnamese communists with substantial military aid in addition to political and economic support, although he opposed any coordinated action with the Soviet Union. When Zhou met Henry Kissinger in 1971 and President Nixon the next year, he insisted that U.S. troops had to be withdrawn from Vietnam. Despite the assistance they received from the People's Republic of China (PRC), North Vietnam's leaders, ever wary of the Chinese, believed that the Sino-American rapprochement would be at their ex-

pense. Zhou died before the deterioration of relations between the PRC and Vietnam culminated in their border war of 1979. Since then, the Vietnamese have often publicly complained about Zhou's 1954 role.

BIBLIOGRAPHY

HAN NIANLONG. *Diplomacy of Contemporary China.* 1990.
KEITH, RONALD C. *The Diplomacy of Zhou Enlai.* 1989.

HAN TIE

Zippo Squads. "Zippo squads" was a slang term for U.S. troops on search-and-destroy missions who searched villages suspected of Viet Cong guerrilla activity. After searching for hidden weapons or other incriminating evidence, the zippo squads set fire to the villagers' thatch huts with their government-issue Zippo lighters or with flamethrowers. In August 1965, CBS News filmed and broadcast a zippo squad in action, inciting much negative public reaction to the search-and-destroy tactic.

BIBLIOGRAPHY

OLSON, JAMES, and RANDY ROBERTS. *Where the Domino Fell.* 1991.

KELLY EVANS-PFEIFER

Zumwalt, Elmo R., Jr. (1920–), admiral, U.S. Navy; U.S. Navy commander, Vietnam, 1968–1970; chief of naval operations, 1970–1974. "Bud" Zumwalt commanded the "brown water navy" of small river boats that patrolled the Mekong Delta and coastal areas of South Vietnam. He planned and executed Operation SEALORDS, which cut riverine supply lines from Cambodia to the Viet Cong guerrillas, and he ordered heavy spraying of Agent Orange defoliant over the Mekong Delta to deprive guerrillas of cover. Chosen ahead of thirty-three senior admirals to be chief of naval operations in 1970, Zumwalt advocated U.S. withdrawal from Vietnam to meet the rising challenge of Soviet sea power. But he sternly criticized the Paris peace accords for abandoning a U.S. ally. "There are at least two words no one can use to characterize the outcome of that two-faced policy," he said. "One is 'peace.' The other is 'honor.' " In 1988, Zumwalt's son died of cancer possibly linked to Agent Orange exposure in Vietnam.

BIBLIOGRAPHY

MAROLDA, EDWARD J., and G. WESLEY PRYCE. *A Short History of the United States Navy and the Southeast Asian Conflict, 1950–1975.* 1984.

ZUMWALT, ELMO R., JR. *On Watch: A Memoir.* 1976.

ZUMWALT, ELMO R., JR. "The War is Over." *New York Times,* 7 February 1994.

ZUMWALT, ELMO R., JR., and ELMO ZUMWALT III. "Agent Orange and the Anguish of an American Family." *New York Times Magazine,* 24 August 1986.

ZUMWALT, ELMO R., JR., and ELMO ZUMWALT III. *My Father, My Son.* 1987.

GLEN GENDZEL

Bibliographic Guide

The already vast body of literature on the Vietnam War continues to grow, and the improvement of relations between the United States and Vietnam can only aid in its expansion. This bibliographic guide is intended merely to point out selected further readings in English on significant topics addressed in the *Encyclopedia of the Vietnam War* and is by no means an exhaustive listing.

Vietnam. Among English-language general histories of Vietnam, Joseph Buttinger's works are perhaps the best available. Most notable is his classic three-volume *The Smaller Dragon: A Political History of Vietnam* (1958), written well before Vietnam became a household word in the United States. Buttinger's also-useful other works include his two-volume *Vietnam: A Dragon Embattled* (1967), *Vietnam: A Political History* (1968), and *Vietnam: The Dragon Defiant: A Short History of Vietnam* (1972).

Vietnam's early history is both ethnographically and politically complex, traditionally dominated by Chinese intervention and colonial rule but also influenced by seafaring South Asian groups. Keith Weller Taylor, *The Birth of Vietnam* (1983), details the origins and early history of the Vietnamese from the third century BC to the tenth century. Georges Coedès' *The Making of Southeast Asia* (1967) and *The Indianized States of Southeast Asia* (1968) are also useful, the later clarifying the history of Vietnam's Cham ethnic minority. Useful reference works include Danny J. Whitfield, *Historical and Cultural Dictionary of Vietnam* (1976), and William J. Duiker, *Historical Dictionary of Vietnam* (1989).

Significant texts covering early French colonialism in Southeast Asia include John Cady, *The Roots of French Imperialism in Asia* (1954); Thomas E. Ennis, *French Policy and Developments in Indochina* (1956); and Milton E. Osborne, *The French Presence in Cochinchina and Cambodia: Rule and Response (1859–1905)* (1969). Ngô Viñh Long's *Before the Revolution: The Vietnamese Peasants Under the French* (1991) is also illuminating, as is his *Vietnamese Women in Society and Revolution* (1974). The era of French imperialism in Indochina also saw the growth of Vietnamese nationalism and the rise of communism as the predominant anticolonialist movement in Vietnam; important texts include John T. McAlister, *Vietnam: The Origins of Revolution* (1969), and, with Paul Mus, *The Vietnamese and Their Revolution* (1970); David G. Marr, *Vietnamese Anticolonialism, 1885–1925* (1971) and *Vietnamese Tradition on Trial, 1920–1945* (1981); William J. Duiker, *The Rise of Nationalism in Vietnam, 1900–1941* (1976); Douglas Pike, *History of Vietnamese Communism* (1978); and Huynh Kim Khanh, *Vietnamese Communism, 1925–1945* (1982).

The Indochina War. Sparked by the 1946 French bombardment of Haiphong, the war of Vietnamese independence against French colonial rule has been extensively covered. Key works include Bernard Fall, *Street without Joy* (1989), first published in 1961; Edgar O'Ballance,

649

The Indo-China War, 1945–1954: A Study in Guerrilla Warfare (1964); Ellen Hammer, *The Struggle for Indochina, 1940–1955* (1966); and Lucien Bodard, *The Quicksand War: Prelude to Vietnam* (1967). McAlister, *Vietnam,* noted above, focuses on the August Revolution and the outbreak of the war, while Peter M. Dunn, *The First Vietnam War* (1985) provides a rare look at the 1945 occupation of southern Vietnam, and attempts to suppress the local Viet Minh, by British forces sent in to disarm the Japanese.

Among the works covering the United States' early involvement in Vietnam is Archimedes L. A. Patti's *Why Vietnam? Prelude to America's Albatross* (1980), written by one of the OSS agents who met with Ho Chi Minh during World War II. Other texts useful to understanding the United States' policies during the the Indochina War, including its commitments to France, include Ronald E. Irving, *The First Indochina War: French and American Policy, 1945–1954* (1975); Robert M. Blum, *Drawing the Line: The Origins of the American Containment Policy in East Asia* (1982); Ronald H. Spector, *Advice and Support: The Early Years, 1941–1960* (1983); Gary R. Hess, *The United States' Emergence as a Southeast Asia Power, 1940–1950* (1987); Andrew J. Rotter, *The Path to Vietnam: Origins of the American Commitment to Southeast Asia* (1987); and Lloyd C. Gardner, *Approaching Vietnam: From World War II through Dienbienphu* (1988).

Dien Bien Phu and Geneva. The climactic battle of the Indochina War and the negotiations that put an end to it are intertwined in history. The battle itself has been covered by its victor, Vo Nguyen Giap, in his *Dien Bien Phu* (1962), while an alternate account is presented in *The Battle of Dienbienphu* (1965), by Jules Roy, a senior French air force officer who served in Indochina. The most scholarly work on the battle is Bernard Fall's *Hell in a Very Small Place: The Siege of Dien Bien Phu* (1966), while Melanie Billings-Yun, *Decision against War: Eisenhower and Dien Bien Phu, 1954* (1988), gives insight into the U.S. refusal to intervene militarily. The battle has also been placed in its wider context, including its impact on the Geneva negotiations, in such works as Melvin Gurtov, *The First Vietnam Crisis: Chinese Communist Strategy and United States Involvement, 1953–1954* (1967); Philippe Devillers and Jean Lacouture, *End of a War: Indochina 1954* (1969); and Denise Artaud and Lawrence Kaplan, eds., *Dienbienphu: The Atlantic Alliance and the Defense of Southeast Asia* (1989). Other works that focus on the negotiations themselves include Robert F. Randle, *Geneva, 1954: The Settlement of the Indochinese War* (1969) and James Cable, *The Geneva Conference of 1954 on Indochina* (1986).

The Vietnam War. The most important published documentary source for the Vietnam War is perhaps the *The Pentagon Papers* (1971), not least for its historical significance. Among the most important general histories of the Vietnam War are George C. Herring, *America's Longest War: The United States and Vietnam, 1950–1975* (1986), which concentrates on U.S. strategy and policy during the war. *Vietnam: A History* (1991), written by journalist and old Indochina hand Stanley Karnow and first published in 1983 to accompany the PBS special of the same name, is also important. Another significant work is Frances FitzGerald, *Fire in the Lake: The Vietnamese and the Americans in Vietnam* (1972); timely, lauded, and influential during the war, the book has been criticized in later years for its sometimes oversimplified portrayals of both the U.S. and the communists. The war as seen by the North Vietnamese and the National Liberation Front is depicted by William J. Duiker, *The Communist Road to Power in Vietnam* (1981). Other useful works include James Pinckney Harrison, *The Endless War: Fifty Years of War In Vietnam* (1982); William S. Turley, *The Second Indochina War: A Political and Military History* (1986); Gary R. Hess, *Vietnam and the United States: Origins and Legacy of War* (1990). Both Gabriel Kolko's *Anatomy of a War: Vietnam, the United States, and the Modern Historical Experience* (1985) and Marilyn B. Young's *The Vietnam Wars 1945–1990* (1991) are strong indictments of U.S. intervention. Works that place the Vietnam War into a broader international context include Ralph B. Smith, *An International History of the Vietnam War* (1983), and Daniel S. Papp, *Vietnam: The View from Moscow, Peking, Washington* (1981).

The event that propelled the United States into the war in Vietnam, the Gulf of Tonkin incident, also prompted several books, among them Joseph Goulden, *Truth is the First Casualty: The Gulf of Tonkin Affair—Illusion and Reality* (1969); John Galloway, *The Gulf of Tonkin Incident* (1970); Anthony Austin, *The President's War* (1971); and Eugene Windchey, *Tonkin Gulf* (1971). U.S. escalation in the war is covered in George McT. Kahin, *Intervention: How America Became Involved in Vietnam* (1986). Other significant works on this period include Robert Scigliano, *South Vietnam: Nation under Stress* (1963); Bernard Fall, *Viet-nam Witness* (1966) and *The Two Viet-nams: A Political and Military Analysis* (1967); Robert Shaplen, *The Lost Revolution: The United States in Vietnam, 1946–1966* (1966); Chester A. Bain, *Vietnam: The Roots of Conflict* (1967); Jean Lacouture, *Vietnam: Between Two Truces* (1966); Leslie Gelb and Richard Betts, *The Irony of Vietnam: The System Worked* (1978); and Larry Berman, *Planning a Tragedy: The Americanization of the War in Vietnam* (1982).

Strategy and Tactics. Critics of U.S. strategy in the Vietnam War often divide over the nature of the war, debating whether it was primarily a conventional war or an insurgency. The most influential strategical examination of the war, Harry G. Summers Jr.'s *On Strategy: A Critical Analysis of the Vietnam War* (1982), holds the former, contending that the United States could have triumphed through a more effective application of conventional military force. Andrew F. Krepinevich Jr., in *The Army and Vietnam* (1986), holds the latter, maintaining that by neglecting pacification in favor of conventional operations, the U.S. effort doomed itself to failure.

Other significant works include Dave Richard Palmer, *Summons of the Trumpet: A History of the Vietnam War from a Military Man's Viewpoint* (1978); Allan R. Millett, ed., *A Short History of the Vietnam War* (1978); Timothy J. Lomperis, *The War Everybody Lost—and Won* (1984); Bruce Palmer Jr., *The 25-Year War: America's Military Role in Vietnam* (1984); Thomas D. Boettcher, *Vietnam: The Valor and the Sorrow* (1985); Shelby Stanton, *The Rise and Fall of an American Army: U.S. Ground Forces in Vietnam, 1946–1975* (1985); Thomas C. Thayer, *War without Fronts: The American Experience in Vietnam* (1985); Norman B. Hannah, *The Key to Failure: Laos and the Vietnam War* (1987); and Phillip B. Davidson, *Vietnam at War: The History, 1946–1975* (1988). Particularly notable is Douglas Kinnard's *The War Managers* (1977), a survey of more than one hundred generals who served in Vietnam. Jeffrey J. Clarke, *Advice and Support: The Final Years, 1965–1973* (1988), covers the U.S. advisory effort during the war. An invaluable resource is Shelby Stanton, *Vietnam Order of Battle* (1981), which details the units of the U.S. Army in Vietnam.

Works covering communist strategies and tactics include Vo Nguyen Giap, *People's War, People's Army* (1962) and *Big Victory, Big Task* (1967); George K. Tanham, *Communist Revolutionary Warfare* (1967); Patrick J. McGarvey, ed., *Visions of Victory: Selected Vietnamese Communist Military Writings 1965–1968* (1969); Jon M. Van Dyke, *North Vietnam's Strategy for Survival* (1972); the official history issued by the Socialist Republic of Vietnam, *Vietnam: The Anti-U.S. Resistance for National Salvation 1954–1975: Military History* (1980); Tran Van Tra, *Vietnam: History of the Bulwark B2 Theater* (1982); Duiker, *The Communist Road to Power*, previously cited; Douglas Pike, *Viet Cong: National Liberation Front of South Vietnam* (1986) and *PAVN: People's Army of Vietnam* (1986).

Among the works on specific battles and campaigns of the war are Robert W. Rogers, *Cedar Fall—Junction City: A Turning Point* (1974); Don Oberdorfer, *Tet!* (1971); Robert Pisor, *The End of the Line: The Siege of Khe Sanh* (1982); Ronald H. Spector, *After Tet: The Bloodiest Year in Vietnam* (1993); Nguyen Duy Hinh, *Lam Son 719* (1979); Ngo Quang Truong, *The Easter Offensive of 1972* (1980); and Dale Andradé, *Trial by Fire: The 1972 Easter Offensive, America's Last Vietnam Battle* (1995). Works on the most notorious atrocity committed by U.S. forces during the Vietnam War include Seymour M. Hersh, *My Lai 4* (1970) and Michael Bilton and Kevin Sim, *Four Hours in My Lai* (1992). The testimony of numerous U.S. veterans of atrocities is contained in Vetnam Veterans against the War, *The Winter Soldier Investigation* (1972), while Guenter Lewy, *America in Vietnam* (1978), is defends U.S. military actions against charges of atrocities. The war's extension into Vietnam's ostensibly neutral neighbors is covered in William Shawcross, *Sideshow: Kissinger, Nixon, and the Destruction of Cambodia* (1979) and Timothy N. Castle, *War in the Shadow of Vietnam: United States Military Aid to the Royal Lao Government, 1955–1975* (1993). The final years of the Republic of Vietnam are detailed in Stuart A. Herrington, *Peace with Honor? An American Reports on Vietnam, 1973–1975* (1983). Among the best works on the collapse of South Vietnam are William E. LeGro, *Vietnam from Cease-Fire To Capitulation* (1981) and Arnold R. Isaacs, *Without Honor: Defeat in Vietnam and Cambodia* (1983), while Van Tien Dung, *Our Great Spring Victory: An Account of the Liberation of South Vietnam* (1977), gives the communist account of the end of the Vietnam War.

The Ground War. Vast numbers of books detail the experiences of U.S. soldiers in Vietnam combat. Perhaps the best is the widely acclaimed work by Harold G. Moore and Joseph L. Galloway, *We Were Soldiers Once . . . And Young* (1992). John A. Cash, *Seven Firefights in Vietnam* (1993), is highly useful for understanding the vast diversity of combat that took place in Vietnam. Other significant books include Al Santoli, *Everything We Had: An Oral History of the Vietnam War by Thirty-Three American Soldiers Who Fought It* (1981); Shelby Stanton, *Green Berets at War: U.S. Army Special Forces in Southeast Asia, 1956–1975* (1985) and *Rangers at War: Combat Recon in Vietnam* (1992); J. D. Coleman, *Pleiku: The Dawn of Helicopter Warfare in Vietnam* (1988); Thomas J. Cutler, *Brown Water, Black Berets* (1988); Eric Hammel, *Khe Sanh: Siege in the Clouds An Oral History* (1989); R. D. Camp and Eric Hammel, *Lima-6: A Marine Company Commander in Vietnam* (1989); R. L. Schreadley, *From the Rivers to the Seas: The U.S. Navy in Vietnam* (1992); and Wallace Terry, *Bloods: An Oral History of the Vietnam War by Black Veterans* (1992). Works covering the Vietnam War experiences of women in the U.S. military include Lynda Van Devanter with Christopher Morgan, *Home Before Morning: The Story of an Army Nurse in Vietnam* (1983); Kathryn Marshall, *In the Combat Zone: An Oral History of American Women in Vietnam, 1966–1975* (1987); and Elizabeth Norman, *Women at War: The Story of Fifty Military Nurses Who Served in Vietnam* (1990). Ian McNeill, *The Team: Australian Army Advisers in Vietnam 1962–1972* (1984), covers the little-known role of a key U.S. ally, while Michael Lee Lanning and Dan Cragg, *Inside the VC and the NVA: The Real Story of North Vietnam's Armed Forces* (1992), give considerable insight into the experiences of communist soldiers.

Pacification. As noted above, debate continues over the importance of the "other war." Important works include George K. Tanham, *War without Guns: American Civilians in Rural Vietnam* (1966); British counterinsurgency expert Robert Thompson, *No Exit from Vietnam* (1969) and *Peace Is Not at Hand* (1974); Jeffrey Race, *War Comes to Long An: Revolutionary Conflict in a Vietnamese Province* (1971); Douglas S. Blaufarb, *The Counterinsurgency Era* (1977); Charles R. Anderson, *Vietnam: The Other War* (1982); Stuart A. Herrington (who from 1972–1973 served as an adviser to South Vietnamese territorials) *Silence was a Weapon: The Vietnam War in the Villages* (1982); Francis West, *The Village* (1985); Michael E. Peterson, *The Combined Action Platoons: The U.S. Marines' Other War in Vietnam* (1989); and Dale Andradé, *Ashes to Ashes: The Phoenix Program and the Vietnam War* (1990). Important works detailing the communist view of pacification are Truong Nhu Tang, with David Chanoff and Doan Van Toai, *A Viet Cong Memoir* (1985), and David Chanoff and Doan Van Toai, *Portrait of the Enemy* (1986). For works on the experiences of U.S. POWs, see *The Air War*, below.

The Air War. One of the most controversial aspects of U.S. military involvement in the Vietnam War has been the bombing campaign. Important critiques include Drew Middleton, *Air War: Vietnam* (1978); William W. Momyer (who commanded the U.S. Seventh Air Force during the Vietnam War), *Airpower in Three Wars (WW II, Korea, Vietnam)* (1978); James Clay Thompson, *Rolling Thunder: Understanding Policy and Program Failure* (1980); Mark Clodfelter, *The Limits of Air Power: The American Bombing of North Vietnam* (1989), which gives particular insight into the LINEBACKER II Christmas bombings of Hanoi and Haiphong; and Earl Tilford, *Setup: What the Air Force Did in Vietnam and Why* (1991). Official histories include Carl Berger, *The United States Air Force in Southeast Asia* (1977); John Schlight, *The United States Air Force in Southeast Asia: The War in South Vietnam—The Years of the Offensive, 1965–1968* (1988); and Jacob Van Staaveren, *The United States Air Force in Southeast Asia: Interdiction in Southern Laos, 1960–1968* (1993). Two complementary works that cover the air war from the viewpoint of the pilots are John B. Nichols and Barrett Tillman, *On Yankee Station: The Naval Air War Over Vietnam* (1987), and Ken Bell, *100 Missions North: A Fighter Pilot's Story of the Vietnam War* (1993), which focus respectively on the U.S. Navy's carrier war and the U.S. Air Force's war from bases in Thailand. Earl Tilford's *U.S. Air Force Search and Rescue in Southeast Asia* (1980) covers a little-known but crucial aspect of the air war. The majority of U.S. prisoners of war were pilots; an important text is John G. Hubbell et al., *P.O.W.: A Definitive History of the American Prisoner of War Experience in Vietnam, 1964–1973* (1976); while a moving personal memoir is James and Sybil Stockdale's *In Love and War* (1984).

The United States. [For the United States' early involvement in Vietnam, see above, *The Indochina War*. For U.S. intervention in Vietnam, see above, *The Vietnam War*. For the U.S. military role in Vietnam, see above, *Strategy and Tactics*.]

The Vietnam War caused social, political, and generational upheaval unprecedented in American history, and continues to affect the United States.

The Antiwar Movement. The communist precept that war is inherently political in nature was borne out by the Vietnam War's hugely divisive effect on U.S. society and politics. Contemporary accounts of the American antiwar movement include Samuel Lubell, *The Hidden Crisis in American Politics* (1971); William O'Neill, *Coming Apart: An Informal History of America in the 1960's* (1971); Thomas Powers, *The War at Home: Vietnam and the American People, 1964–1968* (1973); Alexander Kendrick, *The Wound Within: America in the Vietnam Years 1945–1974* (1974); Irwin Unger, *The Movement: A History of the American New Left, 1959–1972* (1974); and Sandy Vogelsanger, *The Long Dark Night of the Soul: The American Intellectual Left and the Vietnam War* (1974).

Among the most influential post-Vietnam works is *Chance and Circumstance: The Draft, the War and the Vietnam Generation* (1978) by Lawrence M. Baskir and William M. Strauss; however, the work's reliance on anecdotal sources has perpetuated within the literature several myths about the Vietnam War, particularly about the Vietnam-era draft program Project 100,000. Other notable post-war works include Charles Meconis, *With Clumsy Grace: The American Catholic Left, 1961–1977* (1979); Lawrence S. Wittner, *Rebels against War: The American Peace Movement, 1933–1983* (1984); Nancy Zaroulis and Gerald Sullivan, *Who Spoke Up? American*

Protest against the War in Vietnam, 1963–1975 (1984); Randall M. Fisher, *Rhetoric and American Democracy: Black Protest through Vietnam Dissent* (1985); Kathleen Turner, *Lyndon Johnson's Dual War: Vietnam and the Press* (1985); John Dumbrell, ed., *Vietnam and the Antiwar Movement* (1987); James Miller, *"Democracy is in the Streets:" From Port Huron to the Siege of Chicago* (1987); Melvin Small, *Johnson, Nixon and the Doves* (1988); Charles DeBenedetti and Charles Chatfield, *An American Ordeal: The Antiwar Movement of the Vietnam Era* (1990); Mitchell K. Hall, *Because of Their Faith: CALCAV and Religious Opposition to the Vietnam War* (1990); David W. Levy, *The Debate over Vietnam* (1991); Melvin Small and William D. Hoover, eds., *Give Peace a Chance: Exploring the Vietnam Antiwar Movement* (1992); Tom Wells, *The War Within: America's Battle over Vietnam* (1994); and Adam Garfinkle, *Telltale Hearts: The Origins and Impact of the Vietnam Antiwar Movement* (1995). For the impact of the media on the antiwar movement, see Gitlin, *The Whole World is Watching* (1980) and Small, *Covering Dissent* (1994), cited below.

The Media. The influence of the media upon the conduct and the outcome of the Vietnam War has been hotly debated. Important works on the subject include Peter Braestrup, *Big Story: How the American Press and TV Reported and Interpreted the Crisis of Tet in Vietnam and Washington* (1977); Todd Gitlin, *The Whole World is Watching: Mass Media in the Making and Unmaking of the New Left* (1980); Montague Kern, Patricia W. Levering, and Ralph B. Levering, *The Kennedy Crises: The Press, The Presidency, and Foreign Policy* (1983); Martin F. Herz and Leslie Rider, *The Prestige Press and the Christmas Bombing, 1972: Images and Reality in Vietnam* (1985); Daniel C. Hallin, *The "Uncensored War:" The Media and Vietnam* (1986); William M. Hammond, *The United States Army in Vietnam: Public Affairs, The Military and the Media, 1962–1968* (1988); Robert J. Donovan and Ray Scherer, *Unsilent Revolution: Television News and American Public Life* (1992); Clarence R. Wyatt, *Paper Soldiers: The American Press and the Vietnam War* (1993); and Melvin Small, *Covering Dissent: The Media and The Anti-Vietnam War Movement* (1994).

Memoirs, biographies, and accounts by and about Vietnam War journalists include Nick Mills, *Combat Photographer* (1984); Hugh Lunn, *Vietnam: A Reporter's War* (1986); Heinz-Dietrich Fischer, ed., *Outstanding International Press Reporting*, vol. 3, *Pulitzer Prize-Winning Articles in Foreign Correspondence, 1963–1977: From the Escalation of the Vietnam War to the East Asian Refugee Problems* (1986); Robert Shaplen, *Bitter Victory* (1986); Michael Herr, *Dispatches* (1987); David Halberstam, *The Making of a Quagmire: America and Vietnam During the Kennedy Era* (1988); Tim Page, *Page after Page: Memoirs of a War-Torn Photographer* (1988); Robert Sam Anson, *War News: A Young Reporter in Indochina* (1989); Haney Howell, *Roadrunners: Combat Journalists in Cambodia* (1989); Morley Safer, *Flashbacks: On Returning to Vietnam* (1990); Roberta Ostroff, *Fire in the Wind: The Life of Dickey Chapelle* (1992), who was killed in Vietnam while on patrol with her beloved U.S. Marines; Peter Arnett, *Live from the Battlefield: From Vietnam to Baghdad, 35 Years in the World's War Zones* (1993); and Liz Trotta, *Fighting for Air: In the Trenches with Television News* (1994). Collections of Vietnam War photography include Tim Page, *Tim Page's Nam* (1983); Joel D. Meyerson, *Images of a Lengthy War: The U.S. Army in Vietnam* (1986); Dick Durrance, *Where War Lives: A Photographic Essay from Vietnam* (1986); and Owen Andrews, C. Douglas Elliot, and Laurence L. Levin, *Vietnam: Images from Combat Photographers* (1991).

Biographies. As customary throughout history, important Vietnam War decision makers have used memoirs or other retrospective works to explain, celebrate, or defend their actions.

Among the most important works by U.S. decisionmakers are those by Undersecretary of the Air Force Townsend Hoopes, *The Limits of Intervention: An Inside Account of How the Johnson Policy of Escalation Was Reversed* (1969); President Lyndon Baines Johnson, *The Vantage Point: Perspectives on the Presidency, 1963–1969* (1971); General Edward G. Lansdale, *In the Midst of Wars* (1972); General Maxwell D. Taylor, *Swords and Plowshares* (1972); national security adviser W. W. Rostow, *The Diffusion of Power: An Essay in Recent History* (1972); General William C. Westmoreland, *A Soldier Reports* (1976); Secretary of State Henry Kissinger, *White House Years* (1978) and *Years of Upheaval* (1982); President Richard M. Nixon, *RN: The Memoirs of Richard Nixon* (1978); General J. Lawton Collins, *Lightning Joe: An Autobiography* (1979); Undersecretary of State George W. Ball, *The Past Has Another Pattern: Memoirs* (1982); Ambassador to Laos William H. Sullivan, *Obbligato: Notes on a Foreign Service Career* (1984); Ambassador to the Republic of Vietnam Frederick Nolting, *From Trust to Tragedy: The Political Memoirs of Frederick Nolting, Kennedy's Ambassador to Diem's Vietnam* (1988); CIA director William Colby, with James McCargar, *Lost Victory: A Firsthand Account of America's Sixteen-Year Involvement in Vietnam* (1989); Secretary of State Dean Rusk, as told to Richard Rusk, *As I Saw It* (1990); Secretary of Defense Clark Clifford, with Richard Holbrooke, *Counsel to the President: A Memoir* (1991); and Secretary of Defense Robert S. McNamara with Brian VanDeMark, *In Retrospect: The Tragedy and Lessons of Vietnam* (1995).

Useful interpretive accounts of major U.S. figures include Doris Kearns, *Lyndon Johnson and the American Dream* (1976); Herbert Y. Schandler, *The Unmaking of a President: Lyndon Johnson and Vietnam* (1977); Vaughan Bornet, *The Presidency of Lyndon Johnson* (1983); Neil Sheehan, *A Bright Shining Lie: John Paul Vann and America in Vietnam* (1988); Stephen E. Ambrose, *Nixon: Triumph of a Politician, 1962–1972* (1989); Larry Berman, *Lyndon Johnson's War* (1989); David Di Leo, *George Ball, Vietnam and the Rethinking of Containment* (1991); Lewis Sorley, *Thunderbolt: General Creighton Abrams and His Times* (1992); and Deborah Shapley, *Promise and Power: The Life and Times of Robert McNamara* (1993).

Memoirs by former officials of the Republic of Vietnam include those by Prime Minister Nguyen Cao Ky, *Twenty Years and Twenty Days* (1976); Defense Minister General Tran Van Don, *Our Endless War* (1978); head of the Joint General Staff General Cao Van Vien and Dong Van Khuyen, *Reflections on the Vietnam War* (1980); and Ambassador to the United States Bui Diem, with David Chanoff, *In the Jaws of History* (1987). Biographies of Ngo Dinh Diem include Dennis Warner, *The Last Confucian* (1963), and Anthony Bouscaren, *The Last of the Mandarins: Diem of Vietnam* (1965). A satiric contemporary portrait of Bao Dai can be found in S. J. Perelman, *Westward Ha!* (1948), in which the emperor is described as "a short, slippery-looking customer rather on the pudgy side and freshly dipped in Crisco."

Norodom Sihanouk and Wilfred Burchett, *My War with the CIA: The Memoirs of Prince Norodom Sihanouk* (1973), gives the views of wartime Cambodia's ruler.

Works on the two central figures of Vietnamese communism include Jean Lacouture, *Ho Chi Minh: A Political Biography* (1968) and Peter Macdonald, *Giap: The Victor in Vietnam* (1993). William Duiker, *History of Vietnamese Communism, 1925–1976* (1978), contains much useful information on important communist leaders.

STEVEN J. TIRONE

The Gulf of Tonkin Resolution

[Introduced on 5 August by Rep. Thomas E. Morgan (D-Pa.), chairman, Committee on Foreign Relations, after President Lyndon B. Johnson requested "appropriate congressional action" that same day. Passed the House of Representatives 6 August after testimony by Secretary of State Dean Rusk, Secretary of Defense Robert S. Mcnamara, and General Earle G. Wheeler, chairman, Joint Chiefs of Staff; passed the Senate on 7 August. Source: *U.S. Code Congressional and Administrative News,* 88th Congress–Second Session, 1964.]

PUBLIC LAW 88–408; 78 STAT. 384

[H. J. Res. 1145]
JOINT RESOLUTION

To promote the maintenance of international peace and security in southeast Asia.

Whereas naval units of the Communist regime in [North] Vietnam, in violation of the principles of the Charter of the United Nations and of international law, have deliberately and repeatedly attacked United States naval vessels lawfully present in international waters, and have thereby created a serious threat to international peace; and

Whereas these attacks are part of a deliberate and systematic campaign of aggression that the Communist regime in North Vietnam has been waging against its neighbors and the nations joined with them in the collective defense of their freedom; and

Whereas the United States is assisting the peoples of southeast Asia to protect their freedom and has no territorial, military or political ambitions in that area, but desires only that these peoples should be left in peace to work out their own destinies in their own way: Now, therefore, be it

Resolved by the Senate and House of Representatives of the United States of America in Congress assembled,

That the Congress approves and supports the determination of the President, as Commander in Chief, to take all necessary measures to repel any armed attack against the forces of the United States and to prevent further aggression.

Sec. 2. The United States regards as vital to its national interest and to world peace the maintenance of international peace and security in southeast Asia. Consonant with the Constitution of the United States and the Charter of the United Nations and in accordance with its obligations under the Southeast Asia Collective Defense Treaty, the United States is, therefore, prepared, as the President determines, to take all necessary steps, including the use of armed force, to assist any member or protocol state of the Southeast Asia Collective Defense Treaty requesting assistance in defense of its freedom.

Sec. 3. This resolution shall expire when the President shall determine that the peace and security of the area is reasonably assured by international conditions created by action of the United Nations or otherwise, except that it may be terminated earlier by concurrent resolution of the Congress.

Approved August 10, 1964.

Repeal of the Gulf of Tonkin Resolution

[Passed the Senate 30 June 1970 as the twelfth of thirteen amendments to Public Law 91–672; the House bill contained no comparable provision. The amendment repealing the resolution was added in conference committee on 31 December 1970 and passed the same day. Source: *U.S. Code Congressional and Administrative News,* 91st Congress—Second Session, 1970.]

PUBLIC LAW 91–672; 84 STAT. 2053

[H.R. 15628]

An Act to amend the Foreign Military Sales Act, and for other purposes. Be it enacted by the Senate and House of Representatives of the United States of America in Congress assembled, That:

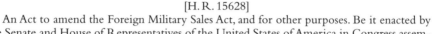

Sec. 12. The joint resolution entitled "Joint resolution to promote the maintenance of international peace and security in Southeast Asia", approved August 10, 1964 (78 Stat. 384; Public Law 88–408), is terminated effective upon the day that the second session of the Ninety-first Congress is last adjourned.

Approved January 12, 1971.

Paris Peace Accords
27 January 1973

[Source: *U.S. Treaties and Other International Agreements.* Vol. 24. (1973).]

AGREEMENT ON ENDING THE WAR AND RESTORING PEACE IN VIET-NAM

The Parties participating in the Paris Conference on Viet-Nam,

With a view to ending the war and restoring peace in Viet-Nam on the basis of respect for the Vietnamese people's fundamental national rights and the South Vietnamese people's right to self-determination, and to contributing to the consolidation of peace in Asia and the world,

Have agreed on the following provisions and undertake to respect and to implement them:

Chapter I

THE VIETNAMESE PEOPLE'S FUNDAMENTAL NATIONAL RIGHTS

Article 1

The United States and all other countries respect the independence, sovereignty, unity, and territorial integrity of Viet-Nam as recognized by the 1954 Geneva Agreements on Viet-Nam.

Chapter II

CESSATION OF HOSTILITIES—WITHDRAWAL OF TROOPS

Article 2

A cease-fire shall be observed throughout South Viet-Nam as of 2400 hours G.M.T., on January 27, 1973.

At the same hour, the United States will stop all its military activities against the territory of the Democratic Republic of Viet-Nam by ground, air and naval forces, wherever they may be based, and end the mining of the territorial waters, ports, harbors, and waterways of the Democratic Republic of Viet-Nam. The United States will remove, permanently deactivate or destroy all the mines in the territorial waters, ports, harbors, and waterways of North Viet-Nam as soon as this Agreement goes into effect.

The complete cessation of hostilities mentioned in this Article shall be durable and without limit of time.

Article 3

The parties undertake to maintain the cease-fire and to ensure a lasting and stable peace.

As soon as the cease-fire goes into effect:

(a) The United States forces and those of other foreign countries allied with the United States and the Republic of Viet-Nam shall remain in-place pending the implementation of the plan of troop withdrawal. The Four-Party Joint Military Commission described in Article 16 shall determine the modalities.

(b) The armed forces of the two South Vietnamese parties shall remain in-place. The Two-Party Joint Military Commission described in Article 17 shall determine the areas controlled by each party and the modalities of stationing.

(c) The regular forces of all services and arms and the irregular forces of the parties in South Viet-Nam shall stop all offensive activities against each other and shall strictly abide by the following stipulations:

- All acts of force on the ground, in the air, and on the sea shall be prohibited;
- All hostile acts, terrorism and reprisals by both sides will be banned.

Article 4

The United States will not continue its military involvement or intervene in the internal affairs of South Viet-Nam.

Article 5

Within sixty days of the signing of this Agreement, there will be a total withdrawal from South Viet-Nam of troops, military advisers, and military personnel, including technical military personnel and military personnel associated with the pacification program, armaments, munitions, and war material of the United States and those of other foreign countries mentioned in Article 3 (a) Advisers from the above-mentioned countries to all paramilitary organizations and the police force will also be withdrawn within the same period of time.

Article 6

The dismantlement of all military bases in South Viet-Nam of the United States and of the other foreign countries mentioned in Article 3 (a) shall be completed within sixty days of the signing of this Agreement.

Article 7

From the enforcement of the cease-fire to the formation of the government provided for in Article [sic] 9 (b) and 14 of this Agreement, the two South Vietnamese parties shall not accept the introduction of troops, military advisers, and military personnel including technical military personnel, armaments, munitions, and war material into South Viet-Nam.

The two South Vietnamese parties shall be permitted to make periodic replacement of armaments, munitions and war material which have been destroyed, damaged, worn out or used up after the cease-fire, on the basis of piece-for-piece, of the same characteristics and properties, under the supervision of the Joint Military Commission of the two South Vietnamese parties and of the International Commission of Control and Supervision.

Chapter III

THE RETURN OF CAPTURED MILITARY PERSONNEL AND FOREIGN CIVILIANS, AND CAPTURED AND DETAINED VIETNAMESE CIVILIAN PERSONNEL

Article 8

(a) The return of captured military personnel and foreign civilians of the parties shall be carried out simultaneously with and completed not later than the same day as the troop withdrawal mentioned in Article 5. The parties shall exchange complete lists of the above-mentioned captured military personnel and foreign civilians on the day of the signing of this Agreement.

(b) The parties shall help each other to get information about those military personnel and foreign civilians of the parties missing in action, to determine the location and take care of the graves of the dead so as to facilitate the exhumation and repatriation of the remains, and to take any such other measures as may be required to get information about those still considered missing in action.

(c) The question of the return of Vietnamese civilian personnel captured and detained in South Viet-Nam will be resolved by the two South Vietnamese parties on the basis of the principles of Article 21 (b) of the Agreement on the Cessation of Hostilities in Viet-Nam of July 20, 1954. The two South Vietnamese parties will do so in a spirit of national reconciliation and concord, with a view to ending hatred and enmity, in order to ease suffering and to reunite families. The two South Vietnamese parties will do their utmost to resolve this question within ninety days after the cease-fire comes into effect.

Chapter IV

THE EXERCISE OF THE SOUTH VIETNAMESE PEOPLE'S RIGHT TO SELF-DETERMINATION

Article 9

The Government of the United States of America and the Government of the Democratic Republic of Viet-Nam undertake to respect the following principles for the exercise of the South Vietnamese people's right to self-determination:

(a) The South Vietnamese people's right to self-determination is sacred, inalienable, and shall be respected by all countries.

(b) The South Vietnamese people shall decide themselves the political future of South Viet-Nam through genuinely free and democratic general elections under international supervision.

(c) Foreign countries shall not impose any political tendency or personality on the South Vietnamese people.

Article 10

The two South Vietnamese parties undertake to respect the cease-fire and maintain peace in South Viet-Nam, settle all matters of contention through negotiations, and avoid all armed conflict.

Article 11

Immediately after the cease-fire, the two South Vietnamese parties will:

- achieve national reconciliation and concord, end hatred and enmity, prohibit all acts of reprisal and discrimination against individuals or organizations that have collaborated with one side or the other;

- ensure the democratic liberties of the people: personal freedom, freedom of speech, freedom of the press, freedom of meeting, freedom of organization, freedom of political activities, freedom of belief, freedom of movement, freedom of residence, freedom of work, right to property ownership, and right to free enterprise.

Article 12

(a) Immediately after the cease-fire, the two South Vietnamese parties shall hold consultations in a spirit of national reconciliation and concord, mutual respect, and mutual non-elimination to set up a National Council of National Reconciliation and Concord of three equal segments. The Council shall operate on the principle of unanimity. After the National Council of National Reconciliation and Concord has assumed its functions, the two South Vietnamese parties will consult about the formation of councils at lower levels. The two South Vietnamese parties shall sign an agreement on the internal matters of South Viet-Nam as soon as possible and do their utmost to accomplish this within ninety days after the cease-fire comes into effect, in keeping with the South Vietnamese people's aspirations for peace, independence and democracy.

(b) The National Council of National Reconciliation and Concord shall have the task of promoting the two South Vietnamese parties' implementation of this Agreement, achievement of national reconciliation and concord and ensurance of democratic liberties. The National Council of National Reconciliation and Concord will organize the free and democratic general elections provided for in Article 9 (b) and decide the procedures and modalities of these general elections. The institutions for which the general elections are to be held will be agreed upon through consultations between the two South Vietnamese parties. The National Council of National Reconciliation and Concord will also decide the procedures and modalities of such local elections as the two South Vietnamese parties agree upon.

Article 13

The question of Vietnamese armed forces in South Viet-Nam shall be settled by the two South Vietnamese parties in a spirit of national reconciliation and concord, equality and mutual respect, without foreign interference, in accordance with the postwar situation. Among the questions to be discussed by the two South Vietnamese parties are steps to reduce their military effectives and to demobilize the troops being reduced. The two South Vietnamese parties will accomplish this as soon as possible.

Article 14

South Viet-Nam will pursue a foreign policy of peace and independence. It will be prepared to establish relations with all countries irrespective of their political and social systems on the basis of mutual respect for independence and sovereignty and accept economic and technical aid from any country with no political conditions attached. The acceptance of military aid by South Viet-Nam in the future shall come under the authority of the government set up after the general elections in South Viet-Nam provided for in Article 9 (b).

Chapter V

THE REUNIFICATION OF VIET-NAM AND THE RELATIONSHIP BETWEEN NORTH AND SOUTH VIET-NAM

Article 15

The reunification of Viet-Nam shall be carried out step by step through peaceful means on the basis of discussions and agreements between North and South Viet-Nam, without coercion or annexation by either party, and without foreign interference. The time for reunification will be agreed upon by North and South Viet-Nam.

Pending reunification:

(a) The military demarcation line between the two zones at the 17th parallel is only provisional and not a political or territorial boundary, as provided for in paragraph 6 of the Final Declaration of the 1954 Geneva Conference.

(b) North and South Viet-Nam shall respect the Demilitarized Zone on either side of the Provisional Military Demarcation Line.

(c) North and South Viet-Nam shall promptly start negotiations with a view to reestablishing normal relations in various fields. Among the questions to be negotiated are the modalities of civilian movement across the Provisional Military Demarcation Line.

(d) North and South Viet-Nam shall not join any military alliance or military bloc and shall not allow foreign powers to maintain military bases, troops, military advisers, and military personnel on their respective territories, as stipulated in the 1954 Geneva Agreements on Viet-Nam.

Chapter VI

THE JOINT MILITARY COMMISSIONS, THE INTERNATIONAL COMMISSION OF CONTROL AND SUPERVISION, THE INTERNATIONAL CONFERENCE

Article 16

(a) The Parties participating in the Paris Conference on Viet-Nam shall immediately designate representatives to form a Four-Party Joint Military Commission with the task of ensuring joint action by the parties in implementing the following provisions of this Agreement:

- The first paragraph of Article 2, regarding the enforcement of the cease-fire throughout South Viet-Nam;

- Article 3 (a), regarding the cease-fire by U.S. forces and those of the other foreign countries referred to in that Article;

- Article 3 (c), regarding the cease-fire between all parties in South Viet-Nam;

- Article 5, regarding the withdrawal from South Viet-Nam of U.S. troops and those of the other foreign countries mentioned in Article 3 (a);

- Article 6, regarding the dismantlement of military bases in South Viet-Nam of the United States and those of the other foreign countries mentioned in Article 3 (a);

- Article 8 (a), regarding the return of captured military personnel and foreign civilians of the parties;

- Article 8 (b), regarding the mutual assistance of the parties in getting information about those military personnel and foreign civilians of the parties missing in action.

(b) The Four-Party Joint Military Commission shall operate in accordance with the principle of consultations and unanimity. Disagreements shall be referred to the International Commission of Control and Supervision.

(c) The Four-Party Joint Military Commission shall begin operating immediately after the signing of this Agreement and end its activities in sixty days, after the completion of the withdrawal of U.S. troops and those of the other foreign countries mentioned in Article 3 (a) and the completion of the return of captured military personnel and foreign civilians of the parties.

(d) The four parties shall agree immediately on the organization, the working procedure, means of activity, and expenditures of the Four-Party Joint Military Commission.

Article 17

(a) The two South Vietnamese parties shall immediately designate representatives to form a Two-Party Joint Military Commission with the task of ensuring joint action by the two South Vietnamese parties in implementing the following provisions of this Agreement:

- The first paragraph of Article 2, regarding the enforcement of the cease-fire throughout South Viet-Nam, when the Four-Party Joint Military Commission has ended its activities;

- Article 3 (b), regarding the cease-fire between the two South Vietnamese parties;

- Article 3 (c), regarding the cease-fire between all parties in South Viet-Nam, when the Four-Party Joint Military Commission has ended its activities;

- Article 7, regarding the prohibition of the introduction of troops into South Viet-Nam and all other provisions of this Article;

- Article 8 (c), regarding the question of the return of Vietnamese civilian personnel captured and detained in South Viet-Nam;

- Article 13, regarding the reduction of the military effectives of the two South Vietnamese parties and the demobilization of the troops being reduced.

(b) Disagreements shall be referred to the International Commission of Control and Supervision.

(c) After the signing of this Agreement, the Two-Party Joint Military Commission shall agree immediately on the measures and organization aimed at enforcing the cease-fire and preserving peace in South Viet-Nam.

Article 18

(a) After the signing of this Agreement, an International Commission of Control and Supervision shall be established immediately.

(b) Until the International Conference provided for in Article 19 makes definitive arrangements, the International Commission of Control and Supervision will report to the four parties of matters concerning the control and supervision of the implementation of the following provisions of this Agreement:

- The first paragraph of Article 2, regarding the enforcement of the cease-fire throughout South Viet-Nam;

- Article 3 (a), regarding the cease-fire by U.S. forces and those of other foreign countries referred to in that Article;

- Article 3 (c), regarding the cease-fire between all the parties in South Viet-Nam;

- Article 5, regarding the withdrawal from South Viet-Nam of U.S. troops and those of the other foreign countries mentioned in Article 3 (a);

- Article 6, regarding the dismantlement of military bases in South Viet-Nam of the United States and those of the other foreign countries mentioned in Article 3 (a);

- Article 8 (a), regarding the return of captured military personnel and foreign civilians of the parties.

The International Commission of Control and Supervision shall form control teams for carrying out its task. The four parties shall agree immediately on the location and operation of these teams. The parties will facilitate their operation.

(c) Until the International Conference makes definitive arrangements, the International Commission of Control and Supervision will report to the two South Vietnamese parties on matters concerning the control and supervision of the implementation of the following provisions of this Agreement:

- The first paragraph of Article 2, regarding the enforcement of the cease-fire throughout South Viet-Nam, when the Four-Party Joint Military Commission has ended its activities;

- Article 3 (b), regarding the cease-fire between the two South Vietnamese parties;

- Article 3 (c), regarding the cease-fire between all parties in South Viet-Nam, when the Four-Party Joint Military Commission has ended its activities;

- Article 7, regarding the prohibition of the introduction of troops into South Viet-Nam and all other provisions of this Article;

- Article 8 (c), regarding the question of the return of Vietnamese civilian personnel captured and detained in South Viet-Nam;

- Article 9(b), regarding the free and democratic general elections in South Viet-Nam;

- Article 13, regarding the reduction of the military effectives of the two South Vietnamese parties and the demobilization of the troops being reduced.

The International Commission of Control and Supervision shall form control teams for carrying out its tasks. The two South Vietnamese parties shall agree immediately on the location and operation of these teams. The two South Vietnamese parties will facilitate their operation.

(d) The International Commission of Control and Supervision shall be composed of representatives of four countries: Canada, Hungary, Indonesia and Poland. The chairmanship of this Commission will rotate among the members for specific periods to be determined by the Commission.

(e) The International Commission of Control and Supervision shall carry out its tasks in accordance with the principle of respect for the sovereignty of South Viet-Nam.

(f) The International Commission of Control and Supervision shall operate in accordance with the principle of consultations and unanimity.

(g) The International Commission of Control and Supervision shall begin operating when a cease-fire comes into force in Viet-Nam. As regards the provisions in Article 18 (b) concerning the four parties, the International Commission of Control and Supervision shall end its activities when the Commission's tasks of control and supervision regarding these provisions have been fulfilled. As regards the provisions in Article 18 (c) concerning the two South Vietnamese parties, the International Commission of Control and Supervision shall end its activities on the request of the government formed after the general elections in South Viet-Nam provided for in Article 9 (b).

(h) The four parties shall agree immediately on the organization, means of activity, and expenditures of the International Commission of Control and Supervision. The relationship between the International Commission and the International Conference will be agreed upon by the International Commission and the International Conference.

Article 19

The parties agree on the convening of an International Conference within thirty days of the signing of this Agreement to acknowledge the signed agreements; to guarantee the ending of the war, the maintenance of peace in Viet-Nam, the respect of the Vietnamese people's fundamental national rights, and the South Vietnamese people's rights to self-determination; and to contribute to and guarantee peace in Indochina.

The United States and the Democratic Republic of Viet-Nam, on behalf of the parties participating in the Paris Conference on Viet-Nam, will propose to the following parties that they participate in this International Conference; the People's Republic of China, the Republic of France, the Union of Soviet Socialist Republics, the United Kingdom, the four countries of the International Commission of Control and Supervision, and the Secretary General of the United Nations, together with the parties participating in the Paris Conference on Viet-Nam.

Chapter VII

REGARDING CAMBODIA AND LAOS

Article 20

(a) The parties participating in the Paris Conference on Viet-Nam shall strictly respect the 1954 Geneva Agreement on Cambodia and the 1962 Geneva Agreements on Laos, which recognized the Cambodian and the Lao peoples' fundamental national rights, i.e., the independence, sovereignty, unity, and territorial integrity of these countries. The parties shall respect the neutrality of Cambodia and Laos.

The parties participating in the Paris Conference on Viet-Nam undertake to refrain from using the territory of Cambodia and the territory of Laos to encroach on the sovereignty and security of one another and of other countries.

(b) Foreign countries shall put an end to all military activities in Cambodia and Laos, totally withdraw from and refrain from reintroducing into these two countries troops, military advisers and military personnel, armaments, munitions and war material.

(c) The internal affairs of Cambodia and Laos shall be settled by the people of each of these countries without foreign interference.

(d) The problems existing between the Indochinese countries shall be settled by the Indochinese parties on the basis of respect for each other's independence, sovereignty, and territorial integrity, and non-interference in each other's internal affairs.

Chapter VIII

THE RELATIONSHIP BETWEEN THE UNITED STATES AND THE DEMOCRATIC REPUBLIC OF VIET-NAM

Article 21

The United States anticipates that this Agreement will usher in an era of reconciliation with the Democratic Republic of Viet-Nam as with all the peoples of Indochina. In pursuance of its traditional policy, the United States will contribute to healing the wounds of war and to postwar reconstruction of the Democratic Republic of Viet-Nam and throughout Indochina.

Article 22

The ending of the war, the restoration of peace in Viet-Nam, and the strict implementation of this Agreement will create conditions for establishing a new, equal and mutually beneficial relationship between the United States and the Democratic Republic of Viet-Nam on the basis of respect for each other's independence and sovereignty, and non-interference in each other's internal affairs. At the same time this will ensure stable peace in Viet-Nam and contribute to the preservation of lasting peace in Indochina and Southeast Asia.

Chapter IX

OTHER PROVISIONS

Article 23

This Agreement shall enter into force upon signature by plenipotentiary representatives of the parties participating in the Paris Conference on Viet-Nam. All the parties concerned shall strictly implement this Agreement and its Protocols.

Done in Paris this twenty-seventh day of January, one thousand-nine hundred and seventy-three, in English and Vietnamese. The English and Vietnamese texts are official and equally authentic.

[separate numbered page]

FOR THE GOVERNMENT OF THE
UNITED STATES OF AMERICA:

William P. Rogers
Secretary of State

FOR THE GOVERNMENT OF THE
REPUBLIC OF VIET-NAM:

Tran Van Lam
Minister for Foreign Affairs

[separate numbered page]

FOR THE GOVERNMENT OF THE
DEMOCRATIC REPUBLIC OF
VIET-NAM:

Nguyen Duy Trinh
Minister for Foreign Affairs

FOR THE PROVISIONAL
REVOLUTIONARY GOVERNMENT
OF THE REPUBLIC OF
SOUTH VIET-NAM:

Nguyen Thi Binh
Minister for Foreign Affairs

Protocol to the Agreement on Ending the War and Restoring Peace in Viet-Nam Concerning the Return of Captured Military Personnel and Foreign Civilians and Captured and Detained Vietnamese Civilian Personnel

The Parties participating in the Paris Conference on Viet-Nam,

In implementation of Article 8 of the Agreement on Ending the War and Restoring Peace in Viet-Nam signed on this date providing for the return of captured military personnel and foreign civilians, and captured and detained Vietnamese civilian personnel,

Have agreed as follows:

The Return of Captured Military Personnel and Foreign Civilians

Article 1

The parties signatory to the Agreement shall return the captured military personnel of the parties mentioned in Article 8 (a) of the agreement as follows:

- all captured military personnel of the United States and those of the other foreign countries mentioned in Article 3 (a) of the Agreement shall be returned to United States authorities;

- all captured Vietnamese military personnel, whether belonging to regular or irregular armed forces, shall be returned to the two South Vietnamese parties; they shall be returned to that South Vietnamese party under whose command they served.

Article 2

All captured civilians who are nationals of the United States or of any other foreign countries mentioned in Article 3 (a) of the Agreement shall be returned to United States authorities. All other captured foreign civilians shall be returned to the authorities of their country of nationality by any one of the parties willing and able to do so.

Article 3

The parties shall today exchange complete lists of captured persons mentioned in Articles 1 and 2 of this Protocol.

Article 4

(a) The return of all captured persons mentioned in Articles 1 and 2 of this Protocol shall be completed within sixty days of the signing of the Agreement at a rate no slower than the rate of withdrawal from South Viet-Nam of United States forces and those of the other foreign countries mentioned in Article 5 of the Agreement.

(b) Persons who are seriously ill, wounded or maimed, old persons and women shall be returned first. The remainder shall be returned either by returning all from one detention place after another or in order of their dates of capture, beginning with those who have been held the longest.

Article 5

The return and reception of the persons mentioned in Articles 1 and 2 of this Protocol shall be carried out at places convenient to the concerned parties. Places of return shall be agreed upon by the Four-Party Joint Military Commission. The parties shall ensure the safety of personnel engaged in the return and reception of those persons.

Article 6

Each party shall return all captured persons mentioned in Articles 1 and 2 of this Protocol without delay and shall facilitate their return and reception. The detaining parties shall not deny or delay their return for any reason, including the fact that captured persons may, on any grounds, have been prosecuted or sentenced.

The Return of Captured and Detained Vietnamese Civilian Personnel

Article 7

(a) The question of the return of Vietnamese civilian personnel captured and detained in South Viet-Nam will be resolved by the two South Vietnamese parties on the basis of the principles of Article 21 (b) of the Agreement on the Cessation of Hostilities in Viet-Nam of July 20, 1954, which reads as follows:

"The term 'civilian internees' is understood to mean all persons who, having in any way contributed to the political and armed struggle between the two parties, have been arrested for that reason and have been kept in detention by either party during the period of hostilities."

(b) The two South Vietnamese parties will do so in a spirit of national reconciliation and concord with a view to ending hatred and enmity in order to ease suffering and to reunite families. The two South Vietnamese parties will do their utmost to resolve this question within ninety days after the cease-fire comes into effect.

(c) Within fifteen days after the cease-fire comes into effect, the two South Vietnamese parties shall exchange lists of the Vietnamese civilian personnel captured and detained by each party and lists of the places at which they are held.

Treatment of Captured Persons During Detention

Article 8

(a) All captured military personnel of the parties and captured foreign civilians of the parties shall be treated humanely at all times, and in accordance with international practice.

They shall be protected against all violence to life and person, in particular against murder in any form, mutilation, torture and cruel treatment, and outrages upon personal dignity. These persons shall not be forced to join the armed forces of the detaining party.

They shall be given adequate food, clothing, shelter, and the medical attention required for their state of health. They shall be allowed to exchange post cards and letters with their families and receive parcels.

(b) All Vietnamese civilian personnel captured and detained in South Viet-Nam shall be treated humanely at all times, and in accordance with international practice.

They shall be protected against all violence to life and person, in particular against murder in any form, mutilation, torture and cruel treatment, and outrages against personal dignity. The detaining parties shall not deny or delay their return for any reason, including the fact that captured persons may, on any grounds, have been prosecuted or sentenced. These persons shall not be forced to join the armed forces of the detaining party.

They shall be given adequate food, clothing, shelter, and the medical attention required for their state of health. They shall be allowed to exchange post cards and letters with their families and receive parcels.

Article 9

(a) To contribute to improving the living conditions of the captured military personnel of the parties and foreign civilians of the parties, the parties shall, within fifteen days after the cease-fire comes into effect, agree upon the designation of two or more national Red Cross societies to visit all places where captured military personnel and foreign civilians are held.

(b) To contribute to improving the living conditions of the captured and detained Vietnamese civilian personnel, the two South Vietnamese parties shall, within fifteen days after the cease-fire comes into effect, agree upon the designation of two or more national Red Cross societies to visit all places where the captured and detained Vietnamese civilian personnel are held.

With Regard to Dead and Missing Persons

Article 10

(a) The Four-Party Joint Military Commission shall ensure joint action by the parties in implementing Article 8 (b) of the Agreement. When the Four-Party Joint Military Commission has ended its activities, a Four-Party Joint Military team shall be maintained to carry on this task.

(b) With regard to Vietnamese civilian personnel dead or missing in South Viet-Nam, the two South Vietnamese parties shall help each other to obtain information about missing persons, determine the location and take care of the graves of the dead, in a spirit of national reconciliation and concord, in keeping with the people's aspirations.

Other Provisions

Article 11

(a) The Four-Party and Two-Party Joint Military Commissions will have the responsibility of determining immediately the modalities of implementing the provisions of this Protocol consistent with their respective responsibilities under Articles 16 (a) and 17 (a) of the Agreement. In case the Joint Military Commissions, when carrying out their tasks, cannot reach agreement on a matter pertaining to the return of captured personnel they shall refer to the International Commission for its assistance.

(b) The Four-Party Joint Military Commission shall form, in addition to the teams established by the Protocol concerning the cease-fire in South Viet-Nam and the Joint Military Commissions, a subcommission on captured persons and, as required, joint military teams on captured persons to assist the Commission in its tasks.

(c) From the time the cease-fire comes into force to the time when the Two-Party Joint Military Commission becomes operational, the two South Vietnamese parties' delegations to the Four-Party Joint Military Commission shall form a provisional sub-commission and provisional joint military teams to carry out its tasks concerning captured and detained Vietnamese civilian personnel.

(d) The Four-Party Joint Military Commission shall send joint military teams to observe the return of the persons mentioned in Articles 1 and 2 of this Protocol at each place in Viet-Nam where such persons are being returned, and at the last detention places from which these persons will be taken to the places of return. The Two-Party Joint Military Commission shall send joint military teams to observe the return of Vietnamese civilian personnel captured and detained at each place in South Viet-Nam where such persons are being returned, and at the last detention places from which these persons will be taken to the places of return, the examination of lists, and the investigation of violations of the provisions of the above-mentioned Articles.

Article 12

In implementation of Articles 18 (b) and 18 (c) of the Agreement, the International Commission of Control and Supervision shall have the responsibility to control and supervise the observance of Articles 1 through 7 of this Protocol through observation of the return of captured military personnel, foreign civilians and captured and detained Vietnamese civilian personnel at each place in Viet-Nam where these persons are being returned, and at the last detention places from which these persons will be taken to the places of return, the examination of lists, and the investigation of violations of the provisions of the above-mentioned Articles.

Article 13

Within five days after signature of this Protocol, each party shall publish the text of the Protocol and communicate it to all the captured persons covered by the Protocol and being detained by that party.

Article 14

This Protocol shall come into force upon signature by plenipotentiary representatives of all the parties participating in the Paris Conference on Viet-Nam. It shall be strictly implemented by all the parties concerned.

Done in Paris this twenty-seventh day of January, one thousand nine hundred and seventy-three, in English and Vietnamese. The English and Vietnamese texts are official and equally authentic.

[separate numbered page]

FOR THE GOVERNMENT OF THE
UNITED STATES OF AMERICA:

William P. Rogers
Secretary of State

FOR THE GOVERNMENT OF THE
REPUBLIC OF VIET-NAM:

Tran Van Lam
Minister for Foreign Affairs

[separate numbered page]

FOR THE GOVERNMENT OF THE
DEMOCRATIC REPUBLIC OF
VIET-NAM:

Nguyen Duy Trinh
Minister for Foreign Affairs

FOR THE PROVISIONAL
REVOLUTIONARY GOVERNMENT
OF THE REPUBLIC OF SOUTH VIET-
NAM:

Nguyen Thi Binh
Minister for Foreign Affairs

Protocol to the Agreement on Ending the War and Restoring Peace in Viet-Nam Concerning the Cease-Fire in South Viet-Nam and the Joint Military Commissions

The parties participating in the Paris Conference on Viet-Nam, In implementation of the first paragraph of Article 2, Article 3, Article 5, Article 6, Article 16 and Article 17 of the Agreement on Ending the War and Restoring Peace in Viet-Nam signed on this date which provide for the cease-fire in South Viet-Nam and the establishment of a Four-Party Joint Military Commission and a Two-Party Joint Military Commission,

Have agreed as follows:

Cease-fire in South Viet-Nam

Article 1

The High Commands of the parties in South Viet-Nam shall issue prompt and timely orders to all regular and irregular armed forces and the armed police under their command to completely end hostilities throughout South Viet-Nam, at the exact time stipulated in Article 2 of the Agreement and ensure that these armed forces and armed police comply with these orders and respect the cease-fire.

Article 2

(a) As soon as the cease-fire comes into force and until regulations are issued by the Joint Military Commissions, all ground, river, sea and air combat forces of the parties in South Viet-Nam shall remain in place; that is, in order to ensure a stable cease-fire, there shall be no major redeployments or movements that would extend each party's area of control or would result in contact between opposing armed forces and clashes which might take place.

(b) All regular and irregular armed forces and the armed police of the parties in South Viet-Nam shall observe the prohibition of the following acts:

(1) Armed patrols into areas controlled by opposing armed forces and flights by bomber and fighter aircraft of all types, except for unarmed flights for proficiency training and maintenance;

(2) Armed attacks against any person, either military or civilian, by any means whatsoever, including the use of small arms, mortars, artillery, bombing and strafing by airplanes and any other type of weapon or explosive device;

(3) All combat operations on the ground, on rivers, on the sea and in the air;

(4) All hostile acts, terrorism or reprisals; and

(5) All acts endangering lives or public or private property.

Article 3

(a) The above-mentioned prohibitions shall not hamper or restrict:

(1) Civilian supply, freedom of movement, freedom to work, and freedom of the people to engage in trade, and civilian communication and transportation between and among all areas in South Viet-Nam;

(2) The use by each party in areas under its control of military support elements, such as engineer and transportation units, in repair and construction of public facilities and the transportation and supplying of the population;

(3) Normal military proficiency training conducted by the parties in the areas under their respective control with due regard for public safety.

(b) The Joint Military Commissions shall immediately agree on corridors, routes, and other regulations governing the movement of military transport aircraft, military transport vehicles, and military transport vessels of all types of one party going through areas under the control of other parties.

Article 4

In order to avert conflict and ensure normal conditions for those armed forces which are in direct contact, and pending regulation by the Joint Military Commissions, the commanders of the opposing armed forces at those places of direct contact shall meet as soon as the cease-fire comes into force with a view to reaching an agreement on temporary measures to avert conflict and to ensure supply and medical care for these armed forces.

Article 5

(a) Within fifteen days after the cease-fire comes into effect, each party shall do its utmost to complete the removal or deactivation of all demolition objects, mine-fields, traps, obstacles or other dangerous objects placed previously, so as not to hamper the population's movement and work, in the first place on waterways, roads and railroads in South Viet-Nam. Those mines which cannot be removed or deactivated within that time shall be clearly marked and must be removed or deactivated as soon as possible.

(b) Emplacement of mines is prohibited, except as a defensive measure around the edges of military installations in places where they do not hamper the population's movement and work, and movement on waterways, roads and railroads. Mines and other obstacles already in place at the edges of military installations may remain in place if they are in places where they do not hamper the population's movement and work, and movement on waterways, roads and railroads.

Article 6

Civilian police and civilian security personnel of the parties in South Viet-Nam, who are responsible for the maintenance of law and order, shall strictly respect the prohibitions set forth in Article 2 of this Protocol. As required by their responsibilities, normally they shall be authorized to carry pistols, but when required by unusual circumstances, they shall be allowed to carry other small individual arms.

Article 7

(a) The entry into South Viet-Nam of replacement armaments, munitions, and war material permitted under Article 7 of the Agreement shall take place under the supervision and control of the Two-Party Joint Military Commission and of the International Commission of Control and Supervision and through such points of entry only as are designated by the two South Vietnamese parties. The two South Vietnamese parties may select as many as six points of entry which are not included in the list of places where teams of the International Commission of Control and Supervision are to be based contained in Article 4 (d) of the Protocol concerning the International Commission. At the same time, the two South Vietnamese parties may also select points of entry from the list of places set forth in Article 4 (d) of that Protocol.

(b) Each of the designated points of entry shall be available only for that South Vietnamese party which is in control of that point. The two South Vietnamese parties shall have an equal number of points of entry.

Article 8

(a) In implementation of Article 5 of the Agreement, the United States and the other foreign countries referred to in Article 5 of the Agreement shall take with them all their armaments, munitions, and war material. Transfers of such items which would leave them in South Viet-Nam shall not be made subsequent to the entry into force of the Agreement except for transfers of communications, transport, and other non-combat material to the Four-Party Joint Military Commission or the International Commission of Control and Supervision.

(b) Within five days after the entry into force of the cease-fire, the United States shall inform the Four-Party Joint Military Commission and the International Commission for Control and Supervision of the general plans for timing of complete troop withdrawals which shall take place in four phases of fifteen days each. It is anticipated that the numbers of troops withdrawn in each phase are not likely to be widely different, although it is not feasible to ensure equal numbers. The approximate numbers to be withdrawn in each phase shall be given to the Four-Party Joint Military Commission and the International Commission of Control and Supervision sufficiently in advance of actual withdrawals so that they can properly carry out their tasks in relation thereto.

Article 9

(a) In implementation of Article 6 of the Agreement, the United States and the other foreign countries referred to in that Article shall dismantle and remove from South Viet-Nam or destroy all military bases in South Viet-Nam of the United States and of the other foreign countries referred to in that Article, including weapons, mines, and other military equipment at these bases, for the purpose of making them unusable for military purposes.

(b) The United States shall supply the Four-Party Joint Military Commission and the International Commission of Control and Supervision with necessary information on plans for base dismantlement so that those Commissions can properly carry out their tasks in relation thereto.

The Joint Military Commissions

Article 10

(a) The implementation of the Agreement is the responsibility of the parties signatory to the Agreement.

The Four-Party Joint Military Commission has the task of ensuring joint action by the parties in implementing the Agreement by serving as a channel of communication among the parties, by drawing up plans and fixing the modalities to carry out, coordinate, follow and inspect the implementation of the provisions mentioned in Article 16 of the Agreement, and by negotiation and settling all matters concerning the implementation of those provisions.

(b) The concrete tasks of the Four-Party Joint Military Commission are:

(1) To coordinate, follow and inspect the implementation of the above mentioned provisions of the Agreement by the four parties;

(2) To deter and detect violations, to deal with cases of violation, and to settle conflicts and matters of contention between the parties relating to the above-mentioned provisions;

(3) To dispatch without delay one or more joint teams, as required by specific cases, to any part of South Viet-Nam, to investigate alleged violations of the Agreement and to assist the parties in finding measures to prevent recurrence of similar cases;

(4) To engage in observation at the places where this is necessary in the exercise of its functions;

(5) To perform such additional tasks as it may, by unanimous decision, determine.

Article 11

(a) There shall be a Central Joint Military Commission located in Saigon. Each party shall designate immediately a military delegation of fifty-nine persons to represent it on the Central Commission. The senior officer designated by each party shall be a general officer, or equivalent.

(b) There shall be seven Regional Joint Military Commissions located in the regions shown on the annexed map [not reproduced] and based at the following places:

Regions	*Places*
I	Hue
II	Danang
III	Pleiku
IV	Phan Thiet
V	Bien Hoa
VI	My Tho
VII	Can Tho

Each party shall designate a military delegation of sixteen persons to represent it on each Regional Commission. The senior officer designated by each party shall be an officer from the rank of Lieutenant Colonel to Colonel, or equivalent.

(c) There shall be a joint military team operating in each of the areas shown on the annexed map [not reproduced] and based at each of the following places in South Viet-Nam:

Region I
Quang Tri
Phu Bai

Region II
Hoi An
Tam Ky
Chu Lai

Region III
Kontum
Hau Bon
Phu Cat
Tuy An
Ninh Hoa
Ban Me Thuot

Region IV
Da Lat
Bao Loc
Phan Rang

Region V
An Loc
Xuan Loc
Ben Cat
Cu Chi
Tan An

Region VI
Moc Hoa
Giong Trom

Region VII
Tri Ton
Vinh Long
Vi Thanh
Khanh Hung
Quan Long

Each party shall provide four qualified persons for each joint military team. The senior person designated by each party shall be an officer from the rank of Major to Lieutenant Colonel, or equivalent.

(d) The Regional Joint Military Commissions shall assist the Central Joint Military Commission in performing its tasks and shall supervise the operations of the joint military teams. The region of Saigon-Gia Dinh is placed under the responsibility of the Central Commission which shall designate joint military teams to operate in this region.

(e) Each party shall be authorized to provide support and guard personnel for its delegations to the Central Joint Military Commission and Regional Joint Military Commissions, and for its members of the joint military teams. The total number of support and guard personnel for each party shall not exceed five hundred and fifty.

(f) The Central Joint Military Commission may establish such joint sub-commissions, joint staffs and joint military teams as circumstances may require. The Central Commission shall determine the numbers of personnel required for any additional sub-commissions, staffs or teams it establishes, provided that each party shall designate one-fourth of the number of personnel required and that the total number of personnel for the Four-Party Joint Military Commission, to include its staffs, teams, and support personnel, shall not exceed three thousand three hundred.

(g) The delegations of the two South Vietnamese parties may, by agreement, establish provisional sub-commissions and joint military teams to carry out the tasks specifically assigned to them by Article 17 of the Agreement. With respect to Article 7 of the Agreement, the two South Vietnamese parties' delegations to the Four-Party Joint Military Commission shall establish joint military teams at the points of entry into South Viet-Nam used for replacement of armaments, munitions and war material which are designated in accordance with Article 7 of this Protocol. From the time the cease-fire comes into force to the time when the Two-Party Joint Military Commission becomes operational, the two South Vietnamese parties' delegations to the Four-Party Joint Military Commission shall form a provisional sub-commission and provisional joint military teams to carry out its tasks concerning captured and detained Vietnamese civilian personnel. Where necessary for the above purposes, the two South Vietnamese parties may agree to assign personnel additional to those assigned to the two South Vietnamese delegations to the Four-Party Joint Military Commission.

Article 12

(a) In accordance with Article 17 of the Agreement which stipulates that the two South Vietnamese parties shall immediately designate their respective representatives to form the Two-Party Joint Military Commission, twenty-four hours after the cease-fire comes into force, the two designated South Vietnamese parties' delegations to the Two-Party Joint Military Commission shall meet in Saigon so as to reach an agreement as soon as possible on organization and operation of the Two-Party Joint Military Commission, as well as the measures and organization aimed at enforcing the cease-fire and preserving peace in South Viet-Nam.

(b) From the time the cease-fire comes into force to the time when the Two-Party Joint Military Commission becomes operational, the two South Vietnamese parties' delegations to the Four-Party Joint Military Commission at all levels shall simultaneously assume the tasks of the Two-Party Joint Military Commission at all levels, in addition to their functions as delegations to the Four-Party Joint Military Commission.

(c) If, at the time the Four-Party Joint Military Commission ceases its operation in accordance with Article 16 of the Agreement, agreement has not be[en] [sic] reached on organization of the Two-Party Joint Military Commission, the delegations of the two South Vietnamese parties serving with the Four-Party Joint Military Commission at all levels shall continue temporarily to work together as a provisional two-party joint military commission and to assume the tasks of the Two-Party Joint Military Commission at all levels until the Two-Party Joint Military Commission becomes operational.

Article 13

In application of the principle of unanimity, the Joint Military Commissions shall have no chairmen, and meetings shall be convened at the request of any representative. The Joint Military Commissions shall adopt working procedures appropriate for the effective discharge of their functions and responsibilities.

Article 14

The Joint Military Commissions and the International Commission of Control and Supervision shall closely cooperate with and assist each other in carrying out their respective functions. Each Joint Military Commission shall inform the International Commission about the implementation of those provisions of the Agreement for which that Joint Military Commission has responsibility and which are within the competence of the International Commission. Each Joint Military Commission may request the International Commission to carry out specific observation activities.

Article 15

The Central Four-Party Joint Military Commission shall begin operating twenty-four hours after the cease-fire comes into force. The Regional Four-Party Joint Military Commissions shall begin operating forty-eighty hours after the cease-fire comes into force. The joint military teams based at the places listed in Article 11 (c) of this Protocol shall begin operating no later than fifteen days after the cease-fire comes into force. The delegations of the two South Vietnamese parties shall simultaneously begin to assume the tasks of the Two-Party Joint Military Commission as provided in Article 12 of this Protocol.

Article 16

(a) The parties shall provide full protection and all necessary assistance and cooperation to the Joint Military Commissions at all levels, in the discharge of their tasks.

(b) The Joint Military Commissions and their personnel, while carrying out their tasks, shall enjoy privileges and immunities equivalent to those accorded diplomatic missions and diplomatic agents.

(c) The personnel of the Joint Military Commissions may carry pistols and wear special insignia decided upon by each Central Joint Military Commission. The personnel of each party while guarding Commission installations or equipment may be authorized to carry other individual small arms, as determined by each Central Joint Military Commission.

Article 17

(a) The delegation of each party to the Four-Party Joint Military Commission and the Two-Party Joint Military Commission shall have its own offices, communication, logistics and transportation means, including aircraft when necessary.

(b) Each party, in its areas of control shall provide appropriate office and accommodation facilities to the Four-Party Joint Military Commission and the Two-Party Joint Military Commission at all levels.

(c) The parties shall endeavor to provide the Four-Party Joint Military Commission and the Two-Party Joint Military Commission, by means of loan, lease, or gift, the common means of operation, including equipment for communication, supply, and transport, including aircraft when necessary. The joint Military Commissions may purchase from any source necessary facilities, equipment, and services which are not supplied by the parties. The Joint Military Commissions shall possess and use these facilities and this equipment.

(d) The facilities and the equipment for common use mentioned above shall be returned to the parties when the Joint Military Commissions have ended their activities.

Article 18

The common expenses of the Four-Party Joint Military Commission shall be borne equally by the four parties, and the common expenses of the Two-Party Joint Military Commission in South Viet-Nam shall be borne equally by these two parties.

Article 19

This Protocol shall come into force upon signature by plenipotentiary representatives of all the parties participating in the Paris Conference on Viet-Nam. It shall be strictly implemented by all the parties concerned.

Done in Paris this twenty-seventh day of January, one thousand nine hundred and seventy-three, in English and Vietnamese. The English and Vietnamese texts are official and equally authentic.

[separate numbered page]

FOR THE GOVERNMENT OF THE
UNITED STATES OF AMERICA:

William P. Rogers
Secretary of State

FOR THE GOVERNMENT OF THE
REPUBLIC OF VIET-NAM:

Tran Van Lam
Minister for Foreign Affairs

[separate numbered page]

FOR THE GOVERNMENT OF THE
DEMOCRATIC REPUBLIC OF
VIET-NAM:

Nguyen Duy Trinh
Minister for Foreign Affairs

FOR THE PROVISIONAL
REVOLUTIONARY
GOVERNMENT OF THE REPUBLIC
OF SOUTH VIET-NAM:

Nguyen Thi Binh
Minister for Foreign Affairs

PROTOCOL TO THE AGREEMENT ON ENDING THE WAR AND RESTORING PEACE IN VIET-NAM CONCERNING THE INTERNATIONAL COMMISSION OF CONTROL AND SUPERVISION

The parties participating in the Paris Conference on Viet-Nam,

In implementation of Article 18 of the Agreement on Ending the War and Restoring Peace in Viet-Nam signed on this date providing for the formation of the International Commission of Control and Supervision,

Have agreed as follows:

Article 1

The implementation of the Agreement is the responsibility of the parties signatory to the Agreement.

The functions of the International Commission are to control and supervise the implementation of the provisions mentioned in Article 18 of the Agreement. In carrying out these functions, the International Commission shall:

(a) Follow the implementation of the above-mentioned provisions of the Agreement through communication with the parties and on-the-spot observation at the places where this is required;

(b) Investigate violations of the provisions which fall under the control and supervision of the Commission;

(c) When necessary, cooperate with the Joint Military Commissions in deterring and detecting violations of the above-mentioned provisions.

Article 2

The International Commission shall investigate violations of the provisions described on Article 18 of the Agreement on the request of the Four-Party Joint Military Commission, or of the Two-Party Joint Military Commission, or of any party, or, with respect to Article 9 (b) of the Agreement on general elections, of the National Council on National Reconciliation and Concord, or in any case where the International Commission has other adequate grounds for considering that there has been a violation of those provisions. It is understood that, in carrying out this task, the International Commission shall function with the concerned parties' assistance and cooperation as required.

Article 3

(a) When the International Commission finds that there is a serious violation in the implementation of the Agreement or a threat to peace against which the Commission can find no appropriate measure, the Commission shall report this to the four parties to the Agreement so that they can hold consultations to find a solution.

(b) In accordance with Article 18 (f) of the Agreement, the International Commission's reports shall be made with the unanimous agreement of the representatives of all the four members. In case no unanimity is reached, the Commission shall forward the different views to the four parties in accordance with Article 18 (b) of the Agreement, or to the two South Vietnamese parties in accordance with Article 18 (c) of the Agreement, but these shall not be considered as reports of the Commission.

Article 4

(a) The headquarters of the International Commission shall be at Saigon.

(b) There shall be seven regional teams located in the regions shown on the annexed map [not reproduced] and based at the following places:

Regions	Places
I	Hue
II	Danang
III	Pleiku
IV	Phan Thiet
V	Bien Hoa
VI	My Tho
VII	Can Tho

The International Commission shall designate three teams for the region of Saigon–Gia Dinh.

(c) There shall be twenty-six teams operating in the areas shown on the annexed map [not reproduced] and based at each of the following places in South Viet-Nam:

Region I
Quang Tri
Phu Bai

Region II
Hoi An
Tam Ky
Chu Lai

Region III
Kontum
Hau Bon
Phu Cat
Tuy An
Ninh Hoa
Ban Me Thuot

Region IV
Da Lat
Bao Loc
Phan Rang

Region V
An Loc
Xuan Loc
Ben Cat
Cu Chi
Tan An

Region VI
Moc Hoa
Giong Trom

Region VII
Tri Ton
Vinh Long
Vi Thanh
Khanh Hung
Quan Long

(d) There shall be twelve teams located as shown on the annexed map [not reproduced] and based at the following places:

Gio Linh   (to cover the area south of the Provisional
            Military Demarcation Line)
Lao Bao
Ben Het

Duc Co
Chu Lai
Qui Nhon
Nha Trang
Vung Tau
Xa Mat
Bien Hoa Airfield
Hong Ngu
Can Tho

(e) There shall be seven teams, six of which shall be available for assignment to the points of entry which are not listed in paragraph (d) above and which the two South Vietnamese parties choose as points for legitimate entry to South Viet-Nam for replacement of armaments, munitions, and war material permitted by Article 7 of the Agreement. Any team or teams not needed for the above-mentioned assignment shall be available for other tasks, in keeping with the Commission's responsibility for control and supervision.

(f) There shall be seven teams to control and supervise the return of captured and detained personnel of the parties.

Article 5

(a) To carry out its tasks concerning the return of the captured military personnel and foreign civilians of the parties as stipulated by Article 8 (a) of the Agreement, the International Commission shall, during the time of such return, send one control and supervision team to each place in Viet-Nam where the captured persons are being returned, and to the last detention places from which these persons will be taken to the places of return.

(b) To carry out its tasks concerning the return of the Vietnamese civilian personnel captured and detained in South Viet-Nam mentioned in Article 8 (c) of the Agreement, the International Commission shall, during the time of such return, send one control and supervision team to each place in South Viet-Nam where the above-mentioned captured and detained persons are being returned, and to the last detention places from which these persons shall be taken to the places of return.

Article 6

To carry out its tasks regarding Article 9 (b) of the Agreement on the free and democratic general elections in South Viet-Nam, the International Commission shall organize additional teams, when necessary. The International Commission shall discuss this question in advance with the National Council of National Reconciliation and Concord. If additional teams are necessary for this purpose, they shall be formed thirty days before the general elections.

Article 7

The International Commission shall continually keep under review its size, and shall reduce the number of its teams, its representatives or other personnel, or both, when those teams, representatives or personnel have accomplished the tasks assigned to them and are not required for other tasks. At the same time, the expenditures of the International Commission shall be reduced correspondingly.

Article 8

Each member of the International Commission shall make available at all times the following numbers of qualified personnel:

(a) One senior representative and twenty-six others for the headquarters staff.

(b) Five for each of the seven regional teams.

(c) Two for each of the other international control teams, except for the teams at Gio Linh and Vung Tau, each of which shall have three.

(d) One hundred sixteen for the purpose of providing support to the Commission Headquarters and its teams.

Article 9

(a) The International Commission, and each of its teams, shall act as a single body comprising representatives of all four members.

(b) Each member has the responsibility to ensure the presence of its representatives at all levels of the International Commission. In case a representative is absent, the member concerned shall immediately designate a replacement.

Article 10

(a) The parties shall afford full cooperation, assistance, and protection to the International Commission.

(b) The parties shall at all times maintain regular and continuous liaison with the International Commission. During the existence of the Four-Party Joint Military Commission, the delegations of the parties to that Commission shall also perform functions with the International Commission. After the Four-Party Joint Military Commission has ended its activities, such liaison shall be maintained throughout the Two-Party Joint Military Commission, liaison missions, or other adequate means.

(c) The International Commission and the Joint Military Commissions shall closely cooperate with and assist each other in carrying out their respective functions.

(d) Wherever a team is stationed or operating, the concerned party shall designate a liaison officer to the team to cooperate with and assist it in carrying out without hindrance its task of control and supervision. When a team is carrying out an investigation, a liaison officer from each concerned party shall have the opportunity to accompany it, provided the investigation is not thereby delayed.

(e) Each party shall give the International Commission reasonable advance notice of all proposed actions concerning those provisions of the Agreement that are to be controlled and supervised by the International Commission.

(f) The International Commission, including its teams, is allowed such movement for observation as is reasonably required for the proper exercise of its functions as stipulated in the Agreement. In carrying out these functions, the International Commission, including its teams, shall enjoy all necessary assistance and cooperation from the parties concerned.

Article 11

In supervising the holding of the free and democratic general elections described in Articles 9 (b) and 12 (b) of the Agreement in accordance with modalities to be agreed upon between the National Council of National Reconciliation and Concord and the International Commission, the latter shall receive full cooperation from the National Council.

Article 12

The International Commission and its personnel who have the nationality of a member state shall, while carrying out their tasks, enjoy privileges and immunities equivalent to those accorded diplomatic missions and diplomatic agents.

Article 13

The International Commission may use the means of communication and transport necessary to perform its functions. Each South Vietnamese party shall make available for rent to the International Commission appropriate office and accommodation facilities and shall assist it in obtaining such facilities. The International Commission may receive from the parties, on mutually agreeable terms, the necessary means of communication and transport and may purchase from any source necessary equipment and services not obtained from the parties. The International Commission shall possess these means.

Article 14

The expenses for the activities of the International Commission shall be borne by the parties and the members of the International Commission in accordance with the provisions of this Article:

(a) Each member country of the International Commission shall pay the salaries and allowances of its personnel.

(b) All other expenses incurred by the International Commission shall be met from a fund to which each of the four parties shall contribute twenty-three percent (23%) and to which each member of the International Commission shall contribute two percent (2%).

(c) Within thirty days of the date of entry into force of this Protocol, each of the four parties shall provide the International Commission with an initial sum equivalent to four million, five hundred thousand (4,500,000) French francs in convertible currency, which sum shall be credited against the amounts due from that party under the first budget.

(d) The International Commission shall prepare its own budgets. After the International Commission approves a budget, it shall transmit it to all parties signatory to the Agreement for their approval. Only after the budgets have been approved by the four parties to the Agreement shall they be obliged to make contributions. However, in case the parties to the Agreement do not agree on a new budget, the International Commission shall temporarily base its expenditures on the previous budget, except for the extraordinary, one-time expenditures for installation or for the acquisition of equipment, and the parties shall continue to make their contributions on that basis until a new budget is approved.

Article 15

(a) The headquarters shall be operational and in place within twenty-four hours after the cease-fire.

(b) The regional teams shall be operational and in place, and three teams for supervision and control of the return of the captured and detained personnel shall be operational and ready for dispatch within forty-eight hours after the cease-fire.

(c) Other teams shall be operational and in place within fifteen to thirty days after the cease-fire.

Article 16

Meetings shall be convened at the call of the Chairman. The International Commission shall adopt other working procedures appropriate for the effective discharge of its functions and consistent with respect for the sovereignty of South Viet-Nam.

Article 17

The Members of the International Commission may accept the obligations of this Protocol by sending notes of acceptance to the four parties signatory to the Agreement. Should a member of the International Commission decide to withdraw from the International Commission, it may do so by giving three months notice by means of notes to the four parties to the Agreement, in which case those four parties shall consult among themselves for the purpose of agreeing upon a replacement member.

Article 18

This Protocol shall come into force upon signature by plenipotentiary representatives of all the parties participating in the Paris Conference on Viet-Nam. It shall be strictly implemented by all the parties concerned.

Done in Paris this twenty-seventh day of January, one thousand nine hundred and seventy-three, in English and Vietnamese. The English and Vietnamese texts are official and equally authentic.

[separate numbered page]

FOR THE GOVERNMENT OF THE
UNITED STATES OF AMERICA:

FOR THE GOVERNMENT OF THE
REPUBLIC OF VIET-NAM:

William P. Rogers
Secretary of State

Tran Van Lam
Minister for Foreign Affairs

[separate numbered page]

FOR THE GOVERNMENT OF THE
DEMOCRATIC REPUBLIC OF
VIET-NAM:

Nguyen Duy Trinh
Minister for Foreign Affairs

FOR THE PROVISIONAL
REVOLUTIONARY
GOVERNMENT OF THE REPUBLIC
OF SOUTH VIET-NAM:
Nguyen Thi Binh
 Minister for Foreign Affairs

Vietnam War Medal of Honor Recipients

†Maj. William E. Adams, USA	25 May 1971
†Pfc. Lewis Albanese, USA	1 December 1966
†Pfc. James Anderson Jr., USMC	28 February 1967
†L.Cpl. Richard A. Anderson, USMC	24 August 1969
Sfc. Webster Anderson, USA	15 October 1967
†Sfc. Eugene Ashley Jr., USA	6–7 February 1968
†Pfc. Oscar P. Austin, USMC	23 February 1969
Sp4c. John P. Baca, USA	10 February 1970
S.Sgt. Nicky Daniel Bacon, USA	26 August 1968
Sgt. John F. Baker Jr., USA	5 November 1966
HC2c. Donald E. Ballard, USN	16 May 1968
†L.Cpl. Jedh Colby Barker, USMC	21 September 1967
†Pfc. John Andrew Barnes III, USA	12 November 1967
Capt. Harvey C. Barnum Jr., USMC	18 December 1965
Sgt. Gary B. Beikirch, USA	1 April 1970
†Sgt. Ted Belcher, USA	19 November 1966
†Pfc. Leslie Allen Bellrichard, USA	20 May 1967
S.Sgt. Roy P. Benavidez, USA	2 May 1968
†Capt. Steven L. Bennett, USAF	29 June 1972
†Cpl. Thomas W. Bennett, USA	9 February 1969
†Sp4c. Michael R. Blanchfield, USA	3 July 1969
†2d Lt. John P. Bobo, USMC	30 March 1967
S.Sgt. James Leroy Bondsteel, USA	24 May 1969
†S.Sgt. Hammett L. Bowen Jr., USA	27 June 1969
Maj. Patrick Henry Brady, USA	6 January 1968
†Pfc. Daniel D. Bruce, USMC	1 March 1969
†Sfc. William Maud Bryant, USA	24 March 1969
Capt. Paul William Bucha, USA	16–19 March 1968
†Sgt. Brian L. Buker, USA	5 April 1970
†Pfc. Robert C. Burke, USMC	17 May 1968
†Lt. Vincent R. Capodanno, USN	4 September 1967
†HC3c. Wayne Maurice Caron, USN	28 July 1968
†Pfc. Bruce W. Carter, USMC	7 August 1969
S.Sgt. Jon R. Cavaiani, USA	4–5 June 1971
Pfc. Raymond M. Clausen, USMC	31 January 1970
†Pfc. Ronald L. Coker, USMC	24 March 1969
†S.Sgt. Peter S. Connor, USMC	25 February 1966
†L.Cpl. Thomas E. Creek, USMC	13 February 1969
†Cpl. Michael J. Crescenz, USA	20 November 1968
†Sp4c. Nicholas J. Cutinha, USA	2 March 1968
†Sp4c. Larry G. Dahl, USA	23 February 1971
†Sgt. Rodney Maxwell Davis, USMC	6 September 1967
Sgt. Sammy L. Davis, USA	18 November 1967
Col. George E. Day, USAF	26 August 1967
†L.Cpl. Emilo A. De La Garza Jr., USMC	11 April 1970
Maj. Merlyn Hans Dethlefsen, USAF	10 March 1967
†Sp4c. Edward A. Devore Jr., USA	17 March 1968
†Pfc. Ralph E. Dias, USMC	12 November 1969
†Pfc. Douglas E. Dickey, USMC	26 March 1967
†S.Sgt. Drew Dennis Dix, USA	31 January—1 February 1968
†1st Lt. Stephen Holden Doane, USA	25 March 1969
Sgt. David Charles Dolby, USA	21 May 1966
Capt. Roger Hugh C. Donlon, USA	6 July 1964
Maj. Kern W. Dunagan, USA	13 May 1969

†2d Lt. Harold Bascom Durham Jr., USA	17 October 1967
†S.Sgt. Glenn H. English Jr., USA	7 September 1970
†Capt. Michael J. Estocin, USN	20 and 26 April 1967
†Sp4c. Donald W. Evans Jr., USA	27 January 1967
†Sgt. Rodney J. Evans, USA	18 July 1969
CWO Frederick Edgar Ferguson, USA	31 January 1968
†Sp4c. Daniel Fernandez, USA	18 February 1966
Maj. Bernard Francis Fisher, USAF	10 March 1966
Sp4c. Michael John Fitzmaurice, USA	23 March 1971
†Sgt. Charles Clinton Fleek, USA	27 May 1967
Capt. James P. Fleming, USAF	26 November 1968
Capt. Robert F. Foley, USA	5 November 1966
†Cpl. Michael Fleming Folland, USA	3 July 1969
†Sgt. Paul Hellstrom Foster, USMC	14 October 1967
†1st Lt. Douglas B. Fournet, USA	4 May 1968
†Pfc. James W. Fous, USA	14 May 1968
Capt. Wesley L. Fox, USMC	22 February 1969
†Cpl. Frank R. Fratellenico, USA	19 August 1970
Capt. Harold A. Fritz, USA	11 January 1969
†1st Lt. James A. Gardner, USA	7 February 1966
†S.Sgt. John G. Gertsch, USA	15–19 July 1969
†Sgt. Alfredo Gonzalez, USMC	4 February 1968
†Capt. James A. Graham, USMC	2 June 1967
†P.Sgt. Bruce Alan Grandstaff, USA	18 May 1967
†Capt. Joseph Xavier Grant, USA	13 November 1966
†2d Lt. Terrence Collinson Graves, USMC	16 February 1968
†Sp4c. Peter M. Guenette, USA	18 May 1968
Sp5c. Charles Cris Hagemeister, USA	20 March 1967
†1st Lt. Loren D. Hagen, USA	7 August 1971
†S.Sgt. Robert W. Hartsock, USA	23 February 1969
†Sp4c. Carmel Bernon Harvey Jr., USA	21 June 1967
Sp4c. Frank A. Herda, USA	29 June 1968
†2d Lt. Robert John Hibbs, USA	5 March 1966
†Sgt. John Noble Holcomb, USA	3 December 1968
S.Sgt. Joe R. Hooper, USA	21 February 1968
†M.Sgt. Charles Ernest Hosking Jr., USA	21 March 1967
G.Sgt. Jimmie E. Howard, USMC	16 June 1966
1st Lt. Robert L. Howard, USA	30 December 1968
†L.Cpl. James D. Howe, USMC	6 May 1970
†Sp4c. George Alan Ingalls, USA	16 April 1967
Lt. Col. Joe M. Jackson, USAF	12 May 1968
Capt. Jack H. Jacobs, USA	9 March 1968
S.Sgt. Don J. Jenkins, USA	6 January 1969
†Pfc. Robert H. Jenkins Jr., USMC	5 March 1969
S.Sgt. Delbert O. Jennings, USA	27 December 1966
†L.Cpl. Jose Francisco Jimenez, USMC	28 August 1969
Sp6c. Lawrence Joel, USA	8 November 1965
Sp5c. Dwight H. Johnson, USA	15 January 1968
†Pfc. Ralph H. Johnson, USMC	5 March 1968
†Sp4c. Donald R. Johnston, USA	21 March 1969
†Col. William A. Jones III, USAF	1 September 1968
†1st Lt. Stephen Edward Karopczyc, USA	12 March 1967
†Cpl. Terry Teruo Kawamura, USA	20 March 1969
Pfc. Kenneth Michael Kays, USA	7 May 1970
†Sp5c. John J. Kedenburg, USA	13 June 1968
†L.Cpl. Miguel Keith, USMC	8 May 1970
Sgt. Leonard B. Keller, USA	2 May 1967
Lt. Comdr. Thomas G. Kelley, USN	15 June 1969
G.Sgt. Allan Jay Kellog Jr., USMC	11 March 1970
Lt. (jg) Joseph R. Kerrey, USNR	14 March 1969
Sp4c. Thomas James Kinsman, USA	6 February 1968
S.Sgt. Paul Ronald Lambers, USA	20 August 1968
Sp4c. George C. Lang, USA	22 February 1969
†Pfc. Garfield M. Langhorn, USA	15 January 1969
†Sp4c. Joseph G. LaPointe Jr., USA	2 June 1969
Lt. Clyde Everett Lassen, USN	19 June 1968
†Pfc. Billy Lane Lauffer, USA	21 September 1966
†Sp4c. Robert D. Law, USA	22 February 1969
Maj. Howard V. Lee, USMC	8–9 August 1966

†Pfc. Milton A. Lee, USA	26 April 1968
†2d Lt. Robert Ronald Leisy, USA	2 December 1969
Sgt. Peter C. Lemon, USA	1 April 1970
†P.Sgt. Matthew Leonard, USA	28 February 1967
Sgt. John L. Levitow, USAF	24 February 1969
Capt. Angelo J. Liteky, USA	6 December 1967
Sfc. Gary Lee Littrell, USA	4–8 April 1970
Capt. James E. Livingston, USMC	2 May 1968
†Sgt. Donald Russell Long, USA	30 June 1966
†Pfc. Carlos James Lozada, USA	20 November 1967
†Lt. Col. Andre C. Lucas, USA	1–23 July 1970
Sgt. Allen James Lynch, USA	15 December 1967
P.Sgt. Finnis D. McCleery, USA	14 May 1968
†Pfc. Phill G. McDonald, USA	7 June 1968
2d Lt. John J. McGinty III, USMC	18 July 1966
†Sgt. Ray McKibben, USA	8 December 1968
†Sp4c. Thomas J. McMahon, USA	19 March 1969
1st Sgt. David H. McNerney, USA	22 March 1967
†Sp5c. Edgar Lee McWethy Jr., USA	21 June 1967
1st Lt. Walter Joseph Marm Jr., USA	14 November 1965
†Pfc. Gary W. Martini, USMC	21 April 1967
†Cpl. Larry Leonard Maxam, USMC	2 February 1968
†Sp4c. Don Leslie Michael, USA	8 April 1967
S.Sgt. Franklin D. Miller, USA	5 January 1970
†1st Lt. Gary L. Miller, USA	16 February 1969
Maj. Robert J. Modrzejewski, USMC	15–18 July 1966
†S.Sgt. Frankie Zoly Molnar, USA	20 May 1967
†Pfc. James H. Monroe, USA	16 February 1967
†Cpl. William D. Morgan, USMC	25 February 1969
S.Sgt. Charles B. Morris, USA	29 June 1966
†S.Sgt. Robert C. Murray, USA	7 June 1970
†Pfc. David P. Nash, USA	29 December 1968
†Pfc. Melvin Earl Newlin, USMC	4 July 1967
†L.Cpl. Thomas P. Noonan Jr., USMC	5 February 1969
Lt. Thomas R. Norris, USN	10–13 April 1972
CWO Michael J. Novosel, USA	2 October 1969
Sgt. Robert E. O'Malley, USMC	19 August 1965
†Pfc. Milton L. Olive III, USA	22 October 1965
†Sp4c. Kenneth L. Olson, USA	13 May 1968
†Seaman David G. Ouellet, USN	6 March 1967
Sgt. Robert Martin Patterson, USA	6 May 1968
†L.Cpl. Joe C. Paul, USMC	18 August 1965
Sgt. Richard A. Penry, USA	31 January 1970
†Cpl. William Thomas Perkins Jr., USMC	12 October 1967
†Sgt. Lawrence David Peters, USMC	4 September 1967
†Sp4c. Danny J. Petersen, USA	9 January 1970
†Pfc. Jimmy W. Phipps, USMC	27 May 1969
†Sgt. Larry S. Pierce, USA	20 September 1965
Sgt. Richard A. Pittman, USMC	24 July 1966
†Capt. Riley L. Pitts, USA	31 October 1967
Maj. Stephen W. Pless, USMC	19 August 1967
†Sgt. William D. Port, USA	12 January 1968
†1st Lt. Robert Leslie Poxon, USA	2 June 1969
†L.Cpl. William R. Prom, USMC	9 February 1969
†S.Sgt. Robert J. Pruden, USA	29 November 1969
†S.Sgt. Laszlo Rabel, USA	13 November 1968
†HC2c. David Robert Ray, USN	19 March 1969
Capt. Ronald Eric Ray, USA	19 June 1966
†1st Lt. Frank S. Reasoner, USMC	12 July 1965
†Sgt. Anund C. Roark, USA	16 May 1968
Sgt. Gordon R. Roberts, USA	11 July 1969
†Sgt. James W. Robinson Jr., USA	11 April 1966
WO Louis R. Rocco, USA	24 May 1970
Lt. Col. Charles Gavin Rogers, USA	1 November 1968
†Capt. Euripides Rubio, USA	8 November 1966
†Sp4c. Hector Santiago-Colon, USA	28 June 1968
†1st Lt. Ruppert L. Sargent, USA	15 March 1967
Sp5c. Clarence Eugene Sasser, USA	10 January 1968
†Sgt. William W. Seay, USA	25 August 1968

†Pfc. Daniel John Shea, USA	14 May 1969
†CB3c. Marvin G. Shields, USN	10 June 1965
†Capt. Lance P. Sijan, USAF	9 November 1967
†S.Sgt. Clifford Chester Sims, USA	21 February 1968
†Sgt. Walter K. Singleton, USMC	24 March 1967
†1st Lt. George K. Sisler, USA	7 February 1967
†Sgt. Donald Sidney Skidgel, USA	14 September 1969
†Cpl. Larry E. Smedley, USMC	21 December 1967
†P.Sgt. Elmelindo R. Smith, USA	16 February 1967
Capt. James M. Sprayberry, USA	25 April 1968
†1st Lt. Russell A. Steindam, USA	1 February 1970
†S.Sgt. Jimmy G. Stewart, USA	18 May 1966
Rear Adm. James B. Stockdale, USN	4 September 1969
†Sgt. Lester R. Stone Jr., USA	3 March 1969
†Sgt. Michael W. Stout, USA	12 March 1970
†Sp4c. Robert F. Stryker, USA	7 November 1967
S.Sgt. Kenneth E. Stumpf, USA	25 April 1967
Capt. James Allen Taylor, USA	9 November 1967
†S.Sgt. Karl G. Taylor Sr, USMC	8 December 1968
1st Lt. Brian Miles Thacker, USA	31 March 1971
PO Michael Edwin Thornton, USN	31 October 1972
Lt. Col. Leo K. Thorsness, USAF	19 April 1967
Maj. M. Sando Vargas Jr., USMC	30 April–2 May 1968
†1st Lt. John E. Warren Jr., USA	14 January 1969
†Maj. Charles Joseph Watters, USA	19 November 1967
†Sp4c. Dale Eugene Wayrynen, USA	18 May 1967
†L.Cpl. Lester W. Weber, USMC	23 February 1969
Sp4c. Gary George Wetzel, USA	8 January 1968
†L.Cpl. Roy M. Wheat, USMC	11 August 1967
†Cpl. Jerry Wayne Wickam, USA	6 January 1968
†Capt. Hilliard A. Wilbanks, USAF	24 February 1967
†Pfc. Louis E. Willett, USA	15 February 1967
1st Lt. Charles Q. Williams, USA	9–10 June 1965
†Pfc. Dewayne T. Williams, USMC	18 September 1968
PO1c. James E. Williams, USN	31 October 1966
†Pfc. Alfred M. Wilson, USMC	3 March 1969
†Pfc. David F. Winder, USA	13 May 1970
†L.Cpl. Kenneth L. Worley, USMC	12 August 1968
Sp4c. Raymond R. Wright, USA	2 May 1967
†1st Sgt. Maximo Yabes, USA	26 February 1967
†Sfc. Rodney J. T. Yano, USA	1 January 1969
†Sgt. Gordon Douglas Yntema, USA	16–18 January 1968
Capt. Gerald O. Young, USAF	9 November 1967
†S.Sgt. Marvin R. Young, USA	21 August 1968
Sfc. Fred William Zabitosky, USA	19 February 1968

†Posthumous award.

Number of Medal of Honor Recipients by Rank and Year

	Year									
Rank	1964	1965	1966	1967	1968	1969	1970	1971	1972	Total
Rear Adm.						1				1
Col./Capt.				2	1					3
Lt. Col./Comdr.				1	2		1			4
Maj./Lt. Comdr.			3	3	2	2		1		11
Capt./Lt.	1	1	4	8	6	2			2	24
Lt./Lt.(jg)		3	3	5	3	6	1	2		23
WO					1	1	1			3
Sgt./PO		2	12	16	19	12	9	1	1	72
Specialist—Cpl.		3	1	14	18	18	7	2		63
Pfc./Seaman		1	2	10	7	10	3			33
Total	1	10	25	59	59	52	22	6	3	237

Number of Posthumous Medal of Honor Recipients by Rank and Year

Rank	1964	1965	1966	1967	1968	1969	1970	1971	1972	Total
Col./Capt.				1	1					2
Lt. Col./Comdr.							1			1
Maj./Lt. Comdr.				1				1		2
Capt./Lt.			2	5					1	8
Lt./Lt.(jg)		1	2	5	2	5	1	1		17
Sgt./PO		1	5	11	12	8	4			41
Specialist—Cpl.		2	1	11	12	17	5	1		49
Pfc./Seaman		1	2	10	7	10	1			31
Total	0	5	12	44	34	40	12	3	1	151

Army, Air Force, and Marine Corps ranks are listed first, followed by equivalent Navy rank separated by a slash. Not every possible equivalent rank is listed, only ranks held by medal recipients. Note that the Marine Corps did not employ specialist rank.

Abbreviations to List of Medal of Honor Recipients

Adm.	Admiral
Capt.	Captain
CB3c.	Construction Mechanic Third Class
Col.	Colonel
Cpl.	Corporal
CWO	Chief Warrant Officer
G.Sgt.	Gunnery Sergeant
HC2c.	Hospital Corpsman Second Class
HC3c.	Hospital Corpsman Third Class
L.Cpl.	Lance Corporal
Lt.	Lieutenant
Lt. Col.	Lieutenant Colonel
Lt. Comdr.	Lieutenant Commander
Lt.(jg)	Lieutenant (junior grade)
Maj.	Major
M.Sgt.	Master Sergeant
Pfc.	Pfc.
PO	Petty Officer
PO1c.	Boatswain's Mate First Class
P.Sgt.	Platoon Sergeant
Sfc.	Sergeant First Class
Sgt.	Sergeant
Sp4c.	Specialist Fourth Class
Sp5c.	Specialist Fifth Class
Sp6c.	Specialist Sixth Class
S.Sgt.	Staff Sergeant
USA	U.S. Army
USAF	U.S. Air Force
USMC	U.S. Marine Corps
USN	U.S. Navy
USNR	U.S. Naval Reserve

Synoptic Outline of Contents

The synoptic outline provides a general overview of the conceptual scheme of the encyclopedia, listing the entry term of each article.

The outline is divided into seven sections:

Overview Articles
The Vietnam War
Armed Forces
Society and Politics
Countries and Places
Diplomacy
Biographies

Several of these sections are divided into subsections. Because the section headings are not mutually exclusive, certain entries in the encyclopedia are listed in more than one section.

OVERVIEW ARTICLES
American Perspectives
Antiwar Movement
Art and Literature
Colonialism
Diplomacy
Media and the War
Prelude to U.S. Combat Intervention
Strategy and Tactics
Vietnam
Vietnamese Perspectives

THE VIETNAM WAR
STRATEGY AND TACTICS
Amphibious Landing Operations
Atrocities
Attrition Strategy
Barrier Concept
Body Count
Chemical Warfare
Clear and Hold
Counterinsurgency
Domino Theory
Enclave Strategy
Flexible Response
Free-Fire Zones
Harassment and Interdiction Fire
Ho Chi Minh Trail
Mine Warfare
   Naval Mine Warfare
Monsoon
Navarre Plan
Nuclear Weapons
Pacification
Rules of Engagement

Search and Destroy
Strategy and Tactics
Ten-pin Theory
Vietnamization
Zippo Squads

WEAPONS
Antiaircraft Defenses
B-52
Booby Traps
Chemical Warfare
Claymore Mines
Cluster Bombs
F-111
Helicopters
Mine Warfare
   Land Mine Warfare
Napalm
SAM Missiles
Smart Bombs
Tunnels
Weapons
   Infantry Weapons
   Artillery and Air Defense
   Armored Vehicles and Transport

BATTLES AND MILITARY ACTIONS
An Loc
Ap Bac
Ap Bia
A Shau Valley
Ban Me Thuot
Ben Suc
Ben Tre
Binh Gia

Cambodian Incursion
Cao Bang
Con Thien
Dak To
Daniel Boone Operations
DeSoto Missions
Dien Bien Phu
Easter Offensive
Hamburger Hill
Ho Chi Minh Campaign
Ia Drang
Iron Triangle
Khe Sanh
LAM SON 719
Loc Ninh
Mayaguez Incident
My Lai
Song Be
Son Tay Raid
Tet Offensive
Trang Sup
Xuan Loc

THE AIR WAR
Air Force, U.S.
Antiaircraft Defenses
ARC LIGHT
B-52
Cluster Bombs
COMMANDO HUNT
FLAMING DART
F-111
Hanoi Hilton
LINEBACKER and LINEBACKER II
MENU

Index

Numbers in boldface refer to the main entry on the subject. Numbers in italic refer to photographs and maps. The letter a following a page number refers to the left column, the letter b to the right column. When both columns are noted, a hyphen indicates that the reference continues across the columns, while a comma indicates that the reference appears separately in each column.